A HISTORY OF
MODERN EUROPE

A HISTORY OF MODERN EUROPE

Second Edition

From the Renaissance to the Present

JOHN MERRIMAN

Yale University

W. W. NORTON & COMPANY

New York · London

For Laura Merriman and
Christopher Merriman

All rights reserved
Printed in the United States of America
Composition by Binghamton Valley Composition
Manufacturing by Courier, Westford
Book design by Charlotte Staub
Director of Manufacturing/College: Roy Tedoff
Production editor: Lory A. Frenkel
Frontispiece: *The Market of Saluzzo.* Left Section. Detail. by P. Borgomano
(17th–18th c.) © Alinari/Art Resource, NY.

Library of Congress Cataloging-in-Publication Data

Merriman, John M.
    A history of modern Europe : from the Renaissance to the present / John
Merriman.—2nd ed.
        p. cm.
    Includes bibliographical references and index.
    ISBN 0-393-97910-5
    1. Europe—History—1492–   I. Title.

D228.M485 2004
940.2'1—dc22   2003063986

W. W. Norton & Company has been independent since its founding in 1923,
when William Warder Norton and Mary D. Herter Norton first published lectures delivered at the People's Institute, the adult education division of New
York City's Cooper Union. The Nortons soon expanded their program beyond
the Institute, publishing books by celebrated academics from America and
abroad. By mid-century, the two major pillars of Norton's publishing program—trade books and college texts—were firmly established. In the 1950s,
the Norton family transferred control of the company to its employees, and
today—with a staff of four hundred and a comparable number of trade, college,
and professional titles published each year—W. W. Norton & Company stands
as the largest and oldest publishing house owned wholly by its employees.

W. W. Norton & Company, Inc., 500 Fifth Avenue, New York, N.Y. 10110
                            www.wwnorton.com

W. W. Norton & Company Ltd., Castle House, 75/76 Wells Street, London
W1T 3QT

2 3 4 5 6 7 8 9 0

CONTENTS

PART ONE   FOUNDATIONS

Maps

PREFACE

With the initiation of a new single currency in most of the member states of the European Union and the planned expansion of that organization, Europe has entered a new and exciting era. The collapse of communism in 1989–1990 and the subsequent break-up of the Soviet Union redrew the map of Central and Eastern Europe, leading to the independence of some existing states and the creation of some new ones. The dissolution of the Soviet Union also ended the Cold War, leaving the United States as the world's only superpower, and altering international relations and the role of Europe in some significant ways. The second edition of this survey of modern European history brings the remarkably rich, dramatic history of Europe up to date. Some of the chapters on the nineteenth century, in particular, have been condensed, and the entire text has been bolstered by incorporating very recent scholarship, for example in the case of Russia in the late nineteenth century. I have also expanded coverage of the long history of the influence of the Ottoman Empire in Europe, and of Eastern Europe and the Balkans in general. It remains essential to explore the roots of the economic and political problems that continue to beset Western and Eastern Europe, for example by demonstrating how the simmering ethnic tensions that burst into bloody civil war in Bosnia after the disintegration of Yugoslavia echoed the quarrels that eroded the stately Habsburg monarchy a century earlier. I remain committed to drawing on the exciting studies in the social history of ideas, approaches that stand at the intersection of intellectual, social, and cultural history. To take examples from early chapters, the text explains how artistic patronage during the Renaissance and the Golden Age of Dutch culture reveals some of the social foundations of art. Recent studies on the family economy, village and neighborhood life, and the changing structure of work have all enriched this book's account of the transformation of European society from an overwhelmingly peasant society into an increasingly urban and industrial world. The account of the emergence of mass politics in the nineteenth century draws on recent studies of popular culture and the symbolism and power of language. The second edition of *A History of Modern Europe* retains a narrative framework with the goals of both analyzing the central themes of the European experience and telling a story. Additionally, the book stresses the dynamics of economic, social, political, and cultural change within the context of the amazing diversity of Europe. The story of the emergence of modern Europe and its influence in the world presents extraordinary characters, whom the text brings to life, presenting portraits of men and women who have played major roles in European history: religious reformers such as Martin Luther and Jean Calvin; Queen Elizabeth I, who solidified the English throne, and Maria Theresa, who preserved the Habsburg monarchy; King Louis XIV of France and Tsar Peter the Great, two monarchs whose reigns exemplified the absolute state; great thinkers like Kepler and Voltaire; Napoleon, both heir to the French Revolution and despot in the tradition of absolute rulers; and the monstrous Adolf Hitler and Joseph Stalin. But ordinary men and women have also played a significant role in Europe's story, and they are present in this book as well, making their own history. These chapters evoke the lives of both leaders and ordinary people in periods of rapid economic and political change, revolution, and war.

The first important central theme in our story is the politics of both states and people. The growth of strong, centralized states helped shape modern Europe. Medieval Europe was a maze of overlapping political and judicial authorities. In 1500, virtually all Europeans defined themselves in terms of family, village, town, neighborhood, and religious solidarities. Dynastic states consolidated and extended their territories while increasing the reach of their effective authority over their own people. Great Powers emerged. Then, with the rise of nationalism in the wake of the French Revolution and the Napoleonic era, demands of ethnic groups for national states encouraged the unification of Italy and Germany and stirred unrest among Croats, Hungarians, and Romanians, who were anxious for their own national states. Ordinary people demanded freedom and political sovereignty, with revolution both a reflection of and a motor for political change. The emergence of liberalism in the nineteenth century and the quest for democratic political structures and mass politics have transformed Europe, beginning in Western Europe. Even the autocracies of Russia and Central and Eastern Europe were not immune to change, and there the quest for democracy still continues. While discussing dynastic rivalries and nationalism, the book also considers how wars themselves have often generated political and social change. French financial and military contributions to the American War of Independence further accentuated the financial crisis of the monarchy of France, helping spark the French Revolution. French armies of military conscripts, replacing the professional armies of the age of aristocracy, contributed to the emergence of nationalism, the origins of which, thanks to very recent studies, we can now date in Britain and France earlier in the eighteenth century. The Japanese defeat of the Russian army in 1905 brought political concessions that helped prepare the way for the Russian Revolution of 1917. The

German, Austro-Hungarian, Ottoman, and Russian empires disappeared in the wake of the bloodbath of World War I; the economic and social impact of that war generated political instability, facilitating the emergence of fascism and communism.

Like politics, religion has also been a significant factor in the lives of Europeans and in the quest for freedom in the modern world. Catholicism was a unifying force in the Middle Ages; for centuries European popular culture was based on religious belief. However, religion has also been a frequently divisive force in modern European history; after the Reformation in the sixteenth century, states extended their authority over religion, while religious minorities demanded the right to practice their own religion. Religious (along with racial and cultural) intolerance has scarred the European experience, ranging from the expulsion of Jews and Muslims from Spain at the end of the fifteenth century, to Louis XIV's abrogation of religious toleration for Protestants during the seventeenth century, to the unsurpassed horror of the Nazi Holocaust during World War II. While religion has become less politically divisive in modern Europe, endemic religious conflict in Northern Ireland and the bloody civil war and atrocities perpetuated in Bosnia recall the ravaging of Central Europe during the Thirty Years' War.

The causes and effects of economic change are a third thread that weaves through the history of modern Europe. The expansion of commerce in the early modern period, which owed much to the development of raising investment capital and obtaining credit, transformed life in both Western and Eastern Europe. The Industrial Revolution, which began in England in the eighteenth century and spread to continental Europe in the nineteenth, was related to a rise in population and agricultural production, but also manifested significant continuities with the past and drew in part on technology that had been in place for centuries. It ultimately changed the ways Europeans worked and lived.

A fourth major theme that runs through this history is Europe's interaction with the rest of the world. Europe cannot be studied in isolation. Europeans, to be sure, have learned from Muslim, Asian, and African cultures. Through commercial contact, conquest, intellectual, religious, and political influence, and, finally, decolonization, the European powers and cultures have affected the histories of non-Western peoples. European history remains crucial to understanding the contemporary world. The political, religious, economic, and global concerns that affect Europe and the world today can best be addressed by examining their roots and development. Globalization has carried movement between the continents to new levels. For centuries Europe sent waves of emigrants to other parts of the world, particularly North and South America. Now the pattern has reversed, and the arrival of millions of migrants from other continents, particularly Africa and Asia, has posed challenges to European states and their inhabitants, frequently generating intolerance. Moreover, the poverty of some of the states of Eastern Europe and the Balkans and the tragedy of the events in Bosnia have increased immigration in Western European countries. Immigrants have added to the religious and cultural complexity of many of European states and as globalization continues to transform Europe and the world, it becomes even more important and exciting to study the continent's history. This second edition, like the first, seeks to bring the past alive and enhance our understanding of Europe and the world today through our understanding of Europe's fantastically rich history. We will contemplate not only the distressing failures and appalling tragedies of the past, but also the exhilarating triumphs that have been part of the European experience.

ACKNOWLEDGMENTS

While I was in graduate school at the University of Michigan, Charles Tilly, now at Columbia University, encouraged me to keep my eye on the dynamics of economic, social, and political change, and their effect on ordinary people. I have tried to do so in this book. I have also always believed that meaningful detail and color reveal the rich texture of the past, and that history can be vivid and compelling. I have tried to write this history with that in mind. Bertolt Brecht's poem "A Worker Reads History" poses questions that I still think are important to answer:

Who built the seven gates of Thebes?
The books are filled with the names of kings.
Was it kings who hauled the craggy blocks of stone?
And Babylon, so many times destroyed,
Who built the city up each time? In which of Lima's houses,
The city glittering with gold, lived those who built it?
In the evening, when the Chinese wall was finished
Where did the masons go? Imperial Rome
Is full of arcs of triumph. Who reared them up? Over whom
Did the Caesars triumph? Byzantium lives in song,
Were all her dwellings palaces? And even in Atlantis of the legend
The night the sea rushed in,
The drowning men still bellowed for their slaves.
Young Alexander conquered India.
He alone?

Caesar beat the Gauls,
Was there not even a cook in his army?
Philip of Spain wept as his fleet
Was sunk and destroyed. Were there no other tears?
Frederick the Great triumphed in the Seven Years War. Who
Triumphed with him?

Each page a victory,
At whose expense the victory ball?

Every ten years a great man,
Who paid the piper?

So many particulars.
So many questions.

As I complete this second edition of *A History of Modern Europe*, I remain indebted to many colleagues and friends who shared their knowledge, expertise, and suggestions with me, including those at Yale, Roberto González-Echevarría, Ivo Banac, Vincent Moncrief, Laura Englestein, Geoffrey Parker, David Underdown, Laura King, Piotr Wandycz, and Richard Brodhead; Daniel Orlovsky of Southern Methodist University; Mark Steinberg, John Lynn, and Mark Micale of the University of Illinois, Champagne-Urbana; Linda Colley of Princeton University; David Marshall of the University of California, Santa Barbara; David Bell of Johns Hopkins University; and my late colleague Robin Winks, a valued friend for decades, whom I miss greatly. I also want to thank Jeffrey Burds of Northeastern University; Harold Selesky of the University of Alabama; Leslie Page Moch of Michigan State University; Richard Stites of Georgetown University; David Cannadine, director of the Institute for Historical Research in London; Jim Boyden of Tulane University; Paul Hanson of Butler University; Robert Schwartz and Michael Burns, emeritus, of Mount Holyoke College; and Thomas Kaiser of the University of Arkansas; Christopher Johnson of Wayne State University; Louise Tilly, emerita of the New School for Social Research; Paul Monod of Middlebury College; Peter McPhee of the University of Melbourne; Judy Coffin and Mark Lawrence of the University of Texas, Austin; John Sweets of the University of Kansas; General (ret.) Harold Nelson; David Large of Montana State University; Kathleen Nilan and Henry Hyder; and Elinor Accampo of the University of Southern California; Jim McClain of Brown University; Alan Forrest of York University; George Behlmer and Mary O'Neal of the University of Washington; Mary Jo Maynes of the University of Minnesota; Thomas Head of Hunter College; Jonathan Dewald of the University of Buffalo; Johan Åhr of Hofstra University; Margaret McLane, Jan Albers, Martha Hoffman-Strock, Tom Maulucci and Michael Levin; Daryl Lee of Brigham Young University; Max Oberfus of Washington University, and several anonymous readers. In preparing this second edition, I have been particularly grateful to Joel Mokyr of Northwestern University for his many helpful suggestions. Special thanks also to Jeffrey Brooks of Johns Hopkins University, Eric Jennings of the University of Toronto, Christopher Reid of Warwick University, and Aristotle Kallis of the University of Edinburgh. I also greatly appreciate suggestions offered by Doron Ben-Atar of Fordham University; Robert Brown of the University of North Carolina at Pembroke; Alexander Ganse; Brad Woodworth; David Goldfrank of Georgetown University; Ivan Marcus, Jay Winter, Adel

Allouche, Timothy Snyder, Keith Wrightson, Frank Snowden, Marco Duranti, Laura Engelstein, Kenneth Loiselle and Carlos Eire of Yale University; Michael Sibalis of Wilfrid Laurier University; James McMillan of the University of Edinburgh; Steven Wheatcroft of the University of Melbourne; Maarten Ultee of the University of Alabama; and Maya Jasanoff of Yale and now the University of Virginia. Several students who read the book noted small errors, which have been corrected: Jeremy Shimkofsky, Giorgio Piccoli, and Josh Arnold as did Maarten Ultee of the University of Alabama. I greatly appreciate the many inspiring and gratifying e-mails I have received from students who have read this book.

I have the greatest admiration for W. W. Norton and Company, very special publishers. Donald Lamm, former chairman of the board and former president of Norton, has always embodied the best in publishing. He first proposed this project to me. Alan Cameron in Norton's London office has long offered his support. In New York and on his many visits to New Haven (and indeed another to Balazuc, France), Steve Forman took up editorial responsibility. He has been both a wonderful editor and a valued friend. Sandy Lifland's deft and patient work as developmental editor contributed greatly to first edition. Jan Hoeper's close reading of the manuscript and perceptive suggestions have contributed much to this second edition, as have Maura Burnett's careful proofreading and Lory Frenkel's project editing. Sarah England, Steve's assistant, has been extremely helpful throughout the entire process. I also would like to thank the University of Melbourne, its fine Department of History, and in particular Peter McPhee, my close friend for decades, and the Miegunyuh Foundation for having made possible two great months in Australia, where I began the revisions. Very special thanks to Carol Merriman, and to Victoria Johnson. This second edition of *A History of Modern Europe* is dedicated, as was the first, to Laura Merriman and Christopher Merriman, now seven years older, again with much love.

Balazuc (Ardèche), France
July 19, 2003

PART ONE

FOUNDATIONS

As Europe emerged from the Middle Ages, the foundations for a dynamic era of trading, global discovery, and statebuilding developed that would affect the lives of rich and poor alike for centuries. During the Italian Renaissance, which lasted from about 1330 to 1530, humanists rediscovered texts from classical Greece and Rome. Renaissance artists and scholars celebrated the beauty of nature and the dignity of mankind, helping shape the intellectual and cultural history of the modern world. Moreover, after a period when almost all of Western Europe adhered to Roman Catholicism, abuses in the Church would lead to cries for reform that would not be stilled until most of Europe was divided between Protestants and Catholics. Religious conflict and wars would tear Europe apart, leading to reform in the Church but leaving permanent religious divisions where once there had been near-uniformity of belief and worship.

CHAPTER 1

MEDIEVAL LEGACIES AND TRANSFORMING DISCOVERIES

Jacob Fugger (1455–1525) was one of the sons of a weaver who settled in the southern German town of Augsburg. At age fourteen, he joined his brothers as a trader in spices, silks, and woolen goods. He traded, above all, with the Adriatic port of Venice, where he learned double-entry bookkeeping (keeping track of business credits and debits), which was then unknown in the German states. Jacob Fugger amassed a vast fortune, and he began to loan sizable sums to various rulers in Central Europe. At times he counted an annual return of 50 percent or more. Fugger's name soon became known "in every kingdom and every region, even among the heathens. Emperors, kings, princes, and lords sent emissaries to him; the pope hailed him and embraced him as his own dear son; the cardinals stood up when he appeared." When asked if he wanted to retire, Jacob Fugger replied that he intended to go on making money until he dropped dead.

The family history of the Fuggers intersected with economic growth and statemaking in Central Europe. The Fuggers emerged as the wealthiest and most influential of the international banking families that financed warring states, answering the call of the highest bidder. In 1519, the Fuggers helped Charles V become Holy Roman emperor by providing funds with which the scheming Habsburg could bribe electors. The Fuggers raised and transported the money that made possible imperial foreign policy. Loaning money to ambitious rulers, as well as popes and military entrepreneurs, the Fugger family rose to princely status and facilitated the consolidation of territorial states and the emergence of a dynamic economy not only in the Mediterranean region but also in the German states and northwestern Europe by helping merchants and manufacturers find credit for their enterprises.

(*Left*) Jacob Fugger, merchant-banker and creditor of rulers and popes, traded with the port of Seville (*right*), a stepping-off point for colonization of the New World.

The growth of trade and manufacturing ultimately changed the face of Europe. The expanding economy contributed to a sense that many Europeans had in 1500 of living in a period of rebirth and revitalization. In Italy, the cultural movement we know as the Renaissance was still in bloom, and it was spreading along trade routes across the Alps into northern Europe. The Genoese explorer Christopher Columbus's voyages to the New World were causing a great stir in Spain and the Mediterranean region. The by-products of trade and exploration were an increasing exchange of ideas and a growing interconnectedness among European states.

Although famine, disease, and war (horsemen of the apocalypse) still trampled their victims across Europe, significant improvements in the standard of living were emerging. Substantial population growth occurred in the late fifteenth century and continued throughout the sixteenth century. Europe's population stood at about 70 million in 1500 and around 90 million in 1600 (well less than a third of that today). These gains overcame the horrific loss of one-third of the European population to the Black Death (the bubonic plague) in the mid-fourteenth century. The expansion of the population brought a recovery in European commerce, particularly in the Mediterranean region and in England and northwestern Europe, where the Fuggers and other merchant-bankers were financing new industry and trade. Towns multiplied and their merchants grew more prosperous, building elegant houses near markets.

The pace of change was quickened by several inventions that would help shape the emergence of the modern world. Gunpowder, first used in China and adopted by Europeans in the fourteenth century, made warfare more deadly, gradually eliminating the heavily armed knight. The invention of the printing press in the mid-fifteenth century engendered a cultural revolution first felt in religious life, with the Bible and other religious texts now more widely available to be read and debated. And the compass, first used to determine direction by Chinese and Mediterranean navigators in the eleventh or twelfth century, now helped guide European exploration across the oceans.

CONTINUITIES FROM THE MEDIEVAL PERIOD

During the medieval period, England and France emerged as sovereign states, standing as exceptions amid the territorial fragmentation that characterized medieval Europe. Furthermore, smaller territories also began to coalesce into larger units and rulers began to consolidate and extend their authority. European society took on the shape it would exhibit through 1789, with three orders—clergy, nobles, and peasants—standing in relationships of mutual obligation to each other. Material well-being would remain at a subsistence level for most peasants but would start to improve as commercial trade across greater distances began to rise in the eleventh century. Moreover, small-scale textile manufacturing would grow, as would towns, particularly in Italy and northwestern Europe during the twelfth and thirteenth centuries.

The Fragmentation of Europe

With the collapse of the Roman Empire in the fifth century, Europe experienced an influx of new peoples. From the east came the Magyars (Hungarians), who settled in Central Europe, where they were converted to Christianity. From Scandinavia came the so-called Northmen (or Norse or Vikings), who reached Ukraine, and who for the most part became Christians. The Arabs invaded Europe in the eighth century, subsequently expanding their influence into North Africa, as well as Spain. The Mongols poured into what is now Russia and Ukraine, sacking Kiev in the 1230s, before their empire began to collapse in the fifteenth century. This multitude of influences contributed to both the political and cultural fragmentation of Europe.

In 1500, Europe was a maze of about 1,500 fragmented states. Economic, political, and judicial institutions were overwhelmingly local. Territories and cities were subject to a confused array of overlapping jurisdictions. Paris, one of five cities in Europe with more than 100,000 inhabitants, was dotted with enclaves of ecclesiastical authority. The city-states of Italy and trading towns of northern Germany managed to preserve their independence from territorial rulers. Town residents hoped that town walls would protect them against bandits and disease (during times of plague and epidemics) and would preserve their autonomy.

Villages or, within towns, parishes, formed the universe for most Europeans. Local loyalties, and those to churches, took precedence over those to the rulers of states, the effective reach of whom in many places remained quite limited. For example, in the late fifteenth century, an entire Balkan village claimed responsibility for the murder of its lord. Many villages were, for all intents and purposes, virtually self-governing; village councils, for example, established which crops would be planted on common land and set the date plowing was to begin. Such councils coexisted with seigneurial authority (that of lords). England, for example, consisted of thousands of relatively small rural communities, interspersed with towns.

Europe stood at the crossroads between civilizations and religions. After the collapse of the Roman Empire, Christendom itself had been split between the Roman Catholic Church and the Eastern Orthodox Church following the Great Schism between the two churches in 1054. The claim by the bishop of Rome—the pope—to authority over all Eastern Christians (as well as a festering doctrinal dispute over the nature of the Holy Trinity) led to the break, culminating in the pope's excommunication of the patriarch of Constantinople. By 1500, the Eastern Orthodox Church held the allegiance of most of the people of Russia and the Balkans. The Roman Catholic and Orthodox worlds met in the eastern part of Central Europe, with Poland, Bohemia, and Hungary looking to the West.

The Catholic Church, as an alternate source of allegiance and power claiming to be a universal state (with its own language, Latin), presented a potential impediment to state authority. As both the Church and the monarchies became more centralized, conflict between them became inevitable. The Church itself had been a centralized religious authority since the Roman Empire, the collapse of which left the papacy in Rome independent of secular rule. After the middle of the eleventh century, the popes were elected by the cardinals, each of whom had been appointed by a previous pope. Bishops and abbots pledged obedience to the pope in return for tenure over abbey lands and ecclesiastical revenues.

In the Ottoman Empire, religious and political sovereignty rested in the same person, the sultan. In contrast, rulers of territorial states in Europe had succeeded in making themselves largely autonomous from Church authority. Although the Church was wealthy and powerful (owning about 25 percent of the land of Catalonia and Castile, about 33 percent in Bohemia, and perhaps 65 percent in southern Italy), princes were unwilling to let the Church interfere with their secular authority, even though ecclesiastical leaders in many cases had crowned them. During the fourteenth and fifteenth centuries, rulers refused to allow ecclesiastical tribunals in their territories. The pope also commanded his bishops and other clergy to be loyal to the rulers of secular states.

During the medieval period, Western Christians attempted to win back lands conquered by Muslims, especially seeking to recapture and hold Jerusalem. The first of eight "Crusades" that lasted to 1270 began in 1096. In 1204, believing the Eastern Orthodox religion to be heresy, the Crusaders conquered the Eastern Orthodox Byzantine Empire, which had extended from eastern Italy to the Black Sea's eastern end. In doing so, Western Christians had unwittingly eliminated the most effective barrier against Islam. In the fourteenth century, the Ottoman Turks (who were Muslims) conquered two-thirds of Anatolia, much of the Balkan peninsula, and Greece. During the fourteenth and early fifteenth centuries, the Byzantine Empire (which was Greek in culture and Eastern Orthodox Christian in religion) was reduced to a small area straddling the straits between Asia and Europe, which included its capital, Constantinople (modern Istanbul), and some surrounding areas. Finally, the Ottoman Turks captured Constantinople after a lengthy siege in 1453, and by 1481, the Ottoman Turkish Empire extended to the Danube River in Central Europe. Roman Catholic Europe for the next several centuries would view Islam as a perpetual threat to its religion and culture. The Muslim Ottoman Turks would control the Balkans for the next five centuries. Yet a sizable majority of the myriad populations they ruled would remain Christian and were allowed to continue to practice their religion. Indeed, the Russian Orthodox and Greek Orthodox (both Eastern Orthodox churches), Catholic, and Muslim religions coexisted remarkably well throughout most of the long period of Ottoman Turkish rule in the Balkans. Whereas the Islamic Ottoman Turks accepted non-Muslims in their empire—the latter always represented a significant majority of the population—Christian states systematically persecuted and expelled Muslims. For centuries, Western writers outdid each other in describing the Ottoman Turks as barbaric, despotic, and cruel.

Europe thus confronted a huge semicircle of states under direct or indirect Turkish control. The Western powers, which had launched Christian crusades against the Muslims, now were forced into a series of defensive wars against Islam, which Christians believed represented the "scourge of God." The Venetians constructed fortifications along the Adriatic coast against the Turks in the fifteenth and sixteenth centuries.

Part of Europe's fragmentation was due to its three systems of law: civil law, canon law, and customary law. The legal concepts, principles, and procedures of civil law evolved from Roman law, which was based on the rational interpretation of written law applied to human affairs. Civil laws were decreed and thereby sanctioned by rulers, whose authority stemmed in part from their right to make or impose laws. The development of civil law, then, was conducive to the development of sovereign states by closely associating the power of rulers of states with the force of law. Canon law, established by the pope for the Western Church, codified in Latin the canons of Church councils and the revealed authorities of the Bible and Church fathers. As in civil law, canon law helped affirm the authority of rulers, that is, the pope, by closely linking the law to the authority of the ruler, whose subjects owed him personal allegiance.

Customary, or common law, was a codification of established custom, implying a constant reference to decisions taken earlier by judges. It was the usual mode of law in all areas where Roman law was not used. In Western Europe, customary law developed out of the customs of feudalism, a set of reciprocal economic, social, and political relationships that encouraged decentralized power structures.

In England, where common law unified the customary law for the whole land, laws were overseen by local courts, which contributed to the decentralization of royal authority. Unlike Roman law, which helped shape the sense that the ruler was a sovereign lawgiver who could override custom, customary law helped corporate groups (such as guilds) or individuals assert their interests and rights by establishing precedents that, at least in principle, could override the ruler's intervention in the legal process.

Although French customary law also evolved from feudal laws, French kings exploited differences in laws in their kingdom as they gradually increased their influence and authority. In this way, the Parlement (law court) of Paris emerged as a royal court to arbitrate among local laws, while in much of southern France, a unified (if not always written) code based on Roman law existed.

Europe's political fragmentation was accompanied by cultural fragmentation, reinforced by the many languages spoken. Latin, the language of culture, was still spoken in university towns (thus the "Latin Quarter" in Paris). Distances and difficulties in travel and communication were also imposing. It sometimes took months for mail to arrive. The shortest time from Madrid to Venice was twenty-two days, and the longest, in bad weather, was four times that. Some merchants anxiously awaited cargoes that never arrived. Mediterranean storms could come quickly: one of them sank 100 small ships filled with grain.

The Structure of Society

Medieval society was roughly divided into three social groups: the clergy, who prayed and cared for souls; nobles, who governed and fought; and peasants, the vast proportion of the population, who labored. Burghers, town residents whose entrepreneurial activity made possible the economic dynamism of medieval Europe, were, despite their increasing importance, outside this classical typology.

The clergy had many roles, serving as priests, teachers, judges, nurses, landlords, and chaplains. But they could only be tried in ecclesiastical (Church) courts; and, in the evolution of the modern state, their status as a class apart would come into question. The secular clergy ministered to the population as a whole. Most of the lower clergy were as poor as their parishioners, but bishops generally were from noble families. The regular clergy included hundreds of thousands of monks and nuns living in monasteries and convents according to strict religious rules, cut off from the outside world by their vows (and in some places legally considered dead!).

Nobles owned most of the land, with their status and income stemming from this land ownership, as well as from their military function. Noble titles connoted superiority of birth, and noble families usually intermarried. Nobles were not supposed to work; instead, they were to stand ready to defend their monarch, their own interests, and their family honor.

Peasants, who made up about 85 percent of the population of Europe in 1500, lived in villages or in small settlements on the lands of the nobles, dependent on the latter for protection in exchange for labor. Peasants had no legal status, with the exception of those (for the most part in Western Europe) who owned some land. In some places, they were considered barely better than animals by the lords who oppressed them and the clergy who told them their lot in life was to suffer in anticipation of heavenly rewards.

At least a fifth of the European population lived in extreme poverty. For ordinary laborers, three-quarters of their earnings went to purchase food, mainly bread. Towns and cities were crowded with poor people struggling to get by. Pope Sixtus V complained of vagrants in Rome "who fill with their groans and cries not only public places and private houses but the churches themselves; they provoke alarms and incidents; they roam like brute beasts with no other care than the search for food." The poor also wandered everywhere their feet could carry them, begging and sometimes stealing. Acts of charity, encouraged by the Catholic Church, which viewed such acts as essential for salvation, helped many poor people survive. But while poor beggars from within communities were tolerated and sometimes given assistance, townspeople and villagers alike feared the poor outsider, particularly the gypsy.

During the fifteenth century, rebellions—generally protests against new tax impositions—remained small. Such rebels often asked for a return to

The poor man, the artisan, and the lord in late fifteenth-century miniatures.

"ancient rights." But banditry was pervasive most everywhere. Some nobles and urban artisans in medieval times even placed themselves at the head of bandit bands, particularly in regions where the authorities of rulers was weak (for example, between Venice and Turkey, or in the Pyrenees Mountains, or between the Papal States and the Kingdom of Naples). The story of Robin Hood, the English bandit and popular hero alleged to have stolen from the rich to give to the poor, had its counterparts in a good many places.

Feudalism

Feudalism developed during the ninth and tenth centuries in response to the collapse of the authority of territorial rulers. Between about A.D. 980 and 1030, law and order had broken down in much of Europe, and violence had become the norm. This unstable period (of which contemporaries were keenly aware) had been characterized by warfare between clans and between territorial lords, attended by retinues of armed men, as well as the ravages of predatory bands.

Feudalism developed in the context of an overwhelmingly agricultural economy, where great estates were in the possession of rulers or lords. The rigid power structure (king, lords, vassals, peasants) was a reaction against the anarchy and instability of earlier years.

Despite some decline in royal dominion throughout the period and an increase in the power of great lords, there remained a crucial difference between a king and a lord. Kings were anointed by the ecclesiastical authority in a sacred rite, and therefore claimed to rule "by the grace of God" even when, as in the case of the early Capetian monarchs of France, they were incapable of coercing the great lords and their families. While swearing to protect vassals and peasants, even the greatest lords avoided using the language associated with kingship. No one was ever anointed duke or count.

The powerful lords imposed obligations of loyalty and military service on "vassals." Their vassals received, in exchange, use of lands (called fiefs) to which, at least in principle, the lords retained rights, as well as the subsequent protection of heirs under the same conditions, although a vassal had to pay the lord a fee upon inheriting an estate. Vassals also agreed to fight for their lord for a certain number of days a year and to ransom the lord if he were captured. For their part, lords adjudicated disputes between vassals. Vassals could join together to oppose a king who failed to meet his obligations; likewise, a king or lord could punish a vassal who neglected his obligations to his lord. Elaborate ceremonies featuring solemn oaths, sworn before God and blessed by churchmen, specified the mutual obligations of lord and vassal. "You are mine," said one powerful lord in Aquitaine in what is now southwestern France to a lesser lord, "to do my will."

Peasants worked the lands of the lords, giving to the latter not only their labor, but most of what they produced. They were also obligated to mill their grain, brew their beer, and bake their bread (and pay to do so) on the lord's estates. Thus, feudalism was a system in which the more powerful extracted revenue or services from the weak.

Feudalism would finally disappear in the monarchical states in the late fourteenth century with the emergence of stronger state structures and the reimposition of the authority of the Roman Catholic Church in much of Europe. Thus, feu-

In this Italian miniature from 1492, a vassal kneels to formally certify his allegiance to his lord and cement their mutual obligations to each other.

dal relationships dissolved as the strength of rulers increased and the independence of nobles declined in the stronger states. Gradually, royal courts usurped the judicial authority of nobles in some places. Furthermore, economic development contributed to the continued growth of a money economy (payment in gold or silver, or in coins minted by rulers), which increasingly made feudalism obsolete. Some of the signs of an emerging money economy in Western Europe included the ebbing of military and service obligations to rulers and lords, and the shift to cash payment by peasants to lords, instead of payment in services, crops, or animals.

The Black Death of the mid-fourteenth century also helped sound the death knell of feudalism in Western Europe by decimating at least a third of the population. As wages rose because of a shortage of labor in the turbulent wake of the Black Death, peasants were able to improve their legal status. The plague had also killed many lords. When lords tried to reimpose feudal relationships, some spectacular rebellions occurred, particularly from 1378 to 1382. The resentment of royal troops (along with the imposition of new taxes) contributed to peasant rebellions in Flanders (1323–1328), northern France (the Jacquerie of 1358), and the Peasants' Revolt in England in 1381. There was also unrest among the urban poor (as demonstrated by the revolt of the Ciompi in Florence; see Chapter 2), as ordinary people resisted attempts to return to the *status quo ante*. States took advantage of the chaos by assessing new taxes, such as the hearth tax. By increasing their authority, the monarchies of Western Europe gradually brought the feudal era to a close. Yet remnants of feudalism (the existence of serfs, who were peasants legally bound to the land that they worked) remained in Eastern Europe and Russia until the nineteenth century.

The Subsistence Economy

Agriculture lay at the base of the European economy. Farming was the principal activity of between 85 to 95 percent of the population. Land was the most prized possession, a principal determinant of status. People of means probably made up 10 to 15 percent of the population. For most, wealth depended on the possession of great estates (known in England as manors).

Peasants were constantly engaged in a protracted and, more often than not, losing battle against nature. Much land was of poor quality, either hilly or rocky, or it was marshland that could not be farmed. In most of Europe, small plots, poor and exhausted soil, and traditional farming techniques limited yields. Steep slopes had to be cleared and terraced by hand. (The traces of terracing today provide a glimpse of the struggles of poor peasants in earlier times.) Peasants plowed with hand "swing" plows. The "three-field system" left about a third of all land fallow (unplanted) in order that part could replenish itself during the growing season. This mode of agricultural production itself necessitated sizable landholdings, and could not have worked on small peasant plots. Furthermore, villages held some land in common, probably granted originally by lords. This was economically wasteful, but for centuries common lands offered the landless poor a necessary resource for survival. And under the best of circumstances, peasants had to save about one-fifth to one-eighth of their seed for replanting the following year.

Peasants also had to pay part of what meager benefits they managed to extract from the land to lords, by virtue of the latter's status and ownership of land. Lords increasingly found it more advantageous to rent out plots of land, and gradually many commuted labor services to cash, which they spent on goods, including luxuries, available at expanding markets and fairs. These included silk, cotton, and some spices that traders brought from the Levant (countries bordering on the eastern Mediterranean). Peasants (like other social groups) also had to tithe (give 10 percent of their revenue) to the Church. These tithes had traditionally been in-kind, but they were increasingly monetized during the late Middle Ages. In a fundamentally subsistence economy, this left the rural poor—that is, most families—with little to eat.

Yet even with the rise in population, lords in the thirteenth century faced frequent shortages of labor, and were forced to grant favorable terms to peasants. In this way, many peasants in Western Europe succeeded in purchasing their freedom, transforming their obligations into rents paid to the lords. Nonetheless, even free peasants still had to pay feudal dues to lords and fees for the right to mill grain, brew beer, or bake bread, monopolies that the lords retained.

Serfdom began to disappear in France and southern England in the twelfth century, and by 1500 serfdom remained only in parts of eastern France. Rulers had reason to encourage the movement toward a free peasantry in Western Europe, because free peasants could be taxed, whereas serfs (who were legally attached to the land they worked) were entirely dependent on the lords who owned the land. In Western Europe, the free peasantry reflected the growth in the authority of rulers and a relative decline in that of nobles. In the West, most peasant holdings were increasingly protected by custom and by civic law.

In contrast to the emergence of a free peasantry in the West, most peasants in Eastern and Central Europe lost their freedom during the sixteenth century, becoming serfs as landowners sought to assure themselves of a stable labor supply. This in itself was a sign that nobles were carving out territorial domination virtually independent from that of kings and other rulers.

Many people were constantly on the move in Europe. Free peasants moved toward the eastern frontiers of Europe in search of land, which they brought under cultivation. Peddlers, artisans, and agricultural laborers

Peasants jostle each other to be paid in cash, a new development in the subsistence economy.

were obliged to travel in search of work. Shepherds moved distances of up to 500 miles with their sheep from the plains to summer pastures at higher elevations, and back again in the fall ("transhumance"). Hundreds of thousands of rural people migrated seasonally from the Pyrenees, Alps, and other mountainous regions to undertake construction work in towns, or to follow the harvest. Or people moved in the hope of simply staying alive. The roads, particularly during years of dearth, seemed full of vagabonds and beggars.

Most poor families survived by eating bread and not much else. For peasants, meat was something that lords and burghers ate, fruit was rare, and vegetables were poor; rye bread, soup, and perhaps peas and beans were the staples of the peasant's diet. In southern France, grain made from chestnuts (which were themselves eaten in many forms) served as "the bread of the poor." The Mediterranean lands produced olives and wine, as well as wheat. Beer (made from cereal grains and hops) was a drink limited to northern Europe, particularly the German states, England, and Scandinavia.

Agricultural growth, which had been steady until the beginning of the fourteenth century, slowed down until the mid-fifteenth century because of the population losses due to the bubonic plague. But once the population began to grow again, plots that had been abandoned during the Black Death were plowed once more. In general, too, farming techniques and tools improved during the fifteenth century. Innovations such as three-field rotation, the use of mills, and metal harvesting implements were introduced at that time, although not adopted by all peasants until much later. Once adopted, these methods would remain basically the same until the nineteenth century, although a good many refinements contributed to subsequent progress, including the arrival of new crops brought from the New World by Columbus and his successors.

Free peasants contributed to the rise in agricultural production, which, however modest, was sufficient to feed a growing population. Not all peasants were desperately poor. Many could survive (and a minority did quite well) when famine, disease, and war left them alone, selling in the nearest market what produce they had left over after replanting and obligations to lords and the Church were paid up for that year. Many lords became market-oriented farmers in response to increased population. This in itself increased agricultural production.

The growth in the European population during the medieval period depended on these modest increases in agricultural yields. In England, Flanders, northern France, and Sicily (as well as North Africa), grain was intensively cultivated for the market. Urban growth encouraged cash-crop farming, enriching larger landlords, merchants, and wealthy peasants. There were, to be sure, areas of prosperous agriculture, such as the rich valley of the Po River in central Italy, and the plains of Valencia near the

The medieval innovation of the three-field system allowed for the renewal of one field by leaving it fallow for a season.

southern coast of Spain. Landowners brought more land under cultivation, cleared forests, drained marshes and swamps, and where possible, irrigated arid fields.

Religion and Popular Culture

Religion maintained a great hold over the lives of most Europeans in the Middle Ages, permeating everyday life. The Church, its faith and learning preserved during the so-called Dark Ages before the medieval period, viewed itself as an institution necessary for the salvation of souls and a unifying force in Europe. This gave the clergy great importance as counselors and distributors of the sacraments (above all, penance, the forgiveness of sins), without which Christians believed that salvation could not be achieved. Western Christendom was interlocked with Western civilization, although Muslim and Jewish heritages remained strong in Spain and Turkish-controlled areas. One of Europe's most traveled routes took pilgrims from many countries to the shrine of Santiago de Compostela in northwestern Castile.

In many parts of Europe, Jews, some of whom were moneylenders and peddlers, remained outcasts, although in general they did not live apart from the Christian population until the fifteenth century, when they were forced to do so by civil and ecclesiastical authorities. The popes forced Jews in Rome to wear distinctive badges; Venice established the first "ghetto" in 1516. Many Jews, forbidden to enter certain trades, were forced to wander in search of towns "where their weary feet could rest."

Religious themes and subjects permeated virtually all medieval art and much of its music. In the twelfth century, magnificent Gothic cathedrals began to be built. The construction of these colossal churches often lasted as long as a century, absorbing enormous resources, and it was paid for by gifts, large and small, from people of all walks of life. Church bells tolled the hours (clocks would remain novelties until the end of the sixteenth century).

Christianity shaped a general system of belief and values that defined the way most people viewed themselves and the world in which they lived. The clergy had enormous moral authority in village life. When preachers passed through villages, peasants and penitents waited long into the night to have them hear their confessions. The Church also blessed oaths of fealty (loyalty) sworn by vassals to lords and rulers, and it took an important role in the rites of passage (birth, marriage, death) that marked the lives of peasants and nobles alike. The Italian Renaissance (see Chapter 2), to be sure, rediscovered the dignity of humanity, but it did so within the context of Christian belief.

Storytellers, both amateur and professional, kept oral traditions of popular culture alive at a time when most people were illiterate. The most accomplished storytellers passed on their tales during evening gatherings, when villagers, principally women, gathered together to mend garments, tell stories, and keep warm. Many of these stories and tales reflected the fatalism of societies in which most people died relatively young.

There was much of which to be afraid. Most people believed in magic and the presence of the supernatural on earth. By such views, sorcerers or saints could intervene between people and the bad luck that might befall them. Primitive healers were believed to stand between disease and survival. They could maintain equilibrium in the community. People believed that rubbing certain saints' images could bring good fortune. When the wine harvest failed in some parts of France, villagers whipped statues of the saints that had failed them. Superstitions abounded. People believed that it was a good sign to encounter a wolf, deer, or bear, that a stork landing on a house assured its occupants of wealth and longevity, that meeting a white-robed monk in the morning was a bad omen, a black-robed one a good one, that a crow cawing over the house of someone sick meant death was on its way, and that a magpie announced a cure. In some parts of the Balkans, garlic was believed to ward off evil. Such beliefs helped peasants cope with a world in which droughts, harvest failures, accidents, and a myriad of fatal illnesses, could bring personal and family catastrophe.

The belief in the supernatural translated into a belief that conjurers, "cunning folk," and witches could determine earthly events. Magic, it was commonly believed, might help expectant parents determine the sex of their child. Likewise, a "cunning man" might discover the identity of a thief by placing papers with names inside little clay balls; the guilty party's name would be the first to unravel inside a bucket of water. If an accused murderer were forced to touch the body of the victim, it was believed that blood would rush from the corpse if he or she were guilty.

Religious holidays interspersed the calendar year. Festivals marked the cycles of the year, with time still largely governed by the agricultural calendar. At the beginning of Lent in some places in Western Europe, frolicking young men carried torches of blazing straw through the village to ensure villagers of agricultural and sexual fertility. Carnival was the highlight of the year for most people in early modern Europe, particularly in the Mediterranean region where it can be sunny and relatively warm even in February. During Carnival, people ate and drank as at no other time, tossing flour, eggs, and fruit at each other and playing games. Carnival also stood the world on its head, if only briefly. The poor acted out the misdeeds of the wealthy in elaborate plays that were both ritualized and spontaneous. Ordinary people could poke fun at the powerful in elaborately staged farces and parades by spoofing the behavior of judges, nobles, and clergymen. Liberated, however briefly, from their station in life by festivity and disguise, they crowned their own "kings" and "queens" of Carnival.

A peasant village festival.

THE EMERGENCE OF EARLY MODERN EUROPE

The late Middle Ages brought some significant economic, social, and political changes that helped shape the emergence of early modern Europe. Following the devastation of the Black Death, Europe's population slowly revived and then grew. More land was brought into cultivation, providing a somewhat greater supply of food. However, the balance between life and death was precarious indeed; famine, disease, and war still intervened frequently to check population growth.

At the same time, the continent's trade and manufacturing developed rapidly, particularly in the Mediterranean region (especially the Italian city-states) and in northwestern Europe. Prosperous banking families provided capital for traders and manufacturers, as they did for states, and basic mechanisms for the transfer of credit evolved. Trade with Asia and the Middle East developed at a rapid pace. At the same time, towns grew in size, and their merchants became more prosperous, especially in northern and central Italy and in the Low Countries, reflecting the importance of trade and textile manufacturing on urban growth. The growing prosperity of the entrepreneurial elite of many towns in Western Europe reflected their relative independence from territorial rulers. One of the characteristics of this independent status was the proliferation of guilds and other organizations that reflected the dynamism of medieval urban, economic, social, and political life.

Yet some aspects of the modern state system were already in place. During the 1350–1450 period, the rulers of France, Spain, England, Scotland, Denmark, Norway, Sweden, and Hungary consolidated and extended their authority over their territories, eroding the domains of feudal lords and ecclesiastical authorities. Most of the small territorial units were in the German states or in Italy. The Iberian Peninsula was divided between Castile and Aragon—joined through the marriage of Queen Isabella and King Ferdinand in 1469, forming contemporary Spain—and Portugal, arguably the first modern nation-state because its borders have not changed since the late Middle Ages. The basic layout of three Scandinavian states already existed. And important states of Central Europe (Poland-Lithuania, Hungary, and Bohemia) were already reasonably well defined. Even the Swiss cantonal federation had emerged.

A Rising Population

Europe's population had almost doubled between 1000 and 1300, rising from about 40 million to perhaps 75 million people. But early in the fourteenth century, the population began to decline, probably because of rampant disease. Then, in the middle of the century, the Black Death ravaged Europe, killing between a third and half of the European population. Spread by fleas carried by rats, the bubonic plague reached Constantino-

TABLE 1.1. THE EUROPEAN POPULATION IN THE SIXTEENTH AND
SEVENTEENTH CENTURIES (IN MILLIONS)

	1500	1600
Spain and Portugal	9.3	11.3
Italian states	10.5	13.3
France	16.4	18.5
Low Countries*	1.9	2.9
British Isles	4.4	6.8
Scandinavia	1.5	2.4
German states	12.0	15.0
Switzerland	0.8	1.0
Balkans	7.0	8.0
Poland	3.5	5.0
Russia	9.0	15.5

*Currently Belgium, the Netherlands, and Luxembourg.
Source: Richard Mackenney, *Sixteenth-Century Europe: Expansion and Conflict* (New York: Macmillan, 1993), p. 51.

ple from Asia in 1347. It then tore through the Italian peninsula, Spain, and France in 1348, Austria, Switzerland, the German states, the Netherlands, and England in 1349, and Scandinavia and Poland in 1350. Victims died horrible deaths, some in a few days, others lingering in agony, but not for long. Some villages were completely abandoned, as people tried to flee the path of the scourge. In vain, states and cities tried frantically to prevent the arrival of travelers, fearful that they were carriers of the dread disease.

For the next century, births and deaths remained balanced (with higher mortality rates in cities wiping out increased births in the countryside). Europe only began to recover during the second half of the fifteenth century, thanks to a lull in epidemics and the absence of destructive wars. However, the population did not reach the level it had been at in 1300 until about 1550, or somewhat earlier, when it began to rise rapidly, particularly in towns and in northern Europe (see Table 1.1).

Europeans remained perpetually vulnerable to disease and disaster. Epidemics routinely took huge tolls in Europe. The bubonic plague was the worst of these, but influenza, typhus, malaria, typhoid, and smallpox also carried off many people, particularly the poor, who invariably suffered from inadequate nutrition. Moreover, Europeans looked to the heavens not only in prayer but also to watch for the bad weather that could ruin harvests, including rainy periods that brought flooding. Famine still killed regularly, a natural disaster that checked population growth, killing off infants, children, and old people in the greatest numbers. "Nothing new here," a Roman wrote in the mid-sixteenth century, "except that people are dying of hunger."

Life, for most people, was short. Life expectancy was about twenty years and, once one had made it out of infancy and childhood alive, perhaps forty years. Infants born in Paris could expect to live to only twenty-three years of age (a figure that includes infant mortality, and that therefore underestimates the average span of life for those surviving infancy). About a fifth of all babies born died before they reached their first birthday. In France, only about half of the children lived past the age of ten. Women lived longer than men, but many died during childbirth. Of 100 children born, less than half lived to age twenty and only about a fifth celebrated a fortieth birthday. Christ, who died at age thirty-three, was not considered to have died young.

The balance between life and death was precarious. In most towns, deaths outnumbered births almost every year. Prosperous families had more children than the poor (the opposite pattern of today). The exposure and abandonment of newly born infants was common. Furthermore, couples may have been limiting births, with careful sexual abstention one possible reason for relatively low rates of reproductivity. The fact that one partner often died prematurely also served as a check on population. So, too, did the fact that most couples married relatively late. In Shakespeare's great play *Romeo and Juliet,* Juliet, who marries at the age of fourteen, was not at all representative of most brides. Most English men married at between twenty-six and twenty-nine years of age, women between twenty-four and twenty-six years.

The choice of a marriage partner was important for economic reasons (although in parts of Western Europe, up to a fifth of women never married). In every social stratum, marriages were often arranged—that is, parents played a major and often determining role in choosing partners for their children. For families of means, particularly nobles, the promise of a sizable dowry counted for much. Yet some evidence suggests that by the end of the sixteenth century the inclinations of the bride and groom among English families were sometimes difficult to ignore. For the poor, marriage could offer the chance of improving one's situation. Thus, a young woman whose family could provide a dowry, however modest, or who had a skill, was an attractive prospective spouse, as was a young man with a trade.

Wives remained legally subservient to their husbands, although in the "economy of makeshifts" in the poor household their role as managers of income and as workers gave them some degree of equality. Sexual infidelity, while common, ran against the grain of a popular sense of justice, which placed a premium on loyalty and mutual obligation between marriage partners and between parents and children. Such liaisons might also jeopardize the system of inheritance and the protection of family property by leading to the appearance of unanticipated offspring, in an age when contraceptive techniques were rudimentary and not well known. Still,

In this 1523 painting by Lorenzo Lotto, a mischievous cupid yokes a bride and groom together.

about a fifth of English brides were pregnant at the time of their wedding, as sexual relations between couples expecting to marry were very common.

Kinship and neighborhood solidarities defined the lives of ordinary people. In some places, extended families were common; that is, parents and sometimes other relatives lived with couples. In England, however, the nuclear family (a couple and their children) was the most common household. When children of the lower classes began their working lives— usually at the age of fourteen or fifteen, or earlier for some apprentices— their obligations to their parents did not cease. Often, however, they left home in search of work, rarely, if ever, to return. The poor turned to family and neighbors for help in bad times, as well as for help with harvests, if they owned some land.

One of the consequences of the rise in Europe's population was the inflation that characterized the sixteenth century, particularly its last decades. It seemed to one Spaniard that "a pound of mutton now costs as much as a whole sheep used to." Between 1500 and 1600, the price of wheat rose by 425 percent in England, 650 percent in France, and 400 percent in Poland. The expanding population brought price rises before the arrival of silver from Latin America, a cause of continued inflation during the second half of the century. An English author in the middle of the sixteenth century insisted that "the principal cause is the engrossing of things into a few men's hands." A larger population also put pressure on the value of land. The rapid rise in rents led a mid-fifteenth-century Englishman to denounce rich landlords as "men without conscience, men utterly devoid of God's fear, yea men that live as though there were no God at all. . . . They take our houses over our heads, they buy our grounds out of our hands, they raise our rents. . . ."

An Expanding Economy

One of the hallmarks of medieval society had been the marked expansion of trade and manufacture that began in the eleventh century. During the twelfth and thirteenth centuries, merchants greatly increased the amount of products carried on land routes and in the low galley-ships that hugged the Mediterranean coastline, more confident than ever before that their goods would find purchasers. Rivers like the Rhône and Rhine were essential trade arteries. In the markets of Flanders and northern France, olive oil, fruit, and wine from the Mediterranean region were exchanged for timber, cereals, and salted fish from the Baltic region.

With the expansion in commercial activity, a money economy slowly developed. Yet trade and barter remained important, particularly for peasants, most of whom were part of a subsistence economy. Currency still did not penetrate some mountainous regions.

The late Middle Ages brought a significant rise in the availability of credit to states and entrepreneurs. In particular, Italian merchants advanced capitalist techniques during the thirteenth century in their trade with the Near East. Some merchants were no longer itinerant travelers, but rather sedentary entrepreneurs able to raise capital and extend (and obtain) credit. They also developed bills of exchange (see Chapter 5), which were orders drawn upon an agent to pay another merchant money at a future date, perhaps in another country and in another currency.

To raise capital, merchants borrowed from banking families, like the Fuggers, other merchants (or merchant-banking families who did both), moneylenders, or formed temporary partnerships. Here and there, businesses began to work on a commission basis, and some entrepreneurs specialized in transporting goods. They began to keep registers of profits and losses, using double-entry bookkeeping.

Banking families in Venice and other Italian city-states were already well established in the thirteenth century. The powerful merchant-banking families influenced rulers by loaning vast sums to kings and popes alike. On a smaller scale, moneylenders still played an important part in rural economies. Territorial rulers and great lords increasingly required a healthy treasury or at least good credit.

The greater availability of credit facilitated a commercial boom in the sixteenth century. By 1500, with new mechanisms of credit, coins, and other money no longer necessarily had to be carried from place to place in order to purchase goods. At the same time, merchants and manufacturers were able to control the distribution of more products, and merchant-manufacturers could bring various stages of production under their control. Yet the multiplicity of states hindered commerce. Even within France, more than 200 tolls were collected in 120 different spots on the Loire River and its tributaries.

The sixteenth century also brought a marked increase in manufacturing, which in some regions may have multiplied by 500 percent. The extraction of iron, copper, and silver quadrupled, for example, in Central Europe. Large-scale manufacturing was limited to mining and textiles, as well as to arms manufacturing and shipbuilding.

The production of textiles, whether for large, distant markets or only for local consumption, dominated the manufacturing economy. The manufacture of silk, techniques for which had been imported from China into Europe by Arabs in the tenth century, centered in the Italian states. It spread during the second half of the fifteenth century across the Alps to the German states, France, and Spain, which soon produced raw silk and no longer depended on imports from Asia and Persia.

The manufacture of cloth spread rapidly in Tuscany, northern France, Flanders, and the Netherlands. The woolens industry of Flanders, which had developed during the medieval period, boomed, centered in the towns of Ypres, Ghent, and Bruges. England, which continued to export wool to the continent, became a major producer of woolen goods in the fourteenth century, forming a base for English industrialization and for London's prosperity as an exporter of manufactured goods. However, Antwerp emerged as Europe's first important center of trade.

Urban merchants and artisans were organized into guilds, which regulated production and distribution, thus protecting, at least in principle,

Bankers sitting behind their *banco* (counter) doing business.

In the cottage (domestic) industry, merchant-capitalists put out spinning, weaving, and other work into the countryside. Here a woman is spinning in her home.

guild members and consumers. The structure of craft production was organized hierarchically. Apprentices who learned their craft became journeymen and, if all went well, could eventually become masters, joining a masters' guild, and employing journeymen and training apprentices. Most cloth was finished in towns by craft artisans. Through the guilds, masters could preserve the quality of work within their particular trades and, at the same time, the reputations of their town.

During the sixteenth century, a period of great economic dynamism, the gap between rich and poor grew, particularly as the massive inflation of that period, pushed by population increase, reduced the value of wages. During the fourteenth and fifteenth centuries, it had become increasingly difficult for journeymen to become independent master craftsmen. Early in the sixteenth century, some German journeymen refused to work for masters who paid them less than they desired or had been used to receiving.

Many craftsmen avoided restrictions on their work by working outside the walls of cities or in the countryside. In this way, they avoided guild monopolies and guild specifications on wages and piece rates. Likewise, merchant-capitalists who owned raw materials put out spinning, weaving (sometimes renting out looms), and other work into the countryside, where labor was even cheaper. Rural production spread rapidly in northern Italy, the Netherlands, northern France, and England between 1450 and 1550. Hundreds of thousands of peasants produced woolen or linen yarn or wove it into cloth; then urban workers dyed, bleached, or shrunk the cloth, which merchants then sold. This "cottage industry" (also sometimes called "domestic industry") would remain an important part of the manufacturing process well into the nineteenth century.

As they grew richer, some merchant families purchased land and noble titles. Merchants therefore became important figures in every state. Many nobles resented the new status of these commoners, following the old saying, "The king could make a nobleman, but not a gentleman." The rising importance of merchants reflected the fact that, with continued economic growth, the possession of money, the ability to acquire credit and draw up a bill of exchange, and entrepreneurial skill were gradually becoming more important than the military might and distinguished lineage of nobles.

The Growth of Towns

During the twelfth and thirteenth centuries, European towns grew rapidly in both number and size, reflecting improvements in economic development and security in medieval Europe. Fortified stone ramparts, gates, and towers gave each town unique visible characteristics. Towns were the residence of most courts (including municipal courts), hospitals, and fraternal associations, such as religious confraternities, as well as guilds. Administrative and religious buildings were the cornerstones of the medieval towns. In addition to the "bourgeois" or "burghers" (townspeople), most towns had a relatively large number of clergy living within their walls, ministering to the needs of the population or living a cloistered existence in convents and monasteries.

Most major towns in Europe were founded before 1300. In Poland, about 200 new towns were created between 1450 and 1550, adding to the 450 already in existence. Northern Italy and the Low Countries had the densest networks of towns. However, even there town dwellers remained a relatively small minority of the population, no more than about 15 percent of the population. Only about 2 percent of the European population lived in towns larger than 40,000 and in 1500, only about 6 percent of Europeans lived in towns of more than 10,000 people. Most towns were small: in the German states, only about 200 of 3,000 towns had more than 10,000 residents. Only Constantinople, Naples, Milan, Paris, and Venice had more than 100,000 inhabitants.

In Italy, the towns of Venice, Florence, Genoa, Milan, and Pisa became independent city-states in about 1100, free to establish control over surrounding towns and villages. The decline of the Byzantine Empire and the inability of the Holy Roman Empire of Central Europe to establish its authority throughout Italy prevented the development of large territorial states. The prosperity of the city-states, too, impeded the creation of a single Italian state, or even a peninsula divided into two or three major political units. Freed of feudal overlords, the dynamism of these city-states underlay the Renaissance (see Chapter 2). Venetian and Genoese merchants sent trading fleets carrying goods to and from the Levant and beyond, as well as along the spice routes to Central Asia, India, and China (visited by the Italian adventurer Marco Polo during his long voyage from 1275 to 1292).

In northern Europe, as well, the growth of cities and towns was linked to the expansion of commerce and long-distance trade. In northern Germany, independent trading cities were enriched by the Baltic grain trade, as Polish landowners, like their Hungarian and Bohemian counterparts, concentrated agricultural development on the production of grain for export to the Dutch Netherlands and other Western countries. Lübeck and Hamburg, among other northern German trading cities, formed the Hanseatic League, which at first was a federation against banditry. Its towns began to thrive in the mid-twelfth century, establishing networks of trade that reached from London all the way to Novgorod. The Polish port of Gdańsk had its own currency, fleet, army, and diplomats. Likewise, some towns in southern Germany formed leagues to resist territorial lords and to protect trade routes. The fairs held outside the towns of Champagne in northern France, as well as Lyon at the confluence of the Saône and Rhône Rivers, and Beaucaire further south on the Rhône, served as trading points between northern Europe and Mediterranean merchants. The market function of trading towns swelled their populations; merchants and small manufacturers catered to the needs of the local population. Market towns also reflected the fact that the European economy remained closely tied to the land, as landowners, particularly in regions of commercialized agriculture, sold their produce in the town markets.

Medieval Europe boasted major urban centers of learning, dominated by Church teaching. Paris (theology), Montpellier (medicine), and Bologna (Roman law) were major university centers. Oxford and Cambridge Universities were founded in the thirteenth century. Universities existed not in the sense that we know them today. Rather, the term referred to a common, corporately organized body of students or masters in one town. By 1500, dozens of towns had universities. And, in turn, literacy (limited to a small proportion of the population even in the best of circumstances) rose faster in towns than in the countryside, as the equivalent of secondary education shifted from rural monasteries to urban church or grammar schools.

Town governments were dominated by oligarchies of rich merchants, guild masters, and property owners (in Italian towns, nobles were part of these oligarchies). Despite the fact that many peasants still lived in towns ("agro-towns"), working fields outside town walls during the day and returning home before the gates slammed shut at nightfall, town and country seemed in some ways worlds apart.

Municipal Liberties

Towns within the feudal context stood as zones of freedom, because their residents were not, in most cases, bound by service obligations to landowners. Contemporaries held that "town air makes [one] free" (for example, no town person in Western Europe could be a serf). Urban freedoms had to be obtained from lords, however. Towns purchased charters of exemption from taxes in exchange for the payment of lump sums. Urban oligarchs jealously guarded this municipal independence against nobles and rulers who tried to expand to attain revenue and political consolidation. In some cases, rulers actively sought alliances with towns against nobles, sworn enemies of towns. Towns could also loan money to kings waging war against recalcitrant vassals or other rulers, including popes. Where territorial rulers were weak, as in Italy and the German states, towns obtained the greatest degree of freedom. By contrast, towns developed less rapidly in areas where rulers and nobles exercised strong authority.

Traditions of municipal liberties would leave a significant heritage in Western Europe, ultimately shaping the emergence of constitutional forms of government. Whereas social relationships in the countryside were largely defined by personal obligations, in towns these were replaced by collective rights through guilds and other associations. In England, northern France, the Netherlands, Flanders, and Switzerland, urban medieval confraternities and other voluntary associations would spur a democratizing impulse within trading towns as they struggled to maintain their independence from rulers and rural nobles. Lacking the associational infrastructure of many towns in Western Europe, however, Eastern European towns were not able to stem the tide of the increasing power of nobles and, in the case of Russia, the tsars. As the Muscovite state expanded its authority, the tsars ran roughshod over urban pretensions. Towns in the East extracted none of the special charters of rights that characterized towns in the West. Russian rulers considered towns their personal property, and Russian lords demanded the service and allegiance of townspeople.

The Emergence of Sovereign States

Although the term "state" was not yet being used to denote a political entity, by 1500 the largest monarchical kingdoms (see Map 1.1) were taking on some of the characteristics of the modern state. During the sixteenth century, France, Spain, and England would evolve into "new monarchies." What was "new" about them was their growing reach, an evolution begun in the late medieval era. While monarchies grew stronger in Western Europe, however, they were actually weakened in Eastern Europe during the late Middle Ages. Struggles for power, civil war, and the growing domination of lords hindered the emergence of strong states there at least until the late sixteenth century.

Sovereign states emerged in Western Europe during the medieval period as rulers moved toward greater authority and independence. Yet, to be sure, these states were not "nation-states" in the modern sense, in which citizens feel that they belong to a nation by being, for example,

MAP 1.1 EUROPE IN 1500   Europe in 1500 was a maze of fragmented realms although sovereign monarchical states were beginning to emerge.

Spanish, French, or Italian. Such "imagined national communities," defined by ethnic bonds and cultural and linguistic traditions, would only develop beginning in the late eighteenth century and the nineteenth century. In medieval Europe, rulers governed a complex hodgepodge of territories, semi-independent towns, feudal vassals, and corporate institutions such as guilds that were largely independent of the crown, exchanging personal and/or corporate privileges for loyalty.

Yet, between the tenth and fifteenth centuries, the kingdoms of France, England, and Spain grew into sovereign states as their rulers consolidated their territories by establishing their primacy over rivals. Rulers made laws and imposed administrative unity to a degree that was unprecedented. They asserted their authority, but not domination, over the nobles of the territories they claimed. Royal authority directly touched more subjects than ever before. Rulers could raise and command armies, mint money, impose taxes, summon advisers, and appoint officials to represent their will.

The French kings, their territories clustered around Paris, had little real power during the medieval period. Until the mid-fifteenth century, the kings of England held Normandy, Brittany, Maine, Anjou, and Aquitaine, and the counts of Flanders held wealthy lands in what is now northern France and southern Belgium. During the Hundred Years' War (1337–1453), French kings raised the funds and armies necessary to expel the English from France (with the exception of the Channel port of Calais). During the last half of the fifteenth century, the French kings ended the *de facto* independence of large, prosperous provinces that were technically fiefs of the crown. In 1482, France absorbed Burgundy, whose powerful dukes were related to the kings of France, and a decade later the regent for Charles VIII (ruled 1483–1498) invaded Brittany, adding it to France. Through timely royal marriages and warfare, the French monarchs established the foundations for a stronger, more centralized monarchy.

England, too, emerged as a stronger monarchical state during the late medieval period, but with significant differences from its continental counterparts. The vassals of King John (ruled 1199–1216) and the people of London had rebelled against more taxes to finance his attempt to recover continental territories lost to France. In 1215, they forced him to sign the Magna Carta, the "great Charter of Liberties." John agreed to impose major taxes only with the permission of a "great council" that represented the barons and to cease hiring mercenaries when his barons refused to fight. Later in the century, King Edward I (ruled 1272–1307) summoned barons, bishops, and representatives from England's major towns in the hope of obtaining their agreement to provide funds for another war against the king of France. From that "parley," or "parliament," came the tradition in England of consultation with leading

King John of England provoked the ire of his vassals when he
attempted to raise taxes; they retaliated by forcing him to sign
the Magna Carta in 1215.

subjects and the origins of an English constitutional government that
constrained royal authority.

In Central Europe, the Holy Roman Empire was not really a sovereign
state. It dated from 962, the year when German nobles elected a ruler. By
the end of the thirteenth century, the principle that the Holy Roman
emperor would be elected, and not designated by the principle of heredity,
had been established. Considering themselves the successors of the
Roman Empire, the Holy Roman emperors saw themselves as the protectors of the papacy and of all of Christendom, which involved the emperor
in the stormy world of Italian politics.

The Holy Roman Empire encompassed 300 semi-autonomous states,
ranging from several large territories to a whole host of smaller states,
principalities, and free cities that carried out their own foreign policy and
fought wars. The emperor could not consolidate his authority, levy taxes,
or raise armies outside of his own hereditary estates. Increasingly, the
Holy Roman emperors were unable to enforce their will outside of the
boundaries of their hereditary estates at all.

The Austrian Habsburgs, the ruling house in the German Alpine
hereditary lands, had gradually extended their territories in the fourteenth and fifteenth centuries between the Danube River, the Adriatic
Sea, and the Little Carpathian Mountains. Beginning in 1438, when
the first Habsburg was elected Holy Roman emperor, until 1740 (when
the male line was extinguished), only Habsburgs held the ruling title of

Holy Roman emperor. Smaller states, such as the thirteen cantons of Switzerland, struggled to maintain their autonomy against rising Austrian power.

Developing State Structures

The growth of bureaucracies was one means by which rulers consolidated more effective power. Rulers had always had some kind of council, but the importance of their advisers grew in the fourteenth and fifteenth centuries. Chanceries, treasuries, and courts of law represented bureaucratization. Serving as royal officials, some humble men of talent began to reach positions of influence within states.

Rulers still earned revenue from their own lands. But in order to meet the expenses of their states, rulers drew income from taxation, sale of offices (posts in the service of the monarch that were often both lucrative and prestigious), government bonds, and confiscation of land from recalcitrant nobles. (Like other rulers, popes also centralized administration and finances, virtually selling posts.) Rulers also imposed taxes on salt, wine, and other goods, impositions from which nobles and clergy were generally exempt. States themselves in the sixteenth century became the great collectors and distributors of revenue. Moreover, the gradual growth of public debt was another sign of the increased power of states. Royal dependency on the loans of merchant-bankers enriched the latter, providing more capital for their ventures.

As they consolidated their realms in the fifteenth century, rulers could offer lords noble titles and offices (lucrative positions within their households or as government officials). Thus, with the strengthening of sovereign states, which in part entailed the loss of some noble judicial rights and the right to have armies of retainers, nobles depended more on monarchies for power and honor. More of them came to court and served as royal officials. Furthermore, the sale of offices, especially in France and Spain, ultimately encouraged loyalty to the throne.

Royal courts now adjudicated property disputes, gradually eroding noble jurisdiction over the king's subjects. Yet, in France and many of the German states, nobles retained rights of justice over peasants.

Rulers, surrounded by courtiers and councils, became more grand. One of the signs of the ascension of monarchical power was that thrones became hereditary, as rulers worked to consolidate their authority and territories. As people were apt to die young, such succession arrangements, which varied throughout Europe, mattered a great deal.

In the fifteenth century, regular channels for diplomacy emerged among the states of Europe. The Italian city-states were the first to exchange permanent resident ambassadors. By the middle of the fifteenth century, Florence, Milan, Venice, and the kingdom of Naples all routinely exchanged ambassadors, who provided news and other information but also represented the interests of their states. States sent diplomatic representatives to the courts of friend and rival alike.

Limits to State Authority

Significant constraints, however, still limited the authority of rulers. We have seen that the privileges of towns, established through the purchase of royal charters of financial immunity, tempered royal power. Some regions (for example, Navarre in Spain), nominally incorporated into realms, maintained autonomy through representative institutions. And, to be sure, distance and physical impediments such as mountains and vast plains also prevented the effective extension of royal authority.

Even more important was the tradition that assemblies of notable subjects who counseled the king had rights, and had to be consulted, as in the case of England cited above. In the thirteenth century, rulers had convoked assemblies of notable subjects to explain their policies and to ask for help and, in doing so, had strengthened and publicized their rule. Because they depended on those whom they assembled to provide military assistance when they required it, they also heard grievances. From this, parliaments, assemblies, diets, and estates developed, representing (depending on the place) nobles, clergy, towns, and, in several cases, commoners.

Early in the sixteenth century, an Italian exile told the king of France what the monarch would need to attack the duchy of Milan: "Three things are necessary: money; more money; and still more money." The most powerful states—France, Habsburg Austria, and Spain—could raise sizable armies with relative ease. But, to meet the extraordinary expenses of wartime, they increasingly borrowed money from wealthy banking families. Rulers also utilized subsidies from friendly powers, imposed special taxes and forced loans, and, especially in Spain and France, sold offices. Sixteenth-century inflation would make wars even more expensive.

Royal levies to finance warfare through direct taxation could only be imposed with the consent of those taxed. The dialogue between rulers and assemblies, and the strength and weakness of such representative bodies, would define the emergence and nature of modern government in the European states.

The princes of the German states had to ask assemblies of nobles for the right to collect excise taxes. These assemblies thus balanced royal authority. In Poland-Lithuania (a confederation created in 1386) and Hungary the noble assemblies were more important than royal authority. Indeed in Bohemia, the rights of towns partially balanced noble prerogatives. Rulers could suspend decisions of those "sovereign" bodies, yet such assemblies could not be completely ignored because rulers needed their support, or at least compliance, particularly in time of war.

The prerogatives of nobles and churchmen also impeded royal authority. Nobles and churchmen successfully resisted royal taxes, which fell on the poor (the vast majority of the population), whom no one represented. Nobles still had to be convinced or coerced to provide armies. Kings became, at least in principle, supreme judges (though not for the clergy, as ecclesiastics were generally tried in Church courts), royal courts offering litigants and petitioners a final appeal.

The struggle between rulers and the popes dated to the late eleventh century, when the popes and Holy Roman emperors had struggled for primacy. During the "lay investiture crisis," which began in 1060, the popes had contested the right of lay rulers to appoint bishops and invest them with signs of spiritual authority, normally a staff and a ring. (The dispute ended in 1122 when Emperor Henry V relinquished the imperial claim to the power to invest bishops with spiritual authority, and the pope recognized the emperor's right to give fiefs to the bishops once they had been consecrated, which left them with the status of vassals recognizing the lay authority of the emperor.) The clergy generally taught obedience to secular as well as ecclesiastical rulers. Furthermore, in the late medieval period, kings were able to further consolidate their power when popes granted the rulers of France, Spain, and some German towns certain rights over the clergy, including that of naming bishops.

Theodore Galle's *Nova reperta* ("New discoveries") celebrates the discovery of the New World and forms of the new technology (gunpowder, the compass, the clock, the saddle with stirrups).

TRANSFORMING DISCOVERIES

In the late Middle Ages, stunning developments in warfare, printing, and exploration would transform the continent of Europe. The effects of these separate revolutions would be so far-reaching that they can still be seen today.

Gunpowder, Warfare, and Armies

Warfare became more pervasive in the early modern period because of dynastic quarrels between rulers as they sought to consolidate or increase their territories. Although kings still depended on nobles to raise armies and to command on the battlefield, the face of battle was revolutionized in the late medieval period. Invented in China, gunpowder was brought to Europe in the thirteenth century by the Arabs. The use of gunpowder would transform warfare from "chiefly a matter of violent housekeeping" between lords and vassals to sometimes massive struggles between dynastic rivals. First used in battle in the early fourteenth century, gunpowder could propel arrows and, increasingly, lead bullets. Gunpowder soon became the explosive for a new weapon, the musket, which could be standardized in caliber and ammunition and for which clockmakers could produce spring-driven wheel locks that would function as firing mechanisms.

Gradually replacing the lance, sword, crossbow, and longbow in battle, the musket eroded the role of the noble as a privileged warrior since nobles could now be more easily shot off their horses by muskets than unseated by the lances of other nobles or brought down by arrows. Thus, the musket reduced the role of cavalry in battle as well as the advantage of the heavily armored knight. Cavalrymen now wore light armor, and, while they might well carry a lance, they also sometimes were armed with pistols. Pikemen, however, remained essential to any army; their thirteen-foot-long weapons, made of a long wooden pole topped by a sharp iron point, protected the infantry while soldiers reloaded. Furthermore, the furious attack of pikemen could tear apart the rows of riflemen as they knelt to reload.

Artillery also transformed warfare. Exploding shells could wound or kill many people at once. At the battle of Novara (1513) in northern Italy, at which Swiss troops defeated a French army, artillery fire killed 700 men in three minutes. Deadly bombardments during pitched battles had a devastating effect on the morale of the enemy. Naval battles grew fiercer as cannon replaced rams on warships. The sleek galleys that raced along the coast of the Mediterranean during the warm summer months gave way to ships large enough to transport heavy cannon. The threat from enemy artillery forced the construction of massive fortifications around towns, which left the defense with a solid advantage in warfare. Sieges lasted longer than ever before, and civilians were deemed "useless mouths" to feed during a siege. Furthermore, the victorious armies, frustrated by lengthy sieges, sometimes slaughtered the surviving civilian population.

Although frontier garrisons, artillery units, and the king's household guards were virtually the only true standing (permanent) armies, the size of armies during wars increased during the late fifteenth and the sixteenth centuries. During the Hundred Years' War (1337–1453), major battles were fought with between 7,000 and 15,000 troops on each side. During the struggles between the Austrian Habsburg and French Valois dynasties on the Italian peninsula in the fifteenth and sixteenth centuries, armies reached 25,000 in size. In France, some nobles began to serve not as obligated vassals, but as paid volunteers. Some nobles still had private armies but served their kings as commanders and cavalrymen.

Mercenaries, the original "free lances," increasingly replaced feudal levies (and urban militias, where they existed) in armies mobilized by rulers to defend or expand their territorial interests. These might include Albanians, Englishmen, Scots, Greeks, Poles, and especially Swiss pikemen, who won battles through their relentless and ferocious attacks. Mercenaries received modest, though irregular, pay and expected acceptable rations and the opportunity to pillage the towns they conquered. Assuming these conditions were met, they seem to have deserted far less frequently than soldiers recruited by states from their native population.

Yet most states had some kind of conscription, whether a formalized draft of men between the ages of fifteen and sixty or a hasty roundup of men when war approached. Loyal nobles, royal officials, and paid recruiters provided soldiers. Peasants made up more than three-quarters of armies, as they did the European population, followed by urban laborers and craftsmen. Criminals also ended up in armies, often as the price of their release from prison or from execution, though they might well carry with them forever a branded letter as part of their sentence (such as the letter "V" for the French word *voleur*—thief).

Conditions of military service were difficult at best. In addition to barely adequate lodging and food, infractions of rules were dealt with harshly, including the infamous and often fatal "running the gauntlet" through troops lined up on both sides armed with sticks or swords. Commanders dispensed justice without trial or appeal; sentences were carried out immediately. The severed heads of deserters or other serious offenders were impaled on pikes for several days at the entry to a camp, sending a clear message to would-be transgressors.

Except for royal guards, artillery units, and other specialized forces, uniforms were rare in any army, although most soldiers sported some type of identification, such as an armband or a tunic bearing a national or regional symbol like the English red cross, the barred cross of Lorraine, or the lion of Lyon.

Epidemics and disease—dysentery and typhoid, among others—carried off far more than did wounds received in battle. But casualty figures were also alarming, however inaccurately kept. The wounded often died from inadequate—even for the time—medical treatment and from neglect.

The Printing Press and the Power of the Printed Word

The advent of printing in Europe in the fifteenth century in some ways marked the end of the medieval period. The invention of woodblock printing and paper had occurred in China in the eighth century; both reached Europe from the Arab world via Spain in the thirteenth century. Before the arrival of these technologies, monks and scribes had copied books on parchment sheets; a single copy of the Bible required about 170 calfskins or 300 sheepskins. Because it was much cheaper than parchment, paper more readily accommodated merchants, officials, and scholars. But the process of copying itself remained slow. Cosimo de' Medici, the Florentine banker and patron of Renaissance art, hired 200 scribes to copy 200 volumes (most of which had religious themes) in two years' time.

All this changed in the fifteenth century when Flemish craftsmen invented a kind of oil-based ink. This and the innovation of a wooden handpress made possible the invention of movable metal type in the German cathedral town of Mainz in about 1450 by, among several others, Johannes Gutenberg (c. 1395–1468), who printed stunningly beautiful Latin Bibles that are still treasured today.

Printing shops began to spread in the 1460s to other German towns, reaching the Italian states, Bohemia, France, and the Netherlands by the end of the decade, and Spain and England in the 1470s (see Map 1.2). By the beginning of the sixteenth century, more than 6 million books had been printed, with the average edition running between 200 to 1,000 copies. In 1500, about 35,000 books were published each year in Europe, and a century later the number had jumped to between 150,000 and 200,000 books.

Books provided scholars with identical ancient and medieval texts to discuss and critique. Accounts of discoveries and adventures in the New World filtered across Europe from Spain, England, and France. The number of scholarly libraries—which were really just private collections—grew rapidly. New professions developed: librarians, booksellers, publishers, typesetters, and editors. Moreover, with the greater dissemination of knowledge came an increase in the number of universities, rising from twenty in 1300 to about seventy in 1500.

More people learned how to read, although literate individuals remained far in the minority. In Florence and other prosperous cities, the rate of literacy may have been relatively high, although in the Italian city-states as a whole it is unlikely that more than 1 percent of workers and peasants could read and write. The literate population of the German states in 1500 was about 3 or 4 percent. But among the upper classes many more people developed the habit of reading, as Bibles, dictionaries, and other books could be purchased, discussed, and debated.

MAP 1.2 SPREAD OF PRINTING THROUGH EUROPE, 1450–1508 Towns and dates at which printing shops were established throughout Europe.

Not all that was published pleased lay and ecclesiastic leaders, and printing made censorship considerably more difficult. No longer could destroying one or two manuscripts suffice to root out an idea. Thus, Pope Alexander VI warned in a bull in 1501: "The art of printing is very useful insofar as it furthers the circulation of useful and tested books; but it can be very harmful if it is permitted to widen the influence of pernicious works. It will therefore be necessary to maintain full control over the printers so that they may be prevented from bringing into print writings which are antagonistic to the Catholic faith or which are likely to cause trouble to believers."

Exploration and Conquest of the New World

By the last decade of the fifteenth century, the inhabitants of the Iberian Peninsula already had several centuries of navigational and sailing accomplishments behind them. The Portuguese had captured a foothold on the Moroccan coast in 1415, beginning two centuries of expansion. Early in the fifteenth century, they began to explore the west coast of Africa and had taken Madeira and the Azores islands in the Atlantic. Their goal was to break Muslim and Venetian control of European access to Asian spices and silk.

King Ferdinand and Queen Isabella of Spain had initially rejected the request of the Genoese cartographer and merchant Christopher Columbus (1451–1506), who sought financial backing for an ocean voyage to reach the Indies. In 1492, however, fearing that Portuguese vessels might be the first to reach the great wealth of Asia, the royal couple finally consented to give their full support to the expedition.

Late in 1492, Columbus set sail with three ships. He believed the earth was a perfect sphere, and since Africa stood in the way of a voyage sailing to the east, he thought it possible to reach the Orient by sailing west across the Atlantic Ocean, which he believed to be quite narrow. After more than nine weeks on the open seas, the small fleet reached not Asia but rather the small Caribbean island of San Salvador in the Americas. He then also reached Cuba and finally Hispaniola (now the Dominican Republic and Haiti). "What on earth have you come seeking so far away?" he was asked. "Christians and spices," he replied. But he also probably believed that he would find gold, and asked the Indians he encountered on the shore in sign language if they knew where some could be found. Columbus was impressed with the beauty of Hispaniola (although he remained convinced that he had discovered islands near India) and the "docility" of the indigenous people. Yet, in the absence of gold, he suggested that the crown could make Hispaniola profitable by selling its people as slaves, a looming tragedy for native Americans. Columbus, whose greatest contribution was to find a way across the sea using the trade winds, made three subsequent voyages of discovery, the last beginning in 1502, after which he gave up his search for a passage to Asia.

Portugal, a much poorer state than Spain, struggled to defend its fledgling empire and trade routes against Spanish encroachments. In 1498, Portuguese explorer Vasco da Gama (c. 1460–1524) reached India; the cargo of spices he brought back to Lisbon paid for his costly expedition sixty times over. The Portuguese maritime route stretched around the coast of Africa across the Indian Ocean to the South China Sea. This route could now compete with the overland spice and silk routes that had long linked Europe to the markets of the East. An Indonesian ruler remarked of the Portuguese adventurers, "The fact that these people journey so far from home to conquer territory indicates clearly that there must be very little justice and a great deal of greed among them." This had made them "fly all over the waters in order to acquire possessions that God did not give them."

In 1493, Pope Alexander VI divided the non-Christian world into zones for Spanish and Portuguese exploration and exploitation (see Map 1.3). He awarded Portugal all of sub-Saharan Africa and Asia; Spain, the pope's ally, received most of the Americas, although Portugal claimed Brazil, which became the largest colony in the Americas. But the practical problems of drawing boundaries down the middle of oceans with primitive navigational instruments resulted in zones of contested territory. No one asked the indigenous populations what they thought.

Soon more and more Spanish explorers reached the Americas. Vasco Núñez de Balboa (c. 1475–1519) established Spanish sovereignty over what is now Panama. The island of Cuba, in turn, fell to the Spanish, and then served as a staging point for the conquest of Mexico by Hernando Cortés (1485–1547), which opened a new chapter in European expansion. Cortés, after landing on the coast of Mexico in 1519, went to see the Aztec emperor, Montezuma, who sent him away, although he later sent him gifts of gold and silver. Determined to conquer Mexico, Cortés formed alliances with Montezuma's non-Aztec peoples, who naively hoped that Cortés might help them achieve their independence. The Spanish adventurer then conquered Mexico with no more than sixteen horses and six hundred soldiers, but with 100,000 Native American allies. Further south, Francisco Pizarro (c. 1476–1541) led his men in the conquest of the Inca Empire in Peru. Although the Incas were a culturally rich people, they had never seen iron or steel weapons before, nor did they have draft animals. When Pizarro's horses lost their shoes in Peru and there was no iron available to replace them, he had them shod in silver.

The Portuguese arrive in Japan in 1542.

MAP 1.3 EXPLORATION AND CONQUEST, 1492–1542 Pope Alexander VI divided the non-Christian world into zones for Spanish and Portuguese exploration and exploitation. Portuguese, Spanish, French, and English explorers set out to find new routes to Asia, the New World, and around the world.

The victory of the conquistadors (conquerors) was the victory of steel-bladed swords over stone-bladed swords. Moreover, the surprise element of cannon and guns also contributed to their victory in the Americas and in Southeast Asia. A witness to a Portuguese attack in 1511 related, "the noise of the cannon was as the noise of thunder in the heavens and the flashes of fire of their guns were like flashes of lightning in the sky: and the noise of their matchlocks was like that of ground-nuts popping in the frying-pan." In addition to their ability to kill, guns had a dramatic shock effect.

Steeped in tales of crusading chivalry and conquest, the conquerors who followed Columbus to the Americas set out looking for adventure and wealth. Cortés, for example, was the son of a modest Castilian noble family. "We came here to serve God and the king," said one, "but also to get rich." Unlike Columbus, most conquerors died young, far from home, their dreams of wealth shattered by the harsh realities of life in what seemed to them a strange and often inhospitable world. Ferdinand Magellan (c. 1480–1521), the Portuguese-born explorer, was killed by angry islanders on a Pacific beach. His crew nonetheless circumnavigated the globe, having proven that a southwest passage to India did exist and returning in 1522 to Seville.

Although many of the conquistadors died in the New World, many times more of the native people they encountered perished as a result of contact with the Europeans. At one point during his conquests, Cortés and his small army had to fight their way out of the Aztec capital of Tenochtitlán (present-day Mexico City), then larger than any other European city except Constantinople. But even after the Spanish left, the smallpox they had brought with them killed rampantly, bringing massive death on the heels of military conquest. The indigenous population of Mexico fell from about 25 million—or more—in 1520 to perhaps as little as 1 million in 1600. The native population of Peru fell from about 7 million in 1500 to half a million in 1600. Other European diseases, including measles, typhus, and bubonic plague, also decimated the native population. In Guatemala, a Mayan Indian kept a chronicle of the ravages of European disease among his people: "Great was the stench of the dead. After our fathers and grandfathers succumbed, half of the people fled to the fields. The dogs and vultures devoured the bodies. The mortality was terrible. Your grandfather died, and with him died the sons of the king and his brothers and kinsmen. So it was that we became orphans, oh my sons! So we became when we were young. All of us were thus. We were born to die."

In turn, the Indians gave the Spanish syphilis (which may have originated in Asia). It spread with Spanish mercenaries who had fought in Naples two years after Columbus's voyage to America (the French called syphilis "the Neapolitan disease," while the Neapolitans referred to it as "the French disease").

The first meeting between Hernando Cortés and Aztec Emperor Montezuma in 1519.

The exchange of disease was a tragic consequence of the meeting between the Old and New Worlds. But there were beneficial exchanges as well. Before the arrival of Europeans, there were no domesticated animals larger than the llama and alpaca in the Americas, and little animal protein in the Indian diet. Spaniards brought horses and cattle with them. Sheep had accompanied Columbus in 1493 on his second journey. Pigs also were carried on the relatively small ships of discovery and conquest. Taking up little room on board ship, they not only could be eaten but provided the additional benefit of manure for farming once the explorers had gone ashore. The 350 pigs brought to Cuba by Columbus had multiplied to over 30,000 by 1514. But they ate their way through much forest land and also eroded the indigenous agricultural terrace system, upsetting the ecological balance of conquered lands.

Every year the Spanish galleons returned with more riches, as if "the hand of God was guiding them." They returned home filled with tobacco, potatoes, new varieties of beans, cacao, chili peppers, potatoes, and tomatoes (not until the early eighteenth century, however, could the first European recipes with tomato sauce be found in Italy). They brought back to Europe Indian maize, which they planted and which provided feed for farm animals. These crops had significant, positive effects on European demography, leading to the availability of more food and an accompanying population increase. In turn, the Spaniards planted wheat, barley, rice, and oats in their colonies. By 1600, most of the important food plants of Eurasia and Africa were cultivated in the Spanish Americas.

In 1565, a Spanish galleon completed global transoceanic trade by sailing across the Pacific Ocean from Manila to unload cinnamon on the coast of Mexico. Thereafter, Spanish ships returned with silver, which could purchase silks, porcelain, spices, jade, and mother-of-pearl, which Chinese junks carried to the Philippines, and which oceangoing ships carried to Acapulco. Shipping routes led from Seville, which had been part of Moorish Andalusia until the Castilian reconquest, to the Caribbean Sea and to the ports of Veracruz in Mexico and Cartagena in Colombia. They supplied the American colonists with European goods, and on the return route carried Mexican and Peruvian silver that replenished the coffers of European princes and merchants. Saluting Acapulco in 1604, Spanish poet Bernardo de Balbueña wrote, "In thee Spain is joined with China, Italy with Japan, and ultimately a whole world in disciplined commerce." All five continents—Europe, Asia, Africa, North America, and South America—moved closer together in reciprocal economic relationships that represented the beginnings of a globalization of trade.

The Europeans sought not only to trade with the people in the New World but also to acquire permanent territories. Thus, Spanish legal documents affecting the new colonies, drawn up in Spain, declared that Indians would keep all lands they already held, but that all other territories henceforth belonged either to the crowns of Spain or were to be divided up among the conquerors as booty. The conquistadors built new towns, placing the church, town hall, and prison around a central marketplace (*plaza*).

In return for the pope's blessing of the colonial enterprise, missionaries began to arrive, hoping to convert the Indians to Christianity. The harsh reality of the colonial experience for the natives, however, was largely untempered by the good intentions of some of the missionaries. "For this kind of people," snapped a Portuguese priest in Brazil in 1563, "there is no better way of preaching than the sword and the rod of iron." However, at least in principle, the missionary impulse remained strong: one monk argued that souls being lost to Satan by Martin Luther's Reformation (see Chapter 3) were being balanced by conversions in the Americas.

Europeans sought to impose their culture on the peoples they conquered, although Christian teaching made only limited headway in India and virtually none in China. Unlike its view of Muslims, the Church did not consider Indians infidels, but rather as innocents who could be taught Christian beliefs. "Are these Indians not men?" asked a Dominican priest in Santo Domingo in a sermon to shocked colonists in 1511, "Do they not have rational souls? Are you not obliged to love them as you love yourselves?" A papal pronouncement depicted the Indians as "true men . . . capable not only of understanding the Catholic faith, but also, according to our information, desirous of receiving it." In the 1590s, a Franciscan friar boasted that he had built over 200 churches and baptized more than 70,000 Indians. Where Christianity was successful, as it ultimately was in much of Latin America, Christian belief sometimes merged with local religious deities, customs, and shrines to create a distinctive form of Christianity.

Obligatory labor service, enforced more than occasionally by brutality, at first formed the relationship between rulers and the ruled. The Church and the crown periodically tried to protect the Indians against the harsh treatment accorded them by many of their Spanish countrymen in the name of profit. Bishop Bartolomé de Las Casas (1474–1566), whose father had accompanied Columbus on his second voyage to the Americas and who had himself been a conquistador before becoming a priest, spoke out against the treatment of Indians. He saluted the "marvelous government, laws, and good customs" of the Mayas of Central America, whom he wanted placed under the authority of the Church.

As the Indian population was depleted through disease, overwork, and brutality, the Spanish looked for new sources of labor. By the fifteenth century, Portuguese traders along the coast of West Africa had begun to make profits selling Africans as domestic servants in Lisbon or as sugar plantation workers in the Portuguese Atlantic islands. The slave-trading network was based on chieftains and traders in African kingdoms, merchants in Seville and Lisbon, settlers in Mexico and Peru, and Brazilian sugar growers. Domestic slavery still existed in Italy, Spain, and Muscovy in the sixteenth century, as well as in the Arab world, and some Indians in the New World also had slaves. The Spaniards believed that Africans could better survive the brutally difficult work and hot climate of America. By 1600, 275,000 black slaves had been transported to Europe and America, and five times that many would be shipped in the next century.

Gradually, more Spanish settlers arrived to populate the American colonies, including small traders, shoemakers, blacksmiths, swordsmiths, and masons. In Paraguay, the governor asked that no lawyers be allowed to emigrate, "because in newly settled countries they encourage dissension and litigation." In Mexico, Spaniards asked that "his Majesty be pleased not to suffer any scholars or men of letters to come into this country, to throw us into confusion with their learning, quibbling and books." By the mid-sixteenth century, about 150,000 Spaniards had crossed to America and by the end of the century, about 240,000 Spaniards had migrated there, and about the same number of Portuguese had gone to Asia. Most of these emigrants never returned to the Old World.

In 1552, a Spanish official wrote King Charles V (ruled 1516–1556, Holy Roman emperor 1519–1558) that the discovery of the East and West Indies was "the greatest event since the creation of the world, apart from the incarnation and death of Him who created it." But Michel de Montaigne (1533–1592), a French writer who had met Indians brought back from Brazil, offered another view in 1588, when he observed that "so many goodly cities [were] ransacked and razed; so many nations destroyed and made desolate; so infinite millions of harmless peoples of all sexes, states, and ages, massacred, ravaged and put to the sword; and the richest, the fairest and the best part of the world topsy-turvied, ruined and defaced for the traffic of pearls and pepper."

CONCLUSION

The economic and political structures of early modern Europe drew on the dynamism of the medieval period. Demographic vitality finally overcame the catastrophic losses brought by the Black Death. Within Europe, commerce and manufacturing expanded. Mediterranean traders roamed as far as the Middle East and even Asia. And, although much of Central Europe and the Italian peninsula remained a hodgepodge of small states, rulers in France, England, and Spain had consolidated their authority, and sovereign monarchical states began to emerge.

Above all, three salient movements of change brought the Middle Ages to an end. The first was the Renaissance, or cultural rebirth, which began in the mid-fourteenth century in the Italian city-states (see Chapter 2). The commercial prosperity of Florence, above all, but also of Venice and other independent city-states made possible this period of extraordinary accomplishment in literature and painting. The invention of printing began to transform one culture after another. Second, the exploration and colonization of the New World would ultimately help end the Mediterranean Sea's role as the center of European prosperity and would lead to Spain's emergence as a world power (see Chapters 5 and 6). In the meantime, the discovery of gunpowder changed the face of battle. Third, the Reformation (see Chapter 3), which began in the second decade of the sixteenth century, challenged the unity of the Roman Catholic Church and its dominance in Western and Central Europe. Thus, by 1500, in the waning years of the Renaissance, the stage had been set for the trends that would shape early modern Europe.

CHAPTER 2

THE RENAISSANCE

In 1508, Pope Julius II summoned Michelangelo from Florence to the papal city of Rome. He commissioned the artist to paint frescoes (paintings on plaster) on the ceiling of the new Sistine Chapel, a ceremonial chapel next to the papal residence in the Vatican. With some reluctance (since he considered himself primarily a sculptor), Michelangelo agreed to undertake the project. He signed a contract that stipulated a payment of 3,000 ducats and began work that very day in May.

During the long, difficult years of intense creativity, Michelangelo often lay on his back, staring at the ceiling (still the best position from which to study his masterpiece), before climbing up the scaffolding to work. His frescoes, depicting Creation, Original Sin, the Flood, and the ancestors of Christ, are a triumph of religious painting. However, Pope Julius II, offended by the nude figures in the *Last Judgment* frescoes, ordered painters to cover the nudes with fig leaves. As a result, Michelangelo left Rome in disgust. He left behind him what is arguably the most beautiful pictorial ensemble in Western painting.

Michelangelo's work represents the epitome of art during the Renaissance, a time of cultural rebirth. From about 1330 to 1530, the city-states of the Italian peninsula emerged as the intellectual and artistic centers of Europe. It was a period during which classical texts were rediscovered, thereby reviving the ideas, architecture, arts, and values of ancient Greece and Rome. By celebrating the beauty of nature and the dignity of mankind, Renaissance artists and scholars helped shape the intellectual and cultural history of the modern world. During the fifteenth century, Michelangelo, as well as Leonardo da Vinci and many other Renaissance sculptors and painters, enjoyed the patronage of wealthy families and produced some of the immortal works of the European experience. From about 1490 to 1530, Rome was the center of a final period of artistic innovation, the High Renaissance, during which time the popes, including Julius II, commissioned paintings, sculptures, and churches.

Yet, weakened by internal political turmoil, the Italian city-states were ravaged by foreign invaders beginning in 1494. Unable to resist French invasion and then Spanish domination, after 1530 the city-states were no longer able to support artistic glories, and the Renaissance ended in a mood of discouragement.

THE CITY-STATES OF THE ITALIAN PENINSULA

The city-states were the fundamental political unit of the Italian peninsula, the most urbanized part of the Western world, even though the vast majority of the population of the Italian peninsula still lived in the countryside. In 1200, there were several hundred independent city-states on the Italian peninsula; gradually, however, that number was reduced, as many were absorbed as subject territories by more powerful city-states. A century later, at least twenty-three cities in the northern and central parts of the peninsula had populations of more than 20,000. It was within these city-states that the achievements of the Renaissance took place.

Thriving Economies

The economic prosperity and social dynamism of the city-states made the cultural achievements of the Renaissance possible. The city-states had

The city-states of Renaissance Italy were the most urbanized part of the Western world. Pictured here is the Loggia dei Lanzi, the principal gathering place in Florence.

become independent and prosperous because of the expansion of commerce during the eleventh and twelfth centuries. The Italian peninsula formed a natural point of exchange between East and West.

Intensively studied in the twelfth and thirteenth centuries, Roman law provided a framework for order and the development of political life within the Italian city-states. Moreover, the Roman Empire had depended on a network of largely autonomous cities and towns, particularly in the plains of the northern part of the peninsula. These had been linked by a system of roads, unrivaled in Europe, all of which, as the saying goes, did indeed eventually lead to Rome.

The people of the Italian peninsula had suffered the ravages of the Black Death and the other epidemics of the fourteenth and fifteenth centuries, but the ensuing economic recession of the fourteenth century, which led to declines in manufacturing and population in the central Italian region of Tuscany, did not affect much of the northern part of the peninsula, which still prospered. Drawing its wool from England and Spain, Florence's textile industry employed about 30,000 workers. The finished Florentine cloth and woolen goods were then traded throughout the lands of the Mediterranean, Burgundy, Flanders, England, and as far as Asia. Agriculture thrived in the broad river valleys of Tuscany and Lombardy. The production of grains, vegetables, and wine, aided by the drainage of swamps and marshes and by irrigation, not only fed the urban population but also provided an agricultural surplus that could be invested in commerce and manufacturing. The proximity of Mediterranean trade routes bolstered international trade and small-scale manufacturing and brought prosperity to ambitious Italian merchants.

The development of banking during the early fourteenth century helped finance internal trade and international commerce. By the beginning of the fifteenth century, the Church's condemnation of usury no longer was taken to apply to banking, as long as the rates of interest were not considered excessive. Florence's gold florin became a standard currency in European trading centers. The bankers of that city, with agents in Avignon and many other cities throughout the trading network, were central to European commerce and monarchical and papal finances. Unlike traders elsewhere in Europe, Florentine merchants had broad experience with bills of exchange and deposit, which provided credit to purchasers. There were, however, risks to such loans. In the fifteenth century, the king of England forced Florentine merchants to loan him money, or face expulsion from the realm and lose all their assets there. But he defaulted on the loans after his invasion of France failed during the Hundred Years' War, and several major merchant Florentine companies went into bankruptcy.

Venice and Genoa were also major trading and banking cities, as well as centers of shipbuilding and insurance. Each city had long traded with the East Indies and the Far East. Venice, in particular, had been a major center of trade and transcultural exchange between the Christian West and

This miniature depicts the Piazzetta of the Republic of Venice, with all the activity of a major Adriatic port.

Muslim East since the eighth century. Venice linked sea routes with the long overland routes to Constantinople through the desolate mountains of the Balkans. Merchants hedged their bets on whether their shipments would fall victim to the sudden Mediterranean storms, to roving pirates, or to some other mishap on the overland route through Central Asia. The merchants carried fine woolens and linen from the Italian peninsula and northern Europe, as well as metals, to the East. They returned with cotton, silk, and, above all, spices, including pepper, cinnamon, nutmeg, ginger, and sugar, which arrived via Alexandria or Constantinople from the East Indies, luxury goods to awaken the palates of wealthy Europeans. Merchants from both East and West used towns in Crimea, a peninsula extending into the northern Black Sea, as intermediary points for trade from Muscovy, Persia, India, and China (see Map 2.1).

Merchant capitalism eroded the power of the nobility by expanding the ranks and influence of townsmen. The wealth and status of urban merchants—although nobles also engaged in trade—allowed them to dominate the oligarchies that ruled the city-states. Prosperity increased the strong sense of municipal identity and pride; the Florentine political

MAP 2.1 REACH OF TRADE DURING THE FIFTEENTH CENTURY Major trade routes, both by land and sea, led from the Italian city-states of Venice, Genoa, and Florence, as well as from northern Europe and the Baltic regions. The Italian city-states formed a natural point of exchange between East and West. Products that were traded are shown at their source.

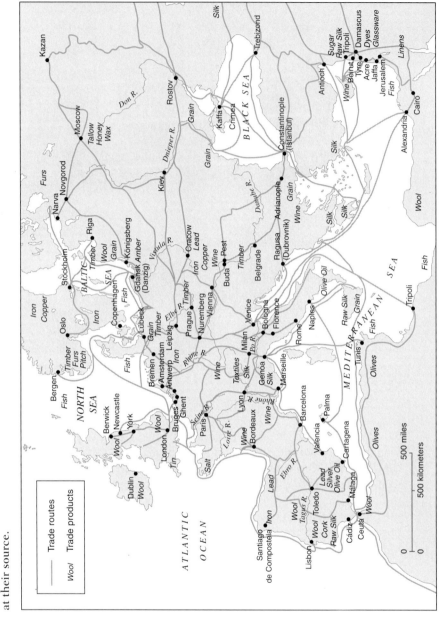

Trade routes
Wool Trade products

theorist Niccolò Machiavelli insisted, "I love my native city more than my own soul."

Social Structure

The social structure of the Italian city-states resembled that of other urban centers of trade and manufacturing in England, France, Flanders, and Holland. In the city-states, the *pòpolo grasso,* or "fat people," were the elite, including nobles, wealthy merchants, and manufacturers. The *mediòcri* were the middling sort, including smaller merchants and master artisans. The *pòpolo minuto,* or "little people," made up the bulk of the urban population. In cities, artisans and laborers were burdened by high taxes on consumption. Urban elites owned much of the richest land of the hinterland, which was worked by tenant farmers, sharecroppers, and agricultural laborers, as well as by peasant landowners. In the northern and central part of the Italian peninsula, most peasants were free to be miserably poor, while in the southern part many still owed obligations to their lords.

The "fat people" of the city-states comprised no more than 5 percent of the population. The great patricians assumed the status of princes of their cities, whether as dukes, cardinals, or, in the case of Rome, as the pope himself. Although social differences remained sharp in Italian city-states, as everywhere, commercial wealth made possible some degree of social mobility, above all in Florence, the wealthiest city. New families, enriched by commerce, rose into the ruling elite, although opportunities to do so had declined noticeably by the end of the fifteenth century.

An elaborate and highly ritualized etiquette based upon mutual flattery maintained social distance. The wealthiest families became even richer despite the recession that extended throughout much of the fourteenth and fifteenth centuries; their prosperity made them even more eager not to be taken for anyone of more modest station. Thus, one of the powerful dukes of Milan insisted that his wife be called *Illustrissima* ("Illustrious One"). Flattery and subservience could be found in every greeting, and in every letter penned to a prince: "Nothing in the world pleases me more than your commands," and the ominous "I live only insofar as I am in your excellency's graces," which was sometimes true enough.

Urban patriarchs dominated their cities through power and patronage. They dispensed titles, privileges, and cash as they pleased. The duke of Ferrara affirmed his power by going door to door once a year to "beg" on behalf of the poor, an inversion of reality that served to define his authority and the subordination of everyone else. But princes and patriarchs also ruled through intimidation, occasionally eliminating enemies with astonishing cruelty.

Renaissance Political Life

The originality of the Italian city-states during the Renaissance lay not only in their remarkable artistic accomplishments but also in their precociously innovative forms of political structure. The organization of some of the city-states into constitutional republics was closely linked to the cultural achievements of the Renaissance. Nonetheless, there was nothing democratic about the city-states of Renaissance Italy, for the elites had brutally crushed the popular uprisings of artisans and shopkeepers that occurred in Siena and a number of other towns during the fourteenth century.

Fourteenth- and fifteenth-century republics were constitutional oligarchies dominated by the most powerful families who filled the executive bodies, legislative or advisory councils, and special commissions that governed each city-state. The percentage of male citizens enjoying the right to vote ranged from about 2 percent in fifteenth-century Venice to 12 percent in fourteenth-century Bologna, the former percentage seeming most representative of the restricted nature of political rights in Renaissance Italy. Venice, Siena, Lucca, and Florence (at least until the waning days of domination by the powerful Medici family) were the most stable oligarchic republics of Renaissance Italy; Genoa, Bologna, and Perugia went back and forth between republican and despotic governments (see Map 2.2).

Some of the other city-states became outright hereditary despotisms (*sig-*

Portrait of Francesco Sforza, one of the elite *pòpolo grasso.*

nori) run by a single family. Milan, a despotism under the control of the Visconti family, had grown prosperous from metallurgy and textile manufacturing. Francesco Sforza, a *condottieri* (mercenary of common origins), who had married the illegitimate daughter of the last Visconti duke in 1447, helped overthrow the republic less than three years later. Sforza imposed his family's rule with the support of Milanese nobles. The Sforza family thereafter skillfully played off rivalries between other powerful families, sometimes implementing their will with sheer force. The duke of Milan tolerated a council of 900 men drawn from the city's leading citizens, but he appointed magistrates and officials—and in general ruled—as he pleased. Likewise, princely families, such as the Este family of Ferrara and the Gonzaga family of Mantua, ran the smaller city-states.

By contrast, Venice, an energetic, prosperous Adriatic port city of lagoons and canals built on a number of small islands, remained in principle a republic. Its constitution offered a balance of political interests: the doge, an official elected for life by the Senate, served as an executive authority whose prerogatives were not that far from those of a monarch. The Great Council, consisting of about 2,500 enfranchised patricians, elected the Senate, which represented the nobility, an increasing number of whom were ennobled merchants living in elegantly decorated houses facing the canals. No one represented the poor, more than half the population of Venice.

Like the monarchies beyond the Alps, the Italian city-states developed small, efficient state bureaucracies, as the despots or oligarchs (a few men or families running the government) of each city improved the effectiveness of state administration. Thus, Florence and Venice had special committees responsible for foreign affairs and commerce. Many offices were sold or filled by members of the leading families linked by marriages. Personal relations between powerful families, for example, between the Medicis and the Sforza, facilitated diplomacy. The Medici engaged financial specialists for the management of the fiscal policies of their city and their family, although the latter, to the detriment of Florence, almost always took precedence. ("Better a city ruined," said Cosimo de' Medici, "than lost.")

The *condottieri* were central to the political and military situation in Italy. A military ethos permeated the courts of the Italian princes. A young prince learned military exercises, including jousting (horseback combat with long lances that could occasionally be deadly), and he began to hunt, sometimes using falcons. Some dukes hired themselves and their private armies out to the highest bidders, such as powerful Italian princes, the king of France, or the Holy Roman emperor.

Renaissance princes and oligarchs surrounded themselves with an imposing retinue of attendants. The court of Urbino, not particularly wealthy compared to some of the others, employed a staff of 355 people. This number included 45 counts of the duchy, 17 noblemen of various pedigrees, 22 pages, 5 secretaries, 19 chamber grooms, 5 cooks, 19 waiters, 50 stable hands, and 125 servants and jacks-of-all-trades, including the *galoppini*, who galloped around on a variety of errands.

Florence, Milan, Venice, Naples, and the Papal States were as aggressive as France and the other monarchies beyond the Alps. They dominated their weaker neighbors through force, intimidation, and alliances, picking them off one by one, as in chess. When they were not battling each other, Florence and Venice combined to limit Milanese control to Lombardy, while establishing their own authority over their respective regions. Venice controlled territory from the Alps to the Po River. Genoa, bitterly divided between merchant factions and nobles living in the hills above the Mediterranean port, struggled to maintain its autonomy because it lay

MAP 2.2 CITY-STATES IN RENAISSANCE ITALY, 1494   The city-state was the fundamental political unit of the Italian peninsula; the number of city-states was reduced as many of them were absorbed by the more powerful city-states.

physically exposed to more powerful Milan, as well as to the kingdom of France.

The Papal States, which bordered Tuscany east of the Apennines and to their south, functioned like any other city-state. The pope, too, was a temporal, as well as a spiritual, prince. He was elected for life by cardinals, the highest bishops of the Church, who were, in turn, appointed by the pope. Like monarchs and urban oligarchs, popes had to contend with the ambitious nobles of the Papal States. They, too, conspired and sought alliances against other city-states. The eternal city was only the peninsula's eighth largest city in the late fourteenth century, ruled by a beleaguered papacy amid distant echoes of past glories. The city-states were increasingly freed from the authority and interference of the papacy. This began with the "Babylonian Captivity" (1309–1378), when the popes lived in Avignon under the direct influence of the king of France and, for a time, a rival pontiff claimed authority from Rome (see Chapter 3). The declining role of the papacy in temporal Italian affairs further aided the rise of Florence, Milan, and Venice.

Florence: Anatomy of a Renaissance City

Florence was the cradle of the Italian Renaissance, fulfilling the prediction of the Tuscan poet Dante Alighieri (1265–1321) that a new civilization would arise on the Italian peninsula. Indeed, early in the Renaissance, the language of the region, Tuscan, emerged as the "courtly language" used by an increasing number of educated Italians beyond Tuscany.

The walled city dominated its rich hinterland of gentle hills and prosperous plains. The Arno River, which flows through Florence, though occasionally turbulent after heavy spring rain, was navigable from the Mediterranean port of Pisa except during the summer months. In 1406, Florence conquered Pisa, another center of textile production, once a worthy challenger of Genoa for maritime trade but now divided into quarreling factions. This window on the sea aided Florentine commerce, enabling the city to become a maritime power.

Several other factors contributed to Florence's success in becoming the center of the revival of classical learning. Roman law and Latin had long

A drawing of Florence in about 1490. Note the Duomo in the center.

been the foundation of training of Florentine ecclesiastics, lawyers, and notaries. Although the influence of the Church remained strong, the Medici rulers encouraged a cultural movement that had strong secular elements. Both Christian and secular traditions, then, infused Florentine civic life.

The combination of a dynamic craft tradition and an economy closely tied to the production of luxury goods made Florence receptive to artistic innovation. The city honored the accomplishments of its citizens—including cultural achievements. Lastly, Florence's reputation as a relatively educated city helped attract talented newcomers from rural Tuscany and other regions. It had many schools, including a university, and boasted a rate of literacy probably unmatched in Europe. In the fifteenth century, at least 8,000 children in a population of 100,000 attended church and civic schools, as well as private academies. It was said that even laborers could recite Dante's verses by heart.

The bell tower of the Palazzo Vecchio, the government building completed early in the fourteenth century, watched over the dynamic center of international banking, commerce, and the manufacture of cloth, woolens, silk, and jewelry. By the middle of the fourteenth century, Florence had become the fifth largest city in Europe. Before the plagues of the 1340s, about 100,000 people lived there. After falling by half, Florence's population revived during the next half-century, equaling that of London and Seville, but not Venice and Naples, each of which then had at least 100,000 inhabitants.

Most Florentine neighborhoods remained relatively heterogeneous in social composition. Increasingly grand patrician palaces were physically set off and protected from the crowded street and the anonymity of medieval buildings that stretched along in rows. Fancy, flamboyant dress also distinguished the wealthy people from those of lesser means. So, too, did the unprecedented quest by patrician families for elegant, crafted furnishings, such as chimney pieces, chests, and sideboards, and other objects, including candlesticks and bird cages. Covered balconies and top-floor terraces opened onto the streets. More modest and poor families lived not far away, yet a world apart, piled into small, sparsely furnished rooms in buildings up to five stories tall.

Wealthy merchants, the *grandi,* governed Florence with the support of merchants, lawyers, and craftsmen of more modest means. Organized into seven major guilds, the merchants and manufacturers, particularly the cloth merchants, kept the fourteen lesser guilds (whose members included artisans and shopkeepers) in a subordinate position. The guilds elected the nine members of government, the *Signoria,* which administered the city. The *Signoria* proposed laws and conducted foreign affairs. Its members led the processions through the narrow streets during the various religious holidays. Two assemblies, the Council of the People and the Council of the Commune, served as a legislature. Citizens wealthy enough

A Florentine council in session.

to pay taxes elected the 600 to 700 members of these councils, which met as needed to approve the decisions of the *Signoria*.

During the fifteenth century, while Florence maintained its leading role in shaping the culture of the Renaissance, the business of government went on in the palaces of the wealthiest citizens of Florence. The elite feared that the poor would revolt as they had in 1378 in the uprising known as the Ciompi, or "the wooden shoes," so named because many of the laborers could only afford such footwear. Suffering from economic hardship and aided by disgruntled members of the lower guilds, the cloth workers had risen up in a bloody insurrection in the hope of expanding the guild system already in power. The possibility of another uprising of the poor thereafter remained in the memory of the "fat people," causing them to keep the workers in a position of resentful subservience.

Timely marriages, and thus alliances, between wealthy families reinforced status and power. A poor choice of allies could bring disaster. New families, some of which had moved to Florence from other parts of Tuscany, managed to enter the ranks of the wealthy ruling families. Enriched by good economic fortune, they replaced those for whom recent years had not been so good.

The renewal, then, of the Florentine elite with new families provided change within continuity, despite no small degree of political turbulence in the fifteenth century. The crowning cultural achievements of the Renaissance were not only rooted in Florence's prosperity but also in the relative social and political stability within that innovative city-state.

In 1434, Cosimo de' Medici (1389–1464) and his family seized control of Florentine political life. The family drew its great wealth from banking and the manufacture and commerce of textiles. Supported by a few patrician families, Cosimo banished prominent members of the most powerful rival clans. The Medici now controlled the offices of government. They manipulated the electoral process masterfully, using their wealth to curry support. Cosimo reflected the marketplace toughness of his family.

Florentine nobles generally accepted Medici rule because stability contributed to prosperity. Wealthy families continued to conspire against each other, even as Florence warred against Venice, but the powerful families remained staunchly patriotic, devoted to their city. Nonetheless, some Florentine nobles continued to oppose the Medici. In the Pazzi conspiracy of 1479, Lorenzo the Magnificent (1449–1492), Cosimo's grandson, survived an assassination attempt during Mass. Several hours later, four of the enemies of the Medici were hanging upside down from a government building, including the archbishop of Pisa. Lorenzo composed verses to be placed under their heads and commissioned Sandro Botticelli (c. 1445–1510) to paint them as they swung. Renaissance culture and the often violent political world of the city-states here converged.

The establishment of a Council of Seventy, which elected committees assigned responsibility for domestic and foreign affairs, helped the Medici tighten their grip on the reins of the Florentine republic. Lorenzo extended the family's banking interests and its influence with the pope in Rome. Among the many honors bestowed on the Medici family, Lorenzo considered the papal nomination of his thirteen-year-old son to the rank of Church cardinal "the greatest achievement of our house."

A DYNAMIC CULTURE

Economically and intellectually dynamic, Florence emerged as the center of the Renaissance. As Florence solidified its leading position on the Italian peninsula, its people rediscovered and celebrated classical learning. While glorifying antiquity, Renaissance poetry, prose, and painting emphasized the dignity of the individual, made in the image of God. It gradually moved concepts like beauty and virtue away from theological constraints.

The Rediscovery of Classical Learning

The Tuscan poet Petrarch (Francesco Petrarca, 1304–1374) was among the earliest and most influential of those who rediscovered and celebrated the classics of Latin antiquity. Petrarch, the son of a Florentine notary, learned Latin from a monk who inspired the boy to pursue his fascination with the classical world, which he came to view as a lost age. As a young man, Petrarch lived in Avignon, among an international community of lawyers and churchmen at the papal court during the "Avignon Papacy" (1309–1378), when the popes were subject to the influence of the kings of France. There he copied ancient works from the manuscripts and books these men had brought with them. Petrarch and his friends searched far and wide for more classical manuscripts. They uncovered the *Letters to Athens* of the Roman orator and moralist Marcus Tullius Cicero (106–43 B.C.), among other texts, stored in the cathedral of Verona. The study of Cicero led Petrarch to see in classical philosophy a guide to life based on experience.

Petrarch's successors found and copied other classical manuscripts. Among them were classical literary commentaries, which provided humanists with a body of information about the authors in which they were interested. Scholars brought works of classical Greek authors, including the playwright Sophocles, from Constantinople and from the libraries of Mount Athos. Knowledge of Greek texts (as well as certain Arabic and Hebrew texts) spread slowly through Italy after the arrival of a number of Greek teachers from Constantinople.

The development of printing (see Chapter 1), following its invention by a German, Johannes Gutenberg, permitted the diffusion of a variety of histories, treatises, biographies, autobiographies, and poems. Printing increased the knowledge of classical texts and the development of textual

(*Left*) Petrarch. (*Right*) A Humanist educator and his charges.

criticism itself. Many Renaissance scholars considered Cicero to represent the model of the purest classical prose (although others considered him too long-winded), and by 1500 more than 200 editions of his works had been printed in Italy, including his influential *On Oratory* and his letters. Libraries were established in many of the city-states, including Florence, Naples, and Venice, and provided scholars with common texts for study.

From Scholasticism to Humanism

The Romans had used the concept of *humanitas* to describe the combination of wisdom and virtue that they revered. The term came to refer to studies that were intellectually liberating, the seven liberal arts of antiquity: grammar, logic, arithmetic, geometry, music, astronomy, and rhetoric (the art of expressive and persuasive speech or discourse). Medieval scholasticism was a system of thought in which clerics applied reason to philosophical and theological questions. Those teachers and students who shifted their focus from the scholastic curriculum—law, medicine, and theology—to the curriculum of Latin grammar, rhetoric, and metaphysics became known as "humanists." They considered the study of the "humanities" to be essential for educating a good citizen.

Renaissance humanists believed that they were reviving the glory of the classical age. They considered their era greater than any since the Roman Empire. They also believed the Italian peninsula, although divided by political units, dialects, and by the Apennine Mountains, shared a common, distinct culture.

Venerating classical civilization, the humanists turned their backs on medieval scholasticism, which they believed was composed of irrelevant theological debates and encouraged the ascetic withdrawal of men and women from the world. Scholastics celebrated the authority of Church texts and revered the saint, the monk, and the knight. Petrarch rejected idle philosophic speculation or even knowledge that seemed irrelevant to mankind. He mocked scholastics, remarking that they can tell you "how many hairs there are in the lion's mane . . . with how many arms the squid binds a shipwrecked sailor. . . . All these things or the greater part of it is wrong. . . . And even if they were true, they would not contribute anything to the blessed life. What is the use, I pray you, of knowing the nature of beasts, birds, fishes and serpents, and not knowing, or spurning the nature of man, to what end we are born, and from where and whither we pilgrimage."

The humanists proclaimed the writers of antiquity to be heroes worthy of emulation. Although virtually all humanists accepted Christianity, and clerical religious culture persisted intact, humanism stood as an alternative approach to knowledge and culture. Humanists believed that a knowledge of the humanities could civilize mankind, teaching the "art of living."

Petrarch insisted that the study of classical poetry and rhetoric could infuse daily life with ethical values.

Unlike the scholastics, humanists believed that it was not enough to withdraw into philosophy. Petrarch rediscovered the classical ideal that the philosopher, or humanist, was a wise man who could govern. Cicero had written that what made an individual great was not the gifts of good fortune, but the use to which he put them. The active life, including participation in public affairs, had formed part of his definition of true wisdom. From the literature of the Greek and Roman past, humanists looked for guides to public life in their own city-states. The first half of the fifteenth century is often referred to as the period of "civic humanism" because of the influence of humanists and artists on the city-states themselves. Like the classic writers of ancient Rome, Renaissance writers were concerned with wisdom, virtue, and morality within the context of the political community. Humanists wrote boastful histories of the city-states, philosophical essays, stirring orations, and flattering biographies, as well as poetry, eagerly imitating classical styles.

The Renaissance and Religion

In rediscovering classic texts and motifs, the Renaissance remained closely linked to religion. Dante's *Divine Comedy* (1321), an allegorical poem, provides the quintessential expression of medieval thought by its demonstration of the extraordinary power that both Latin classical learning and Christian theology exerted on educated thought and literature. In his voyage through Hell, Purgatory, and Heaven, Dante encounters historical figures suffering terrible agonies for their sins, waiting expectantly for admission into Heaven, or reaping the benefits of having lived a good life. Renaissance humanists could reject medieval scholasticism without turning their backs on the Church. Indeed, they claimed that they were searching for the origins of Christianity in the classical world from which it had emerged.

Although not the first to do so, humanists took classic texts, which were pagan, and ascribed to them meanings prophetic of Christianity. For example, the long epic *Aeneid*, written by Virgil (70–19 B.C.), had been commissioned by the Roman emperor Augustus in the hope that it would offer the most favorable image of himself and of the empire, that is, of bringing peace and civilization to the world. The hero of the *Aeneid*, Aeneas, personifies the ideal qualities of a Roman citizen, wanting to fulfill his patriotic duties, seeking glory for the empire but never for himself. The humanists transformed Aeneas's journey into an allegory for the itinerary of the Christian soul, appropriating antiquity into theology by viewing it as a foreshadowing of the true religion.

The place of the Church in Italian life therefore remained strong during the Renaissance, the relative decline in the papacy's temporal power notwithstanding. There was thus considerable continuity between the medieval period and the Renaissance in matters of religion. There were at least 264 bishops in Italy, as many as in the rest of the Christian world. In 1427, Florence had more than 1,400 clerics out of a population of 38,000 living in ecclesiastical institutions. Religious festivals dotted the calendar. The colorful Venetian water processions of elaborately decorated gondolas, jousting, boat races, and the annual horse race (*palio*) sponsored by rival neighborhoods in Siena still bear witness to the playful but intense festivity of the Renaissance city-states, a festivity that gave ritualized religious expression to civic and political life.

The Renaissance Man and Woman

Renaissance literature and poetry, preoccupied with nature, beauty, and reason, placed the individual at the forefront of attention. Renaissance writers praised mankind as "heroic" and "divine," rational and prudent, rather than intrinsically unworthy by virtue of being stained by original sin, as Church theologians held. This, too, represented a revival of the classic vision of the moral greatness of the individual and his or her ability to discover truth and wisdom.

By this view, the lay person could interpret morality through the ancient texts themselves, without the assistance of the clergy. Once someone had learned to read Latin and Greek, neither ecclesiastical guidance nor formalized school settings were necessary for the accumulation of wisdom. Universities in general remained under the influence of the theological debates of scholasticism, although the universities of Florence, Bologna, and Padua gradually added humanist subjects to their curricula. Relatively few humanists emerged from the universities, which remained training grounds for jurists, doctors, and clerics.

"These studies are called liberal because they make man free," a humanist wrote; they are humane "because they perfect man . . . those studies by which we attain and practice virtue and wisdom; that education which calls forth, trains and develops those highest gifts of body and of mind, which ennoble man." The young Giovanni Pico della Mirandola (1463–1494) exclaimed, "O highest and most marvelous felicity of man! To him it is granted to have whatever he chooses, to be whatever he wills." Pico described the individual as an independent and autonomous being who could make his own moral choices and become, within the context of Christianity, "the molder and sculptor of himself."

The political theorist Niccolò Machiavelli (1469–1527), too, found personal fulfillment in the study of the classics. He had been employed in the Florentine chancery, serving as a diplomat. Purged when the Medici overthrew the republic in 1512, he took up residence in the countryside. Machiavelli complained that his days consisted of mundane exchanges with rustics. But "when evening comes I return home and go into my study. On the threshold I strip off my muddy, sweaty, workday clothes, and put on the robes of court and palace, and in this graver dress I enter the antique courts of the ancients and am welcomed by them, and there again I taste the food that alone is mine, and for which I was born. And I make bold to speak to them and ask the motives of their actions, and they, in their humanity, reply to me. And for the space of four hours I forget the world, remember no vexation, fear poverty no more, tremble no more at death: I pass indeed into their world." Machiavelli evoked the exhilaration of the individual discovering the joys of antiquity.

The development of the autobiography in literature reflected the celebration of the individual, however much the genre was limited to public people and the image that they sought to present of themselves, revealing virtually nothing of private life. In the first half of the fifteenth century, the portrait and the self-portrait emerged as artistic genres; princes, oligarchs, courtiers, and other people of wealth joined Christ, the Virgin Mary, and popular saints as subjects of painting.

A growing sense of what it meant to be "civilized" arose in the Italian city-states and highlighted the place of the individual in society. The Italian patrician may have been cleaner and more perfumed than people elsewhere in Europe, and certainly claimed to be so. Books on good conduct and manners emerged. The writer Baldassare Castiglione (1478–1529) urged the person of taste to show that "whatever is said or done has been done without pains and virtually without thought" as if correct behavior

Drawings by Leonardo da Vinci.

had become part of his or her very being. Women, he contended, should obtain a "knowledge of letters, of music, of painting, and . . . how to dance and be festive."

Castiglione's *The Courtier* (1528) described the ideal courtier, or attendant at a court, as someone who had mastered the classics and several languages, and who could paint, sing, write poetry, advise and console his prince, as well as run, jump, swim, and wrestle. This idea of a "universal person," or "Renaissance man," had existed for some time, although, of course, not everyone had the leisure or resources to study so many subjects.

Although he was not a humanist and could not read Latin, Leonardo da Vinci (1452–1519)—painter, sculptor, scientist, architect, military engineer, inventer, and philosopher—became the epitome of the "Renaissance man" in the view of later ages. The illegitimate son of a notary from a Tuscan village, he was apprenticed to a Florentine painter at the age of twelve. Following acceptance into the master's guild in Florence, he remained in the workshop of his master until moving in 1482 to Milan, where he enjoyed the patronage of the Sforza family. Taking the title "Painter and Engineer of the Duke of Milan," Leonardo taught students in his workshop and undertook scientific studies of human and animal anatomy. His drawings were the first modern scientific illustrations. Leonardo began compiling his prodigious notebooks, in which he jotted down his ideas, perceptions, and experiences. He also sculpted an equestrian monument, designed costumes for theatrical performances, worked as a military engineer, and decorated palaces. In 1500, Leonardo returned to Florence, then went back to Milan six years later, beckoned by the governor of Francis I, king of France. When the Milanese freed themselves from French hegemony, he went south to Rome, where Pope Leo X (pope 1513–1521) provided him with a salary. In 1516, the French king brought Leonardo to his château on the Loire River at Amboise, where he sketched court festivals, and served as something of a Renaissance jack-of-all-trades before his death in 1519.

If the Renaissance is often said to have "discovered" mankind in general, this meant, for the most part, men. The Church considered women to be sinful daughters of Eve. Legally, women remained subordinate to men; they could own property and make their wills, but they could not sell property without their husbands' permission. Both rich and poor families continued to value boys more than girls; poor families were far more likely to abandon female babies or to place them in the care of a distant wet nurse. Many families viewed girls as a liability because of the necessity of providing a dowry, however large or small, for their marriage. Some families of means sent daughters off into convents. Because of the strict gender division within the Church, women there could aspire not only to holiness and sainthood, but also to leadership in a world of women. Life in a convent left them free to study.

Some patricians, however, educated their girls as well as their boys in the humanities. These girls studied letters, orations, and poems with tutors. A small number of women went on to write because they could not enter learned professions. Isotta Nogarola, a fifteenth-century humanist from Verona, abandoned secular life for quiet religious contemplation and scholarship. In her discussion of the fall of mankind in the Garden of Eden, she apologized for the weakness of women's nature, and she lamented that she fell short of "the whole and perfect virtue that men attain."

The Renaissance did not bring about any significant loosening in the restrictions placed on women. In the Italian city-states, women had less of a role in public life than they had enjoyed in the courts of medieval Europe. Women presided over social gatherings, but for the most part in a ritualized, decorative role. Overall, the Renaissance era may even have reduced women's social and personal options. Although Renaissance authors idealized love and women, chastity and submission to one's husband remained the reality. When the education of young women clashed with a father's plans for his daughter to marry, the latter won out without discussion. The role of women continued to be to serve their fathers, husbands, or, in some cases, their lovers. Men's feelings were the focus of considerable attention by Renaissance writers; women's feelings and opinions usually were assumed to be unimportant. To be sure, women in large, powerful families like the Sforza, Este, and Gonzaga exerted influence and were patrons to artists. Yet the subjects they commissioned artists and sculptors to portray were essentially the same as those of their male counterparts, and, in patriarchal households, their husbands made the decisions.

RENAISSANCE ART

When the German painter Albrecht Dürer (1471–1528) visited Venice on one of his two trips to the northern Italian peninsula, he was surprised and delighted by the fact that artists there enjoyed considerably more status than in his native Nuremburg: "Here," he wrote, "I am a gentleman, at home a sponger."

The prestige and support given to the Renaissance artist created a nurturing environment for the remarkable artistic accomplishments that characterize that special period's place in history. Great works of Renaissance architecture, painting, and sculpture are still studied by specialists and appreciated by millions of people each year.

Architecture

Despite the Renaissance concept of the "ideal city" of architectural harmony, reflected in the first treatises on architecture, Florence, Siena, Perugia, and other Italian cities retained their medieval cores, which contained their markets and their public buildings, such as the town hall. But during the fifteenth century, the narrow streets and alleys of many Italian cities became interspersed with splendid buildings and dotted with works of art commissioned by wealthy families.

Florence, for example, underwent a building boom during the fifteenth century. Construction of its elegant residences stimulated the economy, providing employment to day laborers, skilled artisans—brickmakers, masons, roofers, tilers, carpenters, cabinetmakers, and joiners—and decorative artists, including goldsmiths, sculptors, and painters. Renaissance architecture emphasized elegant simplicity, an expansion of the simple rustic fronts that had characterized medieval building. Renaissance architects combined plain white walls with colorful, intricate arches, doors, and window frames. In the fifteenth century, expensive palaces of monumental proportions with columns, arches, and magnificent stairways were considered sensible investments, because they could, if necessary, later be sold at a profit.

Like writers and painters, Renaissance architects looked to antiquity for models. Filippo Brunelleschi (1377–1446) first applied theories of classical architecture to the Foundling Hospital in Florence, the earliest building constructed in Renaissance style. Fourteenth-century architects planned churches in the form of circles, the shape they thought was in the image of God, with no beginning and no end. But they may also have drawn on Rome's Pantheon, a round classical temple. After going to the papal city to study the ruins of classical architecture, Brunelleschi solved daunting technical problems to construct the vast dome, or cupola, of that city's cathedral (Duomo). The magnificent structure, completed in 1413 after work lasting more than a century, reflects the architect's rejection of the northern Gothic architectural style, with its pointed arches, vaulting, and flying buttresses that counterbalanced slender vertical columns. Inspired by excavations of classical ruins and the rebuilding of Rome in the late fifteenth century, architects began to copy classical styles closely, adding ornate Corinthian columns and great sweeping arches.

Patronage and the Arts

Renaissance art could not have flourished without the patronage of wealthy, powerful families, though commissions by guilds and religious confraternities were not uncommon. Artists, as well as poets and musicians, were eager, like Leonardo, to be invited into a patrician's household, where there were few or no expenses, and there was time to work. Lesser artists painted coats of arms, tapestries, and even portraits of the prince's pets—dogs and falcons.

Some humanists not fortunate enough to be given the run of a powerful patrician's place found posts as state secretaries, because they could draft impressive official correspondence, and they tutored the children of patrician families. A few worked as papal courtiers. Such humanists penned orations, scrupulously imitating Cicero, for formal state receptions, clamorous festivals, and funerals. Pope Leo X, a Medici who composed and played music himself, brought to his court a number of distinguished

Pope Leo X brought artists and musicians to his court. This portrait was done by Raphael.

artists and musicians, as well as humanists whom he employed as officials and envoys. At the same time, the genres of wit and satire developed and became part of the ribald and "sharp-tongued" life of the political and social world of the city-state. Her well-heeled friends winked and joined in the laughter when Isabella of Mantua dressed one of her dwarfs as a bishop to greet a visiting dignitary; she ordered another to parody the Mass for the amusement of the audience. The biting satires and lampoons of Pietro Aretino (1492–1556), who enjoyed in succession the patronage of a banker, a cardinal, the duke of Mantua, the Medici of Florence, and a Venetian doge and nobleman, spared neither secular nor ecclesiastical leaders from mocking jokes and rhymes. Aretino attacked social climbers and the venality of offices in the city-states with particular venom. He spared the one person he referred to as divine—himself.

Because the classical texts suggested that the active life included playing a salutary role in one's community, families of means believed that they should demonstrate wisdom by making good use of their riches, as they developed their knowledge of the humanities. Commissioning works of art seemed to confirm moral leadership, and therefore the right to govern; in the words of a prosperous Florentine merchant, they "serve the glory of God, the honor of the city, and commemorate myself." Wealthy families also used art to reflect the image that they wished to give of themselves, for example, commissioning portraits to impress the family of a prospective spouse. Portraiture glorified the subject who sat before the artist.

The Medici of Florence, the greatest of the secular patrons of the arts, commissioned buildings, paid for the elaborate decoration of chapels and altarpieces, and restored monasteries. Although wags suggested that he may have been more interested in the expensive bindings of books he purchased than in their contents, Cosimo de' Medici, though himself not a scholar, collected manuscripts and even read some of them. The wealthy banker spent much of his time overseeing the construction of fine palaces and churches. Michelangelo (1475–1564), who designed the Medici tomb in the church of Saint Lorenzo in Florence, was but one sculptor who enjoyed the favor of the Medici. In 1504, he began work on a mural in the city hall commissioned for the city, alongside another undertaken by Leonardo da Vinci.

The long economic recession of the fifteenth century may have actually contributed to the arts. Finding insufficient profits in commerce and manufacturing for their money, patrician families spent considerable sums on paintings and sculpture. This may, in turn, have accentuated the recession by turning productive capital away from economic investments. At the same time, so the argument goes, the recession offered families of means more time to devote to the life of the mind and to culture.

The ruling families of some smaller states were especially lavish in their patronage of the arts. The Gonzaga family of Mantua, for example, carried their enthusiasm for a self-referential courtly life to an extreme that probably was unmatched. To emphasize their might, the Gonzaga brought dwarfs to their court, which was greater in pretension than in might. Venetian envoys arrived to find the syphilitic marquis in 1515 lying on a couch in his favorite room, attended by his favorite dwarf, who was attired

The Gonzaga family of Mantua. Note the dwarf in the foreground.

in gold brocade. Nearby stood three pages, and three greyhounds as well, while the walls were covered with paintings of favorite pets and favorite people, and of the duke himself.

Patrons of the arts often specified not only the subject of the work they were commissioning but certain details as well, requiring, for example, that specific saints be depicted. The size of the work of art and its price of course had to be specified, including the cost of blue pigment or gold for paintings and bronze or marble for sculptures. Cherubs cost more. Although one of the dukes of Ferrara paid for his paintings by their size, increasingly patrons paid the artist for his time—and thus his skill—as well as for the materials he used. The contract for a work of art might specify whether it was to be completed by the artist himself, or if assistants from the master's workshop could be employed for certain parts. Patrons sometimes appeared on the canvas, as in the case of *The Adoration of the Magi* (1426), by Tommaso di Giovanni Masaccio (1401–1428), which includes portraits of the notary who commissioned the painting and his son. Conversely, patricians occasionally commissioned artists to humiliate their enemies, as when a painter in Verona was paid to sneak up to the walls of a rival palace and paint obscene pictures.

Renaissance Artists

Because of its basis in the craft tradition, in the medieval world painting was considered a "mechanical" art. This made the status of the artist ambiguous, because he sold his own works and lacked the humanist's education. Michelangelo's father tried to discourage his son from becoming a sculptor, an art that he identified with stone cutting. Michelangelo himself sometimes signed his paintings "Michelangelo, sculptor," as if to differentiate himself from a mere painter. Yet, in his treatise on painting (1435), the humanist Leon Battista Alberti, irritated by contemporary insistence that painting was a "mechanical art," insisted that the artist was no longer a craftsman but a practitioner of a "high art."

Of the artists whose social origins are known, the majority had fathers who were urban shopkeepers or artisans, most often in the luxury trades. Next in number—surprisingly—came the sons of nobles, perhaps reflecting the relative decline in noble fortunes during the Renaissance. Then came the children of merchants and educated professionals such as notaries, lawyers, and officials. Some artists, like Raphael (1483–1520), were sons of artists. Only a handful were the sons of peasants.

The contemporary association between craftsmen and painters was appropriate, because, like the former, artists entered a period of apprenticeship. Architects and composers lacked such formal training. The architect Brunelleschi belonged to the guild of silk manufacturers and goldsmiths. Composers were usually trained to be musical performers and simply began to write music on their own.

The painters' guild of Venice seems typical of the way in which artists learned their skills. The guild required five years of apprenticeship, followed by two years of journeyman status, requirements similar to those by which silversmiths, shoemakers, cabinetmakers, and other craftsmen were trained. The painters' guilds resembled other craft guilds in that the members were considered brothers in work who passed through life's hurdles together. Some masters had sizable workshops, where apprentices trained and often lived together, sometimes working on the same paintings (which is one reason it is difficult to authenticate some canvases). Because women could neither become apprentices nor attend universities, there were no prominent female artists during the Renaissance, at least until well into the sixteenth century.

By the beginning of the sixteenth century, the artist's status in general had risen so much that a Venetian painter dared propose that only those "noble both by birth and money" be allowed to paint. Michelangelo, Leonardo, Raphael, and Titian (Tiziano Vecellio, c. 1490–1576) lived as gentlemen, the last knighted by Charles V, Holy Roman emperor. Some artists and writers were crowned with laurels—thus the designation of "poet laureate"—by their adoring city-states.

Indeed, artists claimed that they deserved more esteem than a craftsman. Leonardo praised the painter, who sits "at his easel in front of his work, dressed as he pleases, and moves his light brush with the beautiful colors . . . often accompanied by musicians or readers of various beautiful works." The artist's quest for the humanist ideals of beauty and God helps explain the rise of some artists of the Renaissance period from practitioners of a "mechanical art," to the description of Michelangelo offered by a Portuguese painter: "In Italy, one does not care for the renown of great princes: it's a painter only that they call divine." Not all painters ascended to such heights, of course, but in general the status of the artist rose during the Renaissance.

Painting and Sculpture

The rediscovery of antiquity, nature, and mankind transformed European painting. Renaissance artists reflected the influence of the neo-Platonists. In the late fifteenth and early sixteenth centuries, the neo-Platonists appropriated Plato's belief that eternal ideas—such as beauty, truth, and goodness—existed beyond the realm of everyday life. Humanists believed that the mind could transcend human nature and come to understand these eternal ideas. The artist could reproduce the beauty of the soul through imagination and, in doing so, reach out to God. To Dante, art was "the grandchild of God." For Michelangelo, beauty "lifts to heaven hearts that truly know."

Artists sought to achieve the representation of beauty in a realistic way by using the proportions created by God in the universe. It was the supreme compliment to say of a Renaissance painter that his work had surpassed nature in beauty. Leonardo put it this way: "Painting . . . compels the mind of the painter to transform itself into the mind of nature itself and to translate between nature and art."

During the Renaissance, nature ceased to be mere background. Painters now faithfully depicted the beauty of mountains, rocks, and gardens for their own sake. Naturalism was heightened by the removal of the kind of pretty detail that embellished medieval art. It can first be seen in the memorable figures of the frescoes of Giotto di Bondone (c. 1266–1337) in the chapels of Holy Cross Church in Florence. These figures, particularly their facial expressions, reflect humanity, deeply personal emotion, and naturalism, unseen since the classical age. The fame of Giotto, who is usually considered the first great painter of the Renaissance, spread rapidly throughout much of Italy and his style greatly influenced his successors.

Objects of everyday life, reflecting a greater preoccupation with realistic depiction, increasingly appeared in paintings. Take, for example, Raphael's painting of the pudgy Pope Leo X, staring off into space while fiddling with a magnifying glass with which he has been examining a book (see p. 67).

Beauty could be portrayed with extraordinary richness, as in the work of Botticelli, or it could be depicted simply. Raphael, who admired and learned from Michelangelo, eight years his senior, wrote of trying to paint a beautiful woman, "I use as my guide a certain idea of the beautiful that I carry in my mind." Raphael's figures reflect a softness and inner beauty that contrast with the powerful, stirring subjects of the tempestuous Michelangelo. Reflecting neo-Platonist influence, Titian early in the sixteenth century strove to bring the viewers of his paintings closer to the idea of the eternal form of female beauty that he sought to represent with his depictions of Venus.

The Greeks and Romans believed that the painter and sculptor understood and portrayed the soul when they reproduced the human face. Leonardo's famous *Mona Lisa* (1503–1507), with its mysterious, confident half-smile, is a compelling illustration of this

Masaccio's *The Expulsion of Adam and Eve from Eden* (c.1427).

undertaking. "Movements of the soul," wrote Alberti early in the fifteenth century, "are recognized in movements of the body." Leonardo insisted that the rendering of certain gestures indicated the soul or the character of the artist's subject. The artist had to be able to reveal the emotions and passions of the figures he depicted.

Renaissance artists used a large repertoire of stylized portrayals of emotion, the meanings of which were immediately recognized by virtually all viewers of painting. The Florentine Masaccio intended his extraordinary fresco *The Expulsion of Adam and Eve from Eden* (c. 1427) to represent the tortured souls, as well as bodies, of those biblical figures. Masaccio's Adam covers his eyes with his fingers in anguish in this truly gripping depiction of Adam and Eve's crushing grief as they leave the Garden of Eden. Although Renaissance artists generally avoided many of the routine associations of the medieval period (gold for piety, for example), certain colors were used for symbolic purposes. Violet was often a color of reverence, white that of charity, red of fire, and gray of earth. Clear colors, intense light, and ideal proportions were combined in representations of Christ. Deep coloring, more subtle and natural than the blues and golds of medieval painting, enriched the canvas.

Medieval and Byzantine artists painted rigid, unlifelike images on a flat space; linear forms were arranged in order of importance, accompanied by symbols easily identifiable to the viewer. The Renaissance development of perspective theory, in which parallel lines recede from the surface and seem to converge on the vanishing point, facilitated the realistic presentation of figures and movement. Renaissance artists believed that naturalism could only be achieved through the use of perspective. Masaccio first applied the mathematical laws of perspective to painting in his revolutionary *Trinity* (1425), which makes a two-dimensional surface seem to be three-dimensional. The mastery of light also contributed to innovative uses of space; for example, through the technique of foreshortening, artists proportionally contracted depth so as to give the viewer the illusion of projection or extension into space. In his realistic *The Dead Christ* (c. 1506), Andrea Mantegna (c. 1430–1506) utilized this technique, which had been pioneered by Masaccio. This shortcut allowed the artist to create the visual impression of a three-dimensional body on a flat surface. Florentine artists, in particular, used perspective to develop high relief and silhouette, presenting rounded figures on the canvas surface by effective use of tones and shades.

This mastery of perspective by the naturalist painter Masaccio and, above all, the sculptor Donatello (c. 1386–1466), who lived much longer and produced much more, helped Renaissance painters choose difficult, complicated themes and treat them with a more complex realism. Donatello utilized perspective to achieve dramatic action through gradations of relief. In *The Feast of Herod* (c. 1417), sculpted in bronze for the stone basin in the Siena Baptistery, Donatello captures the shocked reac-

Andrea Mantegna's *The Dead Christ* (c. 1506).

tion of the king and guests as John the Baptist's head is presented to Herod. In Leonardo's painting *The Last Supper* (c. 1495–1498), the disciples of Christ crowd around the table. The viewer's eye is drawn along the lines of perspective of the ceiling to the central figure of Christ, whose image stands out in front of a large window. Leonardo identifies Judas, the betrayer of Christ, not by leaving him without a halo nor by placing him alone on the other side of the table from Christ, but by painting him as the only figure in shadow.

To Leonardo, painting was the highest form of science and was based on "what has passed through our senses." He believed that "the scientific and true principles of painting first determine" the components of painting: "darkness, light, color, body, figure, position, distance, nearness, motion, and rest." The work of Michelangelo reflects a mastery of mathematics, anatomy, and optics. Animals, birds, and inanimate objects also took on a lifelike quality based upon artists' discovery of proper proportions.

The quest for the natural representation of beauty led some artists to depict the human body in nude form, which some took to be a more natural and expressive form borrowed from classical paganism. Botticelli's *The Birth of Venus* (c. 1482) represents this trend. Michelangelo believed that the depiction of the human body in sculpture was the ultimate expression of mankind as a divine creation, made in God's image. In his sculptures and paintings of the nude figure, the muscles and sinews of the body are infused with the emotions and passions of humanity.

Religious, public, and private life overlapped, as the people of Renaissance Italy sought religious meanings in everything they saw. Art with religious subjects also served a teaching function for the Church. In many patrician houses, a religious image could be found in every room. Devotional images, known as *ex votos*, were often erected in public spaces to fulfill a vow made to a saint in times of danger or illness. Patricians commissioned paintings with religious themes to realize similar vows. Moreover, the splendid tombs sculpted for patricians and popes may have reflected a preoccupation with glorifying the individual, but they nonetheless also emphasized eternal salvation.

Religious themes continued to dominate painting, accounting for perhaps nine of every ten paintings; the Virgin Mary was the most popular figure, followed by Christ and the saints (above all, Saint John the Baptist, the patron saint of Florence). The visualization of certain episodes in the life of Christ or of the martyrdom of Saint Sebastian were intended to stimulate piety and encourage morality. Thus, artists took on a role similar to preachers, whose orations evoked a powerful emotional response.

Classical symbolism abounded in Renaissance painting and influenced the depiction of religious themes, incorporating images drawn from pagan Rome. Artists used details about history or mythology that patrons insisted grace their canvases. Some of the classical gods stood as Renaissance sym-

Sandro Botticelli's *The Birth of Venus* (c. 1482).

bols of moral or physical qualities. Michelangelo modeled his Christ in *The Last Judgment* (1536–1541) on a classical portrayal of the god Apollo. Mantegna, then the premier painter of northern Italy, drew upon his meticulous study of Roman archaeology.

Yet, along with scenes from classical mythology, paintings with secular themes increased in number, notably portraits of famous men or of wealthy patricians, but also of more ordinary people as well. Aretino, who criticized everything, found fault with the democratization of the portrait, despite the fact that he was the son of a shoemaker, saying, "It is the disgrace of our age that it tolerates the portraits even of tailors and butchers."

High Renaissance Style

During the period of the High Renaissance (1490–1530), the prestige of artists reached its highest level, and the greatest were revered as geniuses. At the same time, the city-states of Italy lost much of their economic and political vitality and faced French invasion and then Spanish domination. In the midst of economic decline as well as internecine political warfare, artists no longer enjoyed the lavish patronage of wealthy patrician families. Instead, the Church became their patron.

The papacy inspired the monumentalism of the High Renaissance. Besieged in the first two decades of the sixteenth century by denunciations of the sale of indulgences—the purchase of the remission of some punishment in Purgatory for one's sins or for those of some family member—the papacy sought to assert its authority and image. Papal commissions in Rome were one attempt to recover public confidence and made possible the artistic achievements of the High Renaissance. Following excavations beginning in the 1470s that heightened interest in the ancient Roman Empire, Raphael himself oversaw the reconstruction of ancient Rome and personally supervised excavations of the Roman Forum. Influenced by and more dependent on the Church, the canvases of the painters of the High Renaissance became even larger as they became less concerned with rational order and more with achieving a powerful visual response in their viewers through large canvases.

Some humanists now began to claim that the papacy was the heir to the glories of classical Rome. Popes took names that echoed the Roman Empire. Julius II (pope 1503–1513) ordered a medal struck that read "Julius Caeser Pont[ifex]. II," a term that meant "high priest" in classical Rome. Wide boulevards and spaces were forged to accommodate waves of pilgrims descending upon the city.

Leonardo's *The Last Supper* is perhaps the first example of the style of the High Renaissance, or what is sometimes called the Grand Manner. Mannerism (a term from the Italian word for style), which particularly characterized the 1520s, is marked by heightened scale, exaggerated drama, and the submersion of detail to a total emotional effect, reflecting

Leonardo da Vinci's *The Last Supper* (c. 1495–1498).

the climate of the times. Donato Bramante (1444–1514), who con-
structed St. Peter's Basilica in Rome in the "grand manner" of the High
Renaissance, designed its grand Byzantine dome, which was completed by
Michelangelo and a successor.

Painters of the High Renaissance increasingly presented large, ambitious, complex, and sometimes even bizarre canvases. Mannerism's imaginative distortions and sense of restlessness offered an unsettling vision in
tune with new uncertainties. Mannerism marked something of a reaction
against the Renaissance ideal of attaining classical perfection. Thus, some
painters ignored the rules of perspective and rationalism, perhaps reflecting the frightening instability of the time. Nature faded into the background again; emotionalism, as well as mysticism and illusionism, won out
over classicism. Toward the end of his career, Michelangelo's work
reflected this influence. His majestic marble *Moses* (1515), sculpted for
the tomb of Pope Julius II, has an immensely prominent head, with an
exaggerated facial expression. It reflects Michelangelo's tragic vision of
human limitations, including his own. Raphael and Titian presented
human figures who seem almost empowered by divine attributes but who
nonetheless retain their humanity.

THE END OF THE RENAISSANCE

Late in the fifteenth century, the Italian city-states entered a period of
economic and political decline, making the peninsula more vulnerable to
foreign invasion. Subsequently, some of the battles between Spain and

France, Europe's two dominant powers, were fought on the Italian penin-
sula. The exploration and gradual colonization of the Americas, first by
Spain, and the increase in trade and manufacturing in northwestern Euro-
pe, helped move the economic and cultural vigor toward the Atlantic
Ocean, to Spain and northwestern Europe, most notably, England,
France, and the Dutch Netherlands (see Chapter 5).

Economic Decline

The economic decline of the northern Italian city-states during the second
half of the fifteenth century undermined the material base of Renaissance
prosperity, indeed the economic primacy of the Mediterranean region.
The Italian city-states lost most of their trading routes with Asia. The
Turks conquered Genoese trading posts in the Black Sea, the traditional
merchant route to Asia, and the Aegean Sea. Turkish domination reduced
Genoa's once mighty commercial network to trade centered on the Aegean
island of Chios. Of the Italian city-states, Venice alone continued to prosper. After the Ottoman conquest of Constantinople in 1453, merchants in
Venice concluded a deal with the Turks by which they received a monopoly on trade with the East, leaving the other city-states without access to
their traditional Asian markets. Venice's economy soon diversified with
small-scale manufacturing, however, particularly as the Turkish threat to
its interests mounted in the eastern Mediterranean and Venetian galleys
no longer could venture into the Black Sea.

Merchants of the Italian city-states sought alternatives. The Genoese
established a trading post in the Muslim city of Málaga on the south coast
of the Iberian Peninsula, although this made them dependent on local
Muslim middlemen. Castile's conquest of Gibraltar and Málaga at the end
of the century made transport between the Mediterranean and Atlantic
ports safer for Christian vessels. Genoese and Florentine merchants
undertook exploratory voyages down the west coast of Africa in search of a
new route to Asia. But most such vessels never returned. The Portuguese
thereafter took up the quest for a southern route to Asia, after acquiring
the Atlantic Ocean islands of Madeira, the Cape Verdes, and the Azores,
which could be used as bases. Portuguese fleets began to monopolize the
spice trade with India and beyond after Bartholomeu Dias (c. 1450–1500)
in 1487 first rounded the Cape of Good Hope, the southern tip of Africa.
From then on, Portuguese crews knew how to reach the Indian Ocean,
and then Calcutta, on the southwest coast of India.

The Florentine silk and woolen industries, long prosperous, now faced
stiff competition from French and Dutch producers and merchants in
northwestern Europe. The dazzling prosperity of the great Italian merchant families ebbed. The economy of Europe—and even of world commerce itself—was changing. Portuguese, Spanish, English, and Dutch
traders looked to the New World for new products and significant profits.

Christopher Columbus, the Genoese explorer, asked an Italian duke to risk funds for his voyages of exploration in 1492, but he refused. Columbus then gained the support of King Ferdinand and Queen Isabella of Spain (see Chapter 1). The rapid growth of Portuguese and then Spanish trade, first down the coast of Africa and then, after 1492, across the Atlantic Ocean to the New World, accentuated the rise of the Atlantic economy. Competition from the larger sailing ships of England, Holland, and Portugal overwhelmed Florence and Genoa and then, more gradually, Venice.

Foreign Invasion

As long as the Italian peninsula remained free from the intervention of France and Spain or other powers, the city-states could continue to prosper while fighting each other and casting wary glances toward the Ottoman Empire as it expanded its influence in the Mediterranean. But the city-states, divided by economic interests and with a long tradition of quarreling among themselves, became increasingly vulnerable to the expansion of French interests.

Threats to the Italian peninsula mounted from the French and the Turks. France had adhered to an alliance of Milan and Florence against Venice, signed in 1451. But the three city-states recognized the threat the aggressive French monarchy posed to the peninsula. Furthermore, following the capture of Constantinople in 1453, Turkish ships now appeared more frequently in the Adriatic Sea. It seemed imperative to end the wars between two leagues of city-states. The Peace of Lodi (1454), signed by Florence, Milan, and Venice, established a new political order. Helping discourage Turkish or French aggrandizement, the peace brought four decades of relative peace, which saw some of the crowning artistic glories of the Renaissance.

The establishment of this Italian League formalized this balance of power—it was already called that—between the strongest city-states. Whenever one or two of the states became aggressive—as when Venice and the Papal States attacked Ferrara—the others joined together to restore the status quo. Such wars were fought for the most part by mercenaries, imported and organized by *condottieri* paid for the task. For the moment, Milan's strong army served as a barricade against French invasion.

Perhaps accentuated by the ebbing of prosperity, political life within the city-states deteriorated. In Florence, the Medici despotism faced opposition from republicans. In the 1480s, Perugia had become a warring camp, torn between two rival families. In 1491, 130 members of one faction were executed on a main square and hanged from poles for all to see. Then, in repentance, the oligarchs erected thirty-five altars on that same square, and ordered priests to say Mass for three days in atonement. In a number of the city-states, some patrician families tried to outdo each other in their violence, crushing their opponents with brutality, then praying over the bodies. The leading Florentine families faithfully attended church, even as they undertook murders of vengeance in defense of family honor. Considerable tension, then, remained between two parallel codes of conduct, one religious, the other defined by family loyalties.

The Italian peninsula then became a battleground for the dynastic ambitions and rivalries of the French kings and the Holy Roman emperors, powerful rulers who could mobilize considerably larger armies than those of the city-states. The absorption of the wealthy and strategically important duchy of Burgundy into the Holy Roman Empire accentuated the struggle between the Habsburg dynasty and Charles VIII (ruled 1483–1498) of France. The latter decided to press his dubious claim to the throne of Naples, encouraged by the Sforza family of Milan, the enemy of Naples. In response, Naples allied with Florence and Pope Alexander VI (pope 1492–1503), himself a Florentine member of the Borgia family, against Milan.

In 1494, Charles VIII invaded the Italian peninsula with an army of 30,000 men. His French cavalry, Swiss mercenary infantry, and Scottish bowmen tore through northern Italy. In Florence, the Medici ruler offered Charles some Florentine possessions in exchange for leaving. This angered Florentine republicans, who drove the Medici from power in 1494 (after sixty years of rule), backed by the army of France. The new government, establishing the Great Council as a legislative assembly, contributed to the city's artistic splendors by commissioning works of art that symbolized republican independence and ideals. Leonardo and Michelangelo painted scenes of Florentine military victories for the meeting hall of the Great Council. Seven years later, the city government commissioned Michelangelo's great statue *David*. Michelangelo's conscious imitation of a Donatello bust of the same name from early in the fifteenth century referred back to the republic's successful resistance to challenges at that time.

In the meantime, the army of Charles VIII moved toward Naples, devastating everything in its path. It marched into the city to cheers from Neapolitans who opposed the harsh taxes that had been levied by their rulers. But an anti-French coalition that included King Ferdinand of Aragon—whose dynastic territories included Sicily, Venice, the Papal States—and the Holy Roman emperor rallied to defeat the French force. Although the French army left the Italian peninsula, the city-states' troubles had only just begun.

In Florence, Girolamo Savonarola (1452–1498), a charismatic Dominican monk who had predicted the French invasion, opposed both the Medici in Florence and the papacy on the grounds that both were worldly and corrupt. He had welcomed Charles VIII of France as "an instrument in the hands of the Lord who has sent you to cure the ills of Italy," including the sinfulness of the Florentines. With the Medici driven from power,

Savonarola took virtual control of the Florentine republic. His denunciation of abuses within the Church led to his excommunication by Pope Alexander VI. Savonarola also incurred the enmity of patrician families by appealing for support to all ranks of Florentine society. With the pope's blessing, Savonarola's enemies first hanged and then burned him—the penalty for heresy—in 1498.

The next year, Louis XII (ruled 1498–1515), the new French king, invaded the Italian peninsula, intent on making good his claim on the duchy of Milan. He did so with the support of the corrupt Pope Alexander VI, who wanted French assistance as he tried to solidify papal territorial claims, as well as to look after the extended interests of his children. To encourage the French king, the pope annulled Louis's marriage, so that he could marry his predecessor's widow, thereby keeping Brittany within his domains. When Julius II, who had been a bitter enemy of Alexander VI, became pope in 1503, he drove the powerful Borgia family from Rome. Then the dissolute pope set about trying to restore territorial holdings taken from the Papal States by Venice and its allies, constructing an alliance against the Venetians and becoming the last pope to lead his troops into the field of battle. That year the Spanish army defeated the French army and the Habsburgs absorbed the kingdom of Naples. Milan remained a fief of Louis XII until French forces were driven from the city in 1512, the same year that a Spanish army defeated the Florentines and

The burning of Girolamo Savonarola in Florence.

the Medici overthrew the republic. Three years later, French troops overwhelmed Swiss mercenaries and recaptured Milan. After the intervention of Emperor Charles V in 1522 and French defeats, the Lombardy city became a Spanish possession in 1535.

Machiavelli

A mood of vulnerability and insecurity spread through the Italian peninsula as the city-states battled each other. Peasants, crushed by taxes and hunger, ever more deeply resented the rich. In turn, wealthy people were increasingly suspicious of the poor, viewing them as dangerous monsters capable of threatening social order.

The devoted Florentine Niccolò Machiavelli was among those people seeking to understand why the once proud and independent city-states of Italy now seemed virtually helpless before the invasion of foreign powers. Machiavelli's view of politics reflects his experience living in Florence during these tumultuous decades. The turmoil in Florence led him to write his *Histories* in 1494, which described the decline of the city-states. Influenced by his experience in government, Machiavelli, who had served as a Florentine diplomat at the court of the king of France and in Rome, believed himself to be a realist. He considered war a natural outlet for human aggression. But he also preferred the resolution of disputes by diplomacy. He believed that the absence of "civic virtue" accounted for the factionalism within and rivalries between the city-states. By civic virtue (not the same thing as Christian virtue in the sense of distinguishing between and acting on the difference between right and wrong), Machiavelli meant the effective use of military force.

In 1512, the Medici overthrew the Florentine Republic, returning to power with the help of the papal army and that of Spain. Following the discovery of a plot, of which he was innocent, against the Medici patriarchs, Machiavelli was forced into exile on his country estate outside of the city. Florence had changed. A Medici supporter wrote one of the family heads: "Your forefathers, in maintaining their rule, employed skill rather than force; you must use force rather than skill."

A year later, Machiavelli wrote *The Prince* (1513). In it he reflected on the recent history of the Italian peninsula and offered a pessimistic assessment of human nature, marked by his belief that a strong leader—the prince—could arise out of strife. By making his subjects afraid of him, the prince could end political instability and bring about a moral regeneration that Machiavelli believed had characterized antiquity. Drawing on Cicero, he studied the cities of the Roman Republic and the Roman Empire. Machiavelli can be considered the first political scientist, because his works reflect a systematic attempt to draw general, realistic conclusions from his understanding of the recent history of the Italian city-states. This

The pensive Niccolò Machiavelli.

preoccupation with the past in itself reveals the influence of the Renaissance.

Machiavelli put his faith in political leadership. Regardless of whether the form was monarchical or republican, Machiavelli believed that the goal of government should be to bring stability to the city. A sense of civic responsibility could only be reestablished through "good laws and institutions," but these, for Machiavelli, depended completely on military strength. He called on the Medici to drive away the new barbarians. Machiavelli's *The Art of War* (1521) expressed hope that the brutish mercenaries who had devastated the Italian peninsula would give way to soldier-citizens who would restore virtue. But for the Italian city-states, it was too late.

Machiavelli's invocation of "reasons of state" as sufficient justification for political action and as a political principle in itself, and his open admiration of ruthless rulers, would leave a chilling legacy, reflected by his belief that the "ends justify the means." While it is unlikely that Machiavelli had a sense of the state in the impersonal, modern sense of the term, he held that "good arms make good laws."

The Decline of the City-States

Thus, for much of the first thirty years of the sixteenth century, foreign armies fought against each other and against alliances formed by the city-states. The army of France in Italy reached 32,000 men by 1525, that of Spain 100,000 soldiers. Only Venice could resist the two great powers. In 1521, the first war broke out between Holy Roman Emperor Charles V (King Charles I of Spain) and King Francis I of France, who became the first Western ruler to ally with the Ottoman Turkish sultan. The former's armies decimated the French at Pavia, Italy, in 1525, carting the French king off to Madrid, where he remained until his family paid a ransom. In 1527, Charles V's mercenary army, angry for lack of pay, sacked Rome. By the Peace of Cambrai (1529), France gave up claims to Naples and Milan. But with the exception of Venice, the Italian city-states were in one way or another dependent upon Charles V, the Holy Roman emperor, as the Spanish army repulsed new French invasions. In Rome, in which Spanish merchants already had a significant presence, the pope increasingly depended on Charles V for defense against the Turks just as Charles V added to his resources by taxing a quarter of the considerable ecclesiastical revenues.

The long wars drained the city-states of financial resources and men, devastating some of the countryside. Nobles, whose political power had been diminished by the wealthy merchants of the fourteenth and fifteenth centuries, took advantage of the chaos to return to prominence in some cities. Patrician families struggled to maintain their authority against newcomers, including wealthy merchants who had married into poorer noble lines and who began to ape the styles of nobles. The Medici, after having once again been expelled by republicans, reconquered their city in 1530 after a siege of ten months. But in Florence, too, the Renaissance was over.

Artistic styles had already begun to reflect the loss of Renaissance self-confidence that accompanied the devastating impact of the French invasion. For example, Botticelli seemed to abandon the serenity and cheerful optimism that characterized the Renaissance. To his painting *Mystical Nativity,* completed in 1500, Botticelli added an anxious inscription: "I Sandro painted this picture at the end of the year 1500 in the troubles of Italy . . . after the time according to the eleventh chapter of St. John in the second woe of the Apocalypse in the loosing of the devil for three and a half years. Then he will be chained in the twelfth chapter and we will see him trodden down as in this picture." Botticelli thereafter became preoccupied with suffering and the Passion of Christ, reflecting the fact that the High Renaissance was more closely tied to ecclesiastical influence. The deteriorating political situation, combined with the expansion of Spanish influence after 1530, made it more difficult for artists to find patronage in the Italian city-states.

Soon in Italy only Venice, the city of Titian, remained a center of artistic life. Machiavelli, who died in 1527, the year Charles V's troops pillaged Rome, sensed that the humiliation of the Italian city-states by foreign armies brought to a close a truly unique period in not only the history of Italy but in Western civilization. Of the great figures of the High Renaissance, only Michelangelo and Titian lived past 1530.

Impulses Elsewhere

The cultural glories of the Renaissance ebbed even as different kinds of discoveries by Europeans opened up new possibilities for mankind. Columbus's transatlantic voyages were signs that the economic and cultural vitality of Europe was shifting away from the Mediterranean to Spain and, to a lesser extent, England. The economic interests of these states would increasingly be across the Atlantic Ocean. The mood of optimism associated with the Renaissance seemed to have moved to central and northern Europe as Italy lapsed into a considerably less happy period. Many humanists and artists began to emigrate north of the Alps to lands considered by most cultured Italians to have been barbarian only in the last century. Now new universities in northern Europe beckoned them.

Other dramatic changes had already begun to occur across the Alps. Relentless calls for reform of the Catholic Church led to a schism within Christendom: the Reformation. In northern Europe, the Dutch monk and humanist Erasmus expressed the exhilaration many men of learning felt when he wrote, "The world is coming to its senses as if awakening out of a deep Sleep."

CHAPTER **3**

THE TWO
REFORMATIONS

Afterpaying a handsome sum to Pope Leo X in 1515, Albert
of Hohenzollern received a papal dispensation (exemption from canon
law) that enabled him to become archbishop of Mainz, a lucrative and
prestigious ecclesiastical post. Otherwise, under canon law, the twenty-
three-year-old Albert would have been ineligible due to his age (archbishops were supposed to be at least thirty years old) and because he already
drew income from two other ecclesiastical posts. As part of his payment
to the pope and in order to repay the large sum of money loaned to him by
the Fugger banking family, the new archbishop authorized the sale of the
St. Peter's indulgence, which would release a sinner from punishment for
his sins. Johann Tetzel, a Dominican friar who was in charge of the sale
of papal indulgences in the archbishopric of Mainz, was commissioned to
preach the indulgence. Half of the proceeds were to go to the papacy, and
half to Albert and the Fuggers. In his tour of parishes, Tetzel emotionally
depicted the wailing of dead parents in Purgatory, pleading with their
children to put coins in the box so that they could be released from their
suffering.

The sale of indulgences, particularly their commercial use to allow clergymen to obtain multiple posts, had drawn increasing criticism in some of
the German states. Indeed, no other ecclesiastical financial abuse drew as
much passionate opposition as did indulgences. More than this, the
Roman papacy itself faced considerable opposition in the German states,
as the pope had appointed foreigners to many key ecclesiastical posts and
had attempted to force the German states to provide him with money for a
war against the Turks. The young German monk Martin Luther was
among those denouncing Tetzel, the sale of indulgences, and the role of
the Roman papacy in the German states.

This opposition to the papacy created a schism that would tear Christendom apart beginning in the second decade of the sixteenth century.
Originating in the German states and Switzerland, a movement for

(*Left*) The young Martin Luther by Lucas Cranach. (*Right*) The pope selling indulgences.

religious reform began to spread across much of Europe, in part reflecting the influence of Renaissance humanism in northern Europe. Reformers rejected the pope's authority and Church doctrine itself. The movement for reform, or of "protest," came to be called the "Reformation." It led to the establishment of many "Protestant" denominations within Christianity. The followers of the German priest Martin Luther became Lutherans, while those of the Frenchman Jean Calvin in Switzerland became known as Calvinists. King Henry VIII established the Church of England (Anglican Church). Under attack from many sides, the Roman Catholic Church undertook a Counter-Reformation, also known as the Catholic Reformation, which sought to reform some aspects of ecclesiastic life, while reaffirming the basic tenets of Catholic theology and belief in the authority of the pope.

By 1600, the pattern of religious adherence had largely been established for the future in Europe. Catholicism remained the religion of the vast majority of people living in Spain, France, Austria, Poland, the Italian states, Bavaria, and other parts of the southern German states. Protestants dominated England and much of Switzerland, the Dutch Netherlands, Scandinavia, and the northern German states. Wars fought in the name of religion broke out within and between European states, beginning in the late sixteenth century and culminating in the Thirty Years' War (1618–1648). These conflicts shaped the next century of European history, with religious divisions affecting the lives of millions of people.

THE NORTHERN RENAISSANCE

Until the middle of the fifteenth century, the Renaissance had been limited to the Italian peninsula. Northern Europe enjoyed very little of the economic and cultural vitality of the Italian city-states. The country estates of noble families were rarely centers of learning. The future Pope Pius II claimed in the mid-fifteenth century that "literature flourishes in Italy and princes there are not ashamed to listen to, and themselves to know, poetry. But in Germany princes pay more attention to horses and dogs than to poets—and thus neglecting the arts they die unremembered like their own beasts." France and the German states also lacked the Italian peninsula's network of city-states, whose wealthy merchant and banking families patronized humanists and artists.

But in about 1460, Renaissance humanism began to influence scholars in northern Europe. As in Italy, humanism changed the way many people thought about the world. Humanists were interested in morality and ethics, as well as in subjecting texts to critical scrutiny. Therefore, debates over religion, and the Bible itself, attracted their attention. Humanists began to criticize Church venality and corruption, and the seeming idleness of monastic life. They also called into question scholasticism and its influence on religious theology, as well as criticizing parts of religious practice that they considered illogical and therefore superstitious. The spread of humanism in northern Europe was gradual, often influencing isolated scholars. In the beginning, it posed no immediate threat to the Church; humanists could not imagine organized religion beyond Roman Catholicism. But the cumulative effect of the Northern Renaissance, and humanism in particular, helped engender a critical spirit that by the first decades of the sixteenth century directly began to challenge Church practices and then doctrine.

Northern Art and Humanism

The Northern Renaissance, which began in the late fifteenth century, reflected considerable Italian influence. Italian ambassadors, envoys, and humanists brought Renaissance art and humanistic thought to northern Europe. Yet, much of the artistic creativity in northern Europe, particularly Flanders, emerged independent of Italian influence. Like the Italian city-states, the Dutch Netherlands, which had a well-developed network of trading towns, had wealthy urban families who patronized the arts. Lacking the patronage of the Church, which so benefited Florentine and other Italian painters, Flemish painters did few church frescoes (which a generally wet climate also discouraged). They emphasized decorative detail, such as that found in illuminated manuscripts, more than the spatial harmonies of Italian art. Dutch and Flemish painters favored realism more than Italian Renaissance idealism in their portrayal of the human body. They began to break away from religious subject matter and Gothic use of dark, gloomy colors and tones. In contrast to Italian painting, intense religiosity remained an important element in Flemish and German painting, and it was relatively rare to see a depiction of nudes.

Albrecht Dürer's visits to Italy reflect the dissemination and influence of the Italian Renaissance beyond the Alps. The son of a Nuremberg goldsmith, Dürer was apprenticed to a book engraver. As a young man, Dürer seemed irresistibly drawn to Italy as he wrestled with how to depict the human form. During two visits to Venice—in 1494 and 1505–1506—he sought out Italian painters, studying their use of mathematics in determining and representing proportion.

Many of the Italian envoys to northern Europe had studied the classics and carried on diplomacy with oratorical and writing skills learned by reading Cicero and other Roman authors. Literary societies, academies, and universities contributed to the diffusion of Renaissance ideals in northern Europe. Francis I established the Collège de France in 1530 in Paris, which soon had chairs in Greek, Hebrew, and classical Latin. Northern universities became centers of humanistic study, gradually taking over the role royal and noble households had played in the diffusion of education. In Poland, the University of Crakow, which had its first printing press in 1476, emerged as a center of humanism in the late fifteenth and early sixteenth centuries. But some universities were quite slow to include humanists; only one humanist taught at Cambridge University in the early sixteenth century.

Some nobles now sent their children to humanist schools or employed humanists as tutors, as did a number of wealthy urban bourgeois. Some Italian artists and scholars found employment in northern courts. Leonardo da Vinci, Renaissance artist and scientist, was employed by King Francis I of France and died in the château of Amboise on the Loire River. Kings and princes also hired humanists to serve as secretaries and diplomats.

Albrecht Dürer's *Self-Portrait* (1500).

Latin gradually became the language of scholarship beyond the Alps. A German scholar emphatically asserted that the German language was "the noblest, most distinguished, most humane of tongues," but he expressed his view in Latin. German, French, Spanish, and English historians borrowed from the style of the Roman historians to celebrate their own medieval past. Unlike Italian historians, they viewed the medieval period not as a sad interlude between two glorious epochs but as a time when their own political institutions and customs had been established.

In England at the end of the sixteenth century, Latin became the language of high culture, arguably as important as English. There Machiavelli's *The Prince* was widely read and debated in Latin. When continental scholars traveled to England, they could discuss common texts with their English counterparts. Sir Thomas More (1478–1535), English lawyer and statesman, reflected the influence of Renaissance humanism, writing poetry in Latin. In his *Utopia* (1516), a satire of contemporary political and social life, More asked readers to consider their own values in the context of their expanding knowledge of other societies, including those of the New World.

The spread of the cultural values of Renaissance humanism across the Alps into the German states and northern Europe helped prepare the way for the Reformation. Like the Renaissance, the Reformation was in some ways the work of humanists moving beyond what they considered to be the constraints of Church theology. Humanists, who had always been concerned with ethics, attacked not only the failings of some clerics but also some of the Church's teachings, especially its claim to be immune to criticism. They also condemned superstition in the guise of religiosity. Northern Renaissance humanists were the sworn enemies of scholasticism, the medieval system of ecclesiastical inquiry in which Church scholars used reason to prove the tenets of Christian doctrine within the context of assumed theological truths. By suggesting that individuals who were not priests could interpret the Bible for themselves, they threatened the monopoly of Church theologians over biblical interpretation.

Erasmus's Humanistic Critique of the Church

One energetic Dutch cleric contributed more than any other person to the growth of Renaissance humanism in northern Europe. Born to unmarried parents and orphaned in Rotterdam, Desiderius Erasmus (c. 1469–1536) spent seven years in a monastery. Ordained a priest in 1492, he taught at the universities of Cambridge and Louvain, then worked as a tutor in Paris and in Italy. As a young man, Erasmus may have suffered some sort of trauma—perhaps a romantic attachment that was either unreciprocated or inopportunely discovered. Thereafter compulsively obsessed with cleanliness, he was determined to infuse the Church with a new moral purity influenced by the Renaissance.

The patronage of Holy Roman Emperor Charles V and several other statesmen permitted Erasmus to apply the scholarly techniques of humanism to biblical study. Erasmus's *In Praise of Folly* (1509) is a satirical survey of the world as he saw it but also a clear call for a pure Christian morality shorn of the corruption he beheld in the monastic system. Thus, he wrote

Portrait of Desiderius Erasmus by Hans Holbein the Younger.

that priests claimed "that they've properly performed their duty if they reel off perfunctorily their feeble prayers which I'd be greatly surprised if any god could hear or understand." He believed that the scholastics of the Middle Ages had, like the barbarians, overwhelmed the Church with empty, lifeless theology.

Erasmus's attacks on those who believed in the curing power of relics (remains of saints venerated by the faithful) reflected his Renaissance sense of the dignity of the individual. His *Handbook of the Christian Soldier* (1503), which called for a theology that de-emphasized the sacraments, was Erasmus's guide to living a moral life. The little book went through twenty Latin editions and was translated into ten other languages. He wrote at length on how a prince ought to be educated and how children should be raised. The most well-known intellectual figure of his time in Europe, Erasmus greatly expanded the knowledge and appreciation of the classics in northern Europe. Erasmus and other major Northern Renaissance figures forged a Christian humanism focused on the early Christian past. Following his lead, northern humanists turned their skills in editing texts in Greek and Latin to the large body of early Christian writings. "All the scholars are Erasmians," a humanist had asserted in 1518, "except for a few skulking monks and petty theologians."

THE ROOTS OF THE REFORMATION

In principle, the pope governed the Church in all of Western Christendom. But in reality, the emergence of the monarchical states of France, England, and the kingdoms of Spain in the late Middle Ages had eroded papal authority. Gradually these rulers assumed more prerogatives over the Church in their states. This expansion of monarchical authority itself provided the impetus toward the development of churches that gradually took on a national character as monarchs bargained for authority over religious appointments and worked to bring ecclesiastical property under their fiscal control by imposing taxation.

In the Italian and German states and in Switzerland, where many smaller, independent states ruled by princes, urban oligarchs, or even bishops survived, the very complexity of territorial political arrangements served to limit the direct authority of the pope. For in these smaller states, too, the ability of the pope and his appointees to manage their own affairs depended on the cooperation of lay rulers. Furthermore, the territorial expanse of Western Christendom and daunting problems of transportation and communication made it difficult for the papal bureaucracy to reform blatant financial abuses. That the papacy itself increasingly appeared to condone or even encourage corruption added to the calls for reform.

Yet, although Erasmus and other northern humanists were among those criticizing the Church, they were unwilling to challenge papal authority. The papacy, however, had other, more vociferous critics. First, the monarchs of Europe's strongest states claimed even greater authority in religious affairs. The monarchs of France, Spain, and England had repudiated the interference of the pope in temporal affairs and reduced his effective authority within their own states by creating what were, for all intents and purposes, national churches. Second, religious movements deemed heretical by the Church rejected papal authority. Some people sought refuge from the turmoil in spiritualism. Others based their idea of religion on personal study of the Bible, turning away from not only papal authority but also the entire formal hierarchy of the Church. Third, within the Church, a reform movement known as conciliarism sought to subject the authority of the popes to councils of cardinals and other Church leaders. Fourth, as the Church seemed determined to protect its authority, to critics it also seemed more venal, even corrupt, than ever before. More and more calls echoed for the reform of clerical abuses. By questioning fundamental Church doctrine and the nature of religious faith, the resulting reform movement, culminating in the Reformation, shattered the unity of Western Christendom.

The Great Schism (1378–1417)

In the fourteenth century, the struggle between the king of France and the pope put the authority of the papacy in jeopardy. The French and English kings had imposed taxes on ecclesiastical property. In response, Pope Boniface VIII's bull *Unam Sanctam* (1302) threw down the gauntlet to lay rulers. It asserted that "it is absolutely necessary for salvation for everyone to be subject to the Roman pontiff." King Philip IV of France ordered Boniface's arrest, and he died in 1303, shortly after his release from captivity. Philip then arranged the election of a pliant pope, Clement V (pope 1305–1314). In 1309, he installed him in the papal enclave of Avignon, a town on the Rhône River. During the "Avignon Papacy" (1309–1378), the popes remained under the direct influence of the king of France. At the same time, they continued to build up their bureaucracies and, like the monarchs whose authority they sometimes contested, to extract ever greater revenues from the faithful.

In 1377, Pope Gregory XI (pope 1370–1378) returned to Rome, in the hope that his presence there might calm the political situation in the Italian states. When Gregory XI died a year later, a group of cardinals in Rome, most of whom were French, elected Pope Urban VI (pope 1378–1389), popularly believed to be faithful to the Avignon Papacy. After a Roman mob invaded the proceedings, most of the cardinals fled. Upon their return several months later, a smaller group of thirteen cardinals was vexed by the new pope's denunciation of their wealth and privileges. Furthermore, they now viewed him as temperamentally unstable, unfit to be pope. They elected another pope, Clement VII, who claimed to be pope between 1378 and 1394. He returned to set up shop in Avignon, leaving his rival, Urban VI, in Rome. The Great Schism (1378–1417) began with two men now claiming authority over the Church.

The two popes and their successors thereafter sought to win the allegiance of rulers. The Avignon popes, like their pre-Schism predecessors, were under the close scrutiny of the king of France, and the Roman pope was caught up in the morass of Italian and Roman politics. France, Castile, Navarre, and Scotland supported the Avignon popes; most of the Italian states, Portugal, the Holy Roman Empire, and England obeyed the Roman popes. In 1409, Church dignitaries gathered at the Council of Pisa to resolve the conflict, and they elected a third pope. However, neither of the other two would agree to resign. And, in the meantime, secular rulers forced the popes to make agreements that increased the authority of the former over the Church in their states. The Great Schism enabled lay rulers to construct virtual national churches at the expense of papal power.

Heretical and Spiritual Movements

The chaos of two and then three popes claiming authority over the Church, along with the ruthlessness and greed of the claimants, greatly increased dissatisfaction with the organization of the Church. For many people loyal to the Church, the Great Schism cast disrepute on papal authority itself. From time to time, heresies (movements based on beliefs deemed contrary to the teaching of the Church) had denied the authority of the papacy and demanded reform. In the twelfth century, the Waldensians in the Alps and the Albigensians in the south of France had defied the papacy by withdrawing into strictly organized communities that, unlike monasteries and convents, recognized neither Church doctrine nor authority.

An undercurrent of mysticism persisted in Europe, based on a belief in the supremacy of individual piety in the quest for a knowledge of God and eternal salvation. William of Occam (c. 1290–1349), an English monk and another critic of the papacy, rejected scholastic rationalism. Scholasticism had become increasingly linked to the theology of Thomas Aquinas, who had deduced the existence of God from rational proofs that moved from one premise to the next. Occam, in contrast, posited that the gulf between God and man was so great that scholastic proofs of His existence, such as those of Aquinas, were pointless because mankind could not understand God through reason. "Nominalists," as Occam and his followers were known, believed that individual piety should be the cornerstone of religious life. Nominalists rejected papal authority and the hierarchical structure of the Church. Their views reflected and accentuated the turn of more clergy and laymen toward the Scriptures as a guide for the individual's relationship with God, emphasizing the importance of leading a good, simple life. The Great Schism may have increased the yearning for spirituality as well as for the institutional reform of the Church.

The English cleric and scholar John Wyclif (c. 1328–1384) also questioned the pope's authority and claimed that an unworthy pope did not have to be obeyed, views that drew papal censorship. For Wyclif, the Church consisted of the body of those God had chosen to be saved, and no more. Stressing the role of faith in reaching eternal salvation, he insisted that reading the Scriptures formed the basis of faith and the individual's relationship with God. Wyclif also put himself at odds with Church theology by rejecting transubstantiation (the doctrine that holds that during Mass the priest transforms ordinary bread and wine into the body and blood of Christ).

Wyclif's de-emphasis of rituals and his advocacy of a religion based on faith suggested the significantly reduced importance of the Church as intermediary between man and God. Wyclif, who had powerful English noble and clerical protectors, called for Church reform. But the Peasants' Revolt of 1381 in England, in which wealthy churchmen were targets of popular wrath, gave even Wyclif's powerful protectors pause by raising the specter of future social unrest. An English Church synod condemned Wyclif, but he was allowed to live out his remaining years in a monastery. Some of his English followers, poor folk known as the Lollards, carried on Wyclif's work after his death. They criticized the Church's landed wealth and espoused a simpler religion. Led by gentry known as "Lollard knights," the Lollards rose up in rebellion in 1414, but the revolt was brutally crushed.

In Bohemia in Central Europe, Jan Hus (c. 1369–1415), a theologian, had learned of Wyclif's teaching. He, too, loudly criticized the worldliness of some clerics, and called for a return to a more unadorned religion. Rejecting the authority of the papacy and denouncing popes as "anti-Christs," Hus held that ordinary people could reform the Church.

The Challenge of Conciliarism to Papal Authority

The doctrine of conciliarism arose not only in response to the Great Schism but also to growing demands from many churchmen that the Church must undertake reform. The Council of Constance (1414–1418) was called to resolve the Great Schism and to undertake a reform of the Church. Many of the ecclesiastical dignitaries who attended also wanted to limit and define the authority of the papacy.

There were at least four significant parties to conciliarism: the popes themselves; bishops who supported councils as a way of resolving Church problems; secular rulers, particularly French kings, but also Holy Roman emperors, intervening in the Great Schism; and finally heretics condemned at Constance, who were far more radical than the mainstream conciliarists in their challenge to papal authority.

The Council of Constance first turned its attention to Jan Hus. Holding a safe-conduct pass given to him by the king of Bohemia, Hus travelled to the Council of Constance in 1414 but was arrested and put on trial for heresy. Hus refused to recant Wyclif's views, defending his own belief that the faithful, like the priest saying Mass, ought to be able to receive communion, the Church's rite of unity, in the two forms of bread and wine. The council condemned Hus, turning him over to the Holy Roman emperor, who ordered him burned at the stake as a heretic. The Hussites, the only major fifteenth-century dissidents within the Church, fought off several papal armies. They finally won special papal dispensation for the faithful to take communion in both bread and wine; their "Utraquist" ("in both kinds") church lasted until 1620.

The council resolved the ongoing conflicting claims to papal authority by deposing two of the claimants and accepting the resignation of the third. In 1417, the council elected Martin V (pope 1417–1431). But the Great Schism, with its multiple papal claimants, by delaying any serious attempts at reform, had reinforced the insistence of some prelates that councils of Church bishops ought to have more authority than the pope.

Convoked by the pope, at least in principle, councils brought together leading ecclesiastical dignitaries from throughout Europe. These councils deliberated on matters of faith, as well as on the organization of the Church. But some councils began to come together in defiance of papal authority. Those holding a "conciliar" view of the Church conceived of it as a corporation of cardinals that could override papal authority. William of Occam had argued a century earlier that, when confronted by a heretical pope, a general council of the Church could stand as the repository of truth and authority. Some reformers wanted to impose a written constitution on the Church, as the papacy moved to reassert its authority. At the Council of Basel, which began in 1431, exponents of unlimited papal authority and their counterparts favoring conciliarist positions both presented their views. A break occurred in 1437, when the pope ordered the council moved to Ferrara, and then to Florence in 1438. At that time and until 1445, some of the participants, mostly conciliarists, continued to meet in Basel, although the pope declared that council schismatic. Fifteen years later, Pope Pius II (pope 1458–1464), who had earlier been active in the conciliar movement, turned against it, declaring it a heresy and reestablishing the absolute authority of the pope.

The assertion by some churchmen that councils had authority over the papacy merged easily with those who called for the reform of blatant abuses within the Church. Some monasteries were mocked as hypocritical institutions no more saintly than the supposedly profane world monks and nuns sought to leave behind. Several new religious orders had been founded at least partially out of impatience if not disgust with ecclesiastical worldliness.

Clerical Abuses and Indulgences

Critics of the papacy attacked with particular energy what they considered to be ecclesiastical financial and moral abuses. They claimed that the papacy seemed to have become an investment trust run by the priests who administered the papacy's temporal affairs. No clerical financial abuse was more attacked than indulgences. Indulgences were based on the idea of transferable merit. Through granting indulgences, the Church

Jan Hus being burned at the stake as a heretic.

supposedly reduced the time a soul would have to suffer punishment in Purgatory (that halfway house between Hell and Heaven that had emerged in Church belief early in the Middle Ages) for sins committed on earth. The practice of selling indulgences began during the Crusades as a means of raising revenue for churches and hospitals. Those seeking the salvation of their souls did not purchase God's forgiveness (which could only be received in the confessional) but rather cancelled or reduced the temporal punishment (such as the pilgrimages, prayers, or charity) required to atone for their sins. In 1457, the pope had announced that indulgences could be applied to the souls of family members or friends suffering in Purgatory. Some people had the impression that purchasing indulgences rather than real repentence was an immediate entry to Heaven for oneself or one's relatives. "The moment the money tinkles in the collecting box, a soul flies out of Purgatory," went one ditty. The implication was that wealthy families had a greater chance of opening the doors of Heaven for their loved ones than poor people. One papal critic interpreted all of this to mean that "the Lord desireth not the death of a sinner but rather that he may live and pay." In his *In Praise of Folly,* Erasmus wrote, "What should I say of them that hug themselves with their counterfeit pardons; that have measured Purgatory by the hourglass, and can without the least mistake demonstrate its ages, years, months, days, hours, minutes, and seconds, as it were in a mathematical table? And now suppose some Merchant, Soldier, or Judge, parts with some small piece of ill-gotten money. He at once conceives . . . his whole life quite cleansed . . . so bought off that [he] may begin a new score."

Another clerical practice that was much criticized was that of the sale of Church offices, or positions, known as simony. Despite a deluge of indignant criticism, in 1487 the pope put twenty-four posts up for sale. More than ever before, those who participated in—and benefited from—this practice were Italian clerics. Most popes appointed Italians as cardinals, many of whom lived in Rome while accumulating great wealth from ecclesiastical sees (areas of a bishops' jurisdiction) they rarely if ever visited. Some prominent families looked to the Church to provide lucrative sinecures (offices that generated income but that required little or no work) for their children. Reformers decried the appointment of unqualified bishops who had purchased their offices.

Many priests were resented because they charged exorbitant fees for burial. Resentment also mounted, particularly in the German states, because clerics were immune from civil justice and paid no taxes. It seemed symbolic of the time that Pope Leo X allegedly effused to his brother, "God has given us the papacy—let us enjoy it!" Indulgences and pardons were swapped for gold or services; since about 1300, they had become a papal monopoly. Commenting on Leo's death in 1521, one wag remarked, "His last moments come, he couldn't even have the [Last] Sacrament. By God, he's sold it!"

The papacy also came under attack for moral abuses. In the diocese of Trent in the early sixteenth century, about a fifth of all priests kept concubines. Nepotism, the awarding of posts to relatives or friends, seemed to reign supreme. In the fifteenth century, Pope Paul II was mocked as the "happy father," not revered as the Holy Father. Alexander VI (pope 1492–1503) looked after his own children with the care of any other father. Paul III (pope 1534–1549) made two of his grandsons cardinals. (Their expensive hats were far bigger than the young heads upon which they occasionally sat.)

The sacrament of penance generated some degree of popular resentment against the clergy. Since 1215, the faithful were required to confess their sins each year to a priest. This sacrament originated in the context of instruction to encourage good behavior—the Ten Commandments gradually replacing the Seven Deadly Sins as the foundation of Christian ethics. But for many people, penance had become the priest's interrogation of the faithful in the confessional, during which the confessor sought out details of misdeeds in order to determine one of the sixteen stated degrees of transgression. Specific confessional questions found in priests' manuals included, "Have you dressed proudly, sung and danced lustily, committed adultery, girl-watched, or exchanged adulterous glances in church or while walking on Sundays?" Church's call for sinners to repent seemed ironic in view of popularly perceived ecclesiastical abuses.

Given a boost by the conciliar movement, calls for reform echoed louder and louder. The representatives of the clergy who had gathered at the Estates-General of France in 1484 criticized the sale of Church offices. In 1510, the Augsburg Diet, an imperial institution of the Holy Roman Empire, refused to grant money to the pope for a war against the Turks unless he first ordered an end to financial abuses. The imperial representative Assembly (Reichstag) had increasingly served as a forum for denunciations against the papacy. In 1511, King Louis XII of France, whose armies had backed up his territorial ambitions in northern Italy, called a council with the goal of reasserting the conciliar doctrine and ordered reforms in the monastic houses of his realm. The Fifth Lateran Council, which met from 1512 to 1517, urged more education for the clergy, sought to end some monastic financial abuses, and insisted that occupants of religious houses keep their vows of chastity. The council also suggested missions to carry the Church's influence into the Americas. Pope Leo X, however, emphatically insisted that he alone could convoke Church councils, and the council itself forbade sermons denouncing the moral state of the Church.

Martin Luther

Martin Luther (1483–1546) was born in the small town of Eisleben in central Germany. He was the son of a miner whose family had been prosperous peasants for several generations. His peasant background could be seen in the coarseness of his language, song, and humor. The pious, determined, stocky Luther went off to a nearby town to attend school. In 1501, he began his studies at the University of Erfurt, where he took courses in philosophy and then began the study of law.

In July 1505, Luther was engulfed in a violent storm as he returned to Erfurt after a visit home. As a bolt of lightning struck not far from where he stood in terror, the young student cried out to the patron saint of travelers, "Help me, Saint Anne, I will become a monk." Returning safely to Erfurt, he gathered his friends together, treated them to a nice meal, and told them, "Today you see me, henceforth, never more." They escorted him to the nearby monastery of the Augustinian monks, which he entered against his father's wishes. Luther prayed, fasted, and, outside the monastery, begged for charity. In 1507, he was ordained a priest and soon became a doctor of theology, administrator of eleven Augustinian monasteries, and dean of the theological seminary in the town of Wittenberg.

Luther had, for some time, been wracked with gnawing doubt concerning his personal unworthiness. Was he not a sinner? He had been saved from the storm, but would he be saved from damnation on Judgment Day? Was there really any connection between good works effected on earth and salvation? Even if he confessed all of the sins on his conscience, were there not sins omitted unintentionally that blotted his soul? If mankind was so corrupted by sin, how could charity, fasting, or constant prayer and self-flagellation in the monastery earn one entry to Heaven? He later recalled, "I tried hard . . . to be contrite, and make a list of my sins. I confessed them again and again. I scrupulously carried out the penances that were allotted to me. And yet my conscience kept telling me: 'You fell short there.' 'You were not sorry enough.' 'You left that sin off your list.' I was trying to cure the doubts and scruples of the conscience with human remedies. . . . The more I tried these remedies, the more troubled and uneasy my conscience grew."

Luther's lonely study of theology in the tower library of the monastery did not resolve his doubts. Like other Augustinians, he had been influenced by the nominalism of the followers of William of Occam. This led Luther closer to his contention that faith, not good works, was the key to salvation. Indeed, the teachings of Saint Augustine himself also suggested to him that each person could be saved by faith alone through the grace of God. Believing man is saved "not by pieces, but in a heap," Luther became obsessed with a phrase from the Bible (Romans 1:17), "The just shall live by faith." Such a conclusion broke with the accepted teachings of the Church as defined by medieval scholasticism. But more than faith was troubling Luther. He was also especially troubled by the abuse of the ecclesiastical sale of indulgences.

On October 31, 1517, Luther tacked up on the door of the castle church of Wittenberg "Ninety-five Theses or Disputations on the Power

An allegorical painting of the dream of Frederick the Wise wherein Martin Luther uses an enormous quill to tack his Ninety-five Theses to the door of the castle church at Wittenberg.

and Efficacy of Indulgences." Other critics before him had denounced the sale of indulgences, but Luther attacked the theoretical underpinnings of the papal granting of indulgences out of the "treasury of merits" accumulated by Christ and the saints. "The true treasure of the Church," Luther declared, "is the holy gospel of the glory and the grace of God." He had his theses printed and distributed in the region and invited those who might want to dispute his theses to present themselves to debate with him, as was the custom. In February 1518, Pope Leo X demanded that Luther's monastic superior order him to cease his small crusade. Luther refused, citing his right as a professor of theology to dispute formally the charges now leveled against him. And he found a protector, Frederick III, elector of Saxony.

In April, as denunciations against Luther poured into Rome, he successfully defended his theses before his Augustinian superiors. Pope Leo was trying to remain on good terms with Frederick III, a strong candidate for election as Holy Roman emperor. Instead of immediately summoning Luther to Rome, he therefore proposed that a papal legate travel to Augsburg to hear Luther out. At their meeting, the legate warned Luther to desist or face the consequences. Luther's friends, suspecting that the pope had authorized his arrest, whisked him away to safety.

Luther sought a negotiated solution. He agreed to write a treatise calling on the German people to honor the Church, and promised neither to preach nor publish anything else if his opponents would also keep silent. At this point Luther did not seek to create a new church, but merely to reform the old one. A papal representative sent to meet with Luther in Leipzig in June 1519 accused him of being a Hussite, that is, of denying the pope's authority. There Luther admitted that he did not believe the pope to be infallible.

Luther crossed his Rubicon, but unlike Caesar moved not toward Rome but away from it. "Farewell, unhappy, hopeless, blasphemous Rome! The wrath of God come upon thee, as you deserve," he wrote a friend, "We have cared for Babylon and she is not healed; let us then leave her. . . ." Luther would not be silenced. "I am hot-blooded by temperament and my pen gets irritated easily," he proclaimed, pouring out vigorous tract after tract, each more adamant than the one before.

Three treatises published in 1520 marked Luther's final break with Rome. Here Luther developed his theology of reform, one that went far beyond the prohibition of indulgences and the sale of ecclesiastical offices. He argued his view that faith alone could bring salvation, that good works follow faith but do not in themselves save the soul. Nor does the absence of good works condemn man to eternal damnation, he claimed. Upon reading one of these tracts, Erasmus, loyal critic of the Church, stated emphatically, "The breach is irreparable."

Developing the theological concept of "freedom of a Christian," Luther's immediate goal was to free German communities from the strictures of religious beliefs and institutions that seemed increasingly foreign to their faith. He called on the princes of the German states to reform the Church in their states. In doing so, he argued that the Scriptures declared the Church itself to be a priestly body that was not subject to the pope's interpretation. Luther acknowledged only two of the seven sacraments, those instituted by Christ, not the papacy: baptism and communion. After first retaining penance, he dropped it, arguing that faith was sufficient to bring about a sinner's reconciliation with God. If this was true, the monastic life no longer seemed to Luther to provide any advantage in the quest for salvation. And he rejected what he called the "unnatural" demands of poverty, chastity, and obedience.

On June 15, 1520, Pope Leo X excommunicated Luther from the Church, accusing him of forty-one heresies, "offensive, erroneous, objectionable to pious ears, misleading to simple minds, and contrary to Catholic teaching." The papal bull called Luther "the wild boar who has invaded the Lord's vineyard." In Wittenberg, a crowd burned papal bulls and documents. Luther defiantly tossed the writ of excommunication into the flames.

Charles V had been elected Holy Roman emperor following his father's death in 1519. He had promised before his election that no one would be excommunicated within the empire without a proper hearing. Through the influence of Frederick III of Saxony, Charles summoned Luther to the town of Worms in April 1521 to confront the imperial Diet (assembly).

Before the assembled Diet, Luther was asked if he had written the imposing number of treatises and books placed on the table. Acknowledging them all, Luther told the Diet: "I am bound by the Scriptures I have quoted and my conscience is captive to the Word of God. I cannot and I will not retract anything, since it is neither safe nor right to go against conscience. I cannot do otherwise, here I stand, may God help me. Amen." The Diet condemned Luther's beliefs. Charles V, in agreement with the pope, signed the Edict of Worms in May 1521, placing Luther under the "ban of the empire." This forbade him from preaching and declared him a heretic, thus promising to stamp out his influence. In the meantime, Luther had left Worms. Several men loyal to Frederick III of Saxony, Luther's protector, kidnapped him, escorting him to safety. In Wartburg Castle, the reformer took shelter from the storms of controversy, translating, despite moods of depression, Erasmus's critical edition and retranslation of the Bible into German.

By declaring Luther an outlaw and forbidding any changes in religion in the Holy Roman Empire, the Edict of Worms made religious reform an issue of state. But Luther could not have survived the ban of the empire if his influence had not already spread, convincing many that through Luther they had now discovered the true Gospel.

Social Background of the Reformation in the German States

Challenging the ways people in Central Europe had thought about religion for centuries, the movement for reform, spread by preachers, found converts in the German states. During the early 1520s, the proponents of Martin Luther's reform convinced many clergy and lay people to reconsider their religious beliefs and to restructure their communities. Social and political unrest, perhaps encouraged by the quest for religious reform, began to stir in the central and southern German states as peasants rose up against their lords. These events, although roundly condemned by Luther, left no doubt that the Reformation would shake the foundations of the German states.

Urban Centers of Reform

At first the Reformation was overwhelmingly an urban phenomenon in the German states and then Switzerland. The decentralized political structure of the Holy Roman Empire and traditions of popular participation in urban government aided the movement for reform. There were free cities in the northern German states, such as the still powerful Baltic trading city of Lübeck, leader of the Hanseatic League, and self-governing towns in the southern German states. Some towns were under pressure from princely neighbors who wanted them to contribute to the cost of imperial government. But even towns that had not maintained their independence enjoyed municipal privileges (such as autonomous administration or exemption from certain forms of taxation) that had already been eroded or had disappeared in France and Spain as monarchies consolidated and extended their authority. Each German town had its own elite of prosperous burghers. Reformers found these communities fertile ground for Luther's ideas. Complaining of incompetent or lazy priests, members of some towns had endowed posts for preachers in order to attract vigorous, effective priests, a good many of whom now followed Luther.

German towns also had a particularly well-developed sense of civic solidarity that included a belief that all citizens of the town shared a common fate in the material world—vulnerability to bad times, and a certain degree of prosperity in good times—and that salvation itself was something of a group enterprise. Erasmus had asked, "What else is the city but a great monastery?" Many German townspeople, then, tended to see their community as a miniature of Christendom. Luther sought to spark a more personal religion that would make people not only better Christians, but better citizens of their communities as well. In many towns, urban leaders and ordinary people may also have accepted reform because it appeared more promising than unreformed Catholicism for the maintenance of local order.

An engraving of Lübeck, Germany.

No simple formula could predict how the Reformation would fare in specific parts of the German states. In some towns in the southern German states, wealthy town leaders such as urban nobles, merchants, and bankers remained staunchly Catholic. These property-owning groups were more conservative by instinct and often had a vested interest in the survival of, for example, stained-glass church windows financed by their ancestors. Here, also, the role of personality and the configuration of local social and political life came into play; so did pure chance, including such factors as whether preachers and reform literature arrived, how both were received, and by whom.

The Process of Reform

Social and political factors thus helped shape religious outcomes. While the embrace of the Reformation did not constitute a social revolution, in many cases clergy supporting religious reform were drawn from the middle and lower middle classes, groups with some possibility of social mobility. The "middling sort," in turn, brought reform to the lower classes. This process might be marked by the spontaneous singing of Lutheran hymns by those sitting in Mass, or by some other signs of a turn to reform. While archbishops and bishops in general opposed Luther, the lower clergy, particularly those of recent ordination, became influential converts in their towns. Communities accepted reformers by consensus, as local governments began to bow to the wishes of townspeople.

Thus, a crowd cheered in Basel when a priest carried the Bible instead of the communion host during the feast of Corpus Christi. Priests began to wear simpler clothes instead of rich robes. They attempted to change the liturgy of the Mass, for the first time saying some of it in German. Some began to give the faithful both bread and wine during communion. Some crowds mocked Church rituals in angry ways: ringing cow bells outside churches to disrupt Mass; heckling priests trying to deliver sermons; smashing stained-glass windows, crucifixes, statues, and other images of the saints; and occasionally destroying relics considered sacred. Such largely spontaneous actions bewildered Luther, who remained in most ways a very conservative man.

Luther and his followers denied the special status of the clergy as a group marked off from the rest of the population. In the early days of the Reformation, some reformers undertook expeditions to "rescue" nuns from convents. A number of former priests began to take wives, which at first shocked Luther, since this represented the end of clerical celibacy, which the Church had proclaimed in the eleventh century. Luther asserted in 1521, "Good Lord! Will our people at Wittenberg give wives even to monks? They will not push a wife on me!" But by 1525 he changed his mind, and married a former nun. The marriage of clerics further broke down the barrier between the priest and the people, symbolizing the

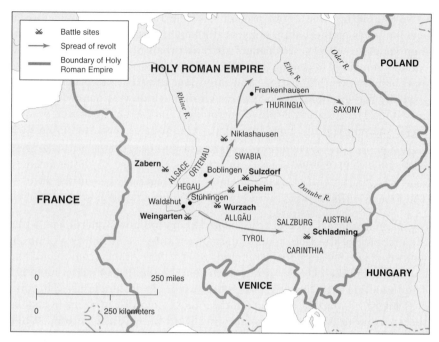

MAP 3.1 THE PEASANTS' REVOLT, 1525–1526   Sites of peasant uprisings in parts of the central and southern German states. The revolt began in Waldshut and Stühlingen in the southern German states and spread east to the Tyrol and Salzburg in Austria, and north to Thuringia and Saxony.

"priesthood of all believers" by eliminating the clerical distinction of celibacy. Nonetheless, Luther limited the task of interpreting the Scriptures to professors of theology.

The Peasants' Revolt

The gap between rich and poor seemed particularly great at the beginning of the sixteenth century. In the southern German states, some burghers worried that law and order would collapse, and that the poor might rise up. News of several strange and alarming prophecies circulated. Some lords and burghers expressed concern that the villagers might "turn Swiss," referring to the Swiss towns that lived without lords and were self-governing and independent.

In 1524–1525, peasants rose up against their lords in parts of the central and southern German states (see Map 3.1). They demanded the return of rights (such as to hunt freely and to pasture their animals on the common lands) that the lords had usurped. They also asked for the abolition of serfdom and the tithe, which they declared to be against God's will. Bands of poor people burned castles and monasteries.

The peasants' revolt spread into Austria and Carinthia, and up into Thuringia and Saxony. Pamphlets called for social as well as religious reform. Thomas Münzer (c. 1491–1525), a priest and theologian, merged religious reform with social revolution. He preached against the Church and Luther with equal fury, for he believed that both the Church and Luther had humbled themselves to lay authorities. Münzer led a peasant army in Thuringia, where Luther's reform movement had made many converts.

In the northwestern German states, also in 1525, some towns that had been won over to religious reform rose up against Catholic princes. Swabian peasants promulgated twelve articles against their lords, princes, and bishops, requesting that communities have the right to choose their own pastors. But here, too, the demands of the rebels had a social content. They asked for an end to double taxation by both lay and ecclesiastical lords and the "death tax" by which heirs had to give up the deceased's finest horse, cow, or garment. They demanded the end of serfdom, the return of common lands to their use, and free access to forests and streams.

Luther had some sympathy with the plight of the poor. But he rejected the idea that his central theological idea of "Christian freedom," which he believed applied only to the spiritual realm, could be extended into the relationship between lord and peasant. As nobles and churchmen began to accuse him of fomenting insurrection, he denounced the peasants in extravagant language. In *Against the Murdering, Thieving Hordes of Peasants,* he advised the German princes to "brandish their swords. . . . You cannot meet a rebel with reason. Your best answer is to punch him in the face until he has a bloody nose." Catholic and reformed princes put aside their differences to crush the revolt, in which more than 100,000 peasants perished. Münzer was defeated, captured, tortured, and beheaded.

Yet, some of Luther's followers began to see in his teaching a means of resistance against the powerful. Luther asked lords to "act rationally" and "try kindness" when confronted by peasant demands. He asked Christian rulers to "offer the mad peasants an opportunity to come to terms, even though they are unworthy of it." But, when all was said and done, Luther was "opposed to those who rise in insurrection, no matter how just their cause."

THE SPREAD OF THE REFORMATION

Because of the intertwining of religion and politics, what began as a movement for Church reform became entangled in princely rivalries in the German states. As the breach between Catholic and reformed princes widened, religion became a source of division rather than of unity. Although Luther had never intended to bring about a permanent division within Christianity, his followers gradually created a new church in many of the German states. The Reformation then spread beyond the German states.

Divisions within Christendom

The Augsburg Confession, a summary of beliefs presented by Luther's friends to the Diet that gathered in that city in 1530, became the doctrinal basis of the Lutheran Church. It was implemented by princes and prelates in the reformed states and towns, and in some places by a council, known as a consistory, of ministers and lawyers.

Some humanists influenced by the Renaissance were attracted by Luther's writing. Erasmus appreciated Luther's call for simple piety and his denunciation of superstition and corruption within the Church. Furthermore, some humanists, in the tradition of their predecessors who had rediscovered the classics, admired Luther's return to the Scriptures as an original source of knowledge. One of Luther's converts later wrote that his own excitement at the new teaching was so great that he studied the Bible at night with sand in his mouth so that he would not fall asleep. Humanists transformed some monasteries into schools. The first reformed university began in the German town of Marburg in 1527.

But as the gap between reformers and the Church grew larger, Erasmus was caught in the middle. His own criticism of the Church did not go far enough for reformers, but it went too far for churchmen. Erasmus, who had condemned ecclesiastical abuses, remained loyal to Church doctrine. Similarly, Luther and the humanists parted ways by 1525. For the latter, humanistic knowledge was an end in itself; for the reformers, rhetoric was

The Augsburg Confession read before Charles V in 1530.

a method for teaching the Scriptures and for arguing in favor of ecclesiastical reform. Many reformers were less committed than humanists to the belief that man is a rational and autonomous being. Luther himself did not share the humanists' Renaissance optimism about mankind. He was not interested in rediscovering mankind but was instead preoccupied with an individual's relationship to God, arguing that people depend on grace alone to obtain salvation. Furthermore, Luther opposed attempts by philosophers to intrude in theological questions. Nonetheless, a humanist curriculum continued to influence the training of reform ministers.

Luther's followers gained their first martyrs in 1523, when two former monks were executed in Brussels for their beliefs. German princes requested from the Holy Roman emperor Charles V that a "free general council or at least a national council" consider the growing religious division within the Holy Roman Empire. The Diet of Speyer (1526) proclaimed that each German prince was "to live, govern, and bear himself as he hopes and trusts to answer to God and his imperial majesty." This truce gave reformers time to win even more converts. In 1529, German princes again gathered in Speyer. Some of them prepared a "protest" against the policies of Charles V and the Catholic princes, who had declared themselves against Luther. The followers of Luther became known as "Protestants."

Luther's writing, translated into Latin, then spread east and west beyond the German states, following trade routes. The reformers easily revived the anti-papal Hussite traditions of Bohemia and Moravia and that of the Waldensians in the southwestern Alps. Turkish military victories over Habsburg armies in Hungary left Lutheran missionaries an open field. German merchants carried reform not only to the Baltic states but also north to Scandinavia. In Denmark, King Christian II adopted Lutheranism for his state. In Sweden, the king's conversion and his break with Rome led to a similar reform. When Lutheranism was declared its official religion in 1527, Sweden and its territory of Finland had the first national reformed church.

Charles V and the Protestants

Holy Roman Emperor Charles V, the pope's most powerful potential advocate, was a pious man who first denounced Luther with passion. But extensive Habsburg imperial interests kept him fighting a war in Western Europe against King Francis I of France, which prevented him from acting against those who supported Luther. The French king, for his part, was pleased that religion was dividing the German princes, thereby weakening the imperial crown that he had coveted and failed to gain. Charles was away from his German states between 1521 and 1530, for the most part in Italy. These were the crucial years during which the Reformation spread within the Holy Roman Empire; as early as 1524, the first Protestant leagues were formed between states in which reform had won wide appeal.

The Christian crusade against the Turks in Eastern Europe and the Mediterranean preoccupied Charles and other Catholic princes as well. In 1526, the Turks defeated the Hungarian king at Mohács in Hungary. A subsequent Turkish advance forced Charles to offer concessions to Lutheran princes in exchange for assistance against the Turks. (Luther's hymn "A Mighty Fortress Is Our God" began as a martial song to inspire soldiers against the Ottoman forces.)

For a time, Charles V held out hope for conciliation with the Protestants. In 1531, however, the princes of Hesse, Saxony, and other states and cities that had adopted religious reform formed the Schmalkaldic League. Although first and foremost a defensive alliance, the princes intended that the league would replace the Holy Roman Empire as the source of their political allegiance. Up until this time, Charles had accepted temporary truces, and thus toleration of Protestants. He had suspended the Edict of Worms (which had condemned Luther as a heretic), until a general council of the Church could be held. When the pope announced that it would be held in the Alpine town of Trent (see p. 124), the stage was set for confrontation with the Protestants. Meanwhile, however, Charles was still preoccupied by hostilities with Francis I of France, who shocked many Christians by allying with the Turks against the Habsburgs. After Charles forced an end to the wars by launching an invasion of France from the Netherlands, he was finally ready to move against Protestants, routing the Schmalkaldic League in battle in 1547, and subsequently forcing reconversion on the people in about thirty German cities. By that time, however, Protestantism had established itself definitively in much of Central Europe.

The Peace of Augsburg

With his attention no longer distracted by war against the Turks and French, Charles tried to bring more of the German princes and their people back into the Catholic fold. He tried without success to impose in Central Europe moderate Catholic reform in order to answer some of the criticism of the reformers. But some of the Catholic princes who had been allied with Charles now left the fold, and three of them took up arms against him in a short war in 1551. The political complexity of the myriad German states militated against a general settlement. The Holy Roman emperor gave up the idea of restoring Catholicism in all of the German states.

The Peace of Augsburg of 1555 was a compromise. It was agreed upon by the imperial representative assembly after Charles, worn down by the complexity of imperial politics, refused to participate. It stipulated that the religion of the ruler of each of the empire's states would be the religion of the state (*cuius regio, eius religio*) (see Map 3.2). Although it excluded reformed groups other than Lutherans, Protestants living in states with a Catholic ruler were free to emigrate, as were Catholics in the same

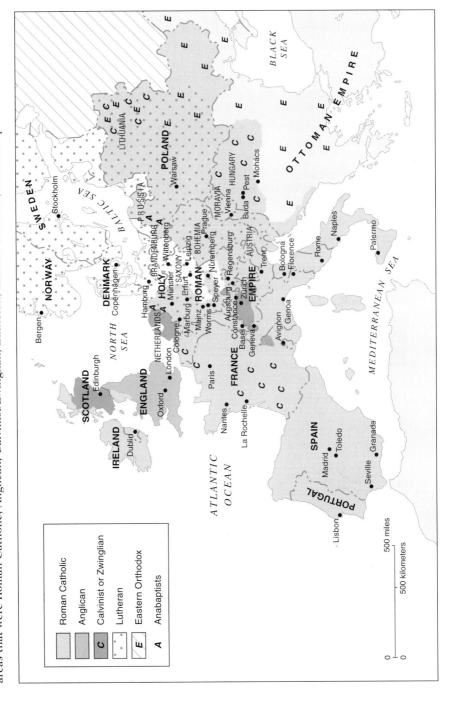

MAP 3.2 THE RELIGIOUS SITUATION IN EUROPE AFTER THE PEACE OF AUGSBURG, 1555   The Peace of Augsburg stipulated that the religion of the ruler of each of the Holy Roman Empire's states would be the religion of the state. The map indicates areas that were Roman Catholic, Anglican, Calvinist/Zwinglian, Lutheran, Eastern Orthodox, and Anabaptist.

situation. The Peace of Augsburg thus recognized that the institutions of the Holy Roman Empire could not provide a solution to what now appeared to be lasting religious divisions in Central Europe. It acknowledged that the Reformation in the German states was an accomplished fact, leaving a religious division in Germany that has lasted until this day. Thus, what had begun as a "squabble among monks" shaped the territorial and political history of Germany. Through the compromise that allowed each prince to determine the religion of his state, the Peace of Augsburg reaffirmed the independence of many German states (German particularism).

THE REFORMATION IN SWITZERLAND AND FRANCE

The next stage of the Reformation occurred in Switzerland, a land of rugged peasants, craftsmen, and mercenary soldiers. The sparsely populated cantons of Switzerland (then about a million people) were loosely joined in a federal Diet. In some ways, the thirteen fiercely independent Swiss cantons were closer in organization and in spirit to the Italian city-states than to the German states. Unlike in the German states, where the conversion of a powerful prince could sway an entire state, there were no such territorial rulers in Switzerland. The reformers in Switzerland, then, would be even more closely tied to privileged residents of towns of relatively small size. The Swiss reformers believed that it was imperative to establish the kingdom of God on earth. Their movement would also soon spread to parts of France.

(*Left*) Woodcut of Huldrych Zwingli. (*Right*) Burning church ornaments and religious statues in Zurich.

Zwingli and Reform

In Zurich, then a town of about 6,000, Huldrych Zwingli (1484–1531) preached salvation through faith alone. Drawing on his strong humanist training, he began preaching from Erasmus's edition of the Greek New Testament. In 1522, several citizens of Zurich publicly munched sausages during Lent in defiance of the Lenten ban on eating meat. Zwingli published two tracts on their behalf in which he insisted that the Scriptures alone should be the basis of religious practice, and that as there was nothing in the Bible about sausages, they could be eaten at any time. This scriptural test also led Zwingli and his followers to iconoclasm (the stripping of images and altar decorations from churches because nothing about them could be found in the Bible). The Zurich municipal council then embraced reform. It ordered the canton's priests to preach only from the Bible, and two years later it forbade the saying of Mass. Zwingli convinced the town's magistrates that tithes should be used to aid the poor, whom he believed represented the real image of God.

A doctrinal conflict among reformers helped define the character of the Swiss Reformation. Luther maintained that communion represented the physical presence of Christ. In this he had not diverged far from the Catholic Church, which insisted that through the miracle of transubstantiation (which the pope originally formulated in 1215), the priest transformed bread and wine into the actual body and blood of Christ, the sacrament of the Holy Eucharist. But to Luther, who condemned Catholic worship of the Eucharist, the bodily presence of Christ in the Eucharist came from the fact that Christ and God were universally present. Zwingli, by contrast, believed that communion was a *symbol* of Christ's real presence in the Eucharist and that Luther's refusal to abandon this idea demonstrated that he still stood with one foot in Rome. Luther accused Zwingli of reducing Christ's presence to a mere symbol. The "Sacramentarian Controversy" emerged as the first major doctrinal dispute among Protestants. The Augsburg Confession of 1530 sealed the rift by excluding reformers who rejected Lutheranism, such as Zwingli and his followers.

Between 1525 and 1530, some German-speaking parts of Switzerland and regions of the southern German states accepted Zwingli's reforms. In 1531, Catholic forces attacked Protestant cantons. Zwingli, carrying a sword and a Bible, led the Protestant forces into the Battle of Kappel and was killed in the fighting. Both Catholics and Lutherans claimed Zwingli's death to be divine judgment against his religious positions. The peace that followed, however, specified that each canton could choose its own religion, which amounted to a victory for Protestantism.

Radical Reformers

Some Zurich reformers had even more radical changes in mind. Believing that neither Luther nor Zwingli had sufficiently transformed religious

MAP 3.3 RADICAL RELIGIOUS MOVEMENTS   Areas in which there were Hussites, Utraquists, Anabaptists, and Mennonites.

morality and communal life, several radical groups, some of whose members were quite poor, formed communities in which they sought to implement "godly living" (see Map 3.3).

Millenarian groups, whose members believed that the end of the world was near, began to spring up. One group of radical reformers who had broken with Zwingli became known as Anabaptists. They rejected the baptism of infants because no reference to it could be found in the Bible. They believed that only adults could manifest true faith and therefore be worthy of baptism. Starting their own church in 1525, Anabaptists began to rebaptize adults—"anabaptism" means rebaptism in Greek.

The Anabaptists were sectarians, because for them membership was through free will or voluntary self-selection, rather than through territorial organization of churches as was true for Catholics, Lutherans, and Zwinglians. Anabaptists formed communities of believers in Switzerland and southern Germany, seeking isolation—"separation from iniquity," as they put it—from the struggles and temptations of the sinful secular world. They would not participate in political life and did not believe in having ties with temporal governments. They rejected secular agreements and refused to take civil oaths, pay taxes, hold public office, or serve in the army.

Catholic and Protestant states moved to crush these dissidents who rejected state authority. At the Diet of Speyer in 1529, Charles V made Anabaptism punishable by death, usually by—with intentional irony—drowning, "the third baptism." Many of these groups of radical reformers sought refuge in the mountains of the Tyrol and Moravia, and in Poland. Persecution increased the number of millenarians. Following the Peasants' Revolt of 1525, unsuccessful insurrections in Frankfurt, Cologne, and several other German towns merged social and political goals with opposition to the Catholic Church.

In 1532, a radical group of Anabaptists, millenarians who believed the second coming of Christ was close at hand, took over the town government of Münster by election. The old patrician families left town. The Anabaptists established a council of twelve that expropriated Catholic Church property, then abolished private property and banned the use of money, establishing a system of barter and communally held property.

Their prophet, John of Leyden, convinced the ministers and elders of Münster to allow polygamy (the taking of more than one wife) in the town, ostensibly to solidify the basis of the new theocracy based on endless links of kinship, but perhaps also because there were four times more women than men in the city. John led the way by taking sixteen wives. Under his orders, all books in Münster were burned except the Bible. The Münster Anabaptists then began to kill Catholics and Lutherans. The Anabaptist kingdom of the "New Jerusalem" lasted but sixteen months. Troops sent by Lutheran and Catholic princes alike stormed the town and then tortured to death the leaders, including a number of women, placing their mutilated corpses in an iron cage that still hangs in the church steeple.

Dutch Anabaptists included a group representing the pacifist strand of Anabaptism, which was largely a reaction to the events in Münster. They became known as Mennonites, after their leader, Menno Simons (1492–1559). Some of them emigrated to the Americas more than a century later in search of religious toleration. Likewise, the Unitarian religion has roots in this period, deriving from Anti-Trinitarian views of God as being one, not three.

Jean Calvin and Reform

France, too, provided fertile ground for reform. In 1520, a Swiss visitor wrote from Paris that "no books are more eagerly bought up than those of Luther. . . . One book shop has sold 1,400 copies. . . . Everywhere people speak highly of Luther. But the chains of the monks are long."

The French monarchy had traditionally maintained a stubborn independence from Rome. Pope Leo X had signed the Concordat of Bologna (1516) with King Francis I, giving the king the right to appoint bishops and abbots in France. Initially the Valois ruler was far more preoccupied with his wars against Charles V and the Habsburgs than with the stormy tracts of an obscure German monk. The threat of heresy, however, convinced him in 1521 to order Luther's writings confiscated and burned. Yet Protestant propaganda arrived in France from Germany through Strasbourg and evangelical attitudes spread during the next several years. In 1534, reformers affixed placards against the Mass in Paris and on the king's bedroom door in his château on the Loire River at Amboise. The "affair of the placards" convinced the king to combat reform in earnest.

Jean Calvin (1509–1564) embodied the second major current of the Reformation. He was born in the small town of Noyon in northern France, where his father worked as a secretary to the local bishop. Calvin's mother died when he was about five years old, and his father sent him to Paris to be trained as a priest. He then decided that his son should become a lawyer, because he might earn more money.

Late-Renaissance humanism and particularly the teachings of Erasmus helped stimulate in the pious young Calvin an interest in religious reform during the legal studies that helped to make him a systematic thinker. In 1534, the Catholic hierarchy and the king himself moved to crush this movement. Finding exile in the Swiss town of Basel, Calvin probably still considered himself a follower of Erasmus within the Catholic Church. In Basel, he penned tracts denouncing the papacy and calling on the king of France to end religious persecution.

Throughout his life, Calvin was overwhelmed by anxiety and self-doubt, compounded by his virtual abandonment by his father and his forced exile. He was also terror-struck by the power of nature and, in particular, by storms as manifestations of God's power—rather like Luther who made his vow to become a monk in a thunderstorm. Humanity seemed to Calvin to be poised before an abyss, a metaphor he frequently used. He feared that oceans might rise and sweep humankind away. Around him Calvin saw only the absence of order. The world was such that "we cannot be otherwise than constantly anxious and confused."

Like other thinkers of the early sixteenth century, Calvin believed that he lived in a time of extraordinary moral crisis. He assessed the world around him pessimistically: "Luxury increases daily, lawless passions are inflamed, and human beings continue in their crimes and profligacy more shameless than ever." It seemed to Calvin that the sense of community that ought to bind people together was dissolving.

Calvin argued that the Catholic Church had made the faithful anxious by emphasizing the necessity of good works in achieving salvation: the anxiety came from never knowing how many good works were enough. This had, Calvin insisted, turned Catholics to seek the intercession of saints. He attacked the sacrament of penance with particular vehemence:

> The souls of those who have been affected with some awareness of God are most cruelly torn by this butchery . . . the sky and sea were on every side, there was no port of anchorage. The more they had crossed over, the greater was the mass ever looming before their eyes, indeed it rose up like high mountains; nor did any hope of escape appear. . . . And at last no other outcome but despair was found.

Calvin also rejected the increasingly human-like images given God and Christ over the previous century. Unlike Luther, Calvin emphasized not reconciliation with God through faith, but obedience to his will. He sought to provide a doctrine that would reassure the faithful of God's grace and of their own salvation. There was hope in Calvin's thought, faith that the labyrinth—another of his frequent images—of life could be successfully navigated. The imposition of order, based upon the morality dictated by the Bible, would put an end to some of life's haunting uncertainties.

With this in mind, Calvin developed in his *Institutes of the Christian Religion* (1536–1559) the doctrine of election or predestination: "God's

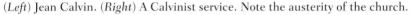

(*Left*) Jean Calvin. (*Right*) A Calvinist service. Note the austerity of the church.

eternal decree. . . . For all are not created in equal condition; rather, eternal life is foreordained for some, eternal damnation for others." The belief in predestination called into question the efficacy of good works. If one's fate were predestined and if good works in themselves (as the Catholic Church claimed) did not bring eternal salvation, why lead a righteous life? Calvin believed that good works were signs of having been chosen by God for eternal salvation, though they did not in themselves guarantee Heaven.

Whereas medieval theologians had condemned lending money for profit, Calvin, unlike Luther, distinguished between usury and productive loans that would raise capital and increase the well-being of the entire community. Replacing penance as a means of imposing individual discipline, Calvin preached collective, communal discipline in the pursuit of holiness. Validating economic activity, later Calvinists came to view prosperity, along with "sober living," as a sign of election by God. In the late nineteenth century, this came to be known as the "Protestant ethic."

Late in 1536, Calvin went to the Swiss lakeside city of Geneva, a town of about 13,000 people. With the first successes of the Reformation, word of which had originally been carried there by German merchants, Geneva broke away from the domination of the Catholic House of Savoy. Earlier that year, troops of the Swiss canton of Bern to the northeast, which had embraced Zwinglian reform, occupied the city. Bern established a protectorate, with Geneva retaining its nominal independence. Citizens elected magistrates and members of two representative councils.

Calvin had become, like Zwingli, convinced that reform must transform not only the individual but society as well. In 1537, he persuaded the smaller and most powerful of the two councils to adopt a Confession of Faith, swearing that the people of Geneva "live according to the holy evangelical law and the Word of God." Residency in Geneva would be contingent on formal adherence to the document. The Mass was banned, and priests were informed that they had to convert to reformed religion or leave the city.

Calvin's plans for Geneva were far-reaching. He hoped to impose Christian discipline and asceticism on the city in order to construct a righteous society. His "Ecclesiastical Ordinances" would provide for the organization of religious life in reformed Geneva, but they threatened the powers of the councils. Calvin insisted that the Consistory, the judiciary of the reformed church made up of lay elders (called presbyters), would have the right to discipline all citizens and to dispense harsh penalties against those who transgressed Geneva's religious laws. These penalties would include excommunication from the church, exile, imprisonment, and even execution. (The councils wanted to reserve the right to dispense such sanctions for themselves, not the Consistory, however, and the issue would only be resolved a decade later in favor of Calvin.) Pastors were to "admonish, exhort, deprecate"; citizens were to "listen to them as to God Himself," and in doing so, they would learn to lead better lives. Calvin wanted municipal supervisors to monitor the religious behavior of the people, but the councils hesitated to surrender their authority to Calvin—who, like most of the proponents of radical reform, was French—or to assume such a supervisory role. In 1538, the councils asked Calvin to leave Geneva.

In 1540, the majority of citizens of Geneva, believing that the town's ties to Bern limited its sovereignty, elected new magistrates, who executed the leaders of the pro-Bern faction. The two councils then invited Calvin to return to oversee reform in Geneva, and they adopted his "Ecclesiastical Ordinances." Feeling himself called by God to undertake the reform of the city he had called "a place so grossly immoral," Calvin returned. He insisted that "the church cannot stand firm unless a government is constituted as prescribed to us by the Word of God and observed." He created separate, autonomous ecclesiastical institutions that, unlike those of Luther and Zwingli, did not depend on governmental institutions. Although he did not become a citizen of Geneva until many years later, Calvin played a determining role in structuring religious life and simplifying the liturgy in his adopted city.

To John Knox, a Scottish reformer, Geneva seemed "the most perfect school of Christ that ever was on earth since the days of the Apostles." But many citizens of Geneva resisted the close scrutiny of the Consistory. One man named his dog "Calvin" in protest. Always on the alert for the "many ambushes and clandestine intrigues Satan daily directs against us," Calvin forced another man who had publicly criticized him to wear a hair shirt (a shirt made of coarse animal hair) and walk slowly through town, stopping at street corners to pray and acknowledge Calvin's authority. Calvin took it upon himself to decide whether future bridegrooms were free from venereal disease and could marry in Geneva. He determined the punishment of merchants who cheated their clients. Drinking establishments were permitted (indeed part of Calvin's salary was paid in barrels of wine) if no lewd songs were sung or cards played, a Bible was always available, and grace was said before meals. The Consistory imposed penalties for laughing during a sermon, having one's fortune told, or praising the pope.

Calvin's uncompromising nature could be seen in his dispute with the Spanish humanist and physician Michael Servetus, who publicly rejected the concept of the Holy Trinity. The stern reformer warned that if Servetus ever appeared in Geneva, "I will not suffer him to get out alive." He made good on his promise when Servetus foolishly turned up in disguise to hear Calvin preach and was recognized. During his trial in 1553, Servetus at one point so irritated Calvin that the latter blurted out: "May little chickens dig out his eyes a hundred thousand times!" Calvin also cautioned, however, that some pastors were too strict, "pretending zeal . . . terrifying sinners so inhumanely, without any sign of anguish or sympathy, they make God's Word seem insulting and distasteful." Calvin's death in

1564 was brought on by a variety of illnesses that were probably compounded by his chronic state of exhaustion and his fretful anxiety about the possibility of reforming a fallen and sinful world.

Calvinist Conversions

Calvinism proved the most aggressive version of the reformed religions. It confronted Catholicism more systematically and over a longer period of time than did Lutheranism. In France, Calvinism made some inroads among all social classes during the 1530s, following the flow of reform literature coming from Switzerland and the German states. Clergy who converted to Calvinism found eager followers, some of whom, distraught by hard times, may have been attracted by Calvinist sermons offering the assurance of the predestination of eternal salvation. People who could not read could nonetheless listen to the Bible being read aloud. In Lyon, a prosperous banking and commercial center, printers were prominent among Calvinists, and they used their ability to read to convert others.

Henry II, who came to the throne of France in 1547, denounced the "common malady of this contagious pestilence which has infected many noble towns." The Parlement of Paris created a special chamber to hear heresy cases—"the Burning Chamber"—and tried about 500 people. The king, a sadist, attended many of the executions himself. A magistrate from Bordeaux described the courage of the Protestant martyrs:

> Fires were being kindled everywhere . . . the stubborn resolution of those who were carried off to the gallows . . . stupefied many people. Because when they saw innocent, weak women submit to torture so as to bear witness to their faith, facing death calling out only to Christ . . . men exulting upon seeing the dreadful and frightful preparations for and implements of death that were readied for them, and half charred and roasted, they looked down from the stakes with invincible courage and the blows incurred from the hot pincers, bearing a brave mien . . . they died smiling.

The judicial system could try some heresy cases, but it could not keep up with the rapid pace of conversion, including the conversion of many nobles. By 1560, there were more than 2,000 Protestant, or Huguenot (perhaps named after a leading French reformer in Geneva, Besançon Hugues), congregations in France.

Calvinism became the dominant religion of reform in the Netherlands. There Protestant conversions set the stage for an inevitable clash with the ruling Catholic Habsburg dynasty. To root out Protestants in the Dutch Netherlands, Philip II expanded the Inquisition (which had been set up by the Spanish crown after the expulsion of the Moors and Jews from Spain in 1492 and later extended to the Spanish Empire in the Americas). When

(*Left*) Henry VIII. (*Right*) Anne Boleyn.

the Dutch declared independence from Spain in 1581, Calvinism quickly became part of the Dutch national movement during the long war of independence that followed (see Chapter 5).

THE REFORMATION IN ENGLAND

Unlike continental reform, the English Reformation began with a struggle between the king and the Church. But this dispute must be placed in the context of discontentment with ecclesiastical venality and the distant rule of Rome. Lollard influence persisted among the middle and lower classes, which resented the wealth of the high clergy and papal authority. Merchants and travelers returned to England from the continent with Lutheran tracts. Among Luther's small group of followers at Cambridge University was William Tyndale, who published the first English translation of the New Testament. Burned at the stake as a heretic in 1536, his last words were "Lord, open the eyes of the king of England."

Henry VIII and the Break with Rome

King Henry VIII of England (ruled 1509–1547) was a religious conservative who published a book in 1521 defending the Catholic view of the sacraments against Martin Luther, prompting the pope to grant him the title of "defender of the faith." The Catholic Church in England already enjoyed considerable autonomy, granted by the pope in the fourteenth century, and the king had the authority to appoint bishops.

The issue of royal divorce led to the English break with Rome. Henry's wife, Catherine of Aragon (1485–1536), had given birth five times, but only an extremely frail girl, Mary Tudor, survived. Henry not only urgently desired a male heir for the prestige of the dynasty but he also desired Anne Boleyn (1507–1536), a lady-in-waiting with long black hair and flashing dark eyes.

Henry had obtained a special papal dispensation to marry Catherine, who was his brother's widow, and now sought the annulment of this same marriage. Obtaining an annulment—which meant, from the point of view of the Church, that the marriage had never taken place—was not uncommon in sixteenth-century Europe and was an escape clause for those of great wealth. Henry justified his efforts by invoking an Old Testament passage that placed the curse of childlessness on any man who married his brother's widow. He furthermore claimed that English ecclesiastical authorities, not the pope, had the authority to grant an annulment. Pope Clement VII (pope 1523–1534), the second Medici pope, was at this time a prisoner of Charles V, the Holy Roman emperor, whose armies had occupied Rome, and who happened to be Catherine of Aragon's nephew. In addition to these political circumstances, the pope opposed the annulment as a matter of conscience. At Henry's insistence, Thomas Wolsey (1475–1530), who had been named at the king's demand as archbishop of

Sir Thomas More, painted by Hans Holbein the Younger. More, who is here shown as lord chancellor, was later executed for his beliefs.

Canterbury and hence head of the Church in England, opened a formal church proceeding in London in 1529 to hear the king's case. But Pope Clement ordered the case transferred to Rome, where the English king had no chance of winning.

Furious, Henry blamed Wolsey for this defeat. Stripped of his post, Wolsey died a shattered man in 1530 on the way to his trial for treason and certain execution. The king had named Thomas More to be his lord chancellor in 1529. But More, a lawyer and a humanist, was a vigorous opponent of the reform movement. Although a layman, each Friday More whipped himself in memory of Christ's suffering at the hands of Roman soldiers.

As a committed Catholic, More balked at Henry's plan to have his marriage to Catherine of Aragon annulled. In 1533, Henry secretly married the pregnant Anne Boleyn. He then convoked Parliament, which dutifully passed a series of acts that cut the ties between the English church and Rome. The Act in Restraint of Appeals (1533) denied the pope's authority. Thomas Cranmer (1489–1556), who succeeded Wolsey as archbishop of Canterbury, showed himself a loyal servant of the throne by mobilizing opinion against Rome and simply declaring Henry's marriage to Catherine, who was sent to a convent, annulled. The Act of Succession in 1534 required all of the king's subjects to take an oath of loyalty to the king as head of the Church of England. Thomas More refused to do so, and Henry ordered his execution. In Henry's eyes, More was a traitor, but he was a martyr and saint to the Catholic Church. When Pope Clement named another cleric languishing in the Tower of London a cardinal, Henry scoffed, "Let the pope send him a [cardinal's] hat when he will, but I will provide that whensoever it cometh, he shall wear it on his shoulders, for his head he shall have none to set it on."

The Act of Supremacy, also passed in 1534, proclaimed the king "supreme head of the Church of England." Another law made possible the execution of anyone who denied the king's authority over the clergy, or who supported "the bishop of Rome or his pretended power." Parliament limited fees that the clergy could assess for burials and forbade bishops of the Church of England from living away from their sees. Reforms brought the clergy under civil law and enhanced the rights and prestige of Parliament. The lack of resistance to Henry's usurpation of ecclesiastical authority reflected the pope's unpopularity, as well as the growing strength of the English monarchy.

After the Break with Rome

Henry VIII's nascent Church of England remained doctrinely conservative in contrast to some of the continental reform churches. Several dozen people were burned at the stake for heresy in the 1530s after Henry broke with Rome, including twenty-five Anabaptists. In 1536, in the Church of England's first doctrinal pronouncement, Ten Articles affirmed the essential tenets of Lutheran reform: salvation by faith alone (although good works were still advised), three sacraments, and rejection of the concept of Purgatory and the cult of saints. However, six more articles promulgated two years later reaffirmed some aspects of orthodox Catholic doctrine, including transubstantiation and clerical celibacy.

Thomas Cromwell (1485–1540), Wolsey's ambitious protégé, oversaw the dissolution of England's 600 monasteries, which was completed in 1538 despite a northern insurrection (the "Pilgrimage of Grace") in defense of the Roman Catholic Church. Members of the clergy who were dispossessed by the dissolution of the monasteries were pensioned off.

Two-thirds of the monasteries were sold within ten years, the largest transfer of land in England since the Norman Conquest of 1066. The appropriation of Church lands doubled royal revenue, allowing the construction of forts along the troublesome border with Scotland and on the Channel coast, and financing the purchase of new ships of war. Nobles, particularly those living in the more prosperous south, were the chief purchasers of monastic lands. Many turned their acquisitions into pastureland for sheep, or undertook more intensive agricultural production.

A few months after she married Henry, Anne Boleyn gave birth to a daughter, Elizabeth, a future queen of England. But Henry then had Anne tried on charges of adultery with one of his courtiers, claiming that she had coyly dropped her handkerchief in order to attract him. Anne was executed in 1536, insisting to the end that "a gentler nor a more merciful prince [than Henry] was there never." Next the king married Jane Seymour, who died shortly after giving birth to a son. Another Anne, this one from a small German state, was next in line, as Henry sought allies against Spain and the other Catholic powers. But this Anne did not please Henry—he claimed he had never consummated his marriage to this woman he disparaged as a "Flemish mare," and he divorced her, too. Catherine Howard became Henry's fifth wife, but in 1542 he ordered her dispatched for "treasonable unchastity." Henry's sixth wife, a pious older woman named Catherine Parr, managed to outlive her husband.

THE CATHOLIC REFORMATION

By 1540, the Reformation had carved out large zones of allegiance in central and northern Europe, as well as parts of France and most of England. It reached into Scotland, where, following the efforts of the fiery reformer John Knox, the Scottish Parliament accepted Calvinism in 1560 as the national religion. More than 90 percent of Protestants were Lutheran, Calvinist, or Anglican; the remainder were scattered among smaller sects.

The Catholic Church responded to the schism within Christendom by reasserting the pope's authority and strengthening its own organization. The Catholic Reformation (sometimes called the Counter-Reformation) was both a defensive response by the Church to the success of Protestantism and an aggressive attempt to undertake reform within the limits dictated by Catholic theology.

Retreat to Dogmatism

In 1536, Pope Paul III (pope 1534–1549) designated a commission to report on possible reforms in the Church. This commission documented the lack of education of many clergy and the scandalous cases of bishops and priests earning benefices from sees and parishes they never visited. At least eighty bishops resided in Rome, most far from their sees.

But the papacy held firm on matters of Catholic Church doctrine. Paul III rejected a last-ditch attempt in 1541 by one of his cardinals and several German bishops to reach agreement on the thorny theological issue of salvation by faith alone. Luther, too, vehemently refused to accept compromise. The papacy then went on the offensive. The next year, the pope ordered Cardinal Gian Pietro Carafa to establish an Inquisition in Rome to root out Protestantism in Italy. Carafa went so far as to build jail cells in his private residence.

Carafa became Pope Paul IV (pope 1555–1559) despite the veto of Holy Roman Emperor Charles V. He once declared, "If our own father were a heretic, we would gladly carry the wood to burn him!" Recognizing that the break with the reformed denominations was definitive, the new pope retreated into doctrinal orthodoxy and aggressive repression. He formalized pre-publication censorship, establishing a list—the Index—of forbidden books in 1559. Censors ordered other books altered, and refused to authorize the printing of publications they deemed controversial.

As part of the Catholic Reformation's efforts to combat, contain, and eliminate "error" in all forms, Paul IV invented the "ghetto," ordering Jews living in the Papal States to reside in specific neighborhoods, which they could leave only at certain times. In a 1555 bull, he stated that the Jews were guilty of killing Christ, and therefore ought to be slaves. In much of Catholic Europe, Jews had to wear yellow caps to identify themselves, could not own land, and were excluded from most professions.

Ignatius of Loyola and the Jesuits

Ignatius of Loyola (1491–1556), a dashing Basque noble, became one of the leading figures of the Catholic Reformation. While recovering from a grave injury suffered in battle, Loyola read an account of the life of Christ and a book on the lives of saints. He vowed to help rekindle Catholic orthodoxy throughout Europe. Loyola made a pilgrimage to a Spanish monastery, left his sword in a chapel, gave his rich robe to a poor man, put on a sackcloth, and travelled through Spain and Italy.

Gradually Loyola attracted followers. The Inquisition came to suspect him because his claims to help people through "spiritual conversion" seemed dangerously close to heresy. He defended himself ably, however, receiving only a short prison sentence.

Loyola wanted to establish a new order that could inculcate the same kind of intense religious experience that he had undergone while lying wounded. He travelled to Rome, offered his services to the pope, and organized the Society of Jesus, which was officially approved by the pope in

1540. Under Loyola's military-style leadership, the Jesuits, as the order's members became known, grew rapidly in number and influence as aggressive crusaders for the Catholic Reformation.

The Jesuit order provided a model for Church organization, orthodoxy, and discipline. Jesuits underwent a program of rigorous training and took a special oath of allegiance to the pope. They combined the study of Thomas à Kempis's mystical *Imitation of Christ* (1418) and Loyola's own intense devotional reflections, with the examination of conscience and prayers intended to shape the will of the individual to the service of the Church.

"I can find God whenever I will," became the motto of the charismatic Loyola. When he died in 1556, there were more than a thousand Jesuits. Counselors to kings and princes and educators of the Catholic elite, the Jesuit religious order contributed greatly to the success of the Catholic Reformation in Austria, Bavaria, and the Rhineland. Jesuits also contributed to the Church's reconquest of Poland, where some landowners had converted to Lutheranism. In the service of the Catholic Reformation, Jesuits began to travel to North America, Latin America, and Asia, eventually establishing a presence even in the court of the Chinese emperors. They led "missions," delivering fire-and-brimstone sermons, which were aimed at rekindling loyalty to the Church. The resourceful German Jesuit Peter Canisius (1521–1597) carried the new Catholic crusade to some of the German states, teaching at universities and establishing Jesuit communities there.

The Council of Trent

In 1545, at the insistence of Holy Roman Emperor Charles V, Paul III convoked the Council of Trent (1545–1563) to assess the condition of the Catholic Church and to define its doctrines. While such an internal reckoning had seemed inevitable for some time, the papacy had long viewed conciliarism as a potential threat to its authority and invoked every possible reason for delay. Once convened, the Council of Trent, which met off and on for eighteen years, made the split within Western Christendom irreparable. Most of the prelates who came to the Alpine town of Trent believed the central goal of the council was a blanket condemnation of what the Church viewed as heresy, as well as the reaffirmation of theological doctrine. Although the pope himself never went to Trent, the Italian delegates dominated the proceedings, coughing and sneezing during the speeches with which they disagreed.

The council rejected point after point of reformed doctrine, declaring these positions "to be anathema." It reaffirmed the authority of the pope and of the bishops, the seven sacraments, and the presence of Christ in the Eucharist. It also unequivocally opposed the marriage of clerics and

The Council of Trent.

reaffirmed belief in Purgatory and in the redeeming power of indulgences, although the practice of selling them was abolished.

In 1562, Pope Pius IV (pope 1559–1565), who had fathered three children as a young man before becoming the inquisitor general in Rome, convoked the last session of the Council of Trent. The council ordained the creation of seminaries in each diocese in order to increase the number and quality of priests. The priests were henceforth to keep parish registers listing the births, baptisms, and deaths of the faithful, which in recent times have provided historians with extraordinarily useful demographic information. Some monastic houses undertook reforms. The infusion of better educated clergy in the southern German states and Austria aided the Church's efforts to maintain its influence in those areas.

The papacy emerged from the Council of Trent much more centralized, better organized and administered, and more aggressive, like the most powerful European states themselves. Gradually a series of more able popes helped restore the prestige of the papacy within the Church.

Putting Its House in Order

"The best way," one churchman advised, "to fight the heretics is not to deserve their criticisms." Some leaders within the Catholic Church reasoned that the Church should put its own house in order and seek to reconvert people who had joined the reformed religions. Pius V (pope 1566–1572) declared war on venality, luxury, and ostentation in Rome. But abuses still seemed rampant. In 1569, the Venetian ambassador to

France reported that the French "deal in bishoprics and abbeys as merchants trade in pepper and cinnamon." But Pius sent some bishops living in Roman luxury packing to their sees, putting those who refused to leave in prison.

Reformers wanted to bring order and discipline to members of religious orders and the secular clergy. "No wonder the Church is as it is, when the religious live as they do [in monasteries and convents]," Teresa of Avila (1515–1582) exclaimed in response to the demeaning battles between religious houses in Spain, struggles that she tried to end. Some churchmen, however, now rejected monastic life as irrelevant to the activist missionary tasks of the Church, another sign of the influence of Protestant reform. New orders, such as the Capuchins—an offshoot of the Franciscans—and the female order of the Ursulines, worked to bring faith to the poor and the sick. Seeing the success Reformation preachers had with mass-produced pamphlets, the Catholic Church also produced catechisms that spread Church teachings. Thus, catechisms, devotional books (including those by the Jesuits), and accounts of the lives of the saints circulated widely. Jesuits used drama to renew faith by portraying episodes from Church history. The Catholic Reformation encouraged other new devotional confraternities (religious brotherhoods of people who heard Mass together), some bringing together laymen of various social classes. The missionary work of Vincent de Paul (1581–1660) also helped restore faith among the poor.

The interior of the Gesú Church in Rome with its false cupola in the baroque style.

The Protestant Reformation had emphasized the religious life of the individual and the development of his or her personal piety through Bible study and personal reflection. The Catholic Reformation, too, now encouraged individual forms of devotion and spirituality. In Spain, where reform had made few inroads, there was a deep spiritual revival, one that extended throughout Spanish society. Nobles, artisans, and peasants joined religious confraternities. A spirit of idealism and contemplative self-reflection merged with the intensely emotional religious devotion and piety that had characterized medieval monasticism in its purest form. Teresa of Avila, later canonized as a saint, believed that in order for spiritual values to survive, "mystical theology," a belief that the individual could have direct access to God through prayer and contemplation, had to be restored, and monasteries and convents reformed, as well.

CULTURE DURING THE TWO REFORMATIONS

The Protestant Reformation began as a religious reaction against established abuses within the Church. But it also reflected profound changes in European society. The Reformation followed not only the discovery of the printing press but also the expansion of commerce, the arteries of which became the conduits of reform. Both the Protestant and Catholic Reformations affected art, architecture, print culture, education, popular culture, and family life.

Print Culture

The printing press did not cause the Reformation, but it certainly helped expand it. There was, to be sure, nothing about the rapid increase in print culture that would aid the cause of religious reform and not the Roman Catholic Church. But a rapid expansion in the publication of pamphlets, books, and other printed material occurred at a time when reformers were challenging Church doctrine and papal authority. The printing of Luther's works facilitated their rapid diffusion, with perhaps a million copies circulating through the German states by the mid-1520s. In 1521, a papal ambassador wrote that "daily there is a veritable downpour of Lutheran tracts in German and in Latin . . . nothing is sold here except the tracts of Luther." The German reformer called the printing press "God's highest and ultimate gift of grace by which He would have His Gospel carried forward." Luther's Wartburg translation of the Bible went through fifty printings in two years. He wrote 450 treatises and delivered more than 3,000 sermons, in addition to thousands of letters; his collected works fill more than 100 volumes and 60,000 pages. Luther also published a hymnal containing many

Private devotion: an old woman reading the Bible.

hymns that are still sung today. Catechisms became his major instrument of religious education. Luther directed many of his dialogues, poems, and sermons to ordinary Germans, and even to children, adopting popular religious themes and images. Luther's book *A Simple Way to Pray, Written for a Friend* was intended for his barber.

Since about 1480, the diffusion of printing had contributed to the expansion of a lay culture in the German states. Much of what was printed was published in the vernacular, that is, German, as opposed to Latin. Although religious literature was the greatest output of early printing presses, other favored themes of books and pamphlets included nature, the discoveries of the explorers, the acquisition of technical skills (such as medical skills from self-help medical handbooks), manuals of self-instruction (such as how to defend oneself in court, or how to make beer and wine), and everyday morality. Visual, often satirical images such as woodcut illustrations and broadsheets, directed at those who could not read, probably reached far more people than did printed tracts, however. Caricatures and cartoons portrayed Luther as Hercules, as an evangelical saint doing battle with wretched animals representing the Church, as a new Moses, as a miracle worker, and, in one popular legend, as the inventor of bratwurst sausage.

Lay Education and Reading

The Reformation, drawing on printing, also profited from increased educational opportunities for laypeople in Europe, which engendered a critical spirit among students and scholars. The number of universities rose steadily during the last half of the fifteenth century. More people could read than ever before—although in most places this still amounted to no more than 5 to 10 percent of the population. Lutherans and Calvinists stressed the importance of education as essential to individual and critical study of the Scriptures, and de-emphasized the clergy's role in religious instruction.

During the Reformation, princes and ecclesiastical leaders intensified their efforts to secure religious conformity by controlling what people read. The "blue library" (so called because small books or pamphlets were wrapped in blue paper) helped diffuse orthodoxy through pamphlets deemed acceptable and sold at a low price by itinerant peddlers. Each Western European country had such a "literature of bits and pieces." Didactic stories were meant to instruct people about religious events, saints, and ideals approved by the Church, and to distance them from the "superstitions" of popular culture. Yet many people living in England probably still knew far more about Robin Hood than they did about the Bible. A chapbook (a small book of popular literature) published in Augsburg in 1621 told the story of Saint George slaying the dragon. The Catholic hierarchy removed the dragon from the story, while Protestants left out Saint George.

Popular Rituals and Festivals

Protestant ministers, like their Catholic counterparts, tried to root out such rituals as baptizing a child by dunking her three times for good luck. Songs rife with pagan imagery had survived virtually unchanged since medieval times. Religion and magic remained closely intertwined; the Catholic Church had been unable to eradicate the difference in the popular mind between prayer and good luck charms, for example. Archbishops and papal legates undercut the cult of some popular saints.

Many a village became the site of an elaborate tug-of-war between state and ecclesiastical authorities and ordinary people, with the local priest caught in the middle. The clergy, often previously active participants in festive occasions, moved away from what they considered "profane" amusements.

The Catholic hierarchy also tried to suppress some popular festivals and rein in others, returning them to the control of the clergy by imposing a religious purpose that seemed to have been lost in all the fun. A dance known as the "twirl" in southern France was banned in 1666 because boys tossed girls into the air "in such an infamous manner that what shame obliges us to hide most of all is uncovered naked to the eyes of those taking part and those passing by."

Ecclesiastical and lay hierarchies, Catholic and Protestant, came to view popular festivity as immoral, or at least licentious. *Combat between Carnival and Lent* (1559), a painting by Pieter Brueghel the Elder (see p. 130), depicts Carnival as a fat man and Lent as a thin woman. Under the twin assault of absolutism and ecclesiastic hierarchy, Lent won. The clergy also condemned the role in Carnival and other festivals of the lay confraternities. These brotherhoods had had their origins in religious devotion, but they now were often fiercely independent and more like festive clubs. The clergy began a long—and often unsuccessful—struggle for control over these lay confraternities. Carnival was largely eradicated in Protestant countries, but it survived in some Catholic ones, although often much transformed. Cults such as that of the Virgin Mary became more popular.

Social and political elites contrasted the "civility" of their beliefs, conduct, and manners with the "barbarity" or "savagery" of popular beliefs and customs. Didactic literature stressing polite comportment and etiquette became popular among people of wealth, further separating them from the poor. The Church tried to impose strict sexual mores on ordinary people, while encouraging gestures of deference toward social superiors.

The Role of Women

Although convents and nunneries were abolished in Protestant states, reformers nonetheless encouraged women to take an active role in the

Pieter Brueghel the Elder's *Combat between Carnival and Lent* (1559).

religious process of being saved. Protestant women, like men, were encouraged to read the Bible themselves, or, as most could not read, to have it read to them. In the case of Anabaptists, women appear to have made decisions about not baptizing their children; most Anabaptist martyrs were female. More women than men seem to have converted to Calvinism in France, perhaps because their legal position was deteriorating—for example, with regard to their dowries and possessions. Perhaps they were attracted by special catechism classes, or by the fact that in Calvinist services, men and women sang psalms together.

Yet Protestant reformers still believed women were subordinate to men. Although a few women published religious pamphlets in the early 1520s and others undertook devotional writing and publishing later, women could not be ministers nor could they hold offices within the new churches. Calvin himself believed that the subjugation of women to their husbands was crucial for the maintenance of moral order. Protestant denominations provided a domestic vision of women, emphasizing their role in the Christian household. The rights of women to manage their own property and undertake legal transactions in their own name were gradually withdrawn.

The fact that a Protestant minister could now marry, however, reflected a more positive view not only of women but of the family as a foundation of organized religion. One pamphleteer admonished husbands that their wives were "no dish-clouts . . . nor no drudges, but fellow-heirs with them of everlasting life, and so dear to God as the men."

Because they no longer considered marriage a sacrament, Protestants also reluctantly accepted divorce in limited cases. Luther viewed adultery, impotence, and abandonment as reasons for divorce, but he counseled bigamy over divorce in the case of Philip of Hesse, and condemned Henry VIII's effort to divorce Catherine of Aragon. Divorce remained quite rare and occurred only after a long, expensive legal process.

In Catholic areas, women could still rise to positions of importance in convents, or in the new charitable orders. But the Council of Trent reaffirmed the Catholic Church's ideal of female chastity, reinforced by the widespread cult of the Virgin Mary. The chapbooks of the Catholic Reformation still taught that the female body was a source of sin, and therefore had to be controlled.

Witches came to symbolize superstitious aspects of popular religion. Catholic and Protestant churchmen identified and persecuted witches as part of the campaign to acculturate the masses with "acceptable" beliefs. Witch hunts peaked during the first half of the seventeenth century. In the southwestern states of the Holy Roman Empire alone, more than 300 witch trials resulted in the execution of 2,500 people between 1570 and 1630, almost all women (in itself not surprising, as Church authorities and priests were all male).

Theologians and judges sought to demonstrate that accused witches embodied the kingdom of the devil. To some extent, the Catholic Reformation wanted to create the idea of a satanic realm of evil on earth with which to juxtapose orthodoxy. "Witches," identified by common reputation, sometimes stood accused of saying Latin prayers backward or performing "black Masses" while standing facing their "congregations," instead of facing the altar, defiantly inverting the kingdom of God. One woman was accused of "consuming" several husbands. Often "witches" were blamed for evil that had befallen villagers: a fire, the unexplained death of a cow, or a male suddenly smitten with impotence.

Most of those accused of being witches were rural, poor, and single women who were victims of other villagers, particularly small town officials and wealthy peasants (it was the opposite in 1692 in Salem, Massachusetts, where many of the women accused of witchcraft had just inherited property, and therefore were resented by the community). Some "witches" confessed under pain of torture, such as one woman in southern France, who was "scorched like a pig" and cooked alive, having been accused of spreading an "evil powder" while committing crimes.

Women were targets for repression because they were transmitters of the collective memory of popular culture. They were genealogists, storytellers, and healers, but almost always without formal education. Women were in many ways the guardians of tradition. But they were also regarded by the Catholic hierarchy as the source of sin. The social exclusion or even execution of women had a social value for those in power, affirming authorities' position and role as interpreters of beliefs and customs deemed appropriate.

After the persecution of witches virtually ended, some lay authorities then turned their attention to outcasts, the socially marginal. In the Austrian Netherlands, a sign "useless to the world" was hung above the head of a beggar. Monarchies increasingly demonstrated their authority in carrying out sentences of royal justice and, therefore, the justice of God. Those found guilty of capital crimes—at least those of the lower classes— were tortured and then executed in public, often before throngs, their mutilated bodies exhibited for some time for all to see.

The Baroque Style

The monumentalism, flamboyance, and theatrical religiosity of the baroque style complemented the Catholic Reformation. "Baroque" refers to a style of extravagant and irregularly shaped ornamentation (the term itself comes from Old French for "irregularly shaped pear"). As an architectural, artistic, and decorative style, the baroque triumphed in southern Germany, Austria, Flanders, and other Catholic regions during the first decades of the seventeenth century (but was also popular in Protestant England, where it merged with the classical style).

Gianlorenzo Bernini's *The Ecstasy of Saint Theresa* (1645–1652).

As in the Renaissance, in Rome the Church remained a major patron of the arts, expressing religious themes through visual representation. Its goal was to impress—indeed, to overwhelm— the emotions through awe-inspiring dimensions, opulence, movement and, in painting, lurid color. Baroque style emphasized the metaphysical side of humanity, seeking to express the experience of the soul. Baroque palaces and churches featured exuberant curves and ornate decoration and were cluttered with lustrous marble altars, ornate statues, golden cherubs, and intensely colorful murals and ceiling paintings. The baroque merged easily with neoclassicism—the revival of an architectural design dominated by

Greek and Roman forms. The Gesú Church of the Jesuits in Rome (see p. 126) is a masterpiece of baroque style. With its vast ceilings and enormous paintings of the ascension of Christ and the assumption of the Virgin Mary, it symbolizes the spirit of the Catholic Reformation. The baroque style used optical illusions such as Gesú's false cupola to achieve the impression that the viewer was reaching for Heaven.

The work of Venetian sculptor Gianlorenzo Bernini (1598–1680) best represents the period of high baroque of the Catholic Reformation. His monumental fountains were constructed throughout Rome. He planned the piazza outside the entrance to St. Peter's Basilica and sculpted the magnificent canopy over the high altar of St. Peter's. Bernini sought to communicate the intensity of religious experience. In the altarpiece *The Ecstasy of Saint Theresa* (1645–1652), Bernini depicted the saint's convulsions of joy when an angel stabs her with a spear as beams of sunlight engulf the scene. Bernini wrote, "It pleased the Lord that I should see this angel in [this] way. . . . In his hands I saw a long golden spear and at the end of the iron tip I seemed to see a point of fire. With this he seemed to pierce my heart several times so that it penetrated to my entrails." This highly sexual description stands in marked contrast with the puritanical impulse that had seen Renaissance popes order the painting of fig leaves on nudes.

THE LEGACY OF THE TWO REFORMATIONS

In 1600, more than half of Europe remained primarily Catholic, including Spain, France, and Habsburg Austria, three of the four most powerful states in Europe. The fourth was England, and it was overwhelmingly Protestant. The Dutch Netherlands, at war with its Spanish overlords, was largely Protestant as well. Yet, of all of the European states, the Reformation failed to influence directly only Ireland. It generated a strong missionary impulse among Protestants and Catholics alike. With the gradual opening up of the world to European commerce and colonization, the Jesuits, particularly, ranged far and wide. Some made converts, and a few found martyrdom in Asia and Latin America.

In Central Europe, the complexity of the state system facilitated reform. The Peace of Augsburg of 1555 reinforced German particularism, the persistence of small, independent states. In contrast, the larger, centralized, and more powerful states like Spain and France most successfully resisted the reform movement. That France and Spain already were large states with relatively strong monarchies helped the Catholic Church remain the dominant religion there, despite the inroads of reform and subsequent wars of religion in the former. Yet, in both states, the Catholic Church remained subordinate to the monarchy, with both the French and Spanish kings retaining considerable authority over ecclesiastical appointments.

The Protestant reformers accepted a separation of functions within the community, what Luther called the "realm of the spirit" and the "realm of the world." Henceforth, the political institutions of the Protestant states remained relatively secularized. In the German states and in Scandinavia, Lutheranism was introduced as a state church, in part because reformers originally needed the protection of princes against Catholic rulers, notably Charles V, the Holy Roman emperor. In England, Anglicanism also took on the status of a state religion. Both Lutheran and Anglican reforms rigorously subordinated the church to the state, separating the spiritual and temporal realms. Whereas Zwingli had called for the complete fusion of church and state, Calvinism alone provided for the institutional separation of both, although in practice the magistrates of Geneva restricted the church's autonomy. Anabaptist sectarians, in contrast, wanted their communities to have nothing at all to do with the state. All reformers called on their rulers to do God's work on earth, arguing that the papacy and the Catholic monarchs had failed to do so.

The Lutheran and Calvinist states were thus not necessarily any more tolerant of religious dissent than those that remained Catholic. Following the Peace of Augsburg in 1555, German princes used their control of the reformed churches to consolidate their political authority. Lutheranism remained wedded to a patriarchal structure of society, which appealed to property owners at all social levels.

In an attempt to obtain religious adherence, some princes declared that church attendance would be mandatory and those who were absent would be punished. Nonetheless, compelling people to attend Sunday services did not guarantee what or even if they believed. One can never know how typical were the thoughts of one girl who related that the sermon she had just sat through was "such a deale of bible babble that I am weary to heare yt and I can then sitt downe in my seat and take a good napp." In one English parish in 1547, it was reported that "when the vicar goeth into the pulpit to read what [he] himself hath written, then the multitude of the parish goeth straight out of the church, home to drink."

Finally, the Peace of Augsburg and the Council of Trent did not end the rivalry between Catholics and Protestants, nor, for that matter, the rivalry between different Protestant denominations. Religious conflict would, to a great extent, help define the first half of the seventeenth century, the age of the wars of religion.

CHAPTER 4

THE WARS OF RELIGION

On May 23, 1618, a crowd of protesters carried a petition to Prague's Hradcany Palace, where representatives of the royal government of Bohemia were gathered. The crowd stormed into the council chamber, engaged Catholic officials in a heated debate, organized an impromptu trial, and hurled two royal delegates from the window. The crowd below roared its approval of this "defenestration" (an elegant term for throwing someone out a window), angered only that neither man was killed by the fall. Catholic partisans construed their good fortune as a miracle, as the rumor spread that guardian angels had swooped down to pluck the falling dignitaries from the air. The Protestants liked to claim that the men had been saved because they fell on large dung heaps in the moat below.

The different reactions to the Defenestration of Prague illustrate how the Reformation left some of Europe, particularly the German states, a veritable patchwork of religious allegiances. Religious affiliation, like ethnicity, frequently did not correspond to the borders of states. The Peace of Augsburg in 1555 ended the fighting between German Protestant and Catholic princes. It stated that the religion of each state would henceforth be that of its ruler. Hundreds of thousands of families left home and crossed frontiers in order to relocate to a state where the prince was of their religious denomination.

By contrast, in France in 1572, the Huguenots (the popular name for the French Protestants) rebelled against Catholic domination. This set off a civil war that led to great instability in France. Moreover, after years of mounting religious and political tension, Dutch Protestants led the revolt against Spanish Catholic authority in 1572, beginning a bitter struggle that lasted until the middle of the next century.

From 1555 until 1618, the German states were for the most part at peace. But religious wars then broke out again with unparalleled intensity. The Thirty Years' War (1618–1648) devastated Central Europe, bringing into the conflict, in one way or another, almost all of the powers of Europe. Armies reached unprecedented size, and fought with a cruelty that may also have been unprecedented.

The wars of religion in France and the Thirty Years' War began because of religious antagonisms, but the dynastic ambitions of French princes lay not far behind the rivalry between Protestants and Catholics. In the Thirty Years' War, the dynastic rivalry between the Bourbons of France and the Habsburgs of Austria—both Catholic dynasties—came to the fore, eventually dominating religious considerations.

The wars of religion resulted in the strengthening of the monarchies of France, Austria, and the smaller German states as well. Kings and princes further extended their administrative, judicial, and fiscal reach over their subjects in the interest of maintaining control over their populations and waging war. In France, particularly, a stronger monarchy emerged out of the trauma of religious struggles and competing claimants to the throne. Germany, in contrast, remained divided into several strong states and many smaller ones. Competing religious allegiances reinforced German particularism, that is, the multiplicity of independent German states and strong regional loyalties.

THE WARS OF RELIGION IN SIXTEENTH-CENTURY FRANCE

Early in the sixteenth century, France was divided by law, customs, languages, and traditions. Under King Francis I (ruled 1515–1547), the Valois monarchy effectively extended its authority. Of Francis I, it was said, "If the king endures bodily fatigues unflinchingly, he finds mental preoccupations more difficult to bear." Yet, the French monarch ruled with an authority unequaled in Europe, however much he was still dependent on the good will of nobles. When the king sought loans to continue a war, a Parisian noble assured him that "we do not wish to dispute or minimize your power; that would be a sacrilege, and we know very well that you are above the law."

When the Reformation reached France in the 1540s and 1550s, Calvinism won many converts. At a time when nobles were resisting the expansion of the king's judicial prerogatives and the proliferation of his officials, religious division precipitated a crisis of the French state and brought civil war.

A Strengthened Monarchy

Francis I and his successors became more insistent on their authority to assess taxes on the towns of the kingdom, many of which had held privileged exemptions granted in exchange for loyalty. Kings had asked for tax levies to help out the monarchy in exceptional circumstances, above all, in time of war. Like his medieval forebears, Francis did not automatically command the allegiance of a large standing army with which he could enforce his will. Raising an army or royal revenue depended on the willingness of the most powerful nobles to answer the king's call. The monarchs had justified such requests with an appeal to the common good in tactful language that also held out the possibility of the use of force. Now the French king wished to tax the towns even when there was no war.

Francis reduced the authority of the Catholic Church in France. The Concordat of Bologna (1516), signed between Francis and Pope Leo X, despite the resistance of the French clergy, established royal control over ecclesiastical appointments. Many more royal officials now represented and enforced the royal will in the provinces than ever before. Francis confirmed and enhanced Paris's iden-

Francis I, painted by Jean Clouet.

tity as the seat and emerging symbol of royal power. The sale of offices originated in Francis's desire for the allegiance of nobles and for the revenue they could provide the monarchy. His successors would depend increasingly on the sale of offices and titles for raising revenue.

The political and religious crises in the middle decades of the sixteenth century threatened monarchical stability. They pushed the country into a period of chaos brought by the lengthy, savage war of religion during which the four Valois kings who succeeded Francis I proved unable to rule effectively.

Economic Crisis

The end of a period of economic expansion provided a backdrop for the political and religious struggles of the French monarchy. The population of France had risen rapidly between the late fifteenth century and about 1570, reversing the decline in population resulting from plagues and natural disasters in the fourteenth and fifteenth centuries. Land under cultivation increased, particularly near the Mediterranean, where landowners planted olive trees on hills and terraces. But by 1570, the increase in cultivable land slowed down in much of France. The European population, which had risen to about 100 million people during the sixteenth century, outstripped available resources. Prices rose rapidly in France, as in most of Europe, pushed upward relentlessly by population increase. Beginning in the late 1550s, the purchasing power of the laborer declined dramatically, whereas that of landowners remained stable, fed by high prices. As agricultural income fell, nobles demanded vexing services from peasants, such as repairing roads and paths on their estates. Many wealthy nobles rented out land to tenant farmers, then took the proceeds back to their luxurious urban residences. Nobles of lesser means, however, did not do as well as the owners of great estates, because the rents they drew from their land failed to keep pace with rising prices.

One sign of the growing power of the monarchy was that nobles lost some privileges of local jurisdiction to the royal law courts. Finding nobles unwilling to provide all the funds the king desired, the monarchy, in turn, put the squeeze on peasants, extracting more resources through taxation.

As the price of profitable land soared, peasant families tried to protect their children by subdividing land among male offspring. Many peasants with small parcels of land became sharecroppers at highly disadvantageous terms—working someone else's land for a return of roughly half of what was produced. Both trends worked against increased agricultural efficiency, reducing land yields. Landless laborers were barely able to sustain themselves.

Taxes and tithes (payments owed the Catholic Church—in principle, 10 percent of income) weighed heavily on the poor. Peasants, particularly in the southwest, sporadically revolted against taxes, and against their landlords, during the period from 1560 to 1660. The popular nicknames of some of the groups of rebels reflect their abject poverty and desperation: the "poor wretches," who rose up against the nobles in central and southern France in 1594–1595, and the "bare feet." Many of the rebels espoused the popular belief that their violence might restore an imagined world of social justice in which wise rulers looked after the needs of their people.

French Calvinists and the Crisis of the French State

Protestantism first found a smattering of French converts during the two decades following Luther's posting of his theses on the church door in Wittenberg in 1517. Followers of John Calvin arriving in France from nearby Geneva attracted converts in the 1540s and 1550s. Henry II (ruled 1547–1559), who succeeded his father Francis I, began a religious repression that created Calvinist martyrs, perhaps further encouraging Protestant dissent. The spread of Calvinism led the king to sign the Treaty of Cateau-Cambrésis in 1559, ending the protracted struggle between France and Spain. After decades of reckless invasions, Henry II agreed to respect Habsburg primacy in Italy and control over Flanders. King Philip II (ruled 1556–1598) of Spain, in return, promised that Spain would desist in its attempts to weaken the Valois kings. These two most powerful kings in Europe ended their struggle for supremacy not only because their resources were nearly exhausted but also because as pious Catholic rulers they viewed with alarm the spread of Calvinism in Western Europe, both within the Netherlands (a rich territory of the Spanish Habsburgs) and within France itself. After signing the treaty, Henry II and Philip II could now turn their attention to combating Protestantism.

Some nobles in France, wary of the extending reach of the Valois monarchy and tired of providing funds for the war against Spain, had resisted the monarchy, which had vigorously embraced the Catholic Reformation. Perhaps as many as 40 percent of French nobles had converted to Calvinism, some of them nobles of relatively modest means squeezed by economic setbacks. The conflict between the monarchy and the nobility thus compounded religious divisions in the last half of the sixteenth century.

In 1559, King Henry II was accidentally killed by an errant lance during a jousting tournament celebrating peace with Spain. He was succeeded by his fifteen-year-old son, who became Francis II (ruled 1559–1560). Catherine de' Medici (1519–1589), Henry II's talented, manipulative, and domineering widow, served as regent to the first of her three sickly and incapable sons. Catherine was reviled as a "shopkeeper's daughter," as her Florentine ancestors had been merchants, bankers, and money changers, all things incompatible with the French concept of nobility (but not with the Italian one). That she was the daughter of the man to whom Machiavelli had dedicated *The Prince* added to the "legend of the wicked Italian queen" in France.

The throne immediately faced challenges to its authority by three powerful noble families, each dominating large parts of France. Religious differences sharpened the rivalry between them. The Catholic Guise family, the strongest, concentrated its influence in northern and eastern France. In the south, the Catholic Montmorency family, one of the oldest and wealthiest in the kingdom, held through marriage alliances the allegiance of some of the population there. And the influence of the Huguenot Bourbon family extended into central France and also reached the far southwest corner.

In 1560, Louis, prince of Condé (1530–1569), a member of the Huguenot Bourbon family, conspired to kidnap Francis II and remove him from the clutches of the House of Guise, who were related to Francis's wife, Mary Stuart, queen of Scotland. The Guise clan, who discovered the plot, killed some of the Bourbon conspirators, which understandably damaged relations between these powerful families. Francis died after a stormy reign of only eighteen months, succeeded by his ten-year-old brother Charles IX (ruled 1560–1574), under the regency of their mother, who remained influential throughout Charles's brief reign.

The rivalry between the Guise, Montmorency, and Bourbon families undermined royal authority. Henry II's lengthy war with Spain had drained the royal coffers, and the economic downturn made it almost impossible to fill them again. Catherine's efforts to bring some of the nobles who had converted to Protestantism to the royal court and to effect a rapprochement between the two denominations failed utterly. Such attempts only infuriated the House of Guise, several of whose members held important positions within the Catholic Church hierarchy. For their part, Philip II of Spain and the Jesuit religious order backed the Guise family. The political crisis of France, then, became increasingly tied to the struggle of the Church with the Huguenots.

Taking advantage of the confusion surrounding the throne, French Calvinists had become bolder in practicing their religion. Religious festivals occasioned brawls between Catholics and Huguenots. Calvinists seized control of Lyon in 1562, forcing the rest of the population to attend their services. Where they were a majority, Calvinists desecrated Catholic cemeteries, smashed ornate stained-glass windows, shattered altar rails of churches, mocked Catholic ceremonies, and covered statues of saints with mud. Catholics replied by slaughtering Calvinists, more than once forcing them to wear crowns of thorns, like Christ, to their death. Both sides burned the "heretical" books of the other denomination. The violence of a holy war was accentuated by rumors that the Huguenots indulged in orgies, while Protestants accused Catholics of idolatry and of doing the devil's work.

In 1562, the first full-scale religious war broke out in France. It began when Francis, the duke of Guise (1519–1563), ordered the execution of Huguenots who had been found worshipping on his land. In the southwestern town of Toulouse, more than 3,000 people were killed in the fighting; the bodies of Protestants were tossed into the river, and their neighborhoods were burned as part of a "purification." Members of the Catholic lay confraternities took oaths to protect France against "heresy" and erected crosses in public places as a sign of religious commitment. Catholics won back control of several major cities.

This first stage of the war, during which a Huguenot assassinated the duke of Guise, ended in 1563. A royal edict granted Huguenots the right to worship in one designated town in each region, as well as in places where Calvinist congregations had already been established. Intensifying the eagerness of the

Catherine de' Medici, widow of Henry II, served as regent to Francis II.

powerful quarreling noble families to impose their will on the monarchy was the fact that young King Charles IX and his two brothers were all childless. There was no clear heir to the throne of France.

In 1567, war between French Protestants and Catholics broke out again. It dragged on to an inconclusive halt three years later in a peace settlement that pleased neither side. In 1572, Catherine and Charles, though Catholics, first agreed to provide military support to the Dutch Protestants, who had rebelled against Spanish authority. The goal was to help weaken France's principal rival. This convinced the duke of Guise that Protestants slowly but surely were taking control of France. Pressured by his mother, Charles renounced assistance to the Dutch and agreed to accept instead the guidance of the Catholic House of Guise. With or without the king's knowledge or connivance, the Guise family tried but failed to assassinate the Protestant leader Admiral Gaspard de Coligny (1519–1572), a Montmorency who had converted to Protestantism and whom they blamed for the earlier murder of the Catholic duke of Guise.

The marriage between Charles's sister, Margaret, a Catholic Valois, and Henry of Navarre, a Bourbon Huguenot, was to be, in principle, one of religious reconciliation. The negotiations for the wedding had specified that the Huguenots in Paris come to the wedding unarmed. But the king's Guise advisers, and perhaps his mother as well, convinced him that the only way of preventing a Protestant uprising against the throne was to strike brutally against the Huguenots in Paris. Therefore, early in the morning on August 24, 1572, Catholic assassins hunted down and murdered Huguenot leaders. During what became known as the Saint Bartholomew's Day Massacre, the (new) duke of Guise killed Admiral Gaspard de Coligny, whose battered corpse was thrown through a window, castrated, and then dragged through the dusty streets of Paris by children. For six days Catholic mobs stormed through the streets, killing more than 2,000 Protestants. The Parlement of Toulouse, one of the twelve judicial courts of medieval origin that combined judicial and administrative functions, made it legal to kill any "heretic." Outside of Paris, another 10,000 Protestants perished. The pope had a special Mass sung in celebration, and Protestants claimed that he danced for joy when he heard the news, rewarding the messenger with a large sum of money. Thousands of Huguenots emigrated or moved to safer places, including fortified towns they still held in the southwest.

Charles IX died in 1574 and was succeeded by his ailing brother, Henry III (ruled 1574–1589). At his coronation, the crown twice slipped from Henry's head, a bad omen in a superstitious age. The new king was a picture of contradictions. He seemed pious, undertook pilgrimages, and hoped to bring about a revival of faith in his kingdom. He also spent money with abandon and enjoyed dressing up as a woman, while lavishing every attention on the handsome young men he gathered around him.

The Saint Bartholomew's Day Massacre, 1572, in which more than 2,000 Huguenots perished in Paris.

Along with the bitter religious factionalism that had been exacerbated by the massacre, Henry III also had to confront a worsening fiscal crisis compounded by a series of meager harvests. But when he asked the provincial estates (regional assemblies dominated by nobles) for more taxes, the king found that his promises of financial reform and of an end to fiscal abuses by royal revenue agents were not enough. The estates deeply resented the influence of Italian financiers at court, the luxurious life of the court itself, and the nobles who had bought royal favor.

The Catholic forces around the king were not themselves united. A group of moderate Catholics, known as the *politiques,* pushed for conciliation. Tired of anarchy and bloodshed, they were ready to put politics ahead of religion. The *politiques* therefore sought to win the support of the moderate Huguenots, and thereby to bring religious toleration and peace to France.

In 1576, Henry III signed an agreement that liberalized the conditions under which Protestants could practice their religion. Concessions, however, only further infuriated the intransigent Catholics, who became known as the "fanatics" (*dévots*). Angered by these concessions to Huguenots, a nobleman in the northern province of Picardy organized a Catholic League. More extensive than smaller local anti-Protestant organizations that had sprung up in the 1560s, the Catholic League (despite an insincere oath of loyalty taken to the king) posed a threat not only to Huguenots but also to the monarchy. It was led by the dashing Henry, duke of Guise (1550–1588), who was subsidized by Philip II of Spain, and vowed to fight until Protestantism was completely driven from France. But another military campaign against Protestants led to nothing more than a restatement of the conditions under which they could worship.

Henry III's reconciliation with the House of Guise did not last long. The death of the last of the king's brothers in 1584 made Henry of Navarre, a Protestant, heir to the throne. This was the Catholics' worst nightmare. The Catholic League threw its full support behind the aged, ambitious Catholic Cardinal de Bourbon, who was next in line after Henry of Navarre.

Henry of Navarre

Henry of Navarre (1553–1610) was born in the town of Pau on the edge of the Pyrenees Mountains in southwestern France. The son of Antoine of Bourbon, patriarch of the powerful Bourbon family, and Jeanne d'Albret. Henry inherited the keen intelligence of his mother and his father's indecisiveness. His mother was a committed Huguenot and raised Henry in that faith. When his father, who was notoriously unfaithful to his wife, sent her back to the southwest in 1562, Henry converted to Catholicism, his father's nominal religion. After his father's death in battle, Henry re-embraced Protestantism. Taken to the royal court as a hostage by Catherine de' Medici, he was permitted to have Huguenot tutors. Among his friends at court were the future Henry III and Henry, duke of Guise.

Henry consulted a fortune teller, who predicted that he would one day be king of France. A member of the Parlement of Bordeaux described the precocious boy: "A charming youth. At thirteen years of age, he has all the riper qualities of eighteen or nineteen; he is agreeable, polite, obliging and behaves to everyone with an air so easy and engaging that wherever he is there is always a crowd. He mixes in conversation like a wise and prudent man, speaks always to the purpose . . . and never says more nor less than he ought." It was after Henry's wedding in Paris in August 1572 to Margaret, Catherine de' Medici's daughter, that the Saint Bartholomew's Day Massacre occurred. Henry then was given the choice of embracing Catholicism or being executed. He chose the former. When the fighting temporarily ended, Henry had more time for his favorite pursuits—pursuing women and hunting.

The Huguenots had every reason to be wary of a young man who seemed to change faiths with such ease. Furthermore, he seemed to have reconciled himself to the Saint Bartholomew's Day Massacre, still counted the "fanatic" duke of Guise among his friends, had accompanied the Catholic army, albeit under guard, to the siege of La Rochelle, and had written the pope begging forgiveness for past misdeeds.

But having left Paris and the watchful eye of the Catholic dukes, Henry then formally abjured Catholicism and took up residence as royal governor in the southwest, where Protestantism was strong. There he tried to steer a path between militant Catholics and Huguenots, and his endorsement of mutual religious toleration won wide approval. After Henry of Navarre became heir to the throne in 1584, the Catholic League rallied its forces, drawing its muscle from the artisans of Paris and other northern towns. In defiance of the king, it forced the Parlement of Paris to withdraw the toleration afforded the Huguenots. The Catholic League's goal was to put the Cardinal de Bourbon on the throne, although the duke of Guise wanted it for himself.

The struggle between the "three Henrys" now began in earnest. Henry (Valois) III first allied with Henry (Bourbon) of Navarre and with the duke of Montmorency against Henry, duke of Guise. The Guise family provocatively accused the king in 1585 of destroying the kingdom through inept rule and called for a rebellion that would bring the duke of Guise to the throne and drive Protestantism from the kingdom.

Henry III then switched partners, joining the duke of Guise against Henry of Navarre. The Treaty of Nemours (1585) between Catherine de' Medici and Henry, duke of Guise, abrogated all edicts of religious toleration and turned over a number of towns to the Catholic League. Now the odd man out, Henry of Navarre prepared for a new war. He denounced Spanish meddling and in a quintessentially *politique* statement, called on soldiers "to rally around me . . . all true Frenchmen without regard to religion." Although he himself increasingly depended on German and Swiss mercenaries for his army and benefited from the intervention of a German Protestant force, Henry's denunciation of foreign influence was a shrewd piece of political propaganda aimed at moderate Catholics—the

Henry III (*left*) and Henry of Navarre, later King Henry IV (*right*).

politiques—and the Catholic clergy. The Catholic League replied with a warning that French Catholics would suffer the fate of English Catholics (who had been executed) should Henry win.

In 1587, Henry of Navarre defeated the combined forces of the king and the Catholic League at Coutras, near Bordeaux. Here his defensive position and use of artillery and cavalry proved decisive. But instead of following up his surprising victory by pursuing the Catholic army, Henry went back to hunting and making love. As a contemporary put it, "All the advantage of so famous a victory floated away like smoke in the wind."

That year, 1587, Queen Elizabeth I of England put to death Mary Stuart, the Catholic queen of Scots and the niece of the duke of Guise (see Chapter 5). Angered by Henry III's inability to prevent the execution of his niece, Guise, at the urging of the king of Spain, marched the next year to Paris, where he and the Catholic League enjoyed great support. The Spanish king hoped to keep the French king from contemplating any possible assistance to England as the Spanish Armada sailed toward the English Channel. When Henry III sent troops to Paris to oppose the duke of Guise, the Parisian population rose in rebellion on May 12, 1588, stretching barricades throughout the city center. The king ordered his troops to withdraw. The "Day of Barricades" marked the victory of a council led by clergymen known as the *Seize*, or Sixteen, then the number of neighborhoods in Paris.

For several years, the Sixteen had been energetically supporting the League, while denouncing the king, the Catholic *politiques*, and Huguenots with equal fervor. The hostility of the population of Paris convinced the king to accept Cardinal de Bourbon as his heir, the duke of Guise as his lieutenant-general, and to convoke the Estates-General (representatives of the provincial estates, which the monarch could summon in times of great crisis).

Later, in 1588, the delegates to the Estates-General, many of them members of the Catholic League, gathered in the Loire Valley town of Blois. Scathing written grievances were submitted to the delegation, including one from Paris that denounced the king as a "cancer . . . filled with filth and infectious putrefaction" and called for "all heretics, whatever their quality, condition or estate, [to] be imprisoned and punished by being burned alive." By now, however, the English fleet had defeated Philip II's Armada in the Channel (see Chapter 5), and the nobles found Henry III less intimidated than they had anticipated. When the duke of Guise heard a rumor that the king was planning his assassination, he replied, "He does not dare." But Henry's bodyguards attacked Henry, duke of Guise, shortly before Christmas 1588 in the Château of Blois, as Catherine de' Medici lay dying in a room underneath the bloody struggle that resulted in the duke of Guise's death. The Valois king had the Cardinal de Bourbon and other prominent members of the Catholic League arrested.

The duke of Guise's assassination drove the Catholic League to full-fledged revolt against Henry III. The theologians at the Sorbonne declared that the people were no longer obliged to obey the Valois monarch, who had become a "tyrant." More than 300 towns, most of them in the north, now joined the "Holy Union" against Henry III. As Catholics prepared to fight Catholics, Henry of Navarre (now Protestant) appealed for peace: "We have been mad, senseless and furious for four years. Is that not enough?"

Henry III was then forced to make an alliance of convenience with Henry of Navarre against the Catholic League. As their combined armies besieged Paris, a monk assassinated Henry III. The king's Swiss guards, who had not done a terribly good job protecting their king, threw themselves at the feet of Henry of Navarre, telling him, "Sire, you are now our king and master."

The Catholic League, however, had proclaimed Cardinal de Bourbon, whom Henry was holding in custody, to be king. Henry's forces defeated Catholic League armies twice in Normandy, in 1589 and in 1590. His able artillery and fearless cavalry carried the day against an army swollen by Spanish reinforcements. But once again Henry failed to take advantage of the situation his shrewd generalship had made possible. He dawdled before finally laying siege to starving Paris.

The arrival of a Spanish army from Flanders to provision Paris helped win Henry further support from moderate Catholics, who resented Span-

Assassination of Henry, duke of Guise.

ish intervention that might prolong the siege. Fatigue began to overcome religious conviction. Henry also played on resentment at the involvement of the pope in French affairs (Henry had been excommunicated in 1585 and, for good measure, a second time six years later). As Henry's army besieged Paris, Spanish troops defeated forces loyal to him in several provinces. Henry captured Chartres in April 1591, more for reasons of the heart—the family connections of one of his lovers—than for strategic reasons. The death of Cardinal de Bourbon led Philip II to proclaim the candidacy of the late Henry II's Spanish granddaughter as heir to the throne of France, and then to suggest that he might claim it himself. In the meantime, Henry's continued successes on the battlefield and conciliatory proclamations furthered his popularity.

Henry of Navarre, a man of changing colors, had another major surprise up his sleeve. In 1593, Henry astonished friend and foe alike by announcing that he would now again renounce Protestantism. This move, however, more reflected his shrewd sense of politics than indecisiveness. Paris, as he put it, was worth a Mass, the price of the capital's obedience. Following his coronation as Henry IV at Chartres the following year, Paris surrendered after very little fighting. Henry's entry into his capital was a carefully orchestrated series of ceremonies that included the "cure" of hundreds of people afflicted with scrofula (a tuberculous condition) by the royal touch, a monarchical tradition in France and England that went back centuries. Henry nodded enthusiastically to the women who came to their windows to catch a glimpse of the first Bourbon king of France.

Catholic League forces gradually dispersed, one town after another pledging its loyalty to Henry, usually in return for payments. Henry's declaration of war on Spain in 1595 helped rally people to the monarchy. The pope lifted Henry's excommunication from the Church. Henry invaded Philip's territory of Burgundy, defeating his army. In 1598, the last Catholic League soldiers capitulated. Henry, having secured the frontiers of his kingdom, signed the Treaty of Vervins with Philip II to end the war that neither side could afford to continue.

Restoring Stability to France

Henry IV reasoned that after years of civil war, "France and I both need to catch our breath." But bringing stability to France would be no easy matter. The wars of religion had worsened the plight of the poor. Disastrous harvests and epidemics in the 1590s compounded the misery. The wars of the Catholic League caused great damage and dislocated the economy in many parts of France. The indiscriminate minting of coins by both sides worsened inflation.

Henry's emissaries gradually restored order by promising that "the Well-Loved," as the king became known, would end injustices. Henry once said that he hoped to live long enough to see "a chicken in every pot." He did slightly reduce the direct tax, of which the peasants bore the brunt. Henry also rooted out some of the corruption in the farming of taxes, whereby government officials allowed ambitious middlemen to collect taxes in exchange for a share. But he shifted even more of the tax burden to the poor.

Gradually Henry succeeded in putting the finances of the monarchy on a firmer footing. In 1596, he convinced an Assembly of Notables to approve a supplementary tax. A new imposition (the *paulette*) permitted officeholders, through an annual payment to the throne, to assure that their office would remain in the hands of their heirs. The *paulette* gave the wealthiest nobles of the realm a greater stake in the monarchy. But while increasing royal revenue, it intensified the phenomenon of the venality of office (the purchase of offices and the noble titles that went with them).

Henry could rarely rest at ease. In 1602 and again two years later, he uncovered plots against him formed by nobles in connivance with the Spanish monarchy. He survived nine assassination attempts and at least twenty-three assorted other plots against him. The first followed his expulsion of the Jesuits, whose pamphleteers had called for his assassination. Small wonder that he carried two loaded pistols in his belt and that some nervous soul tasted his food and drink before he did.

In 1598, Henry's Edict of Nantes made Catholicism the official religion of France. But it also granted the nation's 2 million Protestants (in a population of about 18.5 million) the right to worship at home, to hold religious services and establish schools in specified towns—almost all in the southwest and west—and to maintain a number of fortified towns. The Edict of Nantes also established chambers in the provincial parlements, or law courts dominated by nobles, to judge the cases of Protestants (see Map 4.1).

But careful to placate powerful sources of Catholic opposition, a series of secret decrees also promised Paris, Toulouse, and other staunchly Catholic towns that Protestant worship would be forbidden within their walls. The Edict of Nantes thus left the Protestants as something of a separate estate with specified privileges and rights, but still on the margin of French life. "What I have done is for the sake of peace," Henry stated emphatically. The former Catholic Leaguers howled in protest. By registering royal edicts, the parlements gave them the status of law. In this case, they only gradually and grudgingly registered the edict, which provided the Huguenots with more secure status than any other religious minority in Europe.

Many Huguenots, however, who found the Edict of Nantes unduly restrictive, distrusted the king who had already abjured their religion several times. Henry's foreign policy, which appeared pro-Protestant, supporting the Dutch rebels against Spain and certain German states against the Catholic Habsburgs, was, in fact, based on dynastic interests. But this

MAP 4.1 WARS OF RELIGION IN FRANCE IN THE SIXTEENTH CENTURY   France at the time of the Edict of Nantes, 1598. The map indicates neutral provinces, Huguenot provinces, and Catholic League provinces during the wars of religion, as well as Huguenot and Catholic League towns and battle sites during the wars.

support of Protestant rebels and princes made it impossible for Henry to consider further concessions to the Huguenots.

At the same time, the Catholic Reformation bore fruit in France. The Church benefited from a revival in organizational zeal and popularity. Henry allowed the Jesuits to return to France in 1604, a sign that religious tensions were ebbing, and he admitted several Italian religious orders.

With various would-be assassins lurking, Henry had to think about an heir. He sought a papal annulment of his marriage to Margaret of Valois, whom he had not seen in eighteen years. While waiting, he prepared to marry one of his mistresses, but she died miscarrying their child. With the blessing of the Church, he then arranged to marry Marie de' Medici (1573–1642), a distant relative of Catherine de' Medici. This second marriage of convenience brought a sizable dowry that Henry used, in part, to pay off more international debts.

Henry's charismatic and somewhat contradictory personality has always attracted considerable interest. In contrast to the portraits he encouraged depicting him as Hercules or Apollo, or arrayed in a splendid white plume and a warrior's helmet, the king of France was extremely slovenly, sometimes wearing torn or ragged clothes. He became renowned for his physical vigor on the battlefield and in his travels. He gambled large sums, with a notorious lack of success.

Although he knew nothing of music or poetry, and regularly fell asleep at the theater, Henry IV nonetheless was a patron of new architectural projects that added to the beauty of the city of Paris and imprinted his rule upon it. He oversaw the construction of the Great Gallery joining his residence in the Louvre Palace to that of the Tuileries. He ordered the construction of four quays facilitating the docking of boats along the Seine River. He initiated the splendid Place Dauphine, ringed by elegant buildings on the west end of the island of Cité, where his equestrian statue now stands. And he orchestrated the construction of the Place Royale, with pavilions of symmetrical arcades, brick construction, and steeply inclining roofs in the northern architectural style. The new square lay close to the eastern edge of Paris, which was then near many noble residences.

Intelligent and well organized, Henry kept abreast of events throughout his vast kingdom. But he had little sense of protocol, often rushing out of

The Place Dauphine, seen here from Pont-Neuf, was one of Henry IV's grand architectural projects.

the Louvre by himself as his guards scurried to catch up, once knocking down a messenger as he rushed out a side entrance. His wit was well known: when formally welcomed by a long-winded representative of the town of Amiens, who began "O most benign, greatest and most clement of kings," Henry interjected, "Add as well, the most tired of kings!" When a second spokesman began his official greeting, "Agesilaus, king of Sparta, Sire," Henry cut him short, "I too have heard of that Agesilaus, but he had eaten, and I have not."

Marie de' Medici bore the constant burden of her husband's various infidelities and occasional bouts with gonorrhea. Henry produced six illegitimate children by three mistresses, along with the three born to the queen. His nine offspring made up what he proudly referred to as his "herd." His ease was such that he formally introduced one of his mistresses to his wife, demanding that the latter repeat her curtsy so that she bow a bit lower, and the three dined together in what must have been an uncomfortable meal.

Statemaking

Restoring monarchical prestige and authority in France, Henry IV laid the foundations for what would become the strongest power in seventeenth-century Europe. His reign was an exercise in early modern European statemaking as he reimposed royal authority throughout the realm. Henry was suspicious of any representative institutions, which he believed threatened the exercise of royal authority: he never convoked the Estates-General; he ignored the parlements; and he scorned the provincial law courts.

Henry IV made the monarchy more powerful by dispensing privilege, favors, and, above all, money with a judiciousness that earned loyalty. Provincial governors represented the interests of the monarchy in the face of the privileges and resistance to taxes maintained by the provincial parlements and estates. The difficulties of extracting resources for the state were complicated by the division of the provinces into more peripheral "state provinces" (*pays d'état*) like Languedoc, Burgundy, and Provence, which had been recently added to the realm and retained more of their traditional privileges, and the "election provinces" (*pays d'élection*). In the former, the noble estates assessed and collected taxation; in the latter, royal officials assumed these functions.

Much of Henry's success in achieving the political reconstruction of France can be credited to his arrogant minister of finance, Maximilien de Béthune, the baron and, as of 1604, the duke of Sully (1560–1641). Sully was the son of a prosperous Protestant family whose great wealth had earned ennoblement. His influence, deeply resented by many nobles, was such that he was the only male admitted to the king's bedchamber, where he received the day's instructions.

Sully established budgets and systematic bookkeeping, which helped him eliminate some needless expenses. The monarchy gradually began to pay off some international debts, including those owed to the English crown, and the Swiss cantons, whose good will Henry needed to counter Spanish influence in the Alps. These repayments allowed Henry to contrast his honor in the realm of finances with that of the Spanish monarchy, whose periodic declarations of bankruptcy left creditors grasping at air.

Meanwhile, the nobles reaffirmed their own economic and social domination over their provinces. In 1609, Charles Loyseau, a lawyer, published a *Treatise on Orders and Plain Dignities* that portrayed French society as a hierarchy of orders, or three estates: the clergy, the nobility, and everyone else. He portrayed the king as the guarantor of this organic society. Henry restored the hierarchy of social orders based upon rank and privilege while imposing his rule. But the boundaries between and within these estates were fairly fluid. A few newcomers ascended into the highest rank of dukes and peers who stood above even the "nobles of the sword," the oldest and most powerful nobles traditionally called on by the monarchy to provide military support. The "nobles of the robe," while not a coherent or self-conscious group, were men who claimed noble status on the basis of high administrative and judicial office, for example, in the parlements. Henry strengthened the social hierarchy by bolstering established institutions, including the parlements, the treasury, the universities, and, ultimately, the Catholic Church.

At the same time, conciliatory royal language began to disappear when it came to asking for money, however. Royal governors, whose influence had grown during the wars of the Catholic League, strengthened the monarchy at the expense of towns that prided themselves on their ancient privileges, further eroding their fiscal independence.

The royal privy council, some of whose members were chosen, like Sully, from the ranks of lesser nobles known for their competence and dedication, strengthened the effectiveness of state administration and foreign relations. The king personally oversaw this council, excluding troublesome nobles. Henry monitored the activities of his ambassadors and his court, whose 1,500 residents included the purveyors of perfume, of whom he might have made greater use.

Henry also took an intermittent interest in encouraging French manufacturing, particularly of silk and tapestries. To promote internal trade, he encouraged investment in the construction of several canals linking navigable rivers. He was the first king to take an active interest in supporting a permanent French settlement in the New World, thereby increasing the prospects of French fishermen and trappers following Jacques Cartier's exploration of the St. Lawrence River in 1534. Samuel de Champlain founded the colony of Québec in 1608. This settlement became a base for further explorations by Champlain and those who followed him. Two years later, the first two French Jesuit missionaries arrived in what became known as New France.

On May 14, 1610, Henry set out from the Louvre in a carriage for Sully's residence, accompanied by horsemen and guards. The carriage became ensnared in traffic in central Paris. When some of the guards dashed forward to try to clear the way, a crazed monk named François Ravaillac jumped up to take revenge for the king's protection of Protestants. He stabbed the king three times, as Henry sat listening to a letter being read to him. Henry IV died before the carriage could return to the Louvre.

Louis XIII and the Origins of Absolute Rule

Henry's sudden death left Marie de' Medici, his widow, as regent for his young son, Louis XIII (ruled 1610–1643), who was eight years old at the time. Neither Philip III (ruled 1598–1621) of Spain nor James I of England, nor any of the princes of the German states, were in a position to try to intervene in France on behalf of either Huguenots or Catholics. Marie put aside Henry's planned campaign against the Habsburgs and adopted a policy that considered Catholic powers to be friends.

Marie foiled several nobles' plots against her in 1614–1616. The convocation of the Estates-General accentuated the eagerness of noble rivals to gain influence with the young king. One of them, Charles d'Albert, duke of Luynes, an expert falconer and flatterer who shared his passion for training hawks with the young king while using his position to enhance his family's fortune, convinced Louis to impose his own rule. The king ordered the murder of one of his mother's confidants; Louis then exiled his unpopular mother, hoping to restore calm. When a group of nobles took this as occasion to raise the standard of revolt, the king's army defeated them at Ponts-de-Cé near Angers in 1620. The royal army then defeated a revolt by Huguenot nobles in the southwest and west.

Emotionally, the stubborn, ill-tempered, and high-strung boy-king Louis XIII never really grew up. Throughout his life, he demonstrated the psychological burdens of having been regularly whipped as punishment on his father's orders when he was "stubborn or does something bad." His father's murder when he was young also marked him. As his father's body was carried up the stairs of the Louvre, the chubby eight-year-old had shouted, "Ha! If I had been there with my sword, I would have killed [the assassin]." Louis XIII's marriage to an Austrian princess began with a wedding-night fiasco that, whatever happened between the precocious young couple, led to a six-month period in which they did not even share a meal. Finally, things went better. After suffering several miscarriages, the queen produced an heir in 1638, but the royal couple was otherwise unhappy.

Cardinal Richelieu at the sea wall of La Rochelle in 1628, in the midst of the Thirty Years' War.

Louis XIII was intelligent, though not particularly interested in ideas. He preferred sketching and music, the latter calming him when he fell into a rage. He enjoyed hunting and winning at chess, once hurling the offending pieces at the head of a courtier who had the bad grace to checkmate him.

Louis was a pious man who attended church every day. But he was also invariably willful, ruthless, and cruel, lashing out savagely at his enemies; indeed, no other ruler of France ordered as many executions as Louis XIII. Among those executed were a number of nobles convicted of dueling, a practice that the king detested because it represented to him the possibility that nobles could raise private armies against the throne.

During Louis XIII's reign, Cardinal Armand Jean du Plessis de Richelieu (1585–1642) expanded the administrative authority and fiscal reach of the crown, dramatically increasing tax revenues. Richelieu's family, solidly entrenched in the west of France, had long served the monarchy in court, army, and church. Ordained bishop of Luçon, near the Protestant stronghold of La Rochelle, the gaunt, clever Richelieu staked his future on and won the patronage of the queen mother. He perfected the art of political survival during the court struggles of the next few years. Richelieu was a realist. His foreign and domestic policies reflected his *politique* approach to both. Although he was made a cardinal in 1622, he nonetheless always put reasons of state ahead of any consideration of religious principles.

In 1629, Richelieu prepared a long memorandum for his king. "If the King wants to make himself the most powerful monarch and the most highly esteemed prince in the world," he advised that "[The estates and the parlements] which oppose the welfare of the kingdom by their pretended sovereignty must be humbled and disciplined. Absolute obedience to the King must be enforced upon great and small alike." Richelieu divided France into thirty-two districts (*généralités*), organizing and extending the king's authority. Officials called intendants governed each district, overseen by the king's council and ultimately responsible to the king himself.

In order to enhance the authority of the monarchy and the Church, Richelieu turned his attention to the Huguenots. After forcing the surrender of insurgent Protestant forces at La Rochelle in 1628, he ordered the destruction of the Huguenot fortresses in the south and southwest, as well as the châteaux of other nobles whose loyalty he had reason to doubt.

During the Thirty Years' War (1618–1648, see below), Louis XIII, influenced by Richelieu, reversed his mother's pro-Spanish foreign policy, returning to the traditional French position of opposition to the Habsburgs. The dynastic rivalry between the two powers proved greater than the fact that both kings were Catholic. Louis XIII thus surprised and outraged the Spanish king by joining England and the Dutch Republic, both Protestant powers, against the powerful Catholic Austrian Habsburgs during the Thirty Years' War. And in 1635, France declared war against Spain itself.

Richelieu's successes, however, did not stand well with his resentful enemies within France. His toleration of Huguenot worship drew the wrath of some Catholic nobles, as did continuing costly wars against the Catholic Habsburgs, which included French subsidies to Protestant Sweden. Revolts occurred in Dijon and Aix, both seats of provincial parlements, where local notables resented having to bow to the authority of royal officials.

One of the most conservative Catholic nobles, a royal minister, briefly turned the king against Richelieu. Marie de' Medici, returned from brief disgrace, tried to convince her son to dismiss the cagey cardinal. The "Day of Dupes" (November 10, 1630) followed, which amounted to little more than a high-stakes family shouting match between Marie de' Medici, Louis XIII, and Richelieu. Marie left thinking she had won the day, but awoke the next morning to find that the king had ordered her exile. The king's own brother led a second plot against Richelieu from 1641 to 1642, backed by the king of Spain.

Philippe de Champagne's portrait of the sad-eyed Louis XIII.

After decades of religious wars, the assassination of Henry IV, and a fragile, temperamental young monarch around whom plots swirled, the monarchy of France had nonetheless been greatly strengthened. Louis XIII's sometimes decisive and brutal actions enhanced the reputation of the king who was known to many of his subjects as "The Just," whether fitting or not. A hypochondriac whose health was even worse than he feared, Louis XIII died of tuberculosis in 1643 at the age of forty-two. Philippe de Champagne's portrait of the king preserves his sad eyes and premature aging. But the man-child monarch had, with Richelieu, laid the foundations for absolute monarchical rule in France.

THE THIRTY YEARS' WAR (1618–1648)

In Central Europe, religious divisions led to the Thirty Years' War, a brutal conflict during which the largely mercenary armies of Catholic and Protestant states laid waste to the German states. Dynastic rivalries were never far from the stage, bringing the continental Great Powers into the fray. When the war finally ended, the Treaty of Westphalia (1648) established a territorial and religious settlement that lasted until the French Revolution.

Factionalism in the Holy Roman Empire

The Holy Roman Empire was a loose confederation of approximately 1,000 German autonomous or semi-autonomous states. These states ranged in size from powerful Habsburg Austria to Hamburg, Lübeck, and other free cities in the north, and even smaller territories no more than a few square kilometers in size run by princes or bishops. It would have been almost impossible for a traveler to determine where one state stopped and another began had it not been for the frequent toll stations, which provided much of the revenue for each. The southwest German state of Swabia, for example, was divided between sixty-eight secular and forty ecclesiastical lords and included thirty-two free cities.

Geographic factors further complicated the political life of the German states. A few of the largest states included territories that were not contiguous. The Upper Palatinate lay squeezed between Bohemia and Bavaria; the Lower Palatinate lay far away in the Rhineland. The former was predominantly Lutheran, the latter Calvinist.

Since 1356, when the constitutional law of the Holy Roman Empire had been established, seven electors (four electoral princes and three archbishops) selected each new Holy Roman emperor. The empire's loose federal structure had a chancery to carry out foreign policy and negotiations with the various German princes. But only in confronting the threat of the

Turks from the southeast did the German princes mount a consistent and relatively unified foreign policy.

Other institutions of the Holy Roman Empire also reflected the political complexity of Central Europe. An imperial Diet brought princes, nobles, and representatives of the towns together when the emperor summoned them. An Imperial Court of Justice ruled on matters of importance to the empire. The Holy Roman Empire, once the most powerful force in Europe had been weakened by its battles with the papacy in the thirteenth century. Yet for some states the empire offered a balance between the desire for a figure of authority who could maintain law and order and their continued political independence.

The Peace of Augsburg (1555), which ended the war between the Holy Roman Emperor Charles V and the Protestant German states, had stated that, with the exception of ecclesiastical states and the free cities, the religion of the ruler would be the religion of the land (*cuius regio, eius religio*). This formula, however, did not end religious rivalries or the demands of religious minorities that rulers tolerate their beliefs. The Peace of Augsburg, in fact, reinforced German particularism. It also helped secularize the institutions of the Holy Roman emperor by recognizing the right of the German princes to determine the religion of their states.

The Origins of the Thirty Years' War

Rudolf II (1557–1612), king of Bohemia and Holy Roman emperor (he succeeded his father Maximilian II as Holy Roman emperor in 1576), wanted to launch a religious crusade against Protestantism. He closed Lutheran churches in 1578, reneging on an earlier promise to Bohemian nobles that he would tolerate the religion to which a good many of them had converted. Moreover, Rudolf's brother Archduke Ferdinand II (1578–1637) withdrew the religious toleration his father Maximilian II had granted in Inner Austria.

Rudolf's imperial army, which had been fighting the Turks on and off since 1593, had annexed Transylvania. The emperor moved against Protestants both there and in Hungary. But in 1605, when Rudolf's army undertook a campaign against the Turks in the Balkans, Protestants rebelled in both places. A Protestant army invaded Moravia, which lies east of Bohemia and north of Austria, close to the Habsburg capital of Vienna. In the meantime, Emperor Rudolf, only marginally competent on his best days (he was subject to depression and later to fits of insanity), lived as a recluse in his castle in Prague. His family convinced his brother Matthias (1557–1619) to act on Rudolf's behalf by making peace with the Hungarian and Transylvanian Protestants and with the Turks. This Peace of Vienna (1606) guaranteed religious freedom in Hungary. Matthias was then recognized as head of the Habsburgs and heir to Rudolf.

Most everyone seemed pleased with the peace except poor Rudolf, who concluded that a plague that was ravaging Bohemia was proof that God was displeased with the concessions he had been forced to grant Protestants. He denounced his brothers Matthias and Ferdinand for their accommodation with the Protestants and with the Turkish "infidels." Matthias allied with the Protestant Hungarian noble Estates and marched against Rudolf, who surrendered. Rudolf ceded Hungary, Austria, and Moravia to Matthias in 1608, and Bohemia to him in 1611. Rudolf was forced to sign a "Letter of Majesty" in 1609 that granted Bohemians the right to choose between Catholicism, Lutheranism, or one of two groups of Hussites (see Chapter 3). Protestant churches, schools, and cemeteries were to be tolerated.

The decline in the effective authority of the Holy Roman emperor, after four centuries of power, contributed to the end of a period of relative peace in the German states. In the last decades of the sixteenth century, these states had become increasingly quarrelsome and militarized. "The dear old Holy Roman Empire," went one song, "How does it stay together?" Rulers of some member states began to undermine imperial political institutions by refusing to accept rulings by the Imperial Supreme Court and even to attend the occasional convocations of the Diet. "Imperial Military Circles," which were inter-state alliances responsible for defense of a number of states within the empire, had become moribund because of religious antagonisms between the member states.

For a time, the Catholic Reformation profited from acrimonious debates and even small wars between Lutherans and Calvinists. But increasingly Protestants put aside their differences, however substantial, in the face of Catholic determination to win back territories lost to Protestantism.

Acts of intolerance heated up religious rivalries. In 1606, in Donauwörth, a south German imperial free city in which Lutherans held the upper hand and Catholics enjoyed toleration, a riot began when Protestants tried to prevent Catholics from holding a procession. The following year, Duke Maximilian of Bavaria sent troops to assure Catholic domination. This angered Calvinist princes in the region, as well as some Lutheran sovereigns. The imperial Diet, convoked two years later, broke up in chaos when Holy Roman Emperor Rudolf II refused to increase Protestant representation in the Diet. The political crisis now spread further when some of the German Catholic states sought Spanish intervention in a dispute over princely succession in the small Catholic territories of Cleves-Jülich, which Henry IV of France threatened to invade. In 1609, Catholic German princes organized a Catholic League, headed by Maximilian of Bavaria. Six Protestant princes then signed a defensive alliance, the Protestant Union, against the Catholic League.

Matthias, who had been elected Holy Roman emperor in 1612, wanted to make the Catholic League an institution of Habsburg will. He also hoped to woo Lutherans from the Protestant Union, which was dominated by the Calvinists. But Matthias's obsession with Habsburg dynastic ambitions, his history of having fought with the Protestant Dutch rebels against Spain (see Chapter 5), and his opportunistic toleration of Lutheranism cost him the confidence of some Catholic princes. Archduke Ferdinand, ruler of Inner Austria, waited in the wings to lead a Catholic crusade against Protestantism. Ferdinand, who had inherited the throne of Hungary in 1617 and that of Bohemia in 1618, became Holy Roman emperor upon Matthias's death in 1619. Ferdinand was a pious man who had been educated by the Jesuits and whose every decision followed consultation with his confessor, who convinced him that he could save his soul only by launching a war of religion. In the meantime, Protestant resistance in Bohemia mobilized, seeking Protestant assistance from Transylvania and the Palatinate.

Conflict in Bohemia

In Bohemia, Ferdinand, backed by many nobles, imposed significant limitations on Protestant worship. In Prague, Calvinists and Lutherans, including university professors and students and members of literary societies, began to look outside of Bohemia for potential support from Protestant princes. Protestant leaders convoked an assembly of the Estates of Bohemia, citing rights specified by Rudolf's "Letter of Majesty" of 1609, and petitioned Emperor Matthias to order the withdrawal of the repressive dictates. Ferdinand ordered the assembly to disband.

Following the Defenestration of Prague in 1618, Protestant leaders established a provisional government in Bohemia. "This business of Bohemia is likely to put all Christendom in combustion," predicted the English ambassador to the Dutch capital of Amsterdam. It began a destructive war between Catholic and Protestant forces that would last thirty years, lay waste to many of the German states, and finally bring a religious and territorial settlement that would last for two centuries.

Bohemia rose in full revolt against not only the Church but the Habsburg dynasty as well. With almost no assistance from the nobles, the rebels turned to the Protestant Union, promising the Bohemian crown to Frederick, the young Calvinist elector of the Palatinate and the most important Protestant prince in Central Europe. In their desperate quest for support, the Bohemian Protestants also attempted to woo three other rulers with exactly the same promise, but in 1619, the Estates offered Frederick the crown. He accepted, saying this was "a divine calling which I must not disobey."

The Protestant cause, like that of the Catholics, became increasingly internationalized and tied to dynastic considerations (see Map 4.2). After his brother Matthias died in 1619, the Catholic Archduke Ferdinand received enough votes from electors to become Holy Roman Emperor Ferdinand II. He then learned that Protestant rebels had refused to recognize his authority in Bohemia and had offered his throne to Frederick. Even more determined to drive Protestants from his realm but lacking an army, Ferdinand turned to outside help. The Catholic king of Spain agreed to send troops he could ill afford; the price of his intervention was the promise of the cession of the Rhineland state of the Lower Palatinate to Spain. The Catholic Maximilian I of Bavaria also sent an army, expecting to be rewarded for his trouble with the Upper Palatinate and with Frederick's title of elector in the Holy Roman Empire.

MAP 4.2 THE THIRTY YEARS' WAR, 1618–1648   Protestant and Catholic armies clashed in battles that ranged back and forth across Europe.

The Expansion of the Conflict

In the meantime, Protestant armies marched on Vienna, the Habsburg capital, and laid siege to it. Catholic armies lifted this siege in 1619. Had news of this not been so slow to reach Spain, Philip III of Spain might have changed his mind about intervention. But with Spanish armies and monies already on the way, the internationalization of the Bohemian crisis had reached the point of no return. The Dutch could not provide assistance, as they were fighting for independence from Spain. Several of the German Protestant states also declined, fearing Catholic rebellions in their own lands.

During a short-lived truce brought about by the arrival of a seemingly neutral French army in 1620, the Catholic League raised a largely Bavarian army of 30,000 troops. Count Johannes von Tilly (1559–1632) commanded the Catholic forces. The depressed, indecisive count from Flanders managed to subdue Upper Austria and then defeated the main Protestant Union army at the brief but significant Battle of White Mountain, near Prague in November 1620. With the Catholic forces now holding Bohemia, Tilly's army then overran Silesia, Moravia, Austria, and part of the Upper Palatinate. The extent of the Catholic victory expanded the war, increasing the determination of the Catholic League to crush all Protestant resistance and, at the same time, of the Protestant forces to resist at all costs.

Frederick's Protestant forces fought on, counting on help from France and other states who had reason to fear an expansion of Habsburg power in Central Europe. He also hoped to convince James I of England that a victory of the Catholic League would threaten Protestantism. But the English king had placed his hopes on the marriage of his son, Charles, to the sister of Philip IV of Spain (who had succeeded Philip III in 1621), an alliance that could bring about a diplomatic settlement to the complicated crisis (see Chapter 5). Again dynastic rivalries outweighed those of religion.

The war went on, and Tilly's army won a series of small victories. In 1622, the Spanish won a victory over the Dutch at Jülich in the Rhineland, eliminating any possibility of English armed assistance to Frederick through Holland. For the moment, Frederick's only effective force was a plundering mercenary horde in northeastern Germany. Tilly's victory over a Protestant army in 1623 and conquest of most of the Palatinate forced Frederick to abandon his claims to Bohemia's throne after having been king for all of one winter. But encouraged by the renewed possibility of English assistance after James's plans for the marriage of his son to the Spanish princess fell through, Frederick turned north to Scandinavia for assistance.

The Danish Period

Christian IV (ruled 1588–1648), the Protestant king of Denmark, had ambition and money, but not a great deal of sense. Also duke of the northern German state of Holstein, the gambling, hard-drinking Dane wanted to extend his influence and perhaps even territories in the northern German states. Frederick's difficulties seemed to offer the Danish sovereign the opportunity of a lifetime. In 1625, he led his troops into the northern German states, confident that the English and the Dutch, and perhaps the French as well, would rush to follow his leadership against the Habsburgs.

But King James I of England had died and was succeeded by Charles I, who was even more beset than his father by opposition to his policies. Moreover, Louis XIII of France, who was besieging Protestants at La Rochelle (see Chapter 6), provided the Danes with only a modest subsidy to aid the fight against the Habsburgs. England and the Netherlands did no more than send some money and a few thousand soldiers to help the Danish king. Christian, essentially left to his own devices, was unaware of the approach of a large imperial army commanded by one of the most intriguing figures in the age of religious wars.

Albrecht Wallenstein (1583–1634) was a tall, gaunt Bohemian noble who, after marrying a wealthy widow, had risen to even greater fortune as a supplier of armies. Raised a Lutheran, he converted to Catholicism at age twenty and became the most powerful of the Catholic generals. The fact that a convert could rise to such a powerful position again reveals how a religious war evolved into not only a dynastic struggle between the rulers of France, Spain, and Austria, as well as Sweden and Denmark, but also into an unprincipled free-for-all in which mercenary soldiers of fortune played a major part. Wallenstein, an ardent student of astrology, was ambitious, ruthless, and possessed a violent temper. His abhorrence of noise was obsessive—and odd, for a military person. Because he detested the sound of barking or meowing, he sometimes ordered all dogs and cats killed upon arriving in a town, and forbade the townspeople and his soldiers from wearing heavy boots or spurs or anything else that would make noise. He alternated between extreme generosity and horrible cruelty, and was always accompanied by an executioner awaiting his master's command. Wallenstein, entrusted by Ferdinand with raising and commanding an army drawn from the myriad nationalities fighting for the Catholic cause, marched north with 30,000 men.

Tilly defeated the Danes in 1626, aided by some of Wallenstein's mercenaries and King Christian's inept generalship. The Catholic army then marched to the Baltic coast and crossed into Denmark, devastating the peninsula of Jutland. But Wallenstein's successes engendered nervous opposition within the Catholic states. Furthermore, his troops devastated the lands of friend and foe alike, extracting money and food, plundering, and selling military leadership positions to any buyer, including criminals.

Christian, who had spent much of his personal fortune and bankrupted his kingdom during this ill-fated excursion, signed the Treaty of Lübeck in 1629, whereby he withdrew from the war and gave up his claims in northern Germany. The treaty was less draconian than it might have been because the seemingly endless war was wearing heavily on some of the Catholic German states. They feared an expansion of Habsburg power, and some of them did not want to add Protestants to their domains. The Danish king lost no territory in Denmark, but he agreed that he would never again interfere in the affairs of the Holy Roman emperor.

Ferdinand II now implemented measures against Protestants without convoking the imperial Diet. He expelled from Bohemia Calvinist and Lutheran ministers and nobles who refused to convert to Catholicism and ennobled new men, including foreigners, as a means of assuring Catholic domination. He confiscated the property of nobles suspected of participating in any phase of the Protestant rebellion. With Frederick's electorship now transferred to Maximilian I of Bavaria, the Habsburgs could count on the fact that a majority of the electors were Catholic princes. Captured Habsburg dispatches in 1628 made clear that Ferdinand sought to destroy the freedom of the Protestant German cities of the Hanseatic League in the north in the interest of expanding the Habsburg domains. These revelations alarmed Louis XIII of France.

Ferdinand found that it was not easy to impose Catholicism in territories where it had not been practiced for decades. In the Upper Palatinate, the first priests who came to celebrate Mass there were unable to find a chalice. Until the 1640s, half of the parishes in Bohemia were without clergy. Italian priests brought to Upper Austria could not be understood by their parishioners, some of whom rebelled against their authority and were executed on the emperor's command. The Edict of Restitution (1629) allowed Lutherans—but not Calvinists, who were few in number in the German states except in the Palatinate—to practice their religion in certain cities, but ordered them to return to the Catholic Church all monasteries and convents acquired after 1552, when signatories of the Peace of Augsburg had first gathered. Because the Edict of Restitution also gave rulers the right to enforce the practice of their religion within their territories, the war went on.

The Swedish Interlude

In the meantime, England, the Dutch Republic, the northern German state of Brandenburg, and the Palatinate asked the Lutheran king Gustavus Adolphus (ruled 1611–1632) of Sweden to intervene on the Protestant side. The possibility of expanding Swedish territory, a kingdom of

King Gustavus Adolphus of Sweden in battle.

barely a million inhabitants, was more than Gustavus, who had an adventurer's disposition, could resist.

Gustavus, the "Lion of the North," who survived a shipwreck at the age of five, had been tutored in the art of war by mercenary soldiers. He also played the flute, composed poetry, and conversed in ten languages. The Dutch ambassador described him as "slender of figure, well set up, with rather a pale complexion, a long-shaped face, fair hair, and a pointed beard which here and there runs into a tawny color." Gustavus retained, as did a disproportionate number of rulers in his century, a violent temper. Once, coming upon two stolen cows outside an officer's tent, he dragged the thief by the ear to the executioner. His courage was legendary; he barely paused as cannonballs exploded nearby and as his horses were shot out from under him or fell through the ice.

Gustavus, influenced by an appreciation of Roman military tactics, formed his battle lines thinner—about six men deep—than those of rival commanders. This allowed battle lines to be more widely spread out; the king personally demonstrated to his men the proper way of firing in such a formation. Gustavus organized his army into brigades of four squadrons with nine cannon to protect them, sending the unit into battle in an arrow-shaped formation. Superior artillery served his cause well, hurling larger shot further and more accurately than that of his enemies.

The dashing young Swedish king subdued Catholic Poland with his army of about 70,000 men. Swedish intervention and the continuing woes of Spain, now at war in the Alps, Italy, and the Netherlands, gave Protestants reason for hope. After defeating a combined Polish and Habsburg army in 1629, Swedish troops occupied Pomerania along the Baltic Sea.

In 1630, sure of a Catholic majority, Emperor Ferdinand convoked the imperial electors to recognize his son as his heir. He also wanted them to support his promise to aid Spain against the Dutch in exchange for Spanish assistance against the Protestant armies. But the electors of Saxony and Brandenburg, both Protestants, refused even to attend the gathering. Catholic electors demanded that the powerful Wallenstein be dismissed; even the king of Spain feared the general's powerful ragtag army. Ferdinand thereby dismissed the one man whose accomplishments and influence might have enabled the Habsburg monarchy to master all of the German states.

Despite a sizable subsidy from the king of France, Gustavus Adolphus enjoyed only the support of several tiny Protestant states. Some Lutheran German states still hoped to receive territorial concessions from the Habsburgs. The Catholic dynasty preferred Lutherans to Calvinists, viewing the latter as more radical reformers. Ferdinand now sent Tilly to stop the invading Swedes. He besieged the Protestant city of Magdeburg in Brandenburg, forcing its surrender in 1631. The subsequent massacre of the population and accompanying pillage had an effect similar to that of the Defenestration of Prague; the story of the atrocities spread across Europe. Protestant Brandenburg and Saxony now allied with Sweden.

That same year, the combined Protestant forces under Gustavus Adolphus defeated Tilly's imperial Catholic army at Breitenfeld near Leipzig. The Swedish army, swollen by German mercenaries, then marched through the northern German states, easily reversing Habsburg gains over the previous twelve years.

The expansion of Swedish power generated anxiety among both Protestant and Catholic states, including France, although Louis XIII had helped finance Gustavus Adolphus. In Bavaria, the Swedes defeated Tilly, who was killed in battle in 1632. The rout of the Catholic imperial forces seemed complete. Spain, its interests spread too far afield in Europe and the Americas, could not then afford to help. The plague prevented another Catholic army from being raised in Italy; even the pope begged off a request for help by complaining that the eruption of Mount Vesuvius was preventing the collection of taxes. Upon learning that the Swedes had taken yet another city, an imperial official wrote, "We cry 'Help, Help!' but there is nobody there!"

In April 1632, Ferdinand turned once again to Wallenstein to save the Catholic cause, the latter agreeing to raise a new imperial army in return for almost unlimited authority over it. Wallenstein reconquered Silesia and Bohemia. Against him, Gustavus led the largest army (175,000) that had ever been under a single command in Europe. Although reason dictated that the Swedish army should dig in for the winter of 1632, Gustavus took a chance by attacking Wallenstein in the fog at Lützen in Saxony in November. The two sides fought to a bloody draw, but a draw amounted to a Catholic victory. Gustavus Adolphus fell dead in the battle, facedown in the mud, shot in the arm, back, and head.

Wallenstein's days were also numbered. His new army had accomplished little, and was now living off the land in Central Europe, engendering peasant resistance. Furthermore, Wallenstein, who was ill, demanded command of a Spanish army that had subsequently arrived to help the Catholic forces. In the meantime, it became known that Wallenstein had considered joining Gustavus after the Battle of Breitenfeld in 1631, and that he was offering his services to both France and the German Protestants. Ferdinand dismissed Wallenstein for the final time, and then ordered his murder. In February 1634, an Irish mercenary crept into Wallenstein's room, speared him, wrapped his body in a rug, and hauled it down the stairs for all to see.

With the aid of the remnants of Wallenstein's forces, the Spanish army defeated the combined Swedish and German Protestant army in 1634 in the southern German state of Swabia. The elector of Saxony abandoned the Protestant struggle, making peace in 1635 with Ferdinand. One by one, other Protestant princes also left the war. The Catholic forces now held the upper hand.

The Armies of the Thirty Years' War

The Thirty Years' War was certainly one of the cruelest episodes in the history of warfare. A contemporary described the horror of the seemingly endless brutalities that afflicted Central Europe: "[The soldiers] stretched out a hired man flat on the ground, stuck a wooden wedge in

Soldiers pillaging a farmhouse during the Thirty Years' War, some torturing the farmer over his hearth while others rape the women and steal the food.

his mouth to keep it open, and emptied a milk bucket full of stinking manure droppings down his throat—they called it a Swedish cocktail. . . . Then they used thumb-screws, which they cleverly made out of their pistols, to torture the peasants. . . . They put one of the captured bumpkins in the bakeoven and lighted a fire in it. . . . I can't say much about the captured wives, hired girls, and daughters because the soldiers did not let me watch their doings. But I do remember hearing pitiful screams in various dark corners."

Several factors may have contributed to the barbarity of soldiers during the Thirty Years' War. Mercenaries and volunteers were usually fighting far from home, knowing they had to live off the land to survive. Strident propaganda against other religions may have contributed to the brutality. In response, Gustavus Adolphus and other leaders, however, imposed harsh penalties, including execution, for atrocities, not wanting to so frighten the local population that ordinary channels of provisioning the army would disappear.

During the Thirty Years' War, at least a million men took arms. The armies were enormous for the time. Even Sweden, where there was no fighting, felt the impact of the death of at least 50,000 soldiers between 1621 and 1632 from battle wounds and, more often, disease. Yet, considering the number of troops engaged in the long war, relatively few soldiers perished in battle, particularly when compared to those who succumbed to illness and to civilians who died at the hands of marauding troops. Armies came and went through the German states, Catholic and Protestant, speaking many languages, taking what they wanted, burning and looting. Marburg was occupied eleven different times. Atrocity followed atrocity.

The armies themselves remained ragtag forces, lacking discipline and accompanied by, in some cases, the families of soldiers. The presence of large numbers of women (including many prostitutes) and children as camp followers may have contributed to the length of the war, making life in the army seem more normal for soldiers.

Although Gustavus ordered that troops "provide themselves with proper attire instead of their long smocks and peasant attire" so that people would judge them well, the reality was quite the opposite. Soldiers, for the most part, wore what they could find. Some, if they were lucky, had leather clothes, carried rain cloaks against the damp German climate, and wore felt hats. Some Habsburg troops sported uniforms of pale gray, at least at the beginning of a campaign. As the months passed, and uniforms disintegrated, soldiers were forced to disrobe the dead, friend and foe alike, or to steal from civilians. At best, soldiers wore symbols indicating their regiment and fought behind banners bearing the colors of the army—thus the expression "show your colors." The Swedes wore a yellow band around their hats. The imperial forces placed red symbols in their hats, plumes, or sashes if they could find them.

Drawn from a bewildering number of nationalities, most armies also lacked a common language. The Habsburg army included Saxons, Bavarians, Westphalians, and Austrians; Maximilian's Bavarian army counted various other Germans, Italians, Poles, Slovenes, Croats, Greeks, Hungarians, Burgundians, French, Czechs, Spaniards, Scots, Irish, and Turks.

Some soldiers may have joined regiments because they were searching for adventure; others joined out of religious conviction. Yet a multitude of soldiers fought against armies of their own religion. Some states and armies changed sides when a better opportunity arose. Army recruiters gave religion not the slightest thought in their search for soldiers to fill quotas for which they were being handsomely paid. In any case, recruits on both sides were attracted by the strong possibility that they would be better clothed and fed—bread, meat, lots of beer, and occasionally some butter and cheese—than they were at the time they joined up.

The Wars of Religion and Dynastic Struggles (1635–1648)

Between 1635 and 1648, what had begun as a religious war became a dynastic struggle between two Catholic states, France and Habsburg Austria, the former allied with Sweden, the latter with Spain. France declared war on Philip IV of Spain in 1635. Richelieu had planned for the struggle for some time, hoping to force Habsburg armies away from the borders of France. He took as a pretext the Spanish arrest of a French ally, the elector of Trier. Alliances with the Dutch Republic and Sweden had prepared the way, as did reassurances given by neighboring Savoy and Lorraine, and by French protectorates in Alsace.

The French incursions into the Netherlands and the southern German states did not go well. Louis XIII's army found itself short on capable commanders and battle-experienced troops, largely because France was already fighting in Italy, the Pyrenees, the Netherlands, and the northern German states. But France's involvement, like that of Sweden before it, did provide the Protestant states with some breathing room. French forces joined the Swedish army, helping defeat the imperial army in Saxony.

The wars went on. When the pope called for representatives of the Catholic and Protestant states to assemble in Cologne for a peace congress in 1636, no one showed up. Four years later, another combined French and Swedish force defeated the Habsburg army. Maximilian I of Bavaria then sought a separate peace with France. Devastating Spanish defeats in northern France in 1643, as well as in the Netherlands and the Pyrenees, and the outbreak of rebellions inside Spain, left the Austrian Habsburgs with no choice but to make peace.

At the same time, unrest in France, including plots against Richelieu, and the English Civil War, which began in 1642, served to warn other rulers of the dangers that continued instability could bring. The Swedish population was tiring of distant battles that brought home nothing but news of casualties. In the German states, calls for peace echoed in music and plays. Lutheran ministers, in particular, began to inveigh against the war from the pulpit. Among the rulers of the great powers, only Louis XIII, hoping to help further diminish his Habsburg rival's power, wanted the war to go on. He helped subsidize an invasion of Hungary by Transylvanian Protestants in 1644. As Swedish and Transylvanian forces prepared to besiege the imperial capital of Vienna, Ferdinand III (ruled 1637–1657), who had succeeded his father, concluded a peace treaty with the prince of Transylvania. The Holy Roman emperor promised to tolerate Protestantism in Hungary. After Habsburg armies suffered further defeats in 1645, Ferdinand realized that he had to make peace and offered an amnesty to princes within the empire who had fought against him.

The preliminaries for a general peace agreement had begun in 1643 and dragged on even as a Franco-Swedish army drove the imperial army out of the Rhineland and Bavaria in 1647. Following another French victory early in 1648, only the outbreak of the Fronde, a rebellion of nobles against the king's authority in France, forced the young Louis XIV to seek peace.

The Treaty of Westphalia (1648)

The Treaty of Westphalia was unlike any previous peace settlement in history, which had invariably been between two or three states, rarely more. Its framers believed that they could restore international stability and diplomatic process in a Europe torn by anarchy by eliminating religious divisions as a cause of conflict. The treaty proved almost as complicated as the Thirty Years' War itself. Two hundred rulers converged in Westphalia. Thousands of diplomats and other officials shuttled back and forth between two towns. Letters took ten to twelve days to reach the courts of Paris and Vienna, at least twenty to Stockholm, and a month to arrive in Madrid. In the meantime, the French tried to delay any treaty, hoping to force Spain to surrender. In the summer of 1648, the Swedes reoccupied Bohemia, hoping to win a larger indemnity and toleration for the Lutherans. When, by the separate Treaty of Münster, Spain finally formally recognized the *fait accompli* of Dutch independence, the Spanish Army of Flanders fought against France in a last-ditch effort to help Ferdinand III. In August 1648, the French defeated a Spanish force a month after the Swedes had captured part of Prague. His back to the wall, Ferdinand signed the peace treaty, finally concluded on October 24, 1648.

The Treaty of Westphalia redrew the map of Europe, confirming the existence of the Dutch United Provinces and Switzerland. The treaty did not end the war between Spain and France, but it did end the wars of the German states and in doing so put an end to one of the most brutal, ghastly periods in European history. Sweden absorbed West Pomerania

MAP 4.3 EUROPE AFTER THE TREATY OF WESTPHALIA, 1648   The treaty ended the Thirty Years' War.

and the bishoprics of Verden and Bremen on the North Sea (see Map 4.3). France, by an agreement signed two years earlier, annexed the frontier towns of Metz, Toul, and Verdun, and parts of Alsace. Maximilian I of Bavaria kept the Upper Palatinate, and therefore the status of elector. Frederick's Protestant son ended up with the Lower, or Rhine Palatinate, and was restored to the status of elector. With this addition of an elector, eight votes would now be necessary to elect the Holy Roman emperor.

With minor exceptions, the territorial settlement reached in Westphalia remained in place until the French Revolution of 1789. For the most part, the treaty ended wars of religion in early modern Europe. It encouraged religious toleration. The Treaty of Westphalia reinforced the strong autonomous traditions of the German states, which emerged from the long nightmare of war with more independence from the considerably weakened Holy Roman Empire. Member states thereafter could carry out their own foreign policy, though they could not form alliances against the empire. The Habsburg dynasty's dream of forging a centralized empire of states fully obedient to the emperor's will had failed, although the emperor emerged from the wars with more control over most of Austria. Bohemia lost its independence. Bohemian Protestant landowners recovered neither their lands nor their religious freedom.

By the Treaty of Westphalia, German Calvinists gained the same rights as those previously granted to Lutherans. The settlement granted religious toleration where it had existed in 1624. But it also confirmed the Peace of Augsburg's establishment of territorial churches—Catholic, Lutheran, or Calvinist—still to be determined by the religion of the ruler. Sects were often forbidden, and their followers were persecuted. Generally speaking, Lutheranism remained dominant in the northern half of the Holy Roman Empire, Catholicism in the southern half, with many Calvinists in the Rhineland.

Before his death in battle, Gustavus Adolphus noted "all the wars of Europe are now blended into one." More than 200 states of varying sizes had fought in the war. The devastation brought by thirty years of war is simply incalculable. Catholic Mainz, occupied by the Swedes, lost 25 percent of its buildings and 40 percent of its population. In four years, the predominantly Protestant duchy of Württemberg lost three-quarters of its population while occupied by imperial troops. Almost 90 percent of the farms of Mecklenburg were abandoned during the course of the war. Many villages in Central Europe were now uninhabited. Although devastation varied from region to region during the Thirty Years' War, German cities lost a third of their population, and the rural population was reduced by two-fifths. Central Europe, like the rest of the continent, may have already been suffering from the economic and social crisis that had begun in the 1590s. But the wars contributed to the huge decline of the population of the states of the Holy Roman Empire from about 20 million to 16 million people during the ghastly period of the wars of religion.

A year before the Treaty of Westphalia, a Swabian wrote in the family Bible: "They say that the terrible war is now over. But there is still no sign of peace. Everywhere there is envy, hatred and greed; that's what the war has taught us. . . . We live like animals, eating bark and grass. No one could have imagined that anything like this would happen to us. Many people say there is no God . . . but we still believe that God has not abandoned us."

War was not alone in taking lives: epidemics, the worst of which was the bubonic plague, and other diseases, including influenza and typhus, also took fearsome tolls. This was chiefly so in towns, which were often clogged with starving, vulnerable refugees from the fighting and marauding. The flight of many peasants from their lands reduced agricultural productivity. Relatively little fighting took place in the northwestern German states, so there, at least, less devastation occurred. On the other hand, Mecklenburg and Pomerania, among other states that endured considerable fighting and the coming and going of armies, lost about half of their populations. It would be decades before the German states recovered from the Thirty Years' War.

Although much of the religious settlement of the Treaty of Westphalia and the reinforcement of German particularism would prove enduring, dynastic rivalries still raged. France had emerged from its religious wars with a stronger monarchy; Louis XIII had made his state more centralized and powerful. France's rivals, too, would extend their authority within their own states. In the mid-seventeeth century, Europe would enter the era of monarchical absolutism. The most powerful European states—above all, Louis XIV's France—would enter a period of aggressive territorial expansion. Dynastic wars would help shape the European experience from the mid-seventeenth century to the French Revolution of 1789.

PART TWO

STATEMAKING

During the last half of the fifteenth century, the balance of economic and political power in Europe began to shift away from the Mediterranean region and the Italian city-states. The discovery and then colonization of the Americas contributed greatly to the development of the Atlantic economy, adding to the strength of Spain and England and transporting their rivalry across the Atlantic Ocean. The surprising English naval victory over the Spanish Armada in 1588 symbolized the subsequent shift in power from southern to northern Europe, even if Spain remained militarily stronger until the 1630s.

In the seventeenth century, when aggressive European monarchs were running roughshod over noble prerogatives and town privileges, England and the Dutch Republic both maintained their representative governments. The English Civil War led to the defeat and execution of the king in 1649, the fall of the monarchy, and in 1688, to the "Glorious Revolution," which affirmed the civil liberties of the English people and the rights of Parliament. In the largely Protestant Netherlands, which earned its independence after a protracted struggle against Catholic Spain, the prosperous merchants retained a republican form of government and helped generate the golden age of Dutch culture. In contrast, many European rulers relentlessly extended their power between 1650 and 1750, becoming absolute rulers. In principle, they were above all challenge from within the state itself, affecting the lives of more people than ever before through taxation, military service, and the royal quest for religious orthodoxy.

CHAPTER **5**

THE RISE OF THE ATLANTIC ECONOMY: SPAIN AND ENGLAND

In 1585, Protestant England went to war with its longtime rival, Catholic Spain. Three years after the start of the war, on July 30, 1588, English observers on the cliffs above the English Channel first caught sight of the supposedly invincible Spanish Armada, with its 130 ships and 30,000 men. On the night of August 7, the English fleet attacked King Philip II's Armada in battles along the English coast. After the Armada anchored near Calais, the English sent ships set on fire against the Armada, which caused the Spanish ships to break their tight tactical formation. With the help of strong winds, the English then pinned the Spanish ships against the shore, and destroyed six Spanish ships in the longest and most intense artillery battle that had yet occurred at sea, much of it at such close range that the sailors could hurl insults at each other. Superior English cannon, shot, and gunners took their toll on the Armada. More than 1,000 Spaniards died during the long battle that day. The captain of one Spanish ship that had failed to answer the flagship's call for help was hanged from a yardarm, and his body was hauled from ship to ship to reestablish discipline.

The English ships failed to follow up their advantage, however, letting the Spanish galleons escape. The rough winds of the Channel carried the Spanish ships away from the dangerous Flemish shoals toward the North Sea and then on a long, northern voyage up to the straits between the Orkney and Shetland Islands. This was decidedly the long way to reach the safety of Spanish ports. More than thirty Spanish ships sank in gales off the western coasts of Scotland and Ireland. When some of the ships of the Armada limped into port in Spain, the fleet's captain wrote King Philip II, "I am unable to describe to Your Majesty the misfortunes and miseries that have befallen us, because they are the worst that have been known on

The English defeat of the Spanish Armada, 1588.

any voyage; and some of the ships that put into this port have spent the last fourteen days without a single drop of water." Of the 130 ships that had sailed against England, only 60 could now be accounted for. At least a third had been sunk or wrecked, and many others were severely damaged.

Victory over the Spanish Armada accentuated England's rise to international dominance, enormously boosting English self-confidence. When English armies crushed an Irish rebellion in 1595, fears of an effective Irish alliance with Catholic Spain ended. Despite the defeat of the Spanish Armada, however, Philip did not make peace with England, and the war between the two nations dragged on until 1604.

ECONOMIC EXPANSION

The rise of Spain, England, and the Netherlands must be seen in the context of the sixteenth-century expansion of the European economy. By 1450, the European population had begun to recover slowly from the Black Death, the disastrous plague that had swept the continent a century earlier. In general, the population continued to rise until the mid-seventeenth century, when religious and dynastic wars and new plagues led to such devastation that the period has become known as "the age of crisis." These cataclysms particularly struck Central Europe. But the Mediterranean region, too, suffered population decline, and the European population of the Turkish Ottoman Empire remained extremely sparse, about half that of France and Italy in 1600.

During the 1600s, the commercial and manufacturing center of Europe shifted from the Mediterranean to northwestern Europe. By 1700,

Venice—which, alone among the Italian city-states, had managed to retain significant trade links with Asia—had become a virtual backwater because it had failed to adapt to the global economy that was expanding across the Atlantic Ocean to the Americas. Spain, France, England, and (after its long, successful war of independence from Spain) the Dutch United Provinces emerged as major European powers in the late sixteenth century as they explored new trade routes to Asia.

Spain's preeminence did not survive the end of the seventeenth-century economic crisis, however. Its merchants lacked the flexibility shown by the English and Dutch to adjust to the varying demand for colonial products such as pepper and to create new trading opportunities. Furthermore, merchants in Amsterdam and London, not those in the Spanish city of Seville, expanded trade by using innovative commercial techniques. Spanish merchants proved less able than their northern rivals to lower costs of transportation from the New World. In contrast, English textile merchants found new markets in Spain and the Mediterranean for their cloth.

Increased Agricultural Productivity

Populations cannot grow unless the rural economy can produce enough additional food to feed more people. During the sixteenth century, farmers brought more land into cultivation at the expense of forests and fens (marsh lands). Dutch land reclamation in the Netherlands in the sixteenth and seventeenth centuries provides the most spectacular example of the expansion of farm land; the Dutch reclaimed more than 36,000 acres between 1590 and 1615 alone. Modest agricultural progress was, however, limited to Western Europe. In Russia and Eastern Europe, hundreds of thousands of serfs who were legally bound to the land labored to produce enough grain to feed the population and to generate a surplus that their lords could sell to Western European traders.

Much of the potential for European economic development lay in what at first glance would seem to have been only sleepy villages. Such villages, however, generally lay in regions of relatively advanced agricultural production, permitting not only the survival of peasants but the accumulation of an agricultural surplus for investment. They had access to urban merchants, markets, and trade routes.

Rural industry was an intrinsic part of the expansion of industry. Woolens and textile manufacturers, in particular, utilized rural cottage (domestic) production, which took advantage of cheap and plentiful rural labor. In the German states, the ravages of the Thirty Years' War further moved textile production into the countryside. Members of poor peasant families spun or wove cloth and linens at home for scant remuneration in an attempt to supplement meager family income.

Expansion of Trade

More extended trading networks helped develop Europe's economy. English and Dutch ships carrying rye from the Baltic states reached Spain and Portugal. Population growth generated an expansion of small-scale manufacturing, particularly handicrafts, textiles, and metallurgy in England, Flanders, parts of northern Italy, the southwestern German states, and in parts of Spain. Only iron smelting and mining required marshaling a significant amount of capital.

The development of banking and other financial services contributed to the expansion of trade. By the middle of the sixteenth century, financiers and traders commonly accepted bills of exchange in place of gold or silver or other goods. Bills of exchange, which had their origins in medieval Italy, were promissory notes that could be sold to third parties. In this way, they provided credit. At mid-century, an Antwerp financier only slightly exaggerated when he claimed, "One can no more trade without bills of exchange than sail without water." Merchants no longer had to carry gold and silver over long, dangerous journeys, nor did they have to identify and assess the approximate value of a variety of coins issued by mints here and there. Thus, an Amsterdam merchant purchasing soap from a counterpart in Marseille could go to an exchanger and pay him the equivalent sum in guilders, the Dutch currency. The exchanger would then send a bill of exchange to a colleague in Marseille, authorizing him to pay the Marseille merchant in his own currency after the actual exchange of goods had taken place.

The money changer's office.

Bills of exchange contributed to the development of banks, as exchangers began to provide loans, profiting from the interest attached to them. Not until the eighteenth century, however, did banks such as the Bank of Amsterdam and the Bank of England begin to provide capital for business investment. Their principal function was to provide funds for the state.

The rapid expansion in international trade increased the role of merchant capitalists, particularly in northern Europe, in the emerging global economy. The infusion of capital stemmed largely from gold and silver brought by Spanish vessels from the Americas. This capital financed the production of goods, storage, trade, and even credit across Europe and overseas. Moreover, an increased credit supply was generated by investments and loans by bankers and wealthy merchants to states and by joint-stock partnerships, an English innovation (the first major company began in 1600). Unlike short-term financial cooperation between investors for a single commercial undertaking, joint-stock companies provided a permanent funding of capital by drawing on the investments of merchants and other investors who purchased shares in the company.

Amsterdam and then London emerged as the banking and trading centers of Europe. Merchant towns in Castile, Catalonia, Italy, Holland, and England, as well as the Hanseatic cities of northern Germany, each had their own merchant dynasties.

The Global Economy

Trade with the Americas and Asia provided new outlets for European goods. It also brought from the New World products such as tomatoes, corn, bell peppers, rum, and spices to those who could afford them. The construction of larger ships, weighing as much as eighty tons, a size that would not be surpassed until the middle of the nineteenth century, facilitated oceangoing trade. From seaports, trade continued along the major rivers—principally the Rhine, which flows from Switzerland to the North Sea; the Danube in Central Europe; the Seine, which links Paris to the English Channel; and the Rhône, which carries boat traffic from Lyon to the Mediterranean. The Scheldt River estuary led from the North Sea to the powerful trading and manufacturing city of Antwerp, which already had a population of more than 100,000 people. There, vast quantities of English and Flemish goods were traded for goods from the German and Italian states. Land trade routes also remained important—for example, the route from Marseille to northern France and the Netherlands, that from Valencia on the Mediterranean to Madrid and Toledo in the heart of Castile, and that from Piedmont to the western German states and Holland.

England and the Dutch Netherlands, as well as France, benefited from a new and complex colonial trading system that linked entrepreneurs with the political strategies of each state. In each case, specially chartered East

Indian trading companies helped mobilize investment capital and, enjoying monopolies issued to them by each state, set out to make money. When Hugo Grotius published his treatise on the freedom of the seas, he subtitled it *The Right which Belongs to the Dutch to Take Part in the East India Trade* (1609). Although officially independent of each government, trade companies represented the interests of the state. Yet only in England did colonial trade play a major role in the development of the national economy, principally because England's manufactured goods increasingly found markets in its bustling settlement colony of North America.

Overseas trading remained a risky business, however; storms, wars, and pirates all posed considerable risks. Appropriately enough, the first English company to receive royal authorization for a monopoly on colonial trade was called the London Merchant Adventurers, which exported wool to Antwerp. Spanish kings, in particular, were notorious for declaring bankruptcy and thus repudiating all debts after borrowing money from wealthy subjects based on the expectation—sometimes in vain—of the arrival of valued colonial goods or bullion.

Price Revolution and Depression

The rise in population and the economic boom of the sixteenth century brought a considerable rise in prices. During this "price revolution," the cost of living far outdistanced wage increases. Real income thus fell for ordinary people. Those who suffered included small landholders in England, many of whom fell into the ranks of landless laborers; relatively poor nobles in France and Italy, whose tenants had long-term leases; and landless laborers and wage earners in city and country alike.

Those affected adversely by the price revolution were quick to blame rapacious landlords, greedy merchants, hoarders of grain, selfish masters, usurers, and the spirit of acquisition engendered, some people believed, by the Reformation. Basic long-term causes included the infusion of gold and particularly silver brought principally by the Spanish from the New World, currency debasement undertaken by monarchs to help fund their dynastic wars, and the population increase itself, which placed more pressure on scarce resources.

A long depression followed the economic expansion of the sixteenth century. This in itself reflected the relative decline of Mediterranean trade, symbolized by the end of Venetian supremacy in about 1600. The Thirty Years' War (1618–1648) also disrupted trade and manufacturing. International trade fell off dramatically, and manufacturing suffered. Furthermore, Spaniards had begun to exhaust the gold and silver mines of Latin America, disrupting the money supply. A leveling off of the population probably compounded the saturation of European markets. Urban growth slowed, and many of Europe's old ecclesiastical, administrative, and commercial centers stagnated. By contrast, ports such as Amsterdam,

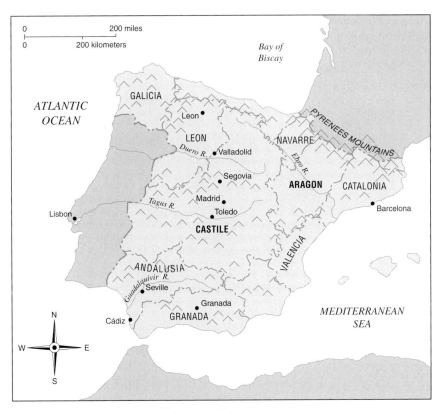

MAP 5.1 SPAIN IN THE LATE FIFTEENTH CENTURY.

Hamburg, and Liverpool grew with the expansion of the Atlantic trading system.

THE RISE OF SPAIN

Sixteenth-century Spain, the most powerful state of its time, was not one kingdom but two: Castile and Aragon. Castile was by far the larger and wealthier; its vast stretch of mountainous land across much of the center of the Iberian Peninsula contained a population of about six million people, five-sixths of the population of Spain as a whole. Aragon, lying in northern Spain, had prospered during the Middle Ages because of its flourishing Mediterranean trade. It became a federation of dominions, including Catalonia and Valencia, and was greatly influenced by Mediterranean peoples and cultures (see Map 5.1). In contrast, Portugal was a poor Atlantic state of mariners lying on the western edge of Iberia. It had a population of about 1 million people (roughly equivalent to that of

Aragon) and was merged into the Spanish kingdom from 1580 until 1640, when Portugal broke away and again became independent. Following the death of the Portuguese king without a male heir, Philip II of Spain claimed the Portuguese throne by virtue of being the only son of Isabella, daughter of King Manuel I of Portugal.

Centralization and the Spanish Monarchy

In 1469, Isabella of Castile married Ferdinand, heir to the throne of Aragon. But even a happy royal marriage could not in itself forge a unified kingdom; other aspects of the state had to change as well. Castilian policies were successfully implemented to create a relatively centralized monarchy. In Castile, the crown centralized the system of justice and made the municipalities more subservient. The Castilian dialect gradually emerged as the language of Spain, giving some truth to the old saying that "a language is a dialect with an army."

Ferdinand and Isabella and their successors were known as the Catholic kings because of their devotion to the Church. But like other monarchs, they brought the Church, its privileges, and some of its income from tithes and the sale of indulgences under royal control. While the Reformation shook the foundations of the Church in much of Europe, it barely challenged Spanish religious orthodoxy. The Spanish Inquisition, whose original purpose had been to enforce the conversion of Islamic Moors and Jews in the late fifteenth century, served the Catholic Reformation in the late

(Left) King Ferdinand II of Aragon was devoted to the Catholic Church. *(Right)* Isabella the Catholic of Castile, wife of Ferdinand II of Aragon.

sixteenth century. Its tribunal interrogated and punished those accused of questioning Church doctrine. Housed in Castile, the Inquisition became a respected agent of royal as well as Church authority in some parts of Spain. Elsewhere—in Sicily and the Dutch Netherlands, above all—local people resisted the Inquisition, believing it to be another aspect of Spanish/Castilian domination.

In Castile, Ferdinand and Isabella stripped the Castilian nobles of some of their privileges and power while dispensing titles and positions. In Catalonia and Valencia, on the other hand, nobles resisted any attempts by the monarchy to reduce their privileges, and therefore most of their noble prerogatives were left intact. Nonetheless, because they feared a revolt of the lower classes against them, the Catalan and Valencian nobles did become willing allies with the crown in maintaining social hierarchy and order.

Parliamentary traditions in the Spanish principalities limited the reach of the Castilian monarchy. The rulers of Spain were not able to tamper with Catalonia's traditionally less centralized constitutional traditions, which dated from the late thirteenth and fourteenth centuries, when Catalonia itself had been a Mediterranean power. Thus, the territories of Catalonia and Valencia maintained their political institutions, principally their *Cortes* (assembly), which continued to limit the authority of the monarchy and which had to be consulted in order to achieve compliance with royal edicts. The Spanish monarchy therefore was less a "new monarchy"—at least outside of Castile—than that of France, because particularly strong institutional limits on its effective authority remained.

In Castile, disagreements between the monarchy and the Cortes were frequent during the middle decades of the sixteenth century. The Cortes excluded nobles and had representatives from only the governments of the eighteen most important cities and towns of Castile. The Castilian Cortes, which maintained the right to approve special taxes, continued to refuse taxes to subsidize the monarchy for thirty-five years (1541–1575). Despite the crown's efforts, this battle between monarchy and the Cortes over taxes led to an inefficient royal fiscal apparatus. But Philip II, whose reign began (1556) and ended (1598) in royal bankruptcy, abided by the Roman law adage that described the medieval customs of his domains: "What touches all must be approved by all."

The Spanish Economy

Although income from its American colonies never accounted for more than about 10 percent of the crown's total income, Spain's colonial empire in the Americas contributed to its expanding economy. During the first years of the Spanish colonial period, Mexican gold helped finance the next wave of conquests. In 1545, Spaniards discovered the rich silver mines of

Potosí (then in Peru), and a year later they uncovered more deposits in Mexico. A new refining process helped Spain triple the silver resources of Europe to its own profit. Mules carried silver extracted at Potosí on a fifteen-day journey down 12,000 feet and many miles to the port of Arica in northern Chile; then the sea voyage of several months by convoy began. The Spanish Empire contributed considerably to the sixteenth-century European trading boom. Spain shipped colonial products and Spanish woolens to France and the Italian city-states. Spanish ships also supplied the colonies with wine, oil, European grain, shoes, and clothing.

The Castilian economy developed rapidly. The mountain ranges and central plateaus of Castile were divided between land for agricultural production, areas for raising sheep for the woolens industry, and rocky outcrops. The wool trade formed the basis of the Castilian export economy. The mining of silver, lead, iron, and mercury also developed in sixteenth-century Castile. Agricultural production was closely linked to manufacturing, as were sheep to the production of woolen goods. Nonetheless, 85 percent of the land of Spain could not be plowed because it was too mountainous or rocky, or could not be irrigated because of the high elevation.

Spanish royal revenue came from peasant obligations owed on royal domains as well as from taxes on commerce and manufacturing, import and export taxes, levies assessed for moving sheep through specific mountain passes, and payment from the Church for collecting tithes (the ecclesiastical tax of 10 percent of revenue). The crown imposed protectionist measures against foreign goods, banned the export of gold and silver, and attracted Italian and Flemish craftsmen to Spain.

In northern Spain, the mountains and valleys of the rainy Cantabrian coast were populated by farmers and fishermen. To the south, the Castilian provinces of Andalusia and Granada benefited from relatively rich land, producing wheat, olives, and wine. Castilian farmers expanded production by terracing hillsides and planting them in perennials, including grapevines and olive trees. Demand for textiles increased, and farmers planted flax, hemp, and, in Andalusia, mulberry trees. Farm towns built irrigation works and processing facilities such as wine and olive presses, flax-soaking ponds, and grist and fulling mills to turn these crops into market commodities. Wealthier farmers used plow animals to transport these goods to the most attractive markets, where they sold them to wholesale merchants.

Spanish nobles incurred no social stigma by engaging in wholesale or international commerce until the eighteenth century. Many nobles capitalized on their revenues from farm products by building facilities to store and process the products—including flour mills, tanneries, and wine cellars, which often doubled as taverns. Several wealthy dukes became shipping magnates. They earned fortunes because they owned the tuna fishing rights on Castile's Mediterranean shore, exporting fish preserved in salt or olive oil all over Europe.

The Expansion of the Spanish Empire

Through marriage and inheritance, Spain's territorial interests reached far and wide. The Spanish throne passed to the Austrian branch of the Habsburg dynasty in 1496, with Ferdinand and Isabella's daughter, Princess Joanna, marrying Philip the Fair, the Habsburg duke of Burgundy, who was the son of Maximilian, the Holy Roman emperor. A year after Isabella's death in 1504, Ferdinand, hoping to produce an heir to the Spanish throne, married a niece of King Louis XII of France. But three years later, their infant son died; royal families, as well as ordinary people, were subject to the harsh demographic realities of the age. In 1516, the Flanders-born son of Joanna and Philip the Fair inher-

Charles V was the grandson of Ferdinand and Isabella. This portrait is by Titian.

ited the throne of Castile and Aragon as Charles I of Spain. In 1519, he became Holy Roman Emperor Charles V (ruled 1519–1558) upon the death of his grandfather, Maximilian I. Along with his Spanish possessions, including Spain's American territories, he also inherited Aragon's Italian possessions. The emperor only briefly resided in Catalonia and rarely visited Castile. But with far-flung dynastic interests, he demanded extraordinary taxes from his Spanish subjects to pay for his wars abroad, including the defense of the Spanish-Italian possessions of Naples, Sicily, and Sardinia against France during the 1520s.

The king's departure from Spain in 1520 was followed by open revolt against royal taxation. The revolt of the *Comuneros* (urban communities) began in Toledo and spread to other towns of northern Castile. Bourgeois and artisans opposed the royal officials Charles had imported from Flanders, but the revolt was also directed against Castilian nobles. After royal forces burned the arsenal and town of Medina del Campo in north-central Castile in August 1520, Charles's regent suddenly switched tactics. He suspended supplementary tax collections and agreed not to appoint any more foreigners to office in Spain. When uprisings continued, Charles's army gradually restored order. One of the leaders of the revolt, the bishop of Zamora, was later tortured and garroted (slowly strangled with a wire),

MAP 5.2 HABSBURG LANDS AT THE ABDICATION OF CHARLES V, 1558.   The division of the Habsburg lands between Philip II (who had already begun to rule Spain in 1556) and Ferdinand I.

and his body was hung from a tower as a warning to those who would challenge royal authority.

With an eye toward his succession, Charles V arranged the marriage of his son, Philip, to the English princess Mary Tudor of England in 1554. Charles formally abdicated as Holy Roman emperor in 1558, dividing the Habsburg domains between his son Philip and his brother Ferdinand (see Map 5.2). Philip II (ruled 1556–1598) inherited Spain, the Netherlands, the Spanish colonies in the Americas, and parts of Italy. Ferdinand I (ruled 1558–1564), who was elected Holy Roman emperor, inherited the Habsburg ancestral domains, including Austria. This ended the period when one ruler held all Habsburg territories and also eliminated any remote possibility that a single Catholic monarch would rule all of Europe. It did not, however, end the cooperation and strong family ties between the two branches of the Habsburg dynasty. Mary Tudor's death in 1558 eliminated the intriguing prospect that England might have become part of the Spanish Empire.

Despite the separation of the Habsburg domains, Philip II inherited the problem of ruling a vast empire. Like its rivals France and England, the

Spanish state developed a large, centralized bureaucracy, including royal councils, essential to the operations of the empire. The council of state and the council of war offered the king advice on matters of internal and colonial policy. Royal secretaries handled correspondence and busied themselves with the operations of the royal household. Most such officials were commoners, for whom such positions provided financial and social advantages. Many of them were extremely able and devoted to the daunting task of maintaining the Spanish Empire.

The monarchy sent officials, many trained in law, from Spain to represent its interests in America. It could take two years for administrative instructions or correspondence to reach distant officials in Latin America and for their response to arrive in Spain. One official awaiting instructions put it this way, "If death came from Madrid, we should all live to a very old age."

The Age of Philip II

Spanish power peaked during the reign of Philip II. He chose as his capital the centrally located Castilian town of Madrid, which became a capital city of nobles and bureaucrats, many of whom, in one way or another, lived off the court. The city grew from a town of about 30,000 people in the 1540s to well over 150,000 inhabitants in the 1620s. Madrid survived through a "command economy"; royal commissioners paid government-fixed prices for what they wanted from the capital's hinterland. As Spain's capital grew, it had to import supplies, which were transported from distant regions by countless mule trains that traversed rough mountain ranges and deep valleys.

Like Francis I of France several decades before him, Philip decided that he needed a permanent royal residence that would provide an elegant symbol of his power. Outside of Madrid, Philip built the magnificent Escorial Palace between 1563 and 1584. Virtually the king's only public appearances after he became crippled by gout were elaborate religious ceremonies at the palace. These were carefully orchestrated to uphold the sanctity of the throne.

Philip II of Spain ruled during the height of Spanish power.

The Ottoman Empire of Suleiman the Magnificent threatened Spanish rule during the sixteenth century.

Complex rituals of court etiquette affirmed a sense of authority, social hierarchy, and order that were supposed to radiate from the Escorial through Spain and to the far reaches of the empire. Once the king had ridden a horse, it could never be ridden again by anyone else except the king. The king received visitors in a room determined by the status of the visitor.

Philip II led a tragic life marred by the premature death of four wives and a number of children. Perhaps because of sadness, he wore only black. The king himself may have contributed to the misfortunes of his offspring. In 1568, he ordered Don Carlos, his bad-tempered and irresponsible twenty-three-year-old son by his first marriage, placed under lock and key. Don Carlos seemed unfit to rule; furthermore, detesting his father, he may have even entered into contact with Dutch leaders who had begun to denounce Spanish policies in their land. Don Carlos's death six months later haunted Philip, inevitably generating stories that he had ordered him murdered. The introverted, sometimes indecisive king thereafter lived among the whispers of intrigue and storms of aristocratic rivalries of the noble families and factions.

With Habsburg domination of Italy secured by the 1559 Peace of Cateau-Cambrésis with France, Philip turned his attention to fighting the Turks. The Ottoman Empire had expanded into Europe following the conquest of Constantinople in 1453. Suleiman the Magnificent (ruled 1520–1566) took advantage of the dynastic and religious rivalries of the European states to expand his domain in the Balkans, where some of the Ottoman cultural heritage endures today, and into the rich plains of Hungary. The Turks also became bolder in their attacks on Spanish ships in the central and western Mediterranean. When the Turks took the Venetian island of Cyprus in 1571, the pope helped initiate the Holy League, an alliance with Venice and Spain. The long naval war against the Ottoman Empire, during which Turkish ships raided the coast of Spain, lasted from 1559 to 1577. With southern Spain virtually undefended and with the

Moriscos (Moors who had been forced to convert to Christianity) rebelling (1568–1570) against taxes, the Turks might well have captured Grenada. But a Spanish-Austrian Habsburg fleet defeated the sultan's larger navy in the Adriatic Sea at the Battle of Lepanto (1571), a monumental struggle in which more than 200 galleys fought, taking the lives of thousands of combatants. The Turkish threat in the western Mediterranean ended. Yet overexpansion had already planted the seeds of Spanish imperial decline.

THE RISE OF ENGLAND

The consolidation and then the extension of the authority of the Tudor monarchy facilitated England's emergence as a power late in the sixteenth century. From the reign of Henry VII to that of Elizabeth I, the Tudor monarchs held in check the great landed magnates, putting down rebellions and extending the reach and prestige of royal government. During the same period, the English state expanded its control over Wales and Ireland while holding at bay Scottish threats to the Tudor dynasty.

The House of Tudor

Victorious in the long War of the Roses between the Lancaster and York families, Henry Tudor, the last claimant to the throne of the Lancasters, became the first Tudor monarch as Henry VII (ruled 1485–1509). Like Isabella of Castile and Ferdinand of Aragon, the ambitious Henry VII set out to make the Tudor state so powerful that it could resist any challenge from noble factions and "overmighty subjects."

Thomas Wolsey, who was archbishop of York and adviser to the king, brought to the King's Council loyal officials drawn from the ranks of the nobility and high clergy. These men met in a room known as the Star Chamber because its blue ceiling, like the night sky, was spangled with stars. The Star Chamber became one of the highest courts in the land, generating revenue for the crown by assessing fines and other monetary penalties.

Henry VII strengthened royal authority in England. At the expense of Parliament, which enacted the laws of the land and attempted to restrict monarchical authority, Henry imposed tariffs protecting the cloth and wool industries, decreed acts unifying weights and measures, and put forth edicts punishing vagabondage and begging. He reduced expenses by disbanding his army, while filling royal coffers by selling monopolies (the exclusive right to import and market foodstuffs or commodities). Monopolies were extremely unpopular, however, among the middle and lower classes because they kept the prices of some products artificially high.

The king won the loyalty of most nobles. When selling offices failed, he resorted to the sheer coercive power of the throne. The Star Chamber enforced compliance, exacting fines and sometimes arresting the recalcitrant for real or imagined offenses. Henry obtained from Parliament writs of attainder and forfeiture, by which he could declare anyone guilty of treason, order their execution, and seize their property.

Henry VII depended not only upon the personal loyalty of local elites but also on the efficiency and prestige of about 600 unpaid justices of the peace. These men, largely drawn from prosperous landed families, dispensed justice, collected taxes, enforced troop levies, and maintained local order. Their judicial authority covered every criminal offense except treason. While maintaining a strong tradition of decentralized government in England, the justices of the peace also strengthened the efficiency and prestige of the monarchy. Gradually, the royal Assize Courts took responsibility for felony cases. Charged with enforcing parliamentary statutes and the orders of the Privy Council, which administered the Tudor state, they also helped extend the state's effective authority.

Henry VIII became king upon his father's death in 1509 and married Catherine of Aragon, who was Ferdinand and Isabella's daughter, as well as his brother's widow. Beneath Henry's proud and impetuous character lay a deep-seated inferiority complex that he tried to overcome with grand deeds. The single-minded Henry dreamed of standing at the head of an empire. The new king spent vast sums fighting against France for more than a decade, beginning in 1512. Cardinal Wolsey, who had been his father's trusted adviser, sought to restrain Henry's ambition. But when the House of Commons refused to provide the king with more funds, Henry simply debased the currency, giving the state more spending power at the cost of higher inflation.

Foreign wars had devastated royal finances. To raise money, the spendthrift monarch heaped more financial obligations on the backs of the poor. Wolsey utilized the cynically named "amicable grant," a royal assessment first imposed in 1525 on lay and ecclesiastical revenues. Peasants in southeastern England, sometimes led by local gentry (the rural elite, whose status came from the ownership of land and who dominated the House of Commons), rebelled against these new levies. Henry responded to the threat by forcing landowners to loan money to the crown, imprisoning some of the wealthiest, confiscating their estates, selling off property that had belonged to the Roman Catholic Church on unfavorable terms, and further debasing the currency, adding to inflation.

To make his monarchy more efficient, Henry shifted royal government, including control of the state's finances, from the royal household of the king's servants to a small but able bureaucracy of officials and their clerks, who were loyal to both the king and Parliament. He reduced the size of the king's advisory council and formalized its structure. The Privy Council assumed oversight functions and routinized communication with the local justices of the peace. The king appointed new administrative officials and established new revenue courts. At the same time, the general acceptance of the "king's law"—common law—gradually helped generate a sense of national unity.

Henry extended the power of his monarchy by breaking with Rome in the 1530s over his divorce of Catherine of Aragon. He established the Church of England (see Chapter 3), which kept some of the ritual and doctrine of the Catholic Church. Henry became head of the Church of England, dissolving monasteries and confiscating and selling ecclesiastical lands. But while leading the break with Rome, Henry planted the seeds for conflicts between Protestants and Catholics in England.

Fearing that the Welsh or Irish might assist Holy Roman Emperor Charles V in an attempt to invade England to restore Catholicism, Henry established English domination over Wales and direct rule over Ireland. Since the late twelfth century, English lords had gradually increased their military colonization of Ireland, pushing back the Gaelic tribes and claiming the finest land by virtue of ancient titles. The English kings delegated authority to English nobles. Yet effective English authority remained fragile in Ireland as long as the crown's continental interests took precedence and disorders in Ireland did not compromise English authority. After the English Reformation, the crown selected English Protestants for all posts in Ireland. And after a minor rebellion against royal authority, which was put down with great cruelty, in 1541 Henry proclaimed himself king of Ireland and head of the Irish Church. In exchange for the Gaelic chieftains' recognition of Henry as their king and acceptance of English law, the crown recognized them as Irish lords. Thereafter, however, the costs of administering Ireland increased rapidly, requiring more troops, as the Irish continued to chafe at English rule.

Scotland also proved to be a thorny problem for England. Although in 1503 the Scottish King James IV had married Henry VII's daughter, Margaret Tudor, relations between Scotland and England deteriorated when Henry VIII became king. When James invaded England in 1513 in support of the French, Henry responded by ordering a major military campaign against the Scots. This ended with the wounding or death of more than 10,000 Scots at the battle of Flodden (where James IV was killed). Nonetheless, Catholic Scotland remained an ally of Catholic France. In 1542, an English army again invaded Scotland, defeating the Scots at Solway Moss. Following James V's sudden death a month after the battle, Mary Stuart (James's six-day-old daughter and the granddaughter of Henry VII of England) became queen of the Scots. In 1546, after Henry's war with France dragged to a halt, another English army laid waste to Scotland, sacking the capital and university town of Edinburgh.

Henry VIII died in 1547. On his deathbed, the originator of the English Reformation hedged his bets, leaving money to pay for Catholic Masses to be said for the eternal repose of his soul. The nine-year-old son of Henry and Jane Seymour became King Edward VI (ruled 1547–1553), governing under the tutelage of his uncle, the duke of Somerset, who served as Lord Protector. Again, rebellions sparked by economic hardship broke out. While seeking accommodation with Protestant dissenters, the young Edward undertook an aggressive campaign on behalf of the Reformed Church of England.

Wars against Catholic Scotland and France continued. The Lord Protector was intent on destroying Catholicism in Scotland. After English troops defeated a French force sent to help the Catholic cause, the young Catholic queen of Scots, Mary Stuart (1542–1587), fled to safety, marrying Francis, the son of Henry II, the king of France.

In England, tensions between Protestants and Catholics grew worse. Landowners began to resist paying more taxes to finance new wars. Allied with fearful Catholic nobles, the duke of Warwick became the new Lord Protector in 1549, taking the title of duke of Northumberland.

Northumberland quickly betrayed the Catholic lords who had supported him. He tightened the crown's control over the Church of England and undertook a repressive campaign against Catholicism. Northumberland's influence over the sickly young king whetted his desire for power. He plotted for Lady Jane Grey (1537–1554; niece of Henry, she stood third in line to the monarchy) to ascend the throne after she married his son. After Edward's death, Northumberland proclaimed his daughter-in-law queen of England. But most nobles rallied to the cause of Mary Tudor (ruled 1553–1558), the daughter of Henry VIII and Catherine of Aragon. She seemed to them the rightful heir to the throne, despite the fact that she was Catholic.

Mary Tudor, later queen of England.

Mary Tudor succeeded her half brother and attempted to return England to Catholicism. She restored all rituals and doctrines of the Catholic Church and she acknowledged the primacy of the pope over the Church of England. The queen abrogated Henry VIII's reforms and began to persecute Protestants, some of whom fled to France. "Bloody Mary" embellished the macabre heritage of the Tower of London with the heads of Northumberland, his son, and Lady Jane Grey, who had ruled for only nine days. Mary married Philip II, who ascended the Spanish throne in 1556. England joined Spain in its war against France, which had long rivaled the Habsburgs in Italy.

Queen Elizabeth dancing with Robert Dudley.

Calais, the last English outpost in France, was soon lost. Sparked by wide-spread opposition to her Catholicism, which was popularly identified with France and Spain, a rebellion broke out against the queen. When Mary died in 1558, few in England grieved.

Elizabeth I (ruled 1558–1603), Anne Boleyn's daughter, restored Protestant rule to England when she became queen at age twenty-five, succeeding Mary, her half sister. Elizabeth's throne was threatened by religious division, which was compounded by antagonism with the Catholic powers, France and Spain. Not many people could have expected the young queen to succeed.

Elizabeth was a woman of intelligence, vanity, sporadic fickleness, and an occasional flash of temper. She enjoyed music, dancing, hunting, and the company of men. Tall, with reddish hair and an olive complexion, she was cautious, even suspicious, having been raised in a world of conspiracy. The queen preferred to wait out many pressing problems in the hope that they would just go away. Educated in the tradition of Italian humanism, Elizabeth learned French, German, and Italian, as well as Latin, and enjoyed translating texts from these languages into English.

Elizabeth never married. It was not uncommon for women to remain unmarried in early modern Europe—in England, about 10 percent of all women remained single throughout their lives—but it was unusual for a monarch to remain single. The question of whether Elizabeth would ever marry preoccupied the other rulers of Europe, as well as her subjects.

In response to a parliamentary petition that she marry and produce a direct heir, Elizabeth responded that she trusted God to ensure that "the realm shall not remain destitute of an heir." As for her, it would be enough that at the end of her life "a marble stone shall declare that a queen, having reigned such a time, lived and died a virgin." Elizabeth rejected one continental hopeful after another, beginning with the handsome but dull Philip II of Spain, Catholic widower of Mary Tudor. Nor was marriage the outcome of a two-year romance with the handsome Lord Robert Dudley, the death of whose wife in 1560 from a suspicious fall down a flight of stairs understandably fueled rumors for some years.

Elizabeth was an able administrator who chose capable people to serve the crown. She appointed as her principal adviser the clever, loyal Sir William Cecil (Lord Burghley, 1520–1598). A Protestant, Cecil served as royal secretary for nearly as many years as Elizabeth was queen. Nonetheless, in the later years of her reign, bitter battles for influence and power within Elizabeth's inner circle belied the appearance of relative harmony.

Religious Settlement and Conflict under Elizabeth I

When Elizabeth took the throne, she was determined to find a means to resolve religious conflict within England, for she recognized that unless the conflict was resolved, it might one day threaten her reign. Elizabeth had been raised a Protestant, but she did not hold particularly strong religious convictions and rarely attended church services. Although she was thought to be favorable to some Catholic rituals, when she first encountered a procession of monks with candles and incense at Westminster Abbey, she cried out, "Away with these torches, we see very well." In the quest for unity, she dismissed many Catholic advisers.

Queen Elizabeth oversaw the religious settlement, which at first aimed to please a wide spectrum of religious beliefs without resorting to heresy hunting or persecution. In 1559, Parliament passed the Act of Uniformity and the Act of Supremacy, which established the lasting foundations of the Church of England, reorganizing it to have Protestant dogma but essentially Catholic structure. The Uniformity Bill imposed the *Book of Common Prayer* (1550) on religious services of the Church of England and required attendance at public worship and imposed fines for not attending services. The bill barely passed the House of Lords (which was primarily composed of Catholics), and probably would not have passed at all had two bishops not been imprisoned in the Tower of London and thus were unable to vote. The Act of Supremacy required all officials, clergy, and candidates for university degrees to take an oath acknowledging the queen as "governor" of the English Church. This title replaced that of "head" of the Church and suggested that the queen would not interfere in matters of doctrine. The Thirty-Nine Articles, enacted in 1563, provided an institutional framework for subsequent relations between state and church in England. The landed elite, strengthening its control of Parliament during Elizabeth's reign, generally supported the Church of England.

Some English Protestants wanted to carry the reforms further than Elizabeth's religious settlement. They sought to eliminate from the Church of England what some members considered vestiges of elaborate Catholic ceremonies, such as baptismal crosses, altar rails before which Catholics knelt while receiving communion, elaborate priestly garb, and stained-glass windows that they associated with Catholicism.

Puritanism, the English version of Calvinism, first took hold among English exiles on the continent during Queen Mary's reign. It emerged in the late 1550s as a dissident force within the Church of England. Puritans could be found in every social stratum, but they were drawn primarily from the middle and lower classes. They drew hostility by insisting on a simplified but more intense religion based on individual conscience, the direct authority of the Holy Scriptures, and a community of belief in which preaching played a preeminent role. Although a few Puritans served as bishops in the Church of England and some fiercely defended Elizabeth's royal supremacy, other Puritans wanted the Church of England to be separate from the English monarchy. The Tudor monarchy, on the other hand, wanted to make the Church serve its secular goals of national glory, prosperity, and public order.

A modest Catholic revival, aided by the arrival of Catholic Jesuit missionaries from the continent, accentuated religious divisions in England. Royal religious policies became more harsh. Dissident Protestants suffered persecution along with Catholics. A Jesuit missionary was tortured to death on the rack in 1581, and six years later the first Puritan was executed for having spoken in Parliament on behalf of free speech in the name of his religion.

Since Elizabeth had no heirs, the Catholic Mary Stuart, niece of Henry VIII, stood next in line for succession to the English throne. After her husband King Francis II of France died in 1560, Mary returned to her native Scotland to assume the power that her mother wielded as regent until her death that same year. The Scottish Reformation had begun in earnest when the theologian John Knox (c. 1505–1572) returned home from Geneva to preach reform. Soon after coming to the throne of England, Elizabeth had made peace with Scotland and France. But Elizabeth and Protestants worried that if Mary became queen of England, she would restore Catholicism to England. When Protestants forced Mary to abdicate the Scottish throne in 1568, she fled to England. There Elizabeth kept her potential rival under virtual house arrest.

In 1569, Catholics in the moors and bogs of the isolated English north rebelled in the hope of putting Mary Stuart on the English throne, precipitating Elizabeth's order for her rival's imprisonment. The Catholic force marched southward, but hastily retreated upon learning that sizable English

Mary, Queen of Scots.

forces loyal to Elizabeth awaited them. English troops defeated a second Scottish army gathered near the border between the two countries. Elizabeth ordered the execution of over 500 of the rebels. This "Northern Rising" ended in complete failure, and the Catholic Church's hopes for a successful Counter-Reformation in England were finally dashed. Pope Pius V excommunicated Elizabeth in 1570 from the Church to which she did not wish to belong, removing the queen's Catholic subjects from the obligation of obedience to her and encouraging several further plots against her. Two years later, French Catholics undertook the Saint Bartholomew's Day Massacre of Protestants in Paris (see Chapter 4), the horror of which firmed Elizabeth's resolve to resist Mary's claims to the throne at all costs. She then vowed to support the Dutch, most of whom were Protestant, in their rebellion against Catholic Spain. In 1583, she foiled a plot, which involved the Spanish and French embassies, to depose her in favor of Mary Stuart. Four years later, under pressure from Parliament and fearing new Catholic plots against her, Elizabeth ordered Mary Stuart's execution.

Elizabeth's Statemaking

The reach and efficiency of the English state increased under Elizabeth's guidance. Lords and other wealthy gentlemen served on the Privy Council, which consisted of between twelve and eighteen members drawn from the nobility, gentry, and officers in the royal household. It oversaw the lord-lieutenants, a new office that gave noblemen control of local militia. Patronage flowed downward from the monarch. England's queen, like her predecessors, used patronage to foster loyalty to the crown. The most desirable posts were at court, including those in the royal household. Some of these carried life tenures; a few were hereditary. More than 500 men were employed in government departments. The most powerful officials at court, such as the Lord Chancellor, also dispensed patronage by selecting officials and filling local positions in the counties. Closely tied to the satisfaction of the private interests of the landed elite, the office of the Exchequer resembled similar offices created by continental monarchs who did not have to contend with a representative body as powerful as the English Parliament. Although it met during only three of the forty-five years of Elizabeth's reign, Parliament retained an important role in government because the crown needed its assent for new laws and new taxes.

Upon ascending the throne, Elizabeth found the crown's financial situation bleak. Revenues raised through taxation and customs dues were inadequate to finance the war against Spain and the Irish campaigns. The sale of some royal lands, forced loans, the occasional seizure of a Spanish ship laden with silver or gold, and purveyance (the right of agents of the monarchy to buy food at below-market prices) could only be temporary expedients. The collection of "ship money" (a tax on ports, which the crown with dubious logic extended to inland towns as well) was extremely unpopular and generated resistance during the hard times of the 1590s. But by exercising frugality in the expenses of government and increasing taxation, the crown managed to replenish its coffers, another sign of a stronger and more efficient state, despite a decade and a half of expensive warfare against Spain. The English monarchy in the Elizabethan Age was relatively more efficient than that of Spain or France.

In Elizabethan England, unlike in France, churchmen did not serve in the highest offices of the realm. Although English nobles still had retainers, by the 1590s they no longer had full-fledged private armies that could threaten the throne's monopoly on force. This contrasted with the situation in France during the same period, when the Guise and Bourbon families, among others, sent their own armies to fight in the wars of religion. English noble violence was instead channeled into service to the crown, and into dueling.

Foreign wars also served to increase the reach of central government in England. The second half of the sixteenth century brought regular training for the militia, which provided the bulk of troops as needed, along with gentlemen volunteers and cavalrymen still recruited by summons. But in the last eighteen years of Elizabeth's reign, more than 100,000 soldiers were impressed into service for wars on the continent and to maintain English hegemony in Ireland. Lord-lieutenants assumed responsibility for troop levies in the counties. The vast majority who were conscripted as soldiers were the poorest of the poor—unfortunate men who happened to be at the wrong place at the wrong time when the press-gangs turned up to roll them out of taverns or out of church and into the queen's service.

The monarchy imposed English law on northern England, Ireland, and Wales, which Henry VIII had absorbed into England. The emergence of a national market economy that was increasingly tied to London also played an important part in the nationalization of English political institutions. Within England, the sense of belonging to a nationality was certainly more advanced than anywhere on the continent. With the exception of part of

Cornwall in southwestern England (where the Cornish language was spoken by many), the people of England spoke English, however great the variation in dialect and accents. A somewhat Anglicized Welsh gentry had even begun to send their sons to Oxford and Cambridge Universities.

The fact that Britain is an island may have made the English more xenophobic and precociously nationalistic than their continental counterparts. Strong traditions of local government and loyalties persisted in England, however, fueled by social differences and the overwhelming influence of wealthy local landed families. The county and parish remained the economic, social, and political universe of most people in England. The state remained an abstraction until the tax collector or the press-gang came to intrude in an individual's life.

Demographic and Economic Expansion

In the last half of the sixteenth century, England emerged as a commercial and manufacturing power. The population of England and Wales—its vassal—grew rapidly, from about 2.5 million in the 1520s to more than 3.5 million in 1580, reaching about 4.5 million in 1610. Reduced mortality rates and increased fertility, the latter probably generated by expanding work opportunities in manufacturing and farming (leading to earlier marriage and more children), help explain this rapid rise in population. While epidemics and plague occasionally took their toll, the people in England still suffered less than did those on the continent. Furthermore, despite the wrenching effects of the English Reformation, the country had been spared the protracted wars of religion that occurred in France and Central Europe during the same period.

England provides the primary example of the expansion of agricultural production well before the "agricultural revolution" of the eighteenth and nineteenth centuries. A larger population stimulated increased demand for food, as well as for manufactured goods, particularly woolens. Through crop specialization, English agriculture became more efficient and market oriented than almost anywhere on the continent. Between 1450 and 1650, the yield of grain per acre increased by at least 30 percent. In sharp contrast with farming in Spain, English landowners brought more dense marshes and woodlands into cultivation.

The great estates of the English nobility largely remained intact, and many wealthy landowners aggressively increased the size of their holdings, a precondition for increased productivity. Marriages between the children of landowners also increased the size of landed estates. Primogeniture (the full inheritance of land by the eldest son) helped keep land from being subdivided. Younger sons of independent landowners left behind the family land to find other respectable occupations, often in the church or in urban trades. Larger farms were conducive to more commercialized farming at a time when an expanding population pushed up demand and prices. Some landowners turned a part of their land into pastureland for sheep in order to supply the developing woolens trade.

Some of the great landlords, as well as yeomen (farmers whose holdings and security of land tenure guaranteed their prosperity and status), reorganized their holdings in the interest of efficiency. Open-field farmers selected crops in response to the growing London market. In their quest for greater profits, many landlords put the squeeze on their tenants. Between 1580 and 1620, landlords raised rents and altered conditions of land tenure in their favor, preferring shorter leases and forcing tenants to pay an "entry fee" before they would agree to rent them land. Landowners evicted those who could not afford their new, more onerous terms. They also pushed tenants toward more productive farming methods, including crop rotation. Many peasants had difficulty competing with their wealthier neighbors. During bad years, the peasants might be forced to sell their land, while wealthy neighbors could survive with relative ease.

Many landowners utilized "enclosure" to expand their holdings. Enclosure included buying up and hedging wastelands, fencing off one's own land, consolidating arable strips of land and enclosing them, and dividing common lands and pasture areas. The enclosure of common lands, sold by villages to the highest bidders, over the long run would spell the end of the common rights of villagers—rich or poor—to use the land, and the removal of tenants in order to consolidate estates marked a push toward "agrarian individualism." Enclosure in this sense drew considerable

In this seventeenth-century woodcut, a country wife engages in domestic industry, part of the expansion of textile manufacturing that transformed England's economy.

resistance, for it left many of the rural poor fenced out of common land on which they had depended for firewood, gleaning, and pasturing. Thomas More's *Utopia* (1516), which describes an imaginary island where all people live in peace and harmony, blamed England's economic inequities on enclosure. Riots against enclosure were widespread in the 1590s, a decade in which popular tax rebellions shook France, Spain, Austria, and Ukraine, among other places, and again in the 1620s and 1630s.

England's exceptional economic development also drew upon the country's natural resources, including iron, timber, and, above all, coal, extracted in far greater quantities than anywhere on the continent. New industrial methods expanded the production of iron, brass, and pewter in and around Birmingham.

But, above all, textile manufacturing transformed the English economy. Woolens (which accounted for about 80 percent of exports), worsteds (sturdy yarn spun from combed wool fibers), and cloth found eager buyers in England as well as on the continent. Moreover, late in the sixteenth century, as English merchants began making forays across the Atlantic, these textiles were also sold in the New World. Cloth manufacturers undercut production by urban craftsmen by "putting out" work to the villages and farms of the countryside. In such domestic industry, poor rural women and girls could do spinning and carding (combing fibers in preparation for spinning) of wool in their homes.

The English textile trade was closely tied to Antwerp, in the Spanish Netherlands, where workers dyed English cloth. Sir Thomas Gresham, a sixteenth-century entrepreneur, became England's representative in the bustling river port. Wining and dining the city's merchants and serving as a royal ambassador, he so enhanced the reputation of English business that English merchants could operate on credit, no small achievement in the sixteenth century. At home, he convinced the government to end special privileges accorded the Hanseatic cities of northern Germany and to authorize lucrative English trading monopolies. Gresham's shrewd sense of finance saved the relatively meager royal coffers from bankruptcy on several occasions through the negotiation of timely loans.

Gresham advised the crown to explore the economic possibilities of the Americas. This led to the first concerted English efforts at colonization. Even more than Spanish colonialism, English overseas ventures were undertaken with commercial profits in mind. When the Spanish, hoping to crush the Dutch rebellion that began against their rule in 1566, closed the Scheldt River, which leads from the North Sea to Antwerp, English merchants responded by seeking new, more distant outlets for trade. From 1577 to 1580, Sir Francis Drake (1540–1596), explorer and privateer who stole treasures brought back by Spanish galleons, sailed around Cape Horn in his search for a passage that would permit commercial ties with Asia. Sir Walter Raleigh (1554–1618; a Renaissance scholar, poet, historian, and explorer) said of Drake, "A single purpose animates all his exploits and the chart of his movements is like a cord laced and knotted round the throat of the Spanish monarchy."

London came to replace Antwerp as Europe's leading center of trade. London's Merchant Adventurers competed with Spanish and Portuguese rivals for spices and other products that fetched increasingly handsome prices at home. They traded textiles and other manufactured goods for slaves, gold, and ivory from the African and Brazilian coasts. West Indian sugar and Virginian tobacco entered the English domestic market in lucrative quantities. English merchants traded in India and Indonesia. In 1600, Queen Elizabeth chartered the East India Company with the goal of competing with Dutch traders. To compete with the Spanish, who already had a colonial empire that stretched several thousand miles from what is now the southern United States to Tierra del Fuego at the southern tip of South America, Raleigh sought to establish a colony in Virginia between 1584 and 1587. Despite the failure of a first settlement, a permanent colony finally succeeded in Virginia, largely because of the popularity of tobacco, which began to reach England in the first decades of the seventeenth century.

English towns grew as migrants arrived in sufficient numbers to overcome high mortality rates caused by catastrophic health conditions stemming from poor sanitation. London became the largest city in the world, its population rising from about 50,000 in the 1520s to 200,000 in 1600, and jumping its walls to 375,000 in 1650. The next biggest towns in England

A British East India Company trading post in Surat, part of the English effort to expand trade into India, among other places.

lagged far behind: Norwich, Newcastle, and Bristol boasted only about 25,000 people each. On the average, about 6,000 people moved to London each year. Including its developing industrial suburbs, about 8 percent of the population of England lived in London by the mid-seventeenth century.

English Society in the Tudor Period

English society under the Tudors reflected what William Harrison, writing in 1577, called "degrees of people," that is, sharply defined social groups. Contemporaries sometimes simplified English social structure by dividing people into the ranks of "gentlemen," "the middling sort," and "the poor." Ownership of land in the form of estates—inherited or acquired—conferred status, or "gentility," in England. All nobles (that is, with a noble title passed on by inheritance) were gentry, but the vast majority of gentry were not nobles. In order to administer the realm and maintain public order in every corner of the country, the crown required the allegiance and the assistance of the landed elite.

In exchange for military service, the crown granted titles that were inherited by the eldest son. The nobility and gentry had enormous social and political influence, and they dominated England for more than the next three centuries. Country manors literally commanded the surrounding countryside. One contemporary exuded, "Nobility is a precious gift, which so glittereth in the eyes of all men that there is no one corporal thing in this world, whereof we make a greater account."

The lord and his family dominated regional economic, social, and political life through ties of kinship and patronage. Ordinary people addressed the nobleman as "your lordship" and the wealthy gentleman as "sir"; poor women curtsied to them as a mark of respect. Village bells were rung in their honor when they passed through. Wealthy landowners mediated in village disputes and provided some charity in exchange for deference. (One man of means chatted with "his people" in the street: "I asked a poor woman how many children she had. She answered 'Six.' 'Here,' I said, 'is a sixpence for them.' 'No, sir,' she said proudly, not realizing the gentleman was offering a gift, 'I will not sell my children.' ")

The Privy Council and Elizabeth's court were remarkably homogeneous from the early 1570s, with few newcomers breaking into the inner circle of like-minded aristocrats. The borders between public and private life within this upper circle of relatives, friends, enemies, and acquaintances were hard to distinguish. The education of gentlemen at Oxford and Cambridge Universities or through private tutoring helped shape common cultural values and social homogeneity among what was increasingly becoming a national elite.

Yeomen stood beneath the gentry on the social ladder, but they could move up if they were able to purchase and maintain large estates. In any case, they possessed "a certain preeminence and more estimation" among

Longleat at Wiltshire, one of the great early-Elizabethan manor houses, which is depicted as a bustling center of activity for the surrounding countryside.

the common people. They had political rights and could vote in the parliamentary elections. They improved their houses, bought or built solid furniture, purchased silver and pewter accoutrements, wore nice clothes on Sundays and holidays, and were able to assure the education of their children.

Within the upper reaches of the "middling sort" were men considered "of sufficiency," even if they were not lords or gentlemen. They were believed by virtue of steady income to be worthy of assuming some kind of public responsibility. England's precocious commercial and manufacturing boom in the sixteenth century increased the wealth and status of merchants and manufacturers. Wealthy merchants and artisans served on town councils, perpetuating their influence from generation to generation. Members of these councils led the way in the pageant-like processions during municipal and national celebrations, such as that of Midsummer Eve, followed by guild members, each wearing the decorative costume of their various trades. Most craftsmen were much better off than the urban and rural poor.

Originally intended to maintain the highest standards in the training of craftsmen and in production, the guilds' influence waned as towns became larger and more complex. Yet some guilds, particularly in London, held monopolies over specific trades. They could control production and therefore the prices of certain commodities. Since guild regulations and ordinances had to be approved by the civic authorities, disagreements between guilds and municipal governments were frequent.

Lower on the social scale were smallholders, farmers who owned just enough land to get by ("husbandmen"), poor clergymen depending for survival upon small fees rendered for their services, and ordinary craftsmen. The majority of the population owned neither land nor skills, and thus lay at the bottom of the social hierarchy. Most laboring families lived in rented one-room cottages and owned little—if any—furniture. Cottagers, employed as farmhands but also often employed as spinners, weavers, carders, or nailmakers, lived on bread, cheese, lard, soup, beer, and garden greens, occasionally supplemented by harvest-time feasts provided by their employers. Farm servants lived in spartan accommodations provided by landlords. In London and smaller towns, the urban poor struggled to survive as common laborers, porters, sweepers, and in other menial occupations, living in squalor in whatever pitiful lodgings they could afford, or, for many, living without shelter.

Social divisions in English society were reflected in how people lived, dressed, and even spoke. During the sixteenth century, the rich got richer—and lived that way, dressing and eating differently from those who were poor. Responding to complaints that "a Babylon of confusion" might blur class lines because anyone with money could purchase the most elegant clothing, Parliament had earlier in the century decreed that only dukes, earls, and barons could wear sable cloth woven of gold and embroidered with gold and silver. Gentlemen with land bringing an income of 100 pounds a year could wear velvet in their doublets but not in their gowns and coats. Ben Jonson (1572–1637), author of scurrilous satires on London life, wrote that to become recognized as a gentleman, a man had to go to London, "where at your first appearance 'twere good you turned four or five hundred acres of your best land into two or three trunks of apparel."

Cardinal Wolsey had earlier attempted to moderate the dietary excesses of wealthy people, including the high clergy. Copying sumptuary regulations that could be found throughout Europe since the Middle Ages, he specified the number of separate dinner courses that people of various ranks might consume, with the largest number—nine—reserved for cardinals like himself. But to no avail. A critical commentator wrote toward the end of the century, "Nowadays, if the table be not covered from the one end to the other as thick as a dish can stand by another . . . and to every dish a several sauce appropriate to his kind, it is thought unworthy of the name of dinner." The poor ate no such meals. The condition of life of some artisans, landless cottagers, rural laborers, and unskilled and underemployed workers declined; soaring food and lodging costs sapped their meager earnings.

There was, to be sure, some degree of social mobility in Tudor England: new economic opportunities brought greater prosperity to gentry, yeomen, merchants, and manufacturers. By the end of the century, the economic gap between nobles and wealthy gentry landowners had been reduced.

Some yeomen achieved gentry status, and merchants and manufacturers made money. The interests and lifestyles of the middling sort gradually moved closer to those of gentlemen and their families as English society became more polarized. And, to be sure, some farm servants were able to save enough money to become husbandmen, or even yeomen; likewise, some apprentices became independent masters within their trades. But social advancement remained relatively rare among the poor, whose numbers were rapidly expanding along with their impoverishment.

The Quest for Public Order

After almost a century of inflation accentuated by a rising population, harvest failures in the 1590s brought the period of economic expansion to an abrupt halt in England. Never had there seemed to be so many poor and hungry people on the roads, dressed in rags, sleeping in fields, searching for wild berries or edible roots, and begging, just trying to get by. "They lie in the streets," reported one observer, "in the dirt as commonly is seen . . . and are permitted to die like dogs or beasts without any mercy or compassion showed them at all."

Ordinary people sometimes took matters into their own hands. Food riots spread throughout much of England, as the poor seized grain and sold it at what they considered a reasonable price. Women usually made up the majority of participants in the food riots because it fell to them to try to make ends meet at the market. Such disturbances increased the resolve of the state to maintain order at all costs.

The prosecution of serious crimes increased rapidly during Elizabeth's reign, peaking between 1590 and 1620. Vagrancy was the most prevalent of these offenses, as people took to the road in search of food. Vagrants were arrested and placed in stocks for three days, before being sent home. Thefts rose rapidly. A contemporary estimated that there were twenty-three different categories of thieves and swindlers, including "hookers," who snatched linen and clothes with a long pole from windows, "priggers of prancers" (horse thieves), and "Abraham men," who "feign themselves to be mad." The theft of goods worth more than twelve shillings could bring the death penalty, but more often offenders were publicly whipped, branded, mutilated by having an ear cut off, or sent to serve as oarsmen in the galley ships. Women were often treated more harshly than men, unless they were pregnant. Although only about 10 percent of those convicted of capital crimes were actually executed, such punishment was particularly brutal, including slow strangulation by hanging and being slowly crushed to death by weights.

The English upper classes, convinced that most crimes went unpunished, became obsessed with maintaining order, a fact reflected in several of Shakespeare's plays, in which ordinary people appear as potential threats to social order. To some people, society seemed on the verge of being overwhelmed by lawlessness and sin. Many Elizabethans believed that social order depended on the maintenance of social hierarchy and the securing of obedience to the moral authority of government. Thus, the Tudors formulated a doctrine of obedience to authority, basing their arguments on religious teaching. A homily warned the English of the consequences of challenging social hierarchy:

> There reigneth all abuse, carnal liberty, enormity, sin and Babylonical confusion. Take away kings, princes, rulers, magistrates, judges, and such estates of God's order, no man shall ride to go by the highway untroubled, no man shall sleep in his own house or bed unkilled, no man shall keep his wife, children or possessions in quietness, all things shall be common; and there needs must follow all mischief and utter destruction both of souls, bodies, goods and commonwealths.

Elizabethan literature and drama constantly returned to the theme of a moral law based upon the necessity of social order. In Shakespeare's *The History of Troilus and Cressida,* Ulysses proclaims:

> The heavens themselves, the planets, and this centre
> Observe degree, priority, and place,
> Insisture, course, proportion, season, form;
> Office, and custom, in all line of order;
> [. . .]But when the planets

Whipping a man arrested for vagrancy and expelling him from town. In view of what has happened to his friend in the upper left corner, he is lucky to have escaped with his life.

In evil mixture to disorder wander,
What plagues and what portents, what mutiny!
What raging of the sea, shaking of earth!
[. . .]Take but degree away, untune that string,
And hark what discord follows. . . .

Many in the middle and upper classes believed that the slightest offense against the monarchy contained the seeds of rebellion; in 1576, a woman was burned at the stake for saying that Elizabeth was "baseborn and not born to the crown." Fear of disturbances and challenges to authority contributed to the development of a sense of national consciousness of England's elite, just as the defeat of Spain's Armada in 1588 led to pride in being both Protestant and English.

In 1598, Parliament passed the first "poor law," followed by another in 1601. These laws recognized for the first time the principle that the needy ought to receive some sort of assistance from the community in which they live. Justices of the peace, under the supervision of the clergy, were to oversee the distribution of assistance to the poor. The poor laws also specified the establishment of poor houses for the incarceration of the poor who could not or would not work (including the aged, sick, and insane).

The poor laws, then, reflected a combination of concern for and fear of the wandering poor. Ministers denounced the poor from the pulpit and trumpeted the virtues of sobriety, submission, obedience, and social deference. Local elites began to take an active role in enforcing ordinances against begging and vagrancy. Landed gentlemen and the merchants and manufacturers of the towns found that they now had more in common than wealth—a fear of the poor.

The Elizabethan Theater

The arts reflected the prosperity of the middle and upper classes in England. In 1576, two theaters opened in London, followed by others in a number of provincial towns. Putting aside the repertory of religious allegories and miracle and morality plays that had been staged in royal castles, country manor houses, or entire towns, they staked their survival on their ability to attract audiences that would pay to see the actors perform. More than 2,000 different plays were staged in London between 1580 and 1640, mainly romances and dramas. During that period, more than 300 playwrights produced enough work to keep 100 acting companies working in London or touring provincial towns.

William Shakespeare (1564–1616) wrote plays that reflected uncertainty, ambivalence, and even disillusionment about contemporary English society. Historians know little about his life, despite the fact that he is perhaps the most revered Western author of all time. He was born in

(Left) William Shakespeare. *(Right)* The Swan Theater, an Elizabethan playhouse that closely resembled Shakespeare's Globe Theater.

Stratford-on-Avon, where his father made gloves and was able to provide him with a primary school education. Shakespeare moved to London with his wife to become an actor, and in the late 1580s he began to write plays. He found first patronage and then unparalleled success, angering rivals, one of whom referred to him as "an upstart crow beautified with our feathers." He became part owner and actor in the Lord Chamberlain's Men, an acting company of the Globe theater, which held an audience of 3,000 and hence was the largest of London's six private theaters. Seats at such private theaters cost at least six times more than the cheapest tickets at the public theaters, which included places for the "penny stinkards" who stood in the uncovered pit below the stage.

Audiences shouted for what they liked and hooted at what they did not. Fights were not infrequent, both inside and outside of the theater. The playwright Christopher Marlowe (1564–1593) died in a brawl in an inn under mysterious circumstances; the actor and playwright Ben Jonson killed another actor in a duel. Because of their rowdy reputations, most London theaters stood outside the city walls. London officials tried to close down the public theaters because they thought that disease spread easily among assembled crowds and because of complaints about profanity and lewdness on stage.

Despite the problems of religious division, warfare, and the struggles for influence that were reflected in the drama of the times, England under the Tudors became a power that would influence the world. Elizabeth died in peace on March 24, 1603, in the forty-fifth year of her reign, leaving England a substantially more unified, effectively ruled, and powerful state.

THE DECLINE OF SPAIN

The "decline" of the overstretched Spanish Empire was first noted in 1600. Had the Spain of the Catholic kings fallen from God's favor? Castilians themselves still regarded Spain as a haven of peace and prosperity compared to the rest of Europe, which was wracked by religious wars.

The Dutch Revolt

The decline of Spanish power began with the Dutch revolt. In the Netherlands, Dutch nobles and officials resented higher taxes imposed by the Spanish crown. Above all, many of the Dutch were angered by the Spanish king's attempt to promote the Catholic Reformation by imposing the Inquisition in a land where most people were Calvinists. In the early 1560s, resistance first began against the presence of Spanish border garrisons and then against the unpopular governor.

In 1567, Philip II appointed the arrogant duke of Alba (1507–1582) to restore order in the north with 10,000 Spanish troops. The ruthless Castilian executed prominent Calvinist nobles on the central square of Brussels, established military courts, imposed heavy new taxes, and virtually destroyed self-government in the Netherlands. But Alba's reign of terror as governor also helped transform the resistance of Dutch nobles and officials, led by William of Orange (1533–1584), into a national revolt.

Alba believed that "everyone must be made to live in constant fear of the roof breaking down over his head" and warned that he was "resolved not to leave a creature alive, but to put them all to the sword." Alba's Council of Troubles, known to the Dutch as the "Council of Blood," executed thousands of people from 1567 to 1573, leading a Catholic bishop to claim that in six years Alba had hurt the Church more than Luther and Calvin combined.

In 1572, rebellion became full-fledged insurrection. Spanish troops dominated on land, but the Dutch controlled the sea. When a Spanish army undertook a siege of Leiden, southwest of Amsterdam, the people of the town opened the dikes, and Dutch ships sailed over the rushing waters to drive the Spaniards away. But Alba's successor earned victories in the Southern Netherlands. There Catholic nobles began to have second thoughts about continuing a struggle launched by Dutch Protestants. They detached the southern provinces from the rebellious federation. In 1579, the Dutch provinces formed the Union of Utrecht, and two years later they declared their independence from Spain as the Dutch United Provinces.

For the moment, Spain could supply its armies because Alba's armies had recaptured some of the Southern Netherlands, while Philip maintained peace with England. As the Dutch revolt wore on, however, the problems of fighting a war a thousand miles away plagued the Spanish

Prince William of Orange leading the revolt in the Netherlands against higher taxes from the Spanish crown. The Dutch revolt signified the decline of Spanish power.

king. Military contractors or entrepreneurs recruited mercenaries, and Italians, Burgundians, Germans, and Walloons made up much of the Spanish army.

Spanish routes for troops, supplies, and bullion to the Netherlands had to be maintained through a combination of diplomatic charm, cunning, and coercion. As allegiances and the fortunes of war eliminated first the Palatinate and then Alsace and Lorraine as routes through which armies could pass, the Spanish forged the "Spanish Road" as a military corridor (see Map 5.3). It began in Genoa, went overland across the Alps, and then passed through Lombardy and Piedmont, Geneva, Franche-Comté, Lorraine and, finally, the Duchy of Liège, with Spanish agents assuring supplies along the way.

Compared to other armies fighting in Europe at the same time, the Spanish army seemed better only in terms of medical attention. Spain's acute problems of recruiting and supply were exacerbated by dubious efforts to save money—for instance, charging sharpshooters for powder and shot. The army's guarantee to carry out the written wills made by soldiers also seems to have been a curiously self-defeating approach to inspiring confidence. Mutinies—the largest involving non-Spanish troops—occurred with ever more frequency as troops demanded payment of back wages, better and more regular food, and decent hospital conditions. Soldiers deserted, encouraged and aided by Dutch agents, as well as by those of France, against whom Spain was also warring. By 1577, the Spanish army in the Netherlands, unpaid for months, had dwindled in size from 60,000 to no more than 8,000 men.

Throughout the long war, the superior Dutch fleet kept the Spanish ships in port, while the English navy, allied with the Dutch in 1586, controlled the English Channel. When the Spanish fleet sailed north in 1588, the result was the disastrous defeat of the Armada. The ships of "sea beggars," as they were called, fighting under William of Orange (until his assassination in 1584), then harassed Spanish ships.

At the beginning of the seventeenth century, the Dutch gradually fell back behind protective town fortifications and natural barriers formed by rivers. The war became a series of long Spanish sieges against frontier towns defended by brick fortifications, bastions, and moats—a defensive system that had its origins with the Italian city-states. With the defense

MAP 5.3 THE SPANISH ROAD   The route taken by the Spanish armies, supplies, and money to the Netherlands was long and difficult, as it passed through mountainous terrain and many states.

having a marked advantage, towns could be conquered only by being starved out.

France withdrew from the war in 1598, and England withdrew six years later. But a truce between the Spanish and the Dutch, signed in 1609, ended in 1621. In Holland the "war party" won the upper hand. Led by Maurice of Nassau (1567–1625), who was the son of William of Orange, the war party appealed to Calvinist religious orthodoxy by calling for a crusade against Catholicism that would also free the Southern Netherlands from Spanish rule. Army officers and merchant traders wanted to keep the struggle against Spain going as long as possible. It dragged on, an expensive drain on the Spanish economy.

Economic Decline

Economic decline—above all, that of Castile in the middle decades of the seventeenth century—underlay Spain's fall from a position of European domination. But decline is, of course, relative. Spain remained an important state even though its population, which had risen to well over 6 million people during the last half of the sixteenth century, fell by almost a quarter to about 5.2 million by the middle of the seventeenth century, as harvest failures, plague, smallpox, and emigration took their tolls.

The "price revolution," a sharp rise in the level of inflation during the sixteenth century in Europe, may well have affected Spain less than some parts of northern Europe, but it still had adverse effects on the Spanish monarchy. Gold and silver from the Americas accelerated inflation by increasing the supply of money, as did royal monetary policies of currency debasement. The monarchy, which had declared bankruptcy in 1557, suspended payments in 1575, and again in 1596, renegotiating loans at more favorable rates. From 1568 to 1598, Spain had five times the military expenditures of the Dutch, English, and French combined. One of the results of so many expensive wars was that Spain lost its margin of safety when it experienced a series of epidemics, plagues, and harvest failures beginning in 1576 and continuing for most of the last quarter of the century. The economy slipped into stagnation. To one noble it already seemed that "the ship is sinking."

Forced to take out large loans from foreign bankers at disadvantageous interest rates, the state attempted to find new sources of revenue. To raise funds, the crown imposed a tithe, or assessment of a tenth of the most valuable piece of real estate in each parish, and in 1590 the Castilian Cortes agreed to an extraordinary tax assessed on towns. An excise (sales) tax was imposed on consumption. This undermined the economy by encouraging the middle class to abandon business in favor of the acquisition of perpetual privileges—and thus tax exemptions—as they obtained noble status. The monarchy's massive expulsion of the Moriscos in 1609 proved counterproductive. The king succumbed to pressure from the

Catholic Church and from wealthy families eager to seize Moorish land. The region of Valencia lost one-third of its population, including many skilled craftsmen and some of the most able and advanced farmers.

Nobles added the lands of indebted peasants to their large estates (*latifundia*), but they showed little interest in increasing the productivity of their land, in contrast to their English counterparts. They turned fields into pastureland or simply left them untended. Royal policies may also have damaged the agricultural economy. Farmers were hampered by a state-imposed fixed maximum for grain prices, which discouraged ambitious agricultural initiatives. Toward the end of the sixteenth century, Spain had become dependent on imported grain. Royal policies also favored sheepherding over farming—because it was easier to collect taxes on sheep than on agricultural produce—and many landowners converted marginal land into pasture for sheep and expanded their home textile manufacturing (as occurred in the Netherlands at the same time). But fine woolens manufacturing suffered from competition with foreign textile imports, especially the lighter cloth brought from France and the Netherlands.

"Conquered by you, the New World has conquered you in turn, and has weakened and exhausted your ancient vigor," a Flemish scholar wrote a friend in Spain. The Spanish colonies became something of a financial drain on the crown because of the cost of administering and defending them. The flow of Latin American silver, which had paid less than a quarter of the crown's colonial and military expenses, slowed to a trickle beginning in the 1620s. The colonial market for Spanish goods shrank with the precipitous decline in the Indian population (caused, above all, by disease; see Chapter 1). Furthermore, the colonies had also developed their own basic agricultural and artisanal production and relied far less on Spanish goods. The Atlantic ports of northern Castile endured competition in shipbuilding and commerce not only from Seville and Cádiz, but from Spain's own colonies, and above all, from England and the Netherlands.

Although the burden of taxes in Castile increased by four times between 1570 and 1670, the Spanish crown proved less efficient in collecting taxes than the monarchs of France and England. More than this, increased taxes on the poor generated more discontent than income. Spain's Italian subjects resisted contributing money for distant wars that did not concern them. Charles V had largely financed his wars through fiscal impositions on the Netherlands, his wealthiest province. But the Dutch revolt, in addition to dramatically raising royal expenses, stopped the flow of money from the Dutch subjects to the crown and thus drastically reduced royal revenue.

Contemporary Spaniards, particularly Castilians, lapsed into a morose acceptance of decline. The novelist Miguel de Cervantes (1547–1616) had fought with the king's armies at the Battle of Lepanto (1571), where he received a wound that permanently crippled his left hand. Several years

The painting *A Soldier's Dream* allegorizes Spanish feelings of morose despair and fatalism as the Spanish Empire begins to crumble.

later, he was captured by Turkish pirates. After five years as a slave, he managed to return to Spain. The first part of *Don Quixote* was published in 1605, the second in 1615. On one level it is a humorous tale of a zany noble intent on bringing true chivalry back to Spain, accompanied by his sensible, subservient squire, Sancho Panza. On a deeper level, however, *Don Quixote* is the story of national disillusionment in the face of perceived national decline. Among the next generation of great Spanish writers, the dramatist Pedro Calderón de la Barca (1600–1681) tragically portrayed in his plays the floundering Spanish aristocracy struggling to preserve its honor. Nobles and churchmen, the two pillars of Spain, purchased the work of the increasingly gloomy Greek-born artist El Greco (1541–1614). His *Burial of the Count Orgasz* (1586) shows figures gazing up at a vision of celestial glory, the splendor of which is heightened by the dismal scenes below them on earth.

An Empire Spread Too Thin

Spain's mounting economic problems were exacerbated by the fact that the empire's interests, some of which were defended in costly wars, were spread so widely, not only in Europe, but across the seas. Philip IV (1605–1665), who succeeded to the throne in 1621, was intelligent, strong-willed, lazy, and had a keen interest in the arts. He chose as his chief adviser Gaspar de Guzmán, the duke of Olivares (1587–1645), an Andalusian noble whose family had, like Spain itself, suffered reverses. The short, fiery, and increasingly obese Olivares sketched ambitious plans to shape the rebirth of Spanish might. Confronted with the growing economic strength of the Dutch rebels, as well as that of the English, Olivares sensed that Spain could not remain a power without a marked economic resurgence. "We must devote all our efforts," he had written, "to turning Spaniards into merchants." The Count Duke, as he was called, mastered his master, convincing the lazy king that only hard work and reform could restore the glories of the not-so-distant past. He would tutor the king, whose chamber pot he once ceremoniously kissed, in the fine art of monarchy.

The Count Duke espoused the growth of monarchical power and state centralization. His motto "one king, one law, one money" generated resistance, in the latter case because of the by then notorious instability of the Castilian currency. At a time when complaints mounted against the extraordinary excise taxes, Olivares sought to subject all of Spain to the laws and royal administration of Castile, promising the king that, if he did so, he would become the most powerful prince in the world.

Olivares wanted to force Dutch capitulation to restore the monarchy's reputation, afraid that the Dutch rebellion might begin a chain reaction that would destroy the empire. He persuaded the king to allow the truce with the Dutch to lapse in 1621, thus necessitating massive expenses for land and sea warfare. Olivares concluded from the Dutch surrender of the fortress town of Breda in 1625 that it was God's will that the fight against the Protestant rebels in the north continue. To preserve the "Spanish Road," Olivares sought to bolster Spanish interests in northern Italy and in Austria, the same expensive strategy employed earlier by Philip II. But France cut the Spanish supply routes in Savoy in 1622 and then in Alsace nine years later. Intermittent hostilities with France lasted from 1628 to 1631, and made more likely a full-scale conflict between the two powers.

Spain could ill afford such conflicts. In 1628, Dutch pirates captured a Spanish fleet loaded with silver. This enormous loss made it imperative that the crown find new resources with which to wage war.

The Count Duke of Olivares.

But for the first time, Castile's monarchs could not establish credit with foreign investors to finance Spain's foreign wars. Increased taxation, the floating of short-term loans through bonds, the sale of yet more privileges, and the imposition of new financial obligations on Aragon and the Italian territories all proved inadequate to the task of financing an expensive, distant war.

Its interests gravely overextended, Spain's position weakened. English ships began to nip at its imperial interests in the Americas. Dutch ships fought the proud Spanish galleons in the West Indies. Three decades of intermittent warfare with France began in 1635, as the Thirty Years' War (see Chapter 4) became a struggle between competing dynasties. As more and more bullion from the Americas had to be diverted to pay military expenses in the Netherlands and Italy, the monarchy demanded new contributions from Catalonia and Portugal, as Spain had assumed the expensive and ultimately extremely damaging responsibility for protecting Portuguese shipping around the world. Tumultuous tax riots broke out in Portugal. The Portuguese upper classes began to resist Spanish authority.

Olivares's decision to demand more taxes from Catalonia proved fateful. Faced with resistance, he ordered the arrest of several Catalan leaders, amid riots in the countryside. Catalan nobles put aside their differences, and a full-scale revolt against Castilian rule began in 1640. Catalan and French forces together defeated the Spanish army. A year later, Andalusian nobles were foiled in a plot to create an independent kingdom there. Nobles in Madrid hatched plots against Olivares. When Portugal proclaimed its independence, there were few Spanish troops there to protest. The vigorous assertion of localism reflected the disillusionment of provincial elites with Castilian power. Philip sent the despondent Olivares into exile in 1643.

However, the illusion of Don Quixote was maintained—that the restoration of traditional aristocratic and ecclesiastical values would restore Spanish power and prestige. Olivares established two court academies intended to train young nobles in the art of government. Heeding the advice of churchmen, he also attempted to ban prostitution and take other such measures in what he considered the interest of traditional morals, censoring the theater and books, prohibiting certain kinds of fancy clothing and long hair. These measures, however, would prove ineffective.

By the 1660s, the Cortes was no longer an impediment to monarchical authority in Castile, and thereafter it was convoked only on ceremonial occasions. Although the Spanish monarchy was damaged by its inability to reform its financial apparatus, the crown continued to extend its reach and solidify its authority against possible provincial rebellions. Over the long run, Spanish rulers weakened parliamentary traditions. Yet enhanced centralization was not matched by more efficient tax collection.

Ironically, amid such signs of decline, the last years of Philip IV and the reign of his pathetic successor, Charles II (ruled 1665–1700), sustained a

Diego de Velazquez's *Surrender of Breda* (1634–1635).

period of considerable cultural accomplishment in the arts and in literature. But this, too, may have been generated by the prevailing mood of
introspection. Olivares put dramatists and a small host of other writers to
work in the name of glorifying the monarchy and imparting a sense of purpose that he hoped would revive Spain.

King Philip IV added more than 2,000 canvases to what already was a
rich royal art collection, including many by Italian masters. He covered
the palace walls with grandiose paintings of battle scenes. Diego
Velázquez (1599–1660), the court painter, undertook forty portraits of the
vain king. Their sharp realism stands as a commentary on the Spanish
monarchy's fading glory and disillusionment. Velázquez also commemo-
rated the badly needed—but ultimately fruitless—victory over the Dutch
in *The Surrender of Breda* (1634–1635).

In the meantime, the Dutch rebels, aided by increased commercial prosperity, had fought the Spanish armies to a draw. The Treaty of Münster,
which was part of the Westphalia settlement of 1648 that ended the Thirty
Years' War, officially recognized Dutch independence after a struggle that
had lasted three-quarters of a century. The provinces of the Southern
Netherlands (modern-day Belgium), which were overwhelmingly Catholic,

remained a Habsburg possession. In Catalonia, Barcelona surrendered to royal troops in 1652. Catalan nobles accepted the supremacy of the crown in exchange for an affirmation of social hierarchy and royal protection against ordinary Catalans who resented their privileges. The Aragonese nobles, too, accepted this compromise.

The Spanish monarchy never learned that it could not fight effectively on a variety of fronts. In contrast, the French monarchy, concentrating its efforts in Italy, for the moment realized the wisdom of fighting on one front at a time. Thus, subsequent Spanish victories in the north against French armies were not enough, for when the French turned their attention to the Spanish front they easily held their own. The Treaty of the Pyrenees, signed between France and Spain in 1659, established the border between these countries that has lasted, with only a few minor changes, until this day. Spain also gave up Milan to Austria, and Naples and Sicily to the Italian Bourbon dynasty. The Portuguese, aided by the English, turned back several halfhearted invasions by Spanish armies, and in 1668 Spain recognized Portugal's independence. Ten years later, France occupied the Franche-Comté, the last major Spanish holding in northern Europe.

By 1680, when the depression that had lasted almost a century ended, Spain had become a second-rate power. This was because of agricultural and manufacturing decline, to be sure, but, above all, because the Spanish crown had overreached its ability to maintain its vast and distant empire.

CONCLUSION

The development of trade across the Atlantic Ocean to the Americas was part of European economic expansion during the sixteenth century. Following the union of the crowns of Castile and Aragon, Spain grew into a great power. Philip II expanded the Spanish Empire, which, in the Americas stretched from what is now the southern United States to the southern tip of Latin America, and in Europe included the Netherlands and several Italian states. The Tudor monarchy in England overcame the country's religious divisions in the wake of the English Reformation to strengthen its authority. In this, it resembled the ruling Valois dynasty of France, another "new monarchy" in that it enhanced its reach, efficiency, and prestige. The burgeoning of English trade, manufacturing, and agriculture in the Elizabethan Age underlay England's relative prosperity, even as social polarization, reflected in the crises of the 1590s, became more apparent.

The surprising English naval defeat of the Spanish Armada in 1588 symbolized not only the rise of England but in some ways anticipated the decline of Spanish power. Spain's rulers had expanded their vast empire and imperial interests beyond the ability of the state to sustain them.

When silver from the Americas slowed to a trickle, Spain's own limited natural resources, combined with demographic stagnation that began early in the seventeenth century, undercut Spanish Habsburg power. The inability of the Spanish monarchy to impose fully its authority on Aragon and Catalonia, or to collect taxes efficiently, prevented a revival of Spanish preeminence. The long revolt of the Netherlands ended with recognition of Dutch independence in 1648. That the Dutch Republic and England, two trading nations, had emerged as European powers reflected the shift of economic primacy to Northwestern Europe.

CHAPTER 6

ENGLAND AND THE DUTCH REPUBLIC IN THE SEVENTEENTH CENTURY

England and the Dutch Republic were anomalies in the seventeenth century. At a time when aggressive European monarchs were forging absolute states, these two seafaring, trading nations maintained representative governments.

The Stuart monarchs' flirtation with absolutism in England brought bitter discord, resistance, and civil war. In the Dutch Republic, which had earned its independence in 1648 after a long war against Spanish absolute rule, the prosperous merchants who dominated the economic and political life of the country brushed aside the absolutist challenge of the House of Orange, which wanted to establish a hereditary monarchy.

In both England and the Netherlands, religious divisions accentuated the struggle between absolutism and constitutionalism. Both the protracted revolt of the largely Protestant Dutch against Catholic Spain and the English Civil War echoed the religious struggles between Catholics and Protestants during the Thirty Years' War (1618–1648) in Central Europe (see Chapter 4). The Dutch had risen up in open rebellion in 1566 in part because the Spanish Habsburgs attempted to impose the Catholic Inquisition on what had become a Protestant country. In England, Kings James I and Charles I attempted to return the English Church to the elaborate rituals that many people associated with Catholicism, thereby pitting the monarchy against Parliament. This constitutional crisis led to the defeat and execution of Charles I in 1649, the fall of the monarchy, and in 1688, to the "Glorious Revolution," which brought King William III and Queen Mary to the throne. Parliament, which historically represented

Illustration of the Council of Delegates in the Netherlands; in the seventeenth century both the Dutch Republic and England supported constitutionalism and the Parliament in opposition to Catholic absolutism.

landed interests, succeeded in balancing and constraining royal authority. By virtue of Parliament's victory in the English Civil War, England remained a constitutional monarchy. England's new monarchs agreed to a Bill of Rights, which affirmed the civil liberties of English people and the rights of Parliament.

Some historians have associated the success of England and the Dutch Republic, two largely Protestant countries, with the "Calvinist ethic" of hard work. Yet the emergence of England and the Dutch Republic as great powers reflected the vitality of the "middling sort" in both nations, the relative unity of the two states, and the location of both rising powers on the Atlantic. Aided by governments quick to realize the benefits to their states of an expansion of international trade, the Dutch Netherlands and England mobilized the resources of their middle classes. England's international commerce developed rapidly. And as Amsterdam emerged as a banking center and first port of call for international trade, the Dutch Republic enjoyed the golden age of its culture.

CONFLICTS IN STUART ENGLAND

Conflicts between the Stuart kings and Parliament, as well as religious conflicts, led to the English Civil War, which helped define the constitutional and political institutions of modern Britain. The monarchy tried to enhance its authority at the expense of Parliament by attempting to impose extralegal taxes without the consent of Parliament. But the English gentry, whose status and influence came from ownership of land, emerged from the period with their parliamentary prerogatives intact. The nature and extent of royal prerogatives were at issue, as well as religious, social, and ideological divisions. These were played out through the English Civil War and its aftermath.

Conflicts between James I and Parliament

King James I (1566–1625) succeeded his cousin Queen Elizabeth to the English throne in 1603. As King James VI of Scotland, he had overcome court factionalism and challenges from dissident Presbyterians. After he became king of England, the two countries were joined in a personal union because he ruled both. The first Stuart king of England, James was lazy, frivolous, and slovenly, particularly enjoying hurling jelly at his courtiers. But there was more to him than that. He was an intelligent and well-read blunderer, once described as "the wisest fool in Christendom." Before coming to the throne, James had sketched out a theory of divine right monarchy. And in a speech to Parliament in 1609 the king had called "the state of monarchie . . . the supremest thing upon earth: for Kings are not only God's Lieutenants upon earth, and sit upon throne, but even by God himselfe they are called Gods." James described Parliament as nothing but "cries, shouts, and confusion." Relations between the monarch and Parliament degenerated rapidly.

The English monarchy was in a precarious financial position. Queen Elizabeth's war debts were at least partially to blame, but so was James's inability to tax efficiently. James brought to court like-minded dandies, most of whom proved not only unpopular with Parliament but incompetent and provocative as well. In the last years of his reign, James became increasingly dependent on his young, handsome favorite, George Villiers, the duke of Buckingham (1592–1628). A relative newcomer to court circles, Buckingham convinced the king to sell peerages and titles, offices, monopolies, and other privileges to the highest bidder. Opposition to the monarch's attempts to raise money in such ways mounted within Parliament.

Although it met only sporadically and at the king's pleasure, Parliament transformed itself from a debating society into an institution that saw itself as defending the rights of the English people. The House of Commons, lashing out at the beneficiaries of royal monopolies, impeached on charges of bribery Lord Chancellor Francis Bacon (1561–1626), philosopher of science and once the king's friend. Here, too, there was a principle at stake: the accountability of ministers to Parliament.

English foreign policy contributed both to the monarchy's mounting debt and to the emerging political crisis. Queen Elizabeth had denied that Parliament had the right to discuss matters of foreign policy unless invited by the monarch to do so. Parliament, however, still insisted on that right. Thus, for example, James favored peace with Spain, but Parliament clamored for war because Catholic Bavaria, an ally of Habsburg Spain, had invaded the Protestant Upper Palatinate. And in 1621, asserting its right to influence foreign policy, Parliament refused to provide more funds for the conflict, setting the stage for the greatest constitutional crisis in English history.

Parliament also denounced the monarch's attempt to arrange a marriage between his son, Charles, the heir to the throne, and the daughter of Philip IV of Spain. As dynastic marriages were an essential part of foreign policy, cementing or building alliances, members of Parliament objected to a royal foreign policy that seemed pro-Spanish and therefore pro-Catholic. Parliament declared its right to discuss the proposed marriage, and thus foreign affairs. But James defied Parliament by stating that it could not discuss matters of foreign policy, denying that the privileges of Parliament were "your ancient and undoubted birthright and inheritance." Rather he described them as "derived from the grace and permission of our ancestors and us."

James's wedding plans for his son fell through in 1623, however, when the Spanish king refused to allow Charles, who had gone to Madrid with the duke of Buckingham, even to set eyes on his daughter. But two years later, James arranged Charles's marriage to another devout Catholic, Henrietta Maria of France. The secret price of this liaison included the king's promise that he would one day allow English Catholics, who numbered 2 or 3 percent of the population, to practice their religion freely. In a country in which anti-Catholicism had been endemic since the English Reformation of the mid-sixteenth century, James seemed to be taking steps to favor Catholicism.

James was succeeded upon his death by his son, Charles I (ruled 1625–1649). The young king was indecisive and painfully shy, traits compounded by a stammer. Even more than his father, Charles rejected the view that his appointments to ministries and other important offices should represent a wide spectrum of political and religious views. Charles stubbornly refused to oust the duke of Buckingham, even as Parliament began impeachment proceedings against the royal favorite.

RELIGIOUS DIVISIONS

King Charles I once claimed, "People are governed by the pulpit more than the sword in time of peace." In the seventeenth century, no other realm of life so bitterly divided Europeans as religion. In England, religious divisions helped accentuate and define the political crisis. The Established or Anglican Church faced a challenge from the Puritans, a dissident religious group of Calvinists that had emerged during Elizabeth's reign.

It is difficult to define what exactly it meant to be a Puritan in early seventeenth-century England. Many Puritans were more sure of what they were against than what they were for. Puritans were strongly attracted by the Calvinist idea that each individual was predestined by God through His grace to be saved or not to be saved. They emphasized preaching and the individual's personal understanding of the Bible, spiritual devotion, discipline, and sacrifice as the basis of religion. Because they emphasized the personal worth of the individual minister, not the value of an ecclesiastical title, Puritans opposed the role of bishops in the Church of England. They wanted authority to be taken away from bishops and given to local synods (ecclesiastical councils made up of clerical and lay leaders). They de-emphasized the sacraments (such as baptism and Communion) and wanted worship to be simpler than the contemporary Anglican Church services. Relentlessly hostile to Catholicism, Puritans held that elaborate church accoutrements—such as stained-glass windows and ornate altar rails—smacked of the Roman papacy.

Puritans could be found in all social groups, not only among the "middling sort"—including merchants, shopkeepers, and artisans—but also among the gentry at one end of the social spectrum and weavers at the other. Puritans did not choose the name by which they came to be known in the late sixteenth century, which was originally intended as a term of abuse. Considering themselves "the godly," they believed that they represented the true Church of England, and they worked for change and moral improvement within it. They remained a minority, probably not more than 10 percent of the population, and perhaps a third of all gentry. As Puritan numbers increased, however, their influence grew. University graduates

(Left) King James I. *(Right)* The young Charles, heir to the throne and later Charles I.

who had embraced Puritanism formed "a godly preaching ministry" in many parishes, with endowed lectureships providing opportunities for Puritans to preach and win converts.

The Puritans were increasingly hostile to those who espoused a kind of Protestantism known as Arminianism. At first no more than a handful of ecclesiastics with the king's ear, Arminians soon came to wield considerable power. Charles I became an Arminian, and so did the duke of Buckingham. English Arminians, like their Dutch counterparts, rejected the Calvinist idea of predestination, which Puritans accepted, and, unlike the latter, believed that an individual could

William Laud, bishop of London and later archbishop of Canterbury.

achieve salvation through free will. Arminians also accepted rituals that to the Puritans seemed to replicate those of the Catholic Church. Charles himself believed deeply in the traditions and rituals of the Church. Arminians also emphasized the authority and ceremonial role of bishops, which Puritans opposed with particular vehemence. The Arminians emphasized royal authority over the Church of England because they depended on it, and thus at least seemed to be proponents of royal absolutism.

The king's aggressive espousal of Arminianism enhanced the influence of William Laud (1573–1645), bishop of London. In 1633, Charles named Laud to be the head of the Established Church as Primate of England (archbishop of Canterbury). The pious, hard-working, and stubborn son of a draper, Laud warned Charles that the religious extremes of Catholicism and radical Puritanism both posed threats to the Established Church, and that "unless your Majesty look to it, she will be ground to powder." An Arminian, Laud espoused High Church rituals, and because of this, the Puritans viewed him with suspicion, believing that he was secretly working to make Catholicism the established religion of England. Under Elizabeth I and James I, Catholics had remained a force in some sectors of English life. Fear of a "popish plot" to restore Catholicism as the religion of the English state existed at all levels of English society. Landowners whose families had purchased ecclesiastical lands during the Reformation now worried that Laud might return them to the Catholic Church. Most people in England identified Catholicism and "popery" with the Spanish Inquisition, the Saint Bartholomew's Day Massacre in

France, and the duke of Alba's Council of Blood in the Netherlands. They also viewed with alarm the reconversion of some families to Catholicism, including a third of the gentry families of Yorkshire.

Charles I and Parliament Clash

Charles's fiscal policies deepened popular dissatisfaction with his reign. In 1625, the king decreed a forced loan on landowners, demanding that they provide him with subsidies, which he levied without Parliament's consent and which he insisted be paid within three months, an unprecedentedly short period of time. The next year, he ordered the imprisonment of seventy-six gentlemen, including five prominent knights, who refused to meet the royal demand. Parliament refused to consent to the levies unless Charles met its demands for fiscal reform. The king convoked three Parliaments in four years, but dissolved each when it refused to provide him with funds. Parliament continued to demand that Charles appoint ministers it could trust and began impeachment proceedings against the duke of Buckingham. However, Buckingham disappeared as a source of irritation to Parliament when a disgruntled naval officer who had not been paid assassinated him in 1628.

After Buckingham's death, Charles again asked Parliament to provide him with more funds. In response, Parliament promulgated the Petition of Right, which it forced Charles to accept in return for the granting of a tax. This constrained the king to agree that in the future he would not attempt to impose "loans" without Parliament's consent, and that no "gentlemen" who refused to pay up would be arrested—nor would anyone else be imprisoned without a show of just cause. The Petition of Right, which was initially put forward in 1628 by Sir Thomas Wentworth (1593–1641), then an opponent of the crown and one of the men imprisoned for refusing to pay the forced loan, was a significant document in the constitutional evolution of England. It defined the rights of Parliament as inalienable and condemned arbitrary arrest, martial law, and taxes imposed without Parliament's consent.

Angered by the Petition of Right and by Parliament's insistence that customs duties were a violation of the Petition, Charles ordered Parliament's dissolution in 1629. Because it was the role of the speaker of the house to communicate with the king on behalf of Parliament, members of the Commons physically held the speaker in his chair so he could not leave. They proceeded to declare that anyone who attempted to collect funds not levied with the approval of Parliament would be considered "a capital enemy to the kingdom and commonwealth," as would anyone who sponsored "innovation of religion," which is what Puritans considered Laud's espousal of elaborate High Church ceremonies. A defiant Parliament then disbanded.

For the next eleven years, Charles ruled without Parliament and tried to raise monies in new and controversial ways. Inflation had increased not only the royal debt but also the cost of ships and arms for waging war. The monarchy had exhausted its credit. Unlike James, Charles had some scruples about peddling privileges, but none at all about other means of raising funds. He fined gentlemen who did not attend his coronation. Most controversially, Charles ordered that "ship money" again be imposed on inland towns beginning in 1634. Ship money also raised the question of royal prerogatives because the tax seemed an affront to English common law and had been imposed without Parliament's consent.

Charles's high-handed royal policies led to a rebellion in Scotland. The king had seized lands from Scottish nobles, and, at Laud's instigation, in 1637 he ordered the imposition of the Anglican Book of Common Prayer on the Scottish Presbyterian Church (established as the Scottish national church in the 1560s). The Scots had never been pleased with the union with England that had been weakly forged in 1603 when James VI of Scotland ascended the English throne as James I. They demanded that Charles allow a general church assembly to consider the prayer book. In 1638, some Scottish leaders signed the *National Covenant,* attacking the pope and the prayer book and swearing to defend their religion and liberties. Faced with the resolution of Scots to maintain the Presbyterian Church, Charles convoked the church assembly in Scotland, but he also began to prepare for an invasion of Scotland. In the meantime, Scottish nobles and landowners began evicting Anglican bishops and taking over churches, and the Scots rose up in arms.

This was a turning point in the dramatic reign of King Charles I. Desperately needing funds to defeat the Scots, in 1639 the king demanded that the city of London help pay for the war. After several allocations, insulting in their modesty, London finally consented to lend the crown a large sum, but only on the condition that Charles convene Parliament. Furthermore, London would provide the bulk of the loan only when Charles had proven good faith by permitting Parliament to sit for a sufficient period of time.

Nobles and gentry led resistance to royal policies from the beginning; some were already in touch with the rebellious Scots, who in 1640 occupied the northeastern English port of Newcastle without resistance. Running short of cash and facing mutinies in the royal army, in April 1640 the king summoned Parliament for the first time in eleven years. But when it refused to allocate money for the war against Scotland until Charles agreed to consider a list of grievances, the king dissolved this "Short Parliament" after less than two months. Charles I's defiance of Parliament turned political division into a full-fledged constitutional crisis.

THE ENGLISH CIVIL WAR

The political crisis of the Stuart monarchy became a constitutional conflict about how England was to be governed. To the king's opponents, Parliament existed to protect fundamental English liberties that had been established under the Magna Carta in 1215. By this reasoning the king did not have the right to dispense with its counsel and its traditional authority to allocate royal finances, nor did he have the right to impose taxes without historical precedent. While Parliament, led by Puritans, was not yet claiming sovereignty, it was clearly asserting its traditional role as a balance to royal authority.

Defenders of Parliament and local prerogatives were upset at the king's effort to expand his reach. They believed Laudian religious reforms and the collection of ship money to be the work of power-crazed men perhaps manipulated by the pope. Justices of the peace resented the usurpation of their authority by various decrees of martial law and by royal courts that had impinged on regional courts. Local officials believed that the king's lieutenants were exceeding their traditional authority over military affairs by bypassing established routines of local approval of military levies. Some Londoners felt particularly aggrieved, especially those merchants who were not able to export cloth because of royal control over cloth exports through the monopoly of the Merchant Adventurers (see Chapter 5). The monarchy alienated other Londoners by allowing some craftsmen to operate outside the structure of the London guilds, by trying to regulate construction in London and its growing suburbs, and by attempting to force the city to provide more money for the war with Scotland. The sale of the right to collect royal customs generated controversy as well, particularly as the government sold more privileges to pay off those who collected or "farmed" taxes on its behalf.

Riot in St. Gile's Cathedral, Edinburgh, when the bishop begins to read from the Anglican Book of Common Prayer.

Charles surrounded himself with confidants, advisers, artists, and musicians, whose sense of royal decorum and aesthetic tastes seemed to suggest the influence of continental Catholicism. The queen brought to the court Flemish artists who emphasized the religious themes of the Catholic Reformation, serving to convince critics of royal political policy that a plot was afloat, as a contemporary put it, "to seduce the King himself with Pictures, Antiquities, Images & other vanities brought from *Rome.*"

John Pym.

Those who consistently supported Parliament became known as the supporters of "Country," while those who supported virtually unlimited monarchical prerogatives were identified with "Court." While the terms "Court" and "Country" are something of a simplification and virtually disappeared in the 1640s, they do reflect essential political differences during the political crisis.

Titled nobles, of whom there were about 1,200 in the country, generally supported the king. Gentry formed the core of the political opposition to the king. Nonetheless, not all of those in the gentry supported Parliament against the king. During the previous century, many gentry had extended their landholdings, and men enriched by commerce or service in the law or army had become part of the gentry through the purchase of land. The roots of confrontation may have come from the struggle of these economically dynamic gentry to obtain political power commensurate with their rising station in English life. And their economic success may have affronted the wealthiest nobles, most of whom supported the king. Some gentry of lesser means who had fallen upon hard times may have blamed the monarchy for their plight and hence supported Parliament. On the other hand, gentry in the economically less advanced north of England may have supported the king as a conservative force for stability.

The English Civil War has been called the "Puritan Revolution," even though its causes extended beyond the question of religion and Puritans were not alone in resisting the monarchy. There were many Puritans in Parliament, including the body's leader, John Pym (1584–1643). A brilliant speaker and debater, Pym was a zealot, an impetuous and perhaps even paranoid man whose strong convictions were in part defined by an obsession that a "popish plot" existed to restore Catholicism to England.

Puritans dominated the ranks of the lesser gentry in eastern England, areas that took the side of Parliament during the Civil War.

As the political crisis grew in the 1630s, the authority of Anglican bishops, their appointment as state officials, and their right to nominate ministers also smacked to many of "popery." Charles I echoed the famous statement of his father, James I, "No bishops, no king!"—an assertion that would come back to haunt him. Laud expanded the power of ecclesiastical courts, which tried people accused of offenses against the Church of England. This reminded some people of the Spanish Inquisition.

Moving toward Conflict

Having dissolved the "Short Parliament" in May 1640, Charles again convoked a newly elected Parliament the following October. That summer brought religious and social turmoil. Ordinary people smashed altar rails and shattered stained-glass windows. The crown's strengthening of the army with Catholic Irish regiments, commanded by Thomas Wentworth, who was now a supporter and adviser of the king and had been named the earl of Strafford, confirmed to credulous ears that a "popish plot" was in the works. The English army suffered defeat in Scotland, and the war required yet more funds. Led by Pym, Parliament turned its wrath upon Charles's advisers, perpetuating the half-truth that the "eleven years of tyranny" had been the fault of bad advice. It indicted Strafford, who was tried and executed in London before a rejoicing throng. Parliament denounced as illegal the most unpopular royal acts during the previous eleven years (including many of the new taxes introduced by the king) and abolished some of the courts controlled by the monarchy. Parliament proclaimed that it could only dissolve itself, and that in the future the king would have to summon it every three years.

In the meantime, Irish peasants, who were overwhelmingly Catholic, rose up against the English in 1641 and killed many Protestant landlords. Furthermore, many believed that the king could not or would not repress the insurgents. The Irish rebellion highlighted crucial questions about the rights of Parliament by making urgent the issue of who controlled the militia.

In November 1641, Parliament passed the Grand Remonstrance. Presenting what Parliament considered a history of royal misdeeds, the document denounced "a malignant and pernicious design of subverting the fundamental laws and principles" of English government and called for religious and administrative reforms. Its passage by a narrow margin indicated that Parliament remained divided over how far to carry its opposition to royal policies. Puritans, who narrowly controlled the House of Commons, now wanted to reform both church and state. Wealthy nobles began to form a solid bloc around the cause of the king, fearing that reform might weaken their influence. Shortly after the passage of the

Grand Remonstrance, the high sheriff of Lancashire called upon "gentlemen" to take arms with their tenants and servants on behalf of the king "for the securing of our own lives and estates, which are now ready to be surprised by a heady multitude." In some places, fighting began that month, as both sides fought for control of the militias.

Emboldened by an intransigent faction in his court, the king attempted a bold coup against Parliament in January 1642. He personally led several hundred armed soldiers into Parliament and ordered the arrest of Pym and several other leaders. Forewarned, Pym and other leaders had left the House of Commons before Charles arrived, and they were protected in London by artisans and craftsmen. Fearing for his safety in London, where people had become more forceful in their support of Parliament and their demands for radical reform, Charles and his family headed north to more friendly country, and his supporters left Parliament. In June, Parliament promulgated the "Nineteen Propositions," which denounced the confrontational royal policy. In August 1642, Charles mobilized his forces at Nottingham.

Taking Sides

As civil war spread, Parliament's soldiers came to be known as "Roundheads" for the short, bowl-shaped haircuts many of them wore. The king's "Cavaliers" liked to think of themselves as fighting the good fight for God and king against those who would shatter social harmony by making "subjects princes and princes slaves." But so far as civil wars go, there was little actual fighting. Relatively short "campaign seasons" were interrupted by winter. There were only four major battles, and only one was very far from London (see Map 6.1). The two sides fought to a draw on October 23, 1642, at Edgehill, south of Birmingham. When a royal military advance on London was turned back, Charles set up headquarters in Oxford, fifty miles northwest of London. In February 1643, the king rejected Parliament's terms for a settlement. When a second royal march on London failed, both sides intensified massive propaganda campaigns to win support. The war became a war of words, among the first in history. More than 22,000 newspapers, newsletters, pamphlets, broadsides, sermons, and speeches were published between 1640 and 1661. At least 2,000 pamphlets were published in 1642, an average of almost 6 a day.

Life in thousands of villages was disrupted, if not by actual fighting and the death of conscripted or volunteer soldiers, then by requisitions, plundering, and general hardship. About 10 percent of the English population was forced to leave home during the war. Many counties—perhaps most—were neutral, as local leaders struggled to maintain control and keep their counties free of fighting and devastation.

Each side had to organize the pursuit of the war. In regions of royalist allegiance, the Cavaliers utilized existing administrative hierarchies, above

MAP 6.1 THE ENGLISH CIVIL WAR   Major battles during the English Civil War, as well as Cavalier and Roundhead strongholds.

all the justices of the peace. Lacking London's credit institutions, Charles financed the war by selling more titles and with gifts and loans from nobles, but he also sought approval for forced levies by calling meetings of freeholders or grand juries.

The Roundheads, in keeping with Parliament's insistence on local pre-rogatives and resistance to monarchical centralization, kept civil, fiscal, and military authority relatively decentralized in regions under its control. A regional military structure developed, based on associations of counties pledging mutual assistance in the parliamentary cause. Parliament raised funds through heavy excise and property taxes, confiscating the property of some prominent families supporting the king's cause.

Patterns of allegiance in the English Civil War were influenced by local economic and social considerations. Parliament drew considerable support from the most economically advanced regions—the south and east—while King Charles I retained the allegiance of most of northern and western England. Parliament found support where commercial agriculture had entailed changes in land use. Cultivation for the urban market had flourished in the aftermath of deforestation, the draining of marshlands, and the privatization of common lands through parliamentary acts of enclosure, some of which the monarchy had opposed. Districts in which cloth manufacturing had developed during the previous hundred years were also particularly likely to support Parliament, perhaps because people were no longer totally dependent on wealthy landowners for work. Regions of rich but traditional agriculture, such as in the west, often supported the king, perhaps because economic and social hierarchies survived intact.

Villages became sites for religious and political struggle. Festivals served a social function, bringing villagers together to celebrate the holidays of the year. Puritans, however, considered such festivals frivolous, disruptive, and ungodly. Puritans believed that village festivals eroded social hierarchy and family life with drinking, dancing, and sexual freedom. Puritans particularly disliked those festivals called "church ales," which were drinking bouts often overseen by gentry and even clergy, raising money for the Anglican Church. Puritans considered bat-and-ball games and a game resembling American football to be unsightly free-for-alls that defamed the Sabbath. In regions where traditional festive rituals survived the Puritan assault against them, support was strong for the King and for the wealthy country gentlemen who encouraged the merriment of village festivals.

Oliver Cromwell and the New Model Army

In 1643, Parliament allied with the Scots, many of whom were Presbyterians delighted to participate in what they considered a holy war against the Anglican episcopacy. John Pym's sudden death at the end of that year did not lessen Parliament's resolve to force the king to capitulate. In July 1644, Parliament's army combined with the Scots to defeat the Cavaliers at Marston Moor, near York. About 45,000 men fought in this battle, the largest of the English Civil War. This gave Parliament control of northern England. Scottish participation only added to the determination of the "war party" faction to whom Charles listened.

Oliver Cromwell (1599–1658), who led the Roundheads to victory at Marston Moor, emerged as the leader of Parliament. Cromwell was born into a gentry family, "by birth a gentleman living neither in considerable height nor yet in obscurity," as he put it. He never lost what well-heeled gentry considered his rough edges. Several years before being elected to

Oliver Cromwell.

Parliament in 1640, he had undergone—perhaps during serious illness—a deep spiritual conversion. Cromwell became convinced that God had chosen him to be one of the elect, and his strong Puritan views led him into politics. Cromwell displayed idealism as well as the stubbornness of someone who can easily convince himself that he is right all the time.

Combining three existing armies, Parliament formed the New Model Army in 1645. Cromwell instilled strict discipline, and the Roundhead soldiers' morale improved with regular wage payments. Unlike its predecessors, the New Model Army won grudging good will in the counties by paying for supplies and not plundering, in contrast to the king's army, which was short on funds.

Divisions within Parliament

Two political groups emerged in Parliament: Presbyterians and Independents. Presbyterians, a majority within Parliament, were moderates in the sense that they were initially reluctant to fight the king to the finish. Originally a pro-Scottish group that had rallied behind John Pym, most (despite the name "Presbyterians") were Puritans. Opposed to the bishops' authority, they rejected religious toleration and wanted an established national Calvinist Church in which lay elders would select ministers. They supported the execution of Archbishop Laud at the beginning of 1645. But they were ready to accept a negotiated settlement with the king.

The Independents were militant Puritans who desired more drastic changes than the Presbyterians. They wanted the church to be a loose alliance of congregations that would choose their own ministers, in the context of the seventeenth century a more radical position than that of the Presbyterians. The Independents were less willing to compromise with the king on the issue of parliamentary prerogatives. They favored state toleration of some religious dissent and opposed an established church. Some of them even desired more far-reaching political reforms that would protect individual rights. Cromwell's rise to leadership reflected the ascendancy of the Independents in Parliament.

Cromwell began to purge Presbyterian commanders within the New Model Army, replacing them with Independents who were loyal to him. Singing psalms as they rushed fearlessly into battle, Cromwell's "Ironsides," as his troops were called, maintained an air of invincibility. In June 1645, the New Model Army routed the royalists. Charles surrendered to the Scots a year later, hoping to obtain a less draconian peace than if he capitulated directly to Parliament. But the Scottish army soon cleared out of England, leaving the king in the custody of Parliament in February 1647.

Crowds watch Puritan soldiers leaving London, c. 1647. Note the "roundheads" and the armed preacher urging them on.

Radicals

As the war dragged on, England fell into virtual anarchy amid growing resentment over the billeting of soldiers, food shortages, and rising prices. The English Civil War unleashed forces that seemed to challenge the foundation of social and political order. During the siege of royalist Oxford, a hungry sentry called down to the besieging forces, "Roundhead, fling me up half a mutton and I will fling thee down a lord!" At times the Roundheads appeared to hold back as if wary of the consequences of victory. Even some gentry who had taken the side of Parliament feared that a crushing victory might unleash "turbulent spirits, backed by rude and tumultuous mechanic persons [i.e., ordinary people]" and attacks against property by the mob, "that many headed monster."

In such an uncertain climate, new, more radical religious groups proliferated. Baptists did not believe that children should be baptized, reasoning that only adults were old enough to choose a congregation and hence be baptized. Some Baptists permitted couples to marry by simply making a declaration before the congregation.

"Levellers" were far more radical, demanding major reforms. They called for new laws that would protect the poor as well as the wealthy. Levellers, many of whom had been Baptists, found adherents among small property owners, including many London artisans, as well as great support in the New Model Army, "wherein there is not one lord." Other Levellers may have begun as staunch Puritans before becoming more radical. Royalists and Presbyterians both held that the Levellers wanted "to raise the servant against the master, the tenant against the landlord, the buyer against the seller, the borrower against the lender, the poor against the rich."

Yet, while the Levellers proposed a new English constitution and demanded sweeping political reforms that would greatly broaden the electoral franchise, they still based these rights on property ownership, which they defined as men having "a permanent fixed interest in this kingdom," excluding wage laborers and servants. Women were also prominent in Leveller petition campaigns, but calls for female enfranchisement were extremely rare.

Smaller groups of radicals soon went even further. The "Diggers," who called themselves the "True Levellers," denied the claim of Parliament to speak for Englishmen and opposed the private ownership of land. They espoused agrarian reform and even began a brief colony that began to share wasteland with the poor and the landless. Another group, the "Ranters," rejected the idea of heaven, hell, and sin, and postulated that true salvation could be found only in drink and sex.

To some people in mid-seventeenth-century England, the world indeed seemed "turned upside down." Some radicals opposed not only hierarchical authority within the state, but also paternal authority within the family. The assumption that the king ruled his nation as a husband and father directed his wife and children had been prominent in early modern political theory. The expansion in the number of literate people in southern England, in particular, exposed more people not only to the writings of the New Testament but also to radical ideas propagated in pamphlets. Some of these pamphlets demanded education for women and denounced the subjugation of women to their husbands. Conservatives railed against such claims, echoing what seemed to be a growing anxiety about patriarchal order and an increasing concern about "unruly women" defying their husbands.

Parliament's Victory

Pressured by the Presbyterians, who feared the radicals of the New Model Army, Parliament ordered the disbandment of part of it without paying the soldiers. The army, however, refused to disband, and instead it set up a general council, some of whose members were drawn from the lower officer corps and the rank and file. This reflected Leveller influence within a body that had been previously loyal only to Cromwell.

The New Model Army considered Parliament's attempts to disband it to be part of a plot against the Independents. A few regiments mutinied and prepared a political platform, the *Agreement of the People*, written by London Levellers. This text anticipated later theorists by claiming that "freeborn Englishmen," not just property owners, were the source of political authority and that "every man that is to live under a government ought first by his own consent to put himself under that government; and . . . that the poorest man in England is not at all bound in a strict sense to that government that he hath not had a voice to put himself under." Cromwell ruthlessly restored order in the New Model Army, subduing mutinous Leveller regiments and ordering several leaders shot.

In November 1647, King Charles escaped the custody of Parliament and fled to the Isle of Wight. At the beginning of the new year, against the opposition of Presbyterians who hoped that some compromise could still be reached with the king, the House of Commons passed a motion that no further addresses should be made to the king. The implication was that Parliament alone should proceed to establish a new government without Charles's participation or consent, probably indicating that Cromwell and many other members of Parliament had already decided that Charles I should be put to death and a republic declared.

In May 1648, a group of Presbyterian moderates joined Cavalier uprisings in southern Wales and southern England. Charles had been secretly negotiating with the Presbyterian Scots, hoping that they now would join an alliance of Anglicans and members of Parliament who had become disillusioned with Cromwell's radicalism. But the New Model Army turned back a Scottish invasion in August and besieged royalist forces in Wales surrendered after eight weeks. The king was now being held on the Isle of Wight, "more a Prisoner," as an observer put it, "than ever . . . and could not goe to pisse without a guarde nor to Goffe [to play golf]."

Believing itself the virtuous repository of English liberties, a detachment of the New Model Army, under Colonel Thomas Pride, surrounded the Parliament house and refused to let Presbyterians—and some Independents as well—enter. "Pride's Purge," which took place without Cromwell's consent or knowledge, left a "Rump Parliament" of about a fifth of the members sitting.

The Rump Parliament, dominated by Independents, then appointed a High Court to try the king on charges of high treason. Charles refused to defend himself and was found guilty. Charles I was executed at Whitehall on January 30, 1649, the first monarch to be tried and executed by his own subjects. Charles's beheading had immediate international repercussions; one power after another severed diplomatic relations with England, and the tsar of Russia ended the exclusive trade privileges of English merchants in his realm.

The Puritan Republic and Restoration

The Rump Parliament abolished the monarchy and the House of Lords. It established a Puritan republic, the Commonwealth of England, with Cromwell as its leader. In 1649, Cromwell brutally put down the Irish uprising, that had gone on for eight years. The Act of Settlement in 1652 expropriated for English colonists the land of two-thirds of the Catholic property owners in Ireland and assured the ascendancy of English Protestants in that strife-torn land for the next 300 years. The Scottish Protestants did not fare any better for having supported Charles, however belatedly, as Cromwell in 1650–1651 then conquered Scotland. Having defeated both the Irish and the Scots, Cromwell fought the Dutch Republic from 1652 to 1654 and Spain from 1655 to 1659, with an eye toward reducing the power of both these economic rivals.

The Rump Parliament met until 1653. It would not dissolve itself and so Cromwell, torn between his determination to assure a "godly reformation" in England and a mistrust of political assemblies, dissolved it in a military coup. The Long Parliament (if the Rump session is counted) had lasted since 1640. Cromwell now picked 140 men to serve as a new Parliament. This body came to be called the Barebones Parliament, named after one of its members, a certain "Praise-God Barbon," a leather merchant.

England became a military dictatorship. The army council dissolved the Barebones Parliament six months later and proclaimed a Protectorate under a new constitution, the Instrument of Government. That year, 1653, Cromwell took the title "Lord Protector" and held almost unlimited power. Thomas Hobbes's description two years after the execution of Charles I of the natural state of mankind as being one of war, "everyone against everyone," seemed to apply to England. What could save England?

Eyewitness depiction of Charles I's execution, January 30, 1649.

To Hobbes, England could be saved only by a powerful state, "that great Leviathan . . . to which we owe . . . our peace and defense."

The Puritan republic turned out to be as oppressive as the monarchy of the Stuart kings. Cromwell imposed taxes without parliamentary approval and purged Parliament when it disagreed with him. When Parliament produced its own constitution, Cromwell sent its members packing in 1655. But, like Charles I before him, he was obliged to recall Parliament the following year to vote money for war, this time against Spain.

Although Cromwell granted *de facto* religious freedom to all Puritan sects (including the Presbyterians, Independents, and Baptists), he continued to deny such freedom to both Anglicans and Catholics. He did, however, allow Jews, who had not been allowed in England since 1290, to return in 1655. Dividing the country into twelve districts, he developed a more efficient civil service. But Cromwell lost support as a result of many financial impositions made in order to fight the Dutch and supply an army of 50,000 men in England. The Lord Protector proved to be a better military administrator than a civilian one. Cromwell also alienated people through his exhortations that people behave in "godly" Puritan ways, as set forth in a code enforced by the army. Cromwell began to wear armor under his clothes and took circuitous routes in order to foil assassins who might be stalking him.

Cromwell claimed to be a humble caretaker of government who would keep order until godly righteousness prevailed. In 1657, a newly elected Parliament produced another constitution and offered Cromwell the throne of England. He refused, perhaps because he believed God had spoken to him against the monarchy and because a monarchy would alienate elements in the army. But he accepted the terms of the "Humble Petition and Advice," introducing a second house of Parliament (a nominated House of Lords) and a quasi-monarchical position for the Lord Protector, including the right to name his successor. Cromwell then dissolved Parliament because republicans in it were hostile to what seemed a drift in a monarchical direction. A year later, Cromwell died, succeeded by his considerably less able son, Richard, the New Protector (1626–1712). Then several military successors stumbled on, backed by remnants of the New Model Army.

Increasingly, however, it seemed to the upper classes that only the restoration of the Stuart monarchy could restore order in England. Charles (1630–1685), the heir to the throne of his executed father, lived in exile in Holland. Armed force would play a deciding role in this tumultuous time. General George Monck (1608–1670), a former royalist officer who now commanded the army in Scotland, had shrewdly kept Scottish tax money to pay his soldiers. His army became the only reliable force in England. After Parliament tried to assert control over the army, Monck marched with his forces on London and dissolved Parliament. New elections returned an alliance of royalists and Presbyterians, giving Parliament a moderate majority inclined to accept a restoration. When Charles issued a conciliatory proclamation, Parliament invited him to assume the throne of England. Eleven years after the execution of his father, he crossed the English Channel in May 1660 and was crowned King Charles II on April 23, 1661.

Preoccupied with protecting his throne against future challenges, Charles II also manifested considerable charm, energy, courage, unfailing good humor, and loyalty to those who had remained loyal to him (with the notable exception of the queen, to whom he was anything but faithful). He could also lash out vindictively when he believed himself betrayed. He earned the affection of most of his subjects because the return of monarchy seemed also to end the extended period of division and chaos.

The English Civil War had been a victory for parliamentary rule. Yet in some ways the Restoration turned the clock back to before the conflict. The Church of England again became the Established Church; the crown refused to extend official toleration to other religions. The Church of England expelled Presbyterian ministers in 1661–1662. Once again the king was chronically short of money and depended on Parliament for funds. Parliament demobilized the New Model Army, the last remnant of Cromwell's rule.

With the Civil War over and the monarchy restored by a victorious Parliament, the way seemed clear for England to continue to expand its commerce and influence in a climate of social and political peace. Between 1660 and 1688, the tonnage hauled by English ships more than doubled, as the merchant fleet established trade routes to Newfoundland, Virginia, and the Caribbean. In 1664, a small English force seized the Dutch colony of New Amsterdam, which became New York. Although it was retaken by the Dutch, it became an English colony again in 1674. England's colonies gradually developed in North America, and settlements took hold on the coasts of India and Africa, where slaves were the principal commodity. Tobacco, calico, furs, sugar, chocolate, and rum began to arrive in England, changing tastes and habits of consumption. London became a booming port, and the East India Company emerged as a powerful force in shaping royal policy. Lloyd's of London began to insure vessels sailing to the New World in 1688. By then almost half of England's ships were trading with India or America. Exports and imports increased by a third by 1700.

England's foreign policy entered a new, aggressive period in support of English manufacture and commerce. To undermine Dutch commercial competition, Parliament passed a series of Navigation Acts between 1651 and 1673, requiring that all goods brought to England be transported either in English ships or in those belonging to the country of their origin. This led to three wars with the Netherlands (1652–1654, 1665–1667, and 1672–1674).

THE GLORIOUS REVOLUTION

The struggle for sovereignty between Parliament and the Stuart kings had been manifested in parliamentary opposition to new taxes and fears that Arminianism would lead to the restoration of Catholicism in England. The issues of royal authority and Catholicism led to another constitutional crisis and planted the seeds for what became known as the Glorious Revolution of 1688, when Parliament summoned a new king to rule England. Moreover, Parliament would also pass the Bill of Rights, which would enshrine the rights of Parliament and of the English people, above all, property owners.

Stuart Religious Designs

After the return of the Stuarts to power, religion once again surfaced as a divisive issue in England, threatening to shatter the political unity seemingly achieved with the Restoration in 1660. Charles II had returned from France if not with strong Catholic sympathies at least with the conviction that he owed toleration to Catholics, who had supported his father. Again, a Stuart king's seemingly provocative policies generated determined opposition from Parliament, which asserted its prerogatives.

Charles favored Catholics among his ministers and tried to appeal to Dissenters in order to build a coalition against the Church of England. In response, Parliament passed a series of laws against Dissenters (1661–1665), known as the Clarendon Code. The Act of Corporation (1661) required all holders of office in incorporated municipalities to receive communion in the Anglican Church. The Act of Uniformity (1662) stated that all ministers had to use the Anglican Book of Common Prayer. Nonconformists had to take an oath that they would not try to alter the established order of church and state in England. Hundreds of Quakers, members of a pacifist group formed in 1649, refused to pay tithes or take oaths and were incarcerated, left to die in prison.

In 1670, Charles II signed a secret treaty of alliance with Louis XIV of France. He promised the king of France that he would declare himself a Catholic when the political circumstances in England were favorable. In return, he received subsidies from the French monarch. Charles ended restrictions on religious worship and laws that had been directed at Catholics and Dissident Protestant groups. The hostile reaction to his decision, however, forced the king to reinstate the restrictive measures. In 1673, Parliament passed the Test Act, which largely superseded the Clarendon Code and excluded non-Anglicans from both military and civil office.

Many people in England suspected that there were plots afoot to restore Catholicism as the state religion. Although Charles II's agreement with

England's Memorial of its Wonderful Deliverance from French Tyranny and Popish Oppression, c. 1688. King Charles II made a secret agreement with Louis XIV of France to declare himself a Catholic, but the English people's overwhelming suspicion towards Catholicism, as illustrated in this 1688 engraving, made that impossible.

Louis XIV remained secret, in 1678 a strange man called Titus Oates loudly claimed the existence of a plot by the Catholic Church against England. Oates claimed that the Jesuits, who were popularly identified with Rome, were preparing to assassinate the king and slaughter all English Protestants. They then would proclaim James, Charles's devout Catholic brother, king. (James was heir to the throne since Charles had no legitimate children, although he had a good many who were illegitimate.) Oates had made it all up, as the king knew perfectly well. But he could not speak up because of his own secret promise to Louis XIV of France to restore Catholicism to England.

In the 1670s, two factions had emerged in Parliament that in some ways echoed the split between "Court" and "Country" before the Civil War. Members of Parliament who supported full prerogatives of the monarchy, some of them trumpeting the theories of divine-right monarchy, became known as Tories, corresponding to the "Court" faction. Those members of Parliament who were critical of the king's policies and who espoused parliamentary supremacy and religious toleration became known as Whigs (corresponding to "Country"). Whig leaders orchestrated a plan to exclude James from the royal succession because of his Catholicism. During the ensuing Exclusion Crisis (1678–1681), the Tories defended James as the legitimate heir to the throne of England. When in 1679 some members of Parliament tried to make Charles's illegitimate son heir to the throne, Charles dissolved Parliament. In three subsequent parliamentary elections, Whigs profited from the mood of anti-Catholicism to win a majority of seats.

Parliament's passage in 1679 of the Habeas Corpus Act reflected Whig ascendancy. This forced the government to provide a quick trial for those who were arrested. By establishing the legal rights of individuals accused of crimes, it further limited monarchical authority. The Habeas Corpus Act was thus part of the successful century-long struggle of the House of Commons for the maintenance of its constitutional role in England's governance.

In 1681, Charles II attempted, like his father before him, to rule without Parliament. Two years later, a number of Whigs were charged with plotting to kill both the king and his brother. Charles had them executed. On his deathbed two years later, Charles proclaimed his Catholicism.

Thus, in 1685, Charles II's brother assumed the throne as James II (1633–1701). In Scotland and in western England, royal armies crushed the small insurrections that rose up in favor of Charles's illegitimate son (who was executed). Naive as he was devout, James forgot the lessons of recent history and began to dismiss advisers who were not Catholics.

In 1687, James made Catholics eligible for office. The Dissenters also benefited from toleration, because the new king needed them as allies. The king did not denounce Louis XIV's revocation of the Edict of Nantes in 1685, ending toleration for Huguenots (French Protestants, see Chapter 7). This made English Protestants even more anxious. In 1687, when it became apparent that the queen was pregnant, James boldly predicted the birth of a son and Catholic heir to the throne. For the enemies of the king, the timing of the birth of a son and the fact that the only witnesses were Catholics inevitably sparked rumors that the newborn was not really the king's son but a surrogate baby.

Royal prerogative remained the central constitutional issue. James may have entertained visions of implanting monarchical absolutism in England, a tide that approached from the continent. Certainly he sought to restore Catholicism as the state religion. In April 1688, he issued a declaration of toleration and ordered the Anglican clergy to read it from the pulpit. When seven bishops protested, James put them in prison. The tide was against James, however. When the bishops were tried in court, a jury found them to be not guilty.

The "Protestant Wind"

One of James's Protestant daughters by a previous marriage, Mary (1662–1694), had married the Protestant Dutchman William of Orange (1650–1702). A group of Tories and Whigs now worked together to invite

William to restore Protestantism and, from their point of view, the English constitution. William prepared to invade England from Holland. His followers flooded England with propaganda favorable to his cause.

The context of European international politics seemed favorable to William. Louis XIV's revocation of the Edict of Nantes had outraged the Dutch. Furthermore, the Dutch worried that James's successful restoration of Catholicism to England might make the Dutch Republic more vulnerable to Catholic France. They believed that England was an indispensable partner in helping resist Louis XIV's grand ambitions. The Dutch hoped that a friendly Protestant monarch on the throne of England might even reduce tensions stemming from the trade rivalry between the Dutch Republic and England.

The Catholic continental monarchs would not aid James II. Louis XIV's principal interest remained continental territorial expansion. Despite declaring war on the Dutch Republic, Louis limited his attacks to verbal bluster and the seizure of several Dutch ships in French ports. Emperor Leopold of Austria, another powerful Catholic monarch, was tied up fighting the Turks in the east.

Despite ample evidence that William was planning an invasion of England, James did little to prepare military defenses except to appoint Catholic officers in his new regiments and to bring more troops from Ireland. He relied on his navy to protect his throne. Hoping for a last-minute compromise, he promised to summon a "free" Parliament. But it was too late.

William III of England and Queen Mary, joint rulers of England.

In a declaration promulgated early in October 1688, William accused James of arbitrary acts against the nation, Parliament, and the Church of England. Aided by a munificent wind—later dubbed the "Protestant wind"—that blew his ships to the southwestern coast of England while keeping James's loyal fleet away in the Channel or in port, William landed at Torbay with a force of 15,000 men on November 5, 1688. William marched cautiously to London, encouraged by defections from James's cause. Uprisings on William's behalf occurred sooner than expected in several northern towns, further isolating the king. James was in a state of virtual physical and psychological collapse. At the end of November, he promised to summon Parliament and allow William's supporters to sit. But riots broke out in other towns against his rule and against Catholics. In December, James left England for exile in France. Parliament, victorious again, declared the throne vacant by abdication and invited William and Mary to occupy a double throne.

The Bill of Rights

This "Glorious Revolution" of 1688, less dramatic than the English Civil War, was arguably of more lasting importance in the constitutional evolution of England. Parliament passed a Bill of Rights in 1689 that ratified the Revolution of 1688 and put an end to decades of constitutional battles. Accepted by William and Mary, it became a milestone in English history. It was passed at a time when the rights and influence of representative bodies lay in shambles throughout much of the continent as absolute monarchs—above all, Louis XIV of France—consolidated their power (see Chapter 7). The Bill of Rights reaffirmed the rights of Parliament and guaranteed the rights of property owners to self-government and of the accused to the rule of law. In particular, it reasserted Parliament's financial authority over government by enumerating what a monarch should not do and by reducing royal control over the army. The Toleration Act (1689) stipulated that Protestant Dissenters could hold public services in licensed meeting houses and could maintain preachers. Anglicanism, however, remained the Established Church of England, and only those who were Anglican could hold office. Catholics faced discrimination. They could not occupy the throne and, like Dissenters, they were excluded from government positions.

The English philosopher John Locke (1632–1704), friend of some of the wealthy landowners who sent James II into exile, was specific about the ways in which the power of monarchs ought to be limited. "The end of government," he wrote, should be "the good of mankind," above all, the protection of the right of property. Thomas Hobbes agreed, writing, "The greatest and chief end therefore of men uniting into Commonwealths, and putting themselves under Government is the preservation of their property." But whereas Hobbes, who supported Charles I against Parliament, held that individuals should surrender their rights to the absolute state of unlimited sovereignty in exchange for protection from the "state of nature," Locke argued that the rights of individuals, including the ownership of property, found protection when Parliament's rights limited monarchical prerogatives. Remembering the turmoil of the Thirty Years' War on the continent, Locke also advocated religious toleration and espoused the right of subjects to rise up against tyranny as the English had against Charles I.

The Glorious Revolution also reaffirmed the political domination of the gentry, whose interests Parliament represented above all. The monarchs named nobles to hereditary seats in the House of Lords, but wealthy landowners elected members to the House of Commons. The gentry's economic and social position was more secure than during the inflationary years of the first half of the century. Order and social hierarchy reigned, and the fear of popular disorder ebbed. Benefiting from the consensus of 1688, the elite of wealthy landowners, increasingly more open to newcomers than its continental counterparts, would continue to shape British political life in the eighteenth century.

THE GOLDEN AGE OF THE DUTCH REPUBLIC

The Dutch Republic of the United Provinces (usually known today as the Netherlands, or sometimes simply as Holland, its most populated and prosperous province) was the other European power that defied the pattern of absolute and increasingly centralized rule that characterized seventeenth-century Europe. Spain ruled the Netherlands from 1516, when Holy Roman Emperor Charles V, who had inherited the territories of the dukes of Burgundy, became king of Spain. After a long, intermittent war that had begun in 1566 against Spanish rule (Chapter 5), the Dutch Republic officially became independent in 1648 (see Map 6.2 and above pp. 211–14). The United Provinces, a confederation of republics, had been federalist in structure since the Union of Utrecht in 1579, when the provinces and cities of the Dutch Netherlands came together to form a defensive alliance against the advancing Spanish army. The federalist republic, from which William of Orange had launched his successful invasion of England, resisted the aspirations of the House of Orange for a centralized government dominated by a hereditary monarchy. Like their English counterparts, most people in the Netherlands did not want absolute rule, which they identified with the arbitrary acts of the Catholic Spanish monarchy.

The Structure of the Dutch State

The States General served as a federal legislative body of delegations from each of the seven provinces of the Dutch Republic. Each of the provinces

MAP 6.2 THE NETHERLANDS, 1648   At the conclusion of the Thirty Years' War, the Dutch war of independence also ended, with the northern United Provinces becoming the Dutch Republic and the southern provinces remaining under Spain as the Spanish Netherlands.

held to traditions of autonomy, provincial sovereignty, and religious pluralism. Nobles received automatic representation in the States General. But their economic and political role in the Republic was relatively weak, except in the overwhelmingly agricultural eastern provinces.

The Dutch Republic was in some ways less a republic than an oligarchy of wealthy families who monopolized political power. No republican ideology existed until at least the second half of the seventeenth century. But Dutch citizens enjoyed some basic rights unavailable in most other states at the time. Provincial courts protected the Dutch against both occasional arbitrary acts of the central government and those of town governments. Solid fiscal institutions generated international confidence, permitting the Republic to raise sizable loans as needed.

The princes of the House of Orange served as *stadholders* (chief officials) of the Republic. Through patronage, the Orangists also dominated some high federal appointments, naming sons of nobles to important positions in the army and navy. After the revolt of the Netherlands against Spanish rule, the stadholder had influence, but not authority. He was not a ruler, and could not declare war, legislate, or even participate in the important decisions of the Republic. Many of the Orangist stadholders chafed under the restrictions on their authority, dreaming of establishing a powerful hereditary monarchy. In 1650, William II (1626–1650), stadholder of six of the seven provinces, arrested six leaders of Holland and sent an army to besiege Amsterdam. A compromise reinforced the power of the stadholder. But with William's sudden death two years later, the balance of power swung back to the regents (wealthy merchants and bankers) of the provinces, particularly Holland. Any possibility of the Netherlands becoming an absolute state ended.

Expanding Economy

Despite the war of independence against Spain, the Dutch economy developed more rapidly during the first two-thirds of the seventeenth century than did the economies of its competitors, England and France. In 1609, following the signing of a truce between Spain and the Netherlands, the Amsterdam Public Bank opened its offices in the town hall. The bank's principal function was to facilitate Amsterdam's burgeoning foreign trade with other European countries and overseas by encouraging merchants to make payments in bills drawn on the bank. Foreign merchants were attracted to Amsterdam, particularly after mid-century, when bills of exchange became acceptable as currency. The increased affluence brought by foreign trade helped the Dutch carry on the war against Spain.

Amsterdam's banking, credit, and warehousing facilities were soon unmatched in Europe. Although an ordinance in 1581 had included bankers among those occupations considered disreputable—along with actors, jugglers, and brothel keepers—and therefore excluded them from receiving communion in the Dutch Reformed Church, bankers came to be respected by the beginning of the seventeenth century. Good credit allowed the United Provinces to raise loans by selling negotiable bonds at low interest rates.

The United Provinces, small in territory and population, expanded its agricultural resources during the first half of the seventeenth century. Thousands of workers and horses reclaimed much of the country's most fertile land from the sea. Increased productivity generated an agricultural surplus that was invested in commerce or manufacturing, and a greater food supply sustained a larger population. Commercial livestock raising and capital-intensive farming became lucrative.

The Dutch Republic's population rose by a third between 1550 and 1650, to almost 2 million people, which made it Europe's most densely populated country after several of the Italian states. More than half of the population lived in towns. As Amsterdam became a major international port of trade and London's primary rival, its population rose from about 50,000 in 1600 to about 150,000 by mid-century.

Early in the seventeenth century, construction of three large canals expanded Amsterdam's area by almost four times. These canals permitted boats to dock outside merchants' warehouses, where they were loaded with goods, which they then carried to the large ships of the port. Handsome, tall townhouses reached skyward above new tree-lined streets along the canals. Built for bankers and merchants, the townhouses had narrow and increasingly ornamented facades, dauntingly steep staircases, and drains and sewers. The city spread out from the port along the semi-radial canals. Thus, the Dutch Republic benefited not only from relatively good roads, which expedited internal trade, but also from 500 miles of canals dug during the middle decades of the century.

Dutch traders steadily expanded their range and the variety of goods they bartered. They specialized in bulk goods carried by specially designed long, flat vessels that could be cheaply built and operated. The Dutch Republic's merchant fleet tripled during the first half of the century. Dutch shipbuilding boomed, aided by wind-powered sawmills. The Dutch Republic's 2,500 ships in the 1630s accounted for about half of Europe's shipping. Amsterdam became the principal supplier of grain and fish in

The Amsterdam Bourse in the seventeenth century. Merchants had fixed places at the Stock Exchange where they met to arrange various financial matters.

Canals and rivers expedited internal trade in the Dutch Republic. These boats along the Spaarne at Haarlem carried goods to the port, where they were loaded for distant trade.

Europe as the Dutch dominated the lucrative Baltic trade. Dutch ships carried wheat and rye from Poland and East Prussia, dropping off what was needed for local consumption and then carrying what was left to France, Spain, and the Mediterranean. Dutch fishing boats ousted their English competitors from the rich North Sea fishing grounds and from the whaling waters of the Arctic Sea. Dutch ships hauled most of the iron produced in Sweden. Dutch merchants traded products in Russia, the West Indies, Brazil, Japan, Southeast Asia, and the West African coast. Herring caught by Dutch fishermen and salted for preservation became available in much of Europe, exchanged for salt, wine, and other commodities. When the Thirty Years' War and a Spanish embargo on Dutch commerce reduced some continental trade, Dutch traders successfully developed trade overseas with India, Ceylon, and Indonesia, establishing a vast network of company settlements.

In 1602, a group of investors had founded a private trading company, to which the government of the Dutch Republic granted a monopoly for trade in East Asia. During the 1620s and 1630s, Dutch merchants extended their reach in the East Indies, where cinnamon, nutmeg, and other valuable spices were produced. The Dutch East India Company proved to be stiff competition for the English company of the same name.

Tolerance and Prosperity

In contrast to England, where religious division led to civil war, the Dutch Republic remained a relative haven of toleration in an era of religious hatred. During the last decades of the sixteenth century, perhaps 60,000 Huguenots fled to the Dutch Republic to escape persecution in France and the Spanish Netherlands. In 1631, about a third of the wealthiest residents of Amsterdam had moved there from the Spanish Netherlands. Published works circulated throughout the Netherlands defending the rights of religious dissidents, including Mennonites, Lutherans, Quakers fleeing England, and Dutch Collegiants (a dissident Protestant group). By 1672, Amsterdam's Jewish community numbered 7,500 in a city of 200,000 people. Most were immigrants from the German states, and they spoke Yiddish among themselves, as well as German and Dutch. Many other Jewish families had come from Spain. The municipal government rejected a request by Christian merchants that their Jewish competitors be restricted, as in many European cities, to a specific neighborhood, or ghetto. The Amsterdam regents built 1,000 dwellings for refugees, and the town of Haarlem established a home for widows and daughters of men who had come to the Republic to flee persecution. Refugees from religious persecution in other countries contributed to the prosperity of the Dutch Republic.

Nonetheless, despite the religious toleration generally accorded in the Dutch Republic, the Dutch Reformed Church, a strict Calvinist religion, did persecute and discriminate against some religious groups. Dutch Arminians asked for protection from persecution in a Remonstrance (which gave them their most common name, the Remonstrants). Catholics, most of whom lived in the eastern provinces, also faced Calvinist hostility,

Etching of Jews in an Amsterdam synagogue.

Dike breach at Caevarden. Because so much land had been reclaimed from the sea, many of the Dutch lived in chronic fear of flooding.

although many had fought for Dutch independence. Jews were excluded from most guilds, and gypsies were routinely hounded and persecuted. Overall, however, toleration seemed less divisive to the Dutch than intolerance, and it seemed to make economic sense as well.

The Dutch Republic blossomed like the famous tulips that were so popular in Holland (which, in fact, had been originally imported from Turkey). To the eyes of a French visitor, Amsterdam was "swollen with people, chock-full of goods, and filled with gold and silver." The Dutch in the middle decades of the seventeenth century reached a level of prosperity unmatched in Europe at the time. Real wages rose in the Republic during the last half of the century while falling elsewhere. Dutch families enjoyed a relatively varied diet, consuming more meat and cheese—as well as, of course, fish—than households elsewhere in Europe. The smell of fruit that had ripened on voyages from southern Europe and of expensive tobacco filled the air of Amsterdam. Europe's finest market offered a plethora of colonial goods, such as coffee, tea, cocoa, ginger, and other spices, dried and pickled herring and other fish, a wide range of grains, finished cloth from Antwerp and Florence, Silesian linens, and English woolens. Dutch manufacturers, with windmills providing power, found lucrative outlets for draperies, worsteds, papers, books, and jewels. At the beginning of the century, Amsterdam had almost 200 breweries and more than 500 taverns.

Although prosperity reached far down the social ladder, the Dutch Republic also had its poor, who lived in the narrow streets around the

Bourse (Stock Exchange), in poor farmhouses in the eastern flatlands, and in the huts of ethnic Frisian fishermen exposed to the brutal waves and wind of the North Sea. The urban poor occasionally rioted and sometimes stole in order to survive. The proliferation of charitable institutions demonstrated Dutch compassion but also the desire to confine vagrants and beggars, as well as a capacity to lash out in brutal repression when patience with the poor grew thin. Beatings, floggings, branding, and even death remained common forms of punishment, and gallows stood at the main gates of large cities.

Yet despite prosperity, a sense of precariousness and vulnerability permeated the Republic. The armies of the ambitious king of France camped across the low-lying Southern Netherlands (now Belgium). The Republic had almost no natural resources and was subject to sudden calamities brought by weather. A good part of the Dutch Netherlands would have been under water were it not for the famous dikes. These occasionally broke with catastrophic consequences long remembered (a flood in 1421 had claimed over 100,000 lives). A sense that disaster might be looming was reflected by the popularity in the Republic of novels and histories about disasters. This may explain the sense of solidarity and duty that brought people of various classes together against Spanish rule.

Seventeenth-Century Dutch Culture

Dutch painting in the golden age of the seventeenth century reflected not only the Republic's commercial wealth, but also its toleration and openness to secular styles and subject matter. The Dutch press, too, enjoyed relative freedom; books were printed in the Republic that could not have been printed elsewhere. The first English and French newspapers were both published in 1620, not in London and Paris, but in Amsterdam. Dutch publishers diffused knowledge of the Scientific Revolution (see Chapter 8). Dutch writers and poets discovered their own language, translated Latin authors, and popularized Dutch accounts of the revolt against Spain.

Dutch painting reflected Dutch society, particularly the wealth and taste of the middle class. Like the artists of the Renaissance, Dutch painters depended on the patronage of people of means, particularly wealthy Amsterdam merchants. Although Delft and several other towns each claimed their own style, the great port of Amsterdam dominated the art market. Some shopkeepers and craftsmen were prosperous enough to buy a painting or two, and some well-off peasants did so as well.

Holland's regents, in particular, patronized Dutch painting. In contrast, the princes of Orange and some nobles patronized French and other foreign artists whose work reflected baroque themes associated with the Catholic Reformation found in the Southern Netherlands. Flanders became a northern outpost of the Catholic Reformation, encouraging religious themes with emotional appeal. By contrast, in the Dutch Republic ecclesiastical artistic patronage was generally absent, and the Dutch Reformed Church ordered the removal of paintings from its churches.

For the most part, Dutch painters looked to picturesque urban and rural scenes within their own country for inspiration. The Dutch school retained much of its cultural unity at least through the first half of the seventeenth century for several reasons. Until 1650, the Republic remained relatively isolated from outside cultural influences, despite the arrival of refugees and immigrants. Very few Dutch artists and writers had the resources to travel as far as Italy or even France; even those who earned a comfortable living showed little inclination to go abroad. The group paintings of merchants or regents and municipal governments were usually commissioned by the subjects themselves, as in the case of Rembrandt van Rijn's *The Syndics of the Cloth Guild* (1662, see below) and his *The Night Watch* (1642), a theatrically staged masterpiece presenting a group of city officials in uniform.

Rembrandt (1606–1669) was the son of a miller from Leiden and the grandson of a baker. He was one of a handful of Dutch painters who amassed a fortune, allowing him to marry the daughter of a municipal official. Certainly few artists have so successfully portrayed human emotions through the use of color, light, and shadow. Despite his posthumous fame, in his own time the brooding Rembrandt was in some ways a tragic figure, a loner isolated from other painters. He bickered with his patrons and squandered most of what he made. He lost his investments in the Dutch

Rembrandt's *The Syndics of the Cloth Guild* (1662).

East India Company. Rembrandt increasingly became his own favorite subject, and he thereafter undertook little more than self-portraits, of which there are at least eighty, revealing a thinly disguised sadness.

Dutch painters depicted everyday life. The prolific Jacob van Ruisdael (c. 1628–1682) mastered the visual effects of light on figures, trees, and household objects. Delft-born Jan Vermeer (1632–1675) was less productive and less well known. But his remarkable ability to place simple scenes of ordinary people in astonishing light exemplifies the Golden Age of Dutch painting. Within the Dutch school of the seventeenth century, only Rembrandt frequently turned to the classical biblical themes that were so predominant in Flemish art. Although seascapes and naval scenes proliferated, there were few canvases depicting battles, a favorite subject in absolute states, and those took their place on the large walls of noble châteaux, not in the narrow houses of Amsterdam.

The Dutch considered the household a place of refuge and safety from the struggles of the outside world, as well as the basis of economic, social, and political order, and therefore worthy of artistic representation. Frans Hals (1580–1666) brought middle-class subjects and militia companies to life in remarkably composed individual and collective portraits. The popularity of household scenes in Dutch painting also reflected the Republic's prosperity. Paintings of families at work, at play, or eating were particularly popular. Jan Steen (1626–1679) portrayed boisterous revelers of different means. Still lifes of platters of food became staples for Dutch artists, as in such paintings as *Still Life with Herring* and *Jug Still Life with Lobster*. The banquet became a favorite subject, with all of its accoutrements, such as oak table and chairs, iron cooking pans, elegant plates and drinking vessels, and its rituals, such as the prayer, the careful carving of the meat, and the rounds of toasts.

The relationship between parents and children emerged as another familiar domestic theme. The Dutch painters also frequently portrayed servants, furniture and other household goods, and domestic pets. Women on Dutch canvases appear more equal to men than they were in reality, however.

Like Renaissance painters, Dutch artists considered themselves craftsmen and were apprenticed to a master and then became members of a guild. The majority were of modest means. Most painters were harried by creditors, haunted by debts, and sometimes sold their works at reduced prices. Some painters managed only by dealing in the work of other painters, others by holding another job, such as Steen, who operated a brewery and inn in Delft when he was not working at his easel. Even in the prosperous and sophisticated Dutch Republic, painting proved to be a tough way to earn a living.

THE DECLINE OF THE DUTCH REPUBLIC

The relative decline of Dutch power is perhaps not surprising, given the greater economic resources and population of France and England, its chief rivals. England emerged in the second half of the century as the world's dominant commercial power, although the decline of Dutch trade was not complete until the second or third decade of the eighteenth century.

The Dutch Republic tried to steer a course between England (its greatest commercial rival) and France. But this proved impossible. Wars against England in defense of Dutch commercial interests drained resources. Furthermore, Louis XIV of France had designs on the Netherlands. In 1667, France imposed damaging tariffs on Dutch goods and also forced the Dutch out of the cinnamon-producing island of Ceylon in the Indian Ocean. In Brazil, the Dutch West India Company failed to dislodge the Portuguese. Few Dutch demonstrated much enthusiasm for these distant places, and the Republic's colonial empire lagged behind those of England and Spain, to be sure, but also behind that of France.

With Spain weakened, Louis XIV coveted the Southern Netherlands, the conquest of which would place the Dutch in direct danger. The Dutch Republic therefore had a vested interest in the survival of the Spanish Netherlands as a buffer against the French threat. Should France be able to open the Scheldt River (closed by the Spanish in 1585 with the goal of breaking the Dutch rebellion) to international trade, Antwerp's return to its former prosperity would be at Amsterdam's expense. In 1672, Louis XIV invaded the Dutch Republic, having signed a secret treaty with King Charles II of England (see Chapter 7). French armies quickly occupied all of the Republic except for Holland and one other province. But the Dutch successfully defended the Republic by land and sea, defeating the English fleet and pushing back the French army.

Taking advantage of the invasion, William of Orange (who became King William III of England in 1688) forced the States General to name him stadholder in 1672. He ordered the dikes opened, literally flooding the French into retreat. Royalist mobs murdered the leading official of the Republic, several influential regents of Holland who had dedicated themselves to keeping the stadholders in place, and other leaders of the province of Holland. Supporters of the House of Orange eased into important political positions in that province. The Orangists controlled the Republic's foreign policy until the end of the century, but they still could not impose a monarchy on the provinces. With William's death in 1702, the main Orange dynastic line ended.

After the Glorious Revolution in England in 1688, the United Provinces allied with England and Sweden, fearing that Louis XIV of France might invade the Netherlands again. The alliance helped stave off the French threat in the last decades of the century, but at the same time it dragged

The Siege of Maastricht by the armies of King Louis XIV. The Netherlands, weakened by damaging tariffs, became vulnerable to attacks by France and England.

the small country into a series of wars with France that lasted until the mid-eighteenth century, necessitating considerable spending on armies and southern fortifications.

Although the Dutch remained successful traders through the first decades of the eighteenth century, the relative decline of Dutch influence in Europe could be first seen by about 1670 or 1680. Some luxury products, such as linen and Delft porcelain, continued to sell abroad, but Holland's textile industry and shipbuilding failed to keep pace with those of its rivals, above all England. Higher wages in the Republic and a lack of technological innovation were at least partially to blame. Furthermore, some Dutch entrepreneurs invested in the colonies, land, government stocks, or even in English manufacturing, not in Dutch industry. Businessmen reduced investment in agriculture and land reclamation as prices fell.

Spain's golden age of art coincided with its decline as a great power. In contrast, Dutch painting languished with the nation's decline. Painters began looking abroad for inspiration and, in doing so, lost some originality. In the 1650s, the Amsterdam regents ignored the influence of the Dutch school when planning the construction and decoration of the new town hall, which combined Italian classicism and the Flemish baroque flamboyance. Some Dutch leaders now took pride in speaking French, believing it the language of good taste. French classicism overwhelmed Dutch literature and poetry. Although the French military invasion of

1672 failed, a cultural invasion succeeded. Dutch artists began to offer pale imitations of French classical works.

The originality of Dutch political life also waned with relative economic decline. The great merchant families maintained increasingly tight control over the position of regent and other influential posts. A form of municipal corruption ("contracts of correspondence") allowed them to divide up or even purchase lucrative government positions. Spectacular cases of social mobility became rarer. More regents were now landowners, who had little in common with merchants who had vital interests in government policies. After 1650, no major cultural figures emerged from regent families. There were fewer paintings of attentive and hardworking municipal and provincial officials. Their simple style of life disappeared.

Government became more rigid, more distant from the Dutch people, and less tolerant, persecuting religious dissenters and undertaking a witch hunt against homosexuals. The Dutch army became increasingly one of mercenaries, not citizens. The Dutch Republic's loss of vitality and economic primacy was accompanied by its decline in international affairs.

CONCLUSION

At the dawn of the eighteenth century, England and the Netherlands remained the only non-absolutist states among the major European states. Whereas elsewhere in Europe the kings of Spain and the rulers of France, Prussia, Austria, Russia, and Sweden increased their authority over their subjects. The victory of Parliament in the English Civil War and the Glorious Revolution of 1688 confirmed parliamentary rule in England, defeating the assertion of royal prerogatives that verged on absolute rule. The Bill of Rights of 1689, accepted by the monarchy, guaranteed the rights of Parliament and the rule of law. While the Netherlands entered a period of decline, as had Spain, Great Britain (as England became known in 1707 after the formal union with Scotland) would remain a great power in the eighteenth century, enriched by commerce and empire.

CHAPTER 7

THE AGE OF ABSOLUTISM, 1650–1720

In Louis XIV's France, architects and artists were paid to glorify the monarch. In 1662, the king chose the sun as his emblem; he declared himself *nec pluribus impar*—without equal. To Louis, the sun embodied virtues that he associated with the ideal monarch: firmness, benevolence, and equity. Henceforth, Louis XIV would frequently be depicted as Apollo, the Greek and Roman sun god.

The rulers of continental Europe, including Louis XIV, relentlessly extended their power between 1650 and 1750. The sovereigns of France, Prussia, Russia, Austria, and Sweden, in particular, became absolute rulers, in principle above all challenge from within the state itself. To the east, the power of the Ottoman Empire was itself already absolute. Rulers extended their dynastic domains and prestige. They made their personal rule absolute, based on loyalty to them as individuals, not to the state as an abstraction. Absolute rulers asserted their supreme right to proclaim laws and levy taxes, appointing more officials to carry out the details of governance and multiplying fiscal demands on their subjects. They ended most of the long-standing municipal privileges, which had survived longer in Western Europe than in Eastern Europe, such as freedom from taxation, or the right to maintain independent courts. The absolute state affected the lives of more people than ever before through taxation, military service, and the royal quest for religious orthodoxy.

Absolute rule thus impinged directly on the lives of subjects, who felt the extended reach of state power through, for example, more efficient tax collection. A Prussian recalled that in school no child would question "that the king could cut off the noses and ears of all his subjects if he

The illustration for the cover of Thomas Hobbes' *Leviathan* (1651) depicts the absolute state. Note how the ruler's body is made up of the masses over whom he rules.

wished to do so, and that we owed it to his goodness and his gentle disposition that he had left us in possession of these necessary organs."

Absolutism was, at least in part, an attempt to reassert public order and coercive state authority after almost seventy years of wars that had badly disrupted trade and agricultural production, contributing to social and political chaos. England and Spain had been at war in the last decades of the sixteenth century. Wars of religion had raged through much of Europe on and off for more than a century—above all, the Thirty Years' War (1618–1648). The Dutch war of independence against Spain began in 1572 and did not officially end until 1648. The tumultuous decade of the 1640s was particularly marked by political crises. The wars had led to often dramatic increases in taxes, which quadrupled in Spain under Philip II, and five times in France between 1609 and the end of the Thirty Years' War in 1648. During the 1640s, the English Civil War led to the execution of King Charles I in 1649 (see Chapter 6). In France, the period of mid-century rebellion known as the Fronde included a noble uprising against the crown and determined, violent peasant resistance against increased taxation. The multiplicity and seemingly interrelated character of these crises engendered considerable anxiety among social elites:

"These are days of shaking, and this shaking is universal," a preacher warned the English Parliament.

THEORIES OF ABSOLUTISM

The doctrine of absolutism originated with French jurists at the end of the sixteenth century. Like absolutism itself, this doctrine arose in part as a reaction to the chaos of religious wars, which came to an end in the German states with the Peace of Augsburg (1555). This treaty stated that the religion of the ruler would become the religion of the land (*cuius regio, eius religio,* see Chapter 4).

The emergence of theories of absolutism reflected contemporary attempts to conceptualize the significance of the rise of larger territorial states whose rulers enjoyed more power than their predecessors. France was a prime example of this trend. The legal theorist Jean Bodin (1530–1596) had lived through the wars of religion. "Seeing that nothing upon earth is greater or higher, next unto God, than the majesty of kings and sovereign princes," he wrote in the *Six Books of the Republic* (1576), the "principal point of sovereign majesty and absolute power [is] to consist principally in giving laws unto the subjects in general, without their consent." The ruler became the father, a stern but benevolent figure. Bodin, who like many other people in France longed for peace and order, helped establish the political theory legitimizing French absolute rule.

Almost a century later, the political philosopher Thomas Hobbes (1588–1679) emerged as the thundering theorist of absolutism. Although Hobbes lived in England, the least absolute state in Europe and one of the few nations in which the rule of law was separated from the will of the ruler, he had experienced the turmoil of the English Civil War (see Chapter 6). In *Leviathan* (1651), he argued that absolutism alone could prevent society from lapsing into the "state of nature," a constant "war of every man against every man" that made life "solitary, poor, nasty, brutish, and short." People would only obey, Hobbes insisted, when they were afraid of the consequences of not doing so. Seeking individual security, individuals would enter into a type of social contract with their ruler, surrendering their rights in exchange for protection. A ruler's will thus became the almost sacred embodiment of the state. In France, Jacques Bossuet (1627–1704), bishop and tutor to Louis XIV, postulated that kings ruled by "divine right," that is, by virtue of the will of God. Unlike Hobbes's notion of authority based on a social contract, Bossuet held that the ruler's authority stemmed from God alone.

Yet theorists of absolutism recognized the difference between absolute and arbitrary power. Inherent in their theories was the idea that the absolute ruler was responsible for looking after the needs of his people. As Bossuet wrote: "It is one thing for a government to be absolute, and quite another for it to be arbitrary. It is absolute in that it is not liable to constraint, there being no other power capable of coercing the sovereign, who is in this sense independent of all human authority." But he went on, "it does not follow from this that the government is arbitrary, for besides the fact that all is subject to the judgment of God . . . there are also laws, in states, so that whatever is done contrary to them is null in a legal sense; moreover, there is always an opportunity for redress, either at other times or in other conditions." Thus, even according to one of the most determined proponents of absolutism, the monarch, whose legitimacy came from God, nonetheless was subject to limits imposed by reason through laws and traditions. Western monarchs recognized, at least in theory, the necessity of consulting with institutions considered to be representative of interests such as the Church and nobility: parlements (noble law courts), estates, or the Assembly of Notables in France, the Cortes in Spain, and Parliament in non-absolutist England.

CHARACTERIZING ABSOLUTE RULE

Absolute states were characterized by strong, ambitious dynasties, which through advantageous marriages, inheritance, warfare, and treaties added to their dynastic domains and prestige. They had nobilities that accepted monarchical authority in exchange for a guarantee of their status, ownership of land, and privileges within the state and over the peasantry, whether peasants were legally free, as in Western Europe, or serfs, as in Prussia, Poland, and Russia. The absolute states of Central and Eastern Europe—Prussia, Austria, and Russia—shared similar social structures: a strong nobility with ties to rulers who granted concessions and privileges in exchange for cooperation; a subservient peasantry in the process of losing remaining rights to rulers and landlords, including—through progressive enserfment—that of personal freedom; and a relatively weak and politically powerless middle class. Unlike England and the Dutch United Provinces, these states had no representative institutions and few towns of enough size and importance to stand in the way of absolute rule.

Absolute states contained an increasingly centralized and efficient bureaucracy able to extract revenue. And above all, the absolute state was characterized by the deployment of a large standing army capable of maintaining order at home and maintaining or expanding dynastic interests and territories in the context of European power politics.

Although some Western sovereigns were somewhat limited by representative bodies—diets, parlements, estates—absolute monarchies nonetheless created an unprecedented concentration of governing power. Between 1614 and 1788, no king of France convoked the Estates-General, an assembly of representatives from the three estates—clergy, nobility, and commoners—that had been created early in the fourteenth century as an advisory council to the king. The Portuguese assembly of nobles did not meet at all during the eighteenth century.

Monarchs and Nobles

Absolute rulers depended on some degree of compliance by nobles. In each absolute state, the relationship between ruler and nobles determined the specific character of absolutism. This delicate balance is reflected in the oath of loyalty sworn to the king of Spain by the Aragonese nobility: "We who are as good as you swear to you who are no better than we to accept you as our king and sovereign lord, provided you observe all our liberties and laws; but if not, not."

Monarchs negotiated compromises with nobles, awarding titles and privileges for obedience, or at least compliance. In some cases, nobles asserted independence vis-à-vis royal authority. But emphatic assertions of royal authority reduced nobles to the role of junior ruling partners in governance. With some nobles frightened by the social and political turmoil that shook Europe during the first half of the century, they now more willingly served rulers as royal officials and military commanders.

But sovereigns needed to woo nobles to gain their compliance. In exchange for loyalty and in many cases service, rulers confirmed noble privileges and allowed them to continue to dominate state and local government. "Tables of ranks" dividing nobles into distinct grades or ranks were established at the turn of the century by the kings of Sweden, Denmark, Prussia, and Russia, making it clear that noble privileges were bestowed by monarchs. Louis XIV of France (ruled 1643–1715) asserted the right to monitor the legitimacy of all titles and even to confiscate noble estates. In 1668, he ordered the investigation of "false" nobles holding dubious titles. These measures helped the king maintain the loyalty of nobles, some of whom resented those who held titles they considered suspect. The great noble families thereafter enjoyed an even greater monopoly over the most lucrative and prestigious royal and ecclesiastical posts.

Using the augmented power of the state, rulers also placated nobles by ending a turbulent period of peasant uprisings against taxes, obligations to lords, and the high price of grain. Monarchs reduced the vagrancy and petty criminality that had increased since the difficult decade of the 1590s. Insurrections occurred less frequently and were savagely repressed by kings.

The gradual centralization of authority in Eastern Europe left nobles with even more autonomy than they had in the West, allowing Russian lords, Polish nobles, and Prussian nobles (the Junkers) the possibility of further increasing their wealth and power through the extension of their estates, which were worked by serfs. Beginning in the late sixteenth century, such seigneurs made fortunes shipping grain to the West, where prices of cereal and food had risen dramatically in response to population growth. Royal decrees in Prussia and Russia and assembly legislation in Poland progressively limited the right of peasants to move from the land they worked, or even to inherit property. Ravaged by hard times, peasant proprietors had to sell their land to nobles. Impoverished and virtually powerless to resist, peasants lost their personal freedom, a process most marked in Russia. Thus, as feudalism gradually disappeared in Western Europe, it became more prevalent in the East as lords dispossessed peasants from their land. The economic crises of the seventeenth century, including the disruptions of the Thirty Years' War and the decline in Western demand for grain imported from the East because of increased production in the West, only made conditions of life harder for serfs.

In the Ottoman Empire, absolutism was even more despotic. All lands were considered the sultan's private imperial possessions. He granted landed estates to those who served him, but because the sultan recognized no rights of property, no hereditary nobility could develop, in sharp contrast to other European states, to challenge his authority. No representative institutions existed. Towns in the overwhelmingly rural empire had neither autonomy nor rights.

Expanding State Structures

Absolute monarchs extended their authority within their territories by expanding the structure of the state. To fill the most prestigious offices, they chose nobles for their influence and wealth more than for their competence. But they also began to employ commoners as officials to collect vital information, for example, projected revenues or the anticipated number of soldiers available in times of war.

The Renaissance city-states of Italy had created relatively efficient civil administrations and had set up the first permanent diplomatic corps. During the seventeenth century, the apparatus of administration, taxation, and military conscription gradually became part of the structure of the absolute state. The result was that in Europe as a whole, the number of government officials grew about fourfold.

One result of these expanding ranks of officials was the tripling of tax revenues between 1520 and 1670 in France and Spain, and in non-absolutist England as well. To raise money, absolute rulers sold monopolies (which permitted only the holder of the monopoly to produce and sell particular goods) on the production and sale of salt, tobacco, and other commodities, and imposed taxes on the trading towns of their realms. The rulers of France, Spain, and Austria also filled the state coffers by selling hereditary offices. James I of England doubled the number of knights during the first four months of his reign. Queen Christina of Sweden doubled the number of noble families in ten years. In addition, as royal power and prestige rose, the monarchs more easily found wealthy families to loan them money, usually in exchange for tax exemptions, titles, or other privileges.

Absolutism and Warfare

The regular collection of taxes and the expansion of sources of revenue increased the capacity of absolute rulers to maintain standing armies, maintain fortifications, and wage war. By the end of the sixteenth century, Philip II of Spain had allocated three-quarters of state expenditures to pay for past wars or to wage new ones. Appropriately enough, the bureau in Prussia that a century later would oversee tax collection itself evolved from the General War Office, making explicit the close connection between the extraction of state revenue and the waging of dynastic wars.

Absolutist statemaking and warfare had direct and indirect consequences for most of the European population. Kings no longer depended on troops provided by nobles or conscripted by military contractors, thereby avoiding the risk that private armies might challenge royal power. Standing armies continued to grow in size during the eighteenth century (see Table 7.1). During the 1500s, the peacetime armies of the continental powers had included about 10,000 to 20,000 soldiers; by the 1690s, they reached about 150,000 soldiers. For the first time, uniforms became standard equipment for every soldier. The French army, which soon stood at about 180,000 men in peacetime, rose to 350,000 soldiers during the War of the Spanish Succession (1701–1714). The Russian army grew from 130,000 in 1731 to 458,000 in 1796. In contrast, England and the Dutch Republic, two non-absolutist powers, had relatively small armies, and, as sea powers, both depended on their navies.

As absolute monarchs consolidated their power, the reasons for waging international wars changed. The wars of the previous century had been fought, in principle, over the rivalry between the Catholic and Protestant religions, even if dynastic interests were never far from the surface. Now, although religious rivalries still constituted an important factor in international conflict (as in the case of the long struggle between the Muslim

TABLE 7.1. THE SIZE OF EUROPEAN ARMIES, 1690–1814

	1690	1710	1756/60	1789	1812/14
Britain	70,000	75,000	200,000	40,000*	250,000
France	400,000	350,000	330,000	180,000	600,000
Habsburg Emp.	50,000	100,000	200,000	300,000	250,000
Prussia	30,000	39,000	195,000	190,000	270,000
Spain	na	30,000	na	50,000	na
Sweden	na	110,000	na	na	na
United Prov.	73,000	130,000	40,000*	na	na

*Drop reflects peacetime and non-absolutist character of the state.
na Figures not available.
Source: Paul Kennedy, *The Rise and Fall of the Great Powers* (New York: Vintage, 1989), p. 99.

Ottoman Empire and the Catholic Habsburg Empire), "reasons of state" became a prevalent justification for the rulers of France, Prussia, and Russia to make war on their neighbors.

Warfare both encouraged and drew upon the development of credit institutions, further expanding the capacity of the state to raise money to wage war. But as the British and Dutch cases demonstrated, a state did not have to be absolutist in order to marshal sufficient resources to fight sustained wars. English colonial trade generated excise and customs taxes, permitting the expansion of the Royal Navy. The crown's reputation for repayment facilitated raising money through loans at home and abroad. Amsterdam's stature as a great banking center contributed to the ability of the Dutch government to fight extended wars. In contrast, the French monarchy lacked the confidence of wary investors, and despite the sale of privileges, found itself in an increasingly perilous financial situation. Moreover, the French monarchy often had to pay higher rates of interest than private investors because it was a bad credit risk.

Even in peacetime, military expenditures now took up almost half of the budget of the European state. In times of war, the percentage rose to 80 percent, or even more. Inevitably, there came a point even in absolute states when noble and other wealthy families upon which monarchies depended for financial support began to grumble.

Absolutism and Religion

Absolute monarchs intruded in matters of faith by both aiding established churches and limiting ecclesiastical authority within their states. An alliance with established churches helped monarchs achieve and maintain absolute rule. In particular, in Catholic states, the Church's quest for uniformity of belief and practice went hand in hand with the absolutist monarch's desire to eliminate challenges to his authority. Absolute monarchs lent their authority and prestige to the Church, the support of which, in turn, seemed to legitimize absolute monarchical power. The Church helped create an image of the king as a sacred figure, benevolent but strict, who must be obeyed because he served God's interests on earth. In turn, absolute monarchs obliged the Church by persecuting religious minorities.

At the same time that they supported established churches, however, absolute rulers also reduced ecclesiastical autonomy in their realms. Although the Catholic Church was a significant economic, social, and political force in the Catholic absolutist states—France, Spain, Austria, and Portugal—it lost authority to their absolute monarchs. The Church owned as much as two-thirds of the land of Portugal, at least one-tenth of the land in Spain, Austria, and France, half the land of Bavaria and Flanders, and considerable holdings in all of the Italian states. The Church claimed the right to the tithe. But absolute monarchs maintained authority over ecclesiastical appointments, in effect creating national churches to the consternation of the papacy in Rome.

Signs of the victory of absolute rulers over the Catholic Church included eliminating the Inquisition in France and Spain, closing monasteries and expelling religious orders in France and Austria, assuming control over censorship, reducing ecclesiastical authority over marriage, and establishing the principle of state supervision over education.

In France, the very existence of the French, or Gallican Church, defied papal claims to complete authority over the Church. By the Concordat of Bologna in 1516, the pope had given the kings of France virtual control (subject to papal confirmation) over the appointment of bishops and other high ecclesiastical officials in France. It also had allowed the French kings to overrule the judgments of ecclesiastical courts. This irritated French "ultramontane" clergy, who rejected the Gallican Church, recognizing only the authority of the pope "beyond the mountains," that is, over the Alps in distant Rome. The provincial noble parlements, or law courts, by contrast, remained defiantly Gallican. The Gallican Church itself was far more likely to remain loyal to the monarchy that defended its prerogatives. Yet Gallicans themselves insisted that the pope and bishops retain spiritual authority, with the king having a monopoly only on temporal power.

The Turks invading Greece, from a sixteenth-century manuscript.

In Russia, the Orthodox Church—independent of the Greek Orthodox Church since the fifteenth century—and the tsarist autocratic state closely supported each other. The Church taught the faithful to obey the tsar. But in 1716, Peter the Great forced bishops to take an oath that they would not interfere in state affairs. And by the end of the century, the Russian clergy lost the right to be tried in their own courts and became subject to those of the state.

Recognizing no distinction between church and state, the Turkish Ottoman Empire remained a theocracy. The sultan's subjects believed his despotic authority was divine. The Muslim religious hierarchy, which included judges, theologians, and teachers, provided officials for the imperial administration. The supreme religious dignitary occasionally invoked religious law, of which he was the main interpreter, to counter some orders of the sultan, although the latter's political authority remained absolute.

The expansion of the Ottoman Empire had been based upon the concept of the crusading "Holy War" against infidels, or non-Muslims. As the Turks destroyed the Byzantine Empire, capturing Constantinople in 1453, they confiscated many of the resources of the Orthodox Church and other Christian denominations. The Ottoman Turks enslaved prisoners of war, purchased slaves abroad, and imposed slave levies upon the Christians of the empire. Many Christian children had been trained as officials or soldiers and had converted to Islam. The empire also depended on the contributions of nonslave Christians, including skilled Greek sailors who made Turkish galleys feared in the Mediterranean. Some joined the "janissary" infantry, a military corps that assumed police duties in periods of peace.

Yet the Ottoman Empire tolerated religious diversity. As long as non-Muslims did not resist Turkish authority, they were free to practice their religion and to become officials within the empire. In Albania (where alone conversions seemed to have been forced), Bosnia, and Herzegovina, many people, including some nobles, converted to the Muslim faith. Young Christians captured by Turkish fleets could convert to Islam in order to escape a life chained to benches as galley slaves. In contrast, Muslims captured by Christian powers remained galley slaves, even if they converted.

Monumentalism in Architecture and Art

Absolute monarchs utilized the extravagant emotional appeal of monumental architecture. They designed their capitals to reflect the imperatives of monarchical authority. Madrid, Berlin, St. Petersburg, and Versailles outside of Paris were planned, shaped, and invested with symbols of absolute rule. These cities were laid out according to geometric principles. In contrast to the narrow, winding streets of trading cities that had evolved organically from medieval times, straight, wide boulevards were created in one fell swoop. These symmetrical boulevards symbolized the organized and far-reaching power of absolutism and the growth of the modern state. Royal armies paraded down the boulevards to squares or royal palaces, around which were grouped government buildings and noble residences. Barracks housing standing armies also became a prominent feature of the new urban landscape.

Monarchs paid artists and architects to combine baroque elements with a more restrained, balanced classicism, influenced by the early sixteenth-century Roman style of the High Renaissance. This became known as the Louis XIV style. Thus, the facade completing the Louvre palace in

Hyacinthe Rigaud's *Louis XIV* (1701).

Paris, the work of Gianlorenzo Bernini (1598–1680), drew on the architectural style of Roman temples, thereby linking Louis to the glories of Julius Caesar and other victorious generals. In fact, with the Royal Academy laying down the classical rules painters were to follow, myriad sculptures and paintings represented the king during the early part of his reign as a Roman commander. Later on, artists were asked to produce historical representations of Louis's own triumphs. Hyacinthe Rigaud's full-length portrait of Louis XIV in 1701 shows a supremely confident and powerful king standing in a regal pose, wearing luxurious coronation robes, clutching his staff of authority, and looking with condescension at the viewer—his subject.

Absolutism in France

Absolutist France became the strongest state in Europe. In the sixteenth century, Francis I and Henry IV extended the effective reach of monarchical authority (see Chapter 4). Louis XIII, aided by his invaluable minister Cardinal Richelieu, had crushed Protestant resistance. Richelieu piled new administrative structures on old ones, using provincial "intendants" (noble royal officials) to centralize and further extend monarchical authority. Richelieu's policies led to the doubling of taxes between 1630 and 1650, sparking four major waves of peasant resistance, including one uprising in the southwest in 1636 in which about 60,000 peasants took arms, some shouting the impossible demand, "Long live the king without taxes!" At Louis XIII's death, the stage was set for Louis XIV to rule as a divine-right king of an absolute state. But before the young Louis could take control of the government, France would first experience the regency of his mother and the revolt known as the Fronde.

The Fronde: Taming "Overmighty Subjects"

Louis XIV was four years old at the time of his accession to the throne in 1643. His mother, Anne of Austria (1601–1666), served as regent. She depended on Cardinal Jules Mazarin (1602–1661) for advice. Mazarin, a worldly, charming, and witty Italian, always dressed in the finest red silk and was well known for his love of money. A master of intrigue, rumor had it that he and Anne had secretly married.

During the Regency period, Anne and Mazarin kept French armies in the field, prolonging the Thirty Years' War, which had become a struggle pitting the dynastic interests of France against the Austrian and Spanish Habsburgs (see Chapter 4). Most nobles, with much to lose from civil disturbances, remained loyal to the monarchy. But Mazarin's prolongation of the victorious struggle against Spain generated a political crisis. Peasants, already weighed down by payments in cash, kind, and labor owed to nobles (an increasing number of whom were becoming absentee lords) and suffering the effects of poor harvests, resisted the additional wartime financial burdens imposed by the state.

Resistance to royal authority culminated in a revolt that shook the Bourbon monarchy at mid-century. Between 1648 and 1653, powerful "nobles of the sword" (those nobles who held ancient titles and whose forebears had gathered retainers to fight for the king) tried to regain the influence lost during the reign of Louis XIII. Ordinary people entered the fray, demanding lower taxes because of deteriorating economic conditions. The revolt became known as the Fronde—named for a slingshot the boys of Paris used to hurl rocks.

Mazarin, whom many nobles considered a "foreign plotter" and an outsider like Anne of Austria, had borrowed money for the state from financiers. He did so against expected revenue from new taxes or the sale of offices. Nobles were willing to suffer extraordinary levies in times of war. But now they complained bitterly that supplementary impositions in peacetime were needless. Furthermore, some of the oldest noble families had claimed for some time that they had been systematically excluded from the highest, most lucrative, and most prestigious offices. In fact, there was some truth in this claim, as the king feared the power of disloyal "overmighty subjects," preferring lesser nobles for military offices and skilled bureaucrats for some civil posts. Now nobles of the sword denounced Mazarin, his system of patronage, and his financier friends, some of whom had made fortunes supplying the royal armies.

In 1648, Mazarin attempted to secure the approval of the Parlement of Paris for increased taxes. The Parlement of Paris, the chief law court in France, was made up of nobles who had purchased their positions from the crown. Wanting to safeguard their privileges and power, the Parlement of Paris defied the Regency by calling for an assembly of the four sovereign courts of Paris to consider the financial crisis. Meeting without royal permission, the assembly proposed that the courts elect delegates to consider financial reforms in the realm. The provincial parlements joined the protest against what seemed to be unchecked royal authority. Financiers who had earlier purchased titles from the crown now refused to loan the state any more money.

When Mazarin ordered the arrest of some of the defiant members of the parlement in August 1648, barricades went up in Paris and ordinary Parisians rioted in support of the parlement. From inside the Louvre palace, Louis XIV, then a boy of nine, heard the angry shouts of the crowds. At one point the mob burst into Louis's bedroom. Popular discontent forced the court to flee Paris in January 1649.

The role of the prince of Condé (Louis de Bourbon; 1621–1686), head of the junior branch of the Bourbon family, was crucial in the Fronde. Condé's great victory in 1643 over the Spanish at the battle of Rocroi in

(Left) Louis, prince of Condé. *(Right)* Jules Mazarin, the Italian cardinal and royal chancellor.

northern France, which ended any possibility of a successful Spanish invasion of the country, earned him the name of "the Great Condé." But as long as Mazarin had met Condé's demands for money and offices, the latter remained loyal to the young king and in 1648 marched to Paris with his army to defend him. Minor, short-lived tax reforms bought time. But major uprisings against taxes, which had doubled in two decades as Richelieu and Mazarin had in turn raised money in order to wage war, broke out in several provinces. Relatively poor nobles, who resented that wealthy commoners were able to purchase titles with the proceeds of tax-farming and various services to the court, led other revolts. Condé himself changed sides in 1649 and supported the *frondeurs*.

Fearing Condé's influence, a Spanish invasion, and further insurrections, Anne and Mazarin found noble allies against Condé and early in 1650 ordered him imprisoned. Condé's arrest further mobilized opposition to Mazarin, whose enemies forced the minister to flee the country early the next year. More revolts broke out in the provinces, notably in Bordeaux, where the parlement joined the rebellion. A year later, Condé was released from prison at the demand of the Parlement of Paris. In September 1651, Louis XIV declared his majority and right to rule, although he was only thirteen. But he faced an immediate challenge from Condé, who, controlling Bordeaux and its region, marched to Paris in 1652 with the goals of reestablishing the great nobles' political influence and of getting rid of Mazarin (who continued to sway royal policy from his exile in Germany). However, finding insufficient support from the parlement, the municipal government, or ordinary Parisians, Condé fled to Spain. King Louis recalled Mazarin to Paris.

The young Louis XIV restored monarchical authority by ending the nobles' rebellion and putting down peasant resistance against taxation. He exiled ten members of the Parlement of Paris who had been disloyal to the crown and agreed to give amnesty to others if they would submit to royal authority. Louis made clear that henceforth the Parlement of Paris could not meddle in the king's business. To make the point, in 1652 the king summoned the parlement to the Louvre for a formal ceremony that confirmed its humiliation by leaving no doubt about the king's victory and authority. And in 1673 the king deprived the twelve parlements of their right to issue remonstrances (formal objections to the registration of new royal ordinances, edicts, or declarations, which could be overridden by the king) before they registered an edict. The king also disbanded the private armies of headstrong nobles and tightened royal control over the provincial governors.

Even at the height of the revolt, when the *frondeurs* were demanding that the king abolish the posts of intendants except in frontier regions, most of them would have been hard pressed to describe the kind of government they wanted. They were also divided by personal rivalries. Unlike the English Parliament's successful rebellion against the crown in defense of constitutional rule (see Chapter 6), royal victory in the Fronde broke French noble resistance to absolute rule. The king's predecessors, particularly Francis I, had frequently consulted with prominent nobles about important matters. Louis XIV felt no obligation to do so. Yet the Fronde also demonstrated that the crown had to rule more subtly, even as the young Louis XIV kept the reins of power for himself.

Mercantilism under Louis XIV

Following Mazarin's death in 1661, Louis XIV, now twenty-two years of age, assumed more personal responsibility for the running of the monarchy. The state's firmer financial footing owed much to the cool calculations of Jean-Baptiste Colbert (1619–1683), controller-general of the realm, who directed administration, taxation, and public works. The grandson of a provincial merchant of modest standing, Colbert suffered the hostility of the old noble families. His frosty personality led him to be dubbed "the North." He employed surveyors and mapmakers to assess the economic resources of the provinces. Royal agents who "farmed" or collected taxes for the state kept part of it for themselves. Whereas formerly only about a quarter of these revenues reached royal coffers, now as much as four-fifths of what was collected poured into the royal treasury. Even though the royal tax on land (the *taille*) had been reduced, state revenues doubled, despite abuses and privileged exemptions (nobles and clergy did not pay the *taille*).

Mercantilism provided the financial basis for absolutist France. Mercantilists posited that all resources should be put into the service of the state and that a state's wealth was measured by its ability to import more gold and silver than it exported to other countries. Jealous of English and Dutch prosperity, Colbert became the chief proponent of French mercantilist policies, which emphasized economic self-sufficiency. He founded commercial trading companies to which the king granted monopolies on colonial trade, levied high protective tariffs on Dutch and English imports, and reduced or eliminated—where possible—tolls within France itself. He established the royal Gobelins tapestry manufacture on the edge of Paris and encouraged the textile industry and the manufacture of other goods that could be exported. He improved roads and oversaw the extension of France's network of canals, including the Languedoc Canal linking the Mediterranean to the Garonne River and thus to the Atlantic Ocean.

Yet despite the growth of the French merchant fleet and navy, the French East India Company, established by Colbert in 1664, could not effectively compete with its more efficient and adventurous Dutch and English rivals. The monarchy had to bail out the company and later took away its trading monopoly. Trade within France remained hamstrung by a bewildering variety of restrictions and internal tariffs that in some places

King Louis XIV (on the left) visiting the royal Gobelins tapestry manufacture on the edge of Paris.

were not much different from those that characterized the hodgepodge of German states.

While the king was a master of extracting revenue from his subjects, his greatest talent was for emptying the royal coffers with dizzying speed. Louis XIV and his successors plunged the monarchy into an ever-deepening and eventually disastrous financial crisis.

The Absolute Louis XIV

As Louis XIV grew into manhood, he looked the part of a great king and played it superbly. Handsome, proud, energetic, and decisive, Louis built his regime more on ceremony than on intelligence and sense. His love of gambling, hunting, and women sometimes took precedence over matters of state. But he also supervised the work of the high council of his prominent officials, and, though a spendthrift, he closely monitored the accounts of his realm.

The king became a shrewd judge of character, surrounding himself with men of talent. He consciously avoided being dependent on any single person, the way Louis XIII had been on Richelieu, or his mother on Cardinal Mazarin. During a visit to the château of Vaux-le-Vicomte, built by the unpopular minister of finance Nicolas Fouquet, Louis was served with solid gold tableware and viewed pools filled with seawater and large saltwater fish. The king, who was ready to get rid of Fouquet anyway, promptly ordered him arrested and took the magnificent château for himself.

Having affirmed his authority over Paris, Louis dissolved any remaining pretensions of autonomy held by the elites in the major provincial towns. One result of the Fronde was that the monarchy expanded the narrow social base on which state power had previously rested. Louis selected governors, intendants, and bishops who would be loyal to him. The king made mayors into officials of the state who had to purchase their titles in exchange for fidelity to the king. Wealthy merchants and other townsmen now preferred to seek ennoblement rather than try to maintain municipal privileges that seemed increasingly archaic. The presence of royal garrisons, which towns once resisted, not only affirmed the sovereign's authority but were welcomed by local elites as protection against plebeian insurrection. By the early eighteenth century, towns practically begged for garrisons because troops were good for local business. In 1667, Louis took another important step in affirming his authority by appointing a lieutenant-general of police for Paris. He gave him extensive authority over a wide range of policing activities, ranging from powers of arrest to responsibility for street cleaning and fire fighting. And thanks to the lieutenant-general of police, Paris soon had street lighting—thousands of glass-enclosed candles—during the early evening hours.

Louis XIV portrayed himself as God's representative, charged with maintaining earthly order. During his long reign the monarch was identified with the state itself: "*L'état, c'est moi*" ("I am the state"), he is said to have remarked. The royal propaganda machine provided ideological legitimacy by cranking out images of the king as a glorious monarch. During the military disasters and hard times of the War of the Spanish Succession (1701–1714), the emphasis shifted toward a view of the king as the father of his people, while hammering home the necessity of obedience. At the same time, royal censors suppressed publications (especially after the Fronde), prohibited imported books, and limited the number of printers.

Louis XIV created the first French ministry of war and shaped it into an effective bureaucracy. The king and his ministers brought the noble-dominated officer corps under royal control, making seniority the determinant of rank and charging wealthy nobles handsome sums for the privilege of commanding their own regiments or companies. The ministry of war ordered the construction of military academies, barracks, drilling grounds, and fortified key border towns.

Louis XIV described himself as first seigneur of the realm. Nobles still insisted more than ever—though more quietly than at the time of the Fronde—that institutionalized noble privileges were necessary to counter the excesses of absolute authority. In exchange for acknowledgment by the nobles of monarchical legitimacy, the king confirmed their privileges, including titles, ownership of land, and seigneurial rights over peasants. Nobles were almost completely immune from royal taxes (basically paying only indirect taxes) until Louis made them subject to two additional taxes (the *capitation*, a head tax, and the *vingtième*, a tax of 5 percent, usually only on land). They benefited from the economic development the monarchy could encourage, such as by building better roads and networks of canals that were largely underwritten by the state. Greater efficiency in the collection of taxes on wealth also benefited nobles, since taxes provided money for the salaries of various royal officers and for the trips of nobles to Versailles to offer homage to the king, and financed the construction of official buildings.

The king awarded ever more titles, ecclesiastical offices, and government and military positions to those who served him. This was the easiest way for the king to raise money, as well as to enhance loyalty. As one minister put it, "as soon as the crown creates an office God creates a fool willing to buy it."

Since the time of Henry IV, offices had effectively become forms of hereditary property. Louis XIV's lavish sale of offices and titles—500 sold with a single edict in 1696—expanded the nobility. Few noble families now could trace their titles back more than several generations. This accentuated differences between nobles of the sword (some of whom could trace their noble lineage back centuries) and nobles of the robe (many of whom had purchased their offices). The nobles of the sword dominated court life, but the king did not hesitate to dip into the ranks of commoners to find efficient, loyal officials, exempting them from taxation and providing lucrative posts for their offspring. Louis de Rouvroy, the duke of Saint-Simon, a noble of the sword, denounced the "reign of the vile bourgeoisie," that is, nobles of recent title whom he viewed as upstart newcomers unworthy of prominent posts.

Louis XIV at Versailles

Louis XIV never forgot hearing the howling Parisian mob from his room in the royal palace. Resolving to move his court to Versailles, twelve miles west of Paris, he visited Paris only four times during the seventy-two years of his reign. Realizing that an adequately fed population would be less likely to riot, Louis XIV and his successors worked to assure the sufficient provisioning of the capital.

The Sun King followed Colbert's admonition that "nothing marks the greatness of princes better than the buildings that compel the people to look on them with awe, and all posterity judges them by the superb palaces they have built during their lifetime." The staging ground for royal ceremonies was the fabulous château of Versailles (constructed 1669–1686), surrounded by geometrically arranged formal gardens, interspersed by 1,400 fountains supplied by the largest hydraulic pumps in the Western world. Sculptures in the gardens made clear the identification of Louis XIV with the Greek and Roman sun god Apollo.

The château, with hundreds of splendidly decorated rooms, is monumental in scale. The royal dining room was so far from the kitchen that the king's food often arrived at his table cold and, during one particularly cold winter, the wine froze before Louis could taste it. The château's corridors were so long that some nobles used them as urinals, instead of continuing the lengthy trek to the water closet.

Louis summoned the greatest nobles of the realm to Versailles to share in his glory. There they could be honored, but none could become too powerful. More than 10,000 nobles, officials, and servants lived in or near the château. Intricately detailed etiquette governed royal ceremonies. Each day began with the elaborate routine of dressing the king in the company of the richest and most powerful nobles. As in the king of Spain's palace near Madrid, court rituals at Versailles were orchestrated to inspire a sense of the majesty and power of the monarch, but also to maintain differences in rank and privilege. The ultimate reward for a loyal noble was to be named to a post within the royal household. Louis XIV allowed the nobles to form cabals and conspire, but only against each other.

For nobles at Versailles there was little else to do except eat, drink, hunt—in the company of the king, if they were favored—gamble, and chase each other's wives and mistresses. Nobles also attended the expensive theatrical and operatic productions put on at royal expense. These included the works of the great Jean-Baptiste Molière (1622–1673) and Jean Racine (1639–1699), both of whom wrote effusive praise for the king into some of their plays.

The château of Versailles, built by Louis XIV between 1669 and 1686.

Social struggles mark the plays of Molière. The son of an upholsterer, the playwright started a travelling theatrical company before settling in Paris. The lonely, unhappy Molière poked fun at the pretensions of aristocratic and ecclesiastical society, depicting the private, cruel dramas of upper-class family life. But his popular works also helped reaffirm the boundaries between social classes. He ridiculed the burghers, whose wealth could purchase titles but not teach them how to behave as nobles. In *The Bourgeois Gentilhomme* (1670), the parvenu gives himself away with a social gaffe. Molière also detested hypocrisy, which he depicted in *Tartuffe* (1664), a tale of the unfortunate effects of untempered religious enthusiasm on a family. *Tartuffe* brought Molière the wrath of the Church, but he had an even more powerful protector, Louis XIV.

Nobles sustained an aristocratic culture tied to notions of civility, and codes governed how nobles and other people of means ought to behave in public. A guide to manners published about twenty years after Louis XIV became king advised: "Formerly . . . it was permitted to spit on the ground before people of rank, and was sufficient to put one's foot on the sputum. Today that is an indecency."

Louis XIV believed that his court stood as the center and apex of civilization. Indeed, French arts and literature had an enormous influence in Europe, particularly during the first thirty years of his reign. Foreign monarchs, nobles, and writers considered French the language of high culture. In 1700, advertisements placed in London newspapers by private teachers promised that their pupils would soon speak the French spoken at the court of Louis XIV. The château of Versailles encouraged imitation. Philip V of Spain and Frederick the Great of Prussia, among others, ordered similar palaces built. The duke of Saxony rebuilt his capital of Dresden along neo-classical lines. The château also served as a model for noble estates and townhouses built in the classical style.

Louis XIV's Persecution of Religious Minorities

One of the most salient results of the victory of absolute rule in Catholic states was the persecution of religious minorities. Such campaigns in part served to placate the papacy and the Church hierarchy in each Catholic state. Louis XIV had little interest in theology, although he was relatively pious. But as he grew older, the king brought into his inner circle a number of extremely devout advisers, and into his bedroom a fervently religious mistress.

Reversing the tolerant policies of Henry IV and Louis XIII, in the late 1670s Louis XIV launched a vigorous campaign of persecution against Huguenots, closing most Protestant churches and initiating attempts to force conversions to Catholicism. In 1685, Louis XIV revoked the Edict of Nantes, by which Henry IV in 1598 had extended religious tolerance to Protestants. This pleased the provincial estates in regions where Protes-

(Left) The symbol of the sun used to glorify the absolute ruler, Louis XIV. *(Right)* This caricature shows Louis XIV, the Sun King, as the exterminator of Protestantism.

tants were a forceful minority and memories of the wars of religion were still fresh. But the economic cost to France was in the long run considerable. Although the king forbade Huguenots from leaving France, many merchants and skilled craftsmen were among the 200,000 Huguenots who emigrated during the next forty years. Many went to England, Prussia, the Dutch United Provinces, and even South Africa.

With the motto "one king, one law, one faith," Louis XIV also persecuted Jansenists in his quest for religious orthodoxy. Jansenists were followers of Cornelis Jansen, bishop of Ypres in the Southern Netherlands (Belgium), who had died in 1638. They could be found in France, the Netherlands, Austria, and several Italian states. Seeking reforms within the Church, Jansenists emphasized the role of faith and divine grace in the pursuit of salvation. Believing mankind to be fallen and hapless, incapable of understanding the will of God, Jansenists came close to accepting a Calvinist doctrine of predestination. Their enemies called them "Calvinists who go to Mass." There were differences in the beliefs of Calvinists and Jansenists, however. Calvinists had developed the notion of "vocation," whereby one was to throw oneself into secular life and live as a saint, as if one had the certainty of salvation. Jansenists, in contrast, believed that one should completely withdraw from the world, given the certainty of sin and mankind's ignorance of God's will. Jansenists, who were notoriously ascetic and disapproved of the frivolity of Versailles, criticized the Church for encouraging a lax morality by holding out the possibility of repeated penance, indeed deathbed conversion.

The pope had condemned Jansenism in 1653, perhaps at the insistence of the Jesuits, the Jansenists' most determined enemy. Louis XIV continued to tolerate them for several decades. But he began to persecute them in the name of "one faith" in 1709 when, influenced by Jesuit advisers, he ordered the Jansenist community at Port-Royal outside of Paris evicted and its abbey burned to the ground. He convinced Pope Clement XI to issue a papal bull, *Unigenitus* (1713), which condemned Jansenism. The Parlement of Paris, however, refused to register the edict. Louis was still trying to force compliance two years later when he died. The king's attempt to impose religious orthodoxy in France fell short, indicating that absolute rule had its limits.

The Limits of French Absolutism

France, like other countries, was far from being a nation-state in which most people thought of themselves as French, as well as or instead of Norman, Breton, or Provençal, or from other regions with their own traditions. More than half the population did not speak French. Inadequate roads isolated mountain regions, in particular, limiting the effective reach of absolute rule.

The absolute monarchy stood at the top of a complex network of patronage based on personal ties that reached into every province and every town. But Louis XIV's intendants still had to take local networks of influence into consideration, using intimidation, cajoling, and negotiating to gain their ends in what was then Western Europe's most populous state.

The king played off against one another the jurisdictions and interests of the estates, parlements, and other provincial institutions dominated by the nobles. The provincial estates were assemblies of nobles of the *pays d'état* (regions retaining a degree of fiscal autonomy, including Brittany, Provence, Burgundy, and Languedoc), which represented each province. The estates oversaw the collection of taxes and tended to details of provincial administration and spending. They met annually amid great pageantry and carefully orchestrated ceremony that, like those at Versailles, reaffirmed social hierarchy. In principle, the estates could refuse to provide the crown with the annual "free grant" (a subsidy provided by each region to the monarch), which was hardly "free," since the king informed the estates of the amount of money he wanted. Louis XIV abolished the custom of allowing the estates to express grievances before voting the amount of their "gift" to the monarchy.

The interests of the nobles also prevailed in the parlements, which were the sovereign law courts that registered, publicized, and carried out royal laws. The parlements, most of whose members were nobles, claimed to speak for their province in legal matters, asserting the right to issue binding commands in cases of emergencies. But, unlike the English Parliament, no national representative political institution existed in France.

Even the king of France was not as omnipotent or omniscient as he would have liked to think. Jean Bodin, theorist of absolutism, expressed the view that a ruler would be wise to avoid exercising full power—for example, to avoid interfering with his subjects' property. This seeming paradox is perhaps best symbolized by the king's phrase to the estates of a province: "We entreat you but we also command you. . . ."

Even the powerful and influential Bourbons were bound by the so-called fundamental laws of the realm, as well as by those they believed God had established. They therefore were responsible for any crimes they might commit. More than this, an absolute monarch could not stem the tide of change. Louis XIII had markers placed around the city of Paris, even beyond the city walls, warning that anyone who built beyond would have his house razed and be slapped with a stiff fine. But Louis XIV had to surrender to spontaneous population growth, finally ordering the walls torn down in 1670.

THE BALANCE OF POWER

During the century beginning about 1650, the concept of a balance of power between states gradually took hold in many of the courts of Europe. Like the evolving European state system itself, the emergence of the concept arose in part out of the decline of religious antagonisms as a dominant cause of warfare. The quest of absolute rulers to add to their dynastic territories and the growing global commercial rivalry between the great powers increasingly shaped European warfare.

A diplomatic concept dating from the time of the Renaissance city-states of fifteenth-century Italy, the balance of power held that great powers should be in equilibrium, and that one power should not be allowed to become too powerful. The decline of one power could threaten the balance of power if, as a result, another power considerably enhanced its strength. Now the main threat to peace ceased to be religious division but rather French expansionism.

The Origins of International Law

Horrified by the Thirty Years' War, two northern European political theorists systematically analyzed questions of international relations, drawing on the recent history of Europe. They helped lay the foundations for the evolution of modern diplomacy. In 1625, the Dutch jurist Hugo Grotius (1583–1645) sought to establish the foundations of international law by arguing that laws to which nations were subject followed from nature and not from God. Samuel von Pufendorf (1632–1694), a German Protestant who tutored the family of a Swedish diplomat in Copenhagen, found himself under arrest for eight months when he was caught up in the war between Sweden and Denmark. Pufendorf's *Of the Law of Nature and Nations* (1672) postulated legal principles for times of peace—which he argued should be the natural state—and for times of war. He claimed that only a defensive war was justified, pending international arbitration to resolve crises. The problem was, of course, that unless there existed some powerful, impartial body to adjudicate disputes between nations, each side in any conflict invariably claimed that its cause was just. But European power politics swept away such theoretical considerations.

THE HABSBURG MONARCHY

The eighteenth-century French philosophe Voltaire only somewhat exaggerated when he dismissed the Holy Roman Empire, that cumbersome federal structure of Central European states that once served as a powerful protector of the papacy, as having ceased to be holy, Roman, or an empire. The Holy Roman Empire included almost 300 German states. Until 1648, seven electors (four princes and three archbishops) picked the Holy Roman emperor, invariably the Habsburg ruler (after 1648, there were eight electors). But in a Europe increasingly dominated by absolute monarchs, the Holy Roman Empire seemed an anomaly.

In principle, the Holy Roman emperor still commanded the allegiance of the states of the empire. These included sizable states such as Austria, Bavaria, and Saxony, whose rulers oversaw elaborate courts modeled after Versailles, maintained standing armies, and paid for all this by levying taxes on their subjects and customs duties and tolls on merchandise being carried through their territories. The Holy Roman Empire also included many small principalities, duchies, and even archbishoprics barely extending beyond the walls of towns like Mainz and Trier. But in reality the empire had increasingly only a shadow existence, despite its mystique as the defender of Catholicism. The Treaty of Westphalia (1648), which concluded the Thirty Years' War, reflected the inability of the Holy Roman Empire to enforce its will, conduct foreign policy, or effectively maintain an army. During the long war, some German princes, with powerful allies outside the empire, had gone their own way. Indeed, the Treaty of Westphalia specifically empowered each member state to carry out its own foreign policy. The imperial Assembly of the Holy Roman Empire, the Reichstag, thus had virtually no authority to conduct foreign policy with other states. The imperial army was too small and difficult to mobilize to be effective. The imperial court of law was powerless to enforce its decisions, depending entirely on the good will of the individual states.

The strongest state within the Holy Roman Empire, Habsburg Austria, extended beyond the boundaries of the empire itself. The Habsburgs had ruled Austria without interruption since the thirteenth century. The old Habsburg principle was "Let others wage war. You, happy Austria, marry [to prosper]." Advantageous marriages brought the dynasty the wealthy territories of Burgundy and the Netherlands in the fifteenth century.

Charles V, who became Holy Roman emperor in 1519, added Hungary and Bohemia. Counting Spain and its far-flung possessions, he reigned over perhaps a quarter of the population of the European continent, as well as the vast Spanish Empire of the Americas.

When Charles V gave up his power in 1556 and formally abdicated as emperor in 1558, he divided the Habsburg domains into two parts. His brother Ferdinand I inherited the Austrian Habsburg lands (including Austria, Hungary, and Bohemia) and succeeded him as the elected Holy Roman emperor. Charles's son Philip II became king of Spain with his empire including the Netherlands, dependencies in Italy, and colonies in the Americas. The Spanish and Austrian branches of the Habsburgs were henceforth two separate dynasties, although the interests of both as Catholic states and also as rivals of France sometimes converged.

The Austrian Habsburg monarchy exercised foreign policy and directed the armed forces, but it had less effective authority within its territories than the kings of France had within their realm. Nobles oversaw the court system and police apparatus. When confronted with threats to their traditional prerogatives, nobles put aside differences, such as those between the great landowners and the lower nobility, and formed a common front to preserve their privileges against monarchical erosion.

Austria was the only power able to exercise its influence equally in both Western and Eastern Europe. The Austrian Habsburgs successfully implemented an effective state administration, expanded educational opportunities for the upper classes, and brought resistant or even rebellious nobles under dynastic control. But timely marriages were no longer enough. Throughout the sixteenth century and during the first half of the seventeenth century, the Habsburgs had been almost constantly preoccupied with politics within and between the German states. During the Thirty Years' War, however, the Habsburgs were unable to expand their domination throughout Central Europe. While still seeking a major role in the German states, the Habsburgs remained vulnerable to French expansionism and to Turkish incursions, forcing the monarchy to address threats on two fronts.

The Habsburg empire's polyglot structure of territories of different nationalities, including fifteen major languages, was a source of weakness. Leopold I, elected Holy Roman emperor in 1658 (ruled 1658–1705; Louis XIV was the opposing candidate), was simultaneously Holy Roman emperor, duke of Upper and Lower Silesia, count of Tyrol, archduke of Upper and Lower Austria, king of Bohemia, prince of Transylvania, king of Hungary, Slavonia, Dalmatia, and Croatia, and titular ruler of Lombardy, Styria, and Moravia (see Map 7.1). The monarch did not rule through a single administration, but rather in each case through local political institutions. The Hungarian and Croatian provincial diets, or noble estates, impeded Habsburg absolutism. Hungarians also resented German-speaking administrators and tax collectors, as well as the Habsburg armies

MAP 7.1 THE HOLY ROMAN EMPIRE UNDER LEOPOLD I, 1658   The Holy Roman Empire was a polyglot state, made up of territories of different nationalities.

stationed in Hungary to help protect the empire from the Turks. In Bohemia, the scars of the religious conflicts between Catholics and Protestants during the Thirty Years' War healed very slowly. Bohemia and Moravia remained centers of Protestant intellectual ferment. Furthermore, many Bohemian nobles resented the fact that a decree in 1627 had abolished the elective monarchy and made the Bohemian crown a hereditary Habsburg possession.

Hungary had been part of the Habsburg domains since the sixteenth century. The Hungarian crown included Hungary, Transylvania, and Croatia. The Hungarian nobles, proud of their defense of the Habsburg empire against Turkish incursions, seized every opportunity to extract concessions from the Habsburgs. Unlike their Austrian counterparts, most of the Hungarian, or Magyar, nobles had become Protestant during the Reformation. Habsburg persecution of Hungarian Protestants helped spark an insurrection in 1679 against Habsburg rule that spread into Moravia, Slavonia, and Silesia. This led Leopold to promise the Hungarian Estates to restore some landowner privileges that had been suppressed. But dissatisfied Protestants then called for Turkish assistance at a time when the Turks were preparing to attack Habsburg territories. The

Ottoman army besieged Vienna, the Habsburg capital, in 1683. It was saved after two months by the arrival of a combined relief army of Austrians, Germans, and Poles under the command of the crusading King John Sobieski (ruled 1674–1696), Catholic ruler of Poland. Pope Innocent XI succeeded in convincing Leopold I, who had been trained for the priesthood before becoming emperor and who saw himself as a prince of the Catholic Reformation, to lead a "Holy League" in 1684 against the Ottoman Turks. In the War of the Holy League (1686–1687), and in subsequent fighting, Habsburg armies recaptured most of Hungary and the eastern province of Transylvania from the Turks, as well as much of Croatia. The Peace of Karlowitz (1699) ratified the Habsburg victory over the Turks. Although Ottoman garrisons remained only eighty miles from Vienna and Turkish galleys still roamed the Mediterranean, the Ottoman threat to Central Europe had passed.

The Habsburg victory over the Turks had also been, for all intents and purposes, over Hungary. In 1687, the Hungarian Estates were forced to declare that the Hungarian throne (the crown of Saint Stephen, named after Hungary's patron saint) would henceforth be a hereditary possession of the Habsburgs and no longer elective. Hungary thereby recognized the sovereignty of the Habsburg dynasty in exchange for several promises: the Hungarian Diet would be convened at regular intervals; Hungary would have its own administration; and Magyar nobles would continue to be exempt from royal taxation. Although he consolidated Habsburg authority within the dynasty's domains, Leopold failed to impose centralized rule on Hungary. Thus, Hungary's special position within the monarchy revealed the limits of Habsburg absolutism and Austrian power.

The Habsburg monarchy, the least absolute of Europe's absolute states, was less successful than France in maintaining its power. In 1700, Austria's Habsburg dynasty lost its long-standing ties to Spain when that country passed from the Habsburg dynasty to the Bourbon dynasty with the death of the childless Charles II (ruled 1665–1700). France's defeat in the War of the Spanish Succession (1701–1714), which had been fought to determine who would inherit the Spanish Habsburg territories, enabled the Austrian Habsburgs to pick up some of the remaining pieces of the decimated Spanish Empire in

Leopold I, the Holy Roman emperor.

The siege of Vienna, the capital of the Habsburg empire, by the Ottoman army in 1683.

Europe. However, Austria ceded its preeminence in Central Europe to Prussia during the eighteenth century.

THE RISE OF PRUSSIA

The presence of all the essential components of absolutism explain Prussia's rise as a major European power: a proud, ambitious dynasty, the Hohenzollern family of Brandenburg; privileged but loyal nobles, the Junkers, whose estates formed the base of the economy and who dominated a downtrodden peasantry devoid of rights; an increasingly centralized and efficient bureaucracy; and, above all, the emergence of a large standing army. Austrian defeats in the Thirty Years' War and vulnerability to French and Turkish challenges left the way open for a rival to emerge among the German states. Bavaria and Saxony were weak claimants for primacy among the German states. Both had relatively weak nobilities, and their rulers had not developed either a strong bureaucracy or sizable army. The Catholic clergy undermined the authority of the Bavarian dukes. The attention of Saxony, subject to Swedish influence, was often turned away from German affairs eastward toward the volatile world of Polish politics.

The small north-central German state of Brandenburg-Prussia, stretching across the sandy marshes between the Elbe and Oder Rivers, seemed an unlikely candidate to rival Austria and to grow into a powerful absolute state. In 1618, Brandenburg's ruling Hohenzollern dynasty inherited East Prussia, which lay 100 miles to the east of Brandenburg along the Baltic Sea and was bordered by Poland. It then absorbed several smaller territories in the Rhineland, more than 100 miles to the west (see Map 7.2). Consisting of three diverse, noncontiguous realms, Brandenburg-Prussia lacked not only defensible frontiers but also the developed network of prosperous trading towns of other regions in Germany. During the Thirty Years' War, Swedish and Austrian armies took turns ravaging it. But it gained territory with the Treaty of Westphalia (1648), which ended the war and permitted Prussia to absorb much of Pomerania, on the coast of the Baltic Sea.

In one of the typical trade-offs that built absolute states in early modern Europe, Prussian nobles accepted Hohenzollern authority as a guarantee of their privileges. At the same time that nobles were securing their privileges, Prussian peasants were losing their freedom, including their rights to free movement and often to inheritance. During the late fifteenth and the sixteenth centuries, they became serfs, legally bound to a lord's estate,

MAP 7.2 THE RISE OF PRUSSIA, 1648–1720   Territories acquired by Brandenburg-Prussia.

and could be sold with the land on which they worked. A burgher in a Prussian town in 1614 described serfdom as "this barbaric and Egyptian servitude . . . in our territory serfdom did not exist fifty or a hundred years ago, but lately, it has been brought in on a large scale, with the help of the authorities." The authority of the Hohenzollerns, however, stopped at the gate of the manor: Junkers retained rights of seigneurial justice over their peasants. The burghers, including merchants and skilled craftsmen, also stood powerless before the Junkers, in contrast to the middle class in England and the Dutch United Provinces, where they presented an imposing obstacle to the growth of absolutism. In Prussia, the middle-class burghers could not export grain freely and had to pay tolls, duties, and taxes.

Frederick William (ruled 1640–1688), the "Great Elector" of Brandenburg (so named because the ruler of Brandenburg had the right to cast a ballot in the election of the Holy Roman emperor), initially had neither a standing army nor the resources to raise one. Prussian nobles at first resisted the creation of a standing army, fearful that it might aid the elector in reducing their privileges. In 1653, Frederick William convinced the Junkers to grant him funds with which to build an army in exchange for royal confirmation of their privileges over the peasantry and their right to import goods without paying duties. Furthermore, the king agreed to consult the nobles on matters of foreign policy.

Then Frederick William turned to the business of augmenting state authority in his three fragmented territories. He extracted concessions from each of them, including more taxes and the right to recruit soldiers. With his permanent standing army, Frederick William was able to wage war in alliance with various states and thereby to acquire more territory, as well as recruiting peasants to serve as soldiers and Junkers as officers. The Great Elector established a centralized administrative bureaucracy, arguably the first modern civil service in Europe. The Hohenzollern family owned more than half of East Prussia, which provided considerable state revenue. A state official supervised military affairs and the collection of taxes in each district, pulling in twice as much revenue as was extracted by the king of France at the same time. Elected by local nobles, he was responsible to the king, who gradually expanded his duties as a royal representative. The Prussian bureaucracy, which was coordinated by an office with the suitably imposing name of "General Directory Over Finance, War, and Royal Domains," reached a degree of efficiency unmatched in eighteenth-century Europe. The remaining prerogatives of the towns disappeared in the expanding state. Prussian towns, which paid a disproportionate percentage of taxes, lost their representation in the provincial estates. In 1701, the Great Elector's son Frederick III (his title as elector of Brandenburg) took the title of King Frederick I of Prussia (ruled 1688–1713).

Frederick William I (ruled 1713–1740), grandson of the Great Elector, succeeded Frederick III as elector of Brandenburg and king in Prussia. As a boy, Frederick William could not count to ten without his tutor's assistance, but upon his succession he continued the centralizing policies of his grandfather and father. Living modestly, he occupied only several rooms of his palace, with the basement serving as the royal treasury. The bad-tempered "Sergeant-King" wore his officer's uniform around the house and turned the royal gardens into a military training ground. He was known for fits of screaming rage, calling everyone in sight "blockhead," sometimes beating officials with a stick, and

King Frederick William I.

knocking out the teeth of several judges whose sentences displeased him. Officials known as "fiscals" went around to make sure that the king's representatives served him well. But the king was astute enough to break with tradition by employing some commoners; finding state service a means of social mobility, many served with uncommon loyalty and efficiency.

A Prussian official described, with some exaggeration, the feature that defined his country's absolutism and the emergence of Brandenburg-Prussia as a power: "What distinguishes the Prussians from other people is that theirs is not a country with an army. They have an army and a country that serves it." Military expenditures accounted for half of Prussia's state budget. King Frederick William I increased the Prussian army from about 39,000 to 80,000 soldiers. He engaged only tall soldiers for his royal guard, those standing more than six feet in height, virtual giants at the time. One of his first royal acts was to abolish the luxury industries in Berlin, the capital of Brandenburg-Prussia, that catered to court and nobles, and to replace them with workshops that made military uniforms. The king ordered all young men in Prussia to register for military service and organized a procedure by which each regiment was assigned a specific region from which to recruit or conscript soldiers. Prussia established the first system of military reserves in Europe: soldiers drilled in the summer for two months. This meant that far more men in Prussia experienced military life than in any other country.

THE RUSSIAN AND SWEDISH EMPIRES

Early in the sixteenth century, Muscovy was a relatively small state. It stood vulnerable to invasions by the Mongols, who had conquered what is now Russia in the thirteenth century, the Tartars of Crimea on the edge of the Black Sea, and to the kingdom of Poland-Lithuania, a kingdom and grand duchy joined in an enormous confederation in 1386. Twice the size of France, the confederation had only about 8 million people, its capital the modest town of Kraków (Cracow). Gradually, however, the duchy of Muscovy, where Orthodox Christianity had taken hold, emerged as the strongest of the territories of Russia, absorbing Novgorod and other rival states and principalities late in the fifteenth century. Muscovy's ruler Ivan III (ruled 1462–1505) began using the title "lord of all Russia," a title that offended the far more powerful state of Poland-Lithuania. In 1500 and again twelve years later, Ivan brazenly attacked Poland-Lithuania, capturing the fortress town of Smolensk, which guarded the upper Dnieper River.

The Expansion of Muscovy

The rise of Russia as an absolute state and empire began with the further expansion of the state of Muscovy later in the sixteenth century. Tsar Ivan IV (ruled 1533–1584) absorbed parts of the Mongol states to the east,

Ivan the Terrible watching the beggars of Novgorod being tortured to death.

drove back the Muslim Tartars, conquered the Don and Volga river basins to the south, and unsuccessfully battled Poland-Lithuania for control of the Baltic territory of Livonia. Peasants and hunters expanded the influence of Muscovy into the cold and sparsely populated reaches of Siberia.

Ivan truly earned his sobriquet "the Terrible." He was raised in a world of violence marked by the bloody feuds of the Muscovite nobles, some of whom poisoned his mother when he was eight years old. Five years later, Ivan ordered a noble ripped apart by fierce dogs; as an adult, he had an archbishop sewn into a bearskin and thrown to hungry wolves. His goals were to assure himself a reliable military force and sufficient revenue. His means was to create a "service state" in which Muscovite nobles—called *boyars*—would serve him while receiving protection against peasant insurrections or other nobles. Allying with a group of military retainers, he decimated noble families he viewed as too powerful or too slow to obey. Ivan alternated between moods of religious fervor, drunken passion, and stormy brutality. After being defeated in Lithuania in 1564, Ivan became even more paranoid, subjecting his people to an eight-year reign of terror. He killed his own son with a massive blow to the skull and routinely ordered anyone who displeased him tortured to death.

Ivan's death in 1584 led, almost unimaginably, to an even worse period for Muscovy, the "Time of Troubles," a period of intermittent anarchy. Weak successors allowed nobles to regain control of the sprawling country. In 1613, the Assembly of Nobles elected the first Romanov tsar. The next two tsars restored order, regaining some of the lands lost to Poland-Lithuania and Sweden.

For most peasants, life itself was an endless "time of troubles" in the face of state taxation and brutalization at the hands of their lords. Revolts seemed endemic, some led by men who claimed to be the "true" tsar who would restore justice. One of the latter, Stephen Razin, whose symbol was a horsetail, led a huge force of peasants on a march to the cry of "To Moscow against the landlords!" The peasant army captured several cities before being decimated in 1670, its leader publicly tortured in Moscow.

Serfdom emerged as one of the fundamental characteristics of Russian absolutism. In times of dearth or crisis, many peasants traditionally had fled the region of Moscow to settle on the frontierlands of Siberia in the east or on land in Ukraine, an extensive, thinly populated territory standing between Russia, Poland, and a Tartar state on the Crimean peninsula—the word *Ukraine* itself means "border region." The resulting chronic shortage of rural labor, and the need to provide landed estates to loyal nobles, led the state in 1649 officially to establish serfdom, which had become widespread by the end of the sixteenth century. The chronically indebted Russian peasants gave up their freedom in exchange for loans from the crown and from landlords. The Orthodox Church, a major landowner, also contributed to the expansion of serfdom. Nearly 90 percent of the peasants were now bound to the land, assuring the state and nobles of a relatively immobile labor supply. In exchange for the tsar's support of this system, Russian nobles, like their counterparts in Prussia, pledged their service to the state.

The Romanov dynasty enjoyed the good will of the Orthodox Church. By the early sixteenth century, the Russian Orthodox Church had become centered in Moscow, which now claimed the title of the third Rome (the second Rome was Constantinople). But after a mid-seventeenth-century schism, the Orthodox Church faced the hostility of the Old Believers, dissidents who claimed authority over the tsars and disliked changes in Church ritual that reformers had implemented. Old Believers participated in violent peasant uprisings until the end of the eighteenth century.

Several neighbors blocked Muscovy's further expansion. The Commonwealth of Poland and Lithuania (the union of which had been formalized in 1569) stood to the west, and Swedish territories were to the north. The northern port of Archangel on the White Sea, its harbor frozen solid much of the year, offered Muscovy its only access to the sea. Turks, Cossacks (a warrior people living in southern Russia), and Crimean Tartars were among the southern peoples resisting incorporation into Muscovy and Poland-Lithuania. Polish territories included much of Belarus and Ukraine. The rest of Ukraine was subject to the influence of Poland, Russia, and Cossacks, and was further divided by religion. Most landowners in Ukraine were Polish Catholics. Most Ukrainian peasants were, like Russians, Orthodox Christians and spoke a language similar to Russian, but were a separate people. Peasant revolts rocked Ukraine in the late 1640s, and, after an uprising that drove back the Polish army, Ukraine accepted Russian sovereignty in 1654. Under the Treaty of Andrussovo (1667), which concluded a war with Poland, Russia absorbed Ukraine east of the Dnieper River.

The Rival Swedish Empire

In the 1640s and 1650s, Swedish kings added to their dynastic holdings the regions of Denmark and Norway, Estonia and Lithuania, and West Pomerania and Bremen in northern Germany. Like the Habsburg empire, the kingdom of Sweden encompassed a farraginous set of languages, including Swedish, Finnish, Latvian, Estonian, and German, the language of administration. Sweden was a relatively poor state, but revenues from lucrative copper mines, the sale of Swedish iron and steel—the finest in Europe—and trade with Muscovy and the West generated enough revenue to finance expansion. But expansion also had its costs: Queen Christina (ruled 1632–1654) raised money by selling almost two-thirds of royal lands, with Swedish nobles becoming the main beneficiaries. Swedish peasants, who had their own estate in the Swedish Diet (or assembly), complained of the "unheard-of state of servitude . . . since private persons took hold of the country." Specifically, they demanded, in vain, the return

Sweden's King Charles XII *(left)*, ruled from 1697 to 1718, and Queen Christina *(right)* ruled from 1632 to 1654.

of all alienated lands to the throne. The lower estates did not dare challenge royal prerogatives, "We esteem Your Majesty's royal power as the buttress of our liberties, the one being bound up in the other, and both standing or falling together."

Emboldened by his fledgling empire, King Charles XI (ruled 1660–1697) in the 1680s established absolute rule in Sweden. He overcame the resistance of the wealthiest nobles by winning the support of their jealous colleagues of lesser means, as well as that of the burghers, clergy, and peasants, who sought royal protection against the wealthiest nobles. His son Charles XII (ruled 1697–1718) became king at the age of fifteen and refused even to take the coronation oath when he came of age in 1700. Symbolically, he snatched the crown and placed it on his own head, and never convoked the estates. Having been instructed only in warfare as a youth, he remained a headstrong military man who acted by impulse, not reflection. Instead of diplomacy, he relied on military force to achieve Swedish ends. Instead of turning Sweden's full military attention toward Denmark, which sought to recapture lost provinces from Sweden, he spent five years campaigning against Russia (see below), a quest that took him into the Ottoman Empire, where he sought assistance against Russia. But during Charles XII's reign, the crown added to its wealth by reclaiming land that had been sold to nobles in the previous decades. Gradually the Swedish monarchy established a bureaucracy and increased state revenue. But when Charles XII was killed in a war in Norway, leaving no heir, the Swedish nobility succeeded in imposing a parliamentary regime based on the prerogatives of the estates and marked by political struggles among the nobility, clergy, burghers, and peasants. In 1772, however, King Gustavus III (ruled 1771–1792) overthrew the parliamentary system, supported by some nobles, and reimposed absolute rule. By then, however, Sweden's empire was a fading memory.

Peter the Great Turns Westward

In Western Europe so little was known about "barbaric" Russia that Louis XIV sent a letter to a tsar who had been dead for twelve years. Peter the Great (ruled 1682–1725) first imposed order on a state torn by bloody uprisings; then he transformed Muscovy into the Russian Empire. Whereas Ivan the Terrible and several of his successors had been turned back by Poland and Turkey, Peter aggressively and successfully moved Russian interests toward Europe. Wars brought territorial acquisitions at the expense of Sweden, Poland, and the Turks.

As a boy growing up in the violent world of Russian court politics, Peter was schooled in all manner of guns, ballistics, and fortifications. Wearing a military uniform, he became tsar at the age of ten after a bloody struggle, which he witnessed firsthand, between the clans of his father's two widows. Seven years later, Peter killed members of his own family whom he perceived to be a threat to his rule.

The tsar, who wore shabby clothes, worn-out shoes, and very long hair, stood close to seven feet tall and suffered from chronic back problems compounded by frenetic energy. A nervous tic became most apparent when he was anxious or angry, which seemed to be most of the time, as he lashed out with clubs or fists.

When he was twenty-five, Peter visited Western Europe incognito, encouraged to do so by Europeans he had met living in the foreign quarter on the edge of Moscow. Peter undertook his travels dressed as a humble, giant workman. In the West, he shocked statesmen and nobles with his dress and coarse manners. Four months on the Dutch docks taught him ship carpentry. He always preferred the company of artisans and dock-workers to nobles and state officials. In London, the tsar and his entourage virtually destroyed a rented house with wild parties—the tsar loved to dance and drink—leading a bishop to worry aloud that this "furious man had been raised up to so absolute an authority over so great a part of the world."

Peter was not an uncritical admirer of the West. But impressed with the military strength and administrative efficiency of the Western powers, Peter emulated what he considered to be the more "rational" organization of Western monarchies. He borrowed Western technical knowledge, attaching it to the structures of Russian absolutism. This represented a monumental cultural

Peter the Great, Emperor of Russia, founder of St. Petersburg.

change that was secular in character. He ordered nobles to become educated and told his guards and officials to shave off their beards—which the Old Believers believed distinguished Russians from Westerners. He encouraged the use of individual glasses, bowls, and napkins at meals, and ordered a Western book of etiquette to be translated into Russian. Furthermore, he ordered nobles to build Western-style palaces, and he demanded that women wear bonnets, petticoats, and skirts. German and, to a lesser extent, French, became the language of court. Purchasing German and Italian paintings and statues, Peter began the royal collection that would later become the renowned Hermitage Museum in St. Petersburg, and he also created the Russian Academy of Science.

Fearing the military superiority of his rivals, Sweden and Poland, Peter now raised the first Russian standing army, gradually replacing Western mercenary soldiers with Russian troops by implementing military conscription in 1705 to complement Cossack cavalrymen. Thereafter, one recruit (who would serve for life) had to be provided for every twenty peasant households. Peter brought Western commanders to train his army and provided soldiers with uniforms and Western flintlock muskets with socket bayonets.

The bustling docks of Amsterdam and London inspired Peter's interest in building first a river navy and eventually an oceangoing fleet. Skilled workers from Prussia and from the Dutch Republic were hired to build warships, and Russian craftsmen were sent abroad to learn new skills. Russians gradually replaced Western Europeans as designers, builders, and ship commanders. By the end of the century, Russia had a fleet.

Military might, then, also underlay Russian absolutism. Even in peacetime, at least two-thirds of state revenue went to the army and navy. Peter forced nobles to send their sons to new military and engineering schools by decreeing they could not marry unless they did so. In order to pay for his army, the tsar tripled state revenues, imposing a direct tax on each male serf, or "soul." Landlords became responsible for the collection of these new taxes. He established state monopolies on the production and sale of salt, oil, tobacco, rhubarb, and even dice, used for gambling, awarding the profitable right to collect these revenues to his favorite nobles, or to foreigners. Hoping to expand Russian industry and attract gold and silver payments from abroad, Peter oversaw the exploitation of mines and the establishment of a metal industry in the Ural Mountains. But even absolute authority could not overcome the primitive transportation system, the lack of raw materials and capital, and the absence of a sizable merchant class.

Peter succeeded in managing the often volatile politics of the court, namely the traditional ruling elite, the nobles (*boyars*). At the same time, Peter's observations in the absolutist courts of Europe inspired the reorganization of the civil administration. While remaining an autocrat, Peter was nonetheless the first tsar to distinguish between his person as ruler and the state itself. Indeed, he made officials take two oaths, one to him and one to the state whose power he enhanced.

Peter divided his domains into fifty administrative districts, appointing a governor for each. He created a Senate, an administrative body charged with ruling in his absence during wartime and with overseeing state administration in time of peace. He experimented with councils whose members could—if they dared—give him advice. The tsar also put towns under the direct control of provincial governors, although they retained a measure of self-government. Peter created a cadre of nobles to fill positions in the bureaucracy. The Table of Ranks (1722) required all male nobles to enter state service, serving in the army, navy, or bureaucracy, and allowed commoners who rose through the bureaucracy or military to assume noble titles. Thus, the nobility became an instrument of the state, instead of, as in the case of other European absolute states, a social institution that could impede the ruler's will. Peter also placed the Orthodox Church fully under state control by first not naming a new patriarch (the head of the Russian Orthodox Church) upon the death of the incumbent in 1700 and later simply abolishing the patriarchate.

The tsar's turn toward the West angered the old noble families of Moscow, traditional Orthodox Church leaders, and Old Believers alike. Peter executed some nobles who refused his order to provide service to the state. Old Believers considered the reforms sacrilegious and contrary to the historical development of Russia. Many churchmen resented that Peter had subordinated the church to his state. Peter overcame four uprisings and several conspiracies directed against him. When his son announced that he would, on becoming tsar, end the Western reforms and restore old Russian customs, Peter ordered him tortured to death for opposing his will.

Peter the Great expanded Russian territory (see Map 7.3). He did so, for the most part, by pushing back the neighbors who had blocked Muscovy's expansion: Sweden, Poland, and the Ottoman Turks. He added territory beyond the Ural Mountains along the Caspian Sea, at the expense of the Turks. Like his successors, Peter dreamed of conquering the Turkish capital of Constantinople, which would give him control over its straits, the crucial passage between Europe and Asia leading to the Black Sea. Peter's new fleet sailed down the Don River in 1696, conquering the Turkish port of Azov on the Sea of Azov, which gives access to the Black Sea. However, in 1711 he was forced to surrender Azov after a short and unsuccessful war against the Turks (1710–1711).

Russia's role in European affairs, however, had remained minimal, despite its participation, with Habsburg Austria, Poland, and Venice, in the long series of wars against the Turks in the last decades of the seventeenth century. Russia joined Denmark and Saxony in attacking Sweden in the Great Northern War (1700–1721). The Russian ambassador in

MAP 7.3 THE EXPANSION OF RUSSIA   The state of Muscovy was expanded through the acquisitions of Ivan III, Ivan IV (the Terrible), and Peter the Great.

Vienna reported that once the news of Peter's victory arrived, "people begin to fear the tsar as formerly they feared Sweden." Peter's goal was to win a "window on the Baltic Sea" at Sweden's expense. The Swedes did turn back the assault of a much larger Russian army at Narva (1700) in Estonia. But after Charles XII of Sweden passed up the opportunity to pursue the Russian army in order to invade Poland and Saxony, the Russian army conquered the mouth of the Neva River in 1703.

There Peter ordered the construction of a new capital city, where he forced nobles and wealthy merchants to build elegant townhouses. St. Petersburg offered a striking contrast to the chaos of tangled streets and shabby wooden buildings of Moscow, then by far the largest city in Russia. Built on coastal marsh lands, St. Petersburg, from its fortifications to its broad boulevards, reflected architectural ideas borrowed from the West, particularly Amsterdam. State offices, including army and military headquarters, occupied the centrally located islands. Symmetrical facades rose along the Neva River's south bank, near the shipyards, admiralty, and fortresses. Geometrically arranged boulevards, squares, and gardens completed the tsar's capital.

Russia supplanted Sweden as the Baltic region's dominant power. In 1709 at the Battle of Poltava, Peter's army turned back an invading Swedish army in Ukraine, a battle that marked the end of Sweden's status as a great power and its domination of northern Europe. Five years later Russian troops raided Sweden for the first time. After losing its German and Polish territories, Sweden then entered a period of constitutional struggles, marked by attempts by the nobility to reassert economic and social prerogatives lost to the monarchy and allowing Russia to solidify its expansion. The Treaty of Nystadt (1721), after which Peter proclaimed Russia an empire, confirmed Russian primacy in the Baltic region. This settlement added Estonia and Livonia (the southeastern part of modern Finland) to Peter's empire, bringing Russia ever closer to European affairs.

By the time of Peter's death in 1725, the territory controlled by Russia had increased sixfold since the time of Ivan the Terrible. The Russian Empire, thirty times bigger than France, had joined the European state system by virtue of its expanded territorial interests. The accession of Catherine the Great (1729–1796) in 1762 ended a long succession crisis, palace plots, and assassinations. The empress oversaw the next stage of Russian expansion, incorporating Ukraine into the empire.

Louis XIV's Dynastic Wars

The rulers of Russia, Sweden, and Turkey, like France, were seeking to expand their territories. Dynastic interests determined a state's choice of allies. Yet strong states with large standing armies were quite likely to switch sides, in order to gain the most beneficial terms from new allies. For example, in order to expand its influence in Central Europe, France needed an alliance with either Austria or Prussia. But inevitably such a coalition pushed the other German power into opposition, forcing it to look for allies against France. Usually this partner was England (called Great Britain following the union of England and Scotland in 1707), France's rival in North America. Following the conclusion of hostilities that reworked borders, alliances frequently shifted, as rulers anticipated the next opportunity to expand their territories.

Louis XIV was determined that territorial gain and prestige should be the measure of his greatness (see Map 7.4). He sought to expand his kingdom's borders to what he considered to be France's "natural" frontiers, that is, the Pyrenees Mountains to the south and the Rhine River to the east. International conditions seemed conducive to the king's grandiose plans. England had been divided by civil war in the 1640s, and its restored monarch, Charles II, faced mounting political opposition at home (see Chapter 6). To the north, Sweden confronted a Danish threat to its control of the Baltic Sea. In Central Europe, the Austrian Habsburgs faced opposition from other German princes, as well as from the Turks.

Louis XIV's "grand strategy" was to contain the two Habsburg powers, Spain and Austria, by initiating a series of wars. Each conflict followed the king's violation of a previous agreement or formal treaty, and was accompanied by the claim that French aggression was "just." Each war was to pay for itself: French armies would force local populations to offer

MAP 7.4 EXTENSION OF FRANCE'S FRONTIERS UNDER LOUIS XIV   Louis XIV sought to expand his dynastic territories through wars fought between 1643 and 1715.

"contributions." The Treaty of the Pyrenees (1659), ending this round of hostilities with Spain, established the frontier between the two nations that exists today.

France again went to war against Spain in 1667. Louis wanted to annex Spain's French-speaking Franche-Comté to the east and the Spanish Netherlands (Belgium) to the north. When French armies invaded the Spanish Netherlands, England, fearful that Flanders and its Channel ports would fall to France, joined the Dutch Republic, Sweden, and Spain to turn back Louis XIV's armies. By the Treaty of Aix-la-Chapelle (Aachen) in 1668, France extended its frontier further north, annexing Lille and part of Flanders. Four years later, Louis XIV invaded the Dutch Republic after assuring English neutrality by making secret payments to King Charles II. The Dutch fended off the French by opening up the dikes to create a barrier of water. After several more years of indecisive fighting and negotiations, France absorbed Franche-Comté, and tiny parcels of the Southern Netherlands. Still the king of France was not satisfied. He conquered Alsace and Lorraine beyond his eastern frontier by claiming each in turn and then launching an invasion. He annexed Strasbourg and occupied Luxembourg. Despite the opposition of a wary alliance of Habsburg Austria, Spain, Sweden, and Saxony, he ordered the invasion of the Palatinate, intending to secure the Rhine River. This initiated the War of the League of Augsburg (1688–1697). England and the Dutch Republic (an alliance solidified by the fact that William III of Orange now was king of England) and a number of other German states joined the alliance against France.

After hesitating in the face of massive opposition, in 1692 Louis made a foolish attempt to invade England. Dutch and English ships drove the French fleet onto rocks off the coast of Normandy; the two sea powers then enforced an economic blockade of France. Louis XIV retaliated by turning French privateers loose on his enemies' ships. French defeats as well as rising opposition in the Dutch Republic and England to the cost of the war forced both sides to negotiate. The Treaty of Ryswick of 1697 confirmed French gains in Alsace, but also made clear that the other European powers would ally again if necessary to keep France from further territorial acquisitions in the Southern Netherlands and the German states.

The question of the succession to the throne of Spain soon presented Louis XIV with the greatest temptation of all. The Habsburg King Charles II of Spain had no direct heir. Louis opposed the candidacy of the Habsburg Archduke Charles of Austria (son of Holy Roman Emperor Leopold I), hoping to end the virtual encirclement of France by Habsburg powers. Then Louis XIV, whose wife was the daughter of the late Philip IV of Spain, put forth his own claim to the throne.

When Charles II died in 1700, he left a will expressing his desire that his diminished empire remain intact, and that Louis XIV's grandson Philip of Anjou succeed him, but that Philip renounce all claim to the throne of France. However, on ascending the Spanish throne, the Bourbon Philip V (ruled 1700–1746) made clear that he favored the interests of his imposing grandfather. The Austrian Habsburg ruler Leopold I refused to accept Charles II's will as valid and attacked the Italian territories of the Spanish Habsburgs.

Louis XIV refused to rule Philip out of the line of succession to the French throne, so that if Philip's elder brother, the Duke of Bourgogne, died without male issue, Philip would then inherit the throne of France and the kingdoms would be joined. The matter became pressing in 1712, when smallpox struck the French royal family, leaving only Bourgogne's youngest son as heir to the French throne. If the future Louis XV had died then, Philip would have become heir to both kingdoms.

The French king's aggressive action drew Great Britain into the wars of the continent. The Dutch Republic again had reason to fear French occupation of the Spanish Netherlands. If the French opened up the Scheldt River to trade, Antwerp would reemerge as a commercial rival to Amsterdam. This vital link to the English Channel had been closed since the Dutch formally received independence from Spain in 1648, thus preventing ships from reaching Antwerp. The alliance against France also included Austria, Prussia, and Portugal. The War of the Spanish Succession reflected the fact that European wars were gradually taking on a global dimension (see Chapter 6), as the powers fought for markets as well as prestige. As in the War of the League of Augsburg, British and French forces also battled in North America.

France fought with Bavaria and Spain as allies. The English commander, the duke of Marlborough (1650–1722), raised an army of English, Dutch, and mercenary troops. In 1704, at Blenheim in southern Germany, the allied armies, aided by the Habsburg troops of Prince Eugene of Savoy (1663–1736), crushed a combined French and Bavarian force. Louis XIV's armies retreated behind the Rhine River. Winning victories in the Spanish Netherlands in 1708 and 1709, the allied armies also drove the French from the Spanish Netherlands and from the Italian peninsula. The English fleet captured Gibraltar (1704), which guards the entrance to the Mediterranean Sea. During the terrible winter of 1709–1710, France suffered military defeat and famine. The great kingdom of Louis XIV seemed on the verge of collapse.

But the French and Spanish armies revived their fortunes. Dynastic changes, too, helped Louis XIV's cause. In 1711, Archduke Charles of Austria became Holy Roman Emperor Charles VI (ruled 1711–1740). Should France and Philip V of Spain be defeated, the British and Dutch now confronted the possibility that Charles might one day become king of Spain, reviving the dynastic union that had made the Habsburgs Europe's strongest power during the first half of the seventeenth century. It was now in the interests of Great Britain and the Dutch Republic to bring the

The Rock of Gibraltar being captured by the English fleet during the War of Spanish Succession.

war to an honorable conclusion. Louis XIV, weakened by age and illness and suffering the financial burdens of the war, agreed to negotiate.

Under the 1713 Treaty of Utrecht (confirmed by the Treaty of Rastatt in 1714, when Emperor Charles VI accepted peace), Habsburg Austria received the Southern Netherlands as security against future French ambitions and annexed Lombardy and Naples, replacing Spain as the paramount power on the Italian peninsula (see Map 7.5). The decline of Spain, which had now lost all of its European possessions beyond the Pyrenees Mountains, continued unabated. In North America, France ceded Newfoundland, Nova Scotia, and Hudson Bay to Great Britain.

Louis XIV had reigned so long that on his death in 1715 the throne passed to his great-grandson, young Louis XV (ruled 1715–1774), with affairs of state in the hands of a regent. Philip V kept the throne of Spain, but the futures of the monarchies of Spain and France would be separate. Louis XIV was defeated by more than powerful alliances mounted against him. Britain had proved better able to sustain long wars; its more developed commerce and manufactures provided greater tax revenues. The non-absolutist British state collected taxes more efficiently than the absolute monarchy of France, where tax farmers kept part of the take. Britain's interests remained overseas, dominated by lucrative commercial concerns, protected by the Royal Navy. France's foreign policy led to more costly wars on the continent.

France had been the preeminent power in Europe at the time of the accession of Louis XIV; this was no longer true at his death. The king's

MAP 7.5 EUROPE IN 1721 Territorial realignments in Europe after the Treaty of Utrecht (1713), the Treaty of Rastatt (1714), and the Treaty of Nystadt (1721).

reputation had fallen victim to age and untempered ambition. Perhaps a lingering sense of failure explains why Louis XIV tried to burn his memoirs shortly before his death, although they were rescued from the fire by one of his officials. On his deathbed, Louis confessed with uncharacteristic insight that perhaps he had "loved glory too much."

THE MODERN STATE

As they established absolute rule, the sovereigns of continental Europe constructed the modern state. While extending authority over their subjects and expanding their dynastic territories, they developed state bureaucracies and established large standing armies. They broke noble resistance to absolute rule, confirming their privileges in exchange for loyalty to the throne. This relationship between rulers and nobles thus remained essential to the functioning of most European states in the eighteenth century.

Following a period of relative stability and even moderate economic expansion, the structure of Western European society then began to change as the European economy entered a remarkable period of dynamic growth, particularly during the second half of the eighteenth century. This was the case above all in Britain, where the expansion of capital-intensive agriculture techniques, population growth, and a boom in manufacturing combined to begin the Industrial Revolution. The changing structure of society, in turn, would affect the developing state by encouraging demands for political reform. Beginning in the 1760s and 1770s, the monopoly on political power by oligarchies and absolute rule itself would start to crumble.

Also under attack were traditional scientific assumptions, which had already been shaken as scientists expanded their knowledge of the universe. The methodology, discoveries, and culture of the Scientific Revolution helped create modern science.

PART THREE

NEW CULTURAL AND POLITICAL HORIZONS

During the late seventeenth century and the eighteenth century, Europe entered a period of remarkable intellectual and political ferment. Rejecting the weight of tradition, men and women of science developed the scientific method, a means of understanding based on systematic observation of natural phenomena and experimentation regarding their causes and effects. Their successors, the philosophes, the thinkers and writers of the Enlightenment, believed their role was to bring progress to the world through the application of reason to their reflections on the nature of mankind. Influenced by growing religious skepticism and drawing on expanding literacy, the philosophes espoused views of nature, mankind, society, and government that challenged some of the fundamental tenets most Europeans shared.

During this exciting period, Europe also entered a remarkable period of economic and social change. Increased agricultural productivity supported a larger population that, in turn, raised the demand for food and permitted the development of large-scale manufacturing in and around northern English towns.

Changes also came in the realm of political life. The public political sphere was transformed by the emergence of newspapers and learned associations, which facilitated political interest and discussion. Reform-minded people began to denounce unwarranted privilege and "despotism," and they celebrated the British model of constitutional monarchy and the successful rebellion of the American colonists against British rule. In a time of economic and social change, new cultural and political innovations began to transform Europe.

CHAPTER 8

THE NEW PHILOSOPHY
OF SCIENCE

In 1633, ecclesiastical authorities summoned the astronomer and physicist Galileo Galilei (1564–1642) to Rome to face the Inquisition. The stakes were high. Many Church fathers vehemently objected to Galileo's work on physics, for he espoused an atomistic theory of matter that seemed to challenge the Catholic Church's view that during Communion bread and wine become the body and blood of Christ. The Church also opposed Galileo's contention that the earth revolves around the sun. The papacy's political situation forced the Church's hand. Protestant armies had recaptured some of the lands in which the Catholic Reformation had appeared victorious. The papacy, its influence weakened by the Protestant Reformation and eclipsed by powerful dynastic rulers, could ill afford another defeat.

Urban VIII, who before his elevation to the pontificate had been Galileo's friend, accused the astronomer only of supporting the views of Copernicus, not of heresy. This would save Galileo from death but might also put the pope in a bad light for protecting the scientist. Although Galileo agreed to renounce these "errors" as heresies in order to avoid a death sentence, in 1633 he was still sentenced to a lifetime of house arrest. When guards returned him to his house, however, he cast a glance to the heavens and proclaimed of the earth, "See, it's still moving!"

The origins of modern science date to the seventeenth century, a period so marked by innovative thinking that it has been called the "century of genius." In several different corners of Europe, a few people struggled to understand the workings of the cosmos in a new way. Their own observations of the skies seemed to contradict explanations of the universe that had originated with Aristotle in the fourth century B.C. and, having acquired the authority of the Church, had been passed down for centuries. Breaking free of the bonds of tradition, these sixteenth-century thinkers developed the scientific method, a means of understanding based on systematic observation of natural phenomena and experimentation regarding causes and effects. But what we now know as the "Scientific Revolution" owed its impact less to new technology and inventions than to new ways of thinking about the universe.

CHANGING VIEWS OF THE UNIVERSE

The writings of the Greek philosopher Aristotle (384–322 B.C.) dominated European science for centuries. Then, in the sixteenth century, the Polish astronomer Copernicus observed the heavens and concluded that ancient and medieval science could not explain what he saw with his own eyes. Later in the century, his successors—above all, Galileo—made systematic mathematical calculations to explain celestial motion. In doing so, they created scientific methodology, which would also be applied to reach an understanding of the workings of the human body.

Ancient and Medieval Science

Aristotle believed that the earth was located at or near the center of the universe. He envisioned a hierarchical order of the cosmos comprised of a series of spheres that became progressively purer. Aristotle also believed that terrestrial bodies naturally moved toward the earth, the center of the universe, unless they were propelled in another direction. In this view, impetus imparted motion through contact with an object; when the contact ceased, the object simply stopped moving or fell back to earth. The natural tendency of all matter, then, was toward rest, regarded as a nobler state than motion. Because all motion had to be explained, a "mover" therefore had to be found for every motion.

In the second century A.D., the Greek astronomer Claudius Ptolemy (c. 85–165) published a massive work that became known as *Almagest* (from the Arabic for "greatest"), which summarized the conclusions of Greek astronomers and presented his own theories and observations. He described instruments such as the quadrant, invented by the Arabs, with which he tried to measure the orbits (which he believed to be spherical) of the sun, moon, and planets in the sky. Ptolemy accepted Aristotle's contentions, asserting that the earth was encased by a series of clear spheres—about eighty—revolving around it. The most distant sphere contained the furthest stars, which he believed were fixed points of light. Within those spheres, the moon was closest to the earth; next came the planets Mars, Venus, Jupiter, and Saturn. With minor variations, medieval thinkers still held Ptolemy's views.

Within the context of Christian theology, people of learning in the Middle Ages believed that scientific inquiry should serve theological ends by studying nature and explaining the mysterious ways of God. Church savants never raised the possibility that mankind could, with understanding, alter or master nature.

Aristotle's belief that the heavens and earth displayed two different kinds of motion—one toward the center of the earth, which seemed the natural state, but also an unnatural violent motion away from it—nicely fit the medieval Church's view that the universe consisted of good and evil. The earth, standing at the center, was heavy, corrupted not only by its weight but also by original sin and earthly misdeeds. Angels therefore were placed far off in a weightless existence in Heaven. The goal of human beings was to achieve the lightness of Heaven, God's domain, on the exterior edge of the universe.

The writings of the medieval poet Dante (1265–1321) reflected the prevailing influence of Aristotle's physics and Ptolemy's astronomy. Dante held that the universe comprised ten spheres surrounding the spherical, motionless earth. In his *Inferno,* Dante and the Roman poet Virgil travel to the core of the earth, then climb out to the other side, the Southern Hemisphere, where they find Purgatory. Hell lay at the earth's center, with Heaven in the distant tenth sphere. Dante and his contemporaries believed that the earth consisted of four elements: earth, water, air, and fire, the first two of which had a natural tendency to fall toward the center of the stationary earth.

Medieval European scholars seemed little interested in astronomy. Yet, to be sure, some medieval thinkers took significant steps toward modern science by embracing the study of natural phenomena and revering the scholars who studied such problems. Medieval scientists made lasting contributions in such fields as optics—inventing eyeglasses—and biology. They classified objects for study and espoused experimentation based on scientific procedures and the use of mathematics to verify theories. But even the contributions of the most brilliant medieval thinkers remained only in the realm of theory.

As the Renaissance drew on the discovery of classical prose, poetry, art, and architecture, Italian scholars of the period also turned to classical Greek scientific texts that had been recovered, edited, and printed. The Ottoman conquest of Greece during the fourteenth century had brought the Arabs into contact with classical learning. Arab scholars, who also made significant original contributions in astronomy, mathematics, and medicine, preserved many ancient Greek and Roman texts, translating them into Arabic. Some of the manuscripts brought by Greek scholars to the West from Constantinople after its conquest by the Turks in 1453 suggested that mathematics could be applied in the quest for knowledge about the universe. Arab scholars had raised troubling questions challenging age-old views of the earth as they observed and even began to measure the heavenly phenomena they beheld. In this way, the texts of Ptolemy became subjects of renewed interest and study.

Ptolemy's view of the cosmos reflected the domination of Aristotle's theory of motion. Yet there had earlier been at least one dissenting voice. Archimedes of Syracuse (c. 287–212 B.C.) had challenged Aristotle's contention that rest was a natural state for all objects and that only the presence of an "active mover" could generate motion. This view was picked up again in the fourteenth century by thinkers at the University of Paris and Oxford University. They observed that falling bodies move at an accelerating speed and that the accompanying presence of a "mover" simply could not be observed. A few scholars also rejected Aristotle's explanation that air itself served as a natural propellant. They observed that an arrow shot from a bow clearly was not continually propelled by air or anything else, but sooner or later simply fell to earth. The gradual development of a theory of motion, based on an understanding of the role of the mass of the moving object, along with the advances in the field of mathematics itself, provided the basis for new discoveries in astronomy and mechanics.

Copernicus Challenges the Aristotelian View of the Universe

The revolution in scientific thinking moved forward because of a cleric who kept his eyes toward the heavens, but not necessarily in pious contemplation. Nicolaus Copernicus (1473–1543) launched the strongest attack yet on the Aristotelian view of the universe. He was born near the Baltic coast in Poland. After the death of his father, Copernicus's uncle (a wealthy bishop) assumed responsibility for his education. From the University of Cracow, Copernicus went to Italy to study medicine and law. After learning Greek, he read medieval scientific and humanist texts. Also trained as a doctor and portrait painter, he devoted his life to observation and discovery.

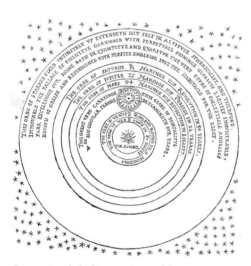

Copernicus's heliocentric world system.

Copernicus's *Concerning the Revolutions of the Celestial Spheres* was not published until he lay dying in 1543, the same year the work of Archimedes was first translated into Latin. Paradoxically, in view of the intense theological debate it would generate, Copernicus dedicated his study to the pope. Copernicus was troubled by the inability of the Ptolemaic system (itself a refraction of the Aristotelian view of the universe) to account for what his own observations, made with the naked eye, told him: that the planets, the moon, and the stars obviously did not move around the earth at the same speed. Nor did they seem to be in the spherical orbits Ptolemy had assigned them. That Mars seemed to vary in brightness particularly perplexed him. What Copernicus observed, in short, contradicted the fundamental assumptions of the Aristotelian and Ptolemaic universe.

Even before Copernicus, some thinkers questioned Aristotelian physics and the Ptolemaic cosmos, but they generally did not venture out of the realm of mere speculation. Nicholas of Cusa (1401–1464), a German bishop and theologian who wrote on astronomy, believed the earth might be in motion, but neither he nor anyone else in the period tried to make mathematical calculations that might prove or reject this bold theory. He had suggested the possibility that the sun stands at the center of the universe and, by implication, that the universe is infinite and nonhierarchical in nature, unlimited by Aristotelian layers of spheres. The extraordinary Renaissance artist and humanist Leonardo da Vinci, who called wisdom "the daughter of experiment," had also suggested that the earth might move around the sun.

Copernicus concluded that the sun, not the earth, lies at the center of the universe and that the earth rotates on its axis once a day and revolves around the sun once every 365 days. "In the middle of all sits the Sun enthroned," he wrote. "How could we place this luminary in any better position in this most beautiful temple from which to illuminate the whole at once?" Copernicus's postulation was, like his critique of some of Ptolemy's conclusions, not totally original. But his assertions were bold, explicit, and, for many, convincing. Furthermore, they suggested that mathematics could verify astronomical theories.

The notion that the earth was just one of many planets rotating in circular orbit around the sun raised shocking questions about the earth's status. This perplexed and angered Catholic, Protestant, and Jewish theologians by seeming to reduce the standing of mankind. It seemed unbelievable that mere mortals peering into the heavens were themselves moving rapidly through the universe. Martin Luther, himself not given to accepting inherited wisdom without skepticism, said of Copernicus, "This fool wants to turn the whole of astronomy upside down!"

Copernicus did just that. Yet he seemed uninterested in carrying out his own systematic observations and made serious errors in some of his calculations. He also could not explain why there was no constant wind from the east, which might be expected based on the assumption that the earth moved in that direction around the sun. Copernicus sometimes sought to answer his own doubts by turning to the teachings of the ancients and did not completely abandon the system of celestial spheres postulated by Ptolemy, whom he continued to revere. Copernicus also continued to accept the notion that the spherical universe was finite, and that it perhaps was limited by the stars fixed in the heavens.

The Universal Laws of the Human Body

As scientists began to chart movements in the heavens, some scholars now began to question old assumptions about the human body. They contended that it is subject to the same universal laws that govern celestial and terrestrial motion. The Renaissance had generated interest in human anatomy. Most assumptions about how the body works had been passed down for centuries from the ancient world. Galen (129–c. 210), a Greek contemporary of Ptolemy, was the first person to develop theories about medicine based on scientific experiments. He carried out a number of experiments on apes, assuming that animal and human bodies were essentially the same in the arrangement of bodily organs. Like Aristotle, Galen believed that disease followed from an imbalance in the four bodily humors—blood, phlegm, yellow bile, and black bile. He held that two kinds of blood initiated muscle movement and digestion, respectively: bright red blood, which flowed up and down through the arteries, and dark red blood, which could be found in the veins. Doubting Galen's view of anatomy, Andreas Vesalius (1514–1564) published *On the Fabric of the Human Body* (1543). Arguably the founder of modern biological science, Vesalius rejected old explanations for the circulation of blood and began to dissect and study cadavers—in the Middle Ages, the Church had considered this to be sinful—and was the first to assemble human skeletons.

The English scientist William Harvey (1578–1657) largely solved the riddle of how blood circulates. Like the astronomers, he adopted a scientific methodology: "I profess," he wrote, "to learn and teach anatomy not

Vesalius dissecting a cadaver.

from books but from dissections, not from the tenets of philosophers but from the fabric of nature." Harvey's accomplishment was in the realm of thought and owed virtually nothing to prior inventions. Indeed, he made his discoveries before the invention of the microscope, and he referred only twice in his experiments to a magnifying glass.

Harvey's theory of blood circulation pictured the heart and its valves functioning as a mechanical pump. Yet Harvey, like medieval thinkers, retained a belief that "vital spirits" were to be found in the blood. The long-term consequence of Harvey's work was, as in the case of Vesalius, to undermine further Aristotelian philosophy and medieval science and to help establish a basis for the development of modern biology and medicine in later centuries.

Brahe and Kepler Explore the Heavens

Tycho Brahe (1546–1601), a Danish astronomer, and Johannes Kepler (1571–1630), his German assistant, carried the search for an understanding of the way the universe works to a new stage of scientific knowledge. While studying philosophy at the University of Copenhagen, Brahe became fascinated with the heavens after observing a partial eclipse of the sun. Brahe, an odd-looking nobleman who had lost part of his nose in a duel and had replaced it with a construction of silver and gold alloy perched above his handlebar moustache, built an astronomical observatory on a Danish island.

Brahe rejected Copernicus's contention that the earth rotated around the sun. He claimed that if this were true, a cannonball fired from west to east (the direction Copernicus thought the earth moved) would travel farther in that direction, and a weight dropped from a tall tower would strike earth to the west of the tower because of the earth's movement. Brahe came up with a cumbersome compromise explanation that had the five known planets rotating around the sun, which in turn moved around the stationary earth.

In 1572, Brahe observed a bright exploding star. This and a comet sighted five years later irrevocably compromised the Aristotelian view of the universe as unchanging. Brahe compiled extensive data based upon his own observations, systematically charting what he could see of the planetary orbits and using mathematics to locate the position of the planets and stars. At the same time, his rejection of the Copernican view that the sun was the center of the universe and the fact that his calculations were often inaccurate remind us that the Scientific Revolution did not develop in a linear fashion. False turns and setbacks were part of the story.

Johannes Kepler, Brahe's assistant, was the son of a German mercenary soldier and an herb dealer with an interest in astrology (his mother would later be condemned to be burned at the stake for her dabblings in astrology; Kepler saved her life by undertaking a lengthy legal process). Kepler was a dazzling but strange individual: a rigorous astronomer and mathematician as well as a religious mystic and astrologer, who took credit for predicting not only a particularly harsh winter but also peasant uprisings in Germany.

Facing persecution from Lutheran theologians in 1596 because of his Copernican beliefs, Kepler briefly found protection from the Jesuits. But four years later, he was forced to leave a teaching position in Austria because he refused to convert from Lutheranism to Catholicism. Kepler moved to Prague and began to work with Brahe in 1600. On his deathbed,

(*Left*) Johannes Kepler. (*Right*) Kepler's depiction of the orbits of the planets.

Brahe implored Kepler to complete his observation tables. Holy Roman Emperor Rudolph II, whose interest in science outweighed any concern that Kepler was Protestant, appointed him to succeed Brahe as imperial mathematician.

Kepler shared Copernicus's belief that observers on earth were moving while the sun stood still. After carefully plotting the orbit of Mars, Kepler concluded that the orbits of the planets were "imperfect"—not circular, but rather elliptical. He also concluded that the planets were affected by some sort of force emanating from the sun. William Gilbert (1544–1603), an English scientist, had published a book on the magnet in 1600, the first study written by a university scholar and informed by laboratory experimentation. Gilbert's investigations of magnetic force provided a model for the development of a modern theory of gravitation. Kepler now decided that it was perhaps magnetic force that attracted the earth and sun to each other. He also determined that tides were the result of the magnetic attraction of the earth and the moon.

Based upon his mathematical calculations, Kepler postulated three laws of planetary motion, which he assumed were determined by the power, or specific magnetic attraction, of the sun. Kepler used observation and mathematical calculations to demonstrate that the planets were a separate grouping with different properties from those of the fixed stars, and that Aristotle's crystalline spheres simply did not exist.

Kepler's discoveries, blows to Aristotelian and medieval science, also suggested that the hand of the prime mover—God—was not required to govern the movement of the planets. Even more than Copernicus's placing of the sun at the center of the universe, Kepler's conclusions challenged the theological assumptions of the Catholic Church. Nonetheless, the

Scientific Revolution still occurred within the system of Christian belief. Kepler himself sought to glorify God by demonstrating the consistency, harmony, and order of divine creation as expressed in the working of the universe.

Francis Bacon and the Scientific Method

From England, Sir Francis Bacon (1561–1626), lawyer, statesman, and philosopher, launched a frontal assault on ancient and medieval metaphysics and science. Calling himself "a bellringer who is first up to call others to church," Bacon helped detach science from philosophy. Medieval scholasticism had focused, he argued, on abstract problems that were without practical consequences, such as the question of how many angels could stand on the head of a pin. So, too, had Renaissance humanism. Bacon rejected outright all arguments based on the weight of traditional authority, calling for "a total reconstruction of sciences, arts and all human knowledge."

Bacon carried out few experiments and made no discoveries that could have been considered significant by his own standards (he died after catching a bad cold while carrying out an experiment of marginal value: stuffing snow into a dead chicken). But Bacon announced the dawn of a new era in which humans would gradually begin to understand and then perhaps even overcome their physical environment. Through inductive reasoning—that is, proceeding from observation and experimentation to conclusions or generalizations—the truths of the universe would be revealed by discovery and scientific experiment, not by religion. "Arts and sciences," Bacon wrote in 1620, "should be like mines, where the noise of new works and further advances is heard on every side." Scientists should divide up the toil by specializing and working in cooperation to "overcome the necessities and miseries of humanity." Bacon's renown—he served for three years as King James I of England's Lord Chancellor (before being dismissed for accepting bribes)—helped create interest in science in England, althrough this was limited to a small number of people.

Galileo and Science on Trial

On the Italian peninsula, Galileo emerged as the dominant figure of the early stage of the Scientific Revolution. The scion of a wealthy family, he studied medicine and mathematics. Like Copernicus, he taught at the University of Padua, the leading center of scientific learning in Europe, at a time when virtually every other university showed little interest in scientific observation. That Padua was under the protection of Venice, which was hostile to the pope, facilitated its university's precocious role in the development of scientific methodology. Scholars in Padua hotly debated Aristotelian explanations of motion as well as the question of the relationship between the natural sciences and metaphysics, or the nature of being. The latter debate was especially crucial, because on it hinged the question of whether scientific investigation could be independent of the Catholic Church, which considered revealed religion the only source of knowledge.

New ways of thinking about the heavens, systematic observation, and scientific measurement had played a more significant role in the early stages of the Scientific Revolution than did the development of new technology. The invention of the telescope, however, led to a further advance in the Scientific Revolution. Upon learning in 1609 that a man in Holland had invented a "spy glass" that could magnify objects many times, Galileo constructed one of his own. This telescope enabled him to study Jupiter's moons, Saturn's spectacular rings, some of the innumerable stars of the Milky Way, and craters on the moon. His observation of spots that seemed to move on the surface of the sun led Galileo to conclude that the sun, too, rotated. That sunspots seemed to change also challenged the traditional view of the static nature of the universe.

Galileo undermined the Aristotelian theories of motion. He demonstrated that the earth was in perpetual rotation and that balls of varying weights will pick up speed at the same rate as they fall, so therefore their speed is not determined by their mass. From such experiments, he developed a theory of inertia: a body moving at a constant speed in a straight line will continue to move until encountering another force. He demonstrated that air and clouds move with the earth as it rotates around the

(*Left*) Francis Bacon at work. (*Right*) The feisty Galileo at age sixty.

sun, while appearing immobile to an observer also moving with the earth. The rooms in his house that he set aside for experimentation served as the first university laboratory.

Unlike other scholars, Galileo did not disdain seeking practical information from craftsmen and artisans. He consulted workers who built cannons, soldiers who fired them, and people who made compasses, astrolabes, quadrants, and other scientific instruments for navigation. He began to investigate water pumps and other means of regulating rivers, as well as planning the construction of stronger military fortresses. Nonetheless, he did not care whether or not his discoveries reached ordinary people. Moreover, he claimed that "the mobility of the earth is a proposition far beyond the comprehension of the common people." And he believed that the "all-too-numerous vulgar" ought to be kept in darkness, lest they "become confused, obstinate, and contumacious."

At first, Galileo tried to reconcile his findings and those of Copernicus with early Church texts. But the feisty Galileo's insistence that the universe was mathematical in its very structure and subject to laws of mechanics that could be discovered left him open to attacks by ecclesiastical authorities. In 1610, he wrote Kepler, "Here at Padua is the principal professor of theology, whom I have repeatedly and urgently requested to look at the moon and planets through my glass, which he obstinately refused to do. Why are you not here? What shouts of laughter we should have at this glorious folly!" In 1616, the pope condemned Galileo's proposition that the sun is the center of the universe and warned him not to teach it. Undaunted, Galileo published his *Dialogue Concerning Two World Systems—Ptolemaic and Copernican,* in which he taunted Aristotelians by presenting a lengthy dialogue between those espousing the respective systems of Ptolemy and Copernicus. A certain Simplicio took the side of Ptolemy in the dialogues; the character's very name outraged the Church by intimating that a farcical character symbolized the pope. This led to Galileo's condemnation by the Inquisition in 1633. But from house arrest in his villa in the hills above Florence, Galileo continued to observe, experiment, and write, publishing his texts in Holland. When he went blind in 1638, the pope refused to allow him to go to Florence to see a doctor. Despite his blindness, he continued his scientific investigations until his death four years later.

DESCARTES AND NEWTON: COMPETING THEORIES OF SCIENTIFIC KNOWLEDGE

Two brilliant thinkers, one French and the other English, both accepted Galileo's revision of classical and medieval systems of knowledge. But they offered contrasting theories of scientific knowledge. René Descartes sought to discover the truth through deductive reasoning. Across the English Channel, Isaac Newton followed his countryman Bacon's insistence that the way to knowledge was through scientific experiment. One amazing discovery after another added to the foundations of the "new philosophy" of science. Science played a major part in the quest for demonstrable truth and authority during and following the period of intense social and political turmoil that lasted from the 1590s until the mid-seventeenth century.

Descartes and Deductive Reasoning

The reclusive French philosopher René Descartes (1596–1650) shared Bacon's and Galileo's critiques of ancient and medieval learning. But he offered a different methodology for understanding the universe, espousing deductive reasoning, that is, deducing a conclusion from a set of premises, not from scientific observation.

In 1637, Descartes published *Discourse on Method*. In this deeply personal account, he discussed his rejection of the scientific teaching he had encountered as a young man. Too much of what he had learned had been handed down from tradition without critical commentary. He defiantly "resolved no longer to seek any other science than the knowledge of myself, or of the great book of the world."

Any person, Descartes claimed, has to begin as a blank slate in order to understand the world through deductive reasoning. "I think, therefore I am" (*Cogito, ergo sum*) was his starting point, the postulation of a self-evident truth and the assertion that the ability to think is the basis of human existence. Then each problem has to be separated, he argued, into "as many parts as may be necessary for its adequate solution," moving from the simplest idea to the most difficult, in the same way as a mathematical proof is formulated. Cartesianism (the philosophy of Descartes and his followers) held that the world could be reduced to two substances: mind and matter, "thinking substance" and "extended substance." Matter—defined as an infinite number of particles that fill all space, leaving neither void nor vacuum—could be discovered and described mathematically, as could the laws of motion. Beginning with the certainty of his own existence, Descartes argued that the existence of the material universe and God could be deduced. "Begin with the smallest object, the easiest to understand," he insisted, "and gradually move to a knowledge of those that are the most complex."

This materialist approach to knowledge left little or no room for ancient or medieval learning. As a sign of this break, Descartes published his works in French, identifying Latin with ecclesiastical doctrine and scholasticism. Like Kepler, Descartes viewed God as a benevolent, infinitely powerful clockmaker, who created the universe according to rules that the human mind could discover with proper reasoning. God then stepped back, according to this view, forever absent from the actual workings of what He had created.

Mathematics, Descartes argued, demonstrates "the certainty and self-evidence of its reasonings." It therefore stood as the foundation of all science. Eventually a rule for every phenomenon could be discovered. Descartes thus subordinated experimentation to reason in the quest for truth. One of the stream of savants who went to meet Descartes recalled that "many of them would desire him to shew them his Instruments . . . he would drawe out a little Drawer under his Table, and shew them a paire of Compasses

René Descartes.

with one of the Legges broken; and then, for his Ruler, he used a sheet of paper folded double."

The Newtonian Synthesis

Sir Isaac Newton (1642–1727) built upon the thought of Kepler, Galileo, and Descartes to effect a bold synthesis of the Scientific Revolution, to which he added his own extraordinary discoveries. Newton's *Principia, The Mathematical Principles of Natural Philosophy* (1687) was the first synthesis of scientific principles. Newton synthesized the empiricism of Galileo and others with the theoretical rigor and logic of Descartes, thereby laying the foundations for modern science, which is based on both theory and experimentation.

Newton conducted some of his experiments while living on his prosperous family's farm. There, sitting under a tree, ruminating about celestial motion, Newton observed a falling apple, which led him to recognize that the force that caused objects to fall to earth was related to planetary motion. Newton demonstrated that earthly and celestial motion are subject to laws that could be described by mathematical formulas, the science of mechanics. Going beyond Kepler's three laws of planetary motion, Newton postulated a theory of universal gravitation, the existence of forces of attraction and repulsion operating between objects. Newton concluded that Kepler's laws of planetary motion would be correct if the planets were being pulled toward the sun by a force whose strength was in inverse proportion to their distance from it. The moon, too, seemed to be drawn to the earth in the same way, while the pull that it exerted determined the ocean tides. Every particle of matter, Newton concluded, attracts every other particle with a force proportional to the product of the two masses, and inversely proportional to the square of the distance that separates them.

Newton combined the insights of his predecessors with his own brilliant discoveries. He correctly calculated that the average density of the earth is about five and a half times that of water, suggested that electrical messages activate the nervous system, and anticipated some of the ideas that two centuries later would form the basis of thermodynamics and quantum theory. Newton was the first to understand that all colors are composed of a mixture of the primary colors of the spectrum. He explained the phenomenon of the rainbow, calculated sound waves, and invented calculus (invented concurrently but separately by Gottfried Leibniz). In the late 1660s, he also constructed the first reflecting telescope (previous telescopes had used a refracting lens). Newton's first paper on optics, published in 1671, proposed that light could be mathematically described and analyzed. Some scientists still consider it to mark the beginning of theoretical physics.

Unlike his predecessors in the development of science, Newton became wealthy and a hero in his own time. He was elected to Parliament in 1689 representing Cambridge University, where he was professor, became warden of the Royal Mint, and was knighted by the king. However, Newton remained a remote, chaste, humorless figure who published his discoveries with reluctance and initially only when it seemed that rivals might first take the credit for a discovery. He brazenly accused those working on similar problems of copying him, and was ungenerous in acknowledging what he had learned from others. His fame marked the victory of the scientific method, however, over ancient and medieval thought. The eighteenth-century English poet Alexander Pope went so far as to compare Newton's accomplishments with those of God on the first day of creation: "Nature and Nature's laws lay hid in night; God said, Let Newton be! and all was light!" Newton was given a state funeral and buried in London's Westminster Abbey.

The Newtonian synthesis of scientific thinking and discovery spread rapidly from England to the continent. Newton's followers clashed with Cartesians, the followers of Descartes. Newton rejected Descartes's materialism, at least partially because it seemed to leave open the possibility that the world was made up totally of

Sir Isaac Newton.

matter and that God did not exist, although the French philosopher never made such an assertion. For his part, Newton believed that God had to intervene from time to time to keep the great clock of creation running, lest it run down. That Newton continued to produce manuscripts on theological questions reflected his own belief that there seemed to be no necessary contradiction between science and religious faith.

Like Descartes, Newton insisted on the explanatory power of abstract reasoning. But despite his postulation of theories that could not be demonstrated by the scientific method, such as his description of gravity as a force that operates between two objects in space, where possible Newton sought to confirm them experimentally. Until at least 1720, some tension remained between the English scientific groups (who insisted on the necessity of experimentation) and their French and German Cartesian counterparts. Yet this was a creative tension, based on a common acceptance of the primacy of scientific inquiry.

The Cartesians found an ally in the Spanish-born Dutch philosopher and mathematician Baruch Spinoza (1632–1677), who also believed that thought and matter formed the two categories of reality. While making his living grinding lenses for glasses, he found both a philosopher's introspective isolation—arguing in a Cartesian manner that human understanding advances through inner reflection—and stimulation from the new physics. Expelled from the Jewish community of Amsterdam in 1656 for refusing to participate in religious ceremonies, Spinoza, a proponent of human liberation, called for toleration of all beliefs.

The northern German philosopher and mathematician Gottfried Leibniz (1646–1716) agreed with Descartes and rejected Newton's suggestion that God had to intervene from time to time in the operations of the universe, believing this idea to be demeaning to the Creator's divinity. For Leibniz, the universe was, like God, infinite in space and time. The bodies of humans and animals ran like clocks, set in motion, like the universe itself, by God. Leibniz's popularity helped perpetuate the Cartesian challenge to Newton, notably in France. His deductive postulation of the infinite nature of the universe and his Cartesian insistence that God created the universe to run without further divine intervention according to the mathematical laws Newton had discovered became the hallmarks of the "new philosophy."

THE CULTURE OF SCIENCE

A "culture of science" developed in Western Europe and very gradually spread eastward. By the 1660s, letters, newsletters, and periodicals linked Europeans interested in science. Gradually a "republic of science" took shape, spawning meetings, lectures, visits by traveling scholars, correspondence, book purchases, personal libraries, and public experiments. Above all, the formation of learned associations provided a focal point for the exchange of scientific information and vigorous debates over methodology and findings, expanding the ranks of people interested in science. Only a few decades after Galileo's condemnation, Louis XIV of France and Charles II of England granted patronage to institutions founded to propagate scientific learning. Attracted by scientific discoveries, rulers realized that science could be put to use in the interest of their states.

The Diffusion of the Scientific Method

Although most scientific exchange still occurred by correspondence, savants of science also traveled widely seeking to exchange ideas and learn from each other. For example, the Czech scholar Comenius (Jan Komensky; 1592–1670), a member of the Protestant Unity of Czech Brethren, left his native Moravia in the wake of religious persecution during the Thirty Years' War. After more than a decade in Poland, he began to visit scholars in many countries. For seven years, he traveled in the German states, Holland, England, Sweden, and Hungary. Publishing hundreds of works, he proposed that one day scientific knowledge should be brought together in a collaborative form.

Learned associations and scientific societies had already begun to appear in a number of cities, including Rome and Paris, in the 1620s. In London, a bequest made possible the establishment of Gresham College, which became a center for scientific discussion and research. In Paris, Marin Mersenne (1588–1637), a monk who had translated Galileo's writings into French, stood at the center of a network of vigorous scientific exchange that cut across national boundaries of states. He organized informal gatherings, attended by, among others, Blaise Pascal (1623–1662), a gloomy young physicist and mathematician who originated the science of probability.

In England, above all, the culture of science became part of public life during the period from 1640 to 1660, with the vocabulary of science joining the discourse of the English upper classes. Newton's prestige further spurred interest in scientific method. In several London coffeehouses, Newtonians offered "a course of Philosophical Lectures on Mechanics, Hydrostatis, Pneumatics [and] Opticks." Exchanges, debates, and even acrimonious disputes reached an ever wider scholarly audience. In England, pamphlets and books on scientific subjects were published in unprecedented numbers.

The Royal Society of London for Improving Natural Knowledge was formed in 1662 under the patronage of Charles II. Its diverse membership, which included merchants, naval officers, and craftsmen, reflected the growing interest in science in England. Members included Edmund

Testelin's tapestry of the establishment of the French Royal Academy of Science, 1666, and the Foundation of the Observatory, 1667.

Halley (1656–1742), an astronomer who catalogued and discovered the actual movement of the stars and who also discovered the comet that bears his name; the philosopher John Locke (1632–1704), founder of British empiricism, who held that laws of society, like those of science, could be discovered; and Christopher Wren (1632–1723), a versatile architect who rebuilt some of London's churches (including St. Paul's Cathedral) in the wake of the fire of 1666, but who was also a mathematician and professor of astronomy.

The Royal Society, to which Newton dedicated *Principia* and of which he served as president, took its motto from one of the letters of the Roman writer Horace: "The words are the words of a master, but we are not forced to swear by them. Instead we are to be borne wherever experiment drives us." The Royal Society's hundred original members doubled in number by 1670, its weekly meetings attracting visiting scholars. One of the latter, who lived in Paris, reported with some astonishment that "no one is in a hurry to speak, nor tries to speak too long, or to tell all that he knows. [The members] never interrupt the speaker and dissension does not rise to the surface, nor even is a tone heard that could displease. One could not find any more civil, respectful or well-organized gathering than this." The *Philosophical Transactions of the Royal Society* published some of the most important work of members and foreign correspondents, especially in the field of mathematics.

The natural philosopher Margaret Cavendish, the duchess of Newcastle (1623–1673), participated in debates about matter and motion, the vacuum, magnetism, and the components of color and fire. The author of books on natural philosophy, as well as a number of plays and poems, Cavendish also hosted the "Newcastle circle," an informal gathering of distinguished scientists that received Descartes. But she worked in isolation, which she attributed not only to the fact that she was shy, but to her sex. Despite the evidence of her own achievements, she accepted, at least in her early years, the contemporary assumptions that women had smaller and softer brains than men, and thus were somehow unfit for science and philosophy. Few men of science would have agreed with the assertion in 1673 by one of Descartes's disciples in France that "the mind has no sex." This bold statement reflected Descartes's belief that thought transcended gender differences—and, therefore, having sense organs equal to men's, women should be recognized as their equals. But although Cavendish was permitted to attend one session, women were formally banned from the Royal Society—this would last until 1945—and they were also excluded from English universities.

In 1666, the French Royal Academy of Science held its first formal meeting in Paris. Like the English Royal Society, the French Academy enjoyed the patronage of the monarchy, which even provided the French Academy with an astronomical observatory. Branches of the Academy began in several provincial cities. Unlike members of its English counterpart, those in the French Academy spent much time eating and drinking—

The Newcastle circle hosted by the duke and duchess of Newcastle. Margaret Cavendish, the duchess, is seated on the far right crowned with laurels.

one of them complained that too much time was wasted at the fancy dinners that preceded scholarly discussion.

Although some writers deliberately had used Latin because they believed that knowledge ought to remain the preserve of the educated few, with the gradual ebbing of Latin as the language of science, language barriers became a greater obstacle to the diffusion of ideas and research. Galileo had written in Italian to attract a wider audience among the elite, but also to remove science from Latin, the language of religious discourse. Newton wrote *Principia* in Latin, in part because only then could his work be read by most continental scholars. Newton's *Optics,* by contrast, appeared first in English, then in Latin and French translations. Gradually during the eighteenth century, each country's vernacular became the language of its scientists.

By the end of the seventeenth century, Descartes's ideas had overcome Calvinist opposition to find their way into Dutch university curricula. But the further east one went in Europe, the weaker was the impact of the Scientific Revolution. Scientific inquiry lagged in Poland, in part because of the success of the Catholic Reformation, which restricted the free flow of scholarly thought. Several printing houses in Gdańsk (Danzig) owned by Protestants began publishing scientific works in the second half of the seventeenth century, however. Leibniz enjoyed popularity in the Habsburg domains, at least partially because he served several German rulers in a diplomatic capacity, and perhaps also because his contagious optimism and belief that God had preordained harmony found resonance in the diverse and scattered kingdom. Nonetheless, theological and devotional literature still dominated the shelves of university, monastic, and imperial libraries. The few publications on science remained strongly Aristotelian.

Some savants in the East did become aware of the debates in the West on the scientific method. Protestant thinkers in Hungary and Silesia, for example, were gradually exposed to the ideas of Bacon and Descartes by traveling scholars from Western Europe, and a few Hungarians and Silesians learned of the new ideas by visiting Dutch universities. Some Bohemian and Polish nobles began to include books on the new science in their private libraries, one of which eventually comprised over 300,000 volumes and 10,000 manuscripts. Theoretical and practical astronomical work spread in the Habsburg lands, carried on in some cases by Jesuits. Mathematics, optics, and problems of atmospheric pressure, too, were the focus of debate. Holy Roman Emperor Ferdinand III (ruled 1637–1657) studied military geometry, constructing arithmetic toys for his children. But Copernicus and Kepler notwithstanding, early modern Central Europe would be far more remembered for its music than for its science.

Russia's distant isolation from Western culture—the Renaissance had absolutely no influence there—was compounded by the Orthodox Church's antipathy toward the West and, therefore, opposition to scientific experimentation. There was, to be sure, acceptance of some practical knowledge from the West, for example relating to the military, mining, or metallurgy, which largely arrived with foreign merchants and adventurous craftsmen. Seventeenth-century Russia had no gifted scientists and no scientific societies. Until the reign of Peter the Great, virtually all books published in Russia were devotional in character, and Russian culture was essentially that of a monastery. Foreign books began to appear at court only after about 1650, many arriving from Poland and Ukraine. At that point, however, the Orthodox Church, having suffered a schism, launched another campaign against Western ideas, denouncing secular knowledge as heresy and science as the work of the Antichrist. But gradually some nobles began to be exposed to ideas from the natural sciences. These were the Russian nobles who were dissatisfied with Church learning and eager to know more, for example, about the geography of their own expanding state. The literate classes in Russia would thereafter in many ways remain divided between those interested in ideas coming from the West (most of what was known in the West was available in Russia by 1725) and those who rejected them in the name of preserving what they considered Russia's uniqueness as the most dominant Slavic state.

The Uses of Science

The seventeenth-century Scientific Revolution was above all a revolution in thought. Technological inventions that would change the way people lived lay for the most part in the future. But during the second half of the seventeenth century, scientific experimentation led to the practical application of some discoveries. Thanks to Newton, longitude could now be easily established and ocean tides accurately charted. Voyages of discovery, commerce, and conquest to the Americas increased the demand for new navigational instruments. Dutch scientists and craftsmen led the way in producing telescopes, microscopes, binoculars, and other scientific instruments.

But gradually, too, physicians, engineers, mariners, instrument makers, opticians, pharmacists, and surveyors, many of them self-educated, began to apply the new discoveries to daily life. Robert Hooke (1635–1703), another member of the Royal Society, improved the barometer, which measures atmospheric pressure, and augmented the power of the microscope by adding multiple lenses. This allowed him to study the cellular structure of plants. Biologists began to collect, categorize, dissect, and describe fossils, birds, and exotic fish, adding to contemporary understanding of the richness and complexity of the world around them.

As Francis Bacon had predicted, governments began to tap science in the service of the state. Absolute monarchs on the continent sought out scientists to produce inventions that would give them commercial and military advantages over their rivals. In France, Jean-Baptiste Colbert, Louis XIV's minister of finance, called on a Dutch scientist to explain his experi-

The University of Padua in Italy, pictured at about the time Galileo taught there.

ments on "the vacuum, force of [gun]powders, steam, wind, and collision." He sought to steer the Royal Academy of Science toward the study of what he considered useful subjects that might benefit French commerce and industry, ordered the collection of statistics, and commissioned people to make reliable maps of the provinces and colonies. English government officials also began to apply statistics to administrative and social problems.

Tsar Peter the Great (see Chapter 7) was convinced by his trip to the West that Russia would have to borrow from the West. He corresponded with Leibniz, who convinced him that empirical science, along with the creation of a system of education, would bring progress. The tsar wanted to refute the Western view that "we are barbarians who disregard science." Peter's campaign of westernization, which included opening his country to Western scientific ideas, made Russia a great power. The sciences that interested Peter were those that were useful in statemaking: mechanics, chemistry, and mathematics aided in building ships and improving artillery.

Science and Religion

As scientific discoveries led more people to doubt religious authority that was based on faith alone, points of tension not surprisingly continued to emerge between science and religion. This was particularly the case with the Catholic and Orthodox Churches. There seemed to be a close association between Protestant countries and advances in science, given the precocious role of England and, to a lesser extent, the Dutch Netherlands in the emergence of a culture of science. This contributed to the debate over whether Protestantism itself was more conducive to scientific inquiry.

Theological concerns still dominated the curricula at most universities, despite the role of the University of Padua, and of the University of Cambridge, where by the 1690s both Newton's theories and those of Descartes were taught. Universities contributed relatively little to the diffusion of the scientific method. During the seventeenth century as a whole, their enrollments declined as the European population stagnated. In Catholic countries, canon law and in Protestant states, civil law, predominated in universities, which trained Church and state officials, respectively. The number of German universities more than doubled to about forty during the seventeenth century. The impetus for their creation came from Lutheranism and Calvinism, however, not from an interest in science.

Catholic universities continued to be the most traditional. Following Descartes's death in 1650, the University of Paris, which had about 30,000 students and was the largest university on the continent, forbade a funeral oration for him. Almost three decades later, the archbishop of Paris declared that "in physics it is forbidden to deviate from the principles of the physics of Aristotle . . . and to attach oneself to the new doctrines of Descartes." The University of Paris continued to exclude the new philosophy until the 1730s. Experimental physics as well as botany and chemistry were absent from university study throughout Europe.

The salient role of Protestants in the diffusion of scientific method reflected differences between the theological stance of the Catholic Church and the more liberal ethos of the Protestant Reformation. Catholic theologians held to dogmas of faith and obedience, leaving little room for innovation or experimentation. The Protestant belief that an individual should seek truth and salvation in his or her own religious experience through a personal interpretation of the Bible encouraged skepticism about doctrinal theology. The emphasis on individual discovery seemed to lead naturally to empiricism. In Protestant countries, the Reformation had undermined the institutional monopoly on truth effectively maintained in Catholic countries. While Protestant theologians also could be rigid and unyielding, there was no Protestant equivalent to the papal Index of Forbidden Ideas or Books or the mechanism of the Inquisition. Although the Massachusetts Bay Puritans may have forced religious attendance and sought to control what church members read, the English colonies, too, generally accepted the principle of toleration.

Scientists in Catholic states, confronted by ecclesiastical denunciations or by reports of miracles that seemed to fly in the face of logic, found support in Protestant lands. The Protestant Dutch Republic, fighting a long civil war against Spanish rule, emerged as a center of toleration, where most books could be published. When Descartes learned of the condemnation of Galileo's work, he fled France for Holland, where he published *Discourse on Method*. Francis Bacon had been among the first to associate the Scientific Revolution with the Protestant Reformation. Indeed, many Protestants believed that scientific discovery would lead to a better world and that the wonders of nature were there to be discovered and to give greater glory to God. Yet Jesuits in Bohemia protected Kepler (who had faced persecution from Protestant theologians), provided he limited himself to speculation about astronomy and mathematics and avoided what they considered to be theological questions.

The development of a scientific view of the world in England may be better understood in the context of decades of social, intellectual, and political crisis during the mid-seventeenth century. The campaigns of Parliament and of Puritanism against Charles I's seeming moves toward absolutism and Catholicism attracted political and religious reformers (see Chapter 6). Many who considered the Catholic Church an obstacle to scientific inquiry opposed Charles I as they sought a climate of freedom. The reformers' triumph in the English Civil War may have emboldened Newton and other proponents of the new philosophy. Moderate Anglicans, like the Puritans before them, insisted that science could bring progress. They encouraged the creation of the Royal Observatory, founded by Charles II at Greenwich in 1675. Newton and other members of the

Astronomers using a telescope at the Royal Observatory of London.

Royal Society almost unanimously supported the exile of the Catholic King James II to France and the Glorious Revolution of 1688. Censorship was relatively rare in England, where political and ecclesiastical authority were not so centralized.

By way of contrast, state censorship, encouraged by the Catholic Church, had formally begun in France in 1623, five years after the sovereign law court of Toulouse had ordered a defrocked monk burned at the stake for denouncing belief in miracles after studying at the University of Padua. Thereafter, each new manuscript had to be submitted to a royal office for authorization to be published. Six years later, separate offices were established for literature, science, and politics, with ecclesiastics having veto power over books treating religious subjects.

Yet, to be sure, not all churchmen in France adamantly waged a war on science. Some French Jesuits were open-minded about the scientific method. Jansenists, forming a dissident movement within the Church, also favored scientific discovery, discussion, and debate, but faced papal and monarchical opposition (see Chapter 7).

CONSEQUENCES OF THE SCIENTIFIC REVOLUTION

The Scientific Revolution seemed to push theology into the background. Even though the earliest exponents of scientific method never doubted God's creation of the universe, the idea that mankind might one day master nature shocked many Church officials. Descartes's materialism seemed to suggest that humanity could live independently of God. His attempt to deduce the existence of God from the laws of motion brought ecclesiastical wrath. Faith in the scientific method indeed had distinct philosophical consequences: "If natural Philosophy, in all its parts, by pursuing this method, shall at length be perfected," Newton reasoned, "the bounds of moral philosophy will also be enlarged." The English poet John Donne had already come to the same conclusion in 1612. "The new philosophy," he wrote prophetically, "calls all in doubt."

The men and women of science espoused the application of the scientific method to the study of nature and the universe. It was but a short step to subjecting society, government, and political thought to similar critical scrutiny. The English philosopher John Locke claimed that society was, as much as astronomy, a discipline subject to the rigors of the scientific method. Moreover, the Scientific Revolution would ultimately help call absolutism into doubt by influencing the philosophes, the thinkers and writers of the eighteenth-century Enlightenment. The philosophes' belief in the intrinsic value of freedom and their assertion that people should be ruled by law, not rulers, would challenge the very foundations of absolutism.

CHAPTER 9

ENLIGHTENED THOUGHT AND THE REPUBLIC OF LETTERS

"What is the Enlightenment?" wrote the German philosopher Immanuel Kant. His response was "*Dare to know!* Have the courage to make use of your own understanding," as exciting a challenge today as in the eighteenth century. During that period of contagious intellectual energy and enthusiastic quest for knowledge, the philosophes, the thinkers and writers of the Enlightenment, espoused intellectual freedom and the use of reason in the search for progress. Unlike most scientists of the eighteenth century, they wanted their ideas to reach the general reading public. Education therefore loomed large in this view of their mission. Their approach to education was not limited to formal schooling, but instead took in the development of the individual and the continued application of critical inquiry throughout one's life.

The Enlightenment began in Paris but extended to much of Western Europe, including the German states, the Dutch Republic, Great Britain, and as far as North America. The works of the philosophes reached Russia. Orthodox Christian intellectuals carried the Enlightenment's celebration of science and humanism into the Balkans. The philosophes' writings helped confirm French as the language of high culture in eighteenth-century Europe. Indeed, it was reported from Potsdam that at the court of Frederick the Great of Prussia "the language least spoken is German." But French was hardly the only language of philosophic discourse. In Italy, those influenced by the new thinking used the ideas of the philosophes to attack clerical and particularly papal influence in political life. In Britain, the philosopher David Hume and economist Adam Smith, father of free-market liberalism, represented the thought of the "Scottish Enlightenment."

The Enlightenment can be roughly divided into three stages. The first covers the first half of the eighteenth century and most directly reflects

John Locke (*left*) and Georges-Louis Buffon (*right*), who both linked the Scientific Revolution and Enlightenment thought.

the influence of the Scientific Revolution; the second, the "high Enlightenment," begins with the publication of *The Spirit of Laws* (1748) by Charles-Louis de Montesquieu and ends in 1778 with the death of François-Marie Voltaire and Jean-Jacques Rousseau; and the third, the late Enlightenment, influenced by Rousseau's work, marks a shift from an emphasis on human reason to a greater preoccupation with the emotions and passions of mankind. This final stage also features new ideas relating the concept of freedom to the working of economies, best represented by the thought of Adam Smith. At this time, too, several monarchs applied the philosophes' principle that rulers should work for the good of their subjects. But these experiments in "enlightened absolutism" were most noted for rulers' organizing their states more effectively, further enhancing their authority. This third period saw popular diffusion of the lesser works of would-be philosophes seeking to capitalize on an expanding literary market. These works, too, were influential in undermining respect for the authority of the monarchy of France and thus indirectly contributed to the French Revolution.

ENLIGHTENED IDEAS

The philosophes espoused views of nature, mankind, society, government, and the intrinsic value of freedom that challenged some of the most fundamental tenets Europeans had held for centuries. Slavery, for example, violated their principle of human freedom. The implications of Enlightenment thought were revolutionary, because the philosophes argued that progress had been constrained by social and political institutions that did not reflect humanity's natural goodness and capacity for material and moral improvement. Although many philosophes saw no or little incompatibility between science and religion, they were skeptical of received truths. Thus, they challenged the doctrinal authority of the established churches and launched a crusade for the secularization of political institutions.

It is to the Enlightenment that we trace the origins of many of our most strongly held political beliefs: the idea that people should be ruled by law, not rulers; the belief that a separation of powers ought to exist within government in order to prevent the accumulation of too much power in a few hands; the concept of popular sovereignty (legal authority should be wholly or at least partly based in the people, reflecting their interests, if not their consent); and the assumption that it is the responsibility of rulers to look after the welfare of the people. The consequences of such modern views of sovereignty, political rights, and the organization of states would be seen in the French Revolution and the era of liberalism in the nineteenth century.

Intellectual Influences on Enlightened Thought

Like all intellectual and cultural movements, the Enlightenment did not emerge spontaneously. Creating what David Hume (1711–1776) called "the science of man," the *philosophes* reflected the influence of the Scientific Revolution, whose proponents had espoused the scientific method in the study of nature and the universe. Sir Isaac Newton, the brilliant English scientist and theoretician (see Chapter 8), emphasized that science—reason and experimentation—holds the key to understanding nature, and that mankind discovers knowledge not through religious teaching but through "observation, analysis, and experiment."

Two thinkers linked the Scientific Revolution and Enlightenment thought: John Locke and Georges-Louis Buffon. Locke (1632–1704) claimed that philosophy was, as much as astronomy, a discipline subject to the rigors of the scientific method and critical inquiry. The son of a landowner and a member of the British Royal Society, Locke maintained a strong interest in medicine. After returning from Holland, where he had gone into self-imposed exile during the political crisis swirling around the throne of King James II, Locke remained close to the government of King William and Queen Mary.

Locke believed that the scientific method could be applied to the study of society. In *An Essay Concerning Human Understanding* (1690), Locke postulated that each individual is a *tabula rasa,* or blank slate, at birth. Believing that all knowledge is sensory, Locke denied inherited abilities and rejected the idea that humanity is stained by original sin. He anticipated that the discovery of more laws of nature would be the basis of secular laws on which society should be based. He was confident that humanity might thereby be able to improve social conditions.

Locke had asserted the dignity of the individual in contending that every person has the right to life, liberty, and property (though he excluded slaves in the Americas from such innate rights). He argued that monarchies were based on a social contract between rulers and the ruled. People had to relinquish some of their liberty in exchange for security. But, unlike Thomas Hobbes, Locke insisted that mankind's liberty and rights stemmed from the laws of nature. He became a leading proponent of educational reform, freedom of the press, religious toleration, and the separation of political powers.

Locke's interest in the relationship between nature and the social order led him to consider issues of gender. The assumption that the king ruled his nation as a husband and father ruled his wife and children had been prominent in early modern political theory, only briefly challenged by a handful of radicals during the English Civil War of the 1640s. John Locke argued against the contemporary vision of the state in which "all power on earth is either derived from or usurped from the fatherly power." He denied the appropriateness of the analogy between the family and the state as patriarchal institutions. Rejecting the contemporary view that Adam held supremacy over Eve, he viewed marriage, like government, to be organized by social contract. However, Locke went no further than that, and his espousal of equality within marriage remained only an ideal. In everyday life, he believed that women should defer to men. But Locke's analysis of the family as an institution nonetheless helped stimulate intellectual interest in studying the social role of women.

More than any of his contemporaries, Georges-Louis Buffon (1707–1788) linked the Scientific Revolution to the Enlightenment. Buffon, whose initial presentation to the French Royal Academy of Science was a study of probability theory applied to gambling on hopscotch, became the curator of the Royal Gardens. Surrounded by monkeys and badgers in his laboratory, he carried out many experiments, some of which worked, such as his study of the burning effect of the sun through glass, and some of which did not, including his study of the emotional life of birds. Buffon's experiments with cooling metals led him to build a large forge near his home in Burgundy.

The philosophes acknowledged their debt to the late-seventeenth-century proponents of the scientific method. Voltaire saluted Newton, whose funeral he attended in London's Westminster Abbey, for having called on scientists and philosophers "to examine, weigh, calculate, and measure, but never conjecture." Hume insisted that all knowledge came from reason and experience—that is, from critical inquiry and scientific discovery—and that the ability to reason distinguished mankind from other animals. Many philosophes, reflecting the influence of the Scientific Revolution, considered religion, the origins of which they found not in reason but in faith and custom, to be a social phenomenon, like any other to be studied scientifically. Hume blasted away at the idea of religious truths revealed through the Bible, and Montesquieu asked, "Is it possible for those who understand nature and have a reasonable idea of God to believe that matter and created things are only 6,000 years old?"

The very universality of their principles led some of the philosophes to suggest that a sense of morality—of what is right and wrong—might vary across cultures, because it emerged from the nature of mankind, but not from religious teaching. Denis Diderot, influenced by Locke, argued that sensory stimulation—or in the case of people who are blind, deprivation—shapes individual moral responses, and that moral principles for a blind man might be somewhat different from those for someone who could see. He described the so-called savages of distant Tahiti as forming a rational social order without the benefit of any ecclesiastical doctrine. Hume called for a "science of morals" to serve the interests of Christians.

The Republic of Ideas

The philosophes' calls for reform were sometimes subtle, sometimes boldly forceful. Yet they did not lead insurrections. Their pens and pencils were their only weapons as they sought to change the way people thought. They communicated their ideas in letters, unpublished manuscripts,

Voltaire presiding (with his arm raised) over a dinner gathering of philosophes, including Denis Diderot, who is sitting on the far left.

books, pamphlets, brochures, and through writing novels, poetry, drama, literary and art criticism, and political philosophy.

The philosophes glorified the collegiality and interdependence of writers within the "republic of letters," what the men and women of the Enlightenment sometimes called the informal international community of philosophes. By the mid-eighteenth century, Voltaire could claim with some exaggeration that the professional writer stood at the top of the social summit. He, Montesquieu, and Diderot accepted election to the prestigious French Royal Academy, revealing their ambivalence toward the monarchy that they attacked, however subtly, in their work. The most famous of the philosophes gained money as well as prestige, although Voltaire and Montesquieu were among the few who could support themselves by writing.

The philosophes may have shared the fundamental ideas of the Enlightenment, but significant differences existed among them. They came from different social classes, generations, and nations. And they often disagreed, like people in any republic, arguing in person, by letter, and in their published work. They could not agree, for example, whether the ideal state was an enlightened, benevolent monarchy, a monarchy balanced by a parliamentary body representing the nobility, or a kind of direct democracy. Their views on religion also varied. Montesquieu, Voltaire, and Rousseau were deists. Because scientific inquiry seemed to have demonstrated that the persistent intervention of God was unnecessary to keep the world in motion, they viewed God as a clockmaker who set the world in motion according to the laws of nature and then left knowledge and human progress to the discovery and action of mankind. In contrast, Diderot, one of the principal spokesmen of the Enlightenment, became an atheist.

For all the variety and richness of the republic of letters, four philosophes dominated Enlightenment discourse with startling ideas about society, religion, and politics: Montesquieu, Voltaire, Diderot, and Rousseau. Each is well worth considering separately.

Montesquieu

Montesquieu (born Charles-Louis de Secondat; 1689–1755) inherited a feudal château near Bordeaux and a small income upon the death of his father. He studied law and later inherited from a wealthy relative more property and the title of baron de Montesquieu, as well as the presidency of the noble parlement, or provincial sovereign law court, seated at Bordeaux.

In 1721, after moving to Paris, Montesquieu published the *Persian Letters*. In the form of reports sent home by two Persian visitors to Paris, his work detailed political and social injustices of life in the West. By casting this critique of eighteenth-century France in the form of a travelogue, Montesquieu was able to dodge royal censorship. The work irritated many people, however, including ecclesiastics who resented its insinuation that the pope was a "magician." As for the king of France, the Persians reported that he "is the most powerful of European potentates. He has no mines of gold like his neighbor, the king of Spain: but he is much wealthier than that prince, because his riches are drawn from a more inexhaustible source, the vanity of his subjects. He has undertaken and carried on great wars, without any other supplies than those derived from the sale of titles of honors." But beneath the satire of the *Persian Letters,* Montesquieu was arguing the point that nature reveals a universal standard of justice that applies for all people in all places at all times, in Islamic Persia as in Christian France.

Montesquieu.

Montesquieu's ideas reflected the increased contact between Europeans and much of the rest of the world. Merchants, soldiers, missionaries, and colonists had followed the first European explorers to, among other places, the Americas and Asia. Published accounts of travel stirred the imagination of upper-class Europeans who were interested in societies and cultures that lay on the fringes of or beyond their continent.

In *Persian Letters,* Montesquieu also offered the first critical examination of the institution of slavery by one of the philosophes. He rejected slavery as an extension of despotism, concluding that "slavery is against natural law, by which all men are born free and independent" because "the liberty of each citizen is part of public liberty." He argued that slavery, in contrast, compromised "the general good of men [and] that of particular societies."

The Spirit of Laws (1748) inaugurated the high Enlightenment. In this important book, Montesquieu applied the principles of observation, experimentation, and analysis, which lie at the heart of scientific inquiry, to the social and political foundations of states. He described the relationship between climate, religion, and tradition, and the historical evolution of a nation's political life. Laws, he argued, are subject to critical inquiry and historical study because they develop over time. Historians, freeing themselves from the influence of the Church, could now study "general causes, whether moral or physical."

The British political system fascinated Montesquieu, who went to England in 1729 for two years. He was impressed by the historical role of

Parliament, a representative body unlike French parlements (law courts), despite the similarity of their names. The English Parliament seemed an "intermediate power" that had during the English Civil War prevented Britain from becoming either a monarchical despotism or a republic, which he identified with chaos. Montesquieu's point was that each political system and legal tradition evolved differently. He feared that the French monarchy was showing signs of becoming despotic because it lacked the separation of powers found in England. Only constitutionalism, he argued, could combine the guarantees for order (offered by monarchy) with those of freedom. Montesquieu believed that noble rights and municipal privileges, which had long been eroded by royal absolutism in France, could stave off monarchical depotism. Moreover, Montesquieu argued that the sovereignty of the king came not from God, but from the people.

Voltaire

Brilliant, witty, and sarcastic, Voltaire (born François-Marie Arouet; 1694–1778) was the most widely read, cited, and lionized of the philosophes. He was the son of a notary who had enhanced his family's position through a favorable marriage. Voltaire's parents, who wanted him to be a lawyer, sent him to Paris to be educated by the Jesuits. Instead, the brash, ambitious young man made a name for himself as a dramatist and poet—though many of these early works are quite forgettable. Voltaire developed a pen as quick and cutting as a sword. Some of his early works were banned in France; everything he ever wrote was forbidden in Spain.

   Like Montesquieu, Voltaire reflected the Anglophilia of the thinkers of the early and high Enlightenment. He extolled Britain, its commercial empire, its relative religious toleration, and its freedom of the press. "The English are the only people on earth," he wrote, "who have been able to prescribe limits to the power of kings by resisting them: and who, by a series of struggles, have at last established that wise Government, where the Prince is all powerful to do good, and at the same time is restrained from committing evil."

   Unlike the noble Montesquieu, who hoped the parlements would balance the power of the monarchy as they did in Britain, Voltaire had little faith in them. Voltaire saw them as representing the narrow and selfish interests of the nobility. He believed that the only representative body that might guarantee the natural rights of the king's subjects in France would be the equivalent of the British House of Commons. Whereas Montesquieu looked to the nobility to protect people from monarchical despotism, Voltaire counted on the enlightened monarchs of centralized states to protect their people against nobles' self-interest.

   Voltaire claimed that the political organization of each state was at least partially determined by its specific history and circumstances. As science should study the world of nature, so should the philosophe trace the separate development of nations. This line of reasoning convinced him that Montesquieu was wrong to think that the British political system could be successfully transplanted to France.

Voltaire reserved his most scathing attacks for the Church, an institution, like the parlements, that seemed to him to block the development of freedom in his own country. His motto was an impassioned cry for a battle against the teaching of the Church—*"Écrasez l'infâme!"* ("Crush the horrible thing!"). Of monks, he once said, "They sing, they eat, they digest." The pope and the Parlement of Paris both condemned his polemical *Philosophical Dictionary* (1764). His attacks were clever and devastating; for example, his pithy description of the Chinese as having "an admirable religion free from superstition and the rage to persecute" was read by virtually everyone as suggesting that in France the opposite was true.

Voltaire, a deist, believed that God created the universe and then let it operate according to scientific laws. He espoused a natural religion based upon reason. At least some of what has often been viewed as his anti-Semitism was, in fact, part of Voltaire's unrestrained assault on what he considered another variety of religious dogmatism built not upon reason but on faith alone.

Voltaire intended *Candide* (1759) to be an indictment of fanaticism and superstition. In the short tale, the cheerful optimist Candide bumbles from disaster to disaster. Here Voltaire confronts the seeming contradiction between the goodness of God and the evil in the world. He writes about the earthquake that ravaged Lisbon in 1755, killing thousands of people and destroying much of the Portuguese capital. If God is all good and omniscient, why, Voltaire reasoned, would He allow such an event to occur? But Voltaire nonetheless believed that religion was beneficial because it offered people hope, and therefore made their lives more bearable. It also kept them in line: "If God did not exist, one would have to invent him. I want my attorney, my tailor, my servants, even my wife to believe in God, and I think that I shall then be robbed and cuckholded less often."

Voltaire's fame spread when he took up the cause of a man who seemed wrongly accused of murder. In 1761, Jean Calas, a Protestant from Toulouse, stood accused of murdering his own son, who had been found hanging in the family basement. The young Calas had intended to convert to Catholicism. Convicted by the Parlement of Toulouse, the father was tortured to death, though it seemed likely that his son had committed suicide. Several years later, the parlement reversed its earlier decision—too late, however, for Jean Calas. But the Calas Affair helped put the philosophes' critique of religious intolerance into the limelight of public opinion.

Voltaire's energetic interest in the Calas Affair reflected his insistence that progress is somehow inevitable without human action. He concludes *Candide* with the famous, though seemingly ambiguous, advice that "one must cultivate one's own garden," as he did at his rural retreat. But Voltaire was counseling anything but a withdrawal into the sanctuary of introspection. He called for each person to follow the path of light and do battle with those institutions that seemed to stand in the way of humanity's potential. The possibility of human action gave Voltaire confidence and hope. In 1764, he predicted, "Everything I see scatters the seeds of a revolution which will definitely come . . . Enlightenment has gradually spread so widely that it will burst into full light at the first right opportunity, and then there will be a fine uproar. Lucky are the young, for they will see great things."

Diderot

Denis Diderot's monumental *Encyclopedia* best reflected the collaborative nature of the Enlightenment, as well as its wide influence. Diderot (1713–1784), the son of an artisan, was something of a jack-of-all-trades, a man of letters who wrote plays, art criticism, history, theology, and philosophy. Educated by the Jesuits (like Voltaire), he flirted with the idea of becoming a priest, and for a time supported himself by writing sermons for bishops. Unlike Montesquieu and Voltaire, Diderot underwent a rugged apprenticeship in the "republic of letters." He penned a pornographic novel to earn enough to indulge the fancies of his mistress. But he also questioned how, through centuries of male domination, women, despite their capacity for reproduction, had come to be considered inferior to men. Diderot claimed that laws that limited the rights of women were counter to nature.

An illustration of various hunting traps from Diderot's *Encyclopedia*.

The *Encyclopedia,* on which Diderot worked for twenty-five years, stands as the greatest monument of the Enlightenment. At the heart of the project lay the philosophes' insistence that knowledge was rational and that it followed laws of nature. Social and political institutions should be submitted to standards of rationality. All things, as Diderot put it, are equally subject to criticism. By elevating mankind to the center of human inquiry, the authors of the *Encyclopedia* sought to achieve Diderot's goal, "to change the general way of thinking," as well as to bring glory to France.

Voltaire had set a goal for the Enlightenment itself: to educate the literate and intellectually curious of the social elite, and perhaps people further down the social scale as well. The *Encyclopedia* at least partially fulfilled that goal. Published over a period of more than twenty years beginning in 1751, it consisted of 60,000 articles and 2,885 illustrations in twenty-eight volumes. Subtitled "A Classified Dictionary of the Sciences, Arts and Trades," this first such compilation in the West was a bold attempt to organize and classify all knowledge gathered from "over the face of the earth." Its authors insisted that by learning more about the universe, men and women could improve the world. This marked a departure from the assumption that mankind's ability to penetrate the secrets of the universe was limited. Montesquieu contributed sections on taste, Rousseau on music, Voltaire on literature, and Buffon on nature. Diderot gave particular credit to the contributions of everyday artisans by describing how and why ingeniously simple tools and machines could make tasks easier.

The *Encyclopedia* generated sufficient excitement that advance sales alone financed its publication. It earned its publishers a handsome profit. After the first edition, subsequent editions with less expensive paper and fewer illustrations became available at about a sixth of the original price. Lawyers, officials, and *rentiers* (people living from property income) were more likely to own a copy than merchants or manufacturers, who could afford the volumes but seemed less interested. What began as a luxury product ended up on the shelves of the "middling sort."

The philosophes wanted the *Encyclopedia* to carry the Enlightenment far beyond the borders of France. Although only about one in ten volumes traveled beyond the country, its pattern of distribution in the 1770s and 1780s reflected the success of the enterprise (see Map 9.1). To contemporaries, the *Encyclopedia* seemed to embody Kant's bold challenge, *"Dare to know!"*

Through Swiss, Dutch, and German booksellers, among others, the *Encyclopedia* reached readers in London, Brussels, Turin, Munich, and St. Petersburg, among other European capitals. The *Encyclopedia*'s prospectus and booksellers' advertisements assured potential buyers that ownership would proclaim one's standing as a person of knowledge, a philosophe. In northern Germany and Scandinavia, customers were described as "sovereign princes" and "Swedish seigneurs." A few copies reached distant African settlements, including the Cape of Good Hope. Thomas Jefferson helped promote the *Encyclopedia* in America, finding several subscribers, among them Benjamin Franklin. King Louis XVI of France himself had a copy purchased for him. There was an Italian edition, despite the opposition of the Church, and a priest was among those taking orders for it. However, in Spain, Inquisition censorship frightened booksellers and buyers alike, and in Portugal only a few copies got by the police.

MAP 9.1 DIFFUSION OF DIDEROT'S *ENCYCLOPEDIA*   Subscriptions to Diderot's *Encyclopedia* throughout Europe.

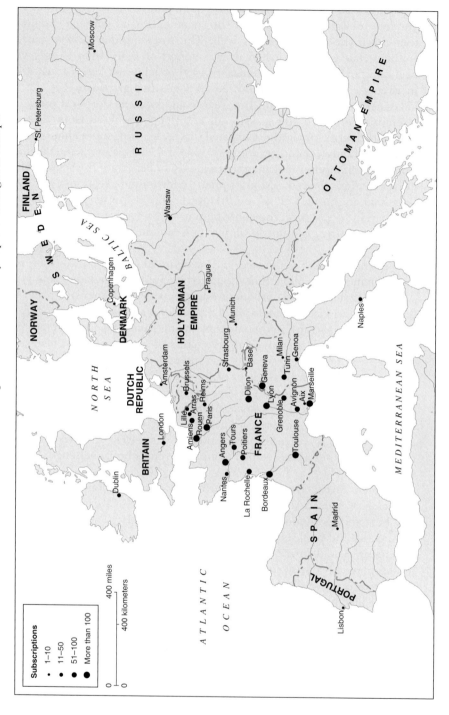

The *Encyclopedia* did implicitly challenge monarchical authority. Jean-Jacques Rousseau and Paul-Henri Holbach (1723–1789) wrote enthusiastically about representative government and even popular sovereignty, though only Rousseau came close to espousing a republic. After initially tolerating the project, French royal censors banned Volume 7 in 1757, after an unsuccessful assassination attempt on Louis XV. Diderot, whose first serious philosophical work had been burned by the public executioner, was briefly imprisoned before being released on a promise of good behavior. Although the philosophes left their skeptical challenge to the Church implicit, disguising the pope in one satire as a figure in Japanese robes, the pope condemned the volumes in 1759.

In the 1770s, the French state again tolerated the *Encyclopedia,* which it now treated more as a commodity than as an ideological threat to monarchy or Church. The small skirmishes fought over the volumes had more to do with rivalries between publishers, between those privileged with official favor and those without. In this way, Diderot's grand project symbolized the ongoing political struggles within the French monarchy itself.

Rousseau

The place of Jean-Jacques Rousseau (1712–1778) in the Enlightenment is far more ambiguous than that of Diderot and his *Encyclopedia.* Rousseau embraced human freedom, but more than any other of the philosophes, Rousseau idealized emotion, instinct, and spontaneity, which he believed to be, along with reason, essential parts of human nature.

The son of a Geneva watchmaker, Rousseau, a Protestant, went to Paris as a young man in the hope of becoming a composer. The arrogant, self-righteous Rousseau received an introduction into several aristocratic Parisian salons, informal upper-class gatherings hosted by noble women at which ideas were discussed, where he became friendly with Diderot. In 1749, the Academy of Dijon (an academy in France was a regular gathering of people to discuss ideas, and, as we shall see below, a way that enlightenment thought spread) sponsored an essay contest on the question of whether the progress of science had strengthened or weakened morality. Rousseau's first-prize essay concluded that primitive or natural humanity had embodied the essential goodness of mankind and that in order for humanity to be happy, new social and political institutions would be necessary.

Rousseau remained a contentious loner, quarreling with other philosophes. Voltaire mocked his insistence that emotion and passion held sway over pure reason. Exiled by the Parlement of Paris because his writings offended monarchy and Church, he moved back to his native Geneva. After being forced to leave Geneva in the early 1770s following the condemnation there of his work, he abandoned his children in an orphanage—

as his father had abandoned him—and set off to visit England. The rest of Rousseau's life was marked by increasingly quarrelsome and paranoid behavior. He assumed that when his former friends disagreed with his ideas, they knew that he was right but simply refused to admit it. Gradually he became overwhelmed with thoughts of revenge against those whom he considered to have wronged him. In his *Confessions* (the first volume of which appeared in 1782), he appealed to future generations to see how contemporary thinkers had misinterpreted or misrepresented him.

In *Discourse on the Arts and Sciences* (1762), Rousseau argued that civilization had corrupted the natural goodness of man, which he called the "fundamental principle" of political thought. The untempered quest for private property had disrupted the harmony that had once characterized mankind in its primitive state by creating a hierarchy of wealth. Rousseau's idealization of relatively primitive, uncomplicated, and, he thought, manageable social and political groupings led him to believe that a republic, such as his own Geneva, alone offered its citizens the possibility of freedom. Its size permitted men wealthy enough to enjoy full political rights to participate directly in decision making. However, Rousseau remained suspicious of representative government, believing that people might ultimately vote themselves into slavery by electing unworthy representatives.

As free people in primitive societies joined together for mutual protection, enlightened people could join together for their mutual development in a kind of direct democracy. This view more than likely reflected his support for artisans' guilds and other small, self-governing groups that charac-

(*Left*) Portrait of Jean-Jacques Rousseau. (*Right*) Rousseau and Voltaire in symbolic battle, a clash of ideas and wills.

terized Old Regime France. In Rousseau's idealized small state, executive authority would be separate from, yet subordinate to, the legislative power. He was, however, vague on how people were to be organized and governed.

The final period of the Enlightenment prefigured nineteenth-century romanticism by giving emotion more free play, as the sensitive individual is awed by nature. Rousseau's *Émile* (1762) became one of the literary sensations of the century. Beginning "Everything is good as it comes from the hands of the Author of nature, but everything degenerates in the hands of man," the novel describes what he considered to be the ideal natural, secular education of the young Émile, who is gradually exposed by his tutor to nature during walks to explore brooks and mills. Rousseau intended such wonders to stimulate Émile's emotions, which were to be developed before his sense of reason, "the one that develops last," Rousseau claims, "and with the greatest difficulty." Émile's primitive virtue must be preserved against the vices of culture, and also developed as an end in itself so that he becomes a developed, autonomous person. Rousseau assigns Sophie, Émile's chosen "well-born" spouse, an education appropriate to what Rousseau considered a woman's lower status in life. Yet even Rousseau's insistence on the capacity of women for intellectual development surprised many contemporaries, and was ahead of its time.

Voltaire also ridiculed Rousseau's espousal of primitiveness as virtue: "I have received, Monsieur, your new book against the human race, and I thank you. No one has employed so much intelligence turning men into beasts. One starts wanting to walk on all fours after reading your book. However, in more than sixty years I have lost the habit."

In *The Social Contract* (1762), Rousseau tried to resolve the question of how people could join together in society to find protection and justice, and yet remain free individuals. Locke had described the relationship between a ruler and his people as a contractual one. Hobbes, in contrast, had argued that individuals could find refuge from the brutality of the state of nature only by surrendering their rights to an absolute ruler in exchange for safety. Rousseau imagined a social contract in which the individual surrenders his or her natural rights to the "general will" in order to find order and security. By "general will," Rousseau meant the consensus of a community of citizens with equal political rights. Citizens would live in peace because they would be ruled by other citizens, not by dynastic rulers eager to expand their territorial holdings.

Although *The Social Contract* remained largely unknown until after the French Revolution of 1789, it offered an unparalleled critique of contemporary society. Rousseau summed up his thinking with the stirring assertion that "men are born free yet everywhere they are in chains." Whereas Voltaire and other philosophes hoped that rulers would become enlightened, Rousseau insisted that sovereignty comes not from kings or oligarchies, or even from God. Sovereignty comes, he argued persuasively, through the collective search for freedom.

THE DIFFUSION AND EXPANSION OF THE ENLIGHTENMENT

The groundwork for the Enlightenment lay not only in the realm of ideas—those of the Scientific Revolution and Locke—but also in gradual social changes that affected the climate of opinion. These changes, especially but not exclusively found in France, included the declining role of religion in the eighteenth century, at least in some regions, and the emergence of a more broadly based culture.

Religious Enthusiasm and Skepticism

During the first half of the seventeenth century, the Catholic Reformation seems to have engendered a slow but steady religious revival in France, Spain, and the Habsburg domains, where the founding of new religious orders, monasteries, and the popularity of the cults and shrines of local saints reflected religious intensity. Moreover, the established churches still retained formidable authority and prestige.

The development late in the seventeenth century of Pietism among Protestants in the northern German states, emphasizing preaching and the study of the Bible, reflected another dimension of both mounting dissatisfaction with established religions and the existence of considerable religious creativity. Disaffected by abstract theological debates and by the Lutheran Church's hierarchical structure, Pietists wanted to reaffirm the Protestant belief in the primacy of the individual conscience. Like English Puritans and French Jansenists (a dissident group within the Catholic Church), they called for a more austere religion. They wanted a revival of piety and good works, and asked that laymen take an active role in religious life. For Pietists, Bible-reading and small discussion groups replaced the more elaborate, formal services of the Lutherans, helping to expand interest in the German language and culture among the upper classes. But by the last quarter of the seventeenth century, Pietist influence had waned, reflecting not only the diffusion of Enlightenment thought but also the fact that Lutheranism remained the state religion in the northern German states, maintaining a hold on the universities. Likewise, the fact that Jansenists were able to win and maintain a wide following in France, despite official proscription, can be taken as evidence of the strength of religious feeling.

In Britain, religious practice seems to have increased among all social classes during the seventeenth century. The Anglican Church of England was the Established Church, but Britain also had about half a million non-Anglican Protestants, or Dissenters, at the end of the eighteenth century.

Some middle-class Presbyterians, Congregationalists, Unitarians, Baptists, and Quakers sent their sons to private academies. Yet Oxford and Cambridge Universities admitted only Anglicans. Moreover, anti-Catholicism was still prevalent in England, where there were about 70,000 Catholics in 1770, most of them in the lower classes.

Although many Baptists, Congregationalists, and Quakers, among other Dissenters, had traditionally been laborers, there was not a particular religion that held the allegiance of ordinary people in England in the eighteenth century until the ministry of John Wesley (1703–1791). An Anglican trained in theology at Oxford University, the intense, brooding Wesley began to be-

John Wesley, who preached Methodist evangelism to the ordinary people of England.

lieve that his mission was to infuse ordinary people (who seemed ignored by the Established Church) with religious enthusiasm.

Wesley never formally broke with the Anglican Church nor claimed to be setting up a new denomination. Yet that was the effect of his lifetime of preaching directly to ordinary people on grassy hills, in open fields, and on highways, and of writing religious tracts directed at ordinary Britons. Wesley attracted about 100,000 followers to Methodism. Stressing personal conversion, Methodism suggested that all people were equal in God's eyes. This offended some upper-class English men and women, not the least because Methodists shouted out their beliefs and sometimes publicly confessed sins that the upper classes thought best left unnamed. A duchess explained that she hated the Methodists, because "it is monstrous to be told that you have a heart as sinful as the common wretches that crawl on the earth. This is highly offensive and insulting and at variance with high rank and good breeding."

Methodist evangelism was both a dynamic and stabilizing force in British society. There was little or nothing politically or socially radical about Wesley, as shown by his unwillingness to break formally with the Established Church. Far from preaching rebellion or revolution, Wesley encouraged work and self-discipline and abstinence from dancing, drinking, and gambling. Popular protest affronted Wesley's sense of respectability.

The Angelican Church, in turn, began to recruit followers among the lower classes. It established associations like the Society for the Promotion of Christian Knowledge and Anglican Sunday schools, which provided poor children with food and catechism. The evangelical Hannah More (1745–1833), the "bishop in petticoats," abandoned the material comforts of upper-class life for the challenges of bringing religion to the poor. In general, although some evangelicals favored improvements in working conditions, most remained politically conservative.

Despite all of the evangelistic efforts, by the middle of the eighteenth century, religion seemed to play a significantly smaller role in the lives of people of all classes, particularly in regions with expanding economies and relatively high literacy rates. The number of men and women entering the clergy in France declined, and male and female monastic orders lost a third of their members between 1770 and 1790 alone. Fewer wills requested that Masses be said for the deceased or for souls in Purgatory. A Venetian theologian at mid-century claimed that the people of his state had become "de-christianized." In France, popular dislike of the exemption of the clergy from taxes increased, although the Church offered the monarchy a sizable yearly contribution from its great wealth. Thus, the philosophes who challenged the role of the established churches in public life were addressing many readers who had lost interest in organized religion.

Expansion of the Cultural Base

The growing influence of the middle class in England and northwestern Europe also began slowly to transform cultural life, expanding interest in literature, music, and the arts. The number of literary associations reflected this change. Lines between the nobility and the wealthy bourgeoisie became less fixed; culture moved from the closed world of court and château into the public domain.

Increasing literacy expanded the size of the potential audience of the philosophes. By the end of the century, perhaps half of the men in England, France, the Netherlands, and the German states could read. A smaller proportion of women—between a third to a half of the female population of these countries—was literate. A far smaller percentage of people could read in southern Europe, and few people indeed in Eastern Europe and Russia. Opportunities for women, even those from noble families, to obtain more than a minimal education remained quite rare, although several German states began schools for girls. Even Marie Antoinette, queen of France and one of the wealthiest people in the world, was so poorly educated that she made frequent grammatical and spelling errors.

Publishers fed the growing appetites of readers eager to know what events were transpiring in their own country and abroad. Newspapers published one or two times a week summarized events transpiring in other countries. The number of English periodicals increased sixfold between 1700 and 1780, reflecting an increasing interest in science and natural history. In the German states, the number of books and magazines published grew threefold during the last decades of the eighteenth century. Novels gained in popularity at the expense of books on theology and popular piety. English female novelists gave women an unprecedented public voice in Britain, presenting their heroines as affectionate companions to their husbands and good mothers. Sentimental novels presented syrupy stories of domestic life and tender love. Diderot, who wrote two mediocre plays, and the German dramatist and critic Gotthold Lessing (1729–1781) called for the theater to portray the lives and passions of ordinary people, instead of only kings and queens, princes and princesses. Traditional literature, such as religious tracts, popular almanacs, and folktales, remained the most widely read literature.

The Enlightenment had a direct influence on the growing popularity of history. Reflecting their interest in understanding human experience, the philosophes helped create history as a modern discipline. Since the classical Greeks, there had been relatively little interest in history in Europe. Church fathers, espousing the primacy of theology and viewing the world as little more than a test to prepare Christians for the afterlife, were generally uninterested in history. But suddenly all human experience, including non-Western cultures, emerged as suitable for historical inquiry. Edward Gibbon (1737–1794) was inspired to undertake his *History of the Decline and Fall of the Roman Empire* (published over a period of twelve years beginning in 1776) by visiting the Colosseum of Rome. Natural science, too, developed a following.

The number of lending libraries, as well as reading circles or clubs, some organized by resourceful booksellers, increased in Western Europe. In Paris, London, Milan, Berlin, and other large cities, lending libraries rented books for as short a period as an hour. Household libraries became more common. Reading, which heretofore had largely been a group activity in which a literate person read to others—in the same way that storytellers spun their yarns—became more of a private undertaking.

While some of the most significant works of the Enlightenment were virtually unknown outside the republic of letters, others became the best-sellers of the age. Montesquieu's *The Spirit of Laws* went through twenty-two printings—approximately 35,000 copies—in the first eighteen months after publication in 1748. Buffon's thirty-volume study, *The System of Nature* (1749–1804)—despite its bulk—also enjoyed prodigious success. Voltaire's *Candide* was reprinted eight times in 1759, the year of its publication. Abbé Guillaume Raynal's *The Philosophical and Political History of European Colonies and Commerce in the Two Indies* (1770) was reprinted seventy times to supply an eager market. It described the colonization of the New World, Asia, and Africa, including the development of the slave trade, which Raynal denounced in no uncertain terms.

Painting

The philosophes sought the same status and freedom for artists that they demanded for writers. They believed that the arts had to be not only unfettered by censorship but also subject to critical inquiry. Critics helped shape public taste with reviews of paintings, circulated as pamphlets, which generated strong debate and comment.

Some philosophes worked toward a philosophy of art, but they did not espouse a single theory. The distinguished English portrait painter Joshua Reynolds (1723–1792), president of the Royal Academy, believed that classical rules preserved from antiquity had to be followed. But David Hume, among other Enlightenment figures, emphasized the aesthetic appreciation of art, rejecting formal rules or standards for art imposed by royal academies or ecclesiastical influence.

The secularization of culture could be seen in the development of rococo, a new and generally secular decorative style. It evolved from the highly ornamental baroque style that had characterized the art and architecture of the Catholic Reformation, particularly in Austria and Bavaria. Closely tied to noble taste, rococo's popularity in France reflected the fact that many nobles now spent more time away from Versailles, in their own

Engraving depicting the grand rococo style that was popular in France in the eighteenth century.

country châteaux or in elegant Parisian townhouses. However spacious, such urban residences afforded them less room than they enjoyed in the countryside. They therefore lavished more attention on decoration.

The rococo style—sometimes called Louis XV style—began in France but also became quite popular in the German and Italian states. Like the baroque, it featured flowing curves, thus suggesting rocks and shells (*rocailles* and *coquilles*), forming its name. Rococo stressed smallness of scale, reducing baroque forms to elegant decorative style, as in gilded molding for theaters or manor bedrooms. It utilized

William Hogarth's *Gin Lane* (1751) is a deleterious commentary on the impact of alcohol on the poor of eighteenth-century London.

different materials, including wood, metal, stucco, glass, and porcelain, brought for the first time from China during the eighteenth century and reflecting the West's growing interest in Asia. It combined texture and color with spirited and even erotic subject matter. Elements drawn from nature, such as birds and flowers, replaced religious objects as decorative elements.

Although Greek mythology and religious themes remained popular, eighteenth-century painters found new sources for artistic inspiration. The French painter Jean-Antoine Watteau (1684–1721) influenced the artistic move away from traditional religious subjects laden with didactic meaning toward lighter, more secular themes. Adopting a more realistic style than baroque painting, he often depicted elegantly dressed noble subjects at leisure. Breaking away from the system of direct patronage, Watteau sold his paintings through an art dealer. Painters adopted the rococo style, emphasizing smallness of scale, as well as elegance and frivolity. As the market for painting widened, scenes of nature and everyday life also became popular.

The expanding middle-class art market and the growing secularization of artistic taste was nowhere more apparent than in Britain. William Hogarth (1697–1764) was the most popular artist of the era. Hogarth portrayed everyday life in London with affection and satire. He was as adept at conveying the elegance of London's parks as the depravation of the city's notorious "Gin Lane." He poked fun at the hearty Englishman putting away pounds of roast beef (it seemed somehow fitting that Hogarth himself died after eating a huge steak), the dishonest lawyer, the clergyman looking for a better post while ignoring his pastoral duties, and the laboring poor drowning their sorrows in cheap gin, a plague that led the government to raise the tax on inexpensive liquor.

In France, the Academy of Painting and Sculpture organized the first public art exhibition in Paris in 1737. A description of one such event suggests that such public exhibitions facilitated some degree of social mingling.

> Here the odd-job man rubs shoulders with the great   noble . . . the fish wife trades her per   fumes with those of a lady of quality,   making the latter   resort to holding her nose to combat the strong odor of cheap brandy drifting her way; the rough artisan, guided only by natural feeling, comes out with a just observation, at which an inept wit nearly bursts out laughing only because of the comical accent in which it was expressed; while an artist hiding in the crowd unravels the meaning of it all and turns it to his profit.

Music

The taste for music also moved beyond the constraints of court, ecclesiastical, and noble patronage. Opera's great popularity in the seventeenth century had been closely tied to ornate opera houses constructed at European courts. Composers and their music passed from court to court, sometimes transported by aristocratic diplomats. In the early 1750s, Jean-Jacques Rousseau penned stinging attacks on French opera. Readers understood his strident language as he intended—he was denouncing court and aristocratic taste itself. Specifically, Rousseau compared the Royal Academy of Music's monopoly on French music to a ruthless Inquisition that stifled imagination. Rousseau's critique generated a storm of controversy because it seemed to be nothing less than a denunciation of the social and cultural foundations of contemporary French society. Like his philosophical works, Rousseau's operatic compositions extolled the simple, unpretentious life of rural people.

Court composers were considered the equivalent of favored upper servants. When someone asked Franz Joseph Haydn (1732–1809), who worked as *kapellmeister* (orchestra director) for the fabulously wealthy Esterházy family of Hungary, why he had never written any quintets, he replied, "Nobody has ordered any." But by the 1790s, Haydn was conducting his symphonies in public concerts in London. The German composer George Frideric Handel (1685–1759) gratefully accepted the patronage of several English aristocrats as well as King George II.

In England, concerts were held at court or in the homes of wealthy families; in Italy, they were sponsored by groups of educated people who gathered to discuss science and the arts; and in Switzerland, concerts were sponsored by societies of music lovers. The public concert also emerged in some German cities early in the eighteenth century. Gradually public concert halls were built in the capitals of Europe. Handel began to perform his operas and concerts in rented theaters, attracting large crowds.

The short life of Wolfgang Amadeus Mozart (1756–1791) reflected the gradual evolution from dependence on court and aristocratic patronage to the emergence of the public concert. Mozart began playing the harpsichord at age three and began composing at five. In 1763, his father took him and his sister on a tour of European courts that would last three years, hoping to make the family fortune. The Mozarts were paid handsomely for their time in Paris and at the court of Versailles, but they were disappointed by the fees they received at the German courts and in London. Mozart returned to Paris in 1778 at his father's insistence that he "get a job or at least make some money." The temperamental Mozart failed to make his way in the social world of Paris: "I would wish for his fortune," a contemporary wrote, "that he had half as much talent and twice as much tact."

Thereafter Mozart resided in his native Salzburg, where he served as unhappy court musician of the unpleasant archbishop. Mozart wrote church music and light music, including a hunting symphony for strings, two horns, dogs, and a rifle, before resigning after quarreling with his patron. Mozart spent money as rapidly as he made it, and was constantly in debt, unable to attract the lavish court, noble, or ecclesiastical patronage he desired. But a list of engagements that he sent his father in 1784 revealed that he had very few evenings free. His schedule included public concerts, which had begun only a year or two earlier. Mozart organized a series of subscription concerts of his own that year, but had only mediocre success, pehaps because his music seemed too innovative and complicated. Opera continued to be the preferred form of music. Unlike Handel, who made a good deal of money during the last ten years of his life, Mozart died a

The young Wolfgang Amadeus Mozart at a pianoforte.

poor man at age thirty-five and was buried in an unmarked pauper's grave in Vienna.

A prolific genius, Mozart moved away from the melodious regularity of his predecessors to more varied and freely articulated compositions. The operas *The Marriage of Figaro* (1786) and *Don Giovanni* (1787) demonstrated Mozart's capacity to present characters from many walks of life, revealing not only their shared humanity but their personal moods and expectations. *The Magic Flute* (1791), Mozart's last opera, expressed his belief in the ability of mankind to develop greater virtue and a capacity for love. He thus shared the confident optimism of the philosophes.

The Spread of Enlightened Ideas

Salons, academies, and Masonic lodges helped spread Enlightenment thought. Salons, which brought together people of means, noble and bourgeois alike, in private homes for sociability and discussion, were concentrated in Paris, but they were also found in Berlin, London, and Vienna, as well as in some smaller provincial towns. The English historian Edward Gibbon claimed that in two weeks in Paris he had "heard more conversation worth remembering than I had done in two or three winters in London." The salons of Paris were organized and hosted mainly by women, who selected topics for discussion and presided over conversations. Women thus became mediators of changing culture. In Warsaw, Princess Sophia Czartoryska's salon played an important role in conveying Western ideas to Polish elites. In London, women hosted similar gatherings, some composed exclusively of women. Sometimes the discussion focused on the place of women in society.

The women of the republic of letters "accustom us to discuss with charm and clarity the driest and thorniest of subject," commented Denis Diderot with admiration but also condescension. Madame Geoffrin in Paris hosted artists on Monday and men of letters on Wednesday. "I well remember seeing all Europe standing three deep around her chair," recalled one of her visitors. Her husband sat silently at the other end of the table while his wife put the philosophes through their paces. One night, a regular guest noted that the place where the silent man usually sat was empty and asked where he was. "He was my husband," came the laconic reply, "and he's dead."

Salon guests could discuss the work of the philosophes without fear of police interference. By the middle of the century, political discussions increasingly captured intellectuals' attention. Not all ideas discussed, of course, were of equal merit. In the 1780s, a German scientist, Franz Mesmer (1734–1815), proclaimed the healing properties of electromagnetic treatments. "Mesmerism" attracted considerable interest in the salons of Paris, where the nature of the "universal fluid" which Mesmer and his

An actor reading from a work of Voltaire at the salon of Madame Geoffrin. Note the bust of Voltaire, then in exile.

disciples believed linked the human body to the universe, was debated. Ironically, the very success of science opened the way for such spiritualist healers to step forward, although the French Academy of Science vigorously denounced Mesmerism as nothing more than resourceful charlatanism.

In France (and in some Italian cities as well), academies, which were organizations of local people interested in science and philosophy, fulfilled a similar role to that of the salons. They were not "academies" in the sense of offering an organized curriculum, but rather formal gatherings taking place about every two weeks of people with similar intellectual interests. Meetings consisted of reading minutes and correspondence, debates, and lectures. The academies helped spread Enlightenment ideas by gathering a literate, upper-class audience, including some clergymen, eager to discuss the works of the philosophes. Unlike the salons, however, women (with several exceptions) were not elected to the academies.

The French academies served two masters: the king and the public. They depended on royal intendants, governors, and other state officials for funding and meeting places. The monarchy believed that the academies served the public interest by bringing together educated people to consider questions of contemporary importance. Some academics sponsored essay competitions on topics of contemporary interest in the arts and sciences, which became an important part of intellectual life in eighteenth-century France;

during the decade of the 1780s, more than 600 such competitions were held. Some of the topics increasingly reflected Enlightenment influence, such as "religious intolerance and the role of magistrates in the defense of liberty."

Many members of the provincial academies by mid-century began to think of themselves both as representing public opinion, serving as informal counselors to the monarchy, and interpreting the sciences and other erudite subjects to a more general audience. The academies contributed to the development in France of a reforming mood. Moreover, some members became increasingly disenchanted with the Church, viewing it as incapable of reforming itself.

Masonic lodges, another medium for the ideas of the philosophes, had begun in Scotland, perhaps as early as the sixteenth century, as stonemasons' guilds. They now brought together freethinkers and others who opposed the influence of the established churches in public life. Masonic lodges proliferated rapidly in Europe during the middle years of the eighteenth century. Members took vows of secrecy, although their meetings, membership lists (which included women), and rituals were widely known. Members held a variety of political opinions, but they shared a general faith in progress, toleration, and a critical spirit about institution-

A gathering of a Masonic lodge in Vienna. Masonic rituals included the use of allegorical symbols, blindfolds, and swords.

alized religion. In Scotland, clubs, coffeehouses, and taverns also provided the setting for discussion of the new ideas.

There were at the same time several obstacles to the dissemination of Enlightenment ideas. Books and even pamphlets were expensive. Censorship, although erratic and varying greatly from place to place, also discouraged publication. All books and pamphlets published or sold in France, for example, first had to be approved by the censorship office in Paris. Censored books were burned, and those who published material officially considered blasphemous could be, at least in principle, sentenced to death. Far more frequently, officials closed printers' shops. Even the relatively tolerant Dutch Republic banned Diderot's *Philosophic Thoughts* as an attack on religion. In the face of a spate of publications critical of monarchy, aristocracy, and Church, Louis XV (ruled 1715–1774) promulgated censorship laws in 1757 that were much harsher than those regulating the book trade in England. The French monarchy also controlled what was published through the licensing of printers, booksellers, and peddlers.

ENLIGHTENED ABSOLUTISM

The philosophes believed that the success of any state depended on the degree of freedom and happiness it was able to assure its people. As David Hume put it, a state is justified by the good that is done in its name. Voltaire and Diderdot, in particular, believed in "enlightened absolutism." They wanted enlightened monarchs to impose reforms that would benefit their subjects. Leopold II of Tuscany (1747–1792), the most significant reformer of his era, went so far as to declare that "the sovereign, even if hereditary, is only the delegate of his people." Rousseau, however, warned that absolutism and enlightened thinking were incompatible.

Reform of Jurisprudence

Cesare Bonesana, the marquis of Beccaria (1738–1794), had the greatest influence on his era as a reformer influenced by the Enlightenment. A noble from Milan, Beccaria became a professor of political philosophy in Habsburg Austria and ended his career advising the state chancellory on such diverse topics as agriculture, mining, and trade. He made his reputation, however, with his ideas on crime and punishment.

In *On Crimes and Punishment* (1764), Beccaria, who had read Montesquieu, Buffon, Diderot, and Rousseau, among other philosophes, applied their analysis to the issues at hand. He argued that the state's task was to protect society while respecting the dignity of all people. This meant that the rights of those accused of crimes, too, had to be protected. Beccaria wanted standard procedures to govern criminal trials, so that rich and poor would stand equal before the law. The Italian philosophe's assumption that the accused was innocent until proven guilty has remained, along with the tradition of English constitutional law and trial by jury, cornerstones of Western judicial systems.

Beccaria argued that the punishment for a given crime should not be linked to the religious concept of sin, but rather rationally determined by an assessment of the damage done to society. He thus rejected the death penalty except in cases when the state itself is threatened by anarchy. Beccaria argued that "it is better to prevent crimes than to punish them." His principles reflected the origins of utilitarianism, the influential social theory of the first decades of the nineteenth century that held that laws should be judged by their social utility.

Beccaria opposed torture to extract confessions or render punishment. He argued that barbarous punishment, instead of protecting society, only encouraged disrespect for the law and hence more awful crimes. This reason, too, led him to object to capital punishment. He lamented the enthusiastic crowds that were attracted to public executions. Leopold II of Tuscany (an admirer of Beccaria), Gustavus III of Sweden, and Frederick the Great of Prussia banned torture—clear examples of the influence of enlightened thought on contemporary rulers. Joseph II of Austria (1741–1790), Leopold's brother, also banned torture and capital punishment, but he substituted many other brutal penalties that he believed would deter crime.

Educational Reform

Education in the widest sense was central to the program of the philosophes. The Empress Catherine the Great of Russia (ruled 1762–1796) admired and read Montesquieu and Voltaire, hosted Diderot, and purchased the latter's library for a handsome price. Born a German princess, she was contemptuous of Russian culture and unwilling to speak either Russian or German, preferring French as the language of learning. She seemed to heed the advice she had received from Diderot: "To instruct a nation is to civilize it." Catherine established a school for the daughters of nobles. Without eliminating censorship, she authorized the first private printing presses and encouraged the publication of more books—on an average only a couple dozen titles were published each year until Catherine's reform, when the annual number increased to almost 400.

A few other monarchs implemented educational reforms. But they did so at least partially in order to assure a supply of able civil servants. In 1774, Joseph II established a structured, centralized system of education from primary school to university, which doubled, for example, the number of elementary schools in Bohemia. Textbooks appeared in the Magyar, German, Croatian, Slovak, Ruthenian, and Romanian languages.

(*Left*) Empress Catherine the Great, and (*right*) brothers Joseph II of Austria and Leopold II of Tuscany.

Religious Toleration

Although the eighteenth century was a period of relative religious peace, intolerance could still be intense. For example, English Dissenters and Catholics both suffered legal discrimination; they were excluded from public offices and some professions. French Protestants had no civil rights; their births, baptisms, and marriages were considered not to have occurred unless registered by a Catholic priest. Protestants suffered discrimination in Hungary and the Catholic Rhineland. In Austria, in 1728 the bishop of Salzburg gave 20,000 Protestants three days to leave their homes, and royal edicts forced Protestants out of Upper Austria and Styria during the next decade.

Europe's 3 million Jews suffered intolerance and often persecution all across Europe—especially in Eastern Europe and Russia. Jews could not take titles of nobility, join guilds, or hold municipal office. In many places, they could own land, although in some of the German states they needed special permission to buy houses. They were excluded from agricultural occupations and certain trades in France, Eastern Europe, and Russia. The Habsburg monarchy required Jews to stay inside until noon on Sundays, and in 1745, it suddenly ordered the thousands of Jews living in Prague to leave. In Vienna and Zurich, Jews were confined to ghettos, and in several German towns they were not allowed inside the city walls.

Although the Swedish government allowed Jews to build synagogues beginning in 1782, they could reside only in certain cities, and were forbidden to marry anyone who was not Jewish, to purchase land, or to produce handicrafts.

Because moneylending had been one of the few professions Jews were allowed to practice, Polish, Russian, and Ukrainian Jews faced resentment from peasants who often owed them money. In Poland the Catholic Church, which condemned usury, often led the way in persecution; rumors that Jews were ritually sacrificing Christian children during Passover found credulous ears. In 1762, Ukrainian peasants killed at least 20,000 Jews in the bloodiest pogrom of the century.

Yet, by about 1750, Western Europe seemed to be entering a more tolerant age. For one thing, intolerance generated periodic rebellions, which took state funds to put down. But a more humanitarian spirit could also be seen. One of Voltaire's disciples in the 1750s achieved great success for his historical novel that denounced religious persecution.

Some of the rulers who undertook what appeared to be religious reforms were inspired less by a Voltarian critique of ecclesiastical authority than by a desire to strengthen their authority. This was the case in the expulsion of the Jesuits from several countries, which highlighted the struggle between the popes and Catholic monarchs. The Jesuits had been closely identified with the papacy since the inception of the order during the Catholic Reformation. They had gained great influence in the Spanish, French, and Portuguese colonies in the Americas, and as tutors to powerful noble families. Furthermore, the order had begun to undertake colonial commercial activity, with mixed results. These factors combined to make Catholic kings perceive the Jesuits as a threat to their authority.

The Austrian Habsburgs expelling the Jews from Prague.

In Portugal, King John V's strong-willed minister, Sebastião, the marquis of Pombal (1699–1782), enhanced the monarchy's authority at the expense of the great noble families and the Church. When Jesuits criticized the regime for, among other things, orchestrating anti-Semitism, Pombal accused them of exploiting the indigenous population of Paraguay, where they virtually ran the colonial state, and of planning to extend their influence throughout the world. After Pombal falsely accused the order of planning the king's assassination, the monarch expelled the Jesuits from Portugal in 1759. Ten years later, Pombal ended the Inquisition's status as an independent tribunal, making it a royal court. Other rulers followed suit, including Louis XV of France in 1764. The expulsion of the Jesuits from some of the most powerful Catholic states reflected the diminishing power of the papacy in the face of absolute monarchs determined to retain control over what they considered to be national churches.

In Spain, Charles III (ruled 1759–1788) ordered universities to include instruction in science and philosophy. He also reduced the feared Spanish Inquisition to a series of legal hurdles governing publishing. In 1781, the last person in Spain was executed after having been accused of heretical religious beliefs. Like the kings of Portugal and France, Charles III in 1776 expelled the Jesuits in part because their near-monopoly on education seemed to pose a threat to the monarchy's control over the Church. In Italy, Leopold II also reduced the authority of the Church in Tuscany, ending the tithe and crippling the Inquisition. Catherine the Great of Russia abandoned persecution of Old Believers, a dissident sect within the Orthodox Church, and granted Jews civil equality. And Louis XVI granted French Protestants most civil rights in 1787, formalizing the *de facto* toleration accorded them for some time.

In Britain in 1788, Parliament passed laws reducing restrictions on Catholics—although they still could not hold public office. Nonetheless, London crowds shouting "no popery!" then attacked the property of Catholics during the "Gordon riots," in which almost 300 people were killed. In 1792, however, the first legal Catholic church in England since the sixteenth century opened its doors in London.

Protestant states seemed most receptive to the philosophes' call for religious toleration. In the northern German states and Swiss cantons, the ideals of the philosophes provided support for traditions of religious toleration that had grown out of the sixteenth-century Reformation. The quest for religious tolerance played an important part in German enlightened thought. In his drama *Nathan the Wise* (1779), Gotthold Lessing argued that people of all religions are members of the human family. In Catholic Austria, Joseph II's relaxation of censorship permitted a spate of pamphlets and brochures denouncing ecclesiastical abuses and calling for toleration of Protestants. The king's Edict of Toleration (1781) extended some toleration to non-Catholics. The edict included Jews, who were now "free" to bear the burden of a "toleration tax" and to pay an assessment on kosher meat. Joseph also ennobled several Jews, incurring the wrath of other nobles. Moreover, for the first time, Protestants could enter the Habsburg civil service.

Frederick the Great

The German states appeared to be the most fertile ground for enlightened absolutism. German philosophes remained closely tied to the existing order, looking to the individual states and to religion for reforms. They were less critical of the state than their French counterparts. For Immanuel Kant (1724–1804), the Enlightenment meant the liberation of the individual intellectually and morally, but not politically or socially. The individual should think critically, but also obey.

Frederick II of Prussia (ruled 1740–1786 and known as Frederick the Great), wanted to be remembered as an enlightened ruler. A man of considerable intelligence, he turned his court into a center of learning for the nobility. Like Catherine the Great, he considered the only worthwhile learning to be French learning. Sans Souci, his rococo château in Potsdam, had French formal gardens and was considered the height of civility. Frederick, who was a flute-playing "philosopher-king," made Voltaire (with whom he had begun corresponding when he was still heir to the Prussian throne) the centerpiece of his palace for two years. Voltaire praised Frederick for having transformed "a sad Sparta into a brilliant Athens." But he soon grew disenchanted with the cynical, manipulative Prussian king, who coolly invaded the Habsburg territory of Silesia in 1740, in the first year of his reign, demonstrating that the needs of his dynastic state would always take precedence over any issue of justice. Voltaire angered Frederick by lampooning a royal favorite, and, when the king ordered his hangman to burn the offending tract publicly, Voltaire took the hint and left Potsdam in 1752.

But Frederick again borrowed Enlightenment discourse in 1770 when he claimed that one of his major tasks was "to make people as happy as is compatible with human nature and the means at my disposal." He once claimed somewhat disingenuously that he was nothing more than the "first servant" of his people as king: "I well know that the rich have many advocates, but the poor have only one, and that is I." Frederick freed the serfs of the royal domains (1763) and ordered the abolition of particularly vexing ties to noble lands, as well as the lords' right to punish their own serfs physically. Judicial reforms ended some flagrant abuses by magistrates. The Prussian king relaxed censorship and abolished capital punishment, except in the army. Yet despite once stating that "everyone must be allowed to go to heaven in his own way," he refused to emancipate Prussian Jews, asserting that they "injure the business of Christians and are useless to the state," while continuing to depend on loans from Jews. Nonetheless, the Prussian Code, finally

Frederick the Great playing the flute at Sans Souci.

completed and promulgated in 1794, eight years after Frederick's death, granted "every inhabitant of the state . . . complete freedom of religion and conscience."

Frederick the Great's "enlightened" reforms were, above all, intended to make the Prussian state more powerful, not more just (see Chapter 11). He made Prussia a more efficient absolutist state. Nobles dominated most of the plum positions as military officers and high officials. Yet because of the needs of the state, some commoners did in fact rise to important posts, including some army officers, who were subsequently ennobled. Frederick improved the state bureaucracy by introducing an examination system to govern entry. In the courts of justice, where candidates had to pass the most complete examinations, the chances of commoners for success were greatest, and in Berlin only a third of all judges were nobles.

Yet Prussian law reinforced the distinction between noble and commoner. The Prussian Code divided Prussian society into noble, bourgeois, and common estates. Frederick bolstered the position of Prussian nobles because he was determined to prevent any erosion of their status as the landowning class. He refused to ban serfdom on private estates, and he created institutions that would provide credit to nobles having financial difficulties. Marriages between nobles and commoners were not recognized. Even if nobles fell on hard times, they were not permitted to sell their lands to non-nobles. Furthermore, Frederick refused to promote civilian bureaucrats into the nobility.

Frederick intended his law code to enhance the reach of the state rather than to make his people equal before the law. When he freed the serfs of the royal domains, it was because he needed them in the army. The Prussian monarch's *Essay on the Forms of Government* (1781) offered a recipe for enhancing the efficiency of the absolute state. Frederick's view of the world bound the state and the individual subject together. When their mutual interests could not be reconciled, however, the Prussian state always took precedence. As Voltaire had discovered for himself, Frederick the Great's reign reflected the limitations of enlightened absolutism.

Rural Reform

Several Central European monarchs tried to improve conditions of rural life. Following the disastrous decade of the 1770s, marked by hunger and disease, Austrian Queen Maria Theresa banned the mistreatment of peasants by their lords and tried to limit seigneurial obligations. As she put it, sheep must be well fed if they are to yield more wool and milk. Her son Joseph II abolished serfdom in 1781, converting peasant labor obligations into an annual payment to the lord. By restricting labor obligations, the Habsburg monarchs thus increased the potential for imposing more taxes on peasants. Joseph also ended obligations of personal service to the lord; henceforth a peasant could marry and/or leave the land without the permission of the lord. Peasants could also turn to the state for support against an oppressive lord; they could even take the lord to court.

Leopold I, Grand Duke of Tuscany (Holy Roman Emperor, 1790–1793), as Leopold II, who promulgated a new code of laws in 1786 and established a new and more independent judiciary, ended some restrictions on the grain trade, freeing the price of grain. These moves were popular among merchants and wealthy peasants, but not among poor people, who depended upon bread to survive.

Enlightened Statecraft

Some rulers applied Enlightenment "rationality" to statecraft. Joseph II of Austria announced that he wanted the Habsburg state to follow "uniform principles," which included a reorganization of the imperial bureaucracy. He taxed Church property, abolished some monastic orders, and forced a reorganization of the Church within the Habsburg domains. But a more efficient government administration did not mean more freedom for subjects. None of the "enlightened" rulers gave up any of his or her monarchical prerogatives. As in the case of Frederick the Great, absolute rulers harnessed Enlightenment rationality to state actions in order to strengthen their own power rather than to improve the lives of their subjects.

Thus, "enlightened" reforms had little effect on the lives of most peasants. Enlightened absolutism benefited the Russian state and nobility, but brought virtually no change to the Russian masses. Millions of serfs were now bound even more formally to their lords. Nobles retained arbitrary rights of justice over their serfs, and lords alone could own land. Within the Habsburg domains, peasants, though legally free, remained indebted to their lords. Reasons of state lay behind even these seemingly enlightened reforms. Peasants now owed the state even more taxes and were subject to a longer term of military service. In any case, determined noble resistance undermined Joseph's reforms in Austria, Hungary, and the Southern Netherlands. In Tuscany, aristocrats and state officials sabotaged Leopold's reforms.

Catherine the Great, influenced by Montesquieu's *The Spirit of Laws,* wanted the nobility to serve as an "intermediary body" standing between the crown and its subjects. Catherine hoped that by clarifying their rights, nobles might contribute to the functioning and glory of her state. The Charter of the Nobility of 1785 formalized the relationship between the autocratic state and the nobles, recognizing the nobility of blood as equal to that of service. It confirmed their security of property, the right to hold serfs, and immunity from arrest and confiscation of property by the state. For the first time, nobles could travel abroad without the permission of the emperor. Local elective councils of nobles could henceforth send petitions to the tsar or empress, but the autocracy had no obligation to respond. Catherine herself turned against Enlightenment thought, however, fearing that it might become a tool of those opposed to absolute rule. Like Voltaire's experience at the court of Frederick the Great, Diderot's confidence in Catherine ended in disappointment when, to his chagrin, he learned that the empress had imprisoned those with whom she disagreed.

CURRENTS OF THE LATE ENLIGHTENMENT

The end of the "high" or "mature" Enlightenment was symbolized by the deaths of Voltaire and Rousseau in 1778. The late Enlightenment was more complex, sharing several currents. British economists applied the concept of freedom for the first time to the workings of the economy. Meanwhile, on the continent, philosophes turned away from the preoccupation with rationality and the laws of nature. The mark of human freedom was no longer the exercise of reason but the expression of the emotions. Rousseau himself had begun this turn toward what he called "reasoned sentimentality" by stressing the importance of emotional development and fulfillment. In a related development, a number of writers began to "discover" and embrace their own national cultures, seeking their origins in medieval poems and songs. And in France, when there were no more Voltaires or Rousseaus, a generation of would-be philosophes, mediocre writers who attacked the institutional structure of the French monarchy, influenced public opinion. All of these developments served to undermine the established order (see Chapter 11). The late Enlightenment's emphasis on the historical roots of national culture provided a way of conceptualizing national identity, a transformation that would, for example, have enormous consequences in Eastern Europe and the Balkans more than a century later.

Enlightened Thought and Economic Freedom

The philosophes' quest to discover the laws of nature and society led several of them to try to establish a complementary set of laws that could explain the working of the economy. This search led away from mercantilism, which had formed the basis of seventeenth- and early eighteenth-century economic theory, and to the emergence of classical economic liberalism. Mercantilist theory held that states should protect their economies with restrictions and tariffs that would maintain a favorable balance of trade, with more gold and silver flowing into a nation than going out.

A group of economic thinkers known as physiocrats believed that land, not gold and silver, was the source of all wealth. They wanted to end state interference in agriculture and the commerce of farm products. Writing in the *Encyclopedia*, François Quesnay (1694–1774), a French doctor and economist, called on the monarchy to free the grain trade. Quesnay wanted the end of arbitrary controls on prices, which states sometimes imposed in order to preserve public order. He and other physiocrats insisted that the initially higher prices for goods would encourage production, thereby bringing about lower prices in the long run. The physiocrats encouraged wealthy landowners to put science to work to increase farm yields, and they recommended that enlightened rulers free the agricultural economy from tolls and internal tariffs. In Britain, where commercial agriculture was already well developed, the physiocrats attracted an interested following. English landowners cheered the physiocrats' exuberant proclamation of the value of land and the sanctity of private property.

However, when the oddly named Anne-Robert Turgot (1727–1781), Louis XVI's controller-general, freed France's grain trade from controls in the early 1770s, disastrous shortages accompanied a series of bad harvests (see Chapter 11). Hoarding contributed to much higher prices; grain riots followed, and the experiment soon ended with the old strictures and controls back in place.

Adam Smith (1723–1790), a Scottish professor of moral philosophy at the University of Glasgow, argued against some of the hallmarks of mercantilism in his *An Inquiry into the Nature and Causes of the Wealth of Nations* (1776). In the name of freeing the economy from restraints, he opposed guild restrictions and other monopolies, as well as trade barriers and other forms of protectionism. Such bold proposals flew in the face of contemporary economic thought, which held closely to regulated monopolies and remained suspicious of free-market competition. Merchants looked to the state to provide financial, political, and military protection. The Scottish philosopher's optimistic doctrine came to be known universally by its French name, *"laissez-faire,"* or "leave alone." Each person, Smith insisted, should be "free to pursue his own interest his own way." If "left alone," Smith argued, the British economy would thrive naturally, generating foreign and domestic markets. The "invisible hand" of the unfettered economy would over time cause the forces of supply and demand to meet, determining the price of a good and clearing markets. By overcoming that "wretched spirit of monopoly," which made people less energetic, the "virtue of the marketplace" would also enhance social happiness and civic virtue. This was a common theme in the Scottish Enlightenment; Scottish philosophes were particularly concerned with how civic virtue and public morality could be inculcated in a society being slowly transformed by commerce and manufacture.

(*Left*) Adam Smith admiring his book, *The Wealth of Nations*. (*Right*) Immanuel Kant, author of the *Critique of Pure Reason*.

German Idealism

While in England the late Enlightenment brought an emphasis on economic freedom, on the continent it was marked by subjectivism and a greater emphasis on emotion, a shift already reflected by Rousseau's "reasoned sentimentality." The basic tenet of German idealism was that we perceive and understand the world through the medium of our ideas, and not through the direct application of our senses. The foremost proponent of this school was Immanuel Kant (1724–1804), born an artisan's son in the Prussian town of Königsberg. In his *Critique of Pure Reason* (1781), Kant affirmed that rational inquiry into nature leads to knowledge. In his memorable analogy, reason is like a judge who "compels the witness to answer questions which he himself has formulated." But for Kant, reason alone was not the basis for our knowledge of the world. He argued instead that each person understands the world through concepts that cannot be separated from his or her unique experience. This philosophy undermined faith in rational objectivity and universalism that had characterized the high Enlightenment and invited the subjectivity and relativism of early nineteenth-century romanticism.

In the eighteenth century, writers became interested in discovering the roots of national cultures; Sweden, Denmark, Russia, and Poland all discovered their "national" literatures, written in their own languages. The first Czech national theater opened in Prague in 1737. Gotthold Lessing proudly wrote in German and called for a national theater. Scottish readers eagerly saluted the "discovery" by the poet James Macpherson (1736–1796) of the work of an imaginary Gaelic bard of the third century, Ossian. Macpherson's publication in the early 1760s of what he claimed were translations of the poet he called the Gaelic Homer set off a bitter debate, one that contributed, despite Macpherson's falsification, to the emergence of Scottish romanticism. Composers began to borrow from popular culture, especially from folk music not necessarily religious in inspiration. The first Jewish periodicals were published in Königsberg in the century's last decades, and the first Jewish school was established in Berlin in 1778. The emotional search for and enthusiastic identification with national cultures contributed, as in the case of Scotland, to the development of romanticism, and though only very gradually, of nationalism. The latter, in particular, helped undermine the established order in several continental states, notably France. In those states, the established order was based on allegiance to a monarchical dynasty and often to established religion as well, and not to national allegiances.

The Enlightenment and Public Opinion

Public opinion, a concept we take for granted, did not always exist. But it began to take shape in French, English, and several other European languages in the eighteenth century (see Chapter 11). During the 1770s, more people in France discussed the pressing political issues of the day than ever before. Barristers helped establish the concept of public opinion when they sought a wide spectrum of support for the parlements. Louis XV had decided to replace these provincial noble law courts in 1768 with malleable institutions more directly under royal control. Public opinion forced the king to restore the parlements six years later and brought about an end to Turgot's attempt to rationalize the administration. Public opinion, to which opponents of the monarchy and increasingly the court itself now appealed, provided a forum in which political ideas were increasingly discussed. These ideas were largely shaped by Enlightenment discourse on political sovereignty and the limits of absolute rule.

A number of the treatises published during the late Enlightenment dealt with contemporary political issues, in the tradition of Voltaire's broadsides at the time of the Calas Affair, which had exposed the consequences of intolerance and persecution to public opinion. As the financial crisis of the French monarchy worsened during the 1780s, such publications would help make the question of reform an increasingly national issue.

Forbidden Publications and the Undermining of Authority

Some of the fringe members of the republic of letters, whom Voltaire had dismissed as mere "scribblers," also undermined respect for the monarchy and the royal family. Whereas the milieu of the philosophes earlier in the century had been elegant salons, the would-be philosophes of the last period of the Enlightenment hung around cheap cafés, lived in rooms high above the street, and dodged creditors by frequently changing addresses, while insisting that royal censorship blocked their ascent to better things. Some made a modest living peddling forbidden publications. A few kept afloat by spying for the police. A few others turned to petty crime, and others, while claiming common cause with the major philosophes against the unenlightened institutions of France, wrote pornography or slandered prominent people, including the royal family. There had been such publications before the 1770s and 1780s, but never so many of them, and never had they been so widely read.

Banned books reached France through the efforts of resourceful shipping agents, transporters, bargemen, dockers, and peddlers, who smuggled books published in Switzerland or the Austrian Netherlands to French booksellers willing to circumvent the controls of the booksellers' guild and the state. In 1783, the crown redoubled its efforts to stem the tide of smuggled books and to still the clandestine presses within France. These publishers undercut the legitimate Parisian book trade because they published banned books and produced cheaper editions of acceptable works. Moreover, royal officials were concerned about the effects of these smuggled satires on public faith in the monarchy.

Was there any connection between the high-minded philosophes and their "successors," who included the authors of *Venus in the Cloister or the Nun in a Nightgown, Christianity Unveiled,* and *Margot the Campfollower*? In fact, the envious and mediocre descendants of the philosophes continued their predecessors' work by undermining respect for the authority of the Church, the aristocracy, and, above all, the monarchy, however much their attacks by character assassination and defamation followed from ambition and financial need more than from adherence to Enlightenment ideals.

Moreover, certain themes of the Enlightenment did find their way into their work. They joined their far more illustrious predecessors in attacking the foundations of the French monarchy. Frustrated authors attacked the privileges, for example, of the printing and booksellers' guild, which they blamed for keeping them on Grub Street. Their identification of censorship with despotism, though self-serving, was nonetheless effective. As they denounced the bureaucratic system of state censorship, they argued that only its abolition could permit the free exchange of ideas. Political events and scandals kept the presses of the literary underground turning, fanning popular hostility to monarchy, Church, and nobility.

LEGACY OF THE ENLIGHTENMENT

The Enlightenment philosophes celebrated reason, while acknowledging the passions, and were suspicious of pure faith. Steeped in respect for science and reason and confident that humanity would discover the truths of nature, they were optimistic about human potential. The philosophes' belief in progress, which Kant insisted was a sign of modernity, separated them sharply from the Catholic Church. Yet, they were not as naive, uncritical, or foolish as Voltaire's Candide, who thought progress inevitable. The philosophes believed that the combination of thought, study, education, and action would lead to a better future. States, they thought, were not ordained by God, but by mankind and, like other phenomena, should be subject to critical scrutiny.

The philosophes' belief in human dignity led them to oppose all forms of despotism. Most spoke out against religious intolerance, torture, and slavery (although an effective campaign against slavery, launched by the English abolitionists of the Society for the Abolition of the Slave Trade in 1787, stood independent of the Enlightenment). Furthermore, some Enlightenment thinkers and writers recognized that contemporary assertions about the inequality of women contradicted their understanding of nature. Diderot, Montesquieu, and Voltaire favored divorce, but they opposed equal status for women.

Some philosophes had strong reservations about the ability of individuals to develop equally. "As for the rabble," Voltaire once said, "I don't concern myself with it; they will always remain rabble." Those with power and influence first must be enlightened, they reasoned, so that eventually everyone could develop through education.

The philosophes in their commitment to individual freedom influenced the subsequent history of the Western world. Whereas most people in the eighteenth century still considered the monarchy to be the repository of the public good, the philosophes proclaimed that the public had rights of its own and that freedom was a good in itself. Enlightenment thought helped create a discourse of principled opposition to the foundations of absolutism. If the philosophes themselves were not revolutionaries, many of their ideas in the context of eighteenth-century Europe were revolutionary indeed.

CHAPTER 10

EIGHTEENTH-CENTURY ECONOMIC AND SOCIAL CHANGE

The great English landowners did as they pleased in the eighteenth century. More than one gentleman had an entire village demolished or flooded because it stood in the way of his landscaping plans. Another wrote, "It is a melancholy thing to stand alone in one's own country. I look around, not a single house to be seen but for my own. I am Giant, of Giant's Castle, and have ate up all my neighbors." Fences and servants kept venturesome interlopers far away. Some men of great means gambled fantastic sums on horse races. Sir Robert Walpole's estate guests drank up £1,500 of wine a year, the combined annual wages of more than 100 laborers. English nobles seemed particularly vulnerable to overeating. A certain Parson Woodforde carefully entered in his diary the day of his death, "Very weak this morning, scarce able to put on my clothes and with great difficulty get downstairs with help. Dinner today, roast beef, etc."

At about the same time, in Switzerland, a peasant lived a very different and arguably more productive life. Jakob Gujer, who was called Kleinjogg (Little Jake) by his friends, inherited an indebted small farm and transformed it into something of a model enterprise, where he grew vegetables and new crops and raised cattle. It is said that when the Prince of Württemberg came to see the famous peasant, Kleinjogg told him how flattered he was that a prince should pay a visit to a humble peasant. The prince, teary eyed, replied, "I do not come down to you, I rise up to you, for you are better than I." To which Kleinjogg is alleged to have answered with tactful deference, "We are both good if each of us does what he should. You lords and princes must order us peasants what to do, for you have the time to decide what is best for the state, and it is for we peasants to obey you and work with diligence and loyalty." But there were few peasants with the means and initiative of Kleinjogg on the continent; in England, there were relatively few peasants left at all.

Although in some ways society remained the same as in earlier centuries, economic, social, and political change began to transform parts of Europe during the last half of the eighteenth century. To be sure, these transformations were uneven and regionally specific, affecting England and northwestern Europe the most, while bypassing much of Central and Eastern Europe. In economically advanced regions, some of the traditional checks on population growth became less imposing. Increased agricultural productivity supported a larger population that, in turn, expanded the demand for food. Large-scale manufacturing developed in and around northern English towns, leading to the beginnings of what we know as the "Industrial Revolution."

In a related change, distinctions within the highest social estates or orders were becoming less marked in Western Europe. Moreover, increased wealth generated some fluidity between social groups, contributing, in particular, to the dynamism that made Britain the most powerful state in the world. In France, too, wealth increasingly blurred lines of social class without, however, eliminating them entirely. Distinctions in title no longer necessarily corresponded to patterns of wealth distribution. By contrast, social barriers remained much more rigidly defined in Central and Eastern Europe.

THE SOCIAL ORDER

In much of early modern Europe, social structure was marked by birth into particular estates, or orders, which conferred collective identities and privileges. Each order was legally defined, with specific functions and rights conferred to it by virtue of being part of the order, not through individual rights. The nobility was a privileged order, with special rights accorded by rulers and law, such as exemption from taxation. Noble titles were hereditary, and stemmed in principle from birth (although in reality many families during the century were able to purchase titles). The clergy was also a privileged order, and, like the nobility, was generally exempt from taxation. The "third estate" in France was simply everyone who was neither noble nor a member of the clergy, and included both peasants and townspeople, all of whom were subject to taxation. Within and between these estates, or orders, some degree of social movement was possible, particularly in Western Europe. The extent of social mobility that existed within the "societies of orders" was debated by contemporaries, as it has been subsequently by historians.

Nobles

"In all states of Europe," a noble remarked in 1770 about his estate, "there are a sort of men who assume from their infancy a preeminence independent of their moral character." In most of the continental European states (with the exception of the Dutch Republic and Switzerland), nobles dominated political life during the eighteenth century, although in most of these states they numbered no more than 2 to 3 percent of the population. They accounted for a much larger percentage in Russia, Spain, Poland, and Hungary, which together may have accounted for almost two-thirds of the nobles in Europe. In Spain's northern provinces, more than 10 percent of the male population, and in Poland perhaps even 15 percent (about 1 million men), claimed noble titles. Sweden's 9,000 nobles owned about a third of the country's land. In Hungary, what may have been the first accurate census in European history in 1784 counted more than 400,000 people claiming to be nobles, about 5 percent of the population. In France, by contrast, there were only somewhere between 25,000 and 55,000 noble families, about 125,000 to 300,000 people claiming noble title. In Britain, there were only about 200 nobles, called peers, whose titles and lands were inherited by only their eldest sons and whose younger sons were thus no longer considered nobles.

The vast majority of nobles drew their wealth from land they owned but that other people worked ("I am idle, therefore I am," went a Hungarian saying about Magyar nobles that spoofed the words of the French philosopher Descartes). Social status came from ownership of land. Noble landlords owned between 15 and 40 percent of the land, depending on the country, and an even higher percentage of productive land. In Prussia, only nobles could own land that was exempt from taxes; in Poland, commoners could not own any land at all. In Russia, non-nobles lost their right to own property to which serfs were legally bound. Austrian nobles held half of the arable land in the Habsburg domains, hiring agents to collect what peasants owed them. In the Italian states, the nobility's share of the wealth was even more than that of the Catholic Church.

Hungarian noblemen in the eighteenth century.

Many continental nobles retained specific rights, often called seigneurial rights, over the peasantry. Nobles drew income in rent (cash), kind (crops), and dues (often labor) owed them by virtue of their social status and ownership of land. Some dispensed justice in their own courts. Peasants were obligated to pay to have their grain ground in the lord's mill, to bake bread in his oven, and to squeeze grapes in his press. The burden of seigneurial dues and debts left peasants with little or sometimes nothing left to pay state taxes and church taxes (tithes), or to feed their families.

Nobles proved remarkably adept at maintaining their privileges while adapting to the challenges and possibilities resulting from the growth of the centralized state. Such privileges included being exempt from virtually all taxation, as were nobles in Prussia, Poland, Hungary, and Russia, or exempt from the direct tax on land. Some French nobles paid the direct tax on land (the *taille*), but most did not. In contrast, British nobles had to pay property taxes and the only special privileges that peers retained (besides their vast wealth) were the rights to sit in the House of Lords and, if accused of a crime, to be tried there by a jury of their colleagues. On the continent, however, other noble privileges included the nobles' right to bear a family coat of arms, to wear certain clothing and jewelry, to occupy special church pews near the altar (in some places Mass could not start until the local nobles had taken their accustomed place), to receive communion before anyone else, and to sit in specially reserved sections at concerts and on special benches at the university. To affirm the deference of social inferiors, commoners were expected to bow or tip their hats when a noble walked by, gestures upon which nobles increasingly insisted. The right to duel over family "honor" in some states and the right to wear a sword were honorific privileges that served to distinguish nobles from their social inferiors.

There were significant differences in the wealth and status of European nobles, however. The wealthiest, most powerful nobles considered themselves "aristocrats." They were proud possessors of the most ancient titles (in France, they were the nobles of the sword, whose titles originated in military service to the king), and many of them were members of the court nobility, although "aristocrat" was not a legal category. The *grands seigneurs* in France and the *grandees* in Spain were identified by their great wealth and ownership of very large estates. But the wealthiest nobles may have been the great landed magnates of Eastern Europe. Prince Charles Radziwill of Poland was served by 10,000 retainers and a private army of 6,000 soldiers. Another Polish nobleman's property included 25,000 square kilometers of land, territory about four-fifths the size of today's Belgium. A single Russian prince owned 9,000 peasant households.

On the other hand, in every country there were also nobles of modest means who eagerly, even desperately, sought advantageous marriages for their daughters, and state, military, and church posts to provide a living for their sons. Demographic factors put pressure on poorer nobles, because now more noble children survived birth and childhood. Most Sicilian, Polish, and Spanish nobles owned little more than their titles. About 120,000 Polish nobles were landless, many so

A baptism performed in Italy, a religious ritual that maintained its importance in most places.

poor that they were referred to as the "barefoot nobility." The *hobereaux* were the threadbare nobles of France. Spanish *hidalgos* depended on modest state pensions, and some were so poor that it was said that they "ate black bread under the genealogical tree." In Spain, these impoverished nobles retained such privileges as immunity from taxation, the right to display their coat of arms and to be called "Don" ("Sir"), and freedom from arrest for debt. But they were not permitted to engage in manual work, and hence they had few ways to emerge from poverty. In 1773, the Spanish king changed this when he ordered the poorest of the *hidalgos* to take up manual work.

Nobles tried to maintain an aristocratic lifestyle. Those with great wealth were able to live lives of privilege and excess. They generally maintained large châteaux (manor houses) on their rural estates, some also owning elegant townhouses with gardens designed to recreate the illusion of a rural manor. Although some nobles had fallen on hard times and wished their fortunes were the equal of their privileges, they still attempted to have an aristocratic lifestyle, often going into debt as a result. Aristocrats viewed themselves as the epitome of integrity, honor, and personal courage, and the embodiment of elite culture.

The British Landed Elite

Although only nobles could sit in the House of Lords, the British ruling elite of great landowners was considerably broader than the aristocracy. Membership in the elite was consistently augmented by wealthy newcomers who had large land holdings, whether or not they were nobles (see below, p. 000). The ownership of landed estates conferred "gentry" status, which a broad range of families claimed. At the time of the Glorious Revolution of 1688, when the rights of Parliament were reaffirmed by the accession of William III to the throne of England, the landed elite numbered about 4,000 gentry families. British landowners became even more prosperous during the eighteenth century, particularly after about 1750, when they raised rents on their estates and amassed fortunes selling agricultural products. The percentage of English land owned by nobles rose from about 15 to 25 percent, a far larger percentage than in either France or the German states.

Because in Britain only the eldest son inherited his father's title and land, younger sons had to find other sources of income. One such source was the Anglican Church and its twenty-six bishoprics, the plums of which were reserved for the younger sons of peers and which offered considerable revenue and prestige. Whereas in the previous century, about a quarter of Anglican bishops had been commoners, by 1760 only a few were not the sons of nobles.

The wives of gentlemen oversaw governesses and domestic servants while instructing them in the responsibilities of family, religion, and social status—to behave politely, but confidently. The young had to learn the prevailing social codes. It was considered poor form to show too much emotion, to be too enthusiastic, and, above all, to be overly passionate, sensual or, worse, licentious. One did not seek openly to convert the lower classes to better manners and virtue, but rather to set a good example. The writer Horace Walpole (1717–1797) once claimed he attended church only to set a good example for the servants.

Young gentlemen were tutored at home, or they attended secondary schools, such as Westminster and Eton, boarding schools that characterized the shift to out-of-home education throughout Europe. Oxford and Cambridge Universities then beckoned some, though few actually graduated. Scottish universities, in contrast, offered more dynamic thought and research. Young gentlemen were expected to know something about the classics and contemporary poets. Yet, to many if not most wealthy families, academic knowledge seemed superfluous, even suspect. When Edward Gibbon (1737–1794), the historian of ancient Rome, presented one of his books to a duke, the latter exclaimed, "Another damned thick square book! Scribble, scribble, scribble, eh Mister Gibbon?" A wealthy dowager offered her grandnephew and heir a handsome annual stipend if he would "chuse to travel" and thus forsake "one of the Schools of Vice, the Universities," still blamed by some for causing the English Civil War. The goal of the "grand tour" of the continent, servants in tow, was to achieve some knowledge of culture and painting. Such trips further enhanced the popularity in Britain of the classical style of architecture, so called because it emulated classical Greek and Roman edifices.

Clergy

Although in France, Prussia, and Sweden, the clergy was technically the first order or estate, the clergy did not really form a separate corporate entity, but rather reflected the social divisions between rich and poor that characterized European life in general. Most village priests and ministers had prestige and local influence, but they shared much of the poverty of their parishioners. Yet in many places, for example the principalities of Wallachia and Moldavia in southeastern Europe, the material advantages of being a priest (including exclusion from some taxes) attracted the sons of poor peasant families. On the continent, the members of the French clergy were likely to be the most literate, Russian Orthodox priests the least.

The lower clergy, drawn from the lower middle class, artisans, or the relatively prosperous peasantry, resented the undisguised ambition, greed, and arrogance of the bishops. Wealth and rank, not piety, usually determined such selections, as in the Italian states, where bishops were overwhelmingly drawn from the families of the great landowners. Even so, few monarchs were as brazen as King Philip V of Spain, who named his eight-year-old son to be archbishop of Toledo. Many bishops did not take their episcopal responsibilities seriously: one French cardinal never visited the diocese from which he drew his income. Moreover, in the 1760s at least forty bishops resided in Paris, only one of whom was, in principle, supposed to live there.

Although some parts of Europe, especially regions in France, had already become "de-christianized," meaning that religious practice and presumably belief had declined (see Chapter 9), in most places religion still played an important part in village life. The clergy baptized children, registered their births, married couples, and buried the dead. Priests and ministers supervised charitable activities and provided certificates of good behavior for those leaving in search of work elsewhere. Religion offered consolation to many impoverished people: everyone could go to church, even if the poor were restricted as to where they could sit or stand. In general, the quality of the parish clergy seems to have been quite high in the eighteenth century (when compared to the next century), due in part to efforts to improve clerical training. Nonetheless, many parish priests were still caught between the liturgical demands of Catholic Church law and the persistence of popular superstitions shared by all social groups—for example, the duchess of Alba in Spain tried to cure her son's illness by having him ingest powder from the mummified finger of a saint.

The "Middling Sort"

Most of those people who engaged in commerce, trade, and manufacturing were known as the "middling sort" by the English and the "bourgeoisie" by the French, a term whose complexity makes definition difficult. The term "bourgeois" evolved from the medieval sense of "privileged townsmen" (in earlier times they had been exempt from having to pay taxes to territorial rulers; see Chapter 1).

Triumphant merchants at table. Note that one of the merchants is smoking tobacco, a new fad. Note also the aristocratic wig on the dog on the right.

The middle classes ranged from wealthy entrepreneurs, who had developed the economies of trading and manufacturing cities, to struggling retail merchants, craftsmen, and innkeepers who made barely enough to hang on to their businesses. Purchasing land and often titles, the wealthiest commoners "lived nobly." They owned about a quarter of the land in France and most of the cantons of Switzerland. *Rentiers* forced their tenants to pay more, and they increased rural rents as well. Great Britain had already become the proverbial "nation of shopkeepers," with one shop for every thirty or forty people.

In Western Europe, the middle decades of the eighteenth century brought an expansion of the liberal professions, particularly in the number of lawyers, who became closely linked to political life in France. Men trained in law took positions in state bureaucracies and law courts. In England and France, some of the best students, or at least the best connected, became barristers; this gave them the right to plead in court, which their subordinates, attorneys (solicitors), could not do. Distinguished medical schools produced few physicians, not yet a profession viewed with great respect. Beneath them were surgeons, some of whom were former barbers. Military surgeons tended to be a cut above the others, their skills honed in the heat of battle. Despite the fact that some universities taught anatomy, surgical techniques were learned on the job.

To some nobles, "bourgeois" was an expression of contempt, seen in the sense of a seventeenth-century play in which a protagonist is jeered by a young nobleman: "Bourgeois is the insult given by these hooligans to anybody they deem slow-witted or out of touch with the court." In the eighteenth century, the term had not lost the sense provided by a seventeenth-century dictionary: "Lacking in court grace, not altogether polite, overfamiliar, insufficiently respectful."

Peasants

Peasants, the vast majority of the population, lay at the bottom of the social hierarchy of early modern Europe. In 1787, the peripatetic Englishman Arthur Young was traveling in Champagne in northern France when he encountered a peasant woman who looked to be about sixty or seventy years of age. To his astonishment, she gave her age as twenty-eight, a mother of seven children who survived by virtue of "a morsel of land, one cow and a poor little horse." Each year her husband owed 42 pounds of wheat to one noble, and 168 pounds of oats, one chicken, and a cash payment to another noble. He also owed taxes to the state. The woman, old before her time, stated simply that the "taxes and seigneurial obligations" were a crushing burden, one that seemed to be getting worse.

Peasants still formed the vast majority of the population on the continent: from about 75 percent (Prussia and France) to more than 90 percent (Russia). Peasants were the source of the wealth that sustained the incomes of crown, nobility, and church.

Peasants stood at the bottom of society, condemned as "a hybrid between animal and human" in the words of a Bavarian official. A Moldavian called peasants "strangers to any discipline, order, economy or cleanliness . . . thoroughly lazy, mendacious . . . people who are accustomed to do the little work that they do only under invectives or blows." Such cruel images were particularly prevalent in regions where lords dominated peasants of another nationality, as in Bohemia, where German landowners drew on the labor of Czech peasants.

The village was the center of the peasant's universe. Villagers viewed outsiders with suspicion; their solidarities helped them pull through as best they could in hard times, through harvest failures, epidemics, and wars. Folk songs celebrated peasant wisdom and wiliness, as humble rural people outfoxed naive and bumbling outsiders, whose wealth could not impart common sense.

All peasants were vulnerable to powerful outsiders in the overlapping and interdependent systems of domination that characterized early modern Europe. The state, nobles, and churchmen extracted taxes, produce, labor, and cash. The proportion of peasant revenue in kind or cash that disappeared into the pockets of nobles, officials, and clergy ranged from about 30 percent (France) to 70 percent (Bohemia). Rulers extracted money, commodities, and labor payments, imposing new taxes when their states were at war.

The peasantry was not, however, a homogeneous mass. In Western Europe, where almost all peasants were free, a peasant's status depended upon the amount of land, if any, owned or controlled through leases. In France, Flanders, southwestern Germany, Switzerland, and Sweden, many peasants owned or rented plots of sufficient size and productivity to do well enough in most years. Swedish peasants owned about a third of the cultivable land in their country. Recognized formally as a fourth estate, the Swedish peasantry maintained a degree of independence perhaps unique in Europe. Charles XII of Sweden bragged that he would rather be the most miserable Swedish peasant than a Russian noble unprotected by law from the whims of the tsar. Rural industry— for example, linens—provided supplementary income for peasant families in parts of France, Switzerland, and a number of German states. In Zurich's hinterland in the 1780s, about a quarter of the population spun or wove at home for the cotton and silk industries.

Many landowning peasants were constantly in debt, borrowing against the often empty hope of the next harvest. Sharecroppers worked land owned by landlords in exchange for one-third to one-half of what was produced. Landless laborers scraped by, if they were lucky, working on rural estates. All over Europe, some peasants took to the road as peddlers. Seasonal migrants left their homes in the Alps, Pyrenees, and other mountain regions each year for construction work in Milan, Lyon, Barcelona, or other large cities, or to work in the grain fields in the summer or in the vineyards in the fall.

Serfdom had largely died out in Western Europe. Yet many free peasants continued to be subject to some kind of seigneurial justice. In France, thousands of manorial courts still existed in 1789, providing lords with additional income by virtue of legal fees and fines assessed on peasants. Most of these courts, presided over by nobles, occupied themselves with minor offenses such as poaching and trespassing, civil suits for debt, and family matters such as inheritances and guardianships.

Flogging a Russian serf.

In addition to taxes on land and salt, peasants also owed obligatory labor service, usually work on roads, in France, Denmark, Sweden, Switzerland, Poland, Russia, and some German states. Obligations varied from only a couple of days in parts of France to as much as 200 days per year in Denmark. In Eastern Europe, peasant children were sometimes required to work in the service of the seigneur. Other obligations included the duty to provide the lord's household with a certain amount of food—for example, a chicken or goose on a holiday, or even just a few eggs—to provide food for the lord's dogs, or to spin or weave cloth for the lord's household. To these were added mandatory payments to the seigneur upon transfer of land held by peasants with hereditary tenure. When a peasant with such tenure died, the lord claimed both money and the best animals the peasant owned.

The conditions of peasant life became worse the further east one travelled. Peasants in Russia and Eastern Europe lived in hovels made of earth, clay mixed with straw, branches, twigs, and sometimes caked manure. Floors were of mud and beds of straw. Only peasants of relative wealth could afford wood as building material.

The further east one went, too, the more authority lords wielded over peasants. Most peasants east of the Elbe River were serfs, some of whom had to take an oath of loyalty to their seigneur, as during the Middle Ages. There were some free peasants in the Habsburg domains and in Poland, but very few in Russia. The number of people who lost their freedom by becoming serfs had increased so much in eastern Prussia and Brandenburg that the German term for serfdom had become the same word for slavery.

Gallows stood near some Prussian manor houses, symbolizing the judicial prerogatives nobles held over serfs, including the right to dispense corporal punishment. In Poland, nobles could have their serfs executed (at least until late in the eighteenth century). Russian lords could torture serfs, as long as they did not die immediately from such treatment, or they could send them into exile in Siberia. In Poland, a noble convicted of murdering a peasant paid only a small fine.

In Russia, proprietary serfs remained personally bound to the land of the nobles and, after Catherine the Great's Charter of 1785, to the nobles themselves. Lords could sell serfs, give them away—for example, as part of a dowry—or lose title to them through gambling. Serfs could be sold individually or as a family to another noble, or be exchanged for animals. Lords could refuse permission for their serfs to marry or to choose a certain occupation. A good number of serfs took their chances in setting out to seek their freedom in the vast expanses on the edge or east of the empire. In Russia, as well as in Central and Eastern Europe, a few serfs managed to put together enough money to purchase their freedom.

A poll tax on males (called "souls" in Russia), from which only nobles were excluded, added to the dependence of the "bonded people" to the state.

Villages were collectively responsible for the payment of taxes. Moreover, all male peasants could be conscripted into army service for terms of twenty-five years, a life sentence for most soldiers.

Possibilities for peasant resistance were limited; yet the "weapons of the weak" were not insignificant. These ranged from sullen resentment and foot-dragging to arson, or even insurrection. All nobles in an idle moment—and there were many—pondered the possibility of a massive uprising of "the dark masses." As the legal and material conditions of the serfs deteriorated, rebellions were endemic in eighteenth-century Russia. During the reign of Catherine the Great, the Cossack Emelian Pugachev appeared on the Siberian frontier claiming to be the pre-

Emelian Pugachev, leader of a peasant rebellion, in his cage after he was apprehended.

tender, "Tsar Peter III" (the real Peter III had spoken of reforms but had been dethroned and then murdered). He led several million peasants against their lords in 1773 and 1774. Pugachev's followers included Cossacks, Old Believers (dissidents persecuted by the Orthodox Church and doubly taxed), the miners of the Ural Mountains, and desperate serfs. About 3,000 landowners perished in the Pugachev rebellion before it was crushed. Rebels were hanged by having hooks stuck through their ribs.

In Bohemia and Moravia in 1775, 40,000 royal soldiers were required to put down peasant uprisings. And in the middle of the next decade, about 30,000 Transylvanian peasants rose up after a false rumor spread that those enlisting in the Habsburg army would gain freedom from serfdom. They demanded the abolition of the nobility and burned several hundred manor houses to make their point. The uprising ended with the torture of several of their leaders, parts of whose bodies were nailed to the gates of four towns.

THE BEGINNINGS OF THE INDUSTRIAL REVOLUTION

The Industrial Revolution began in England during the eighteenth century. For the most part, its early stages brought an intensification of forms of production that already existed: small workshops and cottage-industry manufacturing (producing goods at home). Technological innovation played a part, but its role was not as large as has sometimes been assumed. Ultimately, however, a new source of power, the steam engine, would replace animal and human power, and in the nineteenth century manufacturing increasingly would be characterized by factory production.

The growth in manufacturing itself depended on two interrelated factors: agricultural productivity, then the principal source of wealth, and population growth. The two were so closely linked that it is sometimes difficult to know which followed which. An increase in agricultural productivity permitted the European population to increase during the century. At the same time, greater demand for food encouraged capital-intensive farming, including specialization of cash crops (such as olives, grapes, and raw silk) and the raising of cattle and poultry. Greater profits from agriculture generated a surplus of funds that could be invested in manufacturing. In turn, a larger population, some of the growth concentrated in and around cities and towns, increased the demand for manufactured goods, and provided a labor supply for town-based and rural industry.

Stagnation and Growth in Agriculture

New agricultural methods, first applied in the middle of the seventeenth century, helped raise farm yields in England, aided by the application of natural and artificial fertilizers. Gradually the practice of leaving part of the land fallow every other or every third year gave way to crop rotation. This helped regenerate the soil. Landowners planted fodder and root crops, such as clover and turnips, instead of periodically leaving land fallow. This provided food for animals as well as for human beings, in addition to enriching the soil by helping it absorb and retain nitrogen.

By 1750, English agricultural yield had increased to the point that almost 15 percent of what was produced could be exported abroad (although about a third of the population still did not have enough to eat). On average, at the end of the seventeenth century, an acre of agricultural land yielded perhaps 2.5 times more food in England than in France. Agriculture's contribution to the British gross national product reached a peak of 45 percent in 1770, and then only slowly was overtaken by English manufacturing as it rose in remarkable increments. Increased farm profits provided capital not only for further investment in agriculture but also in manufacturing (although most landowners were more likely to invest in government bonds than in speculative ventures).

One of the impediments to the expansion of agricultural production in England had been the widespread existence of open fields or common lands, which made up about half of the arable land in 1700. Beginning in the sixteenth century, on request from landowners, acts of Parliament permitted the "enclosure" of common land, transforming open fields or land that was communally owned into privately owned, fenced-in fields that could be more intensively and profitably farmed by individual owners (see Chapter 5). Between 1760 and 1815, 3,600 separate parliamentary acts enclosed more than 7 million acres of land, more than one-fourth of the farmland of England. Over two centuries, enclosure acts forced perhaps half of English small landholders from the land, swelling the ranks of agricultural laborers. Small tenant farmers, too, suffered, as many could not afford to pay rents that rose rapidly after about 1760. The poorest members of the rural community lost their age-old access to lands on which they had gleaned firewood, gathered nuts and berries, and grazed animals. Before enclosure, it was said, a "cottager" was a laborer with land; after enclosure, he was a laborer without land. The Irish-born writer Oliver Goldsmith commented with playful, bitter irony:

> The law locks up both man and woman
> Who steals the goose from off the common,
> But lets the greater felon loose
> Who steals the common from the goose.

Agricultural change came far more slowly on the continent and barely at all in much of the Balkans and Russia. Most producers remained at the subsistence level, farming small plots without an agricultural surplus that they might have used to expand their holdings or improve farming techniques. Primitive farming techniques (wooden plows that barely scratched the surface of rocky terrain) characterized the mountainous and arid land of southern Italy and Sicily, the Dalmatian coast, southern France, much of Spain, and the Balkans. Peasants lacked farm and draft animals and therefore fertilizer, meat, and milk. Markets and transportation networks, too, remained inadequate to the task of agricultural modernization.

In Central and Eastern Europe, an old adage went "there is no land without a lord" because in most places only a noble, the crown, or the Church could own land. Serfdom and the absence of independent peasant proprietors left a formidable obstacle to agricultural development in Prussia, much of the Habsburg lands, and Russia.

Measuring land in preparation for enclosure.

On the continent, a bewildering variety of land tenures and agricultural practices under which they were held seemed to set rural poverty in stone. Most continental farmland remained divided into small strips, and each year more than one-third of arable land may have lain fallow, with crops rotated between fields. Traditional peasant agricultural methods also blocked a major expansion of production. "Slash and burn" tillage survived in some parts of Europe where peasants simply burned the stubble on their land once the harvest had been taken in, replenishing soil with ash.

The studied attention many English country gentlemen gave to their lands may be contrasted with the approach of many French and Prussian nobles, content to sit back and live from revenue extracted from peasants. While the state had an interest in increasing farm output to generate additional tax revenue, most royal officials, seigneurs, and churchmen looked first to better ways of extracting peasant surpluses, not to improving yields. Nobles resisted occasional royal attempts to reduce the peasants' obligations, or to change them, such as by commuting labor service to payments in cash or in kind. Furthermore, much of what peasants managed to produce they owed to landlords, the state, and to a lesser extent, the Church. "Why should I build a better house" asked a Bavarian peasant, "so that my seigneur can line his pockets with the requisite fees to be paid?" Serfs had even less interest than other peasants in innovation.

Changes on the continent comparable to those taking place in England were mainly confined to northwestern Europe. In northern France, Flanders, the Dutch Republic, and Schleswig-Holstein, parts of northern Italy, and Spanish Catalonia, the fertile land and sufficient capital facilitated investment in commercial agriculture. Moreover, these were regions generally farmed by people who owned the lands on which they worked, and who therefore had more incentive to augment production. But even in the less densely populated countryside of eastern and southern Europe, more land was brought into cultivation, as in Russia where the population pushed into the steppes of the eastern frontier lands.

Other factors, too, contributed to improvements in Western European agriculture. During the eighteenth century, Europe as a whole experienced warmer, drier weather, particularly in the summers, in stark contrast to the unusually cold and damp seventeenth century. This had a salutary effect on population, agricultural yields, and commerce. Land reclamation projects helped expand the amount of land under cultivation. The Dutch continued to reclaim land from the sea, an ambitious endeavor that benefited their small country greatly. In Schleswig-Holstein, arable lands increased by almost a quarter by the elimination of fens and heaths. Land reclamation added significantly to the amount of land under cultivation in the Southern Netherlands and as well as in Brandenburg. Even in densely settled France, farmers recovered wastelands for pasture, cereal crops, and vines.

Though not to the same extent as in England, the enclosure of separate strips of land and the sale or consolidation of common lands in northwestern Europe permitted the development of "agricultural individualism," as more land passed to peasant-owners. Beginning in the 1760s, state policies created small farms owned by peasants, helping transform Danish agriculture from the stagnation of serfdom to relative prosperity. Royal decrees abolished serfdom, encouraged enclosure, and forced the commutation of labor obligations to rent payments.

Gradually some techniques that characterized agricultural improvements in England reached the continent. Innovative landowners and tenant farmers began to implement crop rotation (growing foliage crops to improve the fertility of fields), replacing the old three-field system so that little or no land lay fallow. As in England, turnips, potatoes, and rice enhanced dietary nutrition. Yet many peasants remained prisoners of tradition, refusing to plant or eat potatoes (Russian peasants called them "apples of the devil"), despite the fact that they can grow almost anywhere under any conditions. Nonetheless, the cultivation of the sugar beet (from which sugar could be made), the tomato (which some peasants believed to be poisonous), and chestnuts (the "bread of the poor") also spread in France.

Animal husbandry also benefited from improved techniques. Oxen, mules, and especially horses could pull plows more easily than peasants. More cattle provided manure for fertilizer, and meat and milk for nutrition. Sheep-raising developed rapidly, providing both food and wool.

Some landowners formed societies to discuss agriculture, and a few began model farms. Such groups included nobles, wealthy bourgeois, clergymen, and an occasional university professor. In France, "physiocrats," economic thinkers who believed that land was the source of all wealth, urged landowners to make their property more profitable and encouraged state policies to free the price of grain. Publications on agriculture increased dramatically.

A few rulers took steps to intervene in the interest of agricultural progress. The elector of Bavaria in 1762 offered farmers an exemption from taxes for ten years in the hope that they would plant foliage crops in their fallow fields. Several princes in the German Rhineland encouraged the selective breeding of cattle. In 1768, Queen Maria Theresa of Austria ordered the division of common pasture lands in some parts of the Habsburg territories and the establishment of agricultural societies.

Population Growth

The European population rose from about 120 million to about 190 million people during the eighteenth century (see Table 10.1). Historians have long debated the causes and consequences of this demographic revolution, studying parish registers of births, marriages, and deaths. Europe's birthrate increased, particularly after about 1740, and the number of deaths each year—the mortality rate—declined even more rapidly. These changes came first and foremost in densely settled regions of soaring agricultural productivity: England, the Netherlands, Flanders, northern Italy, and northern France (see Map 10.1). This suggests that an increase in agricultural production was the most important factor in explaining why the European population began to rise.

Plagues and epidemics, as well as chronic malnourishment, still intervened periodically to check population growth. Many monarchs ascended the throne because elder siblings had died, as did Frederick II of Prussia, who came to the throne because his two elder brothers did not live past their first birthdays. Poor people were particularly vulnerable to infection, and rates of infant mortality remained high. Epidemics such as influenza, typhus, smallpox, and the plague occasionally ravaged populations. In 1719, 14,000 people in Paris died of smallpox. Malaria epidemics occurred in Spain in 1784–1787, and then again in 1790–1792. During the plagues of 1781–1783 in Salonika in the Ottoman Empire, more than 300 people died every day. Whooping cough alone killed at least 40,000 children in Sweden during a period of fifteen years in the middle of the century, and more than 100,000 people died of bacillary dysentery in Brittany in one year. In Moscow, half the population died of disease early in the 1770s. Some states tried to close their frontiers and ports to prevent the arrival of disease, or to put those arriving into quarantine, but usually to no avail. Famine, following several successive harvest failures, accentuated disease, particularly for those at opposite ends of the life cycle, infants and the elderly. Hardship turned into calamity. In 1769 alone, as much as 5 percent of the population of France may have died from

TABLE 10.1. EUROPEAN POPULATION, 1700–1800 (MILLIONS)

	1700	1750	1800
Great Britain	9.0	10.5	16.5
France	19.0	21.5	28.0
Habsburg Empire	8.0	18.0	28.0
Prussia	2.0	6.0	9.5
Russia	17.5	20.0	37.0
Spain	6.0	9.0	11.0
Sweden	1.5*	1.7	2.3
United Provinces	1.8	1.9	2.0

*Data for Sweden is from Franklin D. Scott, *Sweden: The Nation's History* (Carbondale, Ill.: University of Southern Illinois Press, 1988), p. 260.
Source: Paul Kennedy, *The Rise and Fall of the Great Powers*. (New York: Vintage, 1989), p. 99.

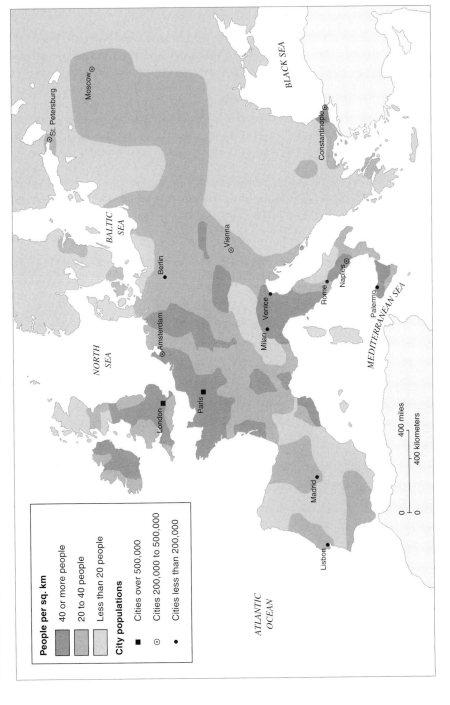

MAP 10.1 POPULATION IN 1780   Distribution of the European population in 1780.

People per sq. km

- 40 or more people
- 20 to 40 people
- Less than 20 people

City populations

- ■ Cities over 500,000
- ⊙ Cities 200,000 to 500,000
- • Cities less than 200,000

400 miles

400 kilometers

ATLANTIC OCEAN

NORTH SEA

BALTIC SEA

BLACK SEA

MEDITERRANEAN SEA

Moscow ⊙

⊙ St. Petersburg

Constantinople ⊙

Vienna ⊙

Berlin •

Rome •

Naples ⊙

Venice •

Milan •

Palermo •

■ Amsterdam

London ■

Paris ■

Madrid •

Lisbon •

hunger. Cities and towns remained unhealthy places where more people died than were born.

Yet life expectancy gradually rose as diseases and epidemics ravaged the population less often and less murderously. In general, people of means lived longer than the poor. But the average life expectancy for French men and women during the last half of the century still was only twenty-nine, and in Sweden, a country of relative longevity, it stood at about thirty-three years for men and thirty-six for women during the same period. Vaccinations against smallpox gradually proved effective, at least in Western Europe, although mass inoculations were not yet available. Quinine water helped people survive fevers. Scientific and medical societies encouraged towns to supervise waste removal and to take greater care when burying the dead, forbidding inhumations within town walls. The expansion of the cotton industry provided clothing, especially underwear, that was more easily washed than wool and other materials.

Warfare, which had checked population growth during the seventeenth century, became less devastating. Armies became professionalized, and more under the control of stronger dynastic states. Military discipline and supply improved, sparing civilians the long, bloody conflicts (such as the Thirty Years' War) that had taken a heavy toll in earlier centuries. Eastern Europe and the New World offered new sites for battles between the great powers.

Economic opportunity, such as the expansion of cottage industry, encouraged couples to marry earlier—in their early twenties in England—and to have more children. Many contemporaries were aware of the rise in population. For the English clergyman Thomas Malthus (1766–1834), the rise of the European population was alarming. Malthus predicted in his *Essay on the Principle of Population* (1798) that natural checks on population growth—plague and disease, famine, war, and infant mortality, what he called "nature's auditing with a red pencil"—would become less significant. He believed that population would "increase beyond the nourishment prepared for it," that is, food supply would grow only arithmetically (2-3-4-5, and so on), whereas population would henceforth multiply exponentially (2-4-8-16-32 . . .). To be sure, the rise in population put more pressure on the land, particularly in France and other places where most land holdings were small and often too subdivided to be profitably farmed. Yet Malthus did not take into consideration rising agricultural productivity, nor the fact that some people had already begun to limit the size of their families, although it is extremely difficult to measure the diffusion of birth control. We have only hints of this, such as when the British writer James Boswell referred delicately to his sexual encounters "in armor." In France, coitus interruptus is credited with bringing about a small decline in the birthrate after 1770. But birth control was unreliable, to say the least.

Manufacturing: Guilds and Domestic Industry

The workshop remained the basis of manufacturing in eighteenth-century Europe. In most countries, merchants and artisans were organized into corporate guilds by the product they sold. Guilds were a type of privilege, because rulers awarded them monopolies over the production or sale of certain products, particularly luxury goods. Masters' guilds and journeymens' associations conferred rights and status on craftsmen; they limited and oversaw the training of boys as apprentices, beginning at the age of twelve or thirteen. In France, journeymen perfected their skills while completing a "tour of France," the origin of the modern bicycle race, the Tour de France. A journeyman stopped in a number of cities over a period of several years; he was housed in the craft association's "mother house" before returning home with skills acquired from serving many masters, and with hopes of one day becoming a master himself.

It was, however, becoming increasingly difficult for a journeyman to become a master, particularly if he did not have a father or other relative to smooth the way with money. By the 1770s, Spanish and French skilled trades, in particular, had become glutted. Moreover, Parisian guilds faced competition from outsiders who escaped corporate controls. "Free" or "illegal" workers lived on the outskirts of the city, beyond the barrier, where a tax on goods brought into town had to be paid. Such craftsmen could produce cabinets and other products more cheaply than their Parisian rivals, whose goods were taxed.

Since at least the sixteenth century in England, partially to circumvent the guilds, some merchant-manufacturers had looked to labor in the countryside to produce goods. This shift to domestic industry (also known as proto-industrialization, the cottage industry, or the putting-out system) contributed to what would eventually become a worldwide revolution in manufacturing. The early stages of the Industrial Revolution showed an increase in domestic industry rather than a shift to new forms of production. New technology would only gradually lead to the mechanization and the standardization of tasks previously done by hand.

Britain's manufacturing base expanded early in the eighteenth century. Indeed, if in 1500 about a quarter of the people of England worked in non-agricultural occupations, by 1750 the proportion had increased to about half. The quest for profit was considered perfectly respectable, the manufacturer worthy of emulation. In 1720, Daniel Defoe (1680–1731) described the Yorkshire countryside as "one continuous village" with a "manufactory or workhouse" attached to each house or farm. Among the houses of the manufacturers "scattered an infinite number of cottages or small dwellings, in which dwell the workmen which are employed, the women and children of whom are always busy carding and spinning." Home workers carded, spun, or wove with equipment (spinning wheels and looms) that they either owned or, in most cases, rented. Hand spinning

Carding and spinning at home.

continued throughout the century to be the largest source of female employment. Master clothiers, or merchant-manufacturers, provided domestic workers with raw materials, such as wool or Indian cotton purchased at one of the cloth halls, later coming back to collect and pay for the goods that had been completed. He would then carry these goods to the next stage in the production process, for example, to a dyer. Low pay rates in the countryside encouraged the persistence of rural industry. At the end of the eighteenth century, hand-knitted stockings produced by rural Scottish families still cost less than those knitted on a power loom.

As the cottage industry was organized by household, women had a major, even determining, role in the organization of the household economy, including training young children. There were both male and female "journeymen" wool spinners. One man, later a successful inventor of textile machinery, recalled, "my mother taught me [while too young to weave] to earn my bread by carding and spinning cotton, winding linen or cotton weft for my father and elder brothers at the loom, until I became of sufficient age and strength for my father to put me into a loom." Many families of home spinners, weavers, glove-makers, and shirt-buttoners also worked the land—theirs or someone else's—part time. Rural industry paused at harvest time.

Inventions

Technological change also contributed to the Industrial Revolution. Between 1660 and 1760, 210 new inventions were patented in England;

during the next twenty-nine years, there were 976. But inventions at first had very little to do with increased productivity. They were probably less important than the infusion of investment capital into manufacturing and the expansion of the number of workers in the textile industry. Some inventions were only gradually diffused, or their importance was not recognized until later. No invention, however, was of greater long-term significance than the steam engine, invented by James Watt (1736–1819), a Scot who made musical instruments. Watt added a separate condenser to a primitive steam engine, resulting in a more powerful engine, which he patented in 1769. Yet, like its predecessor, Watt's costly invention was first used only to drain mines, making it possible to dig deeper shafts, and its use was only slowly expanded.

Inventions eventually transformed the production of iron. In 1709, Abraham Darby, a foundryman, came up with a process to smelt iron ore into cast iron by using coke (coal residue) instead of charcoal. But this process spread only slowly; in 1775, there were still only thirty-one blast furnaces in Britain. Moreover, charcoal smelting continued to be important, further depleting Britain's forests. In 1784, Henry Cort (1740–1800), an ironmaster, invented the "puddling and rolling" process in iron casting. Molten metal in a furnace was raked to remove carbon and other impurities from the iron, producing wrought iron which was far stronger than cast iron. Iron bridges replaced their flimsy predecessors. Iron made new buildings sturdier and basically fire-resistant. Cast-iron railings and gates began to appear on landed estates and in elegant townhouses. Low-cost iron made possible sturdier plows and other farm implements that, in turn, significantly increased the demand for iron. The export of iron increased by nine times in the course of the eighteenth century, helping British foreign trade triple during its last two decades.

(*Left*) James Watt. (*Right*) The steam engine.

Each major invention was the result of the ingenious application of technology already available to production, rather than of brilliant discoveries by genius-inventors. Improvements in the spinning wheel and basic looms accelerated textile production in the late seventeenth and early eighteenth centuries. The stocking frame produced lighter and more fashionable cotton and silk stockings that replaced the heavier woolen hose of the upper classes. John Kay (1704–1764) invented the "flying shuttle" (patented in 1733 but not diffused for more than twenty years), which ultimately made it possible to weave at a much greater speed, doubling productivity. But Kay's invention, too, has to be seen in the context of traditional manufacturing: its principal effect was to increase the productivity of hand-loom weavers.

Gradually machines powered by water and then by steam eliminated bottlenecks in textile production. In about 1764, James Hargreaves (c. 1720–1778), a carpenter and weaver, invented an apparatus known as the spinning jenny, which wrapped fibers around a spindle (a long, slender pin). Drawing on medieval technology, Hargreaves multiplied the number of thread spindles a worker could operate from one to eight, and then soon to eighty spindles. In 1769, Richard Arkwright (1732–1792), a former barber turned entrepreneur, borrowed some money from a publican to finance his research and patented a mechanized "water frame," which, combining spindles and rollers, became the first spinning mill. The water frame turned out a strong, coarse yarn that transformed the cotton industry and increased production of wool worsteds (combed wool). With the exception of its water-powered rollers, Arkwright built his power spinning machine out of the same components as the ordinary spinning wheel that had been found in Europe since medieval times. Using the new technology, Arkwright set up large textile mills and earned half a million pounds in just twenty years. He had his portrait painted with his hand touching his famous spinning machine, as the same painter might have formerly depicted a country gentleman standing with his hand touching a fence, his hunting dogs sitting submissively at his feet. The resourceful manufacturer emerged in Britain as someone considered worthy of emulation. A decade later, a farmer combined features of Hargreaves's spinning jenny and Arkwright's water frame to produce a "spinning mule" that could provide sturdier yarn of consistent quality while further increasing the number of spindles a single spinner could operate.

Cottage industry, artisanal workshops, and factory production often coexisted, not only within the same region, but within industries. With the gradual mechanization of spinning, weaving could only keep pace with the rapid expansion of the number of hand-loom weavers. Even a rudimentary power loom, invented in 1784, was too expensive to compete with domestic industry, which continued to be based on the availability of an inexpensive workforce. Mechanization may first even have increased the demand for production of goods that could best be provided by domestic industry.

Hand-loom weavers survived well into the middle decades of the nineteenth century.

In any case, the clever inventions that slowly revolutionized the textile industry did not inevitably lead to factory production. Like framework knitting, the first spinning jennys and mules were small enough to be adaptable to workshops and even some houses. Manufacturing remained largely based in small workshops, where skilled workers and their apprentices used stronger, more reliable hand-operated machinery or tools. Many small textile entrepreneurs, who had begun as yeoman farmers, rural artisans, or innkeepers, continued to prosper although they owned little more than a single spinning frame.

Richard Arkwright with his famous invention at his fingertips.

The factory, however, slowly became the symbol of the new industrial age in England. One of Arkwright's textile mills in the early 1770s had 200 workers, and ten years later it had four times that number. An ironworks employed more than 1,000 workers by 1770, a concentration previously seen only in great shipyards. In 1774, James Watt and Matthew Boulton (1728–1809), a toymaker, went into business in Birmingham producing engines and machine parts in the largest factory in the world. It was not a single structure but rather a number of adjacent workshops, employing about 20,000 men, women, and children in the countryside around Birmingham.

The development of the factory at first had little to do with technological imperatives. Manufacturers preferred bringing workers under one roof so that they could more easily supervise them, imposing the discipline of factory work on people used to having their schedule defined by the rise and fall of the sun and the passing of the seasons. When a defective piece of pottery emerged from the kilns, the pottery manufacturer Josiah Wedgwood would storm over and stomp on it with his wooden leg, chiding his workers. "Thou shalt not be idle" was Wedgwood's eleventh commandment. "Everything gives way to experiment" was his favorite maxim. His goal was to train his workers so thoroughly as "to make such machines of the men as cannot err." Boulton fined workers a part of their wages if they were late. One of his colleagues took deductions from his workers' wages for "being at taverns, alehouses, coffee houses, breakfast, dinner, playing, sleeping, smoking, disputes or anything foreign to my business, or in any way loitering."

By the middle of the eighteenth century, factory manufacturing had begun to alter the northern English landscape. "From the Establishment of Manufacturers, we see Hamlets swell into Villages, and Villages into Towns," exclaimed a gentleman in the 1770s. The locus of English manufacturing shifted from the south and southeast to the north and northwest, around cities like "old smoky Sheffield."

Expanding British Economy

The production of manufactured goods doubled during the last half of the eighteenth century in Britain. Cotton manufacturing led the way; between 1750 and 1770, British cotton exports doubled. The production of iron followed in importance, along with wool and worsteds, linen, silk, copper, paper, cutlery, and the booming building trades. Coal was substituted for wood as fuel.

Despite its relatively small size, Britain's significant economic advantages over the nations of the continent help explain why the manufacturing revolution first began in Britain. Unlike the German or Italian states, Britain was unified politically. People living in England spoke basically the same language. France and the Italian and German states still had internal tariffs that made trade more costly, whereas in Britain there were no internal tariffs once the union between England and Scotland had been achieved in 1707, creating Great Britain. Moreover, the system of weights and measures in Britain had largely been standardized.

Great Britain was by far the wealthiest nation in the world. Its colonies provided raw materials for manufacturing and markets for goods produced by the mother country. The amount of raw cotton imported from India increased by twenty times between 1750 and 1800. English merchants supplied slaves snatched from the west coast of Africa for the plantations of the West Indies in exchange for cotton. And, beginning in the 1790s, the United States provided Lancashire manufacturers with cotton picked by southern slaves.

England's stable banking and credit arrangements facilitated the reinvestment of agricultural and commercial profits in manufacturing. London's banks, particularly the giant Bank of England, were profitable and respected. Merchants and manufacturers accepted paper money and bills of exchange with confidence. Gentry invested in overseas trade expeditions and in manufacturing without the reticence of continental landowners. London's financial market could provide information twice a week on what investments were worth in Amsterdam and Paris. Joint-stock companies, which had begun in the late seventeenth century, offered limited personal liability, which meant that in the case of a company's financial disaster, individual investors would be liable only to the extent of their investments.

Expanded demand for manufactured goods led to a dramatic improvement in Britain's roads. A new process of road surfacing—macadamization—improved travel on the main routes. Turnpikes were extended and improved; investors formed "turnpike trusts," repairing the highways and turning a profit by charging a toll. In 1700, it took fifty hours to travel from Norwich to London by coach; by 1800, the journey could be achieved in nineteen hours. The daunting trek to the Scottish city of Edinburgh from London had been reduced to a mere sixty hours of travel.

England's water transportation was also unmatched in Europe, a gift of nature. Rich sources of coal and iron ore lay near water transportation. By 1800, Britain was extracting about 90 percent of the world's coal. The coal extracted in northeastern England could be transported with relative ease along the coast. No part of England stands more than seventy miles from the sea. Navigable rivers facilitated the transportation of raw materials and manufactured goods; so did canals built in the middle decades of the century, including a ninety-mile-long canal linking Manchester to the Mersey River and the Irish Sea.

The British government offered businessmen more assistance than any continental rivals could anticipate from their own governments. The powerful Royal Navy protected the merchant fleet, which tripled during the first three-quarters of the century. Navigation Acts forced foreign merchants to ship export goods to Britain in British ships. Bowing to pressure from woolens producers, the British government in 1700 had imposed protective tariffs on imported silk and calico. Agreements with the Dutch Republic and France in the late 1780s reduced trade tariffs with those states, which helped British exports. Other British strategies were even more imaginative: a law dating from the late seventeenth century required that all corpses be dressed in woolens for burial, a clever way of helping manufacturers. Furthermore, the political influence of businessmen kept taxes low.

Yet the British government rarely interfered in operations of the economy in ways that businessmen might have considered intrusive. Adam Smith (1723–1790) emerged as the first economic theorist of capitalism (see Chapter 9). In his landmark work, *An Inquiry into the Nature and Causes of the Wealth of Nations* (1776), Smith rejected the prevailing theory of mercantilism and extolled economic liberalism. He also observed that the greater division of labor was increasing productivity. Taking a famous example, he argued that a single worker could probably not make a single common pin in one day, but that ten workers, each repeating the same task, such as straightening the wire, or grinding its point, could make hundreds of pins in a workday. Smith's logic anticipated the age of factory manufacturing.

Expanding Continental Economies

On the continent, too, particularly in the West, manufacturing expanded rapidly in the workshops of large cities and small towns. Moreover, spinning, weaving, and the finishing of artisanal products like knives increased in the countryside. Banks provided more capital and credit to manufacturers and merchants. Despite bewildering differences in, for example, weights and measures, currencies (even within some states), and calendars (Russia's was eleven days behind that of the West), European commerce developed rapidly during the eighteenth century. The development of larger-scale commerce within Europe—for example, the Baltic trade—was very important to the growth of European economies. In addition, trade with the wider world brought new products—Chinese silk and porcelain, Indian cotton, West Indian sugar and rum, East Indian tea, South Seas spices, and much more. In the chancy sweepstakes of the globalization of colonial trade, traders and their investors could make considerable fortunes, but they could also easily be ruined when a sudden storm or pirate attack destroyed a ship and its cargo.

The great successes—and failures—of colonial trade were those in Britain and the Dutch Republic, but global trade also contributed to the economies of the Italian and German states, and to those of Spain, Portugal, and France (see Map 10.2). France benefited enormously from a dramatic influx of capital, mainly profits from the sugar plantations of Haiti.

Bankers, investors, shipbuilders, wholesale and retail merchants, insurance underwriters, transporters, and notaries profited from the marked increase in international trade. Some of the prosperity trickled down to more ordinary folk as well, particularly in port towns: carpenters built and repaired ships, dockers unloaded them, public criers announced their safe return, haulers carried their products, and artisans supplied luxuries for wealthy merchants.

Considerable obstacles remained, however, to further economic development on the continent. Traditional suspicion of paper money, the problems of obtaining credit and raising investment capital, and periodic government debasing of currencies created hurdles for those undertaking long-distance commerce. London and Amsterdam were alone in having respected banks, credit facilities, relatively low interest rates, and insurance companies. Even in Western Europe, Britain's South Sea Bubble (see Chapter 11) and the collapse of John Law's bank in France in 1720 scared off investors. Capital remained for the most part in the hands of wealthy families and small groups of associates who loaned money to states, pushing up the cost of credit. The absence of investment capital led the Prussian and Austrian states to supply capital for some manufacturing enterprises.

France did not lag far behind Britain in the production of manufactured goods, and it remained the principal supplier of Spain and its empire.

Continental European manufacturing was characterized by small-scale production and cottage industry (taking advantage of an almost endless supply of laborers). Manufacturing drew upon few technological innovations and very little mechanization. Water, wind, and human and animal motion provided power.

There remained several stubborn obstacles to more rapid industrial development: guilds held monopolies on the trade and production of certain products; international tariffs and tolls complicated trade between the vast number of small states in Central Europe; and internal tariffs frustrated the movements of goods and ideas. Furthermore, as we have seen, relatively few nobles took an active interest in manufacturing, although exceptions were to be found in France, the Austrian Netherlands, and Russia, where nobles developed coal mines and invested in the iron industry. In the Russian Empire, despite the development of the copper and iron industry of the Ural Mountains, the possibilities for increased manufacturing were limited by the monumental distances between population centers and natural resources, as well as an inadequate transportation network that had barely changed since the time of Ivan the Terrible in the sixteenth century.

SOCIAL CHANGES

Economic growth and population increases would ultimately transform Europe into a new industrial world, one in which there would be larger cities and greater social mobility. Urban growth, particularly after 1750, was one of the most visible changes engendered by population growth and the expansion of trade and manufacturing, as well as the continuing centralization of state power. Other changes included the rise of the "middling sort" and the greater vulnerability of the laborer who was displaced by enclosure and forced to move from place to place in search of work.

The Growth of Towns and Cities

Although Europe remained overwhelmingly rural, cities and towns grew faster than the population as a whole, meaning that Europe, particularly the West, slowly urbanized. Cities grew as people moved to areas where there was work, or for the poorest of the poor, where they might benefit from charity. New manufacturing centers served as magnets to which those who had no land or prospects were drawn. By the end of the century, Europe had twenty-two cities with more than 100,000 people (see Table 10.2).

The British urban population (any settlement of more than 2,500 people qualified as "urban") grew from slightly less than 20 percent of the population in 1700 to more than 30 percent in 1800, when London's

MAP 10.2 TRADE FROM COLONIES TO EUROPE, C. 1775   Exports from the colonies to Europe, including the value of the trade.

Legend:
- Exports to Britain
- Exports to France
- Exports to Spain
- Exports to Dutch United Provinces
- Exports to Portugal

ASIA

AFRICA

EUROPE

Glasgow
Liverpool
Amsterdam
London
Bristol
Nantes
La Rochelle
Bordeaux
Lisbon
Cádiz

NORTH AMERICA

SOUTH AMERICA

£5.6 million
£5.2 million
£4.9 million
£1.8 million
Value unknown
£1.4 million
£2.3 million
£2.2 million

population reached nearly a million people, nearly twice that of Paris. London was the world's largest port, the center of banking, finance, insurance, manufacturing, exports, and empire. In the eighteenth century, fully one-fifth of the British population spent part of their lives in London. Two-thirds of the residents of London had been born outside of the city and were migrants who had come to the capital in search of opportunity. Indians and blacks had also begun to appear in the imperial capital.

Some contemporaries believed that wickedness and crime increased almost inevitably with growth and prosperity. The book *Hell Upon Earth, or the Town in an Uproar* (1729) was subtitled "The Late Horrible Scenes of Forgery, Perjury, Street-Robbery, Murder, Sodomy, and Other Shocking Impieties." It denounced "this great, wicked, unwieldy, over-grown Town, one continued hurry of Vice and Pleasure, where nothing dwells but *Absurdities, Abuses, Accidents, Accusations.*"

London's emerging social geography reflected the paradox that Britain was both an aristocratic and commercial society. Bloomsbury Square and Bedford Square, elite districts in West London, near Westminster, the seat of Parliament, were largely aristocratic creations, as nobles developed some of the land they owned. At the same time, commercial London also expanded rapidly along with the British Empire. Near the burgeoning docks of the East End on the River Thames, dilapidated buildings housed the poor.

As England's economic dynamism began to shift northward with increased manufacturing, Liverpool, teeming port on the Irish Sea, "the emporium of the western world," and Manchester, a northern industrial

Elegant shops on Capel Street in Dublin.

TABLE 10.2. EUROPE'S LARGEST CITIES AT THE END OF THE EIGHTEENTH
CENTURY

City	Population	City	Population
London	950,000	St. Petersburg	270,000
Paris	550,000	Vienna	230,000
Naples	430,000	Amsterdam	220,000
Constantinople	300,000	Lisbon	180,000
Moscow	300,000	Berlin	170,000

town, grew rapidly. In the 1720s, Daniel Defoe flattered Manchester, already a small center of textile manufacturing, as "the greatest mere village in England," and by 1760, 17,000 people lived there. By 1800, Manchester had become the "metropolis of manufactures," with 75,000 inhabitants and growing industrial suburbs as well.

Paris, Lille, Bordeaux, and other French cities, too, continued to grow, although in France only about 10 percent of the population lived in towns of more than 5,000 people in 1789 (compared to 25 percent in England). In the German states, there had been but twenty-four cities with more than 10,000 people in 1500; by 1800, there were sixty of them.

After the middle of the eighteenth century, the small towns that were centers of regional trade accounted for most urban growth. Royal officials, courtiers and attendants, tax collectors, lawyers, and soldiers swelled the population of state and regional capitals. In Berlin, these groups and their families accounted for about 40 percent of the Prussian capital's 140,000 inhabitants in 1783.

In southern Italy, Naples was barely able to support its impoverished population of more than 400,000 people. No other town in southern Italy had 10,000 inhabitants. Other towns languished in stagnation, without sufficient trade, manufacturing, or administrative functions to infuse them with dynamism. In Rome, the clergy constituted about half the population of 160,000 people. The Spanish town of Valladolid housed forty-six monasteries among a population of little more than 20,000 people. Eastern Europe and the Balkans had few cities. By the middle of the eighteenth century, only three cities within the vast Russian Empire had more than 30,000 inhabitants: Moscow, St. Petersburg, and Kiev, each growing at a relatively rapid pace. Bucharest, the largest town in Wallachia (now Romania), may have had as few as 20,000 inhabitants in the last decades of the century, and no town in Moravia had half that number.

People with money and leisure time had more to do in cosmopolitan cities. The largest English towns sported theaters and concert halls, gentlemen's clubs, scientific societies, and racetracks. Private clubs thrived. Cafés took their name from the coffee served there, a drink only people of some means could afford. In contrast, cabarets and taverns offered cheap alcoholic drink.

Towns took pride in their development. Some began publishing guides for visitors and directories listing the names of shops. Elegant buildings of brick and stone replaced tottering wood-beamed structures dating from medieval times. Streets were widened, paved, and frequently cleaned. Dublin, Boston, and Calcutta offered smaller versions of English urban society, sporting private clubs and municipal pride, at least for English residents.

Wealthy merchants and bankers lived in elegant townhouses near the docks in Hamburg, Nantes, and Genoa, bustling port cities of international trade. Expanded trade and urban growth engendered consumerism. As the French language spread throughout the courts and upper classes in Europe, Paris became the European capital of luxury goods. French nobles established standards of conspicuous consumption. The sober frugality of the past disappeared. Some nobles went broke after borrowing vast sums to provide lavishly for themselves and their families.

Noble and wealthy bourgeois alike insisted on the personal prerogatives of taste, for example, in decoration and food. It became a compliment to say that someone or something reflected "urbanity." Three-cornered hats, along with wigs, which wealthy commoners as well as nobles increasingly favored, and stockings emerged as recognizable symbols of respectability.

Upper-class men and women became concerned as never before with modesty; "water closets" became more common. Social relations became something of an extension of the fenced-in noble château of the countryside, or the walled townhouse with a private garden. A code of conduct served—with income and private space itself—as a barrier between wealthy and ordinary people.

The eighteenth-century consumer revolution extended to the urban poor, as well. The number of ordinary families able to acquire household utensils and even books and cheap prints increased dramatically. For those with a little money or some credit, the tavern and cabaret provided sociability. For people with neither, there was the street.

Social Movement within the Elite

With the growth of manufacturing, trade, and cities came concomitant social changes, including mobility of the "middling sort." In Paris, wealthy merchants purchased elegant townhouses and mingled with nobles. In Barcelona, members of the trading oligarchy earned the right to carry swords like nobles. That Catalan city's sparkling new town hall and aligned, paved streets reflected bourgeois prosperity and urban pride. The bourgeoisie of the Austrian Netherlands demanded privileges granted by the Habsburg rulers to Belgian nobles.

Bankers and wealthy merchants aspired to social distinction and to live the life of the aristocrat. When possible, they would use their wealth to buy their way into the nobility, or to marry a daughter into it. Noble titles

Notice the marked contrast between the poor worker and the elegant member of the gentry in this English etching from the eighteenth century.

could be purchased in most European states, providing a relatively easily obtained means of social ascension, without eliminating the distinctions between nobles and commoners. As the rising cost of warfare (larger armies to equip, train, and send into battle, and expensive fortifications to maintain) and reduced tax revenue during hard economic times weighed heavily on royal coffers, the sale of titles and offices swept more commoners into the nobility in France, Austria, and Castile. The number of French nobles doubled between 1715 and 1789, and relatively few noble families could trace their origins back more than a couple of generations.

In Britain, on the other hand, it was rare for commoners to move into the nobility. The sale of offices had never been as widespread in England as on the continent, at least not since the English Civil War in the mid-seventeenth century, and the purchase of noble titles was nonexistent. But the crown occasionally elevated spectacularly successful, wealthy commoners into the peerage with hereditary noble titles (baron, viscount, earl, marquess, and duke), which carried with them a seat in the House of Lords. The monarchy rewarded other landed gentlemen with other titles, including knight (a nonhereditary title) and baronet (a hereditary title, granted less frequently), both of which carried the title of "Sir." Very few people, however, ever rose from trade into a peerage, or even to the upper gentry.

Entry into the British elite, however, was generally more open than into its continental counterparts. Gradual shifts in social structure in English society, beginning in the seventeenth century, contributed to the nation's social stability. Those who were wealthy enough to purchase estates became part of the landed elite and were considered gentry. Hence, membership in the elite consistently reflected the advent of wealthy newcomers. No legal or cultural barriers in Britain prevented bankers, manufacturers, merchants, and urban professionals from ascending through wealth to social and political predominance as "country gentlemen" through the purchase of landed estates. With national and local influence, these country gentlemen dispensed social and political patronage, as Parliament defended their interests.

Daniel Defoe, who wrote *Robinson Crusoe* and other novels for an expanding middle-class readership, claimed that "men are every day starting up from obscurity to wealth." Trade and manufacturing in England were honored occupations. Unlike on the continent, where second and third sons often were automatically relegated by their fathers into Church or military posts, many of these sons marched proudly into business. A Manchester cobbler wrote in 1756:

> See, as the Owners of old Family Estates in your Neighborhood are selling off their patrimonies, how your townsmen are constantly purchasing; and thereby laying the Foundation of a new Race of Gentry! Not adorn'd, its true, with Coats of Arms and a long Parchment Pedigree of useless Members of Society, but deck'd with Virtue and Frugality.

In France, Denmark, and Sweden, tensions between the oldest noble families and those more recently ennobled remained strong. The wealthiest nobles were ever more eager to maintain social distance from poorer nobles and those recently ennobled, whom they viewed as boorish newcomers, little better than merchants. The number of ennobled commoners in the eighteenth century may not have been significantly greater than that in the previous century, but those who were ennobled were wealthier. By the eighteenth century, few noble families could trace their lineage as nobles of the sword back more than a few generations. But those who could still controlled the most

This painting depicts a socially mobile French merchant and banker receiving envoys from Joseph II, the Holy Roman Emperor, requesting a loan.

important and lucrative offices in the royal bureaucracy, the Church, and the army.

The French army began to phase out the purchase of commissions in the late 1770s, and early in the next decade nobles demanded and received royal assurance that their monopoly over the most significant military titles would be respected by the crown. Directed against *parvenu* nobles, the Ségur Law of 1782 asserted that no one could be appointed to a high post in the army who could not demonstrate at least four generations of nobility on his father's side. A year later, the marquis of Ségur quarreled with a recently ennobled secretary of state and threatened to resign from the royal council: "It is war to the death," he insisted, "between the *robe* [nobles who had purchased their titles] and people like us."

However, barriers between the bourgeois and nobles in many places were starting to break down. In some states, a small number of nobles entered commerce or manufacturing. The expansion of trade and manufacturing led more continental nobles to seek new sources of wealth. French nobles were the principal owners of mines. Swedish nobles contributed to the modest expansion of manufacturing in their country. In eighteenth-century Spain, little stigma was attached to noble commercial ventures, perhaps because there were so many nobles. Russian nobles were particularly noteworthy for undertaking mining projects. In contrast, in Prussia, Poland, and Hungary most nobles still considered participation in commercial activity (above all, retail commerce) or manufacturing to bring derogation, implying a loss of status and honor. Such derogation also, in principle, existed in France, although such was often not the case in reality.

The Changing Condition of the Poor

For millions of people, only a thin line stood between having enough to eat and hunger or starvation, between occasional employment and begging, and between relatively good health and sudden illness and death. Unskilled workers, including male chimney sweeps and market porters, and female domestic servants, seamstresses, embroiderers, braid weavers, and common day laborers, had no protection against the vicissitudes of the market.

If both partners were young, healthy, and could occasionally find work, marriage increased one's odds of survival. But economic crisis often pulled a couple apart, and one partner might be forced to leave to look for work elsewhere. In one village in central France, the priest reported that "in this place there are twenty-four poor families, who have about fifty children begging for the family bread."

At the end of the eighteenth century, almost 30 percent of the British population depended on some sort of poor relief and more than a million people were classified as "paupers" in England and Wales. Laborers, some of whom had been chased from village common lands by parliamentary acts of enclosure, wandered in search of manufacturing work. Thus, the chronically impoverished were constantly on the move, trying to find work. Yet residents of a given village or neighborhood were far more likely to benefit from local charity than outsiders, who were feared as thieves or worse. Local officials and residents wanted beggars who were not from their community to move on. For this reason, beggars in Austrian law were referred to as "push people," because authorities always sought to push them away.

Meager harvests and bitter winters periodically took terrible tolls on the poor (in France, for example, 1709–1710, 1739–1740, 1756–1757, 1766, 1775, and 1781–1788), when indigents were found frozen to death in church doorways, barns, or fields in the depth of winter. When a severe food shortage occurred or the police expelled beggars from large cities, country roads swarmed with young children who had been abandoned or told by their parents to make their way as best they could. The elderly, particularly widows, were often the poorest of the poor, unable to move elsewhere, depending on neighbors little better off than themselves.

Unlike peasants, who often could find solidarity and some material support in their villages, or upon occasion, from their lords, the urban poor were even more vulnerable to unrelenting misery. In Paris during the 1770s and 1780s, about one person out of six lived—and died—in a state of absolute impoverishment. However, in good times, market "strongmen," or porters, water-carriers, chimney sweeps, and ditchdiggers could get by in "the economy of makeshifts."

The urban and rural poor were perpetually undernourished. Bread remained the basis of the diet of the vast majority of Europeans, consuming well more than half the family income—white bread for people of means; black bread (especially in the East), porridge or gruel made from rye, potatoes, or buckwheat (in Brittany and Russia) for everybody else. Vegetables—peas and beans, and cabbage in Central and Eastern Europe—were prized as occasional additions to soup or porridge. The consumption of meat by poor people was rare, except for heavily salted meat that could be preserved. Yet, the orphanage of Amsterdam, a relatively prosperous city, served meat and fish twice a week and vegetables once a week. But dried peas, beans, porridge, or gruel comprised most meals there. Fish and shellfish were common only at the sea's edge for people of ordinary means (especially because they were not allowed to fish in most rivers and ponds). Water, often not very clean, was the drink of necessity; wine and beer were beyond the budget of most people. Swiss peasants prosperous enough to drink coffee and eat chocolate were the exception in Europe. Yet ordinary people experienced a modest improvement in housing conditions, diet, and health during the eighteenth century.

Charitable works, however impressive, fell far short of relieving crushing poverty. In France, where about 40 percent of the population lived in poverty, charity could provide less than 5 percent of what was needed. During the Catholic Reformation of the second half of the sixteenth century, the Church had emphasized the importance of charitable works in the quest for eternal salvation. Most Protestants, too, believed in the importance of good works—after all, Christ had washed a beggar's feet. Parishes and, in Catholic countries, monasteries and convents, regularly provided what relief they could afford to the poor, particularly around Christmas and during Lent. Hospices and other charitable institutions cared for the sick, invalids, and the elderly as best they could. But during hard times, the number of abandoned infants increased dramatically, far beyond the capacity of institutions to care for them. Invariably the numbers of the desperately impoverished far exceeded the charitable resources available.

SOCIAL CONTROL

By the middle of the eighteenth century, many upper-class Europeans believed that they had entered an age of clamoring crowds and even riots. In the 1770s and 1780s, particularly, the lower orders seemed increasingly less deferential. The poor protested the purchase and removal of grain from their markets at prices they could not afford. They stopped wagons, seized grain, and sold it at what they considered to be the "just price," a sum that would permit even the poor to buy enough to survive.

Artisanal work stoppages, too, became more widespread. Following a London strike by journeymen tailors protesting cuts in their pay, the British Parliament passed the first Combination Act in 1721. The law established wages and working conditions for tailors and allowed the jailing of striking workers without benefit of a trial. Seeing that many craftsmen and skilled workers were leaving Britain, some for the colonies, Parliament then passed legislation forbidding their emigration.

Protecting Property

In Britain, Parliament represented the interests of wealthy landowners who consolidated their property during the eighteenth century and alone could elect members of the House of Commons. The philosopher John Locke summed up the relationship between government and landed property in early modern England: "The great and chief end . . . of men uniting into commonwealths, and putting themselves under government, is the preservation of their property." Thus, in 1723, Parliament passed without discussion a law that added fifty separate offenses against property for which the death penalty could be imposed, although it rarely was.

Hunting was a badge of living nobly. It was a domesticated, usually nonlethal—at least for the hunters—version of warfare. The exclusive right to hunt was a vigilantly guarded prerogative of any and all who could claim noble status. But acts against poaching were invoked more often to protect the property of middle-class and even poor land-owners. They were not simply measures taken by the rich against the poor.

Wealthy English landowners set brutal mantraps—including trap-guns—and snares that maimed poachers who snuck onto their property, including the "deer parks" established on land that had once been common land. The felonies listed under the

A gamekeeper snags a poacher.

Black Act, among them the blackening of one's face as a form of disguise—hence the law's name—included poaching game or fish, or chopping down trees or gleaning branches blown down in storms. Henry Fielding (1707–1754) called attention to such a felony in his novel *The Adventures of Joseph Andrews*: "Jesu!" said the Squire, "would you commit two persons to bridewell [prison] for a twig?" "Yes," said the Lawyer, "and with great leniency too; for if we had called it a young tree they would have been both hanged."

The concern for protecting property could be seen in legislation affecting marriage. The Marriage Act (1753) forbade clandestine marriages. While its central goal was to extend the uniformity of the law, it specifically sought to protect property against ambitious men who might be tempted to try to elope with the daughters of wealthy property owners. Parliament also passed a law permitting divorce by parliamentary act—which none but the very wealthy and well-placed could seek—at least partially because gentlemen wanted to be free to divorce wives who shamed them with adultery or who could not produce heirs to inherit their estates.

Subordination and Social Control

People of means debated strategies of social control with increasing urgency as economic crises in the 1770s and 1780s widened the gap between rich and poor. During 1724–1733, the French state undertook a "great confinement" of paupers, beggars, and vagrants in workhouses, where they were to learn

A public hanging at Tyburn in London.

menial trades under conditions of strict discipline. The subsequent reorganization and expansion of royal efforts at policing the poor during the 1760s represented a marked increase in the reach of the state into rural life, as well as into cities and towns. Some states established temporary programs of poor relief while enhancing the repressive capacity of the police and of hospitals and other institutions that took in vagrants and beggars. Milan's government began locking up beggars. Since the beginning of the seventeenth century, English parishes or townships provided charity to those wearing the requisite "P" for pauper. In order to keep indigents off the road, some towns established workhouses, where the poor would be forced to work in exchange for subsistence. Such places were notoriously unhealthy: of more than 2,300 children taken into London's workhouses during the 1750–1755 period, only 168 were alive at the end of the period (although some might have been discharged). A 1782 English law replaced workhouses with somewhat more humane "poorhouses." In 1795, the Speenhamland system, so called after the parish in which it was conceived, provided for a sliding scale of assistance, determined by the current price of bread and wage rates. But such programs merely scratched the surface as the problem of poverty entered public discourse to an unprecedented degree.

On the continent, the eighteenth century witnessed a largely successful campaign to limit the number of capital crimes to those that threatened life or the state. In contrast, Britain's Parliament added almost two hundred capital offenses to the law between 1688 and 1810, sixty-three of them between 1760 and 1810. About mid-century, two young men were arrested for poaching. Their wives went to the landlord's estate to beg his merciful intercession. The lord, moved to tears, said that their husbands would be returned to them. True to his word, he sent the two corpses to the wives.

But English juries, in particular, hesitated to convict those accused; only about two hundred criminals were executed each year. Executions—including that of a peer who claimed that his marriage had led him to murder his steward and who had asked to be hanged in his wedding suit—drew huge throngs at London's Tyburn. Domestics convicted of stealing from their masters or mistresses or workmen from their employers could be executed, but corporal punishment, such as branding or being exhibited in stocks to public contempt, was far more common. Children were worked and punished as adults, though not all as harshly as the seven-year-old girl who was hanged in Norwich for stealing a petticoat. England was relatively underpoliced, particularly when compared to France (Paris had four times more policemen than London, which was twice its size).

The vocabulary adopted by the French police reflected the tendencies of authorities everywhere to lump the poor into one of two broad categories—"deserving" and "undeserving," that is, whether they were considered worthy of pity and charity. Other less general designations included the poor, the truly poor, the shameful poor, the disabled poor, the false poor, the indigent, the miserably poor, the beggar of good faith, the shameful beggar, the professional beggar, and the wandering beggar. The false beggar simulated horrifying wounds or injuries with the skill of a makeup artist and, clutching at the clothes of the wealthy passing by, received a few cents as his benefactors scurried away as rapidly as possible. These categories reflected the belief that many, if not most, of the poor were destitute because they were lazy and that stiff punishment would be enough to end begging.

In small bourgs, villages, and the countryside, people feared bands of thieves, who by setting a fire could intimidate and rob by virtue of their number, and who could destroy a harvest or a farm in a matter of minutes. Brigandage was rampant in southern Italy and in Sicily. In France, some of the most infamous bands were in the grain-rich Beauce region south of Paris. There some bandits were known as *chauffeurs* because they held their victims' feet to the fire to force the victims to reveal the hiding place of their valuables, a tactic borrowed from marauding soldiers in the Thirty Years' War. Yet many poor people considered some bandits as heroic, Robin Hoods, who stole from the rich and gave to the poor.

A CENTURY OF CONTRASTS

The eighteenth century was a period of contrasts. Musical performances at court and in châteaux and elegant townhouses took place while peasants and day laborers struggled to survive, toiling in fields they rarely owned, in forests belonging to the state or nobles, or working as dock or market porters, chimney sweeps, or common laborers in town. These contrasts were, to be sure, also geographic. The well-heeled financier, wholesale merchant, manufacturer, or lawyer of Paris, Amsterdam, Barcelona, Vienna, or Milan lived in a vastly more cosmopolitan world, increasingly shaped by consumerism, than did the middle classes of Prussia, Poland, Russia, and the Balkans, lands in which towns were few and far between. In the northern Italian states and the Austrian Netherlands, prosperous merchants and manufacturers were blurring the lines between nobles and wealthy commoners.

In many ways a century still dominated politically by nobles, the eighteenth century also was a dynamic period of economic and social transformation, beginning with the Industrial Revolution in England, and with the increase in commerce and manufacturing in northwestern Europe as well. These developments had political consequences during the 1760s and 1770s. The country gentlemen who invariably supported court policies and those who often opposed them began to look and act like political parties. And the domination of political life by an oligarchy of landowners came under challenge from ordinary people without the right to vote. British colonists in North America protested the fact that they were taxed without representation, and they rebelled against British rule.

On the continent, denunciations of unwarranted privilege began to be heard. Calls for reform of the French absolute monarchy came even from one of the ministers of the king, who then tried to abolish guilds and institute free trade. During the political crises in the early 1770s, public opinion gradually began to see parlements as blocks against absolute rule and defenders of the rights of the "nation," a term that increasingly came into use. Elsewhere on the continent, too, opposition to entrenched privilege became more and more insistent.

CHAPTER **11**

EIGHTEENTH-CENTURY DYNASTIC RIVALRIES AND POLITICS

King George III (ruled 1760–1820) proclaimed that he "gloried in the name of Britain." Indeed during his reign, despite his personal failings, a nationalist cult developed around the British monarchy, significantly after the empire suffered its biggest loss, that of the thirteen American colonies.

The king projected the image of an ordinary family man, surrounded by his homely wife and fifteen children. Less interested in goings-on in Hanover, his family's dynastic home, than his predecessors, he won popular affection in Britain. "This young man," wrote Horace Walpole, "don't stand in one spot with his eyes fixed royally on the ground, and dropping bits of German news; he walks about and speaks to everybody." The king's domesticity also made him a target for the gentle spoofs of caricaturists. His nervousness led him to bombard almost everyone he encountered with questions, ending with "hey, hey?" By the last decade of the century, symptoms of a hereditary disease made George III appear to be quite mad.

Early in his reign, King George III had strong ideas about monarchical prerogatives, even within the context of the British constitutional monarchy. Yet during his reign, not only did British nationalism develop rapidly, but the idea developed in and beyond Parliament that a party of parliamentary opposition formed an essential part of the parliamentary system of representation.

The nature of the European state system itself also underwent fundamental change in the eighteenth century as the rivalries between Great Britain, France, Spain, and the Dutch Republic (the United Provinces) broadened to a global scale. Whereas Europe in the period of Louis XIV had been marked by frenetic war-making and the pursuit of alliances against France, Europe's

The young King George III in saner days.

dominant power, the wars fought between the great powers in the middle of the eighteenth century reflected a more even distribution of power. This balance of power was increasingly affected not only by events overseas but also by those in Eastern Europe. There, Russia expanded its empire at the expense of the Ottoman Empire, and Russia, Prussia, and Austria dismembered Poland.

The increasingly global nature of conflicts between the great powers put strains on the structures of states in Europe. They were forced to reorganize themselves to become more efficient, either by granting more power to representative bodies combined with stronger mechanisms for raising money, as in the case of Great Britain, or through some variant of enlightened despotism, as in Prussia. In Britain, where monarchs depended on Parliament, the role of the House of Commons expanded and political parties emerged. Newspapers and societies for discussing politics created public opinion, which transformed the political sphere as more people demanded political reform. Patriotism, and by extension, a sense of national identity, emerged in Britain. Some allegiance was transferred from the ruler to Parliament, which was seen as representing the interests of all Britons (directly or indirectly).

Reform movements and uprisings alarmed rulers and intrigued intellectuals, who in increasing numbers denounced unwarranted privilege and despotism. Reformers celebrated the British model of constitutional monarchy but then American colonists rose up against British rule. Public opinion on the continent challenged absolute rule; in France, the parlements began to defend the "nation" against monarchical despotism. As contemporaries sought explanations for movements that sought to limit monarchical authority, the Bavarian envoy in Vienna went so far as to claim in 1775 that "the spirit of revolt has become universal." Although the diplomat exaggerated, these movements for reform to some degree influenced and encouraged each other.

THE EIGHTEENTH-CENTURY STATE SYSTEM

Eighteenth-century Europe consisted of states dancing together in temporary partnership until the music changed and old partners were deserted and new ones embraced. The eighteenth-century state system was a pattern of rivalry and alliance in which each state vied for global and dynastic power. Few borders or thrones were secure from challenge by other states and rulers coveting more territory and more power. Rulers sought to expand their power through marriage, inheritance, or warfare. Each state looked out for its own self-interests and forged alliances that would help further those interests. Global and dynastic rivalries led to conflicts and ultimately to wars as states tried to add more territory and other states sought to maintain the balance of power, so that one state did not grow more powerful at the expense of the others. Spain, the Dutch Republic, Sweden, the Holy Roman Empire, and the Ottoman Empire found themselves with far less power than in the seventeenth century, while Britain, Russia, and Prussia continued to extend their reach.

The emergence of a global economy increasingly linked to colonial trade engendered rivalries and conflicts between England, France, Spain, and the Dutch Republic, as each battled for commercial and colonial advantage. The wars that resulted were motivated by the hope of economic gain and reflected the primacy of the economic theory of mercantilism, which assumed that there was a finite amount of wealth available in the world, and that the might of any state depended on its success in bringing in more gold than it paid out.

Dynastic rivalries remained a major source of conflict. In England, George I from the German state of Hanover succeeded to the throne in 1714, but his German origins and interests complicated British foreign policy and led to unsuccessful attempts by the Catholic Stuart pretenders to take back the British throne. Meanwhile, on the continent, Frederick the Great of Prussia and Maria Theresa of Austria locked horns in a battle of expansion for the former and survival for the latter. The other great powers lined up in alliances on the side of each.

Global Rivalries

As voyages of discovery opened up new horizons to Europeans, the stakes of colonial rivalry between the great powers rose. During the seventeenth century, England, the Dutch Republic, France, Spain, and Portugal had gradually expanded their trading routes across the seas. Coffee, tea, molasses, ginger, indigo, calicoes, tobacco, and other colonial products— for the most part luxury goods—fetched high prices. The discovery of gold in Brazil in 1694 and 1719 further whetted the appetites of commercial companies. China also began to fascinate some Europeans. By the end of the seventeenth century, Dutch and French traders began to go there in greater numbers. The land trade routes that stretched through the Middle East and Central Asia still continued to reward the ambition and persistence of merchant-traders, who returned with spices and fine silks. Chinese prints, porcelain, gardens, silk, and Oriental rugs became popular in Western Europe.

In the eighteenth century, the British East India Company carried its trading interests to more distant places, establishing new posts in South India and Bengal. Parliament licensed the company to operate as a military force. British traders exchanged slaves taken from West Africa and textiles and other manufactured goods for colonial products. The British East India Company's ships carried Chinese porcelain, silks, spices, and tea to England in exchange for silver and, increasingly, opium grown in India. An Englishman in the middle of the eighteenth century exclaimed that "the Interests and Commerce of the British Empire are so inseparably united that they may be very well considered as one and the same."

Spain still had the largest empire. It included the largest Caribbean islands, the Philippines in the Pacific, and most of South America except for Brazil, which belonged to Portugal. The Dutch had bases on the coast of South America, West Africa, South Africa (their colony at the Cape of

The European appetite for luxury goods spurred the expansion of trading routes into Asia. In this eighteenth-century print, tea is being packed up in China for its journey to Europe.

Good Hope was the only permanent European settlement at the time in Africa), the island of Mauritius in the Indian Ocean, the Indian subcontinent, Indonesia, and Japan.

The British colonies in the New World differed from Spanish colonies and, even more, from French colonies. Many people had migrated to the British colonies seeking economic opportunity, or in the case of Massachusetts Puritans and Maryland Catholics, religious toleration. These settlement colonies also welcomed emigrants from the German states, who hoped to make a living as farmers, artisans, and day laborers. Unlike in the towns and villages they left, men far outnumbered women, although entire families, too, took passage on ships bound for America, where as much as possible they sought to recreate the way of life left behind.

French forts and settlements dotted the North American colony of Nouvelle (New) France. French trappers established posts on the Mississippi River, with the port of New Orleans at its mouth far to the south. The territories claimed by the French, on which they had only scattered military and trading posts, almost tripled in size by the middle of the eighteenth century, but by the 1760s the French population of Nouvelle France stood at only about 80,000 people.

Global rivalries led to conflicts between the great powers, both on the seas and in the colonies themselves. French and British armies and navies battled in North America, the West Indies, and India, believing that the gain or loss of Canadian furs, Caribbean spices, or Indian jewels might be a damaging blow to dynastic prosperity and prestige. Spanish colonial rivalry with Britain led to the only war ever fought over an ear. Both Spain and England insisted that their colonies ship goods only on vessels flying their flag. Since 1713 the Spanish had granted the right to Britain to supply its colonies with 4,800 slaves each year; in exchange for this sale, a single English ship each year could trade at one Spanish colonial port. Illegal trade, however, continued as before. The Spanish navy sank several English ships, and in 1731 one of its vessels accosted an English frigate suspected of smuggling. A Spanish sword cut off one of the ears of the captain, Jenkins. The incident led to the "War of Jenkins's Ear" in 1739 after a member of Parliament whipped up anti-Spanish sentiment by waving the severed ear in the air during a speech.

The Hanoverians and the Stuarts in Great Britain

In 1702, Queen Anne (1665–1714), the Protestant daughter of James II, succeeded her brother-in-law, William III, to the throne of England. Despite eighteen pregnancies and five live births, Anne had no surviving children. The House of Commons had passed the Act of Succession in 1701 to prevent any future restoration of the Catholic Stuart line to the throne. By this act, which broke the strict rules of dynastic succession, the Protestant ruling dynasty of Hanover, related by blood to the English royal family, would become the English royal line upon Anne's death.

In 1707, the Act of Union created the Kingdom of Great Britain, which took the Union Jack as its flag, and linked Scotland to England and Wales. Scotland received seats in the House of Commons, but fewer than its population should have warranted. Parliament's goal in formalizing the existing dynastic union was fear that Scotland might seek to summon Queen Anne's exiled Catholic half-brother (James III) to be king of Scotland, instead of going along with England and Wales's awarding of the throne to the house of Hanover. Ireland, in which English Protestants owned seven-eighths of the land, continued to pay dearly for having supported the Catholic monarch James II after the Glorious Revolution of 1688 had sent him from the throne. Legal restrictions prevented Catholics from being merchants, lawyers, or members of the Irish Parliament, the power of which was strictly limited by the English Privy Council. In England itself, Parliament had not extended the Toleration Act of 1689 to Catholics. British Catholics could not vote, be elected to Parliament, or hold state offices; they also were subject to special taxes, could not possess weapons, be admitted to Oxford or Cambridge Universities, or worship freely, at a time when Protestant Dissenters—that is, Protestants not belonging to the Church of England—were able to rise to respectable positions within the British state.

The Hanoverian George I (1660–1727), a distant cousin of Queen Anne, became king in 1714. He never learned English, brought some of his own advisers from Hanover, was stubborn and obese (some of his subjects referred to their monarch as "King Log"), and may have ordered the murder of his wife's lover in Hanover. All of this was more easily forgiven by wealthy Englishmen than his apparent indifference toward the crown he wore, seemingly demonstrated by the fact that he spent long periods of time in his beloved Hanover.

The Hanoverian dynasty's accession to the throne in 1714 complicated British foreign policy. The Treaty of Utrecht (1713), the first of two treaties that concluded the War of the Spanish Succession (1701–1714, see Chapter 7), confirmed Britain's colonial supremacy, adding Newfoundland, Nova Scotia, the Hudson Bay territory, and New Brunswick, as well as Gibraltar and the island of Minorca, and it also granted the right to trade in Spanish colonial ports. But George I, who became king the year after the treaty, looked with disfavor on the Utrecht treaty because it had not furthered the interests of Hanover. Furthermore, some in Parliament viewed the compromise treaty as a humiliation for England. It was ratified by the House of Lords only because Queen Anne had created enough new peers to assure passage.

The new Hanoverian dynasty was threatened by remaining support for the Catholic Stuart dynasty. Some conservatives still claimed that James III, the Stuart son of James II, was the legitimate heir to the throne. In 1715, the intransigent supporters (Jacobites) of James III began an uprising in Scotland. Although by the Treaty of Utrecht the king of France had

George I, the Hanoverian king of Great Britain who never learned English.

officially renounced support for James, Catholic France still wanted him on the British throne. But troops loyal to George I quickly quelled the rebellion.

George II (1683–1760) became king in 1727. Like his father, he was courageous and had led troops into battle in Germany. But unlike his father, he took the time to learn English (although it remained decidedly his second language). He spoke it with a strong German accent that his subjects mocked ("I hate bainting and boetry!" he once announced). He had a stiff, tedious personality, displaying impatience and a bad temper. On one occasion he bellowed, "I am sick to death of all this foolish stuff, and wish with all my heart that the devil may take all your bishops, ministers, Parliament, and the devil take the whole island—provided I can get out of it and go to Hanover!"

In 1745, the dreamy pretender Charles Edward Stuart (1720–1788) planned an invasion of England, similar to the one his father had undertaken thirty years earlier. "Bonnie Prince Charlie" landed in Scotland with a small army of enthusiasts, while British troops were engaged on the continent. Adding Scottish clansmen from the Highlands to his force, he then marched southward into England with about 9,000 men. The threat to the throne was serious enough to give birth to the British anthem "God Save the King," which dates from this time.

But Charles Edward found in England almost no support for his cause. Commercial and manufacturing centers, in particular, rallied against any possibility of a Stuart restoration. The young pretender hesitated a hundred miles from London and then retreated to Scotland.

Many highlanders deserted his ranks as English troops ravaged their country. William Augustus (1721–1765), the duke of Cumberland and third son of George II, overtook and defeated Bonnie Prince Charlie at Culloden Moor near Inverness in April 1746. He earned the nickname of "the butcher" through his ruthless treatment of the defeated rebels. It was the last battle fought on British soil to this day. The pretender high-tailed it back to France. The government ordered the execution of two Scottish peers who had thrown their support to the pretender and for-bade the wearing of kilts or tartans, symbols of the highlanders. There-after, only a handful of Jacobites continued to celebrate Stuart birthdays. They toasted "the king over the water" living in French exile by holding their glasses of spirits over another glass filled with water.

The Prussian-Austrian Dynastic Rivalry in Central Europe

The increased power of Prussia threatened Habsburg interests in Central Europe. Charles VI (ruled 1711–1740), the decent but mediocre Holy Roman emperor, had never recovered from the Habsburg loss of Spain in the War of the Spanish Succession. He remained obsessed with keeping the remaining Habsburg lands together. As Charles had no son, he spent years during his reign trying to bribe or otherwise convince the other European powers to recognize the integrity of the Habsburg inheritance upon his death. In 1713, he sought to get them to recognize the Pragmatic Sanction, which asserted the indivisibility of the Habsburg domains and recognized the right of female as well as male succession, should Charles have no sons.

When Charles VI died without a male heir, his twenty-three-year-old daughter Maria Theresa (ruled 1740–1780) assumed the Habsburg throne. While Maria Theresa could, as a woman, be Archduchess of Austria and Queen of Hungary and Bohemia, she was barred from becoming Holy Roman empress, thus opening up the question of imperial succession. The young queen had little money, no army, almost no bureaucracy, and bad advisers, and hence was in a poor position to defend her throne against hostile powers. Worse, France and Prussia, despite having pledged to uphold the Pragmatic Sanction, were each preparing to dismember the Habsburg empire.

The immediate threat to Maria Theresa came from the Prussian King Frederick II (ruled 1740–1786, see Chapter 7). As a young man, Frederick had little in common with his raging father, Frederick William I. The royal son was intelligent, played the flute, enjoyed reading, preferred the French language to his native German, and as a boy expressed little interest in the army. At the age of eighteen, he tried to run off to England to catch a glimpse of his intended English bride. When young Frederick's scheme, planned by his best friend—and perhaps his lover—was foiled, the furious Frederick William decided to have his son executed. When dissuaded by his officials, Frederick William made the young prince watch from a prison cell the decapitation of his friend. Forced by his father to serve in the royal bureaucracy and as an army officer, Frederick became an aggressive absolute monarch.

Frederick, called "the Great" by his subjects, worked twelve hours a day lovingly overseeing minute details of army administration. His own physical courage was legendary—six times, horses were killed beneath him in battle. At the same time, he eschewed the extravagant court life of the French Bourbons, allocating a mere 3 percent of state revenue to the court, in contrast to perhaps a third of the budget of the French monarchy.

Frederick the Great's "enlightened" reforms (see Chapter 9) made Prussia a more efficient absolutist state. His intent was to extend the reach of the state rather than to improve the lot of his people. Frederick improved the state bureaucracy by introducing an examination system. Through these examinations, talented commoners could be awarded positions in the courts of law. Thus, talent as well as birth determined who served the state.

"Old Fritz" strengthened the Prussian economy by establishing state-operated iron- and steelworks, ordering the construction of more canals to haul goods, and encouraging the establishment of workshops in Berlin to produce textiles, glass, clocks, and porcelain. Because he ordered officials to accumulate stocks of grain in good times, Prussia never suffered the desperate periods of dearth that occurred in eighteenth-century France.

Maria Theresa and her family at the Schönbrunn Palace outside of Vienna. The future emperor Joseph II stands at her right.

Frederick the Great rides into battle.

With careful budgeting and relative frugality, Frederick the Great managed to pay for his wars. He closely monitored state tax revenues and expenses. He refused to undertake expensive loans, sell noble titles and privileges, or impose levies on the peasantry, policies that were wreaking financial and social havoc in France.

Frederick continued the exemptions of the Junkers (nobles) from many taxes and preserved their domination of the bureaucracy and army. He personally planned educational reforms with an eye to improving the performance of his officials. Nobles oversaw regional government, as well as the collection of taxes. But Frederick also wanted to keep the Junkers in a position of subordination to the crown. Noble army officers could not marry or travel abroad without the king's authority, a constraint that would have been unthinkable in France. Frederick's response to the hint of any disagreement from nobles, officials, officers, or anyone else was "Don't argue!" He tolerated no appeals of royal decisions. In a society with a relatively rigid social structure, aristocratic and military virtues were henceforth inseparable in Prussia, a fact fraught with significance for modern German history.

CONFLICTS BETWEEN THE GREAT POWERS

While the rivalry between Great Britain and France assumed global dimensions, the rise of Prussia and Russia (see Chapter 7) carried European dynastic rivalries and warfare into Central Europe. The War of the Austrian Succession (1740–1748), which began when King Frederick II of Prussia invaded Silesia (a Habsburg territory), revealed the fundamental principle in eighteenth-century power politics: the balance of power. The unchecked success of any one power seeking to expand its territory inevitably brought a combined response from the other powers to maintain a rough balance between the states. The expansion of Prussian power, then, engendered the "Diplomatic Revolution" of 1756, when Austria and

France put their long-standing rivalry aside to join forces against Prussia and Britain in the Seven Years' War (1756–1763). The long, costly war between France and Britain was truly global in extent, as both powers battled in North America (where the war become known as the French and Indian War), the Caribbean, and India. Armies were larger and better drilled than ever before. At the same time, the French and British navies played a greater role in transporting troops and supplies, as well as guarding commercial vessels in the global struggle.

The War of the Austrian Succession

The War of the Austrian Succession reflected naked absolutist aggression. Frederick the Great coveted Silesia (now part of Poland), a Habsburg territory south of Prussia and squeezed between Saxony, Poland, and Austria. With its textile, mining, and metallurgical industries, Silesia was a relatively wealthy province within the Habsburg domains. Frederick II had come to the throne in the same year as Maria Theresa and quickly sought to take advantage of the lone queen in a world of kings. Confident that the recent death of the Russian empress would preclude Russian assistance to Austria, Frederick sent his army into Silesia.

Frederick was the latest in the line of aggressive Prussian kings who identified the interests of the state with a powerful army complemented by a centralized bureaucracy able to raise money through taxes. The Habsburg monarchy embodied, by contrast, the complexity of Central Europe. Austrian Germans dominated the administrative structure of the empire of many different peoples and languages. The multiplicity of privileges (particularly those of Magyar and Croatian nobles), traditions, and cultures undermined the authority, resources, and efficiency of the state. The Habsburg empire also lacked the trading and manufacturing base of Great Britain and the Dutch Republic, foremost among the non-absolutist states, or of France or even Prussia. Mercantilists in Austria hoped that foreign trade would add to the coffers of the state, but the overwhelmingly rural Habsburg lands had little to export, despite the development of manufacturing.

The new empress's troubles were not limited to Silesia. The nobles of Bohemia, the richest province, rebelled against Habsburg rule, offering the throne to the ruler of Bavaria, Austria's rival in southern Germany. Dependent upon the good will of the provincial Diets, no Habsburg monarch could be sure of having either sufficient support from the estates or money with which to raise an effective army.

Now, with Prussian troops occupying Silesia, Maria Theresa travelled to Hungary to ask for the support of the Hungarian Diet, which had agreed to the Pragmatic Sanction in exchange for recognition of Hungary's status as a separate kingdom. Dressed in mourning clothes following the recent death of an infant daughter and clutching one of her sixteen children to her, Maria Theresa convinced the Diet to provide an army of 40,000 men and cavalry. The Magyar nobles held out their swords to her, shouting their promise to give "life and blood" for her. The gesture could not restore Silesia to the Habsburgs, but it may have saved the Habsburg monarchy. Aided by Hungarian troops, imperial forces put down the Bohemian revolt.

Fearing a disproportionate expansion of Prussian power in Central Europe, other states joined in the alliance against Frederick. Yet, confronted by an alliance of Austria, Russia, Sweden, and Denmark, states with a combined population twenty times that of Prussia, the Prussian army more than held its own, with the help of France as well as Spain and Bavaria, each hoping to help bring about the disintegration of the Habsburg empire. France joined the anti-Austrian coalition because it coveted the Austrian Netherlands; Spain participated because it wanted to recapture influence in Italy; and the king of Piedmont-Sardinia cooperated because he coveted Milan. Frederick, satisfied for the moment with the acquisition of Silesia, withdrew from the war in 1745 after the Peace of Dresden. But Britain was drawn into the conflict by its need to protect the dynastic territory of Hanover from Prussia and France. Indeed, at Dettingen in 1743, King George II became the last British monarch to fight in battle. His horse was spooked and rode off with its frightened royal rider still astride. France's army defeated the combined Dutch and British forces in the Battle of Fontenoy in 1745, the bloodiest battle of the century until the French Revolution. Two years later in the United

Aristocratic officers safely above the carnage at the Battle of Fontenoy, 1745.

MAP 11.1 THE WAR OF THE AUSTRIAN SUCCESSION, 1740–1748   Major battles and territorial changes at the end of the war.

Provinces, with the war going badly, a coup gave William IV of Orange almost monarchical authority as stadholder, making the post hereditary. In 1748, the inconclusive Treaty of Aix-la-Chapelle ended the War of the Austrian Succession (see Map 11.1). French forces withdrew from the Austrian Netherlands in return for the English abandoning the captured fort of Louisbourg on the St. Lawrence River (in present-day Canada). Parma (in northern Italy) was given to a branch of the Spanish Bourbons, and Piedmont-Sardinia absorbed parts of the Duchy of Milan.

The Seven Years' War

Since the development of absolute states during the seventeenth century, warfare in Europe had been driven by absolutism, specifically the territorial interests of absolute rulers. Wars had dragged to a halt when rulers and states no longer could raise enough money through the sale of offices and titles or by undertaking loans. The Seven Years' War (1756–1763) was remarkable for several reasons. First, it was arguably the first truly global conflict. The commercial interests of France and Britain clashed in North America (where the two powers had been at war since 1754), the Caribbean, and in India (see Map 11.2). The war intensified the Anglo-French struggle for control of North America. Second, for the first time we can speak of a war not just of kings but self-consciously of nations, at least in the cases of Britain and France. Both states underwent a surge of patriotic enthusiasm, marked, for example, in the case of France by calls for "patriotic gifts" to support the war. In Britain, the sense of being "Britons," as opposed to subjects of the king, developed among all classes, accentuated by an overwhelmingly popular war against Catholic France. In both Britain and France, there were calls for the more efficient management of the war, seen as part of pursuing the interests of the country.

Prussia's gains in the War of the Austrian Succession helped engender the Diplomatic Revolution of 1756. This ended more than a century of intermittent warfare between France and the Austrian Habsburgs. Alarmed by the expansion of Prussian power, Austria allied with France, and then Russia, with the goal of recapturing Silesia. The result of France's support would be its future annexation of the Austrian Netherlands (Belgium) and Austrian neutrality in the war between Britain and France (which in 1756 had been going on in North America for two years). Frederick the Great, determined to keep Silesia, now turned to Britain, France's enemy, for an ally. To France and Russia, Britain's sudden and shocking alliance with Prussia seemed a betrayal, even as France reversed its century-old opposition to Habsburg interests. The great powers changed partners, then went to war again.

In 1757, Frederick first defeated a large French army and then a Habsburg force. But a Russian army attacked from the north, occupying Berlin, while more Austrian troops marched on Prussia from the south. Both the French and Russian armies benefited from infantry tactics first implemented by Frederick the Great's army. Prussia's situation seemed desperate, leading the king to compare his state to "a man with many wounds who has lost so much blood that he is on the point of death." But as luck would have it, Peter III became tsar of Russia in 1762, succeeding Empress Elizabeth, Frederick's determined enemy. The new tsar admired the Prussian king and called the Russian troops home. At the cost of perhaps 300,000 soldiers, Prussia had preserved its full independence.

In India, the rivalry took the shape of a struggle between the British and French East India Companies against the background of intrigues and warfare among Indian rulers. In India, where there were only about 5,000 British residents (and 20,000 soldiers), Robert Clive (1725–1774), the son of a provincial gentleman and lawyer, led troops of the East India

MAP 11.2 THE SEVEN YEARS' WAR, 1756–1763   Areas of conflict, including battle sites, during the Seven Years' War, as well as territorial changes at the end of the war.

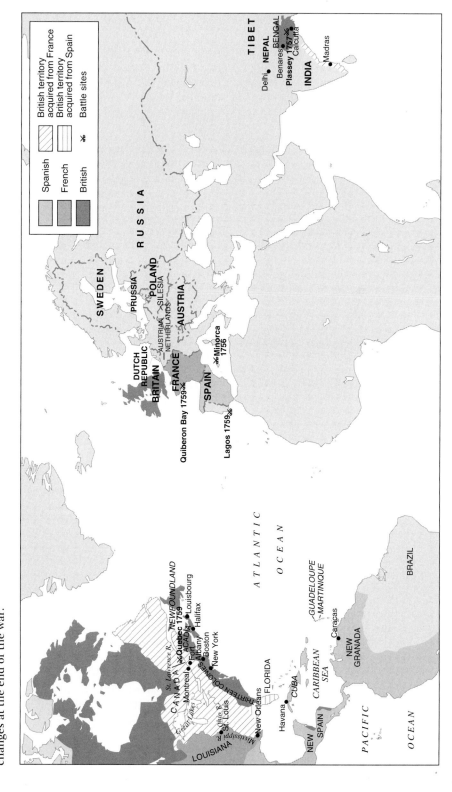

Company and Indian mercenaries into Bengal. There the prince preferred French to British traders and in 1757 had incarcerated more than a hundred British subjects in a room so small and stuffy that most of them died—the "Black Hole of Calcutta." That same year, Clive's force defeated the prince's army at Plassey, a Bengali town north of Calcutta. After putting a pliant puppet on the Bengali throne, Clive continued to use British troops to further not only the interests of the British East India Company but also his own interests (which included becoming very rich through imperial acquisitions and securing a British peerage). By 1761, the stage was set for British control of most of the Indian subcontinent, with the British navy preventing French traders and soldiers from receiving sufficient supplies.

In what became Canada, there was much more at stake because both powers were fighting for control of a vast territory. In this struggle, France had a decided disadvantage. Even after more than a hundred years as a colony, New France had a French population of only about 80,000 people, for the most part clustered in three towns along the St. Lawrence River—Montreal, Quebec, and Trois-Rivières—and otherwise scattered over an immense land. By contrast, the thirteen British colonies already had more than 2 million residents. British incursions into their territory led Native Americans to ally informally with the French. During what Americans call the French and Indian War (1754–1763), British troops forced over 10,000 French-speaking Acadians (that is, people living in Nova Scotia and New Brunswick) to emigrate. Many of them settled in the French colony of New Orleans, where the word "Cajun" emerged as a corruption of the French "*Acadien*."

The British navy accentuated its advantage on the seas by seizing 300 French merchant ships and capturing 8,000 sailors even before hostilities formally began. Despite the capture by French troops of several forts in the Great Lakes region, British ships reduced French reinforcements and supplies to a trickle, also defeating a French fleet at Quiberon Bay off the coast of Brittany in 1759.

In 1759, General James Wolfe (1727–1759) led an audacious, successful British attack on the French near Quebec, his forces climbing up the cliffs from the St. Lawrence River to surprise their enemy. A year later, the British captured Montreal and then drove the French from the Ohio River Valley. In the Caribbean, the British picked off the French islands and their small garrisons one by one.

War left all the combatants exhausted. The British national debt had doubled. The financial crisis of the French monarchy worsened as well, and its capacity to wage war diminished. By the Treaty of Paris of 1763, Austria recognized Prussia's absorption of Silesia in 1740 in exchange for Saxony's retention of independence. The Southern Netherlands, however, would remain an Austrian Habsburg territory. The settlement in North America and the Caribbean was much more far-reaching. Canada became

General Wolfe's forces scale the heights of the Plains of Abraham in Quebec.

British, although France retained fishing rights on the Grand Banks off Newfoundland. But France gave up to Britain all claims to territory east of the Mississippi River, and to Spain all territory west of the Mississippi. This enormous western region, known as the Louisiana Territory, stretched from the almost tropical climate of New Orleans to the freezing plains of central Canada. France retained the Caribbean islands of Martinique and Guadeloupe, only because English colonists feared competition from sugar produced on those islands if they became British. Spain ceded Florida to Britain (though only, as it turned out, until 1783) but reclaimed the fortress of Havana in Cuba.

Britain then tried to mend fences in Europe, where the balance of power had been preserved. However, Joseph II of Austria wanted to incorporate Bavaria into the Habsburg domains. Austrian troops occupied Bavaria, leading to the brief War of Bavarian Succession (1778–1779). The resistance of Prussia and that of various smaller German states foiled Joseph II's plan. Like Franco-British emnity, Austro-Prussian rivalry continued unabated.

Armies and Their Tactics in the Eighteenth Century

Long after monarchs succeeded in putting an end to private noble armies, warfare remained part of noble culture. Military schools in France, Russia, and several of the German states trained the sons of nobles in the skills of war. In Prussia, Frederick William I believed that any attempt to allow commoners to become officers would be "the first step toward the decline and fall of the army." Noble officers had much more in common with the officers of the enemy than with their own troops, conscripted or impressed from the lower classes. Moreover, the Habsburg state often appointed foreign nobles as officers in its army. Officers captured during a war were treated to a nice glass of wine and a good meal, and then exchanged for their own officers who had fallen into enemy hands. War was fought over territory. In some ways, it seemed like a game of chess played between aristocrats in a manor house parlor. It is said that the French officers at the Battle of Fontenoy in 1745 gallantly shouted to their British counterparts, "Fire first, *messieurs les anglais!*"

Recruitment practices differed in the various European states. The Prussian army's military recruitment system was the most comprehensive. Each of its regiments was assigned a district from which to draw recruits, and Prussians were not allowed to serve as mercenaries in other armies. In France, military recruitment was placed directly under the control of the state bureaucracy, which relieved officers of the responsibility for filling a quota of recruits. Villagers now drew lots to see who would be drafted into the reserve force. In Russia, each commune (*mir*) had to provide at least

Siege warfare was still conducted during the eighteenth century. Lines of troops approach and fire on a town.

one soldier. Throughout Europe, certain categories of the population were exempt from service, including prosperous farmers, the servants of French nobles, Russian merchants, and, in many countries, men with families. England was alone among the major powers in not having a standing army, at least in principle.

Yet mercenaries still sometimes provided the bulk of eighteenth-century European armies, the notable exception being the French army. Military service provided those who joined up with regular meals, shelter, and adventure. Swiss guards served the French royal family as well as the popes in Rome, and their countrymen fought with a variety of armies. The Dutch army included a brigade of Scottish highlanders. However limited the possibilities of social ascension through the army, military service could still provide respectability. Criminals and other men with something unpleasant in their pasts often turned up as soldiers.

Desertion remained widespread, affecting up to 35 percent of an army, despite threats of mutilation for those caught leaving. During the Seven Years' War, about 62,000 soldiers deserted the Habsburg army, 70,000 left the army of France behind, and 80,000 Russian soldiers disappeared into the night. Tightly packed formations served to discourage desertions, as they were intended to do, because soldiers were under more constant control. Harsh, even brutal, discipline in army camps complemented that in the field. Frederick the Great was not alone in believing that "[the soldier] must be more afraid of his officers than of the dangers to which he is exposed." Although strategies for supplying troops improved during the century, armies rarely moved far from their supply camps. The lack of commitment and unreliability of mercenary and levied troops often helped end fighting.

Military technology had evolved slowly since the invention of gunpowder. In the seventeenth century, the soldier wielding a bayonet, a musket topped with a razor-sharp knife, had pushed the pikeman, a foot soldier armed with only a spearlike weapon, off the battlefield. Other significant changes in warfare in the seventeenth century included improved flintlock muskets, with cartridges and iron ramrods that permitted riflemen to fire three times per minute and increased their range to 200 meters. Handheld firearms became practical weapons for the first time. Artillery pieces were now also lighter and more mobile, with somewhat greater range. The training of artillery officers, too, improved. Thus, Frederick the Great made exemplary use of artillery to complement infantry during the Seven Years' War.

Soldiers in the eighteenth century were now far better trained and disciplined than in the previous century; armies were far larger than ever before. The discipline and efficiency of troops in formation won or lost battles. Rifles, inaccurate beyond a short distance, were fired in deadly volleys by rows of soldiers taking turns reloading. Cavalry charges, which generally took place on the flanks with the goal of neutralizing the enemy's cavalry, usually were over quickly.

New tactics had brought greater maneuverability in the sixteenth and seventeenth centuries, including linear formations involving coordinated movements that required well-trained and disciplined troops. And in the eighteenth century, even greater troop mobility was achieved by combining line and column formations in a "mixed order." Moreover, the British and Prussian armies were the first to create a light infantry division that could move and engage the enemy more rapidly, often fighting with bayonets. Yet defense still dominated in battle, as symbolized by the impregnable fortresses along the northern frontier of France built in the late seventeenth century. Line formation, the basis of contemporary warfare, was more conducive to defense than offense.

Following the unrestrained carnage of the Thirty Years' War (1618–1648), warfare became somewhat more civilized, or at least somewhat more predictable, with fewer civilian casualties. Prisoners of war, even commoners, were kept in relatively decent conditions and were sometimes exchanged for their counterparts. The development of logistical support and professionalized, well-drilled armies meant that soldiers no longer had to "live off the land." The goals of warfare were now generally restrained by traditions of monarchical and aristocratic civility. Once victory was achieved, there seemed no reason to pursue one's enemy to finish him off. Civilians were now generally spared in times of war.

Navies

British statesmen knew that to maintain superiority over France on the seas, their enemy had to be kept busy on the continent, whether by direct military operations or by large subsidies paid to France's enemies among the German states. The Royal Navy had begun to grow in size during the second half of the seventeenth century. As its role in protecting commerce increased, the Royal Navy expanded further, from 105 ships in 1750 to 195 in 1790, while the smaller French navy increased only modestly in size to 81 warships, 9 more than those of the Spanish navy.

Building on earlier improvements in sails, rigging, charts, and navigational techniques, the size and quality of ships improved. The British first added copper to hulls, which made their ships more sturdy. Short-barreled cannon of greater caliber proved deadly in close combat. Shipbuilding drew on scientific assistance from experts in mathematics and navigation.

Navies were beset by problems of desertion. Almost one-fourth of the men who joined the British navy between 1776 and 1780, many of whom had been dragged to the docks by press-gangs, deserted. Shipboard disease killed many sailors, despite the use of lemon juice to counter scurvy, a malady caused by a vitamin C deficiency.

There were few decisive naval confrontations in the eighteenth century. But the British navy did defeat a Spanish fleet in 1718, thereby preventing an invasion of Sicily, and it defeated a French fleet in 1759. "Do you know what a naval battle is?" asked a French minister. "The fleets manoeuvre, come to grips, fire a few shots, and then each retreats . . . and the sea remains as salty as it was before." The cost of full-fledged battles seemed too high; ships were enormously expensive to build and maintain. Thus, fifteen times more British sailors died of disease between 1774 and 1780 than succumbed to battle wounds.

POLITICAL CHANGE IN GREAT BRITAIN

In England, the Glorious Revolution of 1688 had put an end to fifty years of social and political turmoil. The Bill of Rights of 1689 guaranteed Parliament's right to approve taxation and prohibited the monarch from suspending or dispensing with laws. Parliament also maintained control of military funding and the size of the army. Only with the consent of Parliament could a standing army be raised in peacetime (even though this in itself was technically unconstitutional and the House of Commons had to annually approve funding). Thus, the political struggles of the seventeenth century had demonstrated that the king had to work with Parliament in governing the nation. In turn, the state served as a guarantor of rights of property and patronage. The rights of Parliament and the elective nature of the House of Commons, even if based on an extremely narrow electoral franchise, distinguished British political life from that of its continental rivals.

The period of "aristocratic consensus" that followed the Glorious Revolution was not as free from political contention as the term suggests. But it brought major changes in British political life. The interests of wealthy property owners were represented in the House of Commons, which gradually became a far more important political forum than the House of Lords, which only represented peers. It also became more difficult for the king to manage the House of Commons.

Political differences between Tories and Whigs became more consistent. The former were now clearly identified with the prerogatives of the throne, the latter with the rights of Parliament. Whigs believed that the role of Parliament was to defend liberty, property, and the rule of law and thereby preserve the British constitution against possible abuses of power by the throne. In the words of the Irish-born political theorist Edmund Burke (1729–1797), the British "mixed constitution" (which balanced the institutions of monarchy, the House of Lords, and the House of Commons), stood as an "isthmus between arbitrary power and anarchy." During this period, there emerged a sense that opposition within Parliament to government policies was an intrinsic part of a political process in which competing interests were struggling for primacy. Moreover, during the eighteenth century, political life began to spill beyond the narrow confines of the British political elite as ordinary people demanded a voice in political life with increasing insistence. In Britain's North American colonies, a similar and in some ways parallel struggle for liberty began, leading to the American War of Independence.

Expanding Central Government in Britain

During the eighteenth century, Britain, justly famous for its political pre-occupation with liberty, saw the powers of central government expand. The increasingly global nature of trade and warfare made greater demands on the state's administrative abilities. The growth, greater centralization, professionalization, and efficiency of military and civilian administration permitted Britain to remain the strongest power on the globe.

Between 1680 and 1780, as the British built and consolidated their empire, their army and navy tripled in size. The power and reach of the Treasury also increased. As the economy grew rapidly, the British state raised taxes and efficiently collected them (the latter in dramatic contrast with the monarchy of France, whose financial plight continued to grow). These included land taxes, excise taxes (on commodities), and customs taxes, which provided an increasing percent of revenue.

Britain's bureaucracy, though still quite undersized compared to that of France, also grew in size and complexity. A single French province had more officials than the entire government of Britain at the beginning of the century. By the end of the century, this was no longer the case. Limited venality, too, provided Britain with an advantage over its rivals. As the British state increased in size, its officials became more professional (technical expertise became more important), and departments within the bureaucracy became more clearly defined. Posts in the civil service for educated men offered chances for social advancement.

The British government, like its continental rivals, faced the problem of paying off the massive national debt amassed by loans that financed dynastic and trade wars. The government spent more than three-quarters of its expenditures on the army, navy, or paying back debts from previous wars. In 1719, the government had awarded the South Sea Company the right to take over the national debt. The South Sea Company had been founded in 1711 with the backing of a number of Queen Anne's advisers. Two years later, the government had awarded it a monopoly over the slave trade with Latin America and with favorable conditions for European trade. But because of the intermittent fighting with Spain during the War of the Spanish Succession, any profits from such trade seemed in the distant future. Needing a rapid infusion of capital, the directors of the company offered stock for sale on attractive terms. They bribed some potential purchasers and developed ties with high government officials.

With the help of un-scrupulous investors, many of whom were holders of part of the national debt who wanted to get their money back, the company converted the debt owed them by the state into company shares. The directors parlayed the price of the stock higher. The scam worked as long as there were enough investors whose funds could be used to pay dividends to those who had bought shares earlier. But the profits were all based on the sale of the stock rather than on real commercial gains.

A fever of speculation seized England. Smaller companies started up overnight, most of them insolvent or strangely organized, such as one literally limited

Woodcut of Change Alley during the aftermath of the "South Sea Bubble" speculative crash.

to women dressed in calico. One joint-stock company (made up of shareholders who would divide profits according to the amount of their investments) had been set up for "a purpose to be announced." The speculative craze ended with a jolt in 1720. With no gains of any kind forthcoming, the "South Sea Bubble" burst in September of that year. It was the first great financial crash (and coincided with the bursting of smaller speculative "bubbles" in Amsterdam and Paris). Political careers were ruined in the resulting financial chaos.

The financial scandal hung over political life when Robert Walpole (1676–1745) became chancellor of the Exchequer in 1721, a post he would hold for more than twenty years. The son of a landowner of modest means, the short, ruddy-cheeked Walpole was energetic and ambitious. And he was determined to restore political confidence to Britain. The king quietly replaced several of his ministers who had been most compromised in the South Sea Bubble. Parliament passed a law that allowed only companies chartered by the government to sell stock shares to the public. Walpole created a sinking fund (intended to "retire" the debt by paying off, or "sinking," part of it each year), which helped restore confidence.

George II trusted Walpole's judgment, and the queen's regard for Walpole contributed to his ability to weather political storms. He survived the wrath of some Members of Parliament (MPs) who disliked his unpopular financial reforms, including greater taxes on imports and on salt, and his goal of keeping Britain out of war.

Walpole perfected the system of political patronage, virtually managing the House of Commons. He placed MPs loyal to him—"placemen"—in well-paying governmental positions, some of which were veritable sinecures. In return, they voted with the government. On the local level, the bigger fish became county lord-lieutenants and the smaller fry became justices of the peace. One tombstone epitaph flaunted the harvest of political patronage reaped by a well-connected lady lying therein: "By means of her alliance with the illustrious family of Stanhope, she had the merit to obtain for her husband and children twelve appointments in church and state," not a bad haul.

However, Walpole's support in Parliament eventually began to crumble. His attempt to reform the excise tax by extending it to wine and tobacco failed in 1733 after generating riots. William Pitt (1708–1778) led a coalition of "boy patriots" against Walpole. Specifically, they objected to his inaction against Spain, whose ships were harassing British ships in the Atlantic. After being forced by public outcry to declare war on Spain in 1739—the perfectly trivial War of Jenkins's Ear—Walpole resigned in 1741.

Lesser lights continued Walpole's policies of building a political coalition based upon patronage. The duke of Newcastle (Thomas Pelham-Holles; 1693–1768), whose notorious incoherence led him to be known as "Hubble-Bubble," succeeded Walpole and ably manipulated the patronage of his position. Then Pitt came to power. The "Great Commoner" Pitt was a lonely, unstable man who alternated between feverish excitement and dark depression. He was demagogic, arrogant, and ruthless, commanding respect through fear.

The Role of the House of Commons

The British monarch could declare war or make peace, call or dissolve Parliament, and appoint whomever he or she wanted to serve as cabinet minister, officer, bishop, general, or admiral; the cabinet and government officials carried out the functions of state. But they did the latter against the backdrop of ongoing practical compromises between Parliament and the monarch.

During the early decades of the eighteenth century, the House of Commons gradually emerged as an epicenter of political life. Unlike the House of Lords, all of whose members were nobles, members of the House of Commons were elected by Britain's narrow electoral franchise based on landed wealth. Although still dominated by "gentle," or landed, interests, the number of merchants elected to the Commons increased, for families that had made fortunes in business, whether they were titled nobles, nontitled gentry, or commoners, invested their money in land. Wealthy MPs could easily control blocs of votes in their countries through patronage. In 1776, only 5,700 men in Britain elected half of the members of Commons, most of whose members were routinely re-elected every seven years. In only three boroughs did more than 4,000 men have the right to vote and in several, fewer than 15 men could cast ballots. Thus, one lord confidently assured his son in 1754, "Your seat in the new Parliament is at last absolutely secured and that without opposition or the least necessity of your personal trouble or appear-

Sir Robert Walpole observing the House of Commons.

ance." Some MPs were returned from "rotten" and "pocket" boroughs. Rotten boroughs ranged from the infamous "Old Sarum," which had no inhabitants but two representatives in Commons, and another that had been under water for centuries, to those with several hundred voters almost as easily managed. Pocket boroughs were in the pocket of the MP because his election was uncontested.

Some of England's growing industrial towns were not represented in Parliament. Many urban elites no longer accepted the idea that their interests were "virtually represented" by MPs from districts represented in the House of Commons. Furthermore, emerging political discontent reflected alarm that the role of the House of Commons as the defender of the constitution against possible tyrannical abuse was being compromised by institutionalized corruption, symbolized by rotten and pocket boroughs.

The Development of Party Politics in the 1760s: Whigs and Tories

Whigs and Tories had governed in reasonable harmony during the Robert Walpole era. But after Walpole, many Whigs came to believe that ministers ought to be acceptable to Parliament as well as to the king. In contrast, Tories traditionally took the view that the prerogatives of king and Church had to be maintained at all costs.

After coming to the throne in 1760, George III gave the impression that he intended to rule without Parliament. When George refused to declare war on Spain in 1761 during the Seven Years' War, William Pitt resigned as chief minister. Subsequently, the king appointed his former tutor, the aristocratic, aloof Scotsman John Stuart, the earl of Bute (1713–1792), as secretary of state and then as chief minister of the government. But Bute was an unpopular choice because he was not a Member of Parliament, had little political experience and even less influence, and did not want Britain to undertake hostilities against Spain.

The king's appointment of his "dearest friend" seemed to Whigs to violate the unwritten agreement that the king act with Parliament's consent. Determined opposition merely served to strengthen the king's resolve. The press castigated Bute, and crowds in the street howled against him. Rumor insisted that he owed his controversial appointment to having been the lover of the king's mother. On the verge of a nervous breakdown, Bute resigned in 1763.

Bute's appointment raised the question of ministerial responsibility, dividing the House of Commons along ideological lines. George III sought to diminish the decisive role that the parliamentary Whigs had played during the reigns of his grandfather and great-grandfather. He turned against the Whig country gentlemen who no longer could be counted upon to support him on all matters. The king insisted on the monarchy's independence and particularly on his right to choose whomever he wished as minister.

Members of Parliament representing the interests of the "country gentlemen" began to use the term "party," but without the trappings of formal organization that would come late in the next century. Although they traditionally upheld the rights of Parliament, Whigs, to be sure, remained loyal to the throne. George accused them of being otherwise. While the issues dividing Tories and Whigs remained in some ways the same as those that had characterized the Walpole period, or even the Civil War, the emerging notion of political parties was perhaps of more lasting significance than the political groupings themselves.

The term "party" had existed since the time of the Glorious Revolution of 1688; it had the sense of a group of people sharing a belief on a specific matter of political controversy. It had been somewhat synonymous with "faction," which since the 1670s had the negative connotation of a cabal of individuals working for their own interests.

Edmund Burke.

With the exception of the Jacobite Tories, however, the differences between Whigs and Tories were vague and uncertain during the reign of the first two Georges. George III's seeming determination to create a government above parties helped the old Whigs revive their party solidarity. The idea developed that a party of parliamentary opposition formed an essential part of the parliamentary system of representation.

George III insisted that it was his duty to defeat the forces of "faction." Edmund Burke, for one, rejected the king's efforts to discredit the concept of "party." In *Thoughts on the Cause of the Present Discontents* (1770), he defined a party as "a body of men united for promoting by their joint endeavors *the national interest* upon some particular principle in which they are all agreed." He believed that political parties stood as the basis of representative government and therefore of political order. A newspaper article in 1770 went even further: "Opposition, in parliament, to the measures of government, is so far from being in itself an evil, that it has been often productive of good to the state." Parties alone could ensure the preservation "of responsible government," specifically, the notion that ministers ought to be acceptable to Parliament. This concept of a loyal parliamentary opposition did not exist in France or anywhere else on the continent. Nor, for that matter, did it exist in all constituencies within Britain; in many, politics, dominated by family ties and outright patronage, went on as before.

George III could count on about a third of the members of Commons for unconditional support, at least partially because they held court-appointed posts. Unfailing voters for "court" became increasingly known as "Tories," particularly to the Whig opposition. Supporters of the government rejected the term, as they did all labels, but at the same time they lent credence to the concept by cohesively defending a patriarchal society based on monarchy, titled aristocracy, and the Anglican Church.

In 1766, Pitt returned to power for two years. King George depended on the political leadership of the "Great Commoner," but Pitt lost support even among his political friends by accepting a peerage, becoming duke of Chatham. Vigorous debates among Whigs, principally between the imperious Pitt and the duke of Newcastle and his followers, however, did not diminish the emerging notion of "party" that most Whigs now accepted. For Whigs, the most significant issue remained the extent to which Parliament could limit the will of the monarch.

The Rise of British Nationalism

Although king and Parliament were bitterly divided during the crises that led to the English Civil War and the Glorious Revolution, they were thereafter unified in the quest for British commercial and international predominance. During the eighteenth century, a strong sense of nationalism developed in Great Britain. This included pride in the nation's high degree of freedom and reverence for Parliament as the Protestant institution that had turned back the threat of Catholicism and successfully impeded absolute rule.

The fear of Catholicism, endemic in England since the Reformation, fired British nationalism. During the Anglo-French wars, faced with the threat of French invasion, British patriots across the social spectrum embraced the British Isles as the chosen land of God. They boasted of Britain's prosperity and social stability while belittling France, the strongest Catholic power. French support of the American rebels and the French Revolution of 1789 would, of course, bring these feelings to a head.

William Pitt the Elder, in particular, was an empire builder. Believing that the throne's Hanoverian interests were dominating foreign policy, and having made his reputation attacking Walpole's seeming indifference to British interests abroad, Pitt turned his attention to expanding the colonies. "Who will laugh at sugar, now?" he thundered in 1759 to nobles who had scorned colonial trade. Horace Walpole (1717–1797), Robert Walpole's youngest son, who was a novelist as well as the beneficiary of lucrative posts that left him plenty of time to write, was among the few who had some doubts about all of this. "No man ever went to the East Indies with good intentions," the younger Walpole said, adding sarcastically that "it really looks as if we intended to finish the conquest of the world during the next campaign."

The lure of empire and commercial profit thus helped define British nationalism. A financial community of investors in London closely followed not only the vicissitudes of the economy but the ups and downs of British warfare. A good many financiers had, after all, loaned money to their state and therefore eagerly watched what was done with it. Their foreign and colonial trade often depended on naval protection, further linking their interests to the Union Jack. The state itself depended on expanding commercial activity for tax revenue. Economic interest groups and lobbies developed, learning their way around the London financial community and the corridors of government to represent their views on excise and customs taxes. New patriotic societies, some of them drawing ordinary people into the wave of nationalist enthusiasm, sprang up in many places, with mottoes like "For our country."

The generally harmonious relationship between the landed elite and the commercial community was a source of social and political stability in Britain, and of British nationalism. Nobles and gentry benefited from the expansion of state activity, diversifying their investments with loans to the crown. Unlike the continental powers, in Britain all subjects paid taxes. This afforded all social groups the sense of being Britons. At the same time (in contrast to the case in France), improved communications and the development of a national market aided the process of national integration in Britain.

Their commitment to the nation also enabled the British elite, proud of their freedoms and their country's more decentralized form of government, to accept a stronger state apparatus without complaining about infringements on their liberty. Thus, they did not feel the need for constitutional guarantees (based upon equality before the law) against arbitrary tyranny. The stronger state did not diminish the status of British landowners, and it in no way infringed on their personal freedoms within civil society. Monarch and Parliament joined hands in the pursuit of empire, with the eager support of London's burgeoning financial community. English peers sought to prove, in Burke's words, that "a true natural aristocracy is not a separate interest in the state, or separable from it."

Anglo-Irish, Scottish, and Welsh landowners became more integrated into a national British elite, with increasing intermarriage a revealing indication of this process. Many Scots, though hardly all, began to see themselves as British, just as fewer English people considered Scots or Welsh to be outsiders who were potentially disloyal to the crown. The prerogatives of Parliament notwithstanding, the British monarchy and its armed forces became increasingly revered and celebrated as a rallying point for the nation.

CHALLENGES TO ESTABLISHED AUTHORITY

In the 1760s and 1770s, movements for reform emerged in several countries. In Britain, "liberty" became the watchword of political opposition to the government. In a parallel struggle on the other side of the Atlantic Ocean, the American colonists of Britain's thirteen colonies demanded "no taxation without representation," and then, when rebuffed, the "patriots" rebelled against British rule in the War of American Independence. Elsewhere, similar reform movements on the European continent sought to reduce the strength of absolute rule, as in Denmark, or wanted to prevent the imposition of a stronger centralized authority, as in France and the Dutch Republic. Other movements for reform challenged what seemed to be unwarranted privileges, again most notably in France. In every Western country, more information about political events in other states was available through newspapers and gazettes, as well as from merchants, travelers, and diplomats, who exchanged correspondence in an increasingly literate culture. In Britain and parts of Western Europe, political clubs also reflected greater preoccupation with politics. These reform movements, then, influenced each other, however indirectly.

British Radicals

In the 1760s in Britain, ordinary people (called "the swinish multitude" by Edmund Burke) demanded electoral reform, and some even called for universal male suffrage. Reformers asked that constituencies be redrawn so that rapidly growing industrial regions in the north of England be appropriately represented in Parliament, and that London, which was grossly underrepresented, elect more Members of Parliament. Moreover, outside the small, formal political arena defined by the right to vote, shouts for freedom swelled among ordinary people.

John Wilkes (1727–1797), the son of a successful London malt distiller, was a Member of Parliament of modest means and a Protestant Dissenter. Charming, witty, and reckless, Wilkes leapt into the public eye in 1763 with the publication of his newspaper, the *North Briton*. Issue number 45 attacked the government—and the king himself directly—for signing the compromise Treaty of Paris with France that year, ending the Seven Years' War. The king ordered "that Devil Wilkes, a trumpet of sedition," arrested for libel. Wilkes announced that he considered his arrest a blow against liberty and the constitution by the unjust, arbitrary power of government; it was "a question of such importance," as he declared at his trial, "as to determine at once, whether English Liberty be a reality or a shadow." The court freed Wilkes after a week in jail on the basis of parliamentary immunity. Wilkes triumphantly boasted that his fate was tied to "that of the middling and inferior set of people" in Britain.

Fearing prosecution for pornography, as the government had dug up a bawdy old poem he had written (and the House of Commons had lifted parliamentary immunity), Wilkes left for France in 1764. He was arrested, tried, and convicted upon his return to Britain four years later, and then freed after thousands of people demonstrated on his behalf. Wilkes then stood for election in Middlesex, the county making up most of metropolitan London north of the Thames and outside of the "City." With the support of many merchants and small manufacturers wealthy enough to be eligible to vote, Wilkes was reelected to Parliament. Four times he was elected, and four times Parliament refused to seat him because of his previous conviction.

Wilkes claimed that Parliament's action threatened "the first principle of our constitution," the freedom to stand for election. Cloaking himself in a patriot's garb, he became a rallying symbol for the campaign for the rights of the unrepresented in a time of economic hardship, grain riots, and work stoppages.

The phrase "Wilkes and Liberty" was echoed in speeches, conversation, and song. In 1769, the Society of the Supporters of the Bill of Rights invoked the name of Wilkes as it called for the government to "restore the constitution." The number 45—the libelous issue of the *North Briton*—became a rallying cry. Wilkes's rather misshapen face appeared on posters, handbills, verses, cartoons, tea mugs, and dinner plates. He was elected sheriff of London in 1771, and even lord mayor three years later, though he was not allowed to occupy either position.

Reformers now began to demand greater freedom of the press, specifically a redefinition of libel laws (so that the government could be criticized) and the right to publish parliamentary debates. They further demanded that Parliament meet each year and that MPs be required to live in the districts from which they were returned. However, in general, Whigs disassociated themselves from Wilkes, wary of demonstrations for universal male suffrage. Few Whigs were willing to go beyond insisting on the principle of ministerial responsibility within the confines of the existing constitution.

Literary and "philosophical" societies, which had sprung up in most large towns, facilitated the emergence in England of an even wider political culture than that which had developed during the political crises of the seventeenth century. Interest in politics was now such that some inns and coffeehouses added special reading rooms to accommodate their clientele. By 1760, London printing presses, the number of which had increased from seventy-five in 1724 to about two hundred at the time of Wilkes's first arrest, churned out eighty-nine newspapers, four of which were dailies. Another thirty-five newspapers were published outside London. By 1790, there were fourteen London daily newspapers (Edmund Burke wrote for four of them), and the number of provincial papers printed each day had multiplied by four times.

(*Left*) John Wilkes, in an etching by William Hogarth. (*Right*) Wilkes's supporters take to the streets.

Political pamphlets, handbills, and caricatures inundated the capital and the larger provincial towns. By the 1760s, artists had stopped omitting the names of the targets of their satirical wit. Like its Whig opponents and the extra-parliamentary radicals, the government found itself obliged to utilize newspapers, pamphlets, brochures, and handbills to argue its case before public opinion.

American Revolutionaries

During the 1760s, another challenge to the British crown was smoldering far across the Atlantic Ocean in North America. The thirteen American colonies, many times the size of England, had become ever more difficult for the British government to administer. The population of the colonies, which accounted for about 20 percent of British exports and supplied 30 percent of its imports, had grown by tenfold in just seventy years, from about 250,000 in 1700 to more than 2.5 million in 1775, compared to about 6.4 million in England at the same time. Philadelphia had by that time become the second largest city in the British Empire, with 30,000 residents. Those arriving on the shores of the Americas found a land of opportunity. Many were able to purchase land that would have been beyond their means at home. Artisans and even common laborers commanded relatively high wages because of the shortage of labor in the colonies.

Over the decades, the residents of the colonies had developed a sense of living in a separate society. Merchants, a heterogeneous group that stood atop the social hierarchy, lawyers, and wealthy landowners like the Virginians George Washington (1732–1799) and Thomas Jefferson (1743–1826) led the colonists. They resented the continued presence of the British army and the attempt of British officers to try to impose on the colonial forces the same standards of discipline that applied in Britain. They believed that they had the right to resist unjust laws in the name of liberty.

For radicals in Britain, "rotten" boroughs symbolized the threat to liberty; for the American colonists, as expressed by John Adams, "liberty can no more exist without virtue and independence than the body can live and move without a soul." Some British Whigs began to identify themselves with the colonists, who took the name Whigs themselves, claiming that corruption was threatening Britain's constitutional balance between monarchy and Parliament. They saw the two movements as parallel struggles.

The quest of George Grenville (1712–1770), who had succeeded Pitt in 1763 as prime minister, for supplementary revenue aggravated the strained relations between the colonists and the mother country. The king's new favorite also ordered massive efforts to stop smuggling. In 1765, Parliament passed the Stamp Act, which forced Americans to pur-

Paul Revere's depiction of the Boston Massacre.

chase stamps for virtually anything printed. A year later, Benjamin Franklin (1706–1790) of Philadelphia made the colonists' case to the House of Commons. He argued that the act represented the unfair domination of England over another part of the empire. The House of Commons repealed the Stamp Act, but the government then initiated other taxes. Furthermore, Parliament proclaimed a Declaratory Act in 1766, which asserted its right to tax the colonies as it pleased. A year later, the Townshend Acts levied duties on colonial imports of paper, tea, and other products.

The American colonists' determined protests encouraged British reformers. The colonists' claim that they were being taxed without having the right to representation played nicely into the hands of political radicals in Britain. The shout "Wilkes and Liberty!" found resonance on both sides of the Atlantic. American political pamphlets and brochures found an eager audience among British merchants, manufacturers, artisans, and other people eager for representation in Parliament. Colonists lobbied in Britain to demonstrate that "the cause of America is the common cause of the realm . . . both countries have the same complaint, and therefore claim the same friends."

The British government was at first divided and uncertain in the face of an upsurge of demonstrations at home and agitation in the colonies. In

March 1770 in Boston, British soldiers fired on a crowd that was vociferously protesting the quartering of British troops in that city. The "Boston Massacre," which took five lives, outraged colonists. That year, George III appointed Frederick Lord North (1732–1792) prime minister. North, an amiable, sensible man who got along well with the king, was skilled at putting together political coalitions and was a brilliant debater in the House of Commons. He sponsored the Tea Act of 1773. North hoped to aid the East India Company by allowing the company to ship a surplus of tea to the colonies, with the British government collecting its tariff only when the tea arrived in American ports. The move would reduce the price colonists paid for tea but would maintain the British government's assertion that it could tax goods imported into the colonies. It would also threaten the interests of American smuggling, a widespread money-making operation.

On December 16, 1773, colonists dressed as Native Americans forced their way aboard British merchant ships docked in Boston and dumped the cargo of tea into the harbor. Parliament responded to the Boston Tea Party by passing the repressive "Intolerable Acts." These acts specified that the port of Boston be blocked until the colonists had reimbursed the merchants and government for the tea dumped into the harbor. In September 1774, representatives from the colonies met in the First Continental Congress. Benjamin Franklin drew a distinction between "uncorrupted new states," by which he meant the colonies, and "corrupted old ones," one of which seemed to be waging war on liberty. The British sent more troops to North America. In April 1775, in the first open fighting between colonists and British regulars, the colonial militia held its own against British troops searching for weapons at Concord and Lexington, Massachusetts, and then in the pitched battle at Bunker Hill near Boston, when 1,500 colonists, holding the higher ground, turned back two British attacks until running out of ammunition.

In his pamphlet *Common Sense* (1776), some 100,000 copies of which circulated in the colonies, Thomas Paine (1737–1809) launched a devastating attack on the king. *Common Sense* reflected the influence of the Enlightenment, particularly Rousseau's notion of the "social contract." Furthermore, it reiterated Locke's argument that governments received "their just powers from the consent of the people." All laws, Paine wrote, "are laws of nature." Paine helped convince delegates to the Second Continental Congress to adopt Thomas Jefferson's Declaration of Independence on July 4, 1776. It declared the equality of all people, based on "inalienable rights," and it asserted that the authority of government stems from the consent of the governed. It also stated that when governments violated the "unalienable rights" to "life, liberty, and the pursuit of happiness" of their people, the latter had the right to rebel.

The war now became a fight for independence. The Continental Congress appointed George Washington to command its troops. The British government hoped to recover the colonies at the lowest possible cost; military campaigns were therefore compromised by halfhearted and often inept leadership by the British commanders. The initial British policy, that of isolating and punishing the rebels, quickly failed. There were too few British troops to fight a war on unfamiliar territory against an increasingly determined foe. Next, the British undertook conventional military operations. But the colonial troops simply scattered. In 1776, Washington's army managed to cross the Hudson River into New Jersey. Washington captured Trenton that December, wintering with his ragtag army in freezing temperatures at Valley Forge, Pennsylvania.

In contrast to British soldiers, each of whom required the transport of a third of a ton of food across the Atlantic each year, the colonial army was virtually self-sufficient and broadly supported by the colonists. Trained in part by an officer in the army of Frederick the Great, it became far more than what a loyalist (someone who supported the British cause) dismissed as "a vagabond Army of Raggamufins, with Paper Pay, bad Cloathes, and worse Spirits." The most significant battles of the war were fought in the classic European style of confrontations, not as engagements between hit-and-run patriots and British regulars. Some of the colonists fought with an almost evangelical fervor that reflected the fact that many of them saw the struggle as one of good against evil. The brutality of the British soldiers in requisitioning goods and maintaining order in the territories they

Benjamin Franklin was a favorite of the French, a relationship that was representative of the alliance between America and France against the British.

controlled was self-defeating. By the time General Richard Howe (1726–1799), discouraged by the failure of the British government to send promised reinforcements, tried to negotiate with the rebels at the end of 1776, the colonists refused to listen because they had no reason to negotiate.

France signed an alliance with the American rebels in February 1778, agreeing to provide substantial loans in gold. The French monarchy realized that favorable commercial treaties with an independent United States might more than compensate for having in 1763 lost all rights to territory east of the Mississippi River. Thereafter, the French navy harassed British supply routes. In 1779, Spain joined the war on the American side, hoping to profit from Britain's colonial war by recapturing Gibraltar and the island of Minorca, off the east coast of Spain. Seeking to prevent the North American colonies from purchasing Dutch supplies, the British fought the Dutch Republic. Britain also confronted the refusal of Russia, Sweden, Prussia, Portugal, and Denmark to curtail trade with the rebellious Americans.

Great Britain had overextended its capacity to wage war. Its naval advantage, the basis of its strength in modern times, had been eroded. Despite swelling the army to 190,000 men, campaigns on land went badly. On October 19, 1781, Lord Cornwallis surrendered his outnumbered army at Yorktown, Virginia, to a combined force of American and French troops. "Your armies are captured," George III was informed, "the wonted superiority of your navies is annihilated; your dominions are lost." Two years later, Britain officially recognized the independence of the American colonies. News of the struggle of the colonists for freedom from British rule spread throughout much of Europe, reported in newspapers. As the public became surprisingly well informed about events across the Atlantic Ocean, the American victory encouraged movements for reform in other places.

Britain, which had lost its richest colony, did not want to lose any others. In 1774, as the resistance in the thirteen colonies became more determined, Parliament had passed the Quebec Act, in an effort to prevent tensions between the British Anglican conquerors and the Catholic population of Quebec from boiling over. The Test Act, which required all officials to take communion in the Anglican Church, was abolished in Quebec, and the Catholic Church was given the status of an established church by being permitted to levy tithes. The British government also strengthened its control over its other colonies. The India Act (1784) created a board responsible to Parliament to which the East India Company had to report, beginning in 1773, while establishing the jurisdiction of British courts in cases of fraud or other transgressions. Another parliamentary act in 1791 created more centralized administration in Canada, with a governor-general exercising far more authority than two colonial assemblies elected by restricted suffrage.

The advent to power in 1784 of William Pitt the Younger (1759–1806) restored political stability in Britain. The next year, Pitt introduced a wide-ranging bill for political reform. It proposed to reduce the minimum tax required for the electoral franchise and to abolish thirty-six rotten boroughs, awarding their representation to manufacturing regions and cities. Opposition among the country gentlemen, as well as that of the king himself, however, led to the bill's defeat. But Pitt did manage to eliminate useless offices that had become sinecures, introduce more accurate accounting methods into government, facilitate the collection of excise taxes, and encourage further foreign trade. Despite the personal failings of George III, Britain, which remained the world's premier commercial and manufacturing power, emerged from the turbulent decades of the 1760s and 1770s with its constitutional monarchy strengthened.

The Parlements and the French Monarchy

Two interrelated struggles in the early 1770s challenged the nature of absolute rule in France. The first was against the seemingly unwarranted privileges held by nobles and other corporate groups. The second opposed royal policies and pretensions that seemed to transcend absolute rule and verge on despotism. In a way, this debate somewhat paralleled political issues in Britain.

In France, those seeking reforms that would limit royal authority had a much more daunting task because of the absolute nature of monarchical rule. The kings of France nonetheless depended on the support of the parlements. These law courts were made up primarily of nobles and were seated in Paris and in twelve provincial cities. Their principal function was to give royal edicts the force of law by registering them. By refusing to register them, the parlements could impede the functioning of the absolute state. Thus, when the king's edicts had to do with increased or new taxation, political opposition to royal policies sometimes emerged in the parlements.

The increased centralization of the French state had in itself helped create contact between more people and the officials of the king. The concept of a "public" emerged, to which the monarch was in some sense responsible and before which the layers of privilege in French society no longer seemed acceptable. The crises that embroiled the king and the parlements from the 1750s to the 1780s helped shift public opinion toward the view that the parlements represented the rights of the "nation," threatened by a monarchy that seemed to be lapsing from absolute to despotic rule.

The issue of Jansenism set the parlements against royal absolutism by raising the constitutional issue of the right of the monarch to circumscribe the parlements' traditional prerogatives. The Jansenists (see Chapter 7) were a dissident group within the Catholic Church. The pope had condemned Jansenism in 1713 with the papal bull *Unigenitus,* which Louis XV supported. But Jansenists, with a considerable following in Paris, found support within some of the parlements, which identified with Jansenist resistance to what seemed to be the absolute monarch's despotic rule. Louis XV's support of the papal bull angered some nobles and magistrates, who were inclined to resist what they considered the papacy's undue interference in French affairs.

The period of conflict between the parlements and the crown really began in 1749. The controller-general attempted to make the *vingtième* tax (a tax applying to both nobles and commoners) permanent, drawing heated opposition from the parlements. And the Church again sought, without success, to force the French clergy to accept *Unigenitus.* Many bishops threatened that sacraments would be refused to laymen who did not have a certificate signed by a priest attesting that the person had made his or her confession to a priest who had accepted the papal bull. Seven years later, the pope tried to defuse the crisis by banning these certificates.

But this concession did not placate the Parlement of Paris. Many of the parlements were manipulated by a handful of Jansenist magistrates and lawyers who managed to convince their colleagues that French acceptance of the papal edict amounted to an abandonment of French sovereignty over the temporal affairs of the Church. The king, refusing to hear the parlements' grievances, made clear that he considered the parlements nothing more than rubber stamps, a means of promulgating his will. When the Jesuit order continued to crusade against Jansenism, the Parlement of Paris responded by ordering Jesuit schools closed in 1761, citing the fact that members of the order took a vow of obedience to the pope.

The successive crises over Jansenism may have weakened the authority of the French monarchy by allowing the Parlement of Paris, and several provincial parliaments as well, to claim they were defending constitutional liberties and the independence of the Gallican (French) Church—since Jansenists saw themselves as part of it—against royal encroachment and against Rome. By weakening the authority of the Catholic Church in France, the crisis over Jansenism also eroded the prestige of the absolute monarchy. Jansenism ceased being a political issue after 1758, when the Parlement of Paris won judicial authority over many ecclesiastical matters. But the self-proclaimed role of lawyers and magistrates as representatives of public opinion and protectors of the sovereign political will of the nation against abuses of power was an important legacy from the Jansenist crisis.

The layers of economic privilege in France had proliferated with the extension of state power, as each monarch sought revenues with increased desperation. Despite increasing calls for reform, even critics who vociferously challenged monopolies (for example, those maintained by guilds) did not intend to end privileges per se. Rather, many of them wanted a share of the privileges and wanted to eliminate "unjust" monopolies that seemed to benefit others unfairly. Wealthy commoners, enriched by the economic changes, sought the kind of privileges nobles enjoyed—above all, exemption from many kinds of taxation. Thus, the issue of taxation would mobilize some of the parlements against the monarchy because it raised questions about the layers of privilege within the French state and about the limits of absolute authority.

In 1771, Chancellor René-Nicolas de Maupeou (1714–1792) provoked the parlements by again attempting to make the *vingtième* tax permanent. Many nobles feared that general tax increases might lead to dangerous peasant uprisings, in which nobles stood to lose the most. Facing mounting resistance, Louis XV effectively abolished the parlements. He then created new, more docile law courts that would not resist royal authority, staffed by magistrates who did not own their offices.

Both sides in the conflict between the parlements and Chancellor Maupeou appealed to public opinion. A declaration of high-ranking nobles stated that the king had abused "the constitution of the government and the rights of the people" by trying to establish "a despotism without bounds, without limits, and consequently without rights." The nobility asserted its "right of assembly," recalling that "the nation, in its assemblies, had charged the parlements with defending its rights." Influenced by the ideas of the Enlightenment, lawyers called for judicial reform, religious toleration, and the end to the abuse of privilege. When the monarchy tried to silence the lawyers, the latter turned courtrooms into forums for political opposition. Lawyers explored notions of national sovereignty and put forward the case of the parlements against the crown.

As the idea of the nation gradually entered political discourse, the possibility emerged that when the interests of the monarchy and the nation clashed, popular allegiance could pass exclusively to the nation. Some degree of popular identification with parlements as defenders of the nation against despotism would not be effaced. The Maupeou "coup" lasted only three and a half years, but it had far-reaching effects on the nature of the opposition to the monarchy. It demonstrated that the parlements were not powerful enough to protect "the nation" against royal despotism, suggesting that only a body such as the Estates-General, which had not been convoked since 1614, could do so.

Louis XV was no stranger to unpopularity. He was held to be lazy and indifferent, and rumor had him obediently following the orders of his favorite mistress and advisers. The Seven Years' War had exhausted the treasury, and the king seemed incapable of restoring public confidence. Furthermore, France had lost Canada and several Caribbean islands to Britain, its hated rival. This loss of prestige, as well as income, increased the number of the king's critics. The structures of absolute rule seemed inadequate to the task of managing the cumbersome French state; inefficient tax

Chancellor René-Nicolas de Maupeou (*left*) and his supporter, Anne-Robert Turgot (*right*).

collection and the weight of growing expenses left the state coffers inadequately filled.

Louis XV's death in 1774 did not resolve the crisis. Following popular demonstrations and a spate of publications in support of the parlements, the twenty-year-old Louis XVI (ruled 1774–1793) dismissed Maupeou and recalled the parlements. Public opinion seemed to have helped turn back what was popularly conceived to be a despotic assault on the restraints on absolute rule.

Convinced that the financial difficulties of the monarchy stemmed from the stifling effect of privileges on the economy, a new minister, Anne-Robert Turgot, undertook ambitious reforms. His goal was to cut away some of the web of privileges, making the absolute monarchy more efficient. Turgot convinced the young king to issue royal edicts, despite the opposition of the Parlement of Paris. These ended noble and clerical tax exemptions, abolished the guilds, freed the internal commerce of grain (the price of which had been first set free in the 1760s), and exempted peasants from having to work a certain number of days each year repairing roads. Economic liberalization would, he hoped, increase agricultural production and manufacturing, thereby augmenting tax revenue.

But like Louis XV's attempts to override the traditional role of the parlements, Turgot's reforms aroused vociferous opposition. Nobles—with some significant exceptions—rallied against proposed financial reforms intended to extricate the country from its growing financial morass. The parlements, still smoldering over their treatment by Maupeou and Louis XV several years earlier, refused to register—and thereby give the status of law to—the reforms of Turgot, who had supported Maupeou. Grain merchants and guilds, among other privileged groups, voiced strident opposition. Ordinary people rose up in protest, blaming the freeing of the grain trade for the higher prices of flour and bread in a period of dearth. Accusations of hoarding abounded. Grain riots, in which women played the leading roles, swept across the country during the spring "flour war" of 1775. The significance of these events was that an increasing number of the king's subjects lost the habit of obedience to him. Lawyers, once again insisting on the difference between absolute and despotic rule, would emerge as leaders as the political crisis of the monarchy accelerated in 1788.

The king dismissed Turgot in 1776, ending the most significant reform effort on the continent. That same year, the American colonists declared their independence from Britain. France allied with the colonial rebels, forcing Louis XVI to borrow ever more money at high interest rates and to sell more offices and titles to those who could afford to pay for them. This helped shift power within the nobility from the embittered "nobles of the sword" to the "nobles of the robe," who had been ennobled through the purchase of office or title. The unreformed French monarchy then slid into an even deeper financial crisis.

Other Movements for Reform

Although the influence of the Enlightenment varied in different places, the philosophes all put forward the claims of freedom against privilege and absolutism. Some rulers, principally those of Prussia, Tuscany, and Austria, introduced reforms inspired by Enlightenment thought, putting into practice reforms that seemed to reflect the "enlightened absolutism" that Voltaire and other philosophes had expected (see Chapter 9).

In other cases, movements for reform came from below. In the Swiss Republic of Geneva, native-born artisans during 1765–1768 exerted pressure for the right to vote, meeting in assemblies and demanding equality with the citizens possessing political rights. They were rebuffed by wealthy Genevans, who tried to placate them with reductions in their taxes. An uprising in 1782 unseated the ruling oligarchy before the intervention of France, Sardinia, and the Swiss canton of Bern put an end to it.

There were also insurrections. In 1761, an uprising on the Mediterranean island of Corsica in the name of "fatherland and liberty" ended rule by Genoa, a northern Italian port dominated by bankers and merchants, although the French occupied Corsica seven years later. In 1770, the Greeks, with the assistance of Russia, rose up against Turkish domination. Russia, the Turks' enemy, was eager to enter the world of Mediterranean politics because it desired ultimately to conquer Constantinople. Empress Catherine the Great sent soldiers and a small fleet in the hope that Greek success might encourage other peoples to rise up against Ottoman rule. Turkish troops crushed the revolt, but the Greek movement for independence, by virtue of the special place of classical Greece in the development of Western civilization, helped ignite pan-Hellenism. Yet, to be sure, many who supported the cause of Greek independence had reservations about the role of Russia, a state as despotic as that of the Ottoman Turks.

Peasant uprisings in Bohemia and Moravia in 1775 (see Chapter 10) led Maria Theresa and her son Joseph II to enact reforms that gradually abolished feudal dues. Each of these uprisings was a movement for freedom, but also a return to traditional privileges that seemed imperiled by the centralized absolute state.

In Denmark, where the king had imposed absolute rule in 1660 by suppressing the parliament and refusing to consult with the estates, a current of reform emerged early in the 1770s. In part, it was the inspiration of Johann Struensee (1737–1772), a German doctor, who convinced the ailing King Christian VII (ruled 1766–1808) to undertake reforms to strengthen the state economically so that, with Russian support, Swedish Baltic ambitions could be thwarted. The king abolished censorship and the death penalty for thieves, extended religious toleration, and promised to undertake more agricultural reforms in the interests of creating a free peasantry. But the king's widowed mother and nobles conspired against the reforms. Struensee was tried and convicted of, among other things, living "without religion or morality," and he was executed in 1772. But after little more than a decade of reaction, the reforms Struensee had encouraged became part of a program for the future, a sign of the times.

In Sweden, the reforms of the 1760s and 1770s were swept away, as in the case of France and Denmark. A virtual coup d'état by King Gustavus III (ruled 1771–1792) imposed absolutism. Thus, while presenting himself as a "patriot king" protecting Swedish peasants from the nobility while reassuring the "intermediary powers," or estates, the king imposed a new constitution in 1772. It reduced the power of the Senate and the Diet. The king's cabinet became the principal arm of Swedish government.

Political struggles in the Dutch Republic—like the struggles between Whigs and the crown in Britain—were followed by the emergence of extra-parliamentary demands by ordinary people for political reform. The regents of the Dutch cities, defending the republic's federalism embodied by the Estates-General, which represented the seven provinces, opposed the policies of the bumbling Stadholder William V of Orange (ruled 1751–1795). The regents declared war on Britain in 1780 in the hope of weakening their commercial rival. As the war dragged on, they also sought to weaken the monarchical pretensions of William V, who wanted to augment executive authority at the expense of the provinces.

In 1785, in the midst of political crisis, the Dutch Republic had allied with France to counter the Austrian plan to reopen the Scheldt River and restore Antwerp to some of its former commercial glory, which would have undercut Amsterdam's prosperity. The possibility that France might annex the Southern Netherlands (Belgium) made the British government anxious, further irritating the pro-British William V.

In the meantime, a radical "Patriot Party," primarily drawn from the middle class and artisans, had begun to demand democratic reforms. Influenced by the success of the American revolutionaries, they demanded more democratic representation in the Estates and the right to have urban militias. These Dutch reformers unseated the stadholder. Prussian King Frederick William II (ruled 1786–1797), whose sister was the stadholder's wife, sent an imposing army in 1787, occupying Amsterdam and putting down the challenge to William V's authority as stadholder. France seemed on the verge of offering the Patriots assistance, but distracted by a mounting political crisis, it backed down against the opposition of Prussia and Britain, which supported William V. The balance of power had once again been preserved. Dutch patriot refugees poured into the Austrian Netherlands and France.

The Austrian Netherlands, too, experienced political turmoil. The state's powerful nobles opposed Austrian King Joseph II's enlightened reforms, which threatened their privileges, and they succeeded in driving out Austrian troops in 1789. There, too, a movement for democratic reform emerged, calling for the transformation of the Estates into a representative assembly. The Dutch mood seemed to be catching. The prince-bishop of Liège stressed the importance of preventing "the evil schemes of the majority of the Liègois, who would like to become a republic and to join the United Provinces as other provinces . . . only troops and fortresses can hold them to obedience." Dutch patriots invaded the Southern Netherlands in October 1789, driving away the Austrians. But a popular movement appealed to the nobles even less than did Austrian rule. Nobles, backed by the clergy and with the tacit support of most peasants, wrested control of the short-lived state from the urban-based reformers. The return of Austrian troops in 1790 occurred without resistance.

FADING POWERS: THE OTTOMAN EMPIRE AND POLAND

The structure of international power in eighteenth-century Europe was not fundamentally changed by the quest for reform during the 1760s and 1770s. But in the new, more competitive European environment of the late eighteenth century, two states that did not have access to the fruits of international trade and that were unwilling to restructure themselves lost their power in Europe: The Turkish Ottoman Empire began to decline slowly but surely, and Poland literally disappeared as an independent state, at least until after World War I. The Ottoman Empire, its power overextended and lacking a centralized structure of government, saw its territories in the Balkans and Caucasus eaten away by Austria and Russia. Poland, in contrast, had become a power without becoming an absolute state; weakened by noble domination of the monarchy, it fell prey to its aggressive absolute neighbors: Russia, Prussia, and Austria, which divided up the state in three partitions.

The Decline of Ottoman Turkish Power in Europe

In contrast to other absolute sovereigns, the Ottoman Turkish sultans ruled indirectly, governing through church or village officials. Indirect rule itself may have hastened the decline of Ottoman absolutism. The Turkish economy, army, and navy could not keep pace with the Western powers. Turkish cavalrymen, with curved swords and magnificent horses, fell before Western artillery and rifles.

Like the Spanish Empire at its peak, the Ottoman domains were so extensive that they defied effective control. Insurrections, including some by the janissaries, the once-loyal court militia, challenged the authority of the sultans. Imperial officials, Muslim and Christian Orthodox alike, became notoriously corrupt, including the Greek-educated Phanariots, based in Constantinople, who served the sultans by, among other things, collecting taxes, while making their families very wealthy. As the system of indirect rule declined in effectiveness, some local Christian and Muslim leaders now commanded their own military forces, virtually independent of the sultan's authority in Constantinople. Sultans awarded large estates to those who served them well. This was precisely the same phenomenon that the absolute monarchs of France, Prussia, Russia, and Austria had overcome. Unlike the rest of Europe, territories forming part of the Ottoman Empire did not have a hereditary aristocracy. And unlike Russia and parts of Central Europe, peasants within the empire were free. But Turkish authority virtually collapsed in mountainous Montenegro and Bosnia, where the Turks battled Habsburg and Venetian forces. The government began to run out of money. Stop-gap measures, such as the debasement of the currency, failed to provide the empire with sufficient revenue.

Incapable sultans, who were unable or unwilling to impose reforms, further weakened the Turkish cause. As boys they lived in virtual isolation in a world of uncertainty among court eunuchs and palace intrigue. No regular pattern of succession had ever been established. Whereas Peter the Great of Russia undertook Western military reforms, the sultans did not. The advice of officials who had been sent to Vienna and Paris to study methods of state went unheeded in Constantinople. There was not a single printing press in the Ottoman capital until well into the eighteenth century. Long wars fought against Persia in the east made it less easy to repress disturbances in the Balkans. In some parts of the empire, a system of land inheritance replaced the old system; new landowners began to force peasants into serfdom. The haphazard and inefficient collection of taxes, increasingly by dishonest tax farmers, engendered peasant resis-

Sultan Selim III in his palace in Istanbul, with a line of followers stretching in front of him. The Turkish sultans ruled indirectly over a vast network of domains, a tactic that may have hastened the decline of Ottoman absolutism.

tance. The long decline of Ottoman power in Europe, which began in the last decades of the seventeenth century and culminated in Austria's conquest of Hungary and Croatia, facilitated the rise of Russia. In 1774, following its destruction of the Turkish fleet in the Black Sea, the Ottoman state granted Russia the right to oversee Turkish authority in the Danubian principalities and to serve as the official protector of Christians living within the Ottoman Empire.

The Disappearance of Poland

While the Ottoman Empire survived, Poland did not endure as an independent state (at least until the end of World War I). Poland had been a strong state in the seventeenth century. But during the early decades of the eighteenth century, the kingdom, its population reduced by wars and bubonic plague to only 6 million people, had become increasingly dependent on Russia. Poland's eclipse made possible Russia's gains in Ukraine.

Polish nobles (the *szlachta*) not only maintained their prerogatives, they relegated the king to virtual political impotence. Nobles, who made up 8 percent of the population because of the inflation in noble titles that had begun in the early sixteenth century, elected the king. They considered this period of domination one of "golden liberty," marked by an unworkable political system by which a single vote in the noble assembly (Sejm) would bring about its dissolution (the *liberum* veto). Deputies were forbidden to make speeches in what became known as the "silent Sejm." Furthermore, Poland lacked a standing army and an efficient bureaucracy.

The War of Polish Succession (1733–1735) began when Russia attempted to impose its candidate on the Polish throne over the opposition of the Polish nobles. Because of France's interest in maintaining Sweden, the Ottoman Empire, and Poland as checks against Austrian Habsburg domination of Central Europe, Louis XV proposed a candidate for the throne, his father-in-law, Stanislas Lesczinski, who had reigned as king of Poland from 1704 to 1709 and now had the support of most Polish nobles. But a Russian army forced the election of Augustus III of Saxony (ruled 1733–1763), who was the Austro-Russian candidate.

When the Polish throne again fell vacant in 1763 with the death of the king, Russian influence led the Polish nobles to elect as king the cultured, cosmopolitan Stanislas Poniatowski (ruled 1764–1795), one of the insatiable Russian Empress Catherine the Great's many lovers ("many were called, and many were chosen," as one wag put it). Stanislas was somewhat influenced by Enlightenment thought. Sensing the necessity of reform, he hoped to advance manufacturing in Poland and looked to Britain as a model. He tried to end the *liberum* veto and to curtail the right of seigneurial courts to impose death sentences. He also established a number of schools. Only by such measures, he believed, could Poland escape poverty and backwardness. Voltaire and Rousseau were among those philosophes who viewed Poland as fertile ground for Enlightenment-based reform, and who concerned themselves with the fate of the "most unhappy realm." But some of the more powerful Polish nobles, who resented Russian influence, now opposed Stanislas and his reforms. They hoped that the French monarch or the Ottoman sultan might intervene on their behalf.

Catherine, like the Prussian king, feared that Stanislas's reforms might lead to a stronger, less subservient neighbor. Since 1764, Russia and Prussia had been allies in the attempt to prevent an expansion of French influence in the Baltic, while preventing Poland from reviving its fortunes. Furthermore, Polish nobles had begun to persecute non-Catholics. Catherine, in the interest of the Orthodox Church, demanded that all non-Catholics be granted toleration in Poland. When Polish nobles formed an anti-Russian and anti-Orthodox confederation, Catherine sent troops into Poland. Ukrainian peasants took advantage of the chaos to rise up against their Polish lords. When they burned a Turkish town while chasing out Poles, Turkey entered the war against Russia. Catherine annexed Crimea, Wallachia, and several territories along the Black Sea, at Turkish expense.

Alarmed by an expansion of Russian power, Austria and Prussia demanded territorial compensation. Catherine suggested that the three concerned powers might help themselves to parts of beleaguered Poland. The First Partition in 1772 reduced Poland by about a third (see Map 11.3). Maria Theresa of Austria "wept and then took her share," the large province of Galicia, which lay between Russian Ukraine and Austria.

MAP 11.3 THE PARTITIONS OF POLAND Poland at its greatest extent in 1660–1667, and the loss of territory to Austria, Prussia, and Russia during the Partitions of 1772, 1793, and 1795.

Prussia absorbed West Prussia, which had formed a corridor separating East Prussia from the rest of the kingdom. Russia snatched large chunks of territory of eastern Poland.

Stanislas proclaimed a liberal constitution in 1791 that established a hereditary monarchy, abolished the unworkable system of noble veto, and proclaimed that all authority stemmed from the nation. This remarkable document reflected the influence of the French Revolution (see Chapter 12). Poland became a constitutional monarchy, with the king naming ministers but with the parliament and Poland's few major towns retaining privileges.

But Poland's days were numbered. When Poles rose up in 1792 against Russian authority in the part of Poland that had been absorbed by Russia twenty years earlier, Russian troops intervened. They were backed by Polish nobles, the grave diggers of Polish independence, who opposed the liberal constitution. Prussia refused to come to Poland's aid, receiving in exchange for looking the other way its own annexation of more Polish territory in the Second Partition in 1793. With the Third Partition in 1795, Prussia and Russia ended Poland's independence for more than a century. The Constitution of 1791, perhaps the most progressive constitution of the century, was torn to shreds. "Poland was but a breakfast," wrote Edmund Burke, "where will they dine?" Russia's new gains drew its interests further into Central Europe, and it now shared a border with the Habsburg monarchy. As for the Poles themselves, their incorporation made them subject to the power of the state in which they had been incorporated. For example, in the lands acquired by Prussia, serfs gained some protection against abuses by landlords, but, as in the case of lands absorbed into the Habsburg empire, the Polish secondary-school system was ended, with the German language imposed.

CONCLUSION

Some historians have argued that movements against absolutism and against privilege, such as the political unrest in Great Britain and the successful rebellion of its North American colonies, constituted a general Western "democratic revolution." But despite the quest for political change in several Western states, demands for universal male suffrage were rare, and calls for the extension of political rights to women even more so (an exception being Geneva in the early 1780s). Even in Britain, after a contentious decade marked by demonstrations for political reform, the most widespread riots of the 1780s were the anti-Catholic Gordon riots. In France, calls for reform were less an attack on the nobles, per se, than on privilege. The institutions of the Old Regime in continental Europe demonstrated not only resiliency, but also a capacity to undertake reform.

Nonetheless, denunciations in France against privilege, shaped in part by Enlightenment thought, would be revived in the late 1780s. The Seven Years' War and assistance to the Americans had considerably worsened the financial crisis of the French monarchy, as the increasingly global dynastic rivalries and wars placed further strains on European states. France entered a serious political crisis when critics of the monarchy accused the king of ruling despotically and attacked the layers of economic and social privilege that seemed to constrain effective government and constrict freedom. Demands for sweeping reform led to the French Revolution of 1789, which proclaimed the principle of the sovereignty of the nation. Once again, the eyes of Europe turned toward France.

PART FOUR

REVOLUTIONARY EUROPE, 1789–1850

The French Revolution of 1789 struck the first solid blow in continental Western Europe against monarchical absolutism on behalf of popular sovereignty. The roots of revolution extend back to the second half of the seventeenth century, an era of hitherto unparalleled absolute monarchical authority. The monarchs of France, Russia, Prussia, Austria, Spain, and Sweden had reinforced their authority to the extent that they stood clearly above any internal challenge to their power. Compliant nobles served as junior partners in absolutism, acknowledging the ruler's absolute power to proclaim laws, assess taxes, and raise armies, in exchange for royal recognition of their noble standing and protection against popular revolts. The governments of Great Britain and the Dutch United Provinces stood in sharp contrast to absolute states. In the English Civil War in the 1640s, Parliament had successfully turned aside the possibility of absolute monarchy in England, leading to the execution of King Charles II, followed after some years of turmoil by the Restoration of constitutional monarchy. In the Netherlands, the Dutch revolt against absolutist Spain led to the establishment of the Dutch Republic. The theory of popular sovereignty developed not only as an alternative to absolute rule but also as an extension of constitutional rule. In the dramatic events of the French Revolution that began in 1789, the theory of popular sovereignty became reality as ordinary people helped bring about the downfall of absolute rule and then, three years later, the monarchy itself.

True popular sovereignty was a short-lived experiment, however, as counter-revolution and foreign intervention led to the dramatic centralization of state authority. In 1799, Napoleon

Bonaparte helped overthrow the Directory, the last regime of the revolutionary era in France. An admirer of the Enlightenment, Napoleon claimed that he was the heir of the French Revolution. But while Napoleon saw himself as a savior who carried "liberty, equality, and fraternity" abroad, his conquest of much of Europe before his final defeat left a mixed legacy for the future.

Following Napoleon's defeat in 1815 at the Battle of Waterloo, the Congress of Vienna created the Concert of Europe, the international basis of Restoration Europe, in the hope of preventing further liberal and nationalist insurrections in Europe. But liberal and nationalist movements could not so easily be swept away. During the subsequent three decades, "liberty" became the watchword for more and more people, particularly among the middle classes, who came to the forefront of economic, political, and cultural life. Liberal movements were in many places closely tied to the emergence of nationalism, the belief in the primacy of nationality as a source of allegiance and sovereignty.

In the meantime, during the first half of the nineteenth century, the Industrial Revolution slowly but surely transformed the way many Europeans lived. Dramatic improvements in transportation, notably the development of the railroad but also road improvements, expanded the market for manufactured and other goods. Rising agricultural production, increasingly commercialized in Western Europe, fed a larger population. Migrants poured into Europe's cities, which grew as never before. Contemporaries, particularly in Western Europe, sensed profound economic, social, political, and cultural changes.

CHAPTER **12**

THE FRENCH
REVOLUTION

In 1791, King Louis XVI decided to flee Paris and the French Revolution. A virtual prisoner in the Tuileries Palace by the first months of the year, he had secretly negotiated for possible intervention on his behalf by the Austrian king and other European monarchs. The royal family furtively left the Tuileries Palace late at night on June 20, 1791, disguised as the family and entourage of a Russian baroness riding in a large black coach with yellow trim. But in the eastern town of Sainte-Menehould, the postmaster recognized the king, whose image he had seen on a coin. He rode rapidly to Varennes, where the National Guard prevented the king's coach from going on. Three representatives of the National Assembly brought the royal family back to Paris. Near the capital, the crowds became threatening, and National Guardsmen stood by the roadside with their rifles upside down, a sign of contempt or mourning.

The French Revolution mounted the first effective challenge to monarchical absolutism on behalf of popular sovereignty. The creation of a republican government in France and the diffusion of republican ideals in other European countries influenced the evolution of European political life long after the Revolution ended. Issues of the rights of the people, the role of the state in society, the values of democratic society, notions of "left" and "right" in political life, the concept of the "nation at arms," the place of religion in modern society and politics, and the question of economic freedom and the sanctity of property came to dominate the political agenda. They occupied the attention of much of France during the revolutionary decade of 1789–1799. The political violence of that decade would also be a legacy for the future.

The revolutionaries sought to make the French state more centralized and efficient, as well as more just. Napoleon Bonaparte, whom some historians consider to be the heir to the Revolution and others believe to be its betrayer, continued this process after his ascent to power in 1799.

The arrest of Louis XVI.

Modern nationalism, too, has its roots in the French Revolution. The revolutionaries enthusiastically proclaimed principles they held to be universal. Among these were the sovereignty of the nation and the rights and duties of citizenship. The revolutionaries celebrated the fact that the Revolution had occurred in France. But wars intended to free European peoples from monarchical and noble domination turned into wars of French conquest. The revolutionary wars, pitting France against the other great powers, contributed to the emergence or extension of nationalism in other countries as well, ranging from England, where the sense of being British flourished in response to the French threat, to central and southern Europe, where some educated Germans and Italians began to espouse nationalism in response to the invading French armies.

THE OLD REGIME IN CRISIS

The French Revolution was not inevitable. Yet difficult economic conditions in the preceding two decades, combined with the growing popularity of a discourse that stressed freedom in the face of entrenched economic and social privileges, made some sort of change seem possible, perhaps even likely. When a financial crisis occurred in the 1780s and the king was forced to call the Estates-General, the stage was set for the confrontation that would culminate in the French Revolution.

Long-Term Causes of the French Revolution

The increasing prevalence of the language of the Enlightenment, stressing equality before the law and differentiating between absolute and despotic rule, placed the monarchy and its government under the closer scrutiny of public opinion (see Chapter 11). Adopting Enlightenment discourse, opponents accused Louis XV of acting despotically when he exiled the Parlement of Paris in 1771 and tried to establish new law courts that were likely to be more subservient than the parlements had been. Opponents believed that the king was trying to subvert long-accepted privileges. He was forced to relent and restore the parlements, which maintained their right to register royal edicts.

Enlightenment literature was not in itself revolutionary. But as complaints mounted about noble privileges, guild monopolies, and corrupt royal officials, the implications of Enlightenment thought led to political action. In 1774, Controller-General of Finances Anne-Robert Turgot drew up a program to eliminate some monopolies and privileges that fettered the economy (see Chapter 11). However, the decree abolishing the guilds, among other decrees, generated immediate hostility from nobles, the Parliament of Paris, and from ordinary people, who rioted in Paris in 1775 because the freeing of the grain trade had brought higher prices in hard times. Two years later, Turgot's experiment ended. But some writers now began to contrast the freedoms Turgot had in mind with the corporate privileges that characterized the economy and society of eighteenth-century France.

The social lines of demarcation between the nobility and the bourgeoisie had become less fixed over the course of the eighteenth century. Despite increasing opposition from the oldest noble families who believed their ranks were being swamped by newcomers, in the fifteen years before 1789 almost 2,500 families bought their way into the nobility. Yet many people of means continued to resent noble privileges, above all the exemption of nobles from most kinds of taxes. The disgruntled bourgeoisie did not make the French Revolution, but their dissatisfaction helped create a litany of demands for reform. The monarchy's worsening financial crisis accentuated these calls.

France remained a state of overlapping layers of privileges, rights, traditions, and jurisdictions. Nobles and professional groups such as guilds and tax farmers (who generally had bought their offices and could pocket some of the taxes they collected) always contested any plan to eliminate privileges.

The sharpest resistance to reform came from the poorer nobility. Among the "nobles of the sword," the oldest noble families whose ancestors had proudly taken arms to serve the king, some had fallen on hard times and clung frantically to any and all privileges as a way of maintaining their status. They resented the fact that the provincial parlements, in particular, had filled up with new nobles who had purchased offices—the "nobles of the robe"—and that power had shifted within the nobility from the oldest noble families to those recently ennobled.

The monarchy depended upon the sale of titles, offices, and economic monopolies for revenue and long-term credit. But by creating more offices—there were more than 50,000 offices in 1789—it risked destroying public confidence and driving down the value of offices already held.

Economic hardship compounded the monarchy's financial problems by decreasing revenue while exacerbating social tensions. Rising prices and rents darkened the 1770s and 1780s. A series of bad harvests—the worst of which occurred in 1775—made conditions of life even more difficult for poor people. The harvests of 1787 and 1788, which would be key years in the French political drama, were also very poor. Such crises were by no means unusual—indeed, they were cyclical and would continue until the middle of the next century. Meager harvests generated popular resistance to taxation and protests against the high price of grain (and therefore bread). A growing population put more pressure on scarce resources.

Many peasants believed that landowners were increasing their hardship. Some historians have argued that a "seigneurial reaction" was underway as smaller agricultural yields diminished noble revenues, while inflation raised the costs of noble life. By this view, noble landowners hired estate agents, lawyers, and surveyors to maximize income from their lands, reasserting old rights over common lands, on which many poor peasants depended for pasturing animals and gathering wood for fuel. Landlords raised rents and tried to force sharecropping arrangements on peasants who had previously rented land.

Although the feudal system of the Middle Ages had long since passed, remnants remained. Peasants were still vexed by seigneurial dues and cash owed to their lords. Many nobles still held some rights of justice over their peasants, which meant that they could determine guilt and assess penalties for alleged transgressions; seigneurial courts were often used to enforce the landlord's rights over forests, lakes, and streams, and his exclusive rights to hunt and fish on his estate. The political crisis that led to the French Revolution would provide ordinary people with an opportunity to redress some of these mounting grievances.

The Financial Crisis

The serious financial crisis that confronted the monarchy in the 1780s was the short-term cause of the French Revolution. France had been at war with Britain, as well as with other European powers, off and on for more than a century. The financial support France had provided the rebel colonists in the American War of Independence against Britain had been underwritten by loans arranged by the king's Swiss minister of finance, Jacques Necker (1732–1804). Almost three-fourths of state expenses went to maintaining the army and navy, and to paying off debts accumulated from the War of the Austrian Succession (1740–1748) and the Seven Years' War (1756–1763), as well as from the American War of Independence. The monarchy was living beyond its means.

Where were more funds to be found? Nobles had traditionally enjoyed the privilege of being exempt from most, and the clergy from all, taxation. There was a limit to how many taxes could be imposed on peasants, by far the largest social group in France. In short, the financial crisis of the monarchy was closely tied to the very nature of its fiscal system.

The absolute monarchy in France collected taxes far less efficiently than did the British government. In Britain, the Bank of England facilitated the government's borrowing of money at relatively low interest through the national debt. In France, there was no central bank, and the French monarchy depended more than ever on private interests and suffered from a cumbersome assessment of fiscal obligations and inadequate accounting. French public debt already was much higher than Britain's would be a century later, and it continued to rise as the monarchy sought financial expedients. Public confidence rose and fell, as debt charges sometimes absorbed two-thirds of royal revenues. Even when public confidence waned, however, invariably the market for offices and titles bounced back.

The hesitant and naive Louis XVI was still in his twenties when he became king. Louis knew little of his kingdom, venturing beyond the region of Paris and Versailles only once during his reign. He preferred puttering around the palace, taking clocks and watches apart and putting them back together. He excelled at hunting. The unpopularity of Louis's elegant, haughty wife, Marie Antoinette (1755–1793), accentuated the public's lack of confidence in the throne (whether or not she ever really snarled "Let them eat cake!" when told that the people had no bread). The

(*Left*) Louis XVI. (*Right*) Marie-Antoinette.

daughter of the Austrian queen Maria Theresa, Marie Antoinette was married to Louis to strengthen French dynastic ties to Austria. She never felt really at home in France. Unhappy in her marriage, Marie Antoinette lived extravagantly and was embroiled in scandal. Thus, for example, in 1785, she became entangled in a seamy scandal when a cardinal, the former ambassador of France to the Habsburg court in Vienna, gave her a fabulous diamond necklace in the hope of winning favor. The necklace and some of the prelate's money were then deftly stolen by mysterious plotters, a strange scenario that included a prostitute posing as the queen. The "diamond necklace affair," as it was called, seemed to augment the public image of the king as a weak man, a cuckold. The queen's reputed indiscretions and infidelities seemed to undercut the authority of the monarchy itself. Her detractors indelicately dubbed her the "Austrian whore."

In the meantime, Necker continued to float more loans. But in 1781, some ministers and noble hangers-on convinced the king to dismiss Necker. The following year, Necker produced a fanciful account of the royal finances that purported to demonstrate that more revenue was coming to the state than was being spent. Necker hoped to reassure creditors that reform was unnecessary. Bankers, however, did not believe Necker's figures. Some refused to loan the monarchy any more money until the state enacted financial reforms. The new finance minister, Charles-Alexandre de Calonne (1734–1802), demonstrated that Necker's calculations of royal finances were far-fetched. Yet Calonne spent even more money and put the royal treasury deeper in debt by borrowing from venal officeholders in order to pay off creditors now gathered at the royal door.

The parlements, or sovereign law courts, were certain to oppose fiscal reform, which they believed would lead to an increase in taxation through a general tax on land. They distrusted Calonne, whom they identified with fiscal irresponsibility and governmental arrogance that some believed bordered on despotism.

To sidestep the parlements, Calonne asked the king in February 1787 to convoke an Assembly of Notables consisting of handpicked representatives from each of the three estates: clergy, nobility, and the third estate (everybody else). The crown expected the Assembly to endorse its reform proposals, including new land taxes from which nobles would not be exempt. Believing that the monarchy's policy of borrowing from Peter to pay Paul could not go on, Calonne suggested that France's financial problems were systemic, resulting from a chaotic administrative organization, including the confusing regional differences in tax obligations. The monarchy's practice of selling the lucrative rights to collect, or "farm," taxes worsened the inefficiency. Calonne knew that the crown's contract with the tax farmers would soon have to be renegotiated, and that many short-term loans contracted by the monarchy would soon come due.

Denouncing "the dominance of custom" that had for so long prevented reform and encumbered commerce, Calonne proposed to overhaul the entire financial system. The Assembly of Notables, however, rejected Calonne's proposals for tax reform and refused to countenance the idea that nobles should be assessed land taxes. Moreover, the high clergy of the first estate, some of whom were nobles, also vociferously opposed Calonne's reforms. They, too, feared losing their exemption from taxation. The privilege-based nature of French society was at stake.

Nobles convinced the king to sack Calonne, which he did on April 8, 1788. Louis XVI replaced Calonne with the powerful archbishop of Toulouse, Étienne-Charles de Loménie de Brienne (1727–1794). Like his predecessor, Loménie de Brienne asked the provincial parlements to register—and thus approve—several edicts of financial reform, promising that the government would keep more accurate accounts. But the Parlement of Paris refused to register some of the edicts, including a new land tax and a stamp tax, which evoked the origins of the American Revolution.

THE FIRST STAGES OF THE REVOLUTION

Some members of the Assembly of Notables had been willing to accept fiscal reform and to pay more taxes, but only with accompanying institutional reforms that would guarantee their privileges. They wanted the king to convoke regular assemblies of the Estates-General—made up of representatives of the three estates—which had not been convoked since 1614. The king was in a difficult position. He needed to reduce the privileges of the nobles in order to solve the financial crisis, but to do so without their approval would lead to accusations of tyranny. On the other hand, capitulating to the demands of the privileged classes in return for new taxes would compromise his absolute authority and suggest that his word was subject to the approval of the nation, or at least the nobility. The resolution of this dilemma would lead to the events that constituted the first stages of the French Revolution.

Convoking the Estates-General

The "noble revolt" began the French Revolution. In response to the refusal of the Parlement of Paris to register the land and stamp taxes, in August 1787 Louis XVI exiled its members to Troyes, a town east of Paris. Nobles and high clergymen protested vigorously. The provincial parlements backed up the Parlement of Paris. The Parlement of Grenoble refused to register the new stamp and land taxes and convoked its provincial estates (the assembly of nobles that represented the interests of the region) without royal authorization. The "revolt of the nobility" against the monarchy's attempt to force nobles to pay taxes spread. Provincial parlements continued to demand that the Estates-General be convoked. This revolt was not directed against the institution of the monarchy itself, but against what the nobles considered abuses of the rights and privileges of the nation committed by an increasingly despotic crown. In this, the revolt of the nobles recalled the revolt known as the Fronde, vanquished by the young Louis XIV in the mid-seventeenth century (see Chapter 7).

The monarchy sought compromise. Loménie de Brienne agreed to withdraw the new land and stamp taxes in exchange for maintaining the tax on income (the *vingtième* tax), which nobles and other privileged people had first been assessed in the late 1750s to pay for the Seven Years' War. He made clear, however, that the crown would be forced to settle its debts in paper money backed by royal decree. Louis XVI recalled the Parlement of Paris from exile in November 1787. But the king ordered new loan edicts registered without giving the parlement a chance to be heard. When the duke of Orléans, the king's cousin, interjected that such a procedure was illegal, Louis replied, "That is of no importance to me . . . it is legal because I will it." Louis XVI thus seemed to cross the line between absolutism and despotism.

In May 1788, as hostilities between the monarchy and the Parlement of Paris continued, the king ordered the arrest of two of its most radical members. He then suspended the parlements, establishing new provincial courts to take their place and creating a single plenary court that would register royal edicts. Resistance to the king's acts against the parlements came quickly. The Assembly of the Clergy, which had been summoned to decide on the amount of its annual gift to the crown, protested the abolition of the parlements. Riots in support of the parlements occurred in several towns, including Grenoble, where crowds expressed support for their parlement by pelting soldiers with stones and roof tiles.

On August 8, 1788, Louis XVI announced that he would convoke the Estates-General on May 1 of the following year. He hoped that it would avert royal bankruptcy by agreeing to the imposition of the new taxes. Two weeks later, he reappointed Necker as minister of finance, a measure he believed would appease the nobles, investors, and holders of government bonds, who had never objected to unrestrained borrowing. But the convocation of the Estates-General helped coalesce public opinion against the king. That the nobles forced the crown to convoke the Estates-General became the first act of the French Revolution. Many people believed that the Estates-General, more than the parlements, would represent their interests and check royal despotism.

The question of how voting was to take place when the Estates-General met assumed increasing importance. The issue highlights tensions between conservatives, many of whom were nobles, and reformers, some of whom were bourgeois but who also included some liberal nobles. Would each of the three estates—clergy, nobles, and the third estate— have a single vote (which would almost certainly quash any reform since

(*Left*) The Marquis de Lafayette. (*Right*) The Abbé Sieyès.

the majority of nobles and clergymen were against reform), or would each member of the Estates-General be entitled to his own vote?

On September 25, 1788, the Parlement of Paris, which had been reinstated amid great celebration, supported the king's insistence that voting within the Estates-General would take place by estate instead of by head. This meant that when the Estates-General met, as in 1614, each of the three estates would have the same number of representatives and be seated separately. Henceforth, the parlements would be seen by many people as defending the prerogatives of their privileged members against the interests of the third estate, losing their claim to defend the nation against the king's despotism for having registered the royal decree that voting would be by estate.

Popular political writers now began to salute the third estate (which made up 95 percent of the population) as the true representative of liberty and of the nation against royal despotism. Others asked for some sort of representative assembly that would reflect "public opinion." The "patriot party," a coalition of bourgeois members and some liberal nobles, began to oppose royal policies, which they contrasted with those of the "nation." "Patriots" denounced the vested interests of the court and the nobles close to it. Political publications began to inundate France, transforming these debates into national political issues. The Society of the Thirty, a group that included liberal nobles from very old families—for example, the Marquis de Lafayette (1757–1834), French hero of the American War of Independence—as well as a number of commoner lawyers, met to discuss, debate, and distribute liberal political pamphlets. They proposed that the third estate, which represented everyone not belonging to the first two estates, be entitled to twice as many representatives in the Estates-General as the nobility and clergy.

In January 1789, Abbé Emmanuel Joseph Sieyès (1748–1836), an obscure priest, offered the most radical expression of a crucial shift in political opinion. "We have three questions to ask and answer," he wrote, "First, What is the Third Estate? Everything. Second, What has it been heretofore in the political order? Nothing. Third, What does it demand? To become something therein." He contrasted the "nation" against royal absolutism and noble prerogative. Sieyès's polemic represented a radical current of opinion that had revolutionary implications, for he demanded a predominant role for the third estate in political life.

The vast majority of the men elected to the Estates-General were residents of cities and towns, and two-thirds of these had some training in the law. Two-thirds of those elected to the first estate were parish priests, many of whom were of humble origin and resented the privileges of the bishops and monastic orders. Some of the younger noble representatives elected to the second estate were liberals. They wanted institutional reforms in the organization of the French monarchy that would permit them to check the power of the king, in much the same way as the Parliament in England served as a check on the English crown. In December 1788, the king agreed to double the number of representatives of the third estate but declined to give all members an individual vote.

The king asked the local electoral assemblies, along with the first two estates, to draw up lists of grievances (*cahiers de doléances*), which the Estates-General would discuss. Thousands of grievances offered the monarchy a wide variety of opinions, ranging from concrete suggestions for reform to the considered opinion that the foul breath of sheep was ruining pasture land in Lorraine. More important, *cahiers* criticized monarchical absolutism and the intransigence of seigneurs, asked for a more consistent and equitable tax structure, and called for the creation of a new national representative body. A few of the *cahiers* denounced as an abuse of royal power the so-called *lettres de cachet,* documents issued in the name of the king that allowed a person to be arrested for any reason and imprisoned indefinitely. For example, one *cahier* demanded "that no citizen lose his liberty except according to law." However, some *cahiers* also reflected continued reverence for the king, while denouncing the rapacity and bad faith of his advisers and ministers. Most never reached the king.

On May 5, 1789, the nearly 1,200 members of the Estates-General (about 600 of whom represented the third estate) assembled at Versailles. The king greeted the first two estates, but kept the commoners waiting for two hours. When he finished his speech, members of the third estate violated protocol by boldly putting their hats back on, a right reserved for the two privileged orders. When it became apparent that representatives would vote not by head but by estate, the third estate stalled the proceedings for weeks by insisting that all three estates register their delegates together. On June 17, the third estate overwhelmingly approved a motion by Sieyès that declared the third estate to be the "National Assembly" and the true representative of national sovereignty. The third estate now claimed legitimate sovereignty and an authority parallel, if not superior, to that of the king of France.

But, on June 20, as rumors circulated that the king might take action against them, representatives of the third estate found that their meeting hall had been locked for "repairs." Led by their president, Jean-Sylvain Bailly (1736–1793), an astronomer, the members of the third estate took the bold step of assembling in a nearby tennis court. There they took an oath "not to separate, and to reassemble wherever circumstances require, until the constitution of the kingdom is established and consolidated upon solid foundations." With principled defiance, the third estate demanded that defined limits be placed on the king's authority.

The king declared the third estate's deliberations invalid. Yet, on June 23, he announced some substantial reforms, agreeing to convoke periodically the Estates-General, to abolish the *taille* (the tax on land) and the *corvée* (labor tax), to eliminate internal tariffs and tolls that interfered with trade, and to eliminate the *lettres de cachet*. He also agreed that the Estates-General would vote by head, but only on matters that did not concern "the ancient and constitutional rights of the three orders." To the

The Tennis Court Oath, June 20, 1789.

radicalized members of the third estate, the king's concessions were not enough.

Louis XVI had dismissed Necker on June 22, but reversed himself after learning that thousands of people in Paris had invaded the courtyard of the Tuileries Palace in Paris to demand that Necker stay on. During these days, most of the clergy and a number of nobles had joined the third estate. Now, after threatening to dissolve the Estates-General by force, on June 27 the king ordered the remaining clergy and nobles of the first two estates to join the third. The new gathering began to constitute itself as a National Constituent Assembly.

Storming of the Bastille

Many ordinary people now believed that a conspiracy by nobles and hoarders lay behind the shortage of food and high prices. Furthermore, there seemed to be an increase in the number of royal troops around Paris and Versailles. Rumors spread that the National Assembly would be quashed. On July 11, the king once again ordered Necker into exile. Bands of rioters attacked the customs barriers at the gates of Paris, tearing down most of the toll booths.

On the morning of July 14, 1789, thousands of people—mostly tradesmen, artisans, and wage earners—seized weapons stored in the Invalides, a large veterans' hospital. Early that afternoon, the attention of the Paris crowd, now numbering perhaps 80,000 people, turned toward the Bastille, a fortress in the eastern part of the city, where the crowd believed powder and ammunition were stored. For most of the eighteenth century, the Bastille had been a prison, renowned as a symbol of despotism because some prisoners had been sent there by virtue of one of the king's *lettres de cachet*, summarily and without a trial. On that hot summer day, the Bastille's prisoners numbered but seven, a motley crew that included a nobleman imprisoned upon request of his family, a renegade priest, and a demented Irishman, who alternately thought he was Joan of Arc, Saint Louis, and God.

The crowd stormed and captured the Bastille, which was defended by a small garrison. More than 200 of the attackers were killed or wounded. A butcher decapitated the commander of the fortress, and the throng carried his head on a pike in triumph through the streets. The Bastille's fall would be much more significant than it first appeared. The king entered "nothing new" in his diary for that day, July 14. But the crowd's uprising probably saved the National Assembly from being dissolved by the troops the king had ordered to Versailles and Paris. Now unsure of the loyalty of his soldiers, Louis sent away some of the troops he had summoned to Paris, recognized both the newly elected municipal government, with Jean-Sylvain Bailly serving as mayor, and a municipal defense force or National Guard

The taking of Bastille, July 14, 1789.

(commanded by the Marquis de Lafayette), and capitulated to the popular demand that he recall Necker to office.

On July 17, 1789, the king came to Paris to be received by the municipal council at the town hall, accepting and wearing an emblem of three colors, red and blue for the city of Paris, and white for the Bourbons. By doing so, Louis XVI seemed to be recognizing what became the tricolor symbol of the French Revolution.

The Great Fear and the Night of August 4

News of the convocation of the Estates-General had brought hope to many rural people that the king would relieve their crushing fiscal burdens. They had expressed their hopes in the grievances they sent with their third estate delegates to Versailles.

Encouraged by the gathering of the Estates-General and the news of the fall of the Bastille, between July 19 and August 3 peasants attacked châteaux. In some places they burned title deeds specifying obligations owed to lords. These peasant rebellions helped cause a subsequent general panic known as the "Great Fear." Fueled by the rumor of an aristocratic "famine plot" to starve or burn out the population, peasants and townspeople

mobilized in many regions of France. To repel the rumored approach of brigands sent to destroy crops, townspeople and peasants formed armed units to
defend themselves and save the harvest. New local governments and
National Guard units were established to institute reforms and to restore
order as the effective authority of the state disintegrated. These events
brought to local influence lawyers, merchants, and other "new men" who
had formerly been excluded from political life.

News of peasant violence and the panic engendered by the "famine plot"
galvanized members of the National Assembly. On August 4, 1789, in an
effort to appease the peasants and to forestall further rural disorders, the
National Assembly formally abolished the "feudal regime," including
seigneurial rights. This sweeping proclamation was modified in the following week: owners of seigneurial dues, or payments owed by peasants who
worked land owned by nobles, would receive compensation from the peasants (although, in general, such compensation was not forthcoming and
was subsequently eliminated). The Assembly abolished personal labor
servitude owed to nobles, a vestige of medieval serfdom, without compensation. The members of the National Assembly thus renounced privilege,
the fundamental organizing principle of French society during the Old
Regime. Other reforms enacted the following week included the guarantee of freedom of worship and the abolition of the sale of offices, seigneurial justice, and even of the exclusive right of nobles to hunt. The provinces
and cities, too, were required to give up most of their archaic privileges. In
these ways, the National Assembly enacted a sweeping agenda that proclaimed the end of the Old Regime.

CONSOLIDATING THE REVOLUTION

The Assembly's decrees destroyed absolutism by redefining the relationship between subject and king. No longer would the king rule by divine
right, or buy allegiance by dispensing privileges to favorites. Instead, he
would be constrained by powers spelled out in a constitution. The Assembly then began to create the new regime. It began by promulgating the
Declaration of the Rights of Man and Citizen, a remarkable document
that proposed universal principles of humanity. It next established a new
relationship between church and state, creating a national church, making
Catholic Church property "national property," and compelling the clergy
to swear allegiance to the nation. The National Assembly then turned to
the long process of framing a constitution for the new regime, and is
therefore sometimes also known as the Constituent Assembly.

In the meantime, however, Marie Antoinette denounced the revolutionaries as "monsters," and some of the king's most influential advisers
balked at accepting any weakening in royal authority. Fearing the influence of nobles at the court, crowds early in October marched to Versailles,

returning to Paris with the king and the royal family. Henceforth, while many nobles, among others, fled France for exile and sought the assistance of the monarchs of Europe against the Revolution, the king himself became vulnerable to the tide of Parisian popular radicalism. As nobles and clergy led resistance to the Revolution, the Parisian radical clubs moved further to the left. The days of Louis and of the monarchy itself were numbered.

The Declaration of the Rights of Man and Citizen

As it set out to create a constitutional monarchy, the Assembly promulgated the Declaration of the Rights of Man and Citizen on August 26, 1789. This set forth the general principles of the new order and intended to educate citizens about liberty. It would become the preamble to the new constitution that was being formulated by the Assembly. One of the most significant documents in Western political history, the Declaration reflected some of the ideas that Thomas Jefferson had enshrined in the American Declaration of Independence of 1776. Article One proclaims, "Men are born and remain free and equal in rights." The Enlightenment's influence is apparent in the document's concern for individual freedom, civic equality, and the sense of struggle against corporatism, unjust privilege, and absolute rule, a discourse based upon a belief in the primacy of reason. All people were to be equal before the law. All men were to be "equally eligible to all honors, places, and employments . . . without any other distinction than that created by their virtues and talents." No person could be persecuted for his or her opinions, including those concerning religion.

The English Bill of Rights, passed by Parliament in 1689, had proclaimed the rights of those accused of crimes to the rule of law and the rights of property-owners to self-government, while asserting the rights of Parliament. Now, proclaiming universal principles, the Declaration of the Rights of Man and Citizen clearly placed sovereignty in the French nation. The notion of rights stemming from membership in the "nation," as opposed to that in any corporate group or social estate, was a fundamental change. Laws were to reflect the notion of the "general will," an Enlightenment concept, which would be expressed by national representatives. The nation itself, not the monarch alone, was to be "the source of all sovereignty." The assertion of equality of opportunity, however, was not intended to eliminate all social distinctions. The preservation of property rights assured that differences due to wealth, education, and talent would remain and be considered natural and legitimate. The Declaration thus helped make wealth, not birth, blood, or legal privilege, the foundation of social and political order in modern France.

The Declaration invoked "universal man," meaning mankind. But at the same time, its authors excluded women from the Declaration and did not espouse or foresee equality of the sexes. Nonetheless, many men and women now began to greet each other as "citizen." Indeed, some calls for women's rights arose from the beginning of the Revolution.

The abolition of feudalism and the proclamation of the Declaration of the Rights of Man and Citizen were such monumental achievements that already in 1790 people were referring to the Old Regime as having been that which existed before the representatives of the Estates-General constituted the National Assembly. It remained, however, for Louis XVI to accept the Assembly's work.

"The Baker, the Baker's Wife, and the Baker's Little Boy"

The political crisis was by no means over. The National Assembly's actions challenged the authority of the crown. On one hand, the king's closest advisers, the "court party," rejected any constitutional arrangement that would leave the monarch without the power of absolute veto. Royal authority was at stake. On the other hand, speaking for the patriot party, Sieyès insisted, "If the king's will is capable of equalling that of twenty-five million people . . . it would be a *lettre de cachet* against the general will." The majority of the Assembly, having defeated a motion that an upper chamber like the British House of Lords be created, offered the king on September 11, 1789, the power of a "suspending" veto over legislation. The king would be able to delay a measure passed by the Assembly from becoming law for up to four years.

When the king failed to accept these provisions and the decrees of August 4, a flood of pamphlets and newspapers attacked his intransigence. The radical journalist Jean-Paul Marat (1743–1793) quickly found a popular following for his new newspaper, *The Friend of the People*. A physician beset by financial woes, Marat was like one of the ambitious, frustrated "scribblers" whom Voltaire, forty years earlier, had scathingly denounced as hacks. Marat captured with stirring emotion and the colorful, coarse slang of ordinary Parisians the mood of those for whom he wrote. The rhetoric of popular sovereignty, some of it borrowed from the philosophe Jean-Jacques Rousseau, came alive in the outpouring of political pamphlets that undermined popular respect for Louis XVI and even for the institution of monarchy itself.

By October, some "patriots" were demanding that the king reside in Paris, echoing a number of *cahiers*. Like many of the most important events in the French Revolution, the "march to Versailles" began with a seemingly minor event. The officers of the Flanders Regiment insulted the newly adopted tricolor emblem at a reception in their honor attended by the king and queen. According to rumor, they shouted, "Down with the National Assembly!"

On October 5, women from the neighborhoods around the Bastille, having found the market insufficiently provisioned, gathered in front of the à Versailles à Versailles *du 5 Octobre 1789*

Women of Paris leaving for Versailles.

town hall. From there, some 10,000 people, mostly women, proceeded to walk to Versailles, hoping to convince the king to provide them with bread. Some of them occupied the hall of the National Assembly, where they claimed power in the name of popular sovereignty. Later in the day, a large force of National Guardsmen led by the Marquis de Lafayette also arrived at Versailles, hoping to keep order and to convince the king that he should return with them to Paris. Louis cordially greeted the women in the late afternoon, promising them bread. That night the king announced his acceptance of the Assembly's momentous decrees of the night of August 4.

Nonetheless, violence followed at dawn. When people tried to force their way into the château, royal guards shot a man dead, and the crowds retaliated by killing two guards and sticking their heads on pikes. The crowd insisted that the royal family join it on the road to Paris. Some of the women sang that they were returning to Paris with "The Baker, the Baker's Wife, and the Baker's Little Boy," reflecting the popular notion that the king was responsible for providing bread for his people. The National Assembly, too, left Versailles for Paris. By putting the king and the Assembly under the pressure of popular political will, the women's march to Versailles changed the course of the French Revolution.

Reforming the Church and Clergy

In Paris, the National Assembly set about creating a constitution that would limit the authority of the king. The Assembly proclaimed Louis "the king of the French," instead of the king of France, a significant change that suggested that he embodied the sovereignty of his people. Alarmed by such changes, the king's brother, the count of Artois, went into exile after the October Days, and was soon followed by more than 20,000 other émigrés, most of whom were nobles, other people of means, and clergymen.

The Assembly turned its attention to reforming the Church. The decrees of August had ended the unpopular tithe payments to the Church, and now the Assembly looked to the Church's wealth to help resolve the state's mounting financial crisis. On October 10, Charles-Maurice de Talleyrand (1754–1838), bishop of Autun in Burgundy, proposed that Church property become "national properties" (*biens nationaux*). After the Assembly narrowly passed Talleyrand's measure on November 2, some 400 million francs in Church property—roughly 10 percent of the nation's land—began to be offered for sale at auction. The primary beneficiaries of the sale were urban bourgeois and prosperous peasants who could marshal enough cash to buy the land put up for sale.

To raise funds immediately, the Assembly issued paper money (known as *assignats*), which was backed by the value of the Church lands. Although the law required everyone to accept *assignats* in payment of debts, their value would fall dramatically because of a lack of public confidence, and those who used the assignats to purchase Church lands or pay debts received a windfall. Even poor peasants were thus able to reduce their debts with inflated currency. Among the consequences of the sale of Church lands (and, later, lands owned by noble émigrés) was that in some parts of France more land was brought under cultivation by peasants. The clearing of lands also put increased pressure on the environment as trees and brush were cleared to make room for crops and small-scale farming.

The Assembly also altered dramatically the status of the Church itself. On February 13, 1790, it decreed the abolition of the religious orders, deemed useless and politically suspect by many reformers. On July 12, the National Assembly passed the Civil Constitution of the French Clergy. The Assembly redefined the relationship between the clergy and the state, creating, in effect, a national church. Bishops, who could now only publish pronouncements with the authorization of the government, were to be elected by the electoral assembly at the departmental level. Ten days later, the king reluctantly accepted these measures affecting the Church.

The Church became essentially a department of the state, which henceforth would pay clerical salaries, the expenses of worship, and poor relief. In November 1790, the National Assembly proclaimed that all priests had to swear an oath of loyalty to the Revolution, and thus accept the Civil Constitution of the French Clergy. His authority directly challenged, Pope Pius VI denounced the Declaration of the Rights of Man and Citizen in March, and in April 1791 he condemned the Civil Constitution.

The Civil Constitution of the French Clergy altered the course of the Revolution, largely because it was widely resisted and contributed directly to the growth of a counter-revolutionary movement. Between one-half and two-thirds of parish priests refused the oath, and the Assembly prohibited these disloyal, "non-juring" priests from administering the Church sacraments. Nonetheless, many continued to do so with popular support. The issue of the oath split dioceses, parishes, and some households. In some provinces, violence mounted against "non-juring" priests; in others, refractory priests received popular support and protection. Generally speaking, the clergy of the west of France (particularly Brittany), the north, Alsace, and parts of the south, refused the Civil Constitution; in the rest of France, the clergy evinced at least formal acceptance of the Revolution. Such issues were no small matter, as many Catholics, Louis XVI among them, believed themselves obliged by faith to refuse to take sacraments from the "juring" clergy, that is, those who had taken the oath.

The Reforms of 1791

The Constitution of 1791 formalized the break with the Old Regime by substituting a constitutional monarchy for absolute rule. Although the king retained only the power of a suspending veto, he would still direct foreign policy and command the army. Acts of war or peace, however, required the Assembly's approval.

But France was far from being a republic. In sweeping away the Old Regime, the Revolution had redefined the relationship between the individual and the state by stripping away hereditary legal privileges. Although all citizens were to be equal before the law, the Assembly having in June 1790 abolished titles of hereditary nobility, the Assembly carefully distinguished between "active" and "passive" citizens. Only "active citizens,"

The three estates hammering out the next constitution.

men paying the equivalent of three days' wages in direct taxes, had the right to vote in indirect elections—they would vote for electors, wealthier men, who in turn would select representatives to a new legislature (see Map 12.1). Critics such as Marat and the populist orator Georges-Jacques Danton (1759–1794) denounced the restrictive franchise, claiming that the Assembly had merely replaced the privileged caste of the Old Regime with another by substituting the ownership of property for noble title as the criterion for political rights. Rousseau himself would have been ineligible to vote.

In Europe, religious discrimination still characterized many states. In Britain, English Dissenters and Catholics could not hold public office and were excluded from certain professions; in Hungary and the Catholic Rhineland, on the other hand, it was Protestants who faced discrimination. Jews faced intolerance and persecution in much of Europe, excluded, for example, from certain occupations or forced to live in specially designated places. In some parts of Eastern Europe and Ukraine, they suffered violence as well.

Now the National Assembly granted citizenship and civil rights to Protestants and Jews by laws in 1790 and 1791 (Protestants had already been granted civil rights in 1787). The Assembly abolished guilds, declaring each person "free to do such business and to exercise such profession, art or trade as he may choose." It subsequently passed the Le Chapelier law on June 14, 1791, prohibiting workmen from joining together to refuse to work for a master. This law was a victory for proponents of free trade. The Assembly also passed laws affecting the family: establishing civil marriage, lowering the age of consent for marriage, permitting divorce proceedings, and specifying that inheritances be divided equally among children.

The National Assembly abolished slavery in France, but not in the colonies. This exception led to a rebellion by free blacks on the Caribbean island of Hispaniola in October 1790 against the French sugar plantation owners, many of whom were nobles. It was led by Toussaint L'Ouverture (1743–1803), himself a former slave who had fought in the French army. The National Convention (which would replace the Assembly in September 1792) abolished slavery in the colonies in 1794, hoping that the freed slaves would fight against Britain. Half of Hispaniola—modern-day Haiti—became the first free black state.

In 1791, the call for equal rights for women was first made explicit in France when Olympe de Gouges (1755–1793), the daughter of a butcher, published *The Rights of Women*. "The law," she wrote, "must be the expression of the general will; all female and male citizens must contribute either personally or through their representatives to its formation." Encouraging women to demand their natural rights—and thereby evidencing the influence of the Enlightenment—she called on the Assembly to acknowledge women's rights as mothers of citizens of the nation. She

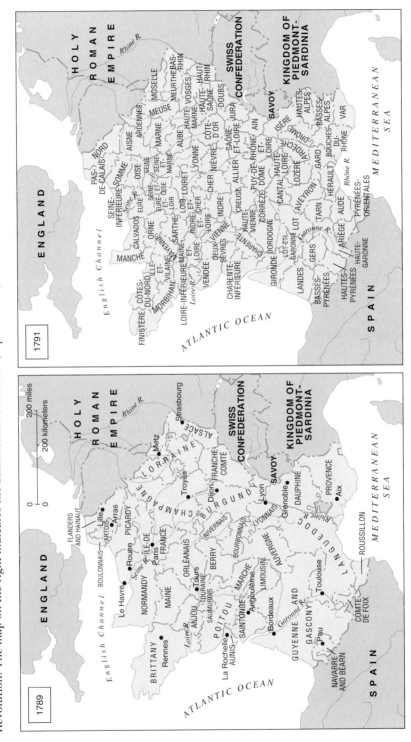

MAP 12.1 FRANCE BEFORE AND AFTER 1789 The map on the left indicates the provinces and provincial capitals in France before the Revolution. The map on the right indicates the administrative districts (*départements*) created in France in 1790.

insisted on women's right to education and to control property within marriage and to initiate divorce proceedings. She defined the nation as "the union of Woman and Man." She suggested that men would remain unfree unless women were granted similar rights: "Enslaved man," she wrote, "has multiplied his strength and needs recourse to yours to break his chains." The concept of "republican motherhood" emerged, stopping short of demanding full political rights for women.

Resistance and Revolution

On July 14, 1790, the first anniversary of the fall of the Bastille, an imposing Festival of General Federation took place on the Champ de Mars, a royal parade ground in Paris. But there was no revolutionary consensus in France. In the south, nobles had already begun to organize resistance against the Revolution, and militant Catholics attacked Protestants, who tended to support the Revolution. By the summer of 1791, as the Assembly promulgated its constitution, open resistance to the Revolution had broken out in parts of the south and west, and in Alsace in the east.

Such resistance prompted further calls for even more radical changes. Some of the revolutionaries, who did not accept the distinction between active and passive citizens, called for more democratic participation in political life. From where did this democratic thrust come? We have seen that the monarchical state had rested on an intertwining network of groups—each with a set of privileges—at virtually every level of society. These included judicial, professional, administrative, and clerical groups, ranging from provincial estates to artisanal guilds. Participatory and sometimes even democratic procedures within such bodies (or *corps*), may have instilled a tendency towards democracy that affected the course of the Revolution and pushed France toward a republic.

A female sans-culotte.

The first clubs were established by political factions among the deputies to the National Assembly. Some of the Assembly's most radical members split off to form the Jacobin Club, so-called because it met in the house of the religious order of the Jacobins. The Cordeliers Club brought together the radicals of Paris, while supporters of the cause of constitutional monarchy, whose members had broken with the Jacobins in July 1791 gathered at the Club of the Feuillants. Monarchists formed royalist clubs. Moreover, some women began their own political clubs, such as the Club of Knitters, or joined the Fraternal Society of Patriots of Both Sexes. By 1793, there were at least 5,000 clubs in France, struggling to help determine the political course of the Revolution in each region.

During the first years of the Revolution, there was little in France that was not political. The political clubs were not the only place where political debate occurred. In Paris, there were also meetings of neighborhood "sections," which had first been defined as electoral districts for the convocation of the Estates-General.

Parisian revolutionaries became increasingly known as sans-culottes. They defined themselves by what they were without—the fancy knee britches, or *culottes*, which were associated with the aristocracy. The sans-culottes were shopkeepers, artisans, and

King Louis XVI wearing the Phrygian cap.

laborers who were not opposed to private property, but who stood against unearned property, and especially against those people who seemed to have too much property, or who, living from rents, did not work for a living. They demanded that a maximum price be placed on bread, which alone absorbed more than half of the earnings of the average working family. Sans-culottes were for the Revolution, for "the people," as they put it. They were defined by their political behavior. Even aristocrats could be sans-culottes if they supported the Revolution. Likewise, laborers or peasants could be called "aristocrats" if they seemed to oppose the Revolution. In a world in which symbols played a crucial political role, sans-culottes could be identified by the Phrygian cap, a symbol of freedom drawn from the Roman Republic—close-fitting, red in color, with a tricolor emblem—in contrast to the three-cornered hat that had been worn by urban social elites. The language of the sans-culottes also quickly indicated who they were; they called everyone "citizen," and used the familiar (*tu* and never *vous*), egalitarian form of address. The political ideal of the sans-culottes was that popular sovereignty had to be practiced every day in direct democracy, in revolutionary clubs and in the sections.

The Flight to Varennes

Fearing the growing violence of the Revolution and counting on the support of the other monarchs of Europe, Louis XVI and his family tried to flee France in June 1791. The king's goal was to throw his support behind the foreign enemies of the Revolution and return to France to dismantle the concessions that had been made. Apprehended by the National Guard in Varennes after being sighted near the French border, however, the royal family was prevented from continuing their journey into exile and freedom.

The king's attempt to flee turned public sentiment further against him, and strengthened support for a republic. The day after his flight, the Cordeliers Club called for the establishment of a republic, but the majority of the Assembly feared civil war. On July 17, 1791, at the Champ de Mars in Paris, people came to sign (or put their "X" on) a petition resting on the "Altar of the Fatherland" that called on the National Assembly to replace the king "by all constitutional means." The National Guard opened fire, killing fifty people. Jean-Sylvain Bailly, the moderate mayor of Paris, and the Marquis de Lafayette, the increasingly disenchanted commander of the National Guard in Paris, declared martial law; Jean-Paul Marat and Georges-Jacques Danton went temporarily into hiding. Even Louis XVI's formal acceptance of the Constitution on September 14, 1791, could not stem the popular tide against the monarchy.

WAR AND THE SECOND REVOLUTION

The Revolution now entered a new, more radical phase. The king's flight seriously weakened the constitutional monarchists within the Assembly. The leaders of the Parisian population—Danton, Marat, and Maximilien Robespierre—were Jacobins who had given up on the idea that a constitutional monarchy could adequately guarantee the liberties of the people.

(*Left*) Georges-Jacques Danton. (*Right*) Maximilien Robespierre.

The newly elected Legislative Assembly met on October 1, 1791, replacing the Constituent Assembly, which had dissolved following the proclamation of the Constitution the previous month. Republicans—now identified with the "left" as monarchists were with the "right," due to the location of the seats each group occupied in the Assembly—became a majority in March 1792.

In the meantime, French émigrés at the Austrian and Prussian courts were encouraging foreign intervention to restore Louis XVI to full monarchical authority. The republican followers of Jacques-Pierre Brissot (1754–1793), former radical pamphleteer and police spy as well as a flamboyant orator, called for a war to free Europe from the tyranny of monarchy and nobility. The members of this faction became known as the Girondins because many were from the department, or district, of the Gironde in which the Atlantic port of Bordeaux is located. Under Girondin leadership, the Assembly's proclamations took on a more aggressive tone. The French declaration of war against Austria led to the Second Revolution, the formation of a republic, and, ultimately, a Jacobin-dominated dictatorship, which imposed the "Terror."

Reactions to the French Revolution in Europe

The French Revolution had a considerable impact on the rest of Europe even before French armies marched into adjoining states proclaiming the dawning of an era of "liberty, equality, and fraternity." The early work of the National Assembly, particularly the abolition of feudal rights and the establishment of a constitutional monarchy, attracted immediate attention and found considerable favor among educated people in Britain, the Netherlands, and some German and Italian states. Some lawyers and merchants in other lands applauded, for example, measures taken to reduce the independence of the Catholic Church. The promulgation of the principles of national sovereignty and self-determination, however, threatened the monarchies of Europe. The European powers had often gone to war against France over the past century, beginning with Louis XIV's relentless wars in pursuit of dynastic territorial aggrandizement. The threat posed by the French Revolution brought about a rapprochement between Austria and Prussia, rivals for domination in Central Europe, as well as a wary alliance between Great Britain and Russia.

The Prussian government's first reaction to the Revolution had been to try to subvert the alliance between France and Austria and to undermine Austrian authority in the Southern Netherlands (Belgium). In Vienna, the Habsburg Emperor Leopold II was initially preoccupied with demands from the Hungarian nobility for more power. In 1789, a rebellion drove Austrian forces out of the Southern Netherlands and led to the establishment of a republic that survived only until Austrian troops invaded as winter approached in 1790.

Olympe de Gouges (*left*), whose book *The Rights of Women* was published in France in 1791. It detailed the notion of equal rights that Mary Wollstonecraft (*right*) would take up the next year in England with the publication of her *Vindication of the Rights of Woman*.

In London, some radical Whigs greeted with enthusiasm the news of the fall of the Bastille and the first steps toward constitutional monarchy in France. But in 1790, the British writer Edmund Burke attacked the Revolution in *Reflections on the Revolution in France*. He contended that the abstract rationalism of the Enlightenment threatened the historic evolution of any nation by undermining its monarchy, its established church, and what he considered the "natural" ruling elite.

The Englishman Thomas Paine (1737–1809; see Chapter 11) wrote pamphlets denouncing monarchical rule and unwarranted privilege. *The Rights of Man* (1791–1792) defended the Revolution against Burke's relentless attack. Political societies supporting the Revolution sprang up in Britain during the early 1790s, composed mainly of artisans.

A small group of English women also enthusiastically supported the Revolution. Mary Wollstonecraft (1759–1797), a teacher and writer, greeted the Revolution with optimism, traveling to France to view events firsthand. She expressed confidence that the Revolution would lead to a republic that would respect the rights of men and women alike. Angered that the Assembly limited the right to education to men only, she published *Vindication of the Rights of Woman* (1792), the first book in Britain that demanded the right for women to vote and hold elected office. The book was an opening salvo in Britain in the struggle for equality of the sexes.

The rulers of the other European states felt threatened by the proclamation of universal principles embodied in the Declaration of the Rights of Man and Citizen. The Revolution also posed the threat of French expansion, now on behalf of carrying the revolutionary principles of "liberty, equality, and fraternity" to other lands. Besieged by exiles from France eager to tell tales of their suffering, the rulers of Prussia, Austria, Naples, and Piedmont undertook the suppression of Jacobin sympathizers in their states. In Britain, the seeming threat of foreign invasion helped forge, principally but not exclusively among the upper classes, a sense of British national identity (see Chapter 11). Popular respect for the British monarchy and probably also for the nobility seems to have soared as anti-French and anti-Catholic feelings came to the fore as scarcity increased fear of revolution. Pitt the Younger's government lashed out at the development of popular politics in Britain, suspending the freedoms of association, assembly, and the press, as well as the writ of *habeas corpus*. "Coercion Acts" facilitated the arrest of those advocating parliamentary reform.

Thus, Louis XVI's virtual imprisonment in the Tuileries Palace in Paris and the thunderous speeches in the Assembly proclaiming the necessity of "a war of peoples against kings" worried the crowned heads of Europe. On August 27, 1791, Emperor Leopold II of the Holy Roman Empire (brother of Marie Antoinette, who had not seen him in twenty-five years) and King Frederick William II of Prussia promulgated the Declaration of Pilnitz. It expressed their concern about the plight of the French monarchy and stated the common interest of both sovereigns in seeing order restored in France. Despite Robespierre's speeches warning the deputies that the Revolution must first deal with its enemies within France before waging war abroad, the Assembly, egged on by General Charles François Dumouriez (1739–1823), who was minister of foreign affairs, in April 1792 declared war on Austria. The stated reason was fear that an Austrian invasion from the Southern Netherlands was imminent. The declaration of war soon seemed a rash move, as the army had been devastated by the desertion of two-thirds of its officers (85 percent of its officers had been nobles before the Revolution) and Prussia soon joined with Austria in fighting the French. The early stages of the war produced French defeats at the hands of Austrian and Prussian armies.

A Second Revolution

The war greatly influenced the course of the Revolution by sealing the fate of the monarchy and the royal family. As France faced the possibility of foreign invasion by Austria and Prussia, the popular fear that aristocrats and clergymen were betraying the Revolution eventually brought down the monarchy. Early defeats on the northern frontier by Austrian troops and soaring bread prices (in part due to the requisitioning of food for the army) compounded popular anxiety and led to a new revolutionary groundswell, particularly in Paris.

In early April 1792, women from the plebeian districts of Paris marched through the capital demanding the right to bear arms. On June 20, a crowd stormed into the Tuileries Palace and threatened the royal family, shouting, "Tremble, tyrants! Here come the sans-culottes!" Strident calls for the end of the monarchy echoed in clubs and in the sections. On July 11, the Assembly officially proclaimed the *patrie,* or nation, to be "in danger," calling on all citizens to rally against the enemies of liberty within as well as outside of France. The Assembly encouraged the sections to admit the "passive" citizens who had previously been excluded because they had failed to meet tax requirements. Troops from Marseille, among federal volunteers called up to defend the front, sang a new revolutionary song, "The Marseillaise," penned by Rouget de Lisle for the Army of the Rhine. It became the anthem of the Revolution. In the meantime, the Jacobins pressed their attack against the monarchy.

In the Brunswick Manifesto (July 1792), Austria and Prussia warned the French that they would be severely punished if the royal family were harmed. All but one of the forty-eight sections of Paris responded by demanding that the king be immediately deposed. Popular discontent and Jacobin agitation came together in August. A radical committee overthrew the city council and established a revolutionary authority, the Commune of Paris, on August 9, naming Antoine-Joseph Santerre, a brewer, commander of the National Guard. On August 10, sans-culottes from the Paris sections attacked the Tuileries Palace. The invaders killed 600 of the king's Swiss Guards and servants after they had surrendered. The royal

The September Massacre of 1792 in the abbey of Saint-Germain-des-Prés in Paris.

family escaped and found protection in the quarters of the Legislative Assembly. The Assembly immediately proclaimed the monarchy suspended and ordered the royal family's imprisonment. A radical municipal authority, or "commune," constituted itself in Paris.

The popular revolution doomed France's first experiment in constitutional monarchy. On September 2, 1792, a Prussian army entered French territory and captured the eastern fortress town of Verdun. The proximity of the allied armies and the fear of betrayal at home led to the imprisonment in Paris of many people suspected of plotting against the Revolution. When a rumor circulated that the prisoners were planning to break out of prison and attack the army from the rear, mobs dragged the prisoners from their cells and killed them. During these September Massacres, more than 1,200 people, including 225 priests, perished at the hands of crowds who acted as judges, juries, and executioners.

But just as Paris seemed vulnerable to foreign invasion, a ragtag army of regular soldiers and sans-culottes stopped the Prussian and Austrian advance with effective artillery barrages on September 20, 1792, near the windmill of Valmy, east of Châlons-sur-Marne. The German poet Johann Wolfgang von Goethe, amazed by the victory of such ordinary people over a highly trained professional army, wrote, "From this time and place a new epoch is beginning." An officer trained under the Old Regime called the resultant warfare of the revolutionary armies a "hellish tactic," which saw "fifty thousand savage beasts foaming at the mouth like cannibals, hurling themselves at top speed upon soldiers whose courage has been excited by no passion."

The Revolution had been saved by the same people who had first made it. Delegates to a new assembly called the National Convention were selected by universal male suffrage in elections dominated by Jacobins (with a very low turnout, perhaps because the radicals had used scare tactics to keep moderates and royalist sympathizers from voting). The delegates arrived in Paris to draft a republican constitution. Their first act was unanimously to abolish the monarchy and proclaim the republic on September 21, 1792, before news of Valmy had been learned.

The revolutionary armies of proud, loyal citizen-soldiers, however badly armed, pushed Prussian troops across the Rhine and entered Mainz on October 21. On November 6, Dumouriez defeated the Austrians at Jémappes, north of Mons in the Austrian Netherlands. The French revolutionary armies soon controlled all of the Austrian Netherlands (see Map 12.2).

Emboldened by these unexpected military successes, the National Convention on November 19, 1792, promised "fraternity and assistance to all peoples who want to recover their liberty." French troops captured Frankfurt and occupied much of the Rhineland. The Convention also declared the outright annexation of the Alpine province of Savoy, belonging to the Kingdom of Sardinia, and the Mediterranean town of Nice, captured at the end of September. They declared them within the "natural frontiers"

MAP 12.2 EXPANSION OF REVOLUTIONARY FRANCE, 1792–1799   The map indicates French revolutionary army offensives and foreign anti-revolutionary army offensives. It also shows areas annexed by the French, areas occupied by the French, and dependent republics established by revolutionary France.

of France—a claim that contradicted the principles of popular sovereignty and self-determination contained in the annexation decrees themselves. In the Austrian Netherlands, the imposition of the new French administrative structure and the creation of Jacobin Clubs failed to win much support, despite the fact that an insurrection against Austrian rule had occurred there in 1791. On December 15, 1792, the Convention abolished all feudal dues and tithes in those territories occupied by French armies.

The governments of Britain and the Dutch Republic viewed the occupation of the Austrian Netherlands as a great threat to their interests. When it appeared that both states were considering joining Austria and Prussia in taking action against France, the Convention on February 1, 1793, declared war on Britain and the Dutch Republic. Spain and the Kingdoms of Sardinia and Naples joined this First Coalition against France.

When correspondence between the king and the Austrian government was discovered, the trial of Louis XVI became inevitable. Accused of treason, the king defended himself with grace and dignity. He called on the Convention to look after the needs of his family as he had tried to watch over those of France. But with the words "one cannot reign innocently" ringing in the hall, the Convention condemned the king to death. On the morning of January 21, Louis XVI was guillotined on the Place de la Révolution (as the Place de la Concorde was then called). The huge throng roared its approval as the executioner held up the severed royal head, symbol of the Old Regime, for all to see.

As the Convention and the Paris Commune vied for authority, the French Republic, under continuing attack from beyond its borders, began to split apart. In Paris and the provinces, the Girondins and the Jacobins quarreled bitterly. The Girondins were popularly identified with the economic liberalism that characterized the port cities and with the desire to carry the Revolution aggressively beyond the frontiers of France. Opposed to centralizing power in Paris, they wanted a significant degree of local

The execution of Louis XVI.

political control. The deputies of the far left, principally the Jacobins and their followers, sat on the raised side of the Tuileries Hall where the Convention met. The far left became known as "the Mountain" (their followers the *Montagnards*). The political center became known as "the Plain." Backed by the Parisian sans-culottes, the Jacobins insisted on the necessity of centralizing authority in the capital to save the Revolution from internal treason and foreign defeat. The Girondins were moderates who believed that the Revolution had gone far enough. The Jacobins accused the Girondins of secretly supporting the monarchy and demanded swift punishment for traitors.

From the point of view of the Jacobins, those who were not for them were against the Revolution. The sense of vulnerability and insecurity was heightened by reverses in the field. The armies of the First Coalition defeated the French in the Austrian Netherlands in March 1793. Dumouriez then betrayed the Revolution, preparing to march his soldiers to Paris to put Louis XVI's son on the throne as Louis XVII. When his army refused to follow him, Dumouriez fled across the border to join the Austrians and other émigrés. In the meantime, the allies recaptured the left bank of the Rhine River.

Counter-Revolution

The Counter-Revolution began in regions where religious practice still seemed strong and where the Civil Constitution of the French Clergy had met with considerable resistance (see Map 12.3). A full-scale insurrection against the Revolution began in March 1793. This revolt in the western part of France became known as the Vendée, after the name of one of the most insurrectionary districts. In August 1793, the revolutionary government decreed mass conscription, the *levée en masse*, which initiated the concept of the nation at arms: "Young people will go to battle; married men will forge arms and transport supplies; women will make tents, uniforms, and serve in the hospitals; children will pick rags; old men will have themselves carried to public squares, to inspire the courage of the warriors, and to preach hatred of kings and the unity of the Republic." The unpopularity of military conscription in defense of the republic also generated resistance. Both sides fought with a brutality, including mass executions and systematic pillage, that recalled the Thirty Years' War (1618–1648) in Central Europe.

South of the Loire River, the counter-revolutionary forces principally emerged from the relatively isolated bocage, or hedgerow country, where the old noble and clerical elites had been relatively unaffected by the economic changes of the past few decades, specifically the expansion of the market economy. In Brittany, which had enjoyed a relatively light tax burden during the Old Regime, the revolutionary government was hated for

MAP 12.3 THE COUNTER-REVOLUTION   The map indicates areas of federalism and counter-revolutionary activity, including major uprisings.

having ended that privilege, thereby increasing taxes. Under such conditions, the Counter-Revolution won the allegiance of many people.

The Terror

Facing foreign invasion and civil insurgency, the Jacobins further centralized government authority and implemented the "Terror" against those considered enemies of the Revolution. The Convention set aside a planned Constitution of 1793 (which was to have replaced the Constitution of 1791). The apparatus of the Terror included laws reducing the rights of the accused, the establishment of special courts, and the prosecution of those considered disloyal. On March 19, 1793, the Convention passed a law permitting the immediate trial of armed insurgents without a jury. A week later, the Convention established a Committee of Public Safety of nine and then twelve members, which gradually assumed more and more power as it oversaw the Terror. The Convention also decreed a special war tax, including a forced levy on wealthy people, and in May 1793 imposed a maximum price on grain. These measures of centralization and government interference in the economy led to an irreversible break between the Jacobins, who believed in state controls, and the Girondins, who believed in economic freedom.

Military requisitions of foodstuffs accentuated hardship. Poor people rioted against the high price of grain. More Jacobin Clubs sprang up in the provinces. In Paris, the Society of Revolutionary Republican Women took to the streets, demanding laws against hoarding and calling for women to be granted citizenship. Another group, called the "enraged" (*enragés*), demanded that bakers be penalized if they charged more than the maximum price for bread.

In June, pushed on by crowds from the radical sections of Paris, the Convention expelled twenty-nine Girondin deputies, accusing them of supporting hoarders, and it ordered the arrest of some of them. In Paris, Dumouriez's betrayal of the revolutionary cause added to the tension. Insurgents in Toulon turned over half of the French fleet to the British. In July, Charlotte Corday, a royalist noblewoman, stabbed Jean-Paul Marat to death in his bathtub. Tax revenue and foreign trade fell by half. *Assignats*, more of which had rolled off the government presses as the financial crisis continued, plunged further in value.

Two young radical Jacobin leaders strode forward to take charge of the Terror. Louis Antoine Saint-Just (1767–1794), a precocious, icy young deputy whose mother had once had him incarcerated by *lettre de cachet* in Paris for running off with the family silver, waged war on royalists, hoarders, and Girondins. "Those who make revolutions by halves dig their own grave," he warned.

Maximilien Robespierre (1758–1794) emerged as the leading figure on the Committee of Public Safety. He knew that the Mountain drew its support from the sans-culottes, some of whom supported the Terror. But he also believed that the popular movement remained a threat to the orderly transformation of political life in France. Historians have offered interpretations of Robespierre that range from the view that he was a popular democrat who saved the essence of the Revolution from counter-revolutionaries to the suggestion that he was actually a precursor of twentieth-century totalitarianism.

Robespierre was the son and grandson of lawyers from the northern town of Arras. After his irresponsible father abandoned his family, Robespierre depended on scholarships for his schooling. At age eleven, he was chosen to read an address in Latin to the royal family at his school in Paris. It was raining and the royal family, it was said, without acknowledging the young student, ordered their driver onward. The royal coach splashed Robespierre with mud.

After completing his law degree, Robespierre defended a number of poor clients, including a man unjustly accused of stealing from an abbey. After he was elected to the third estate, Robespierre gradually established a reputation in Paris for his well-organized and thoughtful but colorless speeches. Contemporaries noted the prissiness of the impeccably dressed, slight man with very pale skin and chestnut hair always perfectly powdered. A favorite of the Parisian sans-culottes, the man they nicknamed "the Incorruptible" called in 1793 for "a single will" of the nation to save the Revolution; he would go on to play a dominant role in the Terror.

Insurrections by supporters of the Girondins against the Jacobins and the authority of the Convention broke out in Lyon, Marseille, Bordeaux, and Caen, where unlike in the counter-revolutionary west, merchants and lawyers played prominent roles in "federalist revolts" against centralized revolutionary authority emanating from Paris. Merchants and lawyers viewed the radicalization of the Revolution as a threat to their own control of political life. Lyon, France's second largest city, fell to Jacobin troops on October 9, 1793, and bloody reprisals followed.

The "Law of Suspects" promulgated by the Convention in September deprived those accused of crimes against the nation of most of their remaining rights. The Convention specifically banned clubs and popular societies of women. Olympe de Gouges was among the Girondins

Jacques-Louis David's representations of *The Death of Marat* (*left*) and Marie-Antoinette (*right*) awaiting her execution. Both the Jacobin leader and the Queen were ultimately victims of the Revolution.

A revolutionary tribunal during the Terror.

guillotined. Marie Antoinette, though hardly a feminist, also went to the scaffold.

The Jacobins were so intent on destroying the Old Regime and building a new political world that they instituted a new calendar in October 1793. The old calendar of twelve months and fifty-two weeks of seven days gave way to a new republican calendar based upon "weeks" or cycles of ten days and "months" taking their names from more secular notions of the changing of the seasons (such as *Germinal*, meaning "the budding," *Ventôse*, meaning "windy," and so on). September 22, 1792, the first year of the republic, became, retroactively, day one of the "year I."

The Jacobins adopted new revolutionary symbols to take the place of Old Regime symbols and to help maintain revolutionary enthusiasm. Following the execution of Louis XVI, the revolutionaries chose a female image for liberty and the republic, which was ironic in light of their denial of political rights to women. Unlike lusty and even pornographic images of Marie Antoinette, the female image of the republic appears gentle, nonthreatening, and virtuous, representing the abstract virtues of liberty, popular sovereignty, community, and nation. Contemporaries contrasted republican virtue with the abuses of power that seemed to have characterized the Old Regime. They did so even as Jacobin representatives of the Revolution imposed their will wherever they were resisted in the provinces.

During the "year II" (which began in September 1793), radical revolutionaries undertook an ambitious campaign of "de-christianization," a war on religious institutions and symbols. They closed down churches and removed crosses standing in public places. The campaign failed, unable to overcome centuries of firmly implanted traditions and beliefs, even among many people who supported the Revolution. "De-christianization" also turned many clergy who had accepted the Civil Constitution away from the Revolution, generating further resistance.

Outside of Paris, "representatives on mission," armed with dictatorial authority in the name of the Convention, tried to maintain order. They worked with local "surveillance committees" and "revolutionary tribunals" of Jacobins. Some of these revolutionary officials sent counter-revolutionaries to the guillotine. "Revolutionary armies" of artisans and day laborers guarded requisitioned provisions for the military and oversaw the melting down of church bells for war use.

Yet the Terror was never uniformly implemented. Between 11,000 and 18,000 people perished at the hands of the Committee of Public Safety (a fraction, by comparison, of the deaths that had resulted from the Thirty Years' War or the American Civil War). About 300,000 royalists, Girondins, or other "enemies of the Revolution" were imprisoned for some period during the Terror. About 15 percent of those killed were nobles or clergy. Thus, nobles and clergy suffered disproportionately in terms of their number in the population as a whole (5 to 8 percent). However, artisans and peasants constituted by far the largest number of those dispatched by the revolutionary tribunals. The majority of these were arrested near the northern and eastern frontiers that had been invaded by foreign armies or in the counter-revolutionary west where civil war raged. During the winter of 1793–1794, perhaps as many as several thousand prisoners—including priests and nuns—captured from the counter-revolutionary armies of the Vendée were taken out into the swirling waters of the Loire River in boats that had holes bored in them and drowned at the orders of a cruel revolutionary official.

In the meantime, the tide of the war had turned in favor of the aggressive French armies. Some significant French victories on the battlefield undercut the argument that the Terror was necessary because of the immediate external threat to the Republic. A French army defeated the Austrians in the Austrian Netherlands in June 1794, forcing them out of Belgium. Another French force reached the Rhine River and captured Mainz. A third French army recaptured Savoy from the kingdom of Sardinia. The Spanish army retreated across the Pyrenees Mountains.

The Terror struck the *enragés* leaders in March 1794 after they demanded even more economic controls and an intensification of the "de-christianization" campaign. They were brought before the Revolutionary Tribunal, condemned, and guillotined. The Committee of Public Safety then went after Danton and his followers, who believed that the Terror was no longer necessary, and thus had been labeled the "Indulgents." They too were condemned and guillotined. Real and imagined conspiracies provided the justification for the Terror, which now seemed without end. "Who will be next?" was whispered among even those loyal to the most radical members of the Committee of Public Safety. In May, Robespierre, the mastermind of the Terror, survived an assassination attempt.

Besides eliminating his enemies both at home and abroad, Robespierre sought to establish a secularized "Cult of the Supreme Being" that would serve as a "constant reminder of justice" to bind the people to the new values of republicanism. With the elimination of the *enragés* and the Dantonists, he was able to devote his energies to his Republic of Virtue. Thus, early in June 1794, the republic celebrated the "Festival of Reason." The cathedral of Notre Dame in Paris became a "temple of reason." A popular female opera singer, dressed as Liberty—the image of the republic—wearing a Phrygian cap and holding a pike, bowed down before the flame of reason. The painter Jacques-Louis David constructed huge statues of monsters like Anarchy and Atheism made of pasteboard. After Robespierre set fire to them, a statue of Wisdom rose out of the ashes. The Terror seemed to have taken on a momentum of its own. Saint-Just warned, "We must punish not merely traitors, but also the indifferent."

The Jacobins arrested the Marquis de Condorcet (1743–1794) for alleged counter-revolutionary activity and condemned him to death. Condorcet, an influential philosophe of the late Enlightenment, had been elected to the Assembly in 1791. He believed that all people should have a voice in approving acts of government, albeit indirectly, and that all citizens should be equal before the law. He had campaigned against the death penalty and slavery, and he defended political equality and the rights of women because he considered women fully capable of participating in political life. Condorcet died of apoplexy—or committed suicide—in his cell in the spring of 1794, shortly before he was to be executed. The Revolution seemed to have turned on and destroyed the enlightened reason that had arguably helped bring it about.

THE FINAL STAGES

Moderate Jacobins and other members of the Convention, fearing that they might be next in line to be purged, overthrew the Jacobin dictatorship. They established a new government called the Directory, which ended the Terror. Caught between staunch Jacobins on the left and monarchists on the right, the period of the Directory was marked by great political instability, shaped by ongoing wars abroad and economic hardship at home. Although the Directory consolidated some of the gains of the Revolution, it too would be overthrown by conspirators led by the Abbé Sieyès and one of the rising stars of the revolutionary army, General Napoleon Bonaparte.

Thermidor

The Revolutionary Tribunal was given new powers in June 1794, and it used them to send 1,300 people to their deaths over a period of six weeks. Afraid that they would be next on Robespierre's list, moderates in the Convention began to plot against Robespierre and his friends. They were led by Paul Barras (1755–1829), a follower of Danton, as well as by Joseph Fouché (1758–1820), an ultra-revolutionary Jacobin whom Robespierre did not trust. On July 27, 1794 (the 9th of Thermidor), he haltingly addressed the Convention, calling for one more purge. But, anticipating his own downfall, Robespierre also murmured, "I ask for death." That night, Robespierre, his brother Augustine, and Saint-Just were arrested at the virtually unguarded town hall of Paris. In an attempt to die the classical, stoic death of a hero, Robespierre shattered his own jaw with a shot.

Robespierre and the others were arrested, outlawed by the Convention, and executed without trial, their fate as swift and pitiless as that of the Terror's victims. They were followed to the scaffold by more than a hundred of their cohorts. Lazare Carnot (1753–1823), a talented military engineer, brilliant administrator ("the organizer of victory"), and one of the twelve members of the Committee of Public Safety, survived because he had opposed Robespierre. Moreover, the continuing war effort desperately required his administrative talent. In the provinces, particularly in the south, the revenge against the Jacobins by their enemies was swift and brutal.

After dismantling the Paris Commune, the victors of Thermidor—the name taken from the period in the revolutionary calendar in which Robespierre fell—set about establishing a new national government. Order was only slowly and incompletely restored in the countryside. The Thermidorians greatly reduced the powers of the Committee of Public Safety on July 31, 1794, and then abolished it completely. In November 1794, Jacobin Clubs were banned.

The Directory: Politics and Society

In 1795 the Thermidorians produced a Constitution, creating a bicameral (two-house) legislative assembly and a collective executive of five directors. The latter provided the name "the Directory" for this period of the Revolution. The two assemblies included the Council of the Ancients (250 members), which discussed and voted on legislation proposed by the second assembly, the Council of Five Hundred. Two-thirds of the members of the new councils were elected from among the members of the existing Convention. The two councils elected the five directors who formed the collective executive authority, or Directorate. Beginning in 1797, one-third of the members of each council and one of the five directors were to be replaced each year.

People of property benefited from the Thermidorian reaction. By the Constitution of 1795, all male taxpayers could vote, but they selected electoral assemblies for which only about 30,000 men were eligible, a smaller group than in the indirect elections of 1789–1791. But although about 2 million men could vote (out of some 7 million men of voting age), the system of indirect election favored the selection of the wealthiest citizens to serve in the assemblies.

The period of the Directory was marked by a decided turn against the asceticism associated with Robespierre's Republic of Virtue. The *jeunesse dorée,* or gilded youth, drawn from the bourgeoisie and old nobility, set the social and cultural tone of the day. Wearing square collars and fancy clothes, wealthy young men smashed busts of Marat and shut down theatrical performances favorable to the Jacobins. The red-colored symbols of the sans-culottes—such as the Phyrgian cap—quickly disappeared. Women who could afford to do so wore long flowing white robes of opulence and sensuality, with plunging necklines that would have horrified Robespierre. The familiar (*tu*) form of address, identified with section and club meetings, gave way to the formal *vous* more characteristic of the Old Regime. Crowds in which women played a prominent part demanded that churches be reopened. Boisterous social events amused the middle class; among them was the macabre "Dance of the Victims," a ball to which only those with a relative who had perished in the Terror could be admitted. Some revelers turned up with their hair cut away from the back

The return of high society during the Directory.

of their neck, mimicking the final haircut of those about to be sent to the guillotine.

Under the Directory, the comforts of the wealthy, some of whom had made their fortunes during the Revolution (by buying Church lands or supplying the military), contrasted sharply with the deprivations of the poor. The economy lay in shambles. The winter of 1795 was cruelly harsh. The abolition of the Maximum—the maximum price that could be charged for grain, set in May 1793—spelled the end of cheap bread, and the price of basic commodities soared. A load of firewood that cost 20 francs in 1790 required 500 francs in 1795. The price of bread rose by thirteen times in Paris that spring. Near Paris, people scrambled to eat the carcasses of dead army horses, and in mountainous areas people searched for berries and edible roots while trying to stay warm. The military requisition of food supplies weighed heavily on peasants.

Instability

The Directory may have ended the Terror, but it did not bring stability to France. Nor did the Directory bring peace. France remained at war despite the conclusion of peace agreements with Prussia in April 1795, in which the latter tacitly accepted the French annexation of the left bank of the Rhine River, the Austrian Netherlands, and the Dutch United Provinces, which became the "Batavian Republic." French armies continued to press forward against the Austrian armies in Central Europe and Italy. Meanwhile, mass desertion and heavy casualties drastically reduced the size of the French army, which, after reaching a million men in the summer of 1794, fell to less than 500,000 a year later.

War compounded the Directory's social and political instability in 1795. That spring, the Directory repressed two small popular demonstrations by crowds demanding a return to controls on the price of bread. Encouraged by the Convention's move to the right, royalists also tried to seize power. The king's son had died in a Paris prison in June 1795, and so the count of Provence, Louis XVI's brother, was now heir to the throne. He denounced the Revolution, making clear that he would never compromise with reforms enacted since 1789. An army of nobles supported by the British landed at Quiberon Bay in Brittany on June 27, but French forces turned back the invaders with ease. On October 5, 1795, royalists attempted an insurrection in Paris, where they found support in the more prosperous districts. The government called in Napoleon Bonaparte (1769–1821), a young Corsican general, who defeated the insurgents with a "whiff of grapeshot."

Instability continued nonetheless. François-Noël Babeuf (1760–1797), who was called Gracchus, plotted to overthrow the Directory. Influenced by Rousseau and espousing social egalitarianism and the common ownership of land, Babeuf concluded that a small group of

Napoleon's whiff of grapeshot disperses royalist insurgents, October 5, 1795.

committed revolutionaries could seize power if they were tightly organized and had the support of the poor. Some Marxist historians have considered him an early proponent of twentieth-century revolutionary political tactics. Following Thermidor, Babeuf organized the "Conspiracy of the Equals," finding support among a handful of Parisian artisans and shopkeepers. But the Directory's police were on their trail. In May 1796, Babeuf and his friends were arrested; they were guillotined a year later after a trial. The Directory took advantage of the discovery of this plot to purge the Jacobins once again.

Caught between the intransigent, dogmatic followers of Robespierre and the Jacobins on the left and the royalists on the right, and lacking effective and charismatic civilian leaders, the Directory's difficult tightrope act grew more precarious. Its leaders were caught in an atmosphere of intrigue and rumors of coups d'état, fraught with tensions between the directors themselves and the councils.

In 1797, elections returned a good many royalists to the Council of Five Hundred. Fearful that they might press for peace with France's enemies in the hope of obtaining a restoration of the monarchy, the Directory government annulled the election results. The coup d'état of the 18th of Fructidor (September 4, 1797) eliminated two of the directors, including Lazare Carnot. In May of the next year, the directors refused to allow recently elected deputies to take their seats on the Council of Five Hundred.

The wily Abbé Sieyès (who once replied "I survived" to the question of what he had done during the Revolution) became a director in the spring of 1799. He believed France needed a government with stronger executive authority. Because one revolutionary government after another had maintained an aggressive foreign policy, it had gradually become clear to Sieyès that the army would emerge as the arbiter of France's political future.

For all of its failures, the Directory did provide France with its second apprenticeship in representative government. The Constitution of 1795 was an important transition between the political system of the Old Regime, based primarily upon monarchical absolutism and noble privilege, and modern representative government grounded in the sanctity of property. It further preserved the centralized administration of the French state and made efforts to centralize education.

The Directory had rejected cautious British suggestions that a workable peace might be forged without France having to give up its conquests of the Rhineland and the Austrian Netherlands. Perhaps fearful that a more bellicose ministry in Britain might replace that of William Pitt the Younger if such a peace were signed, the French fought on.

Under the Directory, France's financial situation deteriorated even further. Inflation was rampant, and the collection of taxes was sporadic at best. *Assignats* were now virtually worthless. Many bourgeois were dissatisfied, having lost money when the Directory cancelled more than half of the national debt in 1797.

Napoleon Bonaparte, the victor over the royalist insurrection, now commanded the Army of Italy, checking in with Paris only when it suited him. His armies overwhelmed the Austrian troops in northern Italy. The fighting ended with the Treaty of Campo Formio (October 17, 1797), which left France in the position of having supplanted Austria as the dominant foreign power in Italy. This victory, and Napoleon's boldly independent diplomatic negotiations in the Italian campaigns, made him the toast of Paris. The Austrians joined the Prussians in recognizing French hegemony on the left bank of the Rhine River and in the Austrian Netherlands. Reorganized in July 1797 as the Cisalpine Republic, much of the north of Italy became a feeble pawn of France.

Despite these victories, years of war had exhausted the French nation and damaged the economy. Peace proved short-lived. In May 1798, Napoleon sailed with an army to Egypt, over which Turkey was sovereign; he hoped to strike at British interests in India. Fearing that France sought to break apart the Ottoman Empire and extend its interests in an area it had always wanted to dominate, Russia allied with Britain. Austria also joined the alliance, which became the Second Coalition (1799–1802). Austria hoped to undo the Treaty of Campo Formio and to prevent further French expansion in Italy, where French forces had sent the pope into exile and established a Roman Republic.

The combined strength of the Coalition powers for the moment proved too much for the overextended French armies in Italy. In Switzerland, a combined Russian and Austrian army defeated a French force. When Irish rebels rose up against British rule, France sent an invasion force that failed to reach Ireland—the logical jumping-off point for an invasion of England. In 1798, British troops crushed a series of Irish rebellions in a bloody struggle in which 30,000 people were killed, and British forces captured one of the French ships sent to aid the insurgents, turning back the rest.

Coalition members began to quarrel over strategy and eventual goals. Russian Tsar Paul (ruled 1796–1801) withdrew from the Second Coalition in October 1799, as he was irritated with the British for insisting that the Royal Navy had the right to stop and search any vessel on the seas. Nonetheless, after repelling an attack by a Russian and British force, French armies still held the Netherlands and the left bank of the Rhine River.

The Eighteenth Brumaire

In the face of endemic instability, Sieyès decided in 1799 to overthrow the Directory in a coup d'état. The go-between was Talleyrand, the foreign minister. The career of the former bishop provides another remarkable example of revolutionary survival; a detractor once claimed that Brie cheese was "the only king to whom he has been loyal." Sieyès contacted General Napoleon Bonaparte, whose successes and attention to the needs

A contemporary British caricature of the 18th of Brumaire. "The Corsican Crocodile dissolving the Council of Frogs!!!"

of his soldiers seemed to assure their support. Napoleon returned to France in October. On November 9, 1799 (the 18th Brumaire), General Bonaparte (who had been appointed military commander of the Paris region) announced to the hastily convened councils that another Jacobin conspiracy had been uncovered and that a new constitution had to be framed to provide France with a stronger executive authority. The deputies were justly dubious. Some demanded his immediate arrest. Napoleon's response was incoherent and ineffective, but the quick thinking of his brother, Lucien, president of the lower assembly, saved Bonaparte from one of his few moments of indecision. Lucien rejected the call for a vote to outlaw Napoleon, and he ordered troops to evict members who opposed him. Those who remained delegated complete power to Sieyès and General Bonaparte.

Many people believed that this latest coup would preserve a moderate republic. Others hoped that Bonaparte would provide an authoritarian government that would end the quarreling factions that dominated the political life of the Directory. To a contemporary, "The Revolution of the 18th Brumaire . . . appeared as pure and brilliant rays of sunshine after long and disastrous storms. One can even say that it has begun a new era."

PERSPECTIVES ON THE FRENCH REVOLUTION

The French Revolution, which began in Paris, swept across Europe. In France, it marked a significant break with the past, although, to be sure, important continuities from the Old Regime helped shape the modern world. In other countries, too, the Revolution effected major changes. These included in some places the abolition of feudalism, curtailment of clerical privileges, and a more centralized governmental structure. But while some people welcomed the export of the French Revolution, others did not. To the latter, liberation by the French seemed indistinguishable from conquest. The French presence engendered a patriotic response in Russia, Spain, and in some of the German and Italian states, contributing to the emergence of nationalist feeling there.

Like contemporaries viewing the Revolution, historians also have had a variety of different interpretations of it. Many of them still disagree as to the causes, effects, and significance of the Revolution, debating the dramatic events with some of the same passion as those who experienced it firsthand.

European Responses to the Revolution

Soldiers in the French revolutionary armies liked to think of themselves as liberating the rest of Europe from feudalism and oppression. During 1793–1794, at least, military successes and political propaganda convinced many if not most soldiers that they carried the cause of freedom on their shoulders along with their backpacks. But, at the same time, French soldiers accepted Thermidor with barely a murmur of regret for the end of the Jacobin period.

In other countries, some people at first viewed the French as liberators who would free them from the domination of nobles and the clutches of kings, nobles, and clergy. But, in fact, the line between a "liberator" and a "conqueror" was quite thin. Enthusiastic shouts for "liberty, fraternity, and equality!" echoed in German, Dutch, and Piedmontese, disappeared in a sea of French muskets, military requisitions, and even vandalism.

The revolutionary wave did bring about sweeping changes in some of the "liberated" territories, and these changes would continue as Napoleon consolidated his authority in France (see Chapter 13). Thus, in Piedmont, French control reduced the influence of the nobility and left a heritage of relative administrative efficiency. The abolition of feudalism in some of the conquered German states, northern Italy, and the Kingdom of Naples increased the number of property owners. The French conquerors proclaimed the rule of law and curtailed some of the influence of the clergy.

But the French faced the realities of almost constant warfare and, increasingly, resistance from the local population. As the wars dragged on and the economic situations of the "republics" grew worse, the benefits brought by the French seemed increasingly less important. Ruined merchants and former officials joined nobles and clerics in opposing rule by France or its puppets. As the Civil Constitution of the French Clergy led to a violent reaction against the Revolution in France, anticlerical measures in the occupied territories had the same effect. The peoples of the Rhineland, the Netherlands, and Flanders bitterly resented the revolutionaries' de-christianization campaign. Increasingly, the French presence bred contempt and hatred. Bavarian, Dutch, Piedmontese, Austrian, and Swiss patriots found willing listeners, while French propagandists heaped abuse on the local populations for their apparent disloyalty. Thus, the French occupation gave rise to general opposition and a new wave of national feeling among the conquered. Although Great Britain had not been directly threatened by French ambitions on the continent, the French Revolution also contributed to the accentuation of British nationalism in the face of a perceived threat by its old Catholic enemy in a new guise.

The French conquests in Europe were themselves an exercise in statemaking, largely unanticipated and unwanted by the local populations. Between 1795 and 1799, the Directory established satellite "sister republics" directly administered by France. The Helvetic Republic (Switzerland), the Batavian Republic (the Netherlands), the Cisalpine Republic (Milan), and the Parthenopean Republic (the Kingdom of Naples) were founded with the goal of shoring up alliances against the other great powers. But in the Italian states, only the Cisalpine Republic generated any local enthusiasm for the French invaders, and then only briefly. People "liberated" from the rule of kings and princes found themselves governed by a revolutionary bureaucracy controlled in Paris.

The French found support and hired officials principally from the middle class, which had already provided officials in the old state structure. But the French invasions gradually generated a hatred for the revolutionary invaders and in some places a concomitant nationalist response. This was especially true within the German states, where many writers and other people in the upper classes hoped one day that "Germany"—300 states, 50 free cities, and almost 1,000 territories of imperial knights of the Holy Roman Empire—would one day be politically unified.

Historians' Views of the Revolution

Marxist historians long dominated the historiography of the French Revolution. They have described the Revolution as the inevitable result of a bourgeois challenge to the Old Regime, dominated by nobles. Thus, Marxists have interpreted the Revolution in terms of the rise of the bourgeoisie and its struggle for social and political influence commensurate with its rising economic power during the eighteenth century. Marxists have insisted that the nobility compromised the authority of the absolute monarchy by refusing to be taxed; then, according to this interpretation, the emboldened bourgeoisie allied with urban artisans and workers to bring down the absolute monarchy. They have described the emergence of the bourgeoisie as the dominant social class in France, insisting on its growing role in the country's increasingly capitalist economy.

This traditional Marxist economic interpretation of the French Revolution has been widely criticized if not discredited. Some historians have noted that differences between aristocrats and bourgeois, and within both social groups, had become considerably blurred during the eighteenth century; that most of the "bourgeois" members of the Estates-General were not drawn from commerce and manufacturing but rather from law; and that, in any case, the upper middle class and nobles by the time of the Revolution shared a common obsession with money, not privilege. Thus, one cannot accurately depict the Revolution as having been simply a victory for the bourgeoisie. Moreover, revisionists have argued that the Revolution did not expedite capitalism but even retarded it, by launching France and Europe into a long series of costly wars.

Views critical of the "bourgeois revolution" thesis have also emphasized that within France the complex nature of local political power, divided among provincial estates and parlements, and among various groups enjoying formal privileges or monopolies and municipalities, served to limit the actual prerogatives of absolute monarchy. Many historians now see the Revolution as affirming the victory of men of property—a rubric that included both nobles and bourgeois—over titled nobles born into status and power.

A related interpretation has seen the Revolution as part of an essentially democratic "Atlantic Revolution" stretching across the Atlantic Ocean. By this view, the American War of Independence was the first manifestation of an essentially political quest for popular sovereignty. It influenced, in turn, the French Revolution and subsequent attempts in other European countries to gain political rights, as well as movements for independence in Spain's Latin American colonies early in the nineteenth century.

More recently, another revisionist school has argued that a new political culture was already in place in the last decades of the Old Regime. An extreme version of this interpretation sees the French monarchy as a state well on the way to reforming itself through the collaboration of liberal nobles before the Revolution interrupted this process. One view looks to the 1750s and 1760s for the origins of this new, revolutionary political culture, seen in the political and ideological opposition to Louis XV and particularly in the rhetorical violence of the Revolution's first year.

None of these varying interpretations, however, diminishes the significance of the French Revolution in transforming the Western world by providing its first modern democratic experience. This is why its origins and nature continue to generate excitement and debate today well more than 200 years after the fall of the Bastille.

CHAPTER 13

NAPOLEON AND EUROPE

The royalist, religious writer François-René de Chateaubriand once called his enemy Napoleon "the mightiest breath of life which has ever animated human clay." In a rare moment of introspection, Napoleon once said, "It is said that I am an ambitious man but that is not so; or at least my ambition is so closely bound to my being that they are both one and the same."

Yet, far more than his imposing will, Napoleon's career was shaped by and reflected the breathtaking changes brought by the French Revolution. Statemaking and the emergence of nationalism, accompanied by the increased secularization of political institutions, slowly but surely transformed the European continent. Because Napoleon helped overthrow the Directory (1794–1799) and transformed France into an empire, the question of whether Napoleon was the heir or the undertaker of the French Revolution is an important one.

An admirer of the Enlightenment, Napoleon claimed that he was the true son of the French Revolution. He personally supervised the writing of the new constitution, which made wealth, specifically propertied wealth, the determinant of status. Napoleon's reign was also a watershed in French statemaking: he further centralized the French state and extended its reach, making it more efficient by codifying laws and creating new bureaucratic structures and a new social hierarchy based upon state service.

Napoleon saw himself as a savior who carried "liberty, equality, and fraternity" abroad, freeing the European peoples from sovereigns who oppressed them. From his final exile on the distant Atlantic island of Saint Helena, Napoleon claimed to have created European unity. But in the process of "liberating" other nations from the stranglehold of the Old Regime, he also conquered them.

Antoine-Jean Gros's painting of the young Napoleon in *Bonaparte at Arcole* (1796).

NAPOLEON'S RISE TO POWER

Napoleon's rise to power would have been unthinkable had it not been for the Revolution. With the emigration of most of the officer corps during the early stages of the Revolution, a generation of talented generals had risen rapidly through the ranks by virtue of their remarkable battlefield accomplishments during the revolutionary wars that had raged across much of Western and Central Europe since 1792. During the Directory, generals became increasingly powerful arbiters in political life. Napoleon manipulated the consuls and ultimately overthrew the Directory.

The Young Bonaparte

Of the strategically important Mediterranean island of Corsica, Jean-Jacques Rousseau in *The Social Contract* (1762) wrote, "I have a presentiment that one day this small island will astonish Europe." The year before, the Corsican patriot Pascale di Paoli (1725–1807) had managed to evict the Genoese from Corsica. But in 1768 the French took Corsica. Carlo Buonaparte, one of Paoli's followers, remained on the island rather than join Paoli in exile in England.

On August 15, 1769, Buonaparte's wife, whose family could trace its noble origins back to fourteenth-century Lombardy, gave birth to a son, Napoleon, named after a cousin who had been killed by the French. It is one of the strange ironies of history that Napoleon would have been British had his father followed Paoli into exile. In 1770, the French government accepted the Buonaparte family as nobles. The island's governor arranged for the young Buonaparte to receive an appointment to the royal military school at Brienne, in Champagne, which Napoleon entered as a boy in 1779. There he was exposed not only to a rigorous program of study but also to the humiliating condescension of the other students. They mocked his strong Corsican accent and his relatively humble economic situation. He fought back. Even in the winter snowball fights, Napoleon showed a remarkable determination to succeed. Napoleon had gray eyes, chestnut-colored hair, and a pale complexion. Of average height and barrel-chested, he became increasingly corpulent as the years passed.

Unusually bright, he earned appointment to the artillery section of the national military academy in Paris, passing the examinations in a single year.

Napoleon and the Revolution

With the outbreak of the Revolution, Napoleon returned in September 1789 to Corsica. There he helped organize the National Guard and drew up a petition to the National Assembly in Paris asking that Corsica formally become part of France, with its people enjoying the rights of citizenship. In this way, Napoleon clearly distanced himself from those Corsicans who wanted independence, thus parting ways with his hero Paoli, who had returned from England and joined the island's royalists. Napoleon favored the Revolution for three reasons: he wanted to see a curtailment of the abuses of the Old Regime; he hoped that the Revolution might end his island's status within France as little more than a conquered territory; and he thought the Revolution might provide him with an opportunity for promotion.

Napoleon became a Jacobin. He commanded a volunteer force that on Easter Sunday, 1792, fired on rioters supporting the cause of the Catholic Church. When Paoli's victorious forces turned the island over to the English, the Buonapartes were forced to flee. Sent by the Committee of Public Safety to fight federalist and royalist rebels and their British allies in the south, in December 1793 Napoleon planned the successful artillery siege of the port of Toulon, which was held by British forces.

Useful political connections and the lack of direct involvement in the bitter factional struggles in Paris may have saved Napoleon from execution in the Terror or during Thermidor. The result was that Napoleon's star continued to rise, while some of his Jacobin friends went to the guillotine. In the Paris of Thermidor, Napoleon helped put down a royalist uprising on October 6, 1795, with a "whiff of grapeshot." He attracted the attention of—and soon married—Joséphine de Beauharnais, the lover of the corrupt Paul Barras, one of the directors, and the widow of a member of the National Assembly who had been guillotined during the Terror. In 1796, the directors made Napoleon commander of the Army of Italy. It now seemed appropriate to eliminate the Italian spelling of his name; Buonaparte became Napoleon Bonaparte. Spectacular successes against the Austrians and their allies in Italy made him the toast of Paris. He later recalled that after victory over Austrian forces at the battle of Lodi, which opened the way to Milan, "I realized I was a superior being and conceived the ambition of performing great things, which hitherto had filled my thoughts only as a fantastic dream. I saw the world flee beneath me, as if I were transported in air."

Napoleon was now conducting military and foreign policy virtually on his own. His forceful and virtually independent pursuit of the war and subsequent peace arranged with Austria at Campo Formio (October 18, 1797) gave France control of the Austrian Netherlands, Venetia, and the satellite Cisalpine Republic in northern and central Italy. For the moment, only Great Britain remained as an enemy.

Napoleon thus turned his attention to the Middle East, setting off on a spectacular voyage to Egypt, part of the Ottoman Empire. He was accompanied by 35,000 soldiers and a shipload of scientists, a few of the latter already dreaming of carving a canal through the Isthmus of Suez that would give the French an overwhelming advantage in trade with the Far East. After pausing en route long enough to capture the island of Malta, Napoleon defeated Egyptian forces at the Battle of the Pyramids in July 1798. But the tiny British admiral Horatio Nelson (1758–1805), who could see out of only one eye, had lost an arm, and had few teeth left, trapped and destroyed the French fleet on August 1, 1798, in the Battle of the Nile. Russia and Austria, their respective interests threatened by French campaigns in the east, now formed a Second Coalition against France, which Turkey also joined. Temporarily stranded in Egypt because of the naval defeat, and with his officers having to use the Greek historian Herodotus's *Histories* as their guide to Egypt, the undaunted Napoleon set off to conquer Syria, before being forced back by dwindling supplies and disease. After a final victory in Egypt over the Turks, Napoleon returned to France.

In Paris, Abbé Emmanuel Sieyès was plotting to overthrow the Directory. Such a venture now virtually required the participation of one of the powerful, popular young generals whom the incessant warfare had catapulted to prominence. One of them nodded toward Napoleon when approached by Sieyès about undertaking such a plot, "There is your man, he will make your coup d'état better than I." Napoleon helped piece

Horatio Nelson on the *Vanguard* after being wounded during the Battle of the Nile.

together a political constituency from among the quarreling factions of the Directory. With the coup d'état of the 18th of Brumaire, 1799 (November 9, 1799), Sieyès and Napoleon overthrew the Directory.

CONSOLIDATION OF POWER

After the overthrow of the Directory, the conspirators established a new government, the Consulat, which brought political stability to France. It did so by concentrating strong executive authority in the eager hands of Napoleon, who oversaw the drafting of a constitution and made peace with the Catholic Church. Designated "consul for life" in 1802, Napoleon crowned himself emperor two years later. In the meantime, he continued to wage wars against Britain, Austria, Russia, and Prussia, four rivals driven into coalitions by French expansion. By 1809, although he had failed in his goal of bringing Britain to its knees, a series of remarkable victories confirmed his brilliance as a military strategist and tactician. Napoleon had forged a great empire, the largest in Europe since that of Rome.

Establishment of the Consulat

With the fall of the Directory in 1799, Napoleon Bonaparte, at the age of thirty, became first consul, the most powerful man in France. He named Sieyès and Roger Ducos to fill the remaining posts in the new, stronger executive of three consuls, replacing the five directors. The Constitution of 1799, promulgated in December, gave lip service to universal suffrage, but reflected the authoritarian character Sieyès intended. Indirect election for each political institution reduced the political body of the nation to a small number of notables. A Senate, appointed by the consuls, chose men from a list of 6,000 "notabilities" to serve in a Tribunate. A Council of State, whose members were appointed by the first consul, would propose legislation. The Tribunate would discuss the proposed legislation, and a legislative body would vote on the laws but could not debate them. There was more than a little truth to the oft-repeated story that one man who asked what was in the new constitution received the reply, "Napoleon Bonaparte." The constitution was submitted to voters in a plebiscite (voters could vote either yes or no). More than 99 percent of the all-male electorate approved the document. The plebiscite became a fundamental Napoleonic political institution, embodying his principle of "authority from above, confidence from below."

The Consulate provided political stability by institutionalizing strong executive authority. France's districts (*départements*) each received an appointed prefect, whose powers, delegated by the central government in Paris, far surpassed those of the intendants of the Bourbon monarchs. Napoleon's brother Lucien, as minister of interior, helped extend effective executive authority to the most distant corners of the nation, curtailing royalist and Jacobin opposition. Napoleon ruthlessly suppressed the press, reducing the number of newspapers in Paris from seventy-three to thirteen, cowing survivors with threats, or winning their allegiance with bribes.

The Concordat

Napoleon made peace with the Catholic Church, bringing it under state supervision. Deep hostility remained between priests who had sworn allegiance to the nation during the Revolution—the "juring" clergy—and those who had refused. Influenced by Enlightenment secularism, Napoleon believed the Church should not have an institutional role in the affairs of state. But he was also a cynical pragmatist. "There is only one way to encourage morality," he once said, "and that is to reestablish religion. Society cannot exist without some being richer than others, and this inequality cannot exist without religion. When one man is dying of hunger next door to another who is stuffing himself with food, the poor man simply cannot accept the disparity unless some authority tells him, 'God wishes it so . . . in heaven things will be different.' " An agreement with the Church would also undercut popular support for the monarchist cause by restoring some of the Church's prerogatives, but not any that would threaten the government's authority. Napoleon thus shrewdly sought to detach the Church from the quest for a restoration of the monarchy.

With the death in 1799 of Pope Pius VI (pope 1775–1799), who had refused any accommodation with the Revolution, his more liberal successor, Pius VII (pope 1800–1823), was eager to end a decade of religious turmoil. In 1801, Napoleon signed a Concordat with the papacy that helped solidify some of the changes brought by the Revolution, declaring Catholicism "the religion of the majority of citizens" in France. A majority of bishops refused to accept the Concordat. The pope would henceforth appoint new bishops, but on the recommendation of the first consul, that is, Napoleon. The Church also abandoned all claims to those ecclesiastical lands that had been sold as "national property" during the first years of the Revolution. The Concordat helped restore ecclesiastical influence in France, reflected by an increase in religious observance and in the number of people entering the clergy. Napoleon also pleased the Church by abandoning the confusing official calendar put in place in 1793, reestablishing Sundays and religious holidays.

The Organic Articles, which Napoleon promulgated without consulting the pope, regulated the Gallican (French) Church's status in France and reduced the pope's authority. The Church would now be subject to virtually the same administrative organization and policing as any other organization; a "minister of religion" would sit with the other ministers in Paris. The state would pay clerical salaries. No papal bull could be read in

Napoleon and Pope Pius VII signing the Concordat in 1801, reconciling the Catholic Church with France after the Revolution.

France's churches without permission of the government; the clergy would have to read official government decrees from the pulpit. Under Napoleon, the Church gained the freedom of religious practice, but at the expense of some of its independence. A new catechism required primary-school students to memorize:

> *Question:* What are the duties of Christians with respect to the princes who govern them, and what are, in particular, our duties toward Napoleon . . . ?

> *Answer:* . . . Love, respect, obedience, fidelity, military service. . . . We also owe him fervent prayers for his safety and for the spiritual and temporal prosperity of the State.

Napoleon granted Protestants and Jews state protection to practice their religion. An article of the Concordat guaranteed freedom of worship for people in both religions (who together made up less than 5 percent of the population, the vast majority being Protestant). One set of Organic Articles supervised Calvinists, another Lutherans. An imperial decree in 1808 organized Judaism into territorial consistories, although rabbis, unlike priests and Protestant ministers, would not be paid by the state.

Napoleon's settlement with the Church alienated some of his cautious supporters on the left, notably the group known as the Ideologues. After a solemn ceremony at Notre Dame Cathedral in Paris celebrating the

Concordat, one general put it bluntly to Napoleon—"A fine monkish show. It lacked only the presence of the hundred thousand men who gave their lives to end all that."

Napoleon's Leadership

One of his staff would later describe Napoleon as an "ever-restless spirit." He ate rapidly and could work days on end with very little sleep, dictating more than 80,000 letters in his extraordinary career. He seemed to absorb every bit of information that arrived in his office or field headquarters and rapidly mastered subjects related to military or administrative concerns. But he often ignored matters that did not really interest him, such as economics and naval warfare, in which France lagged behind Britain.

Napoleon was more than just an optimist. He believed that his wildest dreams of conquest and empire would inevitably become reality. Everyone feared his rages, although he could be surprisingly understanding and generous toward subordinates when he believed they erred. A man of monumental stubbornness, he sometimes succeeded in reconciling others of opposing temperaments and views. He delegated very little meaningful authority, mistrusting even his closest advisers, but he tolerated opposing viewpoints. Napoleon's style of leadership became ever more tyrannical. He made up his own mind, and that mind invariably chose war.

Wars of Conquest and Empire

Napoleon had brought stability to France, but France was still at war with the Second Coalition: Great Britain, Austria, and Russia. In February 1800, when Austria turned down his overtures for peace on the basis of the Treaty of Campo Formio, Napoleon returned to the battlefield, retaking Milan and defeating an Austrian army in June 1800. With the Treaty of Lunéville (February 1801), Austria reaffirmed the conditions of the Treaty of Campo Formio, accepting French gains in Italy, as well as French control over the Southern Netherlands (Belgium).

With Austria defeated and Russia tied up by a war against the Ottoman Empire, the British government signed the Peace of Amiens in March 1802. France kept all of its significant gains on the continent, and Britain returned all the French colonies it had captured. Great Britain gained only the end of hostilities.

In Central Europe, Napoleon was now free to dismember the Holy Roman Empire and to dictate the territorial reorganization of the small German states. France had absorbed the left bank of the Rhine River, fulfilling the nationalistic dreams of a France extending to its "natural frontiers." Since this expansion came at the expense of Prussia and Austria, these two powers had to be compensated. By the oddly named Imperial Recess of 1803, the two most powerful German states absorbed a number of small, independent German states, ecclesiastical territories, and most of the free cities. The rulers of Baden, Bavaria, Hesse-Kassel, and Würt-temberg, the other largest German states, also added to their domains. France's position in Italy also was solidified. Piedmont remained a French possession, with Napoleon naming himself president of the Italian Cisalpine Republic. After imposing a Federal Constitution on the cantons of Switzerland that transformed them into the Helvetic Republic, Napoleon forced a defensive alliance on that strategically important coun-try. By 1802, France was at peace for the first time in a decade. Napoleon had brought his nation to a position of dominance in Europe not seen since the time of Charlemagne a thousand years earlier.

No longer satisfied with the title "first consul," in 1802 Napoleon became "consul for life," a change approved by plebiscite. Napoleon then prepared the establishment of a hereditary empire in France. Although thousands of émigrés took advantage of a declared amnesty to return to France, an alleged conspiracy against Napoleon's life by a group of royal-ists in 1804 led him to act against the Bourbons and to expedite his plan to become emperor. Napoleon accused Louis de Bourbon-Condé, the duke of Enghien (1772–1804)—a member of the Bourbon family who had emi-grated to Baden—of involvement in the conspiracy. French troops moved into Baden to arrest him. The duke was hurriedly tried and executed near Paris, despite the lack of any evidence of his involvement in plans to assas-sinate Napoleon. Public opinion throughout much of Europe was out-raged. The German composer Ludwig van Beethoven crossed out the

Jean-Louis David's *Emperor Napoleon Crowning the Empress Joséphine in the Cathedral of Notre Dame* (1805–1808).

dedication to Napoleon of his Third Symphony ("Eroica," meaning "Heroic") shouting "So he is also nothing more than an ordinary man? Now he will trample on the rights of mankind and indulge only his own ambition; from now on he will make himself superior to all others and become a tyrant!" One of the royalist conspirators, before his own execution, lamented, "We have done more than we hoped to do; we meant to give France a king, and we have given her an Emperor."

The Tribunate, Senate, and the people (through another plebiscite) quickly approved the change from the Consulat to an empire. On December 2, 1804, Napoleon was anointed emperor by Pius VII. Instead of waiting for the pope to crown him, Napoleon snatched the crown from the pontiff and placed it on his own head. A new constitution presented a telling contradiction: "The government of the republic is entrusted to an emperor." An unknown officer who had scraped by with little money amid the spendthrift glitter of Thermidor, Bonaparte began to wear a coat of red velvet that would have been fit for Louis XIV.

Napoleon was no more temperamentally suited to live with peace than with defeat. Jealous of Britain's naval and commercial supremacy in the Mediterranean and the Western Hemisphere, he began to goad Britain into a new war. A government-controlled newspaper boasted that France would conquer the road to British India.

Haiti, the western side of the island of Hispaniola, had proclaimed its independence from France in 1801 under the leadership of a former slave, Toussaint L'Ouverture. In 1802, Napoleon restored French control of Haiti and reinstituted slavery in the French colonies, in response to pressure from sugar planters. French troops captured Toussaint L'Ouverture and took him to France, where he soon died. Tropical disease killed most of the French troops occupying Haiti, and the British prevented the arrival of reinforcements. The French army surrendered, and in 1804 Haiti again became independent. With his plans to extend France's empire to the Caribbean having come to naught, Napoleon shouted "Damn sugar, damn coffee, damn colonies!"

Seeking to recoup the financial losses France had incurred from war, Napoleon sold the huge Louisiana Territory to the United States in 1803 for 60 million francs (then about 11 million dollars). In retrospect, this was a paltry sum for territory that virtually doubled the size of what was then the United States. Napoleon's hope that its former colony would emerge as a rival to Britain also lay behind the sale.

In July 1805, Russia and Austria joined Britain to form the Third Coalition against Napoleon. Alexander I (ruled 1801–1825) had succeeded his assassinated father, Paul, as tsar of Russia. Undaunted, Napoleon readied an army and ships of all sizes at the port of Boulogne on the English Channel for an invasion of Britain. In 1805, a French decoy fleet lured Horatio Nelson's fleet into pursuit, hoping to inflict a crushing defeat on the Royal Navy. But the hunter soon became the hunted. When the French fleet

The Battle of Trafalgar.

sailed from the Spanish Mediterranean part of Cádiz on October 21, 1805, it sighted the Royal Navy. Turning to sail back to port, the French vessels were left vulnerable to attack by two columns of ships that succeeded in breaking the French line. As Nelson lay dying of a wound (which might have been avoided, had he agreed to cover up his medals and epaulets that attracted a French marksman's eye), his fleet earned one of naval history's most decisive victories at Cape Trafalgar, not far from Gibraltar. Any chance for a French invasion of England evaporated. Great Britain controlled the seas.

The French armies were more successful on the continent. They defeated the Austrians at Ulm in October 1805, capturing 50,000 troops. Napoleon finally coaxed the Russians and Austrians into the open. At Austerlitz on December 2, 1805, Napoleon tricked his opponents into an attack on his intentionally weakened right flank. He then divided the two armies with a crushing attack at their vulnerable center. When the dust cleared after the battle, the Russians and their Austrian allies had suffered 30,000 casualties, the French less than 9,000. Austria asked for peace, giving up the remnants of imperial territories in Italy and Dalmatia. Napoleon's allies, Bavaria, Baden, and Württemberg, once again gained Habsburg territories. Alexander limped back to Russia with his broken armies.

In the wake of Austerlitz, the hesitant King Frederick William III (ruled 1797–1840) of Prussia abandoned his tentative agreement to join the

Third Coalition, instead signing an alliance with France. In July 1806, Napoleon organized the Confederation of the Rhine, composed of sixteen German states, excluding Prussia and Austria (see Map 13.1). Napoleon named himself "Protector" of the Confederation, whose members agreed to accept French garrisons in southern Germany and to support Napoleon if war broke out again. This made the Holy Roman Empire even more irrelevant than it had been for a very long time. Emperor Francis II of Austria simply dissolved the clumsy entity.

As French power in central Europe grew, the British government convinced Frederick William to join the alliance against Napoleon. But Napoleon's forces humiliated the Prussian army at Jena near Nuremberg on October 14, 1806, and then occupied Prussia's capital, Berlin. In February 1807, the French and Russian armies fought to a bloody draw in a Polish snowstorm. Had Austrian and British troops been sent to support the Russians, Napoleon might well have been soundly defeated. But Austria was still reeling from the defeat at Austerlitz, and the English were preoccupied with defending their commercial interests in the Western Hemisphere. Napoleon sent for fresh troops from France and added 30,000 Polish soldiers, some attracted by speculation that the emperor might create an independent Polish state.

After defeating the Russian army at the Battle of Friedland (June 1807), Napoleon met with Tsar Alexander on a raft in the middle of a river. Frederick William, the king of Prussia, paced anxiously on the shore as he awaited the outcome. The news was the worst. By the Treaty of Tilsit (July 1807), Prussia lost territory in western Germany and in Poland, which became, respectively, the Kingdom of Westphalia and the Grand Duchy of Warsaw, the latter annexed by Napoleon's ally, Saxony. Russia suffered only the loss of its Ionian Islands in the Aegean Sea, but was forced to accept the territorial settlements in Western Europe as definitive. In return, the tsar received a promise of French support in Russia's current quarrel with the Ottoman Empire. France thus tacitly agreed to back Russia's long-standing ambitions in southeastern Europe. Finally, the tsar agreed to close Russian ports to British ships.

Two years later, when Austria challenged Napoleon by invading Bavaria in 1809, Napoleon moved rapidly against Vienna, capturing the Habsburg capital. He then crossed to the left bank of the Danube River, and, after avoiding being pinned against the river by Austrian forces, earned a great victory in July 1809 at Wagram. Defeat forced Austria to surrender Illyria to France and other territory to Bavaria, the Grand Duchy of Warsaw, and Russia, which was still technically but uneasily allied to France. With Austria defeated and weakened, Prussia discouraged and dismembered, Russia neutralized, and Britain once again left alone to challenge France, Napoleon's position in Europe seemed invincible. Through conquest, the establishment of satellite states, and alliances with smaller powers, Napoleon had constructed a vast empire.

MAP 13.1 THE EMPIRE OF NAPOLEON   This map shows the areas conquered by Napoleon, including dependent states and states incorporated directly into France or ruled by Napoleon's relatives.

The Corsican Warrior

Napoleon has been considered one of the most brilliant military leaders in modern history. Yet his talents lay not in originality but in his stunningly innovative adaptations of military strategies and tactics developed in the eighteenth century and during the Revolution. Before mass military conscription, warfare had usually involved relatively limited numbers of soldiers. Armies had not moved rapidly. Since the beginning of the Thirty Years' War (1618–1648), wars had been fought over dynastic honor, commercial rivalry, and disputed territories (see Chapters 7 and 11). Old Regime armies had consisted largely of mercenaries commanded by nobles. Most battles had been fought in precise, drilled ranks, by two relatively small armies in line formation directly facing each other.

In the eighteenth century, technological and tactical improvements in artillery augmented its importance in warfare. Artillery pieces became lighter and therefore could be moved more easily. Improvements in roads also helped expedite the movement of cannon, as well as troops. Properly positioned artillery, launching powerful shells, could now play a decisive role against infantry. The artillery became a more respected part of the army; talented officers, Napoleon not the least of them, found a chance for promotion that they would not have had elsewhere.

Warfare changed when armies were no longer made up of mercenaries but rather of "citizen-soldiers" with greater commitment to their cause. Thus, during the French Revolution, committed sans-culottes were first mobilized as citizen-soldiers in the *levée en masse* proclaimed in August 1792. They fought to defend the nation, winning the stunning victory over the Austrian army at Valmy (September 1792, see Chapter 12). The Revolution inaugurated a period of warfare in Europe in which more soldiers entered battle than ever before. Between 1800 and 1815, perhaps as many as 2 million men served in or allied with Napoleon's armies. Napoleon harnessed French nationalism to win the commitment of his armies.

The Prussian general and military writer Karl von Clausewitz (1780–1831) described how warfare, which he defined as "an extension of state policy by other means," had changed. Whereas the wars of most of the eighteenth century had been those of kings and of states, not entire peoples, now "war had again suddenly become an affair of the people, and that of a people numbering thirty million, every one of whom regarded himself a citizen of the state."

Napoleon's genius was his ability to organize, oversee, and assure the supplying of and communication between larger armies than had ever before been effectively assembled, and to move them more rapidly than anyone before him. "Everything is in the execution," as he put it. He built on the French innovation in 1792–1793 of using combat divisions that combined infantry, cavalry, and artillery, and he subdivided his armies into corps, each with its own sense of pride and morale.

Citizens drawing lots to determine who would be conscripted to fight in Napoleon's wars.

Napoleon's ability to select and promote able marshals, and to inspire officer and foot soldier alike, drew the admiration of even his most bitter enemies. He founded a military school in 1803 that produced 4,000 officers by 1815—there were lots of vacancies as endless wars took their toll. As in the administration of the empire, however, Napoleon refused to delegate responsibility for crucial strategic and tactical decisions to his subordinates. In the long run, this would cost him dearly.

The infantry remained the heart of Napoleon's armies and his military planning (there were never more than 4 artillerymen for every 1,000 foot soldiers). Napoleon perfected the "mixed order" formation developed in the eighteenth century, which combined stretching troops across the field in a thin line about three men deep and bunching them in columns not only for marching but also for attack. Napoleon kept some battalions in columns, others in lines, which allowed battlefield flexibility. When he saw the opportunity, he launched an attack by outflanking his opponent and striking against the enemy's lines of communication. When he confronted an army stretched out before him, skilled marksmen threw the opponent's advance forces into disarray. Napoleon then brilliantly assessed the opposing army's weakest point. The concentration of deadly artillery fire—Napoleon once referred to the twelve-pound cannons as his "beautiful daughters"—prepared the way for the assault of the infantry columns. The speed of his army's movements was such that

Napoleon could rapidly attack and defeat part of an enemy army before reinforcements could arrive. Instead of stopping to celebrate victory, Napoleon sent his troops, particularly the cavalry, to pursue the enemy. Victory became a rout.

Napoleon's armies, unlike the professional armies of the Old Regime, lived off the land, simply requisitioning what they needed. This did not make the French troops very popular, even in those lands officially incorporated into the empire. But it did allow the imperial army to travel far afield, in great numbers, marching up to twenty miles a day. Such speed seemed incredible for the period, since each infantryman carried with him about sixty pounds of equipment.

Finally, Napoleon enjoyed intense loyalty from his officers and troops, even up to the bitter end. He took to the field with his troops and rewarded good work with promotions and decorations, sometimes given on the field of battle. The emperor's own courage was also a source of inspiration to his troops. He had the good fortune to be wounded only twice in his long military career (a slight bayonet cut at the siege of Toulon in 1793 and a wound when he was hit by a spent musket ball at Wagram in 1809). During one battle, the Imperial Guard refused to fight until Napoleon had moved to a safer place. He treated his soldiers with demonstrable respect and even affection because they seemed willing to die for him. At least 400,000 did just that.

The Napoleonic adventure offered even the most humble soldier a chance for glory. Yet the risks of injury and death were considerable. Dis-

Napoleon used titles and awards as pillars of the empire. Jacques-Louis David's *Oath of the Army after the Distribution of Standards* shows the eagerness of the army to defend Napoleon and the empire.

ease sometimes killed more soldiers than battlefield wounds. Soldiering was a tough life. In good times, soldiers ate reasonably well—bread, vegetables, even some meat, and drank wine or rum. But after defeat, or when they were far inside inhospitable territory, soldiers were fortunate just to find enough to eat. Medical care remained inadequate, despite the improvements brought by a talented and dedicated doctor, Dominique Larrey. He arranged for the wounded to be cared for while the battle was still raging, rather than afterward when it often was too late. Major surgery—countless amputations occurring after each major battle—was often fatal. Napoleon remained far more concerned with able-bodied soldiers than with the wounded or sick.

Incessant warfare was the most fundamental characteristic of Napoleon's empire. The emperor used nationalistic appeals to mobilize the resources of his centralized state and to deploy them in the war effort. Military genius or not, Napoleon dragged his country and much of Europe into a protracted, damaging series of wars. These stretched across the continent, lasting almost from the very beginning of his empire to his final defeat.

THE FOUNDATIONS OF THE FRENCH EMPIRE

The Napoleonic empire was a significant episode in the long story of statemaking in Europe. Continuing the tradition of eighteenth-century monarchs, Napoleon sought to make state administration more efficient and uniform. His aggressive conquests brought centrally controlled, bureaucratic government and a property-based legal system to much of the continent. For this reason, it is possible to see him as the embodiment of "enlightened absolutism" awaited by the philosophe Voltaire.

Napoleon created a new social hierarchy based not on blood but on service to the state, particularly in the army and bureaucracy, and on ownership of property. Beyond French borders, the empire was based on an imperial system in which Napoleon made his relatives and marshals heads of state. Thus, he gave the throne of Westphalia to his brother Jérôme, as earlier he had transformed the Cisalpine Republic in northern Italy into a monarchy ruled by his stepson, Eugène de Beauharnais. He made his brother Louis king of Holland. His brother Joseph became king of Naples and later king of Spain. Everywhere that French armies conquered, Napoleon's daunting will imposed change.

Institutional Foundations: Imperial Centralization

Napoleon's Council of State, the most prestigious and important administrative body of the empire, oversaw finance, interior affairs, and war.

Members advised the emperor and drew up laws and regulations for approval by the Legislative Body. Napoleon attached to the council a corps of young, bright, apprentice bureaucrats, trained to assume important administrative posts in the future. The Senate, Legislative Body, and Tribunate lost all but their ceremonial roles, and Napoleon completely eliminated the Tribunate in 1807. Even the members of the Council of State found their influence on the emperor increasingly reduced.

Napoleon established the Bank of France in 1800, which facilitated the state's ability to borrow money. He followed the Directory's policy of abandoning the grossly inflated paper money of the Revolution, which stabilized France's currency. He facilitated the assessment and collection of taxes, ordering a land survey of the entire country upon which direct taxes were to be based. And he expanded the number of indirect taxes collected on salt (which had also been a principal source of revenue for the Old Regime monarchy), tobacco, and liquor, as well as on goods brought into any town of over 5,000 inhabitants.

The empire followed the Revolution, and particularly the Directory, in making higher education the responsibility of the state. In a country in which about half the population was illiterate, Napoleon believed that schools could create patriotic and obedient citizens through teaching secular values that would ultimately link education to nationalism. In 1802, Napoleon established state secondary schools called *lycées,* thirty-seven of which were operating six years later, for the relatively few boys who went beyond primary school. Students read only textbooks approved by the emperor. In 1808, Napoleon created France's first public university system, charging it with "direct[ing] political and moral opinions." Education in-creasingly became seen as a value in itself, as well as a means of social ascension.

Napoleon's imperial family, with Empress Joséphine above the wives of his relatives, Queens Marie Julie of Naples, Augusta Amelia of Bavaria, Frederica Catherine of Württemberg, and Hortensia Eugene of Holland.

Legal Foundations: The Napoleonic Code

Napoleon wanted to be known to history as the new Justinian, the Roman lawgiver. The Civil Code of 1804, which became known as the Napoleonic Code, may have been the emperor's most lasting legacy. Many of the *cahiers,* or lists of grievances submitted to Louis XVI on the eve of the Revolution, had asked that French laws be uniform. During the constitutional monarchy, the Convention had begun the process of codifying French laws, but it had been interrupted by the vicissitudes of the Revolution. While the fundamental division in French law had been between the written Roman Law in the south and customary law based upon regional and local traditions in the north, there were many different legal codes in France. Napoleon ordered the Council of State to seek advice from a battery of lawyers to codify the laws of the land. Napoleon personally participated in the most critical discussions and debates. The Napoleonic Code made the rights of property owners sacrosanct: the majority of the articles concerned private property.

The code, over 2,000 articles long, enshrined the equality of all people before the law and the freedom of religion. The subsequent Penal Code of 1810 proclaimed the "freedom of work," reaffirming the Le Chapelier law of 1791 that forbade associations of workers' or employers' associations (the latter were extremely rare). The "freedom" guaranteed in relations between employers and workers left workers legally subordinate to their employers and unable to strike. Furthermore, workers were required to carry small passports that had to be handed over to municipal officials, police, or employers when requested.

The Napoleonic Code reflected Napoleon's traditional attitudes toward the family. He considered the family the most important intermediary between the state and the individual, a means of guaranteeing social order. Rejecting scattered demands during the Revolution for the equality of women, the code reaffirmed the patriarchal nature of the traditional family. It made women and children legally dependent on their husbands or fathers. The code granted men control of family property. A woman could not buy or sell property or begin a business without her husband's permission, and any income she earned would pass to his descendants, not hers. A woman worker's wages, too, went to her husband, and women had no control over their children's savings. As during the First Republic, the state recognized divorce, but it was now more difficult to obtain. More articles in the Napoleonic Code established conditions for the sale of cattle than addressed the legal status of women. In cases of adultery, women risked penalties that were far more severe than those for men. Only adult males could officially witness a legal document. Napoleon complained: "In France women are considered too highly. They should not be regarded as equal to men. In reality they are nothing more than machines for producing children."

As in the Old Regime, parents could put their offspring in jail and retained authority over their children's marriages. The code required equal inheritance of all children (the parents could dispose of a certain percentage, based on a sliding scale, as he or she wished), ending primogeniture (inheritance by the eldest son) in northern France, where it still existed. Yet siblings often found ways to keep the family property together; one brother could buy out his brothers' shares in an inherited property. The end of primogeniture also may have provided an impetus for French couples to have fewer children in an effort to avoid further division of property.

The Napoleonic Code—despite its obvious inequities, imperfections, and the fact that it was sometimes promulgated by a conquering army—served as the basis for the codification of laws and the reorganization of judicial systems in Switzerland, Piedmont-Sardinia, and the Netherlands. At the end of his life, Napoleon claimed, "My glory is not to have won forty battles . . . but what nothing will destroy, what will live eternally, is my Civil Code."

Social Foundations: The Imperial Hierarchy

Napoleon once wrote, "My motto has always been: a career open to all talents." He considered the end of social distinctions by birth to be one of the most lasting accomplishments of the French Revolution. The empire favored the aspirations of the middle classes. The elimination of legal barriers to social ascension left wealth, largely defined by the ownership of property and service to the state (rewarded by grants of property, titles, and pensions), as the main determinant of status. Yet imposing obstacles to social mobility remained. It took wealth to acquire the background, education, and reputation to take one's place in the imperial hierarchy.

The army and the bureaucracy were the two pillars of the empire. Napoleon created an elite of "notables," as they were called, rewarding those who served him well with prestigious titles and lucrative positions. At the pinnacle of the new hierarchy were eighteen marshals, appointed in 1804 from the ranks of the Senate and including generals who had earned fortunes waging war. Napoleon began to restore titles abolished by the Revolution: prince in 1804, duke two years later, followed by count, baron, and chevalier. But unlike the titles of the Old Regime, these titles, which could be heridtary, did not stem from the ownership of a certain estate or château, but rather were awarded for service to the state.

Between 1808 and 1814, Napoleon created 3,600 titles. Yet Napoleonic notables totaled only one-seventh of the number of the nobles in France on the eve of the Revolution. Some of the new notables had already become rich through purchase of ecclesiastical and émigré lands sold during the Revolution. More than half of all men granted titles by the emperor had rendered service in the military. The emperor often repeated that "in the backpack of each soldier, there is a marshal's baton." The civil service was the second most important avenue to a Napoleonic title. Some Italians, Dutch, Germans, and others from conquered lands found that the French Empire offered them dignified and sometimes even lucrative careers.

In May 1802, Napoleon established the Legion of Honor to reward those who served the nation with distinction. It was, predictably enough, organized along military lines, with commanders, officers, and knights. Yet a former Jacobin member of the Council of State complained that the award, a decorated cross that could be displayed prominently on one's coat, was nothing more than a "bauble." Napoleon replied, "You may call them baubles, but it is by baubles that mankind is governed." The subjects of territories incorporated into the empire were eligible to receive the Legion of Honor. When Rome became part of Napoleon's immense empire, the following parody on the Legion of Honor appeared on the walls of the Eternal City:

> In fierce old times, they balanced loss
> By hanging thieves upon a cross.
> But our more humane age believes
> In hanging crosses on the thieves.

THE TIDE TURNS AGAINST NAPOLEON

Almost inevitably, French rule generated resistance in countries absorbed into Napoleon's empire through conquest. Napoleon manipulated factional splits in some countries, co-opted local elites where he could, brushed aside rulers as he pleased, and tried to establish compliant new regimes, some of which he handed over to his brothers. But ultimately French rule over such an extended empire collapsed. Napoleon's failure to force British submission by strangling its economy with his "Continental System," which aimed to cut off Britain from its continental markets, kept his major enemy in the field, or more appropriately, on the high seas. Spanish resistance against French rule became a full-fledged rebellion (the Peninsular War) that, with British assistance, sapped imperial resources. Moreover, French occupation of some of the German states gave rise to German nationalism, solidifying resistance. Prussian and Austrian military reforms led to stronger opponents in the field. And in a final ill-considered expansion of imperial aggression, Napoleon in 1812 decided to invade Russia. The destruction of his "Grand Army" in the snowdrifts and howling winds of Russia was the beginning of the end.

Prime Minister William Pitt the Younger and Napoleon carve up the world.

The Continental System

Knowing that the war was costing the British government huge sums (between 60 and 90 percent of the state's annual revenue), the emperor devised a plan he was sure would force his rival to end the conflict. In November 1806, Napoleon announced his Continental System, which prohibited trade with Britain and which he hoped would strangle the British economy by closing all continental ports to British ships. French merchants and manufacturers, as well as the state, would earn fortunes supplying the captive markets of the continent. Increased hardship might cause popular disturbances in Britain.

But the blockade of the continental ports was far easier said than done. The continental coastline is enormous, the British navy was strong (despite the loss of 317 ships between 1803 and 1815), and the merchants and smugglers were resourceful. British merchants continued to find American markets for their goods. The banning of British imports did lead to the development of some important innovations in France (for example, the Jacquard loom for silk weaving and the planting of the sugar beet to compensate for the loss of sugar from the West Indies). But France's relative lack of available coal and iron ore, its lack of capital accumulation and investment, and the overwhelming allocation of the nation's material and human resources to war prevented French merchants from taking up the slack left by the absence of British goods in continental markets.

In response to Napoleon's Continental System, the British government's "Orders in Council" in November and December 1807 demanded that trading ships under all flags purchase a license in a British port. This decision placed Britain at loggerheads with the United States, one of France's principal trading partners. Napoleon retaliated with the Milan Decrees, threatening to seize any ship that had traded with Britain or that had even allowed itself to be searched by British ships. Yet, in 1809, British imports could still be readily found on the continent. The French, suffering a sharp decline in customs revenue, began tolerating violations of the Continental System, even selling special licenses and placing hefty taxes on the importation of British goods to bring in more revenue. The blockade came completely apart in the midst of an economic depression that began in 1811.

Napoleon counted on Britain's deepening crisis with the U.S. government, which opposed the boarding and searching of its vessels by British inspectors, to bring Anglo-American relations to a breaking point. But even the War of 1812 between the British and the United States, which ended with the exhausted British capitulating, could not destroy the British economy. Moreover, the fact that French agents had encouraged an Irish insurrection against British rule in 1798 lingered in the memory of the British upper class, adding to their resentment of France. Tory governments, which governed Britain throughout the entire revolutionary and Napoleonic periods, remained committed to defeating Bonaparte (and repressing dissent at home), despite the staggering economic cost of the war.

The Peninsular War

Napoleon's obsession with bringing Britain to its knees led him into the protracted, bloody, and disastrous Peninsular War (1808–1813) in Spain. In 1807, Napoleon had reached an agreement with Charles IV (ruled 1788–1808), the incompetent king of Spain, that permitted French troops to pass through his kingdom to conquer Portugal, Britain's perpetual ally (an arrangement that had functioned to guarantee Portugal's independence from Spain and had also provided Portuguese wine with a ready market for thirsty British people of means). A French army marched on Lisbon, and the Portuguese royal family fled to Brazil. An insurrection in March 1808 led to the abdication of Charles IV and the succession of his son Ferdinand VII (ruled 1808, 1814–1833) to the throne. Believing that the kingdom of Spain was on the verge of falling like an apple into his hands, Napoleon forced Ferdinand to abdicate that same year, summoned his older brother, Joseph Bonaparte (1768–1844), from his wobbly throne in Naples, and made him king of Spain.

But Napoleon did not count on the resistance of the Spanish and Portuguese people. Ecclesiastical reforms imposed by Joseph and Napoleon, including the reduction in the number of monastic convents by two-thirds and the abolition of the Inquisition, angered the Church, which remained a powerful force in Spanish life. Napoleon found some allies among the urban middle class, but the Spanish nobility joined their old allies, the clergy, in opposition to the invaders. French forces were easy targets for the small, mobile groups of Spanish guerrillas, who attacked and then quickly disappeared into the Spanish landscape. British troops led by Arthur Wellesley, later duke of Wellington (1769–1852), arrived to help the Spanish and Portuguese fight the French. By 1810, about 350,000 French troops were tied up in the Iberian Peninsula. Fighting for "Church and king," Spaniards sustained what arguably was the first successful guerrilla war in modern Europe. Napoleon's "Spanish ulcer" bled France.

Stirrings of Nationalism in Napoleonic Europe

One of the lasting effects of the Napoleonic period was the quickening of German and, to a lesser extent, Italian national identity. The French revolutionaries had called for a war against the tyrants of Europe. But Napoleon seemed blind to the fact that the exportation of the principles of the French Revolution might encourage resentment and even nationalist

Francisco Goya's *The Third of May, 1808*, depicts the execution of citizens of Madrid by French soldiers after the fall of the city during the Peninsular War.

feeling against the French in those countries conquered by his armies. Gradually the French discovered that nationalism was a double-edged sword. Many people in states conquered by French armies not only resented the occupation of their lands but they also began to long for the existence of a territorial state organized around their own nationality.

In any case, Napoleon sought to curry favor in each conquered state in exchange for support against his enemies. Napoleon may indeed have intended that Westphalia, created by the Treaty of Tilsit (1807) out of former Prussian territories and other smaller states that had fought against him, would become a model state. He ended serfdom and gave peasants the right to own land, to move through the kingdom as they pleased, and to send their children to school. But his principal goal was to bolster the Confederation of the Rhine's north flank against possible attacks against his interests.

Napoleon considered conquered territories sources for military conscripts and raw materials, or as potential markets for French goods. In Italy, French authorities forbade the importation of textile machinery and imposed disadvantageous tariffs on the local population, fearful of competition with their own industries. With the exception of Jacobin anticlericals, intellectuals, and merchants who stood to profit from the French occupation, most people expressed little enthusiasm for the Napoleonic regime. In the Netherlands, the French occupation virtually brought the prosperous Dutch trading economy to a standstill. Poles soon began to doubt Napoleon's promise to reestablish Polish independence; some Polish nobles began to look to the Russian tsar for help, others to the king of Prussia. Among those territories conquered by Napoleon, open insurrections were relatively rare, although in the Austrian Tyrol, peasants sang nationalist songs as they fought against the French in 1813.

The impact of the French invasions on nationalism was perhaps clearest in the German states. At first, some German intellectuals had praised Napoleon. The philosopher Georg Wilhelm Friedrich Hegel (1770–1831) described the emperor, of whom he caught a glimpse after the Battle of Jena in 1806, as "this world soul . . . dominating the entire world from horseback. . . . It is impossible not to admire him."

But the French invasions carried German nationalism beyond the small ranks of writers and intellectuals. Attacks by German writers against French occupation mounted in 1807. That year, the French executed a Nuremburg bookseller accused of selling anti-French literature. Two years later, Napoleon escaped an assassination attempt by a young German student, the son of a Lutheran minister, who shouted "Long live Germany!" as he was executed.

Gradually German writers discovered, or even invented, the idea of Germany by arguing forcefully that the people of the German states shared a common culture based upon language, tradition, and history. Only in the middle of the eighteenth century had German writers begun to write in their own language; before then, they considered French the language of culture. Like some composers, they began to discover elements of a common culture, drawing on language, literary texts, folk traditions, and other German cultural traditions to express themselves. This emotional quest for cultural and political institutions that would define "Germany" reflected some rejection of the rational tradition of Enlightenment thought identified with France.

German nationalists knew that the multiplicity of states in Central Europe stood in the way of eventual German unification. Hegel, for one, believed that Napoleon had helped the cause of German nationalism by eliminating hundreds of tiny states. About 60 percent of the population of the German states passed from one ruler to another during the revolutionary and Napoleonic eras. Still, forty separate German states survived. Among them, Baden, Bavaria, and Württemberg, although much smaller and less powerful than Austria and Germany, emerged from the period with their independence and separate traditions for the most part intact.

Even though any possible political unification of Germany seemed distant, if not impossible, German nationalism nonetheless contributed to the determination with which the people of the German states resisted Napoleon. Johann Gottlieb Fichte (1762–1814) called on "the German nation," which he defined as including anyone who spoke German, to discover its spiritual unity. Fichte thundered at a university lecture in February 1813, "This course will be suspended until the close of the [military] campaign, when we will resume it in a free fatherland or reconquer our liberty by death!"

In Spain, as we have seen, people of all classes came to view the French as invaders, not liberators. A constitution proposed by the Spanish Cortes in 1812 at Cádiz, which was not under French control, nonetheless reflected the influence of the French Revolution. It proclaimed freedom of the press, established an assembly to be elected by a relatively wide electorate, and abolished the Inquisition. But the constitution, although never implemented because of the eclipse of Spanish liberals in the wake of conservative reaction, was also a self-consciously nationalist document. Some Spaniards, too, were becoming more aware of their own shared linguistic, cultural, and historical traditions, particularly as the French conquerors tried to make their language that of administration. In Illyria, the Napoleonic occupation encouraged the creation of a Croat national party.

Military Reforms in Prussia and Austria

Just as the French invasion engendered a nationalist response in some of the Italian and German states, so did the successes of Napoleon's armies lead Prussia (particularly in view of the devastating Prussian defeat at

The retreat of the Grand Army in Russia, November 1812.

Jena in 1806), and, to a lesser extent, Austria, to enact military reforms. In 1807, a royal decree abolished serfdom, permitting peasants to leave the land to which they had been attached and to marry without the lord's permission. A decree three years later allowed peasants to convert some of the land they worked into their own property. Other reforms removed class barriers that had restricted the sale of land between nobles and non-nobles and that had served to keep middle-class men from assuming the military rank of officer (and had also prevented nobles from taking positions considered beneath their status). The Prussian military commander Baron Heinrich Karl vom und zum Stein (1757–1831) appointed some commoners to be officers and cashiered some of the more inept noble commanders. Stein established a ministry of war, taking away some important decisions from the whims of the king and his inner circle. The abolition of serfdom improved the loyalty of peasant-soldiers to the state. The elimination of most forms of corporal punishment enhanced troop morale, as did the rewarding of individual soldiers who served well.

Stein also organized a civilian militia, which provided a proud, patriotic reserve of 120,000 part-time soldiers. Napoleon, upon learning of the Prussian reformer's plans, forced the Prussian king to dismiss his minister in 1808 (at the time, the Prussians were still bound by the terms of the Treaty of Tilsit, signed the previous year, to limit the size of their army). But henceforth the Prussian army would be much larger and more efficient than the army that Napoleon had previously defeated with ease.

The Empire's Decline and the Russian Invasion

Napoleon now confronted the fact that he still had no legitimate children to inherit his throne. Although he admired his wife Joséphine, and may even have loved her, he was as unfaithful to her during his lengthy absences as she was to him. Napoleon arranged for a bishop in Paris to annul his marriage—the pope having refused to do so—allowing him to remarry with the Church's blessing. Napoleon then considered diplomatically useful spouses. When the Russian tsar would not provide his younger sister, Napoleon arranged a marriage in 1810 with Marie-Louise (1791–1847), the daughter of Austrian Emperor Francis I. She had never even met Napoleon, but that in itself was not as unusual as the fact that the French emperor had an old enemy, the Archduke Charles (brother of Francis I and Napoleon's opponent during the 1809 war with Austria), stand in for him at the wedding ceremony, while he remained in Paris. Napoleon thus entered into a *de facto* alliance with the Habsburgs, Europe's oldest dynasty. Within a year, Napoleon had a son and heir.

For the first time since Napoleon's remarkable rise to power, dissent also began to be heard openly inside France. Deserters and recalcitrant conscripts dodged authorities in increasing numbers beginning in about 1810. Royalist and Jacobin pamphlets and brochures circulated, despite censorship. Royalists objected to Napoleon's disdainful treatment of the pope, who excommunicated the emperor after France annexed the Papal States in 1809. Napoleon responded by simply placing Pius VII under house arrest, first near Genoa, and then near Paris in Fontainebleau.

Napoleon had become increasingly unable to separate options that were feasible or possible from those that were unlikely or indeed impossible to achieve. One of the emperor's ministers remarked: "It is strange that Napoleon, whose good sense amounted to genius, never discovered the point at which the impossible begins. . . . 'The impossible,' he told me with a smile, 'is the specter of the timid and the refuge of the coward . . . the word is only a confession of impotence' . . . he thought only of satisfying his own desires and adding incessantly to his own glory and greatness . . . death alone could set a limit to his plans and curb his ambition."

Napoleon's advisers increasingly expressed their doubts about the emperor's endless plans for new conquests. Charles Maurice de Talleyrand, the former bishop who had loyally served as minister for foreign affairs since 1799, had resigned in 1807, after the execution of the duke of Enghien. Talleyrand now symbolized the "party of peace," which opposed extending the empire past limits that could be effectively administered. In 1809, he began to negotiate secretly with Austria about the possibility of a monarchical restoration in France should Napoleon fall.

Napoleon's interest in expanding French influence in the eastern Mediterranean and his marriage to a Habsburg princess virtually assured war with Russia. In 1808, he had put the issue succinctly: "Ultimately, the question is always this, who shall have Constantinople?" and thus control access to the Black Sea. Russia had reopened its ports to British and neutral vessels carrying English goods. Believing that he could enforce the continental blockade by defeating Russia, Napoleon prepared for war, forcing vanquished Austria and Prussia to agree to assist him. In the meantime, the tsar signed a peace treaty with the Ottoman Empire, freeing Russia to oppose Napoleon. Alexander I lined up the support of Sweden. There Jean-Baptiste Bernadotte (1763–1844), once one of Napoleon's marshals, had been elected Crown Prince in 1810 and thus heir to the Swedish throne by the Swedish Estates (he would succeed the childless Charles XIII in 1818 as King Charles XIV). In return, the tsar offered Sweden a free hand in annexing Norway.

In June 1812, Napoleon's "Grand Army," over 600,000 strong, crossed the Niemen River from the Grand Duchy of Warsaw into Russia. Napoleon hoped to lure the Russian armies into battle. The Russians, however, simply retreated, drawing Napoleon ever farther into western Russia in late summer.

The Grand Army may have been the largest army ever raised up to that time, but the quality of Napoleon's army had declined since 1806 through casualties and desertions. Some of his finest troops were tied up dodging guerrilla attacks in Spain. Half of the Grand Army consisted of Prussian, Italian, Austrian, Swiss, or Dutch conscripts. A general complained in 1813, "Some [cavalrymen] had only mounted a horse for the first time in their lives two weeks previously. . . . it was all they could do to hold the reins in one hand and a saber in the other." Officers now were by necessity more hurriedly trained. As the Grand Army was almost constantly at war, there was no chance to rebuild it to Napoleon's satisfaction.

In Russia, disease, heat, and hunger took a far greater toll on Napoleon's army than did the rearguard action of enemy troops. The Grand Army finally reached the city of Smolensk, 200 miles west of Moscow, in the middle of August; there the emperor planned to force the tsar to sign another humiliating peace. The Russian troops continued to retreat deeper into Russia. Napoleon's marshals begged him to stop in Smolensk and wait there. Yet, tempted by the possibility of capturing Moscow, Napoleon pushed on until his army reached Borodino, sixty miles from Moscow. There the two armies fought to a costly draw in the bloodiest battle of the Napoleonic era, with 68,000 killed or wounded before the Russian army continued its retreat. Napoleon entered Moscow on September 14, 1812. He found it virtually deserted. Fires, probably set by Russian troops, spread quickly through the wooden buildings. Almost three-quarters of the city burned to the ground. The tsar and his armies had fled to the east.

Over 1,500 miles from Paris, without sufficient provisions, and with the early signs of the approaching Russian winter already apparent, Napoleon decided to march the Grand Army back to France. The retreat, which began October 19, was a disaster. Russian troops picked off hundreds of the retreating forces, forcing them to take an even longer route to Smolensk, 200 miles away. The Russians were waiting for Napoleon's beleaguered armies at the Berezina River, where they killed thousands of French soldiers. The emperor himself barely escaped capture by the Cossacks. The freezing winter then finished off most of what was left of Napoleon's Grand Army.

The retreat from Moscow was one of the greatest military debacles of any age. A contemporary described some of the French troops: "a mob of tattered ghosts draped in women's cloaks, odd pieces of carpet, or greatcoats burned full of holes, their feet wrapped in all sorts of rags . . . skeletons of soldiers went by, their gaunt, gray faces covered with disfiguring beards, without weapons, shameless, marching out of step, with lowered heads, eyes on the ground, in absolute silence. . . ." Of the more than 600,000 men who had set out in June from the Grand Duchy of Warsaw (Napoleon's defeat ended hopes for Polish nationalists of independence), only about 40,000 returned to France in December. (Indeed, a mass grave of frozen soldiers of the Grand Army was discovered in Lithuania in 2003.) After racing ahead of the groans of the dying and the frozen corpses, Napoleon issued a famous bulletin that was sent back to Paris: "The health of the emperor has never been better."

Napoleon arrived at the Tuileries Palace on the night of December 18, 1812. In the wake of a military disaster of such dimensions that press censorship and duplicitous official bulletins (the expression "to lie like a military bulletin" became current) could not gloss over it, the mood of the French people soured.

Undaunted, Napoleon demanded a new levy of 350,000 more troops. This call, coming at a time of great economic hardship, was greeted with massive resentment and resistance. Instead of negotiating a peace that could have left France with the left bank of the Rhine River, Napoleon planned new campaigns and further expansion.

The Defeat of Napoleon

Napoleon now faced allies encouraged by his devastating defeat. In February 1813, Russia and Prussia signed an alliance, agreeing to fight Napoleon until the independence of the states of Europe was restored. Napoleon earned two costly victories over Russian and Prussian troops in the spring of 1813, but his casualties were high. Great Britain, still fighting the French in Spain, formally joined the coalition in June. Napoleon rejected Austrian conditions for peace, which included the dissolution of the Confederation of the Rhine, and Austria joined the coalition in August 1813. Napoleon's strategy of winning the temporary allegiance, or at least neutrality, of one of the other four European powers had failed.

In August 1813, Napoleon defeated the allies at Dresden, but then learned that Bavaria had seceded from the Confederation of the Rhine and joined the coalition against France. In October, his troops outnumbered two to one, Napoleon suffered a major defeat at Leipzig (in the Battle of the Nations) and retreated across the Rhine River into France. His armies, ever more filled with reluctant, raw recruits, lacked adequate supplies. Napoleon's military inspiration now seemed less apparent. An insurrection in the Netherlands followed by an allied invasion restored the prince of Orange to authority there. Austrian troops defeated a French army in northern Italy. The duke of Wellington's English forces drove the French armies from Spain and back across the Pyrenees. Forced to fight on French soil for the first time, Napoleon's discouraged armies were greeted with hostility when they tried to live off the land as they had abroad. Opponents of Napoleon, including some churchmen for whom a Bourbon restoration now seemed a possibility, now spoke more openly in France.

Early in 1814, the allies proposed peace (perhaps insincerely, assuming the French emperor would refuse) if Napoleon would accept France's natural frontiers of the Rhine River, the Alps, and the Pyrenees. Napoleon stalled. An allied army of 200,000 moved into eastern France. In Paris, the Legislative Body approved a document that amounted to a denunciation of the emperor, though it never reached the public. Even Napoleon's normally dutiful older brother Joseph encouraged the members of the Council of State to sign a petition calling for peace.

Demonstrating that they had learned a key lesson from Napoleon on warfare, the allies were determined not to stop until they had captured Paris. After overcoming stiff French resistance (in February, Napoleon

(*Left*) Arthur Wellesley, the duke of Wellington. (*Right*) Charles Maurice de Talleyrand.

won ten battles in twenty days), the main allied force swept into the French capital in March 1814. Tsar Alexander I of Russia and King Frederick William III of Prussia rode triumphantly into the city. At Fontainebleau, Napoleon's marshals refused to join in his frantic plans for an attack on the allies in Paris and pressured him to abdicate. Talleyrand called the Senate into session. It voted to depose Napoleon. The allies refused to consider Napoleon's abdication in favor of his three-year-old son. Without an army and, perhaps for the first time, without hope, Napoleon abdicated on April 6, 1814, and then took poison, which failed to kill him. The long adventure finally seemed at an end.

MONARCHICAL RESTORATION AND NAPOLEON'S RETURN

The allies sought the restoration of the Bourbon monarchy. The French Senate, too, expressed its wish that Louis XVI's brother, the Count of Provence, return to France as Louis XVIII. By the Treaty of Fontainebleau (April 11, 1814), the allies exiled Napoleon to a Mediterranean island off the coast of Italy. Bonaparte would be emperor of Elba alone. Marie-Louise refused to accompany him, preferring to be duchess of Parma, receiving the title by virtue of being a member of the Austrian royal family. As Napoleon travelled to the Mediterranean to sail to Elba, he saw himself hanged in effigy; to conceal his identity, he donned an old blue coat and a white Bourbon cockade, later trying to look like an Austrian officer. In the meantime, although in most places the news of the restoration of the monarchy was not greeted with wild outbursts of enthusiasm, there nonetheless seemed to be a palpable sense of relief that the long Napoleonic Wars would be over.

The Bourbon Restoration

The count of Provence entered Paris on May 3, 1814, as King Louis XVIII (ruled 1814–1815; 1815–1824). With more than a little wishful thinking, he announced that this was the nineteenth year of his reign (counting from the death of the son of Louis XVI, who had died in 1795 in a Paris prison without ever reigning). The allies worked out a surprisingly gracious peace treaty with France, largely thanks to Talleyrand's skilled diplomacy. The Treaty of Paris, signed May 30, 1814, left France with Savoy, and small chunks of land in Germany and the Austrian Netherlands—in other words, the France of November 1, 1792. France could now rejoin the monarchies of Europe.

Louis XVIII signed a constitutional "Charter" that granted his people "public liberties," promising that a legislature would be elected, based on a very restricted franchise. Although the document affirmed monarchical rule by divine right, it confirmed some of the important victories of the Revolution, including equality before the law and freedom of expression and religion, although Catholicism would be the religion of the state (see Chapter 15). A coterie of fanatical nobles and their followers (the Ultra-royalists) convinced the king to enact some measures, however, that were highly unpopular. Many in France disapproved of the substitution of the white flag of the Bourbon family for the tricolor, the description of the Charter as a "gift" from the king to the French people, the retiring of 14,000 officers at half pay, the restoration of returned émigrés to high positions in the army, and the return to their original owners of national lands that had not been sold. But most of the French were simply exhausted from years of wars and sacrifice, and even Napoleon's most fervent supporters did no more than occasionally shout "Long live the emperor!" and disappear into the night.

The 100 Days

In March 1815, just months after his exile, Napoleon boldly escaped from Elba and landed near Antibes on the French Mediterranean coast. He knew that he retained considerable popularity in France. Furthermore, so much time had passed and so many dramatic events had occurred since the execution of Louis XVI that one of the monarchy's staunchest supporters claimed, with some exaggeration, "The Bourbons were as unknown in France as the Ptolemies."

The word that Napoleon had landed in France and was marching north with a small band of followers stunned everyone. Marshal Ney, who had offered his services to the Bourbons, promised to bring Napoleon back to Paris in a cage. But upon seeing Napoleon, Ney fell into his arms. Regiment after regiment went over to Napoleon as he marched north. With Bonaparte nearing Paris, Louis XVIII, his family, and advisers fled for Belgium (as Louis XVI had attempted to do in 1791), which had become part of the Kingdom of Holland. Soon Napoleon again paced frenetically through the Tuileries Palace, making plans to raise armies and defend him-self against the inevitable allied response, and dreaming of new conquests.

It was not to be. The allies quickly raised an enormous army of more than 700,000 troops. Napoleon led an army of 200,000 men into the Austrian Netherlands, engaging Prussian and British forces south of Brussels on June 16, 1815. He forced the

Louis XVIII, king of the French. Note the perhaps unconscious Napoleonic pose.

The Battle of Waterloo, June 18, 1815.

Prussians to retreat and ordered one of his generals to pursue them with his army. Napoleon then moved against the British forces commanded by Wellington, his old nemesis. The armies met near the village of Waterloo on June 18, 1815. Wellington had skillfully hidden the extent of his superior infantry behind a ridge. Napoleon watched in horror as a Prussian army arrived to reinforce Wellington. The general sent in pursuit of the Prussians, like all Napoleon's commanders, had been taught to follow Napoleon's directives to the letter and not to improvise. He held back until it was too late. When the imperial guard broke ranks and retreated, much of the rest of the French army did the same. The defeat was devastating and total.

Napoleon abdicated a second time. He surrendered to British forces near the western coast of France, while hoping to find a way to sail to America. This time the exile would be final. The allies packed Napoleon off to the small island of Saint Helena, in the South Atlantic, 1,000 miles away from any mainland. The closest island of any size was Ascension, a British naval base, some 600 miles distant. Louis XVIII returned to take up the throne of France a second time, 100 days after fleeing Paris.

On Saint Helena, Napoleon's health gradually declined. He died on May 5, 1821, his last words being "France, army, head of the army, Joséphine." He died of an ulcer, probably a cancerous one, despite stories to this day that he was poisoned by arsenic.

NAPOLEON'S LEGACY

Napoleon's testament, a masterpiece of political propaganda, tried to create a myth that he saved the Revolution in France. "Every Frenchman could say during my reign,—'I shall be minister, grand officer, duke, count, baron, if I earn it—even king!' " And in some ways, Napoleon was indeed the heir to the French Revolution. He guaranteed the survival of some of its most significant triumphs. Napoleon considered his greatest achievement "that of establishing and consecrating the rule of reason." His Napoleonic Code proclaimed the equality of all people before the law (favoring, however, men over women), personal freedom, and the inviolability of property. Napoleon furthered the myth, and to some extent the reality, of the "career open to talent," which aided, above all, the middle class, but even peasants in some cases. He consolidated the role of wealth, principally property ownership, as the foundation of the political life of the nation. This increased the number of citizens eligible to participate in political life, however limited by imperial strictures. Furthermore, Napoleon helped turn nationalism into an aggressive secular religion, manipulating this patriotic energy and transforming it into an ideology inculcated by French schools.

Napoleon's reforms, built upon those of the French Revolution, extended into states conquered by his imperial armies. The French imposed constitutions and state control over the appointment of clergy, standardized judicial systems, and abolished ecclesiastical courts. Throughout the empire, Napoleon created new tax structures, standardized weights and measures, ended internal customs barriers, abolished guilds, and established state bureaucracies that were extensions of French rule in the "sister republics" founded by the Directory. In addition to abolishing serfdom and proclaiming equality before the law in Poland, the French occupation also ended residual peasant seigneurial obligations (such as the requirement to provide labor services to the lord) virtually everywhere, and abolished noble and ecclesiastical courts in northern Italy and the Netherlands. The Napoleonic Code proclaimed freedom of worship, and the French conquest of other European states, including Baden, Bavaria, and the Netherlands, helped remove onerous restrictions on Jews. But under pressure from French planters, Napoleon also reestablished slavery in Haiti in 1802.

Yet Napoleon's success in implementing reforms varied from place to place, depending on existing political structures, the degree of compliance by local elites, and the international situation. In southern Italy, for example, which Napoleon's armies conquered relatively late and where the structures of state authority had always been particularly weak, the French presence had little lasting effect. As the Napoleonic wave subsided, nobles and clergy regained domination over the overwhelmingly rural, impoverished local population.

Napoleon claimed from Saint Helena that he was trying to liberate Europe, but he had actually replaced the old sovereigns with new ones—himself or his brothers. "If I conquered other kingdoms," he admitted, "I did so in order that France would be the beneficiary." Wagons returned from Italy full of art and other treasures, which became the property of

Napoleon and his family, his marshals, or the state. French conquests helped awaken nationalism in the German states and Spain.

To the writer Germaine de Staël (1766–1817), the daughter of the Swiss banker Jacques Necker, Louis XVI's minister, Napoleon "regarded a human being as an action or a thing . . . nothing existed but himself. He was an able chess player, and the human race was the opponent to whom he proposed to give checkmate." In the end, his monumental ambition got the best of him. About 2 million men served in Napoleon's armies between 1805 and 1814; about 90,000 died in battle and more than three times that number subsequently perished from wounds or disease; over 600,000 were later recorded as prisoners or "disappeared." In all, Napoleon's armies may have suffered as many as 1.5 million casualties. The Napoleonic Wars killed about one in five of all Frenchmen born between 1790 and 1795.

Napoleon's final legacy was his myth. From Saint Helena, he claimed, "If I had succeeded, I would have been the greatest man known to history." The rise of romanticism helped make the story of Napoleon, the romantic hero, part of the collective memory of Western Europe after his death. Long after Waterloo, peddlers of songs, pamphlets, lithographs, and other images glorified Napoleon's life as earlier they had the lives of saints. "I live only for posterity," Napoleon once said. "Death is nothing, but to live defeated and without glory is to die every day." Rumors of his miraculous return to France were persistent long after his death. So powerful was his legend that even the most improbable seemed possible.

Of the changes in the post-Napoleonic period that profoundly transformed the way Europeans lived, none arguably had more important social, political, and cultural consequences than the Industrial Revolution. Having begun in England in the middle decades of the eighteenth century, it accelerated in that country during the first decades of the nineteenth century. Furthermore, it spread to Western Europe in particular, but affected regions in other places as well. Amid the rapid expansion of manufacturing, many workers began, for the first time, to see themselves as a separate class exploited by their employers. The Industrial Revolution and its critics would help shape the modern world.

CHAPTER **14**

THE INDUSTRIAL
REVOLUTION,
1800–1850

Manufacturing on a small scale had been part of the European experience for centuries. The economy of virtually every region had depended to some extent on the production of clothes, tools, pots, and pans. Most production was carried out by men and women working in small workshops, hammering and shaping household goods, or by country women weaving or knitting clothes.

During the first half of the nineteenth century, the Industrial Revolution slowly but surely transformed the way many Europeans lived. In Western Europe, it became easier for entrepreneurs to raise money for investment as banking and credit institutions became more sophisticated. Dramatic improvements in transportation, notably the development of the railroad but also the construction of more and better roads, expanded markets. Rising agricultural production, increasingly commercialized in Western Europe, fed a larger population. Western Europe underwent a period of rapid urbanization: the number of people living in cities and towns grew more rapidly than did the percentage of people residing in the countryside, although the latter still predominated.

As the population expanded, demand increased for manufactured goods. The percentage of the population involved in industry rose. Mechanized production slowly revolutionized the textile and metallurgical industries, increasingly bringing together workers under the same roof. Manufacturers now frequently concentrated workers in large workshops and factories. Workers who had been used to setting their own schedule at home were now summoned to arrive and leave by the bell. Rural industry gradually declined and, in some regions, it had disappeared by the end of the nineteenth century. Rural producers in much of France, the uplands of Zurich in Switzerland, and Ireland, among others, lost out to more

A factory town in Germany in the 1830s.

efficient urban, factory-based competitors. Slowly but surely, factory production transformed the way Europeans worked and lived.

While many contemporaries were amazed and impressed by factory production of goods and watched and rode trains in wonderment and appreciation, others were shocked at what seemed to be the human costs of such a transformation. Poor migrants flooded into towns and cities, which burgeoned as never before. Conditions of life in the gritty industrial towns of northern England and Scotland, Lille and Saint-Étienne in France, and towns in the German Rhineland appalled some visitors. The Industrial Revolution also threatened artisans, who lost protection when guilds were abolished under the influence of the French Revolution. Mechanization, too, undercut their livelihood. At the same time, lurid but not inaccurate accounts of the awful conditions of workers (men, women, and children) in factories and mines began to reach the public. Calls for state-sponsored reform from state officials and middle-class moralists echoed far and wide. Moreover, many skilled workers in Western Europe not only protested harsh conditions of work and life but began to see themselves as a class with interests defined by shared work experience. During the 1830s and 1840s, workers began to demand social and political reform. Proclaiming the equality of all people, the dignity of labor, and the perniciousness of unrestrained capitalism, the first socialists challenged the existing economic, social, and political order.

PRECONDITIONS FOR TRANSFORMATION

We have come to call the transformation of the European economy the "Industrial Revolution." It began in England and parts of northwestern Europe during the eighteenth century (see Chapter 10), and during the first half of the nineteenth century it spread through Western Europe. Fundamental changes transformed the way goods were produced. In some industries, machines gradually replaced manual labor. Factory manufacturing accentuated the division of labor, the specialization of manufacturing tasks first described by the Scottish economist Adam Smith in the 1770s. It also increasingly gathered workers who had spun or woven at home or in small shops into the same workplace under the immediate direction of employers or their representatives, ultimately foremen, shop stewards, and managers.

The early histories of the Industrial Revolution tended to emphasize the suddenness of these changes; historians sought to identify the exact period of industrial "take-off" in each country, underlining the role of inventions, mechanization, and factories in the process. This led to an emphasis on "victors" and "laggards," "winners" and "losers" in the quest for large-scale industrialization, a preoccupation that blinded historians to the complexity and richness of the manufacturing revolution.

Recent work, however, has de-emphasized the suddenness of these changes. Despite the importance of inventions such as those that gradually transformed textile manufacturing, first in England and then on the continent, the first Industrial Revolution was largely the intensification of forms of production that already existed. Most industrial work still was organized traditionally, using non-mechanized production. Rural industry and female labor remained essential components of manufacturing. Not until the mid-nineteenth century, when steam power came to be used in many different industries in Western Europe, did industrial manufacturing leave behind traditional forms of production. Handicraft production remained fundamental to manufacturing, as did domestic industry (such tasks as spinning, weaving, and product finishing done for the most part, but not exclusively, by women in the countryside). For example, the growth of the linen industry in Porto, Portugal, stemmed not from factories, but from the work of villagers in the countryside who were paid for spinning and weaving per piece. Even in England, the cradle of large-scale industrialization, craft production and rural "outwork" (work being farmed out to cheap labor) remained important until the second half of the nineteenth century. In the Paris region in 1870, the average manufacturer still employed only seven people. At mid-century, the majority of British industrial workers were not employed in factories. Moreover, in Germany there were twice as many "home workers" as workers employed in German factories.

Regardless of whether goods were produced in homes or factories, by hand or steam power, more goods were certainly being produced in the early nineteenth century. This could not have occurred without increased agricultural productivity, which sustained a dramatically larger population. In turn, an increase in population generated greater consumer demand for manufactured goods. And with the introduction of new modes of transportation, such as trains and steamships, even more goods could be produced and exported to markets that were far beyond the local bounds. The timing and degree of economic change in Europe during the first half of the nineteenth century may be debated, but its impact on European society and politics over the long run seems undeniable.

Demographic Explosion

The rise in population in Europe that began in the eighteenth century accelerated during the first half of the nineteenth century. It is still debated whether this increase marked the beginning of modern population growth, or if it was part of a traditional cyclical pattern of demographic revival following yet another period of high mortality. Europe's population grew from an estimated 187 million in 1800 to about 266 million in 1850, an increase of 43 percent. Europe was then the most densely populated of the world's continents, with about 18.7 people per square kilometer in 1800 (compared to approximately 14 in Asia and less than 5 in Africa and the United States), rising to about 26.6 fifty years later.

Industrializing northwestern Europe—Britain, Belgium, and northern France—had the greatest population increases (see Table 14.1). Britain's population tripled during the nineteenth century. The population of predominantly agricultural societies rose, as well. Sweden's population more than doubled over the course of the nineteenth century. Russia's also rose substantially, from about 36 million in 1796 to about 45 million in 1815 to at least 67 million in 1851. The population of the Balkans rose from about 10 million in 1830 to four times that ninety years later.

Nonetheless, disease and hunger continued to interrupt cycles of growth well into the twentieth century. Cholera tore a deadly path through much of Europe in the early 1830s and reappeared several times until the 1890s. During the Irish potato famine in the late 1840s, between 750,000 and a million people died of hunger in Ireland. Tuberculosis (known to contemporaries as "consumption") still killed off workers, particularly miners.

Overall, however, the mortality rate fell rapidly in the first half of the century. Vaccination made smallpox, among other diseases, somewhat rarer. Municipal authorities in some places paid more attention to cleanliness, sewage disposal, and the purity of water supply, although the most significant improvements did not come until later in the century. Sand filters and iron pipes helped make water more pure; in 1851, engineers com-

TABLE 14.1. ESTIMATED POPULATIONS OF VARIOUS EUROPEAN COUNTRIES
FROM 1800 TO 1850 (IN MILLIONS)

Country	1800	1850
Denmark	0.9	1.6
Norway	0.9	1.5 (1855)
Finland	1.0	1.6
Switzerland	1.8	2.4
Holland	2.2	3.1
Sweden	2.3	3.5
Belgium	3.0	4.3 (1845)
Portugal	3.1	4.2 (1867)
Ireland	5.0	6.6
Great Britain	10.9	20.9
Spain	11.5	15.5 (1857)
Italy	18.1	23.9
Austria-Hungary	23.3	31.3
The German states	24.5	31.7
France	26.9	36.5

Source: Carlo M. Cipolla, *The Fontana Economic History of Europe: Vol. 3, The Industrial Revolution* (London, 1973), p. 29.

pleted the first English reservoir near Manchester, although it would not be put into full use until fifteen years later.

Life expectancy increased in all classes. Individuals surviving their first years could anticipate living longer than their predecessors. Fewer women died young, thus prolonging the period during which they could bear children. Furthermore, wives were less likely to suffer the loss of their partner during this same period, and therefore were more likely to become pregnant. Yet poor people—above all, urban residents—remained far more vulnerable than people of means to early death because of illness. In Liverpool, the average working-class life expectancy was only fifteen years, although that fact is somewhat misleading because it includes infant and child mortality—half of all children born to the poorest families died before the age of five. In eastern and southern Europe, mortality and birthrates continued to be quite high until late in the century.

Despite the fact that infant mortality rates remained high until the 1880s, the gradual decrease in the death of children created a younger population. The chances of a baby surviving his or her first year of life rose because of rudimentary improvements in sanitation, such as a safer water supply and waste disposal. The practice of "wet-nursing," in which urban families farmed out babies to women in the countryside to nurse them and which traditionally took a heavy toll on infants because of illness and accidents, slowly declined. Among the factors that explain this evolution are the increased availability of fresh milk (with, toward the end of the century, the awareness that it must be sterilized).

The decline in mortality, particularly among infants, preceded and encouraged a fall in the birthrate in Western Europe. With more adults surviving childhood, the subsequent decline in birthrates had much to do with choice. The French birthrate, in particular, gradually fell, then plunged dramatically beginning with the agricultural crisis of 1846–1847. Many farming families had fewer children so that inheritance would not be spread too thin.

Europe also enjoyed nearly a century of relative peace, broken only by brief and limited wars: the Crimean War (1853–1856), the Franco-Austrian War of 1859, and the wars of Prussia against Denmark (1864), Austria (1866), and France (1870–1871). A Swedish bishop, then, was not wrong to describe the causes of his overwhelmingly rural country's rise in population during the first half of the century as "peace, vaccine, and potatoes."

The Expanding Agricultural Base

Agricultural production sustained the rise in population (although more easily in western than in eastern or southern Europe). It also permitted the accumulation of capital, which could be reinvested in commercialized farming or in manufacturing. Capital-intensive production (larger-scale and market-oriented farming) underlay the agricultural revolution. More land gradually came under cultivation as marshes, brambles, bogs, and heaths gave way to the plow. Between 1750 and 1850, 6 million acres—or one-fourth of all the country's cultivatable land—were incorporated into larger farms in Britain. In France, migration to the city by peasants from economically marginal rural regions facilitated the consolidation of plots, as the smaller parcels of land they left behind often were bought up by neighbors.

Farm yields increased in most of Europe. England produced almost three times more grain in the 1830s than in the previous century. The elimination of more fallow land (land left untilled for a growing season so that the soil could replenish itself) also increased agricultural productivity. Some farmers did well by raising cattle or specializing in vegetables and fruits for the burgeoning urban market. Farmers increased yield by using more intensive agricultural techniques and fertilizers, which, in turn, accentuated demand for sturdier manufactured agricultural tools.

During the first half of the century, continental visitors to England were surprised to find that, in contrast to the world they knew, relatively few small family farms remained. With the ongoing consolidation of plots, the number of rural people dependent on wage labor for survival rose. Farm work in 1831 remained the largest single source of adult male employment in Britain, employing almost a million men. Thus, the English countryside was peopled by a relatively small number of "gentlemen" of great wealth who owned most of England, many yeomen (independent landowners and tenant farmers of some means), and a vast proletariat (workers depending upon wage labor) of landless laborers.

On the continent, there was not as much consolidation of land as in England, but there too productivity rose as more land was brought into cultivation and fertilizers became more widely used. French agricultural production rose rapidly after 1815, as northern farmers with fairly large plots began to rotate their crops three times a year. In the south, where the soil was of a generally poorer quality, the land more subdivided, and much of it rocky, many landowners planted vineyards near the Mediterranean coast, although the wine they produced hardly caused the owners of the great vineyards of Burgundy or the Bordeaux region to lie awake at night worrying.

In Central Europe and parts of Eastern Europe, too, a modest increase in agricultural production occurred with the gradual commercialization of agriculture. In the German states, agricultural productivity rose more than twice as fast as the population between 1816 and 1865, although large-scale capitalist agriculture could be found only in Prussia and Hanover. Prussian agricultural productivity rose during the first half of the century by 60 percent, at least partially because of improved metal plows and other farm implements, as well as because of information disseminated by the agricultural societies that had been formed there by mid-century. As in Western Europe, reclamation expanded the amount of land under cultivation; and as in Britain and France, root crops, such as turnips and the potato, added nutrition to the diet of the poor. Even in the impoverished Balkans, some peasants began to grow corn, potatoes, and tomatoes.

Yet in much of Europe, including Portugal, where two-thirds of the land was not cultivated, and the Balkans and Greece, subsistence agriculture continued as it had been for centuries. In Russia, agriculture developed only very slowly. In Russia, the rich Black Earth region, covering the middle Volga River area and much of Ukraine, still was undeveloped. During the first half of the nineteenth century, some of the larger estates, benefiting from fertilizer and even some farm machinery, began to produce and export more wheat and rye. The yield of potatoes and sugar beets (and wine in the south) increased dramatically during the 1830s and 1840s. Yet Russian farms could barely feed the empire's huge population in good times, and their output was grossly inadequate in bad times. Serfdom still shackled Russian farm productivity.

Trains and Steamboats

Besides the growth in population and the expansion of the agricultural base, remarkable improvements in transportation—including the development and use of railroads and steamboats—also contributed to the transformations of the Industrial Revolution. The first railroad train began hauling coal to the northern English town of Stockton in 1820, and the first passenger train began service between Liverpool and Manchester in 1830. (It was macabre testimony to the novelty of the train that the British minister of commerce was run down and killed by a train after stepping out of a carriage.) Britain had about 400 miles of rail in 1830, 6,600 in 1852; the number of railroad companies doubled between 1844 and 1850. In 1846, railway construction already employed 200,000 men and by the end of the century the railways employed well over 600,000 people (only about 5 percent of them women). Gradually, embankments, tunnels, and bridges transformed the countryside; railway stations became centers of urban life (see Map 14.1).

The railroad's development served as a significant catalyst for investment, catching the imagination of the middle classes, which identified the railway with progress that could be seen, heard, and experienced. Private investment completely financed British railways during this period. Whereas earlier investments in businesses had been largely the preserve of patricians, smaller companies undertaking railroad construction attracted middle-class investors. Railway booms accustomed more middle-class people to the benefits (up to 10 percent annually in 1846), as well as the risks, of investment. The value of the stock-in-trade of the London and North Western Railway had outstripped that of the East India Company by the mid-nineteenth century.

The opening of the Stockton and Darlington Railway in 1825.

MAP 14.1 PRINCIPAL BRITISH RAILWAY LINES, 1851   Railway lines crisscrossed Britain in 1851.

The construction and operation of railroads also brought other benefits to the expanding economy. Railroad construction provided many jobs, and it spurred the metallurgical industry, since every line required bridges, railway cars, and other materials. It also entailed the destruction of large swaths of the center of major cities, displacing about 50,000 people in

Manchester during a seventy-five year period, and many times that in London. Rail transport reduced shipping costs by about two-thirds, dramatically increasing consumption and, in turn, production. Trains quickly carried frozen meat from the port of Southampton to London, and they brought in "railway milk" from the countryside. The relatively rapid pace of travel arguably helped spread the sense of being "on time," and in the 1850s Greenwich time, or "railway time," had become standard in Britain. Railway construction also brought continental states into the realm of economic decision making; in France, the government and private companies cooperated in building a railway system. In Belgium and Austria, the railway system was state-owned from the beginning (see Map 14.2).

Railroad companies were quick to divide their cars into first-, second-, and third-class service, although at first luxuries were limited to footwarmers in winter. For people of more modest means, second- or even third-class carriages (called "penny a mile" travel in Britain, with train wagons not even sheltered from the elements until the mid-1840s) had to suffice. English seaside resorts lured middle-class visitors and some craftsmen and their families. Trains ran to German health spas and casinos, whose clientele a century earlier had been limited to princes and noblemen.

There was also good news on the oceans and rivers. In 1816, a steamship, combining steam and sail power, sailed from Liverpool to Boston in seventeen days, halving the previous time for the journey. Steamboats, which began to operate on Europe's rivers in the 1820s and 1830s, also revolutionized travel and transport. By 1840, the transport of Irish cattle and dairy products to England alone fully engaged eighty steamships. A constant procession of steamships travelled the Rhine River from Basel, Switzerland, to the Dutch seaport of Rotterdam.

The Great Western leaving Bristol in 1838 for its maiden voyage to New York. Steam power reduced the trip to nineteen days.

MAP 14.2 PRINCIPAL CONTINENTAL RAILWAY LINES, 1851 More railway lines existed in the north than in the south of Europe, as industrialization proceeded more quickly in northern France, Belgium, the German states, and the northern Italian states than in southern France or southern Italy.

At the same time, the contribution of improved roads to the Industrial Revolution should not be forgotten. Here, too, the story of European economic development involved continuity as much as innovation, reminding us that in some significant ways the Industrial Revolution was based upon an innovative expansion of technologies and ways of doing things that were already in place.

A VARIETY OF NATIONAL INDUSTRIAL EXPERIENCES

During this period, the Industrial Revolution affected western Europe, and particularly northwestern Europe, more than the countries in southern or eastern Europe. Furthermore, within states some regions underwent significant shifts toward a manufacturing economy: Catalonia, but not Castile in Spain; the Ruhr and Rhineland in the German states, but not East Prussia; Piedmont and Lombardy in northern Italy, but not southern Italy and Sicily (see Map 14.3).

Some regions that developed modern industries had the advantage of building on long-standing economic bases (see Table 14.2). This was true in Belgium, a small, newly independent (1831) country that emerged with continental Europe's greatest concentration of mechanized production and factories. While Belgium's northern neighbor, the once-great trading power of the Netherlands, continued its relative economic decline, Belgium seemed to offer a blueprint for rapid industrial development. Like the Netherlands, it was densely populated and urbanized, which provided demand for manufactured goods and an available labor supply. Flanders had for centuries been a center of trade and the production of fine textiles. Antwerp, linked to the North Sea by the Scheldt Estuary, remained one of Europe's major ports, generating capital for investment in industry. In 1816, the textile industry of Ghent employed more than 12,000 workers at home and in workshops. Blessed with rich coal deposits, Belgium's railroad construction advanced rapidly, thriving by transporting goods from North Sea ports toward Central Europe. Belgian manufacturing boomed.

In the Vanguard: Britain's Era of Mechanization

Why did the Industrial Revolution begin in England? Britain was well on the way to becoming the "workshop of the world" in the second half of the eighteenth century. Capital-intensive commercialized farming began to transform English agriculture earlier than anywhere else, feeding Britain's growing population. Britain was blessed with coal and iron ore deposits located near water transportation, which made it possible for raw materials to be transported to factories with relative ease. British commercial domination, built in part on its rich colonial trade, provided capital for investment in manufacturing. British entrepreneurs relied heavily on

MAP 14.3 THE INDUSTRIAL REVOLUTION IN EUROPE, 1815–1860 Areas of industrial concentration and growth in Britain and on the continent.

TABLE 14.2. MANUFACTURING CAPACITY THROUGHOUT EUROPE (THOUSANDS OF HORSEPOWER OF STEAM POWER)

Country	1800	1850
Great Britain	620	1,290
The German states	40	260
France	90	270
Austria	20	100
Belgium	40	70
Russia	20	70
Italy	10	20
Spain	10	20
The Netherlands	—	10
Europe	860	2,240

Source: Carlo M. Cipolla, ed. *The Fontana Economic History of Europe: Vol. 4(1), The Emergence of Industrial Societies* (London, 1973), p. 165.

self-finance, and at first banks played relatively little role in long-term investment. However, the government did encourage a precocious banking system that would assume a great role later in the century. It was far easier to begin a company in Britain than on the continent; after 1840, any number of people could form a company in Britain simply by registering with the government.

The structure of British society also proved conducive to economic development. There were fewer social barriers between wealthy landowning nobles, prosperous gentry, and eager entrepreneurs. Dissenters (non-Anglican Protestants) were afforded basic toleration and some became manufacturers.

The British government adopted a general policy of non-interference in business. However, Parliament protected British manufacturers by enacting tariffs on goods imported in the eighteenth century and, when no foreign economic challenge seemed too strong, by reducing tariffs in the 1820s. Parliament also allocated funds for improving England's transportation network, which helped merchants and manufacturers. Parliamentary acts of enclosure (facilitating the consolidation of arable strips of land and the division of common lands) helped wealthy landowners add to their holdings, augmenting the productivity of their land and permitting the accumulation of investment capital.

English cotton manufacturing, gradually transformed by mechanization, led the Industrial Revolution and carried along other industries in its wake. The popularity of cotton clothing spread rapidly, allowing poor people to be more adequately clothed. Cotton fabric could be more easily cleaned and was less expensive than wool, worsted, and other materials. Cotton clothing joined silks and linens in the wardrobes of the wealthy.

Power looms in a British cotton factory, 1830.

The cotton manufacturer became the uncrowned king of industrial society in Britain, revered as the epitome of the successful entrepreneur who was enriching himself while embellishing Britain's reputation. Between 1789 and 1850, the amount of raw cotton imported into Britain (much of it picked by plantation slaves in the southern United States), increased by more than fifty times, rising from about 11 million pounds per year to 588 million pounds. During the same period, British production of cotton textiles increased from 40 million yards per year to 2,025 million yards. Cotton goods accounted for about half of all British exports through the first half of the nineteenth century.

In the British textile industry, spinning (the operation by which fibrous materials such as cotton, wool, linen, and silk are turned into thread or yarn) gradually had become mechanized during the last decades of the eighteenth century (see Chapter 10). The advent of power looms and power weaving (the process by which threads are interlaced to make cloth or fabric) removed the last bottleneck to fully mechanized production. The number of power looms in England multiplied rapidly: 2,400 in 1813, 55,000 in 1829, 85,000 in 1833, and 224,000 in 1850.

Industrialization in France

France was the world's second leading economy, although the wars during the revolutionary and Napoleonic periods had interrupted economic development. The revolutionary government had eliminated some hurdles for French businessmen by ending the tangle of regional customs barriers and tax differences. But in comparison with Britain, France's coal deposits were less rich and more dispersed and were far from iron ore deposits and from canals. Thus, transportation costs kept up the price of raw materials. Demand was also less in France than in Britain because the French population rose by only 30 percent during the first half of the nineteenth century, compared to that of Britain, where the population had doubled during the same period. Yet many French manufacturers benefited from extremely high protective tariffs, which kept out some lower-cost British goods. French agricultural production developed more slowly than that of Britain; small family farms remained common in much of France. High agricultural tariffs and considerable village common land did not encourage agricultural efficiency.

French banking facilities remained relatively rudimentary compared to those in Britain and the Netherlands. The primary function of the Bank of France, created by Napoleon in 1800, was to loan money to the state. The handful of private banks, which were run out of the deep pockets of wealthy families, preferred to make what appeared to be safer loans to governments. Furthermore, banks—like investors—faced unlimited liability in the event of bankruptcy. Deposit banks were specifically denied the

A rural Joiner's workshop in France.

right to invest in private industry, except for investment in companies enjoying state concessions—such as those building the railways. Even normal business transactions were complicated by the fact that more than 90 percent of payments had to be made in specie (gold or silver). Until the late 1850s, the smallest banknote was worth 500 francs (the equivalent of almost a year's earnings for an unskilled worker). Banks thus had considerable difficulty attracting ordinary depositors.

The French state shared investors' suspicions of companies of any size, limiting the number of investment "joint-stock companies" that could be created. Furthermore, many companies were cautious family firms that invested profits in land rather than in the expansion of their businesses. With many peasant families still hiding their money in their mattresses or burying it in their gardens, it was difficult to raise investment capital.

In France, as in England, textile production (primarily of woolens, cotton, and linen) provided the catalyst for industrial development. At the same time, between the end of the Napoleonic Wars in 1815 and the beginning of the economic crisis of 1846–1847, the production of coal tripled, and that of pig iron doubled.

The reputation of French industry, and that of Paris, in particular, still proudly rested on the production of quality items, "articles of Paris" such as gloves, umbrellas, and boots, as well as furniture, the demand for which had been accentuated by the consumer revolution in the eighteenth century. During the 1830s and 1840s, workshop production—for example of barrels, pipes, and watches—expanded into many rural areas in response to increased demand, spurred by a modest level of growth in cities and market towns. Rural industry, characterized by low capital investment, remained essential to French economic growth.

French manufacturers benefited from increased state assistance. The July Monarchy (1830–1848) encouraged business interests, sometimes maintaining high tariffs that protected special interests—for example, those of textile manufacturers, who feared outside competition. Taxes on commerce and industry remained extraordinarily low. The government provided a decisive push in the launching of railways in France, purchasing the land and bridges along which the tracks were to pass and guaranteeing a minimum return on investments in railway development. Bankruptcy laws became less onerous, eliminating the humiliation of incarceration as a penalty. New legislation made it easy for investors to join together to form new companies with people to whom they were not related, or, in some cases, did not even know—hence their name, "anonymous societies" (*sociétés anonymes*). The government also pleased businessmen by crushing insurrections by republicans and by silkworkers in Lyon in the early 1830s. Furthermore, strikes, legalized in Britain with the repeal of the Combination Acts in 1824, remained illegal in France until 1864.

Industrialization in the German States

In the German states, industrialization lagged behind that of Britain and France. There were three main factors that undercut manufacturing in the German states: the multiplicity of independent states; the labyrinth of tolls and customs barriers, a veritable financial gauntlet through which any wagon or boat carrying merchandise had to pass; and virtual monopolies held by guilds over the production and distribution of certain products. The German states remained as a whole overwhelmingly rural, with the percentage of rural population barely declining at all between 1816 and 1872. Furthermore, the harvest failure and subsequent agricultural depression of 1846, compounded by the Revolutions of 1848 (see Chapter 16), temporarily halted German economic development, like that of France, cold in its tracks.

Yet beginning in the mid-1830s, textile manufacturing developed in the three most demographically dynamic regions—the Rhineland, Saxony, and Silesia (see Map 14.3). Berlin emerged as a center of machine production. Coal mining and iron production developed in the Ruhr Basin in western Prussia, which had half of the coal riches of the entire continent. The Prussian state appointed directors to serve on the boards of private companies, brought technical experts from Britain to help develop industries, encouraged technical education, and founded associations for the encouragement of industrialization. In the 1840s, the Bank of Prussia began operating as a joint-stock credit bank, providing investment capital, the lack of which limited industrial development in the other German states.

The German states took a major step toward an expansion of commerce and manufacturing when they formed the Zollverein, a customs union, in 1834 (see Map 14.4). The Zollverein was the brainchild of economist Friedrich List (1789–1846), a tanner's son who became an outspoken proponent of railway building. Calling a customs union within the German states and railway construction the "Siamese twins" of economic expansion, List proposed in 1819 the abolition of all tariffs within the German states, although, unlike many other liberal economists, he insisted that protective tariffs be raised to shield German industries from British imports. List, a fiery advocate for the political unification of the German states, believed that only through tariff reform could Germans save themselves from being "debased to be carriers of water and hewers of wood for the Britons . . . treated even worse than the downtrodden Hindu." The Zollverein included four-fifths of the territory of the German states. It contributed modestly to German economic and industrial growth, expanding markets for manufactured goods.

In the Ruhr Basin, young Alfred Krupp (1812–1887) began to manage his late father's small steel manufacturing firm in Essen at the age of four-

MAP 14.4 THE ZOLLVEREIN (GERMAN CUSTOMS UNION), 1834 States and cities within the German Customs Union. Led by Prussia, it was the first attempt by the German states to reduce customs duties and to coordinate economic activity.

teen. Krupp travelled through other German states to study manufacturing. Returning to his factory, he served, in his words, as "clerk, letter-writer, cashier, smith, smelter, coke-pounder, [and] night watchman at the converting furnace." In 1832, his firm nearly closed for lack of business. Even after visiting France and Britain in search of new ideas, business was so bad in 1848 that he melted down the family silver in order to pay his workers. Finally, an order from Russia arrived for machinery to produce knives and forks, followed by another for steel springs and axles for a German railway. Krupp's company produced high-quality machine parts and steel tools. In 1851 at the Crystal Palace in London, he exhibited axles for train coaches and a cannon with a gleaming cast-steel barrel (his newest and ultimately most successful product). Thereafter, Krupp's steelworks became enormously and ominously successful, turning out guns of increasing size and quality. Krupp employed 72 workers in 1848, 12,000 in 1873.

Sparse Industrialization in Southern and Eastern Europe

Eastern and southern Europe remained sparsely industrialized, hampered by inadequately developed natural resources and insufficient government attention. Entrepreneurs faced the difficulty of raising investment capital in what were overwhelmingly poor agricultural societies. There were regional exceptions, to be sure: the increasingly mechanized textile production of Piedmont and Lombardy in northern Italy and Catalonia in Spain, and pockets of industrialization in Bohemia and near Vienna.

Industrialization in Spain was slowed by inadequate transportation and laws that discouraged investment. Lacking navigable rivers, Spain also suffered the absence of a railway system until after the middle of the nineteenth century. A commercial code in 1829 established the right of the state to veto any proposed association of investors. Following the continent-wide economic crisis in 1846–1847, the state placed banking under the control of the Cortes (assembly) and forbade the creation of new companies unless investors could demonstrate that they would serve "public utility."

Russia had a relatively tiny middle class—with only about 160,000 merchants out of a population of about 57 million people in 1854. State-owned serfs had been emancipated beginning in the 1840s and could till the land to which they had previously been attached. However, the majority of the population of the Russian Empire remained until emancipation in 1861 (see Chapter 18) bound for life as serfs to land owned by lords or the state. Although some serfs were skilled artisans, their bondage made it difficult for entrepreneurs to recruit a stable labor force since industrial laborers were among the hundreds of thousands of serfs who fled toward the distant eastern reaches of the empire.

Transportation in the Russian Empire remained rudimentary. One short railway line linked St. Petersburg to the Baltic Sea in the late 1840s and another longer route served the iron works of the Urals. The minister of finance from 1823 to 1844, a crucial figure in state economic policy, had opposed the building of railway lines, believing that they would encourage needless travel. Moscow and St. Petersburg were joined by rail only in 1851. Serviceable roads—only about 3,000 miles of them—had been built with military considerations in mind, not for commercial or industrial purposes. Rivers were used for transportation, but the boats were not steam-driven and travel was slow. Early in the nineteenth century several important canals were constructed, including that joining St. Petersburg to the Volga River. Internal and foreign trade expanded markedly in the first half of the nineteenth century, the latter, including grain and timber, probably by three times, much of it through Black Sea ports. However, coal and iron ore deposits lay thousands of miles from St. Petersburg, Moscow, and Kiev and could be transported to manufacturing centers only with great difficulty and at daunting cost.

Some hostility toward industrialization—and toward the West in general—remained entrenched in Russia, in part orchestrated by the Orthodox Church. In the 1860s, there still was no generally accepted word in Russian for "factory" or even "worker." Industrial workers remained closely tied to village life. The state undertook only feeble efforts to encourage industrial development. The Council of Manufacturers, created in 1828, included several merchants, industrialists, nobles (characteristic Russian entrepreneurs), professors, and a technical adviser. Trade councils were organized in the largest towns, and several national technical schools were established.

Yet, despite these factors, the growth of Russian industry was significant during the first half of the nineteenth century, if only in and around St. Petersburg, Moscow, and the Ural Mountains. The cotton industry developed rapidly, as did a number of traditional manufacturing sectors in response to population growth. There were even some remarkable success stories. The entrepreneurs of the small town of Ivanovo, northwest of Moscow, were almost all peasants. The most successful of all was a serf who with his master's permission had constructed a textile factory late in the eighteenth century. Adding power looms and lodging his peasant workers in dormitories, he created what was by far the largest industrial enterprise in Russia, with 2,600 employees by 1852. Another serf set up a textile workshop in a village near Moscow in 1797 and then, after purchasing his freedom, moved the operation into Moscow, adding power looms early in the 1850s.

The number of Russian industrial workers (of whom about a fifth were serfs) increased from 201,000 in 1824 to 565,000 in 1860. At the same time, Russia began to import and construct more machinery. However, many spinners and weavers labored by hand without the benefit of the new machines in textile production, which remained overwhelmingly a cottage industry. Hundreds of thousands of other workers labored as tailors, shoemakers, and in other trades essential for urban and rural life, including 300,000 boatmen who pulled barges up the Volga River, a trip of seventy-five days.

IMPACT OF THE INDUSTRIAL REVOLUTION

The Industrial Revolution, to be sure, changed the way people lived. Yet one should not overestimate either the speed or the extent to which these fundamental changes occurred in the nineteenth century. Even in Britain, France, and Prussia, the three most industrialized powers, factory workers comprised between only 2 and 5 percent of the population in 1850. In many places, industrial workers—particularly miners—were also part-time peasants, who went home to work in the fields part of the year, or even part of the day.

Continuities on the Land

Most rural people in Europe were not landowners. Landless laborers far outnumbered any other category of the rural population, and their numbers increased dramatically in nineteenth-century Europe. Agricultural wages were falling, and rural under- and unemployment became chronic. Landlords hired on shorter-term contracts. The abolition of serfdom on the Prussian great estates east of the Elbe River increased the number of rural laborers scrambling to find low-paid farm work. The increase in population put more pressure on the rural poor. Many landless peasants were forced to sign disadvantageous leases with their landlords. Yet, even when peasants owned land, they were by no means guaranteed a decent life, because many plots were too small to be profitable, or the land was of poor quality. In Prussia and southern Spain, the number of landless laborers soared as owners of small farms were unable to survive and sold off their land.

Rural protest increased in the first two decades of the nineteenth century. In 1830, a hard year, travelers found people who had died of hunger on the roads, nothing in their stomachs but dandelions. In southern and eastern England, wealthy landowners had begun to use threshing machines, which left many hired hands without work. Grain passed through the rollers of these portable machines and then into a revolving drum. Threshing machines could be set up in any barn or field and operated by one or two horses. Farm workers, whose labor as threshers or "flailers" was no longer needed, began to smash threshing machines. Sometimes local artisans supported the protesters, and they sometimes

Bread riots in England, 1830.

also benefited from the tacit support of smaller landowners who could not afford the machines and were being driven out of business by their wealthier colleagues who could.

Some of the scrawled threats landowners received were signed "Captain Swing" (for example, "Revenge for thee is on the wing, from thy determined Captain Swing!"). Swing emerged as a mythical figure symbolizing popular justice, created to give the impression that the laborers were numerous and organized enough to force the landowners to renounce—as some did—use of the machines. Authorities weighed in to make arrests, exiling some people to Australia, and executing nineteen men. Incidents of machine breaking ended in September 1832. But other similar attacks occurred between 1839 and in Wales when poor people attacked tollgates and tollhouses in the "Rebecca riots," which were also named after an imaginary redresser of social wrongs. In Portugal, women played a major role in an uprising in 1846 that followed a government attempt to enclose land and force peasants to register the land they owned. Like Captain Swing in England, the mythical "Mary by the Fountain" became a symbol of revolt.

Rural poverty weighed heavily on the continent. The Prussian political theorist Karl von Clausewitz, travelling in the Rhineland during the brutal winter of 1817, came upon "ruined figures, scarcely resembling men, [prowling] around the fields searching for food among the unharvested and already half rotten potatoes that never grew to maturity." A traveler described the hovels in which Romanian peasants lived: "holes dug in the earth, over which a propped roof is thrown—covered rarely with straw, generally with turf." The further east one went in Europe, the more peasants remained fettered by obligations to lord and state. More than a hundred Russian landlords or their stewards were murdered by their peasants and serfs in two decades beginning in 1835. In 1846, peasants in Galicia in Central Europe rose up and slaughtered nobles in a bloodbath.

Russian serfs needed permission to leave their villages. In Silesia, peasant families still owed lords more than a hundred days of labor a year, for which they were to provide a team of animals; they were also obligated to repair roads and to make various payments in kind. Such peasants paid the equivalent of a third of their produce to the lord or to the state in taxes. Even when entrepreneurial landlords began commuting such payments in labor and in kind into cash, some of which they put back into their lands, such reforms did not end subsistence agriculture in parts of Central Europe and most of Eastern Europe and the Balkans.

Conditions of rural life in Eastern Europe may even have worsened since the eighteenth century. Balkan peasants and Russian serfs still lived in wooden huts. In Sweden, the small red cottages of farming families were notoriously cramped and many people depended on their parishes to provide assistance in hard times. Rural people drew warmth from fireplaces during the day and from animals with whom many shared quarters at night. There were few windows because they let in wind and rain (in Sweden, some windows were still covered with animal membrane), or because farmhouses had been built that way to reduce the tax on doors and windows, as in parts of France.

The rural poor of Ireland, Spain, Portugal, Italy, Russia, and the Balkans ate rye bread, porridge, and vegetables such as potatoes in northern Europe, cabbage in Portugal, Eastern Europe, and Russia, and onions and garlic in France. For many people meat was little more than a distant memory of a wedding feast. When they could afford to eat meat at all, poor people were most likely to eat tripe, pigs' ears, or blood sausage. Most peasants who owned animals could not afford to slaughter them. Fish was relatively rare on peasant plates, unless the peasants lived by the sea, or near a lake or pond in which they were allowed to fish or could get away with it (although even the English and Scandinavian poor could afford herring, fished in enormous quantities in the Baltic Sea). Water, however contaminated, remained the drink of necessity for the poor. People in southern Europe drank poor quality wine; northern Europeans drank beer when they could, or cider, although both were relatively expensive.

Urbanization

The first half of the nineteenth century brought about a marked urbanization of the European population, as the percentage of people living in towns and cities rose rapidly (see Table 14.3). In 1750, two British cities had more than 50,000 inhabitants (London and Edinburgh); in 1801, there were eight, and by mid-century, twenty-nine. London's population rose from about 900,000 in 1800 to 2,363,000 in 1850. At mid-century, half of the population of Britain resided in towns. French and German urbanization proceeded at a significantly slower pace than that

TABLE 14.3. POPULATION OF MAJOR EUROPEAN CITIES

City	1800	1850
London	900,000–1,000,000	2,363,000
Paris	547,000 (1801)	1,053,000 (1851)
Vienna	247,000	444,000
Naples	350,000	415,000 (1871)
St. Petersburg	200,000	485,000
Moscow	200,000	365,000
Berlin	172,000	419,000
Liverpool	77,000	400,000
Birmingham	73,000	250,000
Leeds	53,162	172,023
Manchester	25,000 (1772)	367,000

of Britain and Belgium. In 1851, only a quarter of the French population lived in urban areas, which were defined as settlements of at least 2,000 people.

Yet Paris grew from about 550,000 in 1801 to a million inhabitants in 1846. Stockholm's population multiplied by four, from only 75,000 in 1800 to 350,000 at the end of the century. Smaller towns grew rapidly, as well, such as Porto in Portugal, which doubled in size in sixty years. Industrial towns grew most rapidly, but commercial and administrative centers, too, gained population.

The further east one went in Europe, the fewer and smaller the towns. This was because rural nobles retained control over agricultural exports and over people through serfdom, which tied peasants to the land. Furthermore, there was in general less manufacturing in Eastern Europe, and therefore fewer manufacturing towns and fewer trading ports. In Austria, more than four of every five people lived in the countryside; in Sweden, nine of ten. The Russian Empire had only three cities of any size—St. Petersburg, Moscow, and Kiev; parts of Moscow were still indistinguishable from the rural world, dotted with wood or even mud huts inhabited by peasant workers. Yet even in the Russian Empire, the percentage of people living in towns and cities grew during the first half of the century from 4.1 percent to 7.8 percent.

Hundreds of thousands of migrants, most of whom were poor, swarmed into cities, which had difficulty providing needed services for the mass of people and where living conditions in general were abysmal. Streets may have been better illuminated than ever before, thanks to gas lighting, but working-class districts became much more crowded. Only a fifth of the buildings in Paris were connected to the city's water supply. And even in those, few apartments above the first floor had running water (carriers hauled tubs of water up and down staircases). Crimes against property increased rapidly with urban growth, especially during periods of hardship. Between 1805 and 1848, indictable offenses in England and Wales multiplied by six, although part of this dramatic jump may reflect the result of better policing, and thus reporting, as many towns established police forces for the first time. To the upper classes, rapid urban growth itself seemed threatening during the first half of the century.

As urban centers became ever more densely packed, industrial suburbs also developed. The urban periphery offered more available land, proximity to railways, canals, and rivers, and a ready labor supply perched on the edge of the city, where the cost of living was cheaper. Shortly before the Revolution of 1830, one of French King Louis-Philippe's ministers warned that the factories and industrial workers of the periphery "will be the cord that wrings our neck one day." Several years later, a member of the Chamber of Deputies warned "the barbarians who now threaten society are not in the Caucasus, nor in the steppes of the [Russian] Tartary; they are in the suburbs of our manufacturing cities." Within cities, the European middle classes withdrew into privileged elite quarters, leaving workers and other poor people in separate, disadvantaged neighborhoods.

Immigration

As more people died than were born in most large cities, immigration of peasants and unskilled workers (usually young people from regions of marginal agricultural production) accounted in almost every case for urban growth. Thus, only about half of the residents of London and Paris and only about a quarter of those in the even more rapidly growing northern English industrial towns had been born there.

Most migrants moved to town because they knew someone there, usually relatives or friends from home who might be able to help them find a job, and perhaps put them up until they found a job and their own place to live. Within large cities, people tended to live in the same neighborhood as others from their regions, such as the sooty "Little Ireland" in the midst of the largest factories of Manchester in which many of the 35,000 Irish of the city lived in cellars, or the infamous Irish "rookery" of St. Giles in central London. The discrimination faced by the Irish in London was reflected in literature, such as in Elizabeth Gaskell's *North and South* (1855), in which the villains are Irish.

Between 1816 and 1850, at least 5 million Europeans booked passage across the seas, particularly during the "hungry forties," which struck Central and Eastern Europe, as well as Ireland, particularly hard. One and a half million people of Ireland's population of approximately 8 million left their homeland between 1835 and 1850, particularly during the potato famine in the late 1840s. An Irish migrant to London remembered:

> I had a bit o' land, yer honor, in County Limerick. Well, it wasn't just a farrum, nor what ye would call a garden here, but my father lived and died on it—glory be to God!—and brought up me and my sister on it. It was about an acre, and the taties was well known to be good. But the sore times came, and the taties was afflicted, and the wife and me—I have no children—hadn't a bit nor a sup, but wather to live on, and an igg or two. I filt the famine a-comin'. I saw people a-feedin' on the wild green things. . . . The wife and me walked to Dublin . . . and we got to Liverpool. Then sorrow's the taste of worruk could I git, beyant oncete 3 [shillings] for two days of harrud porthering, that broke my back half in two. I was tould, I'd do betther in London, and so Glory be to God! I have—perhaps I have.

Following the Irish, the largest group of emigrants were Germans. After 1820, Norway sent more emigrants to the United States than the number of people living in the country in that year. Many more families and individuals began the trek toward a port of departure, such as Bremen or Le Havre, than actually sailed for a new life. At the same time, hundreds of

HERE   AND   THERE;
Or, Emigration a Remedy.

This British cartoon from 1850 depicts the expectations of migrants.

thousands of Russian migrants pushed toward the eastern reaches of the empire in the quest for land.

The growth in manufacturing and improvements in transportation expanded the distance people could travel to find work. Seasonal migration took men greater distances to work in towns and cities during the warmer months of the year, while their wives cared for the children and whatever land they might have at home. Before the middle of the nineteenth century, seasonal workers may have accounted for as much as a third of the workforce.

INDUSTRIAL WORK AND WORKERS

The English novelist Charles Dickens dubbed the grim, sooty industrial cities of England "Coketown." After completing his novel *Hard Times* (1854), an account of working-class life, Dickens wrote that "one of Fiction's highest uses" is to "interest and affect the general mind in behalf of anything that is clearly wrong—to stimulate and rouse the public soul to a compassionate or indignant feeling that *it must not be.*"

Middle-class socialists and workers themselves began to criticize passionately some of the consequences of large-scale industrialization. The growing awareness among some workers that they formed a class apart followed directly from their growing sense that they were vulnerable to the vicissitudes of capitalism.

Gender and Family in the Industrial Age

Not only men found jobs as industrialization proceeded, but women as well were employed in many of the industries, both rural (where their labor had long been predominant in cottage industry) and urban, that were expanding during the industrial age. Female labor remained central to large-scale industrialization. While there were a number of important predominantly male industries, such as iron production, the leather trades, building, and mining, women did work in these industries as well. Thus, in the 1840s, about 6,000 women worked in English mines. In Lancashire in northern England, more than a third of all married women worked in textile mills. The workforce in the textile industry (above all, lacemaking) was to a great extent female. In France, women accounted for 35 percent of the industrial workforce in 1856 and about half of textile workers.

Although important social continuities from the pre-industrial age remained, wage labor altered family life and the structure of local communities. Wage labor made young women and men less dependent on their parents, enabling many to marry earlier. But marriage still remained to some extent an economic relationship and some couples delayed wedlock until both partners could accumulate the skills or assets to maintain an independent household. A sharp rise in illegitimate births (in Paris, about 33 percent of all births, 45 percent in Stockholm) seems to have been another effect of the rise in employment opportunities and wages for unmarried couples in "free unions," or common-law marriages.

In Western European nations, domestic service remained the largest category of female occupations at the middle of the nineteenth century, employing in Britain 1.3 million women, nearly 40 percent of women workers. The second largest employer of women was the textile industry, which employed 22 percent of women workers. Working up to eighteen hours a day, servants slept under staircases and in attics, but ate relatively well. They had a higher rate of literacy than did working-class women in general and better prospects of marrying above their social class.

Country women spun and wove wool, linen, and cotton; sewed, embroidered, and knitted stockings by hand; and worked in fields or gardens, while looking after children. On the continent, even in areas of relative agricultural prosperity, cottage industry still provided women with work during the winter, allowing country people to maintain the traditional rural family economy well into the nineteenth century. Rural women also continued to work as wet nurses for babies sent to them from the cities. Urban women worked as laundresses, seamstresses, street merchants and peddlers, and some kept boardinghouses. Some middle-class women worked in commerce, as unpaid clerks in their husbands' shops or as receptionists and secretaries in their spouse's law, medical, or notarial offices.

Although only a relatively small percentage of women's work was organized in factories, a gradual shift to larger textile and clothing workshops and factories occurred in England, above all, as well as in parts of France, Belgium, and several German states. With the expansion in power-loom weaving, many women with experience as cottage laborers found employment in textile mills. Factories expanded work opportunities during the 1830s and 1840s. Women worked for about half of what their male counterparts earned. As in the pre-industrial period, many, if not most, women workers were young and single (including widows and spinsters).

Working-class families were presented with a dilemma: with the growth of factories and the consequent separation of home and work, women had to balance the need for the additional income factory work could provide with that of caring for young children. Many mothers would withdraw from the workforce to care for children for at least a time. But since the family economy also depended on their wages, they generally returned to work as quickly as possible.

Hundreds of thousands of European women worked full- or part-time as prostitutes. Prostitution presented a hierarchy of conditions of life and wages, ranging from confident high-class courtesans to poor girls beckoning clients from dark doorways. Some women, including many who were married, were able to earn much more money selling sexual favors than they could earn in textile mills or in domestic service.

To middle-class moralists, prostitutes symbolized moral failure and the dangers of modern life. Yet the increase in middle-class male demand for prostitution helped swell the number of prostitutes in Europe's burgeoning cities. Governments therefore accepted prostitution as a "necessary evil." They sought to police brothels and the comportment of prostitutes in order to keep the profession hidden as much as possible from public view, while trying, by ordering prostitutes to have regular medical checkups, to limit the ravages of venereal disease. The number of prostitutes in London was so difficult to determine that estimates for the 1840s vary from 7,000 to 80,000. In St. Petersburg, there were over 4,000 registered prostitutes in 1870. In France, many prostitutes were former servants who, after an inopportune pregnancy, now walked the streets or beckoned from doorways, trying to avoid humiliating, obligatory medical inspections because they knew they would be incarcerated if it was demonstrated that they had contracted venereal disease, which they could pass on.

Child Labor

Children had always worked in agriculture in such tasks as caring for farm animals, scaring birds away from crops, and gleaning at harvest time. At a very young age, many had also learned to assist in domestic textile production, preparing wool for spinning, and raising silkworms. With industrialization, children came to be employed in factories, where their compact size made them useful for certain tasks, such as mending broken threads, or climbing on machinery to extract something impeding its operations. Teenage girls were considered particularly adept at calico printing. In 1850, 28 percent of girls between ages ten and fifteen were employed; in Britain during the early 1830s, youths less than twenty-one years of age made up almost a third of the workforce.

As in cottage industry, factory work often employed entire families, with adult males supervising other family members. Children's low wages— about a quarter of what their fathers earned—nonetheless represented a significant contribution to the family economy. One man recalled "being placed, when seven years of age, upon a stool to spread cotton upon a breaker preparatory to spinning," an elder brother turning the wheel to put the machine in motion.

Factory work was often dangerous. An English factory inspector reported that the children working at a punching machine risked losing their fingers. " 'They seldom lose the hand,' said one of the proprietors to me, in explanation, 'it only takes off a finger at the first or second joint. Sheer carelessness . . . sheer carelessness!' " An eight-year-old girl who worked as a "trapper" in the mine pits, opening ventilation doors to let coal wagons pass, related, "I have to trap without a light, and I'm scared. I go at four and sometimes half-past three. . . . Sometimes I sing when I've light but not in the dark. I dare not sing then."

Some reformers believed that long days of labor instilled discipline, whereas idleness would turn children into sinners and criminals. But British evangelical Protestants (such as Methodists who aggressively taught the necessity of a personal conversion experience and the authority of the Bible), among others, wanted to save children from exhausting and sometimes dangerous work. A British law passed by Parlia-

Young children working in a factory.

ment in 1833 forced employers to start part-time schools in factories employing children, although in some cases the owners simply designated a worker to be "teacher," whether or not he could read or write very well. The 1833 Factory Act in Britain limited labor by very young children to eight hours (subsequent legislation in 1847 limited older children and women to a ten-hour day). In 1841, France's first child labor law banned factory work for children under eight years of age, limited the workday to eight hours for those eight to thirteen years old and to twelve hours for those thirteen to sixteen years old, and banned child labor at night

The satanic mills of Manchester.

and on Sundays and holidays. The law, however, was extremely difficult to enforce, and was routinely circumvented by employers and ignored by parents who needed the additional family income.

Standards of Living of the Laboring Poor

In 1838, a British member of Parliament described a cotton mill:

> [It was] a sight that froze my blood. The place was full of women, young, all of them, some large with child, and obliged to stand twelve hours a day. Their hours are from five in the morning to seven in the evening, two hours of that being for rest, so that they stand twelve hours a day. The heat was excessive in some of the rooms, the stink pestiferous, and in all an atmosphere of cotton flue. I nearly fainted. The young women were all pale, sallow, thin, yet generally fairly grown, all with bare feet—a strange sight to English eyes.

The northern industrial cities of England attracted the attention of horrified observers. "The entrance to hell realized!" wrote the general sent to Manchester in 1839 when the government expected disturbances from thousands of unemployed and hungry workers. After seeing Manchester, an American visitor wrote in 1845, "Every day that I live I thank Heaven that I am not a poor man with a family in England." There were, to be sure, people of means in Manchester, but Friedrich Engels (1820–1895), a German Rhinelander, believed "that a [middle-class] person may live in it for years, and go in and out daily without coming into contact with a working-people's quarter or even with workers . . . by unconscious, tacit agreement."

Engels sought and found the grim face of unrestrained capitalism in Manchester:

> At the bottom flows, or rather stagnates, the Irwell, a narrow, coal-black, foul-smelling stream, full of debris and refuse. . . . Above the bridge are tanneries, bonemills, and gasworks, from which all drains and refuse find their way to the Irk, which receives further the contents of all the neighboring sewers and privies . . . here each house is packed close behind its neighbor and a bit of each is visible, all black, smoky, crumbling, ancient, with broken panes and window-frames. The background is furnished by old barrack-like factory buildings. . . . [Beyond] the background embraces the pauper burial ground, the station of the Liverpool and Leeds railway, and, in the rear of this, the Workhouse, the "Poor-Law Bastille" of Manchester, which, like a citadel, looks threateningly down from behind its high walls and parapets on the hilltop, upon the working people's quarter below.

Elizabeth Gaskell's popular novel *Mary Barton* (1848) has the subtitle "A Tale of Manchester Life." The novel was criticized when it was published for being hostile to mill owners, but a magazine recommended the novel to its middle-class readers: "Do they want to know why poor men . . . learn to hate law and order, Queen, Lords and Commons, country-party and corn-law league alike—to hate the rich, in short? Then let them read *Mary Barton*. . . . Do they want to get a detailed insight into the whole science of starving? . . . Let them read *Mary Barton*."

In 1846, a visitor described the environs of Saint-Étienne in France as "monotonous and without charm; the countryside is furrowed with railroads. One encounters factories of various kinds almost everywhere, and especially coal mines with smoking obelisks, forges of coke that give off a thick, black smoke which can be seen from afar; it paralyses all vegetation and gives everything a black tint. At night these blast furnaces offer a truly astonishing spectacle, infernal to all who see the city for the first time."

Historians have long debated whether the standard of living for workers increased or fell as large-scale industrialization transformed society during the first half of the nineteenth century. The "cheerful" school of historiography has argued that the Industrial Revolution, at least during the first half of the century, by increasing employment and lowering the price of some goods, almost immediately improved the way ordinary people lived. By contrast, other historians have embraced the view that industrial capitalism was making conditions of life even worse for workers and their families as the number of people depending on wage labor increased faster than did job possibilities and pay.

During the first half of the century, the incomes of many artisans, as well as women workers, fell as trades were flooded with the end of guild restrictions and increasing mechanized production. Women workers, such as spinners, were often the first to experience unemployment because of the new technology. Wages in many industries were extremely volatile; boom periods could come and go with numbing suddenness. Even good years were broken in many industries by "dead seasons" when there was no work. In England, women who had been gradually displaced from farm work and rural spinning could not be absorbed into factories, which already had enough employees.

Despite the fact that improved transportation made more goods available to more people, the gap between the rich and the poor increased. In England, many middle-class heads of household earned three or four times as much as even a skilled worker. In the late 1820s in Paris, more than three-quarters of people who died left virtually nothing to heirs, because they had nothing to leave in a will and, in any case, they could not afford to have one drawn up by a lawyer.

On the continent, the poorer a family was, the greater the percentage of its income that still was spent on food, primarily bread. Poor Belgian workers in 1850 spent two-thirds of their income on food. Clothing accounted for the second largest category of expense, followed by housing. All other expenses, including heat, light, tools, supplies, and recreation, had to come out of less than 10 percent of the family income.

Yet even fairly reliable data on wages and the cost of living leave us without a full appreciation of the vulnerability to hard times of working-class families. Fluctuations in wage levels were part of life. Industrial workers remained susceptible to the effects of economic crisis; furthermore, many manufacturing jobs were interrupted by seasonal layoffs. Most migrants no longer benefited from the kind of community support they had received during hard times in their villages. Recourse to the neighborhood pawn shop was part of the experience of the majority of urban working-class families until at least the middle of the nineteenth century.

English workers tended to be better off than most of their continental counterparts. However, within England, a gap existed between the situation of skilled British workers drawn from the "aristocracy of labor," such as printers, cabinetmakers, and blacksmiths, and that of unskilled workers, such as dockworkers or agricultural workers, who made their tea from used tea leaves and burnt crusts.

The nineteenth-century urban poor probably lived in more miserable housing than their counterparts in the previous century. Buildings in industrial cities, built as hurriedly and as cheaply as possible, quickly became dilapidated tenements. A fifth of all Liverpool residents lived in cellars; in St. Petersburg, an inspector found 40 percent of cellar housing flooded when he came around.

Many workers lived amid terrible smells from raw sewage, garbage, industrial pollution such as sulfurous smoke, and putrid rivers and streams. Warm summers brought outbreaks of serious diseases like typhus and dysentery. In Britain, one of every three people still died of contagious diseases between 1848 and 1872. Despite attempts to improve water supplies and construct sewer systems in several large British cities, the decline in mortality was barely felt in the heart of industrial cities, where tuberculosis and lung diseases were great killers. Inadequate diet and crowded, unclean housing both added to the urban death toll.

Under these circumstances, many children either died or were abandoned at an early age. The most fortunate of the abandoned were left at the doors of charitable organizations, sometimes with a note such as that found in Rouen in 1831: "It is with the greatest pain that I separate myself from my son, after the great suffering I have gone through to keep him in his present state. . . . I hope to see him again as soon as I can take him back for good." Sadly, this would usually not be the case. Furthermore, foundling homes were overcrowded and notoriously unhealthy. In four towns in one Russian province, more than 90 percent of all of the children taken in by orphanages died within a few years. Human tragedy lay behind grim statistics.

A poor family blocks their landlord from invading their cellar apartment, which they share with a donkey and some rats.

Poor Relief

Paternalism, the tradition by which employers took some responsibility for helping their workers by providing some supplementary assistance in addition to their salaries, seemed rare in the new factory towns. But some factory owners took pride in paying higher wages, providing decent housing, and insisting that their workers' children attend school. However, such laudable efforts affected the lives of relatively few workers.

Great Britain was the first state to have a national policy of poor relief. Against the background of the French Revolution, the Speenhamland system established in 1795 supplemented the wages of laborers with funds generated from property taxes ("poor rates"). Doles were based on the price of bread and the number of dependents for whom each head of a poor family had to provide. But this arrangement had the drawback of encouraging landowners to pay lower wages, while assuring them of an inexhaustible supply of cheap field hands. It also may have encouraged poor families to have more children, as payments were adjusted to family size.

The Poor Law Amendment Act of 1834 ended the Speenhamland system. It established residential workhouses in which poor people without jobs would be incarcerated. Its rationale was "to make the workhouses as much like prisons as possible . . . to establish therein a discipline so severe and repulsive as to make them a terror to the poor." Towns enforced laws against begging in order to force the unemployed poor into workhouses. When families were taken in, husbands were separated from their wives, children from their parents, and all were herded into dormitories. Inmates were forced to work at simple tasks, wearing clothes someone else had worn, eating dreadful food, and chafing under the biting commands of little tyrants. The stigma of being poor was such that one influential official even tried to stop the ringing of church bells at pauper funerals. Seven years later, despite organized opposition and although application of the law varied greatly, more than 200,000 people were workhouse inmates in Britain. Still, charitable institutions dispensed more assistance in Britain than the workhouses established by the Poor Law of 1834.

The Question of Class Consciousness

During the first half of the nineteenth century, many workers began to consider themselves members of the working class. They began to think of themselves as having interests that were different from those of their employers. They began to have a sense of community based on a belief in the dignity of labor. This class consciousness did not spring up overnight, and it is difficult to fix a certain point in time when it did develop. Moreover, some recent historians have even questioned the entire concept of a unified class consciousness, given the fact that there were great differences in skills and work experience among workers in different countries and even among workers in the same country, region, or industrial city, and between male and female workers. They stress the other identities that continued to be important to workers, such as those of family and motherhood, cultural identities (Flemish, Venetian, Welsh, etc.), religious adherence, village and neighborhood solidarities, or use of leisure time, most of which had little or nothing to do with a worker's conditions of work or material interests. Nonetheless, it is useful to discuss class consciousness as a way of understanding the perceptions of many workers and the emergence of workers' movements, even if all workers were not conscious of themselves as a class.

Urban artisans were the first workers to begin to express class consciousness, in the sense of identifying themselves as part of a community, sharing the frustrations and goals of other workers. This process occurred very early in the nineteenth century in England, in the 1830s in France, in the 1840s in the German states, and later in other countries.

Large-scale industrialization had deleterious consequences for those in many trades, threatening the control craftsmen had maintained for centuries over their work. Changes in artisanal production were a Europe-wide phenomenon. Artisans had traditionally organized themselves by trades into guilds, which enabled them to control entry into their trades, as well as controlling the training of apprentices and production. Guild controls could not protect all workers from market forces (for example, from rural cottage production and from workers who avoided corporate controls by working just outside city walls). Shoemakers, masons, and tailors, among those in other trades, each had their own craft organizations, some on a national basis, some within a given city. Rival associations within the same trade sometimes engaged in bitter, violent battles. Furthermore, even within trades, despite some trade solidarity (for example, the handing down of "trade secrets" from master to journeyman to apprentice), all artisans did not necessarily share the same interests. Hierarchies of skill and remuneration remained.

As a number of states followed France's lead in 1791 by banning guilds in the name of economic liberalism, the number of artisans expanded rapidly because there were no legal restrictions to entering a given craft. Journeymen, having completed their apprenticeships, were more uncertain than ever before that they would become masters and would employ their own journeymen and take on their own apprentices. In Prussia, the number of masters increased by only about half between 1816 and 1849; the number of journeymen and apprentices aspiring to a mastership more than doubled during the same period. Artisans' confraternities and trade associations (some of which governments tolerated, even if they were technically illegal) facilitated the emergence of working-class consciousness (although where they helped to maintain trade exclusiveness, they may have delayed its emergence).

"De-skilling" reduced the income and status of workers like tailors and skilled seamstresses by taking away opportunities for them to work for piece rates and wages they had once earned. Competition buffeted artisans such as tailors as never before. Merchant-manufacturers, some of them former tailors who had been able to save some money, put work out to master and journeymen tailors, who performed a single task, such as making sleeves in return for less money than if they had tailored an entire suit. In Paris, tailors' incomes plunged during the 1830s and 1840s. Many master tailors were driven out of business or forced by necessity to become subcontractors in their trade. Mechanization also gradually began to undercut tailors.

Indeed the gradual mechanization of some trades brought protest. Already in 1811 and 1812, glove makers in Nottingham, England, had smashed a thousand stocking-frames that deprived them of work. One of their leaders—perhaps fictitious—was a man called Ned Ludd, a legendary figure. Machine-breaking "Luddites" yearned for a return to the old economic and social order, before mechanization.

In 1836, a mob burned down a textile factory in Barcelona, Spain, denouncing machinery as "the devil's invention." Silesian hand-loom weavers were reduced to desperate poverty by mechanical looms. Movements of social protest and gradual political involvement infused communities of workers with a sense of moral struggle against economic and political forces they could not control.

Workers' views of themselves drew upon the corporate language of the Old Regime that gave primacy to the idea of work as a value in itself and of the community of workers as a moral entity. Many workers concluded that workers, not entrepreneurs with capital, were the source of wealth and were being exploited. Other workers also began to feel a sense of class consciousness because they suffered unemployment or reduced wages. The likelihood that the children of laborers would advance beyond their origins was remote. Residential patterns and leisure haunts (pubs, cabarets, music halls) contributed to solidarities among such workers.

Workers' Associations and Social Protest

Workers' associations helped shape working-class solidarity and militancy. In Britain, craft-based "friendly societies" had more than a million members in 1815. Almost 10,000 such societies existed in 1803 and more than 32,000 in 1872. Their counterparts were "mutual aid societies" (most of which banned women) or journeymen's associations in France and in the German states.

Fledgling trade unions developed in Britain, particularly after Parliament repealed the Combination Acts (1799–1800) in 1824, which had forbidden unions. Members sought to protect wage rates and conditions within their trades. Yet, even in prosperous periods when workers could

Socialism as a symbol of hope for the working poor, about 1848.

afford dues, less than 20 percent of workers belonged to such associations during the first half of the century, and the vast majority of these were workers in the more skilled, better-paid trades. Many of these men believed they had little in common with unskilled workers who, in any case, could not afford union dues and who lacked job stability.

Some trade associations, including a minority organized by and for women, provided assistance when a member fell sick (paid out of membership dues) and assured members that they would be spared the indignity of a pauper's grave. They also provided funds to assist workers who refused to agree to conditions imposed by employers or masters. These payments had to be made covertly because strikes remained illegal in most places.

Artisans led movements of social protest, first in Britain, and then in France and the German states. They had a much higher level of literacy than did unskilled workers—printers were an obvious example, but tailors and shoemakers were often literate, as well as many seamstresses, who were often self-educated. Literate workers read newspapers and brochures and related the news to those who could not read. The emergence of political movements seeking universal male suffrage (or even universal suffrage) and significant social reforms aided the development of a sense of class by emphasizing the language of "liberty, fraternity, and equality," a heritage of the French Revolution.

The period from 1820 to 1850 was arguably the most socially turbulent period in modern British history. Francis Place (1771–1854), a tailor who had been a member of one of the workers' associations sympathetic to the French Revolution, became a leader of the English workers' movement. In part influenced by the industrialist Robert Owen's cooperative philosophy (see below), some workers began cooperative stores, hoping to put aside enough money to finance cooperative villages. Also influenced by Owen, trade unionism made considerable headway between 1829 and 1836. In the latter year, the first national union, made up of spinners, was founded. Some trade union members undertook producers' cooperatives within their trades, but most of these were short-lived.

Skilled workers joined with middle-class radicals to demand political reform. William Cobbett (1763–1835) helped galvanize radical opinion with his journal, the *Political Register*. Artisans and skilled workers led massive demonstrations in 1831 and 1832, which pressured Commons and the House of Lords to pass the Reform Bill of 1832 (see Chapter 15). By expanding the number of those eligible to vote, the Reform Bill temporarily diffused middle-class dissatisfaction. At about the same time, middle-class and working-class support for factory reform, marked by public meetings, petitions, and demonstrations, led to the acts of Parliament in the 1830s limiting work hours for children and then women. The economic depression in Britain that began in the middle of the decade, however, brought hardship, popular disturbances, and more calls for political reform.

Yet, even in Britain, the most industrial nation, major impediments limited working-class militancy. Methodism (see Chapter 9), which won thousands of converts among workers, preached discipline and the acceptance of one's fate on earth, although the total number of adherents probably was not great enough to have made much of a difference. More important, solidarities within specific trades remained stronger than those that cut across trades. Furthermore, unskilled workers lacked the organization and resources of craftsmen. Gradually, too, the utopian vision of rebuilding British political life while bringing social justice faded. Many if not most workers came to accept capitalism as inevitable, while demanding a fairer share of its benefits.

French and German artisans were arguably more militant than their British counterparts, who accepted the tradition of the politics of reform. German craftsmen desperately struggled to try to protect their trades from being flooded by newcomers. Many French workers, now seeing themselves as members of a "confraternity of proletarians," struck against employers during the July Monarchy. They also supported bourgeois republicans in their push for electoral reform, in the hope that a republic would enact reforms on their behalf.

THE ORIGINS OF EUROPEAN SOCIALISM

As large-scale industrialization gradually transformed economy and society in Western Europe, the 1830s and 1840s brought lively discussion, heated debate, and startling transformations in thought. Many contemporaries believed that the miserable conditions of the laboring poor in much of Europe brought increased social protest. The rapid increase in wage labor influenced the emergence of new political forces that, proclaiming the equality of all people, sought dramatic social and political change. One of the most salient results of the growing preoccupation with the condition of workers was the birth of the movement known as socialism.

Utopian Socialists

Utopian socialists, most of whom were French, provided an original and far-reaching critique of the changes brought by the Industrial Revolution. Their ideas were in part shaped by their reaction against the social consequences of economic liberalism. The name "utopian" reflected their dreams of creating a perfectly harmonious way of life. But their importance comes not from their sometimes quirky theories, however intriguing they may be, but from the fact that many workers, above all in France, found an explanatory power in the critical reaction of the utopians to liberalism and capitalism. This accentuated their determination to put forward demands for social and political reform.

Utopian socialists agonized over the living conditions of the laboring poor. They doubted the willingness of those enriched by the Industrial Revolution to solve what was often called "the social question," that is, the miserable living conditions of many if not most workers. Rejecting the "egotistic" individualism of the spirit of acquisition, utopian socialists envisioned a gentle world of cooperation. In some ways children of the Enlightenment, utopian socialists were optimistic champions of the power of science and technology to construct new social and political institutions.

Count Claude-Henri de Saint-Simon (1760–1825) posited a "religion of humanity," arguing that religion should "direct society toward the great end of the most rapid amelioration possible of the lot of the poorest class." In 1820, Saint-Simon published a provocative parable. Speaking hypothetically, he asked what the consequences for France would be if all of its dukes and duchesses, princes and princesses, bishops and priests, and other luminaries of altar, throne, and château sank in a terrible shipwreck. As tragic as that event would be, he had to admit that the loss to society would be inconsiderable. However, if France, in a similar tragedy, were to lose all of its most learned men, talented bankers, artisans, and productive farmers, the result, Saint-Simon argued, would be disastrous. The timing of his parable was unfortunate, because soon after its publication in 1820 the heir to the throne of France, the duke of Berry, fell to an assassin's knife (see Chapter 15). Saint-Simon was charged with offending the royal family, but he was acquitted by a jury.

Saint-Simon postulated a hierarchy, or order of status, based not on blood, but on productivity. Believing that history moves through discernible stages, Saint-Simon asserted that mankind could anticipate a future in which science would solve the material problems of humanity in harmony with an era of moral improvement. For this to happen, people of talent must be freed from the fetters of restraint imposed by uncaring, unproductive monarchs, nobles, and priests.

Contemporary and historical appraisals of Charles Fourier (1772–1837), Saint-Simon's mystical rival, have ranged from sanctifying him as a genius of great insight to ridiculing him as a paranoid crackpot. Born to a commercial family in Besançon, Fourier claimed that at a very early age he discovered that the art of selling was the practice of lying and deception. At his father's insistence, he went off to Lyon as a young man to start a business that quickly failed. Fourier spent the rest of his life preparing a grand scheme for improving the condition of humanity. His cosmology rested upon his conclusion that history moved in great cycles toward a more perfect future. This planet's next stage would be based upon mankind's discovery that the principles of cooperation and harmony would free everyone from the repression of bourgeois individualism. Having determined that there were 810 distinct personality types, Fourier proposed that they be organized into "phalanx" communities made up of 1,620 people, one man and one woman of each personality type. The phalanx would channel the "passions" of each person in socially productive ways, while individuals would benefit from the opportunity to express their deepest proclivities. In the "phalanstery," the place where the utopians would live, crime would become a distant memory, because criminals' supposed penchant for blood would be safely fulfilled in certain occupations, such as by becoming butchers. With everyone so satisfied, it would

A drawing of a phalanstery contemplated by Charles Fourier.

not matter that differences in wealth would remain. Fourier sat in his apartment everyday at noon, awaiting the wealthy man who would come, he hoped, to finance the first phalanstery. No one ever showed up.

While Fourier dreamed and waited, the wealthy British industrialist and philanthropist Robert Owen acted. Believing that education and environment could shape a spirit of cooperation, Owen built a mill in New Lanark, Scotland. He provided sturdy, clean housing for his workers and established schools for their children. Like Fourier, for whom human progress demanded the emancipation of women, Owen espoused the equality of women, although he emphasized not political rights but rather the special qualities of motherhood.

No utopian socialist had a greater popular following than Étienne Cabet (1788–1856) in France. Cabet, too, sought to apply the principles of Christianity to the extreme social problems of the day. His novel *Voyage to Icaria* (1840) described an imaginary city of wide streets, clean urinals, and social harmony, a vision of organized economic and social life so attractive that even the bourgeoisie would be converted peacefully to the principles of cooperation and association. Cabet's "communist" newspaper had 4,500 subscribers in the early 1840s, and almost certainly reached twenty times that number. Artisans, their livelihoods threatened by the abolition of the guilds and mechanization, were particularly intrigued by Cabet's ideas. A few of them set sail with Cabet for the New World, founding several utopian colonies in Texas and Iowa.

Another group of utopian socialists represented the scientific, or technocratic and even authoritarian tendencies inherent in Saint-Simon's overwhelming respect for science and insistence that the state lead the way toward material progress. One Saint-Simonian, Prosper Enfantin (1796–1864)—called "Father" by his followers—left Paris for Egypt with a small group in search of the Female Messiah; one of the travelling party, Michel Chevalier, came back with the idea of building a canal through the Isthmus of Suez, thus joining the Red Sea and the Mediterranean, a project later achieved in 1869 by Ferdinand de Lesseps, another Saint-Simonian.

Practical Socialists

Some utopian socialists carried Saint-Simon's analysis a crucial step further. They relegated the bourgeoisie into the category of nonproducers, because they contributed capital, while workers seemed to them to be the real producers by virtue of their labor. In France, a group of Saint-Simonian women in 1832 founded a newspaper, *La Tribune des Femmes,* that vowed only to publish articles by women, proclaiming that the emancipation of women would come with the emancipation of the worker. Although two years later the newspaper ceased publishing, utopian socialist women undertook another newspaper with republican leanings during 1836–1838, which called for political and civil rights for women.

Gender discrimination led Flora Tristan (1801–1844) to socialism. When the French government confiscated her Peruvian father's fortune upon his death and declared Flora to be illegitimate because it refused to recognize her parents' marriage in Spain, she had to take a series of makeshift jobs. When she separated from her abusive husband, French law decreed that he receive custody of their children, although she later won custody when he started to abuse them, too. Tristan campaigned against women's inequality within marriage and before the law. Linking feminism and socialism, she campaigned for female

Proudhon destroying property as seen by a hostile caricaturist.

emancipation with impassioned speeches and forceful prose. Tristan also called for a union of workers that would establish throughout France "workers' palaces," where workers could be educated and victims of industrial accidents cared for.

Louis Blanc (1811–1882) looked to the French state for the improvement of the condition of the working class. Governments must, he argued, give scientists a free hand in applying their talents to the betterment of the human condition. The state should also guarantee workers the "right to work," that is, employment in times of distress and a decent wage in the face of unchecked competition. The state should provide credit to workers so that they could form producers' associations within their trades, thereby eliminating the middleman who skimmed off profits that he had not earned. Blanc believed that these workshops would serve as the basis for the reorganization of society along cooperative lines. Blanc's socialism was predicated on increasing working-class influence on government through the establishment of universal suffrage.

In sharp contrast to Blanc, Pierre-Joseph Proudhon (1809–1865) looked not to the strengthening of the state but to its abolition to create a better world. Proudhon, a typesetter, had grown up among landowning peasants in eastern France. He believed that the existence of the state itself was a principal reason why capitalism exploited workers. In 1840, he published a pamphlet that answered the question "What Is Property?" with the resounding reply "Theft." Not surprisingly, this provocative work frightened property owners in France, even though Proudhon defined property as unearned profit that came to employers from the labor of their workers, and not property per se. Suspicious of political movements, which he argued merely substituted one elite for another, Proudhon wanted workers to organize themselves into small, autonomous groups of producers that would govern themselves. By preaching the abolition of the state, Proudhon was arguably the first anarchist.

Karl Marx and the Origins of "Scientific Socialism"

The economic and political theorist Karl Marx (1818–1883) also read the utopian socialists, but although admiring their critique of capitalist society he found them naive and "unscientific." Born in 1818 in the Rhineland, Marx studied philosophy at the University of Berlin. When in 1843 his career as a journalist came to an abrupt halt after his radical newspaper ran afoul of the Prussian government, he went to Paris. There he read the histories of the French Revolution and the utopian socialists.

After Marx lambasted the French monarchy in a series of articles, the French police expelled him. He befriended Friedrich Engels, the Rhineland German whose prosperous, conservative family owned a cotton mill in Manchester, England. Marx visited industrial Lancashire, then having the greatest concentration of industry in the world. Marx's observation of evolving capitalist society led him to conclude that capitalism was but a stage in world history, which was marked by stages of class struggle. His theories of revolution were rooted in his attempts to understand the revolutions that he saw around him in Europe.

Marx applied the concept of dialectical stages of the development of ideas and institutions, developed by the German philosopher Georg Wilhelm Friedrich Hegel (1770–1831), to the progression of world history. The French Revolution had marked the definitive overthrow of feudal society, represented by the power of the aristocracy and the Church; for Marx, this was a bourgeois revolution. Just as the nobility and the bourgeoisie had battled in the eighteenth century, so the victorious bourgeoisie, who controlled the means of production (capital, raw materials, and equipment needed to produce goods), and the proletariat were in the process of fighting it out in the middle decades of the nineteenth century. English commercial capitalism had brought the bourgeoisie to power, which in turn had facilitated the growth of industrial capitalism. By creating a proletariat, however, capitalists had sown the seeds of their demise. Proletarians would be the "grave diggers" of the bourgeoisie. Inevitably, socialism would replace capitalism when the proletariat would seize power. The end of private property and pure communism would follow.

But that moment, Marx thought, lay in the future, awaiting the further concentration of capitalism and the development of a larger, class-conscious proletariat aware of its historical role. Marx called his socialism "scientific socialism" (in contrast to utopian socialism), because he thought that it was inevitable, based on what he considered the scientific certainty of class struggle.

Marx believed that a revolution by workers would be prepared by the organizational efforts of a group of committed revolutionaries like himself. Gradually winning followers, Marx formed the Communist League. In 1848, he published the *Communist Manifesto,* which resounds with the provocative exclamation, "The proletarians have nothing to lose but their chains. They have a world to win. Working men of all countries, unite!"

CONCLUSION

Europeans could not help but be impressed with the rapid pace of economic change during the first half of the nineteenth century. Trains truly revolutionized commerce and travel. The population of cities grew even more rapidly than did the population in general. Agricultural productivity increased in northern Europe with capital-intensive farming. In some places, property-owning peasants gave up rural life, moving to the cities in search of industrial work. More people worked in industry than ever before. Factories now dotted the landscape, although traditional workshop and cottage production, too, continued strong.

Yet many upper-class contemporaries were worried by what seemed to be teeming, increasingly disorderly cities that were being overwhelmed by new inhabitants. The Industrial Revolution, to be sure, had generated material progress—indeed, opulence for some people—but it also seemed to have increased wrenching poverty among laborers.

In the meantime, having defeated Napoleon at Waterloo, the European powers—Britain, Prussia, Austria, and Russia—set about trying to restore the prerogatives of ruling dynasties, nobles, and the established churches. Liberal and national movements struggled against conservative ideology in Restoration Europe. Liberalism, above all, seemed to reflect the desires of the middle classes, whose numbers and influence expanded rapidly in the decades following the end of the Napoleonic era.

CHAPTER 15

CHALLENGES TO RESTORATION EUROPE: THE MIDDLE CLASSES IN THE AGE OF LIBERALISM

At the Congress of Vienna of 1815, representatives of the allies who had defeated Napoleon—Austria, Russia, Prussia, and Great Britain—came together to reestablish peace in Europe. They hoped that by imposing a treaty on France and creating an international mechanism, the Concert of Europe, they could prevent Europe from again being shaken by revolution in France or elsewhere.

Early nineteenth-century Vienna was a perfect setting for a gathering of the representatives of Europe's sovereign powers. The Schönbrunn Palace on the outskirts of the Habsburg capital and Vienna's own elegant baroque buildings still reflected the grandeur of absolutism and traditional court life, despite the fact that years of warfare had virtually bankrupted the Austrian monarchy.

At the Congress, which met between September 1814 and June 1815, the Austrian hosts revived the aristocratic court life of the pre-revolutionary period. Elaborate dinners, elegant balls, festive fireworks displays, and organized hunts helped relieve boredom. Artists stood ready to paint the portraits of the members of the diplomatic delegations. Aristocratic guests amused themselves by trying to guess which of the hundreds of maids and porters were spying for the Austrians; and by trying to be the first to catch a glimpse of the dashing duke of Wellington, who had defeated Napoleon at Waterloo. The British prime minister and his wife took dancing lessons. The antics of some representatives provided as much comic relief as irritation. A Spanish diplomat put forth the claim that his country should have the right to several small Italian states. The other representatives were so annoyed by this demand that they invited him to go on a ballooning excursion, and sent him off in the general direction of the Alps.

What the English poet George Gordon, Lord Byron (1788–1824), called "that base pageant," the Congress of Vienna provided an opportunity for the informal discussions that had always been an important part of traditional European diplomacy. In fact, the Congress met officially but once, to sign the final treaty, which had been negotiated in smaller formal and informal gatherings of the various delegations. And in the wake of the many territorial changes that had occurred during almost twenty-five years of intermittent warfare, the representatives redrew the map of Europe. They established new borders, particularly in Central Europe, putting old rulers back in power in some places, assigning territories to the rule of one power or another.

After Napoleon's final defeat in 1815, a protracted struggle between the conservative forces, monarchies, nobles, the established churches, and liberals took place in Europe. The struggle between liberals and conservatives stretched across much of Europe, revealing an interconnectedness of experience that transcended the particular histories of individual states, despite the unevenness of economic development. "Liberalism" as an economic and political philosophy implies the absence of government constraints that could interfere with the development of the individual. It was a philosophy perfectly suited to the middle classes in what has been called "the bourgeois century." The middle classes were an extremely diverse

The Congress of Vienna.

social group that ranged from merchants and manufacturers of great wealth to struggling shopkeepers and innkeepers. Rapid population growth, particularly in towns and cities, swelled the number of lawyers, notaries, and other middle-class professionals. The entrepreneur replaced the noble as someone to be revered. Moreover, the middle classes' liberal emphasis on individual freedom found expression not only in economics and politics but also in the literature, art, and music of romanticism, which celebrated individual fulfillment through subjectivity and emotion. Boasted one German liberal, "We are the times."

Liberal movements were in many places closely tied to the emergence of nationalism as a source of allegiance and sovereignty. Nationalism is the belief in the primacy of nationality, usually defined by language and cultural traditions, and the resulting quest for national states, whose borders would correspond to patterns of ethnic residence. Nationalism threatened the territorial settlements effected by the Congress of Vienna. The Habsburg Austrian monarchy, for example, ruled at least fifteen peoples without a state of their own, including Poles and Hungarians, who had once had fully independent states. The German and Italian states, where liberalism became increasingly identified with nationalism, lacked the astonishing cultural, linguistic, and religious diversity of the Habsburg domains, and they witnessed increasing calls by nationalists for political unification. The political unification of the German states could threaten the settlement of the Congress of Vienna, which restored territories to Prussia, Austria, and many of the lesser states that had long had their own ruling dynasties. Likewise, Italian nationalism threatened Austria's hold on Lombardy and Venetia, as well as the Bourbon dynasty of Naples and Sicily, the Papal States in central Italy, and petty potentates ruling several smaller states.

THE POST-NAPOLEONIC SETTLEMENT

The allied representatives were determined to ensure that France could not again rise to a position of domination in Europe. Thus, even before Napoleon's first defeat and abdication in 1814, representatives of Prussia, Austria, Russia, and Great Britain had agreed to form a coalition that they hoped would last at least twenty years. The purpose of this "Quadruple Alliance" was to prevent France or any other state or political movement from threatening the legitimate sovereigns of Europe.

The Treaty of Paris

The allies and representatives of the usurped French Bourbon monarchy signed the Treaty of Paris in May 1814. Charles-Maurice de Talleyrand (1754–1838), who had served Napoleon with flexibility rooted in an uncanny sense of survival, became the intermediary. He exploited tensions between the allies, particularly between Prussia and Austria. In the end, the victorious powers agreed to restore the Bourbons to the throne of France in the person of the count of Provence, brother of the executed Louis XVI, who took the throne as Louis XVIII. The allies might well have forced the French to sign a draconian treaty. But they were dealing not with the defeated Napoleon but with the restored Bourbon monarch, whose throne they wanted to solidify. Stripping France of its imperial gains was one thing. But to leave the country too weak could work against the allies by leaving the king vulnerable to Jacobin challenges from within France.

The allies permitted France to keep lands incorporated before November 1, 1792, including parts of Savoy, Germany, and the Austrian Netherlands, as well as the former papal city of Avignon. France gave up claims to the remainder of the Austrian Netherlands, the Dutch Republic, the German states, the Italian states, and Switzerland. It lost the Caribbean islands of Trinidad, Tobago, Santa Lucia, and part of Santo Domingo to Britain. But despite the enormous cost of the Napoleonic Wars to all powers, the allies then demanded no reparations from the French.

Extremely difficult territorial issues remained to be resolved in central and southern Europe, where Napoleon had disrupted the old structure of states by, for example, breaking apart the Holy Roman Empire in 1806.

Diplomatic Maneuvering at the Congress of Vienna

The Congress of Vienna was almost entirely the work of diplomats representing Austria, Prussia, Great Britain, and Russia. The rulers and princes of the smaller German states travelled to Vienna in the hope of maintaining their independence and security, a complicated task for those states that had cast their fate with Napoleon. At least at the beginning, defeated France played only the role of a very interested observer (although French was the official language of the conference). But Talleyrand's wily off-stage negotiations gradually brought France to the position of a full-fledged participant in the deliberations. Russian Tsar Alexander I (ruled 1801–1825) participated personally, but the dominant figures in Vienna were unquestionably the Austrian Chancellor Prince Klemens von Metternich (1773–1859) and, to a lesser extent, British Prime Minister Viscount Robert Castlereagh (1769–1822).

Metternich, born in the German Rhineland, was the son of a noble who had served at the court of the Habsburg monarch. Forced to flee his homeland by the French invasion in 1792, he entered the diplomatic service in Vienna, rising to become the minister of foreign affairs in 1809. Metternich was a handsome and invariably elegantly dressed dandy with immaculately powdered hair; he was at home in the social whirl of formal receptions and magnificent balls, as well as in the petty intrigues of high

British Prime Minister Viscount Robert Castlereagh.

society. Well educated, he could bore people in five languages. But he was also a determined, calculating practitioner of tough-minded diplomacy, unmatched in his ability to understand both the potential consequences of virtually any diplomatic situation. He had great faith in his own ability to set and steer the proper course for the continent, whose international affairs he would dominate until 1848. Like the conservatives he represented, Metternich believed that Europe would find peace only if its legitimate sovereigns were unchallenged by the forces of liberalism and nationalism, and if a single state could no longer threaten the international balance of power by becoming too powerful, as France had during the reign of Louis XIV and again during the Revolution and Napoleonic era.

Britain's aloof, cold, and painfully shy Castlereagh, whose single passion was sheepherding, went to Vienna in the hope of establishing Britain as the arbiter of European affairs. Britain had emerged from the long Napoleonic Wars as Europe's greatest power, with an empire that included one of every five people in the world. Instead of territorial aggrandizement on the continent, the British government sought the elimination of the French threat to its commercial interests as well as security. Castlereagh worked for a declaration to ensure freedom of the seas. Moreover, he and Metternich both viewed the prospect of Russian expansion in Central Europe with anxiety. With France occupied by allied troops and once again ruled by a legitimate sovereign, only Russia seemed in a position to disrupt Europe through unilateral acts.

Russian Tsar Alexander I wanted the allies to affirm formally what he considered the religious basis of the European alliance. A complex and in many ways contradictory figure, Alexander I had been scarred by the hatred between his father, Tsar Paul, and his grandmother, Catherine the Great, and by the assassination of Paul in 1801, because he had previously been at least aware of the plot. Familiar with Enlightenment thought, his advent was welcomed by some liberals who saw him as potentially a charming reformer. He had begun his reign by granting an amnesty to thousands of people condemned by his father, relaxing censorship, abolishing torture in judicial investigations, allowing more Russians to travel abroad, and creating a committee of advisers. Thomas Jefferson sang his praises, "A more virtuous man, I believe, does not exist, nor one who is more enthusiastically devoted to better the condition of mankind." However, in 1809 the tsar rejected a proposed constitution. Alexander I was, above all, a deeply religious man who occasionally lapsed into an intense mysticism and overwhelming unhappiness that made him increasingly reactionary. This greatly disappointed some educated Russians who had idealized his resistance to Napoleon's invasion.

Alexander I drafted a document that became the basis for the Holy Alliance, providing considerable support to European conservatives. It asserted that the relations of the European sovereigns, whom he referred to as "the delegates of Providence," would thereafter be based "upon the sublime truths which the Holy Religion of Our Savior teaches." Emperor Francis I of Austria and Frederick William III of Prussia signed the document, but the British prince regent—the future George IV (ruled 1820–1830)—begged off, confirming the constitutional nature of British government. Lord Castlereagh revealed the British attitude toward the Holy Alliance when he called it "a piece of sublime mysticism and nonsense." Prussia, Russia, and Austria promised mutual assistance whenever religion, peace, or justice was threatened. In the moral claims of the Holy Alliance lay justification for the repression by the allies of any liberal and national movements in Europe.

The Congress System

The Congress of Vienna drew a map of Europe that lasted for several generations (see Map 15.1). Under Metternich's stern leadership, what became known as the Congress system restored the principle of dynastic legitimacy and the balance of international power in Europe. The balance of power would ensure that no one power would come to dominate the rest, and that when a state gave up territory it would receive other land in compensation. Territory was apportioned to create buffers to France, as well as to prevent Russia from wielding too much power.

For neither the first nor the last time in European history, the future of Poland, which had lost its independence when it was last partitioned by Russia, Prussia, and Austria in 1795, stood at the top of the list of contentious issues. Tsar Alexander I's troops occupied much of Poland, and he wanted to annex all of it to the Russian Empire. Great Britain, France, and Austria, fearing increased Russian and Prussian influence in Central Europe, formed an alliance (proposed by Talleyrand, who was trying to improve France's position in the negotiations) to head off any attack in Central Europe by Russia or Prussia. This forced Alexander and his Prussian supporters to moderate their demands. In May, the Kingdom of Poland was proclaimed. It was to include lands Austria and Prussia had

MAP 15.1 EUROPE AFTER THE CONGRESS OF VIENNA, 1815   Changes in boundaries of states after the Congress of Vienna.

seized during the earlier partitions. But "Congress Poland," as it came to be known, was nothing more than a Russian protectorate, with the tsar himself occupying the Polish throne. Russia also held on to Finland, which it had conquered during the Napoleonic Wars. To balance Russian gains in the east, Prussia received the northern half of Saxony, which had cast its fate with Napoleon, as well as Polish-speaking Posen and the port city of Danzig (Gdańsk).

In comparison with the debates over Poland and Saxony, the resolution of remaining territorial issues seemed easy. Prussia received territories on the left bank of the Rhine River in order to discourage French aggression to the east. This left the Prussian Rhineland separated from the eastern Prussian provinces by the states of Hanover and Hesse-Kassel. Prussia also received Swedish Pomerania and parts of Westphalia, but lost its outlet to the North Sea with the return of East Friesland to Hanover. Other buffers against France along its eastern border included Switzerland, reestablished as a neutral confederation of cantons, and the Kingdom of Piedmont-Sardinia (which was enlarged to include Genoa, Nice, and part of Savoy).

Most territorial settlements were made without the slightest consideration of local public opinion. Although the allies emphasized the principle of legitimacy in the territorial settlement, they never hesitated to dispense with a number of smaller legitimate princes whose claims would have interfered with the creation of buffers against France. Thus, the republics of Genoa and Venice disappeared from the map.

The Congress placated Britain by awarding the former Austrian Netherlands (Belgium) to the Dutch, leaving a state friendly to Britain on France's northern border. The former stadholder of the Dutch Republic became King William I. But Castlereagh's plan to link the Dutch throne to the British monarchy by engineering the marriage of a British princess to the Dutch royal family failed, at least partially because the intended groom became royally drunk in the presence of the intended but most unwilling bride.

Austria was well compensated for the loss of the Austrian Netherlands with Lombardy and Venetia in Italy, much of Galicia, and Illyria on the coast of Dalmatia. The grand duchies of Parma, Modena, and Tuscany, too, had close family links to Vienna. The Congress also restored the Bourbon dynasty to the throne of the Kingdom of the Two Sicilies (Naples and Sicily). There, Ferdinand I introduced a constitution, but signed an alliance with Austria and promised not to introduce any reforms without the latter's permission. Austrian garrisons and secret police in each Italian state reporting to Metternich helped assure Austrian domination of northern Italy.

Napoleon's remarkable escape from Elba in March 1815 and the dramatic episode of the 100 Days did not change the most important aspects of the Congress's shuffling of European territories. The second Treaty of

Paris, signed in November 1815, however, pushed France back from its 1792 borders to those of 1790. Furthermore, the allies now exacted reparations totaling 700 million francs from France. Their armies would occupy France until the debt was settled.

Napoleon's victories in Central Europe had led to the end of the Holy Roman Empire in 1806. On June 9, 1815, the Congress created a German Confederation of thirty-five states loosely joined by a Federal Diet (Bundestag) that would meet in Frankfurt. In addition to Prussia and Austria, the Confederation also comprised the so-called middle states of Bavaria, Hanover, Württemberg, the two Hesses, and Baden, and the independent, or "free," cities of Hamburg, Frankfurt, Bremen, and Lübeck. The Confederation did not, however, include the non-German lands of the Austrian Empire. Members of the Confederation pledged to assist each other if any of them were attacked or in any way threatened. But it was unlikely that unanimity could ever be achieved among the member states, or that any state could be compelled to obey a decision made by the Confederation, despite disproportionate Austrian and Prussian preeminence. The Diet merely afforded Metternich a means of bullying the smaller states.

The newly created German Confederation was anything but an affirmation of a move toward German national unification. The German states, large and small, were proud of their traditions of autonomy. By virtue of its Rhineland acquisitions, Prussia emerged as a rival for Austria's leadership of the Confederation and for dominance in Central Europe.

The Concert of Europe

To preserve the settlements enacted at Vienna, the five major European powers (Great Britain, Prussia, Austria, Russia, and defeated France) formed a "Concert of Europe." In this extension of the Congress of Vienna, representatives of the powers would meet annually. If necessary, they would join together to put down movements that could threaten the *status quo*. Metternich's Austria had the most to fear from national claims for independent states. Austria was both a state in the German Confederation and the most important province within its empire of many nationalities. Austria's empire stretched from the stately elegance of Vienna through the plains of Hungary, to isolated, backward Romanian and Croatian villages. German was the language of the imperial bureaucracy, and of many of the towns, but one could find fifteen major languages within the borders of the empire. The Habsburg monarchy depended on the support of the nobles of the favored nationalities—principally Austrian, Hungarian, and Croat—and the German-speaking middle classes. Metternich exploited the fear that the upper classes of the favored nationalities felt toward any awakening from the lower classes. This kept most Magyar (Hungarian) nobles loyal to the Habsburg dynasty, although some desired ultimate independence and resented Metternich's attempt to modernize Hungarian laws and administration.

Tensions remained between the allies. Prussia and particularly Austria feared that Russia was seeking to expand its influence in the Balkans, especially among peoples of the Orthodox faith. Metternich therefore was willing to use Austrian armies to maintain the *status quo,* but he sought to avoid any joint Congress military action that might bring Russian armies into central or southern Europe. He thus wanted to keep alive the Austrian alliance with Britain against any future French, Prussian, or Russian aggression.

Castlereagh, on the other hand, was less concerned by Russia's expanded interests in Central Europe and most concerned about containing France. But, unlike Metternich, he had reservations about the appropriateness of the Quadruple Alliance's intervention in the internal affairs of European states. The British participated in the annual gatherings of representatives of the Concert powers, but gradually withdrew from the Congress system. At Aachen (Aix-la-Chapelle) in 1818, the allies agreed to withdraw their remaining troops from France, which, having paid off the war debts, now joined the Holy Alliance.

RESTORATION EUROPE

The diplomats and monarchs of the Congress of Vienna had worked to restore the state system of Europe. Monarchs and nobles were guided by conservative principles of monarchical legitimacy, with the right to the thrones of Europe determined by hereditary succession, and by close ties to the prerogatives of the established churches. They sought to defend themselves against liberals and nationalists, who espoused organizing states along ethnic or national lines and who demanded reforms in the name of popular sovereignty.

The Restoration of Monarchs, Nobles, and Clergy

Following the fall of Napoleon, in the Kingdom of Piedmont-Sardinia, the members of the ruling House of Savoy came back wearing powdered wigs, in the style of the eighteenth century. The religious orders also returned in force. In Lombardy-Venetia, consultative assemblies were established in Milan and Venice, but they did little more than assess taxes. With the exception of Baden, in the German states such bodies routinely approved legislation without limiting the power of the sovereign. The governments of the German states that had been occupied by France during the Napoleonic period completely purged the remnants of Napoleonic administration, annulled French-inspired legislation, and imposed strict censorship.

When the French left the Papal States, Pope Pius VII immediately tried to exorcise all traces of the influence of his French captors. Administrative reforms undertaken during the occupation ended; so did street lighting and even vaccinations, identified with the godless French. The clergy reclaimed most public offices. The degree to which French influence in Italy was erased could be seen in Tuscany, where the duke ordered the colors of Giotto's portrait of Dante altered, fearing that observers would see in them the French tricolor.

The French Revolution had by no means eliminated noble influence in the states of Europe. Even in Britain, where the lines between landed and business wealth were more blurred than anywhere else, nobles still dominated the House of Commons. In France, the Bourbon monarchy restored nobles to political primacy. Not all nobles were reactionary, but most were, and an electoral system based on landed wealth gave them a disproportionate advantage. In Spain, nobles were particularly numerous, although many of them were relatively poor. Sweden still counted about 12,000 nobles in the middle of the nineteenth century. In Spain until 1836 young men aspiring to an officer's commission in the army had to provide proof of nobility.

In the Italian states, nobles still held sway in declining or stagnant walled towns like Palermo, Naples, and Rome, as they did in the countryside, until at least 1850. Even in industrializing Milan in Lombardy and Turin in Piedmont, nobles dominated the civic administration.

The farther east one went, the more nobles still dominated economic, social, and political life, particularly in states that had been or still were absolute monarchies. Nobles (Junkers) owned 40 percent of the land of Prussia and maintained their social and political connections to the court. They considered entrepreneurs to be crass parvenus, outsiders, despite the fortunes they had accumulated, irritating bourgeois who demanded a strong political voice. In Austria, too, 70 percent of those in the top official posts had titles in 1829, and twenty years later the percentage had grown even more. Austrian Chancellor Metternich warned the Russian Tsar Alexander I about the "intermediate class"—that is, the middle class—which prospered by adopting "all sorts of disguises, uniting and subdividing as occasion offers, helping each other in the hours of danger, and the next day depriving each other of their conquests."

The social composition of the military officer corps remained a telling indicator of the degree to which nobles dominated each state. In Prussia, Junkers retained their stranglehold over the officer corps. The army defiantly brushed aside possible competition from the Landwehr, the civilian reserve force commanded by merchants, teachers, and bureaucrats. In Russia, the officer corps still was a noble stronghold, reinforced by the aristocracy's near monopoly on appointments to military academies and to important posts in the civil service.

During the revolutionary era, the established churches, particularly the Catholic Church, had suffered at the hands of revolutionaries. Conservatives both Catholic and Protestant) insisted that the established churches provided a moral authority that complemented secular authority. Thus, in the German states, Pietism and other revivalist Protestant movements broke with Protestant orthodoxy to teach that mankind was essentially sinful and required a repressive state to keep in line. In Russia, the mystical Tsar Alexander I believed fervently that the Orthodox Church had an important role in keeping his people subservient.

Europe witnessed a marked revival in enthusiasm for organized religion. A largely

Tzar Alexander I.

Lutheran revival of religious enthusiasm occurred in the northern German states. In France, the old religious confraternities revived. Pious families contributed money to rebuild churches, monasteries, and convents destroyed or damaged during the Revolution. In Britain, the Established (Anglican) Church helped shape the conservative view of the world. Although they rejected the notion of divine-right or absolutist monarchy, most British Conservatives believed the existing social order to be God-given and immutable, represented by the Anglican Church, and strongly opposed Dissenters and, above all, Catholics. In 1818, Parliament passed the Church Building Act, which provided government funding for the construction of more than 200 new churches.

Conservative Ideology

Conservatives sought to craft a viable political program for the post-revolutionary world that would preserve the monarchies and nobles of Europe. The conservative ideology of Restoration Europe drew on several sources. A theory of organic change held Christian monarchies to be, as the French writer Louis de Bonald put it, "the final creation in the development of political society and of religious society. The proof of this lies in the fact that when monarchy and Christianity are both attacked, society returns to savagery." Conservatives insisted that states emerged through gradual growth and that monarchical legitimacy stemmed from royal birthright, confirmed by the sanction of religion. Traditional monarchical institutions of government alone could maintain order. This helps explain why the British government, with its limited monarchy, was eager to support a French monarchy that retained a degree of authority that would have been considered unacceptable in Britain. Europe's conservative monarchies, including that of Britain, depended on the support of nobles, and they therefore sought to reestablish the privileges that the French Revolution and the Napoleonic era had swept away. Conservatives admired the British writer Edmund Burke, who during the Revolution had argued that monarchical stability and noble privilege were inseparable, the natural pillars of order, along with religion, on which society must stand.

De Bonald and his fellow French writer, Joseph de Maistre (c. 1754–1821), another émigré during the Revolution, espoused the alliance of throne and altar. Both rejected the concept of "natural rights" associated with Enlightenment thought. De Maistre believed that the Church stood as the foundation of social order. The king's power could never be limited by his subjects, because that power came only from God. De Maistre blamed the Revolution on the philosophes, particularly Voltaire, who had shaken the faith that underlay the absolutism of hereditary monarchy. Monarchies had to re-impose unquestioned obedience through fear. He wrote that "the first servant of the crown should be the executioner." Most conservatives saw no difference between reform and revolution, believing that reform would inevitably lead to revolution and radical change. They stood adamantly opposed to political claims based upon any notion of individual freedom, popular sovereignty, or membership in any particular national group. Liberalism seemed to them to be a political philosophy that set no limits on change, and therefore might open a floodgate of demands and concessions to popular sovereignty. Yet conservatives confronted the problem that their support was limited to a very narrow social and political base in a Europe that was slowly being transformed by the manufacturing revolution. It was testimony to the influence of the revolutionary era that the restored monarchy in France under Louis XVIII granted a Charter to the French people promising essential liberties. Moreover, the French monarchy, as well as those of Piedmont-Sardinia and even the rulers of Metternich's Austria, utilized the bureaucratized state apparatus inherited from Napoleon to repress liberals, instead of restoring the less-centralized ruling structure that had typified Old Regime Europe.

LIBERALISM

Nineteenth-century liberalism was more than an economic and political theory: it was a way of viewing the world. Liberals—the term became current in the late 1830s—shared a confidence that human progress was inevitable, though gradual. From the Enlightenment, the bourgeoisie inherited a faith in science, which they held to be a motor of progress. Liberalism reflected middle-class confidence and economic aspirations.

Liberals and Politics

Liberals believed that all individuals should be equal before the law because—in debt to Enlightenment thought—they believed that individuals are born good, free, and capable of improvement. Economic liberals for the most part believed in "laissez-faire," that the economy should be allowed to operate freely without state interference. Celebrating freedom from constraints inspired by the French Revolution, political liberals wanted government by constitution and by elected legislative bodies (such as the British Parliament and the French Chamber of Deputies) that would reflect some degree of popular sovereignty, with authority resting to some extent in the popular will rather than from monarchical legitimacy. Therefore they insisted on constitutional restraints on existing monarchies. Moreover, liberals demanded such civil liberties as freedom of the press and of assembly. Furthermore, most liberals demanded the extension of education to the lower classes as a means of expanding the number of people capable of participating in political life. Here, too, the goal was to allow each person to develop according to his or her capacities. But most liberals during the first two-thirds of the nineteenth century did not believe that all people should vote, but rather that eligibility to vote should stem from the amount of property owned, and that only such men—and not women—of property should hold the electoral franchise. During the subsequent three decades, "liberty" became the watchword for more and more people, particularly among the increasingly liberal middle classes, who protested their exclusion from political life.

Liberals gradually replaced the discourse on the rights of man—which had emerged from the Enlightenment of the eighteenth century and the French Revolution—with that of the legally defined rights of the citizen or subject. They put their faith in political and social rights embodied in constitutions, defined by law, and guaranteed by the state. Middle-class electors, all of whom were male, trusted elected legislative bodies to ensure that their rights as property owners could not be trampled by monarchs and aristocrats.

However, many liberals wanted the electoral franchise broadened. They denounced electoral systems that were so narrowly constructed that only the wealthiest men were allowed to vote, as in Britain, France, and Prussia, while recognizing that it was better to have some people vote than none at all. Most liberals at the time, however, opposed universal male suffrage (although some, like James Mill, believed that workers, with improved living conditions, would ultimately prove themselves worthy of participation in British political life). Moreover, very few liberals favored

extending the franchise to women. All over Europe, as franchise requirements were gradually loosened in response to pressures from the middle
class, the percentage of members of representative bodies drawn from the
middle class, and particularly from the legal profession, increased rapidly.

Laissez-Faire

As the guiding philosophy of the middle classes, liberalism was less a
clearly defined program than a combination of attitudes, an outlook rather
than an agenda. The origins of liberal thought were closely tied to the Enlightenment's uncompromising assertion of individual freedom. Like their
enlightened predecessors, classic nineteenth-century liberals believed that
humanity could improve itself. But unlike some of the philosophes who
had—at least briefly—placed their faith in enlightened absolutism, the
first generation of economic liberals believed that non-intervention by the
state would bring the greatest degree of prosperity and happiness. Governments were to do little more than protect private property.

Adopting the maxim "that government is best which governs least," liberals therefore sought to place limits on state authority. In particular, they
rejected government interference in the operations of the economy. Many
liberals therefore opposed protectionism—state-imposed duties on
imports. They followed the theories of Adam Smith (1723–1790), author
of *The Wealth of Nations* (1776). Their motto was "laissez-faire" ("let do as
[one] pleases"), which meant government non-interference in the workings of the economy, the "invisible hand" that engendered change. Smith
had argued that the unrestricted functioning of the free economy would
ensure the pursuit of private interests. This would, in turn, serve the public interest by creating more wealth. Smith contended that a new social
hierarchy would emerge if the economy were allowed to follow its natural
course. With their investments augmenting the general good, businessmen would supplant nobles and churchmen as the men to whom ordinary
people deferred.

Along with Smith's theories of laissez-faire, utilitarianism formed
another cornerstone of the entrepreneurial idea, indeed of liberalism in
general. Jeremy Bentham (1748–1832) was its most influential exponent.
In 1776, he had posited that laws should be judged by their social utility,
or whether or not they provided "the greatest good for the greatest number" of people. His famous standard question about any law or government institution was "Does it work?" Bentham's utilitarianism reflected
the relatively decentralized government of Britain and a pervasive belief
among the king's subjects that a government that made few demands and
that served efficiently was an essential part of the "liberties" of freeborn
Britons.

Adam Smith's successors gradually made a science out of specula-
tions about the operations of the economy, insisting that the laws they

postulated about the development of capitalism were based on scientific certainty. They pointed to the continued economic and social transformation of Britain. Both laissez-faire liberalism and utilitarianism were optimistic, secular doctrines based on the belief that society would continue to improve in the manufacturing age. The theories of Smith and Bentham had a great impact on British businessmen. The social status of an individual increasingly came to be measured in terms of utility.

In 1817, the British economist David Ricardo (1772–1823), the son of a Dutch banker, published his influential *Principles of Political Economy and Taxation*. Ricardo assumed the existence of an "iron law of wages," which held that, if wages were left to the laws of supply and demand, they would fall to near subsistence level. This was certainly more cheering news for manufacturers than for workers. Many liberals followed Ricardo in continuing to argue that if manufacturers were permitted to pursue private interests without government intervention or obstruction, the interests of everyone would be served.

Elected to Parliament in 1819, Ricardo became a hero to the middle class. Ricardo reassured liberals by telling them that "invisible hand" of the economy would bring continued economic growth and allocate resources, with the bulk of entrepreneurial profits going into employers' pockets. Through the Political Economy Club, the *Westminster Review* (first published in 1824), and newspapers, the ideas of Bentham and other liberals reached a wide audience. Liberal economists earned academic appointments at the University of Edinburgh and the University of London (founded in 1828 by religious dissenters). Economic liberalism also found proponents in France.

Middle-class entrepreneurs did not necessarily agree on what economic policies they favored, however. In the 1820s, Tory governments in Britain bored the first holes in the wall of protectionism by reducing the duty collected on Baltic timber, which had been kept high to favor Canadian exporters, and by establishing sliding scales for tariffs tied to the price of wheat in England. On the other hand, many French industrialists demanded that the government maintain high tariffs to keep out British manufactured goods and machinery. Merchants living in port cities usually wanted lower trade barriers. Businessmen everywhere demanded improved transportation networks.

Liberals also demanded the "freedom of work," that is, that nothing constrain free agreements between employers and their workers. Many manufacturers concurred, demanding that states keep unions and strikes illegal, despite the decline of wages in many trades. Employers wanted the market to determine wages, because, with the supply of workers far outnumbering demand, remuneration could, as Ricardo predicted, be kept relatively low. A good many industrialists opposed state-imposed limits to their authority within the workplace, including regulations concerning safety and child labor.

Many liberals also believed that a strong state compromised political freedom. British liberals, in particular, held that the French Revolution had culminated in Jacobin state centralization and Napoleonic despotism. Continental liberals remained more "statist," accepting a more active role by government, particularly in the German states, and in Spain, where they relied on a powerful state to counteract the influence of nobles and clerics.

ROMANTICISM

Romanticism, emphasizing imagination and emotion in personal development, had begun to emerge as a literary, artistic, and musical movement late in the eighteenth century. In 1798, the English poets Samuel Taylor Coleridge (1772–1834) and William Wordsworth (1770–1850) journeyed to the rugged Lake District in northern England. There they penned a manifesto of the "new poetry" which appeared in the preface to their *Lyrical Ballads*. They called on poets to abandon the formal rules that defined the classical style based on Greek and Roman models that was characteristic of eighteenth-century court and aristocratic life and instead express their emotional response to nature. Such a contrast may be seen, for example, in the geometrically planned formal gardens of the eighteenth-century English country houses and the more natural, unkempt, overgrown gardens in which nineteenth-century romantic poets sought inspiration. While those inspired by the rationalism of the Scientific Revolution might study a mountain objectively, Coleridge and Wordsworth saw mountains as wonders of nature that should best be appreciated emotionally. During the romantic era, swooning and fainting came into vogue because they seemed to be honest expressions of emotion.

Conservative Origins

Romanticism first contributed to the conservative revival. After initially being intrigued by the French Revolution's apparent victory over the strictures of the Old Regime, the early romantic writers had become disillusioned by its violent turn. Coleridge had been among the first to sing the praises of the Revolution, but he turned against it when French armies began pouring across the frontiers more as conquerors than as liberators.

Many of the early romantic writers were individuals of religious faith who rejected Enlightenment rationalism. "I wept and I believed," wrote the French writer François-René de Chateaubriand (1768–1848), relating his re-conversion to Catholicism after the turmoil of the Revolutionary and Napoleonic eras. Disillusionment with the French Revolution helped German romantic writers discover in nationalism a means of individual fulfillment. Nationalism, too, marked a reaction against Enlightenment rational tradition. Johann Gottfried von Herder (1744–1803), the son of a Prussian schoolteacher, was one of the impassioned leaders of the *Sturm und Drang* (Storm and Stress) movement, a rebellion by young German writers against Enlightenment thought. Calling for the study and celebration of German literature and history, Herder argued that it was through the passionate identification with the nation that the individual reached his or her highest stage of development. All Germans would be bound together by an awareness of and identity in a common history, culture, and above all, language as part of a *Volk*, or living and evolving "national community." Herder thus helped invent the idea of a national culture. But at the same time, his insistence on the existence of different racial types, shaped by climate, history, and cultural traditions, would influence the evolution of racism later in the century. In the meantime, most German romantics glorified the Middle Ages, when kings and nobles, they believed, had undertaken heroic deeds on behalf of a hierarchically organized community of the faithful. Likewise in Britain, the novels of Sir Walter Scott (1771–1832) romanticized the honor, chivalry, and hierarchical society of medieval Scotland.

However, romanticism's espousal of artistic freedom and the development of the individual increasingly became linked to liberalism, but also to nationalism as a force for change. This was particularly true in Central and Eastern Europe, which was constituted in many areas by a patchwork of nationalities. Romanticism celebrated the historical authenticity of the cultural traditions and languages of ethnic peoples. From there it would be a short step to argue that nationalities have their own independent state.

Romantic Literature and Painting

The high Enlightenment of the middle decades of the eighteenth century had emphasized rational inquiry as the means of discovering truth. But in the last stage of Enlightenment thought, Jean-Jacques Rousseau's "reasoned sentimentality" had made emotional development and fulfillment the center of an individual's development. Similarly, German idealism (sometimes called "pre-romanticism") had stressed subjectivity, reflecting a transition away from the rationalism of the early Enlightenment.

Romantic writers saw the arts as embodying the relationship between nature and spirit in the quest for freedom. The German poet and playwright Friedrich von Schiller (1759–1805) put it this way: "If man is ever to solve the problem of politics in practice, he will have to approach it through the problem of the aesthetic, because it is only through Beauty that man makes his way to freedom."

Like romantic poets, painters sought to convey feeling through the depiction of the helplessness of the individual confronted by the power of nature—gathering storms, surging seas, and immense, dark forests,

Théodore Géricault's *Portrait of an Officer of the Chasseurs Commanding a Charge* (1812).

portrayed with deep, rich colors. In France, Théodore Géricault (1791–1824) reached the public eye with his *Officer of the Chasseurs Commanding a Charge* (1812), an almost worshipful painting of a Napoleonic officer in the heat of battle. Géricault became obsessed with shipwrecks, a subject that reflected his volatile personality. He sought out real-life survivors of such tragedies in order to paint his powerful *The Raft of the Medusa* (1818–1819), based upon a shipwreck off the west African coast of what would become Senegal.

German romantics like Schiller defined freedom as the unleashing of the senses and passion of the soul. They searched for the "heroic genius" who fulfills himself in spite of constraints placed on him by the state, religion, or societal convention. Johann Wolfgang von Goethe (1749–1832) evoked the impassioned battle raging in the mind of the heroic individual. Goethe's hero in *Faust* (1790) struggles to make his way against a society that fails to understand him.

Like Faust, romantic writers and artists were, at least at the beginning, literary and academic outsiders. Many were loners, without established professional positions, overwhelmed by what they considered the tragedy of their unrequited search for individual fulfillment because less-gifted people did not comprehend their brilliance. Romantics bared the suffering of their souls. The English poet Percy Bysshe Shelley (1792–1822) penned his loftiest tribute to the poet (and, thus, himself) in the "Hymn of Apollo":

I am the eye with which the Universe
Beholds itself and knows itself divine;
All harmony of instrument or verse,
All prophecy, all medicine is mine,
All light of art or nature;—to my song
Victory and praise in its own right belong.

Romantic Music

The romantics also believed that music, like painting, was poetry capable of releasing torrents of emotion in listeners. Whereas romantic literature sought and achieved a sharp break with the rules of classical literature, romantic musical compositions built on the traditions of the eighteenth-century masters, helping the public rediscover them. The compositions of Ludwig van Beethoven (1770–1827) form a bridge between the classical and romantic periods, with a foot firmly in each. Beethoven's romanticism is reflected by his perhaps unsurpassed capacity to evoke an emotional response. Beethoven, the son of an alcoholic court musician in the Rhineland town of Bonn, was a homely, isolated, brooding individual. As a young man he earned the patronage of Viennese nobles, winning spirited competitions staged by composers and performers for the entertainment of the nobles.

Before he began to lose his hearing, Beethoven's music followed classical rules of structure and harmony. The German romantic composer Richard Wagner would later say that, as Beethoven became increasingly deaf, he was "undisturbed by the bustle of life [hearing only] the harmonies of his soul." Beethoven's audiences struggled to understand his music, which increasingly seemed to defy traditional structures and harmonies. An Austrian monument to Beethoven reflects the duality between classicism and romanticism: the seated figure of the composer wears an unmistakable bourgeois coat that gives way to a Roman toga.

A critic reacted to one of Beethoven's symphonies, "The composer, often bizarre . . . takes the majestic flight of the eagle, then he creeps along rock-strewn paths. After penetrating the soul with a gentle melancholy he immediately lacerates it with a mass of barbarous chords. I seem to see doves put in together with crocodiles!" Beethoven's symphonies and string quartets were widely played in Europe, and his sonatas helped popularize the piano. Whereas only two decades earlier Mozart had struggled to make ends meet, Beethoven enjoyed wealth and fame.

The Viennese-born composer Franz Schubert (1797–1828), whose father was a Moravian peasant, further exemplified romanticism's influence on music. In his more than six hundred *Lieder* (songs), Schubert fused romantic lyric poetry and music, helping to make folk songs part of instrumental musical expression. His music was performed in only one public concert in his brief life, which was cut short by syphilis, but his many operas, masses, symphonies, piano sonatas, and string quartets influenced the subsequent evolution of romantic music.

Although opera remained the most popular form of musical expression, drawing crowds with its extravagant staging and elaborate, expensive costumes, romantic music grew in popularity during the first half of the nineteenth century. Musically educated listeners flocked to public concerts, and more musicians could now make a living from their performances.

The family concert.

During the 1840s in the German states, the conductor (who now no longer played in the orchestra himself) began to stand in front of the musicians, who were grouped in a semicircle around him. The middle classes flocked with unbridled enthusiasm to hear such virtuosos as the Italian violinist Niccolò Paganini (1782–1840). Paganini's performances, the musical effects he produced, and his frenzied appearance suggested to one observer that he was engaging in witchcraft.

Music assumed a greater role in private life. Private concerts in middle-class homes were common: in Vienna during the Carnival season before Lent in 1821, chamber groups and small orchestras played at 1,600 private balls. Choral societies provided opportunities for amateur musical performances. Nonprofessional orchestras and choruses became more common; some were simply gatherings of friends who enjoyed playing and listening to music. Piano playing became far more common in middle-class homes, often accompanied by a voice recital. More musicians earned money giving music lessons to children of middle-class families, for whom musical accomplishment was seen as a social asset.

THE MIDDLE CLASSES

One should not exaggerate either the cohesiveness of the middle class, nor the extent of its dominance. Indeed, middle-class influence varied greatly within Europe, reflecting the economies and political structures of the various states. The size and influence of the middle class was far greater in Britain (where prosperity provided entry into the gentry through the purchase of land), France, Belgium, the German states, and the northern Italian states, whose economies and politics were slowly being transformed by the Industrial Revolution, than in Spain, the Habsburg monarchy, or Russia, still dominated by nobles.

The middle classes emphasized individual freedom and the respectability that came from work and prosperity. In liberalism, they found an economic and political theory that echoed the way they viewed the world. At the same time, for all the frugality sometimes ascribed to the nineteenth-century middle class, bourgeois prosperity found expression in the development of a culture of comfort. The middle class viewed the family as the basis of social order. Within the family—in which men and women occupied, at least in theory, separate spheres—religion and education played privileged roles.

Diversity of the Middle Classes

The middle class included all people who neither held noble title nor were workers or peasants depending on manual labor for economic survival. The terms "bourgeois" and "burghers" had first emerged in the Middle Ages to refer to residents of towns that enjoyed specific rights (such as immunity from some kinds of taxation), or even independence granted by territorial rulers. By the nineteenth century, the middle class made up roughly 15 to 20 percent of the total population in Western Europe but a far smaller percentage in Sweden, Eastern Europe, Russia, and the Balkans. The middle class expanded in size and diversity amid the ongoing economic transformation of Europe.

The nineteenth-century middle class encompassed a great range of economic situations, occupations, education levels, and expectations. It can be imagined as a social pyramid, topped by a small group of well-connected banking families, industrial magnates, and the wealthiest wholesale merchants, as well as a few top government ministers and ambassadors. Below this extremely wealthy group came families drawing more modest incomes from smaller businesses, rental properties, lawyers and notaries (both part of what became known as "the liberal professions") and lucrative government posts. In general it required some resources, connections, and access to credit to make money. Four out of five Berlin entrepreneurs were the sons of bankers, manufacturers, or merchants, with fathers who could bring them into the business or loan them enough money to get started on their own. At the bottom of the pyramid stood the "petty bourgeoisie," at whose expense nobles and wealthy bourgeois made cruel jokes. This stratum included shopkeepers of modest means and expectations, wine merchants, minor officials, schoolteachers, café owners, and some master artisans—craftsmen in the luxury trades, such as goldsmiths and silversmiths—who proudly considered themselves middle class.

Merchants and lawyers had long since been the most prominent citizens of towns in Belgium, the German Rhineland, and northern German trading cities like Lübeck, Bremen, and Hamburg, whose long traditions of political independence stretched back to the Middle Ages. The bankers and shippers of Amsterdam and other commercial centers still set the social and political style of the trading states. In Milan (Lombardy) and Turin (Piedmont), merchants and manufacturers helped convince municipal authorities, following outbreaks of cholera in the early 1830s, to improve the water supply, pave streets, and move slaughterhouses and cemeteries to the edge of town.

The Russian, Eastern European, and Balkan middle classes were minuscule in size and without political influence. The Russian bourgeoisie, which at the beginning of the century accounted for no more than about 2 percent of the population, included Orthodox priests, state officials, and a few intellectuals, but relatively few men whose entrepreneurial instincts and experience were remotely comparable to those of the Western middle class. The state itself managed some industries and, again in contrast with the West, noble domination of business—and of the universities and top ranks of the bureaucracy, as well—continued throughout the century. Some wealthy merchants, including former peasants and freed serfs, gained ennoblement. The Stroganov family, after whom the beef dish is named, was among these privileged few who were wealthy enough to buy meat, sour cream, and pepper for their favorite dinner.

A middle-class couple out on a walk in Vienna.

Sweden, too, had a small middle class, that enjoyed considerable economic and cultural influence. The sons of ministers and businessmen filled most of the posts in the civil service and the army. The powerful merchant families of the west coast trading port of Gothenburg were linked by their credit connections to an international trading network. They included prosperous traders who were Germans, Scots, or Jews.

Wealthy merchants and industrialists still hungered for social prestige and, in Britain, for the status of gentility that came from owning lots of land. The proportion of land owned by the middle class increased rapidly during the first half of the nineteenth century in Britain, France, and the German and Italian states. As ownership of land (specifically taxes paid on it) remained the basis of electoral enfranchisement in much of Western Europe, the political influence of the middle classes increased as well.

The landed elite remained at the pinnacle of social status in Britain, although its share of the nation's wealth fell from about 20 percent to about 10 percent between 1800 and 1850. Some English "country gentlemen" still looked down their noses at those they scorned as mere "calico printers," "shopkeepers," and municipal officials of modest means. Yet sons of wealthy landowners, titled or not, sat alongside the sons of nobles at Oxford and Cambridge Universities. Britain retained a uniquely narrow definition of nobility. Nonetheless, some peers owed their titles to family fortunes made in commerce or industry during the previous century. Likewise, because in Britain the eldest son still inherited the entire family fortune, some second and third sons left country life to become businessmen, without feeling the sense of humiliation that their counterparts might have felt in France or Prussia. Many noble families were delighted to have their offspring marry the sons and daughters of wealthy businessmen.

The remnants of noble political power, perpetuated by patronage and sometimes outright corruption, drew attacks from reformers who believed that self-satisfied indolence could only be constrained by "the wisdom of the middle class." In Western Europe, whereas many nobles still remained loyal to ruling or deposed dynasties, strong feelings of nationalism first developed within the middle class.

The Entrepreneurial Ideal and Social Mobility

In liberal Europe, the entrepreneur emerged more and more as the man to be revered and emulated. Commerce appeared as "the great emancipator." To Lord John Russell (1792–1878), a British prime minister and liberal reformer of the early Victorian period, "The best way in which to encourage social happiness and to spread Christianity and advance morality was to let commerce take its own course."

The middle class identified its status with the common good and fate of each nation, even in Great Britain, Prussia, and Austria, where nobles retained great influence. The Scottish philosopher and economist James Mill (1773–1836) emerged as the political champion of the middle class, which he called "both the most wise and the most virtuous part of the community." Mill's 1820 *Essay on Government* denounced nobles for invariably selfish attention to their own landed interests. "They grow richer as it were in their sleep, without working, risking, or economizing. What claim have they, on the general principle of social justice, to this accession of riches?" In Spain, the middle class—bankers, manufacturers, and merchants in the prosperous port of Barcelona, and lawyers and civil servants in Madrid—were considered "the useful classes," the motors of prosperity. They contrasted their penchant for hard work with noble "idleness." Many middle-class families in England, the Netherlands, and some of the German states were influenced by evangelical Protestantism, which stressed the redeeming nature of hard work. The message was often the same in Catholic France. In 1847, a Parisian newspaper defined what it meant to be bourgeois: "The bourgeoisie is not a class, it is a position; one acquires that position and one loses it. Work, thrift, and ability confer it; vice, dissipation, and idleness mean it is lost." The novels of Honoré de Balzac (1799–1850) depict Paris in the 1820s and 1830s as an economic and social jungle in which everything—even one's family—is sacrificed in the pursuit of money.

The notion of "respectability" gradually changed in Europe. Even in Prussia, still dominated by the landed wealth of the nobility, schoolbooks that had early in the nineteenth century emphasized immutable social hierarchy and the necessity of obedience gradually shifted to discussions of the virtues of hard work, self-discipline, and thrift. Middle-class families viewed the expansion of their fortunes as the best assurance of respectability. Bankruptcy seemed a fate worse than death.

The ideal of the self-made man was born. But, like any myth, it far surpassed the reality. Rapid social ascension remained difficult and fairly rare. There were, to be sure, spectacular success stories. The son of an ironmonger and saddler, the Welshman Robert Owen (1771–1858) began his career as a clerk and then sold cloth. Borrowing £100 in Manchester in 1789 to start up his own textile business, he became part owner of the large and prosperous New Lanark Mills in Scotland. Robert Peel, the British prime minister, is another case in point. His family had been Lancashire yeomen who also produced textiles. Peel's grandfather sold goods door to door; his son, the prime minister's father, became one of the most successful entrepreneurs in Lancashire. By 1790, he sat in Parliament as Sir Robert Peel, one of England's wealthiest men. The younger Peel went on to enjoy extraordinary social and political prominence.

To be sure, some degree of social mobility was possible from the ranks of relatively prosperous master artisans. Yet downward mobility also occurred; hard times could cause petty bourgeois to fall into the working class. The possibility of being afflicted by economic crises or personal disasters—the illness or death of a spouse, or one's own illness—haunted many such families.

Rising Professions

The growth of cities swelled the ranks of lawyers, doctors, and notaries. For the most part, however, the aspirations of those in these professions remained higher than their incomes and prestige. In Balzac's novels, young professionals "kill each other, like spiders in a jar." One French monarchist contended that "it isn't the workers one should fear, rather it is the *déclassés*, doctors without patients, lawyers without briefs, all the misunderstood, the discontented, who, finding no place at the banquet table, try to overturn it." During the July Monarchy (1830–1848) in France, many frustrated lawyers, doctors, and army officers would become republicans, joining forces with workers to demand universal male suffrage.

Lawyers had less than sterling reputations even as their numbers increased. In the 1830s and 1840s, the great French caricaturist Honoré Daumier (1808–1879) depicted lawyers as arrogant, self-satisfied, insensitive men far more interested in extracting fees than serving justice. However, in Britain the "pettifogging attorney" of the eighteenth century gradually was replaced by the "respectable lawyer" of the nineteenth. Notaries, too, gained in wealth and status with the growth of cities. They earned—though some of their clients would not choose that particular verb—fees that sometimes amounted to a tenth of the value of a property by registering and storing deeds of title. They also prepared marriage documents, dowries, and wills. Notaries thus remained in most countries the financial equivalent of father-confessors, knowing—or at least guessing—most of the deepest secrets concerning their clients' fortunes.

Daumier depicts a lawyer pleading his case.

The number of doctors, too, rose rapidly in nineteenth-century Western Europe, although they still struggled to be recognized as professionals rather than members of a trade. While some brilliant researchers labored in obscurity, notorious hacks received public plaudits. Among the latter was the decorated French doctor who claimed that he had proved that syphilis was not communicable—thus reassuring clients who paid considerable sums for his soothing words. A colleague treated mentally disturbed people by strapping them to wooden planks and drenching them with icy water. In some Swedish hospitals in the middle of the nineteenth century the mentally ill were still incarcerated in cages, their feet restrained by iron bars. Doctors were limited in the treatments at their disposal, which also contributed to their profession's minimal prestige. Popular belief in age-old cures, many based upon superstition, persisted throughout the continent.

In Western Europe, doctors began to form professional associations. The British Medical Society began in 1832 with the goal of encouraging standardized training and scientific research, as well as enhancing professional identity. For the first time in some countries surgeons now needed to have studied medicine in order to take up a scalpel, at least legally. The British Medical Act of 1858 standardized credentials for doctors, but did not require them.

Other professions also gradually commanded respect. In 1820, the Scottish writer Sir Walter Scott, assessing the future of a nephew, said that if the young man seemed fit for the army, he might well make his way there, but, if not, "he cannot follow a better line than that of an accountant. It is highly respectable." Newer professions in such field as veterinary science and pharmacology were open to sons of artisans and peasants. Clergymen and schoolteachers were also increasingly drawn from the middle classes. The growing reach of the state also required a growing number of officials and bureaucrats, providing attractive careers for middle-class sons.

MIDDLE-CLASS CULTURE

The many dimensions of the bourgeois experience during the nineteenth century shaped middle-class culture. The middle classes believed that the family offered the best guarantee of social order. Most bourgeois held fast to the idea of separate spheres for men and women. Education and religious practice (however varied) provided a common culture for the middle classes within individual states. Middle-class families sought education and advantageous marriages for their children. Many (and probably most) such families considered religion an important part of their lives. Largely because of the interest of the middle classes, voluntary associations proliferated, including many organized for charitable purposes. At the same time, growing middle-class prosperity generated a quest for comfort that permitted social distinction, reflected in residence, dress, and leisure.

Marriage and Family

An astute choice of a marriage partner could preserve and even enhance a family's wealth and position through the acquisition of handsome dowries and wealthy daughters- and sons-in-law. Although finding a noble spouse for their daughters still remained a prized ambition for French business magnates, there were fewer noblemen to go around. Moreover, the disasters of what were considered ill-advised or inappropriate marriages ("misalliances")—that is, a union between two people far apart on the social ladder—continued to be a popular theme in novels and the theater.

Love could—and increasingly did—play a role in the choice of mates. Prospective partners were more likely to insist that their views be taken into consideration in the arrangement of marriages. One Parisian woman told her father that she could not marry "someone that I do not love, that I am to marry for reason's sake, in order to give myself a lot in life. . . . How could I hold onto him, if I do not love him and desire him?"

With an eye toward assuring the future of their progeny, some middle-class families, above all in France, began to practice contraception after about 1820, limiting their children to two. The economist Jean-Baptiste Say (1767–1832), for one, encouraged family limitation, warning that "one must increase savings accounts more than increase the number of children." Coitus interruptus certainly became more common, as well as other rudimentary forms of birth control.

The concepts of childhood and adolescence developed rapidly within middle-class families. The "children's room" and the "children's hour," when the young came forward to see their parents and sometimes to meet guests, were middle-class concepts. In working-class and peasant households, there was no space for a separate room or quarters for children. Most working-class and peasant children had to begin work as soon as it was physically possible for them to do so. Furthermore, many children who were apprentices did not live with their families, but with the masters of their chosen trade.

Because children, too, were an investment—and much more, of course—parents had to prepare them for the time when they would take on family responsibilities. Parents sought to pass on self-discipline and self-reliance to their sons. Germans called it *Bildung*, the training of cultivation and character, the subject of many nineteenth-century novels.

Separate Spheres

To the nineteenth-century middle class, the family was the basis of order, what the English called the "nursery of virtue." Many men considered

A woman's separate sphere was inside the household and included supervising children and servants.

women "virtuous" when they remained in their domestic sphere, "angels" whose obligation was to provide comfort, happiness, and material order to their families. A woman's status remained closely tied to that of her father and her husband. In France, the Napoleonic Code made all men legally equal but left each woman subordinate to her husband's (or father's) will. A married woman could not freely spend money she earned. On his accession to the throne in 1820, King George IV of Britain (ruled 1820–1830) tried to prevent his wife, Caroline, from becoming queen by blocking her return to England from Italy under threat of prosecuting her for adultery. But the king was forced to abandon his plan and accept his queen when women (particularly middle-class women) petitioned on her behalf, denouncing the king for espousing a double standard, since his own liaisons were notorious. A contemporary ballad urged woman to rally behind Caroline:

Attend ye virtuous British wives
Support your injured Queen,
Assert her rights; they are your own,
As plainly may be seen.

Middle-class women cared for their children, planned and oversaw the preparation of meals, supervised the servants, and attended to family social responsibilities. They exercised great influence over the education of their children, supplementing formal school instruction. They also assumed responsibility for providing guidance about religion.

Many contemporary bourgeois insisted that women should work only when dire necessity left them with no alternative. Yet, although it was unusual for women to play a role in the operation of large businesses, they stood behind the counter to

"Mill's Logic, or Franchise for Females"

Caricature of John Stuart Mill's espousal of voting rights for women.

serve customers in shops. Widows often continued the family business after their husbands' demise. During the first decades of the nineteenth century, British feminists debated the issue of "separate spheres" for women and for men.

Middle-class British feminists began to challenge the legal and political subordination of women. Some demanded the right to vote. In *The Enfranchisement of Women* (published anonymously in 1851), Harriet Taylor Mill (1807–1858) stressed the injustice of considering anyone inferior, and therefore not deserving the right to vote, or other rights, by virtue of gender. Believing her time a period of social and political progress, she espoused the view that now "for the first time in the world, men and women are really companions." Eighteen years later, her long-time companion and later husband John Stuart Mill (1806–1873) published *The Subjection of Women* (1869). Mill argued that women, like men, should be able to compete as equals in a society defined by market relations. By the time of John Stuart Mill's long essay, feminism had emerged as a movement organized by women. Feminists demanded, among other things, that married women be allowed to continue to have control over property they had brought with them into marriage.

Opponents of women's rights identified feminist movements with the violence of the French Revolution, or with surges of working-class militancy. Despite the fact that many women had been active proponents of British nationalism during the revolutionary era and the Napoleonic Wars—such as by organizing patriotic subscriptions—many upper-class Britons still felt feminism to be "unrespectable."

A Culture of Comfort

The European middle classes gradually shaped a culture based on comfort and a quest for privacy that complemented growing prosperity. Most bourgeois families were able to employ one or more servants and had apartments of several rooms. The wealthiest usually occupied the first floors of buildings—but rarely the ground floor, where the concièrge, or building caretaker lived—while less well-off neighbors had to hike further up the stairs. In Balzac's *Old Goriot* (1834–1835), as the retired Goriot gives away more of his fortune to his two spendthrift daughters, he moves up another flight of stairs in the shabby but (barely) respectable rooming house in which he lives.

Kitchens and even dining rooms became separate rooms, as did attached offices for notaries, lawyers, and doctors. A distinct middle-class style of interior design slowly emerged, with national and regional variations. The German decorative style, with wallpaper and sparse, austere furnishings and ornamentation, matched the frugality of many burghers. In Lisbon and Porto, the middle class emulated the middle classes in Britain, which had for well more than a century had enormous influence on Portugal.

The accoutrements of the salon were likely to include an armoire or two, a chest of drawers, an elegant table and chairs, Limoges porcelain in France, Wedgwood china in England, crystal glasses, a clock, candelabras, a painting or print or two on the walls, all passed down from one generation to the next. Very wealthy families had much more, some beginning collections of knickknacks, small statues, and paintings. A Victorian pen manufacturer bought the entire studio collection of the painter J. M. W. Turner to go with his Gainsboroughs. He also possessed a rich collection of musical instruments, but when asked if he wanted to buy a Stradivarius, the finest violin in the world, he replied, "Nay, lad, I shan't buy any more fiddles." Such philistinism, however, was probably unusual. Pianos and other musical instruments became more common in the home and accompanied family singing. Flush toilets with running water would later gradually replace outdoor privies and the chamber pots that had caused many unfortunate mishaps when emptied unceremoniously out windows. Countryside secondary residences, retreats from the bustle of urban life, became considerably more common.

As Europe's large cities grew rapidly during the first half of the century, social segregation intensified, reinforced by the distribution and cost of public transportation. Within industrial towns, the pollution of smoke and other manufacturing smells also altered residential patterns, driving some middle-class families to new quarters. Paris's western neighborhoods became increasingly reserved for families of means, even if many apartment buildings still counted laborers and seamstresses living on the top floors. The wealthy in London enjoyed wide thoroughfares, vast public gardens, comfortable theaters, and elegant shopping arcades, a jolting contrast to the misery of the

East End. In 1856, a minister compared the West and East Ends of London: "There is little communication or sympathy between the respective classes by which the two ends of London were occupied. They differ in external appearance; in the fashion of their clothes, in their pursuits, in their pleasures, and in their toils; and on the rare occasions when they come into contact, they gape at each other with much the same curiosity and astonishment as would nowadays be exhibited by a native of this town at the appearance of an Eskimo in Hyde Park or Regent Street." Public gardens like Copenhagen's Tivoli, and its imitation in Stockholm, Berlin's Tiergarten, and Paris's Champs-Elysées developed at this time and were, for all intents and purposes, domains of the upper classes. Cafés catered to people of means— coffee was expensive—while cabarets, selling cheap drink, attracted a more plebeian clientele.

A cross-section of a Parisian apartment building, about 1850. Note that with the exception of the concierge's apartment on the ground floor, the farther you had to walk up the stairs, the less well off you were.

Expanding readership during the first half of the century encouraged a proliferation of novels, histories, poetry, newspapers, political pamphlets, and literary reviews, reflecting the diversity of middle-class interests. Balzac's novels were first published in France as installments of lengthy serials (particularly as authors were often paid by the word) on the bottom on the front page of newspapers. Charles Dickens (1812–1870), too, first reached his public in monthly installments. *The Pickwick Papers* (1836–1837) attracted 40,000 regular readers. Reading clubs and bookshops flourished in Western Europe.

The old Roman saying that "clothes make the man" rang true of the nineteenth-century bourgeoisie. Middle-class men wore black suits, perhaps enlivened by a cashmere scarf. Their wives dressed only somewhat less simply; besides the quality of the material of apparel, it was left to jewelry to suggest family wealth.

Travel for pleasure, previously relatively rare, became common. It also became a business. In 1835 in the German Rhineland, a young publisher named Karl Baedeker (1801–1859) published a guide to sites along the Rhine River. He soon published similar guides to Paris, several German states, Austria, Belgium, and the Netherlands. In Britain, Thomas Cook (1808–1892) organized his first collective excursion in 1841 when he chartered a special train to transport a group of workers to a temperance meeting. Four years later, he began the first travel agency, building on demand for his services at the time of the Great Exposition of 1851 in London. Soon Cook was transporting groups across the Channel to Paris, and some as far as the classical ruins of Italy and Greece. Middle-class families began to view travel as a means of self-improvement. They took in museums and other sights. In London, the National Gallery first opened its doors in 1824; about the same time, the middle class came to view the exhibits of the Old Museum in Berlin.

Education

Secondary education increasingly provided a common cultural background for the middle classes. Prussia's secondary schools (*Gymnasien*) were arguably Europe's finest, offering a varied curriculum that included considerable religious instruction. In Britain, the victory of the entrepreneurial ideal was reflected in a gradually changing secondary-school curriculum. The English elite had long been exposed to a classical curriculum, as well as to Spartan discipline based upon corporal punishment. Reforms undertaken by Thomas Arnold (1795–1842), headmaster at Rugby School, were intended to spur students on to better performances by stimulating academic competition through examinations and prizes. Arnold's reforms reinvigorated the existing English "public" [in the United States they would be considered private] secondary schools, and new ones were established.

Many businessmen, however, still believed that experience was the best preparation to carry the family torch. Prosperous French shopkeepers sometimes pulled their children out of school at age eleven or twelve, viewing what they learned there as irrelevant to the family tasks that lay ahead. Some entrepreneurs of family firms preferred to send sons to other companies, sometimes even in other countries, in order to obtain practical experience. In Catholic countries, middle-class families sent girls to convent schools to learn about drawing, music, and dance.

Secularized education, sponsored by states, only slowly undermined the role of religion in public life. In France, the Chamber of Deputies approved a law in 1833 (known as the Guizot Law, after the French politician who sponsored it) specifying that each village was to have a primary school. Private schools operated by the clergy continued to exist, and in many places provided the only schooling. But the existence of a state system, staffed by lay teachers, gradually eroded ecclesiastical control of education. Most French liberals and republicans opposed a pronounced role for the Church in public life. Many were staunchly anticlerical, demanding public schools that would teach secular values. In the German states, the same battle went on between ecclesias-

The Reading Lesson, by Jean-François Millet.

tical and secular authorities and proponents, but the established churches retained greater influence over public education. The clergy still controlled schools in Spain and the Italian states, where in 1847 Piedmont was the first European state to establish a ministry of public education. Yet in the region of Belgrade in what would become Serbia, in 1810 there were only two primary schools.

Thus, despite the gradual emergence of state systems of education, only a small percentage of people went beyond primary school to secondary education, and far more men than women could do so because of the lack of opportunities for the latter. The educational systems of early nineteenth-century Europe did provide many more people than ever before with basic reading and writing skills, and the literacy rate in Western Europe moved well above 50 percent. But they also maintained social barriers because relatively few families could afford to send their children to secondary schools, which could provide them with more advanced skills needed for better-paying employment. In France in the early 1840s, only two of every thousand people attended a secondary school. Some working-class families still resisted even sending their children to primary school, not only because they could ill afford the modest costs involved, but because they needed their children's wage contributions, however small, to the family income.

Although their numbers were still relatively small, more young men went to university in order to prepare for careers in law, medicine, the church, or the civil service. Even in Russia, the number of university students tripled, rising from 1,700 in 1825 to 4,600 in 1848—still precious few in a population of more than 50 million.

Religion

Religious ideals still played an important part in the middle-class view of the world, though the extent varied from place to place. If disenchantment with organized religion permeated novels in Britain, France, and the German states, contemporary writing rarely challenged common doctrinal assumptions that closely linked Christianity and morality. Biblical references abounded even in the treatment of secular subjects because they were understood by all literate people. In the German states, as in the Scandinavian countries, the middle classes were more likely to go to church than other social groups. And throughout Europe, women manifested a much higher rate of religious observance than did men.

Many middle-class men and women deplored the materialism that seemed to have lured some of their own away from church. The novels of Jane Austen (1775–1817), the daughter of a clergyman, were highly successful at least partially because she affirmed that character, moral rectitude, and proper conduct, including control of the passions (in short, "respectability"), were not the preserve of wealthy landowners and titled nobles, many of whom were concerned only with wealth and status. Virtue could also be found among the men and women of the middle class. In the end, her characters' behavior is the key to respectability. Austen's remark-

Evening prayer in a Viennese middle-class household.

able wit brought forward compelling characters whose inner struggles and social dramas engaged contemporary readers.

The English middle class also viewed religion as a way of "moralizing" workers by teaching them self-respect. By the mid-nineteenth century, more than 2.6 million children attended Sunday schools. Many Sunday schools were created by the working-class communities they served. They provided the children of workers with educational, social, and recreational opportunities not otherwise available. The middle class did not have a monopoly on "respectability" and the virtues of hard work and discipline.

THE AMBIGUITIES OF LIBERALISM: VOLUNTARISM VERSUS STATE INTERVENTION

Clubs, societies, and other voluntary associations characterized nineteenth-century middle-class life. Some, organized exclusively for leisure activities, manifested an upper-class sense of social distinction, such as the exclusive clubs of west London and the Anglophile Jockey Club of Paris (founded in 1834). Other more modest clubs included the dueling fraternities (*Burschenschaften*) of German universities and the sociable "circles" in French towns. Although most such groups excluded women from membership, middle-class women formed their own clubs, principally charitable associations. Outside the home, such activities were among the few public opportunities open to middle-class women.

Charitable activities emerged as an important facet of middle-class life in nineteenth-century Europe. Growing public awareness of the appalling conditions in which many workers and their families lived engendered impressive charitable efforts among people of means. In England, charity was organized by middle-class women, often through their churches or clubs. Some middle-class associations joined manufacturers, merchants, and members of the professions in northern English industrial towns in seeking to "moralize" the lower classes by shaping their conduct (for example, by encouraging them to attend church and to drink less). In 1860, there were at least 640 charitable organizations in London alone, more than two-thirds of which had been established since the beginning of the century. Moreover, the vast majority of the voluntary hospitals that existed in London at that time had also been founded since 1800.

Despite the growing tradition of voluntarism, gradually many middle-class liberals came to believe that liberty sometimes had to be tempered in a rational way. Fears of popular insurgency, which they identified with the French Revolution, also could outweigh distrust of a strong state. Anxious bourgeois were reassured by the greater professionalization of police forces both in France and in Britain, where Home Secretary Robert Peel (future prime minister) organized the unarmed municipal police, whose members became known as "bobbies" in his honor. Berlin had only 200 policemen in 1848 to watch over a population of 400,000, which they did with military precision and occasional brutality. In British, German, French, and Italian cities, and in the United States, as well, civilian national guards were established, with membership limited to property owners. Such forces on occasion supplemented the police, gendarmerie (national police), and regular army units, and could be called upon to quell local disturbances and protect the propertied classes.

Yet, to be sure, those calling for more state intervention in economic and social matters did not just have the repression of the lower orders in mind. By about 1830, some Western European liberals became aware of some of the unfortunate social consequences of classical liberalism and pure utilitarianism. They did not object to the wealthy becoming even wealthier, but they did worry that the poor were becoming too poor. Some of the English philosopher Jeremy Bentham's followers, among others, began to espouse government-sponsored social reform. Liberals crusaded against slavery, portraying the institution as incompatible with morality and with British freedom. Such campaigns reflected the development of Evangelical Christianity, which had blossomed during the last two decades of the eighteenth century in Britain.

Most liberals considered education an essential means of developing the individual. In contrast, the British writer Hannah More (1745–1833) believed that poor children should learn how to read so that they could study the Bible, but not to write, because such a skill might make them reject their social subordination. For his part, Thomas Malthus (1766–1834), the English clergyman who predicted that the rise of population would rapidly outdistance the ability of farmers to provide enough food, believed that education would make ordinary people "bear with patience the evils that they suffer," while realizing the "folly and inefficacy of turbulence." Middle-class liberal reformers, however, shared far more optimistic views of education. The National Society campaigned for universal education in Britain. Henry Lord Brougham (1778–1868), a key figure in the passage of parliamentary political reform acts, believed that progress would be served if working men were educated. In 1826, he founded the Society for the Diffusion of Useful Knowledge, which made available to ordinary people cheap pamphlets and other publications of "improvement literature." Brougham and his followers founded a number of schools called Mechanics Institutes, most of them short-lived, which hammered home the entrepreneurial ideal to artisans and skilled workers. But educational reform in Britain proceeded slowly, at least partially because the state provided little direction.

Many poor children in Britain attended Sunday schools, charity, or "dame" schools (essentially day-care centers that charged a fee, allowing working women to leave their children), but government intervention seemed necessary in order to upgrade the education poor children received at these schools. The state did no more than provide inspectors for schools built by towns or parishes that could afford to do so or that had received random government grants. On the continent, compulsory primary education existed only in Switzerland, beginning in the 1830s.

Disillusioned by the contrast between liberal ideals of individual self-development and the effects of laissez-faire, the English philosopher John Stuart Mill became a forceful proponent of greater government intervention on behalf of social reform. Mill, who began learning Greek at the age of three at the insistence of his domineering father, James Mill, believed in the capacity of the free individual to develop his or her abilities. "Among the works of man, which human life is rightly employed in perfecting and beautifying," he wrote, "the first in importance surely is man himself." John Stuart Mill's *On Liberty* (1859) argued that the individual is the best judge of his or her own interests, and that the individual develops by expressing free choices; it also marked a retreat from pure economic liberalism even in its spirited defense of individual freedom.

John Stuart Mill's espousal of causes such as women's rights and his participation in union campaigns for economic justice reflected this evolution of liberalism away from laissez-faire principles to a political theory concerned with economic, social, and political justice. Unlike his father, Mill was appalled that relatively few people of means seemed concerned

Charity in the attic. A middle-class woman visits an impoverished family living in an attic apartment without furnishings or comforts. The last thing a poor family would pawn would be their mattress, a symbol of respectability.

about the awful conditions of working-class life. "I confess I am not charmed," he wrote, "with the ideal of life held out by those who think that the normal state of human beings is struggling to get on; that the trampling, crushing, elbowing, and treading on each other's heels, which form the existing type of social life, are the most desirable lot of human kind, are anything but disagreeable symptoms of the phases of industrial progress." In his *Principles of Political Economy* (1848), Mill rejected Adam Smith's cheery optimism about the "invisible hand," called on the state to assist workers by encouraging their cooperative associations.

STIRRINGS OF REVOLT

The Congress of Vienna resembled the Dutch boy gamely trying to dam the deluge by plugging up the holes in the dike with his fingers. During the first half of the century, virtually every country in Europe experienced a confrontation between the old political order reestablished by the Congress of Vienna and nascent liberalism.

In France and many of the German states, liberal bourgeois formed political organizations that demanded political rights for a wider number of people. Newspapers and political pamphlets deftly sidestepped the heavy hand of censorship to challenge the restored prerogatives of conservative princes and the established churches. In Britain, middle-class spokesmen confronted conservatives and what its enemies referred to as "Old Corruption," a political system based upon the patronage and influence of wealthy landowners. In the German states, the Swiss cantons, and in reactionary Spain, the middle classes clamored for constitutions.

In the German and Italian states and Belgium, liberalism was closely associated with fledgling nationalist movements. Groups of nationalists, including intellectuals, students, and lawyers, called for the creation of independent states based upon nationality. Nationalist demands were anathema to the powers represented at the Congress of Vienna, particularly the leaders of the Russian and Austrian Empires, whose subjects included many different peoples. Demands for new states organized around the principle of nationality would threaten the existence of these empires and perhaps also might challenge the hierarchy of social privilege.

Liberal Revolts in Spain, Portugal, and Italy

The first test for the Congress system came in Spain. Upon his return to Madrid in 1814, Ferdinand VII (ruled 1808–1833) declared that he did not recognize the liberal constitution that had been drawn up by the Assembly (Cortes) in 1812. This stillborn document nonetheless formed the basis of Spanish (and Portuguese) liberalism in the nineteenth century. It provided for a "moderate monarchy" with ministers responsible to the Cortes and defined sovereignty as residing "essentially in the [Spanish] Nation," the union of all Spaniards in both hemispheres. It guaranteed the right of property, freedom of the press, and freedom from arbitrary arrest.

King Ferdinand VII may not have been quite the intransigent fanatic that some contemporaries insisted, but he disliked liberals. He repressed Masonic lodges, imposed strict censorship, and welcomed back the Jesuit religious order. Furthermore, he refused to convoke the Cortes, which he had promised to do upon his return. Ecclesiastics and nobles reclaimed land they had lost during the Napoleonic period. Moreover, the Inquisition, the Catholic Church's institutionalized apparatus to maintain religious orthodoxy, returned to Spain, and the police again began to arrest alleged heretics.

The Spanish monarchy remained inextricably allied with ecclesiastical and noble privilege. The clergy accounted for about 30 percent of adult Spanish males, many living in the monasteries that dotted the countryside. The aristocracy and the Church owned two-thirds of the land, much of it as unproductive as its owners, who collected revenue from those tilling the soil. Yet the vast majority of peasants supported the established order, believing the word of the village priest to be that of God. The small number of nobles and bourgeois who read the country's few newspapers—the majority of the population remained illiterate—found little except, as one traveler put it, "accounts of miracles wrought by different Virgins, lives of holy friars and sainted nuns, romances of marvelous conversions, libels against Jews, heretics and Freemasons, and histories of apparitions."

The allies were delighted to have a "legitimate" sovereign back on France's southern flank, although Spain had long since ceased to be a European power. Moreover, its empire had begun to disintegrate. Rebellions against Spanish rule broke out in the Latin American colonies, beginning in Argentina in 1816. Military expeditions, which failed to reconquer the colonies, exacerbated Spain's economic crisis. Simón Bolívar (1783–1830), a fiery Creole aristocrat educated in European Enlightenment ideals, led an army that liberated his native Venezuela in 1821 and defeated Spanish troops in Peru in 1824. Mexico had declared its independence two years earlier. Of the overseas empire that had stretched from North America to the tip of South America in the sixteenth century, Spain retained only the Caribbean islands of Cuba and Puerto Rico, as well as the Philippines in Asia.

Against this background, a revolt broke out in Spain in 1820. Army officers who led the insurrection against Ferdinand were soon joined by merchants and lawyers. The intimidated king agreed to convoke the Cortes and abide by the liberal constitution of 1812. Metternich and Tsar Alexander of Russia, supported by Prussia, demanded armed allied intervention; so did Louis XVIII, who was eager to prove himself a reliable ally. Great Britain, however, with economic interests in Portuguese trade, remained adamantly opposed to any intervention in Spanish internal affairs, first as a matter of principle, and secondly because of fear that the presence of

Latin American liberator Simón Bolívar (standing in the center), meeting with his generals.

foreign troops in Spain might jeopardize British commerce or increase French influence on the Iberian Peninsula.

Meanwhile, the fires of liberalism broke out in Portugal. Liberal army officers took advantage of the continued absence of King John VI, who had fled to Brazil during the Napoleonic Wars, to rise up against the British-backed regent in August 1820. They drafted a liberal constitution, based on that penned in Spain in 1812. That same year, a military coup d'état led to the return of John from Brazil as a constitutional monarch. The constitution proclaimed that year guaranteed religious toleration, civic rights, and the sanctity of property. The influence of this revolution, which undercut the influence of the Church, was to be felt for several decades in Portugal: it led to civil war from 1832 to 1834 between royalists and an alliance of liberals and radicals, and then in 1851, after some forty different governments and a coup d'état, to the establishment of a parliamentary system of government based on a restricted electoral franchise.

In 1820 an insurrection also broke out in Italy. Army officers and merchants in Naples and Sicily revolted against the rule of King Ferdinand I, another monarch who had been restored to his shaky throne by the allies. Some of the revolutionaries were members of a secret society, organized along military lines, known as the "Carbonari." These "charcoal-burners" took their name from their practice of swearing each new member to secrecy by tracing a charcoal mark on his forehead. The Carbonari, originally formed to fight Napoleon's armies, now directed its fervor against the monarch placed on the throne by the Austrians. Another small revolt broke out in the Kingdom of Piedmont-Sardinia. Austrian troops quickly put down these uprisings.

The Russian, Prussian, and Austrian governments signed an agreement at the Congress of Troppau in Galicia in October 1820. Based on the "principles of the [Holy] Alliance," it proclaimed the right of the signatories to intervene militarily in any country in which political changes were brought about by revolution. Following Castlereagh's suicide in 1822, Britain further distanced itself from the Congress system. That same year, the remaining Congress powers reconvened in the northern Italian town of Verona. Britain's withdrawal cleared the way for military action in Spain, where King Ferdinand VII had been deposed. With the support of Russia, Prussia, and Austria, a French army took to the field for the first time since Waterloo, but in very different circumstances and with a very different purpose. It crossed the Pyrenees Mountains in 1823 and captured Madrid. Restored to his throne, the grateful Ferdinand renounced the Constitution of 1812 and ordered the torture and execution of his opponents.

In December 1823, U.S. President James Monroe, fearing that the Concert powers might try to help Spain restore its authority over its former Latin American colonies, issued a proclamation that became one of the bases of subsequent American foreign policy. The Monroe Doctrine stated that "the American continents . . . are henceforth not to be considered as subjects for future colonization by any European powers." Stressing that the political systems of the latter were different from its own, it warned that the United States would "consider any attempt on their part to extend their system to any portion of this hemisphere as dangerous to our peace and safety."

Stirrings in Germany

In the German states, as in the Italian states, liberals and nationalists were often the same people. Members of student fraternities, who had grown up amid the nationalist response to the Napoleonic invasions and who were as much known for their dueling, wanted a united Germany. In 1817, a large convocation of student associations celebrated the three hundredth anniversary of Martin Luther's revolt against the papacy, burning books deemed anti-patriotic. In 1819, a German student murdered an arch-conservative historian and dramatist commonly believed to be in the pay of the Russian tsar. Metternich persuaded the Austrian Emperor Francis I and Frederick William III of Prussia to impose a series of repressive measures, the Carlsbad Decrees, which the Diet of the German Confederation unanimously accepted. These muzzled the press and dissolved the student fraternities. Teachers fired in one state were to be blacklisted in other member states. Metternich used the murder to convince Frederick William to renounce any form of "universal representation" in his kingdom. The

Nationalist German students in 1817 burning books and other objects deemed anti-patriotic.

episode seemed to clinch Metternich's victory over constitutionalism in the German states.

Cracks in the Congress of Europe: The Greek Revolt

The Greek revolt against the Ottoman Turks, which followed in 1821, shattered the alliance. Austria and, above all, Russia hoped to extend their influence in the Balkans at the expense of the Ottoman Empire. In the late eighteenth century, Catherine the Great had seen Russia's role in the Balkans as protecting Christians there against the Turks. Moreover, Russian nationalists coveted Constantinople, the gateway to Asia and the Black Sea. Britain vehemently opposed Russian acquisition of the Ottoman capital, fearing a potential threat to British control of India and influence in Afghanistan. Austria, threatened by Russian interest in the Balkans, also feared Russian designs on Constantinople. The Greek revolt put the Congress powers in a bind. Much of Christian Europe considered the Turks savage infidels. But, at the same time, the Congress powers had to recognize the Ottoman Empire as the historically "legitimate" sovereign of the Greeks, who benefited from commercial privileges awarded them by the Ottoman Turks. Support for the Greeks by the European powers would represent a renunciation of the *status quo*, a principle upon which the Congress system had been based.

Building upon a small Greek nationalist movement that had developed at the end of the eighteenth century, Prince Alexander Ypsilantis (1792–1828), a former general in the Russian army and the son of a Greek provincial administrator, founded a secret nationalist organization in 1814, the "Society of Friends." He recruited members among Greeks living abroad, and counted on the tsar's support for a Greek uprising. Russia had encouraged a Greek insurrection in 1770, one that had been crushed by Turkish forces, as was another by Serbs put down in 1810. In 1821, Ypsilantis organized a revolt in Turkish Moldavia, hoping that Romanians would also rebel against Ottoman domination and that Russia would aid the cause of the insurgents. The Turks crushed the initial Greek uprising, since the Romanians did not rebel and the tsar disavowed the rebels. Several weeks later, however, further revolts against the Turks broke out in mainland Greece and on several Aegean islands. The Congress powers, including Russia, immediately condemned the insurrection.

However, the Greek revolt caught the imagination of writers in Western Europe. Romantic writers now used their literary gifts to challenge the monarchs of Restoration Europe through espousal of national self-consciousness. Members of the Philhellenic movement (scholars and intellectuals who had become passionately interested in classical Greece) embraced the Greek revolt as a modern crusade for Christianity and independence against what they considered Turkish oppression of the birthplace of Western civilization. The English poets Byron and Percy Bysshe Shelley took up the cause of Greek independence. Shelley, who called the poet the "unacknowledged legislator of the world," also supported the quest for Irish independence from Britain. He died in a shipwreck off the coast of Italy in 1822. Byron died of fever in Greece two years later.

The Greek insurgents had massacred thousands of Turks in 1821, but it was the brutal Turkish repression of the Greeks that appalled Western conservatives and liberals alike. In 1822, the Turks massacred the entire Greek population of the island of Chios, after having executed the patriarch of Constantinople in his ecclesiastical robes on Easter Sunday the previous year. The French artist Eugène Delacroix (1798–1863), arguably the greatest romantic painter, celebrated the Greeks' struggle for national sovereignty in his painting *The Massacre at Chios* (1824). The British government also had come to the view that peace could best be maintained by the creation of an autonomous Greek state. In 1827, Britain, France, and Russia signed the Treaty of London, threatening the Turks with military intervention if they did not accept an armistice. When the Turks refused, a combined naval force destroyed the Turkish fleet at Navarino.

Russia, eager to capitalize on the dwindling fortunes of the Turks, declared war on the Ottoman Empire in 1828, quickly occupied the

Balkan territories of Moldavia and Eastern Wallachia, and captured Adri-anople. However, long sieges against a Turkish fortress on the Danube River and another on the Black Sea coast, and the self-interested disap-proval by Britain and France of Russian plans for dismembering the Ottoman Empire, forced Russia to agree to the Treaty of Adrianople (1829). Moldavia and Wallachia became protectorates of Russia, further pushing back the Ottoman Empire's European territories and expanding Russian influence in the Balkans. In 1832, the Greeks finally gained in-dependence from the Turks. The treaty between Britain, France, Bavaria, and Russia placed Greece under the "guarantee" of "protecting powers" and selected a young Bavarian prince to be king of Greece (Otto I; ruled 1833–1862). Greek nationalists began to dream of expanding the coun-try's borders, some hoping to create a much larger state with Constan-tinople its capital.

After the Battle of Navarino, the allies actually apologized to the Ottoman sultan for sinking his fleet. In doing so, they acknowledged a paradox: the allies of the Concert of Europe had intervened militarily on behalf of a nationalist movement against an established power. The Greek revolt had shattered the Congress system. Like Delacroix's painting, the allied inter-vention had sanctioned a nationalist insurrection as a worthy act.

Eugène   Delacroix's
Massacre   at   Chios,
1824.

The Decembrist Revolt in Russia

The sprawling Russian Empire had remained practically immune to change for centuries, despite the flirtations of Peter the Great and Catherine the Great with Western ideas and culture in the seventeenth and eighteenth centuries. At his succession to the throne after the assassination of his autocratic father in 1801, Tsar Alexander I seemed liberal and idealistic. He had initially relaxed the restrictive measures of his father and surrounded himself with advisers who advocated reform.

An enormous social, economic, and legal gulf separated the Russian aristocracy from the millions of destitute serfs bound to the lands of their lords. Most Russian nobles feared that any reform would threaten their prerogatives. Prussia had freed its serfs in the name of military efficiency, but when Alexander I gave permission to the nobles to free their own serfs early in his reign in 1803, few had chosen to do so.

During the Napoleonic Wars, Tsar Alexander had taken steps to make his regime more efficient, including the creation of a council of state, centralized ministries directly responsible to the tsar, a more efficient bureaucracy, and the organization of local governments.

However, Tsar Alexander became increasingly reactionary. Conservative elements regained power and introduced coercive measures. Universities and schools were closely monitored to root out liberals; study abroad was banned; and censorship was applied with ruthless efficiency.

But liberal reform had advocates in Russia, including some young nobles who had been educated in Western Europe (before foreign study was prohibited) and among some army officers who had lived in France during the allied military occupation after Napoleon's fall. Sharing a deep desire to see reforms come to Russia, they were bitterly disappointed by Alexander I's reactionary turn. By 1820, two loosely linked conspiratorial "unions," as they were called, existed. The educated nobles of the Northern Union hoped that Russia might evolve toward British constitutionalism. The military officers of the Southern Union had a more radical goal: to kill the tsar and establish a republic.

Tsar Alexander's sudden death in December 1825 seemed to offer the secret society its chance. The tsar had two brothers. Constantine, the eldest, had quietly yielded his succession to the throne in favor of his younger, more reactionary brother Nicholas. The secret society of the Northern Union nonetheless convinced the St. Petersburg garrison to support the succession of the more liberal Constantine. Troops occupied a central square in the capital, shouting the name of their favorite, until Nicholas ordered troops loyal to him to fire. A hastily planned insurrection by the Southern Union was also put down, and the leaders of the Decembrists, as they were subsequently called, were executed.

Nicholas I (ruled 1825–1855) was nineteen years younger than his brother and, unlike the latter, his education had been limited to military

Tsar Nicholas I.

matters. He drew his top officials and advisers only from military men. A contemporary who knew the cold and uncommunicative tsar assessed, "Nicholas desires to be obeyed whereas others desire to be loved." Hard-working and willful, Nicholas believed that his power to govern came directly from God. Hand-picked men directed the empire, and the new generation of army officers strongly supported the tsar. Nicholas tightened the grip of the police on education in an attempt to exclude Western ideas from Russia. In 1833, the minister of education proclaimed the doctrine of "Official Nationality": autocracy, orthodoxy, and nationality were the intertwined principles of the state, and they were to be defended at all costs. Yet, at the same time, the tsar's coronation manifesto referred to "defects [that will be] remedied and abuses corrected." He did not approve of serfdom because it was inefficient. But he feared insurrection, stating in 1842: "There is no doubt that serfdom . . . is an evil, palpable and obvious to all. But to touch it now would be a still more disastrous evil. . . . The Pugachev rebellion [of the eighteenth century] proved how far popular rage can go." Nicholas did, however, order the codification of Russian laws in the first decade of his reign and encouraged reforms improving the conditions of state peasants. However, Nicholas doggedly held on to the old system, embodied in the doctrine of "Official Nationality." The liberal wind was felt only weakly in Russia. Yet despite censorship, the arrival of liberal ideas from the West encouraged debate and calls for reform within the Russian intelligensia. These trends also encouraged the emergence of a group of reform-minded men within the imperial bureaucracy. Both groups helped expand the perimeters of public opinion within the Russian Empire.

France: The Bourbon Restoration and the Revolution of 1830

In a contemporary French lampoon of the return of the Boubons to the throne, a majestic eagle—the symbol of Napoleon—sweeps out of the Tuileries Palace in Paris as a somewhat plump, unsightly duck waddles in, followed by its ungainly brood. The contrast between the image of Napoleon's bold achievements and the stodgy and pious Restoration was sharp indeed. Former soldiers regaled their families and neighbors with stories of their exploits, real or imagined, during the Napoleonic Wars. The Bourbons, on the other hand, returned "in the baggage of the allies," as it was said.

Upon the return of the Bourbons to power in May 1814, Louis XVIII promulgated a Charter that, in effect, made France a constitutional monarchy. Realizing that he could not ignore liberal opinion, Louis's Charter of 1814 recognized equality before the law and accepted the Napoleonic Civil Code. It established an Assembly consisting of a Chamber of Deputies and a Chamber of Peers. The king would name members (whose appointment would be for life and hereditary) of the Chamber of Peers, as well as ministers, who would be responsible only to him. The Chamber of Deputies would be elected in a complicated two-stage process. The electoral franchise, however, was extremely narrow, limited to France's 50,000 wealthiest men, and only about a third of those would be eligible by virtue of their wealth (in the tradition of the first French republic and the empire) to stand for election to the Chamber of Deputies in a nation of more than 30 million people.

Yet, like the very existence of a Charter itself, Louis XVIII recognized that he could not completely turn the clock back to 1788. He maintained the centralized reorganization of the state bureaucracy, including the division of the country into "départments"; recognized all titles, decorations, and even pensions awarded during previous regimes; and promised that property purchased during the Revolution as "national property" would remain in the hands of the new owners. Moreover, the Charter guaranteed freedom of the press. The government could levy no taxes without the consent of the Assembly. It reaffirmed the Napoleonic Code's guarantee of the free practice of religion to France's Protestants and Jews. The Catholic Church would still be subject to Napoleon's Concordat with the Church (see Chapter 13).

But in other ways, the Church returned to its privileged position, Catholicism again becoming the official state religion. Religious orders returned to France in force. The observance of Sunday and Church holidays became obligatory. The Church also sent a preaching order into most provincial towns to give "missions," several days of intense ceremonies and sermons intended to return the local population to traditional religious values.

Some of the nobles who returned from foreign exile were eager to exact revenge on those who had served the Revolution and Napoleon (whom they considered "the usurper"), dishonored their religion, and even purchased their land in their absence. Ultra-royalists, or "Ultras," the most fanatical royalist enemies of the Revolution, had after Waterloo launched the "White Terror," so called because of the color of the Bourbon flag, against those who had supported Napoleon.

In the election for the Chamber of Deputies in August 1815, the Ultras easily defeated the more moderate royalists sponsored by the government.

Some of the Ultras even referred contemptuously to Louis XVIII as "King Voltaire" because of his Charter, which they viewed as a compromise with the Revolution. They demanded that the "national property" that had been confiscated and sold during the Revolution be returned to its original owners.

Confronted by the intransigence of the Ultra-dominated chamber, Louis XVIII dissolved it in 1816; new elections produced a somewhat more moderate chamber. In 1820, a madman assassinated Charles, the duke of Berry, the king's nephew and the only member of the Bourbon family capable of producing an heir to the throne. France was plunged into mourning. The Ultras cried for revenge, accusing the liberals of being ultimately responsible for the assassination. The king dismissed the moderate government, restored more stringent censorship, and altered the electoral system to reduce the influence of wealthy bourgeois voters living in towns.

Soon, however, the church bells stopped their mournful cadence and rang out in joy. Incredibly enough, it turned out that the duke's wife had been pregnant at the time of his death. Royalist France celebrated the birth of a male heir, "the miracle baby," as he came to be called, the duke of Bordeaux (later known as the count of Chambord). Confident that God was with them, the Ultras, at least for the moment, retained the upper hand.

Upon Louis XVIII's death in 1824, his brother, the count of Artois, took the throne as Charles X (ruled 1824–1830). The new king was one of those intransigent Old Regime nobles who "had learned nothing and forgotten nothing" during the long revolutionary and Napoleonic eras. The French monarchy seemed to be defying the new century. Charles's coronation ceremony in the Reims Cathedral could have come right out of the Middle Ages: the newly anointed monarch attempted to cure crippled subjects with the "healing touch of kings."

Many people believed rumors that the pious king was going to allow the Catholic Church to collect the tithe, that is, require them to pay 10 percent of their income to the Church. The Chamber of Deputies passed a law making sacrilege—any crime committed in or against a church—a capital offense. That no one was ever executed for such an offense did not diminish public outrage. Amid rumors that noble land sold during the Revolution was to be returned to its original owners, the government financed the indemnification of those who had lost land by reducing the interest paid to holders of the national debt, most of whom were middle class. Dissatisfaction and unrest intensified among liberal elements of the population.

Some young men, like Julien Sorel, the antihero of Stendhal's novel *The Red and the Black* (1831), maintained a romantic allegiance to Napoleon's memory. Former Napoleonic soldiers, particularly those officers pensioned off on half pay, looked back on the imperial era as their halcyon days. In 1820–1821, some had joined the Carbonari, a secret society named after

Honoré Daumier's caricature of the less-than-inspiring members of the Chamber of Deputies.

its Italian equivalent, and plotted to overthrow the Restoration. Some merchants and manufacturers believed that the Restoration monarchy paid insufficient attention to commerce and industry, listening only to rural nobles.

Amid an economic crisis that had begun with the failure of the harvest the previous year, elections in 1827 increased liberal strength in the Chamber of Deputies. In August 1829, Charles X threw caution to the wind, appointing as his premier the reactionary Prince Jules de Polignac (1780–1847), one of only two members of the Chamber of Deputies who had refused an oath of allegiance to the Charter granted by Louis XVIII.

The opposition to the government of Charles X received a boost from a new generation of romantic writers. In the preface to his controversial play *Hernani* (1830), the production of which caused a near riot outside the theater, Victor Hugo (1802–1885) clearly set liberalism and romanticism against the established order of the restored monarchy:

> Young people, have courage! However difficult they make our present, the future will be beautiful. Romanticism, so often badly defined, is . . . nothing less than *liberalism* in literature. . . . Literary liberty is the daughter of political liberty. That is the principle of this century, and it will prevail.

In 1828, liberals formed an association to refuse to pay taxes in protest of the government's policies and worked to ensure that all eligible to vote registered to do so. Moreover, Benjamin Constant (1767–1830), Swiss novelist, political essayist, and a member of the French Chamber of Deputies, demanded that the electoral franchise be extended. He espoused a philosophy of liberalism based on a separation of powers and "a government of laws and not men."

In response to Charles's bellicose speech opening the 1830 session of the Chamber, 221 deputies signed an address to the throne that attacked the government in no uncertain terms. When the king dissolved the Chamber, the liberal opposition won a majority in the new Chamber of Deputies. In the meantime, Charles had sent an army to conquer Algeria, whose ruler was a vassal of the sultan of Turkey. But not even news of the capture of Algiers on July 9, 1830, could end vociferous opposition. The king and his minister Polignac then settled on a move that they hoped would bring an end to the crisis. It brought revolution instead.

On July 26, 1830, Charles X promulgated the July Ordinances, shattering the principles of the Charter of 1814. He dissolved the newly elected Chamber of Deputies; disfranchised almost three-quarters of those currently eligible to vote, leaving virtually all political power in the hands of the wealthiest property holders; ordered new elections under the newly restricted franchise; and muzzled the press. Demonstrations on July 27 led to skirmishes with troops the following day. Parisians blocked the capital's narrow streets with barricades. Fired upon in the street and pelted by rocks and tiles thrown from rooftops, the king's soldiers became increasingly demoralized.

King Charles X of France.

On July 31, Charles X named Louis-Philippe, the duke of Orléans, to be Lieutenant-General of the Realm. The family of Orléans was the junior branch of the royal Bourbon family and Louis-Philippe had the reputation for being relatively liberal. He had fought in the revolutionary armies, and his father (known as Philippe Égalité) in the National Assembly had voted for the execution of Louis XVI. He had visited the United States, expanding his horizons by drinking Kentucky bourbon.

When Charles finally realized he could not save his dynasty, he abdicated in favor

Louis-Philippe receiving black-suited members of the Chamber of Deputies, who present him with the act by which they confer the crown on him.

of his grandson on August 2, 1830. The liberals offered the throne to Louis-Philippe (ruled 1830–1848). He became "king of the French" (the title, rather than "king of France," was intended to convey that the king's authority came from the people). The tricolor flag replaced the white flag of the Bourbons, and Louis-Philippe agreed to a revised version of the Charter of 1814.

Despite its revolutionary origins, the new regime won relatively quick acceptance from the other European powers. The Revolution of 1830 marked a victory for French liberals. Catholicism ceased to be the official religion of the state, although it remained the nominal religion of the vast majority of French men and women.

The new Orleanist regime almost doubled the number of voters, but France was still far from being a republic. Many of those enfranchised by the revised Charter were drawn from the middle class. While the continuing influence of France's nobles should not be underestimated, lawyers and men of other professions significantly increased middle-class representation in the legislature. The government helped generate economic growth and industrial development by improving roads and implementing other policies that benefited manufacturers and merchants. "I strongly support the cause of the new society that the Revolution has made," François Guizot, historian and prime minister (1787–1874, prime minister 1840–1848), wrote, with "the middle class as its fundamental element." His rallying cry to the supporters of the July Monarchy was "Enrich yourselves!"

In addition to being known as the "July Monarchy," after the month of its founding, the Orleanist reign also came to be known and lampooned as "the bourgeois monarchy." The portly Louis-Philippe himself contributed to this image. He rose early and went to bed quite late, reading all diplomatic dispatches and working closely with his ministers. "There's no distance between Philippe and me," went one popular though extremely exaggerated refrain, "he's king-citizen, and I am citizen-king." The first official portrait of the monarch includes not only a throne of modest proportions but a number of dark-suited businessmen being shown in to see the new king (see illustration). Eugène Delacroix's *Liberty Leading the People* (see illustration) presents the July Revolution in Paris in a heroic manner, heightening dramatic, even tragic scenes by portraying movement and intense colors intended to overwhelm the emotions of the viewer.

The Orleanists defiantly slammed the drawbridge shut behind them against those who demanded to bring more people into the narrow political arena. Benjamin Constant, vigorous opponent of the Bourbon monarchy, now called Louis-Philippe's constitutional monarchy "our last ark of safety" against revolution. The new monarchy could claim neither the principle of monarchical legitimacy asserted by the Legitimists (supporters of Charles X's Bourbon grandson) or that of popular sovereignty assumed by republicans, who demanded universal male suffrage. Legitimists launched several

Eugène Delacroix's *Liberty Leading the People* (1830). Note the female image of liberty and the presence of the top-hatted bourgeois and the heavily armed street urchin, neither of whom actually fought in the Revolution.

small insurrections in the west against the Orleanists. In Paris, crowds of workers, disappointed by the government's lack of attention to their demands, sacked the archbishop's palace the year after the July Revolution. Silk workers in Lyon rose up in 1831 and 1834. In the latter year, following an uprising by republicans in Paris, the Chamber of Deputies passed a law severely restricting the right to form associations, and the next year it passed another law fettering the press.

Louis-Philippe survived an assassination attempt in 1835; a plot by a secret organization of revolutionaries, the "Society of the Seasons," to overthrow him in 1839; and another attempt to kill him in 1840. Less serious—for the moment—seemed attempts in 1836 and 1840 by Louis Napoleon Bonaparte, Napoleon's nephew, to invade France and rally support. Put on trial, Louis Napoleon told the peers, "There is no quarrel between you and me." The majority of the peers had grown up during, and some had served, the Napoleonic Empire. In 1840, the government brought Napoleon's ashes from Saint Helena to be interred in Paris. Hundreds of thousands of people turned out to pay their tribute to the emperor. The cult of Napoleon, accentuated by the vogue for the literature of romanticism, served only to highlight the weaknesses of the July Monarchy.

MORE LIBERAL ASSAULTS ON THE OLD ORDER

The French Revolution of 1830 directly encouraged liberal and national movements in other countries. Metternich pessimistically called the July Revolution "the collapse of the dam in Europe," fearing that it would eventually lead to his nightmare, popular sovereignty. Liberal successes followed in Belgium and Switzerland. Moreover, the Belgian revolt of liberals was also a nationalist struggle (in which both French and Dutch speakers participated) against the union with the Dutch Netherlands. In Greece, King Otto was forced by a coup d'état undertaken in 1843 by military officers to grant a liberal constitution which included universal male suffrage to his adopted people.

Independence for Belgium

The Dutch Netherlands, largely Protestant, had achieved independence from Spain in the seventeenth century. Catholic Belgium had never been united or autonomous and was divided between Flemish speakers in the north and west and Walloons, French speakers, in its southern and eastern parts (see Map 15.2). Brussels, the largest city in Belgium, lies within Flemish Belgium, but much of its population increasingly spoke French.

What Belgians called "Dutch arithmetic" left Belgium with fewer seats in the Dutch Estates-General than its population should have warranted and far fewer positions in the bureaucracy. Catholics had to contribute to Protestant state schools and paid higher taxes. In the late 1820s, Belgian liberals allied with Catholics against the Protestant Dutch government. Following petition campaigns demanding that ministers be responsible to the Estates-General and that taxes be reduced, Dutch King William I (1772–1843) granted only more press freedom.

Following the arrival of news from France of the July Revolution, the Brussels opera presented a production about an insurrection in Naples in 1648 against Spanish rule. The audience left the theater to demonstrate against a government newspaper and other symbols of Dutch authority. Workers, suffering unemployment and high prices, put up barricades, and were soon joined by units of bourgeois militia from outside Brussels.

MAP 15.2 THE BIRTH OF BELGIUM, 1831–1839   The boundaries of the Dutch Republic and Belgium, including within Belgium the areas that were Protestant and Catholic, as well as Flemish and Walloon areas. The Grand Duchy of Luxembourg was created in 1831 and united with the Netherlands in the person of the grand duke, King William I of the Netherlands.

Revolution in Brussels, 1830s.

The Dutch army could have easily overwhelmed the hastily organized force of several hundred defending Brussels. But having been reassured by nobles that the elite of Brussels still supported the royal cause and fearing that a full-fledged assault would generate more opposition, a halfhearted attack floundered when inexperienced Dutch troops panicked as the ranks of the defenders swelled. After three more days of fighting, the Dutch troops withdrew to the north. The Dutch bombardment of Flemish Antwerp sealed the Dutch defeat, for it led the Flemish of northern Belgium to support the rebels.

In early October, a provisional government declared Belgium an independent state. A Belgian Congress offered the throne to one of Louis-Philippe's sons, but he was forced to decline because Britain would not tolerate such French influence in Belgium. The Congress then offered the throne to a German prince, Leopold of Saxe-Coburg (who was a British subject and the widower of Princess Charlotte of England). Leopold was crowned King Leopold I (ruled 1831–1865) in July 1831. The European powers had guaranteed Belgium's independence, and when the Dutch invaded Belgium in August 1831, taking Antwerp, French military intervention returned that city to the new nation. Belgium became a constitutional monarchy with a parliament of two houses, elected by 50,000 voters (only one of every thirty males).

Liberal Successes in Switzerland

Another liberal success came in Switzerland, which the Congress of Vienna had reestablished as a federation of semi-autonomous cantons, dominated by Zurich, Bern, and Lucerne. Because of Switzerland's long tradition of decentralized government, the allies had been willing to tolerate a constitution that allowed relatively extensive political freedoms. Fearful that some cantons might become havens of liberalism, the Congress powers forced the Swiss cantons in 1823 to restrict freedom of the press and curtail the activities of foreign political exiles.

The 1830 revolution in France inspired the quest for constitutional guarantees of freedom, more efficient government, and limits on the political influence of the Protestant and Catholic clergy. In December 1830 the federal Diet of Switzerland declared its willingness to accept constitutional changes, initiating a period of "regeneration." The constitutions of ten cantons were liberalized, guaranteeing freedom of expression and giving all adult men the right to vote, a victory unique at that time.

But Metternich was not far away. Austria pressured the German-speaking Swiss cantons to oppose secularization. During the winter of 1844–1845, when the canton of Lucerne announced that the Jesuit order would again be welcome within its borders, liberals rebelled. Seven Catholic cantons withdrew from the Swiss Confederation, forming a separate league (*Sonderbund*). In 1847, the other cantons declared war and, in what amounted to little more than a skirmish, defeated the Catholic cantons within a month. In 1848, Switzerland adopted a new liberal constitution, becoming a federal state with universal male suffrage.

NATIONALIST DREAMS

Nationalism also gradually emerged as a force for change in Europe. It was closely tied to liberalism in that exponents of both ideologies demanded far-reaching political change that threatened the state system of Central Europe (see Map 15.3). In 1830–1831, Polish nationalists rose up against Russian domination but were crushed. During the 1830s and 1840s, more people living in the German and Italian states began to favor the political unification of their respective peoples. Many German businessmen believed that the creation of a "Germany" would eliminate some trade barriers. Some of them began to acquire positions of political influence in the Rhineland, Prussia's rapidly industrializing western territory.

Intellectuals representing other ethnic groups demanded that national boundaries correspond to linguistic frontiers; during the 1830s, the first scholarly books written in Czech and in Romanian were published. Polish and Serb nationalism, too, had their respective exponents. And, in Ireland, where the upper class was almost entirely English, Daniel O'Connell (1775–1847), a barrister, stimulated national awareness among Irish peasants.

The Revolt in Poland

The Congress of Vienna had left most of what had been Poland as a kingdom ("Congress Poland") with its own army, but with the Russian tsar as king of Poland. Tsar Alexander I granted the Poles the liberal Constitutional Charter of 1818, which provided for a parliament of two houses—a Senate of appointed members drawn from noble families and Catholic bishops, and a lower house (the Sejm) elected by people of means. Neither assembly, however, possessed much autonomy. In 1820, Alexander forbade the Sejm from meeting for five years as punishment for opposing Russian policies, which included imposing disadvantageous customs barriers on grain.

Many Poles hoped that France, in the wake of the July Revolution, would send forces to help them expel the Russians. However, the issue of Polish independence interested only French republicans, not the liberal monarchists who had brought Louis-Philippe to power.

Polish military cadets rose up in Warsaw in November 1830, capturing the arsenal. Russian troops withdrew from the Polish capital in the hope that its municipal government could restore order. In January 1831, a large crowd surrounded the Sejm, which declared that the Russian tsar (Nicholas I) was no longer king of Poland. A provisional national government formed. The Sejm, however, refused to attempt to mobilize peasants

Polish insurgents who rose up against the Russians in 1830–1831.

MAP 15.3 LIBERAL REVOLTS Liberal or nationalist uprisings in Congress Europe. Arrows indicate intervention by conservative Congress powers to suppress revolts.

in support of the insurrection, fearing that they might demand land reform and attack their lords instead of the Russians. Despite a Polish army that reached 30,000 in size, at the end of August 1832, the tsar's troops surrounded Warsaw. In the Polish capital, tensions between moderates and radicals erupted into violence, making its defense even more difficult. The rebels awaited assistance in vain from France and Britain, but liberals in those countries were not able to convince their governments to intervene. Warsaw fell to Russian troops in the autumn. About 10,000 Poles fled Russian oppression, including artists and musicians who helped infuse Polish nationalism with romanticism, and who (unlike subsequent refugees late in the nineteenth-century) were welcomed in the capitals of Western Europe, where they enriched cultural life, while dreaming of the day that Poland would be free. The composer Frédéric Chopin (1810–1849) had moved to Paris in 1831, hoping to make his fortune. Although he was not really a political refugee, ardent nationalism infused his music, and he drew upon Polish folk themes and dances in his polonaises, which inspired Polish nationalists.

The privileges that had been accorded "Congress Poland" disappeared in a wave of repression overseen by Nicholas I. The tsar abolished the special constitution that Poland had enjoyed within the Russian Empire, as well as the Sejm and the Polish army. Encouraged by the tsar's repressive measures against the Poles, Prussia and Austria withdrew what concessions they had earlier given to the Poles in the territories they had absorbed in the 1790s.

Uprisings in Italy and Spain

Unlike the revolutions in France and Belgium and the ill-fated Polish insurrection, popular stirrings in the Italian states, beginning with movements in Bologna and the Duchy of Modena, started as protests against inefficient and corrupt rule. Several of these uprisings had a comic-opera quality to them, such as when rebels in Parma literally locked Duchess Marie-Louise out of the city by shutting the gates until an Austrian army arrived in March 1831 to let her back in. Several cities in central Italy that proclaimed their independence from the Papal States tried to create the "United Provinces of Italy."

Like the Poles, insurgents against Austrian rule in several towns within the Papal States unrealistically counted on help from French armies, some still believing that France had a mission to free the oppressed peoples of Europe. With Austrian troops approaching from the north, an army of volunteers marched toward Rome, defeating the pope's army, which had been weakened by desertion. But by then the Austrians had taken Modena, Parma, and Ferrara. Three weeks after its creation, the United Provinces surrendered to the Papal States. A papal army mopped up resistance, sacking several towns so viciously that Austrian troops had to return to save the local populations. The Italian insurrections, compromised by tensions between moderates and radicals, collapsed without really winning popular support.

Giuseppe Mazzini (1805–1872), a lawyer by training and an energetic revolutionary by temperament, emerged as a guiding spirit in the quest for Italian unification under a republic. Influenced by the liberal romanticism of Wordsworth and Byron, Mazzini asserted the need to bring peace to Europe by liberating all peoples, imputing to the idea of the "nation" an almost mystical religious quality. He was one of the first to suggest that the states of Europe might evolve into a loose federation of democratic states based on the implementation of the principle of nationality.

Mazzini believed that a defeat of Austria would serve as a first step toward creating a federation of European democratic republics. Rejecting the Carbonari's conspiratorial tradition, he was convinced that he could expand his nationalist organization, Young Italy, whose membership was limited to individuals under forty years of age. Jailed and then expelled from one country after another, he launched futile insurrections in 1834–1836 and again in 1844. In doing so, he legitimized Italian nationalism abroad, keeping it alive in European international relations.

As conspiracies and insurrections failed and brought repression in their wake, some Italian nationalists began to look to the liberal Kingdom of Piedmont-Sardinia, Italy's strongest state, to effect national unification. But for the moment, the Italian peninsula remained dominated by an outside power, as it had been since the early sixteenth century, and divided into small states that were proud of their independence. The dream of Italian unification remained, for the most part, limited to a small number of middle-class intellectuals.

However, the quest for Italian unification began to stir romantic artists and composers. The Italian composer Gioacchino Rossini (1792–1868) represented this change. He had been asked by Prince Metternich in 1822 to attend a meeting of the Congress powers in Verona, as assembled representatives of the Great Powers discussed how to crush national movements. But Rossini soon changed his tune and came to espouse Italian nationalism. His allegoric opera *William Tell,* performed in Paris in 1829, tells the story of a fourteenth-century Swiss patriot, who, refusing to pay homage to Austrian rule, is forced by an official to shoot with bow and arrow an apple off the top of his young son's head, and who eventually kills the Austrian official. "This art of music which is based solely on sentiment and ideals," Rossini wrote, "cannot escape the influence of the times we live in, and the sentiment and ideals of the present day are wholly concerned with steam, rapine, and barricades."

Liberals also failed in Spain. In 1830, Ferdinand VII, a widower, married Maria Christina, a liberal Neapolitan princess. Their daughter Isabella became the heir to the Spanish throne. But nobles and churchmen insisted that a woman could not rule Spain. After the king's death in

1833, civil war broke out between liberals, who placed their hopes in the little girl, and conservatives (the Carlists), who supported the cause of the late king's brother, Don Carlos. Maria Christina, ruling as regent, promulgated a constitution in 1834 modeled on the French Charter of 1814. As liberals quarreled among themselves over the kinds of constitutional changes they wanted, however, Maria Christina in 1840 turned to the army to maintain order. In 1843, General Ramón Narváez (1800–1868), a hot-tempered Andalusian squire who considered himself a liberal, seized power. He implemented a conservative constitution and made peace with the Catholic Church. Narváez soon abandoned his liberal pretensions, stifling the press. On his deathbed he boasted, "I have no enemies, I have shot them all." The struggle of liberals against a powerful general would not be the last in Spain.

German Nationalism in Central Europe

In most German states, conservatives had triumphed after Napoleon's defeat, and liberals seeking economic and political change faced an uphill battle. Constitutions implemented during the Napoleonic period had been gradually weakened or withdrawn. Electoral assemblies in general were selected by limited franchise and had almost no power. Prussian town councils were forbidden to discuss any political matter that did not directly affect their communities.

However, the wave of liberal and nationalist movements unleashed by the Revolutions of 1830 soon reached Central Europe. Revolts broke out against the rulers of several Rhineland states. Popular disturbances forced the rulers of Hanover and Hesse-Kassel to make political concessions. In Saxony, a liberal constitution was enacted following uprisings in Leipzig and Dresden, and liberals won a constitution in the northern German state of Brunswick.

The Polish revolt against Russia in 1831 fueled the imagination of a generation of German university students. The movement culminated in a huge meeting in 1832 of 30,000 people at the ruins of a château near the University of Heidelberg, where speakers saluted popular sovereignty. Police foiled an attempt by students to seize Frankfurt, the meeting place of the Federal Diet of the German Confederation. Metternich berated the rulers of the German states for their permissiveness. The Confederation's Diet responded by passing "Ten Articles," which brought the universities under surveillance, coordinated police repression of liberals in the German states, prohibited public meetings, and stipulated that any state threatened by revolution would be assisted by the others.

Yet, despite a lack of popular support, liberalism in the German states slowly gained momentum among professors, students, and lawyers during what later became known as the *Vormärz* ("Before March") period, that is, the period of ferment that preceded the revolution of March 1848. The

French Revolution of 1830 influenced these "Young Germans." They included the poet Heinrich Heine (1797–1856), who had rushed to Paris after the fall of the Bourbon dynasty. Heine's *French Conditions* sharply contrasted the mood of apparent intellectual freedom and optimism that radiated from Paris with that of the repression and gloomy resignation liberals faced in the German states.

However, German liberals, like German philosophes of the late Enlightenment, shied away from defying the existing structure of state authority. Instead they looked to individual states to undertake reforms in the common interest. Many German liberals considered the state itself, not the people or any representative institution, to be the source of national sovereignty.

The philosopher Georg Wilhelm Friedrich Hegel made explicit the close connection between the development of German nationalism and the reverence for a strong state that characterized some German liberal thought. The son of a bureaucrat in Württemberg, Hegel had first expressed attachment to the liberating possibilities of the French Revolution before recoiling against French expansionism and the Terror. Hegel increasingly considered the state to be the embodiment and potential of a nation. Hegel's state, like that of Edmund Burke before him, develops through history. For Hegel, nationalism was the equivalent of a secular religion that had the potential of shaping a new morality. However much Hegel believed that reason offered the path to truth, he, like Burke, turned against the natural law of the philosophes. Hegel's state is overwhelming, even frightening, subsuming individual rights to its power.

England had had a civil war in the seventeenth century and France its revolution in 1789; the German states had no revolutionary tradition. German liberals remained political outsiders, butting their heads against a particularly pervasive respect for ideological conformity. Alluding to the state, however, a German liberal in 1842 spoke of it in a way that would have seemed strange in Britain: "We all want [the state] to be great, mighty, powerful, and rational. We all have no other wish than to be absorbed into the state, and to devote our strength to it." German liberals were thus both intrigued and frightened by France's Revolution of 1830.

German liberalism became closely tied to the pursuit of German unification. German particularism—the tradition of many independent states, large and small—thus complicated the liberal movement in Central Europe. Liberals did not constitute a party, lacking a precisely defined program for reform. They wanted some sort of constitutional, representative government. But like British and French liberals, they believed that only men who owned property ought to vote because the independence of their vote would be assured.

Liberal economic theory attracted German merchants and manufacturers, who objected to the discouraging complexity of customs tariffs that created a series of costly hurdles along roads and rivers. As German manufacturing developed, particularly in the Rhineland, businessmen demanded an end to these unnatural impediments faced by neither British nor French rivals. They supported a proposed German Customs Union (Zollverein), which, following its creation in 1834, removed many of these tariff barriers from seventeen states. Yet some German states depended on high tariffs to protect local manufacturing. Thus, some merchants and manufacturers denounced any government interference in business, believing that the proposed tariff union would above all serve the interests of Prussia, the largest northern German state.

German liberals who espoused free trade made greater headway than those demanding political reform. To liberal nationalists, the Zollverein seemed to offer a basis for the eventual political unification of Germany, breathing life into the movement for political reform. But those who hoped that Prussia and the other German states would move toward constitutionalism were disappointed. Prussian King Frederick William IV (ruled 1840–1861) disappointed liberals when he refused to establish a Diet representing the entire country. When he finally did convoke a United Diet in 1847, it was not popularly elected and was to serve the king only in an advisory capacity.

CRISIS AND COMPROMISE IN GREAT BRITAIN

In Britain, the continued call for political reform, specifically the expansion of the electoral franchise to include more middle-class voters, would be the true test of the ability of the British elite to compromise in the interest of relative social harmony. Popular protests swept parts of England. At a gathering in London in 1816, speakers demanded a greatly expanded electoral franchise. Poor harvests in 1818 and 1819 led to grain riots, machine breaking, and other protests by poor people. On August 16, 1819, a mass meeting was held at St. Peter's Fields in the burgeoning northern industrial town of Manchester. A crowd of some 50,000 men and women gathered to demonstrate for the right to form political organizations and to assemble freely. Deputized local constables moved in to arrest the main speaker. Then soldiers fired, killing eleven and wounding hundreds of other protesters. The ugly incident entered history as "Peterloo," a shameful victory not over Napoleon at Waterloo but over Britain's defenseless laboring poor. Parliament passed Six Acts that, reviving the repressive legislation of the era of the French Revolution, banned demonstrations, suspended the writ of *habeas corpus,* and placed restrictions on the press.

The late 1820s were also bleak years for the English poor, with hunger following unemployment. In the north, artisans and skilled workers demanded higher wages. In Ireland, violent resistance broke out against the Church's efforts to collect the tithe. In 1830, a wave of food riots and machine breaking spread through southeastern England.

The Peterloo Massacre in Manchester, 1819.

But there would be no revolution in nineteenth-century Britain, despite the prevalence of social tensions in the world's most industrialized society. The landed elite, which dominated Parliament, supported by manufacturing interests, enacted reforms that defused social and political tensions by bowing to middle-class demands for change. The greatest of these were the Reform Act of 1832 and the repeal of the Corn Laws in 1846. The resolution of these crises contributed to the emergence of a liberal consensus in Victorian Britain that lasted throughout the century.

Religious and Electoral Reform

Many Tories, including men of great landed wealth, believed that electoral reform would be a dangerous precedent, perhaps opening up the floodgates of popular protest. But the fear of civil war in largely Catholic Ireland led some Tories to compromise, first making possible religious reform. Despite vociferous opposition from the Established Church, Parliament in 1828 repealed the Test and Corporation Acts, which had forced anyone holding public office to take communion in the Anglican Church.

Catholic emancipation had become a major political issue, at least partly because it was linked to the problem of Catholic Ireland, where a reform movement had begun and where protests against English domination and outright insurrection seemed endemic. Catholics could not vote or stand for election to Parliament, or serve in the army in Britain (although Irish Catholics were recruited in great numbers to serve overseas, particularly in India). In 1829, Parliament passed the Catholic Emancipation Act, which removed the legal restrictions that had kept Catholics from holding office or serving in Parliament.

In Britain, political liberalism continued to be closely linked to the movement led by some Whigs for electoral reform. Businessmen resented being underrepresented in the House of Commons. The electoral system remained a patchwork that reflected the interests of local elites and particular communities that had gradually developed in England since the fourteenth century. The industrial north sent few men to Parliament because electoral districts had not changed since before the Industrial Revolution. No one represented the industrial centers of Manchester and Birmingham in Parliament. Wealthy merchants in those cities were no longer pacified by assurances that they had indirect, "virtual representation" through members of Parliament who had their interests in mind, or that they could personally contact a peer, who might introduce a bill in the House of Lords. On the other hand, some sparsely populated rural districts still were represented in Parliament. Dunwich, the most notorious of these "rotten boroughs," had been covered over by the sea since the twelfth century. "Pocket boroughs" were electoral districts "in the pocket" of a wealthy landowner routinely returned to Parliament (see Chapter 11). In the first half of the century, only one member of the British House of Commons was of working-class origins, and he had become a prosperous manufacturer.

With news of France's Revolution of 1830, the British upper classes rallied together, fearful, as they used to say, that when France sneezed, the rest of Europe might catch a cold. However, amid shows of armed force by constables and troops, organized protest was limited to an enthusiastic rally in the Scottish city of Glasgow to celebrate the news of the French and Belgian revolutions. In England, crowds gathered to hear the popular radical William Cobbett (1763–1835) speak on behalf of the extension of the electoral franchise to all men.

The Reform Bill of 1832

The general election following George IV's death in 1830 reduced the conservative majority in Parliament. A broadly based campaign for electoral reform swept the country; some of the 5,000 petitions that were brought to Parliament attacked in patriotic language the selfishness of the landed elite. The new Whig prime minister, Earl Charles Grey (1764–1845), believed reform inevitable in a country in which only one of every fifteen adult males had the right to vote. But Grey knew that any reform bill that passed the House of Commons would never get through the House of Lords as then constituted. In 1831, the Lords rejected a bill sponsored by the government that would have eliminated many "rotten" and "pocket" boroughs. Public meetings protested this defeat, particularly in the unenfranchised cities of the industrial north and lowland Scotland.

When the House of Lords rejected a second reform bill in October 1831, demonstrators massed in London, and a riot in Bristol ended in twelve deaths.

By this time, more Tories had come around to Grey's view that only the passage of some sort of electoral reform bill could save Britain from a revolution. The Whigs proposed a third bill, which Commons passed in March 1832, and sent it on to the Lords. As the political crisis mounted, the duke of Wellington, commander of British troops at Waterloo, tried and failed to form a ministry. Grey, who again became prime minister, convinced the new king, William IV (ruled 1830–1837), to threaten to create enough new peers in order to get the reform bill through the House of Lords. Wellington agreed not to oppose its passage, and the bill was passed.

The Reform Act of 1832 was a turning point in the history of modern Britain. The peers, who did not want to see their ranks contaminated with "instant lords," wanted to avoid any possible alliance between frustrated businessmen and radicals supported by the workers. This had occurred in France in the last years of the Bourbon Restoration. The historian and statesman Thomas Macaulay warned the peers to keep in mind the fate of some French nobles during the Revolution: "From those magnificent hotels, those ancient castles, they were driven forth to exile and beggary . . . to cut wood in the back settlements of America, or to teach French in the schoolrooms of London." The landed magnates had listened and agreed to a liberal compromise that, by lowering the minimum franchise requirement, almost doubled the size of the electorate. The Reform Act thus greatly contributed to the development of more broadly based political parties.

Still, only about one of every five adult male citizens was able to vote. Britain was far from a democracy, despite fears among the wealthy that reform pointed in that direction. The British Parliament now more accurately reflected the country's economic and social evolution during the age of the Industrial Revolution. In the early 1840s, 15 percent of the members of the House of Commons were businessmen, and 35 percent had some other connection to commerce and industry, such as serving on the board of directors of enterprises. What was gained in France by revolution in 1830 was achieved in Britain through reform in 1832. A larger percentage of men could now vote in Britain than in France, Belgium, the Netherlands, or Spain.

The new electorate, as the Tories had feared, increased Whig strength. Commons passed two reforms in 1833 that would have been inconceivable without the Reform Act. Anti-slavery societies launched a nationwide campaign against slavery in the British Dominions (Britain had withdrawn from the slave trade in 1808, but it still existed in British parts of Africa, Asia, the Caribbean, and in the United States). During the 1820s and 1830s, ladies' associations distributed campaign literature and organized a boycott of sugar produced by slaves in the West Indies. In 1833, about 100,000 women signed petitions against slavery, which was abolished in the British Empire that year. The second reform measure passed that same year prohibited all work by children under nine years of age, limited the workday of children from nine through twelve years to eight hours a day (and a maximum of forty-eight hours per week), and that for "young persons," ages thirteen to eighteen, to twelve hours a day (up to a maximum of sixty-nine hours per week). In 1834, Parliament passed the controversial Poor Law, by which able-bodied individuals would no longer receive assistance from parishes, but would be incarcerated in "well-regulated" workhouses. And finally the Municipal Corporations Act of 1835 eliminated the old, often corrupt borough governments, creating elected municipal corporations responsible for administration. These reforms allowed many more Whigs, including Dissenters, to assume positions of responsibility in local government, another blow to the domination of public life by the old aristocratic oligarchy and the Established Church.

Chartism and the Repeal of the Corn Laws

The Chartist movement reflected the strength of reformism in Britain. Whereas some French and German workers oiled their guns, their English counterparts took out their quill pens. In 1836, William Lovett (1800–1877), a cabinetmaker, founded the London Workingmen's Association for Benefiting Politically, Socially, and Morally the Useful Classes. Two years later, Lovett and Francis Place, a London tailor, prepared a charter that would be signed by millions of people and then delivered to Parliament. The "Great Charter" called for the democratization of political life, including universal male suffrage, annual elections, equal electoral districts, the secret ballot, and salaries for members of Parliament, so that ordinary people could serve if elected. The movement for political reform that had culminated in the Reform Act of 1832 also gave impetus to the New Poor Law, the expansion of the system of police, the refusal of government to sponsor legislation to improve conditions in factories, and action against trade unions, all contributing to a sense of urgency and of moral righteousness to the cause. Chartists objected to the monopoly of wealth and political influence in Britain by a small percentage of the population, wealthy landowners, many of them aristocrats, and the captains of industry. Such a radical criticism of political life in Britain had been voiced in the 1770s. But it also found resonance among many people who were not workers because it drew a distinction between people who had the right to vote and those who did not. The Chartist movement remained overwhelmingly peaceful, its members committed to acting as a "moral force" in British life. Chartism was in some ways a movement that looked back into a past its members imagined as being more religious and moral than the period in which they lived. In 1839, a small "physical force" group emerged within the Chartist movement in northern England, particularly among workers whose livelihoods had been eroded by mechanization. They threatened strikes and even insurrection if Parliament did not yield. But the group remained small and relatively unimportant in the movement itself, which remained for the most part committed to peaceful change.

During the next few years, coinciding with economic hard times, Chartism spread throughout much of industrial Britain. Becoming the largest working-class national political movement in the century, it mobilized not only skilled and organized craftsmen but also unskilled handloom weavers. (However, Chartist leaders rejected feminist pleas that their movement include demands for the rights of women.) In May 1839, Parliament summarily rejected a Chartist petition with almost 1.3 million signatures. Undaunted, the Chartists tried again in 1842 when the National Chartist Association carried a giant scroll with 3.3 million signatures to Westminster. Once again, Parliament rejected the Great Charter. Thereafter, Chartism declined as a movement, despite a revival in 1848.

Passed by a conservative-dominated Parliament in 1815 and 1828, the Corn Laws had imposed a sliding tariff on imported wheat (then known as "corn"). When the price of wheat produced in Britain fell below a certain level, import duties would keep out cheaper foreign grain. Foreign grain could be imported virtually free of import taxes when the price of wheat stood at or above a certain level. The laws protected landowners, but were

The Irish potato famine of 1846.

Photograph of the final Chartist demonstration at Kensington Common, April 10, 1848.

detrimental to the interests of businessmen who imported or sold imported grain, and, above all, to consumers, who were forced to pay higher prices for bread. Failed harvests of 1839–1841 came when an expanding population had created an increased demand for food, even as parishes were cutting back on their allocations to the poor. The "Great Hunger" in Ireland caused by the potato famine that began in 1845 brought mass starvation and sent waves of impoverished Irish emigrants to the United States.

The issue of the repeal of the Corn Laws pitted proponents of laissez-faire economic policies against wealthy property owners, Whigs against Tories. British manufacturers and spokesmen for the poor denounced the entrenched, landed, "bread-taxing" and "blood-sucking" oligarchy. Proponents of repeal cited biblical texts denouncing those enriched by the hunger of the poor. In 1839, the Anti–Corn Law League brought together businessmen, Whig politicians, and political radicals. With strong support among working people, John Bright (1811–1889) argued that the repeal of the Corn Laws would be a major step toward political democracy. The son of a Quaker cotton mill owner, he thundered against aristocratic privilege and its close ties to the Established Church. He warned the aristocracy: "Until now, this country has been ruled by the class of great proprietors of the soil. Everyone must have foreseen that, as trade and manufactures extended, the balance of power would, at some time or other, be thrown into another scale. Well, that time has come."

As with the 1832 Reform Act, it took a change of heart by a Conservative government to get a repeal bill passed. Prime Minister Robert Peel (1788–1850), of whom someone once said that his smile resembled the gleam of silverplate on a coffin, was himself the conservative son of a cotton manufacturer. Believing in free trade, he had pushed through reductions in and even the elimination of a number of tariffs, including those on imported raw cotton for the textile industry. The Irish potato famine helped push him to undertake the dismantling of the Corn Laws. Repeal would be an act of political courage, as he was bound to fall from power, but Peel believed only such a move could forestall a popular insurrection. In June 1846, Parliament repealed the Corn Laws, reducing duties on wheat and other imported agricultural products. Peel fell from office the same day, a victim, his supporters insisted, of angering many conservatives by doing the right thing. The repeal of the Corn Laws again demonstrated the ability of the British government and political elite to compromise to avoid greater crises.

CONCLUSION

Between 1820 and 1850, liberals and nationalists challenged the conservative post-Napoleonic settlement. In France and Belgium, it took revolutions to bring change: in the former, a liberal monarchy; in the latter, independence. In Britain, middle-class men were gradually and peacefully incorporated into the political arena. Political and economic liberalism triumphed within Britain's reformist tradition. Britain remained a constitutional monarchy with representative government, however narrowly based. British workers themselves remained committed to peaceful protest, while assuming a langue of political reform.

　In the German states and in the northern Italian states, liberals gained ground. In Switzerland, more liberal constitutions and educational reforms were implemented. Nationalists, too, gained strength in Europe. Proponents of German and Italian national unification became more vocal. Much of the support for the nationalist groups espousing national unification in the German and Italian states, as well as the massive pressure for an expansion of the electoral franchise in France and Great Britain, came from the burgeoning middle class. Cultural and nationalist movements began to develop among Czechs, Serbs, and other peoples within the Habsburg domains. However, the Prussian and Austrian monarchies, to say nothing of the Russian tsar, whose troops had crushed the Polish insurrection in 1831, stood as formidable obstacles to constitutional change and national movements. Nonetheless, the Concert of Europe no longer existed. Political momentum was with those seeking to break down the bastions of traditional Europe.

　Urban rebellions and full-scale political revolutions suggested that more upheavals and even social revolution might follow. To conservatives, such movements were seen as the unwanted and unsettling consequences of rapid change. Léon Faucher, French politician and keen observer of economic change, offered a prophetic warning in 1846. Claiming that the middle class now occupied the same position as the nobles had in the previous century, Faucher argued that the middle class could hold its place only by "raising little by little the lower classes." He predicted that if his class failed to serve as "an instrument of progress . . . it will have to contend with another 1789."

CHAPTER 16

THE REVOLUTIONS
OF 1848

The year 1848 was the year of barricades in Europe, the "springtime of the peoples." Few took note when an uprising occurred in January 1848 in Palermo, Sicily, against King Ferdinand II of Naples. But when a revolution drove Louis-Philippe from the throne of France in February, nationalists exiled in London, Brussels, Paris, and Zurich excitedly returned to their native lands, convinced that their time had come. Everything seemed possible.

The establishment of a republic in France, reminding people of the vulnerability of monarchical regimes to revolution, became the catalyst for revolutionary movements in Central Europe. In the face of clumsy attempts by governments to repress opposition by force, barricades and street insurgency forced the rulers of Prussia, Austria, and several other German and Italian states to accept more liberal constitutions when confronted by determined crowds. The existence of the Habsburg monarchy was threatened by insurrections against its rule. People in Lombardy and Venetia in northern Italy, and Czechs, Poles, and South Slavs put forth demands for autonomy. In Austria, liberals demanded political reforms, while some German speakers sought inclusion in a unified Germany. Magyar nobles forcefully asserted demands for Hungarian autonomy. Turkish and Russian troops put down an uprising by Romanian nationalists in Bucharest. Of the European powers, only Britain (the most economically and politically advanced) and Russia (the most economically backward) did not experience revolutions. Yet in Britain, the Chartist petition campaign for the extension of political rights revived in 1848 with news from the continent, and the government feared an Irish uprising, searching ships arriving from the United States for weapons. In several countries, monarchs capitulated to liberal demands. In Sweden, the king appointed a new, more popular government. Danish nationalists pressured their king to grant a liberal constitution. The Netherlands received a new

670

constitution in October 1848, and popular pressure forced the expansion of the Belgian electoral franchise.

A common process was present in the revolutions in France, the German states, and in the Habsburg lands: initial mobilizations of liberals, republicans, and nationalists coalesced into movements against existing regimes (see Map 16.1). In each revolution, the hard times of the 1840s, marked by harvest and business failures, had increased popular dissatisfaction with conservative or moderate regimes. Essentially middle-class movements drew on the support of artisans and craftsmen, members of trade organizations who believed that political change would lead to social reforms that would benefit their trades. Following initial victory, ranging from the overthrow of the Orleanist monarchy in France to political concessions in Austria and Prussia, however, the ensuing struggle to implement change led to a split between moderates and radicals. Then followed the gradual but convincing victory of counter-revolution, in which the armies of the reactionary Tsar Nicholas I of Russia would play an important role.

REVOLUTIONARY MOBILIZATION

The late 1840s brought food shortages in Europe, including the tragic Irish potato famine. Unemployment plagued manufacturing towns. Yet, however widespread, economic discontent was not enough in itself to bring about the wave of revolutions that occurred in 1848 (if this was the case, the Irish would have risen up). Rather, hard times provided an impetus to political opponents of existing regimes, which themselves were preoccupied with food riots and other popular protest.

Critics and political opponents included reformers asking for moderate political changes, such as a lessening of restrictions on the press, or, in states with elected assemblies, an expansion in the electoral franchise to allow more people to vote. German nationalists stood ready to push for the unification of the German states. Republicans and socialists demanded more radical reforms, including universal male suffrage and social reforms to ameliorate the condition of the laboring poor. Radical reformers also included nationalists within the Austrian Habsburg lands, principally Czechs and Hungarians, who wanted their own independent states. When a spark ignited the fires of protest, moderates and radicals joined forces in revolution. The sudden overthrow of the July Monarchy provided that spark.

The February Revolution in France

In France, the liberal Orleanist monarchy, which had been established by the Revolution of 1830, seemed to have more enemies than friends. It was

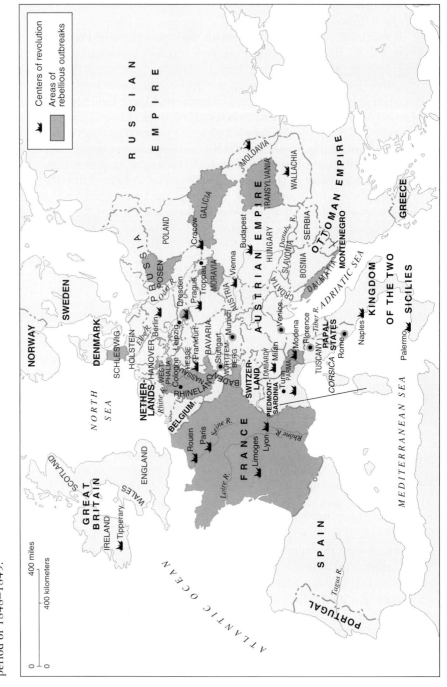

MAP 16.1   MAJOR REVOLUTIONS, 1848–1849   The map shows areas of rebellion and centers of revolution during the turbulent period of 1848–1849.

The February Revolution of 1848 in Paris.

caught between nobles insisting that the monarchy lacked dynastic legitimacy and republicans demanding a regime based on popular sovereignty. Republicans had begun to campaign for electoral reform in 1840–1841, as the country reeled from a disastrous harvest. France had also suffered international humiliation in 1840 after King Louis-Philippe seemed to back the Egyptian pasha, Mehmet Ali, who was rebelling against the Turkish ruler. When the other European powers, particularly Britain, opposed the pasha, fearing that his autonomy and recent conquests threatened the stability of the Ottoman Empire, France had to back down to avoid war.

Republicans mounted another campaign for electoral reform, organizing banquets to rally public opinion in the midst of another cyclical economic crisis that began with the disastrous harvest of 1846. Workers demanded the right to vote and state assistance for their trades.

The electoral reform campaign was to culminate in a giant reform banquet on February 22, 1848, in Paris. François Guizot, King Louis-Philippe's premier, banned the event. Demonstrators marched through the streets of central Paris, shouting for Guizot's resignation. The next day, large crowds assembled in the pouring rain. The Paris National Guard, drawn from the middle class, refused to disperse the demonstrators by force. Louis-Philippe dismissed Guizot. But that evening, amid continuing boisterous protests, troops panicked and fired on a crowd, killing forty people. The crowds carried the bodies through the streets, and workers (primarily craftsmen) began to construct barricades. After insurgents captured government buildings, King Louis-Philippe abdicated, hoping that the Chamber of Deputies would crown his young grandson, the count of Paris. It was too late. The victorious crowd proclaimed the Second French Republic at the town hall.

The Chamber of Deputies selected a provisional government, headed by nine well-known republicans. A crowd at the town hall pressed for the addition of two well-known socialists supported by the radicals: Louis Blanc and a worker, Alexander Martin, known as Albert. The provisional government immediately proclaimed universal male suffrage and abolished slavery in the French colonies.

The revolution spread to the provinces. Enthusiastic crowds planted "liberty trees," intended to commemorate a new era, a ritual borrowed from the French Revolution. Republicans were not the only political group seeking to fill the power vacuum left by the Orleanist regime. "Legitimists" wanted a Bourbon Restoration. Nor could the Orleanists be counted out, for Louis-Philippe had several able sons in exile. Both shades of monarchists could count on the support of local notables (nobles or wealthy bourgeois). Furthermore, Napoleon Bonaparte's nephew, Louis Napoleon (1808–1873), had a coterie of supporters who honored his uncle's memory. At a time when the prominent poet Alphonse de Lamartine (1790–1869) complained that "France is bored," the legend of Napoleon remained strong among many former soldiers, peasants, and students. Popular histories of the French Revolution and the empire extolled French nationalism.

Republicans were themselves divided between staunch republicans, who had opposed the Orleanist regime all along, and moderates, who accepted the republic only after its proclamation. Socialists hoped that the republic would be but the first step toward a "democratic and social republic." Louis Blanc and other socialists were committed to the "right to work," as they put it, believing that the government should assume responsibility for providing employment in times of economic crisis, as well as encouraging or even subsidizing workers' associations.

Because of France's revolutionary tradition, the fledgling republic had to reassure the other powers of Europe that the French would not try to export their revolution, as had occurred in the 1790s. The other powers feared that the new regime might publicly support Polish independence or Italian or German nationalism, spurred on by the presence in Paris of political exiles advocating these causes. Some French nationalists called for the annexation of Savoy and Nice (parts of the kingdom of Piedmont-Sardinia), which France had claimed off and on for centuries. Volunteers formed a ragtag army with this acquisition of territory in mind. But Alphonse de Lamartine, the new republic's minister of foreign affairs, assured the European powers that the French had only peaceful intentions.

With elections for a constitutional assembly approaching, political interest was widespread among people previously excluded from political life. In Paris, more than 200 political clubs, mostly republican and republican-socialist, began to meet and almost that many newspapers began publication, joined by others in the provinces. When George Sand (the pen name of Amandine Dudevant; 1804–1876), a writer and activist for women's rights, was locked out of her apartment, she discovered that all three of the neighborhood locksmiths were at club meetings. Representatives from the clubs went into the provinces with the goal of wooing the overwhelmingly rural electorate away from the influence of local notables who favored a monarchy.

The economic crisis immediately cast a shadow over the new regime and widened the gap between moderate republicans and socialists. Unable to secure credit, many businesses closed. Government bonds plunged in value, and the Paris Stock Exchange temporarily shut down. Artisans were left without clients, laborers without work. More than half of the workforce in the capital was unemployed. Younger and more marginal workers were enrolled in an auxiliary paramilitary police force, the Mobile Guard, organized by the provisional government to help maintain order. Short of funds, the provisional government raised direct taxes on an emergency basis by 45 percent.

With more provincial workers arriving in Paris every day looking for assistance, the provisional government opened "National Workshops," paying unemployed workers to repair roads and level hills. Many well-off Parisians began to grumble about the new government having to support unemployed workers. The government finally agreed to restrict the workday to a maximum of ten hours in Paris and twelve hours in the provinces.

A Paris women's club in 1848.

At the request of the socialists, the government also established the "Luxembourg Commission" to study working conditions.

By undermining existing political structures, the 1848 revolution called into question all social institutions, including the existing gender hierarchy. In Paris, women formed a number of clubs. *The Women's Voice* and several other newspapers begun by women called for reforms, including equality of women before the law, the right to divorce, and better working conditions. Petitioners demanded that the republic extend the electoral franchise to women. This groundswell of demands for change frightened the upper classes.

April elections, in which an astounding 84 percent of the eligible voters (adult males) cast ballots, brought a conservative majority, including many monarchists, to the National Assembly, which would draw up a new constitution. Radical republicans and socialists won only about 100 of 900 seats. The republicans were hurt in the countryside by the provisional government's tax hike. Many rural people resented the demands of urban workers, including low bread prices and the maintenance of National Workshops. In two industrial cities, Limoges and Rouen, workers, angered by the conservative victory, seized power, at least until troops arrived several days later. The euphoria of February gave way to the anxiety of the spring.

Revolution in the German States

Unlike the Revolution of 1789, that of 1848 spread rapidly from France into Central Europe. The composer Richard Wagner (1813–1883), a fervent German nationalist, had predicted in 1846: "The new Germany is ready, like a bronze statue that requires only a single blow from a hammer in order to emerge from its mold." Wagner, however, overestimated popular support for German nationalism. While liberals bided their time, young German radicals, few in number, became more restive. During the "hungry forties," in which perhaps 50,000 people died of disease in Prussian Silesia alone, riots against grain merchants and tax collectors occurred in many German states. Craftsmen formed trade associations and mutual aid societies. Although these organizations offered only minimal assistance during times of unemployment and strikes, they provided an apprenticeship in political ideology.

The differences in tactics between German liberals and radicals were clear and significant. Both groups, sometimes sharing newspaper offices, political clubs, and even associations of gymnasts and rifle enthusiasts, demanded an end to all remaining feudal obligations owed by peasants to nobles, the end of political repression, the granting of a constitution, freedom of assembly and the press, and expansion of the electoral franchise. Liberals, however, rejected universal male suffrage. Radicals, some of whom were socialists, believed that only revolution could move the German states along the path to a new, more liberal political order, and perhaps to unification.

The news in late February 1848 of revolution in France convinced rulers of the German states to make concessions to liberals. In Bavaria, word of the February Revolution arrived at a time when students had begun protesting the rule of Ludwig I (ruled 1825–1848). As Bavarian demonstrators built barricades and demanded a republic, Ludwig granted freedom of the press and other liberties. When this failed to placate his opponents, the king abdicated in favor of his son. The sovereigns of several smaller states, including Hanover, Württemberg, Saxony, and Baden, also named prominent liberals to ministerial positions. These were the "March governments," formed not out of conviction but rather from fear of revolutionary contagion.

Everyone waited to see what would happen in Prussia and Austria, the two largest and most powerful German states. In the Prussian capital of Berlin, demonstrators agitated for liberal political reforms and in favor of German nationalism. Prussian King Frederick William IV responded by convoking the United Diet, or Parliament. On March 18, 1848, he replaced his conservative cabinet with a more liberal one. Addressing a crowd from the balcony of his palace, he promised to end press censorship and grant a constitution. He further stated that the Prussian monarchy would take the lead in pushing for a joint constitution for the German states.

But as troops moved in to disperse the throngs, someone on one side or the other fired shots. Students and workers put up barricades. The next day the army attacked insurgents, killing about 250 people. As in Paris, the shooting of civilians by troops drove the situation out of control. Women were among the casualties. The king sent the troops out of the capital and appealed for calm. Intimidated by the disturbances, he met with representatives of the crowd, authorized the formation of a civic guard, and ordered the release of imprisoned liberals. He paid homage to those killed in the "March Days" and announced that "Prussia is henceforth merged with Germany."

Most of the Berlin insurgents had been journeymen artisans, as in the February Revolution in Paris. Although some of them were vaguely nationalist and wanted Prussia to lead the way toward the unification of Germany, most had economic goals. During the "hungry forties," mechanized production had undercut tailors, whose handmade clothes could not compete with mass-produced wear. Cabinetmakers and shoemakers had lost the security afforded by guilds. Now these artisans demanded state protection. Workers in other German states, too, mounted protests, principally in the more industrialized Rhineland. Transport workers who had been put out of work attacked railroads and steamships on the Rhine River, forcing temporary government concessions.

As in Paris, clubs and workers' associations began meeting in several German cities in March. A Club of Democratic Women and a congress of

Germans putting up barricades in the streets of Altenburg during the Revolution of 1848.

workers both demanded equal rights for women. Workers formed the first All-German Society of Labor. The German political theorist and revolutionary Karl Marx hurried back to the Rhineland from Belgium, convinced that revolution was at hand.

Disturbances broke out in the German countryside. In the Black Forest, peasants attacked noble manors. In early March, the rural poor increasingly defied laws forbidding them to use royal and noble forests, and now hunted game and pastured their flocks as they pleased. Some peasants seized and destroyed old documents that had recorded feudal obligations and forced lords to sign formal renunciations of old privileges. Outbreaks of violence occurred even in Brandenburg, where the iron will of the Prussian nobles, the Junkers, had rarely been tested. Several wary German princes formally relinquished long-held rights. Armies, militias, and police hesitated to enforce the laws or obligations that affected the peasantry for fear of sparking a bloody uprising like that in Polish Galicia in 1846. The revolution in the German states had not only quickly shaken Berlin and other capital cities but had reached the countryside as well.

Revolution in Central Europe

There were relatively few liberals to trouble the sleep of the feeble-minded Habsburg ruler, Ferdinand I (ruled 1835–1848), who could barely sign his name to the reactionary decrees put before him. Liberals, most of whom were Austrians seeking political change or Czechs desiring more rights for their people, opposed Habsburg autocracy, not Habsburg rule itself. They wanted constitutional reform, the complete emancipation of the peasantry, greater efficiency in the administration of Habsburg lands, and, like Western liberals, freedom of the press and expansion of the electoral franchise.

Although Hungary, over which Ferdinand ruled as king, had an even smaller middle class than Austria, it did have several prominent Hungarian nobles who espoused liberalism and supported constitutional reform. Their chief goal, however, was the creation of an independent Hungary. Lajos Kossuth (1802–1894), a lawyer from a lesser noble family, emerged as the leader of Hungarian liberals who had been influenced by British and American constitutional liberalism. Whereas some Magyar leaders believed that Hungary could survive as a nation only within the Austrian monarchy, Kossuth saw Hungary's junior partnership with Austria as an obstacle to liberal reform and to Magyar nationalism. Most nobles were unwilling, however, to support reforms that would inevitably undercut their special privileges. Elsewhere in the Austrian monarchy, small nationalist groups, such as the Polish Democratic Society, Young Italy, and the Italian Carbonari, also demanded national independence from Habsburg rule.

News from Paris encouraged liberals and radicals in the imperial Habsburg capital of Vienna. On March 13, 1848, crowds composed largely of students and artisans demanded reform. Troops opened fire, killing several demonstrators, a familiar scenario. Klemens von Metternich, the seventy-five-year-old Austrian premier, was not optimistic: "I am not a prophet and I do not know what will happen, but I am an old physician and can distinguish between temporary and fatal diseases. We now face one of the latter. We'll hold on as long as we can, but I have doubts about the outcome." The Imperial Council advised Ferdinand to sacrifice Metternich. The guiding light and symbol of the post-revolutionary restoration left Vienna in a rented carriage, beginning his voyage to the safety of London amid the spectacle of joyous crowds parading through the streets in triumph. The crown capitulated to protesters' demands and authorized the formation of a National Guard, with a separate battalion (the Academic Legion) for Vienna's students. Workshops, similar to those in Paris, provided many workers with temporary employment.

The emperor then announced several important political concessions, including freedom of the press and the expansion in the narrow electorate for the Diet. Ferdinand hurriedly granted constitutions to Austria, Moravia, and Galicia, adding lower houses to the Diets that were to be elected indirectly by men wealthy enough to pay taxes. When demonstrators protested these requirements, the crown reversed itself, creating a single house of parliament to be elected by universal male suffrage in each province. In the elected Assembly, the monarchy's ethnic minorities would outnumber German speakers.

Ferdinand then attempted to renege on his promises and ordered the universities closed and abolished the Academic Legion within the National Guard. But again barricades went up in Vienna, and again Ferdinand was forced to relent. Fearing rural rebellions upon which liberals and nationalists might capitalize, the emperor in September decreed the abolition—effective the following year—of all remaining seigneurial obligations. He also abolished the onerous *robot*, the yearly obligation of labor service—sometimes a hundred days working in the fields or on roads—that peasants owed lords. The crown would compensate the lords for their losses. Many landowners had already converted the labor obligation into peasant cash payments.

Meanwhile, the Hungarian nobles proceeded as if the Habsburg monarchy no longer existed. Kossuth, the liberal Hungarian aristocrat, demanded virtually complete Hungarian autonomy. He and his allies proclaimed the "March Laws," under which the delegates to the Hungarian Diet were to be elected by male property holders. The cabinet would be responsible to Hungary's Parliament. The emperor of Austria would remain the king of Hungary, but Hungary would maintain a separate army and conduct its own foreign policy. The Habsburg court, reeling from reverses on all sides, had little choice but to approve the changes. The new Hungarian government immediately proclaimed freedom of the press, established a civilian guard, and affirmed the abolition of the *robot* for peasant landowners, while maintaining it for landless peasants.

Although asserting its own autonomy from the Habsburg empire, the Hungarian Diet virtually ignored the autonomy of the other nationalities

Vienna explodes in Revolution in 1848.

within the Hungarian domains, including Czechs, Poles, Croats, Slovenes, and Romanians, some of whose intellectuals viewed the revolutions of 1848 as the victory of the idea of the nation. Croats, the largest of the non-Magyar nationalities in Hungary, were particularly resentful at not having been consulted. A small insurrection of students in Budapest on March 15 first challenged Kossuth's preoccupation with the interests of Hungarian landowners. The narrow electoral franchise, based on property owned and taxes paid, excluded most people of the poorer nationalities from election to the Diet. So did the requirement that each representative speak Hungarian, one of Europe's most difficult languages (although Latin remained the official language of Hungary until 1844).

The Magyars' problem of national minorities became the Habsburg dynasty's hope for holding its empire together. The imperial government began to mobilize the Croats against the Hungarians, with whom the Serbs and Romanians were also angry. In March, the emperor appointed Joseph Jelačić (1801–1859) as the new governor-general for Croatia. Jelačić refused to cooperate with the Hungarians. In retaliation, the Hungarians refused to send troops to help the imperial army battle Italian insurgents. Ferdinand then withdrew the concessions he had made in March to Hungarian autonomy.

Another challenge to the monarchy, again revealing the complexity of Central Europe, came in Bohemia, populated by both Czechs and Germans. In March, Czech nationalists revolted in Prague, demanding that Bohemia, like Hungary, become an autonomous state only loosely tied to the old monarchy. They wanted the Czech language to be made equal to German, which remained the language of the army, the bureaucracy, and commerce. They also wanted to expand the borders of Bohemia eastward into Moravia, where many Czechs lived. At the same time, many Bohemian Germans looked eagerly toward possible unification with the German states to the north. In the meantime, Emperor Ferdinand left Vienna for Innsbruck in May 1848, fearing that revolutionary students and workers might make him, like Louis XVI during the French Revolution, an ill-fated prisoner in his own palace.

Revolution in the Italian States

In the Italian states, March brought insurrections against Austrian rule in Lombardy and Venetia, and against conservative regimes in the other states, notably the Papal States. In Tuscany, the grand duke bowed to reformers by promulgating a constitution. King Charles Albert (ruled 1831–1849) of Piedmont-Sardinia met some liberal demands by creating a bicameral parliament to be selected by a small minority of adult males, easing press censorship, and establishing a civilian guard in Italy's strongest state. The revolutions in the Italian states were also animated by different goals: bourgeois liberals called for political reform and Italian unification, radicals wanted a republic, and workers demanded some tangible benefits for themselves.

On March 18, 1848, 10,000 people marched to the palace of the Austrian governor-general in Milan carrying a petition calling for liberal reforms, echoing those in Paris, Berlin, and Vienna. Barricades went up, and five days (known as the "Five Glorious Days") of bitter street fighting followed. The poorly armed people of the city, whose arsenal included medieval pikes taken from the opera house, drove away the Austrian army of Count Joseph Radetzky (1766–1858). Radetzky would become a major figure in the counter-revolution at age eighty-one (and was energetic enough to have fathered a child only two years before). Radetzky had overcome an unhappy family life and an earlier career setback brought on by his wife's debts. Now in Milan, as insurgents established a provisional republican government, he found his army weakened by the desertion of many Hungarian, Croat, and Slovene soldiers.

Suddenly, much of Italy, particularly the Austrian-controlled north, seemed on the verge of a liberal and national revolution. Other towns in Lombardy rose up against Austrian rule. Venetians forced Habsburg troops to leave their city and declared a republic. In Naples, liberals forced a constitution on King Ferdinand II (ruled 1830–1859).

Many Italian nationalists now looked to Charles Albert of Piedmont-Sardinia for leadership in the political unification of Italy. Yet, despite pleas for armed assistance from Lombardy and Venetia, Charles Albert hesitated to send his army against the Habsburg forces. He felt that if the Italian peninsula were to be unified, it should be on his terms, not as a result of rioting commoners and armies swollen by ragtag volunteers. The Piedmontese king feared the specter of popular insurgency in northern Italy. He also worried that if Piedmont launched a war against Austria, the new French republic might take advantage of the situation to invade Savoy and Nice.

The outpouring of anti-Austrian sentiment in Piedmont and the opinions of his advisers convinced Charles Albert to change his mind. The Piedmontese army, swollen by volunteers from Tuscany, Naples, and Parma, and even the Papal States, marched unopposed through Lombardy, defeating the Austrian army. But instead of crossing the Po River and cutting off Radetzky from supplies in Venetia, Charles Albert decided to consolidate his gains in Lombardy, with an eye toward annexing that territory to Piedmont.

In Lombardy itself, no one seemed able to agree on what should happen next. Wealthy landowners wanted little more than a loose union of Lombardy with Piedmont. Middle-class nationalists hoped to drive the Austrian army from Italy and establish a unified state, perhaps a moderate republic. Radicals were disappointed when the charismatic nationalist leader Giuseppe Mazzini supported Charles Albert, instead of forcefully arguing in favor of a republic. In a hurried plebiscite, the people of Lombardy approved union with Piedmont.

(*Left*) Giuseppe Mazzini dreaming of a unified Italy. (*Right*) King Charles Albert of Piedmont-Sardinia, who was faced with revolutions in the Italian states.

The other Italian states hesitated. Some rulers mistrusted Charles Albert, fearing that he wanted to expand Piedmont at their expense. Traditional tensions between northern and southern Italy surfaced. Furthermore, the pope helped stymie the movement for Italian unification. Before the revolutions, the new pope, Pius IX (pope 1846–1878), had initiated a few modest reforms in his territories, releasing some liberals jailed by his predecessor. Some nationalists had even begun to think that Italy could be unified around papal authority. But the pope was hardly about to oppose the Catholic Habsburg dynasty on which the papacy had depended for centuries. Pius then tried to recall his army from the north, announcing that he would not support the war against Austria.

Meanwhile, the newly elected French National Assembly unanimously approved a motion calling for the liberation of the Italian states. A French volunteer legion stood ready on the frontier, hoping that its help against Habsburg armies would bring French annexation of Savoy and Nice, as Charles Albert had feared. But facing British opposition and with enough to worry about at home, the new French republic stayed out of the Italian fray. Nonetheless, for the moment the beleaguered Austrian court seemed resigned to losing Lombardy, and willing even to abandon its claim on Venetia, provided that Piedmont would not directly annex either of them.

Benefiting from better troop morale and reinforced by soldiers arriving from Austria, Radetzky believed he could defeat the nationalist armies of the Italian states, which fought with more enthusiasm than experience and lacked effective organization and supplies. One Piedmontese commander complained that the nationalists did "nothing, except to drown themselves with flowers, dancing, singing, shouting, and calling each other 'sublime,' 'valorous,' and 'invincible.'" Radetzky's army defeated the Piedmontese-led army of Italian nationalists at Custoza near Milan in early August 1848. The people of Milan then scornfully turned against Charles Albert, who slipped out of the city late at night and returned to his capital of Turin. From safer ground, the hesitant king negotiated an armistice with Austria, hoping in vain that he could retain Lombardy for his kingdom of Piedmont-Sardinia.

THE ELUSIVE SEARCH FOR REVOLUTIONARY CONSENSUS

The Revolutions of 1848 generated resistance almost immediately from the political and social forces that had the most to lose from their success. In Prussia, the king and nobles feared being toppled from their privileged positions. In the Habsburg lands, where nationalism was the most significant factor in the revolution, resistance came from the emperor and his army. In France, the upper classes generally opposed radical changes. The ultimate success of the counter-revolution throughout Europe was aided by the revolutionaries' mixed aims. The split between liberals and radicals worked to the advantage of those who wanted a return to the way things had been before the spring of 1848.

Crisis in France

In France, where the wave of revolutions had started, the political crisis intensified as the provisional government faced competing demands. On May 15, 1848, an attempt by the political clubs of the far left to dissolve the Assembly and declare a "social" republic of the people failed. The new government now began to arrest radical republicans.

With the provisional government rapidly running out of money and credibility, the Assembly voted to halt enrollment in the National Workshops, which were generating considerable opposition from the upper classes. The workers' associations and radical political clubs protested vigorously. On June 23, 1848, the Assembly announced that the National Workshops would be closed in three days. Enrolled unmarried men were to be drafted into the army and married workers sent to work in the provinces. When word of the dissolution decree leaked out that morning, Parisian workers rose up in rebellion.

For three days the "June Days" raged in the workers' quarters of central and eastern Paris. General Louis Cavaignac (1802–1857) put down the uprising with brutality, using regular army soldiers, the Mobile Guard, and National Guard units, some of whom arrived from conservative provinces by train and steamboat, two symbols of a new age. In the climate of social tension, between 1,500 and 3,000 insurgents were killed, some summarily executed by National Guardsmen. Afterward, the provisional government deported more than 4,000 workers to Algeria or other colonies, and sent thousands of people to prison.

Karl Marx believed that the June Days were a dress rehearsal for a future proletarian revolution that would pit workers against the bourgeoisie. The short, bloody civil war, however, was more complicated than that. Some younger workers, including artisans, fought alongside unskilled proletarians in the Mobile Guard, which helped put down the uprising. Some radical bourgeois supported the workers. The typical participant was a young journeyman artisan, married, and a member of a trade association.

The Assembly immediately passed legislation to curtail popular political movements. New laws limited freedom of the press and assembly and closed political clubs, specifically banning women from membership. The Luxembourg Commission was quickly disbanded. Cavaignac became provisional chief executive of the republic. The government sent new prefects and other officials into the provinces. Many who had begun their administrative careers during the July Monarchy felt only tepid support for the republic they would represent.

Attention now focused on the presidential elections instituted by the new republican constitution that was finally promulgated in November 1848. Louis Napoleon Bonaparte quickly emerged as a leading candidate, largely because of the reputation of his uncle, Napoleon. Although one wag cruelly dubbed him "the hat without the head," it was testimony to the magic of the Napoleonic legend that Louis Napoleon had been elected to the Constitutional Assembly in April 1848, after returning from exile. Many people believed that he could restore political stability. Even those who were against the republic could vote for him because they identified him with the empire. Cavaignac, the other major candidate, was the favorite of those who wanted to combine social order with a very moderate republic. The minister of the interior of the provisional government, Alexandre-Auguste Ledru-Rollin (1807–1874), was the principal candidate of the socialists, while the poet Alphonse de Lamartine, a moderate, also ran, but both were identified with the provisional government and the unpopular forty-five-centimes tax. Outside of Paris many people had never heard of either Ledru-Rollin or Lamartine, while just about everyone had heard of Napoleon. Louis Napoleon also won the support of many people who were for the republic. Like his uncle, he was assumed to have good will toward all people in France and, for that matter, had published a book called *The Extinction of Pauperism* (1844). On December 10, 1848, Louis Napoleon Bonaparte was overwhelmingly elected president of the Second Republic. Some skeptics were already wondering whether he, like his uncle, would serve as the heir to a revolution, or its executioner.

The Frankfurt Parliament

In the German states, liberals and radicals gradually split as conservative forces gathered momentum. Shortly after the February Revolution in Paris, a group of about 50 German liberals, meeting in Heidelberg, invited about 500 like-minded figures to form a preliminary parliament to prepare elections for an assembly that would draft a constitution for a unified Germany. Most liberals among the organizers of the parliament wanted the German states to be united under a constitutional monarchy. Radicals, however, wanted nothing less than a republic based on universal male suffrage, and some of them joined a brief insurrection in the Rhineland state of Baden. To conservatives, and to some of the liberals as well, this insurrection raised the specter of "communism," amid rumors that radicals would divide the great estates among landless peasants.

The remainder of the members of the preliminary parliament announced elections for a German Constituent National Assembly, the Frankfurt Parliament. But, distinguishing their liberalism from that of the departed radicals, only male "independent" citizens in the German states would be eligible to vote, with some states using this vague qualification to exclude men who were propertyless. The Diet of the German Confederation accepted the plans for the election of the Frankfurt Parliament.

In May 1848, more than 800 elected delegates of the German Constituent National Assembly filed into Frankfurt's St. Paul's Church, which was decked out in red, black, and gold, the colors of early German nationalist university student organizations. State, municipal, and judicial officials, lawyers, university professors, and schoolteachers comprised about two-thirds of the Frankfurt Parliament. Since about a third of the delegates had some legal training, many people began to refer to the gathering as a "parliament of lawyers," whose members debated far into the night. Almost giddy with enthusiasm as news of insurrections came from various corners of the continent, delegates spoke from the church's pulpit, confident that their deliberations

The Frankfurt Parliament in 1848.

would shape the future of the German states. Many were oblivious to the fact that poor acoustics rendered their speeches inaudible to people sitting in the back.

In electing Heinrich von Gagern (1799–1880) president, the delegates chose a man who symbolized the liberal and nationalist idealism of 1848. Gagern had fought in the Battle of Waterloo as a boy of sixteen. He had been one of the founders of the nationalist fraternities and a leader of the liberal opposition in his native Hesse. Although not of great intellect, Gagern nonetheless offered an imposing physical presence and carried out his difficult tasks with dignity. He echoed the lofty hopes of nationalists while pushing difficult and perhaps even insoluble problems into the background, confidently giving the false impression that the unity of the delegates was assured and that German unification lay ahead.

The Frankfurt Parliament operated outside any state structure. It lacked the support of the rulers of Prussia and Austria, and, for that matter, of Bavaria and Württemberg. Without an army, it could not impose its will on any of the German states. Furthermore, considerable division existed over what shape the proposed unified Germany would take. Would it be a centralized state, or only an expansion of the German Confederation? How would sovereignty be defined? Who would have electoral rights?

Amid flowery speeches celebrating German national destiny, the problem of nationality immediately surfaced. Some delegates wanted Austria excluded from a united Germany, leery of the problem posed by non-German speakers within their state. Among these exponents of this "smaller German" (*Kleindeutsch*) solution, some wanted German unification around Protestant Prussia, fearing the inclusion of Catholic Austria. The more liberal "greater German" (*Grossdeutsch*) group wanted a unified Germany to include all states and territories within the German Confederation. Some wanted Austria's inclusion to counter possible Prussian domination, as well as that of northern Protestants.

After months of debate, a compromise solution appeared to be a victory for the "smaller German" plan. On October 27, 1848, the Frankfurt Parliament voted that any German state could join the new Germany, but only if it did not bring with it territories having non-German populations. Unless Austria was willing to separate itself from Hungary, it would have to remain outside a united Germany. For the moment, the Austrian government, struggling against resistance to its authority from Hungary and the northern Italian states of Lombardy and Venetia, regarded the Frankfurt Parliament's German nationalism as another threat to its survival.

The Frankfurt Parliament put aside its liberalism when it came to the question of Poland, which had lost its independence following the Third Partition of 1795. When a Polish uprising against Prussian rule broke out, a parliamentary delegate rose to denounce Polish nationalism, insisting on "the preponderance of the German race over most Slav races" and calling for "[German] national egotism" and "the right of the stronger." The

Frankfurt Parliament voted overwhelmingly in favor of armed Prussian repression of the Polish uprising, also expressing support for the Habsburg monarchy's crushing of the rebellious Czechs.

The United Assembly of Prussia (which had been elected by universal male suffrage after the March insurrection in Berlin) had also gathered in May 1848 to begin to draft a constitution for Prussia. Amid urban and rural unrest, the Assembly voted to make the civic guard a permanent institution, which challenged noble control of the army officer corps. It also abolished the Junkers' special hunting privileges and banned the use of all noble titles in anticipation of the abolition of formal class distinctions.

The Junkers, however, were not about to stand by and watch Prussia drift toward a constitutional monarchy or republic. They vowed to defend "God, the King, and the Fatherland," which they identified with their immunity from taxation and other prerogatives. Encouraged by the reaction to the June Days in France, Frederick William dismissed his liberal cabinet, sent troops to Berlin, and then in December dissolved the Assembly. He declared martial law, disbanding the civic guard. Prussian troops crushed opposition in the Rhineland and Silesia.

While counter-revolution gathered momentum in Prussia, the middle-class liberals of the Frankfurt Parliament, powerless to effect German unification on their own, failed to build a base of popular support among workers and peasants. They feared the lower classes perhaps even more than did the Prussian nobles: one member of the Parliament described universal male suffrage as "the most dangerous experiment in the world." Thus, the Frankfurt Parliament rejected craftsmen's demands for protection against mechanization and an influx of new practitioners into their trades as being incompatible with economic liberalism. Since the eighteenth century, German guilds had gradually lost their autonomy to the regulatory authority of the states. The influx of apprentices and journeymen into trades had reduced the opportunity for journeymen to become masters. By turning a deaf ear to workers' demands, the Frankfurt Parliament lost a significant source of popular support. Furthermore, any hope of winning the allegiance of German peasants probably ended when the Parliament proclaimed that peasants must compensate their former lords in exchange for their release from remaining obligations.

Frustrated by the Parliament's moderation and general dawdling, in September 1848 several hundred workers charged into St. Paul's Church and tried to persuade the Parliament to declare itself a national convention of republicans. Austrian, Prussian, and Hessian troops had to rescue the delegates.

After six months of debate, the Frankfurt Parliament proclaimed in December 1848 the Basic Rights of the German People. Influenced by the American Declaration of Independence and the French Declaration of the Rights of Man and Citizen, it proclaimed the equality of "every German" before the law, freedom of speech, assembly, and of religion, the end of seigneurial obligations, and the right to private property. Jews gained legal equality. But the document would remain only a theoretical exercise unless a substantial number of states agreed to put it into effect.

The support of Prussia and/or Austria would be necessary to implement the Basic Rights of the German People and to form a united Germany. "To unite Germany without [Prussia and Austria]," would be, as a contemporary put it, "like two people trying to kiss with their backs turned to one another." But Austria's opposition to the Frankfurt Parliament became even stronger. Nationalism was antithetical to the monarchy's existence. The Frankfurt Parliament could do nothing as the Austrian government executed one of its delegates for having led an uprising in Vienna in October 1848. The Habsburgs encouraged other German states to disregard the Parliament and to proceed with their own counter-revolutions. The emperor made it clear that Austria would only consider joining a united Germany if the entire Habsburg monarchy, with its many non-German nationalities, was included. The Parliament had already rejected such a possibility.

In April 1849, the Frankfurt Parliament promulgated a constitution for a united Germany. It proposed the creation of a hereditary "emperor of the Germans" and two houses of Parliament, one representing the individual German states, the other elected by universal male suffrage. Austria, Bavaria, and Hanover rejected the proposed constitution.

The only chance for the constitution to succeed was to convince the king of Prussia to become king of a unified Germany. Frederick William had occasionally voiced vague support for German nationalism. The Parliament sent a delegation to Berlin to offer Frederick William the German crown. A Prussian noble shouted: "What, you bring an imperial crown? You are beggars! You have no money, no land, no law, no power, no people, no soldiers! You are bankrupt speculators in cast-off popular sovereignty!" When the head of the delegation asked for a glass of water in the royal palace, he was denied even that. Frederick William refused to accept a "crown from the gutter," a "dog collar" offered "by bakers, and butchers, and reeking with the stench of revolution."

Before the Prussian Parliament could approve the constitution proposed by the Frankfurt liberals, the king dissolved it on April 28, 1849, declaring a state of emergency. He then implemented new voting restrictions that greatly favored the conservatives in subsequent parliamentary elections. Henceforth, the wealthiest 3 percent of the Prussian population (paying one-third of all taxes) elected one-third of the representatives; the next wealthiest 10 percent (paying the next third of taxes) elected another third; and the remaining 87 percent of men elected the final third of the Prussian Parliament. Liberal abstentions and popular indifference further assured conservative domination of the new Parliament, which created an upper house of nobles, officials, churchmen, and other members to be selected by the king. Divided by indecision, lacking popular support, and facing Prussian and Austrian opposition, most of the Frankfurt parliamentarians went home. The Frankfurt Parliament, which embodied the hopes of German liberals and nationalists, ended in abject failure. Germany would not be unified by liberals.

COUNTER-REVOLUTION

The high hopes of the revolutionaries of 1848 were thus disappointed by the reality of different aims and a split between liberals and radicals. With the lack of consensus among the revolutionaries, counter-revolution now gained the upper hand in the Habsburg monarchy, the German states, and the Italian states. In the Habsburg monarchy, the initial period of optimism gave way to a grim realization of the complexity of Central Europe. Ethnic conflicts broke out among Hungarians, Croats, and Serbs, as well as between landowners and peasants.

Counter-Revolution in Habsburg Central Europe

The confusion of competing national claims and rivalries within the monarchy eased the task of counter-revolution within the Austrian empire. If freedom was a central concern of the revolutionaries, it meant different things to different people. Magyar nobles wanted more autonomy for Hungary; Viennese journalists wanted freedom from press censorship; artisans wanted freedom from the competition of mechanized production; peasants wanted freedom from labor obligations owed to nobles. Czechs demanded freedom from German domination as well as their own national freedom.

Czechs hosted a Pan-Slav Congress in Prague in June 1848 to promote the rights of and bolster a union of Slavs within the Habsburg empire and Central Europe. The assembled national groups could agree only on their common dislike for Habsburg policies. Each group had a different plan for the reorganization of the empire, one that would favor its own interests. Finally, the Pan-Slav Congress issued a vague statement in June 1848 that condemned the Germans for having oppressed the Slavic peoples and called for the reorganization of the Austro-Hungarian monarchy into a federation that would take into consideration the rights of each nationality.

While the Pan-Slav Congress, like the Frankfurt Parliament, was discussing lofty national questions, ordinary people were hungry. On June 12, 1848, barricades went up in Prague, manned by artisans and the laboring poor. Prince Alfred Windischgrätz (1787–1862), the Habsburg imperial governor, ended the insurrection on June 16, bombarding Prague with cannon fire. Meanwhile, in northern Italy, the Habsburg imperial

Croatian regiments loyal to the Habsberg emperor attack Viennese revolutionaries, October 1848.

army defeated the Piedmontese forces, which had moved to assist the revolutions against Austria-Hungary, and Jelačić's Croatian army defeated Hungarian revolutionary forces.

In August, Ferdinand returned to Vienna, welcomed by the middle classes. When Ferdinand began to shut down the workshops (which had been established to provide work for the unemployed), the workers rose up, as they had in Paris, before being crushed by the bourgeois National Guard. Two months later, workers rebelled again. Expected support from Hungary for the revolutionaries did not materialize, once again demonstrating the seeming incompatibility between the goals of workers and students in Vienna and those of national movements for autonomy. Ferdinand left his imperial capital a second time, taking his court to Moravia. The imperial armies under Windischgrätz bombarded Vienna, killing more than 3,000 people. Once again, enthusiastic revolutionaries proved no match for the professional armies of the established powers. The emperor imposed martial law, closed the political clubs, dissolved the National Guard, and reestablished censorship. Arrests, trials, and twenty-five executions followed. The emperor appointed a council of advisers (the *Reichsrat*), but was under no obligation to consult it.

Emperor Ferdinand appointed the noble Prince Felix zu Schwarzenberg (1800–1852) as head of government on November 21, 1848. This ended the period of political uncertainty within Austria that had followed the March insurrection. Schwarzenberg convinced the hapless emperor to abdicate his throne in December 1848 in favor of his eighteen-year-old nephew, Francis Joseph (ruled 1848–1916), who had fled Vienna during the March insurrection and turned up at Radetzky's camp in northern Italy dressed in military uniform. Placing his faith in the army, the new emperor was determined to assure the dynasty's survival and influence in Central Europe and the Italian states.

Prince Schwarzenberg enhanced the effectiveness of the imperial bureaucracy by appointing able commoners to important posts. In order to confront the Hungarian challenge, he hoped to win the support of Hungarian moderates, albeit without recognizing the rights of nationalities. Alexander Bach (1813–1893), a lawyer of noble origins, was first appointed to be minister of justice and then of the interior and reformed the Habsburg legal system. At the same time, he implemented a system of carefully coordinated bureaucratic surveillance, spying, and repression— known as the "Bach system"—that helped root out political opposition.

But the Schwarzenberg government still had to deal with the Austrian Parliament. That body, from its exile in the town of Kremsier, had produced a draft for a liberal constitution. The constitution approved the emancipation of the peasantry and sought to establish a decentralized, multinational state, under a constitutional monarchy that would recognize all languages. It would have made ministers responsible to Parliament. But the liberal Kremsier constitution was never implemented. Schwarzenberg suddenly dissolved the Parliament in March 1849, ordered the arrest of some of the deputies, and imposed his own constitution. Although it had liberal aspects, it made virtually no concessions to the non-German nationalities within the Habsburg domains and restored Hungary to its pre-1848 position. Furthermore, Schwarzenberg, with the young emperor's consent, intended to delay putting the constitution into effect until the revolutionary crisis had passed.

In April 1849, the Hungarian Parliament refused to recognize Francis Joseph's ascension to the Habsburg throne and thus his sovereignty over Hungary. In turn, the young emperor refused to recognize Ferdinand's concessions to Hungary. The liberal Hungarian leader Lajos Kossuth tried to rally support in Hungary against Austria. Although the Hungarian army fell back at the approach of a Habsburg army, forcing the provisional government to withdraw to the east, the tables then turned. The Hungarians defeated the imperial forces twice in the spring, taking Budapest and driving the Habsburg army out of Transylvania.

On April 14, 1849, the Hungarian Diet proclaimed Magyar independence and made Kossuth president of the newly formed Hungarian republic. As the monarchy's survival was now defiantly threatened, Francis Joseph called on the Russian tsar for help. The European revolutions had made Nicholas I even more reactionary. Having previously granted small reforms (see Chapter 15), he now forbade Russian students from traveling abroad, drastically reduced the number of government scholarships, ordered that philosophy and constitutional law be dropped as university subjects, and reinforced censorship of all publications. Thus without hesitation the Russian tsar sent 140,000 troops into Hungary and Transylvania. Kossuth frantically implored the Frankfurt Parliament for assistance, but that body had no army. The British government disliked the Russian intervention in Central Europe, but it wanted to preserve the Habsburg monarchy as a buffer against French and, above all, Russian interests. Hungarian resistance ended in August as Russian and Austrian forces advanced. Kossuth escaped to Turkey, never to return to Hungary. Austria executed thirteen Hungarian generals for treason, imprisoned thousands of people, and imposed martial law. The "Patent" of December 31, 1851, officially restored imperial absolutism.

One by one in the other German states, the "March ministries" of 1848 fell from power as rulers abrogated constitutions granted that spring. Even where constitutions remained on the books, the counter-revolutions orchestrated by rulers with the help of nobles left parliaments and assemblies with little or no effective power.

Radicals launched scattered insurrections, all of which failed. After being chased from his duchy in June 1849, the grand duke of Baden returned to oversee the trials of more than 1,000 people. Ten thousand people fled Baden, including Karl Marx, many emigrating to the United States. The German Revolution of 1848 was over. On August 23, 1851, the German Confederation annulled the Basic Rights of the German People, the major work of the Frankfurt Parliament.

Prussian-Austrian Rivalry

Prussian King Frederick William IV had grown up with a romantic attachment to the idea of German nationalism, while never losing an iota of his commitment to the interests of the Prussian ruling dynasty. Now that the German revolutionaries had, for all intents and purposes, been swept away by the juggernaut of counter-revolution, he proposed the creation of a "Prussian Union." It would consist of two "unions": the larger would include the states of the defunct German Confederation, as well as non-German Austrian territories; the smaller would be a confederation of all German-speaking lands, including those of Austria. In proposing these clumsy structures, a loose confederation based both on conservative political premises and an expansion of Prussian influence, Frederick William took advantage of the insurrections against Austrian authority in Hungary and northern Italy. Austria, Bavaria, and Württemberg all expressed immediate opposition to the plan. The Habsburg dynasty no more wanted to see an expansion of Prussian influence in Central Europe than it had desired German unification under the liberal auspices of the Frankfurt Parliament. On September 1, 1849, Austria unilaterally proclaimed the revival of the old German Confederation, pressuring member states to withdraw all the concessions to constitutionalism and liberalism they had made in 1848.

As Prussia and Austria both sought to assure the victory of counter-revolution, each seeking a dominant position in Central Europe, relations between the two powers deteriorated to the point that war seemed possible. In September 1849, the prince of Hesse asked the reconstituted German Confederation for assistance when his own people rebelled against the withdrawal of a liberal constitution he had earlier granted. The government of Prussia, however, objected to the involvement of the Confederation in Hesse because Hesse stood between two parts of Prussia. Prussia, which had the right to move troops through Hesse, threatened to send an army there if the Diet tried to intervene. But the Russian tsar, who had become wary of a possible expansion of Prussian power in Central Europe, forced Prussia to back down. In October, the German Confederation, with secret Russian backing, sent Bavarian and Hanoverian troops to Hesse, but Prussian forces blocked their way. Once again, the Prussian government backed away from war, agreeing to drop plans for a Prussian Union. The Prussian government signed the "humiliation of Olmütz" (November 29, 1850), in which Prussia agreed to demobilize its army.

The Counter-Revolution in the Italian States

The counter-revolution in Central Europe and particularly in Austria spelled doom for Italian revolutionaries. And as in the German states and in the Habsburg Empire, those espousing liberal reforms and the cause of nationalism were too few, too scattered, and too divided by divergent and even conflicting goals. When Habsburg forces were fighting in Hungary, a nationalist "war party" in Piedmont-Sardinia pushed King Charles Albert toward a resumption of hostilities with Austria. The Piedmontese army crossed into Lombardy, but Austrian forces under General Joseph Radetzky defeated it at Novara in March 1849. Fearing that Radetzky's strengthened army would invade Piedmont, Charles Albert asked for peace and abdicated in favor of his son, Victor Emmanuel II. The new king signed an armistice with Austria in Milan in August, renouncing Piedmontese claims to Lombardy.

In 1848, revolutionaries had challenged the authority of the pope in the Papal States. In August, workers in Bologna rose up against Pope Pius IX because he had helped the Austrian cause by recalling his army to Rome. But the pope's forces prevailed. The next outbreak of opposition to papal authority came in Rome itself. Fearing an insurrection, Pius named a new, more liberal government, which announced the imposition of a tax on Church property. After one of the government's leaders was assassinated in November 1848, crowds stormed into the streets, calling for a declaration of war against Austria. Pius appointed more liberals to his government and called for parliamentary elections, before fleeing in disguise. From Naples, he called for the overthrow of the government he had appointed under duress.

In Rome, the new cabinet met many of the workers' demands, setting up charity workshops and ending the grain tax. The new government confiscated Church property, turning some buildings into apartments for poor workers. In elections for a Constitutional Assembly, the radicals won an overwhelming victory. On February 9, 1849, the Assembly proclaimed the Roman Republic. The pope immediately excommunicated some of the republic's officials. The republic, in turn, abolished the Inquisition and proclaimed freedom of the press and the secularization of university education.

Some Italian nationalists now were beginning to think of the Roman Republic as a center around which the peninsula could be unified. Giuseppe Mazzini's arrival in Rome in early March 1849 to join the revolutionary government confirmed the pope's fears in this regard. With the armies of the Habsburgs tied up with struggles in Central Europe, the pontiff had to look elsewhere for a strong army to come to his rescue. Although Piedmont, the strongest Italian state, did not want a Roman Republic, the pope did not solicit Piedmontese assistance, fearing that if its forces came to the rescue, they might never leave.

Beset by severe economic shortages and inflation and discouraged by the news of the Piedmontese defeat at Novara in March, leaders of the Roman Republic now learned that the French were coming to try to restore the pope's temporal power. Louis Napoleon Bonaparte was eager to consolidate the support of French Catholics. He also did not want Austrian influence in Italy to go unchallenged. With the approval of the French National Assembly, an army of 10,000 French troops disembarked near Rome, and then, embarrassingly enough, had to retreat when they were met by fierce resistance. Giuseppe Garibaldi (1807–1882), a more strident—and organized— republican nationalist than Mazzini, arrived with a corps of volunteers from Lombardy to help the besieged republic. As pro-papal forces sent by the king of Naples and the Spanish government approached Rome, the

Pope Pius IX puts aside the liberal mask of Christ, revealing his true conservative face.

French army began to shell the eternal city in early June 1849. The Assembly capitulated a month later. French troops then occupied Rome, dissolving the Roman Assembly and the clubs and reviving press censorship. Three cardinals assumed power, preparing for the pope's return in April 1850 and the repression that followed.

Of all of the governments formed by revolutions and uprisings in the Italian states in 1848, only the Venetian Republic survived. But having defeated the Piedmontese in March 1849, the Austrians now blockaded and bombarded Venice. Morale fell inside the hungry city, and disease spread. The Venetian Republic capitulated on August 22, 1849.

The Italian revolutions were over. The only liberal regime that remained was in Piedmont. Austria retained Lombardy and Venetia. The king of Naples, the grand duke of Tuscany, and the pope were back in power. Italian unification remained a dream of northern middle-class nationalists. The multiplicity of states and lack of strong popular support for unification—reflected by the gap between liberals' and workers' goals—had for the moment proven too powerful.

The Agony of the French Second Republic

In France, where the wave of 1848 revolutions had begun, the election of Louis Napoleon as president in December of that year seemed to guarantee a return to political stability. Yet even as better economic times gradually returned, the "democratic-socialists," whose supporters had been primarily drawn from France's largest cities and some smaller market towns, expanded their appeal in the countryside, particularly gaining followers in the south. They won support not only among radical bourgeois and artisans but also among many peasants, for whom the low prices of the agricultural depression had brought hard times. Taking the name of the far left during the French Revolution, the Montagnards called for specific national reforms such as the establishment of progressive taxation, higher wages, the abolition of the tax on wine, the creation of credit banks for peasants, and free and obligatory primary schools.

The democratic-socialists effectively used written political propaganda to reach ordinary people. They also exploited the deep-seated traditions of oral culture in a society in which only somewhat more than half of the people could read and write; stories, songs, lithographs, and engravings spread the popularity of radical candidates. In the legislative elections of May 1849, the left won almost a third of the seats in the National Assembly, harnessing the heritage of the French Revolution in regions in which it had found enthusiastic support.

Encouraged by the strength of the left in the Chamber of Deputies and in Paris, Ledru-Rollin, who had been a candidate in the presidential election, attempted to provoke an insurrection on June 13, 1849. His pretext was the Assembly's readiness to send a French army to support the pope,

Uprooting a liberty tree in Paris.

which the left claimed violated the new constitution, because French troops would be violating the freedom of the Romans. However, intervention in Rome earned Louis Napoleon the gratitude of conservative Catholics; Ledru-Rollin's uprising discredited the left among the upper classes. But by-elections in the spring of 1850 reflected the growing popularity of the democratic-socialist program in some places.

Backed by the "party of order," Louis Napoleon Bonaparte's government claimed that a massive plot threatened social order. Symbols of the French Revolution itself, including singing "The Marseillaise," became illegal. The government also outlawed red caps and belts, because red was identified as the color of the left. The police chopped liberty trees down one by one.

The government curtailed the freedoms of assembly and association. It banned a number of workers' associations, including some that had been granted state funds in 1848 to establish producer and consumer cooperatives. National Guard units in many towns were disbanded. Mayors and schoolteachers were replaced if they supported the left, and cafés identified with the democratic-socialist cause were closed. Many radical republican and socialist leaders were jailed. These included Jeanne Deroin (1810–1894), a socialist seamstress and feminist, who in 1849 had tried to run for election despite the fact that women were ineligible for election and could not vote. In March 1850, the Assembly passed the Falloux Law, which allowed the Catholic clergy to open secondary schools and permitted them to serve on education committees. One of the practical consequences was that villages now could turn operation of their schools over to the clergy.

In May 1850, the National Assembly ended universal male suffrage by adding a residency requirement that disqualified many workers who travelled from place to place. This reduced the electorate by one-third, eliminating 3 million voters. Many of the disenfranchised lived in the larger cities, where Napoleon and his candidates had not fared well. The repression succeeded in smashing the left in much of France.

In some southern and central regions, the repression drove the left into secret societies, whose members, mostly artisans and peasants, swore an oath of allegiance to defend the "democratic and social Republic." These societies, which started in towns, gradually spread into the surrounding countryside. This occurred particularly where economic growth during the preceding two decades, including cash-crop agriculture and rural handicrafts, had brought more rural artisans and peasants regularly into market towns. The precocious politicization of the French Second Republic, through the conduits of voluntary associations and cafés, reflected links between economic growth and political activity.

The constitution limited the presidency to one term of four years. Although Louis Napoleon's term as president was, in principle, nearing an end, he had no intention of stepping aside despite the fact that the Chamber of Deputies had rejected a proposal to allow the president, if re-elected, to serve a second term. In the fall of 1851, the government declared a state of martial law in several regions. On December 2, 1851, the anniversary of the battle of Austerlitz and the coronation of Napoleon Bonaparte as emperor, Parisians awoke to read an official poster that announced the dissolution of the National Assembly. The secret societies then undertook the largest national insurrection in nineteenth-century France. A small uprising broke out in eastern Paris and, while troops easily dispersed demonstrations in several other major cities, more than 100,000 people, principally in the south and center of the country, took up arms in defense of the republic. But the ragged forces of artisans and peasants armed with rusty rifles and pitchforks were easily dispersed by troops before they got very far. Military courts tried over 26,000 democratic-socialists, and almost half that many went into exile.

Support for the coup by Louis Napoleon was overwhelming in France as a whole, however. The plebiscite that followed the coup approved the takeover by more than 10 to 1. The Paris stock market soared. Louis Napoleon proclaimed a new constitution, which made him chief executive of the republic for ten years. On December 2, 1852, he took the title Napoleon III, emperor of the French.

THE LEGACY OF 1848

The glacial winds of reaction brutally chilled the "springtime of the peoples." The wave of repression dashed the hopes of liberals, republicans, and nationalists throughout Europe. It has often been said, with the advantage of hindsight, that in 1848, at least with reference to the German states, European history reached its turning point and failed to turn.

European states became even stronger after the Revolutions of 1848. The revolutions had succeeded at first because the French, Prussian, and Austrian authorities lacked sufficient military preparedness. All three quickly learned their lessons. With the defeat of the revolutionaries came the end of the era of civic or national guards, which had been demanded by the people of Berlin, Vienna, and Paris. Professional armies enforced the counter-revolution: those of Jelačić, Windischgrätz, and Radetzky restored Habsburg authority in Bohemia, Hungary, and northern Italy; the Prussian army crushed the last gasps of revolution in the German states; and the French army put down subsequent resistance to Louis Napoleon's coup d'état. Louis Napoleon's plebiscite reinforced the centralized character of the French state.

Nonetheless, the Revolutions of 1848 marked the first time workers put forward organized demands for political rights. Class antagonisms, already evident in much of Europe during the "hungry forties," would deepen further after the failures of 1848. Moreover, radical peasants in southern France helped dispel the myth of the inevitably conservative peasant.

Although the Revolutions of 1848 ultimately failed, they left crucial political legacies. The period was one of political apprenticeship for

The generals who crushed the insurgency within the Habsburg empire: Jelačić, Radetzky, and Windischgrätz.

republicanism in France and nationalism in the German and Italian states. Portugal completed a liberal revolution begun in 1820 with the establishment of a parliamentary government. The revolutions were not only separate national phenomena but also part of a common process that anticipated the emergence of mass politics in the last decades of the nineteenth century. While many of the goals of the revolutionaries centered on middle-class demands for liberal reforms, such as freedom of the press, the Revolutions of 1848 also had a popular quality characterized by demands for universal male suffrage, as well as by a few calls for political rights for women. Hundreds of thousands of ordinary people participated, if only somewhat briefly, in political life. The mid-century revolutions influenced the subsequent political evolution of each country that had had a revolution in the spring of 1848.

The counter-revolution in Europe scattered a generation of committed republicans, nationalists, and socialists throughout much of the world. Thousands of Frenchmen were exiled to Algeria, while German and Italian political exiles emigrated to the United States. They spread the ideas of republicanism, nationalism, and socialism.

The Habsburg monarchy, too, survived the liberal and nationalist challenges of 1848. The young Habsburg Emperor Francis Joseph bragged to his mother, "We have thrown the constitution overboard and Austria has now only one master." The Austrian government had adroitly manipulated ethnic tensions, using a Croatian army against a Hungarian uprising. The situation was so complicated that a Hungarian noted that "the King of Hungary declared war on the King of Croatia, and the Emperor of Austria remained neutral, and all three monarchs were the same person." Hungary, in which perhaps as many as 100,000 people were killed during the fighting in 1848–1849, remained within the monarchy as Austria's junior partner. But none of the major reforms undertaken within the monarchy in the wake of the revolution were abolished during the counter-revolution. Peasants were now free from labor obligations previously owed to landowners. Although the liberal Kremsier constitution had been tossed aside, the Austrian constitution of March 1849 did establish a parliament. Yet the goals of many Hungarians, Czechs, Poles, and other ethnic groups remained unachieved. On the Italian peninsula, Habsburg control of Lombardy and Venetia, the existence of many other separate states, and the indifference of most people to Italian nationalism remained daunting obstacles to Italian unification. Even in failure, however, the revolutions in the Italian states had only made Italian nationalists more determined to work for national unification. Likewise, the defeat of the Hungarian and Bohemian revolutions, as well as the failure of the radical revolution in Vienna that had first challenged Habsburg rule, by no means ended the threat to the Habsburg monarchy.

The Revolutions of 1848 accentuated support for German nationalism. A Prussian minister recognized that "the old times are gone and cannot return. To return to the decaying conditions of the past is like scooping water with a sieve." The revolution did produce a Prussian constitution and an elected assembly, however, which the king only slightly modified in 1849–1850, when he again took control. The failure of the Revolutions of 1848 in Central Europe suggested to many that German unification could only be achieved under the auspices of either Prussia or Austria. By revealing the complexity of national tensions and rivalries within the Habsburg monarchy, it now seemed even more unlikely that Austria would have an interest in bringing about German unification, although it would oppose an expansion of Prussian power. Prussia would only be likely to support German unification, however, if it would serve to extend its own power within the German states and in Europe. German unification under any auspices would potentially entail a drastic change in the European state system, altering the balance of power, especially in Central Europe.

PART FIVE

THE AGE OF MASS POLITICS

In 1850, Great Britain, France, and Russia were the three major European powers. However, the unification of Italy and Germany during the 1860s and early 1870s shifted the balance of power in Central Europe and dramatically changed international dynamics. Moreover, amid rising national consciousness, ethnic minorities in the Habsburg Empire demanded more rights, setting the stage for further conflict in Europe.

During the nineteenth century's last three decades, much of Europe entered a period of remarkable economic, social, political, and cultural change. During the Second Industrial Revolution, scientific and technological advances ushered in a period of rapid economic growth. Steel and electricity transformed manufacturing. Cities grew rapidly, their wide boulevards lined with department stores, cafés, and newspaper kiosks. The emergence of spectator sports and flashy cabarets symbolized the fin-de-siècle period. However, some of the rebellious writers and artists of the avant-garde worried that Western civilization was moving too rapidly and seemed out of control.

Despite a general improvement in the quality of life, the difficult conditions of the laboring poor encouraged the creation of Socialist parties in France, Germany, Italy, Belgium, and most other Western European states, and Socialist representatives were elected to many European parliaments. Trade unions put forth demands and engaged in strikes. In Britain, the Labour Party came into existence early in the twentieth century, largely supported by workers who demanded social reform. In Russia, liberal critics of the tsarist autocracy became bolder. The humiliating defeat of Russia by Japan led to the

Russian Revolution of 1905. This forced short-lived political reforms and encouraged reformers and revolutionaries alike.

For more than half a century, liberals had championed the interests of the middle class, basing the right to vote on the ownership of property. They did so in the context of constitutional government, pushing for the rights of legislative assemblies. In the three decades following the largely unsuccessful 1848 revolutions, liberalism prevailed in Great Britain, France, Austria, Italy, Greece, and Sweden. The British Parliament, which in 1867 had greatly extended the right of males to vote, approved the secret ballot in 1872, and in 1884 enfranchised almost all remaining adult males. France became a republic in the 1870s, and universal male suffrage subsequently was adopted in Germany, Belgium, Spain, Austria, and Italy. Without the liberals' determination to expand the franchise, the emergence of universal male suffrage in much of Western Europe, followed by political democracy in many states, would not have occurred. Liberal democracy emerged as the dominant form of European politics from the second half of the nineteenth century to the present day.

However, in the last decades of the century, liberalism was on the defensive, attacked from left and right. Nationalism increasingly became part of the expanding contours of political life within states and between them. During the French Revolution and Napoleonic era, nationalism had been an ideology identified with the political left. Liberals had believed that laissez-faire economic policy and parliamentary government combined with an expansion of the right to vote (but not necessarily universal male suffrage) would provide a firm base for the establishment of nation-states. During at least the first half of the nineteenth century, liberalism and nationalism were closely entwined; liberals and nationalists were often the same people, as in Britain, France, and Italy.

By the end of the century, many nationalists, convinced that their people were superior to any other, trumpeted the primacy of the nation over claims of popular sovereignty or belief in human equality. Nationalism became an ideology championed, above all, by right-wing parties. Cheap newspapers glorified the nation for eager readers. "Jingoism" came to define the swaggering self-assurance of nationalists committed to expanding the power of their nation. At the same time, waves of strikes and demonstrations frightened conservatives from Norway and Sweden to Austria and Spain. The fear of socialism, espousing internationalism, pushed social elites and some in the middle class to the nationalist right. Anti-Semitism fed on aggressive nationalism. Nationalism merged easily with imperialism, which was predicated on the assumption that the people of one nation were superior to others, and therefore entitled to dominate "inferior" peoples. The "new imperialism" of the powers began in the 1880s. By 1914, they had divided up three-quarters of the world's surface. Imperialism helped sharpen international rivalries. Entangling alliances led the European powers into two heavily armed camps, linking Germany and Austria-Hungary against Britain, France, and Russia. The growth of nationalism in the Balkans fueled the rivalry between Russia and Austria-Hungary, each backed by strongly committed allies.

CHAPTER **17**

THE ERA OF NATIONAL UNIFICATION

      Born into a family of Piedmontese nobles during the Napoleonic occupation, Camillo di Cavour was educated in a military academy and entered the army, where he became enamored of political radicalism. Upon hearing of the July Revolution of 1830 in France, Cavour ran through his barracks in Genoa with a paper knife, shouting "Long live the Republic! Down with all tyrants!" Cavour came to espouse aristocratic liberalism, and he became determined to effect the political unification of the Italian peninsula. An idealist of vision and courage, Cavour was also capable of ruthlessness and unscrupulous trickery, all of which would be necessary to form one state from the many that existed on the Italian peninsula at that time.

    During the first half of the nineteenth century, small groups of German and Italian nationalists (like Cavour) agitated for the political unification of their respective peoples. Liberals and nationalists in the 1830s and 1840s were often the same people sharing the same goals. Many revolutionaries in 1848 had demanded national unification, notably the lawyers and professors of the Frankfurt Parliament in the German states and the Italian liberals and nationalists opposing Austrian domination of northern Italy. But the outcome of the 1848 revolutions notwithstanding, Germany and Italy were not unified by the popular movements that typified the insurrections and revolutions that in 1848 brought a republic to France, forced constitutional changes in Prussia and Austria, and sparked insurrections against Austrian control of northern Italy.

    Italian unification came, not because of the utopian nationalism of Giuseppe Mazzini nor because of the frenzied dashes of Giuseppe Garibaldi and his followers into the south, but rather largely as a result of the expansion of Piedmont-Sardinia, the peninsula's strongest and most liberal state. Italy was unified politically by Cavour under the liberal auspices of the Piedmont-Sardinian monarchy, the House of Savoy. Thus, the unification of Italy was itself a victory for liberalism, even if Italian liberalism would eventually collapse before the onslaught of fascism in the wake of World War I.

The case of Germany was very different. German unification was effected by autocratic Prussia. Prussian King William I and Chancellor Otto von Bismarck achieved unification through shrewd manipulation of both diplomacy and warfare. "Most countries have an army," it was said, "Prussia is an army with a country." The German Empire, like the Prussia that forged it in "blood and iron," was defiantly reactionary, flying in the face of currents of European liberalism.

Without question, the emergence of Italy in the 1860s and of Germany in 1871 changed the history of modern Europe. Germany emerged as a great power, Italy as a would-be great power. And the Austro-Hungarian monarchy increasingly was confronted by demands from its ethnic minorities for their own independence, which remained a factor for instability in its domestic and international politics. In some ways, the Habsburg monarchy seemed an anachronism, out of place in an age of growing nationalism.

THE POLITICAL UNIFICATION OF ITALY

The Austrian statesman Klemens von Metternich once whimsically remarked that Italy was "a mere geographical expression." Since the end of the Roman Empire, Italy had been politically disunited, a cacophony of competing voices from different regions and peoples.

Marked differences in economic development compounded the problem of political fragmentation. Northern Italy has always been considerably more prosperous than the south. The Habsburg monarchy also presented a formidable obstacle to Italian unification, as it retained Venetia and Lombardy, and dominated Parma, Tuscany, and Modena in north-central Italy (the rulers of the latter two states were members of the Austrian royal family). The pope's influence in all Italian states and temporal control over the Papal States around Rome posed another barrier to Italian unification. Furthermore, Italy lacked a tradition of centralized administration. Powerful local elites dispensed patronage, constituting unofficial parallel governments in much of the south and Sicily. Finally, these structural barriers to unification were accompanied by disagreement among elites and nationalists about whether a unified Italy would be governed by a monarchy (constitutional or not), a republic, or even by the pope.

Although there were many forces working against Italian unification, some factors promoted the ultimate Risorgimento ("Resurgence") of Italy. Nationalist sentiment developed among the liberal aristocracy and the upper middle classes, particularly among northern lawyers and professors. It was fanned by nationalist brochures and newspapers, the memory of the failures of the Revolutions of 1848, and a common hatred of Austria, the

(*Left*) King Victor Emmanuel II of Piedmont-Sardinia. (*Right*) Count Camillo di Cavour.

latest of the outside powers that had held parts of Italy since the end of the fifteenth century. Most Italian nationalists envisioned a Risorgimento independent of the pope and the Catholic Church.

Leadership for Italian Unification

There seemed to be two possible sources of leadership for Italian unification. First, Victor Emmanuel II (ruled 1849–1878) of the House of Savoy, king of Piedmont-Sardinia (the Kingdom of Sardinia), wanted to unify Italy by gradually extending his control over the peninsula. Piedmont-Sardinia was far and away Italy's most prosperous region, boasting a significant concentration of industrial production, fine sources of water power, and accessible markets. It had inherited from the French revolutionary and Napoleonic eras a relatively efficient bureaucracy modeled after that of its conquering neighbor.

King Victor Emmanuel II, poorly educated and uncouth, loved horses and hunting more than anything else, with the possible exception of his sixteen-year-old mistress, the daughter of a palace guard. In 1852, Victor Emmanuel at least had the good sense to appoint Count Camillo di Cavour (1810–1861) as prime minister.

The Piedmontese Cavour was a pampered child who grew up to be headstrong, somewhat lazy, and bad tempered. His older brother inherited the family title of marquis, and Cavour entered a military academy, where he did well in mathematics and engineering. Later he would brag that he liked to reduce political problems to graphs on which he had plotted all possible factors and outcomes. As a young man, Cavour came to espouse political radicalism, a view that was unlikely to win him promotion in the army. He resigned his commission as a military engineer, pleading poor eyesight and bad health, the latter at least partially due to a lifelong pattern of eating and drinking too much.

Cavour read widely in economics and politics and travelled to France and England, both of which impressed him with their prosperity and efficient administration. (Cavour's first language remained French, although his command of Italian improved.) He attributed the well-being of both countries to the same aristocratic liberalism that characterized Piedmont-Sardinia. On his property, he had made a good deal of money by utilizing crop rotation, land drainage, and mechanized farm machinery. Triumphs in banking and business followed, but none brought the morose Cavour happiness. In his early twenties, he wrote in his diary that he thought of suicide because he believed his life "without purpose, without hope, without desire," copying morbid lines from Shakespeare into his diary. Yet he found a compelling goal: the unification of the Italian peninsula.

Elected to the Piedmontese Parliament in 1849 in the new constitutional government, named minister of commerce and agriculture in 1850 and prime minister two years later, Cavour orchestrated the unification of Italy around the constitutional monarchy of Piedmont-Sardinia. He initiated the first of a series of loose coalition liberal governments based on the political center, standing between the noble and clerical right and the republican left.

Cavour's policies helped stimulate the Piedmontese economy. He facilitated the availability of credit for businessmen, helped attract foreign capital by lowering tariffs, built railways, and strengthened the army. Reflecting Piedmontese liberal secular values, Cavour made the clergy subject to the same civil codes as everyone else, limited the income of bishops, and taxed Church property. Like the liberalism of the French Orleanist monarchy and the early Victorians in Britain, however, Cavour's liberalism stopped well short of republicanism. But he could claim that Piedmont-Sardinia was the rightful leader of Italian liberals and nationalists.

A second, more popular nationalist tradition survived the broken dreams of "the springtime of the peoples" in the Revolutions of 1848. Giuseppe Mazzini remained its spokesman. The Genoese-born Mazzini had as a boy watched Piedmontese patriots leave for exile after an ill-fated revolutionary uprising in 1820–1821. Mazzini frequently dressed in black (often surrounded by cigar smoke and in the company of his pet canaries), vowing to remain in mourning until Italian unification could be achieved. The failure of conspiratorial uprisings led him to espouse a nationalist movement that had a wider range of support, with the goal of establishing a republic that would implement social reforms. While he was a determined enemy of monarchism and aristocratic privilege, Mazzini believed that classical liberalism was devoid of moral values and rejected socialism as overly materialistic. He embraced unification as a moral force that would educate and uplift the people of Italy, providing a common faith and purpose that would unlock their great potential and make them worthy of democracy.

Mazzini believed that the unification of Italy had to be the work of the people themselves, and should not be achieved merely through the expansion of the kingdom of Piedmont-Sardinia. Drawing on the conspiratorial tradition of the Carbonari, Mazzini's secret society, "Young Italy," hoped to mobilize the European masses, beginning in the Italian states, to rise up for nationalism and democracy. He thus supported the goals of other nationalist groups in Europe, including Hungarians, Poles, and Slavs in the hope that "Young Europe," a brotherhood of nations, would eventually come into existence.

Mazzini was undaunted by the failures and repression that followed the Revolution of 1848, including the ill-fated attempt to proclaim the Roman Republic in 1849. However, these debacles discredited him and his movement among the middle classes. Four years later, Cavour tipped off the Austrians that Mazzini was planning an insurrection in Lombardy. King Victor Emmanuel II congratulated Austrian Emperor Francis Joseph on the success of the subsequent repression. Yet Mazzini's effective propaganda kept the Italian question alive in European diplomatic circles while attracting the interest of lawyers and liberal landowners in some of the northern Italian states.

Alliances and Warfare to Further Italian Unification

Italian unification would be impossible as long as Austria dominated much of northern and central Italy. Having first concentrated on reforms within Piedmont-Sardinia, Cavour next began a series of diplomatic moves that he hoped would bring the support of Great Britain and France. Specifically, he wanted to form an alliance with France against Austria that would further the cause of Italian unification. Austria was not about to withdraw from Lombardy on its own, and Piedmont-Sardinia was too weak to defeat the Habsburg army alone. Cavour initiated commercial agreements with France, as well as with Great Britain, trying to impress both powers with Piedmont-Sardinia's political and economic liberalism.

In March 1854, France and Great Britain joined the Ottoman Empire in opposing Russia in the Crimean War, which had begun a year earlier. The cagey Cavour worked to make the war serve the interests of Piedmont-Sardinia and Italian unification. In October, while ordering fortresses on the Austrian frontier strengthened, Cavour informed the French and British governments that Piedmont-Sardinia would be willing to join the coalition against Russia in exchange for a role in determining new frontiers in Eastern Europe at the war's end. Knowing that Britain needed more troops for the fight, Cavour sent 15,000 soldiers in January 1855 to Crimea. Mazzini, on the other hand, bitterly opposed intervention as irrelevant to his vision of a united republican Italy.

Piedmont-Sardinia signed the Peace of Paris in 1856, which ended the Crimean War, an occasion Cavour used to focus diplomatic attention on the Italian situation.

Cavour was now eager to ally with imperial France in the interest of working toward Italian unification. Despite a failed assassination attempt against him by an Italian nationalist republican in 1858, French Emperor Napoleon III was eager to extend his country's influence in Italy and hoped to annex Savoy and Nice from Piedmont-Sardinia. He proposed marriage between Victor Emmanuel's fifteen-year-old daughter and his own young cousin, Prince Napoleon Bonaparte. Such an alliance would help cement relations between France and Piedmont-Sardinia, not a happy situation for the Austrians (nor necessarily for the young bride).

Cavour devised an agreement with France against Austria, which was signed in July 1858 at Plombières, a health spa in eastern France. Napoleon III now agreed to support Piedmont-Sardinia in a war against Austria, if such a war "could be justified in the eyes of diplomacy and even more in the eyes of public opinion in France and Europe." Cavour and Napoleon III envisioned an Italy divided into four confederated states: Piedmont-Sardinia as the Kingdom of Upper Italy, which would include Venetia and Lombardy, as well as part of the Papal States and several duchies; a second state in central Italy, with Napoleon III's cousin Prince Napoleon Bonaparte as king; a third state made up of the remaining papal

Pope Pius XI on the special train given to him by Napoleon III, who protected papal temporal independence.

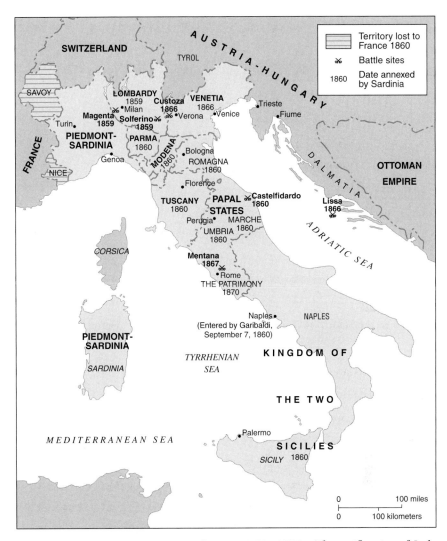

MAP 17.1. THE UNIFICATION OF ITALY, 1859–1870   The unification of Italy by Piedmont-Sardinia included territory acquired in 1859, 1860, 1862, and 1866.

territories; and the Kingdom of the Two Sicilies as the fourth state. The French emperor could only regard such a situation with glee: three of the four proposed states would require French support to survive, and France would receive Nice and Savoy from Piedmont-Sardinia.

In January 1859, Piedmont-Sardinia and France formalized the Plombières agreement in a treaty. Then the ruling dynasties were united in youthful marriage (the princess had agreed to marry the young Frenchman if "he is not actually repulsive to me"). Russia, Austria's rival in the

Balkans, was happy to sit this one out in exchange for French acceptance of a possible revision of the Peace of Paris, which had in 1856 deprived Russia of the right to have a fleet in the Black Sea. In turn, Russia would look the other way if events in Italy altered the settlements enacted by the Congress of Vienna in 1815.

Austria provided an excuse for war, announcing that it would draft men from Venetia and Lombardy into the imperial army. Piedmont-Sardinia, in turn, made it known that it would accept deserters from Austrian conscription, and it mobilized troops in March. But the British government lobbied so effectively for a peaceful solution that Cavour denounced a "conspiracy of peace" and threatened to resign, suggesting to his friends that he would move to the United States, or perhaps even commit suicide. Napoleon III hesitated, asking Piedmont-Sardinia to demobilize its troops. Austria saved the situation for Cavour by issuing an ultimatum to Piedmont-Sardinia on April 23, 1859, hoping that other German states would support it. With Austria now appearing as the aggressor, Prussia and the other German states felt no obligation to come to its aid. After Piedmont-Sardinia rejected the ultimatum, Austrian troops invaded Piedmont, which brought France into the war. Napoleon III himself led 100,000 troops into northern Italy; many of the troops went by train, the first time that a railway played a major part in warfare.

The French and Piedmontese defeated the Habsburg army at Magenta and then at Solferino in June 1859, driving the Austrians out of Lombardy (see Map 17.1). But the French feared that a crushing defeat of Austria might yet bring Prussia and other German states into the war against France, with the bulk of the French armies still in northern Italy. Furthermore, Cavour had sparked several nationalist insurrections against the Austrians in Bologna, Tuscany, Modena, and Parma, whose rulers fled, leaving the duchies under Piedmontese control. Further revolts in the Papal States failed; the pope's Swiss mercenaries recaptured Perugia, looting the city and shooting unarmed civilians. It became apparent to the French emperor that if Piedmont-Sardinia were *too* successful, Victor Emmanuel's expanded kingdom might become a rival instead of a grateful, compliant neighbor. Without consulting Cavour, Napoleon III arranged an armistice at Villafranca with Francis Joseph of Austria in July.

Cavour and Victor Emmanuel now believed that France had betrayed them. Austria had lost Lombardy to Piedmont-Sardinia but would retain Venetia. By the Treaty of Turin on March 24, 1860, Napoleon III agreed to Piedmont-Sardinia's annexation of Tuscany, Modena, Parma, and Bologna, in addition to Lombardy. In exchange, Piedmont-Sardinia ceded Savoy and Nice. With the exception of Venetia, almost all of northern and central Italy had now been united under the constitutional monarchy of Piedmont-Sardinia.

Garibaldi and the Liberation of Southern Italy

The colorful republican revolutionary Giuseppe Garibaldi (1807–1882) now leapt onto the stage. Born in Nice (and, like Cavour, a French speaker by preference), the charismatic and courageous Garibaldi, a man of simple tastes, had joined Mazzini's Young Italy movement in 1833. After twelve years in exile in South America, he fought against the Austrians in Lombardy in 1848 and in Rome in 1849. The war of 1859 provided him with another opportunity to fight Austria. Angered that the Villafranca armistice had cut short what he considered a war for Italian unification, Garibaldi formed an army of volunteers. Cavour tolerated it in the hope of preventing the French from annexing Savoy and Nice. Garibaldi also hoped to drive the Austrians from Venetia and the French from Rome. But his force's ill-prepared attack on Rome failed completely.

In April 1860, a revolt began against Francis II, the Bourbon monarch of the Kingdom of the Two Sicilies (Naples and Sicily), as a protest against the milling tax and the high price of bread. Secretly encouraged by Cavour (who planned to send Piedmont-Sardinia's army later to Rome to rescue the pope) and openly urged on by Mazzini, Garibaldi landed in Sicily with an army of 1,000 "Red Shirts" (a "uniform" that made it possible for virtually anyone to join and feel like he belonged to the force). Sicilians welcomed him as a liberator who would help them obtain their independence and rid them of onerous taxes. Garibaldi's followers outfought the larger

(*Left*) Giuseppe Garibaldi. (*Right*) An exultant reception greets Garibaldi when he lands at Marsalla in Sicily around 1860.

Neapolitan army, taking Palermo on May 27, 1860. This success swelled Garibaldi's ragtag army of nationalists and adventurers.

Garibaldi then announced that he was assuming dictatorial power in Sicily on behalf of King Victor Emmanuel II of Piedmont-Sardinia. In August, Garibaldi's army returned to the Italian peninsula. Aided by an insurrection of craftsmen and day laborers, the Red Shirts took Naples, Italy's largest city, in September. Garibaldi's victories put Piedmont-Sardinia in a difficult situation. If Garibaldi marched against Rome, France might declare war because of the threat to the pope. If Garibaldi moved against Venetia, which seemed inevitable, Austria would almost certainly fight again, perhaps this time with Prussia's support. Cavour sent Piedmontese troops into the Papal States the same day that Garibaldi's troops took Naples. The ostensible goal was to join Garibaldi, but the real intention of the expedition was to stop the adventurer's dramatic independent operations. The combined forces of Piedmontese troops and Garibaldi's army put an end to papal resistance and that of the royal Bourbon family of Naples.

Italy Unified

Plebiscites in October in Naples, Sicily, and the Papal States demonstrated overwhelming support for joining the expanding Italian state of Piedmont-Sardinia. The annexation of these states angered Napoleon III, as Cavour had promised that an international conference would provide arbitration. Now only Venetia—still Austrian—and Rome and its region—the shrinking kingdom of the pope—remained unincorporated into the new Italy.

Victor Emmanuel II of Piedmont-Sardinia triumphantly entered Naples with Garibaldi in November 1860. He took the title King Victor Emmanuel II of Italy in March 1861. Garibaldi, whose daring exploits had made these events possible, retired in semi-exile to his home on a small island. On June 6, 1861, Cavour suddenly died at the age of fifty-one, depriving Italy of his effective decision making and political acumen. Depending on one's point of view, Italy had lost either the great hero of the Risorgimento or a scheming Machiavellian—probably something of both.

Two more conflicts completed the political unification of Italy. In 1866, Austria went to war with Prussia, its rival for the leadership of the German states. The Italian army, allied with Prussia, more than held its own in brief fighting in Italy, and then moved into Austrian Venetia. When Prussian forces defeated the Austrians in July 1866, Venetia became part of Italy.

The final piece in the Italian jigsaw puzzle fell into place when French troops left Rome in 1870 at the beginning of the Franco-Prussian War. Italian troops occupied Rome, making it the capital of the new Italian state. The Roman population approved the city's incorporation into Italy by more than 40,000 votes to just 46. On May 13, 1871, the Italian Parliament passed the Law of Papal Guarantees, which reduced the holdings of the pope to the Vatican, barely larger than Saint Peter's Basilica and its adjoining ecclesiastical buildings.

Despite enormous regional differences in economic, social, and cultural development, especially between north and south, Italy had been unified politically.

Limits to Unification

During the next decades, the limits to Italian unification became increasingly apparent. The Italian state, despite its centralized character, phalanx of civil servants, police, and large army and navy, seemed irrelevant to many, perhaps even most, of the people now called Italians. Most remained loyal to their families, towns, regions, and to the Catholic Church (particularly in central and southern Italy), as well as to powerful local leaders or factions. In a country in which almost 70 percent of the population was illiterate in 1871 and 50 percent in 1900, it mattered little that all parts of the peninsula now shared a common written Italian language. In 1860, almost 98 percent of the population of Italy spoke dialects in daily life and not Italian. Schoolteachers sent to Sicily from the north were taken for Englishmen by the local population. The French writer Maxime du Camp related that in Naples in 1860 he heard people shout "Long Live Italy!" and then ask what "Italy" meant.

Resistance to the Italian state came naturally. In southern Italy, the Camorra of Naples and the Mafia of Sicily and other criminal organizations with similar codes of honor served as the real basis of authority. Family feuds and vendettas, often accompanied by grisly violence, went on as before. "Italy" was seen as a northern ploy to bilk people out of money through taxes, or to draft their sons into the army, or to undercut what seemed to be the legitimate influence of the local notable, landowner, merchant, or mafioso. To the poor property owners and impoverished laborers trying to scratch out a living, local notables at least could provide what they considered "justice" for the poor. Brigands had traditionally received assistance from the local population, who viewed them as fellow resisters to the state, if not Robin Hoods. Although the state managed to drive bands of brigands out of business in the 1870s, crimes against outsiders remained endemic. The savage repression that followed killed more Italians than all the wars of the Risorgimento combined, intensifying suspicion and mistrust of the state.

The liberal free-trade policies of Cavour, who had never been further south in Italy than Florence, further served to concentrate industry in the triangle formed by Milan, Turin, and Genoa by driving out smaller and less efficient manufacturers, accentuating the gap between north and south. Northern large-scale textile production undercut struggling rural industry in other regions. The south became even more dependent on poor agriculture. Northerners dominated Italian politics, as they had Italian unification, treating the people of the south as colonial underlings. Far fewer southerners were eligible to vote than northerners. Mass emigration, principally to the United States and Argentina, could only partially resolve the problems of overpopulation and poverty.

In the meantime, the popes portrayed themselves as Roman prisoners of a godless state. The Church had refused to accept the Law of Papal Guarantees of 1871, which gave it title to the Vatican and the authority to make ecclesiastical appointments within Italy. The popes not only refused to recognize Italy's existence, but they banned the faithful from running for electoral office or even voting. While some Italian Catholics simply ignored such stern papal warnings, others systematically abstained from casting a ballot. The state paid the salaries of the clergy, but it also confiscated Church property. Secular reforms removed the teaching of theology from the universities, closed convents and monasteries, made priests eligible for military conscription, banned public religious processions, and made civil marriage obligatory. The attitude of the Church hierarchy and prominent laymen to the Italian state was reflected by the headline of one Catholic newspaper after the death of King Victor Emmanuel II in 1878: "The king is dead, the pope is well."

Italian Politics

The king of Italy ruled through a premier and parliament. The electoral franchise was small: only about 600,000 men (2.5 percent of the population) were eligible to elect members of the Chamber of Deputies before the expansion of the franchise in 1882, when 2 million voters, or about 10 percent of the population, were enfranchised, and 1912, when the number eligible to vote was doubled. Italian governments lurched from one political crisis to another in the 1880s, buffeted by rampant corruption as well as rapidly changing coalitions—a process that became known to critics as *trasformismo* ("transforming" political opponents into allies). King Umberto I (ruled 1878–1900) stood aside until his intervention became absolutely imperative. Italy's king was lazy, so uneducated that he did not even like to sign his own name if someone was watching, and considered himself above politics.

The arrogant Premier Francesco Crispi (1819–1901) built political alliances between northern industrialists, who were anticlerical and wanted high tariffs, and southern landowners, who also favored protectionism. Crispi used the army against strikers and demonstrators and used the police to cow opponents daring to organize electoral opposition against him. In 1894, he ordered the disfranchisement of nearly a million voters and banned the Italian Socialist Party. His authoritarian methods

(*Left*) The assassination of King Umberto I. (*Right*) Giovanni Giolitti who, as premier, brought relative stability to Italian political life.

angered even the king, who wryly admitted that "Crispi is a pig, but a necessary pig."

In 1901, King Victor Emmanuel III (ruled 1900–1946) signed a decree granting the premier authority over all cabinet posts. Upon becoming premier in 1903, Giovanni Giolitti (1842–1928) brought relative stability to Italian political life. Giolitti was a master of *trasformismo*, making party labels essentially meaningless by building a series of makeshift, though effective, coalitions. Giolitti won the loyalty of enough deputies to keep himself in office with negotiations, cajoling, promises of jobs and favors, threats, and outright bribery. With the motto "neither revolution nor reaction," the premier's balancing act depended on votes from the anticlerical Radicals, a party based in the north, who supported the increased efficiency of state administration and liked the premier's opposition to socialism. But Giolitti also depended on southern Catholic moderates, and therefore opposed any land reform on behalf of the rural poor that would break up large estates. His government also had to appease the Church by declining to meet the anticlerical demands of the Radicals. (In 1904, the Church had relaxed its antirepublican stand enough to allow practicing Catholics to vote in elections if their participation would help defeat a Socialist candidate.) Giolitti also sponsored legislation that turned over education in southern Italy to the clergy. The premier left the Camorra and Mafia alone because they could bring him votes in any region or town they controlled, ordering on one occasion the release of more than a thousand mafiosi from prison in exchange for their votes. But Giolitti also believed that social reforms enacted by his government could "put Marx up in the attic."

The Rise of Italian Nationalism

In a country wrought by political division, aggressive nationalism appeared as one means of bringing Italians together. Francesco Crispi had favored a policy of forceful colonialization, fearful that Italy would be left out while the other powers snatched up territory (see Chapter 21). He prepared an invasion of the East African state of Abyssinia (now Ethiopia) from the Italian colony of Eritrea in 1896, circumventing parliamentary opposition and refusing to heed the warning of generals that such a move might fail. When the Abyssinian tribesmen Crispi had referred to as "barbarians" crushed the Italian army at Adowa, he resigned. Italian nationalists then began to claim the territory of Trentino in the Austrian Tyrol and the Adriatic port of Trieste as "Unredeemed Italy" (*Italia Irredenta*). In 1911, while Giolitti was premier, Italy launched a war of conquest in Libya, establishing a colony called Tripolitania there (see Chapter 22). Giolitti's social reforms had frightened employers and many other conservatives, and the ranks of the anti-parliamentary right swelled. Nationalist candidates demanded further aggressive moves in the Mediterranean. Although the war in Libya went reasonably well for Italian troops, the right objected to the fact that it seemed mismanaged, and the left did not want the invasion at all. Both left and right moved further away from Giolitti's Liberal center. The Libyan War thus directly led to the end of Giolitti's political system. With the Socialists angered by the Libyan War and now standing unwilling to be "transformed" into temporary political partners, Giolitti now had to turn to Catholic leaders, who hated the Socialists. Giolitti convinced Catholic candidates to support his Liberal candidates if the Liberals agreed to end the campaign against Church schools and for legalized divorce. Angered by Giolitti's promises to the clerical candidates, the left tripled its vote, forcing him from office in March 1914. But six right-wing nationalists were elected to the Chamber of Deputies. A nationalist proclaimed that the role of his new party was to teach Italians to respect "international struggle," even if the result was war. The Italian liberal state had survived many challenges, but even greater ones lay ahead.

THE UNIFICATION OF GERMANY

The unification of Germany would not come through liberal auspices. In the German states, too, growing nationalist sentiment had existed, at least within the middle class. Yet, as in the case of Italy, there were also formidable obstacles to German unification. First, in the wake of the Revolution of 1848, the upper classes were wary of any change that might threaten the *status quo*. They particularly feared the strong nationalist feeling unleashed by revolution, the extension of which might lead to, they reasoned, the proclamation of the equality of all citizens. Second, it was still not clear which power, Austria or Prussia, would become the dominant influence in a unified Germany. Some believed in the "small German" solution in which Prussia might effect German unification and exclude Austria. Other German nationalists supported the "big German" ideal, whereby Austria would dominate an expanded German Confederation. Third, in both Prussia and Austria, the 1850s were an extremely repressive period that made it clear to most nationalists that German unification would not come under liberal auspices. The repression following the Revolutions of 1848 had scattered thousands of German democrats and nationalists across Europe and as far as the United States.

As in the case of Italy, where unification had been achieved primarily through the efforts of one relatively strong and prosperous state, in the German states Prussia held several trump cards toward achieving German unification: territorial additions in the industrializing Rhineland after the Napoleonic Wars and a relatively strong economic position, which had been bolstered by the Zollverein customs union. Furthermore, Prussia's population was quite homogeneous, almost entirely German-speaking and Protestant. The Prussian royal family, the Hohenzollerns, benefited from the internal stability brought by an effective administrative bureaucracy and were supported by an ambitious and powerful landed nobility, the Junkers, who dominated the officer corps of Prussia's strong army. In sum, Prussia already represented an example of successful statemaking. The expansion of Prussian power therefore seemed to many Prussians to be perfectly natural. Catholic Austria, on the other hand, dominated a multinational population. The Habsburg monarchy had much to lose by the encouragement of national movements that might catch fire among the varied peoples within the imperial boundaries.

All German nationalists, however, did not agree on what political form a unified Germany should take. Most Prussian Junkers (nobles) had been unrelenting in their opposition to the liberal movements that had championed popular sovereignty during the 1848 revolutions. They rejected the liberalism of Rhineland industrialists who were anxious to enhance their own political power. Many liberals, particularly republicans from the more liberal southern German states, wanted a unified Germany to have a parliamentary government free from the domination by either autocratic, aristocratic Prussia or imperial Austria. Yet, despite Prussia's autocratic and militaristic traditions, some nationalistic republicans still hoped Prussia, not Austria, would lead Germans to unification. Some Prussian Junkers also feared that if the "big German" plan for unification came to be, their influence would be greatly diluted by Austrian strength. Nonetheless, Austria continued to attract the interest of some German nationalists who mistrusted Prussia. Southern Germans wanted the Habsburg monarchy to champion the cause of the smaller German states, leading to a decentralized federation, not domination by Prussia.

William I, Bismarck, and the Resolution of the Constitutional Crisis

The first step in the unification of Germany was the ascension to power of a monarch equal to the task. In 1858, the pious William I (1797–1888) became regent for his brother, Frederick William IV, who was declared insane. Crowned king following Frederick William's death in 1861, William made clear from the outset of his reign that, unlike his predecessor, he would look beyond the small group of reactionary Prussian Junkers and bring some more moderate conservatives into his cabinet. William I promised to rule constitutionally, accepting the restraints to which Frederick William IV had agreed in 1849. Voters—men of at least moderate wealth—responded by turning out in unprecedented numbers to vote. Liberals won a clear victory in the 1858 elections to the Prussian Parliament, which brought to that assembly a good number of men enriched by the economic boom in the early 1850s. Liberals who favored German unification now had a public forum in which to be heard. Many businessmen believed that German unification would be good for them, as the Zollverein customs union had benefited them in the 1840s.

In the meantime, the Austrian war against Piedmont-Sardinia and France in 1859 divided Prussians. Some were torn between dislike for Austria and irritation with French Emperor Napoleon III for helping engineer the outbreak of war. Austria was a member of the loose German Confederation and had the right to expect assistance from fellow members. But Austria was also Prussia's major rival for power within the German states. Prussia remained neutral in the war, but Italy's move toward unification greatly impressed German nationalists. German nationalists who looked to Prussia to forge German unity welcomed Austria's defeat.

In 1858, several "Pan-German" associations formed as pressure groups supporting German unification. The largest and most influential, the National Union (*Nationalverein*), wanted a constitutional and parliamen-

(*Left*) Otto von Bismarck. (*Right*) William I.

tary German state. The Prussian government remained suspicious of the National Union because many of its members favored the extension of political freedom within the German states. As in the old Frankfurt Parliament, its members were overwhelmingly middle class, including intellectuals, lawyers, officials, and small businessmen, but also several industrialists. They even rebuffed an attempt by workers' organizations to join in 1863. The National Union contributed to the resurgence of political liberalism within Prussia, however, by demanding an effective constitution that would limit the power of the monarchy and the Junkers.

The question of army reform raised the issue of parliamentary control over the budget. The Prussian constitutional crisis that followed became a critical step in the unification of Germany along lines that turned out to be anything but liberal. The Prussian military mobilization in 1859 during the Austrian war against Piedmont and France had revealed serious inadequacies in the Prussian army. The minister of war proposed expensive reforms of the army: expansion of the officer corps, increasing the number of recruits, and an extension of the time of service to three years. Prussian liberals wanted all citizens to serve in the army, but also hoped that the National Guard (*Landwehr*) would replace the professional, Junker-dominated army as the foundation of the Prussian military, thus forging a link between the army and the people.

The Prussian Parliament did not enjoy many prerogatives in autocratic Prussia, but it did have the right to approve new taxes. In response to government pressure, in May 1861 the parliament, despite its liberal majority, passed a provisional bill that gave the army the money it needed until the reform could be considered. Liberal approval of the provisional bill was a fateful event in German history because it provided parliamentary sanction to the virtually unchallenged power of the military in Prussia.

Some leaders among the liberal opposition then formed the German Progressive Party. Emboldened by victory in the 1861 elections, three months later liberals declined to vote for the new military budget when the minister of war refused compromise. After William dismissed parliament, new elections returned another liberal majority, which rejected a second army budget. Opposition to the government seemed so strong that the king considered leaving the throne to his more liberal son, Crown Prince Frederick William. Seeking to overcome the parliamentary opposition, the king turned to a strong-willed and intransigently conservative Junker, Count Otto von Bismarck (1815–1898), appointing him prime minister in 1862.

Bismarck was the son of a dull, rather incompetent Junker father and a lively, intelligent mother from a family of middle-class bureaucrats. Rejecting the solemn rural world of the Junkers, Bismarck's mother once related that her single ambition was to have a son "who would penetrate far further into the world of ideas than I, as a woman, have been able to do." In his Berlin school, Bismarck was more noted for dueling scars earned in student fraternities than for academic success. After receiving his law degree, he passed the entrance examination for the Prussian bureaucracy. Bismarck was appointed Prussian representative to the German Confederation in Frankfurt in 1851. He was sent to St. Petersburg as ambassador in 1859, perhaps to mute his noisy denunciations of Austria. Brief stints in London and Paris increased Bismarck's knowledge of European affairs.

As prime minister of Prussia, Bismarck was convinced that he could create a new German state that would not be too large for Prussia to dominate, nor too democratic for the tradition of the Hohenzollern monarchy. For the next three decades, Bismarck's shrewd manipulation of domestic and international politics dominated relations among the European powers. The "iron chancellor" patiently made uncanny assessments of every possible option and then moved with determination to strengthen Prussia's position. Domestic policy occupied just as large a place in Bismarck's plans as did foreign affairs. He wanted to create a modern, bureaucratic state that would be strong and secular. He cleverly used political parties when it suited his purposes, as he doggedly held on to personal power. This type of politics came to be known as *Realpolitik*, the pursuit of a nation's self-interest based on a realistic assessment of the costs and consequences of action. Inherent in *Realpolitik* was an absence of moral or ethical considerations, overrun by Bismarck's unshakable determination to enhance the power of the Prussian monarchy and nobility, and therefore of Germany.

Bismarck evoked contradictory reactions of admiration, respect, and fear among Germans and foreign statesmen alike. He was a very complex man, both a man of iron and one easily moved to tears. He once said of himself: "Faust complains of having two souls in his breast. I have a whole squabbling crowd. It goes on as in a republic." A large man given to excesses of food and drink, he looked like a senior military officer stuffed into a uniform that was too small. At times outgoing and charming, Bismarck could also lapse into moods of intense, gloomy isolation. He was unforgiving toward those who crossed him: "If I have an enemy in my power, I must destroy him." He once said that he sometimes spent whole nights hating. He could also bide his time, always waiting for the most advantageous moment to act, ever willing to choose another strategy when necessary.

Bismarck had been named prime minister to confront the constitutional conflict over the army budget. After first putting parliament in the position of appearing to refuse compromise, in 1862 he linked the ongoing constitutional question to the role of Prussia in German unification. Bismarck could never contain his disdain for parliamentary liberalism: "The position of Prussia in Germany will be determined not by its liberalism but by its power. . . . Not through speeches and majority decisions are the great questions of the day decided—that was the great mistake of 1848 and 1849—but through blood and iron." He then announced that the government would operate without constitutional authorization, which it did for four years, using tax money previously voted to finance army reforms.

In June 1863, Bismarck struck against the liberal Progressives by restricting freedom of the press, refusing to confirm the election of Progressive mayors, and banning discussion of political issues in municipal council meetings. The fact that both public opinion and even Crown Prince Frederick William opposed these measures did not dissuade him in the least. Nor did the election of even more liberals to the parliament in October 1863. Bismarck's stridently anti-Austrian policy helped split the liberal parliamentary opposition. The army budget crisis was to be a harbinger of the unification of Germany, which would be achieved through "blood and iron."

Alliances and Warfare to Establish Prussian Leadership

Russia and France were the two powers that would be most threatened by a unified Germany. The 1863 Polish revolt against Russian domination presented Bismarck with a perfect opportunity to ingratiate himself to the tsar. Whereas the other major powers seemed to side with the Poles, whose insurrection in 1830–1831 had won them great sympathy in Europe, Bismarck immediately voiced support for Russia, going so far as to mobilize troops along the eastern frontier as if ready to spring to the aid of Russian troops. "Hit the Poles so hard that they despair for their lives," Bismarck advised. The Prussian government then signed an agreement with Russia, by which both powers agreed to assist each other in the pursuit of insurgents across their respective frontiers. Austria, which had a sizable Polish population within its borders, found its relations with Russia soured.

Bismarck's first war was fought against the Danes in 1864 over Schleswig and Holstein, two duchies including the Baltic port of Kiel. British Prime Minister Lord Palmerston (Henry John Temple; 1784–1865) once said that only three men truly understood the problem of Schleswig-Holstein: one was dead, one had gone mad, and the third, Palmerston himself, had forgotten it. The provinces were ruled by the king of Denmark although not incorporated as part of the kingdom of Denmark. Holstein, which lies between Prussia and Schleswig, was almost entirely German-speaking, also belonged to the German Confederation, and both German and Danish speakers lived in Schleswig. In 1848, the king of Denmark had declared the union of Schleswig with Denmark, and revolution broke out in both duchies. During the summer, a Prussian army on behalf of the German Confederation had intervened in defense of the revolutionary provisional government in Holstein, which seemed determined to join a unified Germany. International opinion (particularly Britain and Russia) rallied to the cause of the Danes, who were backed by

Prussian coastal battery during the war against Denmark, 1864.

Sweden. After some fighting, the provisional government was dissolved by the Armistice of Malmö (August 1848).

The London Protocol of 1852 placed Schleswig-Holstein under the authority of the Danish king, but forbade their incorporation into Denmark. In March 1863, however, the Danish king enacted a new constitution that seemed to incorporate Schleswig into his kingdom. Bismarck, capitalizing on the wave of nationalistic support from Prussian conservatives and liberals alike, then found an ally in Austria. The latter, also a member of the German Confederation and eager not to be left on the sidelines, prepared to send troops into Holstein to defend the independence of both Holstein and Schleswig.

Bismarck issued Denmark an ultimatum in January 1864, demanding that the new constitution for Schleswig be redrawn. The Danish government, assuming that because of Schleswig's strategic importance, France and Britain would rush to its defense, rejected the ultimatum and found itself at war with Prussia and Austria. To no one's surprise, the Danes were easily beaten. The Treaty of Vienna (October 1864) established the joint administration of Schleswig-Holstein by Prussia and Austria— Austria would administer Holstein, and Prussia would administer Schleswig. This awkward arrangement left Prussia with a military corridor and communications line through Austrian-controlled Holstein and use of the port of Kiel.

Bismarck now viewed a military showdown with Austria as inevitable, even desirable. Yet, while preparing for that eventuality by currying the favor of the smaller German states and working to isolate Austria further from the other European powers, he blithely tried—and failed—to tempt Austria into making an agreement that would formally divide their influence in the German states into north-south spheres. Bolstered at home by victory over Denmark, Bismarck was now free to enhance Prussia's diplomatic position in Europe. He persuaded Napoleon III that France would receive territorial compensation in the Rhineland if it would stay out of an Austro-Prussian war. The French emperor tried to play both sides. Convinced that Austria could defeat Prussia, he signed a secret treaty with the

Habsburg monarchy that would give the French Venetia and establish a French protectorate in the Rhineland after an Austrian victory.

Bismarck then drew Italy into a secret alliance, signed in April 1866, by promising it Venetia in the event of a Habsburg defeat. Italy promised Prussia assistance if there was war with Austria, knowing that a Prussian victory would add the last large chunk of the Italian peninsula to Italy.

Hoping to win the support of the other German states, Bismarck sent a plan for reform to the Diet, calling for the establishment of a national parliament to be elected by universal male suffrage. That the Junker conservative would suggest that male suffrage might form a foundation for the creation of a unified German state surprised liberals. While the leaders of the other German states pondered a response, Bismarck moved to instigate war.

Exaggerating reports of Austria's military preparations, Bismarck denounced Austria's "seditious agitation" against Prussia in Schleswig-Holstein. By this he meant Austria's convocation of the Diet of Holstein to reconsider the duchy's status. After Bismarck had secured the temporary alliance with Italy and assured France's neutrality, Prussian troops entered Holstein. Austria allied with some of the smaller states (including Hanover, Saxony, and Hesse-Kassel) of the German Confederation. Prussia left the German Confederation, which then voted under Austria's leadership to send troops against the Prussian army.

Within three weeks, Prussian troops had defeated the South German and Hanovarian armies in the Austro-Prussian War (1866). Thanks to the timely arrival of a second force led by the Prussian crown prince and the division of the Austrian forces (half of which were fighting against the Italians), the Prussian army defeated the Austrian forces in the Battle of Sadowa (or Königgrätz) in eastern Bohemia on July 3, 1866; almost 1 million soldiers fought in the battle. Superior military planning as well as the rapid mobilization, deployment, and concentration of troops, talented officers, and more modern weapons—particularly the breech-loading "needle gun," which could be fired from a prone position—brought the Prussian army success.

The North German Confederation

In the aftermath of a victory most people did not expect, Bismarck's first accomplishment was to restrain the Prussian officer corps, many of whom wanted to push on to Vienna. Bismarck, however, realized that he would ultimately need the support of the South German states, some of whom had been allied with Austria, if Germany was to be unified under Prussian auspices. He also did not want to provide France or Russia with an opportunity to enter the conflict. The Treaty of Prague (August 1866) eliminated Austria as a rival for the domination of the German states. The German Confederation was dissolved. The Habsburg monarchy recognized the

North German Confederation (see Map 17.2), a new union of twenty-two states and principalities north of the Main River, with a constitution and a parliament (Reichstag), which Prussia would dominate with William I as president and Bismarck as federal chancellor. Bavaria signed an alliance promising to join Prussia if it were attacked by France, which had been surprised and alarmed by the relatively easy Prussian victory. Schleswig-Holstein became part of Prussia. By virtue of the annexation of Hanover, Frankfurt, Nassau, and the electorate of Hesse, Prussia ceased to be divided into two separate provinces. The incorporation of the smaller states into Prussia proceeded rapidly, with the centralized government in Berlin quickly establishing channels of administration. The Berlin government intimidated, bribed, or cajoled the smaller states into compliance.

Bismarck left no doubt that he considered the North German Confederation a provisional solution until Germany could be united under Prussian leadership. In the meantime, the old Zollverein customs union, which included the South German states, was expanded to include an assembly

MAP 17.2 THE UNIFICATION OF GERMANY, 1866–1871   The unification of Germany by Prussia included territory acquired after the Austro-Prussian War (1866) and the Franco-Prussian War (1870–1871).

Prussian troops move to cut a French railway line in the Franco-Prussian War.

of elected delegates. Bismarck hoped that this economic alliance, however loose, would in the future expedite the political unification of the German states. He received support from Prussian businessmen who would profit from the removal of customs barriers and the centralization of railway networks. As long as unification brought material progress, it did not seem to matter to them that the traditional class system and restricted political life that characterized Prussia would form the basis of a united Germany.

Bismarck was the man of the hour, the Prussian state a dynamic force with which to be reckoned. Bismarck's bitter quarrel with the liberals over the military budget disappeared. The Prussian Parliament, elected during the war, overwhelmingly and retroactively approved the budgets of 1863–1866. As one parliamentarian who had previously opposed Bismarck on this issue put it, "The heavenly tribunal of success has cast its decision for the government."

Some members of the Progressive Party and other liberals still espoused "a vigilant and loyal opposition" at home. But liberal newspapers willingly accepted the triumphs of Prussian foreign policy and military might. Bismarck was shrewd enough to realize that German unification would require liberal support, particularly as many of the conservative Junkers were still wary of any change that might threaten Prussian traditions. Some liberals were so elated by the prospect of German unification that they left the more hesitant Progressive Party and formed the nationalistic National Liberal Party, which supported Bismarck. At the same time, some of the South German states were moving closer to Prussia through economic and military alliances.

The Franco-Prussian War and German Unification

Prussian victory in the Franco-Prussian War of 1870–1871 completed the unification of the German states, with the exception of Austria. Napoleon III foolishly seized upon the issue of the Hohenzollern candidacy for the vacant Spanish throne as an occasion to go to war against Prussia (which might have left France with Hohenzollern rulers on two sides). Bismarck fanned the embers of the crisis he had hoped would lead to a war he considered inevitable and necessary (see Chapter 18). His carefully planned diplomacy was never more evident. The Russian tsar warmly remembered Prussian support during the Polish rebellion of 1863. The Austrians had not forgiven France for joining Piedmont-Sardinia in the war of 1859. Italy still resented the loss of Savoy and Nice in 1860 to the French. Bismarck played his real trump card with the British, coolly revealing documents proving that the French emperor had in 1866 demanded Belgium and Luxembourg as compensation for Prussia's increased power. This ended any chance of support for Napoleon III by the British government, which would never tolerate a potentially hostile power in Belgium, just across the English Channel. France went alone to war against Prussia. The ease of Prussia's victory was shocking. Following the surrender of two armies at the end of August and the beginning of September, Prussian forces besieged Paris. French resistance continued until January 28, 1871 (see Chapter 18).

Bismarck signed a convention with the provisional French government, awaiting the election of a National Assembly in France that could conclude a peace treaty. Bolstered by a surge of nationalist sentiment in the South German states as well as in Prussia, Bismarck demanded the annexation of Alsace and much of Lorraine, where German speakers predominated (although they did not necessarily want to be incorporated into a united Germany). The French had to pay war reparations of 5 billion francs, and France also lost a small mining district on its northern frontier.

The German Empire was officially proclaimed in the Château of Versailles on January 18, 1871. King William I of Prussia became Emperor William I of Germany. The North German Confederation and its constitution provided the framework for German unification. But this federalism existed in structure only, despite the rich traditions of German particularism (individual states with histories of independence and religious and cultural diversity). The German Empire took on the autocratic political structure of Prussia, characterized by the influence of Prussian nobles and military officers.

Industrialists and merchants now hoped that unification would provide a boost to large-scale industrialization in the new Germany. Hamburg merchants thus with some apprehension traded the traditional independence of their city for the economic advantages of operating within a centralized state. Unlike Cavour in Italy, who reached liberal political goals by liberal political means, Bismarck had harnessed economic liberalism to the goals of conservative political nationalism.

Germany would be an autocracy based on the alliance of throne and aristocracy, whereas Britain retained its liberal parliamentary government and France became a republic in the 1870s. Although many Germans remained indifferent to unification and others preferred the particularism of their region to the new Germany, over the long run, Germans came to accept with growing enthusiasm the politically unified state that had been forged by Bismarck's spectacularly successful statemaking. The result was a critical shift in the balance of power in Europe.

The empire had a parliament but the Reichstag had little real authority. Its members, elected by a franchise system that in Prussia grossly overrepresented landed interests, could not hold cabinet posts. The chancellor

William I and Bismarck celebrate the proclamation of the German Empire in the Hall of Mirrors at Versailles.

was not responsible to the Reichstag, but rather to the emperor. The Reichstag could not propose legislation. Foreign policy and military affairs remained in the hands of the emperor and the chancellor. The Reichstag's control over the budget could not limit the prerogatives of the throne. Each of Germany's twenty-five states sent a delegate to a federal council (*Bundesrat*), over which the chancellor presided. Although each German state—for example, Bavaria, which had a relatively liberal constitution— retained considerable administrative autonomy, as well as in some cases its own prince, the nature of the German imperial government remained solidly authoritarian. Germany's growing economic power was therefore unaccompanied by an evolution toward effective parliamentary government.

Junkers dominated the army and civil service. In exchange for loyalty, they were exempt from most taxation, receiving what amounted to state subsidies for their immense estates. Inevitably, as in England, noble economic clout declined with the agricultural depression and with the remarkably rapid industrialization of Germany, but Prussian Junkers retained their full measure of political power.

Unlike their counterparts in Victorian England and France, the German middle class largely remained outside political life in the German Empire, as they had been in Prussia before unification. Most middle-class Germans willingly acquiesced to imperial authority and noble influence. The rise of the Social Democrats was, in most cases, enough to keep the German middle class loyal to the empire, even if it meant allying with Prussian nobles. Many German industrialists and other magnates continued to look up to nobles in ways their French counterparts had long since abandoned. Some clicked their heels and tried to look like Junkers—a few dueling in the hope of picking up a stray aristocratic scar—and the emperor awarded some of them noble titles.

Nationalist versus Internationalist Movements

Chancellor Bismarck hated the Catholic Center and Social Democratic Parties. He doubted their loyalty, because he considered them internationalist and anti-nationalist: German socialists, in principle, expressed allegiance to socialists in other countries, and many Catholics expressed some degree of loyalty to the pope in Rome. The Catholic Center Party had been founded in 1870 in order to lobby for the rights of Catholics, who made up 35 percent of the German population, most living in Bavaria and the Rhineland. After the Church's assertion of papal infallibility in 1870, Bismarck believed that one day the pope might order German Catholics to not obey the government. In 1873, Bismarck launched a state campaign against Catholics (*Kulturkampf*). Priests in Germany henceforth had to complete a secular curriculum in order to be ordained, and the state would now recognize only civil marriage.

Subsequent laws permitted the expulsion from Germany of members of the Catholic clergy who refused to abide by discriminatory laws against Catholics. An assassination attempt against Bismarck by a young Catholic in 1874 and papal condemnation of the *Kulturkampf* the following year only hardened the chancellor's resolve. Furthermore, France, intent on regaining Alsace and Lorraine, was overwhelmingly Catholic.

A contemporary image of Bismarck pitted against the pope in his campaign against German Catholics.

Gradually Bismarck realized that he might in the future need the support of the Catholic Center Party against the Social Democrats. The chancellor quietly abandoned the *Kulturkampf*, although Catholics were still systematically excluded from high civil service positions, as were Jews. The state helped German Protestants purchase bankrupt estates in Prussian Poland so that they would not fall into the hands of Catholics, who made up most of the population there. Alsace and the parts of Lorraine annexed from France, where Catholics formed a solid majority, were administered directly from Berlin instead of being considered a separate state of the Reich.

Bismarck became obsessed with destroying the socialists, who had improved their gains in the elections, although they still held only a couple of seats in the Reichstag. Two attempts to kill Emperor William I in 1878 provided Bismarck with an excuse for his war on the socialists, although neither would-be assassin had even the slightest contact with the Socialist Party. The Reichstag obliged Bismarck by passing antisocialist legislation that denied socialists the freedoms of assembly, association, and of the press, and allowed individual German states to force socialist activists to change residence or go into exile. The police arrested socialists, shut down their newspapers and periodicals, and intimidated workers into quitting trade unions.

William II and German Nationalism

Following William I's death, Frederick III, a man of foresight and tolerance, reigned for only 100 days, tragically dying of throat cancer. In 1888, William II (ruled 1888–1918) became emperor. William, a Prussian autocrat who believed that "democratic principles can only create weak and

often corrupt pillars of society," held that "a society is only strong if it rec-
ognizes the fact of natural superiorities, in particular that of birth." Referring to himself as "an instrument of God," he boasted, "We Hohenzollerns
derive our crowns from Heaven alone and are answerable only to Heaven."

The German emperor compensated for a withered left arm with a love of
uniforms and swords. His education had proceeded in a hit-or-miss fashion
that mostly missed. William's favorite reading included the pseudo-scientific racist ramblings of the English writer Houston Stewart Chamberlain.
Like several of his Hohenzollern ancestors, William considered himself an
expert on military affairs, but, unlike them, he was not. He was lazy and
lacked the patience to concentrate on anything very long at all, talking at
great length superficially about any conceivable subject and rushing to conclusions without reflection. The Kaiser thrived on and encouraged unctuous
flattery. His lack of tact—he invariably referred to the diminutive King Victor Emmanuel III of Italy as "that dwarf"—was a common topic of conversation in imperial circles.

Bismarck lasted two years as William's chancellor. When Bismarck in
1890 sought a pretext to launch another campaign of repression against
the Social Democrats, the emperor, wanting to cultivate as much popularity as possible, preferred to win mass support by sponsoring more legislation that would improve working
conditions. After an unpleasant
confrontation in March, Bismarck resigned.

The iron chancellor's less able
successors were unable to keep
William from impulsively antagonizing Germany's rivals. The
emperor's personal foibles became
increasingly important as international relations entered a
new and dangerous stage. The
emperor personally contributed
to the rise of aggressive German
nationalism and the Anglo-German naval rivalry. William zipped
around Germany and the North
Sea eagerly reviewing troops and
christening ships. He enthusiastically supported the expansionist
goals of the Pan-German and
Naval Leagues. He asserted, "I
believe, as it is written in the
Bible, that it is my duty to

William II (*left*) and Franz Joseph (*right*).

increase [the German heritage] for which one day I shall be called upon to give an account to God. Whoever tries to interfere with my task I shall crush."

The alliance between Conservatives, National Liberals, and the Catholic Center Party provided the German emperor with a conservative base within the Reichstag. The National Liberals wanted a strong, secular state, and mistrusted parliamentary democracy. The resulting alliance between industrialists and agriculturists ("iron and rye") led to protectionist economic policies beginning in 1879, culminating in 1902 with a tariff that imposed a 25 percent duty on heavy industrial and food imports.

The German middle class remained considerably more socially conservative—indeed even apolitical—than its counterparts in the rest of Western Europe; no equivalent of the progressive British Liberal Party or the French Radical Party existed in Germany. Liberalism continued to be closely tied to the defense of small-town interests. The German Progressive Party, founded in 1910, earned lower-middle-class support, but it was too small and divided to have much influence.

In the meantime, the German conservatives became increasingly nationalistic and anti-Semitic. Following the economic crash of 1873, two years after Jews had received full legal emancipation with the proclamation of the empire, some newspapers had chosen Jewish bankers, industrialists, and rival publishers as scapegoats. The operatic composer Richard Wagner and his circle of friends were outspokenly anti-Semitic. Wagner believed that the theater (and composers) stood as a center of emotional national culture, which he did not believe included Jews. His works reflected growing right-wing German nationalism. Some Germans identified Jews with liberalism and socialism. In 1892, the German Conservative Party made anti-Semitism part of its party platform, despite the fact that most Jews were fully assimilated into German society. A Jewish industrialist remembered in 1911 that "in the youth of every German Jew there comes a painful moment that he never forgets, the moment when he realizes for the first time that he has entered the world as a second-class citizen and that neither his efforts nor his accomplishments will free him from this status. . . . [It is] the harshest thing one man can tell another. . . . 'Your blood, your soul, your sensibility has no place in our community, you are and will remain different, ignoble, alien.' "

Yet, in 1912, the Social Democrats won more seats in the Reichstag in 1912 than any other party. But many Social Democrats also seemed engulfed in the mood of nationalism that swept much of Germany, heightened by rivalry with Great Britain and the Second Moroccan Crisis of 1911, which brought Germany and France close to war (see Chapter 22). Socialist deputies voted for the prodigious augmentation of funds for naval expansion. Unlike French or Italian socialists, German socialists manifested little anti-militarism, giving every sign that they would support the government in time of war, particularly against Russia. The German Empire embodied the decline of liberalism, and the rise of aggressive nationalism in late nineteenth-century Europe.

NATIONAL AWAKENINGS IN THE HABSBURG LANDS

Whereas Germany and Italy were politically unified when astute leaders mobilized nationalist feeling within the upper classes and successfully carried out an aggressive foreign policy, nationalism threatened the very existence of the Habsburg monarchy. Ethnic tensions within the Austro-Hungarian Empire, the second largest European state, were in many ways those of Europe itself. In the meantime, the unification of Germany, as well as that of Italy, altered the balance of power in Central Europe. Unified Germany, not Austria, was now unquestionably the strongest state in Central Europe. Moreover, the absorption of Lombardy and Venetia into the new Italian state had come at the expense of the Austrian Habsburgs.

Diversity and Cohesion in the Habsburg Empire

The provinces that formed the Habsburg domains represented extraordinary linguistic, cultural, and historical diversity (see Map 17.3). Twenty nationalities lived within the territorial boundaries of the empire; these included Czechs in Bohemia and Slovaks to their east, Poles in Galicia, Slovenes, Croats, and Serbs in the south, Romanians and Ruthenians in the southeast, and Italians in the Alpine Tyrol, as well as Bulgarians, Turks, and Gypsies. But by far the two largest national groups were the Germans (35 percent of the population), living principally in Austria but numerous also in Bohemia, and the Hungarians, or Magyars (23 percent), whose traditional crown lands formed the largest territory in the empire. These lands were divided into five districts: Hungary, Croatia, Transylvania, the Vojvodina, and the Military Frontier. Yet the Germans and Hungarians were outnumbered by the various Slavic groups, who together accounted for about 45 percent of the empire's population. Czechs comprised 23 percent of Austria's population. In Hungary, Romanians (with 19 percent of the population) formed the next largest group after the Magyars (see Table 17.1). Inadequate transportation networks accentuated the insular and overwhelmingly rural nature of many ethnic regions—for example, there was no railroad between Vienna and the Croatian capital of Zagreb.

How did this polyglot empire hold together as long as it did among all of the competing ethnic rivalries and demands? The answers tell us something of the process of statemaking from the point of view of the nonnational state. First, the tradition of the Habsburg monarchy itself was an

MAP 17.3 NATIONALITIES IN THE HABSBURG EMPIRE   The diverse nationalities and lands encompassed by the Habsburg Empire during the 1860s and 1870s.

important force for cohesion, rooted in centuries of Central European history. Emperor Francis Joseph, who was eighteen when he came to power in 1848, had taken the second part of his name from his enlightened ancestor Joseph II in order to invoke the tradition of the House of Habsburg in those revolutionary times. As one Hungarian statesman put it during the Revolutions of 1848, "It was not the idea of unity that had saved the monarchy, but the idea of the monarchy that saved unity."

Second, the Habsburgs depended on the support of the German middle class and of the enormous German-speaking bureaucracy. The most salient cultural traditions (for example, music) of the imperial capital, Vienna, were overwhelmingly German. Viennese liberals celebrated their domination of Austrian political and cultural life during the 1850s and 1860s by building a broad boulevard, the Ringstrasse. The grand artery was built on the traces of the city's fortifications, which Francis Joseph had ordered dismantled in 1857, since they had long since lost all military function except to separate the wealthy center of the city from the proletarian suburbs. The new boulevard also took shape with military motives in mind—troops could be moved rapidly in the event of a working-class rebellion. The architecture of central Vienna reflected the taste of the aristocracy and the Catholic Church. In contrast, public buildings (including the university, the opera, and the parliament building) and residences of manufacturers and bankers that bordered the Ringstrasse reflected the secular cultural tastes of the Viennese upper classes.

The empire's largest towns, even outside of Austria, were largely German-speaking; in Prague, Germans outnumbered Czechs by more than three to one, although the percentage of Germans there declined during the second half of the century with the migration of more Czechs to the city. German was also the official language of the army (and of the secret police); more than half of the officers were native German speakers. To get anywhere, one had to speak German, a fact learned by thousands of non-German migrants to the cities. The German middle class also benefited from free-trade policies, and profited from the beginnings of industrial concentration in Bohemia.

Third, the monarchy enjoyed the support of Austrian and Hungarian nobles, as well as their Croatian, Polish, and Italian counterparts, landed nobles of ethnic groups with long histories of political sovereignty. The latter three nobilities depended on the Habsburg monarchy to maintain their prerogatives vis-à-vis ethnic minorities within their territories and against the peasants of their own nationality. Thus, the small Croatian nobility, which needed the cooperation of the Habsburgs for the retention of their own privileges in Croatia, had a long tradition of military service to the dynasty. (Croatia would in 1868 be given semi-autonomous status.) The monarchy therefore depended on the preservation of the status of the favored nationalities, above all, the Germans and Magyars, from the challenges of other national minorities within the lands of their domination, such as Slovenes, Slovaks, Ruthenians, Ukrainians, Serbs, and Czechs.

Fourth, Catholicism, the religion of the majority of the peoples of the Habsburg domains, was another factor for unity in Austria. The centuries-

TABLE 17.1. ETHNIC COMPOSITION OF THE AUSTRO-HUNGARIAN EMPIRE IN 1910 (IN MILLIONS)

Ethnic Group	Population	Ethnic Group	Population
Germans	12.0	Serbs	2.0
Magyars	10.1	Slovaks	2.0
Czechs	6.6	Slovenes	1.4
Poles	5.0	Italians	0.8
Ukrainians	4.0	Bosnian Muslims	0.6
Romanians	3.2	Others	0.4
Croats	2.9		

A view of Vienna and its Ringstrasse, 1873.

old support of the Catholic Church for the Habsburg dynasty also under-cut nationalist movements among predominantly Catholic nationalities like the Slovaks, Croats, and above all, the Poles. In the newly unified Germany, by contrast, the religious division between the Protestant north and the Catholic south represented a potential force for disunity.

Fifth, the imperial army retained considerable prestige (although, lack-ing adequate funds, it had proved more dashing on the parade ground than on the battlefield, as defeats by the French in 1859 and the Prussians in 1866 had demonstrated). The army helped hold the monarchy together. German speakers dominated the officer corps, as they did the bureau-cracy, holding 70 percent of military positions. Habsburg officers prided themselves on a military esprit de corps (interestingly enough, addressing each other by the familiar *Du* form, and not the more formal *Sie* that per-sisted in the German army). Soldiers, drawn from the different nationali-ties, continued to serve loyally in the army, which rarely was forced to intervene in local strikes, in contrast to the situation in France, where the army was unpopular with many workers. Francis Joseph, whose long rule was shaped by the fact that he had come to power as his monarchy seemed to be breaking apart, was as devoted to the army as it was to him.

Repression of Nationalism in the Habsburg Empire

In the 1850s and 1860s, nationalism among the ethnic minorities remained limited to a relatively small number of intellectuals and people from the liberal professions who had the literacy and leisure to dream of having a national state. As a Czech nationalist put it at a meeting of writers in Prague, "If the ceiling were to fall on us now, that would be the end of the national revival." Most nationalists at first aimed at a cultural and linguistic revival.

The Habsburg monarchy feared that demands for autonomy, or even outright independence, would pull the empire apart. Nationalism, which had frequently been tied to political liberalism, could also challenge the empire's authoritarian structure. German and Italian nationalism threatened the empire's territorial integrity by raising the possibility that the very small Italian and, above all, the German-speaking parts of the empire might prefer inclusion in Italy or Germany, respectively. Furthermore, Hungarians, the second-largest ethnic group within the empire, demanded political influence commensurate with the size of the Magyar territorial domains.

After the mid-century revolutions, the Habsburg monarchy, like the German states and France, continued an unrelenting repression of liberal and national movements. Beginning with Francis Joseph's accession to the Habsburg throne, the monarchy entered a period of "neo-absolutism," codified in the "Patent" of December 1851. Alexander von Bach (1813–1893), the minister of the interior (and essentially prime minister without the title), put some of the most potent tools of the state to work, including a hierarchy of officials and police sent out from Vienna into the imperial provinces. The nobles, some of whom resented the abrogation of peasant obligations after 1848, had in general welcomed the restoration of Habsburg authoritarianism. But they also had lost some of their regional privileges and prerogatives to the state. In 1855, Bach signed a Concordat with the Catholic Church, restoring many of its privileges and extending ecclesiastical authority, including the right of prelates to judge the clergy. As in France, the Church made a comeback. The monarchy eliminated civil marriage and restored the Church's *de facto* control over education. Protestants were not allowed to teach in Catholic schools, and new restrictions limited the right of Jews to acquire property.

A contemporary cynically described the Bach system: "The administration was run by a standing army of soldiers, a kneeling one of those praying in church to be acceptable to the government, and a crawling one of informers."

Political Crisis and Foreign Policy Disasters

In the wake of the defeat of Austrian forces in Italy and amid mounting hostility between Germans and non-Germans and the growing unpopularity of neo-absolutism, in August 1859 Francis Joseph dismissed Bach as the head of government. He then promulgated a new constitution, the October Diploma of 1860, which reestablished a form of conservative federalism. The provincial assemblies received new authority, placating the nobles. Nonetheless, the October Diploma did not satisfy the Hungarian aristocrats, who lacked the influence and political role enjoyed by German speakers who had benefited from the Bach system. One critic assessed this transition with cynicism: "Absolutism in bankruptcy put on a false constitutional nose in order to extract a few more pennies from the public."

Anton von Schmerling (1805–1893), minister of the interior, drafted the February Patent of 1861, a constitution that established a bicameral parliament in which all the empire's nationalities were to be represented. Yet the number of non-German representatives, as elected by the diets of the respective crown lands, would not equal those of the Germans, as electoral restrictions favored urban elites. Magyars, Croats, and Italians refused to participate in the first election, and Schmerling dissolved the regional parliaments. The February Patent perpetuated the most salient elements of Bach's neo-absolutism, including the German-speaking bureaucracy, police, and spies. It placed virtually no constitutional limitations on the emperor's power. One political crisis after another marked the mid-1860s, until Francis Joseph finally suspended the constitution in 1865.

While Bach's neo-absolutism made many internal enemies, foreign policy failures seriously undermined the monarchy's international position. The Habsburg monarchy's status as a power in European affairs declined as relations with Russia and Prussia deteriorated. In 1863, Schmerling expressed sympathy for the Poles in their struggle against Russia (in contrast to Bismarck's response, as we have seen). This pleased the Poles within the Habsburg empire but angered Tsar Alexander II. When his empire went to war with Prussia in 1866, Francis Joseph could not look for support from the tsar, or from the British or French, who were angry that Austria had joined Prussia against Denmark two years earlier.

Prussia's victory over Austria cast doubt on the efficiency of Bach's neo-absolutism and encouraged the other preeminent nationalities—particularly the Magyars, but also the Croats and Poles—to demand a greater share of political power, since the monarchy seemed to be floundering under the domination of German speakers. Humiliated twice in seven years on the field of battle (first by the French and Piedmontese in 1859 and then by the Prussians in 1866), some of Francis Joseph's subjects blamed the authoritarian structure of neo-absolutism for the defeat. Liberals called for the implementation of constitutional government, backing their demands by pointing to the inefficient way in which the wars had been fought.

Creation of the Dual Monarchy

The empire's military defeats heightened Magyar demands for more power. Fearing the possible alliance of German liberals with the Magyars, Francis Joseph had in 1865 met the Magyar demand for the reincorporation of

Transylvania into Hungary. He had already asked Ferenc Deák (1803–1876) to propose a solution that would reconcile Magyar demands with imperial power. Deák, a wealthy Magyar noble and lawyer, believed that Hungary's strength as a nation depended on the continued existence of the Habsburg monarchy. The emperor realized that as long as the Magyars remained dissatisfied and uncooperative, he could not contemplate a war of revenge against Prussia.

The Compromise (Ausgleich) of 1867 created the Dual Monarchy of Austria-Hungary. The Hungarian Parliament proclaimed Francis Joseph constitutional king of Hungary, as well as emperor of Austria. The bureaucracy in Vienna would continue to carry out matters of finance, foreign policy, and defense. Hungarian now became the language of administration in Hungary, and the Magyar domains henceforth had their own domestic bureaucracy, parliament, and constitution. Transylvania was brought within the administration of the kingdom. The halves of the Dual Monarchy would negotiate economic tariffs every ten years. The parliaments of Austria and Hungary elected representatives to the Imperial Assembly, or Delegation. The settlement was a victory for Hungarian liberalism.

The Ausgleich left intact the dominance of German speakers in Austria and Magyars in Hungary. While in principle recognizing the equality of all nationalities, the new constitution nonetheless maintained the disproportionate advantage enjoyed in the empire's parliament by Austria's Germans. The emperor routinely appointed Germans to important ministries, and he could easily circumvent parliamentary opposition by ruling by decree when parliament was not in session, or by refusing to sign any piece of legislation he did not like.

The Hungarian Constitution of 1867 allowed the Magyar nobles to hold sway in the Hungarian Parliament, since the emperor's powers as king of Hungary were now more limited. Hungarian ministers were not responsible to Francis Joseph, but rather to the Hungarian Parliament's lower house, which was elected by leading Magyar property owners. The Nationality Law of 1868 gave the peoples of each nationality the right to their own language in schools, church, and in government offices, but it did not recognize any separate political identity. The Croats and the South Slavs particularly resented the settlement. Growing tensions were reflected by the claim of one of the Austrian architects of the Ausgleich that "the Slavs are not fit to govern; they must be ruled." Many Serbs increasingly identified with Russia, which saw itself as the protector of all Slavs.

Ethnic Tensions and Nationalist Movements in the Dual Monarchy

Whereas most of the crises in France, Germany, Belgium, and Britain centered on the demands of workers for social reform, under the Dual Monarchy ethnic tensions generated continued political division stemming principally from Hungarian resentment of Austrian preeminence within the Dual Monarchy and the demands of the subordinate nationalities.

Beginning in the 1870s, Croatia, which was technically part of Hungary, sent five representatives to the sixty-member imperial Delegation, while the Slovenes, Serbs, and other minorities were left out. The Hungarian government relentlessly carried on with a program of Magyarization, ranging from dissolving non-Magyar cultural societies to banning non-Magyar names for villages and streets. Hungarian remained the official language and the government refused to allow administrative or cultural autonomy of the other nationalities. To an extent, the Magyarization campaign in Hungary was a reaction by Hungarians to this growing Pan-Slavist movement, combined with Hungary's resentment of its junior status in the Dual Monarchy.

Count Eduard von Taaffe (1833–1895), Austrian prime minister from 1879 to 1893, balanced off the competing interests of the varied nationalities. Czech nobles and intellectuals early in the century had worked toward a literary and linguistic revival, compiling and publishing Czech dictionaries and books of Czech grammar. Czech nationalists demanded recognition of the historic Kingdom of Bohemia. But opposition from German speakers in Bohemia, and from Magyars, who feared similar demands from minorities within Hungary, led Francis Joseph early in the 1870s to refuse such recognition. While ignoring demands by Slovaks and other smaller national groups for concessions to their languages, Taaffe placated the Czechs, the third largest ethnic group, by declaring their language on an equal footing with German in the state administration in Bohemia and Moravia in 1880. He also encouraged Czech schools and established a university in Prague (1882). But intellectuals within the "Young Czech" movement wanted national independence. In 1893, Taaffe resigned after the government had to declare martial law when Czechs demonstrated against the withdrawal of an edict, following protests by German speakers, that ordered officials to know both languages.

As movements of cultural nationalism grew, they almost inevitably added the goal of national independence. Since the Third Partition in 1795, Poles had been a subject people in the empires of Germany, Austria-Hungary, and Russia, where troops had crushed the Polish insurrection of 1863. Tsar Alexan-

An image in a Pan-Slav journal published in Vienna.

der II cracked down, forbidding the sale of lands to Poles or Catholics (priests had been among the insurgents), closing most monasteries, and not permitting the creation of *zemstvos* (elected councils) or juries in law courts, reforms applied to Russia. Polish nationalism revived during the 1880s, but the relatively favored position of Poles in Austrian Galicia (where they held sway over Ukrainians in eastern Galicia) and the dispersion of the Polish people in three empires reduced any immediate Polish threat to the Habsburgs.

The absorption in 1878 of Bosnia and Herzegovina into the Habsburg empire added a large Serb, as well as Muslim population, at a time when the Pan-Slav movement was growing in Russia and the Balkans. This increased demands from South Slavs—principally Serbs, Croats, and some Slovenes—that they be allowed to form an integral third part of the monarchy. Serbia had been virtually independent within the Ottoman Empire since 1828, when a Serb official who had put down a Serb insurrection was named hereditary prince of Serbia. Now, with Serbia's independence formalized in 1878, many Serbs wanted to be attached to Serbia, dreaming of a "Greater Serbia."

Hungarians demanded that their language be put on an equal footing with German in the army. At the turn of the century, Emperor Francis Joseph threatened to dissolve Hungary's parliament and to declare universal suffrage, believing that giving in to Hungarian demands would have meant the end of the Dual Monarchy. Relations between the aging Habsburg emperor and the Hungarian Parliament deteriorated, just as the Balkan Wars (1912–1913, see Chapter 22) and rampant South Slav nationalism soured relations between the Austro-Hungarian Empire and Russia. A visitor to the lower house of the Austrian Parliament in March 1914, recalled in amazement: "About a score of men, all decently clad, were seated or standing, each at his little desk. Some made an infernal noise violently opening and shutting the lids of these desks. Others emitted a blaring sound from little toy trumpets; others strummed Jew's harps; still others beat snare drums. And at their head, like a bandmaster, stood a gray bearded man of about sixty-five, evidently the leader of this willful faction, directing the whole pandemonium in volume and in tempo. The sum of uproar thus produced was so infernal that it completely drowned the voice of a man who was evidently talking from his seat in another part of the house, for one could see his lips moving, and the veins in his temple swelling. Bedlam let loose! That was the impression on the whole."

CONCLUSION

The unification of Italy and that of Germany had both largely been effected by the expansion of the most powerful of the states that would become part of the unified state that resulted. Yet the two cases were different, despite appearances. Camillo di Cavour first had transformed Piedmont-Sardinia into a liberal monarchy through reforms, before achieving the unification of Italy. Liberal Italy then struggled from one political crisis to the next, despite reforms, its expanding electoral franchise—which more than doubled in 1912—arguably adding even more division to those provided by the gap between north and south. The advent of Giovanni Giolitti as premier in 1903 stabilized Italian politics. Yet his system of electoral engineering undermined parliamentary politics. At the same time, socialists, growing in strength, opposed the liberal regime from the left, while nationalists attacked from the right. Whereas Cavour had achieved Italian unification through liberal political means, Otto von Bismarck had harnessed economic liberalism to the goals of conservative political nationalism in achieving the unification of Germany. Liberals had little influence in unified Germany. Although having universal male suffrage, Germany remained dominated by reactionary monarchs supported by reactionary Junkers, its Parliament (Reichstag) almost powerless against autocracy, despite the growth of a mass socialist party.

In the wake of the Revolutions of 1848, nationalism had proven itself a major force for unification in both Germany and Italy. In the Habsburg lands, however, nationalism was a force that came to challenge the very existence of the empire. In the age of militant nationalism, ethnic tensions within the Austro-Hungarian Empire would become those of Europe. Moreover, the Habsburg monarchy remained precariously placed between both recently unified states. Russia, the self-proclaimed protector of all Slavic peoples, stood to the east. In contrast, each of Europe's three other powers had been politically unified for centuries. Of the three, Britain and Russia had had no revolution in 1848. In contrast, France, the third, emerged from the tumultuous period with an authoritarian empire. In the next chapter, we will consider Britain, Russia, and France during the great period of change, 1850–1914.

CHAPTER **18**

THE DOMINANT POWERS IN THE AGE OF LIBERALISM: BRITAIN, RUSSIA, AND FRANCE

The Crystal Palace, a vast structure built of glass and iron in London's Hyde Park, housed the Exposition of 1851, the first world's fair. It stood 1,848 feet long, 408 feet across, and 66 feet high, and included a million square feet of glass, 3,300 columns, and 2,300 girders, all of identical size so they could be prefabricated. Gaslight provided illumination, and, for the first time, numerous public toilets were installed for the convenience of visitors. The machinery on exhibit, above all, captured the attention and imagination of observers, including Queen Victoria herself.

To many British subjects of Queen Victoria, the Great Exposition of 1851 stood for the ascendancy of Christianity, the British constitution, and free trade. It symbolized the social and economic transformation of one of the three most powerful states in Europe during the middle decades of the nineteenth century. Besides Britain, the other dominant powers during the age of liberalism were France, which was more slowly entering the industrial age, and Russia, which despite some significant reforms, remained an autocracy antithetical to liberalism. Great Britain was the quintessential liberal state. Britain's long tradition of constitutional monarchy, with the remaining authority of the monarch more than balanced by Parliament, reflected its liberalism and economic prosperity. There had been no revolution in 1848 in Europe's most liberal nation. Nor had there been a revolution in Russia, Europe's most autocratic state. In France and Britain, liberal reforms expanded the number of those eligible to vote in 1852 and 1867, respectively. In Russia, Tsar Alexander II shocked many of his own nobles by emancipating the serfs in

The Crystal Palace, symbol of the new industrial age.

1861. But unlike the political reforms enacted in Britain and France, the tsar's reforms did not significantly alter the autocratic nature of the Russian Empire. France during the period 1852–1870 was a strongly centralized empire, with Emperor Napoleon III determined to bring economic progress through the strong involvement of the state. Following a disastrous war against Prussia (1870–1871), the empire fell, replaced by the Third Republic, another liberal regime in which executive authority was left weak, in this case out of fear that yet another Napoleon might emerge. In contrast, Russia was an autocracy, a state in which the absolute authority of the tsar was limited only by bureaucratic inefficiency and the impossibility of reaching into every corner of the vast empire. Russian nobles dominated the backward peasant masses, and unlike Britain and France, Russia had only a tiny middle class and, despite economic growth, no representative political system. Yet Russia, too, was transformed by new ideas and increasingly courageous opponents of autocratic authority.

VICTORIAN BRITAIN

In 1840, young Queen Victoria (1819–1901) married the German Prince Albert (1819–1861) of Saxe-Coburg-Gotha. They were happily married, although she described sex as "giving way to the baser passions." Indeed, she warned one of her daughters who was about to be married that a bride was "like a lamb led to the slaughter," and that there would be times when she would simply have to submit to her husband's urges and "think of England." Victoria bore children only because she thought it part of her duties as queen. She raised her children with little visible affection, as if managing a business from afar.

Albert's tendency to be narrow-minded, socially awkward, and tactless irritated cabinet ministers and other highly placed people. He hovered about the government, dashing off letters and memoranda when the mood struck him, meddling when he could. Although Victoria made clear from the beginning that she would serve as a queen without a king, her devotion to Albert sparked some anti-German feeling in Britain.

Prince Albert organized the Great Exposition of 1851 in London. In his opening prayers, the Anglican archbishop made the connection between Britain's prosperity and the era of relative peace that had prevailed since the end of the Napoleonic Wars in 1815. More than this, Great Britain seemed special. The historian Thomas Macaulay wrote in the wake of the Revolutions of 1848 on the continent: "All around us the world is convulsed by the agonies of the great nations. . . . Meanwhile, in our island, the course of government has never been for a day interrupted. We have order in the midst of anarchy."

At the Great Exposition of 1851, more than 6 million visitors—most from Britain but a good many from the continent and beyond—could choose among more than 100,000 exhibits (half from Britain and its colonies, put forward by 14,000 exhibitors), divided into raw materials, machinery, manufactured goods, and fine arts, and ranging from useful household items to huge guns exhibited by the Prussian industrialist Krupp. These seemed somewhat out of place on an occasion in which many assured themselves that science and industry offered hope for continued peace in Europe.

The Great Exposition celebrated the industrial age, Britain's primacy in manufacturing, and the "working bees of the world's hive." Its catalogue intoned, "The progress of the human race . . . we are carrying out the will of the great and blessed God." The majority of the six million visitors to the Great Exposition, ranging from the wealthy and famous to poor folk paying just one shilling to enter, arrived by railroad.

When Albert died of typhoid in 1861 at age forty-two, Victoria was devastated. She retreated into lonely bereavement and isolation, spending—particularly in the early years of her widowhood—most of her time in a Scottish castle or on the Isle of Wight, ignoring most public duties. Only gradually did Victoria re-emerge to provide a focal point for a nation in the midst of a great transformation during the second half of the century.

Victoria knew virtually nothing about the lives of her subjects and instinctively disapproved of factory reforms and increased opportunity of education for the lower classes (fearing that it would lead them to want to raise their station in life). But the queen remained the personification of the "respectability" that gave her name to the Victorian age. "Respectability"—inculcated by education and contemporary literature—centered on the family and strict rules about public comportment. But it meant different things to families of different strata: three servants for a comfortable middle-class family, a parlor off the kitchen for breakfast for a lower-middle-class family, avoiding a pauper's funeral for a lower-class family (since to be buried "on the parish" was widely regarded as the ultimate stigma).

The Victorian Consensus

"Victorian," a term first used in 1851, the year of the Great Exposition, evokes a sense of the contentment and confidence that middle-class Britons enjoyed. For Britain, it was a confident time. The Victorian consensus was formed around the capitalist entrepreneurial ethic, emphasizing self-reliance and faith in progress. In the Victorian entrepreneurial ideal, the individual demonstrated his moral worth through hard work, in contrast to the evils of the old system of aristocratic patronage and parasitic behavior. Competition would determine those who were fit to rule, not aristocratic monopoly or unearned privilege, nor working-class demands for a greater share in the prosperity of the nation that middle-class Britons believed their hard work had created.

In 1859, the belief in the virtues of rugged individualism received a boost from the publication of *On the Origin of Species* by Charles Darwin (1809–1882). Darwin, the son of a domineering father, overcame chronic anxiety, self-doubt, and severe depression to undertake determined, systematic research and analysis on the evolution of living organisms. His bold book argued that some animal species survived and evolved by virtue of being better adapted to existing conditions, while others disappeared because they were less "fit." By implication, Darwin's work seemed to suggest that the state should stand back and let individuals alone to compete on the playing field of life. This was more good news for many confident

A contemporary impression of Darwin looking at human ancestry.

Victorians, but not for churchmen, for Darwin's book taught that mankind evolved from other animal forms over millions of years, thus challenging the Bible's description of God having created the world in seven days. Darwin's research and analysis were a major event in the battle between science and religion in nineteenth-century Europe.

Samuel Smiles (1812–1904) popularized these beliefs. "What some men are," the Scotsman insisted, "all without difficulty might be. Employ the same means, and the same results will follow." Trained as a physician, Smiles had published a biography of George Stephenson, the man who invented the first railway without knowing how to read. In 1859, Smiles published Self Help, which sold 20,000 copies in its first year and a quarter of a million copies by 1905. It was translated into Dutch, French, German, Arabic, Turkish, and several Indian languages. Smiles decried state interference in the operations of the economy. Laws, he insisted, could not "make the idle industrious, the thriftless provident, or the drunken sober." Such improvements could only be brought about by "individual action, economy, and self-denial, by better habits rather than by greater rights." Unemployment and low wages could, Smiles reasoned, serve the interests of the poor by forcing them to be thrifty and to save. Smiles's gospel of work nicely complemented *laissez-faire* economics, a cornerstone of Victorian thought.

Religious images and references permeated Victorian social and political discourse. Entrepreneurs believed that they were doing God's work by becoming successful and rich. Many Victorians insisted that the pervasive influence of religion more than prosperity explained the apparent social harmony of their age.

Thus, many Britons were surprised and even shocked by the results of a government survey of every church in England and Wales on a Sunday morning in 1851. The goal was to find out how many people went to church, and which denomination they embraced. Out of a population of almost 18 million people, only slightly more than 7.2 million had attended church. Even when the number of people who could not have attended services because they were infirm, sick, or attended religious services on a different day was taken into account, far more than half the population had stayed home. Moreover, the survey also revealed that if everybody in England and Wales had decided to attend church, only 58 percent of the population and only 30 percent of Londoners could be accommodated. Between 1841 and 1876, the Anglicans built 1,727 new churches and restored more than 7,000 old ones; among their rivals, Congregationalists and Catholics doubled the number of their churches, and Baptists multiplied their churches by five.

The Church of England, closely identified with the British elite, remained a target for liberal reformers. Parliament had repealed the Corporation and Test Acts in 1828, eliminating two significant discriminatory laws that had kept Dissenters (non-Anglican Protestants) who refused to take communion in the Anglican Church from holding office. Parliamentary decrees in 1854 and 1856 allowed non-Anglicans to attend Cambridge and Oxford Universities. Catholics, most of whom were Irish immigrants—in addition to a small number of nobles whose families had converted to Catholicism—still faced popular suspicion, however, reflecting the deep roots of anti-Catholicism in Britain.

Many middle-class Victorians wanted to make the lower classes more "moral." Congregationalist and Baptist evangelicals (as well as Methodists) won converts among the lower classes, perhaps because leaders of these churches demonstrated far more interest in the conditions of the poor than did the Church of England. Temperance movements proliferated in a wave of concern about lower-class drunkenness—one-third of all arrests were for drunk and disorderly conduct. The Charity Organization Society, founded in 1869, promoted charitable giving to those who steered clear of drink. And in 1875, the Salvation Army began its work, offering assistance to those who would participate in religious revival services.

The Crimean War

In 1854, Britain found itself involved in a war that ended the long peace that had lasted almost without interruption since Napoleon's defeat in 1815. Britain entered the Crimean War (1853–1856) to support the Turks against Russia, which had intervened in 1841 against Mehmet Ali, the pasha of Egypt (see Chapter 15). In 1853, Russian forces occupied the Ottoman Danubian principalities of Moldavia and Wallachia (see Map 18.1) in order to solidify the Russian Empire's position in the Balkans.

The Russian Empire had since the eighteenth century sought control over the Straits of Constantinople, which divide Europe from Asia, and could provide the Russian navy with access to the Aegean and Mediterranean Seas. Such ambitions inevitably would bring conflict with the Ottoman Empire, which had controlled virtually the entire Balkan region until the early nineteenth century, and would continue to maintain a foothold there until the first two decades of the twentieth century.

Following defeat after the Greek revolt in the 1820s, Ottoman rulers had undertaken a series of major reforms of the army (after having replaced the janissary corps—the court militia which had originally been formed of Christians who converted to Islam—with an army in 1826) and imperial administration. Sultan Mahmud II (ruled 1808–1839) had reorganized the treasury and ordered a census of the empire (1831). Mahmud II's successors decreed further reforms during the period known as Tanzimat—the "Reorganization"—that lasted from 1839 to 1878. By the Rose Chamber (Gulhane) Decree of 1839, the sultan guaranteed the life and property of all Ottoman subjects and their equality before law, while initiating military conscription and a more organized system of taxation. Penal

MAP 18.1 THE CRIMEAN WAR, 1853–1856   Russian, British-French-Piedmontese, and Austrian troop movements involved in this war between the great powers.

and commercial codes and the reform of justice followed. Such reforms pleased Britain and France, whose governments viewed the stability of the Ottoman Empire as necessary to tempering Russian dreams of further expansion toward Constantinople and the Bosporus and Dardanelles straits. Moreover, the reforms centralized the authority of the sultan's government, reducing the autonomous power of the governors and creating a modern bureaucracy.

A century earlier, perhaps as much as 80 percent of the population of the Ottoman Empire in Europe had been Christian. Each religion had the right to worship freely, a toleration that often was not found in Western Europe, and non-Muslims had access to Islamic courts. Christians and Muslims got along for the most part very well. The structure of the Empire had for centuries encouraged the conversion of Christians to Islam, because Christians were considered second-class subjects and faced a heavier tax burden then did Muslims. Intermarriage was fairly frequent. In the late eighteenth century, the sultans had begun to tighten their control over the various religions in the Empire. Each religious community—Greek Orthodox, Jewish, and Armenian—was organized into what became known as the "millet" system. Now the sultan brought the hierarchy of Muslim religious and cultural leaders (the *ulema*) under administrative control, allowing the state access to some of the wealth of the Islamic empire. In addition, stories of persecution of Muslim minorities in Russia and suspicion of the Western powers contributed to the gradual emergence of Islamism in the Ottoman Empire, and leaders began calling for a return to the fundamental religious values of Islam. Economic development brought the emergence of a group of prosperous merchants who turned away from and even rejected the organization of communities along religious lines. Officials (*memurs*) replaced the old Ottoman ruling class, which had originally been drawn from the servants of the sultan's household, who had held positions in the imperial administration and army. The Ottoman ministries of the interior, finance, and foreign affairs, among others, reflected Western influence. The reorganization of the army extended the reach of the Ottoman state in the provinces.

Yet the relative decline of the Ottoman Empire seemed probable, if not increasingly inevitable. Russia stood poised like a vulture to profit from its once-powerful neighbor's weakness, a situation that came to be called the "Eastern Question." Egged on by nationalists, Russia presented itself as the protector of Slavic and Orthodox Christian interests in the Balkans, encouraging agitation against the Turks.

Britain had opposed expanding Russian interests in the region since the late eighteenth century because the British feared that such expansion threatened the European balance of power. By the 1830s, increased British trade with the Ottoman Empire had become another factor in British support for the Turks. With India its most vital colony and with interests in Afghanistan, Britain was ill disposed to the expansion of Russian influence. Napoleon III of France, eager for a military victory to solidify support for his regime, also stood ready to stop Russian expansion by supporting the Ottoman Empire. More than this, the French emperor saw himself as the protector of the Catholic Holy Places of Judea, which were under Ottoman authority. In particular, to placate Catholic supporters, he demanded at least Catholic equality with the Orthodox religion in the Jerusalem Church of the Holy Sepulcher. This Russia refused, demanding the right to veto any changes in the status not only of the Holy Places but also in the situation of the entire Ottoman Christian population.

The Ottoman Empire declared war on Russia in October 1853. Russian Tsar Nicholas's fleet defeated the Ottoman fleet in the Black Sea, setting fire to the sultan's wooden ships with incendiary shells. But the tsar's confidence that Britain and France would soon quarrel because of conflicting interests proved ill founded. With British public opinion eager for the flag to be shown even after the withdrawal of Russian troops from Moldavia and Wallachia, the British Royal Navy sailed into the Black Sea. Not to be outdone, Napoleon III, too, sent warships.

Britain and France declared war on Russia. British and French forces first moved against the Russian port of Sebastopol on the peninsula of Crimea on the edge of the Black Sea. Invulnerable to sea attack, Sebastopol could only be stormed from land. The rusty invading armies lay siege to Sebastopol, fighting a war that would have been comic in its mismanagement by aged, inept commanders if it had not cost so many lives. The French army seemed vastly better trained, as well as better fed and supplied than that of the British. The senior British commander, a veteran of Waterloo forty years earlier, persisted in referring to the Russians as "the French." Most British officers owed their commissions to the fact that they were aristocrats, not to their competence. One commander spent each night on his private yacht anchored offshore, dining on meals prepared by a French chef while his men shivered in the wind and mud of the Crimean winter.

Far more men died (about 600,000) of disease than in battle, although Alfred Tennyson (1809–1892), Britain's poet laureate, helped make famous the "Charge of the Light Brigade," in which British cavalry rode into "jaws of death." Freezing soldiers trying to eat ghastly rations and those wounded in battle seemed to face almost equal risks. The first war correspondents sent dispatches by telegraph to eager readers in Britain and France, where interest in the distant siege dramatically increased newspaper circulation.

Into this maelstrom ventured Florence Nightingale (1820–1910). The daughter of a prosperous family, she had shocked her parents by declaring

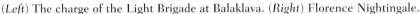

(*Left*) The charge of the Light Brigade at Balaklava. (*Right*) Florence Nightingale.

her intention to become a nurse, an occupation that had a particularly bad reputation as providing a refuge for "disorderly" women. Nightingale volunteered for service in a Constantinople hospital after hearing of the appalling conditions endured by the wounded and those sick with cholera and dysentery. She bombarded the government with highly detailed information on what was wrong and what was needed. Raising funds through private contributions, she succeeded in improving conditions in the hospital, ensuring a sufficient supply of medical equipment and clothing. She had to overcome the conviction of officers that she would "spoil the brutes," that is, the sick and wounded enlisted men, as well as overcoming prejudices against a woman making forceful demands on the government.

The British government several years later enacted a series of reforms to improve food and health care for the men in its army. As a result of Florence Nightingale's highly publicized work throughout the remainder of her career, nursing emerged as a more respected profession.

The Crimean War ground to a halt after Sebastopol finally capitulated in September 1855. The Peace of Paris (March 1856) guaranteed the autonomy of the Danubian principalities of Moldavia and Wallachia (which became independent Romania in 1878), the independence of Turkey, and the neutrality of the Black Sea. The Crimean War left little doubt that Victorian Britain remained Europe's strongest power.

The Liberal Era of Victorian Politics

In Britain, political reform followed compromise, not revolution. Most Victorians of all social classes increasingly felt themselves part of a nation with which they could identify; they were therefore not attracted by political extremes. In contrast to their French counterparts before the Revolutions of 1830 and 1848, English middle-class liberals avoided at all costs prodding workers into street confrontations with authority, fearful of unwittingly unleashing an uncontrollable insurrection. Chartism, the mass petition movement in the 1840s for universal male suffrage, had its last gasp in 1848. The government arrested suspected radicals, sent 8,000 troops into London, and appointed 150,000 civilian "special constables." Businessmen, anticipating trouble from a Chartist demonstration, hauled out hunting rifles and barricaded their offices. In any case, with the exception of a very small radical component in favor of the use of "physical force," the Chartists were gradualists. The Irish nationalist movement, dormant since a failed insurrection in 1798, reawakened in 1848. But the presence of the British army and the emigration of great numbers of Irish to the United States limited Irish nationalists' efforts in that revolutionary year to one minor uprising.

Despite the Crimean War, Britain entered a period of relative social harmony. The repeal of the Corn Laws in 1846 convinced many workers that they could place their trust in political reform. Middle-class reformers had broadened their appeal to include the most prosperous segments of the working class. Most British workers seemed to accept the belief that hard work and savings would inevitably be rewarded.

British workers, including many union members, joined "friendly societies," or as they were increasingly called, "self-help associations." Membership in such groups rose from less than a million in 1815 to 3 million in 1849 and 4 million in 1872, four times that of unions. They provided members with minimal assistance in times of unemployment or illness and a decent burial. Preaching individual self-help and respectability, such organizations did not offer the socialist vision common among workers in France, Belgium, or the Rhineland. They helped inculcate a sense of what the British called "respectability," and they also discouraged militancy.

Like the friendly societies, Britain's "new model unions" also embodied the concept of self-help. Members of these unions first and foremost saw their organizations as representing skilled workers of specific crafts, not the working class as a whole. Most members in Britain lacked the class consciousness found in comparable organizations in France and parts of Germany. Unions brought together craftsmen and skilled workers (such as carpenters and printers) from the "aristocracy of labor," who could afford high dues. Constituting about 15 percent of the working class, these craftsmen and skilled workers stood apart from the mass of unskilled laborers. Some of them taught in Sunday schools, working men's colleges, reading rooms, and improvement societies.

Even when local unions within a single trade joined to form national organizations, there was no talk of revolution or even of eventually restructuring British economic, social, and political life. Strikers in the 1860s were increasingly willing to accept arbitration boards and to compromise to achieve limited goals.

Benefiting from the 1832 enfranchisement of more middle-class men, the Whigs governed Britain for most of the 1850s and 1860s. Henry John Temple (1784–1865), the Viscount Palmerston, who began his political career as a Conservative, led the Whigs in the early 1850s. The notorious philandering of the shrewd and feisty "Lord Cupid," as he was known to his detractors, stood out in an age of public prudishness. Palmerston outraged Queen Victoria by trying to seduce one of her ladies-in-waiting in Windsor Castle.

Palmerston held together a coalition of Whigs who were determined to uphold laissez-faire economic policies. Dissenters, Catholics, and liberal Anglicans wanted the Anglican Church to lose its status as the Established Church of England. Gradually these Whigs began to be referred to as the Liberal Party.

Palmerston's bellicose saber-rattling won him personal popularity. Crowds cheered when he ordered the blockade of the Greek port of Piraeus in 1850 to enforce claims against the Greek government by Don

Pacifico, a British-born Portuguese Jew whose house an Athens mob had destroyed. Palmerston triumphantly defended himself in the House of Commons, boastfully comparing the might of classical Rome and Victorian Britain, which had remained one of the "protecting powers" of Greece since Greek independence in 1832. Following the overthrow of King Otto in 1854, Britain, France, Bavaria, and Russia selected a Danish prince to rule Greece as King George I, while placating Greek nationalists with the awarding of the Ionian islands to Greece.

After glorying in the unjustified credit he received for Britain's victory in the Crimean War, Palmerston then lurched into a short war against China in 1857, after the Chinese government seized a pirate ship that had formerly been registered under the British flag. Considering this a major insult to Britain, but rebuffed by a majority in Commons and opposed by pacifist political radicals outside of Parliament, Palmerston refused to resign and called for a general election. Basing his campaign on an appeal to patriotism, he won the day.

William Gladstone (1809–1898) then became the leader of the Liberal Party. Gladstone was the son of a wealthy and unscrupulous merchant who had made a fortune in trade with India and the West Indies. The young Gladstone was deeply religious and wore his moral vision of the world on his sleeve for all to see, going out into the night to try to convince prostitutes to abandon their trade. Gladstone sought to impose his own self-discipline and sense of Victorian Christianity on the nation. During his early years in government, he worked to assure laissez-faire economic policies, campaigning for the abolition of even the very modest income tax.

As chancellor of the Exchequer, Gladstone had waged war against extravagance and waste in government. In contrast to his Conservative rivals, he opposed colonization as being too expensive. Queen Victoria loathed Gladstone, blaming him for almost every domestic and international problem. She resented his *de facto* campaign to reduce the already limited role of the monarchy in the constitutional government of Britain. Having supported the repeal of the Corn Laws in 1846, he wanted to make the Liberals the party of reform.

Robert Peel had split the Conservatives by supporting the repeal of the Corn Laws in 1846. After Peel's death in 1850, Benjamin Disraeli (1804–1881) became the leader of the Conservatives and Gladstone's great rival. A Jew who had been baptized into the Anglican Church, Disraeli seemed an unlikely leader of a party dominated by landed wealth. But he was an energetic, skilled politician and an impressive orator who had the good sense to realize that further Conservative attempts to revive economic protectionism were doomed. Unlike Gladstone, Disraeli got along famously with the queen, whom he flattered on every possible occasion. Victoria depended upon Disraeli for advice much as she had on Albert. (As Disraeli lay dying, the queen wrote to ask if she might visit the Conservative

(*Left*) William Gladstone, Liberal prime minister. (*Right*) Benjamin Disraeli.

leader. "It is better not," Disraeli replied, "She'd only ask me to take a message to Albert.")

The Reform Bill of 1867

Since 1832, the majority of British subjects had regarded further political reform as virtually inevitable. A growing number of middle-class voters, hoping to end disproportionate aristocratic influence in British political life, supported some expansion of the suffrage. Workers wanted universal male suffrage. As for Queen Victoria, she insisted she "cannot and will not be the queen of a democratic monarchy." John Bright (1811–1889), who represented Manchester and then Birmingham in the House of Commons, campaigned for electoral reform. In 1866, the National Reform Union, whose membership was overwhelmingly middle class, and the Reform League, which many artisans had joined, allied with Bright's parliamentary radicals. Their goal was household suffrage, that is, the right of the adult male head of each family to be able to vote.

Gladstone, typically, was convinced that political reform was not only expedient but also moral. "You cannot fight against the future," the Liberal leader taunted Conservatives in Parliament, "Time is on our side. The great social forces . . . are against you." But he wanted to let down the electoral drawbridge only long enough to let in artisans and skilled workers, the "aristocracy of labor."

Conservatives feared that the enfranchisement of more ordinary people would not only add to the ranks of the Liberals but would eventually lead to subsequent legislation that might weaken the political influence of wealthy landowners. The Liberal government proposed a bill to reduce the minimum amount of tax one had to pay to be eligible to vote both in the countryside and in towns, where the rate would be set lower. The proposed reform, then, would still exclude ordinary workers and other poor people. The House of Lords rejected the bill because a majority of members opposed any change.

Disraeli, who six years earlier had predicted that "pillage, incendiarism, and massacre" would follow universal male suffrage in Britain, now believed that electoral reform that maintained some exclusions was not only inevitable but that his Conservative Party could benefit from it. It might bring about a return to the aristocratic leadership and patronage that seemed to have all but disappeared in the Liberal-sponsored free-for-all of laissez-faire. Disraeli took a "leap in the dark," proposing that the vote be given to each head of a household and that the minimum countryside tax requirement be further lowered. Under Conservative auspices, the Reform Bill of 1867 passed, like that of 1832, again doubling the ranks of voters. This, however, still left Britain short of universal male suffrage.

In France at the same time, every adult male could vote during the Second Empire, to be sure. But there Emperor Napoleon III cynically manipulated universal male suffrage by presenting government-sponsored candidates and utilizing that old Bonapartist tool, the plebiscite. The German Empire, too, had universal male suffrage, but the Reichstag (Parliament) had little real authority. In Russia, there were no national elected bodies at all, and local assemblies (*zemstvos*) initiated in 1864 were elected by local electoral colleges but were dependent upon officials named by the tsar. In Italy, only a tiny percentage of adult males were eligible to vote, by virtue of their ownership of property. In contrast with these other powers, the reformed electoral system in Britain had not only enfranchised many more voters, but gave them power through the vote, because the House of Commons exercised great authority in the context of Britain's constitutional monarchy. Here, too, Britain seemed to lead the way in the gradual emergence of democratic politics.

Disraeli's Conservatives, however, failed to woo many of the new voters, and their leader resigned. The Liberals won a large majority in Parliament, boosted by support from workers who now could vote. The major goal of the Chartist campaign more than two decades earlier had now been reached, giving further impetus to British reform, not revolution.

Another act of reform in 1884 added 2 million more voters to the rolls by enfranchising agricultural laborers, among others excluded by the second Reform Act of 1867. With women still excluded from the vote, the only adult males who could not vote were those without a fixed residence, sons living at home with their parents and not paying rent, and domestic servants. The Redistribution Act of 1885 disenfranchised some underpopulated districts while increasing the representation of many urban areas. However, the establishment of single-member constituencies compensated Conservatives, balancing potential Liberal gains in urban areas.

Early Reform in Victorian Britain

The Victorian consensus rested upon a strong belief that the "invisible hand" of the economy would generate economic growth. Many Victorians therefore believed the Poor Law of 1834 was self-defeating because it provided resources to the poor for which they had not worked. But increasingly aware of the devastating poverty of millions of workers, most middle-class Victorians by mid-century had changed their minds about the role of government in society. Edwin Chadwick (1800–1890), a journalist and associate of Jeremy Bentham, had drafted the Poor Law and served as one of the Poor Law commissioners; he compiled a *Report on the Sanitary Condition of the Laboring Population of Great Britain* (1842). This pathbreaking investigation served as an impassioned plea for government action after cholera had ravaged poorer urban neighborhoods. Largely thanks to Chadwick's efforts, Parliament passed laws facilitating the inspection of rooming houses, where many poor workers resided.

Thereafter, parliamentary commissions began to call upon "experts" to gather information and assess conditions of British life. The age of statistics had arrived. Regulatory agencies began to spring up. In 1848, Parliament passed the first national health act, creating the national General Board of Health.

Chadwick's revelations about public health—or rather, the lack of it—encountered ferocious opposition from those who were against any government intervention in such things as a matter of principle. "We prefer to take our chance on cholera and the rest than be bullied into health,"

Street disinfectors in London, 1875.

groused *The Times*. Yet, by the time Chadwick was driven to resign from the General Board of Health in 1854, the right of the state to intervene in matters of health had been established. Parliamentary acts in the 1860s extended regulations of working conditions in mines and in factories with more than fifty employees and where women and children worked. The Public Health Act of 1866 gave local government more authority to assure a cleaner water supply. Five years later, state inspectors for the first time obtained legal access to workplaces. A year later, Parliament established health boards in towns and country districts, but local business and political interests often combined to foil the efforts of doctors and other reformers. Reform leagues, such as the National Education League, which urged Parliament to act in the interest of education, became part of British political life.

In the wake of the Conservative defeat following the passage of the Reform Act of 1867, the Liberals, with a mandate to enact more reforms, ended the purchase of army commissions; they enacted land reform in Ireland and the government recognized the legal existence of trade unions. When the Conservatives returned to power in 1874, they, too, sought to woo the allegiance of workers from the Liberals by getting Parliament to approve a number of reforms, including a law that forbade labor by uneducated children.

Gradually, Victorian middle-class liberals had come around to the view that social reform was necessary. In part, the acceptance of reform followed the religious view that one should "do unto others," as well as the prevalent belief in progress. Furthermore, hit-or-miss elite assistance to the poor no longer seemed sufficient to address the complex problems engendered by industrialization and urbanization. Samuel Smiles may have been an outspoken proponent of the entrepreneurial ideal and of laissez-faire economic policies, but he, too, came to accept the necessity of minimal reforms.

Yet considerably more than altruism lay behind a shift in middle-class attitudes. An Evangelical reformer put it this way: "The middle classes know that the safety of their lives and property depends upon their having round them a peaceful, happy, and moral population." Manufacturers also knew that demand for their products depended on workers having money to spend. In Great Britain, the "age of optimism" became the "age of improvement."

Queen Victoria once asked someone to define "bureaucracy," a term she did not know. "That, Madam," came the reply, "is something that they have in France." Yet the Victorian state grew in its reach. In 1841, the British government—the least centralized of the major European powers—had employed 40,000 men and 3,000 women; by 1911, 271,000 men and 50,000 women worked for the state. The administration of the Poor Law itself served to strengthen the role of government in local affairs. The municipal councils took over tasks of administering local government from the justices of the peace, who had served in such capacity since the sixteenth century. Municipalities were now responsible for education, as well as for health, housing, roads, and policing. Service in local government, once little more than another honor awarded a landed gentleman, now required the participation of paid officials.

With increased responsibilities, the British civil service became professionalized. The government administered competitive examinations on which appointment and promotion depended. However, competitive examinations did not democratize entry into the civil service. Applicants who had attended one of the expensive elite public schools (so called because they accepted students from all over Britain, provided their families could afford the steep tuition) had a far greater advantage on the examinations than those who had not.

Despite presiding over the Victorian age of reform with crusading zeal, William Gladstone remained convinced to the end, like many Liberals, that the charitable efforts of individuals were preferable to government action. In one of his last letters, he wrote, "Of one thing I am and always have been convinced—it is not by the State that man can be regenerated, and the terrible woes of this darkened world effectually dealt with." But the role of the British state had nonetheless expanded considerably during the middle decades of the century. The era of laissez-faire liberalism ended. Speaking of her father, Gladstone's daughter remembered, "I was accustomed to hear him utter the word 'Government' in a tone that charted it with awe and made it part of my effective religion."

Mass Politics Come to Britain

Out of office following passage of the 1867 Reform Act, Benjamin Disraeli sought to accommodate conservatives to the era of mass political life. Realizing that his party, which had long been almost exclusively based in the British landed elite and closely tied to the Anglican Church, would have to outbid their Liberal rivals for votes or be condemned to oblivion, he created a modern national party organization and expanded the popular appeal of his party, in part by supporting certain reforms. Disraeli made British nationalism and imperialism part of the Conservative Party platform. He affirmed his support for "maintaining the greatness" of the empire and suggested that the Liberals, because of Gladstone's anti-imperialist views, would weaken Britain. When the Turks and Russians began to quarrel over the Balkans, Disraeli supported the Turks, despite the massacre of about 10,000 to 15,000 Bulgarians in 1876 by Turkish troops. Gladstone, however, was horrified by the bloodbath and made a political issue of the Balkans. It was easy enough for him to do so: Britain had less to fear from the Ottoman Empire in decline than from an aggressively expansionist Russia.

The Conservative Party now reflected an important change in modern British political life. The traditional split between "city" and "country," which had characterized politics since the seventeenth century, had largely ended. The Conservatives now found new support among some of the wealthiest businessmen, who abandoned the Liberals. Furthermore, many aristocrats were themselves now actively involved in the management of banks and modern industries. The English business elite that had been formed during the first decades of Victoria's reign became as conservative as the aristocrats they emulated. A contemporary assessed this evolution when he wrote: "Our territorial nobles, our squires, our rural landlords great and small, have become commercial potentates; our merchant princes have become country gentlemen." Some wealthy businessmen deserted the Dissenters to join the Established Anglican Church. This new Conservative political culture, supported by a faithful minority of nationalist "Tory workers," survived the economic and social changes that were transforming Britain.

Gladstone himself embarked on whistle-stop "Midlothian" campaigns—so named for one of his first stops in 1879. His audiences were made up of anyone who wanted to come to the railroad station to hear him. This forced Conservatives even more to put aside their feelings that such appeals to ordinary people were vulgar, too "American."

Yet the Conservative Party remained the party of great landed wealth. The law of primogeniture helped keep huge estates intact. Because of parliamentary districting, the countryside remained overrepresented in Parliament, again to the advantage of landed gentlemen. In 1871, about 1,200 people owned a quarter of the land of England, and the holdings of 7,000 families amounted to half of the country. Landed gentlemen dominated the House of Commons until 1885, the cabinet until 1893, and the aristocratic House of Lords well into the twentieth century.

Irish Home Rule

Despite the reforms achieved by the Liberals, they continued to be faced with the problem of Ireland, which reflected the dilemmas of national identity in late nineteenth-century Europe. In 1868, William Gladstone had announced that the most pressing mission of his new government was to "pacify Ireland." A year later, the Liberal prime minister pushed through both houses of Parliament a bill that disestablished the Church of Ireland (which had become part of the United Church of England in 1800), since Ireland was 80 percent Catholic. This meant that the Episcopal Church no longer received state support. But to many Irish it seemed that only by owning land could Irish peasants reach any degree of prosperity. The Irish Land Act of 1870 provided tenants with compensation for improvements they had undertaken and protected them from being evicted from property without just cause. But English landlords were not about to turn over land in Ireland to the peasants who rented from or worked for them. The fall in the price of agricultural commodities made it more difficult for tenant-farmers to meet their rent payments. In 1879, the Irish Land League, drawing on the remnants of the secret Irish Republican Brotherhood (known in Gaelic as the Fenians) and sworn to win independence, began to pressure Parliament for gradual land reform.

Gladstone's determination to make Ireland his ongoing moral crusade met with opposition within his own Liberal Party, which depended on support from Whig landowners in Ireland to maintain a parliamentary majority over Conservatives. Charles Stewart Parnell (1846–1891), a Liberal Irish Protestant, began to build a small parliamentary coalition in favor of Home Rule, which meant the establishment of a separate Irish Parliament, but not outright independence. The Irish Catholic Church supported Home Rule. Parnell's program, however, fell short of the demands of the Land League, which wanted immediate and sweeping land reform, and the revived Irish Republican Brotherhood, which insisted on complete Irish independence.

During 1879–1882, Irish farmers undertook a "land war" of protest. Irish tenants and laborers began to shun farmers who took over the leases of peasants evicted for nonpayment of rent. A certain Captain Boycott, the agent of a large landowner, was one of the first targets; his name became synonymous with such a strategy. The British government replied with repression, suspending the writ of *habeas corpus* in Ireland in 1881. However, that same year, Gladstone also pushed through a bill (by threatening to dissolve Parliament) protecting any Irish tenant from eviction who could pay one year's back rent. But Irish leaders now wanted independence rather than reform. Parnell was sent to prison for his violently anti-British speeches. Moreover, opposition to Home Rule mounted in Parliament among MPs who argued that concessions had encouraged violence. A year later, the British government ordered Parnell's release from prison, in the hope that he would help end disorder in Ireland in exchange for the future passage of a bill to help tenants.

In 1882, Irish republicans hacked to death two British officials who had been walking in Phoenix Park in Dublin after having just arrived in Ireland. The assassinations shocked the English public. In response to the murders, and to more than thirty other deaths in Ireland at the hands of Irish republicans, a Coercion Act facilitated the British government's repression of the republicans by eliminating some rights of arrested individuals. Five of those responsible for the Phoenix Park assassinations were arrested and hung.

British Liberals remained divided over Home Rule. Gladstone, already under Conservative attack because forces sent to relieve General Charles "Chinese" Gordon in the Sudan had arrived too late to save the popular British hero (see Chapter 21), resigned from government in 1885. But Gladstone returned to power in 1886, convinced that nothing less than

A government reporter being protected by the Royal Constabulary during a raucous meeting of Charles Parnell's supporters.

Home Rule would bring peace to Ireland, as well as keep Irish voters in the Liberal camp. He proposed a Home Rule bill intended to establish an Irish Parliament and allow Irish control over most affairs of government but that stopped short of outright independence. The bill did not pass, and Gladstone's government fell as Home Rule divided the Liberal Party. In 1885, the Liberal maverick Joseph Chamberlain (1836–1914), a successful manufacturer and mayor of Birmingham who wore a monocle in his right eye and an orchid in his buttonhole, led the defection of the "Liberal Unionists" from the Liberal Party over the issue of Home Rule. Obsessed with his fear that Britain's imperial power would decline, he believed Irish Home Rule might start a chain reaction that could bring about the collapse of the British Empire.

After the failure of the first Home Rule bill in 1886, the Conservatives formed a government. When in 1892 the elderly Gladstone became prime minister for the fourth and last time, he again proposed Home Rule. However, he had split with Charles Parnell, who had fallen into public disrepute when it was learned in 1889 that the Irish leader had long been a lover of Kitty O'Shea, the wife of an Irish Liberal MP active in the campaign for Home Rule. Captain William O'Shea had filed for divorce, naming Parnell as co-respondent. The scandal ruined Parnell, taking away his political influence. This tipped the balance against Home Rule. Although the bill passed the House of Commons in 1893, it was tripped up in the House of Lords.

New Contours in British Political Life

Queen Victoria's longevity—she ruled Britain and its vast empire from 1837 until 1901—symbolized British social and political stability. She ruled with dignity, also endearing herself to her people on the occasion of her silver jubilee in 1887 by wearing a simple bonnet (albeit one with diamonds) instead of her crown. The Prince of Wales inherited the throne as King Edward VII (ruled 1901–1910). Edward could not have been more different from his mother, with whom he constantly battled and whom he often embarrassed. He indulged his extravagant tastes in prize horses, good food, fine wines, gambling, and beautiful women.

The Conservatives again came to power in 1895, and retained the reins of government for ten years. Some Liberals now joined the Conservative Party. Like their counterparts in France and Germany, the British Conservative Party became aggressively nationalist, imperialist, and resolutely antisocialist. The Liberal Unionists had allied with the Conservatives over Home Rule. In 1895, their leader Joseph Chamberlain joined the Conservative government as colonial secretary.

Frustrated by the Conservative government's refusal to initiate parliamentary bills of social reform and by employers' attempts to weaken the unions by hiring non-union labor, British trade unionism entered a more aggressive phase during the last two decades of the nineteenth century. British trade unions during the middle decades of the century had been largely limited to craftsmen and skilled workers who shared in the prosperity of the booming Victorian economy and could afford union dues. The Trades Union Congress (created in 1868) had provided a forum for organized labor, although during the long depression, the financial resources of unions—limited in the best of circumstances—became even more depleted. The more militant "new unionism" was characterized by the organization of semiskilled workers, including many iron and steel factory workers.

In 1887, for the first time since the last Chartist marches in London in 1848, English workers went into the streets in great numbers to protest, demonstrating against unemployment and the high cost of living. On November 13—"Black Monday"—store owners slammed their doors shut amid a "red fear" in central London. The police attacked crowds of workers, killing 2 and wounding about 100 protesters.

In 1889, following a victory by gas workers in a London strike that achieved the eight-hour workday, dockworkers struck for a minimum wage. They were led by Ben Tillett (1860–1943). Born in Bristol, Tillett had at the age of seven begun cutting slabs of clay in a brickyard, then ran away with Old Joe Barker's Circus as an acrobat, before joining the merchant marine and then the navy. Finding work as a dockyard laborer, he helped organize thousands of unskilled laborers in a massive strike.

Supporting the unskilled workers, skilled workers marched through central London. A contemporary remembered their "long scarlet coats, pink stockings and velvet caps, with huge pewter badges at their breasts, like decorated amphibious huntsmen." Australian workers sent funds that helped tide the strikers over. After five weeks, the dock companies capitulated. The strike, which succeeded in obtaining a minimum wage for the dockworkers and the right to overtime pay, encouraged union growth and strike militancy in the following decade. Tillett's new dockworkers' union soon had 30,000 members.

Union organization industry by industry—such as that of the miners', gasworkers', and dockworkers' unions—helped bring together skilled and unskilled workers. But hundreds of thousands of casual laborers, particularly the part-time workers living in London's teeming East End, still were not unionized. Most casual laborers were uneducated and did not belong to friendly societies. For them the independence of the skilled worker remained only a dream. While British strikes lacked some of the drama of French work stoppages, strikes in 1897–1898 (including Britain's first national walkout, which ended in the workers' defeat) revealed the growing reach of the new unions.

The state went on the offensive against the unions. In 1901, in resolving a railway case in Wales, the House of Lords made unions and their officers legally responsible for losses sustained by companies during strikes. This Taff Vale decision led to the creation of the Labour Party.

The Labour Party, first organized in 1900, had its origins in the small Independent Labour Party, which had been founded in 1893 by MP Keir Hardie (1856–1915). This rough-hewn Scottish miner had outraged the House of Commons by chiding members for sending a congratulatory message to the queen on the birth of a great-grandson instead of a message of condolence to the families of several hundred miners killed in an accident in a mine shaft in Wales. The Labour Party vowed to represent workers in Parliament and specifically to bring about the repeal of the Taff Vale decision.

A split within the Liberal-Unionist-Conservative bloc brought ten years of Conservative government to an end. Some political leaders, including Joseph Chamberlain, supported protective tariffs, believing that they would increase British prosperity by creating a large imperial market. Chamberlain resigned from the government in 1903 in order to campaign for tariffs. Many Conservatives, including Prime Minister Arthur Balfour (1848–1930), believed that voters preferred traditional free trade policies because they feared protective tariffs would increase food prices. Unable to resolve the split within his party, Balfour resigned in December 1905, and the Liberals swept to a crushing victory in the 1906 elections. Promising to repeal the Taff Vale decision, they garnered many working-class votes, and did well in Wales and Scotland, bastions of Liberal support. The Labour Party, which had managed to win only one seat in 1900, now sent twenty-nine MPs to the House of Commons. Under the Liberal government, Parliament reversed the Taff Vale decision with the Trade Disputes Act of 1906, which legalized picketing and relieved unions of the legal responsibility for financial losses caused by union members during strikes.

In 1908, Herbert Asquith (1852–1928), a wealthy lawyer and the new head of the Liberal Party, became prime minister. Like the Conservatives, he supported British imperial causes. But the dynamic, ambitious, and charismatic Welshman David Lloyd George was the rising star of the Liberals. A man of modest origins who preferred to speak his native Welsh than English, Lloyd George had come into the public eye for his opposition to the Boer War (see Chapter 21), although he supported having an empire. While crusading against the Conservative Party, which he still considered to represent only the interests of wealthy British landlords, Lloyd George worked to continue the Gladstonian reformist tradition. He wanted to counter the drift of union members toward the Labour Party by bringing workers, middle-class men, and businessmen into an alliance that would support social and political reforms supported by the Liberal Party. The Liberal government established local boards to set minimum industrial wages, involving the British government in bargaining between employers and workers to an extent hitherto unseen.

(*Left*) Ben Tillett, organizer of the Docker's Union. (*Right*) James Keir Hardie, founder of the Independent Labor Party.

In 1909, Lloyd George (who was chancellor of the Exchequer) proposed a budget that called for increased public benefits to be partially funded by taxes on inheritance and on unearned income and uncultivated land. These "supertaxes" (which were in fact quite small) would fall on the richest families of the nation. He compared the costs of maintaining "a fully-equipped duke" to that of a new battleship, depicting the aristocratic families as parasitical leeches maintained at public expense.

In the Osborne judgment of 1909, the conservative House of Lords had ruled in favor of a railway worker who had sued his union with the goal of keeping union funds from being used to support Labour candidates for the House of Commons or to pay them while they served so that ordinary people could be elected. Several years later, MPs would receive salaries. Like the Taff Vale case, the Osborne judgment struck a damaging blow against the unions. In a climate of social confrontation, the House of Lords then provocatively vetoed the 1909 budget, which it viewed as being an attack on the wealthy, thus exercising a right that it had not used for decades. Asquith called the House of Lord's veto a "break with the constitution and a usurpation of the rights of the Commons." He dissolved Parliament, confident of winning the new elections.

The Liberals did indeed return to power early the next year with the help of Irish nationalists and the Labour Party. Asquith's Parliament Act of 1911 proposed to eliminate the right of the House of Lords to veto any financial bill. Many Britons viewed the passage of such a bill as a final blow to noble privilege. The act also specified that any bill that the House of Lords did not pass after it had been approved on three occasions by the House of Commons would become law if two years had passed since it had first been introduced in Parliament.

When Asquith threatened to ask King George V (who had succeeded his father as king in May 1910) to create enough new peerages to pass the bill, the House of Lords, despite the opposition of the intransigent "Diehards," approved the Parliament Act in 1911. The House of Lords thus eliminated its own constitutional veto, completing the long revolution in British political life that had begun with the passage of the Reform Act of 1832, which had first reduced the disproportionate power of British nobles. The House of Lords then reversed the Osborne judgment.

In 1911, a walkout by seamen, stevedores, bargemen, and ship repairers spread rapidly in London, Manchester, and Liverpool, where troops shot and killed two strikers during riots. The prospect of a food shortage forced the government's hand. Through binding arbitration, the strikers won raises. A national rail strike ended in compromise settlements. Next, when the Miners' Federation called the first general coal strike, more than 800,000 men went out, which left another 1.3 million without work. The miners gained a minimum wage, but when dockers failed to achieve their strike goals in July 1912, Britain's largest wave of strikes to date ended with the workers' capitulation.

Even Ben Tillett reflected the commitment of almost all British labor leaders and workers to peaceful reform. Denouncing "hare brained chatterers and magpies of Continental revolutionists," he espoused compulsory industrial arbitration as the means of achieving compromise in labor disputes. In any case, collective bargaining had become commonplace in the 1890s, with conciliation and arbitration boards established in many localities. That many strikes ended in defeat may have helped turn British workers further toward parliamentary reformism.

Irish Home Rule, still a major political issue, seemed almost inevitable. Irish politicians, peasants, and poets shared the burst of nationalist sentiment characteristic of the first decade of the twentieth century. The Gaelic League popularized Irish music and encouraged people to speak Gaelic, not English. The great poet William Butler Yeats (1865–1939), who helped create a native Irish theater in Dublin, contributed to a literary nationalism that sometimes glossed over class differences among the Irish: "Parnell came down the road and said to a cheering man: / 'Ireland will get her freedom, and you shall still break stone.' " Such literature also tended to romanticize the Irish as peasants made virtuous by poverty and hard work. In the collection of short stories *Dubliners* (1912) by James Joyce (1882–1941), the countryside appears as an idyllic escape from the confusion of Ireland's rapidly growing, impoverished metropolis, which had once been his home.

If Irish nationalists would accept nothing less than complete independence from Britain, Irish Protestants living in Ulster, who outnumbered Catholics there by two to one, opposed any measure of Home Rule. To them, Home Rule would be Catholic "Rome Rule." In 1913, Ulster Protestants formed a paramilitary army of volunteers. An Irish Republican Army added men and arms. Century-old wounds split open again, and Ireland seemed on the verge of civil war. In September 1914, Parliament passed a Home Rule Bill, despite the intransigent opposition of the House of Lords. But with Britain—and all the powers of Europe—approaching war, the details were left for the uncertain future. Liberal Britain, too, was being swept into international events it could not control.

TSARIST RUSSIA

Autocratic Russia—an absolutist state based upon an alliance of the tsar and the nobles—in the nineteenth century presented a particularly sharp contrast with Great Britain, with its long tradition of parliamentary rule and commercial and manufacturing prosperity. Since the sixteenth century, the Russian tsars had slowly expanded their empire through the conquest of vast stretches of territories and peoples to the south and west. Like the Austro-Hungarian Empire, the much larger Russian Empire was multinational. Ethnic Russians formed less than half of the population. Although there had been relatively fewer nationalist stirrings in the Russian Empire than had occurred within the Austro-Hungarian monarchy, ethnic resistance to the empire and to the Orthodox Church—for example, from Polish Catholics—increasingly challenged Russian domination.

Since the brief and ill-fated Decembrist uprising of 1825 (see Chapter 15), organized by army officers and students, Russia had seen neither major reforms nor revolution. Yet liberal ideas from the West had begun to filter into Russia via intellectuals. Surrounded by and alienated from a society built upon serfdom, which legally bound most peasants to the land, some of them believed revolution inevitable. Serfdom not only was inhumane, it was also economically inefficient. During the Crimean War (1853–1856), the Russian army, largely made up of illiterate serfs who could barely operate the old guns that they had been given, acquitted itself poorly. This helped convince the tsar that only through reform and the emancipation of the serfs could Russia compete with the West. Nonetheless, the basic structure of the state remained the same, with no institutional constraints on the tsar's authority.

Stirrings of Reform in Russia

Serfs lived in villages in which patriarchs served as intermediaries between the lords and the community and, like the gentry, administered harsh physical punishments to serfs who failed to obey. Only about 5 percent of the empire's population resided in towns. In Russia, which had a very small middle class, a tiny group of intellectuals, some nobles, and educated commoners wanted reform. In Britain, the movement for political and social reform championed by the middle class had for the most part been pursued through parliamentary means. In contrast, in Russia many intellectuals believed that only revolution could bring change.

Nicholas I (ruled 1825–1855), who had become tsar just after the Decembrist revolt of 1825, was obsessed with keeping Russia sealed off from Western ideas, which he blamed for the rebellion of military officers. The Revolutions of 1848 in Western and Central Europe increased the determination of the Russian autocracy to stifle internal dissent. The ministry of education oversaw a policy of tight censorship and repression by the fearsome Third Section, the political police. But the police found it impossible to seal off the colossal empire entirely. More than 2 million foreign books entered Russia just in the 1847–1849 period, most ending up in St. Petersburg and Moscow.

Nineteenth-century Russian intellectuals were unique in Europe. Many were gentry who could survive well enough without a university position or government post. Part of a privileged, educated elite, they could thus afford to write, even if the public opinion they wanted to reach was small indeed. Unlike their counterparts in Western countries, they were not

(*Left*) Aleksandr Pushkin. (*Right*) Alexander Herzen.

absorbed into the liberal professions. Some of these intellectuals became professional revolutionaries.

During the 1830s and 1840s, some of the gentry were overwhelmed with guilt that they were well off while the masses suffered. Aleksandr Pushkin (1799–1837), whose mother exiled two serfs to Siberia with a nod of her head after they failed to bow as she passed by, attacked serfdom in his short stories. A few educated commoners joined this group of conscience-stricken gentry, although in all of the empire, there were only 4,000 university students in 1849, about a third of whom were commoners. Steeped in a variety of intellectual currents, the intelligentsia brooded over and debated how Russia might emerge from autocracy and relative backwardness.

Like the philosophes of Old Regime France, the Russian intelligentsia gathered to discuss ideas that censors considered seditious and dangerous. Trying to avoid censorship and dodging the police, they met in small groups, or "circles," in St. Petersburg and in Moscow, where the atmosphere was somewhat freer than in the tsar's capital.

Several important writers emerged from this underground hotbed of intellectual and creative ferment. Fyodor Dostoyevsky (1821–1881), who adhered to populism and the Pan-Slavist cause and whose life was a series of disasters, presented brilliant psychological depictions of his characters. These included most memorably disturbingly accurate portraits of troubled individuals like himself whose actions reflected not rationality but aberration, even madness, in such novels as *Crime and Punishment* (1866) and

The Brothers Karamazov (1879–1880). Sentenced to death by the authorities in 1849 for participation in a reading circle that discussed socialism, he was hauled out of jail early one morning, blindfolded, placed before a firing squad, and then, after a cruelly staged mock execution that understandably shattered his nerves, sent to prison in Siberia. He described his own suffering, but also that of Russian society, in the crucial years following defeat in the Crimean War. The novelist Count Leo Tolstoy (1828–1910), another great Russian realist writer, was a wealthy landowner who served in the Crimean War. He emerged as a moral voice against violence. His monumental *War and Peace* (1869), in harmony with other Russian writers of the time, depicts the struggle between his country and the West.

The intelligentsia also debated the works of Russian writers. Pyotr Chaadayev's *Philosophical Letters* had slipped by the censors in 1836. Chaadayev (1794–1856) presented a thinly veiled condemnation of Russia's cultural history. Officials declared him to be mad, and the police hounded him for the rest of his life. His pessimistic piece provoked heated discussion because it suggested that cultural backwardness would keep Russia from joining the ranks of civilized nations.

Chaadayev's *Philosophical Letters* opened the debate between "Westernizers"—those Russian intellectuals who, like Tsar Peter the Great in the seventeenth century, looked to the West for a model for progress— and "Slavophiles," who believed that Russia could never be reconciled with Western values. Like Westernizers, most Slavophiles were social critics of autocratic Russia. Westernizers like Chaadayev regarded the development of parliamentary institutions and industrialization in Britain, France, and the German states as a model for Russia to emulate. In contrast, Slavophiles cherished the specificity of Russia's defining institutions: the Orthodox Church, the village commune (the *mir*), and even tsardom itself. They did not want Russia to go forward, as did the Westernizers. Rather, they argued that Russia could avoid the traumas of Western industrial development because in the village it already possessed the basis for a future socialist society. The peasant commune, with a variety of communal buildings (a wind or water mill, a grain supply store, tavern, and a workshop), facilitated survival. Peasants adapted their lives to unbelievably difficult conditions imposed by nature, the state, and the lords. The *mir* seemed to provide both a moral vision and revolutionary potential.

Vissarion Belinsky (1811–1848) and Aleksandr Herzen (1812–1870) forcefully made the case that Russia had to follow the example of the West if it were to emerge from backwardness. Belinsky, the son of a doctor, had been expelled from university for writing an article denouncing serfdom. When the writer Nikolay Gogol (1809–1852) refused to criticize the autocracy, Belinsky circulated his *Letter to Gogol* (1847), which helped define the Westernizer position by blasting Gogol's respect for "orthodoxy, autocracy, and nationality," the dominant triad of the Russian Empire:

"Advocate of the knout [whip], apostle of ignorance, champion of obscurantism and reactionary mysticism, eulogist of Tartar customs—what are you doing? Look at what is beneath your feet; you are standing at the brink of an abyss." In Belinsky's view, the inculcation of some Western values and progress would eradicate the superstitions of the past. He argued that in defending Russian political and social institutions, Gogol was betraying all writers.

Herzen, a landowner's son, had vowed following the ill-fated Decembrist revolt to carry on the work of the revolutionary martyrs. Arrested and exiled for participation in a student discussion group, Herzen traveled to France. Returning to Moscow in 1840, he espoused the French Jacobin and socialist tradition and the belief in the inevitability of progress. In *From the Other Shore* (1855), written in voluntary exile in Paris after the Revolution of 1848, Herzen, like the Slavophiles, expressed confidence that Russia, even while following the lead of the West, would take its own path to socialism. It would thus be able to avoid what he considered to be the decadence brought by capitalist social relations. Socialism could be easily established in Russia because the village commune already existed as a community of social equals in the face of autocratic and noble exploitation. Herzen implored Russian officials to struggle for peaceful liberal reform. Interestingly enough, both radical reformers and the men of the tsarist state shared a suspicion of Western "bourgeois" political and social life. The Slavophile current of reformism thus had much more in common with the tsarist autocracy than it cared to admit.

Unlike the Westernizers, the Slavophiles celebrated the religious faith of the Russian masses. Gogol, for one, contended that the Russian people

A Russian religious procession.

were the most religious anywhere, with village life centering around the Russian Orthodox Church. The peasant household, which brought together the extended family (parents, children, grandchildren, and sometimes brothers-in-law and their families) under the stern guidance of the patriarch, was itself a place of worship. Rejecting Western materialism, Slavophiles believed that an era of social harmony and equality had existed in Russia before Peter the Great transformed the Russian state in the late seventeenth century by importing Western ideals and bureaucracy. "We are a backward people," wrote one young Slavophile, "and therein lies our salvation. We must thank destiny that we have not lived the life of Europe. . . . We do not want its proletariat, its aristocratic system, its principles of state, its imperial power. . . . We believe in the strength of Russia because we believe that we are called to bring into history a new principle . . . and not to repeat the stale old lessons of Europe."

The Emancipation of the Serfs

The emancipation of the serfs in 1861 by Tsar Alexander II (ruled 1855–1881) was the most ambitious attempt at reform in Russia during the nineteenth century. Following the failed Decembrist revolt in 1825 some government officials began to think what for most nobles was the unthinkable—that Russia could develop economically only if serfdom were abolished. Serfdom dictated the organization of taxation, the army, courts, and virtually every other institution of government. Because gentry landowners had a virtually unlimited source of labor, many showed little inclination to try to increase agricultural yields.

Alexander II succeeded his father Nicholas I as tsar in 1855. During his father's reign he had shown no signs of being anything but conservative. He was thus an unlikely ruler to undertake the most significant reforms in Russia since the time of Peter the Great. However, Russian defeat in the Crimean War shocked him. The tsar and some of his officials began to believe that his country could not compete with the West if the serfs were not emancipated. Despite an increase in agricultural laborers hired for wages, Russian industrial development and effective agricultural production, he argued, required free wage labor that could be taxed. Even if some lords had attempted to increase the productivity of their land, serfs only worked halfheartedly; most Russian peasants still used the wasteful three-field system (with one field left fallow each year).

Serf rebellions—more than 1,500 during the first half of the century—shook the empire. Many serfs had joined the army during the Crimean War, believing that they would be freed upon returning home. The flight of thousands of serfs toward the open spaces of the east, or to Crimea in the south, undermined the agricultural economy upon which Russia depended. Moreover, as many as two-thirds of all gentry were indebted to the Russian state, even as the great estates had begun to produce and

Peasants hailing Tsar Alexander II after the emancipation of the serfs in 1861.

export more grain. Now, as rumors spread that the tsar, whom many peasants considered the father of his people, would end Russia's "peculiar institution," peasant rebellions became even more widespread. Tsar Alexander told assembled landowners, "It is better to abolish serfdom from above than to wait until serfs begin to liberate themselves from below." Some nobles now believed emancipation inevitable. That Russia could not be considered Europe's most powerful state wounded their nationalist pride. In 1858, a Slavophile noble wrote the tsar that the "abolition of the right to dispose of people like objects or like cattle is as much our liberation as theirs."

On April 5, 1861, Russia became the last European state to abolish serfdom. Alexander II emancipated the 22 million serfs by a proclamation made through the Orthodox Church. For two years, however, the old system remained essentially in place. But serfs then received land through the *mir*, which was administered by male heads of household. Nobles were compensated for their land by the state, and peasants had to repay the state through forty-nine annual redemption payments. Yet nobles lost in the emancipation, as in many cases they received bonds of little value, as well as losing the value of the serfs. Peasants were no longer dependent upon the whims of landlord justice. Yet many peasants, who had wanted complete and immediate freedom without compensation ("We are yours," went an old serf proverb, "but the land is ours.") were bitterly disappointed by the terms of their freedom. Indeed Russian serfs may have had access to more land per family than French peasants—although still not much—and their standard of living, however low, was probably comparable to Western European peasants before 1800. The allotments of land they received were insufficient for them to grow enough to eat and pay taxes and redemption fees. Furthermore, as the villages were collectively responsible for land redemption payments and taxes (although the lords' household serfs were freed without land and owed no payments), former serfs were rather like hostages to their own villages. Instead of owing labor to the lords, former serfs now owed taxes to the state; these would be collected by the communes. They were dependent upon the village patriarchs for permission to go find work elsewhere. Despite restrictions on their movements, peasants flocked to the cities, which grew by leaps and bounds.

In tsarist Russia, the serfs were freed practically without bloodshed, while in the United States the slaves found freedom only after one of the most violent struggles—the Civil War (1861–1865)—anywhere in the nineteenth century. Unlike the southern landed elite in the United States, who went to war in defense of slavery, the Russian nobility capitulated without resistance to emancipation. Despite the vast expanse of the Russian Empire, the tsarist state exercised more centralized authority than did the relatively weak central government in the United States. Moreover, Americans considered private property more of an absolute right than did even Russian nobles, who wanted, above all, to extract services from peasants. After emancipation, the vast wealth of the Russian nobles could still pay for such services.

Many critics of autocracy now expected further reforms. Alexander rooted out some incompetent ministers and officials and asked the ministry of finance to keep regular budgets. In 1864, Alexander decreed the establishment of district or village assemblies called *zemstvos*. These would elect delegates to regional assemblies. Six years later, the tsar created similar urban institutions called *dumas* (councils), with the authority to assess taxes and to organize public education and public services. But the ministry of the interior controlled the *zemstvos*, and provincial governors ignored them, some treating their members as seditious agitators. Moreover, landowners elected the members of the *zemstvos*, and their votes were given more weight than those of landowning townsmen and peasants.

The emancipation of the serfs necessitated an expanded administrative apparatus, since millions of people were no longer subject to the justice of the lord but rather to that of the state. The tsar introduced regional and lower courts modeled on those of Britain, as well as public trial by jury. In 1864, for the first time a separate judicial branch of government came into existence in Russia, although the tsar could override any court decision. Such power remained the essence of autocracy.

Thus, the essential structure of the empire remained the same, even after the emancipation of the serfs. The army was no longer made up of loyal, poorly supplied, illiterate, beaten serfs but rather of loyal, poorly supplied, illiterate, beaten, free peasants. In the past, few soldiers had been expected to survive the twenty-five-year term of service. Indeed, wives of soldiers had the right to remarry three years after their husbands left for military service. With an eye toward reform, the tsar established a Prussian-style general staff, took steps to modernize weapons, and reduced the term of military service to six years, followed by nine years in the reserves and five years in the militia. Alexander also ordered the elimination of some forms of corporal punishment, including the brutal—and often fatal—floggings and beatings.

Yet the arbitrary power of the tsarist state and its Third Section police to repress dissent remained largely intact. Most political cases were gradually removed from the court system and handed over to trial by secret court-martial. Alexander restored the censorship apparatus, which was temporarily weakened in the years before the emancipation, to full strength. The tsar had no intention of creating any kind of national representative institution that would undercut his authority.

The Expansion of the Russian Empire

The prestige of the Russian Empire in Europe fell with the Crimean defeat. By the Peace of Paris (1856), Russia relinquished Moldavia, Wallachia, and Bessarabia and had to accept the neutrality of the Black Sea, further frustrating imperial designs in southeastern Europe (see Map 18.2). After two years of public demonstrations, the Polish rebellion of 1863 followed, proclaiming a "national government" before being crushed by Russian troops. The brutal repression that followed brought the Poles widespread sympathy in Western Europe, but not independence. Russia intervened on behalf of the Bulgarians and Serbs, who were fellow Slavs. In Herzegovina, peasants had rebelled against tax-collectors and the soldiers who accompanied them after a harvest failure. As a Russian army drove toward Constantinople in the Russo-Turkish War (1877–1878), the Austrian army and British navy readied to prevent the tsar from reaching the Dardanelles Strait. Defeat forced the Ottoman Empire to sign the Treaty of San Stefano (1878) with Russia. In the case of Bulgaria, there were few Bulgarian nationalists, and not many decades earlier most educated people there had considered themselves Greek. The fact that Russia would clearly dominate Bulgaria and the rising mood of Pan-Slavism (a movement aimed at promoting the interests and unity of all Slavs) in the Balkans alarmed Britain and Austria-Hungary. They demanded the convocation of an international conference to discuss the matter. The other powers then called a conference in Berlin, over which German Chancellor Otto von Bismarck presided. At Disraeli's insistence, the Congress of Berlin (1878) reduced the size of Bulgaria (giving Greece Thessaly, which it had claimed, thus moving its border to the edge of Macedonia, claimed

MAP 18.2 THE EXPANSION OF RUSSIA   After territorial losses under the Peace of Paris (1856), Russia turned eastward, expanding through Central Asia toward the Far East and its port at Vladivostok.

by Bulgaria, Serbia, and Greece). Bulgaria, which had its own Orthodox Church as of 1870, became a principality, headed by Prince Alexander Battenberg, but it would remain a vassal state of the sultan of Turkey, although Russians held key government posts. The Congress recognized Serbia, Montenegro, and Romania (formed by the union of the principalities of Wallachia and Moldavia) as independent states, thus considerably reducing Ottoman territory in Europe. Russia made some face-saving gains, including a small part of Bessarabia, which allowed it to control the mouth of the Danube River. But Russian Pan-Slavs, in particular, believed themselves aggrieved by Britain and betrayed by Bismarck's Germany. Likewise, Bulgarian nationalists would increasingly feel that they had been cheated out of land in Macedonia that they believed Bulgaria had been promised by Russia.

Alexander II then turned his attention toward Central Asia and the Middle East. Russian armies conquered Turkistan and the other relatively powerless Muslim states in Asia, reaching Afghanistan. Britain now felt threatened by Russian expansion, which seemed to impinge upon British interests near India. In response, the British army invaded Afghanistan, and in 1881 put a puppet ruler on the throne. In the Far East, Russian forces moved across Siberia, giving the Russian navy access to the Pacific Ocean at Vladivostok.

The Russian Empire now included about one-seventh of the world's land mass. Eastward expansion brought contact and eventually conflict with China. The Chinese emperors would be powerless in the face of Russian demands, as they were when confronted by those of Britain. Surprisingly, Japan, which emerged from centuries of isolation following the Meiji Restoration in 1868, would prove to be a far tougher adversary for Russia.

Nihilists and Populists

Revolutionaries replaced the conscience-stricken gentry of the 1830s and 1840s as the principal critics of the Russian autocracy. They were drawn from a variety of social backgrounds, including the sons and daughters of nobles, merchants, peasants, and Orthodox priests. Convinced that one spark might ignite a wave of rebellion, they struck out on their own or in very small groups. They were loners, determined to the point of obsession with what each believed was his or her mission.

Some of the Russian revolutionaries found the old debates between the Westernizers and Slavophiles irrelevant. Nihilists accepted no dogmas. Above all, the nihilists rejected the materialist doctrines of the West. But they also disavowed many Russian traditions, and thus repudiated the Slavophiles. Some of them viewed the Orthodox Church as an institution of oppression, whereas others remained fervent believers.

Some nihilists saw in the Russian masses an untapped revolutionary force. Among them were those who believed that the emancipation of the

(*Left*) Mikhail Bakunin, professional anarchist. (*Right*) Karl Marx, founder of Communism.

serfs had aided their cause by creating an independent peasantry, which might be more likely to rise up against its oppressors. Like the conscience-stricken gentry before them, the nihilists believed in the power of literature to effect change. In 1863, Nikolay Chernyshevsky (1828–1889), a former seminarian, published *What Is to Be Done?*, a novel that had an enormous impact on several generations of intellectuals. Chernyshevsky described committed people of action as "rational egoists" who would form a disciplined vanguard of change. Because nihilists did not feel bound by moral codes, they believed they could take whatever action seemed necessary to achieve their goals. In the 1860s, groups of nihilists turned to violent revolution, plotting the assassination of state officials and the tsar himself. The police infiltrated and drove groups like "Land and Freedom" and "The Organization"—with its central committee called "Hell"—underground, particularly after a student attempted to kill Tsar Alexander II in 1866.

In the meantime, Mikhail Bakunin (1814–1876) became the most famous anarchist of his or any other time. Anarchists rejected the very existence of the state, thereby quarreling bitterly with socialists, who wanted not to destroy the state but to take it over. A professional revolutionary who complained, "Karl Marx is ruining the workers by making theorists out of them," Bakunin left behind his comfortable noble origins. He was a man of enormous energy who slept only a couple of hours a day, eating, drinking, and smoking cigars almost constantly, organizing and plotting between bites, gulps, and puffs. Once calling himself "the devil in the flesh," Bakunin defined the "social question" as "primarily the overthrow of society." That he set out to do. He led the police on a chase from Paris in 1847 to Dresden and other stops in Central Europe in 1848, that year of revolution. Arrested and imprisoned in Russia, he was exiled to Siberia, managed to escape in 1861, reached Japan, and then arrived in London via the United States.

Bakunin believed that "destruction is a creative passion" and, like the nihilists, that the peasant masses had untapped revolutionary potential. Karl Marx, who reserved a special sarcastic contempt for the anarchists, insisted that peasants, unlike the industrial proletariat, could never be truly revolutionary and seize power because they could not be class-conscious. Anarchists, in turn, rejected Marx's belief that a militant working class organized in a centralized party could make a revolution, fearing that Marxists wanted to replace a bourgeois state with a proletarian state, a state all the same.

Unlike revolutionary nihilists and anarchists who dreamed of a spontaneous peasant uprising, Sergey Nechayev (1847–1882) held that a small, tightly organized revolutionary group could seize control of the state. They would begin the peasant revolution that would sweep away autocratic corruption and oppression. "The revolutionary is," Nechayev wrote, "a doomed man. He has no personal interests, no affairs, sentiments, attachments, property, not even a name of his own. Everything in him is absorbed by one exclusive interest, one thought, one passion—the revolution." Dostoyevsky based the character of the hero of his novel *The Possessed* (1871–1872) on Nechayev. After murdering one of his colleagues, Nechayev was arrested and sent to prison, where he died.

During his anguished life, Nechayev had battled the populists (*narodniki*) within the revolutionary ranks. The populists developed their doctrine in response to nihilism and retained the Slavophiles' faith in the Russian peasantry. They were romantic collectivists who idealized the Russian peasant community. In contrast to Chernyshevsky, who wanted to teach the peasants, the populists wanted to learn from them. In the early 1870s, several thousand young Russians went from St. Petersburg and Moscow into the countryside. These upper-class Russians resembled the conscience-stricken gentry of the 1830s and 1840s. But these populists dressed up like peasants; not only did they want to "go to the people," to learn from the masses, but they also wanted to prepare an insurrection. Claiming that revolution was near, they taught their listeners revolutionary songs. Some of those attracted to direct action worried that the emancipation of the serfs might create a class of conservative peasant proprietors. Time seemed to be running out for Russia to take its own path to socialism before capitalism became entrenched in Russia, as it had in Western Europe.

In 1878, a revolutionary populist shot and wounded the governor-general of St. Petersburg. Another attack that year, carried out by the "disorganization section" of Land and Freedom, struck down the head of the Third Section police. A wave of strikes by industrial workers convinced the terrorists that revolution was not far away.

Twice more, Tsar Alexander II escaped assassination attempts. In the hope of placating his enemies without destroying the foundations of the autocracy, Alexander disbanded the Third Section. He dismissed the minister of education, whose restrictive policies on university admission were unpopular, and announced the formation of a new consultative assembly. But in 1881, members of "People's Will" struck, hurling a bomb near Alexander's sleigh. When the tsar foolishly stepped from the sleigh to inspect the damage, another man threw a bomb that killed him. Russian autocracy, however, survived. The assassination did not prove to be the revolutionary spark anticipated by those who carried it out. Millions of the tsar's subjects, among them many who demanded further reform, mourned the ruler who had at least given them freedom.

Alexander III's Empire

Following his father's assassination, Alexander III (ruled 1881–1894) was in no mood to contemplate any liberalization of Russian imperial institutions. Public opinion existed in the Russian Empire, but mass political life did not. The assassination led to a curtailment of the powers of the *zemstvos* and a shifting of judicial authority to the police, putting political trials in the hands of military courts. For the moment, exile was the only safe place from which to criticize the autocracy. Small colonies of political refugees, most of whom were socialists, lived in Geneva, Paris, and London.

Professors and teachers were brought under stricter state control, and tuition was increased to discourage commoners from going to school. The police received carte blanche to arrest and imprison anyone without reason. The resulting political trials may have actually helped the cause of reformers and revolutionaries by serving as tribunals where the autocratic regime was discussed and political issues were brought into the open. What went on in courtrooms helped shape Russian opinion, even when political trials were moved into military courts.

Alexander ordered a vigorous campaign of "Russification," although the Russian people made up only 40 percent of the population. Ukrainians, Poles, and Byelorussians made up the next largest national groups, followed by Lithuanians, Latvians, and Estonians in the Baltic states,

A Russian princess in Tartar costume.

Finns, Romanians (in Bessarabia), Crimean Tartars, Armenians, Georgians, and Azeri in the Caucasus, and the Muslim peoples of Central Asia. The tsar banned the use of languages other than Russian in school, and forbade publication in, for example, the Ukrainian language, despite the fact that it was spoken by 25 million people. At the same time, the Russian Orthodox Church launched campaigns against non-Orthodox religions, which maintained the allegiance of almost a third of the people of the empire.

"Russification" firmed the resolve of nationalist groups to persevere in their demands for recognition, including some Armenians and Finns, who had been loyal to the tsar. In 1899, the Finnish Assembly was reduced to a "consultative" voice, and Russians replaced Finns in most key administrative positions. In Poland, opposition to Russia grew more daring. The Polish League was founded in 1887 as a conspiratorial organization. The National Democrats were a more moderate nationalist group seeking to keep Polish nationalism alive in Russian Poland (where the tsar launched a campaign against wearing Polish national dress), as well as in the German and Austro-Hungarian Empires. Poles were linked by long-standing cultural bonds, based in a single literary language with origins in the sixteenth century. This had survived the end of an independent Poland with the Third Partition of 1795 by Russia, Austria, and Prussia. Moreover, the cause of Polish independence had been kept alive by Poles forced to flee after the ill-fated insurrections of 1831 and 1863. Polish socialists hoped eventually to undermine the tsarist autocracy and create an independent socialist Polish state in which the rights of non-Poles, too, would be recognized.

The Russo-Japanese War (1904–1905)

The Russian Empire, which now reached the Pacific Ocean, began to covet Chinese Manchuria and the peninsula of Korea. The acquisition of Manchuria would permit Russia to construct a more direct rail link to the ice-free Russian port of Vladivostok; that of Korea would protect the new port from possible attack and provide still more ports. In 1894, Japan had goaded China into a war. By the Treaty of Shimonoseki (1895), the victorious Japanese took the island of Formosa (Taiwan) and gained Chinese recognition of Korea's independence. This placed the peninsula under direct Japanese influence. Japan also acquired the Liaodong (Liaotung) peninsula in southern Manchuria but was forced by Russia, Germany, and France to return it.

Russia viewed the expansion of Japanese interests in the Far East with concern. In 1898, Tsar Nicholas II (ruled 1894–1917) signed a treaty with China and obtained a concession to build the Manchurian railway and to construct a port at Port Arthur on the tip of the Liaodong peninsula, setting up a source of conflict between Japan and Russia. Japan, in

Three Manchurian men crouch before the hulks of Russian ships sunk during the Russo-Japanese War.

turn, signed a treaty in 1902 with the government of Great Britain, Russia's rival for influence in Afghanistan. Britain would remain neutral if Japan and Russia went to war against each other. But Britain would join Japan in any conflict that allied Russia with any other power in a war against Japan.

In February 1904, Japanese torpedo boats launched a surprise attack on the Russian fleet at Port Arthur, destroying a number of ships while the Japanese army drove Russian forces away on land. In March 1905, Japanese troops defeated the Russians in the bloody Battle of Mukden where, for the first time, two armies faced each other across trenches dug for protection. Two months later, the Japanese navy pounced on the Russian fleet, which had spent nine months at sea. The battle of Tsushima ended with nineteen Russian ships sunk, five captured, and six forced to neutral ports; only three ships of the Russian fleet reached Vladivostok.

How could the Russian Empire be defeated by a small island nation with no experience fighting a Western power? Only a single-track railway line stretching across thousands of miles supplied the Russian forces. The Russian army was poorly commanded and was fighting with outdated artillery and rifles. By the Treaty of Portsmouth (New Hampshire), signed in September 1905 at a conference hastily arranged by U.S. President Theodore Roosevelt, Japan took over Russia's lease of the Liaodong peninsula and Chinese concessions in Manchuria. Russia accepted Japanese influence over Korea. A new world power was born. At the same time, the Russian defeat was a key factor leading to the Revolution of 1905 in Russia.

Unrest, Reform, and Revolution

The Russian Empire at the end of the nineteenth century was enormous. More than a hundred times the size of Great Britain and three times larger than the United States, its population doubled from about 74 million inhabitants in 1861 to about 150 million by 1905. It was now comprised of almost 200 nationalities who spoke 146 languages. The majority of the population was poor: the average per capita income was more than four times higher in Britain, three times higher in Germany, and twice as high in the Balkan states. If by 1910, 70 percent of children aged 7 to 11 were likely to attend school for at least one year, about 60 percent of the population remained illiterate. In 1897, only 1 percent of the population had attended secondary school for any amount of time. Yet literacy in European Russia, in particular, was rising. The reading public grew dramatically in size around the turn of the century, especially among ordinary people in rapidly growing cities, such as St. Petersburg and Moscow. Even seasonal workers and peasants migrating to Siberia began to carry books with them. The taste for literature expanded from religious books and the emerging classics of the Russian literary tradition (above all, Tolstoy and Gogol) to liberal magazines and newspapers.

Enemies of Autocracy

Liberal constitutionalism had played a role in the expanding domain of Russian public opinion since the heady days of the 1860s and the emancipation of the serfs. The Russian army's poor performance in the war against Turkey (1877–1878) proved that military reforms instituted following the Crimean War had not been enough. Expanding opportunities for education, increased government bureaucratization, and industrial development contributed to an increase in the professional middle class. This, combined with the expansion of heavy and light industry, and urban growth, seemed to make autocracy an anachronism.

Liberals included a smattering of gentry, leaders of local assemblies (the *zemstvos* and the municipal *dumas*), and, above all, members of the expanding professional classes, including economists, *zemstvo* agronomists, physicians, lawyers, teachers, and students. Some state bureaucrats, too, sought a middle way between state and noble intransigence and revolutionary terrorism, hoping that the tsar would grant political reforms to complement the gradual modernization of the Russian economy. Some were encouraged by laws slightly reducing the long work day (1897) and providing the first factory insurance law (1903). Liberals demanded an extension of the powers of the *zemstvos*, whose limited authority had been curtailed in 1890, but imagined little more than active consultation between those bodies and the tsar.

Revolutionary groups, however, still believed the autocracy incapable of reforming itself. They argued that only revolution could bring reform. The populist Socialist Revolutionaries became the largest radical group, with growing support among peasants, whom Socialist Revolutionaries believed would one day overthrow the tsar.

In the meantime, a group of Marxists founded the Russian Social Democratic Workers' Party at Minsk in 1898. They were confident that one day, though probably not in their lifetimes, the Russian proletariat would be sufficiently numerous and class-conscious to seize power. But this seizure of power could only occur, they believed, after a democratic revolution had successfully overthrown the Russian autocracy. Marxists claimed vindication for their view that peasants had no true revolutionary potential when, despite the terrible suffering and deaths of millions of peasants during the famine that followed the severe drought and epidemics of 1891–1892, the countryside remained quiescent.

By 1900, the tsar's police had succeeded in disbanding most of the revolutionary groups within the empire, deporting their leaders to join the groups in exile, sending them to Siberia, or putting them in prison. Most revolutionaries, whether living in Russia or in exile, shared a belief that their country was far from revolution.

Lenin and the Bolsheviks

Vladimir Ilyich Ulyanov, known as Lenin, was born in the Volga River town of Simbirsk on April 22, 1870, more than 400 miles east of Moscow. His father served as the director of primary schools for the province and, as a result of loyal service, he obtained nonhereditary membership in the nobility; Lenin's mother, whose family had originally been German, was the daughter of a doctor. His older brother Alexander, who joined the revolutionary group "People's Will," was executed in 1887 after being arrested for participation in a plot to kill Tsar Alexander III. Lenin briefly attended university, but was expelled for participating in a student demonstration. During the next six years, Lenin read widely in history and philosophy, including the works of Karl Marx and Friedrich Engels, and he returned to receive a degree in law from the University of St. Petersburg. All the while, Lenin was forming the beliefs that would lead him to become a revolutionary committed to the overthrow of the Russian autocracy and world capitalism.

In 1895, Lenin made his first trip abroad. He went to Austria, France, and Switzerland, meeting Russian political exiles and socialists from many countries. Back in St. Petersburg, Lenin was arrested at the end of 1897, charged with organizing and writing articles in a clandestine newspaper (*Iskra,* or *Spark*), and he was exiled to Siberia. When his term of banishment ended in 1900, he moved to Switzerland.

"I know Russia very little," Lenin admitted. With the exception of a brief return during the Revolution of 1905, he remained in exile abroad until 1917. As a virtually penniless exile, he bore his situation with good humor in what seemed to be a strange, somewhat stodgy land. Lenin's few interests outside of politics and revolution included chess, hunting, bicycling, and mountain hiking. But he viewed most recreational activities—even, at times, simple conversation—as interfering with revolutionary struggle.

There was nothing about Lenin's appearance that would have attracted the attention of tsarist spies or Swiss and French police. An Englishman said that "he looked more like a provincial grocer than a leader." He had piercing gray eyes, and his slightly Asian facial features revealed a glimpse of the eastern heritage of his father's family. The American journalist John Reed described him as "a short stocky figure with a big head set down on his shoulders, bald and bulging. Little eyes, a snubbish nose, wide generous mouth, and heavy chin, . . . already beginning to bristle with the well-known beard of his past and future. Dressed in shabby clothes, his trousers much too long for him . . . a leader purely by virtue of intellect; colorless, humorless, uncompromising and detached . . . with the power of explaining profound ideas in simple terms, of analyzing a concrete situation."

Lenin combined a powerful ability to theorize with a facility for adapting to changing circumstances. His steely resolve would carry him to cold fury when colleagues or rivals failed to agree with him. "He who does not understand this does not understand anything!" was a typical Lenin rejoinder. A vigorous polemicist, he could be impatient and churlish in speech, cutting and sarcastic with his potent pen.

In 1902, Lenin, who had taken his name as a pseudonym the previous year, published *What Is to Be Done?* In this pamphlet (with the same title as the work by Chernyshevsky), Lenin established what would become the basic tenets of a new revolutionary party. The long tradition of authoritarian rule in Russia helped shape Lenin's view of how the autocracy could be overthrown. Lenin believed that Marxist analysis could be applied to a backward nation with a relatively undeveloped working class and a small bourgeoisie. "The one serious organizational principle for workers in our movement must be strictest secrecy," he wrote, and "the strictest choice of members and the training of professional revolutionaries." He rejected all compromise with liberals and reform socialists, viewing as self-defeating the struggle of workers for small economic gains, which he viewed as crumbs tossed from the posh table of the ruling class. Rejecting the common Marxist view that the social experiences of workers would lead the entire working class to revolutionary consciousness, Lenin believed that only a minority of workers would achieve consciousness and that these should join with intellectuals in a party that would direct the masses.

At the second congress of the Russian Social Democratic Workers' Party, held in Brussels and London in 1903, Lenin and his followers became known as the "Bolsheviks," or the "majority" (although much of the time in the years that followed they were not), and their rivals were known as the "Mensheviks," or the "minority." The Mensheviks believed that a proletarian revolution lay in the future, but not until a bourgeois uprising had first succeeded in overthrowing the tsarist state. Mensheviks believed that their historic role was to mobilize support for their party through propaganda, while undertaking timely alliances with liberal groups and rejecting terror. They thus sought to become a large party of extreme revolutionary opposition. They also objected to the high degree of party centralization upon which Lenin insisted.

The Revolution of 1905

Many of the tsar's subjects had blamed government inaction for the murderous famine of 1891–1892, which had captured world attention. In 1902, peasants attacked noble property in some districts, and a wave of industrial strikes followed the next year. Liberals organized support for political reform by sponsoring banquets similar to those employed by French republicans just before the Revolution of 1848. Dissent mounted against forced Russification among subject nationalities, most notably the Poles and the Finns. Marxist groups were particularly active in Poland—where the issue of Polish nationalism versus internationalism was hotly debated—and in the Jewish Pale—those provinces where Jews were allowed to settle and where they faced endemic anti-Semitism and occasional bloody pogroms.

Defeats in the ongoing Russo-Japanese War increased calls for liberal reform. A wide-ranging social and political alliance for change extended across classes. Not only were Russian soldiers being killed in a far-off war for reasons that did not concern most of the population, but it soon appeared that the war was being badly fought. After the assassination of his minister of the interior in July 1904 by a Socialist Revolutionary, Nicholas II appointed a more moderate successor in the hope of calming dissent. Moreover, the tsar allowed a national congress of *zemstvos* and *dumas* to take place. It formally asked that it be given powers and called for the establishment of a national parliament.

Liberal and socialist groups, with the exception of Mensheviks and Bolsheviks, began to meet together in the hope of capitalizing on growing dissatisfaction with the tsar's policies. For the first time, liberals and socialists, intellectuals and workers, and Russians and non-Russians came together in common opposition to autocracy, embracing a loose ideology of reform. Reformers within the gentry and professional classes, including some state officials, believed that the tsar could be influenced by a broadly based movement.

In the meantime, the Russian labor movement remained small and faced constant police harassment. The growing number of skilled factory workers supplied the majority of labor militants. At the turn of the century, the police had authorized government-controlled labor associations in the hope of undercutting revolutionaries. By encouraging workers to concentrate on their economic grievances and achieve some small victories through negotiation, those in power believed that the structure of autocracy could be left intact. These organizations were supposed to offer meeting places and welfare assistance to workers and occasionally to help resolve disputes with employers (strikes remained illegal). But such halfway measures further frustrated workers, while giving them useful organizational experience. More workers defied the employers and the state by going on strike.

In January 1905, a strike by 100,000 factory workers brought St. Petersburg to a standstill. On January 22, an Orthodox priest led a march of workers to the tsar's Winter Palace, carrying a petition asking for "justice" and political reform. Troops blocked their way. When the marchers locked arms and refused an order to disperse, a commander barked out the order to fire.

More than 300 marchers, including women and children, fell dead, and perhaps 1,000 or more were wounded. "Bloody Sunday" helped shatter the myth that the tsar was the Holy Father, the people's powerful friend, enacting evil policies because he was manipulated by selfish nobles and

Russian troops fire on the workers, Bloody Sunday, January 1905.

wicked advisers. Bolsheviks and Socialist Revolutionaries, the latter particularly influential in the countryside, encouraged more strikes. The rhetoric of demands for constitutional reform became increasingly revolutionary in tone. Nicholas dismissed his liberal minister of the interior. The tsar's uncle fell to an assassin's bullets. Strikes spread to Poland, Ukraine, Latvia, and Estonia. In some rural areas of Russia and in the Baltic provinces, peasants attacked the homes of wealthy landowners. In the southeastern borderlands, Muslim leaders announced the formation of an All-Russian Muslim League. Workers began to organize trade unions in huge numbers and a free press emerged in open defiance of censorship. The experience—brief as it turned out—of having a free press giving voice to new ideas and information as never before had an important and lasting effect on public opinion.

With the bulk of the army fighting the Japanese in Manchuria, the Russian Empire seemed on the verge of collapse. Nicholas appeared to choose the path of reform, appointing Sergey Witte (1849–1915) as prime minister. Witte was eager to make Russia a modern industrial power, and he believed that he could do so if the tsar granted minimal reforms. He persuaded Nicholas to rescind redemption payments to the state for land acquired in the serf emancipation, to allow Poles and Lithuanians to use their own languages, to allow religious toleration in Poland, to turn political trials back over to the regular courts, and to abolish some restrictions on Jews.

Even more important, Nicholas's October Manifesto of 1905 created a national representative assembly, the Duma, to be chosen by universal male suffrage, and it promised freedom of the press. Some state officials and most nobles, however, viewed these particular reforms as unacceptable, associating them with the parliamentary regimes of the West. But progressive nobles and businessmen were encouraged by the sudden, unexpected turn of events. Some staunch liberals, some of whom had participated in the *zemstvos,* took the name of the Constitutional Democratic Party (known as the Kadets). They demanded constitutional government and put forward the case that the promised reforms left the essential structures of autocracy unchanged. In the meantime, the Mensheviks had championed the establishment of St. Petersburg workers' councils, known as *soviets.* These were neighborhood councils made up of delegates from factories, shops, trade unions, and political parties that helped organize strikes, which became legal in December. The Mensheviks expressed willingness to collaborate with the liberals in order to bring further reforms to workers and peasants.

But a violent uprising in Moscow in December 1905 brought on a vigorous counter-revolution. Witte ordered the arrest of many of the workers' leaders. The *soviets* no longer were free to meet. Army units returning from Manchuria crushed nationalist demonstrations in Poland and Georgia and brutally restored order in the Russian and Ukraine countryside. In the Baltic provinces of Latvia and Estonia, punitive expeditions ordered by the tsar killed over 1,000 people while violently putting down strikes and rural unrest. Fanatical Russian nationalists known as the Black Hundreds, perhaps instigated by Orthodox priests, unleashed a wave of violence against Jews (and against German, Russian, and Polish property owners, as well) which lasted more than a year. The Black Hundreds were led by small traders and agricultural laborers who feared that economic change would cost them what limited security they had and by police who opposed political reform. In the Crimean town of Odessa, drunken mobs aided by the local police murdered 800 Jews, injured more than 5,000 other people, and left twice that number homeless. The tsar himself intervened to prevent Witte from prosecuting the police, praising the "mass of loyal people"; they had struck out against "troublemakers," who could be conveniently blamed for agitating against autocratic rule.

Against this turbulent backdrop, the Duma had met for the first time in April 1906. The U.S. ambassador described the gathering in the Winter Palace of the members of the Duma, who were dressed "in every conceivable costume, the peasants in rough clothes and long boots, merchants and tradespeople in frock coats, lawyers in dress suits, priests in long garb and almost equally long hair, and even a Catholic bishop in violet robes." The majority of the Duma members were Kadets (Constitutional Democrats), largely because the Marxist Social Democrats (both Mensheviks and Bolsheviks) and the Socialist Revolutionaries parties refused to participate in the election. The Kadets wanted to reduce the powers of the tsar.

As the Duma debated land reform, an issue on which the tsar and most lords refused any compromise, Nicholas decreed the establishment of an upper assembly, the State Council. With members to be drawn from the high clergy, the army, or other loyal institutions, it would counteract the influence of the Duma. The tsar then dismissed Witte and announced that he would promulgate any decree he pleased while the Duma was not in session. When the Kadets petitioned Nicholas to abolish the State Council, make ministers responsible to the Duma, and turn over some noble estates to the peasants, he dissolved the Duma.

The Revolution of 1905 had ended in failure, but its memory could not be effaced. The tsar had been forced to grant a parliament and the promise of limited civil rights. Many people within the Russian professional class, particularly bureaucrats and lawyers, remained sympathetic to these reforms after they had been undone by the tsar. These liberals still stood between the autocratic routines of the state and the revolutionaries.

The Revolution of 1905 heightened the divisions among exiled Russian socialists. Mensheviks contended that compromise with bourgeois reformers would increase socialist support within Russia. Lenin and the Bolshe-

Tsar Nicholas II presides over the opening of the Duma.

viks, on the other hand, believed that the failed revolution had clearly demonstrated that the Russian proletariat in the large cities was already a revolutionary force, and that the first stage of Marx's promised revolution could be achieved if workers and peasants joined together.

Nicholas II named Pyotr Stolypin (1862–1911) as prime minister, and in June 1906 he ordered the dissolution of a second elected Duma even though it was more conservative than the first. In the meantime, the police and the Black Hundreds systematically beat up and, in some cases, killed opponents of the tsar. In an August decree, the tsar established military field courts that could summarily convict and sentence civilians accused of violent political crimes. This law resulted in nearly 1,000 hangings before it expired six months later. Liberals dubbed the ropes of the gallows used to execute more than 1,000 people "Stolypin's neckties."

After Nicholas changed the rules of election to increase the power of noble votes at the expense of peasants, workers, and non-Russians, a third Duma was elected in 1907 that was more to the tsar's liking. It was dominated by the "Octobrists," who believed that the tsar's promises in his manifesto of October 1905 represented sufficient reform and wanted to stop at that. The repression and Russification campaign went on.

Stolypin nonetheless undertook some rural reforms beginning in 1906, hoping that they might defuse the political intensity of the agrarian question and reduce agrarian unrest without the confiscation of land owned by the gentry. His goal was to create a class of prosperous peasants (*kulaks*) while increasing agricultural production by allowing peasants to leave the communes and set up independent farms. He hoped that the enclosure of common lands and a consolidation of holdings would expand peasant plots. Indeed a considerable amount of land passed from communal to private ownership. As a result, the number of prosperous peasants increased. Yet prices for farm products fell, and even peasants with fairly large plots of land still had to struggle to survive. Hundreds of thousands of peasants migrated to Siberia in order to obtain land.

In 1911, Stolypin was assassinated. Although the government claimed the assassin was a Jew, the minister may have been killed with the approval of the tsar at the instigation of noble advisers who considered him too liberal and rejected any agrarian reforms.

A surge of industrial strikes and peasant violence over the next three years reflected mounting popular dissatisfaction with the regime. Liberals, Socialist Revolutionaries, and Menshevik and Bolshevik Social Democrats mobilized support against the regime. Indeed, the growing popularity of Bolsheviks among organized urban workers—revealed in their victories in trade union elections—reflected deepening impatience with the path of moderate reform.

FRANCE: SECOND EMPIRE AND THIRD REPUBLIC

In the meantime, Europe's traditionally most revolutionary country remained France. Following the Revolution of 1848, Louis Napoleon Bonaparte had smashed the democratic-socialist movement, jailed or exiled its leaders, and disbanded or harassed workers' organizations. He had completed his destruction of the Second Republic with his coup d'état on December 2, 1851, proclaiming himself emperor (and taking the name Napoleon III) the following year with the overwhelming support of the upper classes and of peasants in many parts of the country.

Emperor Napoleon III was a small man with a prominent nose who appeared lethargic. He reminded some people of a sphinx, and one contemporary of "a melancholy parrot." An unimpressed visitor from the United States described the French ruler as "a long-bodied, short-legged man, fiercely mustached, old, wrinkled, with eyes half closed, and such a deep, crafty, scheming expression about them!" Indeed, like his legendary uncle, Napoleon III consistently demonstrated considerable energy when it came to behind-the-scenes intrigue and the pursuit of women.

During the Second Empire (1852–1870), wealthy businessmen became the equivalent of an imperial aristocracy in France, money standing as the measure of value that blue blood had been in the early modern period. Enjoying access to the emperor, some of them lived in Parisian residences and owned country houses that would have made eighteenth-century aristocrats drool with envy. The empress set the tone for Parisian fashion, while critics condemned the "triumphant vulgarity and appalling materialism" of the "imperial festival."

Yet Napoleon III also set out to pull the nation together. France was the only European power with universal male suffrage, however distorted by government pressure. The emperor promoted economic growth, encouraged urban rebuilding projects, created institutions that provided credit, and constructed more railways so that if all went well not only the rich and middle classes would benefit but also the lower classes. Moreover, in 1859 Napoleon III initiated the "liberal empire," encouraging a series of reforms, including authorizing a liberal trade treaty with Britain in 1860 and permitting the legalization of strikes in 1864.

The Authoritarian Empire

Napoleon III ruled with the help of a handful of worldly, trusted cronies who held ministries or who served on the council of state. Ministers were responsible to the emperor, who alone could propose legislation. The empire's authoritarian phase lasted until 1859.

The Bonapartist state clamped down on the remnants of political opposition, maintained press censorship, and sponsored "official" candidates in the elections held every six years for the Legislative Corps, the lower

A critical cartoon of Napoleon III, shown limping behind a vulture after his defeat in the Franco-German war (*left*), stands in stark contrast to the Bonapartiste propaganda early in his dictatorship declaring "The Glory of Napoleon III" (*right*).

house of the National Assembly. Hand-picked notables made up its upper chamber, the Senate. Napoleon III's men built a Bonapartist party from the remnants of Orleanism, that is, from those conservative bourgeois who had supported the July Monarchy (1830–1848). They rallied to Napoleon III because he promised to maintain social and political order and promoted economic growth.

The French state, more than its decentralized British counterpart, could buy political support by dispensing patronage, for example, by assuring that a railroad under construction would pass through a certain town. The prefect, the most powerful local official, more than the largest landowner, now held the key to patronage. The Second Empire thus further centralized economic and political power in France.

Napoleon III maintained considerable support among peasants, some of whom retained a romantic attachment to the memory of his uncle, Napoleon. A good many Legitimists—that is, the supporters of the Bourbon royal family and its exiled pretender, the count of Chambord—also supported the emperor. Like his uncle, Napoleon III had made peace with the Church. The clergy remained grateful that during the Second Republic over which Napoleon had presided as president and than destroyed, the Falloux Law of 1850 had returned control of education to them, and for the most part continued to be loyal to the regime.

Despite an avalanche of Bonapartist propaganda, many workers still espoused republicanism or democratic socialism. And as the political repression slackened in the early 1860s, socialist activity increased. In 1862, French workers joined some of their counterparts from the German states as delegates of their trades at the London International Exposition to discuss the situation of labor in their countries. In 1864, several French artisans were among the founders of the first international workers' organization, the First International, in the hopes of strengthening socialist movements within individual countries.

Economic Growth

The rate of French economic growth was such during the Second Empire, particularly during the 1850s, that economic historians sometimes use it as an example of an industrial "take-off." French exports doubled between 1853 and 1864. Never before had any state taken such a direct role in stimulating the economy through encouragement and investment. Government officials coordinated the efforts of the ministries of agriculture, commerce, and public works, while keeping in close touch with wealthy bankers and industrialists who backed the regime.

French entrepreneurs had often found it difficult to raise investment capital. Most companies remained family concerns, hesitant to open investment possibilities to outsiders. Napoleon III expanded credit, providing government guarantees to credit companies and thereby stimulating the economy. The emperor encouraged the creation of state mortgage banks. In 1852, the Péreire brothers, who were Protestants like many French bankers, created the Crédit Mobilier, an investment bank. Selling shares to raise capital until its collapse in 1867, it provided loans to many business-men. Other smaller deposit banks, too, attracted large and medium investors. A mortgage bank (the Crédit Foncier), another one of Napoleon III's pet projects, aided the development of the agricultural sector.

At the same time, some major French industries achieved a scale of pro-duction and concentration comparable to that of their British rivals. The metallurgical industry, in particular, underwent unprecedented growth and concentration. But most French industries remained relatively small in scale, producing luxury goods, such as gloves, umbrellas, silk, jewelry, and fine furniture.

France became a major exporter of capital. French investors financed the construction of Russian, Spanish, and Italian railroads, as well as pro-viding other timely loans to Russia, Spain, Portugal, Austria-Hungary, and Mexico. Ferdinand de Lesseps (1805–1894), an engineer, raised enough money through loans (half through public subscription) to finance the construction of his brainchild, the Suez Canal. It opened with suitable fanfare in 1869. Yet the chief beneficiary of the canal was not France but Britain, the world's leading trader, which had by far the most to gain by considerably reducing the journey to and from India and the rest of Asia (see Chapter 20).

The opening of the Suez Canal, 1869.

State encouragement of economic development may be most clearly seen in the French railways. The Bank of France, which had seventy-four branches by 1870, provided financial aid to the companies that for the most part completed the main railway lines that helped stimulate the country's commercial and manufacturing boom. The state guaranteed investors a minimum profit. Between 1851 and 1869, the railway network expanded by five times, reaching almost 10,000 miles of track. French railroads became one of the largest employers in Europe.

Producers could now more easily market their goods; the prices of staples, in turn, fell, aiding French consumers. This encouraged farmers to specialize in one or two crops that they could raise most efficiently. Agricultural specialization and greater integration into the market thereafter created conditions for new kinds of agricultural crises, such as those of overproduction, marked by falling prices. The agriculture crisis of 1854–1855 was the last of the harvest failures that had periodically plunged France into economic crisis. Dearth and skyrocketing prices for staples now lay in the past. Yet, unable to raise enough produce to take advantage of improved access to urban markets and undercut by falling agricultural prices, many peasants sold their small farms and moved to the cities in search of work.

The railway carried France into a new age of increased consumption that gradually included the lower classes. Because of reduced transportation costs, meat became less of a luxury. People who lived a good distance inland—and who were of some means—found that fish reached them before the ice keeping the fish fresh had melted. The diet of ordinary people improved, and as a result of improved nutrition, military records revealed that conscripts gradually became taller. The poor, too, now enjoyed a more varied diet, consisting of more vegetables, fruit, and cheese.

The "Liberal Empire"

In 1859, Napoleon III announced his intention to "crown the [imperial] edifice with liberty." He would diffuse opposition by implementing some of the very reforms his opponents on the left desired. Although some large cities remained defiantly opposed to imperial politics and had elected five republicans to the Legislative Corps two years earlier, the emperor had the support of the majority of people. In 1860, the National Assembly received the right to discuss the emperor's annual address—an exercise in sheer boredom, as he was a notoriously poor speaker. That same year, France and Britain signed a liberal trade agreement lowering tariff barriers between the two nations. In France, the Cobden-Chevalier Treaty of 1860 was the idea of the emperor himself and an adviser, Michel Chevalier (1806–1879), who had been a utopian socialist as a young man. Like the emperor, Chevalier had begun to have doubts about economic protectionism. The treaty of 1860 provided a sliding scale on import duties. It helped some French economic interests, such as Bordeaux wine producers.

Having undone protectionism, Napoleon III then promulgated further liberalizing measures. The National Assembly received the right to approve the imperial budget. Press controls were relaxed, and the right to strike was established in 1864. The liberalization of political institutions helped republicans increase their support. Foreign policy ultimately revealed Napoleon III's weakness as a ruler, despite the fact that the emperor was widely regarded in Europe as an outstanding man of state, a victor of the Crimean War. In 1859, Napoleon III joined with Count Camillo di Cavour of Piedmont-Sardinia to draw Emperor Francis Joseph of Austria into a war (see Chapter 17) under its direction. In June 1859, the French army defeated the Austrians in northern Italy at Magenta and at Solferino, where the emperor himself commanded the French troops on horseback, if at a safe distance from the actual fighting. By the Treaty of Turin (1860), France gained Savoy and Nice, both long coveted. Napoleon III then ordered the expansion of French control in Senegal and sent troops to protect missionaries in Lebanon and distant Indochina, annexing Cochin-China as a colony. At a state dinner in London in 1864, someone voiced the opinion that Napoleon III had been considerably more successful than his famous uncle. Only one of the diners disagreed: the Italian revolutionary Giuseppe Garibaldi cautioned, "We must wait for the end of the story."

An imperial adventure in Mexico, which was in the midst of a civil war, ended in fiasco. The emperor believed that Mexico could become a profitable market for French exports of textiles and wine. In 1861, France sent troops to protect French financial interests there. When order was restored, the French troops stayed. In 1864, Napoleon III proclaimed his protégé, Austrian Archduke Maximilian (1832–1867), the brother of Habsburg emperor Francis Joseph, to be emperor of Mexico. The United States protested that French intervention represented a violation of the Monroe Doctrine (1823), which had declared the Western Hemisphere off limits to the European powers. The Mexicans, understandably enough, did not want an Austrian emperor. Three years later, Mexican patriots defeated the French forces, who disembarked, leaving Napoleon III's hapless protégé to his own devices. Maximilian was executed in June 1867, a blow to Napoleon III's international prestige.

A year earlier, the French emperor had made an error in foreign policy that would come back to haunt him. As Prussia and Austria drew closer to war in 1866, Napoleon III believed that Habsburg Austria would prevail. Bismarck quickly rejected Napoleon III's demand in August 1866 that Prussia compensate France with Rhineland territory. The French emperor then boldly insisted that Prussia go along with a possible French annexation of Belgium and Luxembourg (see Chapter 17). After an international conference a year later guaranteed Luxembourg's independence, Napoleon III's dreams of territorial compensation from Prussia disappeared. But the cagey Bismarck kept the French emperor's written demand tucked away in a drawer.

Edouard Manet's *Execution of Maximilian* (1867).

In June 1868, the emperor's authorization of a law permitting freedom of assembly helped mobilize opposition among monarchists, republicans, and socialists alike. Napoleon III's advisers wondered aloud if he had not sown the seeds of imperial demise by granting liberal reforms. Early in 1870, strikes spread. The emperor invited opponents to join the government and to begin drafting a more liberal constitution, one that would make ministers in some way "responsible" to the Legislative Corps. Napoleon III then reverted to a plebiscite, with a craftily worded statement in May 1870 by which those who wanted more extensive changes were forced to abstain, or to vote "yes" as if they approved of the emperor's policies. The plebiscite, in which "yes" overwhelmed "no," thus partially concealed the depth of opposition to imperial policies.

To the end, Napoleon III manifested a bizarre combination of perceptive foresight and bad judgment. When the Spanish throne fell vacant after a military coup deposed Queen Isabella II of Spain in 1868, one of the candidates was Prince Leopold, a Catholic prince of the ruling Prussian dynasty, the Hohenzollerns (see Chapter 17). If Leopold were to become king of Spain, France would find itself with members of the Prussian royal family across both the Rhine River and the Pyrenees. Napoleon III threatened war with Prussia if it did not withdraw the Hohenzollern candidacy. He then ordered his ambassador to extract a letter from the king of Prussia apologizing to France and promising that Prussia would never revive the candidacy of Prince Leopold.

In July 1870, the French ambassador harangued Prussian King William I in a garden in the spa town of Ems. The king politely dismissed the ambassador and sent Bismarck a telegram stating what had occurred. After learning that the Prussian army was ready to fight, Bismarck embellished the king's telegram (the Ems Dispatch) to make the graceless diplomacy of the French seem positively insulting and the king's response stronger than it had actually been. Prussian public opinion reacted to French demands with anger. Bismarck's expectation that it would "have the effect of a red cloth on the Gallic bull" was justified; the incident increased popular support for France's declaration of war on Prussia on July 19, 1870. Württemberg, Hesse, Baden, and more hesitantly, Bavaria joined the Prussian side. Bismarck pressured Austria, Russia, and Italy to remain neutral. Then he produced the French emperor's written offer for French support of Prussia in 1866 in exchange for the latter's acquiescence in France's absorption of Belgium and Luxembourg. For centuries, Britain had opposed a French presence in the Low Countries. Napoleon III went to war against Prussia without allies.

The Franco-Prussian War and the Siege of Paris

The Franco-Prussian War was a French debacle. Whereas the French mobilization of troops proceeded slowly, the Prussian armies moved quickly into northeastern France (see Map 18.3). The speed of the Prussian attack and the competence of its generals more than made up for superior French rifles and recently developed machine guns. In August, Prussian troops cut off the fortress of Metz from the rest of France. When Marshal Marie-Edme de MacMahon (1808–1893) moved north in an attempt to relieve Metz, the Prussians cut him off. On August 31, 1870, the main French force foolishly retreated to the fortress town of Sedan not far from the Belgian border. Sedan was soon surrounded by Prussians, who captured the emperor, who was so sick that he could barely sit on his horse. In Paris on September 4, 1870, crowds proclaimed a republic, and a provisional government was formed. Prussia allowed Napoleon III to leave for exile in Britain.

The Prussian army besieged Paris. The population of the capital swelled with soldiers and National Guardsmen. As hunger invaded the capital, dogs and cats disappeared from the streets, finding their way to some of the finest tables. Zoo animals, too, were eaten, including two elephants admired by generations of Parisian children. An attempt to break through the Prussian lines north of the city at the end of October failed miserably. Still, Paris hung on.

In the meantime, Louis-Adolphe Thiers (1797–1877), who had served as Orleanist prime minister during the 1830s, wanted Bismarck's help in facilitating the establishment of a very conservative republic at the war's conclusion, or even a monarchy. The provisional government negotiated with Bismarck in the hope of obtaining an armistice on favorable terms. On January 28, 1871, ten days after the proclamation of the German

Empire at Versailles (see Chapter 17), Bismarck and Thiers signed an armistice. France lost Alsace and much of Lorraine to the new German Empire.

Some French leaders protested, demanding that the French army keep fighting. In February 1871, French voters—though only half of those eligible cast ballots—selected a monarchist-dominated National Assembly. It would be charged with making peace with Prussia and with establishing a new government. The newly elected National Assembly officially elected Thiers to be chief executive of the provisional government.

By signing the Treaty of Frankfurt (May 10, 1871), Thiers's provisional government agreed to pay a large indemnity; Prussian troops would occupy Paris and retain garrisons in eastern France until the sum had

MAP 18.3 THE FRANCO-PRUSSIAN WAR, 1870–1871 Troop movements and battles during the Franco-Prussian War show fighting at Metz and Sedan, as well as Dijon and Orléans, with German troops converging on Paris.

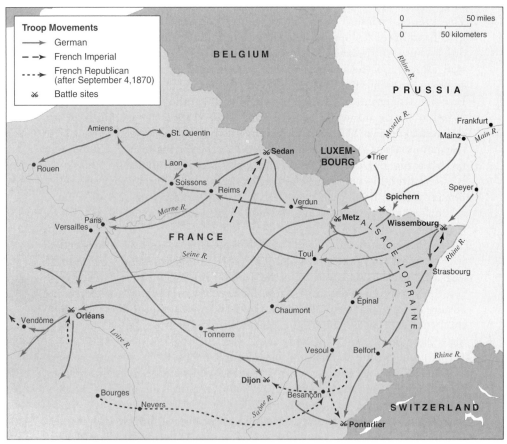

been paid off. The National Assembly's choice of Versailles, the home of the Bourbon monarchs, as the temporary capital stirred popular anger and suspicion. Parisians, who had held out against the Prussians for four months, resented the ease with which the provinces had seemed to capitulate. When the siege ended, wealthy Parisians who had left Paris at the beginning of the siege returned from the safety of the countryside. Landlords insisted that back rents be paid immediately, angering renters, most of whom were workers.

The Paris Commune

Early in the morning on March 18, 1871, Thiers sent a small detachment of troops to Montmartre to seize cannon that had belonged to the National Guard during the siege. Women at the market alerted the neighborhood; a crowd surrounded the detachment and put two generals up against the wall and shot them. Thiers ordered his troops, their number increased by prisoners of war released by Bismarck, to surround the capital. A second siege of Paris began, this one a civil war.

During the Prussian siege, socialists had placed bright red posters on the walls of the capital calling for the establishment of the "Paris Commune." Now surrounded by armies directed by monarchists from Versailles, the Commune set out to defend Paris. The leaders of the Commune were drawn from a variety of political persuasions: Jacobins, socialists inspired by the memory of the French Revolution, and moderate republicans who wanted Paris to become again the capital of an anticlerical republic. Some Communards had been democratic-socialist activists during the Second Republic; others were followers of the revolutionary Auguste Blanqui (1805–1881), who believed that revolution could be achieved only by a small cell of determined men seizing power. There were also a good many anarchists, who hoped that independent Paris would serve as a model for a society of producers existing without the tyranny of the state.

Revolutionary clubs sprang up in Paris. The Communards organized Paris's defense and enacted a number of significant social reforms. These included the creation of a Labor Exchange, the abolition of night baking (long a grievance of bakers), the establishment of nurseries for working mothers, and the rights of workers' organizations to receive preference when the municipality contracted work. The Commune recognized women's unions—indeed the role of women in the Commune exceeded that of any previous revolutionary movement in France. Given the severity of the circumstances, it is remarkable how much the Communards accomplished in such a short time.

Much smaller uprisings occurred in Lyon, Marseille, and in several other towns. These movements reflected a combination of middle-class dissatisfaction with Bonapartist centralization, republican enthusiasm,

Jules Favre, peace negotiator, and Adolphe Thiers, provisional head of the government, accede to the loss of Alsace-Lorraine, France's right arm. They drag the weeping female image of France away from the "social republic."

and socialist mobilization. But the provinces provided no help to the Paris Commune; rather, conservative regions sent volunteers to fight for the Versailles forces.

On May 21, 1871, the troops of Thiers's Versailles government poured into Paris through the western gates, left open for them by monarchist sympathizers. During the "bloody week" that followed, Thiers's army, aided by the recently constructed boulevards, overwhelmed neighborhood after neighborhood, blasting through barricades. Summary executions occurred throughout Paris, particularly after a rumor began that female incendiaries were burning banks and the homes of the wealthy. The Communards retaliated by executing some hostages, including the archbishop of northeastern Paris. The last Communard resistance was finally crushed in one of the most plebeian parts of Paris. At least 25,000 Parisians died at the hands of the provisional government, summarily executed or dispatched after hurried military trials. "In Paris, everyone was guilty," was the way one magistrate coolly put it.

For the left, the Commune seemed to be a glimpse of the future proletarian revolution (although Paris largely remained a city of artisans and skilled workers, not semi- or unskilled industrial workers). To conservatives, the Commune offered a frightening glimpse of plebeian insurrection, and it firmed their resolve to oppose movements for social and political change with armed force. The massacre of the Communards suggested to some people the futility of armed rebellion against modern armies. Many ecclesiastics blamed France's defeat at the hands of Prussia and the Commune itself on religious indifference and anticlericalism. As a form of penance for France's "sins," the Church constructed the basilica of the Sacred Heart on Montmartre, where the Commune had begun.

REPUBLICAN FRANCE

Legislative elections of February 1871 gave monarchists a majority in the National Assembly that was to determine France's political future. The gradual victory of moderate republicanism in France in the years after the Commune reflected the fact that most people in France wanted a republic based upon mass political participation.

In republican France, too, mass politics and fervent nationalism went hand in hand. This nationalism was not that of the French Revolution, when French armies had poured across the frontiers, ostensibly to carry "liberty, fraternity, and equality" to other lands. Nor was it that of the Revolutions of 1848, when France seem poised to "liberate" Savoy from Piedmont. Now, following defeat at the hands of Prussia in 1871 and the proclamation of the powerful German Empire, French nationalists became obsessed with recapturing Alsace and Lorraine from Germany.

Monarchists and Republicans

The Bourbon pretender was the count of Chambord, a lazy man of mediocre intelligence who lived in an Austrian castle and amused himself by playing cards and telling dirty jokes and anti-Semitic stories to his cronies. The Orleanist pretender to the throne was the relatively dashing count of Paris. Yet Chambord seemed to hold the upper hand, for his was

The beginning of the Commune, March 18, 1871: the execution of Generals Lecomte and Thomas. (The photo may be a re-enactment).

the old Bourbon royal line. But, unlike the count of Paris, he was child-less, and his death would bring the end of the direct Bourbon line. A com-promise, by which Chambord would become king with the count of Paris as his heir, fell through when the former refused to be king under the tri-color flag, which he identified with the French Revolution.

The close association of monarchism with the Catholic Church led many people to agree with the assessment of the radical republican Léon Gambetta (1838–1882) that "clericalism, there is the enemy." Republi-cans opposed the political domination of the "notables," the wealthiest men in France. The republic found a groundswell of support from those Gambetta called "the new social strata," the shopkeepers, café owners, prosperous peasants, craftsmen, and schoolteachers. The charismatic Gambetta's whistle-stop tours of the provinces reflected the rise of mass politics in France.

Thiers, who had converted to moderate republicanism, resigned under monarchist pressure as provisional head of state in 1873. Prussian troops marched out of France that year after the French government finished paying off the war indemnity, raised by loans and a public subscription. The monarchists, seeing their majority in the National Assembly eroding with each by-election, elected as president Marshal MacMahon, a hero of the Crimean War and the Italian War of 1859, who favored a monarchist restoration. The new government of "moral order," closely tied to the Church, undertook a massive purge of republican mayors, censored news-papers, closed hundreds of cafés, and banned the public celebration of the French Revolution on July 14.

For the moment, the government of France was a republic with monar-chist political institutions. In January 1874, the National Assembly passed the Wallon Amendment by one vote, stating that henceforth "the presi-dent of the Republic" would be elected by the Senate and the Chamber of Deputies. The lower house drafted a republican constitution in 1875, but one that seemed so indefinite that the state could easily enough have been converted into a monarchy.

Universal male suffrage determined the composition of the Chamber of Deputies. Each district elected a single representative. This gave monar-chists an advantage, as local notables would be the most likely beneficia-ries from last-minute political negotiations before the second ballot of each election. The Senate would be elected indirectly through a system that was radically tilted to overrepresent conservative rural interests. Yet, despite heavy-handed governmental and ecclesiastical pressure on voters, more than twice as many republicans were elected as monarchists to the Chamber of Deputies in 1876. MacMahon was therefore forced to select a moderate republican, Jules Simon (1814–1896), as premier.

The republican majority in the National Assembly sought to limit the power of the president who was, after all, a monarchist. In 1877, MacMa-hon initiated a political crisis (the crisis of May 16) by forcing Simon's res-

The Champs-Élysées in Paris during the Commune.

ignation and naming a monarchist in his place. When the Chamber of Deputies withheld its approval, MacMahon dissolved it and called for new elections. He embarked, with the help of the Church, on a bitter campaign to defeat Gambetta and the republicans.

However, France's voters returned republicans again, although with a smaller majority. MacMahon named a republican premier, and he resigned in 1879. Henceforth the role of the executive authority would be weak because republicans feared that some Napoleonic character might try to impose his rule. With the constitutional privilege of dismissing government cabinets that had lost the confidence of the majority of its members, the Chamber of Deputies would dominate the political life of the Third Republic. In 1881, the Chamber of Deputies passed a controversial bill giving full amnesty to exiled Communards. Towns and villages began to put up statues and busts in honor of the republican tradition.

The Third Republic

The governments of the new republic reflected the center of the political spectrum, that of the "opportunists," so called because many of them accepted a very conservative republic while preferring something more to the center. Resolved to hold the center against the monarchists and the Church on the right and the anti-clerical Radicals, as well as the socialists to their left, the opportunists retained the support of peasant proprietors by implementing high agricultural tariffs. The Méline Tariff, supported by industrialists and farmers, went into effect in 1892.

The opportunist republic guaranteed freedom of the press, legalized public gatherings without prior authorization, and gave municipal councils the right to elect their own mayors (with the exception of Paris, which was not allowed to have a mayor). The president served as something of a chairman of the board to the Chamber of Deputies. He shook hands with everybody, intrigued pleasantly, and helped form coalitions. Governments came and went, giving an exaggerated image of parliamentary impotence and instability.

The educational reforms of the 1880s had the goal not only of making France more literate but also more republican. Jules Ferry (1832–1893) sponsored laws that made primary education free and obligatory. The state allocated money to build village schools. Although some priests and nuns stayed on to teach in what were technically lay schools, the debates ensured the animosity of many prelates and practicing Catholics against the "godless" republic.

General Boulanger and Captain Dreyfus

Amid growing social and political division, during the 1880s the parliamentary center began to melt under pressure from right and left. Nationalism became a potent political ideology. Bonapartists emerged from obscurity to tout Napoleon III's cousin, Prince Napoleon Bonaparte (1822–1891), as a potential savior. Some nationalists began to think that the republic was too weak to ever recapture the lost provinces from Germany. This concern with "revenge" against Germany reflected the passing of nationalism from the liberal left to the right wing in France.

The Boulanger Affair was in some ways the birth certificate of the new right in France, the Dreyfus Affair its baptism. In 1887, French rightists began to place their hopes of overthrowing the republic on the dashing figure of General Georges Boulanger (1837–1891), who had risen rapidly through the ranks to become minister of war. His bellicose noises about recapturing Alsace-Lorraine pleased nationalists while irritating Bismarck. Rightist leaders now were convinced that they had found the man who could overthrow the republic, restore the monarchy, or establish a dictatorship. Flattered by all of the attention, Boulanger allowed his name to be put forward as a candidate for the Chamber of Deputies.

The political movement on behalf of Boulanger was arguably the first mass political campaign in France. Funds provided by a wealthy royalist widow helped inundate the country with electoral posters and busts and statues of the dashing general. His supporters now battled their political enemies in the streets, bringing unprecedented violence into an electoral campaign, drawing on rising nationalist anti-Semitism, although there were only about 80,000 Jews in a population of 40 million in France. For example, Parisian shopkeepers, frustrated by the economic depression, fearful of workers' consumer cooperatives, and losing clients to department stores, swung their support from the Radical Party to right-wing nationalist parties. Many could be convinced by right-wing polemicists that "Jewish capitalists" were responsible for their plight.

Boulanger was elected in by-elections in several districts, but, because he was in the army, he was ineligible to serve in the Chamber of Deputies. At this point, no one was sure what exactly Boulanger represented, no one probably less than the general himself. If his campaign money came from the right, many of his votes at first came from the left. The opportunist government sent Boulanger to central France in order to remove him from the political limelight of the capital.

A political scandal cast a further shadow on the government, giving another twist to the term "opportunist." A prostitute revealed that the Legion of Honor medal was being peddled to the highest bidder. It turned out that one of the most successful salesmen was Daniel Wilson, the ruthless son-in-law of President Jules Grévy, who had used his political connections to make a killing selling these highly coveted awards. Grévy resigned the presidency. When a deputy asked Georges Clemenceau, the feisty anti-clerical Radical, to suggest someone for whom he could vote as a successor, he was alleged to have replied, "Vote for the stupidest!" In this way Sadi Carnot (1837–1894), grandson of the "organizer of victory" during the French Revolution, became president of France.

All of this added to a feeling among some observers that the Third Republic was at the end of its rope. The government declared General Boulanger retired. But this now left him free to run for the Chamber of Deputies. Boulanger was elected deputy from Paris. To his right-wing followers, it seemed that a perfect occasion for a coup d'état had arrived. In January 1889, triumphant crowds gathered in the street, calling out the general's name while he sat in a restaurant quietly eating dinner. But his moment had passed. Two years later, government officials convinced the naive general that

The suicide of General Boulanger.

they held evidence that could lead to his conviction on charges of state treason. Boulanger caught a train to Belgium and, on the grave of his late mistress, took out his army pistol and blew out his brains.

Having survived Boulanger, the republic then received an unexpected boost from its old enemy, the Catholic Church, whose "rallying" to the republic began with an archbishop's toast in 1891 in Tunisia. Henceforth, the moderate republicans could draw on political support from the Catholic right against the socialist parties.

Another scandal gave the anti-parliamentary right a new focus for opposition. In 1881, a French company had begun to dig the Panama Canal under the direction of Ferdinand de Lesseps, who had overseen the construction of the Suez Canal. This canal proved to be even more challenging to build because of difficult terrain and malarial conditions. In order to raise additional funds, company officials bribed government officials in the hope of gathering sufficient support to get the Chamber of Deputies to approve a loan that would be financed by a national lottery. The Chamber of Deputies obligingly approved the plan, but the financial campaign fell short. When the company went broke in 1889, more than half a million investors lost their money.

In 1892, Édouard Drumont's right-wing newspaper *La Libre Parole* published a series of revelations about the scandal. Six years earlier, Drumont had published a book in which he claimed that Jewish financiers were conspiring to dominate France. Now, the fact that some of the directors of the defunct company had been Jewish helped generate support for the League of Patriots, founded in 1892, a nationalist and anti-Semitic organization of the extreme right. The next year an indulgent court acquitted all but one of those implicated in the scandal.

The next scandal was such a series of dramatic events that it became known for years simply as "the Affair." It pitted right against left, the army, Church, and monarchists against republicans and, in time, socialists, and family against family.

Alfred Dreyfus (1859–1935) was the son of an old Jewish family from Alsace. His family had been peddlers and then textile manufacturers. They were assimilated Jews, proudly considering themselves French. Following the annexation of Alsace by Germany in 1871, the Dreyfus family moved to Paris. In 1894, evidence surfaced—from a wastepaper basket in the office of a German military attaché—that someone in the French army had been passing secret information to the Germans about French military operations. Circumstantial evidence pointed to Captain Dreyfus—the writing on a list of documents that had been prepared to be handed over to a German contact resembled Dreyfus's handwriting. Maintaining his innocence, Dreyfus refused the arresting officer's offer of a loaded pistol with which he could kill himself. A hurriedly convened and secret court-martial found him guilty of treason. Dreyfus was stripped of his rank and sent to Devil's Island off the coast of South America.

(*Left*) Edouard Drumont's anti-Semitic newspaper *La Libre Parole* (*The Free Word*), 1893. (*Right*) Captain Alfred Dreyfus.

However, confidential documents continued to disappear from French army offices. Two years later, a new chief of army intelligence, Lieutenant Colonel Georges Picquart, determined to his own satisfaction that the original list of documents had not been penned by Dreyfus, but by Major Walsin Esterhazy. Picquart, who was an unlikely hero in this case because he made no secret of his anti-Semitism, presented his evidence. But high-ranking officers believed that it was better to have an innocent Jew languishing in increasing depression on Devil's Island than to compromise the army's public image. The army packed Picquart off to a post in Tunisia, and a military court acquitted Esterhazy, despite overwhelming evidence of guilt.

The novelist Émile Zola now took up Dreyfus's case. In January 1898, he wrote an article in a daily newspaper with the bold headline *"J'accuse!"* ("I accuse!"), denouncing the army and the government for covering up the reality of the case. The political right and the Church hierarchy jumped in on the side of those now known as the "anti-Dreyfusards," seeing the Dreyfus Affair as a conspiracy of Jews and Freemasons to destroy France by undermining the prestige of its army. The newspaper of the Assumptionist Order demanded that all Jews be deprived of their citizenship. Action Française, a right-wing nationalist and monarchist organization led by Charles Maurras (1868–1952), an anti-Semitic novelist, jumped into the fray against Dreyfus. Gradually, reform socialists began to demand a new trial.

Another officer soon discovered that some new documents had been added to the Dreyfus file. They had been quite badly forged by Lieutenant Colonel Hubert Henry, who hoped they would lead to a new conviction of Dreyfus should the case be reopened. Maurras saluted this "patriotic forgery," but when confronted with the evidence, Henry slit his throat in a military prison. In 1899, the army retried Dreyfus, once again finding him guilty, but this time with "extenuating circumstances." Dreyfus returned, a broken man, to Devil's Island. However, the president of France gave Dreyfus a presidential pardon that year, which allowed him to return to his family, but Dreyfus was not fully exonerated until 1906, when his military rank was restored.

The Radical Republic

Dreyfus's return to France provided the republic with a badly needed period of stability and boosted the Radical Party. The Dreyfus Affair had helped forge a working alliance between the Radicals, who were anticlerical moderate republicans, and socialists, moving the republic to the left. In the Radical government formed in 1899, Alexandre Millerand (1859–1943), a reform socialist, became minister of commerce, despite the bitter opposition of many socialists who objected to a socialist serving in a "bourgeois" government.

The Radicals moved to separate church and state against ecclesiastical and conservative opposition. In 1902, the Chamber of Deputies, with socialist support, passed legislation exiling religious orders from France. In 1905, church and state were formally separated in France. During the next two years, the state took possession of all ecclesiastical property and assumed responsibility for paying the salaries of priests. Despite papal condemnation and the resistance of some clergy and parishioners, a *modus vivendi* evolved, with parish councils leasing churches from the state.

The Radical Premier Georges Clemenceau (1841–1929) embodied aggressive French nationalism. The man who later became known as "the Tiger" had been born into a family of modest noble title; his father was a prominent republican who had been exiled by Napoleon III. Clemenceau was a wealthy bully and a formidable dueler who hated socialists, unions, and the Catholic Church as much as he did his American ex-wife, whom he had followed by a detective, jailed, and deported. In 1907, he sent troops to crush a determined strike by small property owners and vineyard laborers in the southern town of Narbonne.

In 1911, Radical Premier Joseph Caillaux (1863–1944), unlike Clemenceau, sought accommodation with Germany. The French Socialist Party launched a campaign against militarism and particularly against the extension of the term of military service from two to three years. Anti-militarism remained popular among workers because of the role of troops in the repression of strikes. But the Second Moroccan Crisis between Germany and France that same year (see Chapter 22) gave rise to another wave of nationalism. Besieged by the press for his pacific stand, Caillaux's government fell the following year. Raymond Poincaré (1860–1934), an outspoken nationalist who loved reviewing troops while military bands played, became premier in 1912 and then president a year later. He eagerly anticipated the chance to win back Alsace and Lorraine, and he firmed up French support of a Russian role in the Balkans. Poincaré's nationalism seemed in tune with the times.

CONCLUSION

The second half of the nineteenth century brought about significant political change to the three European powers that had been the strongest at mid-century. In Britain, the second Reform Bill of 1867 expanded the electoral franchise. Following the collapse of the Second Empire in 1870 and the Paris Commune the following year, France emerged as a republic. Unlike Britain and France, the Russian Empire had not entered a period of liberal reform. Following defeat in the Crimean War, Tsar Alexander II's emancipation of the serfs in 1861 did not change the fundamental institutions of autocracy. Yet some reforms did follow, even as critics of the tsarist state grew more vocal, contributing to the Revolution of 1905, which challenged the foundations of autocracy. In the meantime, Britain's economic strength and great navy left it in a position to dominate international affairs. Having defeated both Austria and France, Prussia emerged as the leader of a unified and powerful Germany, dominant in Central Europe.

At the same time, remarkable technological advances, increased mass production, and continued urbanization characterized the Second Industrial Revolution, which began about 1870. But as the pace of life seemed to accelerate in a time of material progress, pessimism and anxiety together characterized the remarkable years that brought to a close the nineteenth century and the dawning of the modern world in the first years of the twentieth century.

CHAPTER 19

RAPID INDUSTRIALIZATION AND ITS CHALLENGES, 1870–1914

Jeanne Bouvier was a peasant girl born in 1865 in southeastern France, south of Lyon. In her village, her father earned his living by tilling the fields and as a barrel maker, an occupation closely tied to wine production. But in 1876, disease began to destroy the vineyards of the Rhône River Valley. Jeanne's family was forced to sell its land and possessions and travel to find work, pushed along by poverty and unemployment. From age eleven to fourteen, Jeanne worked thirteen hours a day in a silk mill. Four other jobs in various towns and villages in her region followed until Jeanne's mother took her to Paris, where the first job she found lasted only a week. Like so many other single, female migrants to city life, she then worked as a domestic servant until a cousin showed her how to do hat-trimming work. When that trade collapsed because of changes in style and the economic depression, she became a skilled dressmaker in a Parisian workshop and then developed her own clientele. In this way, Jeanne Bouvier became a Parisian. When she returned home to her native village, Jeanne spoke French, and not the patois in which her old friends conversed. She had become an urban woman.

In 1900, the French Catholic writer Charles Péguy expressed the opinion that Europe had changed more in the previous thirty years than it had since the time of Jesus Christ. The period 1870–1914 was indeed one of rapid economic and social change in much of Europe. Technological advances helped propel the Second Industrial Revolution of the century's last decades. It swept across much of northern, western, and central Europe, as well as the United States, and some of southern and eastern

(*Left*) The Eiffel Tower illuminated at night. (*Right*) The Palace of Electricity at the Paris Exhibition of 1900.

Europe. Machinery transformed industry even in relatively undeveloped countries, from Portugal to Russia. New manufacturing processes spurred the emergence of the chemical, electrical, and the steel industries. "Big business" took shape as larger companies controlled a greater share of markets.

Technological advances and mechanized factory production transformed the way millions of people worked and lived. Electric lights began to turn night into day in rapidly growing cities. Rural areas were changing as well. Agricultural productivity increased. Large, productive farms whose lands were enriched by chemical fertilizers and cultivated with mechanized equipment could be found in Britain, parts of Belgium, northern France, and in Germany. Improvements in agriculture were considerably less evident in the Russian Empire, Eastern Europe, and the Balkans. In Hungary, where the great magnates and other nobles still owned much of the land, the use of agricultural machinery, the rotation of crops, and product specialization also brought greater yields.

Declining mortality rates led to an increase in Europe's population. Longer life expectancy followed better nutrition—a more varied diet with greater caloric consumption—as well as improved sanitation and purer water supplies. Living conditions gradually improved for most people. Wages continued to rise. Mass education elevated rates of literacy. The middle class expanded in size and complexity. An expansion in white-collar jobs—including positions as clerks, tram ticket collectors, and schoolteachers, among many others—offered some peasants and workers chances for social mobility, particularly in Western Europe; new employment opportunities beckoned in cities.

Many workers now had a little money and time left over for leisure activities. Bicycles, sports, and, early in the new century, movies became part of the lives of millions. Nonetheless, in many regions—including much of southern Italy, Spain, Portugal, Russia, and the Balkans—wrenching poverty remained common, and mobility into the middle class remained exceptional at the turn of the century.

The last years of the nineteenth century—the fin de siècle—would be remembered after World War I as the "Belle Époque,"—the "good old days"—a period of material progress and cultural innovation. New inventions like the telephone and automobile promised an even better life ahead. The creation in 1883 of a worldwide system for patenting reflected a veritable torrent of new inventions.

THE SECOND INDUSTRIAL REVOLUTION

Steel led the Second Industrial Revolution. Then, once the problem of the generation of electricity had been solved, electricity accelerated European economic growth, providing, with the century's last two decades, power for industry. It brought a stunning variety of technological innovations that ultimately improved the everyday lives of most Europeans. In large cities, subways and, increasingly, automobiles made people more mobile. At the same time, new discoveries in the physical sciences—particularly chemistry—as well as the development of germ theory and bacteriology led to advances that improved agriculture, as well as public health, making possible longer lives.

The Second Industrial Revolution seemed oblivious to the long economic depression that began in 1873 and lasted until the mid-1890s. It was marked by falling prices and punctuated by financial panics, although not by prolonged unemployment or economic stagnation. Following a fever of speculation, particularly in Germany, banks failed in Vienna. The

TABLE 19.1. ANNUAL OUTPUT OF STEEL (IN MILLIONS OF METRIC TONS)

Year	Britain	Germany	France	Russia
1875–1879	0.90	—	0.26	0.08
1880–1884	1.82	0.99	0.46	0.25
1885–1889	2.86	1.65	0.54	0.23
1890–1894	3.19	2.89	0.77	0.54
1895–1899	4.33	5.08	1.26	1.32
1900–1904	5.04	7.71	1.70	2.35
1905–1909	6.09	11.30	2.65	2.63
1910–1913	6.93	16.24	4.09	4.20

Source: Carlo Cipolla, ed., *The Fontana Economic History of Europe*, vol. 3(2) (London: Collins/Fontana Books, 1976), p. 775.

speed with which the crisis spread to other financial capitals reflected the extent to which improvements in transportation and communication during the middle decades of the nineteenth century had extended the links of an increasingly global economy. Agricultural prices fell virtually everywhere in Europe, in part because imported grain from the United States and Canada flooded markets. In every industrialized country, tariffs became the focus of impassioned political debate, even in Britain, where economic liberalism remained the prevailing credo. Governments responded to the depression by imposing protective tariffs in the interest of native industries and agriculture: Austria (1874), Russia (1875), France (1892), Italy (1887), and Germany (1902).

New Technology and Scientific Discoveries

In 1856, the English inventor Henry Bessemer (1813–1898) developed a new method for forging steel from pig iron by forcing air through the molten metal to reduce its carbon content. The result was steel that was less expensive to produce than it had been by the old method and that could be turned out in greater quantities (see Table 19.1). Other discoveries over the next twenty years permitted the production of steel of a more consistent quality, lowering its price by two-thirds.

Steel's strength, durability, and flexibility gave it a marked advantage over iron. Steel improved the size, quality, standardization, and precision of machinery. Just three years after Bessemer's discovery, the first British ship constructed of steel slid into the sea. Larger, sturdier, and faster than their predecessors, steel ships transformed naval warfare, contributing to the Anglo-German naval rivalry that accelerated dangerously at the dawn of the new century.

Medical advances enhanced the already soaring prestige of science and the professional stature of its practitioners. Thanks to discoveries in medical science, in much of Europe a trip to the doctor was no longer seen as the first step to the undertaker. Anesthesia, which had already been discovered in the United States in the 1840s, had begun to make surgery less painful. The French scientist Louis Pasteur (1822–1895) discovered that just as various types of fermentation were caused by different kinds of germs, so were many diseases. His development of germ theory in the 1860s brought a virtual revolution in health care. His

Louis Pasteur in his laboratory.

experiments demonstrated that the spoilage of food could be avoided by destroying microbes that were already present and preventing the arrival of others (thus, the "pasteurization" of beverages, including milk). Pasteur's studies of specific bacteria and viruses led to the immunization of animals. Wilhelm Röntgen (1845–1923), a German scientist, discovered the X-ray in 1895. Then another German, Robert Koch (1843–1910), discovered and isolated the tuberculosis bacillus, winning the Nobel Prize in 1905.

The development of bacteriology, which infused the hygienic movement with the certitude of science and helped create preventative medicine, had a salutary influence on daily life, reducing mortality by encourag-ing, for example, sewage works. Many towns built sewer systems to ensure a cleaner water supply. This reduced some contagious diseases, and people seemed to become less tolerant of foul smells. Rat poison killed off millions of disease-carrying rodents. Still, the poor continued to die earlier than people of means, even as the European population rapidly increased.

The Electric and Chemical Revolutions

Electricity made possible the invention of the electromagnetic telegraph, the undersea cable, and the telephone. Yet electricity remained little more than a scientific curiosity until late in the century. The bottleneck remained the generation of electricity. Werner von Siemens (1816–1892), a German, invented the first self-excited electromagnetic generator in 1867, which made possible the production of electrical energy, and three years later the first generator of direct current (a ring dynamo) followed. Germany took the lead in the production of power generators. Thomas Edison (1847–1931), an American scientist, invented the incandescent lamp in 1879. Two years later, the first electric power stations began oper-ation in England, and during the following decades electricity gradually entered European homes. Electric alternators and transformers and improvements in cable and insulation provided means by which electric power could be generated and diffused. Yet, well into the twentieth cen-tury, in many parts of Europe electricity still remained a luxury, lighting only magnificent hotels and fancy neighborhoods.

For all their efficiency, water power, coal, and gas had placed limits on the location of factories. Electric power, however, could be transported with relative ease, which ultimately enabled countries not well endowed with natural resources to industrialize partially. The steel, textile, shoe-making, and construction industries, among others, came to depend upon electric power. In Europe, as in the United States, the first results of the electric age were particularly striking in heavy industry—for example in electrochemistry (aluminum) and metallurgy (electric furnaces). Electric-ity also provided a source of power in small workshops. The burgeoning German electrical manufacturing industry helped Germany to challenge Britain for European manufacturing primacy.

Women working on a sewing machine and sewing by hand.

The sewing machine, developed by the American Isaac Singer (1811–1875), began to be found in the 1850s in industry and homes, well before the use of electricity became common. The mechanization of the production of ready-made garments rapidly extended consumer markets, setting styles and reducing the price of clothing. But the impact of the sewing machine also demonstrated continuities in industrial work. For the garment industry—attracting Jewish immigrants to Paris and, above all, New York—remained largely tied to home work. Women, and some men, too, worked sewing machines in their apartments and rooms and in cramped sweatshops, turning out ready-made cloaks and dresses. Machines that could do band stitching, make button holes, or embroider led to a further specialization of labor. Singer marketed his machine as a device that would liberate women from tedious work. But the sewing machine also bound many women to the hectic pace of piecework, and to payments for the machine itself, usually purchased on time-payment plans.

By 1900, electrically powered household appliances—refrigerators, fans, and vacuum cleaners—were generally available to those families that could afford to have their houses wired for electricity and could pay for the appliances.

The development of chemistry also brought lasting advances, particularly in Germany, where research and teaching developed in universities and which by 1900 trained far more chemists than any other country.

German companies benefited from synthetic organic chemistry, manufacturing dyes, soaps, and pharmaceuticals, further improving sanitation and public health. Fritz Haber (1868–1934), another German, discovered the nitrogen-fixing process, by which atmospheric nitrogen could be converted into compounds. By 1913, he and his colleagues were able to transform ammonia into nitric acid by oxidation, which made possible the industrial production of fertilizers and explosives (Germany had previously been dependent on importing nitrates in order to produce explosives). Advances in chemistry helped transform agriculture, the textile industry, and engineering.

In Western Europe, business became bigger. Powerful industrial giants began to emerge. The development of economic cartels dealt a blow to the liberal era of free trade. Cartels are formal agreements by which competitors within the same industry protect profits by sharing markets, regulating output, fixing prices, or taking other measures to limit competition. Cartels permitted a few large companies to dominate production and distribution, enabling heavy industries to protect themselves during periods of falling prices and high unemployment by controlling production and setting prices. In Germany, mining cartels set production goals and kept prices artificially high. In France and Great Britain, informal agreements among industrialists achieved virtually the same results as formalized cartels. The return to protective tariffs aided cartels, protecting them from competition from abroad. Even where there were no cartels, the concentration of business in larger companies continued, in part because in industries such as metallurgy and chemicals, expensive machinery made "start-up" costs prohibitive for smaller firms.

Regional Variations

The industrial boom of the Second Industrial Revolution was perhaps most dramatic in Germany. By 1890, both Germany and the United States had moved ahead of Britain in metallurgical production. By the turn of the century, German factories turned out more steel than Britain and France combined. Germany's chemical industry was the most modern in the world, producing fertilizers, chlorine, and other products for agriculture and industry. In 1900, Britain produced twice as much sulphuric acid as Germany; in 1913, the proportion had been reversed.

How can we explain the German industrial productivity? Germany enjoyed the advantage of starting to industrialize after its rivals, thereby being able to employ the most modern equipment in factories specially built to accommodate technological advances. By contrast, some British factories, most of which had been built early in the century (and some even before), seemed to be crumbling.

German banks played a more direct role in German industrialization than did their counterparts in other countries. While providing investment capital, the Dresdner Bank, Deutsche Bank, and other large investment banks themselves acquired large blocks of industrial shares, particularly in heavy industries like coal mining, electricity, and railways. Having entered industry in order to assure proper business management of companies to which they loaned money, they earned big profits and paid high dividends. German banks themselves became industrial entrepreneurs. This also favored the trend of German industry toward cartels, which controlled production and prices and therefore provided security within heavy industries.

German universities were more numerous and of better quality than any others in Europe at the same time, despite their authoritarian structure and their acquiescence in discrimination against Jews, Catholics, and socialists. They emerged as centers of scientific research. By contrast, English employers tended to look down their noses at academic training as a poor substitute for work experience, just as universities in Britain were relatively slow to adopt a more practical curriculum.

British manufactured goods stacked up at the docks as demand declined abroad and prices fell. By the mid-1880s, some of the countries that had purchased British goods were able to meet consumer demand at home with their own production. Shiploads of foreign-made goods in the century's last decades began to undercut British production, which was unprotected by tariff walls. Instead of depending upon British shipping, German, Italian, and French merchants now took advantage of the Suez Canal, opened in 1869, to send their own ships to Asia to make purchases and sell goods directly. Yet Great Britain remained the world's greatest economic power.

In the Russian Empire, the economy remained overwhelmingly agricultural. The famine of 1890–1891, which killed millions of peasants and to which the novelist Leo Tolstoy helped focus international concern, demonstrated the fragility and limits of Russian agriculture. Absentee ownership of large estates, the many small peasant plots that continued to be farmed at subsistence level as they had been for centuries, and village communal lands hindered agricultural development. Farming remained dependent on peasant-owned machinery and in some places lacked even enough horses to pull plows. Yet Russian agriculture gradually increased its productivity, doing so without the capital-intensive farming that characterized much of Western Europe. Russian increases in harvest yields were comparable to those of France and Germany by 1900. Larger yields made possible the increased export of grain and other foodstuffs. The Peasant Land Bank, created in the 1880s, helped thousands of peasants purchase land and a thriving cooperative movement beginning at the turn of the century helped some prosper.

Russian industries, too, had much to overcome. They faced the serious physical impediment of sheer distance between resources, manufacturers, and markets. Coal deposits lay far from centers of manufacturing. Some

Russians, because of the influence of the Orthodox Church, viewed investment as usurious and therefore dishonest. Weak banking structures limited the accumulation of investment capital and left some Russian manufacturers largely dependent on foreign capital.

Yet Russian industry also developed rapidly beginning in the mid-1890s, benefiting from advanced technology imported from Western Europe (see Map 19.1). Foreign investment in Russia, above all, from France, more than doubled during the 1890s. Although textiles still represented the largest branch of Russian industry, heavy industries, particularly metallurgy, boomed. The state helped develop heavy metals and fuel production, including oil. The output of steel increased fourfold during the last decades of the century (see Table 19.2). At the same time, the growth of light industry and the expansion of the market contributed considerably to the country's economic growth, permitting exports to Asian neighbors. Russian foreign trade tripled between 1885 and 1913. Russia's rail lines increased by three times between 1881 and 1905, and its banks developed in size and scale. By the turn of the century, railroads at last linked Russia's major cities and facilitated the shipping of grain to the empire's northern ports.

The Russian working class grew from about 2 million industrial workers in 1900 to about 3 million by 1914 (compared to over a 100 million peasants). Many Russian industrial workers still labored part-time in agriculture. They retained strong ties to their villages, which remained their legal residences. The rural commune still carried out functions of local authority, including many fiscal obligations (assuring the payment of taxes and redemption payments on land gained at the time of the emancipation of the serfs in 1861), policing (including overseeing the division of communal lands), and rudimentary welfare functions. But one of the key social phenomena of the period was the development of a permanent working class that had broken its ties with the countryside. Even in overwhelmingly rural Bulgaria, the value of industrial production multiplied by three times just between 1904 and 1911, and the railway network increased by almost ten times between 1880 and 1912.

In most of Europe's industrializing countries, the growing manufacturing sector coexisted with small-scale production (see Map 19.2). In France, whose economy still also was dominated by agriculture, the production of high-quality handicrafts, centered in Paris, continued to dominate industry, despite the presence of developing heavy industry. Traditional small-scale manufacturing also persisted alongside regionally specific heavy industries in Spain (Catalonia and the Basque country), Austria-Hungary, and Italy, where little large-scale industry could be found south of the triangle formed by Milan, Turin, and the port of Genoa. As in Russia, most of the investment in Spanish industry came from abroad because agriculture generated inadequate surpluses for significant industrial investment. In the Austro-Hungarian monarchy, the dynamism of Bohemia and Moravia contrasted sharply with the small-market ways of Austria and the Hungarian plain. In the Balkans, where major rail lines were not in place until the late 1880s, poor roads and the daunting impediments posed by nature prevented even the emergence of vibrant regional market economies. In many places, mules remained the best way to transport goods.

MAP 19.1 RUSSIAN INDUSTRIALIZATION, 1870–1914 Areas of industrial concentration, including kinds of industry and resources.

TABLE 19.2. PRODUCTION OF COAL AND STEEL IN RUSSIA (IN THOUSANDS OF TONS)

Year	Coal	Steel
1860	695	257
1880	3,276	289
1890	6,015	857
1900	16,155	2,711
1910	25,000	3,017
1913	36,038	4,918

Source: Arcadius Kahan, *Russian Economic History: The Nineteenth Century* (Chicago: University of Chicago Press, 1989), p. 21.

Travel and Communications

Electric power led to the construction of public transportation systems, first trams and then subways. Mass transportation transformed residential patterns in large cities. The London underground railway had already opened in 1863, making it possible for employees and workers to live farther from their jobs. On July 14, 1900, the first Paris subway—the *métro*—began operation on the right bank of the Seine River, and other lines soon followed, connecting the center city with its periphery. Four years later, the first sections of New York City's subway began operation.

In 1885, Carl Benz (1844–1929), a German engineer, built upon the invention of the internal combustion engine, by adding a primitive carburetor, thus constructing a small automobile. The first automobiles were very expensive, the tires alone costing more than an average worker's annual wages. In 1897, Rudolf Diesel (1858–1913), a German, produced the first successful engine fueled by kerosene, which could power larger vehicles capable of carrying heavy loads. By the turn of the century, four-cylinder engines powered automobiles.

Automobile manufacturing quickly became a major catalyst for industrial growth and the implementation of new production methods, stimulating industries that produced steel, aluminum, rubber, and tools. The petroleum industry, too, gradually developed, although at the time only the oil reserves in Romania were known and exploited (the first oil refinery in Europe had been built there in 1857). Only slowly did some industrialists and statesmen begin to grasp the economic and strategic significance of oil wealth, particularly after the discovery in 1908 of rich oil fields in Persia (Iran).

Automobile manufacturers shifted from the limited production of elite cars, above all, the British Rolls Royce, to less expensive models. Henry Ford (1863–1947), who began his company in Detroit in 1903, produced more than 15 million "Model T" Fords, which even some of his own workers could afford to purchase.

MAP 19.2 AREAS OF INDUSTRIAL CONCENTRATION, 1870–1914 Various regions industrialized more quickly than others, with industrial concentration likely to be found where there were coal fields and rivers.

Areas of industrial concentration

An early automobile assembly line.

Worried by American competition, particularly in its lucrative export market to Britain, the French car manufacturer Louis Renault (1877–1944) looked for ways to cut production costs. Assembly-line production made it possible for his company to construct cars in segments. Workers mounted components on stationary chassis frames lined up along the factory floor. They used hand files to shape engine parts for expensive cars since interchangeable parts were not yet available. Techniques of scientific management of assembly-line production—"Taylorism," after Frederick W. Taylor (1856–1915), the American engineer who developed them—included careful counting of the number of units assembled by each worker in an hour. The assembly line reduced the time it took to produce each car from twelve hours to one and a half hours.

A revolution in communications also slowly transformed life. The telephone, invented by Alexander Graham Bell (1847–1922) in 1876, reached private homes. Germans made 8 million telephone calls in 1883, 700 million in 1900. Fifteen years after Thomas Edison invented the gramophone in 1876, a number of virtuosos had made their first scratchy recordings. The Italian Guglielmo Marconi (1874–1937) pioneered the first wireless voice communication in the 1890s; by 1913, weekly concerts could be heard on the radio in Brussels. Silent motion pictures, first shown in 1895, became an immediate hit. Early viewers watched brief scenes of modern life, such as a train beginning to move. Entrepreneurs soon offered considerably longer films with plots and action, and silent movies were increasingly accompanied by a piano. The Austro-Hungarian army began to experiment with motion pictures, using cameras to study the flight of artillery shells.

The automobile transformed travel even more than had the railway earlier in the nineteenth century. Elegant horses and fancy carriages owned by people of means no longer monopolized travel, although country gentlemen scored an early triumph, convincing the British Parliament to pass the "Red Flag Act." Until it was repealed in 1896, the act restricted the speed of motor vehicles to two miles per hour and required three people carrying red warning flags to accompany each vehicle, a decided inconvenience. In 1896, the speed limit was raised to fourteen miles per hour.

Car travel necessitated better roads. Early drivers required not only thick goggles to protect themselves against dust but also whips to keep away startled dogs. Gradually, government authorities ordered the paving of roads, and gas stations began to dot the landscape. In 1900, the Michelin company in France, one of the first to shift from producing bicycle to automobile tires, first published its guide for travelers, listing garages, hotels, and restaurants in every town of any size in the country. The number of cars in Paris tripled between 1906 and 1912. Traffic jams became a way of urban life. Automobile-taxis and then motorized fire engines raced by their horse-drawn predecessors.

The cult of speed next took to the air, after centuries of dreams had brought only balloon ascents and short glider flights. In 1900, a retired German general, Count Ferdinand von Zeppelin (1838–1917), built the lumbering dirigible airship that still bears his name. After years of experimentation with propellers and small engines, Orville and Wilbur Wright, two American bicycle manufacturers, launched the first successful flight in 1903. They then took their air show to England, France, and Germany, where the crown prince of Prussia began to consider the military uses of the airplane. To the young Swiss architectural student Le Corbusier, the airplane was "the vanguard of the conquering armies of the New Age."

Whether or not they went by car, more Europeans could now travel for leisure than ever before. Middle-class vacations became more common. The travel business boomed. Health spas and resorts, which had developed since the mid-1800s, became even more popular in Western Europe.

Women at work at a telephone switchboard.

Spas claimed that their thermal waters offered healing and sustaining properties, facilitating the circulation of blood, attacking gout—the encumbering malady of people who were too well fed—or in some other way restoring to equilibrium the human body victimized by modern life.

Mediterranean, North Sea, and English Channel resorts offered casinos and beach-front promenades. English coastal towns like Brighton and Blackpool attracted middle-class and working-class tourists, oblivious to the cold, rainy climate. The tourist pier and arcade took shape. English nobles, who could afford to flee the British winter, "discovered" Nice. Upper-class Italians began to frequent their own Riviera. Germans preferred chilly Baltic resorts. Vacationers from many countries discovered the Alps and sent the first postcards back to envious friends. Partially spurred on by tourism, photography emerged as a major visual art, moving from individual poses to mass picture taking. The relatively light Kodak camera appeared in 1888. Before too long Bretons began to refer to French-speaking tourists as "Kodakers."

Further Scientific Discoveries: "A Boundless Future" and Its Uncertainties

The astonishing advances of nineteenth-century science led one researcher to exude that "science strides on victoriously towards a boundless future." But new discoveries revealing nature's complexity began to temper the infectious optimism of the age. Scientists had already concluded that cells form the basis for life, and new knowledge led scientists to a greater awareness of the principles of heredity. Yet, fin-de-siècle scientists realized that the more they understood about the world, the more there was left to know about such basic principles as matter, light, and energy. Mathematicians and especially physicists began to rethink fundamental assumptions about the universe. Radioactivity was discovered in Paris in 1896. Marie Curie (1867–1934), a Polish-born chemist carrying out research with her husband, Pierre Curie (1859–1906), in 1910 isolated radium, a radioactive element. Marie Curie, who was refused entry to the French Academy of Science because of her gender, won two Nobel Prizes. Her rival, Ernest Rutherford (1871–1937), a New Zealander, discovered two kinds of radiation, which he called the alpha and beta rays. He posited the disintegration of radioactive atoms, which is the phenomenon of radioactivity. Rutherford used this discovery to postulate the structure of the atom, with a positively charged nucleus and negatively charged electrons circling around it.

"Particle theories" in physics cast doubt on contemporary assumptions about the universe. They demonstrated the complexity of motion, light, and matter, which appeared to consist of electrically charged particles. Since the time of the great seventeenth-century English thinker Sir Isaac Newton, scientists had believed that any two objects, whether the sun and the earth, or a coffee cup and a bowl of sugar, acted on each other through

(*Left*) An English caricature of Pierre and Marie Curie. (*Right*) Ernest Rutherford, who is holding the apparatus that he used to break up the nucleus of the nitrogen atom.

gravitational force. There seemed no mechanism for transmitting action but rather only empty space between the two. James Maxwell (1831–1879), a British scientist, solved the "action at a distance" problem for the case of electromagnetic forces. His theory of electromagnetic fields postulated that one object creates an electrical field around particles, which in turn exerts forces on electrically charged objects, and that light itself consists of electromagnetic waves. The German scientist Max Planck (1858–1947) discovered that radiant energy is emitted discontinuously in discrete units, or quanta. Planck's quantum theory, not finalized until 1925, challenged the fundamental scientific understanding of energy that had survived almost intact since Newton. More than this, it seemed to add an element of chance to the story of the universe, suggesting that its operations were not absolutely predictable. Here, too, scientists now realized that they knew considerably less about the nature of matter and about the universe than they had thought.

These discoveries were only a beginning. The much more difficult problem of gravity remained. In Switzerland, German-born Albert Einstein (1879–1955), whose modest position as a patent examiner of other people's discoveries belied his genius, sought to carry physics beyond Newton's theory that space and time were absolute quantities. In 1905, Einstein postulated a special theory of relativity, arguing that the velocity of light was both constant and independent of the velocities of the source and observer of light.

Einstein also postulated the relationship between mass and energy in his equation: $E = mc^2$ (energy equals mass multiplied by the square of the speed of light). In the mid-twentieth century, this formula would provide the key for the controlled release of energy from the atom. After becoming a professor in Zurich, Prague, and then Berlin, Einstein's search for an exact description of the laws of gravitation led him in 1915 from his relatively simple special theory of relativity to his general principle of relativity, which postulated that the laws of nature operated in exactly the same way for all observers. His theory supplanted traditional theories of gravitation, which saw gravity as a property of objects interacting with each other. Rather, Einstein believed that they interacted with space. Yet Einstein and other scientists remained ill-at-ease with the element of chance suggested by Planck's quantum theory. Trying to explain his conclusion that the universe could not operate in a random way, Einstein later insisted: "God does not play dice." Both Planck's theory, by suggesting a role for chance, and Einstein's staggering achievements themselves left open as many questions for the future as they resolved, not the least of which would later be terrifying new applications of the German scientist's famous formula to the hydrogen and atom bombs.

Albert Einstein explaining his theories to a stunned audience.

TABLE 19.3. POPULATION GROWTH IN MAJOR STATES BETWEEN 1871 AND 1911 (POPULATION IN MILLIONS)

	c. 1871	c. 1911	% increase
German Empire	41.1	64.9	57.8
France	36.1	39.6	9.7
Austria-Hungary*	35.8	49.5	38.3
Great Britain	31.8	45.4	42.8
Italy	26.8	34.7	29.5
Spain	16.0	19.2	20.0

*Not including Bosnia-Herzegovina.
Source: Colin Dyer, *Population and Society in Twentieth Century France* (New York: Holmes and Meier, 1978), p. 5.

SOCIAL CHANGE

Between 1870 and 1914, the population of Europe increased by half, rising from 290 to 435 million (see Table 19.3). By the end of the nineteenth century, one of every four people in the world was a European. Most countries urbanized; the number of people living in cities and towns increased even more rapidly than the general population as urban births outnumbered deaths. More and more "white-collar" positions, such as clerks and salespeople, became available, and service employment drew migrants to cities. Increased factory production altered the physical structure of industrial cities: they were characterized by greater social segregation within their limits, and working-class suburbs grew rapidly on the edge of town. Overseas emigration, particularly to the Americas, rose rapidly and did not slow down even with the end of the economic depression in the mid-1890s.

Demographic Boom

Europe's population grew rapidly because the continent passed from the traditional pattern of high birthrates and high death rates to low rates of both births and deaths. Mortality rates fell during the second half of the nineteenth century, particularly among children. Births outnumbered deaths, despite the fact that fertility rates fell beginning in the 1860s, or even before. Yet in England, dysentery and diarrhea still carried off about 15 of every 100 infants born. In France, infant mortality declined from about 184 to 159 per 1,000 live births in the last two decades of the nineteenth century. The big decline in infant mortality came to England after 1900. Reasons for such improvement include greater medical knowledge of chest and stomach infections, as well as a general improvement in the standard of living. Poor people could afford to eat more nutritious food and lived in warmer, drier accommodations, although such improvements still lagged behind in large, dirty, industrial cities.

With infant mortality greatly reduced, more couples sought to control the number of children they had (see Table 19.4). The number of families with more than two or three children fell. Although Britain's Queen Victoria had nine children, poor families often had more children than upper-class couples, who seem to have limited births because they wanted to devote more resources to the education and inheritance of each child.

Contraception became more widespread. Coitus interruptus was the most common method, although it was hardly flawless. An upper-middle-class English woman told a friend after she had given birth: "Dear child, you look very pale and must not have another baby for a long time. Henry always withdrew in time, such a noble man!" Rudimentary condoms made of animal intestines were superseded in the 1880s by rubber condoms, although these still were relatively expensive, available mainly in cities, and used primarily for protection against disease rather than for birth control.

In France, officials and nationalists worried about their country's unique plunging birthrate. The reasons for it have continued to baffle demographers. Although regions with many practicing Catholics continued to have high rates of birth, the French population grew by only about 15 percent from mid-century until 1914. In one small area in southwestern France, the birth of a second child—one more mouth to feed—occasioned condolence cards. The division of farmland into small plots may be a partial explanation—another child ultimately meant a further subdivision of land because France no longer had primogeniture (inheritance by the eldest son).

In some places, however, births to unmarried couples or to single mothers increased in number. Young female migrants to the city, no longer constrained by living with their parents, were vulnerable to the advances of men promising marriage or promising nothing at all. Unplanned pregnancies followed. A sizable percentage of the population of most coun-

TABLE 19.4. THE DECLINE IN FAMILY SIZE (NUMBER OF CHILDREN) IN ENGLAND AND WALES

Year	Family Size
1861–1869	6.16
1871	5.94
1876	5.62
1890–1899	4.13
1900–1909	3.30
1910–1914	2.82

Source: E. A. Wrigley, *Population and History* (New York: McGraw-Hill, 1969), p. 197.

tries—about 10 to 15 percent—never married or entered into permanent or long-term relationships. Unmarried women were especially common in Scotland, Ireland, and in Brittany in France, from which more males than females migrated to urban, industrial regions.

Improving Standards of Living

Living standards improved for ordinary people in every industrialized country. Standards of living were far higher in northern Europe than in southern and eastern Europe, greater in Britain than in France, with Germany closing the gap with both of its rivals. In Britain, real wages (taking inflation into account), which had increased by a third between 1850 and 1875, again rose by almost half during the last three decades of the century. Workers enjoyed higher levels of consumption because the price of food declined, principally because of increased agricultural production and improved transportation. Working-class families still spent half of their budget on food, but this was almost a quarter less than during the past several centuries. This left more money to spend on clothes, with something occasionally left over. Small-town shops were better supplied than ever before, and ready-made clothes sold on market day alongside manufactured household utensils.

More grain and meat, arriving in refrigerated ships, reached Europe from Australia, Canada, the United States, and Argentina. Meat ceased to be a luxury. The average German had consumed almost 60 pounds of meat in 1873, 105 pounds in 1912. Germans consumed on average three times more sugar at the end of the century than thirty years earlier. Still, workers almost everywhere remained chronically undernourished and vulnerable to childhood diseases, which is reflected in the fact that the average European laborer was shorter than the average middle-class person.

Migration and Emigration

European migration was part of a worldwide movement of men and women in what was becoming a global labor force. Migration—both permanent and seasonal—within Europe continued to be significant. Seasonal work took hundreds of thousands of laborers across borders for part of the year as construction and harvest workers. Some Italian laborers known as "swallows" spent four weeks a year going to and from Argentina to work the harvests!

Permanent migration to the city did not end the contact between the migrants and their rural origins. In France, many industrial workers still went back to their villages to help with the harvest and many miners were also part-time farmers. In Russia, the peasant-workers of Moscow and St. Petersburg kept one foot in the rural world. They lived on the edge of the cities and dressed like villagers, maintaining legal ties to their rural commune, where they remained responsible for their share of the commune's tax quota. In 1900, peasants made up two-thirds of the population of St. Petersburg, a city of more than 1.4 million people.

Thus, migration was a two-way street, at least when patterns of movement involved relatively short distances. When migrants returned home for visits, they brought with them not only stories about what they had experienced in the cities and towns where they now lived, but different ways of speaking, knowledge of birth control, the habit of reading, a taste for sports, and greater political awareness and interest.

Emigration to other countries emerged as one of the most significant social phenomenon of the age. Peasants and laborers, in particular, left Europe in hope of economic opportunity in the United States, Canada, and Latin America. Ireland, Britain, and Germany had provided most of the earlier waves of emigrants—for example, during the "hungry forties" marked by the Irish potato famine. Overseas emigration increased dramatically during the nineteenth century's last decades, the result of agricultural stagnation, religious persecution, and the hope of finding a better life. Russia and Eastern Europe sent an increasing number of impoverished people abroad. Between 1890 and 1914, about 350,000 Greeks—one-seventh of the population of Greece—left their country, most for good.

With improving economic times in the late 1890s, emigration slowed down from Germany, while remaining high from Ireland and increasing dramatically from Italy. During the first decade of the twentieth century, emigration from Europe rose to between 1 and 1.4 million people each year. Most of those packing themselves onto overcrowded steamers went to the United States: Italians and Irish to New York, Boston, and Philadelphia; Russian and Polish Jews to New York's Lower East Side; Portuguese to Providence and New Bedford; Germans (and Poles) to Chicago, Milwaukee, and Philadelphia (see Table 19.5). In 1907, due to their sheer number, Italian emigrants sent back enough money to cover half the commercial deficit of their native country. Pushed by crop failures and pulled by the U.S. Homestead Act of 1862 (which virtually guaranteed land in the American West), waves

Immigrants from southern Italy arriving in New York City, 1905.

TABLE 19.5. EMIGRATION TO THE UNITED STATES, 1871–1910

	1871–1880	1881–1890	1891–1900	1901–1910
Germany	718,000	1,500,000	505,000	341,000
Ireland	437,000	656,000	388,000	339,000
England/ Scotland/Wales	548,000	807,000	272,000	526,000
Scandinavia	243,000	655,000	372,000	505,000
Italy	56,000	307,000	652,000	2,000,000
Austria-Hungary	73,000	363,000	574,000	2,145,000
Russia/ Baltic states	39,000	213,000	505,000	1,597,000

Source: Leonard Dinnerstein and David M. Reimers, *Ethnic Americans: A History of Immigration and Assimilation* (New York: Harper and Row, 1977), p. 11.

of Swedes, along with Norwegians and Finns, began to emigrate to the northern United States (including Minnesota and Washington State). By the 1930s, 3 million had changed countries, leaving a population of about 6 million at home. Hundreds of thousands of Portuguese left for Brazil in search of jobs as laborers, following the abolition of slavery in that country in 1888.

Between 1871 and 1914, more than 1.5 million Jews left Russia for the United States, fleeing poverty and periodic anti-Semitic violence in search of freedom and jobs. Many left their homes with little more than a few cherished items and great hopes. One Jewish emigrant from a village in Byelorussia (now Belarus) remembered that his family carried empty suitcases as they left home—they did not want the other people they met along the way to know that they owned virtually nothing to carry with them. Tens of thousands of Jews moved westward to European capitals. Unlike their more prosperous predecessors who had been political émigrés in the middle decades of the nineteenth century, they were not welcomed with open arms. Most Jews retained their cultural traditions and religion and spoke Yiddish as their first language, they were considered outsiders by many people in Vienna, Berlin, Budapest, Paris, and other cities (even in some cases by assimilated Jews). The Zionist movement for the establishment of the Jewish homeland in Palestine emerged partially in response to the rising tide of anti-Semitism in Europe. The movement's founder was Theodor Herzl (1860–1904), a gifted journalist and German-speaking Jew from Budapest who had moved to Vienna, then arguably the European capital of anti-Semitism.

Although many families left together for overseas destinations, many married men went alone, hoping either to send for their families when they could afford to do so, or to return after making and saving some money. Single men, too—more than single women—left loved ones on the docks of European ports, or on distant farms. A popular Irish ballad related some of the anguish of leaving one's home:

Oh, farewell to poor old Erin's Isle,
I now must leave you for awhile.
The rent and taxes are so high,
I can no longer stay.
From Dublin Quay I sailed away,
And landed here but yesterday.
My shoes and brogues and my shirt
Are all that's in my kit.
I have just called in to let you know
The sights I've seen before I go.

In new homes, migrants forged new collective identities, a process shaped not only by their own ethnic backgrounds and solidarities but also by conditions in their new homelands. Many never saw their families again. Migrants to the United States from southern Italy were the most likely to return permanently again, with almost two-thirds eventually going back.

The Changing World of Work

By 1900, more than half of all industrial workers in Britain, Germany, and Belgium were employed in firms with more than twenty workers. Although artisans, skilled workers, and unskilled workers often found themselves in the same factory, a larger percentage of workers, many with prior industrial experience in rural workshops or domestic industry, depended on their labor for survival. Most industrial workers came from proletarian families and grew up with few or no illusions about finding a more secure way of earning a living. Working-class families prepared their own offspring for industrial work. But "proletarian" was also a state of mind. Many workers took pride in their work and in their social class. "I was born in the slums of London of working-class parents," a contemporary recalled, "and although I have attained a higher standard of living, I still maintain I am working class."

Enormous differences existed in skill, remuneration, and quality of life among workers. In Britain, above all, workers who were relatively well off insisted on their respectability, viewing many occupations as beneath their dignity.

Nonetheless, one of the effects of "de-skilling" among workers was increased class consciousness and trade union militancy. Indeed, mechanization eliminated or reduced demand for some trades, skilled or otherwise. Skilled glassworkers in France, for example, were no longer needed when the Siemens furnace, which reduced fuel costs and permitted continuous production, was adapted to the production of bottles in the 1880s. Porcelain painters lost their jobs to unskilled female laborers when factory owners started using decals that could be applied to plates and then baked on. Steam laundries left many washerwomen without clients.

At the same time, however, new professions brought some workers higher status. Engineers, capable of designing, overseeing, and repairing machinery, became fixtures in factories. In the 1880s, some engineers still received training as apprentices, but by the first decades of the twentieth century, many had received university training in their chosen profession.

Most female workers were still employed in small workshops or at home, but more women became factory workers. Even in the Habsburg empire, which was much less industrialized than Germany or Britain, about 900,000 women worked in factories, largely in unskilled jobs. Most earned only about half the wages of their male counterparts for, in some cases, the same jobs. Women workers were usually the last hired and the first fired.

Despite harsh working conditions and relatively low wages, some women saw factory work as bringing an improvement in wages and conditions over agricultural labor, cottage industry, or domestic service. A Belfast woman in 1898 remembered her time in a linen mill: "Wonderful times then in the mill. You got a wee drink, got a join [pooled money with others to buy food], done your work and you had your company."

Women's work remained closely tied to their stage of life. Many young, unmarried women became servants upon arrival in the urban world, trying to save enough money for a modest dowry, in the hope of marrying someone of a slightly higher social class. Because upper-class families employed more domestics than ever before, three times more women worked in domestic service in England than in textile factories. By the end of the century, servants accounted for more than half of female workers in Britain.

Some contemporary surveys emphasized the plight of child workers, who already constituted 14 percent of the workforce in the British textile industry in 1874. Although most states had already passed laws limiting the ages of children who could be employed in factories and the hours they could work (see Chapter 14), at the turn of the century many thousands of children, including those between the ages of eight and fourteen, were still working part-time. Above age fourteen, children worked as adults.

In Émile Zola's best-selling novel *Germinal* (1885), the thirteenth of his series of twenty novels about a large working-class family, Étienne

Derbyshire pit boys outside the mines.

Lantier goes to work in the mines of northern France. In the shaft, where the temperature rose to ninety-five degrees and air could not circulate, fifteen-year-old Catherine teaches Étienne the exhausting and dangerous job of digging coal, filling the coal tub, and pushing and steering it on its tracks up the steep incline with his body. Believing Catherine to be about twelve because she was so small, "he was amazed at the child's strength, a nervous strength with much skill in it. She filled her tub [of coal] quicker than he did, with fast, regular little movements of her shovel, then pitched it to the incline with a long, slow push without any hitch, passing easily under the low rocks. . . . She sweated and panted and her joints cracked, but she never complained, for familiarity had brought apathy, and you would have thought that being doubled up like that was part of the normal course of human suffering."

Industrialization and the Working-Class Family

Moralists bemoaned some of the bad effects of industrial work, arguing that the uprooting of families from villages put them at risk in cities characterized by vice and immorality. Some blamed the increasing separation of home and work, claiming that moral degradation and promiscuity almost inevitably accompanied the mixing of the sexes in factories. They believed that only education, marriage, the habit of saving money, and a return to old moral ways could save family life. More than a few viewed single working women as by their very nature promiscuous, representing the worse aspects of modern cities, what one called "the blasts of unspeakable exhalations, the pell-mell of fumes, of evil emanations and bad dreams that hover above our darkened cities." Women, they claimed, were being taken away from their reproductive function, and from family life itself. Working-class families in cities were indeed much less likely to live with their extended families—that is, with parents and sometimes grandparents and in-laws—than were country people. More families tended to be broken up early when children sixteen years or younger left villages in search of work in the cities, leaving aged parents on their own at home. Furthermore, long hours in the factory for parents and children alike seemed to erode parental authority. Moralists blamed increasingly homogeneous working-class neighborhoods, where drinking and domestic violence seemed rampant.

Many women of child-bearing age who could afford to do so, or who had no other choice, tended children full-time. But once their offspring were old enough to care for themselves, many working-class mothers returned to factory work. Others worked at home, doing piecework and caring for their children at the same time. Many women thus alternated between industrial wage labor and child rearing, sometimes leaving factory work once their children had reached fourteen years of age, old enough to bring home minimal wages themselves.

Henri de Toulouse-Lautrec's *In the Salon at the Rue des Moulins* (1894) depicts French prostitutes.

As ever in the European experience, many women still were forced by economic circumstances into prostitution, in large cities, towns of modest size, and even villages. Some of the tens of thousands of prostitutes in Paris, London, Berlin, and Vienna worked in elegant brothels, under the direction of a "madam," who allowed them only a couple days off per year. Others worked on their own, waiting for customers in bars, parks, doorways, and windows. Most prostitutes were working-class women— some of whom were married—unable to find industrial work or, in some cases, having been dismissed from their positions as household servants because they had become pregnant. Many were young, having had to leave school early to support a younger brother or sister, and were already on their own.

Prostitutes began to be perceived more than ever before as a chronic danger to public health. Complaints from the middle class increased (which was ironic, since middle-class men constituted a significant portion of the clientele for prostitutes). Socialist parties, however, expressed little interest in prostitution as an issue of reform. While blaming capitalism for the low wages or unemployment that forced many women into prostitution, socialists criticized the structure of bourgeois family life and middle-class men for subsidizing the trade.

In 1864, the British Parliament passed the Contagious Diseases Act, which required medical examination of prostitutes. The goal was to stop the spread of venereal disease, particularly syphilis, by hospitalizing prostitutes found to be infected. If a woman refused medical examination, she could be prosecuted for prostitution. The Contagious Diseases Act had the ironic effect of transforming prostitution from a temporary profession for many struggling working-class women to a dead-end, permanent job because the law publicly branded them as prostitutes.

Josephine Butler (1828–1906), the devoutly religious wife of a clergyman and president of an association encouraging higher education for women, led a well-organized, determined campaign in Britain and then on the continent against the Contagious Diseases Act. Some opponents of the act objected that the law called only for the inspection of prostitutes, not their clients; others opposed extensive police regulatory authority. Butler espoused the right of women to regulate their own sexuality. Parliament responded by passing a law that banned brothels. It repealed the acts in 1886 but then forced prostitutes to operate in tolerated "red-light" districts, where they were often subject to violence. Almost all of the victims of the still unidentified London killer "Jack the Ripper" were prostitutes.

In France, where prostitutes had for some time been obliged to submit to medical inspection for venereal disease, state officials also implemented laws to bring them under greater regulatory control. The fear of syphilis contributed to the state regulation of prostitution in France, where both officials and the public viewed prostitution as a hygienic and social problem rather than a moral and religious one.

Gradually, the belief that morality could be legislated ebbed in Europe. Charitable institutions more willingly provided assistance to unwed mothers and their offspring, increasingly considering their sad situations as a social, not a moral, problem.

Teeming Cities

In 1899, an American statistician—the profession itself was another sign of the times—noted that "the concentration of population in cities [is] the most remarkable social phenomenon of the present century." Britain and Germany led the way, but France, Austria, Switzerland, Italy, Sweden, and even Spain and Serbia also had high rates of urban growth. Classic "factory towns" such as Manchester, Saint-Étienne, and Essen grew rapidly in size, but so did the population of other towns, swollen by service workers, factory laborers, and commercial employees.

Rural industry, which had provided spinning, weaving, and finishing work for hundreds of thousands of people—above all, women—on a full- or part-time basis, gradually disappeared during the last half of the century. Manufacturing, including home production in the garment industry, now became overwhelmingly concentrated in urban centers. Although farms became larger, mechanized agriculture (which became more prevalent in Western Europe) and falling agricultural prices reduced demand for farm laborers. These changes encouraged temporary and permanent migration to towns. Rural people and immigrants from foreign lands poured into cities, seeking work in the booming service sector or in industry, as employment opportunities in the countryside shrunk. For example, the population of Istanbul doubled in forty years, reaching 850,000 by 1886, swollen by the influx of Muslim refugees from Russia and the Balkans. In the Russian Empire, during the first fourteen years of the twentieth century, about 4 million peasants moved to cities or their outskirts to find urban industrial work, particularly to St. Petersburg, which in 1914 had more than 900 large factories, one of the largest concentrations of industry in Europe.

Although some working-class families now lived in marginally more spacious lodgings, many densely packed neighborhoods in large cities became ghastly slums. London had its infamous "back to back" row houses, with little or no space between the houses and room for little more between the rows than outdoor toilets, if that, and garbage heaps. For most British workers, a parlor (a family room), a sign of "respectability," remained only a dream. In Glasgow, Scotland, a third of the city's families lived in one room, as more and more highlanders crowded into tall tenement dwellings.

As Paris became ever more crowded, Emperor Napoleon III undertook a massive rebuilding project in Paris during the 1850s and 1860s. He entrusted the planning to Baron Georges Haussmann (1809–1891), prefect of the region of the Seine. Although his family had been from Alsace, Haussmann had grown up in the capital at a time when migrants from the provinces seemed to overwhelm the city and revolutionary upheaval appeared endemic. Together they planned the most massive project of

(*Left*) Tenement housing in Glasgow. (*Right*) Company housing near mines in northern France.

Emperor Napoleon III (*left*) and Baron Georges Haussmann, viewed as either the rebuilder of Paris or the "Alsatian Attila," (*right*).

urban renewal since the rebuilding of London following the great fire in
the seventeenth century and that of Edo (Tokyo) in Japan at about the
same time following the great conflagration of 1657.

Napoleon III and Haussmann wanted to facilitate the expansion of commerce and industry through the creation of long, wide boulevards, which
would be lined by symmetrical apartment buildings. The "great crossing,"
then the chief intersection of Paris, was the intersection of major boulevards
along and perpendicular to the Seine River. To the west, the Arc de Triom-
phe became the center of a star-shaped intersection of new boulevards. It
was not a coincidence that some of the new arteries cut through some of the
most traditionally revolutionary neighborhoods, providing troops quick
access into the narrow streets in eastern Paris where ordinary people had
risen up during the June Days in 1848, as well as during the French Revolution, and making it more difficult to erect barricades. The impressionist
painter Auguste Renoir would lament the transformation of these old
Parisian neighborhoods and the new symmetrical buildings that lined the
boulevards, "cold and lined up like soldiers at review." It seemed an appropriate image to accompany the further consolidation of state power.

Glittering department stores and fancy cafés stood along the elegant
boulevards, showcases to imperial monumentalism but also to modern
life. Large structures of iron and glass, in the tradition of the Great Exposition of London of 1851, provided space for Les Halles, the refurbished
market of central Paris.

Napoleon III also wanted to make Paris a healthier place. In central Paris, some of the broad boulevards replaced narrow, winding streets, cutting through dirty, unhealthy neighborhoods. Aqueducts were built to provide cleaner water for residents. Four hundred miles of underground sewers (which emptied into the Seine River northwest of Paris) improved health conditions in a city that had been ravaged by cholera in 1832 and 1849.

Although the massive rebuilding provided jobs for many workers, it also forced many thousands of workers and their families to leave the central city for the cheaper rents of the inner suburbs, particularly those to the north and northeast—which were annexed to Paris in 1860—or to increasingly industrialized suburbs farther out. For the loss of their rental lodgings, they were reimbursed but a single franc, about a third of a day's wages. Property owners then raised rents with impunity. Within a very short walk from Notre Dame Cathedral, more than 14,000 people were displaced from the Ile de la Cité by the construction of a public hospital and the new prefecture of police. The cost of all these projects was enormous and far exceeded original estimates. Speculators made a fortune, tipped off as to where the next demolitions would take place. Financial scandals finally forced Haussmann to resign in 1870.

By 1900, nine European cities had populations of over 1 million people. London dwarfed them all, growing from 1.9 million in 1841 to 4.2 million in 1891. Between one-fifth and one-sixth of the population of Britain lived in London, which was larger than the next seven largest English cities and Edinburgh combined. The sprawling imperial city seemed almost ungovernable, an imposing labyrinth of different jurisdictions with 10,000 people exercising varying degrees of authority. Unlike Paris, which was for the most part administered by the centralized French state, London only had an effective local government after the establishment of the London City Council in 1889.

The largest port in the world, London also remained a center of international banking, finance,

Paris before Haussmann: Charles Marville's photograph of the Rue Traversine. Notice the drainage ditch in the center of the cobblestone street.

and commerce, and the administrative nerve center of the British Empire. Its influence extended around the world, channeling investment capital to innumerable countries within and beyond the empire. The largest merchant marine fleet in the world carried woolens and other textiles to China, machine parts and hardware to Russia, toys to New York, settlers to Canada, and soldiers and sailors to India, and it imported Australian wool, Chicago beef, Bordeaux wines, Portuguese port, and Cuban cigars.

London was also a center of small-scale production and finishing in shops usually employing only a few skilled and semiskilled workers each, such as in the clothing industry, furniture making, engineering, and printing. The bustling East End docks employed a vast force of "casual labor"— that is, semiskilled and unskilled laborers—mostly recent migrants from Ireland and rural England. Two million people lived in the East End; the homeless slept where they could, in empty or half-collapsed buildings, under bridges and railroad viaducts. To upper-class Londoners, the East End, about which they knew nothing except "from hearsay and report," was a morass of tangled slums "as unexplored as Timbuctoo." Residents of these districts spoke a cockney dialect that was difficult for outsiders to understand, with a thick Irish brogue, or Yiddish.

The Hungarian capital of Budapest (formed by the union of Buda, Pest, and another smaller town in 1873) revealed not only the social and ethnic complexity of the Austro-Hungarian Empire but also the increased social segregation characteristic of the modern city. This city on the Danube River grew from a population of about 120,000 in 1848 to 280,000 inhabitants in 1867 and almost 900,000 people in 1914. By then, Hungarian, which had been spoken by a minority of the population of the capital at mid-century, had become the language spoken by the vast majority of people. Many Germans and Jews had emigrated or been assimilated. Rich, middling, and poor people increasingly lived in separate districts; in some parts of town, however, families of means lived on the street side of large rectangular apartments while the poor occupied apartments off dank passageways in the back. The complexity of social differences was such that five forms of salutation were current, depending upon whom one was addressing. These ranged from the ultimate deference of "Gracious Sir," through the only slightly less groveling "Dignified Sir" or "Great Sir," all the way down to the considerably more common "Hey, you!"

Many social theorists were convinced that the rapid growth of cities bred crime (see Chapter 20). But, in fact, urban growth in some places seems to have significantly increased only crimes against property. Crime rates in Glasgow fell during the last half of the century, despite the petty extortion carried out by youth gangs like the Penny Mob, the Redskins, and the Kelly Boys. Many contemporary observers inveighed against cities as promoting an anonymous, alienated mass of people. Yet relatives and friends who had the same dialect or accent or religion encouraged others to move to the city and served as conduits for information about jobs and lodgings. The resulting "chain" migration created "urban villages" that mitigated against uprooting and lawlessness. Neighborhoods of Irish in Liverpool and London, and Italians and Irish in Boston and New York, provided solidarities that made the city seem less anonymous to newcomers.

Social segregation within European cities became more pronounced. Elevators carried wealthy occupants of apartment buildings to refurbished dwellings in the upper stories, where poorer people had once lived. Families of means lived along Vienna's Ringstrasse and near the parks of west London. Suburbs developed around the edge of Europe's larger cities. Some, particularly outside London, catered to middle-class people who could commute into the city, happy to live in small houses that offered more room and more fresh air than in London. These suburbs, unlike most center cities, reflected some degree of planning and improved water and gas supply, among other municipal services.

But European suburbs were, for the most part, a plebeian phenomenon, quite different from suburbs in the United States. Factories were constructed on the edge of cities so that manufacturers could take advantage of more space, proximity to railways and canals, somewhat lower cost of land and raw materials (avoiding the taxes that were still levied on goods brought into some cities), and the availability of cheap labor. Railway lines and factories, whether in old districts or in new ones on the edge of town, were surrounded by poor-quality, low-rent housing, usually owned by absentee landlords. More and more workers commuted daily into town to work—some still on foot, others by train, tram, subway, and, later, bus. Modest suburbs developed around the small Estonian capital of Tallinn in the Russian Baltic provinces, where peasant workers settled on the edge of town.

With urban growth came civic pride. Municipal governments built celebratory historical monuments, constructed new hospitals and town halls, sponsored bands, and created beautiful parks complete with ornate bandstands. They prided themselves on an increasingly diverse municipal cultural life, including occasional music festivals and perhaps even a museum. The proliferation of voluntary associations, such as clubs and choral societies, also came to be taken as symbols of urbanity as cities and towns continued to grow, transforming the lives of millions of Europeans.

Social Mobility

The middle classes swelled during the Second Industrial Revolution, taking their places in Europe's burgeoning cities. Lower-middle-class occupations, in particular, expanded rapidly. (That the lower middle class had some degree of self-awareness was revealed by the fact that in 1899 the first—and last—World Congress of the Petty Bourgeoisie took place in

Brussels.) Architects required draftsmen; companies needed accountants and bookkeepers; and the London underground and Paris subway had to have agents. Furthermore, the expansion of governmental functions generated thousands of jobs in every country: tax collectors, postal workers, food and drug inspectors, and recorders of official documents. The number of schoolteachers increased dramatically in every country between the 1870s and 1914—five times more in Italy, thirteen times more in England. Table 19.6 represents the rapid growth in the number of state employees. In Britain, the proportion of the population classified as lower middle class grew from about 7 percent in 1850 to 20 percent in 1900. Clerks working for banks, railroads, utility companies, and insurance companies considered themselves above the working class and therefore "respectable." With the optimism of the age, they viewed such employment as a first step to one day owning their own store. They did not wear work clothes and did not do manual labor and they made a little more money than did workers.

In European cities, women found jobs as department store clerks, stenographers, and secretaries. There were twelve times as many secretaries in 1901 as there had been two decades earlier; women, who held only 8 percent of post office and government clerical positions in 1861, accounted for more than half in 1911. They now used metal pens that replaced the age-old quill, and then the typewriter, invented in the 1880s. Nursing gradually became a respected profession. Cafés and restaurants employed hundreds of thousands of women.

Gains made by workers seemed paltry when compared to the fortunes being made by industrialists, and even the salaries earned by management personnel. These gnawing disparities aided unions and socialist parties in their quest for the allegiance of workers, who walked to and from work while horse-drawn cabs raced by, carrying well-heeled occupants. In the mid-1890s, real wages, which had risen for several decades, entered a period of decline.

Dizzying "rags to riches" tales (especially popular in the United States and Russia) suggested that hard work could lead to better conditions of life. Emigrants to the United States often arrived with fantastically high expectations of what life would be like. Inflated expectations often brought disap-

Table 19.6. Number of Public Servants (Non-Military)

	1881	1901	1911
Great Britain	81,000	153,000	644,000
France	379,000	451,000	699,000
Germany	452,000	907,000	1,159,000

Source: Norman Stone, *Europe Transformed 1878–1919* (Cambridge, MA: Harvard University Press, 1984), p. 130.

pointment, as social mobility was extremely limited, particularly for first-generation immigrants. During the last decades of the century, 95 percent of American industrialists came from upper- or middle-class families, and not more than 3 percent were the sons of poor immigrants or farmers. Among immigrants and native-born workers in the United States, the most common form of social advancement was within the working class, not into a higher social group.

Clerical work toward the end of the nineteenth century.

Despite movement in Western European countries into clerical and other lower-middle-class jobs, however, there were fewer possibilities of movement by workers into the middle class during the hard years of the 1880s than there had been during the middle decades of the century. Some newer professions, including veterinary science and pharmacology, rewarded sons—and, in the case of teaching, daughters—of artisans and peasants. But everywhere the gap between craftsmen and semiskilled or unskilled workers remained great.

Low wages and periodic unemployment for industrial workers made saving and the ownership of apartments or houses, both essential components of mobility, extremely difficult to achieve. Craftsmen and skilled workers had a far better chance for social ascension than did unskilled workers. However, as in the United States, those who did move up to middle-class employment were the exceptions. The vast majority of marriages in Europe took place between partners considered social equals. Working-class women were more likely than men to achieve some social mobility—for example, by marrying a clerk or railroad station employee.

CULTURAL CHANGES: EDUCATION AND RELIGION

In every country, states took enormous strides to bring education to more people. More children went on to secondary school, now including some girls. The state's increased role in education in Western Europe contributed to a growing secularization of public life. At the same time, the established churches lost the allegiance of many ordinary Europeans.

Education

Literacy rose rapidly during the last decades of the century in Europe as more governments enacted educational reforms. More men could read and write than women, more urban residents than rural people. Literacy rates were higher in western—above all, northwestern Europe—than in southern and eastern Europe, although progress was notable in Russia around the turn of the century.

In Britain, Parliament passed, over Anglican opposition, the Education Act of 1870, which placed education in the hands of the state by permitting local education boards to create schools in districts where neither the Established Church nor its Dissenting Protestant rivals had created one. However, with the help of state grants, the Anglicans had far outdistanced their competitors in building new schools, so that just ten years earlier they had controlled 90 percent of the elementary schools in England and Wales. School boards could now compel children to attend school until they reached thirteen years of age. In 1880, Parliament passed a law requiring that all children between five and ten years of age attend primary school (up to age twelve beginning in 1899) and in 1891 primary education became free. Truancy officers increasingly appeared in working-class neighborhoods, sometimes meeting resistance from parents who preferred the supplementary income from their children's work to their schooling. State inspectors maintained educational standards, requiring villages to provide better facilities for their schools and accommodations for teachers.

In France, the Ferry Laws (passed 1879–1881, named after Minister of Education and then Premier Jules Ferry) made primary schools free, obligatory, and secular for all children from age three to thirteen. Each region was required to operate a teacher-training school. In France, Provençaux, Gascons, Bretons, and peoples of other regions learned French, now spoken by the large majority of the population (although bilingualism remained common, with local languages, dialects, and patois spoken at home). In Italy, Italian ceased to be a language spoken only by the upper class.

The percentage of people able to read and write still varied considerably from country to country. In France, where 40 percent of military conscripts had not been able to read or write at mid-century, the percentage had fallen at the turn of the century to only 6 percent. In contrast, in Dalmatia, on the Adriatic coast, only 1 of every 100 conscripts could read and write in 1870 and in Spain 70 percent of electors were illiterate in 1890. In 1860, 75 percent of Italian men and almost 90 percent of women could neither read nor write and depended on public letter writers to pen what correspondence they required. By 1900, 50 percent of the population could read and write; by 1914, 75 percent of all Italians were literate. School attendance in Italy again revealed the gap between the more prosperous north and the south, where more than half of the children in many places still did not attend school regularly or at all. In Germany, by the turn of the century less than 1 percent of the population remained illiterate. In Russia, illiteracy fell from about 90 percent of the population in the 1860s to about 75 percent by 1910. Whereas the older, illiterate generation of Russians mistrusted education ("You can't eat books"), fearing that literacy would erode village religious culture (and perhaps also deference to elders), younger peasants ridiculed their superstitious parents and welcomed self-improvement through education.

During the 1870s and 1880s, the issue of female education surged to the forefront, at least in Western Europe. But only women whose families were able and willing to pay the required fees received secondary education. In France, women were allowed to teach boys, but men were not permitted to teach girls. Both lay teachers and nuns instructed girls in the domestic mission of women, stressing gender differences and promoting deference to their future husbands. Schooling for boys and girls alike emphasized patriotic, secular, and politically conservative themes. Female teachers of girls were to be morally irreproachable and thoroughly secular mother figures within their communities. Textbooks counseled "patient resignation" to one's economic and social condition, with one book in 1882 showing a picture of a woman desperately trying to persuade her husband not to go on strike.

A protest opposing the admission of women to Cambridge University in 1881 demonstrates the unwillingness of many to erase gender distinctions in education.

In Western Europe, more young people attended secondary schools, the number tripling in Germany and quadrupling in France between 1875 and 1912. During a five-year period in the 1880s, the number of French secondary schools for girls jumped from 3 to 111. A female German Social Democrat later recalled that the education she had received had been so "that I might one day be able to provide my husband with a proper domestic atmosphere." Many families viewed education as a way of improving the employment and marriage possibilities for their daughters.

Yet secondary education in general remained possible only for families of some means. Moreover, existing educational systems reinforced social distinctions of class and gender. Secondary schools taught skills that led to good jobs, but they drew very few children from the lower classes. In England, boarding schools founded in the 1860s and 1870s catered to middle-class students, while the sons of nobles and of other very wealthy landowners attended the nine old elite "public"—that is, private—schools.

Although the number of university students tripled in Europe during this period, university education remained limited to a tiny proportion of the population drawn from the upper classes. In Prussia, for example, only 1 in 1,000 university students had parents who were workers. In Britain, there were only 13,000 university students in 1913 in a total population of 36 million people, although technical colleges began to attract more students. In Russia, the tsars reversed the European trend during the course of the century, making it more difficult for non-nobles to attend secondary school and university. Yet, overall, the number of universities increased— for example, in Hungary, where three new ones opened their doors.

The Decline of Religious Practice

In a century of vigorous state secularization, particularly in Western Europe, many clergy viewed the period of rapid social change at the turn of the century with anxiety. The institutional influence of churches on states had declined dramatically in most of Europe. More than this, in some parts of Europe, the influence of organized religion on society continued to wane. Secular education, espousing the cult of the nation, accelerated this trend, even though many people in Catholic countries still attended Church schools. However, fewer people went to church than earlier in the century. A survey of London's churches at the turn of the century revealed that less than 20 percent of the population regularly attended services, a marked decline. In Spain, Galicia, the Basque provinces, and much of Castile remained devout, while much of southern Spain did not. In some regions of France, many people lived almost completely apart from the Catholic Church. In Marseille, about 50 percent of the people went to church regularly in 1840; in 1901, only 16 percent did so.

The first Catholic sociologists of religion found a sharp rise in "dechristianized" regions, as demonstrated by rates of couples not having

Believers mass around the Grotto of Lourdes.

church marriages or not having their children baptized. By the 1890s, the Church considered some regions in France, and most working-class districts of large European cities, to be "missionary" areas, their populations no more attached to the Catholic Church than those of China or the Congo. The loss of the Church's hold on ordinary people was reflected in the decline in the birthrate, explicable in part by increased use of birth control. Furthermore, an increasing number of French people called upon the clergy only at the time of baptism, marriage, and death (and thus were sometimes referred to as "four-wheeled Catholics," in reference to the wagons that carried an individual to each important occasion).

Yet the decline of religious practice in Europe was neither linear, nor did it occur everywhere. A revival of popular religious enthusiasm occurred in some places between 1830 and 1880, particularly among the upper classes. In Sweden the "Great Awakening" brought the revival of popular religion. In Catholic countries, particularly, lithography and printing presses helped rekindle devotion, spreading the news of religious shrines.

Women were more apt to attend church than men (although in part this resulted from the fact that women live longer than men). The cult of the Virgin Mary also contributed to the feminization of religion in Catholic countries, perhaps encouraging more young women to enter convents. In France, nuns accounted for almost 60 percent of the clergy.

The growing cult of miracles was part of a revival of popular religion, particularly in France, Italy, and Spain. Near the French town of Lourdes in the central Pyrenees, Bernadette, a peasant girl later canonized by the Church, announced in 1858 that the Virgin Mary had appeared to her on the Feast of the Annunciation commemorating Christ's conception. Churchmen and their followers believed that the apparition explained the miraculous cures that seemed to occur at Lourdes, despite the skepticism of scientists and secularizers. Religious pilgrimages by train to sites of miracles became big business. In the first decade of the new century, more than a million people came to Lourdes each year, many hoping to be cured of illness and disease. The popularity of pilgrimages reflected the resiliency of the Catholic Church.

The Consumer Explosion

During the last decades of the nineteenth century, the culture of consumerism developed in the countries of Europe, although with considerable country-to-country variation. The new leisure activities of the Belle Époque themselves reflected the Second Industrial Revolution. Sports—principally soccer and rugby, bicycle and automobile races (although automobiles were far too expensive for ordinary people), and track and field—attracted participants and spectators and encouraged the formation of clubs. In and around cities and towns, cafés and taverns attracted throngs of pleasure-seekers, day and night.

The bedding department in a Parisian department store.

Department stores reflected and helped shape the burgeoning consumer culture. In London, New York, Chicago, and Paris, department stores transformed the way many families shopped. They attracted prosperous middle-class clients in search of quality ready-made clothes that were less expensive than those stitched by tailors. The stores were, in a sense, monuments to the dynamism of bourgeois culture, displaying in their windows products that reflected material progress and a growing emphasis on consumption. Seeking to increase the volume of sales, department stores also stocked more inexpensive clothing, while adding umbrellas, toothbrushes, stationery, and much more. All of this required a remarkable degree of bureaucratization, with organization into departments overseen by trained managers, which typified the Second Industrial Revolution. The expanding clientele of department stores included the families of shopkeepers, civil servants, and clerks of more modest means, and gradually workers as well. On an average day in the 1890s, 15,000 to 18,000 people entered the "Bon Marché"—still a Parisian landmark—and many more when there were sales. Glossy catalogues in color, advancing advertising techniques, permitted middle-class and even working-class shoppers to make purchases from catalogues in the comfort of their homes. Advertisers began to direct their appeals at the "new woman," the housewife of taste, who had the time to create the model home and had some money to spend.

The owners of department stores wanted shopping to become an experience in itself, like a visit to a world's fair—except that one could now buy some of the displayed wonders of human innovation. Architects aimed at monumental and theatrical effects. Department stores were enormous, stately structures topped with cupolas—statues of the gods reclining are part of the decoration of the Bon Marché—with iron columns and an expanse of glass giving shoppers a sense of space and light. Shoppers could walk up grand staircases to observe the crowds below. Department stores became tourist sights; dazzled visitors themselves became part of the spectacle. Émile Zola went so far as to claim that "the department store tends to replace the church. It marches to the religion of the cash desk, of beauty, of coquetry, and fashion. [Women] go there to pass the hours as they used to go to church; an occupation, a place of enthusiasm where they struggle between their passion for clothes and the thrift of their husbands; in the end all the drama of life with the hereafter of beauty."

Leisure in the Belle Époque

During the Belle Époque, there was more to do than ever before for those with time for leisure and money to spend. The French capital set the tone for style in Europe, if not the world. Dance halls, cafés, and café-concerts, the latter offering the performances of musicians, singers,

The actress Sarah Bernhardt dramatically laid out in the Art Nouveau style in a coffin.

poets, comedians, jugglers, acrobats, female wrestlers, and snake charmers, lined the *grands boulevards*, attracting throngs of Parisians and tourists alike. Hundreds of thousands of Parisians went to the theater at least once a week. Europeans danced faster; the tango and the turkey trot, imported from the Americas, were banned in some establishments. German Emperor William II forbade officers from dancing these steps while in uniform.

The talented and beautiful actress Sarah Bernhardt (1844–1923) embodied images of fin-de-siècle Europe. The daughter of a Dutch immigrant, she became famous for her dramatic expressiveness and ability to communicate tears to an audience through her supremely evocative voice. Bernhardt had learned her trade from the traditions of the popular boulevard theater. Renowned for her dramatic gestures (as a young woman she asked a photographer to take a picture of her in a coffin) and for a variety of sexual liaisons, Sarah Bernhardt's worldwide fame was such that the American circus entrepreneur P. T. Barnum, upon hearing that she risked the amputation of a leg, offered her a fortune if she would allow him to take it on the road and exhibit it with his famous circus.

Sports in Mass Society

Participatory and spectator sports emerged as a prominent feature of mass society during the last decades of the century, a phenomenon linked to modern transportation and to a general increase in leisure time. The first automobile race was held in 1894 in France, from Rouen to Paris and back. Some of the cars were powered by electricity, others by gasoline or even steam. Cycling competitions also generated enormous public interest, providing the first heroes of spectator sports. Sporting newspapers catered to riders and fans. Competition between two cycling clubs led to the first Tour de France race in 1903, in which riders covered almost 1,500 miles in nineteen days.

Not only did people watch bicycle races, many rode bicycles themselves, both for leisure and as a source of transportation for those who could not afford horses. The bicycle, in the words of one devotee, represented "the new wheels of the chariot of progress." A simple mechanism, it nonetheless reflected technological innovation and mass production. By the late 1880s, bicycles were lighter, more affordable, and more easily repaired or replaced. Their manufacture became a major industry, with 375,000 produced in France by 1898, and 3.5 million in 1914.

Both men and women rode bicycles. But some men complained that the clothes women wore while riding bicycles were unfeminine. Some worried that female cyclists might compromise the middle-class domestic ideal of the "angel of the house." Moralists were concerned that the jolts of rough paths and roads might interfere with childbearing, or even lead to debauchery by generating physical pleasure. The president of a feminist congress in 1896, however, toasted the "egalitarian and leveling bicycle." It helped free women from the corset, "a new Bastille to be demolished." It may have also changed what some people considered the feminine ideal from plumpness to a more svelte line.

Team sports also quickly developed as a leisure activity during the second half of the nineteenth century. The two most popular team sports in Europe, football (soccer in the United States) and rugby, both began in England. Rugby, which developed at Cambridge and Oxford Universities in the 1860s, was an upper-class sport. Football had much earlier origins, perhaps going back to when Vikings and Russians used to "kick the Dane's head around"—literally. But football, which also had university origins, evolved into a plebeian sport, like boxing, which was to English workers what rowing, cricket, and golf became to the upper classes. Professional football began in England in 1863; eight years later, there were fifteen clubs playing for the championship. The new century brought the first major brawl between supporters of rival teams: a match between the Catholic Celtics and the Protestant Rangers of Glasgow ended with the stadium burned to the ground. In 1901, 111,000 spectators watched the English Cup Final.

Baron Pierre de Coubertin (1863–1937), a French noble who feared that the youth of his country were becoming soft, organized the first modern Olympic Games, held in Athens in 1896 in homage to the Greek creators of the Olympiad. An Anglophile, he revered the contemporary image of hard-riding, athletic upper-class Englishmen playing sports at Eton and Cambridge and then going on to expand the British Empire.

There was more to the rise of sports and the cult of physical vigor than simply games and fun. The development of sports culture also reflected the mood of aggressive nationalism. The popularity of Darwin's theory of the evolution of species led to a growing preoccupation with the comparative characteristics of specific races, or peoples. "Social Darwinists" misapplied the theory of "survival of the fittest" to society, including international sports competition. Games soon became hotly competitive. Moveover, the development of feminism in Western Europe may have contributed to what has been called a "crisis of masculinity," by which many men saw the strengthening of the "weaker sex" as the weakening of men. By this view, growing interest in sports competition was an affirmation of masculinity. Furthermore, the emerging interest in the times it took to run distances may have reflected fascination with scientific management.

The burgeoning interest in sports touched, above all, the young. In Germany, "wandering youth" clubs (*Wandervogel*) became popular, sending young boys out to camp under the stars. In England, Robert Baden-Powell (1857–1941) founded the Boy Scouts. After being rejected for admission to Oxford University and finding his vocation among young men in the army, Baden-Powell in 1908 organized the Boy Scouts in the hope of developing "among boys . . . a spirit of self-sacrifice and patriotism, and generally to prepare them to become good citizens." The uniform Baden-Powell had worn in South Africa—a Stetson hat, neckerchief, and khaki shorts—became that of the Boy Scouts, and their motto, "Be prepared."

Interest in sports touched all classes and, in fact, reflected class differences. The poet Rudyard Kipling, who disliked sports in general, called cricket players (who tended to be from a loftier social class than his own) "fools." Football players, most of whom were from the working class, he

(*Left*) A marathon race at the first modern Olympic Games in Greece, 1896. (*Right*) Robert Baden-Powell, founder of the Boy Scouts.

dismissed as "oafs." Nobles and other people of great means were no longer the only people able to enjoy sports. While the upper classes had their own sporting associations, which retained a preference for horse racing—"the sport of kings"—working-class cycling and gymnastic clubs also began to spring up in the 1880s in Western Europe, particularly as workers won a shorter workweek and workday.

CONCLUSION

The Second Industrial Revolution transformed the way many Europeans lived. Electricity brought light to growing cities and towns, along whose boulevards, dotted with kiosks selling inexpensive newspapers, cars and trams now carried passengers. Most Europeans could now read and write, but they were—at least in Western Europe—less likely to go to church regularly than earlier generations. Most people lived better and longer than ever before. At the same time, economic and social inequalities generated union organization, the growth of mass political parties—notably a variety of socialist movements—and waves of social protest. Nationalism became a political force in many countries during the last three decades of the nineteenth century and the beginning of the twentieth century, engulfing not only the industrialized constitutional monarchies and republics of western and southern Europe but also the empires of central and eastern Europe. Moreover, the rapid pace of scientific and technological advances generated innovative, complex cultural responses in fin-de-siècle Europe.

CHAPTER 20

POLITICAL AND CULTURAL RESPONSES TO A RAPIDLY CHANGING WORLD

As European economies were being transformed by the Second Industrial Revolution, states faced organized challenges from political movements that rejected the economic, social, and political bases of those states and demanded sweeping changes. Government officials, social reformers, and politicians had to confront the difficult conditions of many workers and their families—"the problem of problems," as it was called in Britain. Some states began to enact social reforms to improve the quality of life for workers and other poor people.

At the same time, the growth of large socialist parties that wanted to capture control of the state was one of the salient signs of the advent of mass political life. Marxist socialists believed that inevitably a working-class revolution would bring down capitalism. Reform socialists, in contrast, believed that electoral victories could lead to a socialist state, and that along the way to ultimate victory socialists could exert pressure on states to improve conditions of life for workers. Anarchists did not form political parties. They did not want to seize the state, but rather to abolish it. Believing that violent acts would provide a spark that would unleash a social revolution, a number of anarchists launched a campaign of terrorism at the turn of the century, carrying out political assassinations. In parts of Europe, trade unionists known as syndicalists (from the French word *syndicats* for trade unions) believed that trade unions would provide not only the means by which workers could take control of the state but also a blueprint of how society would be organized after a successful revolution.

The late nineteenth and early twentieth centuries also brought remarkable cultural achievement in Europe from Britain to Russia, as writers and artists reacted to and against changes in the world they saw around them. Beneath the tangible progress and increased prosperity of late-nineteenth- and early-twentieth-century Europe lurked cultural pessimism and artistic rebellion, a modernist critique of the idea of progress itself. In 1904, the German sociologist Max Weber wrote that "at some time or another the color changes, the importance of uncritically accepted viewpoints is put in doubt, the path is lost in the twilight." To some, the fin de siècle seemed to be such a time.

STATE SOCIAL REFORM

In general Karl Marx's gloomy prediction that workers' wages and overall conditions of life would continue to decline had not been borne out in late-nineteenth-century Europe. Yet economic uncertainty and grinding poverty seemed to have engendered a social crisis of unmatched proportions. Descriptions of the dreary slums of blackened manufacturing towns reached many readers through novels and surveys of working-class life. By the 1880s, however, pressure mounted on Western European governments from the political left to enact measures of social reform.

Confronted with the increased militancy of their workers, some Western European employers sought to maintain worker loyalty through paternalistic policies. Here and there, they encouraged workers to form savings associations by matching whatever small sums the working-class families could put aside for the future. A minority of manufacturers started funds for insurance and pension plans, or provided basic company housing (especially in mining communities). Yet such paternalistic policies, largely confined to Western Europe, were far from being generalized. Some social reformers, many politicians, and most workers demanded state intervention to protect workers from some of the uncertainties and hardships of their labor.

Imperial Germany, not republican France or parliamentary Britain, first provided workers some protection against personal and family disaster stemming from work-related accidents. Germany's domineering Chancellor Otto von Bismarck sought to outbid the Catholic Center Party and the Social Democrats for working-class support. Determined to preserve his own power and the autocratic structure of the empire, Bismarck carried out domestic policies based upon compromise and conciliation between middle-class political interests and working-class demands. The German chancellor thus placed Socialists in the delicate position of either opposing bills that would benefit workers or appearing to compromise their ideologically based refusal to collaborate with the autocratic imperial government. The Sickness Insurance Law of 1883 covered all workers for up to thirteen weeks if their income fell below a certain level. Deductions withheld from workers' wages provided most of the funds. A year later Bismarck announced that the state would undertake an insurance program that would incorporate existing voluntary plans. It would compensate workers for injury and illness, as well as provide some retirement funds. Other laws required that all workers be insured against accidents and disability, with half of the funds paid by employers, and provided pensions for workers who lived until seventy years of age. By the turn of the century, many German workers received medical care, small payments when they were ill or injured, and, if worse came to worse, a decent burial. By 1913, 14.5 million German workers had insurance.

In comparison to Germany, Britain's social policies were out of an earlier era. Workhouses, which had been created by the Poor Law of 1834, still carried a social stigma, even if conditions had somewhat improved toward the end of the century. Families were separated, and inmates were forced to wear uniforms, attend chapel, participate in group exercises, and sustain periods of silence, all with the goal of learning "discipline." A contemporary surveyor of working-class life noted that "aversion to the 'House' is absolutely universal, and almost any amount of suffering and privation will be endured by the people rather than go into it." The vast majority of the inmates of the workhouses were not the able-bodied unemployed, but were children, the infirm, single mothers, the aged, or the insane. But although public opinion had already turned against work-

Dinnertime in an English workhouse, which provided relief for unemployed workers experiencing the dislocation and social transformation accompanying the Second Industrial Revolution.

houses, the Poor Law, slightly reformed, remained on the books until 1929.

The first Victorian social reforms had been largely limited to establishing minimum health standards. The Factory Act (1875) then reduced the workweek in large factories to fifty-six hours. The Artisans' Dwelling Act, passed the same year, defined unsanitary housing and gave the state the right to order the demolition of slum buildings that fell below a minimum standard. These laws were, however, only very randomly enforced.

By the turn of the century, many Conservatives, most Liberals, and virtually all members of the new Labour Party (founded in 1901 and taking its name in 1906) accepted the right and the obligation of government to undertake reforms, thus ending classic liberal government non-interference in the working of the economy. The Workmen's Compensation Law (1897) made employers responsible for bearing the cost of industrial accidents; another act extended the same protection to agricultural workers. Liberal governments provided lunches to poor children and passed the Old Age Pension Act (1908), which provided some income for workers over seventy years of age whose incomes fell below the paltry sum of ten shillings a week. As a result of the National Insurance Bill (1911), workers' friendly societies administered insurance payments based on voluntary (and thus unlike the German case) employee wage deductions. The law's most salutary effect was to provide more workers and their families with direct medical treatment. Yet a third of the British poor still received no assistance of any kind. Moreover, government assistance to unemployed workers in Britain was less well organized and less generous than, for example, that in France.

In France, pushed by Radicals and Socialists, the Chamber of Deputies between 1890 and 1904 passed laws that eliminated obligatory special identity papers, or internal passports, for workers (1890), created a system of arbitration for strikes, banned female night work (1892), established employers' legal liability for industrial accidents (1898), reduced the workday to ten hours for women and children (1904), established a minimum age for industrial workers, and mandated an obligatory weekly day of rest. It also affirmed the right of the state to monitor conditions of work and hygiene in factories (although inspection was in many areas nonexistent), passed a workmen's compensation law with modest pension benefits, and provided limited medical care for working-class families. With the exception of Belgium, Sweden, and a smattering of other countries, in most of Europe workers could only dream of such reforms.

The Trade Union Movement

The trade union movement grew rapidly in Western Europe, above all among skilled workers, most of whom were male. The goals of unions were to raise wages and improve conditions, while increasing the number of unionized workers. By 1914, 3 million workers had joined unions in Britain, 1.5 million in Germany, and 1 million in Italy. The number of white-collar unions also increased, such as those organizing schoolteachers and postal clerks. In 1913, there were more than 400,000 union members in Austria, a country of only 6 million inhabitants. French unions had been tolerated in the guise of friendly associations and mutual aid societies; they proliferated after they were legalized in 1884. In 1895, French unions formed the General Confederation of Labor (C.G.T.), with the goal of unifying the trade union movement. The C.G.T., to which about a third of French unions belonged, renounced participation in politics and espoused revolutionary principles. Union membership soared in France, reaching 2.6 million in 1914. May Day demonstrations and festivals, with red flags flying, vigorous political debates, consumer cooperatives, and informal networks provided by factory work and cafés also helped maintain solidarity among workers.

Most European workers did not belong to unions, although they often supported strikes and believed in union goals. The 1875 Trade Union Act ended many limitations on unions in Britain, but by the turn of the century only about 25 percent of British workers were organized. Moreover, the percentage fell to about 10 percent in France and to an even lower percentage in Italy and Russia. Several factors limited the expansion of union membership. Considerable gaps remained between the work experience, salary, organizations, and expectations of skilled and unskilled workers, differences that were most pronounced in Britain. Many workers moved from place to place, following employment opportunities. Those with urban roots were far more easily organized than recently arrived migrants from smaller towns or villages. Differences and tensions between workers of different national groups also served to divide workers, such as between Irish and English workers in London, German and Czech workers in Prague, or Belgian and French workers in northern France.

The union organization of female workers lagged far behind that of men. Women made up 30 percent of the British labor force, but only about 7 percent of union members. Almost all were relegated to relatively unskilled and low-paying jobs and confronted chronic vulnerability to being dismissed. Women also had to take responsibility for their children, something male union members often failed to recognize. Most women worked in unskilled jobs, making boxes, knotting fish nets, making buttonholes, doing food-processing work, and many other tasks. Furthermore, many male workers refused to accept women as equals and claimed that they were taking jobs away from men (a French union, which admitted women as members, included the following regulation: "Women may address observations on propositions to the union only in writing and by the intermediation of two male members"). Yet women workers also struck in the face of tougher working conditions, low wages, and, occasionally, sexual harassment.

Between 1890 and 1914, strikes increased dramatically, particularly in Western Europe. The organized strike became a social fact of modern life as workers learned to protect their interests. Strikes could become political issues when unions pressed the state to intervene on their behalf. Thus, workers hoped that they could force government officials to pressure employers to bargain with them. Workers struck when employers seemed most vulnerable; for example, when they had recently received large orders for products. The vast majority of strikes were undertaken by skilled, organized workers in large-scale sectors such as textiles, mining, and metallurgy, whose unions had resources such as strike funds upon which to fall back. Strike movements reflected a more generalized sense of class consciousness among many—but hardly all—workers.

Strikes reflected not only growth in union membership but also changes in the organization of industrial work. In addition to low wages and the length of their workday, workers also resented factory foremen. Foremen, representing the company's interests, sought to impose industrial discipline on workers, some of whom had worked on farms or in domestic industry and had more or less controlled their own time. Now they were forbidden to enter and leave the factory as they wished when they had nothing to do, or to talk on the job.

Many workers also objected to the implementation of techniques of "scientific management," or "Taylorism," which placed factory workers more directly under the control of factory managers by measuring worker performance, tying pay scales to the number of units produced, which put more pressure on workers. Taylorism wore out workers. Noting that virtually all the factory workers employed by a Philadelphia manufacturer who had become enamored of scientific management were young, a British visitor asked repeatedly where the older workers were. Finally, the owner replied, "Have a cigar, and while we smoke we can visit the cemetery."

Socialists

The Socialist First International was founded in 1864. Members represented a bewildering variety of experiences and ideologies. Karl Marx emerged as the dominant figure within the International. He was convinced that the unprecedented concentration of capital and wealth meant that the final struggle between the bourgeoisie and the working class was relatively close at hand. Marx's inflexible beliefs ran counter to the views of the majority of French members, some of whom were anarchists, and to the moderate, reformist inclinations of the more prosperous British workers.

The First International was dissolved in 1876 amid internal division, the victim of a wave of repression in many states. Nonetheless, socialism emerged as a major political force in every major European nation. In 1889, at the centennial of the French Revolution in Paris, delegates to a socialist congress founded the Second International. At its congresses, socialists discussed strategies for pushing governments toward reform and for coordinating international action (for example, to achieve a shorter workday), while debating differences over doctrine and strategy.

During the last two decades of the nineteenth century, mass socialist parties developed in France, Germany, Italy, and Belgium. By the end of the first decade of the twentieth century, every Western European state had working-class representatives in their national assemblies, some of whom defiantly wore work clothes to parliamentary debates.

Socialists proclaimed themselves internationalists. Contending that workers in different nations shared common interests, they believed a revolution would put the working class in power. But socialists remained divided. For Marxist adherents of his "scientific socialism," emancipation of the workers from capitalism could only be achieved by the conquest of the state through revolution and the subsequent establishment of a socialist society. Reform socialists believed that political participation could win concrete reforms that would improve conditions of life for workers until socialists could take power. Reformists participated in the political process, even at the cost of being accused by revolutionary socialists of propping up "bourgeois" regimes by doing so. Legislation in many countries had brought improvement in conditions of work, however unevenly felt. The extension of the franchise also offered hope that progress might come without a revolution that, given the strength of states, seemed to even some revolutionaries to be increasingly unlikely. Reform socialists were willing to cooperate with non-socialist parties to achieve an extension of the franchise; they concluded that socialism could come through the ballot box.

The emergence of socialists as contenders for political power reflected economic, social, and political changes in individual countries more than the influence of the Second International. Yet the debates and divisions that obsessed European socialists revolved around common questions. What should be the relationship between socialism and nationalist movements? Could socialists, proclaiming international solidarity among workers, support demands for Polish independence from the Russian and German Empires, or those by Czechs and other nationalities for independence from the Austro-Hungarian Empire? Czech socialists with national aspirations for their people challenged the domination of the Austrian Social Democrats by German speakers who seemed oblivious to Czech demands. The Polish-born socialist Rosa Luxemburg (1870–1919) found herself in the minority when she opposed demands of many Polish socialists for the independence of their country because she saw that quest as incompatible with socialism. Imperialism also divided socialists (see Chapter 21). Should socialists oppose imperialism in all its forms, or should they hope that the colonial powers might gradually improve the conditions of life of Africans and Asians, who might become adherents to

The Socialist League at Hammersmith, England, included the craftsman and designer William Morris, who is standing in the second row toward the right, with his hand on his chest.

socialism? Finally, amid rising aggressive nationalism, socialists were divided on what response they should take in the event of the outbreak of a European war. Some socialists believing that a declaration of war should be a signal for a mass general strike that could bring the European state system and capitalism to their knees.

In France, that country's revolutionary tradition and, above all, the Paris Commune of 1871, encouraged some French socialists to believe that revolution would bring them to power. The Parisian socialist Jules Guesde (1845–1922), rigid, humorless, and doctrinaire (he was known as "the Red Pope" or "the Red Jesuit" by detractors and followers alike), espoused Marxist socialism. In 1883, Guesde's socialists, irritated that many members were reformists, formed a defiantly Marxist political party, the French Workers' Party, the first modern political party in France. Guesdists tried to subordinate workers' demands for improvements in working conditions to the political goals of their party. Guesde viewed electoral campaigns as an opportunity to propagate Marxian socialism, although Guesdists joined the battle for an eight-hour workday and other reforms.

In the Russian Empire, Marxists were "Westernizers," in that they looked to "scientific socialism" as a model for political change in their country (see Chapter 18). Westernizers counted on Russia's industrial workers to launch a revolution, but only after Russia had undergone a bourgeois revolution similar to that which they believed had taken place in Paris in 1830, bringing the middle class to political power. In the 1880s, socialists formed reading groups of intellectuals and students—and at least one that was made up of workers—in the imperial capital of St. Petersburg. Exiles began to publish socialist newspapers abroad, smuggling them into Russia.

Reformism dominated socialist movements in much of northern Europe. Great Britain's handful of socialists were virtually all intellectuals and reformists. In 1884, a group of intellectuals formed the Fabian Society, which took its name from the Roman dictator Fabius, known for his delaying tactics. Committed to gradualism, the Fabians took the tortoise as their emblem. The Fabians were influenced by an American writer, Henry George. The author of the best-selling *Progress and Poverty,* George argued that the great gulf in Britain between rich and poor could be lessened by the imposition of a "single tax" on land, which would force wealthy landowners to pay more taxes. The "single taxers" believed that socialism could be gradually implemented through reform. Fabians started reading groups in London and other major cities, and some were elected to municipal offices, where they worked to improve workers' housing conditions.

Some German socialists, too, believed that the state could be influenced to carry out reforms that would improve the lives of workers and that one day socialists might obtain a parliamentary majority. Most did not accept Marx's contention that the working class could only take power through revolution. In 1863, Ferdinand Lassalle (1825–1864), the son of a Prussian merchant, had formed the first independent workers' party in any of the German states. Lassalle only lived a year more—killed in a duel at age thirty-nine by the fiancé of the woman he loved. His socialist party, in principle internationalist in outlook, was small and carried no political weight. In 1875, the German Social Democratic Party (S.P.D.), was founded. Despite official proscription in 1878, it slowly grew into a mass political party. At its party congress at Erfurt in 1891, Karl Kautsky (1854–1938), Marx's determined disciple, convinced the S.P.D. to reject reformism and adopt his revolutionary program. Accepting Marx's materialist view of history that stressed class struggle, Kautsky argued that capitalism's defeat was inevitable. But the S.P.D.'s program also included reformist demands, including proportional representation, political rights for women, and the eight-hour workday for workers. Furthermore, Eduard Bernstein (1850–1932), the son of a Berlin plumber who became a railway engineer, helped the reformists carry the day by forcefully rejecting in his *Evolutionary Socialism* (1898) the Marxists' insistence that capitalist society was on the verge of final collapse.

The S.P.D.'s popular vote in the elections for the Reichstag rose from less than 10 percent in 1884 to almost 35 percent in 1912. It earned the support of most workers and many middle-class voters as well. Women, who could join the party following the passage of a national law on associations in 1908 but who still were not permitted to vote, added to the ranks of the S.P.D., which had more than a million members in 1914. Nonetheless, despite the membership of women, the party showed little interest in movements for women's rights, believing that only the end of capitalism could lead to women's equality.

The S.P.D. worked to build cradle-to-grave social institutions that would give members a sense that they belonged to a special culture, establishing consumer cooperatives, choral societies, and cycling clubs. Unlike French socialists, the S.P.D. not only developed a close alliance with the trade union movement but also helped found some unions.

The S.P.D. became the largest and best-organized socialist party in Europe; it published more than a hundred newspapers and magazines, and it held regular political meetings and social events. The party's organization and reformism influenced the evolution of similar parties in Belgium, Austria, and Switzerland. The S.P.D. remained, however, caught in the paradox of struggling by electoral means for social and political reform in a society that was fundamentally undemocratic.

In France, the reform socialists were known as "possibilists" because they supported the republic and, in that context, espoused political pressure to win all possible social reforms through the ballot box. They disparaged their revolutionary Guesdist rivals as "impossibilists." Yet, during elections, revolutionary and reform socialists often put their differences behind them, winning control over the municipal governments of several predominantly working-class towns. But the results of "municipal socialism," while subsidizing some services for ordinary people, were limited by the strongly centralized French state.

When the reform socialist Alexandre Millerand (1859–1943) accepted a cabinet post in 1899, the split between revolutionary and reform socialists was accentuated. In 1904, the Socialist International, meeting in Amsterdam, supported Kautsky's proposal that the congress condemn reformism and parliamentarianism.

In 1905, Jean Jaurès (1859–1914), a former philosophy professor whose energy, organizational skills, and stirring oratory swept him to national prominence, achieved the unification of French socialists with the formation of the French Section of the Working-Class International (S.F.I.O.), although the differences between the Guesdists and reformists could not be swept under the rug. The support of some shopkeepers, teachers, and peasants, as well as most workers, helped the socialists become the second largest party in France, gaining in 1914 almost one-fifth of the seats in the Chamber of Deputies.

In Italy, socialists had to overcome the entrenched power of local elites, repression (including the jailing in 1887 of the first Italian socialist deputies), and the strong attraction of anarchism, particularly in southern Italy and Sicily. The Italian Socialist Party, founded in 1892, made few inroads in Italy's impoverished south. To many southern workers and peasants, the party seemed just another obtrusive northern institution, although it did win some support among agricultural workers. By 1912, the revolutionary faction had gained control of the party. In Spain, real power still lay in the hands of powerful local government officials and landowners, men of great local influence (the *caciques*) who rigged elections to the Cortes, backed by the Catholic Church and the army. The Spanish Socialist Party, founded in 1879, gained a sizable following only in industrial Asturias and the Basque region. The first socialists were not elected to the Spanish Parliament until 1909.

Christian Socialism

In Catholic countries, the Church still provided an alternative allegiance to the nation-state. However, the secularization of state and social institutions, along with nationalism itself, reduced the Church's influence in Catholic countries. Papal pronouncements seemed to stand steadfastly against social and political change, and particularly against the emergence of the nation-state and parliamentary forms of government. In a papal encyclical, the *Syllabus of Errors* of 1864, Pope Pius IX condemned the very idea that "the Roman Pontiff can and ought to reconcile himself and come to terms with progress, liberalism and modern civilization." In 1870, the Church proclaimed the doctrine of papal infallibility, which stated that in matters of faith and morals the pope's pronouncements would have to be taken as absolute truth. The Church backed monarchical regimes in Spain and Portugal, opposed the newly unified state in Italy, and, at the

(*Left*) A Socialist baptism in Boulogne-sur-Seine, France. (*Right*) Pope Leo XIII.

beginning of the Third Republic, lent tacit support to monarchist movements in France.

Breaking with his predecessors, Pope Leo XIII (pope 1878–1903) accepted the modern age. His encyclical *Rerum Novarum* (1891) called attention to social injustice, recognizing that many workers were victimized by "the inhumanity of employers and the unbridled greed of competitors." One of the unintended effects of *Rerum Novarum* was the development of "Christian Socialist" movements in France, Germany, Belgium, and Italy in the 1890s, although the Church generally repudiated them. Christian Socialists hoped to bring employers and workers back to the Church. Some clergy and laymen and -women organized clubs, vacation colonies, sporting clubs, and charities, and helped workers rent gardens so that they could grow vegetables and fruit. And many Catholics took the pope's encyclical as authorization to participate in national political life. They organized cooperatives, charitable organizations, and even rural banks. Catholic unions tried to counter socialist influence by bringing together workers, employers, and honorary members from local elites. These "mixed" or "yellow" unions drew the unrestrained opposition of most trade unions.

The Anarchists

While most socialists hoped to seize control of the state, anarchists wanted to overthrow it. Anarchism was never more than a minority movement, hampered by distrust of political organization itself.

The dramatic increase in the reach of European states in the nineteenth century encouraged the development of anarchism, a philosophy with few roots in earlier periods. Anarchism was the very antithesis of a philosophy of political organization because anarchists associated politics itself with a tacit recognition of the state's existence. Socialists had expelled the anarchists from the founding congress of the Second International in 1896 even before they could storm out in protest.

While many anarchists believed in the violent overthrow of the state, others believed that voluntary mutualism would eventually make the state superfluous. Pyotr Kropotkin (1842–1921), the son of a Russian prince and himself a geographer, held a vision of a gentle society of equals living in harmony without the strictures of the state. Kropotkin's desire for anarchist communism was rooted in his first-hand views of the misery of the Russian masses and his own experience living in the Jura Mountains of Switzerland and France in the 1860s, where watchmakers and farmers seemed to coexist in relative prosperity and the state seemed distant. Kropotkin, like the philosophe Jean-Jacques Rousseau, espoused the primitive as a natural end in itself, believing that each person was born a *tabula rasa,* or blank slate, and then corrupted by society—above all, by the state.

Anarchism gained some adherents in France, the most centralized state in Europe, but above all in Italy and Spain, two countries in which the nation-state appeared to many people as a foreign intruder, and in Argentina, a Latin American nation influenced by Spanish and Italian migrants. There was also a smattering of anarchists among recent migrants to the United States in the last decades of the century. In contrast, anarchism found almost no following in Germany, where respect for the state seemed endemic among socialists as well as supporters of the imperial monarchy, and in Great Britain, the least centralized, but also one of the most nationalist states in Western Europe.

A loose organization of anarchists, the International Working-Class Alliance, known as the "Black International" because of the color of the anarchist flag, maintained contacts among anarchists in France, Italy, and the United States. But, for the most part, anarchists formed small groups or struck out on their own. Among poor peasants in the rugged southern Spanish province of Andalusia, anarchism took on a millenarian character stripped of most of the trappings of religion. Andalusian anarchists told the story of one of their own who, as he lay dying, whispered to one of his religious relatives to summon a priest and a lawyer. Relieved that the anarchist seemed at the last moment to be accepting the conventions of religion by accepting the last rites of the Church and drawing up a will, relatives sent for both. When they arrived, the anarchist beckoned them to stand on either side of his deathbed. As they leaned forward, one to hear his confession, the other to write down his will, the anarchist proclaimed, "Now, like Christ, I can die between two thieves."

In the 1880s and 1890s, a wave of anarchist assassinations and bombings shook Europe. To violent anarchists, the goal of "propaganda by the deed" was to spark a revolution. Mikhail Bakunin's Italian disciple Enrico Maletesta (1853–1932), who had a following in both Spain and Argentina, expressed the bitter frustration of anarchists who had virtually nothing: "Do you not know that every bit of bread they [the wealthy] eat is taken from your children, every fine present they give to their wives means the poverty, hunger, cold and even perhaps the prostitution of yours?" Bakunin (see Chapter 18) had believed that a single violent act might shock people into a chain-reaction revolution. "A single deed," Kropotkin once said, "is better propaganda than a thousand pamphlets."

Anarchists killed six heads of states beginning in 1881, when members of People's Will assassinated Tsar Alexander II. Other victims included King Umberto I of Italy, who was killed in 1900 and President William McKinley of the United States, gunned down the following year. The assassination of the Italian king revealed anarchism's loose international links: his assassin was sent by a group of Italian anarchists living in Paterson, New Jersey.

From 1892 to 1894, a wave of bombings terrified Paris. Jean Ravachol, an impoverished worker, had thrown one of the bombs. "See this hand,"

(*Left*) The assassination of French President Sadi Carnot by an Italian anarchist, 1894. (*Right*) Pyotr Kropotkins's publication *The Spirit of Revolt.*

Ravachol told the horrified judge and jurors, "it has killed as many bourgeois as it has fingers!" More attacks followed. In March 1893, an unemployed worker unable to feed his family threw a small bomb into the Chamber of Deputies, slightly injuring several members. French President Sadi Carnot (1837–1894) turned down an appeal for mercy for the perpetrator. Next, another worker tossed a bomb into a café near the Saint-Lazare railroad station, killing one man and injuring about twenty other people. "One does not kill an innocent person in striking the first bourgeois one sees," the anarchist told the shocked judge. In June 1894, an Italian anarchist assassinated Carnot. The wave of anarchist attacks subsided in France but continued in Spain, where the government tortured and executed militant anarchists. But with the rise of mass socialist parties and unions, anarchism faded further into the fringes of popular protest.

Syndicalists

As European trade unions grew in number and size, they attracted unskilled workers as well as craftsmen and skilled workers. At the turn of the century, syndicalism developed as an ideology that held that union organization could provide a means for workers to seize control of their industries and of the state itself. In this way, free associations of producers would eventually replace the state. Syndicalists rejected participation in political life. Syndicalism, which was centered in France, Spain, and Italy, was sometimes called anarcho-syndicalism, because of its anti-statist thrust.

A retired engineer who proudly wore the prestigious Legion of Honor awarded by the French state, Georges Sorel (1847–1922) seemed an unlikely candidate to plan any revolution. But Sorel's *Reflections on Violence* (1908) encouraged direct syndicalist action against capitalism and the state, until a "general strike" by workers would bring both to their knees. By the general strike, Sorel meant a series of simultaneous walk-outs that would shut down factories and lead to revolution. This hope—or "myth," in the sense of a widely accepted belief capable of motivating action—firmed the resolve of syndicalist workers to demand concessions from their employers.

The period 1895–1907 is sometimes referred to as "the heroic age of syndicalism" in France because so many strikes spread through so many industries there, as elsewhere in Europe. More than 1,000 strikes in France occurred in 1904 alone. Troops fired on and killed marchers during a peaceful demonstration on behalf of the eight-hour workday on May Day, 1891, in the small northern French town of Fourmies, and during the "revolt of the South" in 1907, when vineyard owners and vine-tenders protested the state tax on drink.

Italy provided particularly fertile ground for anarcho-syndicalism. Italian anarchists participated in the waves of strikes and insurrections in Sicily in 1893–1894. In Milan in 1898, fighting pitted the industrial suburbs against soldiers, and nearly 200 workers were killed and hundreds were wounded. Violent disturbances during "Red Week" shook Ancona in June 1914 after police shot two people to death while preventing a crowd leaving an anti-militarist demonstration from marching into the downtown area. Massive protests and strikes followed in many cities in Italy. Workers poured into the streets, rioted in several cities, built barricades, and raised the red flag over a number of town halls. The government sent in troops, who fired on demonstrators. Even the normally peaceful Swedish capital of Stockholm was stirred by a general strike in 1909. It failed.

Anarcho-syndicalists dominated the labor movement in Barcelona, particularly among dockworkers. In Catalonia's largest city, dockside contacts with Latin American anarchists accentuated anarchist influence; so, too, did the persistence of small-scale industry, the defiance of the wealthiest employers, and police repression orchestrated from Madrid. Waves of strikes took place in Catalonia in 1902, 1906, and 1909, the latter followed by a bloody insurrection ("Tragic Week"). But gradually in Spain, as in France and Italy, revolutionary rhetoric gave way to the pursuit of concrete economic gains.

The Quest for Women's Rights

Everywhere in Europe, women remained subordinate to men in legal rights. They were excluded from most universities, could not vote (in contrast, some states in the United States gave women the vote before 1900), and had limited or no control over family financial resources (not until 1907 in France did a married woman have free access to her own salary). Women made very little progress entering the professions because some men feared the advent of the "new woman," who demanded the same access to education and opportunity as men. The term "new woman" came from the title of a lecture given by the Italian feminist Maria Montessori (1870–1952), a doctor and originator of innovative schools (which still exist) that stress the encouragement of creativity in children. Still, the beginnings were difficult. When a female Greek scientist gave her inaugural lecture at the University of Athens, male students disrupted her lecture with shouts of "back to the kitchen!" The Polish-born French scientist Marie Curie, who discovered radium and won two Nobel Prizes, related the isolation and challenges of her studies in Paris in the early 1890s: "It seems that life is not easy for any of us. But what of that? We must have perseverance and above all confidence in ourselves. We must believe that we are gifted for something, and that [our goals], at what ever cost, must be obtained."

Women demanding equal rights faced considerable opposition. Queen Victoria of England called demands by women for equal rights "on which her poor feeble sex is bent . . . a mad, wicked folly . . . forgetting every sense of womanly feeling and propriety." The biologist T. H. Huxley (1825–1895) insisted that women were less intelligent than men. The claims of such bad science bolstered opposition to the women's movement.

Right-wing political parties opposed women's suffrage on principle. Moderate republicans often claimed that women could not understand political issues; and left-wing socialists in Catholic countries feared that if women had the right to vote, they would support clerical candidates. Socialist parties and unions threw their support to women workers laboring for better wages and conditions. In the meantime, some women, however, contended that social reforms would be inadequate as long as women were without the right to enter universities or vote.

The feminist movement (a name that only gradually took hold in Europe and the United States) developed very slowly in Europe and was most active in Britain, where women had gained the right to vote in municipal elections in 1864 and for county and parish councils six years later. In 1889, at the time of the centennial of the French Revolution, the first International Congresses on Women's Rights and Feminine Institutions took place in Paris. By 1900, more than 850 German associations were working for women's rights, including improved educational and employment opportunities and equal wages.

Near the end of the century, British women's groups presented to Parliament a petition with more than a quarter of a million signatures calling for reform. As more occupations opened up to women, the campaign for women's suffrage widened. The International Women's Suffrage Alliance encouraged organizations in a number of countries. A more militant group of feminists undertook a campaign of direct action. Emmeline Pankhurst (1858–1928) founded the Women's Social and Political Union in 1903. Members protested the lack of female suffrage by breaking shop windows on London's fashionable Oxford Street, tossing acid on golf putting greens (a sport then identified with aristocratic British males), and bombing the house of Liberal party leader David Lloyd George (1863–1945). Other "suffragettes," as they were called, went on hunger strikes upon being arrested. In 1907, British women gained the right to serve in local government, and three years later Parliament considered a bill that would grant the vote to single women who owned property, but Prime Minister Herbert Asquith (1852–1928) simply let the bill drop. In the most dramatic incident, a suffragette carrying a banner proclaiming "Votes for Women" hurled herself in front of a horse owned by King George V at the 1913 Derby at Epsom Downs and was killed.

In 1913, the suffragette Emily Davison throws herself before the king's horse at the Derby at Epsom Downs and is killed.

CULTURAL FERMENT

Europeans had many reasons to be optimistic at the turn of the century. Since the fall of Napoleon in 1815, Europe had enjoyed a relatively long period of peace broken only by short wars with limited goals, although the bloody but short Franco-Prussian War (1870–1871) had spawned lasting hatred. Literacy had risen rapidly, particularly in western and northern Europe. Nation-states, increasingly secular in character, commanded the loyalty of their populations. Advances in science and technology were transforming the way people lived. The standard of living had generally risen, and, at least in most of Europe, white-collar jobs provided hope of better things for more people. Furthermore, somewhat shorter working hours for employees, including many workers, left more time for leisure activities.

During the 1850s and 1860s, the scientific progress and social change was reflected in the emergence of realism as the dominant cultural style for artists and writers. Then, beginning in the last decade of the nineteenth century, technological advances, large-scale industrialization, and the emergence of a more urban world brought both a cultural crisis of previously unparalleled dimensions and remarkable achievements in the arts. New discoveries in science and theories about the functioning of the universe continued to tear away some of the old certainties. Social scientists tried to find explanations for the working of society and the inner world of the individual. At the same time, some writers and artists began to turn away from rationalism, materialism, and positivism. In France, Henri Bergson (1859–1941) emerged as the philosopher of irrationality. Challenging materialism and positivism, Bergson popularized the idea that each individual and each nation had a creative "dynamic energy" or vital force (*élan vital*) waiting for release. The "modernist" culture of the avant-garde turned against the century-old acceptance of rationality as one of the dominant values of Western culture. The notion of an avant-garde, a term taken from military tactics, implies a small group of people who see themselves in the forefront of artistic expression and achievement. Intellectuals and artists began to insist on the irrational basis of human nature, their work reflecting both uncertainty and rebellion.

Realism

Influenced by the widening interest in science and the quickening pace of social change, some writers had earlier in the century broken with literary traditions. The escapist popular science fiction fantasies of the French author Jules Verne (1828–1905) reflected contemporary fascination with developing sciences like geography, science, astronomy, and physics, as well as interest in new means of transportation and communication. *Around the World in Eighty Days*, first published in 1873, was a best-

Charles Baudelaire, "the poet of modern life," in a photograph by Félix Nadar.

seller. In Britain, Sir Arthur Conan Doyle's character of Sherlock Holmes emerged as fiction's first truly scientific detective.

Above all, realism had emerged as the dominant European cultural style during the 1850s and 1860s. Charles Baudelaire (1821–1867) once described himself as the poet of modern life. Best known for his volume of poems *Les Fleurs du Mal* (1857; *The Flowers of Evil*), Baudelaire believed that art had to be the product of an exchange between the individual artist and contemporary society. In this way, the artist's own experience and self-discovery became critical in the emergence of modern literature. Baudelaire was fined in 1857 for "obscene and immoral passages or expressions." *Les Fleurs du Mal* became even more popular as his decadence and overt eroticism—he died of syphilis in 1867—angered officials and critics alike. Baudelaire was the consummate dandy and *"flâneur,"* the observer of modern urban life. Dressed in what modest elegance his small inheritance permitted, the flâneur strolled through Paris, finding beauty in its modern boulevards but also gazing at its hideous, even frightening aspects with objective detachment. The flâneur both reacted to and reflected modern urban life. Baudelaire rebelled against bourgeois culture and conventional assumptions about artistic subjects and style. Rejecting the notion that absolute aesthetic values exist, Baudelaire was a crucial figure in the emergence of modern culture in the middle of the century. He observed, reflected upon, and wrote about the transformation of urban society, particularly the leisure of prosperous bourgeois on the sparkling new boulevards of Paris. Beyond these symbols of urban modernity stood the popular classes threatening a further democratization of politics and culture.

In the 1850s, the Barbizon painters—so called because they gathered in a village southeast of Paris of that name—emphasized the painting of peasants, harvests, animals, and other symbols of village life. In doing so, they broke sharply with many of the long-accepted styles of painting, including romanticism. The development of photography during the 1840s may have contributed to the interest in portraying artistic subjects with a vivid sense of actuality. Jean-François Millet (1814–1875) was among the Barbizon painters. He painted peasants at work in such pieces as *The Gleaners* (1857) and *The Angelus* (1859), giving peasants a kind of dignity that repelled many middle-class viewers who thought them unworthy of being painted.

Artistic style evolved far more rapidly than did official views of what constituted good art. Gustave Courbet (1819–1877), the son of a peasant in eastern France, abandoned the idealization that still characterized painting. "Show me an angel," he scoffed at his critics, "and I will paint one." Taking as a compliment the assessment that he was "a democratic painter," he startled viewers by choosing ordinary workers as his subjects, as in his *The Stonebreakers* (1849). Like Millet, Courbet shocked bourgeois opinion with his realism. *Burial at Ornans* (1849) portrays a family of some means looking rather unattractive, bored, or even indifferent as the body of a relative is being lowered into a grave in Courbet's hometown. *The Bather* (1853) shows a stout naked woman rising from a forest pool. Nudity did not bother many viewers—it was, after all, a staple of classical painting. Rather, viewers were upset by the fact that Courbet portrayed an ordinary-looking woman assuming a classic pose, holding herself up very awkwardly. The artist seemed to be mocking the kind of classical scene painters had been expected to treat with reverence. When Napoleon III saw the exhibited painting, he struck the canvas with a riding-crop. Courbet, a political radical, believed that art should have a social purpose. He exacted some revenge in a later painting by presenting the emperor as a shabby poacher. Like some other artists of his time,

Jean-François Millet's *The Gleaners* (1857).

Gustave Courbet's *The Bather* (1853) in which the subject strikes an awkward pose.

Courbet remained torn between his desire for success—he was a specialist in self-promotion—and his determination to pursue his own realist course.

Realists continued to ruffle some official feathers. The French police hauled the novelist Gustave Flaubert (1821–1880) into court, charging him with obscenity. His novel *Madame Bovary* (1857) evokes with flawless attention to detail the affair of a bored bourgeois housewife living in a dreary Norman town. Flaubert reflected the bohemian underside of bourgeois life. But like most writers and artists at the time, he also depended upon middle-class patronage for his work.

Another writer who drew admiration and protest alike with works of unrelenting realism and concern with women's lives was the Norwegian playwright Henrik Ibsen (1828–1906). His forceful dramas, such as *A Doll's House* and *Hedda Gabler,* offer realistic descriptions of the psychology and interaction of his complex characters. Considered in some ways the father of modern drama, Ibsen privileged the themes of guilt and hypocrisy as he presented families in small-town life.

The French novelist Émile Zola (1840–1902) shocked many critics with his evocation of working-class life not only because the subject itself challenged traditional assumptions about literary worthiness but also because of his unabashed realism in depicting ordinary people as he saw them. Zola believed that naturalistic writing was a form of science. He went down into the mine shafts of northern France so that he could offer a realistic depiction of the work there in his novel *Germinal* (1885).

Artists and writers who espoused the new realism confronted censorship in France. The historian Joseph Ernest Renan (1823–1892) considered himself a proponent of "progressive ideas"—above all, a faith in science. "The triumph of science," he wrote, "is in reality the triumph of idealism." The emperor prohibited Renan, named to the prestigious Collége de France, from giving lectures. Renan then published his controversial, best-selling *Life of Jesus* (1863). It offended the Catholic Church by presenting Christ in a historical way, casting some doubt upon his divinity. More than this, Renan argued that the Scriptures had to be studied like any other historical document. Renan lost his academic chair.

Impressionism

During the French Second Empire, a group of artists developed impressionism, a remarkable artistic movement that lasted until the end of the century. Like the realists of the Barbizon school, impressionist painters rejected traditional religious and historical subjects and formal presentation. Instead, they depicted rural and urban landscapes, offering scenes from everyday existence, but generally integrated individual figures into landscapes. Embracing subjectivity, the impressionists preferred direct observation and the study of nature's effects to studio composition and imitation of classic styles. Édouard Manet (1832–1883), another dandy and flâneur, aspired to create what a contemporary called an art "born of today." The impressionists painted what they saw, and how they saw it at first glance. Their paintings, too, reflected an interest in science, particularly in the effects of light.

Impressionists attempted to capture their initial, fleeting visual sensations, trying to recreate on the canvas nature's wondrous incidents, such as the way sunlight falls on inanimate objects. This distinguished them from the realism of Courbet and his generation. Claude Monet (1840–1926) described what made such painting different: "Try to forget what objects you have before you—a tree, a house, a field, or whatever. Merely think, here is a little square of blue, here an oblong of pink, here a streak of yellow, and paint it just as it looks to you, the exact color and shape, until it gives your own naive impression of the scene before you." The way the impressionists saw what they painted was far more important than what they actually saw. They increasingly put lighter and brighter colors on large canvases (which previously had usually been reserved for historical themes), applying many small dabs of paint to convey an impression of spontaneity, energy, movement, and change. The subjectivity and artistic style of impressionism challenged basic contemporary assumptions about society and culture, while reflecting in important ways the time in which the impressionists lived.

Although the impressionists did not begin to exhibit their paintings with the self-consciousness of an artistic group until 1874 (and chose not to accept any official name when they did), their movement was shaped by official rejection. The Salon was a state-sponsored exhibition on which artists depended in order to attract purchasers. In 1863, the jury for the official Salon turned down, among hundreds of paintings, several by Manet. After certain complaints reached the emperor, he allowed some of the paintings to be shown in other rooms. The "Salon of the Refused" included works by Manet, Pierre-Auguste Renoir, and Paul Cézanne. Some critics raged against what they saw, but at least the public could

Édouard Manet's *Déjeuner sur l'herbe* (1863).

now make up its own mind. Manet's *Olympia* (1863) generated a chorus of complaint. The study of a nude shocked public opinion—the outraged Empress Eugénie, not to be outdone by her husband, Napoleon III, who had attacked a Courbet canvas with a riding-crop, hit Manet's painting with her fan. Manet's *Déjeuner sur l'herbe* (1863), presented at the same time, drew scathing commentary because it showed a nude female sharing a picnic with two fully dressed, upper-class males. Here, Manet, even more than the realists, challenged the hierarchy of subjects imposed by classicism. Manet and his younger followers gradually won public support.

Manet chose provocatively contemporary subjects, including very ordinary people, clients, and café waitresses enjoying themselves. He and his younger friend Monet both painted the Gare Saint-Lazare, the point of entry each day for thousands of commuters, vacationers, and other visitors. A keen observer of urban life, Manet encountered and painted rag-pickers, vagrants, and gypsies in a northern suburb of Paris, where he lived—although he could have afforded to reside in considerably more elegant surroundings—in the 1860s and 1870s.

In Manet's *Bar at the Folies-Bergère* (1882), the barmaid he depicts could be viewed in several ways. She could be merely serving drinks, as countless women did to earn a living. But, more likely than not, she is also arranging a more intimate, paying encounter solicited by the customer in the background. Berthe Morisot (1841–1895), Manet's sister-in-law, placed her subjects, most of whom were women, in private gardens, in the Bois de Boulogne, boating on the Seine, and at the resorts of the Norman coast, which had been "discovered" by wealthy Parisians.

The rebuilding of Paris opened up new possibilities for the understanding of modernity. Camille Pissarro and his colleagues found the great boulevards of Paris, lined with trees and newspaper kiosks, fitting subjects for their portrayal of modern life. The early impressionists were also influenced by the growing commercialization of leisure in Paris. Edgar Degas (1834–1917) followed wealthy Parisians to theaters, racetracks, cafés, and café-concerts. The latter offered entertainment that included vaudeville acts, poetry readings, comedians, and singers renowned for bawdy lyrics. He observed Parisians from a variety of backgrounds, as they smoked, drank, talked, and sought companionship. Degas frequently chose female entertainers, most of whom were drawn from the popular classes, as his subjects. In the shadows of his ballet paintings lurk wealthy gentlemen awaiting their prey, or, like Napoleon III himself, occupying the loges closest to the stage at the opera, or standing in the shadows of the dressing rooms of the dancers, ready to claim their prizes. Degas, whose banking family had lost its money early in an economic depression, forcing him to sell off some favorite paintings to get by, presented unflattering, dark stereotypes of Parisian speculators in *At the Stock Exchange* (1879).

The increasing anonymity of the burgeoning city (by 1891, only about a third of those living in Paris had been born there) was also a frequent impressionist theme. Degas's *L'Absinthe* (1876–1877) shows two disconnected figures in a café. Such encounters with strangers seemed an intrinsic part of modern life.

The great impressionist painter Claude Monet also manifested an uneasy ambivalence toward large-scale industry. In the 1870s, Monet lived in the industrializing Paris suburb of Argenteuil. His paintings of the town reflect a balance between leisure

Edgar Degas's *L'Absinthe* (1876–1877) shows a woman and her companion with a glass of absinthe. Note how the lack of a table support helps draw the viewer's attention to the glass of absinthe.

and industry (seen, for example, in a painting of sailboats on the Seine River with factory smokestacks in the background). Monet eventually tired of the hustle and bustle of urban life and moved down the Seine to the village of Giverny. There his garden and its pond and lily pads provided an ideal rural setting for his work. He never painted the railway tracks that ran through his property.

Social Theorists' Analyses of Industrial Society

Many visible, helpful advances contributed to the diffusion of the belief that human progress was inevitable and that it moved in a linear manner. This optimistic view became known as positivism. Auguste Comte (1798–1857) had already diffused faith in the promise of science. Believing that scientific discovery had passed through three stages of development—the theological, the metaphysical, and the positive (or scientific)—Comte concluded that what he called "the science of society" could do the same. Society itself, he reasoned, like nature could be studied in a scientific manner and its development charted. Comte's positivism called for the accumulation of useful knowledge that would help students of society to understand the laws of social development.

Positivists challenged some of the central tenets of the established churches, particularly those of the Catholic Church, whose theologians held fast to a view of humanity as essentially unchanging. Darwinism denied the literal biblical description of God creating the world in seven days. Clergy of many denominations, and many other people who misinterpreted Darwin's theory, were aghast to think that people could have descended from apes.

Now, in the face of continued rapid social change, intellectuals attempted to understand the structure of contemporary society. They did so by adopting the model of natural science and undertaking objective systematic analysis of observable social data. They gradually developed the science of society, sociology, which asked a fundamental question that in itself revealed social uncertainties: How do societies hold together when confronted by economic and social forces that tend to pull them apart? The question expressed the cultural crisis of the fin de siècle. In 1887, the German Ferdinand Tönnies (1855–1936) published a groundbreaking work, *Community and Society* (*Gemeinschaft und Gesellschaft*), which sought to synthesize and apply historical experience to understand the unique development of modern Western civilization.

Influenced by Tönnies and fascinated by the emergence of industrial society and the growth of the state, Max Weber (1864–1920), one of the fathers of modern social thought and sociology, sought to create an objective and thus "value-free" science of society that he thought held the key to guiding the future. Trained as a professor of law in Heidelberg, Weber became interested in the relationship between religion and society. *The*

Protestant Ethic and the Spirit of Capitalism (1904–1905) defined the "spirit of capitalism" to be the assumption that whoever works hard in the pursuit of gain fulfills a moral obligation. He identified the origins of capitalism with Calvinist entrepreneurship in the sixteenth and seventeenth centuries. Weber observed the contemporary trend toward larger structures of government and the bureaucratization of state, business, and political structures, which he believed marked the victory of Enlightenment rationalism, as well as increased social stratification. But he worried that in the advancing impersonal age of bureaucracy, state officials would ignore political and social ideals. Weber's modern man seemed to be trapped in what he called "the iron cage of modern life." Theorist of a nervous age, Weber had a nervous breakdown before the turn of the century.

Doctors diagnosed more cases of hypochondria, "melancholy," and hysteria, paralyzing nervous disorders that many blamed on the complexities of modern life, which seemed to be overwhelming the nervous system. In particular, neurasthenia seemed to be a sign of the times, with its symptoms of extreme sensitivity to light and noise (two characteristics of urban life), fatigue, worry, and digestive disorders.

Alcoholism was ravaging many countries in Europe. In England, the "habitual soaking" of workers in beer worried reformers. A contemporary investigator claimed that it was not uncommon for some workers to spend a quarter of their earnings on drink. The dramatic increase in the production of wine in France (with the exception of the 1880s and 1890s, when the insect Phylloxera ravaged vineyards), Italy, Spain, and Portugal flooded markets, greatly reducing its price. In parts of France, the average person (and thus the figure for adults would be even higher) consumed well more than sixty gallons of wine a year, in addition to beer, brandies, and absinthe, a licorice-tasting drink made from wormwood that is highly addictive. There were almost half a million establishments licensed to serve drink in France at the turn of the century—one for every 54 people, compared to one British "public house" for every 843 inhabitants at about the same time.

French temperance movements were swept aside like tiny dikes by the torrent of drink. Nationalists, worried about the plunging birthrate, joined some doctors and reformers in claiming that France faced "racial degeneration" since its population

Two elegant morphine addicts, 1891.

might cease to reproduce itself because of the ravages of alcoholism. Only by rallying around nationalist values could France, they argued, avoid total collapse. In Britain, the temperance movement began earlier and was far stronger than in France, and much more closely tied to churches, as was the movement in Sweden, where in 1909 temperance societies had almost half a million members who signed pledges promising not to drink at all.

The use of opium and its derivatives—morphine (the popularity of which increased with its use as an anesthetic), laudanum (a mixture of wine and opium), and heroin—as well as cocaine and hashish, unfortunately became common among the artistic avant-garde, well before most people were aware of their devastating effects. These drugs were brought from Turkey, Persia, and India, with coca (from which cocaine is derived) brought from Peru and Bolivia. When Sigmund Freud (1856–1939), the father of psychoanalysis, was invited to the house of the great French neurologist Jean Charcot (1825–1893) in Paris, before the negative effects of drugs were known, he remembered, "I [was] very calm, thanks to a small dose of cocaine." The painter Pablo Picasso (1881–1973) was also for a period a hashish user, which may have influenced his dreamy rose-colored paintings of 1905–1908.

Only in 1908 did the French government ban such drugs, in the wake of a number of drug-related suicides. Less dangerous, exoticism, mysticism, and a fascination with the occult became more popular than ever before, another sign of the rejection of science and the associated preoccupation with the irrational.

Modern life seemed to provide evidence that industrialization and urban growth had uprooted traditional values. Murder in France rose by about one-third between 1865 and 1890, robberies doubled, and assault and battery increased by four times. Seeking an explanation, the French social theorist Émile Durkheim (1858–1917) came to believe that the rapid, seemingly uncontrollable growth of large cities had destroyed the moral ties that had sustained the individual in traditional society. Durkheim believed that the waning of religious practice had undermined authority and therefore social cohesiveness, and that individuals lost in the faceless urban and industrial world suffered social and moral disintegration—"the state of disorganization, of maniacal agitation"—marked by class conflict and social unrest. Durkheim's quantitative study of suicide led him to believe that the stresses and strains of increasingly urban, industrial life were becoming more debilitating. Durkheim's modern individual now faced "alienation" (*anomie* in French) within his society. Some of Durkheim's theories, however, have not been substantiated by recent empirical studies. Yet he manifested the optimism of the new academic discipline by suggesting that social problems could be solved by studying them in a systematic, scientific manner.

Durkheim was hardly alone in thinking that urban growth, spurred on by the arrival of rural migrants, generated social pathology of

which criminality was but one manifestation. In 1895, Gustave Le
Bon (1841–1931) published *The
Crowd*, in which he worried that
modern life submerged the individual in the "crowd." The mob could
rise up, Le Bon argued, in violent
protest. Riots and strikes, he
warned, were becoming part of the
political process. To conservatives
like Le Bon, crowds threatened traditional elites. He described crowds
as lurching erratically, and sometimes dangerously, like drunks. At a
time of growing awareness that
alcoholism was ravaging France,
this very metaphor was closely tied
to elite perceptions of popular politics.

As some contemporaries became
uneasy about the rapid pace and
tensions of modern life, another
sign of the nineteenth-century erosion of faith in science and

Friedrich Nietzsche, philosopher of the
irrational.

progress was a growing obsession with "decadence." Some nationalists
now worried that their peoples were being undermined by "racial degeneration," which might compromise the natural process of evolution by
hereditary debasement. Some scientists claimed that significant racial differences could be identified within specific peoples, and that they
accounted for soaring rates of crime, alcoholism, insanity, syphilis, and
even popular political action. A degenerate underclass seemed to them to
threaten to compromise the vitality of industrializing countries. An Italian
anthropologist believed that criminals showed inferior physical and mental development. He described them as being like microbes that pollute
society, and he held that they could be identified by measuring their
skulls.

Nietzsche's Embrace of the Irrational

Friedrich Nietzsche (1844–1900) emerged in this period as the most strident philosophical critic of Enlightenment rationalism. The son of a strict
Protestant German minister who died when the boy was young, Nietzsche
was raised by his domineering mother. He became a professor of classics
in Basel, Switzerland. The tormented Nietzsche, forced by illness to leave
the university, moved to the Swiss Alps and thereafter lived by his pen, but

with little success. In increasingly poor health, he suffered a mental collapse at the age of forty-five, after sending off telegrams to some of his friends signed "The Crucified." Nietzsche was briefly confined in an asylum toward the end of his life, leading one wag to comment, "At last, the right man in the right place."

Nietzsche hated all religions equally, believing that they had destroyed the individual's capacity for natural development and fulfillment by imposing uniformity. He became an atheist, proclaiming, "God is dead . . . and we have killed him." He claimed strenuously that religion was incapable of providing ethical guidance and that no single morality could be appropriate to all people.

Espousing "philosophy with the hammer," Nietzsche awaited the heroic superman who, as part of a natural nobility of "higher humanity," would rule through the "will to power." Although indirectly influenced by the contentions of Hegel and Darwin that mankind could continue to develop to a higher stage, Nietzsche's thought marked a total rejection of all previous philosophy. His "vital" force, which he believed could be found only in new philosophers like himself, would be morally ambivalent, idealizing power and struggle. The free man, wrote Nietzsche, "is a warrior." Yet for all of his talk about "master races" and "slave races" in a period marked by a growth of racism, he castigated the herd-like instincts of frenetic German nationalists and anti-Semites. After World War I, impassioned German admirers would invoke Nietzsche, seeking a "Germanic religion" freed from the constraints of Christian humanitarianism and from rationality itself.

Freud and the Study of the Irrational

The Viennese doctor Sigmund Freud stressed the power of the irrational, which he placed in the human unconscious. Freud was born in the small Moravian town of Freiberg (now in the Czech Republic) in the Habsburg monarchy. He was the son of a struggling Jewish wool merchant and his much younger wife. When Sigmund was three, his father's business affairs went from bad to worse, forcing the family to leave its tranquil, small-town existence for Vienna. The younger Freud never felt comfortable in the imposing imperial capital. But he benefited from the period of liberal ascendancy in Austria, where Jews, many of whom had migrated from Galicia, had received full civil rights in 1867. The Viennese middle class had helped make their city a cultural capital of Europe. That reassuring atmosphere changed with the stock-market crash in 1873, which began a period of economic depression and culminated in the election of an anti-Semite, Karl Lueger ("I decide who is a Jew," Lueger insisted), as mayor of Vienna in 1895. (In contrast, Jews confronted considerably less anti-Semitism in Budapest, where they made up over 5 percent of the population.)

After beginning his career as a research scientist in anatomy, Freud fell under Jean Charcot's influence. From his scientific laboratory, Freud moved to the study of the irrational, or the "unconscious," convinced that it could be studied with the same systematic rigor as human anatomy. In the spring of 1886, he opened a small office in Vienna, treating patients with nervous disorders.

Freud developed the method of psychoanalysis, a term coined in 1896. It was based on the premises that the mind is orderly and that dreams offer codes that can unlock the unconscious. To Freud, a dream represented "the fulfillment of a [suppressed] wish"; it was the expression of an unconscious conflict. Freud encouraged patients to dream and to "free associate" in order to break down their defense mechanisms (the means by which individuals repress painful memories from childhood or even infancy). Sexuality, specifically the repression of sexual urges, formed the basis of Freud's theory of the unconscious. One of Freud's followers described the role of his mentor's "dream-work": "The mind is like a city which during the day busies itself with the peaceful tasks of legitimate commerce, but at night when all the good burghers sleep soundly in their beds, out come these disreputable creatures of the psychic underworld to disport themselves in a very unseemly fashion; decking themselves out in fantastic costumes, in order that they may not be recognized and apprehended."

Psychoanalysis became both an investigative tool and a form of therapy, in which, very gradually—from several months to many years and at considerable financial cost—the patient could obtain self-awareness and control over his or her symptoms, such as hysteria.

Freud's theories of human development established the irrational as an intrinsic and sometimes even determining part of the human psyche. This in itself generated further anxiety among some critics. They feared that one of the consequences of the Viennese doctor's views might be a further weakening of the moral codes of church and the laws of states as individuals turned inward in order to understand themselves. Psychoanalytic theory, which Freud claimed as a new science, emerged, along with Darwin's evolutionary theory and Marx's writings on capitalist development and revolution, as one of the foundations of twentieth-century thought.

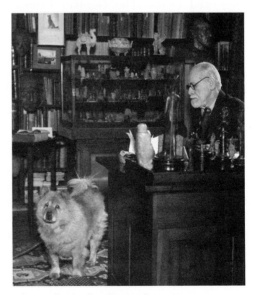

Sigmund Freud in his study.

Artists and the Rapid Pace of Modern Life

Progress seemed to have a price. At the Paris Exhibition of 1900, which celebrated the dawn of a new century, an uneasy visitor noted, "Life seethes in this immense reservoir of energy . . . a too violent magnificence." In *The Wind in the Willows*, published in 1908 by Kenneth Grahame (1859–1932), the motor car threatens stability. Behind the wheel, Toad, the amphibian protagonist, turns into "the terror, the traffic-queller, before whom all must give way or be smitten into nothingness and everlasting night . . . fulfilling his instincts, living his hour, reckless of what might come to him." The airplane, rapidly rising and then swooping dangerously, seemed not only a soaring symbol of scientific advances but also of the uncertainty that unsettled some fin-de-siècle Europeans. Émile Zola claimed that "modern society is racked without end by a nervous irritability. We are sick and tired of progress, industry, and science."

The last ten years of the career of the French impressionist painter and anarchist Camille Pissarro (1830–1903) reflected his growing preoccupation with the rapid trans-formation of modern life, particularly in cities. Perhaps the pre-eminent painter of the countryside, he later took up urban subjects, painting bridges, riverbanks, and boulevards, crowding myriad forms and figures into his panoramic views. Emphasizing the motion of transportation, walking, riding, loading, and unloading, he depicted the light, color, nervous movement, and energy of the city and its seemingly uncontrollable throngs, calling one series of paintings "Social Turpitudes."

Other painters also presented urban scenes in a harsh, jarring light that suggested chaos. The German Expressionist painter Ludwig Meidner (1884–1966) insisted that painters ought to abandon the gentle, almost rural style that characterized impressionist urban scenes: "A street," he wrote, "is rather a bombardment of hissing rows of windows, of blustering cones of lights between vehicles of all kinds and thousands of leaping globes, human rags, advertising signboards and masses of threatening, formless colors."

Artists' Responses to Popular Culture and Mass Production

Avant-garde writers and artists loathed the culture of the public, or what the English aesthete Oscar Wilde called the "profane masses." Popular culture seemed to be eroding the ability of high culture to survive the assault of mass manufacturing and teeming cities.

Sharp reactions against the seeming uniformity of the machine age permeated the arts. The English craftsman and designer William Morris (1834–1896) had already voiced reservations about the triumph of industry and the department store. He believed that mass production was in the process of eliminating the aesthetic control craftsmen had maintained over production. Describing capitalism as a "defilement" and Victorian England as the "age of shoddy," Morris argued that the machine had become the master of both workers and design, instead of the other way around. Only a revolutionary transformation of society could save the working class and only a revolution in aesthetics could save art and architecture. Morris spearheaded the "arts and crafts movement" in Britain, espousing craft production that would create useful but artistic objects for the general public, thereby elevating taste to a new level.

The painter Edward Burne-Jones and the craftsman and designer William Morris.

Symbolism, which began as a literary movement in the early 1870s but had origins a decade earlier—the symbolists revered Baudelaire, aesthete and dandy, as a founding father—also reflected the discontent of writers with the materialism of the industrial age. Symbolists sought to discover and depict aesthetically the reality of human consciousness and identity. They believed that analogies existed between the human mind and the external world, and thus between the natural and spiritual worlds. They believed that the links could be discovered through the exploitation of symbols, particularly through poetry. There thus was some continuity between the romanticism of the early nineteenth century, as symbolists sought to bring emotions to the surface through dreamlike states of consciousness.

The Avant-Garde's Break with Rationalism

In May 1913, the Russian aristocrat Sergey Diaghilev's ballet *The Rite of Spring* opened in Paris. For Diaghilev (1872–1929), who organized major art expositions and outraged conventional society by flaunting male lovers, art and life went hand in hand—they imitated each other. Diaghilev sought liberation in erotic ballets, and in life itself. Hitherto, ballet had retained absolute loyalty to classical subjects and presentation, immune to avant-garde challenge. Diaghilev's Russian Ballet Company helped to revitalize ballet. That night in 1913, aesthetes in the audience hissed the men and women of Parisian high society filing into the theater wearing tails and evening gowns. When the curtain went up and the first notes of music were heard, the dancers were jumping up and down, toeing inward in defiance of conventional ballet. The majority of the audience reacted with catcalls, hisses, and then screams of anger. "Listen first, and then whistle!" shouted one enthusiast, drowned out by the din. An elderly countess scoffed that it was the first time that anyone—in this case, the dancers with their provocative performance—had ever made fun of her. The audience was shocked, too, by the jarring, primitive music of the Russian composer Igor Stravinsky (1882–1971), who dispensed with the sentimental music that had invariably accompanied ballet. The avant-garde, however, cheered; art and life had merged.

Thus, rejecting the idea that rationalism should underlie the arts and that objective standards could exist by which to assess literature, painting, and music, the writers, painters, and composers of the avant-garde rebelled against accepted cultural forms, which they believed threatened to render the individual insignificant and powerless. Mass-circulation newspapers, the popular theater inevitably playing Gilbert and Sullivan in London or soapy popular operas in Paris, music halls, military band concerts in Hyde Park, and the cinema were the stuff of popular culture. The avant-garde wanted none of it.

The artists of the avant-garde accepted nothing as absolute, certainly not the traditional forms of cultural expression or morality. Showing Nietzsche's influence, some sought to transcend the limits of reason and moral purpose. Far more than even impressionist painters, the turn of the century avant-garde artists broke with the past. This was, to an extent, a revolt of the young—because of the rise in population, a larger percentage of the population was indeed young—and self-consciously so. In Austria, the avant-garde called themselves "The Young Ones." They were defiantly "modern," a term they embraced with passion. They paid less attention to their subjects than the response their work would elicit in their audiences.

Scene from *The Rite of Spring*, 1913.

The French playwright Alfred Jarry (1873–1907) staged the play *King Ubu,* a mockery of an authority figure. The story of an avaricious oaf in desperate search of a crown, the farce ran one tumultuous night in December 1896; it began with one of the characters pretending to hurl human waste at the outraged audience.

The avant-garde did not write or paint for everybody. In Paris, a group of artists and writers called themselves "Bohemians"—gypsy wanderers. These avant-garde of young men gloried in the condition of being out-siders, rebels against the dominant culture in the way that romanticism had been a revolt against the classical tastes of court and château.

Some of them rebelled against the strictures of their own middle-class social origins. They sought to surprise with their spontaneity and creativ-ity, and even to offend by creating a scandal. Many of them, including a number who were homosexual, celebrated their individuality and tried to keep themselves in the public eye. The flamboyant Irish-born poet and dramatist Oscar Wilde (1854–1900), whose witty dialogues greatly improved British comedy, became a symbol of contemporary "decadence." When asked by a customs official if he had anything to declare on arriving in France, Wilde replied, "Only my genius." He faced prosecution in 1895 for his sexual orientation, but also on trial, at least implicitly, was his belief in artistic decadence. Wilde, who insisted that "it is personalities, not principles, that move the age," dominated the court proceedings with his performance before he was sentenced to two years' hard labor for "immoral conduct." He died a lonely, premature death in a small Parisian hotel in 1900.

The proponents of cultural modernism believed themselves caught between two forces. They mocked bourgeois "respectability" and popular culture by sporting long hair, strange clothes, and erratic behavior. But, at the same time, they nonetheless sought public acceptance and patronage of their work.

Musical composition reflected the contemporary discovery of the unconscious, and avant-garde composers moved defiantly away from tradi-tional forms, with many abandoning the ordered hierarchical scale, in which certain tones held precedence. The composer Gustav Mahler (1860–1911) sought to release in his audience dreams and fantasies, which he believed could not be distinguished from real life, just as Freud sought to elicit them from the patients on his office couch. The French pianist and composer Erik Satie (1866–1925) composed music by the dim light of lampposts as he returned in an alcoholic haze from his favorite cafés, where he would eat only foods that were white in color. Both Satie and his countryman Claude Debussy (1862–1918) set out to free music from all constraints. Satie's compositions, with fanciful titles like *Three Pieces in the Form of a Pear,* explored new relationships between chords that surprised listeners, outraging some while delighting others with their humor. Satie also sought popularity, to the extent that he wanted to write

Georges Seurat's *A Sunday on La Grande Jatte* (1884).

what he called "furniture music," which he hoped would serve as background for daily life. The Austrian composer Arnold Schoenberg (1874–1951) began to break the patterns of traditional harmonies to write free atonal music, beginning with his String Quartet No. 2 (1908). He believed atonality realistically and subliminally followed the dictates, instincts, and sometimes suffering of his psyche: "What counts is the capacity to hear oneself, to look deep inside oneself. . . . Inside, where the man of instinct begins, there, fortunately, all theory breaks down." For Schoenberg, the self became a refuge from the outside world.

The artists and writers of the avant-garde believed that art could reveal what is hidden in the unsconscious, and thus open up new vistas of experience that could be communicated to viewers and audiences. Alfred Jarry held that all meanings that a reader could discover in poetry or prose were equally valid. The poet Guillaume Apollinaire (1880–1918), whose work defied stylistic convention, wrote reviews of books that only existed in his mind. Master of ambiguity, he abandoned direct statement and even punctuation and conventional word order to encourage readers to find new meanings in his work. One contemporary, affirming the particularly close link between symbolism and music, urged writers to "drop a syllable into a state of pure consciousness and listen for the reverberations."

Post-impressionists painted subjects in ways that even more consciously than impressionism distanced the artist from the subject. Georges Seurat (1859–1891) claimed that painters could evoke emotions through the visual suggestions of discontinuous lines, colors, and tones. Seurat's work was a reaction against impressionism. His paintings intrigued symbolist writers, who believed that symbols would stimulate memory through free association, because they consisted of thousands of dots of color forming figures and landscapes. Seurat's bold style, "pointillism," influenced by the development of photography, left his figures appearing strangely mechanical and separate from each other. This may suggest the alienation, social division, and isolation of modern urban life. His greatest and still most controversial work, *A Sunday on La Grande Jatte* (1884), may be seen in this way. Yet it also may be that Seurat sought to portray social cohesion through the social mix of bourgeois and workers enjoying a Sunday afternoon along the Seine River, all part of the same colorful matrix of light.

Expressionist painters used daring distortions, curious juxtaposition, and bold, unfamiliar color schemes to express what lay deep inside them and to obtain an emotional response in viewers. They were greatly influenced by the art of "primitive" societies. The French painter Paul Gauguin (1848–1903) abandoned a comfortable living as a stockbroker for the uncertainty of a career as a painter. His lengthy stay on the Pacific Ocean island of Tahiti shaped the appearance of his painting. Edvard Munch (1863–1944), a Norwegian artist who came to Paris in 1893, demonstrated Gauguin's influence. Munch's *The Scream* (1893) evokes the viewer's alarm and fear, because the subject's scream seems to fill the entire canvas. In Munich, which along with Dresden was the center of the expressionist movement in Germany, the Russian painter Wassily Kandinsky (1866–1944) moved expressionism by 1910 even further away from surface reality, portraying the inner being in a simplified form with lines, dots, and intense colors.

The Russian artist Kazimir Malevich (1878–1935) exhibited "Black Square" in 1915 as a religious icon would have been presented, and which he had hung over his bed. The painting reflected the painter's belief that the search for ultimate reality—self or God—could be discovered through the transformed consciousness that he believed came through intuition. He promoted the basic shapes, which he used as a new language in art.

Art Nouveau, a sinuous decorative style offering a synthesis between traditional and modern art, also reflected the anxiety and moodiness of the fin de siècle. Art Nouveau evinced contemporary fascination with psychiatry. Jean Charcot, the French neurologist, had opened up the unconscious to investigation through hypnosis. The dreamlike flowing forms and shapes of Art Nouveau, then, complemented the growing awareness of the contours and fluidity of the mind and its dreams and fantasies.

Although drawing upon past decorative traditions in furniture, jewelry, glasswork, and ceramics, Art Nouveau also influenced architecture, seen in the houses and sweeping entrances to subway stations that Hector Guimard (1867–1942) designed in Paris, and in the public park, apartment buildings, and beginnings of a cathedral undertaken (and still unfinished) in Barcelona by Antonio Gaudí (1852–1926).

Leading cultural figures in France identified Art Nouveau's style with the republic, seeing in its highly crafted luxury products something that was very French. At the same time, it could be associated with the conservative republic because the style's rococo origins were rooted in an aristocratic tradition and, perhaps as well, seemed to affirm women's traditional role in household decoration at a time when more feminists were stepping forward to demand equal rights for women.

Vienna became a vital center of avant-garde cultural experimentation. But after first enjoying state sponsorship of their art, the painters and writers of the avant-garde faced rejection in the climate of intolerance. Some intellectuals and painters embraced aestheticism, which emphasized form and beauty as a way of surviving in an increasingly irrational, hostile world.

(*Left*) Antonio Gaudí's Casa Batllo in Barcelona. (*Right*) Gustav Klimt's *Judith II* (*Salome*) (1909).

The painter Gustav Klimt (1862–1918), among other Viennese artists, retreated into subjectivism, attaching primary value to individual experience. In 1897, Klimt and his friends adopted the motto "To our era its art, to art its freedom." Yet in Vienna—and perhaps there alone—the aestheticism of the avant-garde was not a reaction against the resilient cultural values of the middle class. It was a reaction against political intolerance.

Klimt and the "seccessionists," like their counterparts in Munich who in 1892 announced their "secession" from officially approved art, rebelled against what Klimt considered the unsatisfactory values and dangers of mass society. He sought to stimulate and shock viewers by using, for example, classical images in strange, unprecedented juxtapositions, presenting erotic fantasies and other representations of utopian escape.

Following on the heels of Klimt in Vienna emerged a disparate but supremely talented group of younger modern painters in Paris. When in 1905 they exhibited their work together, a critic dismissed the show as "touches of crude colorings juxtaposed haphazardly; barbaric and naive games of a child who is playing with the 'box of colors.' " Another dubbed them the "fauvists," or wild beasts. The name stuck. The fauvists remained committed to experimentation on canvas in their quest for the liberation of both subject and painter. But they also frequently painted landscapes, including some familiar subjects such as coastal resorts, with bright colors and open spaces. One hostile critic in 1905 described a fauvist's brush as having been "dipped in dynamite," affirming the perceived association between artistic and social rebellion in some minds.

Pablo Picasso (1881–1973), a native of southern Spain, is considered by many specialists to be the first painter of the modern movement. Influenced by his homeland, Picasso's work (especially the paintings of his blue period) revealed the gloomy obsession with death that had characterized earlier Spanish painters. As with the other avant-garde artists, Picasso's work drew on his own intense subjectivity. He spent most of his career in Paris, where he became a fixture in the low-life cafés of Montmartre. Because Picasso at first mistrusted art dealers, his work was rarely shown and did not achieve great influence until later.

Picasso's daring *Les Demoiselles d'Avignon* (1907), depicting five nudes, may mark the beginning of modernist art. Abstract painting is a subjective form of expression. "I paint objects as I think them, not as I see them," Picasso asserted. Above all, abstract art abandoned the artist's system of perspective that had endured since the Renaissance. In Picasso's work, one finds a fragmentation of perception and dismantling of realistic depiction in favor of products of the imagination—flat, distorted, and highly simplified geometric patterns of solid forms, and space divided by sharp angles.

Critics called the Spanish painter's style "cubism" because of his preoccupation with basic shapes, particularly the three-dimensional prism.

(*Left*) The young Pablo Picasso in his studio. (*Right*) Picasso's *Les Demoiselles d'Avignon.*

Picasso considered the prism the fundamental component of reality. The inflnence of Georges Braque (1882–1963) on the cubist style contributed to the development of a second, "analytical" phase of cubism with an even greater emphasis on geometric shapes, now constructed from inanimate, pasted materials, as seen in Braque's *Newspaper, Bottle, Packet of Tobacco* (*Le Courrier*, 1914). The cubists became a more cohesive "school" than the fauvists, and relied more on light and shade than color to represent forms.

Futurist artists, most of them Italian, were inspired by technological change. In 1910, a futurist wrote, "All subjects previously used must be swept away in order to express our whirling life of steel, of pride, of fever and of speed." *Dynamism of a Cyclist* (1913) by Umberto Boccioni (1882–1916) depicts the frenetic energy of pedaling without actually showing the cyclist. The poet Filippo Tommaso Marinetti's "Manifesto of Futurism," which was published in 1909 in the aftermath of Wilbur Wright's triumphant airplane flights in France (following his first controlled airplane flight in Kitty Hawk, North Carolina, in 1903), proclaimed "We want to sing the love of danger, the habit of energy and rashness. . . . Beauty exists only in struggle. There is no masterpiece that has not an aggressive character. . . . We want to glorify war—the only cure for the modern world." One critic wrote in 1912, "Art is moving in a direction of which our fathers would never even have dreamed. We stand before the new pictures as in a dream, and we hear the apocalyptic horsemen in the air."

Conclusion

Artists in the early twentieth-century suffered the shrill denunciations of chauvinists. In France, the nationalist press denounced the cubists, several of whom, like Picasso, were not French, for artistic decadence, specifically for importing "foreign perversions" with the goal of weakening French morale. Insisting on eclecticism and experimentation, some Munich artists affronted German nationalists by insisting that art ought to be international in character and by bringing French and Russian artists— including Kandinsky—into their circle. The turn of the avant-garde toward irrationality came at a time when the rational structures that governed domestic political life and international relations seemed to be breaking down amid aggressive nationalism and militarism in Paris, Vienna, Berlin, and other European capitals.

Aggressive nationalism was closely linked to the "new European imperialism." Between the mid-1880s and 1914, the European powers raced each other to increase their domination of the globe. The imperialist powers included Great Britain and France, old rivals for colonies, as well as Germany and Italy, which also sought to extend what each considered its national interests. Imperial rivalries helped solidify international alliances, dividing Europe into two armed camps. The avant-garde had good reason, as it turned out, to be anxious. In the summer of 1914, World War I began.

CHAPTER **21**

THE AGE OF EUROPEAN IMPERIALISM

In one of the odd twists in the long, bloody history of European imperialism, the vast Congo region in Central Africa was colonized by a monarch acting as a private citizen. When he was heir to the Belgian throne, Leopold II (ruled 1865–1909) had given one of his father's ministers a piece of granite with the inscription "Belgium needs colonies." And so when he was king of Belgium, Leopold organized the Congo Company to explore and develop Central Africa.

In 1879, Leopold sent the British-American journalist Henry Stanley (1841–1904) to the Congo. Stanley emerged with treaties signed with local rulers establishing Leopold's personal claim over the Congo. The Belgian king would now have his "piece of that great African cake."

An international congress of representatives of European states held in Berlin in 1884–1885 to discuss claims to African territory declared the Congo to be the "Congo Free State," with Leopold as its head. This "free state," recognized as the private possession of the Belgian king and as part of his business organization, received the status of a "mandate." The Congress of Berlin established this designation to signify that a European power accepted the "mandate" to govern a territory and to provide, in principle, for the welfare of its "backward people." At the Congress of Berlin, the European powers agreed on ground rules governing the race for colonies. Henceforth no power could simply declare a region its colony unless it exercised effective control over the territory.

Despite Leopold's pledge that each colonial power would "undertake to watch over the preservation of the native races, and the amelioration of the moral and material conditions of their existence," the horrors perpetrated on the people of the Congo at Leopold's orders in his quest for ivory and rubber may have been unmatched in the annals of European imperialism. For the indigenous population, the colonial experience was hell on earth.

An American missionary reported a macabre way the Belgian soldiers had of trying to reduce the waste of bullets: "Each time the corporal goes

898

out to get rubber, cartridges are given to him. He must bring back all not used; and for every one used, he must bring back a right hand . . . in six months, they had used 6,000 cartridges, which means that 6,000 people are killed or mutilated. It means more than 6,000, for the people have told me repeatedly that soldiers killed children with the butt of their guns." Another European employed by the king boasted that he could line up several men in such a way that one bullet could kill them all.

The Belgian Parliament, stung by revelations of brutality uncovered by international investigations, demanded more humane standards. In 1908, it took the Congo away from Leopold and made it a colony of Belgium, a country one-eightieth the size of its colony.

FROM COLONIALISM TO IMPERIALISM

Imperialism is the process by which one state, with superior military strength and more advanced technology, imposes its control over the land, resources, and population of a less developed region. Although the repeated extension of Chinese control over the Vietnamese people of Indochina would fit most definitions of the term, imperialism has above all characterized the relations of the European powers with Africa and Asia. At the same time, Japan emerged in Asia as an imperial power itself during the first decades of the twentieth century. From the 1880s to 1914, the European powers expanded their direct control over much of the globe. Imperialism reflected and contributed to the development of a truly

The Congress of Berlin, 1878, included Disraeli (standing center left), Bismarck (center foreground) and Leopold II of Belgium.

global economy: the manufacturing boom of the Second Industrial Revolution whetted the appetite of merchants seeking new markets and manufacturers seeking new sources of raw materials. The expansion of European empires through what has been called the "new imperialism" generally included the exploitation of African and Asian lands with economic and strategic interests in mind.

Imperialism may be differentiated from colonialism, which from the sixteenth to the middle decades of the nineteenth century had entailed economic exploitation and control over territories through settlement by the colonizing power, as in the case of Britain's relationship with its American colony before the War of American Independence. But as the era of colonialism became that of imperialism, relatively few Europeans settled permanently in Africa or Southeast Asia, both of which had difficult tropical climates, or in China, which was an independent though weak state when compared to its European antagonists.

Europeans had long visited, influenced, learned from, and conquered distant lands. Spain and Portugal began the first sustained European quest for colonies in the fifteenth century with excursions along the West African coast. During the sixteenth century, Spaniards built a vast colonial empire that stretched from what is now the southwestern United States to the southern tip of Latin America. In the seventeenth century, French traders, missionaries, and soldiers began small settlements in "New France" (present-day Quebec). France lost New France to Britain in the 1760s. After the loss of New France, France's modest empire included Algeria (conquered in 1830) and a few Caribbean islands.

During the eighteenth and nineteenth centuries, British merchants sought both raw materials and sizable markets for manufactured goods in Africa, India, and as far as Southeast Asia, China, and Japan. The drive for colonies heightened the rivalry between Britain and France in the era of the American Revolution.

During the nineteenth century, many of the original colonies of Spain and Portugal became independent. Thus, following successful drives for independence early in the nineteenth century, the Spanish Empire in the New World had largely disappeared by 1850. But Spain still held Cuba, Puerto Rico, and the Philippines. After Brazil, many times the size of Portugal, proclaimed its independence in 1822, Portugal was left with only toeholds in Africa, India, and East Asia.

The Dutch had established bases on the coast of West Africa (abandoned in 1872) and small island colonies scattered in the Caribbean, the Indian Ocean, and the Pacific. Dutch traders ended Portuguese control of Java, one of Indonesia's islands, and extended their own influence over the island in 1755. Although the Dutch lost Java to the British in 1811, they reestablished control there in 1816 and then gradually extended their political control over the rest of Indonesia, the centerpiece of their colonial empire.

A European colonizer courts a tribe in the Congo.

Britain and France had established bases on the west coast of Africa, despite its lack of natural harbors and estuaries. Both powers began to penetrate the giant continent during the nineteenth century—the British from the tip of South Africa, the French from Algeria and the coast of West Africa. In the early 1850s, merchants in the ports of Bordeaux and Marseille had begun to pressure Emperor Napoleon III to help them expand French trading interests in West Africa beyond several coastal bases. In the 1860s, the governor of the French territory of Senegal, who learned the local language and married an African, established a French protectorate over a wider area.

Only Britain, despite being only about the size of the island of Madagascar, still had a large empire by the middle of the nineteenth century. Despite the loss of thirteen of its American colonies (which became the United States of America after the Declaration of Independence of 1776), the British Empire still extended into so many corners of the world that it was commonly said that "the sun never sets on the British Empire." Britain's strength partially rested on the pillars of settlement colonies. In search of a more secure future or simply adventure, more than a million people emigrated from the British Isles in the 1850s alone, most of them to Australia, New Zealand, and Canada, as well as to the United States. Australia had become the world's largest exporter of wool by 1851, when the discovery of gold in New South Wales and Victoria brought another wave of immigrants

MAP 21.1 COLONIAL EMPIRES UNTIL 1880 Colonies of Britain, France, Russia, the Netherlands, Spain, Portugal, and the Ottoman Empire.

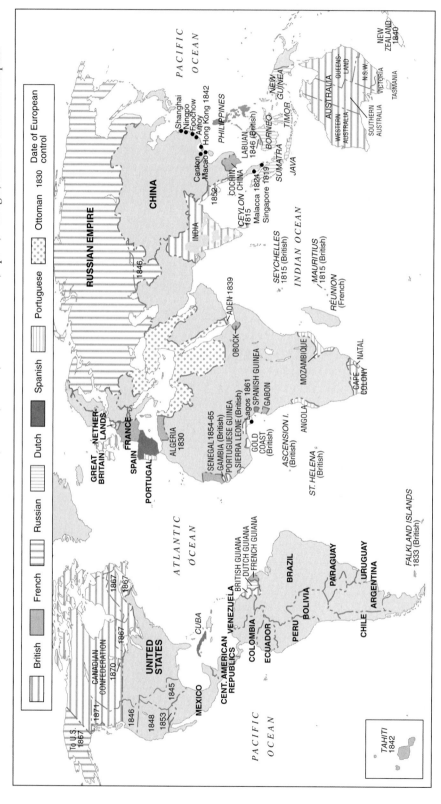

dreaming, like those pouring into California at the same time, of making their fortune. The Australian colonies and New Zealand received the right to maintain their own governments in the 1850s, under the watchful eye of the British Foreign Office, although western Australia remained a convict colony until "transportation" to Australia ceased to be a punishment in England in 1865. Canada achieved Dominion status in 1867 with passage of the British North America Act by the British Parliament. The crown would grant Dominion status to Australia in 1901 and to New Zealand in 1907.

THE "NEW IMPERIALISM" AND THE SCRAMBLE FOR AFRICA

In the early 1880s, the hold of the European powers on the rest of the world was still relatively slight, as Map 21.1 demonstrates. Many leaders could still conclude that the cost of maintaining colonies outweighed the benefits. In 1852, British Prime Minister Benjamin Disraeli, later an outspoken advocate of imperialism, had referred to the colonies as "wretched" and "a millstone round our necks." William Gladstone, Disraeli's great rival, reflected the prevailing liberal view when he pontificated, "The lust and love of territory have been among the greatest curses of mankind."

Distant, underdeveloped lands still seemed remote from urgent European interests. But this changed rapidly. Before the age of imperialism, Shaka, a renowned leader of the Zulus, who had established one of the two dominant African kingdoms in what is now South Africa, prophesied before his death in 1828 that his people would be conquered by the "swallows," the white men who built mud homes. The prophecy came true.

The rapid spread of a contentious nationalism fueled imperialism. The imperialist powers included Great Britain and France, old colonial powers and rivals, and also newly emerged Germany and Italy. Nations no longer necessarily looked to preserve the balance of power, but rather to extend what each considered to be its national interests. Smaller nations, too, participated in the drive for empire, including the Netherlands and Belgium.

Trying to establish the frontier between French and German territory in the Congo, 1913.

A British foreign minister recalled in 1891, "When I left the Foreign Office in 1880, nobody thought about Africa. When I returned to it in 1885, the nations of Europe were almost quarreling with each other as to the various portions of Africa which they should obtain." Another British foreign official would ask incredulously if his country sought to "take possession of every navigable river all over the world, and every avenue of commerce, for fear somebody else should take possession of it?" The colonial race extended even to the North Pole, first reached by the American Robert E. Peary (1856–1920) in 1909.

British and French Imperial Rivalry

A French colonial enthusiast assessed the scramble for Africa that began in the 1880s: "We are witnessing something that has never been seen in history: the veritable partition of an unknown continent by certain European countries. In this partition France is entitled to the largest share." Africa included about one-fourth of the world's land area and one-fifth of its population. Explorers plunged almost blindly into the uncharted and unmapped African interior. The source of the Nile River, the lifeline of Egypt, had been located in the Sudan only in 1862; most Western maps still showed blank spots for much of the continent's interior. Europeans discovered the bewildering complexity of a continent that included about 700 different autonomous societies with distinctive political structures.

France's imperial aspirations reveal some of the motives that fueled the new imperialism. After its humiliating defeat by Prussia during the Franco-Prussian War of 1870–1871, the gnawing loss of Alsace-Lorraine hung over France during the next decade and beyond. German Chancellor Otto von Bismarck subtly encouraged the French government to pursue an interest in distant colonies, hoping it would forget about trying to retake Alsace-Lorraine. Yet French colonialism during the period of the "new imperialism" was closely tied to a nationalist spirit of revenge against Germany, including the desire to recapture Alsace-Lorraine.

At the Congress of Berlin, the French agreed to abandon their claims to the island of Cyprus, while the British gave up claims to Tunisia. The French ambassador to Germany warned his own government in 1881 that if it failed to order bold action in Tunisia, France risked decline as a power, perhaps even "finding itself on a par with Spain." In March 1881, the French government claimed that raiders from Tunisia were harassing their troops in Algeria. French troops invaded Tunisia and crushed resistance there. Tunisia became a French protectorate two months later. Between 1895 and 1896, France also seized the island of Madagascar off the coast of East Africa and made it a colony (see Map 21.2).

French merchants and nationalists dreamed of an empire that would stretch across Africa. Railroads had begun to reach across continental Europe in the 1840s and 1850s. They became a symbol of modernity, but also of conquest, as in the case of the U.S. transcontinental railway. Not

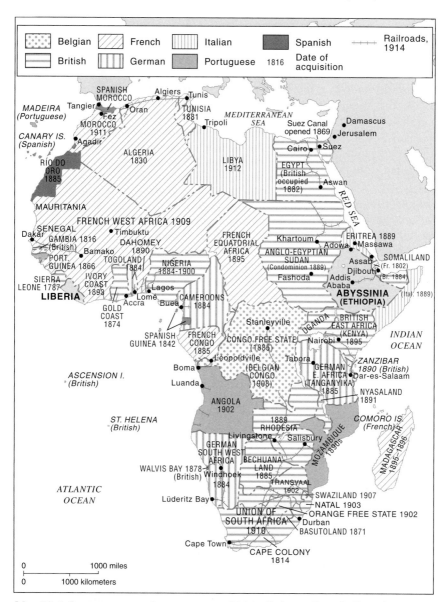

MAP 21.2 IMPERIALISM IN AFRICA BEFORE 1914   Belgian, British, French, German, Italian, Portuguese, and Spanish colonies in Africa and dates of European control.

surprisingly, then, the railroad captured the imagination of imperialists. Cecil Rhodes (1853–1902), British entrepreneur, colonialist, and millionaire, asserted that rails went farther and cost less than bullets. During the late 1870s, the French Chamber of Deputies subsequently approved a series of expensive, far-fetched plans to build railways across the vast

African expanse. A railway network was mapped out to connect Algeria and Senegal by crossing the Sahara Desert. Most of the lines were never built, and, in any case, they could never have generated sufficient revenues to justify their enormous cost. France had little more than a series of forts to show for the expense. Yet British merchants on the coast of West Africa feared that French advances would lead to the loss of products such as palm oil and potential markets for their own goods in the African interior. The Franco-British rivalry in Africa heated up. Further French advances in western Sudan followed.

British and French rivalries in Egypt, a gateway to the markets and products of the Middle East, dated to the British clash with France during the revolutionary years of the late 1790s. In 1869, a French engineer and entrepreneur, Ferdinand de Lesseps (1805–1894), completed a canal through the Isthmus of Suez, which connects the Red and Mediterranean Seas. The canal cut the distance of the steamship voyage from London to Bombay in half by avoiding the treacherous Cape of Good Hope at the southern tip of Africa. The severe financial difficulties of Ismail Pasha, the ruler, or *khedive,* of Egypt, which was a part of the Ottoman Empire, brought Britain a stroke of incredibly good fortune. In 1875, Britain bailed out the bankrupt Ismail Pasha by purchasing a considerable portion of shares in the canal. Under British management the number of ships passing through the canal rose from 486 in 1870 to 3,000 in 1882.

No power had a greater stake in the canal than Britain. The British government traditionally had sought to protect the land and sea routes to

Gunboat diplomacy: the British fleet anchored at Alexandria, Egypt, 1882.

India by supporting the Islamic Middle Eastern states—above all, the crumbling Ottoman Empire—against Russian designs. With continuing social and political chaos in Egypt threatening the interests of British bondholders, in 1882 a British fleet shelled the Mediterranean port city of Alexandria. The British then established a protectorate over Egypt, although the country remained nominally part of the Ottoman Empire. The Egyptian *khedive* henceforth accepted British "advice." Over the next forty years, the British government repeatedly assured the other powers that its protectorate over Egypt would only be temporary. The French, who had loaned the *khedive* as much money as had Britain, were particularly aggrieved at the continued British occupation.

Central Africa became the next major focus of European expansion. In 1869, the *New York Herald* hired Henry Stanley to find the missionary and explorer David Livingstone (1813–1873), from whom there had been no word in almost four years. After a trip of fifteen months, he found the missionary in January 1871 on the shores of Lake Tanganyika and greeted him with that most understated Victorian salutation, "Dr. Livingstone, I presume?" Henry Stanley's subsequent long journey up the Congo River in 1879 to gain treaties for Belgian King Leopold II opened up interior Africa to great-power rivalry. In 1880, Savorgnan de Brazza (1852–1905), a French naval officer, reached Stanley Pool, a large lake Stanley had "discovered" in 1877. ("Stanley didn't discover us," one "native" put it reasonably, "we were here all the time.") Brazza returned with a piece of paper signed with an "X" by a king, which Brazza claimed granted France a protectorate over the territory beyond the right bank of the Congo River.

Although the French government first showed little interest, French nationalists made ratification of Brazza's "treaty" a major issue. Portugal then declared that it controlled the mouth of the Congo River. The British government demanded trade rights with the region. Leopold of Belgium voiced opposition to any French moves near his Congo territory. Amid continued resentment over British control of Egypt, the French Chamber of Deputies eagerly ratified Brazza's treaty. French colonial activity in West Africa continued unabated.

Germany and Italy Join the Race

Germany was the next power to enter the race for colonies. It did so despite the fact that Chancellor Otto von Bismarck at first viewed colonization as an expensive sideshow that distracted attention from the essential questions of power politics in European diplomacy. He once curtly rejected a German colonial explorer's plea for a more aggressive colonial policy: "Your map of Africa is very nice, but my map of Africa is in Europe. Here is Russia, and here is France, and we are in the middle. That is my map of Africa!"

The Germans in Africa. Cartoons originally appearing in the German journal *Jugend* in 1916 show (*left*) an officer arriving to find chaos and (*right*) imposing military order.

The chancellor had routinely rejected pleas that Germany intervene in Africa on behalf of merchants, missionaries, and nationalistic adventurers. The Colonial League, established in 1882, and the Society for German Colonization, a lobby of businessmen and other nationalists formed in 1884, pressured the government to pursue colonies. The German adventurer Karl Peters (1856–1918) sought an outlet for his financial interests and nationalist fervor through his East Africa Company. Peters's chartered company signed commercial agreements, built settlements, and assumed sovereignty over a variety of East African territories. These activities aroused the ire of nationalists in England, exactly what Bismarck had hoped to avoid but, given the sudden intensity of nationalist and colonial fever at home, could not.

Bismarck gradually came to share the imperialist view that colonies might provide new markets for German products. But more than this, he realized that the establishment of colonies would solidify his political support within Germany and might also help defuse domestic social tensions. New markets could create jobs at home or abroad for unemployed German workers. Bismarck concluded that colonies could be administered indirectly at a relatively low cost.

The time also seemed right for the German government to appease its drooling colonial lobby, including merchants. The British Foreign Office was preoccupied with Islamic fundamentalist rebellions in the Sudan. France, with a new protectorate over Tunisia, was embroiled in debate over colonization in Indochina. In April 1884, Bismarck wired his consul in Capetown, South Africa, ordering him to proclaim that the holdings of a German merchant north of the Orange River—the territorial limit of British colonial authority—would henceforth be the protectorate of German Southwest Africa. Britain acquiesced in exchange for Bismarck's acceptance of the British occupation of Egypt. That summer the German chancellor also decided to establish a protectorate over the Cameroons and Togoland in West Africa.

Bismarck, who expertly played British and French interests off against each other, called the Berlin Conference of 1884–1885 in response to an 1884 agreement signed between Britain and Portugal recognizing mutual interests. The Berlin Conference divided up the territory of the Congo basin between the Congo Free State (Leopold's territory) and France (the French Congo), while declaring the Congo River open to all. French merchants penetrated Dahomey and the Ivory Coast, with French troops reaching the ancient trading town of Timbuktu in 1894.

In 1885, Bismarck agreed to protect Peters's commercial enterprises in Tanganyika, which became German East Africa. Germany also established several coastal trading stations and the colony of Angra Pequena in Southwest Africa, which merchants had portrayed with unerring inaccuracy as a territory of untapped wealth just waiting to be extracted.

To placate Britain, Germany recognized British interests in Kenya and Uganda and the protectorate status of Zanzibar in 1890. In exchange, Germany received a small but strategically important island naval station in the North Sea. The German colonial lobby was not happy: "We have exchanged three kingdoms for a bathtub!" moaned Peters. Nonetheless, by 1913, German colonies in Africa, including German East and Southwest Africa, Togoland, and the Cameroons, occupied over 1 million square miles, five times the size of Germany.

Italy was the last of the major European nations to enter the colonial fray. Its ravenous hunger for empire led Bismarck to note sarcastically that it proceeded "with a big appetite and bad teeth." In 1882, Italy established Assab, a small settlement on the Red Sea, and three years later it occupied Massawa, which in 1889 became the capital of the new Italian colony of Eritrea. Italian merchants hoped to force the adjacent African state of Abyssinia (now Ethiopia) to trade through Eritrea. In 1889, the Abyssinian emperor signed a treaty with Italy which the Italian government took to mean that Abyssinia was now an Italian protectorate. When the French began building a railroad that would link Abyssinia to French Somaliland and the Abyssinians attempted to cancel the treaty, Italian troops launched a war (1894). The result was an Italian disaster. In 1896, a general without adequate maps marched four badly organized columns of Italian troops into battle. Abyssinians, some 70,000 strong, with Russian artillery advisers and French rifles, routed the Italian army in the hills near the coast at Adowa; 6,000 Italian soldiers were killed—many more than in the various wars that had led to Italy's unification—and several thousand were captured. The Italians became the first European army to be defeated in the field by Africans. Under the Treaty of Addis Ababa that same year, Italy was forced to renounce Abyssinia as a protectorate, although it kept the territory of Eritrea on the Red Sea.

Standoff in the Sudan: The Fashoda Affair

In 1898, the Anglo-French rivalry in Africa culminated in the standoff between French and British forces at Fashoda on the Nile River in the southern Sudan, nearly bringing the two powers to war. The French government resented the fact that Egypt served as a base for British initiatives in the hot, dry Sudan.

A fundamentalist Islamic and nationalist revolt led by a former Sudanese slave trader who declared himself to be the Mahdi (the Guided One) in the early 1880s challenged the nominal authority of the *khedive* of Egypt over Sudan. After the Mahdi and his followers (the Mahdists) began a holy war against Egypt and defeated Egyptian armies led by British officers, the British sent an expedition to the Sudanese capital of Khartoum to evacuate the Egyptian population. It was led by the dashing, eccentric British adventurer General Charles "Chinese" Gordon (1833–1885), so called because he had commanded troops that assisted the Chinese government in putting down the Taiping Rebellion in the 1860s. Besieged for ten months in Khartoum by the Mahdi's forces in 1884, Gordon was killed when the Mahdists stormed the garrison two days before a relief expedition from Britain arrived in January 1885.

Britain lost interest in the Sudan until the French colonial lobby, still smarting from Britain's occupation of Egypt, sought a strategic foothold on the Nile River. In January 1895, Britain claimed the Sudan. The French government, in turn, announced that it considered the Sudan

The charge of the dervishes (followers of the Mahdi) at the Battle of Omdurman in the Sudan, 1898.

open to all colonial powers. The British government responded that it would consider any French activity in the Sudan "an unfriendly act."

In 1898, a British force commanded by Lord Horatio Kitchener (1850–1916) set out from Egypt for the Sudan with the Upper Nile outpost of Fashoda as its goal. Kitchener and his army took revenge for Gordon's death, using machine guns to mow down 11,000 Mahdists at the Battle of Omdurman (September 1898) and retaking Khartoum. British troops desecrated the Mahdi's grave, playing soccer with his skull. At Fashoda, they encountered a French expeditionary force, which intended to establish a French colony on the Upper Nile. Kitchener handed his counterpart a mildly worded note of protest against the French presence, and the two commanders clinked drinking glasses, leaving their governments to fight it out diplomatically.

In both Britain and France, nationalists demanded war. But the Dreyfus Affair (see Chapter 18) divided French society; furthermore, as the French foreign minister lamented, "We have nothing but arguments and they have the troops." The Fashoda Affair ended peacefully when France recognized British and Egyptian claims to the Nile Basin and Britain recognized French holdings in West Africa. For the moment, there seemed to be enough of Africa to go around. Only Abyssinia and Liberia, which had been settled in the 1820s by freed U.S. slaves, were independent African states.

The British in South Africa and the Boer War

In South Africa, Britain had to overcome resistance to its presence, first from indigenous peoples and then from Dutch settlers. The British had taken the Cape of Good Hope at the tip of South Africa from the Dutch in 1795. British settlers moved in, fighting nine separate wars against the Bantu people in the 1850s and 1860s. In 1872, the Cape Colony emerged from under the wing of the British Foreign Office, forming its own government, but remaining within the empire.

Known as the Boers, the Dutch settlers (Afrikaners) in South Africa were a farming people of strict Calvinist belief. The Boers resented the British abolition of slavery and the fact that the British allowed blacks to move about freely and to own property. In the "Great Trek" from the Cape Colony, which began in 1836 and lasted almost a decade, many Boers began to move inland to carve out states that would be independent of British rule (see Map 21.3). Overcoming Zulu resistance, Boers established the Natal Republic, a strip along South Africa's east coast. When the British intervened in support of the Zulus, the Boers left Natal, which became a British colony in 1843. The Boers crossed the Vaal River in search of new land. Slaughtering Zulus as they went, the Boers founded the Republic of Transvaal (later called the South African Republic) and the Orange Free State, which the British recognized as independent in 1854.

MAP 21.3 SOUTH AFRICA, 1800–1910   The settlement of South Africa by the Boers and English, including the Boers' Great Trek and the 1910 boundaries of the Union of South Africa.

The discovery of diamonds in the late 1860s, first in the Cape Colony and then west of the Orange Free State, attracted a flow of treasure seekers—at least 10,000 people—raising the stakes for control of South Africa. After annexing the Republic of Transvaal against the wishes of the Boers in 1877, the British gradually extended their colonial frontier northward, convinced that more diamonds and gold would be found beyond the Vaal River.

Cecil Rhodes orchestrated British expansion in South Africa, leading to conflict with the Boers, who still bitterly resented annexation into the British Empire. In 1880, the Boers rose up in revolt, their sharpshooters picking off British troops at Majuba Hill a year later. Unwilling to risk further trouble, William Gladstone's Liberal government recognized the political independence of the South African Republic. But, at the same time, the British tried to force the Boers to trade through the port of Capetown by denying them access to the sea, reflecting the primacy of commerce in the British grand scheme.

The Boers in Transvaal were given a boost by the discovery in the mid-1880s of more gold deposits, which enabled them to buy weapons. Constructing their railway to Port Mozambique on the eastern coast, the Boers offered advantageous shipping rates to Natal and the Orange Free State, taking business away from British South Africa, and further souring relations between the Boers and Britain. Rhodes then subsidized an uprising in the Transvaal against the Boers. The British government followed Rhodes's advice to send a military excursion against the Boers in 1895, but the Boers fought off the "Jameson Raid" by 500 British cavalry with ease. The raid discredited Rhodes, but brought the British government even more directly into the crisis, particularly after Emperor William II of Germany sent Transvaal president Paul Kruger a congratulatory telegram after the failed Jameson Raid.

In 1899, the British goaded the Boers into a war that lasted three years. In order to depopulate the farms that supplied the Boer rebels, the British imprisoned farmers' wives and children in camps in which thousands died. Some people in Britain criticized these camps, though there had been few such outcries when the British had killed people of color during the wars against the peoples of India, Burma, and elsewhere in Africa. The outnumbered Boers evoked great sympathy in France and Germany, leaving the British government isolated diplomatically. The war shocked many

(*Left*) British troops in Pretoria, South Africa. (*Right*) Boer Commandos.

people in Britain not only by the extensive, costly military campaigns it required (almost 400,000 British troops were sent), but also because of the hostile reaction the British conduct of the war engendered in other countries. In 1902, the Boers asked for an armistice. Thereafter, they were forced to take an oath of loyalty to the king of England. In 1906 and 1907, Britain granted the Republic of Transvaal and the Orange Free State self-government. In 1910, the Boers joined the British Union of South Africa (which now included the Cape Colony, the Orange Free State, Transvaal, and Natal, and which was given Dominion status by the British at that time).

The new Boer government immediately proclaimed that it would "permit no equality between colored people and the white inhabitants either in church or state." Apartheid—the unequal separation of whites and blacks by law—was the result of the Boer policy of racial domination. It proved to be the most extreme consequence of the "scramble for Africa," which would in the twentieth century leave Africans with daunting challenges.

THE EUROPEAN POWERS IN ASIA

The European powers and the United States divided up the entire Pacific region in their quest for raw materials, markets, strategic advantage, and prestige. (Cecil Rhodes cosmically announced in the same spirit, "I would annex the planets if I could.") From the populous Indian subcontinent, Britain expanded its interests into and beyond Burma, accentuating a rivalry with Russia for influence in the region. In the meantime, the Dutch extended their authority in Indonesia, while the French turned much of Indochina into their protectorate. Russia, too, was an Asian power. Its empire had expanded to the Pacific Ocean and well into Central Asia. By 1900, only Japan, the emerging power in Asia, maintained real independence. Siam (now Thailand) stood as a buffer state between British and French colonial interests, and the Western powers dominated China, forcing trade and territorial concessions on that weakening empire.

India, Southeast Asia, and China

Europe's quest for colonies and domination in Asia had begun even earlier than in Africa. During the Seven Years' War (1756–1763), British troops defeated the French in India. The British East India Company, responsible to the British Parliament, administered India. The Company ruled with the assistance of various Indian princes. The British recognized their local prerogatives in exchange for their obedience and assistance. Britain later expanded east from India into Burma, overcoming Burmese resistance in a war from 1824 to 1826, and then expanded south into Malaya (see Map 21.4).

Using India as a base, British merchants, backed by British naval power, had worked to overcome barriers to trade with East Asia. In the 1830s, British traders had begun to pay for silks, teas, and other Chinese luxury goods with opium grown in India. With opium addiction rampant in southern China, in 1839 the emperor tried to stop trade completely with foreigners. The Royal Navy sent gunboats—hence the origins of the term "gunboat diplomacy"—to Canton (now Guangzhou) to force Chinese capitulation in the short, one-sided Opium War

Chinese men smoking opium.

(1840–1842). By the Treaty of Nanking that followed in 1842, China was forced to establish a number of "treaty ports" open to British trade, including Canton and Shanghai, and it was required to grant Britain formal authority "in perpetuity" over Hong Kong (authority which lasted until 1997). British residents and European visitors received the rights of extraterritoriality, which meant that they were not subject to Chinese law. Britain and France together occupied Canton. In 1858, China opened six more ports to British and French trade.

In 1857, a revolt shook British rule in India, revealing some of the tensions between the colonialists and the colonized. Long-term causes of the mutiny of the Sepoys—Indian troops in the British army—included anger at the British policy of taking direct control over Indian states whose princes died without heirs and the dismissal of an Indian prince whose corruption was well known. The immediate cause was the continued use of animal fat to grease rifle cartridges, a religious affront to both Hindu and Muslim soldiers. Confronted with British intransigence, the Sepoys rebelled over a wide area, in one place killing 200 British women and children. In retaliation, British authorities hanged rebels and burned a number of villages.

Following the mutiny, administration of India passed in 1858 from the East India Company to the British crown, Queen Victoria becoming "Empress of India." British rule became formalized and more direct. Indian princes were guaranteed their lands if they signed agreements accepting British rule. The governor-general of India added the honorific title of "viceroy," as the monarch's personal representative, serving under

MAP 21.4 INDIA AND THE FAR EAST BEFORE 1914   Areas controlled by the British, French, Dutch, Portuguese, Germans, and Americans in Asia.

the secretary of state for India. Lord George Curzon (1859–1925), one of the most forceful proponents of British imperialism, strengthened the northwestern frontier defenses against Russia, reduced the cost of government, and took credit for a modest increase in the Indian standard of living.

The British government enacted educational reforms, initiated irrigation projects, reformed the police and judicial systems, and encouraged the cotton industry, which by 1914 became the fourth largest in the world. Frightened by the Sepoy Mutiny, the British government also expedited railway construction in India in order to be able to move troops rapidly. From less than 300 miles of track in 1857, a network of 25,000 miles was established by 1900. By connecting much of the Indian interior with ports, railway development also encouraged production of Indian cotton, opium, rice, oil, jute, indigo, and tea, which could now reach ports by train and then be exported to Britain.

But while some Indian merchants and manufacturers made money from expanded trading opportunities, others lost out. To assure a lucrative market in India, a country of almost 300 million people in 1900, the British at first banned some Indian manufactures that would compete with British goods produced at home, thereby destroying Indian village handicrafts such as textile weaving. Raw Indian cotton was shipped to England to be made into cloth there, and then re-exported to India. British tax collectors increased the indebtedness of peasants in a vast

(*Left*) Ruins after the Sepoy Mutiny, 1857. (*Right*) Lord and Lady Curzon in Delhi, 1903.

nation beset by rising population, small holdings, and the increasing subdivision of land.

Railroads indirectly aided Indians by helping to reduce the ravages of famine. So did the planting of new crops, such as potatoes and corn. Rapid population growth resulted from the greater availability of food. The Indian subcontinent in the twentieth century would become one of the most populous places on earth.

In Indonesia, the Dutch had maintained a foothold in the jungles since the early seventeenth century, when they fortified their trading posts against marauding sea pirates. Local rulers signed treaties recognizing the Dutch as overlords. The Dutch held the largest islands, Sumatra, Java, and Borneo, dividing New Guinea with Britain. Aggressive Dutch merchants tapped rubber and other natural resources of the region.

France made its first move to colonize Southeast Asia in the late 1850s. French and Spanish forces had bombarded the towns of Da Nang and Saigon (in present-day Vietnam) in joint retaliation for the execution of a Spanish missionary. When the Vietnamese counterattacked, a French admiral annexed three provinces. France attempted unsuccessfully to form a protectorate over northern Annam (the central part of Vietnam).

French traders arrived in Indochina in ever-increasing numbers. In the early 1880s, the Emperor of Annam sought Chinese assistance against the French, invoking China's ancient claims to the region. An anti-foreign movement known as the "Black Flags," which included Vietnamese and Chinese brigands, harassed foreigners, aided by Chinese soldiers. In 1883, a French expedition captured the city of Hanoi in Tonkin in northern Vietnam. French troops sent from Cochin (the southern part of Vietnam) forced the Vietnamese to accept a protectorate that included all of Annam. In 1887, France created the Union of Indochina, which included Tonkin, Annam, Cochin, and Cambodia, and, in 1893, it unilaterally added Laos to French Indochina.

The colonial race extended to the islands of the South Seas. France claimed Tahiti and New Caledonia. Britain held the Fiji Islands, some of which served as refueling ports, but little else. Germany hoisted its flag over the Marshall Islands and Samoa. Smaller islands were sometimes bartered and traded as trinkets by the European powers in the various agreements signed to settle major disputes over the larger colonies.

Japan and China: Contrasting Experiences

In contrast to other Asian countries, Japan maintained real independence and gradually emerged as a power in Asia. Japan built up its army and navy after being opened to Western contact in the 1850s. The 1868 Meiji Restoration, ending a period of chaos, facilitated a remarkable "Westernization" of economic life in Japan. The new centralized state structure encouraged the development of commerce and industry. Military conscription and the implementation of Western technology, assisted by Western technical experts, made it possible for Japan to emerge as a world power at the dawn of the twentieth century. Japan, too, then began to seek colonies in Asia.

In China, the Ching (Qing) dynasty continued to be beset by internal division, as well as by the demands of the imperialist powers, and the government only slowly began to adopt Western technology. In the late 1860s, a few Chinese reformers had begun to favor building railways as a way of modernizing the Chinese state. Yet conservative opposition to modernization continued within the imperial court. Some Chinese scholars believed that railways damaged "the dragon's vein" across the landscape, threatening the earth's harmony. Imperial officials feared that in case of war China's enemies would quickly seize the rail lines.

With colonial rivalries reaching a fever pitch in the late 1890s, the European powers sought to impose further trade and territorial concessions on China. Military weakness made China an easy target for expansion of European influence. The Sino-Japanese War of 1894–1895 led to an independent Korea and China's loss of the island of Formosa (Taiwan) to Japan. Needing loans to pay off a war indemnity to Japan, China was forced the next year to make further trading concessions and disadvantageous railroad leases to Germany and Russia.

Following the murder of two German missionaries in 1897, the German government forced China in 1898 to grant a ninety-nine-year lease on the north Chinese port of Tsingtao (Qingdao) on Kwangchow (Jiaozhou) Bay and to grant two concessions to build railways in Shandong Province. German engineers constructed a line from Tsingtao to Tsinan (Jinan). Russia was eager to complete its own line to Vladivostok through Chinese territories, permitting it to open up the Chinese province of Manchuria, rich in soybeans and cotton. Russia seized and fortified Port Arthur (Lüshun) on the pretext of protecting China from Germany and compelled the Chinese government to lease Port Arthur and Dalian (Lüda) for twenty-five years. The Chinese gave France a lease on Canton Bay and recognized France's trading "sphere of influence" over several southern provinces.

The U.S. government now claimed to seek what it referred to as "an open door" in China, in accordance with the principle of free trade. The powers agreed not to interfere with any treaty port or with the interests of any other power. China agreed to lease Britain some of the Shandong peninsula and several ports, and to guarantee a British trade monopoly on the Yangtze River, the entry to much of central China. These forced concessions further weakened the ruling Ching dynasty.

In northern China, many Chinese resented the foreigners, whom some blamed for floods in 1898 and a drought two years later, events that also were taken to mean that the "mandate of Heaven" of the ruling dynasty was at an end. The "Righteous and Harmonious Fists" was a secret antiforeign society better known as the Boxers after the training practices of

Armed Boxers in Peking, 1900.

its members. Many of the Boxers believed they were immune to foreign bullets. The targets of their wrath were missionaries who sought to convert the Chinese, railroads that took work away from Chinese transporters, foreign merchants who flooded the Chinese market with cheap textiles, bringing unemployment to the local population, and foreign soldiers, who often mistreated the Chinese.

In 1900, the Boxers attacked Europeans, Americans, and Chinese Christians in Shandong Province, cutting the railway line between Peking (Beijing) and Tientsin (Tianjin). These attacks spread quickly to the imperial capital and other parts of northern China. After the Boxers killed several hundred "foreign devils," British, Russian, German, French, Japanese, and American troops put down the rebellion. Their governments assessed the Chinese government a crushing indemnity of 67.5 million pounds.

The scramble for concessions went on. Russia's competition with Japan for Manchuria in northeastern China led to its shocking defeat in the Russo-Japanese War of 1904–1905. Following its victory, Japan took over and expanded the Manchurian railways. This humiliation and subsequent disadvantageous railway concessions granted to the European powers and Japan intensified Chinese nationalist sentiment, and contributed to the overthrow of the Ching dynasty in 1911.

The United States in Asia

The American imperial venture in the Philippine Islands, an archipelago in the Pacific Ocean, was not all smooth sailing. During the Spanish-American War of 1898, fought largely over the Caribbean island of Cuba, the American admiral George Dewey (1837–1917) sailed into Manila Bay and defeated the Spanish fleet, capturing Manila. The United States had been helped by a Filipino nationalist, Emilio Aguinaldo (1869–1964). But once the peace treaty ending the Spanish-American War was signed, President William McKinley announced that it would be "cowardly and discreditable" to leave the Philippines. In 1899, the Filipinos began to fight the Americans to obtain their independence, but U.S. troops defeated Aguinaldo's guerrilla forces after three years of fighting. American soldiers herded Filipinos into prison camps, torturing and executing some of those they captured. Aguinaldo himself was taken prisoner in 1901 and the insurrection, in which perhaps as many as 200,000 Filipinos died, ended the following year. The Philippines became a territory of the United States.

At the same time, the U.S. government did not want to be left out of the scramble for Chinese concessions. In 1899, Secretary of State John Hay announced his country's "Open Door Policy" with regard to China, and tried to convince the other powers to leave China open to all trade. Only the British government publicly expressed its agreement with this principle, but the scramble for advantage in China and elsewhere went on.

Map 21.4 demonstrates the remarkable impact of the scramble for colonies in Asia. Only Japan succeeded in really keeping its independence, with the government of China virtually helpless in the face of the imperial powers and Siam (Thailand) serving as a buffer state between British and French spheres.

DOMINATION OF INDIGENOUS PEOPLES

The eagerness with which many Europeans embarked on or applauded imperial ventures can be partially explained by their assumptions that non-Western peoples were culturally inferior to them. These were not new views, nor were they the only ones held. However, during the sixteenth and seventeenth centuries, non-Western peoples—particularly Islamic peoples—had been viewed as enemies by virtue of their religion (as well as because of the threat seemingly posed by the Ottoman Empire). In the nineteenth century, many Westerners viewed Chinese and Africans with disdain.

Nineteenth- and twentieth-century Western academic and literary attempts to understand the special character of dominated or conquered peoples reflected the intellectual and cultural processes of imperialism. The colonial powers, believing themselves racially and culturally superior

The British image of themselves in Africa, from *The Kipling Reader*, 1908: "A Young man . . . walking slowly at the head of his flocks, while at his knee ran small naked cupids."

to the people they had conquered, assumed the right to exploit conquered territories and to decide what was "best" for the colonized. This made it easier to view their lands as offering opportunities for financial gain, as well as a testing ground or laboratory for European science and technology. It also made it easier for Europeans to justify conquest, domination, and exploitation.

"Orientalism," as this viewpoint was called, began with the assumption that not only were Asian, African, and other colonized peoples different, but they were inferior as well. This was reflected by the Egyptian exhibit at an international exposition in Paris in 1900. An Egyptian visitor was outraged that it seemed "intended to resemble the old aspect of Cairo," the image that the hosts wanted to present, in such a way that "even the paint on the building was made dirty."

The competition for colonies also coincided with the emergence of pseudo-scientific studies that purported to prove the superiority of Western peoples (through, for example, measures of cranium size). Material progress represented by steamboats, railroads, and machine guns was assumed to follow logically from what was considered moral superiority. For one, a French prime minister insisted that "the superior races have rights over the inferior races."

Social Darwinism

In the eighteenth century, some of the philosophes of the Enlightenment had come to view cultural differences of non-Western peoples with detachment and interest, believing that they could learn from people who seemed in some ways different from themselves. In writing about the "propensity to war, slaughter, and destruction, which has always depopulated the face of the earth," Voltaire had noted that "this rage has taken much less possession of the minds of the people of India and China than of ours." Not all of the philosophes, to be sure, had been so enlightened in this respect: David Hume wrote in 1742, "I am apt to suspect the negroes and in general all the other species of men . . . to be naturally inferior to the whites." Likewise, social Darwinists in the nineteenth century did not believe that they could learn anything from non-Western peoples. Social Darwinists argued the natural superiority of some races to justify the conquest of the "backward" peoples of Africa and Asia. They misapplied theories of biological evolution to the history of states, utilizing the principle of "natural selection" developed by Charles Darwin, in which the stronger prevail over the weak. These theories were popularized by another British scientist, Herbert Spencer (1820–1903), who took Darwin one step further by first uttering the chilling phrase "survival of the fittest." Nations, according to this view, must struggle, like species, in order to survive. Success in the international battle for colonies would measure and develop national mettle.

Cultural stereotypes of the peoples of the "mysterious" East or the "dark continent" of Africa held sway. These ranged from "childlike" (and therefore in need of being led) to "barbaric," "depraved," "sneaky," and/or "dangerous" (and therefore in need of constant surveillance). Lord George Curzon called the Indian princes "a set of unruly and ignorant and rather undisciplined school-boys." British doctors contributed to a prevailing juxtaposition of the "African jungle," seen as a "hotbed of disease" (including stigmatized diseases like leprosy) by virtue of a lack of civilization, with the healthier "civilized" colonizers.

Even well-meaning critics of colonial brutality and other reformers assumed the inferiority of those they were trying to help. Josephine Butler, a feminist reformer, denounced the prostitution of Indian women, but believed that Indian women stood lower on a scale of human development than did her British "sisters." Yet, at the beginning of the twentieth century, some feminist activists did begin to learn about and respect Indian culture and work closely with Indian women.

Imperial officials adopted racist ideology to justify colonialism and the brutalization of indigenous peoples. Colonial businessmen, as well as administrators, paid little attention to the damaging effects of colonialism on the indigenous peoples, while simultaneously justifying their presence by claiming to "civilize" the people they dominated.

The experience of the Herero people in what had become German Southwest Africa provides perhaps the most egregious example of this. A German official stated the goal of the colonial administration: "Our task is to strip the Herero of his heritage and national characteristics and gradually to submerge him, along with the other natives, into a single colored working class." Germany put down resistance to its domination with particular barbarity. In 1903, the Herero people, losing their land to German cattle raisers and angered by the unwillingness of colonial courts to punish cases of murder and manslaughter against them, rose up in rebellion. The Germans killed about 55,000 men, women, and children, two-thirds of the Herero people, chasing survivors into the desert and sealing water-holes. The German official report stated: "Like a wounded beast the enemy was tracked down from one water-hole to the next until finally he became the victim of his own environment. . . . [This] was to complete what the German army had begun: extermination of the Herero nation."

Social Darwinism had other implications for the home countries. At the turn of the century, the U.S. historian Frederick Jackson Turner held that the westward expansion of the American frontier helped reduce discontent by providing land and opportunity to the surplus population of the East. A French military administrator, Marshal Lyautey, once referred to Algeria and Morocco as the "French Far West." Some prominent Europeans began to believe that the European powers could "export" their more economically marginal or politically troublesome population to the colonies. By "social imperialism," colonies would help countries easily dispose of their "least fit," such as unemployed or underemployed workers. Social tensions and conflict would be reduced, the ambitions of the working class for political power thus defused. Cecil Rhodes, as usual, put it most baldly: "If you want to avoid civil war, you must become imperialists." The British colonial armies alone absorbed thousands of "surplus" Scots and Irish, the latter making up about 40 percent of the non-Indian troops in India. By this view, colonies, then, could serve as a social safety valve.

Technological Domination and Indigenous Subversion

Europeans employed technological advances in travel and weaponry in their subjugation of indigenous peoples. Railways aided imperial armies in their conquest and defense of colonial frontiers, although horses, mules, and camels still hauled men and supplies across African deserts and bush country. The steamship, like the train, lessened the time of travel to distant places. In 1825, a steamship first supplemented sailpower. By the end of the century, thanks to the completion of the Suez Canal in 1869, linking the Mediterranean and Red Seas, British bureaucrats, soldiers, merchants, and tourists could reach India in about twenty days. The heliograph, which sent messages by means of a movable mirror that reflected sunlight, and then the telegraph speeded up communications and led to better coordination of troop movements.

Advanced military technology invariably overcame open rebellion by indigenous peoples. Observation balloons and later power searchlights aided European armies. Along the South African frontier, Zulu warriors resisted the British advance in the late 1870s, earning several victories with surprise attacks. But by the 1890s, they were no match for the white outsiders with their guns and cannon. The gunboat was the prototypical instrument of European power and enforcement, as it had proven to be in China during the Opium War in the early 1840s. The Gatling, or machine gun, and the single-barreled Maxim gun, which could fire rapidly without being reloaded, proved devastating. A contemporary quip described relations between colonists and the colonized: "Whatever happens we have got the Maxim gun, and they have not." A single gunner or two could fend off a large-scale attack, and British casualties were reduced to almost none. To soldiers, colonial battles now seemed "more like hunting than fighting."

The colonial powers tested new, lighter artillery that could be moved quickly and new, more powerful shells. The British developed the "dum-dum" bullet, which exploded upon impact, with the shooting of attacking "natives" in mind. (It took its name from the arsenal in Calcutta where it was developed.) For the most part, there was little to stop the European onslaught other than malaria and yellow fever carried by mosquitoes, and sleeping sickness, carried by the tsetse fly.

Yet indigenous peoples could express resistance to powerful outsiders in other ways besides risking annihilation in open rebellion. The "weapons of the weak" ranged from riots and individual subversion to foot-dragging and gentle but determined defiance. The latter included pretending not to understand, or sometimes what Chinese called "that secret smile" that suggested not compliance but rather defiance in the guise of deference. Such play-acting in daily life offered only glimpses of the ridicule of Europeans that could be expressed openly in private or hinted at in theatrical productions, songs, dances, or other public expressions of local folklore. Symbols, gestures, double meanings, and images were easily understood by the subordinate population, but sufficiently disguised from Europeans or ambiguous enough to fall short of being considered "seditious." These were small victories of political dissent, but victories nonetheless.

Imperial Economies

Once they had a foothold, the European powers established "plunder economies" in three ways: they expropriated the land of the indigenous people; they used the soil and subsoil for their own profit; and they exploited the population for labor. In British Ceylon (captured from the Dutch during the Napoleonic Wars), Dutch Java, French Algeria, and German East Africa, indigenous people without deeds or titles to their land lost it to the colonial power. They also lost traditional rights to hunt, graze animals, and gather firewood on land they did not own, a process that had also characterized the early stages of capitalist agriculture in Western Europe.

The European powers imposed commercial controls over natural resources, demands that again reflected the evolution toward the arbitrary, centralized control of the "new imperialism" of the century's last two decades and beyond. Imperial powers routinely blocked long-standing trade routes that led to other colonies, preventing commercial exchanges from which their own merchants did not profit. European merchants, protected by high tariffs at home against foreign imports, insisted on maintaining a monopoly on the sale of their manufactured goods in the colonies. Colonialists forced or, in the best circumstances, encouraged local populations to produce for the European market, discouraging or even forbidding the extraction of raw materials or production that would compete with that of the mother country. In Indonesia, for example, the Dutch employed the "culture" or "cultivation" system until 1870, whereby they imposed production quotas on the indigenous population, employed forced labor, and ordered people in West Java to grow coffee when its price rose and to cut down spice-bearing trees and plants when the price of spices fell.

In North Africa, the French government promoted the economic interests of French settlers, giving them the finest Algerian land. The government also ordered land owned collectively by Arabs to be sold as individual plots that only the French could afford to purchase. In Morocco and Tunisia, the French claimed "unexploited" land, such as that belonging to nomad peoples, with French tribunals adjudicating contested cases. Above all, French colonial administrators sought to maintain order and collect taxes. One visitor found that "the head tax is above all a very effective agent of civilization," so that in one district "when a village could not or would not pay its taxes in full, the custom was to seize a child and place him in a village named 'Liberty' until the tax was paid." In some regions, taxes were collected in kind, or through forced labor.

Portuguese colonists imposed conditions of virtual slavery in their African colonies in the nineteenth century. They kidnapped people from their colony of Angola, shipped them to the coastal island of São Tomé, and forced them to work on the cocoa plantations for a "contract" period

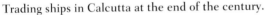

Trading ships in Calcutta at the end of the century.

of five years, which few workers survived. In Angola, villagers who could not pay their taxes were required to work for the government for 100 days a year. The use of forced labor on mine and construction sites by colonial merchants and administrators alike was common; in the German Cameroons, it was estimated that 80,000 Africans hauled goods for Germans on a single road in one year. Forced labor, which might be considered slavery in disguise, was widely practiced throughout most of the French colonies until 1946.

Colonial Administrations

European notions of the organization of states clashed with the way indigenous people lived. Almost all Africans lacked the European obsession with fixing exact boundaries, one that intensified in the age of nation-states and aggressive nationalism. For most Africans living in tribal societies, European notions of "boundaries" and "borders" seemed strange. Boundaries established by colonial powers left many formerly unified societies arbitrarily separated and sometimes interfered with the movements of migratory peoples.

How the European powers maintained control over colonies varied. Historians have distinguished between "formal" and "informal" imperialism, although the distinction is mainly one of degree, not kind. Britain, above all, took the path of informal imperialism by maintaining control through economic and military domination, without taking over political functions. But a "resident," or representative of Britain, retained ultimate authority, which he exercised in international crises. In formal imperialism, the European power assumed "protectorate" status over a territory, administering the colony directly. The colonial powers viewed colonial administration as a problem to be solved and, for the most part, remained oblivious to the moral consequences of their domination. Types of colonial administration included the French policy of leaving pre-existing monarchies intact in Indochina, the initiation of complete assimilation in old French colonies like the island of Réunion in the Indian Ocean, and the British strategy of indirect rule in India.

The nature of a colonial "protectorate" changed during the scramble for Africa. Originally the establishment of a protectorate meant that a colonial power defended its interests by controlling the foreign relations of a territory, leaving it to each ruler or chieftain to control his people. Thus, for example, British colonial administration remained decentralized, like the home government itself. But gradually the colonial powers extended their authority over the local population through indigenous officials. In 1886, Britain assumed full sovereignty over most of its colonies. Not long after a British politician predicted "nothing but endless expense, trouble and disaster" if his country took over Uganda, Britain declared Uganda a protectorate in 1894, when the East African Company became unable to

The King and Queen Mother of the Ashanti humble themselves before members of the British Army in accordance with tribal custom.

administer the territory. Local rulers found earlier agreements broken, and they were increasingly treated as little more than intermediaries between the imperialists and their own people. Local systems of justice were left intact wherever possible—this, too, cost less money—but whites were subject only to the courts of the colonial power.

The British government wanted colonies to pay for themselves, with chartered commercial companies—which had launched British rule in Nigeria, Uganda, and what became Rhodesia—bearing the bulk of expenses in exchange for the right to extract profit. During the height of the colonial mania in the 1890s, the British still wanted colonialism to come cheap. Even after formally establishing sovereignty over some colonies, the British colonial administration continued to rule indirectly, trying to make the colonies pay for themselves by directing railway development and then private capital toward regions where raw materials could be extracted or markets found.

The fate of the Ashanti kingdom, which dated to the early eighteenth century, in West Africa, illustrates how informal control was transformed into more direct authority. In the early 1860s, British forces skirmished with the Ashanti people on the northern frontier of the Gold Coast, over which Britain had established a protectorate. After defeating the Ashanti in 1873–1874, Britain made the Gold Coast a crown colony, imposing more direct control. In 1891, the British proposed that the Ashanti kingdom itself become their protectorate. The king replied "my kingdom of

Ashanti will never commit itself to any such policy; Ashanti must remain independent as of old, at the same time to be friendly with all white men." Five years later, British troops occupied the Ashanti capital and deported the king when he could not come up with a huge sum in gold to buy continued independence. In a bloody sequel in 1900–1901, British troops crushed an uprising when the Ashanti refused to surrender the golden stool they treasured as the symbol of their people. In 1901, the Ashanti kingdom became a British colony.

African imperial ventures often began with the directors and principal shareholders of trading companies forging out territories from the underbrush and jungle. But gradually the states they represented became involved and took over the role of protectors and administrators. For example, the Royal Niger Company, with a charter from Parliament conveying administrative powers in 1886, began to develop what became Nigeria. To counter French moves in East Africa, the British government had authorized the Royal Niger Company to launch an expedition through the rain forests to reach the Sudan. When German merchants, newcomers to Africa, began to establish trading posts to the east in the future Cameroons, the British government declared a protectorate over the Niger Delta.

The French government and the Royal Niger Company settled their respective claims through conventions. But when the Royal Niger Company went bankrupt in 1899, the British government took over administration of the territories. This scenario was common to the colonial experiences of France, the Netherlands, and Germany: merchant companies that had been granted state monopolies established trading interests in a new colony and then ran into financial difficulties, if not bankruptcy, necessitating the intervention of the colonial power itself.

After the government had taken over for the commercial companies, great differences remained from colony to colony as to their status and administration. These ranged from Canada, independent in all but foreign policy, to remote Ascension Island, halfway between Brazil and the west coast of Africa, run "by a captain as if it were a ship" until British interests were directly threatened, at which time formal annexation took place.

Many of Queen Victoria's subjects served in the colonial administration including the army. Given the size of the empire, however, the number was surprisingly small. Near the end of the century, about 6,000 British civil servants governed India's 300 million inhabitants. The British colonial administration provided a career outlet for the sons of aristocrats, who became high-ranking administrators or officers in the navy and army. Eleven of the fourteen viceroys who served in India from 1858 to 1918 were peers by birth.

British officials recruited subordinates selectively from the colonial population, training, for example, upper-caste Indians to work in the administration of the subcontinent. In Nigeria, selected tribal chiefs assumed administrative functions. In the first decade of the twentieth century, at least partially in response to the first stirrings of Egyptian nationalism, the British government expanded the participation of Egyptians in running their country. In Malaya, the British "resident" was responsible for putting down disturbances that might threaten British control, while the local rulers were placed in paid administrative positions but had authority only in dealing with religious matters.

The British mastered the policy of "divide and rule," playing off ethnic rivalries wherever helpful, favoring and choosing officials from the dominant groups to ensure cooperation. In India, the British effectively manipulated age-old tensions between Hindus, Muslims, and Sikhs to keep the Indian component of its army under control, ruthlessly repressing dissent.

In the colonies, the British lived in isolation from the indigenous population. The upper class tried to replicate the world of the common rooms of Cambridge and Oxford Universities (more than a quarter of all graduates of Oxford's Balliol College at the turn of the century served in the empire) and of gentlemen's clubs in London, served by Indian, African, or Asian waiters. British colonial women served only English recipes to their guests. Architects attempted (with considerable success) to duplicate Victorian architectural styles in far-off lands, so that the British felt closer to home. In India, British "hill stations," which had begun early in the nineteenth century as isolated sanitaria where British could recuperate from tropical heat and illness, also provided commanding heights useful for surveillance. They became part of the imperial system, both as centers of power (the commander in chief of the army in northern India lived in one) and closed British communities, "islands of white" that replicated the architecture and lifestyle of the English village. Indeed, in Kenya and Rhodesia, settler communities were organized around the sense of being "white" in unsettling and even dangerous surroundings, and newcomers were discouraged from crossing racial lines because of the fear that such contact could undermine settler cohesion.

Although often drawing on local traditions, colonial urban architecture reflected the attempt to represent Western domination. In what became Vietnam in Indochina, the opera house built in Hanoi was a copy of that in Paris. The French architects who planned the high Gothic vaulting of the cathedral in Saigon ignored the considerable difference in climate between France and Southeast Asia, providing insufficient ventilation. Outsized public buildings and long boulevards extended French authority in the form of architectural modernism into the daily life of French settlers and the local colonial population. In Madagascar, the medical school reflected beaux arts design more appropriate to Lyon than a tropical island.

Many indigenous men who rose to positions of relative responsibility under the British managed to look and sound as much as possible like British gentlemen. But many Victorians disdained the Westernized Indian; they ridiculed the "babu," not because he seemed to be rejecting his own culture, but because they thought he could never be good enough to be British. At the same time, the British government often left intact the hierarchy of indigenous ruling elites, because this seemed more natural and made administrating the colonies easier.

French colonial rule differed from that of the British in ways that revealed contrasts between the British and French states. French colonial administration reflected the state centralization that had characterized France's development over the past century and more. Military control, more than commercial relations, formed the basis of the French colonial empire. The French colonial administration employed relatively more French officials and relied less on indigenous peoples than did its British rival.

The ministries of the navy and of commerce administered French colonies until the establishment of the colonial ministry in 1894. The French colonial ministry then took a much greater role in economic decision making, such as the planning of railroads, than its counterpart in the British Empire. The French colonial civilian administration was staffed by bureaucrats, some trained at the Colonial School created in the 1880s. Africans and Vietnamese, among others, worked for the French governors-general as virtual civil servants. Like their British rivals, French colonial administrators also exploited pre-existing ethnic and cultural rivalries, using dominant groups to control their enemies. Thus, the French government used Vietnamese officials in key posts in Cambodia and Laos, and in Madagascar highland officials dominated the administration of their coastal rivals.

The French government directly ruled Algeria; Algerians could become French citizens, but with only limited rights. The sultan of Morocco and the bey of Tunisia still ruled their subjects, at least in name, although government and the exercise of justice remained in the hands of the French colonial administration. In Southeast Asia, the French government created the Union of Indochina between 1887 and 1893, which included Cochin, Tonkin, Annam, Cambodia, and Laos under a single governor-general. The French government also centralized the administration of West Africa in 1895 by forming the federation of French West Africa, and in 1910 it established the federation of French Equatorial Africa, made up of its Central African colonies. Governors-general, based in Dakar and Brazzaville, served as the highest local administrative authority.

ASSESSING THE GOALS OF EUROPEAN IMPERIALISM

Someone once summed up the reasons for which the European powers expanded their horizons as "God, gold, and glory," or as the geographer, missionary, and explorer David Livingstone put it, "Christianity, Commerce, and Civilization."

In addition, some British imperialists spoke of "the white man's burden," a phrase unfortunately immortalized by Rudyard Kipling's poem

(1899) of the same name: "Take up the White Man's burden— / And reap his old reward: / The blame of those ye better, / The hate of those ye guard." Which, if any, can be singled out as the dominant impulse behind the "new imperialism"?

The "Civilizing Mission"

Most colonists insisted that God was on their side. Lord George Curzon once gushed that the British Empire was "under Providence, the greatest instrument for good that the world has seen." A South African offered a more realistic perspective when he commented, "When you came here we owned the land and you had the Bible; now we have the Bible and you own the land." The "civilizing" impulse still animated some European missionaries during the age of the "new imperialism." Thousands of Catholic and Protestant missionaries went to Africa, India, and Asia in the name of God to win converts, a mission both religious and cultural. In 1900, about 18,000 Protestant missionaries lived in colonial settlements around the world. Some British officials considered Anglican and Methodist missionaries to be nuisances. Most Dutch, Belgian, and Italian clergy made little pretense of bringing indigenous peoples "civilization," tending primarily to the spiritual needs of their troops and settlers. Yet, in some places, the clergy helped force Europeans to end or at least temper abuses carried out against local populations. Missionary societies may have been the "conscience" of European colonization, and a small conscience was better than none at all.

Queen Victoria giving a Bible to a man wearing Central African garb.

One aspect of the "civilizing mission" continued to be the attempt of some reformers to limit or to bring to an end abuses of indigenous peoples. For British reformers, the primary goal of the "civilizing mission" in the early part of the century had been to abolish slavery in the British Empire, which was achieved in 1833. In the 1880s, pressure from the British Liberal Party helped end the transport of Chinese laborers to work as indentured workers in South African mines. The British government was embarrassed by the treatment of Indian workers in what is now Natal, a province of South Africa, which was brought to light by, among others, the young and future Indian leader Mohandas (Mahatma) Gandhi (1869–1948). British officials also protested the brutal labor practices of Portuguese and Belgian entrepreneurs. Britain declined to press a campaign to reduce or eliminate the sale of arms and liquor to Africans, because both commodities were extremely lucrative to British merchants; similarly, it had refused to stop the sale of Indian opium by British traders in China. French religious leaders launched a campaign against the remaining Arab slave trade in Africa, receiving endorsement from Germany and Britain.

Lord Frederick Lugard (1858–1945), a British colonial official, came up with the term "Dual Mandate" to describe what he considered the "moral" and "material" imperatives of colonial powers. The European powers, he believed, had an obligation to "civilize" native populations and also to "open the door" to the material improvements brought by Western technology. They were establishing "trusteeships." In exchange, the Europeans would extract raw materials and other products. While imperialism would become associated with conservative nationalism in Western Europe, a few socialists in Britain and France believed that the establishment of empire might improve conditions of life for colonial peoples. In general, however, European socialists did not view the question of imperialism as one of their central concerns.

Earlier in the century, the French had seen their "civilizing" mission as the assimilation of colonial peoples into French culture: they would, it was commonly thought, become French. By the end of the century, however, the goal of assimilation had given way to a theory of "association," similar to Lugard's British Dual Mandate. This theory of association held that although colonial peoples were not capable of absorbing French culture, French colonialists would help them develop their economic resources, to the benefit of both. Only in urban settlements in Senegal in West Africa did newborn children automatically become French citizens; in 1914, Senegalese voters elected the first black representative to the French Chamber of Deputies.

The Economic Rationale

When missionaries arrived on the shores of Africa or Asia, they usually found that merchants and adventurers were already there looking for gold, ivory, and raw materials. Indeed, Cecil Rhodes once stated that in the business of running colonies "philanthropy is good, but philanthropy at five percent is better." The discovery of new markets seemed absolutely necessary in the 1880s, particularly to British manufacturers, as one continental country after another adopted high protectionist tariffs. "If you were not such persistent protectionists, you would not find us so keen to annex territories," the British prime minister told France's ambassador to London in 1897. In the rather far-fetched opinion of the brother of Cecil Rhodes, "The Waganda [of Uganda] are clamoring for shoes, stockings and opera glasses and are daily developing fresh wants," which would enrich British manufacturers and merchants peddling the products of the Second Industrial Revolution.

Writing in 1902 and influenced by the Boer War in South Africa, the radical British economist J. A. Hobson (1858–1940) called imperialism "the most powerful factor in the current politics of the Western world." He agreed that the great powers sought colonies because their economies required outlets for domestically produced manufactured goods and for capital investment. In Hobson's view, businessmen, particularly the finance sector based in London, virtually determined British imperial policy; missionaries and soldiers helped them accomplish their goals. Hobson believed that the quest for colonies simply deferred the resolution of the central economic problem at home: oversavings of unearned income and resulting underconsumption of industrial goods. He believed that if governments took action to raise wages and impose progressive taxation on wealth, a more equitable redistribution of wealth would allow ordinary people to purchase more goods. The reduction in domestic underconsumption would make imperialism unnecessary and allow countries like China to develop on their own. Hobson's views on imperialism have found an echo in our era, in some ways anticipating contemporary critiques of the economic and social consequences of globalization.

Hobson was not a Marxist, but his views in some ways echoed those of Karl Marx. In *Capital*, Marx, who never used the word imperialism, postulated that the bourgeoisie required "a constantly expanding market for its products." Subsequent Marxists therefore agreed with Hobson's linking of industrial capitalism and imperialism. The Russian revolutionary leader Vladimir Ilyich Ulyanov, better known as Lenin, took Hobson's analysis a step further. He argued that the incessant expansion of capital inevitably brought with it colonial rivalries and war; in this final stage of capitalist development, "international trusts" would divide up the globe.

If Hobson, Rhodes, and Lenin had ever sat at the same dinner table, they would have disagreed about a good many things. But they would have agreed that there was a close connection between the great age of European imperialism and the quest for economic gain. The drive for colonies took on urgency in a period of mounting economic tariffs: there might not be, many thought, enough raw materials and markets to go around.

Merchant traders, like their seventeenth- and eighteenth-century predecessors, counted on finding rich mineral deposits and untapped markets in Africa and Asia. When wildly exaggerated reports of the natural wealth of Africa swept Europe, the competition for colonies increased. In talking to Manchester textile magnates, the journalist and explorer Henry Stanley described the Congo not in terms of square kilometers but as "square yards of cotton stuff to be exported." Gold and diamond discoveries in South Africa in the 1860s and again in the 1880s unleashed a stampede of prospectors and inspired colonists' dreams. Coastal traders generated further colonial expansion in West Africa. Trade in palm oil, used in large quantities for making soap and glycerin, replaced the slave trade.

Ivory from Africa became a valuable item on the European markets.

Was the hope of economic gain the most significant factor in the frenetic European rush for colonies during the last decades of the nineteenth century? Did the colonial powers actually realize great wealth through their exploration and conquest?

To be sure, colonies provided some valued products for European markets. Ivory and rubber from the Belgian Congo, palm oil from Nigeria, Dahomey, and the Ivory Coast, peanuts from French Senegal, diamonds and gold from South Africa, coffee from British Ceylon, and sugar from Malaya proved to be lucrative commodities. The rubber trade of French Indochina, Dutch Indonesia, the Congo, and British Malaya expanded rapidly with the popularity of the bicycle and particularly following the invention of the automobile. The British colonies of Nigeria and the Gold Coast produced 4 percent of the world's cocoa in 1905, 24 percent ten years later. The consumption of tea, most of it from China and Ceylon, increased by almost four times between 1840 and 1900.

Colonies provided an inviting market for manufactured goods from the mother country. In the 1890s, about a third of all British exports and about a quarter of all investment went to its colonies, above all India, which imported cotton cloth and other textiles, iron, hardware, and shoes from Britain. Yet British capital investment abroad was still principally directed toward its lost colony, the United States, as well as toward other independent states such as Ottoman Turkey. British subjects also invested in the settlement colonies, Australia, New Zealand, and Canada, as well as India. The African colonies attracted very little British investment. There was more British trade with Belgium in the 1890s than with all of Africa.

Because colonial investments were risky, only a very small percentage of French and German investment was directed into their respective colonies, along with a trickle into the colonies of rivals. French investment abroad was overwhelmingly directed toward other parts of Europe, particularly Russia. Only about 5 percent of French investment reached its colonies in 1900; in 1914, France bought more goods from its colonies than it sold them in return. Less than 1 percent of German trade was with its colonies. By 1907, German investment in all German colonies fell slightly below the value of investments in a single large bank at home.

Imperial governments, which had to foot the bill for troops, supplies, guns, and administrative and other expenses, therefore became increasingly suspicious of the confident assurances of adventurers that incredible riches lay just a little farther up a barely explored African river or beyond the next oasis. In 1899, a French politician whose ardor for imperialism had waned defined the two stages of colonization as "the joy of conquest," followed inevitably, as after a fine restaurant meal, by "the arrival of the bill." The French colonial lobby, including provincial chambers of commerce in manufacturing cities and ports and geographic societies, had pictured western Sudan as teeming with lucrative commercial opportunities. It turned out that this vast region of desert offered merchants little more than rubber, a little gold, some peanuts, and an occasional elephant tusk. Yet the French government spent vast sums to administer and police an increasingly unwieldy empire.

In the meantime, the exploitation of natural resources by the imperialists contributed to the economic and political underdevelopment of these regions once they became independent nations in the twentieth century.

The economic interpretation of the imperial race for colonies cannot be discounted, however. Key economic sectors did benefit substantially from raw materials and markets provided by the new colonies, as did individual businessmen. Nonetheless, an economic explanation for colonialism was only one factor—often a minor one—and it is difficult to detach from other motives.

Imperialism and Nationalism

The new imperialism was, above all, an extension of the search for security and power on the European continent in a period characterized by aggressive nationalism and bitter international rivalries. Even in the case of Great Britain, the imperialist power with the greatest economic investment in colonies, the international rivalry of the European powers was the strongest impulse for imperialism. Britain expanded its domination into new regions, not only in search of new markets, but simply to keep the French, Germans, or Russians from establishing bases and colonies that might threaten British interests. Britain's definition of its interests in Egypt, the pursuit of which helped launch the landgrab in Africa, had far more to do with fear of competition from its rivals than with economic motives.

Burma, absorbed by Britain after wars in 1824 and 1852 to protect India's eastern frontier against possible colonial rivals, is a case in point. When France declared its economic interest in Burma in the late 1870s, the British expanded their control over Upper Burma as well, fighting another war with Burma in 1885. After this third war, they packed off the reigning king to India, shipped his throne to a museum in Calcutta, turned his palace into a British club, and annexed Burma to the administration of India. Likewise, the establishment of a British protectorate over Afghanistan in 1880 cannot be explained by economic motives, only by a desire to place a buffer state between India and expanding Russian interests in the region. Britain's goal in what contemporary diplomats called "the great game" between Britain and Russia in the Near East and Asia was to prevent Russian troops from occupying the high range of mountains in and adjacent to Afghanistan. Lord Curzon put the issues at stake for Britain succinctly: "Turkistan, Afghanistan, Transcaspia, Persia—to many these names breathe only a sense of utter remoteness. . . . To me, I confess, they are the pieces on a chessboard upon which is being played out a game for the domination of the world."

The nationalism that surged through all the European powers in the 1880s and 1890s fueled the "new imperialism." In 1876, when Britain opposed Russian moves toward the Turkish capital of Constantinople, a popular British song went: "We don't want to fight, / But, by Jingo, if we do, / We've got the men, / We've got the ships, / We've got the money too." The term "jingoism" came into use in English to mean fervent nationalism. Generations of British schoolchildren gawked at maps of the world that displayed colony after colony, however varied the structure and effectiveness of British control, colored red, the map color of Great Britain.

In Britain, the colonial experience became an important part of British national consciousness, pervasive in literature and in material culture. Newspapers, magazines, popular literature, and the publication of soldiers' diaries and letters carried home news from the colonies and made imperialism seem a romantic adventure.

In 1880, the annual Naval and Military Tournament in London began to present reenactments of colonial skirmishes and battles. One play, *Siege of Delhi*, ended with an Irish officer falling in love and dancing a jig, as the curtain falls on Indians about to be shot out of a cannon. In 1911, an Italian writer's enthusiasm for the feats of his army, which established a colony in Libya through conquest (see Chapter 17), included descriptions of the "lustrous" eyes of the Sicilian horses, who seemed, by their neighing, to be attempting to pronounce the word "Italy." "Let the peace-people croak as they please," a general's daughter exclaims in a contemporary novel about Egypt, "it is war that brings out the truly heroic virtues."

From the drawing rooms of country estates to the wretched pubs of Liverpool and Birmingham, the British howled for revenge for the death of General Charles "Chinese" Gordon, killed in the Sudan by the forces of the Mahdi in 1885. Few Europeans wept at the destruction of entire cultures and the death of hundreds of thousands of people at the hands of European armies. "Special artists" and then photographers began to travel with British colonial forces; movie cameras recorded Horatio Kitchener's 1899 campaign against the Boers in South Africa. At a time of political opposition in Great Britain to costly colonial commitments, the romanticization of British expeditionary forces helped win support for spending even more.

Voluntary associations pressured the colonial powers to devote more resources to the building of empire. In Great Britain, Germany, and France, geographic societies, associations that met periodically to listen to talks about exploration in Africa and Asia, sponsored voyages that charted unexplored—at least by Europeans—territories.

In Germany and Britain, naval leagues whipped up enthusiasm for imperialism. The Pan-German League (1891) demanded more expenditures for warships. The champion of colonial lobbying groups, the Primrose League in Britain (founded in 1884), had 1.7 million members by 1906, drawn primarily from business, finance, the military, and government, the groups with the greatest stake in imperialism.

To be sure, strident critics of imperialism could be found. In Britain, anti-imperialists were to be found among Liberal or Labour Party intellectuals, some of the latter, in particular, denouncing the Boer War as orchestrated in the interests of British capitalists with investments in South Africa. Anti-imperialist groups included the "Ethical Union," formed in 1896, whose members believed that imperialism marked a setback on the path of human progress. They rejected the "civilizing mission" arguments for imperialism. Like J. A. Hobson, who frequently addressed their meetings, they had no illusions about the causes or consequences of imperialism, and they disparaged jingoism with passion. They denounced the fact that "imperialists have frightened us . . . into a 'spirited foreign policy,' [with] the bogey of 'Our Trade in Danger,' and the pretense that 'Trade follows the Flag.' " These critics of imperialism wanted moral reason to be applied to international affairs. But with the end of the Boer War, anti-imperialist voices grew fainter in Britain.

In France, anti-imperialists focused on the financial burden of expansion. One member of the Chamber of Deputies complained, "We are being drawn along in an irresistible process, like that of Time, by the mere force of a colonial expansionism which has got out of control." In the United States at the turn of the century, the American Anti-Imperialist

League joined together groups opposing the annexation of the Philippines as a territory. But almost everywhere the strident imperialist roar drowned out dissident voices. It contributed to the aggressive nationalism that fueled the increasingly bitter rivalries between the European great powers and further destabilized the continent.

CONCLUSION

In 1500, the European powers controlled about 7 percent of the globe's land; by 1800, they controlled 35 percent; in 1914, they controlled 84 percent. Between 1871 and 1900, the British Empire, which came to include one-quarter of the world's population, expanded to include 66 million people and 4.5 million square miles, the French Empire 3.5 million square miles, and Germany, Belgium, and Italy about 1 million square miles each. In Spain, with little left from its once mighty empire, the shock ("the Disaster") of losing the Philippines and Cuba to the United States in 1898 led to an intense period of introspection by intellectuals known as the "generation of 1898" who wanted to "regenerate" Spain, looking to other European nations to provide inspiration through art and literature. As for the Spanish government, it took new colonies in Morocco and the western Sahara.

Aggressive nationalism shaped the contours of the new European imperialism from the early 1880s to 1914. A British nationalist put it this way: "Today, power and domination rather than freedom and independence are the ideas that appeal to the imagination of the masses—and the national ideal has given way to the imperial." Imperialism sharpened the rivalries of the great powers, while solidifying international alliances. Competing colonial interests brought France and Britain to the verge of war after the Fashoda Affair of 1898. Subsequent crises, including the emergence of nationalism among the colonized themselves, assumed even more dramatic dimensions. Infused with the same sense of struggle that seemed to engulf Europe, these crises would defy peaceful resolution.

PART SIX

CATACLYSM

The Great War began in August 1914. Germany and Austria-Hungary and their smaller allies fought against Great Britain, France, Russia, and their allies. Although most statesmen, military leaders, and ordinary soldiers and civilians believed that the war would be over by Christmas, if not well before, it raged on for more than four years. A military stalemate, bogged down in grisly trench warfare, particularly in France, took the lives of millions of soldiers. In the war's wake, four empires fell. In 1917, a revolution overthrew the tsar of Russia, and then the Bolsheviks overthrew the provisional government, withdrawing from the world conflict and imposing Communist rule. The German Empire collapsed upon the victory in November 1918 of Britain, France, and their allies (including the United States since 1917). The multinational Austro-Hungarian and Turkish Ottoman Empires, Germany's wartime allies, also collapsed.

The Versailles Peace Treaty, signed by the new German Republic in 1919, carved up the fallen empires, creating successor states in Central Europe—Poland, Czechoslovakia, and Yugoslavia. The treaties signed between the victors and the vanquished left a legacy of nationalist hatred in Europe that poisoned international relations during the subsequent two decades. Out of the economic, social, and political turmoil of the 1920s and 1930s emerged authoritarian movements that swept to power in many European countries, beginning with Mussolini's Italian fascists in 1922. In Germany, Hitler's National Socialist Party grew in strength with the advent of the Great Depression in 1929. The Nazis drew on extreme right-wing nationalism that viewed the Treaty of Versailles as an unfair humiliation to Germany. In the Soviet Union, Joseph Stalin became head of the Communist Party following Lenin's death in 1924; he purged rivals within the party, launched a

campaign of rapid industrialization, forced millions of peasants into collective farms, and ordered the slaughter or imprisonment of those who
resisted. Britain and France retained their parliamentary forms of government, despite economic, social, and political tensions.

In the Europe of extremes, the search for political stability after World
War I proved illusive. After coming to power in 1933, Hitler rearmed Germany and disdainfully violated the Treaty of Versailles by reoccupying the
Rhineland in 1936 and forging a union with Austria. The same year, Hitler
and Mussolini supported a right-wing nationalist insurrection in Spain
against the Spanish Republic. They sent planes, advisers, and war materiel
to aid General Francisco Franco's military forces, which were victorious
three years later. After Hitler's initial aggressive moves against Czechoslovakia were unopposed by Britain and France, the German dictator
brazenly sent German troops to occupy all of Czechoslovakia in 1938.

Just weeks after shocking the world by signing a nonaggression pact
with Stalin's Soviet Union, Hitler began his long-planned invasion of
Poland, which quickly fell. And after a brief "phony war" of inaction in the
West, in the spring of 1940 Hitler invaded France, the Netherlands, and
Belgium. Japan's sudden attack on the U.S. military bases at Pearl Harbor,
Hawaii, on December 7, 1941, brought the United States into World War
II. Over 17 million people were killed in the fighting, and another 20 million civilians perished, including more than 6 million Jews, systematically
exterminated by the Nazis during the Holocaust. The war finally ended in
1945, after the defeat of Germany, Italy, and Japan. Europe and the entire
world entered a new and potentially even more dangerous period, one in
which nuclear arms made the threat of a new war even more horrible.

CHAPTER 22

THE GREAT WAR

"The lamps are going out all over Europe. They will not be lit again in our lifetime." So spoke Sir Edward Grey, the British foreign secretary, in early August 1914, as the Great War began. His last-ditch diplomatic efforts to prevent war having failed, Grey was one of the few to share an apocalyptic vision of a conflict that most people thought would be over by Christmas. Few observers anticipated that this war would be more destructive than any ever fought. International peace conferences, held in The Hague in 1899 and 1907, had considered ways of reducing atrocities in war, but they failed to take into account that future wars might be different from those of the past. Not even Grey could have foreseen the 37.5 million casualties, the downfall of four empires, and shifts in Europe's economic, social, cultural, and political life after the war that made the years before the war seem "the good old days."

The Great War was the first international conflict of great scale since the Napoleonic era. It involved all the great powers, with Italy entering the war in 1915, and the United States in 1917. Before the war ended, it would also draw a host of minor powers into the fray. The catastrophic conflagration was set off by a spark—the assassination of Austro-Hungarian Archduke Francis Ferdinand in Sarajevo, the capital of Bosnia, on June 28, 1914, by a Serb nationalist. In little more than a month, war engulfed the powers of Europe through the decades-old system of entangling alliances that interwove their fates. And while these alliances did not make a general war in Europe inevitable—in fact, the situation in Europe seemed much more precarious in 1905 and 1911 than it did in 1914—most heads of state, diplomats, and military planners expected a major war in their lifetimes. Some were relieved, and others delighted, when it began. Few were surprised.

ENTANGLING ALLIANCES

Among the national rivalries in Europe, none seemed more irreparable than that between Germany and France. However, none was potentially as

Entangling alliances, 1906: Britain, France, and Russia on the left; Austria-Hungary and Germany on the right; and childlike Italy trying to choose between them.

dangerous as that between Russia and Austria-Hungary, which, focusing on the Balkans, was accentuated by the presence within the Habsburg empire of South Slav peoples who looked to Russia as the protector of all Slavs. In the meantime, Russia, with its long-standing goal of increasing its influence in the Balkans, fanned the flames of Pan-Slavism. Germany and Austria-Hungary became firm allies, their alliance directed, above all, against Russia. In 1882, Italy joined the two Central European powers to form the Triple Alliance. By 1905, growing German and British economic and military rivalry helped drive together France and Britain, the oldest rivals in Europe. Now Russia, France, and Britain were allied in the Triple Entente. Entangling alliances left the great powers of Europe divided into two armed camps. Because of these alliances, the outbreak of war between any two rivals threatened to bring all of the powers into the conflict.

Irreconcilable Hatreds

The German Empire, proclaimed at Versailles in the wake of the French defeat in the Franco-Prussian War of 1870–1871, continued to hold Alsace and most of Lorraine after the war indemnity was paid and German occupation troops were withdrawn from the rest of France. The French never reconciled themselves to the loss of two of their wealthiest provinces. Although many Alsatians spoke a German dialect, Alsace had been an integral and strategically important part of France since the seventeenth century. Most people living in the parts of Lorraine absorbed into Germany spoke and considered themselves French. The absorption of Alsace-Lorraine into unified Germany in 1871 alone would have guaranteed animosity between Germany and France.

The growing rivalry between France and Germany over colonial interests added to mutual mistrust. At first, newly unified Germany had no colonies. But Chancellor Otto von Bismarck's successors gradually led Germany into a rivalry with France over colonial interests in the Mediterranean and in North Africa, and with Britain in Africa, Turkey, and the Middle East.

Francis Joseph, the elderly emperor of Austria-Hungary, was a plodding man of integrity who had assumed the throne in 1848 and who had once told Theodore Roosevelt, the president of the United States, "You see in me the last monarch of the old school." Respected by his people, he remained a largely ceremonial figure identified with the survival of the polyglot Habsburg state in an age of nationalism. Francis Joseph bore a series of family tragedies with dignity: the execution in 1867 of his brother Maximilian in Mexico, where he was briefly emperor, his son's suicide in 1889, and his wife's madness. Throughout his reign, which was fifteen years longer than that of Queen Victoria of England, the Habsburg emperor had been determined that the imperial army be strong and that his dynasty maintain international prestige.

Irreconcilable hatreds existed in the Austro-Hungarian Empire, which was made up of a great many different nationalities. The Austrians and the Hungarians, who dominated the other nationalities of their territories, were satisfied, but other peoples were not. Thus, many peoples, such as Czechs and Slovaks in Central Europe, particularly resented Austrian and

(*Left*) An Alsatian woman learning to goose-step in a caricature from the German satirical review *Simplicimus*. (*Right*) The aging Emperor Francis Joseph of the Habsburg monarchy.

Hungarian domination. And Romanians, a Latin people, were unhappy with Hungary's vigorous campaign to "Magyarize" public life at the expense of non-Hungarian minorities.

The South Slavs were the most dissatisfied peoples within the Austro-Hungarian monarchy. The southern territories of Austria-Hungary included South Slav peoples, majorities in some regions, who resented subservience to the monarchy. These included Slovenes, Croats, and, above all, Serbs (see Map 17.3). Russia's ties to the Slavic peoples of the Balkans, reinforced by similarity of language and, in the case of Serbia, the sharing of the Orthodox religion, challenged Austro-Hungarian influence in that region.

During the mid-nineteenth-century revolutions, the Russian army had bailed out the then youthful Emperor Francis Joseph, invading Hungary in 1849 and defeating its rebellious army. But by the turn of the century, the Russian government was eagerly fanning Pan-Slav fervor in the Balkans, stirring ethnic tension in the southern regions of the Habsburg monarchy. In the mountainous Habsburg Balkan territories of Bosnia and Herzegovina, which included Orthodox Serbs, Muslims, and Catholic Croats, many Serbs were committed to joining Bosnia to Serbia. The threat of Russian-oriented Pan-Slavism made the Habsburgs even more dependent on their alliance with Germany, as they contemplated the possibility of one day being drawn into a war against Russia. The implication of Pan-Slav nationalism, that Slavs sharing a common culture ought also to share a common government, threatened the very existence of the Habsburg monarchy.

For centuries Russia had coveted the strategically crucial Dardanelles Strait, as well as the narrow Bosporus Strait of Constantinople, controlled by the beleaguered Turkish Ottoman Empire. Russian mastery over the straits that separate Europe and Asia would allow it to control entry to the Black Sea and afford it free access to the Mediterranean. British policy in the Balkans had long been predicated on keeping the straits from Russian control. Russia's defeat in the Crimean War (1853–1856) by Britain, France, and the Ottoman Empire had only temporarily diminished Russian interest in the region. British governments therefore traditionally tried to protect the Turkish Ottoman Empire, above all, against Russian encroachment.

The Alliance System

The alliance system of late-nineteenth-century Europe, then, hinged on German and French enmity, the competing interests of Austria-Hungary and Russia in the Balkans, and Germany's fear of being attacked from both east and west by Russia and France (see Map 22.1). Great Britain and Italy were more or less free agents: Britain, colonial rival of both Germany and France and opponent of Russian expansion, ultimately came to

Map 22.1 Europe In 1914   Highlighting Alsace and the part of Lorraine occupied by Germany before the outbreak of the Great War.

fear the expanding German navy more than French colonial competition. Italy's support could be purchased by the highest bidder. The foundation of nineteenth-century diplomacy lay in the assumption of each continental power that alliances with other great powers would protect it by forcing any nation considering war to face at least two hostile powers. This system, based upon two counterbalancing alliance systems, had helped maintain peace.

Bismarck captured the urgency the European great powers felt about the necessity of alliances, and the delicate nature of the balance of power itself: "All [international] politics reduces itself to this formula: Try to be *à trois* (three) as long as the world is governed by the unstable equilibrium of five great powers"—Germany, Austria-Hungary, Russia, Britain, and France.

The diplomats of the great powers were the heirs of Klemens von Metternich, the Austrian leader who dominated international relations in the three decades following Napoleon's defeat in 1815. Many of them were nobles who believed that the great powers ought to make decisions in the interest of the smaller ones, and in the interest of peace. Unlike Metternich, they embraced nationalism as a principle, but only when considering the rights of the great powers. If they allowed smaller powers some rights, they ascribed the non-European peoples (with the exception of the United States and Japan, the only non-European powers in the world) none at all.

The details and even the existence of most treaties and agreements remained hidden from public scrutiny. Only gradually, during the final diplomatic crisis that immediately led to the war, did the extent to which national destinies were intertwined by alliances become clear to the mass of the population.

Germany and Austria-Hungary against Russia

Germany at first enjoyed good relations with Russia, another autocratic power. In 1873, Bismarck forged the Three Emperors' League, an alliance between Germany, Austria-Hungary, and Russia; by the alliance, the three rulers pledged to consult each other in order to maintain the peace "against all disturbances from whatever side they might come." But it was difficult to gloss over tensions between Austro-Hungarian and Russian interests in the Balkans. When Russia sought and found occasions to extend its influence in that region, Austria-Hungary reacted with concern. In 1875, a revolt against Turkish rule had broken out in the Balkan provinces of Bosnia and Herzegovina. Following Russian intervention against and victory over Turkey in the bloody Russo-Turkish War (1877–1878), the Congress of Berlin in 1878 left Bulgaria nominally under the authority of the Ottoman Empire but under Russian influence. Moreover, the Austro-Hungarian government would henceforth administer Bosnia and Herzegovina, although they would remain within the

Ottoman Empire. But this had the effect of potentially antagonizing Russia, because both territories had populations of Serbs, who as Slavs looked to Russia for leadership. Moreover, in part because Britain and Austria-Hungary feared that Bulgaria might serve Russian interests, the Congress of Berlin recognized the creation of the independent states of Serbia and Romania as buffers against further Russian ambitions in the Balkans. Montenegro also gained independence and the Ottoman Empire ceded the Mediterranean island of Cyprus to Great Britain. The Ottoman Empire not only lost considerable territory but now faced two new hostile states. Moreover, hundreds of thousands of Muslim refugees fled Serbia, Bulgaria, and Bosnia and Herzegovina, pouring into the diminished Ottoman territories. By 1879, about half of the 1.5 million Muslims who had lived in Bulgaria were no longer there; 200,000 had died, and the others were refugees in Turkey.

In 1879, fearing Russian expansionism, Bismarck forged the Dual Alliance, the cornerstone alliance between Germany and Austria-Hungary, predicated on German support for Habsburg opposition to an expansion of Russian interests in the Balkans. Although the details of the alliance remained secret, its general outlines were well known, and the alliance became one of the central factors of European diplomacy for the next thirty-five years. When Italy allied with Germany and Austria-Hungary in 1882, the Triple Alliance was formed. Italy was not a great power, but it wanted to be one. Italian conservatives, who had recently come to power, were more ideologically attracted to the authoritarian powers than to either republican France or parliamentary Britain. The Italian government also wanted support for its aggressive imperial ambitions, which were directed toward the Mediterranean region, particularly North Africa. There France stood in the way, having occupied Tunisia in 1881 before the Italians could get there (see Chapter 21), and Italy sought support against France.

Germany's alliance with Austria-Hungary made the Three Emperors' League virtually meaningless. Germany and Austria-Hungary each agreed to come to the aid of the other in the event of a Russian attack. Bismarck had intended Germany's alliance with Austria-Hungary to force Russia to seek better relations with Germany. But it had the effect of driving Russia farther away. Moreover, Austria-Hungary's alliance with Germany had the potential to make instability in the Balkans a threat to European peace by putting Russia at odds not only with Austria-Hungary, but with Germany as well.

Germany Encircled: Russia and France Ally

The last thing Bismarck wanted was for his alliance with Austria-Hungary to drive Russia and France together. Such an eventuality might one day leave Germany confronting the necessity of fighting a war on two fronts, Bismarck's nightmare. In 1881, he resurrected the Three Emperors'

In a caricature of the alliance system, Otto von Bismarck is depicted as a puppet-master controlling the emperors of Russia, Austria, and Germany.

League, which again allied the tsar of Russia with the emperor of Germany and the ruler of Austria-Hungary. Despite considerable points of tension with the Habsburg monarchy, the Russian government entered this alliance as a hedge against Austro-Hungarian expansion in the Balkans toward the straits of Constantinople. The result was that Bismarck's resourceful diplomacy left Germany allied, in one way or another, with all of its potential enemies except France. As on the eve of the Franco-Prussian War of 1870–1871, France stood without allies.

Yet several factors seemed to draw Russia and France together, despite the great differences in their political systems. Both France and Russia stood outside the Triple Alliance, which joined the powers of Central Europe with Italy. Russia, too, faced diplomatic isolation, despite the Three Emperors' League, because its Balkan interests clashed with those of Austria-Hungary. Russia hoped that an alliance with France would limit German support for the ambitions of the Habsburgs in southeastern Europe. Cultural ties between the Russian aristocracy and France remained strong, as they had been in the eighteenth century; many Russian nobles still preferred to speak French.

French investment in Russia increased dramatically in the late 1880s and early 1890s. French bankers seized the opportunity to provide capital at attractive interest rates for Russian railway and mining development, and French investors enthusiastically purchased Russian bonds. By 1914, about one-fourth of all French foreign investment was in Russia. In contrast, Bismarck and his successors made it a policy to discourage and even to forbid German loans to Russia, although they invested in the Austro-Hungarian and Ottoman Empires. German private investors, in any case, usually lacked the capital to undertake such loans. At the same time, German and French financial cooperation was extremely limited. French and German capitalists saw each other as bitter rivals.

Franco-Russian ties were further solidified by Tsar Alexander III's visit to Paris during the exposition of 1889, when one of the bridges across the

Seine River was named after him. Yet toasts to Franco-Russian friendship seemed inappropriate to many in France. The French left was outraged by government overtures to the autocratic and often brutal tsarist regime. For their part, Russian Tsar Alexander III and his successor Nicholas II were uncomfortable with close ties to a republic. Still, Nicholas stood while a band played "The Marseillaise," the anthem of the French Revolution, while greeting a French naval squadron at the Russian Baltic base of Kronshtadt.

As the Russian government blamed Austria-Hungary for opposing what they considered its natural influence in the Balkans, the Three Emperors' League lapsed. In 1887, Germany and Russia signed a Reinsurance Treaty, by which each pledged to remain neutral if the other went to war, but it did not cover the most likely contingency of all—war between Russia and Austria-Hungary—because Germany was already committed to aid Austria-Hungary if Russian forces attacked. The young, headstrong Kaiser William II dismissed Bismarck as chancellor in 1890. Bismarck's successors were increasingly anti-Russian and failed to prevent Russia's alliance with France.

In 1892, Russia and France signed a military treaty by which each pledged a military response if the other were attacked by Germany or by one or more of its allies. A secret formal alliance followed in 1894. The alliance was essentially defensive in nature: the French no more encouraged Russian moves in the direction of the Balkans than the Russians wanted to see France embark on a war of revenge to recapture Alsace-Lorraine from Germany. But the Dual Alliance, as it was called, countered the Triple Alliance. It defeated the most essential thrust of Bismarck's foreign policy by ending France's diplomatic isolation.

Anglo-German Rivalry

During the 1890s, the possibility of Britain joining the Dual Alliance of France and Russia seemed remote. Whereas Germany and Britain had some competing colonial interests—for example, in Africa—hostilities seemed most likely to break out between France and Britain. Their respective interests clashed in West Africa and Indochina, and France was jealous of British influence in Egypt. When a French force encountered a British army unit in 1898 on the upper Nile at Fashoda, war between the two seemed a distinct possibility (see Chapter 21). The French government backed down. Furthermore, Afghanistan, lying strategically between British India and Russia, was a particular point of tension between those two powers.

The British government had long made it clear that it sought no alliance with anyone, and that it would stand alone, its empire protected by the great British navy. But the British government signed the Entente Cordiale ("Friendly Agreement") with France in 1904. Britain did so for several reasons. The hostile reaction from every power in Europe to the Boer War (1899–1902, see Chapter 21) fought by British troops in South Africa demonstrated that it was one thing to stand in proud isolation from the continent, but another to have no friends at all. Furthermore, Britain's relations with Germany soured markedly. Germany's pointed criticism of Britain's war with the Boers strained relations between the two powers. In 1895, Kaiser William II, in his inimitably clumsy way, had sent a telegram congratulating the president of the Boer Republic of Transvaal in southern Africa on the Boers' successful stand against a British attacking force. This unleashed a storm of nationalistic fury in both countries. In 1899, British Foreign Secretary Joseph Chamberlain awkwardly responded to German criticism by stating that Britain was waging no more "barbarous" a war than that undertaken by Prussia against France in 1870 (which was not, in any case, true).

Neither Anglo-German cooperation in the suppression of the Boxer Rebellion in China in 1900, nor a joint operation to force Venezuela to pay some of its foreign debts in 1902, significantly improved Anglo-German relations. Gradually, the British began to realize the growing extent of German influence in the Turkish Ottoman Empire. British military planners feared that Germany might be able to move troops more quickly overland into the Middle East than the Royal Navy could by ship.

German economic growth and the doubling of its foreign trade during the last three decades of the nineteenth century had begun to make some in Britain anxious, although Britain still accounted for about 45 percent of world investment. It also inspired a campaign to establish an empire-wide tariff barrier that would encourage trade within the British Commonwealth, while keeping foreign goods out.

Above all, it was the Anglo-German naval rivalry that pushed Britain toward a rapprochement with France. German military spending had already quadrupled between 1874 and 1890 (in a period of little inflation). Germany had never been a naval power, but in 1897 the Reichstag allocated funds for the accelerated expansion of the German navy over the next six years.

William II's uncontrolled enthusiasm provided no small degree of impetus—the vain kaiser loved putting on his military medals, sword, and polished boots, reviewing his sailors and soldiers, and breaking champagne bottles over the bows of powerful warships. Bismarck once remarked, "The kaiser is like a balloon. If you don't hold fast to the string, you never know where he'll be off!"

Admiral Alfred von Tirpitz (1849–1930), trusted adviser to the kaiser, made a speech to the Reichstag, wherein he belligerently cited the strength of the British navy as the *raison d'être* for the passage of the bill to build up the German navy. The nationalistic Pan-German League and the Naval League, organizations whose members included powerful commercial and industrial magnates, whipped up popular enthusiasm for the navy and for German colonialism. The new German fleet, which was to include some of the biggest, fastest, and widest-ranging warships ever built, would be capable of operating aggressively far from Germany's Baltic ports.

Britain reacted quickly when confronted with the sudden and almost unexpected naval competition. In 1906, Britain launched the fastest and most powerful battleship in the world, the Dreadnought. Whereas its predecessors had four heavy guns, the Dreadnought could carry ten. The following year, Germany began to build comparable ships of war. British naval yards were constructing eight more ships of the Dreadnought class in 1908. But rumors and wild estimates had the Germans turning out even more, leading to a brief panic in 1909 that Germany was about to invade Britain.

British-French Rapprochement

The British government took a hesitant step toward ending its diplomatic isolation by signing a treaty in 1901 with the United States, which permitted the latter to construct the Panama Canal. By undertaking an alliance with Japan in 1902, Britain sought to counter Russian ambitions in East Asia. The Russo-Japanese War of 1904–1905 helped push Britain toward France. The conflict itself followed the development of a rivalry between Russia and Japan in Manchuria—in particular, the increasing Russian demands for further Chinese economic concessions there. The hostilities began in February 1904 with a surprise Japanese attack on the Russian naval base of Port Arthur (Lüshun). The Russian Baltic fleet, embarking on a disastrous voyage around the world to confront the Japanese navy in the Yellow Sea, sank several British fishing trawlers in the North Sea, somehow mistaking them for Japanese ships. Germany expected that France would immediately support Russia, with whom it was allied. Yet, to almost everyone's surprise, French Foreign Minister Théophile Delcassé (1852–1923) helped mediate between Russia and Britain. Russia's defeat by Japan ensured that Russia would be unable to launch a war against Germany's eastern frontier for some time. Furthermore, the defeat of Russia in East Asia confirmed that Britain had far more to fear from Germany than from Russia.

In the 1890s, the ogre-enemy of the "future war novels," published in Britain had invariably been France. The French were characterized as untrustworthy and downright sneaky. In one scenario, the French stealthily construct a tunnel underneath the English Channel while the unprepared British doze, and they then send an invading army through the tunnel disguised as café waiters, before the heroic English come to their senses and drive their unscrupulous enemies back to France. But with the Anglo-German naval rivalry, the new enemy in these imaginary future wars became Germany. The Germans were not depicted as sneaking around. Unlike the French, they were portrayed as organized and brutal, sending their feared Dreadnought-class warships up and down the eastern coast of England, blasting military and civilian targets indiscriminately, until the British rallied and defeated their new enemy.

Delcassé was determined to forge a rapprochement with Britain. The Entente Cordiale reached between Britain and France in 1904 had the immediate goal of eliminating points of tension between the two powers: Britain recognized French interests in Morocco in exchange for the French recognition of British control over Egypt; both sides accepted the existence of neutral Siam in Indochina between French Indochina and British-controlled Burma; and they settled a centuries-old dispute over fishing rights off the coast of Newfoundland.

The First Moroccan Crisis

The First Moroccan Crisis (1905) solidified the rapprochement between Britain and France. The British had abandoned their interest in Morocco, which France clearly dominated. But Germany had not, despite the fact that Germany had only modest commercial interests in the North African state. The German chancellor, Bernhard von Bülow (1849–1929), convinced William II to test the recently concluded Anglo-French agreement and perhaps force the British government to leave France to its own devices while casting Germany as defender of Moroccan sovereignty. In March 1905, the German kaiser himself was aboard a German yacht that docked in Tangier. Seeking to emphasize Morocco's independence from France, William II demanded that Germany receive from Morocco the same commercial benefits as any other trading partner.

The French government reacted with fury, but backed down because it seemed unlikely that Britain would then support it in a war against Germany. Delcassé, who had urged a measured French response to the incident,

"For whom Morocco?" William II of Germany, Marianne (the image of the French Republic), Kind Edward VII of England, and King Alphonso XIII of Spain chase the sultan of Morocco, 1906.

resigned as foreign minister. Nationalism and anti-German feeling intensified in France. Earlier in the Third Republic, French nationalism had also been primarily identified with the anti-parliamentary right; now it affected political moderates.

Germany also pulled away from possible conflict, seeing that British support for France had remained firm and that only Austria-Hungary took the German side. The crisis ended with an international conference in the Spanish town of Algeciras in January 1906. Germany recognized the primacy of French interests in Morocco. This left Germany determined that another humiliation must not be suffered. The incident also seemed to confirm the bellicose and bullying nature of German foreign policy to Britain as well as to France. French and British generals and admirals began to draw up joint contingency plans for combined warfare against Germany.

The Algeciras Conference, and particularly the policies of Russian Foreign Minister Aleksandr Izvolsky (1856–1919), also brought Russia and Britain closer together. For Izvolsky, Russian interests were in the Balkans, where they competed with those of Austria-Hungary, not in Asia, where British interests lay. Set on the road to recovery from the disastrous Russo-Japanese War by British loans, Russia was now eager for better relations with Britain. The British government had long viewed Russian economic influence in Persia (Iran) and Afghanistan as threatening to its interests, in the first case because a strong Russian presence in Persia might one day compromise the sea route to East Asia, in the second because Afghanistan served as a buffer between Russia and British India. However, in 1907, the two powers divided Persia into three zones—a Russian zone, a British zone, and a neutral zone—and agreed to respect each other's zone of influence. The Russians accepted British influence in Afghanistan, and both powers agreed to stay out of Tibet. Russia hoped that Britain might support, or at least tolerate, its interests in the Balkans, and its ultimate desire of controlling Constantinople. The elimination of some of the tension between Britain and Russia strengthened the Franco-British Entente Cordiale.

THE EUROPE OF TWO ARMED CAMPS, 1905–1914

The inclusion of Russia in what was increasingly known as the Triple Entente moved Europe toward a clear division into two camps. Cordial relations, however, continued between Tsar Nicholas II and his cousin, German Kaiser William II. As in centuries past, European royal families had intermarried. The German kaiser was the grandson of Queen Victoria of England—a standing joke in Berlin went that William feared no one except God and his English grandmother. But in the Europe of entangling alliances, blood relations were subordinate to the logic of great-power interests and alliances.

The German government could find little reassurance in Italy's nominal alliance with Germany and Austria-Hungary. Italian nationalist goals seemed incompatible with its alliance with Austria-Hungary. Italian irredentism (the absorption of adjacent territories with significant Italian populations) could only be fulfilled at the expense of Austria-Hungary, whose territories included the South Tyrol in the Alps and Trieste on the Adriatic coast. Improved relations between Italy and France confronted Germany with the prospect that Austria-Hungary would be its only dependable ally.

Should Austria-Hungary cease to be a power or, in the worst scenario, completely collapse because of national movements from within, Germany might be left alone, encircled by enemies and vulnerable to annihilation. This fear weighed heavily on William, his advisers, and on German public opinion. The German high command prepared for a possible war against both France and Russia, a war that would have to be fought on two fronts. This left the German government in the position of having to support its troubled Habsburg ally unconditionally in the Balkans.

The Balkan Tinderbox

The Balkans increasingly became the key to maintaining peace in Europe (see Map 22.2). In 1897, Russia and Austria-Hungary had agreed informally to respect the *status quo* in the region. But the development of intense cultural and political nationalism among the South Slavs living within the boundaries of the Austro-Hungarian Empire, in Serbia, or under Ottoman rule, increasingly challenged the *status quo*. In the Balkans, the vast majority of peoples had remained indifferent or ignorant of nationalist identities until at least the beginning of the twentieth century. Religious identities—Muslim; Greek, Russian, or Bulgarian Orthodox; Catholic; Jewish—had always defined a sense of community, along with regional and village identities.

Then, encouraged by the creation of new states carved out of what had been Ottoman territory, national identities began to take hold. This made southeastern Europe a focus of the rivalry between Austria-Hungary and Russia.

When a bloody revolution led to the assassination of the king and queen of Serbia in 1903, Russia quickly recognized the new king, Peter, hoping that Pan-Slav elements would dominate. Fearing any delay would push Serbia further toward Russia, Austria-Hungary recognized the *fait accompli*. The Serb parliament voiced its unqualified support for Russian ambitions in East Asia and its 1904–1905 war against Japan: "Slavic Serbia naturally considers every Russian success as a strengthening of the Slavic cause." Serbian nationalists began to call for union with Serbs in Macedonia. Lying in the southern Balkans, Macedonia, then still part of the Ottoman Empire, was peopled by Macedonians, Serbs, Bulgarians, Sephardic Jews, and Greeks (whose guerrilla fighters operated inside

▨	Absorbed by Romania from Bulgaria, 1913
▨	Absorbed by Bulgaria from Turkey, 1913
▤	Absorbed by Serbia, 1913
▦	Absorbed by Greece, 1913

MAP 22.2 THE BALKANS, 1914   The Austro-Hungarian Empire and the Balkan states, including territory acquired in the Balkan Wars of 1912–1913.

Macedonia, as did Bulgarian and Macedonian nationalists). As Greek and Bulgarian Orthodox churches battled for the allegiance of the peasants, the strident, aggressive calls of various nationalist groups helped create a nationalism that had previously existed on only a superficial level among elites. A Bulgarian described life in the 1870s:

> Turks and Bulgarians got on well together. The women of a village quarter bordering on Turkish houses mixed with the Turkish women in a neighborly way, while the children played with the little Turks as with their own playmates. The Turkish women and children spoke Bulgarian quite well and the Bulgarians, like their children, managed to get by in Turkish . . . those Turks who worked at Bulgarian houses were accepted as close friends. . . . We Bulgarians . . . had our own

dress, our own customs and stuck to our faith, while they lived another way. . . . But all this we took as being in the order of things.

This would change. Provocative addresses to ethnic minorities worsened tensions between ethnic groups, as well as between Serbia and Austria-Hungary and between Russia and Austria-Hungary. Religion became much more identified with emerging national identities. Relations between Serbia and Austria-Hungary further deteriorated. When Serbia tried to lessen its economic dependence on Austria-Hungary (the destination of almost all Serb exports) by signing a commercial treaty with Bulgaria, Vienna responded by forbidding the importation of Serbian livestock. Thus began an economic battle in 1906 that became known to much of Europe as the "Pig War," as the humble pig formed the basis of Serbia's fragile agricultural economy. The Serbs resourcefully found new markets for their pigs. The Habsburg government, despite the lack of Hungarian support for economic retaliation, responded in 1908 by announcing the construction of a new railroad that would further isolate Serbia economically. Izvolsky worked aggressively to expand Russian influence in the Balkans. Serbian nationalists, for their part, viewed Bosnia and Herzegovina as South Slav states that should, with Russian encouragement, become part of Serbia.

Instability in Turkey

Political instability in Turkey in the early 1870s had further whetted the appetites of both Russia and Austria-Hungary for the Balkans, amid financial crisis, poor harvests, and the opposition of religious conservatives to secularization. Following the Crimean War (see Chapter 18), Britain and France had condescendingly invited the sultan "to participate in the advantages of public law and the system of Europe," while insisting on further Western reforms. Sultan Abdülhamid II (ruled 1876–1909) agreed to a constitution upon his ascension to the throne in 1876, consolidating some of the reforms of the past several decades. Furthermore, it established parliamentary rule and guaranteed personal freedom and equality before the law. The sultan's purpose in promulgating this liberal constitution was to discourage the powers from intervening in Ottoman affairs on the pretext of forcing political reform. But in 1878 he suspended the constitution and dissolved the parliament it had established. He directly oversaw government, using the secret police to root out potential opposition. During Abdülhamid's rule, foreign trade increased, agriculture developed, railway lines and paved roads more than doubled, and public schools increased in number. But his reign was also marked by the brutal repression of non-Muslim peoples of the Ottoman Empire. About 200,000 Armenians (who made up about 6 percent of the empire's population) were slaughtered in 1894 and 1895 in eastern Anatolia in response to Turkish fears about rising Armenian nationalism and even revolutionary activity, which Russia was encouraging. Moreover, the empire continued to be beset by financial problems— above all, the high-interest debt owed to foreign bondholders. Influenced by Western political ideas and reflecting the emergence of a generation of Turkish intellectuals, a group of nationalists from a variety of backgrounds had in 1889 founded in Paris the Committee of Union and Progress. In the Ottoman Empire, they found support in the bureaucracy and army despite being the target of police repression. In July 1908, these "Young Turks," as they were called, who had penetrated the army, revolted in the name of

Enver Bey, leader of the Young Turks party, talking with an English military attaché.

"order and progress" and forced the sultan to restore the constitution of 1876. One of their leaders was Mustafa Kemal (later known as Atatürk, 1881–1938), a recent graduate of the imperial War Academy. The goal of the Young Turks was to modernize and unify all of the Ottoman lands, while preventing Western intervention on behalf of the Armenians. Abdülhamid II was deposed in 1909 when he tried to plot a counter-revolution, and gradually a Western-like bureaucracy was put in place.

The chaos within the Ottoman Empire seemed to promise the realization of the Russian dream of opening the straits of Constantinople to Russian ships, and perhaps only Russian ships. The Austro-Hungarian government faced the possibility that lands still held by the Ottoman Empire might be added to Serbia and Romania. This pushed Russian and Austro-Hungarian relations toward a breaking point.

The Bosnian Crisis of 1908

Turkish instability led to the Bosnian Crisis of 1908. In 1878, the Congress of Berlin had authorized Austria-Hungary to occupy Bosnia and Herzegovina, although both territories technically were still part of the Ottoman Empire. Austria-Hungary had done so, at the risk of bringing more Slavs into the empire, not only to solidify its position in the Balkans but also to prevent Serbia from absorbing them. The Russian government had been secretly negotiating with Austria-Hungary to accept the Habsburg absorption of Bosnia and Herzegovina in return for Austria-Hungary's support for the opening of the Bosporus and the Dardanelles Straits to the Russian fleet. In October 1908, the Austro-Hungarian government suddenly announced that it was directly annexing Bosnia and Herzegovina, fearful of the influence of the Young Turks there. The annexation was a clear violation of the agreements reached at the Congress of Berlin in 1878. The Russians reacted with rage at Austria-Hungary's betrayal of their understanding. Serbia, furious that two territories in which many South Slavs lived were to be incorporated into the Habsburg empire, mobilized its army with Russian support. Austria-Hungary responded in kind. The annexation also considerably strained relations between Austria-Hungary and Italy, nominal allies, because of Italian strategic and economic interests on the Adriatic coast.

The resolute opposition to war by Hungarian leaders within the Dual Monarchy, as well as the opposition of the heir to the Habsburg throne, Archduke Francis Ferdinand (1863–1914), helped defuse the crisis. Not only would war be expensive, victory might well add a considerable South Slav population (from Serbia) to Hungarian territories, adding to the potential for instability within the Habsburg lands. Furthermore, despite diplomatic bluster, Russia was not ready to fight, and its ally France was unwilling to go to war over the Balkans, where its own interests were not threatened. Lacking French or British support, the Russian government backed down, forcing Serbia to accept what by now was a *fait accompli* and recognize the annexation.

War had been avoided, but the European powers had drawn significant conclusions from the Bosnian Crisis. The German government clearly supported Austrian policy in the Balkans without reservation. Italy remained allied with both Central European powers, but both Berlin and Vienna viewed Italy's commitment to the alliance as uncertain. Italy's economic and colonial rivalry with France became less intense as Italian business and colonial interests increasingly looked to regions (the Balkans and the eastern Mediterranean) in which the French had no immediate interests. Italy's problematic status as an ally thus firmed up Germany's alliance with Austria-Hungary. German and Austro-Hungarian military commanders met to plan for hostilities with Russia, France, Serbia, and possibly—given its announced interests in Tyrolean Austria and Dalmatia—Italy. Britain and France had discovered that German support for Austria-Hungary was unshakable, even for a potentially dangerous move for which Berlin had received no advance warning. The German government sent a note to the Russian government, demanding that Russia give up support for Serbia and recognize Austria-Hungary's takeover of Bosnia-Herzegovina. The Russian government, viewing itself as a victim of German bullying, now wanted a close relationship with Britain. With German shipyards rapidly producing the most modern and heavily armed fighting ships at a frightening pace,

British officials quickly gave up their reservations about the Entente Cordiale with France.

The Bosnian Crisis left deep scars on Russian relations with Austria-Hungary. Russia, in the wake of its surprising defeat by Japan, urgently began restoring its army and navy to fighting shape. Serbian relations with Vienna worsened. The Habsburg government presented poorly forged documents to support claims that the Serbian government was trying to stir up the Slav populations within and against the Habsburg empire. In fact, several groups of devoted Serb nationalists, including "The People's Defense" and "The Black Hand," received tacit support from the Serb state, as well as Russian encouragement. The Bosnian Crisis passed, but ethnic tensions and Russian and Habsburg rivalry in the region did not.

The Second Moroccan Crisis

Germany provoked the Second Moroccan Crisis (1911). France had established a virtual protectorate in Morocco, which violated the Algeciras agreements of 1906. Using a local rebellion against the new Moroccan sultan as an excuse, a French army marched on the town of Fez, allegedly to protect French settlers. When the French government did not offer to compensate Germany because France had added another protectorate to its empire, the German kaiser sent a small gunboat, the *Panther,* to the port of Agadir. It arrived on July 1, 1911, with demands that Germany receive the entire French Congo as compensation for France's claiming Morocco as a protectorate.

France refused, bolstered by its closer relations with Britain, Russia's increased strength, and a wave of nationalist sentiment at home. David Lloyd George (1863–1945), Liberal British chancellor of the Exchequer and a man usually known for his caution, declared that "the formula of peace at any price is unworthy of a great power." Britain could never accept the possibility of a German port on the coast of North Africa. This response further diminished chances of German-British rapprochement. Even German moderates seemed angered at what appeared to be a British commitment to preventing Germany from finding its "place in the sun."

The Second Moroccan Crisis, like the first, passed without war. William II seemed less willing to follow up bravado with action. The French minister of war's assessment that the army was in no shape to fight forced a moderate French response. On November 4, 1911, Germany agreed to recognize Morocco as a French protectorate in exchange for 100,000 square miles of the French Congo. But the crisis further solidified Europe's antagonistic alliances. Britain and France now formalized the agreement by which each pledged to aid the other in case of an attack by Germany. In April 1912, the British and French admiralties established zones of responsibility for their fleets—the French in the Mediterranean and the British in the English Channel and the North Sea.

The Balkan Wars

The Bosnian Crisis of 1908 had demonstrated that events in the Balkans could carry Europe to war. The Second Moroccan Crisis hardened the increasingly confrontational alliances. Now in 1911, the Turkish Ottoman Empire provided the kindling for another international flare-up. Late in the year, Italy invaded Libya in what became known as the Tripoli War. Italy proclaimed Libya its colony, but the Turks and the Libyan population resisted. The war dragged on until Italy claimed victory in October 1912. France acquiesced to the Italian seizure of Libya in exchange for Italian recognition of Morocco's status as a French protectorate.

Serbia, Bulgaria, Montenegro, and Greece had formed the Balkan League with the intention of completely freeing the Balkans from Ottoman rule. Encouraged by the difficulty the Turkish army had in putting down an insurrection in Albania in 1910 (many Albanians resisted the "modernization" brought by the Young Turks, identifying it with Christian values) and by the Turkish defeat in Libya, they declared war on Turkey in 1912. The First Balkan War lasted less than a month, with the Balkan League emerging victorious. The success of the Balkan states worried the Austro-Hungarian government. Russia and the Austro-Hungarian monarchy seemed on a collision course in the Balkans. Serbia, Bulgaria, and Greece each annexed territory (for Greece, which increased its territory by 70 percent, this new territory included the prize port of Salonika) that had belonged to the Ottoman Empire. This left the once enormous former Ottoman Empire with only a small territory on the European side of the straits of Constantinople (see Map 22.2). Albania achieved its independence, recognized by the great powers.

This time Russia and the Habsburgs had stayed clear of the brink of war. New foreign ministers, Sergey Sazonov (1861–1927) of Russia and Leopold Berchtold (1863–1942) of Austria-Hungary, helped defuse the crisis. Furthermore, both Francis Joseph and Archduke Francis Ferdinand opposed war at this time. Austria-Hungary had, in any case, no commitment of any kind to the Turks. Austria-Hungary's goals were to see that no Balkan state became so strong that it could generate nationalist agitation within its territories, and to prevent Serbia, Russia's friend, from gaining a port on the Adriatic. In the interest of peace, Britain and France supported Austria-Hungary's call for the creation of the independent state of Albania on the Adriatic, which would prevent Serbia from having its port. The German government now also viewed these issues as sufficiently grave to warrant its unconditional support for Austria-Hungary. The Treaty of London of May 1913 divided up most of the remaining Ottoman holdings in southeastern Europe among the Balkan states.

However Bulgaria felt aggrieved by the fact that Serbia and Greece had ended up with large chunks of Macedonia, and it attacked both powers. Serbia and Greece, with the assistance of Romania and the Ottoman

Empire, quickly defeated expansionist Bulgaria in 1913 in the Second Balkan War. With the Peace of Bucharest, Serbia received the parts of what had been Ottoman Macedonia, which Bulgaria was to have received; Greece gained more territory on the Aegean coast as well as Crete, which it tried to occupy in 1897 before being easily defeated by Ottoman forces; and the independent state of Albania came into existence. Turkey regained Adrianople, but following these further territorial losses, the Turkish government evolved into a military dictatorship intent on imposing Turkish culture on ethnic minorities. Serbia emerged from the Balkan Wars larger, stronger, more ambitious, and angry that Austria-Hungary had frustrated its quest for an Adriatic port. It also may have emerged with the impression that there were limits to Germany's support for Austria-Hungary, since the German government had appeared to restrain the Habsburg government's aggressive response to Serbia's demand for a port. Defeated Bulgaria became a target for Austro-Hungarian overtures, although it lay within the sphere of Russian influence by virtue of its cultural and linguistic affinities.

South Slav nationalism gained more adherents in the Balkans. After backing down against Austria-Hungary for the second time (the first having been the Bosnian Crisis in 1908), Sergey Sazonov irresponsibly placated the Serbs by telling them that their promised land lay inside the frontiers of Hungary. Some Serb political leaders sympathized with the young fanatics of "The People's Will" and "The Black Hand" nationalist organizations. In 1910, a boy who had been taught to shoot a gun by a Serb officer attempted to use it on the Austrian governor of Bosnia; the youth committed suicide after failing, becoming a martyr in Serbia. A few Habsburg personages, possibly including the Archduke Francis Ferdinand, may have been willing to consider the South Slavs as partners in a tripartite empire—the mere suggestion of which infuriated almost all

"The Vortex—Will the powers be drawn in?" This image of the Balkan Wars, 1912–1913, had a ring of prophetic accuracy.

Magyars, of whom he was not their champion, and most Austrians. But the government of the Dual Monarchy considered the South Slav nationalists to be threats who would ultimately have to be crushed by force. Because of the Balkan situation, the German military command once again turned its attention to readying its army, a reaction to recent Russian measures of military preparedness. But in 1914 Europe seemed far less close to war than it had been in 1905 and 1911, the years of the two Moroccan Crises. When the final crisis came, however, Britain, France, and Russia found themselves fatefully linked, set against the cornerstone alliance of Germany and Austria-Hungary.

THE FINAL CRISIS

The powers of Europe were poised for conflict, divided into two armed camps by two rival alliances. While the outbreak of war was probably not inevitable—although many nationalists and military planners believed it to be—it was likely. Furthermore, once two powers seemed on the verge of war, the entangling alliances that pitted the Triple Alliance against the Triple Entente seemed likely to bring all of the European powers into the conflict. The crisis that precipitated World War I occurred in the Balkans, when Serb nationalists assassinated the Archduke Francis Ferdinand of Austria. Europe's diplomatic house of cards collapsed and World War I began.

Assassination in Sarajevo

Archduke Francis Ferdinand, sixty years of age, was heir to the Habsburg throne. His first love was his commoner wife, Sophie; his second, hunting—he bragged of having killed 6,000 stags in his lifetime and of having bagged 2,763 seagulls on a single day. The archduke was considered relatively anti-German, and, despite being an intolerant person, he probably had more sympathy for the problems of the South Slavs than any member of the royal family. For this, the Hungarians disliked him, fearing that when he came to the throne, he might eventually award the South Slavs the same status as the Austrians and Hungarians. Nor did the archduke's relatively understanding view of their position win him points with South Slav nationalists, many of whom would accept nothing less than an expanded independent Slavic state, or what they called Greater Serbia. (Ferdinand had once described Serbia as a country of "thieves and murderers and bandits and a few plum trees.")

On June 28, 1914, Francis Ferdinand and his wife were on an inspection tour of the army in Sarajevo, the capital of Bosnia. As the archduke's motorcade approached the center of the city, a bomb exploded under the archduke's car, wounding two Austrian officers. The motorcade continued to the town hall, where a municipal authority stumbled through his speech, and the archduke expressed his indignation at the attempt on his

On an inspection tour of the army in Sarajevo, capital of Bosnia, Archduke Francis Ferdinand and his wife bathe in a warm welcome. They were assassinated a few hours later.

life. When the motorcade departed, the drivers of the cars had not been informed of a change in route chosen to avoid the tangle of streets in central Sarajevo. When the first several vehicles began to turn into a narrow street, the military governor ran ahead, ordering their drivers to back up. Gavrilo Princip (1895–1918), one of seven trained assassins from the "Black Hand" Serb nationalist group, saw his chance, as he happened to be only a few feet from the archduke's car. He opened fire, killing Francis Ferdinand and his wife. Princip, who had been expelled from school in Sarajevo two years earlier for participating in anti-Austrian demonstrations, liked to recite a line written by the German philosopher Nietzsche: "Insatiable as the flame, I glow and consume myself." His actions would, in the end, lead to Europe itself being consumed in flames of war.

Although the Serbian government had been aware of the Black Hand nationalist organization and some individual officials had supported it, the Austrian description of the youthful killers as puppets whose strings were pulled in Belgrade was incorrect. Nonetheless, the Serb response to the assassination only seemed to confirm Austria's interpretation: newspapers virtually celebrated the death of the Habsburg heir. In Vienna, even those who had disliked the archduke for having married a commoner now mourned the couple fervently.

The Ultimatum

Within the Habsburg imperial administration, many officials immediately took the view that the chance to crush Serbia had arrived, and that, unlike

1908 and 1912, this time the opportunity would not be missed. The usually indecisive and ineffective Austrian Foreign Minister Leopold Berchtold, who had opposed war during the Balkan Crisis of 1912, now took a hard line. Unlike the Bosnian Crisis of 1908, the Hungarian leaders now accepted the possibility of war.

Despite its anger and vengeful mood, Vienna delayed its official reaction to the assassination. From Berlin, however, came anything but caution. William II urged retaliation, blaming Serbia for the assassination of Francis Ferdinand, whom he had visited only two weeks earlier. The brooding Theobald von Bethmann-Hollweg (1856–1921) had become chancellor of Germany in 1909. During the Second Moroccan Crisis of 1911, he complained to the British ambassador that he no longer could listen to Beethoven before going to bed: "How can I play my beloved old music with the air full of modern discords?" He stubbornly held the view that Germany's strength must be paramount. ("Necessity knows no law," he once said.) Now he expressed his doubts that Austria-Hungary could remain a great power if it backed down a third time. In Berlin, the German government gave an Austrian official a "blank check" to act with the knowledge of full German support. The German foreign office assured Austria-Hungary that Germany would, if necessary, fight both France and Russia if those two powers intervened once Austria had declared war on Serbia, but expected Britain would remain neutral.

It therefore seemed clear that Germany would maintain its unqualified support for Austria-Hungary at all costs. Bethmann-Hollweg was now determined to stay the course with a numbing fatalism undoubtedly accentuated by the recent death of his wife. He advised his son not to plant his estate with trees that would take a long time to grow, because they would please only the Russians, whom by then he expected to have occupied northeastern Germany. He did not want a war, but he expected one, and he wanted Russia to appear the aggressor.

But for the moment, Austria-Hungary waited. In Vienna, Berchtold convinced the Hungarian leaders to support war against Serbia, promising that no Slavs from territories taken from defeated Serbia would be incorporated into Austria-Hungary. The Hungarian Social Democrats ended their opposition to the war. On July 21, 1914, Russian Foreign Minister Sazonov, encouraged by Maurice Paléologue, the French ambassador, warned that "Russia would not be able to permit Austria-Hungary to make any threat against Serbia, or to take any military measures." The Austro-Hungarian government, however, continued to believe that the French and British governments would convince Russia to pull back before the point of war.

On July 23, 1914, almost a month after the assassination, the Austrian ambassador in Belgrade handed a lengthy ultimatum to Serb officials. It denounced what it claimed was Serbian activity aiming to "detach part of the territories of Austria-Hungary from the Monarchy." Austro-Hungarian demands included the elimination of all anti-Habsburg publications, including schoolbooks, the dissolution of all Serb nationalist organizations, a purge of officials and army officers to be named by Austria-Hungary, and a specific response as to the means by which the Serbian government would submit to these demands. The Serbian reply was expected within forty-eight hours. Edward Grey, the British foreign secretary, called the ultimatum "the most formidable document ever presented by one independent state to another."

The Serb government was in a no-win situation. Even the most optimistic Serb could not help but admit that Serbia's small army was no match for that of Austria-Hungary. Its options were either to capitulate completely to the ultimatum and suffer a humiliating diplomatic defeat, or, as one official put it, to die fighting. This made Serbia almost totally dependent upon Russian intervention.

The ultimatum sent shock waves through the capitals of Europe. Upon learning its contents, Sazonov exclaimed, "It's the European War!" He blamed Germany for having inspired the Austro-Hungarian response and claimed that the ultimatum was part of a German plan to keep Russia from reaching Constantinople.

The tsar's immediate circle was divided over the advisability of going to war. Some advisers saw war as a means of rallying the support of an entire people behind the tsar. Yet others remembered Russia's disastrous defeat in the Russo-Japanese War. This, in turn, had contributed to the outbreak of the Revolution of 1905 (see Chapter 20). Now, Sazonov's first practical concern was to mobilize French support against Austria-Hungary, believing that a united show of strength would force the Central European allies to back down. French President Raymond Poincaré's state visit to St. Petersburg from July 20 to July 23 seemed to indicate that France would stand by Russia, and now Sazonov received quick assurance from the French ambassador of full French support.

On July 25, 1914, two days after the Austro-Hungarian ultimatum, the tsar placed the Russian army on alert, a stage that would normally precede mobilization. Such a step was fraught with consequences for the military planners of each power. Mobilization meant preparing an army for war, calling up reserves, declaring martial law in frontier areas, readying the railways for hauling troops and supplies, and accelerating the production of munitions. In these circumstances, a Russian decision to mobilize would be tantamount to an act of war. Military planners assumed it would take at least two weeks, perhaps more, for the Russian army to be ready to fight.

The Schlieffen Plan

Germany's plan for war against France had been drawn up in 1905 by Count Alfred von Schlieffen (1833–1913) a former chief of the German general staff. Based on the assumption that it would take Russia, France's ally, some weeks to prepare its armies to fight, the Schlieffen Plan called for the German armies in a lightning attack to knock the French out of the war within several weeks. Then the German forces would be able to confront the Russian army attacking in the east. The German attack on France would require its forces to violate Belgian neutrality in order to bypass the sturdy defenses in eastern France. To do this, the German armies would storm around the network of fortifications the French had constructed on their eastern frontier after the Franco-Prussian War of 1870–1871. German troops would march through the flat lands of Belgium and the Netherlands, and turn south once the last soldier on the northern flank had brushed his sleeve against the English Channel. A pincer movement southward would encircle Paris from the northwest, and then turn to trap the French armies struggling in Alsace-Lorraine. It mattered little that the Germans might first have to give ground in Alsace-Lorraine, where the French, as a matter of pride, would surely attack. Schlieffen and his successors all recognized that the plan would probably bring Great Britain into the war because that nation would never accept the violation of Belgian neutrality and the possible presence of an enemy power just across the Channel. But German commanders believed that the war on the continent would be over before the superior British navy could make a difference and that the small, volunteer British army posed little threat. Then, once Paris had fallen and the French armies had been put out of action by the wrenching German headlock, there would still be time to ship enough of the victorious army to the east to defeat the Russians as they rolled slowly toward Germany. This was the solution to Bismarck's nightmare, a simultaneous war on two fronts.

The French high command had its own plan for war. It, too, envisioned a rapid attack, called "Plan XVII," in which two French armies would be sent into Alsace-Lorraine, as the Germans expected. The French planned another thrust to drive German forces back. With the bulk of the German army tied up by French and British troops in Belgium, and, at worst, northern France, the way to Berlin would be open. The French army was itching to redeem itself. Unlike Germany, which had to contemplate fighting a war on two fronts, the French army enjoyed the advantage of being able to focus its full attention on Germany. Marshal Joseph Joffre (1852–1931) had overseen plans for a full-scale assault into Alsace-Lorraine, followed by a march to Berlin. (When asked in 1911 if he thought about war, he replied, "Yes, I think about it all the time. We shall have a war, I will make it, and I will win it.") To the French high command, *élan*, or patriotic energy, was expected to bring victory: "The French army . . . no longer

(*Left*) French Marshal Joseph Joffre. (*Right*) Count Alfred von Schlieffen of Germany.

knows any other law than the offense," announced one of Joffre's disciples; "[we need only] to charge the enemy to destroy him." The plan counted on the Russian army attacking Germany from the east by the sixteenth day of mobilization.

The British government suggested that, following the Russian army's mobilization, the other powers help arrange a peaceful solution. Britain was unwilling to back Russia, a move that at this point might have made both Austria-Hungary and Germany consider backing down. The German government still assumed that the British would remain neutral in a war, even if France and Russia were fighting Germany and Austria-Hungary.

The Russian government continued to believe that its resolute support for Serbia might well be enough to force Austria-Hungary to back down. Austria-Hungary and its ally, Germany, were laboring under the same kind of illusion about Russia. Both believed that a show of unconditional support—Germany's "blank check" to Austria-Hungary—would force Russia to pull back. Yet Germany's aggressive support for its ally, combined with the bellicose prodding of the Russian government by the French ambassador, had just the opposite effect.

The Serb government therefore ordered military mobilization on July 25, 1914, confident of full Russian support. It then presented a formal reply to the Austro-Hungarian ultimatum. This reply, which reached the Austrian government just before the forty-eight hours had elapsed, seemed surprisingly conciliatory. The Serbs accepted five of the demands without reservation; four others they would accept pending discussion and some further explanation. They rejected only one outright, that the

Austro-Hungarian government send representatives to collaborate in the investigation of the Serb "plot" against it.

The Austro-Hungarian government viewed anything less than total compliance as unsatisfactory. It ordered military mobilization against Serbia, but stopped short of declaring war. The British again proposed a meeting of the powers in the hope of avoiding conflict in the Balkans, or at least keeping it limited to the Balkans. Germany rejected such a plan, believing that Britain would not go to war unless it appeared that Germany was intending to conquer and absorb France.

"A Jolly Little War"

Austria-Hungary declared war on Serbia on July 28, 1914, exactly one month after the archduke's assassination. The declaration claimed an unsatisfactory Serbian response to the Austro-Hungarian ultimatum, as well as an attack on Austro-Hungarian troops along the Bosnian frontier, an event that never took place. In a final attempt to avert war, British Foreign Secretary Edward Grey asked if Germany would participate in an attempt to negotiate a settlement to the crisis. Germany accepted, but at the same time did nothing to try to forestall an Austro-Hungarian invasion of Serbia. If anything, Bethmann-Hollweg egged his ally on, recalling the two occasions on which the Habsburg government had backed down, thereby allowing itself to be bullied by Serbia. In St. Petersburg, the Austro-Hungarian declaration of war generated popular support for Serbia. An American diplomat reported tersely, "Whole country, all classes, unanimous for war."

On July 28, the same day as the Austro-Hungarian war declaration, Bethmann-Hollweg sent his own telegram to Vienna, expressing anxiety that, in view of various proposals from Britain that the great powers mediate the conflict, Germany ran the risk of being blamed for a European war. The telegram also suggested that its ally find a way to make it appear that, if war did come, it would be Russia's fault. And finally he warned that if the Russians did not pull back in their support of Serbia, Austria must stay the course, even if it led to war, or forever renounce its status as a great power.

By the time the British cabinet discussed the Serbian crisis on July 24, it was clear that Germany would not, as in 1912, restrain Austria-Hungary. The Liberals, who had come to power in 1905, had long opposed entangling international alliances and large military expenditures, and they were divided over British intervention, at least partially because many Liberals and most Laborites disliked the idea of fighting alongside autocratic Russia. The government was beset by a number of pressing political issues: a revival of labor militancy, the movement for women's suffrage, the refusal of the Conservative-dominated House of Lords to pass the budget, the subsequent reduction of the Lords' powers by the House of Commons, and, last but hardly least, the Home Rule Bill for Ireland. British politicians and the public were principally preoccupied with the Home Rule crisis—on July 16, British troops had fired on rioters in Dublin—and with vacation plans for the unusually sunny summer. The Royal Navy was placed on alert, so that it could fulfill Britain's obligation to France: to protect the Channel from German warships. By July 29, everyone recognized that Britain might well be drawn into the conflict, particularly if Germany marched into Belgium. In Berlin, rumors and then word of Russia's military preparation alarmed Helmuth von Moltke (1848–1916), chief of the German general staff. Should Russia mobilize, Germany would have to move quickly against France.

Bethmann-Hollweg now sent a sealed envelope to the German ambassador in Brussels, which he was to present to the Belgian government when ordered to do so. The envelope contained a demand that German troops be allowed to march through Belgium. But, for the moment, there still seemed to be hope. William II sent a telegram to the tsar, expressing his desire for peace, and assuring him that he was urging Austria-Hungary "to deal honestly and to arrive at a satisfactory understanding with you." He signed it, "your very sincere and devoted friend and cousin, Willy."

Russian ministers and generals had debated since July 28 whether the crisis called for a limited mobilization of a million soldiers on the Polish and Galician frontiers, or a full mobilization. On July 29, word reached St. Petersburg that the Austrians had bombarded Belgrade from the Danube. French Ambassador Paléologue continued to assure Russian officials that France would fight Germany. After twice changing his mind, Nicholas II ordered a full mobilization on July 30 for the following day. The tsar's diary entry for that day read: "After lunch, I received Sazonov. . . . I went for a walk by myself. The weather was hot. . . . I had a delightful bath in the sea." The Russian mobilization put an end to any hope for a negotiated settlement to the crisis. Francis Joseph also succumbed to his generals' pressure, declaring a general Austro-Hungarian mobilization against Russia and Serbia.

A mood of anxious excitement prevailed in Paris. The army had already taken cautious steps to ready France's frontier defenses, but French troops were pulled back several kilometers from the frontier in order to avoid any incident with German units. In France, only the Socialist Party spoke out against the imminent outbreak of the international war that had seemed probable for so long. Many socialists still hoped that French and German workers would lay down their weapons and refuse to fire on fellow proletarians. Anti-militarism ran deep in some of France, not only because the army took sons away from farms, industrial work, and families, but also because the French government used the army to break strikes. The government maintained a list of socialists and other leaders of the left to be arrested in the event that war was declared.

In the meantime, the Russian and French ambassadors were hounding British officials, demanding assurance of British military support. The

French ambassador even asked rhetorically if the word "honor" would be stricken from British dictionaries if Britain refused to join France and Russia against Germany and Austria-Hungary. Britain, which had for centuries wanted to avoid the presence of a hostile power across the Channel in one of the Low Countries, asked both Germany and France for a guarantee that Belgian neutrality (which had been accepted by Britain, France, Austria, Prussia, and Russia in 1839) would not be violated. Germany did not reply, Bethmann-Hollweg having earlier referred to the old guarantee as "a scrap of paper."

In Berlin, even the Social Democratic newspapers now accepted war as inevitable, declaring tsarist Russia the enemy. Moltke pushed for a German attack on France, fearing that should Russian mobilization proceed any further, the Schlieffen Plan for a two-front war might fail. On July 31, 1914, Germany warned Russia to suspend mobilization at once. At the same time, the German ambassador demanded that France guarantee its own neutrality in the event of a Russo-German war, and that German troops be allowed to occupy a number of French frontier forts as a show of French good faith. This no French government could accept. When no response was heard from either Russia or France, the German army began mobilization for war on August 1.

The relentless logic of the entangling alliances and military plans propelled Europe to war, as if the great powers were being pitched forward on an enormous wave. In Britain, Edward Grey's frantic attempts to arrange a direct negotiation between Russia and Austria failed. The struggle of socialists in many countries to rally opposition against the war fell far short. On July 31, a rightist assassinated the popular French socialist leader Jean Jaurès. But Jaurès, too, had apparently just come to the conclusion that he should support the war effort against autocratic Germany. The Austrian socialist leader Victor Adler predicted: "Jaurès's murder is just the beginning. War unchains instincts, all forms of madness."

Of the powers, only Italy, bound to the Triple Alliance if its estranged allies were attacked, was not committed by alliance to fight. France ordered mobilization after receiving the impossible German demands. Germany declared war on Russia that same day, August 1. This obliged France, by virtue of its alliance with Russia, to fight Germany. German troops invaded Luxembourg, claiming falsely that a French attack on them was imminent and that they needed to seize the small duchy's railroads to defend themselves. On August 2, the German ambassador in Brussels handed the Belgian government the sealed letter requesting permission to march armies through its territory. The negative reply came the next morning. Britain assured France that the Royal Navy would defend its Channel ports. On August 3, Germany declared war on France, falsely claiming that French planes had attacked Nuremberg. When Moltke's army marched into eastern Belgium shortly thereafter, the British government formally demanded that the German armies withdraw. German troops kept marching toward the massive Belgium fortress at Liège. On August 4, 1914, Britain declared war on Germany.

Enthusiastic crowds toasted departing soldiers in Paris with champagne, shouting, "*À Berlin!*" Joyful throngs toasted departing soldiers in Berlin with beer, shouting, "*Nach Paris!*" The German crown prince anticipated "a jolly little war."

THE OUTBREAK OF WAR

When war was declared, eager commanders put long-standing military plans into effect. The German general staff counted on a rapid victory against France in the west before the giant Russian army could effectively be brought into action in the east. But anticipating a quick victory, German troops outflanked French defenses by invading Belgium. However, this violation of Belgian neutrality inevitably brought Britain into the war on the side of France and Russia. Thus, the Great War pitted the Triple Alliance (Germany and Austria-Hungary, minus Italy, which for the moment remained neutral) against the Triple Entente (France, Great Britain, and Russia). These alignments had been shaped by the international tensions of the past decades.

Alfred von Schlieffen's last words had been "Keep the right wing [of the attacking armies] strong." Yet, his successor as chief of the German general staff, Helmuth von Moltke, reduced the strength of the attacking

(*Left*) French soldiers depart for war. (*Right*) British men surge toward a recruiting office.

force by bolstering German defenses in Alsace-Lorraine. Moltke also eliminated the Netherlands from the invasion plan for lack of men; the German army would pass through southern Belgium. The French high
command, which had known the basics of the Schlieffen Plan for years,
did not believe the German army could move rapidly through Belgium, in
part because the attacking forces would have to overcome the imposing
fortress at Liège. The French also knew that the plan called for the incorporation of reserves into the main German army, and doubted they could
quickly become an able fighting force. In any case, the French expected a
frontal attack between the Meuse River and the hills of the Ardennes in
northeastern France. But having miscalculated the size of the German
fighting force, the French also underestimated the speed with which their
enemy could mobilize for war and attack.

Opening Hostilities

The Schlieffen Plan dictated the course of the opening hostilities and the
stalemate that followed. It was as if Schlieffen's "dead hand automatically
pulled the trigger" when the Belgian government on August 2 rejected the
German demand that its armies be permitted to march through Belgium.
Although the Belgians fought bravely against vastly superior strength,
Liège fell on August 16 after a massive bombardment, followed by the fall
of Namur. The Germans easily forced King Leopold's army to retreat westward to Antwerp. But Moltke deployed seven divisions to prevent the Bel-
gian army from escaping. This weakened the attacking forces that
Schlieffen intended to drive as rapidly as possible toward the English
Channel.

German armies, supplied by 500 trains that crossed the bridges of the
Rhine River each day, also defeated the French in battles around Metz.
General Alexander von Kluck, commander of the First German army, then
turned his troops toward the Belgian town of Mons. He hoped to force the
French to surrender before they could bring up more troops from the Paris
region. French advances in Alsace, although anticipated by Schlieffen,
now convinced the Germans to divert troops to that border region from
their primary attacking force attempting to encircle the French capital.
Both the French and German high commands considered success in
Alsace critical to their strategies and to morale at home.

The British Expeditionary Force arrived to take its place on the French
flank on August 20, reaching Mons two days later. One British soldier who
went off to war in the summer of 1914 reassured his family, "At least the
thing will be over in three weeks." But by August 24, the Allied (Entente
Powers) armies were rapidly retreating. At Mons and then Le Cateau, the
British army fought its biggest battles since Waterloo in 1815. Its retreat
did not yet spell defeat. The Germans, fatigued by the pace of their march,
also suffered from Moltke's indecision and inadequate communications.

Old and new combat in World War I.

Kluck's army was already spread too thinly across a wide front. Moltke further weakened the attacking force by sending still more troops to defend Alsace. Then, reacting to the news of a preliminary Russian victory on the eastern front, he sent four divisions to the east to confront the surprisingly rapid Russian advance.

Nonetheless, the German armies managed to fight to within thirty-five miles of Paris (see Map 22.3). The French government provisionally withdrew to the safety of Bordeaux on the southwest coast, just as they had been forced to do during the disastrous Franco-Prussian War. But despite heavy losses, French Marshal Joseph Joffre was able to reinforce his defensive positions around Paris. This was possible because the French had concluded a secret treaty by which Italy agreed to remain neutral if Germany attacked France. Germany, unaware of the treaty, hoped to ally with Italy. The Italian government was playing both sides against each other, assuring its Austro-Hungarian and German treaty partners of its loyalty, while telling Britain at the same time that Germany and Austria-Hungary were the aggressors. In any case, the Italian commitment to its allies was defensive. Joffre could thus count on troops that otherwise would have been needed in southeastern France to halt a possible Italian invasion.

The French managed to wear down the German offensive. At the dawn of air warfare, a French reconnaissance pilot noticed Kluck's army changing direction as it swept toward a point southeast of Paris, leaving its flank open. The French army rushed every available soldier into action, some arriving at the front in requisitioned Parisian taxis. When the Germans crossed the Marne River on September 5, the French counterattacked. Two German armies retreated, fearing that the French might take advantage of a sizable gap between their forces. It was the end of the Schlieffen Plan, and of the offensive war that the German generals had planned. The British poured through another gap between the German armies, forcing the Germans to retreat forty miles to the Aisne River. There, on September 14, the Germans fortified their position by digging deep defensive trenches. Like the Battle of Valmy in 1792 during the French Revolution, the Battle of the Marne saved France in 1914.

The Germans then tried to outflank the British and French forces—Schlieffen's strategy in the first place. This led to what amounted to a race for the sea, as the Allied armies kept pace, holding much of Picardy and Flanders, before both sides ran out of space. The British and French, too, dug in.

A series of attacks and counterattacks in the fall took frightful tolls, with neither side able to break through. In November 1914, the last open battle of the western front was fought in the mud around Ypres in Belgium; the British prevented the Germans from reaching the Channel ports in France. By the end of the year, German and French forces had combined casualties of 300,000 killed and 600,000 wounded. The British Seventh Division arrived in France in October with 400 officers and 12,000 soldiers: after eighteen days of fighting around Ypres, it had 44 officers and 2,336 men left. In a special British battalion of football players, originally brought together to play exhibition matches near the front and then sent to fight like everybody else, only 30 of 200 survived.

THE CHANGING NATURE OF WAR

The German and Allied armies stared at each other across a broad front that reached from the English Channel to Switzerland. Two long, thin lines of trenches punctured the dreams of rapid victory based upon a mastery of offensive tactics. Few analysts had considered the possibility of a frozen front that would rarely move more than a few hundred yards in either direction and along which several million soldiers would die.

Besides trench warfare, new weapons dramatically changed the nature of battle. Before the war finally ended, poison gas, hand grenades, flamethrowers, tanks, military airplanes, and submarines had entered the arsenals of both sides. More than this, a new scale of warfare required an unparalleled, total mobilization of the home front to sustain the war effort.

Trench Warfare

In trench warfare, spades for digging trenches and rows of tangled barbed wire became more important than the rifle and bayonet, weapons of attack. Soldiers on both sides dug about 6,250 miles of trench in France. The front-line trenches were six to eight feet deep and about fifty yards to a mile apart. They were supplemented by support trenches several hundred yards to the rear and linked by communications trenches. Small fortress-like "strong points" held the line together even if part of the system was overrun. Sandbags and rows of barbed wire protected the trenches from attack. As the months passed in sectors where the front

MAP 22.3 THE GERMAN ADVANCE, 1914   The Germans moved quickly into Belgium and France, largely following the Schlieffen Plan of 1905.

Paul Nash's *We Are Making a New World*, a tormented painting evoking the pockmarked landscape around Ypres in Flanders.

lines were immobile, the trenches became more elaborate, offering at least electricity and a certain minimal level of comfort. When there was no fighting, the soldiers confronted boredom. The French theater star Sarah Bernhardt, who had herself lost one leg to amputation (because of several bad falls) was carried on a stretcher near the front so she could entertain soldiers by reciting poetry. Some soldiers read voraciously to pass the time; the British poet Siegfried Sassoon was only half kidding when he remembered, "I didn't want to die, not before I'd finished reading *The Return of the Native* anyway." Since they were below ground, the trenches offered soldiers some protection from rifle or pistol fire, but not from direct artillery hits. The periscope, sticking up from the trench below, provided the only safe way of looking across at the enemy lines without being shot by enemy snipers.

The front-line soldier lived amidst the thunder of barrages and the scream of falling shells. Persistent lice, mice, and enormous starving rats were his constant companions in the stagnant water of the trenches. So, for many, was venereal disease, contracted in the brothels near the front. A British soldier described a night in the trenches in January 1916:

> Lights out. Now the rats and the lice are the masters of the house. You can hear the rats nibbling, running, jumping, rushing from plank to plank, emitting their little squeals behind the dugout's corrugated metal. It's a noisy swarming activity that just won't stop. At any moment I expect one to land on my nose. And then it's the lice and

fleas that begin to devour me. Absolutely impossible to get any shut-eye. Toward midnight I begin to doze off. A terrible racket makes me jump. Artillery fire, the cracking of rifle and machine-gun fire. The Boches [Germans] must be attacking. . . . Everything shakes. Our artillery thunders away without pause. . . . I doze off so as to get up at six. The rats and the lice get up too; waking to life is also waking to misery.

The cold and wind tore into the troops, especially in winter. "Before you can have a drink," one soldier wrote home, "you have to chip away the ice. The meat is frozen solid, the potatoes are bonded by ice, and even the hand grenades are welded together in their cases." The German army had been so sure of an easy victory that it had not equipped its men with high lace-up boots or adequate coats. German troops prized the British soldiers' sheepskin coats and removed them from enemy corpses when they had the chance. After battle, the screams of the wounded and dying filled the air; groans in German, French, and English from no-man's-land grew increasingly faint, but sometimes lasted for days.

Death was everywhere. A French soldier remembered, "We all had on us the stench of dead bodies. The bread we ate, the stagnant water we drank, everything we touched had a rotten smell." Death numbed. An Austrian soldier, a violinist, wrote: "A certain fierceness arises in you, an absolute indifference to anything the world holds except your duty of fighting. You are eating a crust of bread, and a man is shot dead in the trench next to you. You look calmly at him for a moment, and then go on eating your bread. Why not? There is nothing to be done. In the end you talk of your own death with as little excitement as you would of a luncheon engagement." Hundreds of thousands of soldiers suffered shell shock, psychologically devastated by the battle raging around them, unable to act.

Massive attacks were preceded by an intensive bombardment of enemy positions. Such bombardments, lasting hours and even days, clearly indicated where the next attack could be expected, allowing the enemy to bring up sufficient reserves to prevent a breakthrough. Both sides adopted the use of "creeping barrages," which moved just ahead of the attacking army to soften resistance. The shelling mangled the terrain, leaving huge craters and dislodging corpses, thereby creating unanticipated obstacles to the attacking troops. The attackers then faced the most effective weapon of trench warfare, the machine gun—it, too, a defensive weapon that mowed down line after line of advancing soldiers carrying rifles, bayonets, and pistols that they often never had a chance to use.

Piles of the dead filled shell craters left by the first barrages. If attacking Allied troops managed to reach, take, and hold the first line of trenches, they confronted fresh reinforcements as well as an even more solid second line of defense, which the Germans had been able to construct at their leisure. The defensive lines had an elastic quality to them; they could bend, but then snap back against attacking forces that soon outran their cover. Joffre's second offensive in Champagne in 1915 illustrated this situation well. The French offensive ran right into the second line of defense, took enormous casualties, and then faced a vigorous counterattack. The Germans lost 75,000 killed and wounded, the French 145,000, for not more than a few miles of ravaged land. Still, Joffre ordered another attack. The result was the same.

Soldiers also faced new, frightening perils. German attacks against British positions around Ypres featured a horrifying new weapon, mustard gas, which was carried by the wind and burned out the lungs of the British soldiers. A member of the British medical corps wrote, "I shall never forget the sights I saw by Ypres after the first gas attacks. Men lying all along the side of the road . . . exhausted, gasping, frothing yellow mucus from their mouths, their faces blue and distressed. It was dreadful, and so little could be done for them." The gas mask soon offered imperfect protection—"this pig snout which represented the war's true face," as one combatant put it.

War in the Air and on the Seas

Airplanes became weapons of combat. In the first months of the war, airplanes were only used for reconnaissance in good weather. But in October 1914, a British plane took off from Antwerp and destroyed a hangar in Düsseldorf with two twenty-pound bombs the pilot dropped over the side. Some pilots kept carrier pigeons in a cage, so that, if they had to ditch

(*Left*) French soldiers wearing gas masks prepare to attack. (*Right*) Victims of a German gas attack lining up at a field hospital.

their planes, they could scribble their approximate location on a paper and send the information back to headquarters with the bird. Pilots fired pistols and hurled hand grenades and even bricks at enemy planes and troops before both sides discovered that machine guns could be mounted and timed to fire between the blades of the plane's propellers.

By the end of 1916, dashing and brave "aces," such as the German Red Baron, Manfred von Richthofen, and later the American Eddie Rickenbacker, chased each other around the skies, cheered on by the trench soldiers. When Richthofen was shot down behind British lines in April 1918, he was buried by his enemies with full military honors. Although the "dogfights" of combat in the skies had a romantic dimension, the airplane soon began to terrorize civilians. Paris and particularly London were bombed several times during the war, as the speed and capacity of the first warplanes increased; the Rhineland German cities suffered heavy bombardments later in the conflict. By the war's end, Germany had produced more than 47,000 aircraft, France more than 51,000, and Britain more than 55,000 planes.

With the European powers fighting a land war unlike any ever seen, and conflict having taken to the skies, the seas remained relatively quiet. There the British navy retained command; the famed and feared German Dreadnoughts, those enormous battleships that had helped fuel the Anglo-German naval rivalry before the war, stayed in port. The British navy won a series of initial encounters as far afield as the coast of Chile, the Falkland Islands near Argentina, and the Indian Ocean. German battleships trapped in the Mediterranean at the beginning of the war took refuge in Constantinople and were turned over to the Turks. The German navy took them back when Turkey entered the war on the side of the Central Powers. The Austro-Hungarian navy, based in Trieste, was small and its influence was limited to the Mediterranean. The British admiralty, which possessed the German code book—plucked from the Baltic Sea by Russian sailors—awaited a major confrontation, another Trafalgar. Certain that the German fleet was going to sail from Wilhelmshaven, the British Grand Fleet lay in wait. At Dogger Bank on January 24, 1915, the Royal Navy sunk a German battleship. For the remainder of the war, the British were able to blockade the principal German ports, effectively neutralizing the kaiser's proud fleet.

Late in the 1880s, several countries had experimented with underwater warfare. At the turn of the century, the U.S. Navy was the first to commission a submarine. Although all of the powers had submarines by the time of the Great War, those of Germany made the greatest impact. The German navy believed that its fleet of submarines, which brought another fearful dimension to warfare, could force Britain to pull out of the war by sinking its warships and by preventing supplies from reaching the British Isles. In September 1914, a German submarine, or "U-boat," sank three large British armored cruisers off the coast of Belgium. U-boats, 188 feet

German and British planes in a dogfight high above the trenches.

long and with a range of 2,400 miles, could slip in and out of port undetected.

Germany came to depend ever more on unrestricted submarine warfare against Allied shipping in the North Atlantic, but this later had the catastrophic effect of bringing the United States into the war as an enemy.

Support from the Home Front

The waging of war on such an unprecedented scale required the full support of the "home front," the very concept of which emerged during the Great War. Sustaining the massive war effort depended first on mobilizing enough soldiers and food to supply the front, and then on producing enough guns and shells. It also depended on maintaining morale at home. With both sides disappointed by the failure to win a quick victory, popular enthusiasm increasingly fed on a deep hatred of the enemy. German propagandists portrayed the war as a fight for German culture, besieged by Russian barbarians and the dishonorable French. A German soldier wrote, "We know full well that we are fighting for the German idea in the world, that we are defending German feeling against Asiatic barbarism and Latin indifference." British propagandists depicted the Allies as defending law, liberty, and progress against German violations of national sovereignty and international law. German harshness in dealing with Belgian civilians in the first months of the war convinced the British population more than ever that their cause was just. French propagandists had the easiest case to make: Germany had, after all, invaded France.

Such propaganda mixed elements of myth and truth, a potent concoction. By the end of 1914, tales of Germans impaling children and raping nuns were horrifying British and French readers. The German execution in Belgium of the British nurse Edith Cavell, accused of helping British prisoners escape, outraged people in Britain and France. Germans shot many civilians in the Belgian town of Dinant and shelled the twelfth-century Cathedral of Reims. ("Better that a thousand church towers fall than one German soldier should fall as a result of these towers," explained one German historian at the time.) These actions foreshadowed a new kind of war—a total war in which civilians were not spared. At the outbreak of hostilities, shops owned by people with German-sounding names were pillaged in Britain and France (in the latter case, many of the victims were French Alsatians for whom the war, at least in part, was supposedly being fought). Not long after the war began, a French teacher told his pupils, "We must eradicate to the last stone and to the last individual this race of vipers that is the Prussian race." A publication for French schoolchildren told a story, "Your little brother in your presence has lied to your mother. You take him aside and tell him, 'Do you want to behave like the Krauts?' " The younger boy confesses, now understanding that "the French don't lie." A publication for girls informed them that "pillage is a German word." German propaganda similarly smeared their enemies, particularly the British, who supposedly used dum-dum bullets that exploded upon impact and who gouged out the eyes of German prisoners. Publications for German schoolchildren emphasized the country's "combat for existence" and the spirit of collective sacrifice in the name of the fatherland.

The outbreak of the war pushed aside bitter political divisions at home. In France, competing parties proclaimed a "sacred union," and Jules Guesde, a socialist, became minister of commerce. There was little public criticism of the way the war was being run until later in the conflict when casualties mounted. In Germany, too, socialist opposition to militarism based on class solidarity quickly turned to patriotic support. In Russia, only the tsar's will seemed to matter. In Austria-Hungary, the ability of the imperial bureaucracy to supply its multinational army, the prestige of which had helped keep the Habsburg empire together, seemed almost miraculous. Tensions between the empire's nationalities remained beneath the surface, at least in the war's early years.

In Britain, the angry quarrels over strategy among the generals, as well as between them and the cabinet, were well hidden from the public. A volunteer army was raised with remarkable enthusiasm and speed, aided by an effective recruitment poster sporting the face of Lord Horatio Kitchener, the secretary of war (leading Prime Minister Lord Asquith to observe, "He is not a great man. He is a great poster"). On a single day in September 1914, 33,000 men joined up. By the end of the year, the

British had 2 million men in uniform. The volunteer force that German Kaiser William II had called "a comtemptible little army" fought very well.

David Lloyd George skillfully oversaw the transition from peacetime to wartime industrial production, using the powers specified by the Munitions of War Act of May 1915. The act forbade strikes and provided for the requisition of skilled workers for labor in factories, which were converted to the production of war materiel. Supplying the front with shells alone was a monumental task. The nineteen-day artillery barrage at the third Battle of Ypres in 1917 expended all the shells carried to the front by 321 trains, the output of a year's work for 55,000 armament workers.

The war spurred other changes in daily life at home. As heavy drinking became more widespread, legislation restricted the operating hours of British pubs. Some complained that the war had brought Britain a loosening of morals, frivolous dress and dancing, and an increase in juvenile delinquency. Daylight savings time was introduced for the first time to conserve fuel. A successful campaign for voluntary rationing of essential commodities such as sugar allowed the British to avoid mandatory rationing until early 1917, when shortages were generated by hoarding. The government instituted a coupon system, but, in fact, price controls on essential commodities served to ration food.

Suffragette leaders, who had put aside their campaign for women's right to vote, threw their support behind the war. Millicent Garrett Fawcett

(*Left*) In the perfect recruitment poster, Lord Kitchener summons British males to join the army. (*Right*) A poster showing support from the home front.

(1847–1929), a leading British feminist, appealed to the readers of a suffrage magazine: "Women, your country needs you. . . . Let us show ourselves worthy of Citizenship." She announced that she considered pacifism almost the equivalent of treason. Some of the members of the Pankhurst family, committed suffragettes, now spoke at bond-selling rallies, and two members urged supporters to beat up pacifists.

In every belligerent country, women made varied contributions to the war. Nurses in every country served heroically at the front and were acclaimed as heroines. With so many men dead, injured, or still at the front, beginning in 1915 over 1 million British women stepped into jobs from which they had previously been excluded, ranging from skilled and semiskilled jobs in munitions factories ("Shells made by a wife may save a husband's life" went one public poster in Britain) to positions as tram conductors and gas-meter readers. A visitor to Berlin in March 1916 reported "no men anywhere, women are doing everything."

THE WAR RAGES ON

Early in 1915, the French general staff predicted that its army would break through the German lines. However French attacks in the spring in Champagne and then in Artois further north brought enormous casualties but little progress (see Map 22.4). A British assault at Neuve Chapelle on March 10 gained 1,000 yards at a cost of 13,000 casualties. The Allied offensives in 1915 demonstrated that neither side could effect a breakthrough against enemy forces. *Élan* was not enough. In 1916 during the murderous Battle of the Somme, a British captain sought to inspire his men by jumping out of the trench and leading the attack by dribbling a soccer ball across no-man's-land. He was shot dead far from the goal.

The British lost almost 300,000 men in 1915 alone; the Germans, who had a much larger army, took at least 610,000 casualties. Both nation's casualties, however daunting, paled alongside those of the French, who suffered 1,292,000 killed and wounded in 1915. French infantrymen were not helped by the fact that their uniform pants were, at least in the early stages of the war, bright red, which could be more easily seen through the morning mists than the German gray.

Fighting also engulfed the eastern front, where the Russian army fought both German and Austro-Hungarian forces. In 1915, Italy entered the war on the Allied side. The struggle between Britain and Turkey— which was also allied with the Central Powers—carried the war into the Middle East. Japan, coveting several German islands in the Pacific and seeking sanction for its interest in a province of northeastern China, entered the war on the Allied side in 1914. What began as a European war became a world war.

MAP 22.4 THE WESTERN FRONT, 1914–1917   Major battles from 1914–1917, and location of trenches at the end of 1915 and at the end of 1917.

The Eastern Front

Having failed to achieve the anticipated quick victory in the west, German forces now fought on two fronts. In the wide-open spaces of the eastern front, the Russian armies had advanced into eastern Prussia despite the incompetence of the Russian general staff, intense animosity among commanders, hopelessly archaic equipment, and communications so inadequate that the Germans could easily listen to Russian officers discussing tactics on the telephone. In late summer 1914, the German army drove the Russians back, inflicting over 250,000 casualties. A Russian general committed suicide in despair. On the more confident German side, sixty-seven-year-old General Paul von Hindenburg (1847–1934), a stolid Prus-

MAP 22.5 THE EASTERN, ITALIAN, AND BALKAN FRONTS Russian and Austro-German advances and battles along the eastern front; Austro-Hungarian and Italian armies face off along the Italian front; and Turkish and Allied armies clash on the Balkan front.

sian who had been called out of retirement, and the determined and organized General Erich Ludendorff (1865–1937) embellished their reputations in these battles.

The Central Powers, with no joint plan of military coordination, eventually found the huge Russian army an imposing foe. In addition, the

Austro-Hungarian army had diverted too many divisions in the punitive invasion of strategically unimportant Serbia. In September 1914, the Russians captured the fortress of Lemberg in Galicia from the Austro-Hungarian armies, and took 100,000 prisoners (see Map 22.5). Many of these were conscripted Slavs, who felt more allegiance to their fellow Slavic Russians than to their German-speaking officers.

In January 1915, the Habsburg forces launched an offensive against the Russian army in the Carpathian Mountains. Although the offensive looked good on a map, the reality was otherwise. Snow-covered mountains posed a daunting obstacle: supplies had to be moved over ice or freezing marsh; low clouds obscured artillery targets; and soldiers had to warm their rifles over fires before they could use them. When the Russians counterattacked, they found "men already cut to pieces and defenseless. . . . Every day hundreds froze to death; the wounded who could not drag themselves off were bound to die; riding became impossible; and there was no combating the apathy and indifference that gripped the men." The Germans had to send troops to support their ally in the Carpathians, and as a result they lost over 350,000 men. With the stalemate in the west, the Germans wanted to beat the Russians before the latter could defeat the Habsburg army. In May 1915, a massive German attack tore into the Russian army, driving it back almost 100 miles. The Russian retreat, which had been orderly in the beginning, turned into "a mad bacchanalia," with Cossacks abducting female refugees. A million civilians moved eastward with the Russian armies; "while thousands of people trudge along the railway lines they are passed by speeding trains loaded with couches from officers' clubs, and carrying quartermasters' bird cages." The Russian retreat from the Carpathian Mountains gave the Austro-Hungarian forces some badly needed breathing room.

The Central Powers could not look to Italy for help. Italy had remained neutral at the outbreak of the war but gave in to street demonstrations and entered the war on the Allied side through the secret Treaty of London, signed in April 1915. Britain and France held out as bait territories many Italian nationalists claimed as part of "Italian Irredenta" ("unredeemed lands"), including the Tyrol in the Alps and Istria along the northern Adriatic coast. Italian nationalism, as well as the desire of powerful Italian businessmen to find new markets in the Balkans, had proved stronger than Italy's pre-war commitment to its former allies. Austria-Hungary now found itself, like Germany, fighting a war on two fronts. The Italians attacked with the port of Trieste as their goal. In the meantime, the German armies reached Brest-Litovsk in August 1915, ending 100 years of Russian control of Poland. In all, about 1 million Russian soldiers were killed or wounded on the front, and another 1 million were captured.

The War in the Middle East, Africa, and the Far East

British military and political leaders were divided between those who believed that victory would have to be won in the west, and others who pushed for a series of dramatic strikes against Germany or its allies on Europe's periphery. The latter included Winston Churchill (1874–1965), the First Lord of the Admiralty, and David Lloyd George, the Liberal politician who headed the wartime Ministry of Munitions. Such victories might also help expand the British Empire, which pleased the colonial lobby at home. This strategy angered the French government, which bitterly opposed any reduction of British support on the western front.

Churchill and Lord Kitchener planned an attack on Germany's ally, Turkey. Since entering the war on the side of Germany and Austria-Hungary in November 1914, the Turks closed off the Dardanelles Strait, which separates the Aegean Sea from the Sea of Marmara. This cut off an important route for supplies to Russia through the Black Sea. Turkish forces also tied up Russian troops in the Caucasus Mountains. Now Turkey posed a potential threat to the Suez Canal. The British high command planned an assault on the Dardanelles Strait. If everything went well, a British success might bring an end to the power of the pro-German faction in Constantinople. With Turkey out of the war,

British troops massing during the ill-fated Gallipoli campaign.

Churchill reasoned, the German effort in the Balkans could be undermined, and Bulgaria would stay out of the conflict.

Following a month-long naval bombardment of Turkish forts, a predominantly British fleet of thirteen battleships entered the Dardanelles Strait in March 1915. After running into a line of mines left along the shore and losing three battleships, the warships retreated. In April, the fleet returned, disembarking five divisions on the beach of Gallipoli (see Map 22.5). The British army hurled itself against the well-defended heights held by the Turks. British troops managed to dig in, and in August launched an assault that failed miserably. After committing more than 400,000 men, half of whom were killed or wounded, the British were fortunate to evacuate their remaining forces in January 1916. Amid harsh criticism of the campaign's humiliating failure, Churchill and Kitchener lost influence. To this day, the Gallipoli Campaign remains controversial. Some historians consider it an imaginative, even brilliant stroke that might have won the war. Others agree with most contemporaries who believed that it was a needless diversion dictated by British colonial interests in the Middle East and for which Australian and New Zealander troops paid a disproportionate price.

Still hoping to knock Turkey out of the war, the Allies tried to coax Bulgaria into the war on their side. But Bulgaria coveted neighboring Serbian Macedonia, and in October 1915 joined the Central Powers, who promised Bulgaria much of Thrace and all of Macedonia, which the Allies could not because of Serbian claims. A month later, a Franco-British force landed in Salonika, Greece, to try to help Serbia. But within two months, the German, Austro-Hungarian, and Bulgarian armies had crushed the Serbian army, which by 1916 had suffered 100,000 deaths of the 450,000 men serving in 1914. The Germans called Salonika their "largest internment camp," since that campaign tied up half a million Allied troops in fighting the Bulgarians. The British also fought a desert war against the Turks in Palestine and Mesopotamia.

Smaller British forces were occupied fighting for the German colonies in Africa (see Map 22.6). Togoland fell in August 1914, German Southwest Africa in 1915, and the German Cameroons in 1916. The fighting in German East Africa (Tanganyika) went on for the duration of the war, pitting German troops against British and South African soldiers, and both sides against mosquitoes and disease. In Asia, Japanese forces captured the fortress and port of Tsingtao (Qingdao) from a German garrison, and the undefended German islands of the Marianas, Carolines, and Marshalls in the North Pacific.

The Western Front

With their failure at Gallipoli, the British again focused on the western front. England was so close to this front that officers who had lunch in

MAP 22.6 THE WORLD WAR   The expansion of the war beyond Europe to the German colonies in Africa and the Far East.

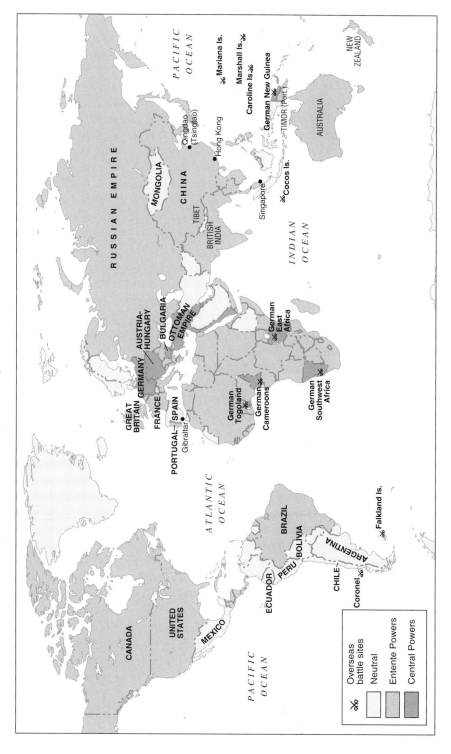

private railroad cars before leaving Victoria Station could be at the front by dinner. When British miners managed to blow up a previously unconquerable ridge near Messines in western Belgium, Lloyd George was said to have heard the explosion at 10 Downing Street in London. General Douglas Haig (1861–1928) was named commander in chief of the British army in France in December 1915. He agreed with Joffre's plan for a mighty offensive in the vicinity of the Somme River. The assault would have to await the arrival of more British soldiers and spring weather. The German army, too, had big plans. The new German commander in chief, General Erich von Falkenhayn (1861–1922), planned an assault on the fortresses surrounding Verdun in eastern France. These had been neglected by the French, who had shipped off some artillery pieces to points of attack further west. Falkenhayn had no illusions about breaking through the French lines. But he believed that with a massive attack on Verdun, the Germans could "out-attrition" the French, who, by virtue of a lower birthrate, could not afford to lose as many soldiers as their more populous enemy. Assuming that France would lose five men for every two German soldiers killed, Falkenhayn's goal was "to bleed France white." Realizing that even more German victories on the eastern front would not necessarily knock Russia out of the war, and doubting the ability of Austria-Hungary to hold off both the Russians on Germany's eastern front and Italy in the south, the German command needed to force the French to sue for peace.

After nine days of delay because of bad weather, the German artillery began to bombard the French forts stretched around Verdun across a front of eight miles on February 21, 1916 (see Map 22.4). Some of the guns weighed twenty tons; it took nine tractors to move each piece to its place and a crane to load the shells. The French prepared to hold Verdun at all costs. Its loss would be a potentially mortal blow to French morale. In the damp, chilling mists of the hills northeast of Verdun, hundreds of thousands of men died, killed by shells that rained from the sky, machine guns that seemed never to be stilled, or bayonetted in hand-to-hand fighting within and outside the massive cement forts.

The French army held. General Philippe Pétain (1856–1951), the new commander, became a hero in France. But the cost of this victory came close to fulfilling Falkenhayn's expectations. The French lost 315,000 men killed or wounded; 90,000 died at the appropriately named "Dead Man's Hill" alone. The Germans suffered 281,000 casualties. A French counterattack in the fall recaptured several of the forts the Germans had taken; again the casualties mounted. In all, the French suffered 540,000 casualties and the Germans 430,000 casualties at Verdun. At one of the forts, Douaumont, one can still see plaques put up by proud, grieving relatives after the war, one of which reads, "For my son. Since his eyes closed mine have not ceased to cry." Verdun was truly a national battle, in part because a new system of furloughs meant that nearly everyone in the French army spent some time in the hell that was Verdun.

The Battle of Verdun merely postponed plans for a massive British offensive on the Somme River, supported by a similar French thrust. The assault began on July 1 after a week's bombardment. British troops attacked in the sector selected by Joffre, not for strategic or tactical reasons, but because it was where the French and British lines met.

Allied troops climbed out of the trenches at dawn to the whistles of their officers, and moved into no-man's-land. Things could not have gone worse along the eighteen miles of front. Artillery barrages had chopped up the terrain over which the attackers had to struggle but left intact most of the German barbed wire, which the British soldiers found was too strong for their wire cutters. German machine gun emplacements had also survived the barrage. Many British soldiers managed only a few yards before falling with the sixty-six pounds of equipment they were carrying. The Germans moved up reserves to wherever their lines were bending. The British commanders sent wave after wave of infantrymen "over the top" to their death; corpses piled up on top of those who had died seconds, minutes, or hours before. Of 752 men in the First Newfoundland Regiment, all 26 officers and 658 men were killed or wounded within forty minutes. Sixty percent of the 10th Battalion of the West Yorkshires were killed in the initial assault. At the end of the first day of the Battle of the Somme, about 60,000 soldiers of the 110,000 British soldiers had become casualties, including 19,000 killed. (There were more British soldiers killed and wounded in the first three days of the Battle of the Somme than Americans killed in World War I, the Korean War, and the Vietnam War combined, and three times as many killed as had been killed in fifteen years of war against Napoleon.) When the disastrous offensive finally ended in mid-November 1916, Britain had lost 420,000 men killed and wounded. The French lost 200,000 men in what was primarily a British offensive. It cost the Germans 650,000 soldiers to hold on. The maximum German retreat was a few kilometers; in most places, Allied gains were measured in yards. A sign left over one mass grave said, "The Devonshires held this trench, the Devonshires hold it still." The British poet Edmund Blunden, who survived the Battle of the Somme, tried to answer the question of who had won: "By the end of the [first] day both sides had seen, in a sad scrawl of broken earth and murdered men, the answer to the question. No road. No thoroughfare. Neither race had won, nor could win, the War. The War had won, and would go on winning."

Futility and Stalemate

Futility and stalemate also prevailed on the mountainous Austro-Italian front, where in 1916 there were *twelve* different Battles of the Isonzo River. The Italian army considered one of these, the sixth, a great victory because it moved three miles forward. After half a million casualties, the Italians were still only halfway to their objective, the Adriatic port of Trieste.

On the eastern front, General Paul von Hindenburg claimed that there was no way of gauging the number of Russians killed with any accuracy: "All we do know is that, at times, fighting the Russians, we had to remove the piles of enemy bodies from before our trenches, so as to get a clear field of fire against new waves of assault." In June 1916, the Russian offensive pushed back the Austrians by combining smaller surprise attacks by specially trained troops, without the preliminary barrages, against carefully chosen targets. But the arrival of more German troops minimized Russian gains. Each side lost over 1 million men in these encounters.

In 1916, the British poet Isaac Rosenberg, who would later die in battle, wrote "Break of Day in the Trenches," one of the most haunting poems to come out of the war.

> The darkness crumbles away.
> It is the same old druid Time as ever,
> Only a live thing leaps my hand,
> A queer sardonic rat,
> As I pull the parapet's poppy
> To stick behind my ear.
> Droll rat, they would shoot you if they knew
> Your cosmopolitan sympathies.
> Now you have touched this English hand
> You will do the same to a German
> Soon, no doubt, if it be your pleasure
> To cross the sleeping green between.
> It seems you inwardly grin as you pass
> Strong eyes, fine limbs, haughty athletes,
> Less chance than you for life,
> Bonds to the whims of murder,
> Sprawled in the bowels of the earth,
> The torn fields of France.
> What do you see in our eyes
> At the shrieking iron and flame
> Hurled through still heavens?
> What quaver—what heart aghast?
> Poppies whose roots are in man's veins
> Drop, and are ever dropping;
> But mine in my ear is safe—
> Just a little white with the dust.

The winter of 1916–1917 was bleak. There seemed few families on either side who had not lost a relative or friend at the front. On the Allied side, there was some cheer when Romania joined the war in exchange for the promise of some Hungarian territory with a significant Romanian population once the Central Powers had been defeated. But Falkenhayn, removed from the western front in disgrace after Verdun, quickly defeated

The devastation wrought by the Battle of the Somme did not lead to a clear victory for either side.

the Romanians. In southeastern Europe, the war eroded the resources and morale of Bulgaria and Turkey. Both issued declarations expressing their willingness to discuss terms for peace on December 12, 1916. The following March, Emperor Charles I (ruled 1916–1918) of the Austro-Hungarian Empire, who assumed the throne after Francis Joseph's death in November 1916, sent the Allies a peace proposal, without having consulted Germany. It included a willingness to recognize French claims to Alsace-Lorraine. But talk of a compromise peace was hushed and, in most quarters, deemed unpatriotic.

Unlike the French and British, the Germans realized that victory by breakthrough was extremely unlikely, if not impossible. To the Allies, a compromise peace seemed out of the question given that enemy troops were occupying much of the north of France. The complete withdrawal of German troops required a total victory that would guarantee France's future security. Increasingly criticized for the staggering casualty rate, Joffre was replaced by General Robert Nivelle (1856–1924) as commander in chief of the French forces in 1916. Nivelle, promoted rapidly through the officer corps, had led the troops who had heroically stormed Verdun's Fort Douaumont. He insisted that similar tactics on a much larger scale would bring the long-awaited breakthrough in the west.

In Britain, Lloyd George became prime minister in December 1916. Even after staggering losses on the Somme, he, too, thought military victory possible if the Allies cooperated more closely, despite now doubting the claims of British commanders that a breakthrough on the western front was possible. The British government thus rejected a peace note sent by Germany on December 12, the aim of which was to force an end to the war by splitting apart Britain and France.

Soldiers and Civilians

In some ways, life in Britain—as in the other countries—seemed to go on as before, which increasingly outraged soldiers returning from the front. The elegantly dressed upper classes dining in the finest restaurants or watching the races at Derby and Ascot contrasted dramatically with the returning trainloads of badly wounded soldiers. A newspaper headline in 1917 gave equal emphasis to its two lead stories: "Battle Raging At Ypres. Gatwick Racing—Late Wire."

Some big businessmen found the war very profitable. Like workers and labor leaders, the men at the front were angered that profiteers amassed fortunes on war supplies: Anglo-Persian Oil, which had lost money in 1914, enjoyed profits of 85 million pounds in 1916, 344 million in 1917, and over 1 billion in 1918. Profits of rubber companies increased fourfold.

Women took over many of the jobs of men who left to fight in the war. But women workers, as in the past, received lower wages than their male counterparts, allowing many employers to reduce expenses and increase their profits. In France and Austria, women workers went out on strike in 1917 and 1918 to protest working conditions. Everywhere, shortages and economic hardship made women's tasks of managing the household economy that much more difficult, including standing in line for hours at stores. Crowds of women protested high prices in Italy in 1917.

Censorship, particularly in the first year, prevented the population from knowing about the staggering death toll, or about the various strategic blunders of the generals. "The war, for all its devastating appearances, only seems to be destructive," one Parisian newspaper assured its readers in November 1914, and in July 1915 it asserted that "at least [those killed by German bayonets] will have died a beautiful death, in noble battle . . . with cold steel, we shall rediscover poetry . . . epic and chivalrous jousting." Other papers emphatically related that "half the German shells are made of cardboard, they don't even burst," and that "Boche corpses smell worse than [those of the] French."

The British poet Robert Graves wrote that "England looked strange to us soldiers. We could not understand the war-madness that ran wild everywhere, looking for a pseudo-military outlet. The civilians talked a foreign language; and it was newspaper language." Newspapers described troops as itching to go over the top, even after the Battle of the Somme. Lord Northcliffe, the press baron named by the government to provide the public with reports of the war, described the trenches, "where health is so good and indigestion hardly ever heard of. The open-air life, the regular and plenteous feeding, the exercise, and the freedom from care and responsibility, keep the soldiers extraordinarily fit and contented." A French newspaper headline in December 1916 read, preposterously enough, "Among the many victims of gas, there is hardly a single death." The poems of Wilfred Owen emphasized the contrast between those who cheered on the war from the home front and knew little about it, and the soldiers who suffered ("Gas! Gas! Quick, boys! . . . the blood / Come gargling from the froth-corrupted lungs"). A French captain wrote to protest newspaper accounts of heroic fighting and glorious death on the battlefield: "How does [the civilian] picture us combatants? Does he really believe we spend our time brandishing great swords with heroic gestures and yelling 'Long live France!' at the top of our lungs? When will these ladies and gentlemen in civilian life spare us their fantasies?"

The men in the trenches forged close bonds to those with whom they served. They bitterly resented senior officers who barked out deadly orders from the safety of requisitioned châteaux behind the front lines, and they detested government propagandists and censors. On leave, soldiers headed together to music halls, cabarets, and bars, hoping to forget a war they felt uncomfortable trying to describe to civilians who knew so little about it.

More than this, embittered soldiers occasionally felt more sympathy for those in the opposite trenches than for the politicians and generals at home. On Christmas Day, 1914, on the western front in France, German

Russian sharpshooters in a trench on the eastern front.

and British soldiers spontaneously declared their own one-day truce, some meeting in no-man's-land to exchange greetings, souvenirs, and even home addresses. A German juggler surfaced to perform, drawing applause from the opposing British trench. In one or two places, soldiers from both sides played soccer. A year later, a British soldier was executed for ignoring orders that such an event was not to recur. There were even occasional informal arrangements between units that had been facing each other across no-man's-land for several months, agreeing not to fire during mealtimes, or entertaining each other in verse or song, with the most talented singers in the trenches booming songs from their home regions across the battlefield. A British writer later recalled calmly discussing Nietzsche with a German he had captured just minutes after almost killing him. One prevalent rumor in both trenches had an entire regiment of German, French, and British deserters living under no-man's-land in tunnels, coming out only at night to rob corpses and steal food and drink from both sides. They, many soldiers said, were the lucky ones.

What were soldiers to think of the contention of the London *Daily Mirror* in 1916 that the British dead lay on the battlefield looking "more quietly faithful, more simply steadfast than others"? Siegfried Sassoon's "The Hero" attempted to offer a more realistic picture:

> "Jack fell as he'd have wished," the Mother said,
> And folded up the letter that she'd read.
> "The Colonel writes so nicely." Something broke
> In the tired voice that quavered to a choke.
> She half looked up. "We mothers are so proud
> Of our dead soldiers." Then her face was bowed.
> Quietly the Brother Officer went out.
> He'd told the poor old dear some gallant lies
> That she would nourish all her days, no doubt.
> For while he coughed and mumbled, her weak eyes
> Had shone with gentle triumph, brimmed with joy,
> Because he'd been so brave, her glorious boy.
> He thought how "Jack," cold-footed, useless swine,
> Had panicked down the trench that night the mine
> Went up at Wicked Corner; how he'd tried
> To get sent home, and how, at last, he died,
> Blown to small bits. And no one seemed to care
> Except that lonely woman with white hair.

It was impossible to hide the effects of the war. In all combatant countries, women in mourning clothes were an increasingly frequent sight, clutching telegrams that began, "Be proud of X, who has just died like a brave man. . . ." Soldiers who had been badly wounded resented the high-living of the wealthy, who seemed unaffected by the rationing of food and coal. At home, illegitimate births rose rapidly. In Germany, state govern-

German and Russian soldiers mingle together during the war.

ments, except for that of Prussia, for the first time allowed "illegitimate" birth certificates and gave unmarried or widowed women the right to call themselves *Frau* (Mrs.) instead of *Fraulein* (Miss).

As casualties mounted and the fighting ground on, opposition to the war emerged in Britain. The most extreme case was that of the Irish Republicans, who opposed Britain in order to gain Ireland's independence. The Germans encouraged Irish Republican preparations for an insurrection in Dublin set for Easter Sunday, 1916, which was later called the Easter Rising. Sir Roger Casement (1864–1916), an Irish nationalist, tried to form an Irish Legion and urged the Germans to send military assistance. But seeing that the Germans had no plans to offer substantial help, he tried to convince the Irish Republicans to call off the insurrection. They went ahead, surrendering after five days of fighting. Casement was among those executed, traitor to the British, hero to many Irish.

Elsewhere in Britain, a relatively small number of pacifists and conscientious objectors protested against the war. Some of them were prosecuted under the Military Services Act and imprisoned. In 1916, when the British abandoned the volunteer army and adopted conscription, pacifists became more vocal in their opposition. In his *No Conscription Leaflet No. 3*, the writer Lytton Strachey (1880–1932) warned, "The Cat kept saying to the Mouse that she was a high-minded person, and if the Mouse would only come a little nearer they could both get the cheese. The Mouse said, Thank you, Pussy, it's not the cheese you want, it's my skin."

In Germany, Clara Zetkin (1857–1933), a militant socialist, went to jail because she refused to stop denouncing the war and tried to mobilize working-class women against a struggle between capitalist states that pitted worker against worker. Rosa Luxemburg, a Polish socialist living in Germany, also went to prison for her efforts to turn more members of her party against the war.

When Dutch socialists initiated a peace conference in Stockholm in December 1917, Britain prohibited British citizens from attending. Siegfried Sassoon, wounded at the front, returned to England and publicly declared, "I believe the War is being deliberately prolonged by those who have the power to end it. I am a soldier, convinced that I am acting on behalf of soldiers." After being incarcerated in a mental asylum, he returned to the front because of his allegiance to friends more than leaders. There he was wounded again.

The French government faced different problems at home than those confronting Britain. The German armies occupied some of France's richest agricultural land and industrial centers of the north and northeast. Refugees from the war zone arrived in Paris and other towns carrying their remaining possessions. But the French home front held together, despite ebbs and flows in morale as the war went on and on. Although there was grumbling about peasants who profited from price rises for commodities, or about skilled workers, exempt from conscription because munitions factories required their skills, and other "shirkers" who escaped service, there were relatively few signs of opposition to the war in France, at least at the start. The government's decision in the war's first month to provide some financial assistance to families with husbands, brothers, and sons in uniform was popular. The French gradually adapted to the war, remaining confident that the Allies would eventually win. With the German army

Berliners hunt for food.

deep inside France, close to Paris, capitulation was unthinkable, as was even a negotiated settlement.

The German home front also held together. An American newspaper correspondent in 1916 found the Germans "amazingly solid" against giving in: "They have the habit, as have no other people, of obeying." German morale remained generally strong despite severe shortages, bringing the rationing of food, coal, and other essentials. Posters showed an ogre-like British "John Bull," with the caption "This man is responsible for your hunger."

In 1917 in Germany, signs of war weariness increased, as casualties reached astronomic levels and rumors spread that the campaign of unrestricted submarine warfare against the Allies was failing. Open criticism of officials became more common, despite the repressive structure of what remained an authoritarian state. In July, the Reichstag passed a resolution by a large majority asking the government to repudiate a policy of annexation and commit itself to seeking a peace of reconciliation. But the Reichstag had little influence in what amounted to a military government. In Germany, the kaiser dismissed Chancellor Theobald von Bethmann-Hollweg in 1917, giving Generals Hindenburg and Ludendorff even more power. The Reichstag, in any case, did not attack the political structures of the empire itself.

Opposition, however, mounted in the streets. Strikes became more common as the lines outside food shops grew longer. In January 1918, 400,000 workers in Berlin went on strike, demanding a democratization of the government and peace without annexation. Berlin, in contrast with Paris and London, had suffered since 1917 increased shortages of fuel and food, social tensions, and demoralization. More Germans began to express candid opposition to government policies as leaflets proclaimed, "Down with the kaiser! Down with the government!"

THE FINAL STAGES OF THE WAR

In 1917, two events of great consequence changed the course of the war. Reacting in part to a German campaign of unrestricted submarine warfare against Allied shipping, the United States entered the war in April on the Allied side. And Russia withdrew from the war after the Bolsheviks seized power in the October Revolution. Meanwhile, the French armies seemed on the verge of collapse, with widespread mutinies occurring within French divisions in response to a series of catastrophic offensives. And a massive German offensive that began in March 1918 pushed Allied forces back further than they had been since 1914, before grinding to a halt in the face of stiff resistance. The stage was set for the final phase of the war.

The United States Enters the War

In 1916, Woodrow Wilson had been re-elected president of the United States on the platform "He kept us out of war." The U.S. government had adopted a declaration of neutrality, but American popular sympathy generally lay with the Allies, even though the German government tried to capitalize on American resentment of the British blockade, which entailed searches of American ships. U.S. bankers made profitable loans to both sides, but far more funds went to the Allies than to the Central Powers.

On May 7, 1915, a German submarine sank the British cruise liner *Lusitania* off the coast of Ireland. The ship was, despite U.S. denials, carrying American-made ammunition to the Allies; 128 U.S. citizens were among the almost 1,200 killed. The United States, already outraged by the recent German introduction of mustard gas into combat, protested vigorously, and on September 1 the German government accepted the American demand to abandon the unrestricted submarine warfare. For the next two years, the Germans, wanting to keep the United States neutral, adopted a policy of warning liners before sinking them, providing for the safety of the passengers.

The fact remained that only with submarines could Germany prevent Britain from maintaining total control of the high seas. In 1916, the German fleet left port to challenge the British Royal Navy. The German admiralty hoped to entice part of the main British fleet into a trap by offering a smaller fleet as a target off the Norwegian coast. German submarines lay in wait, with a sizeable surface fleet, which could strike before a rescue force could arrive. The British, who had broken the German code, hoped to have the last laugh when the entire Grand Fleet suddenly appeared. The German and British fleets stumbled into each other off the coast of Denmark, in the Battle of Jutland, May 31–June 1, 1916. After a heavy exchange of gunfire, the German ships fled. The British lost fourteen ships and about 6,000 men were killed; eleven German ships were sunk and about 1,500 men were killed. Both sides claimed victory, but British losses were heavier, surprising and embarrassing British naval leaders (such that one admiral turned to a junior officer and stammered, "Chatfield, there seems to be something wrong with our bloody ships today!").

The continuing success of the British blockade led Germany to announce on February 1, 1917, that its submarines would attack any ship in "war zones." In March 1916, the U.S. government had forcefully protested the sinking of the British ship *Sussex* in the English Channel, with the loss of American lives. Germany agreed to the "*Sussex* pledge," reaffirming the agreement made after the sinking of the *Lusitania* to give up unrestricted submarine warfare. But pressure came from the German high command to turn loose the submarine fleet, now 120 strong, as the only hope for knocking Britain out of the war. This was a calculated risk, because it would surely entail American intervention. Two weeks earlier, the United States had intercepted a coded telegram from the German foreign secretary, Arthur Zimmermann, to his ambassador to Mexico. The

(*Left*) Allied tanks become stuck in the mud. (*Right*) A German U-boat surfaces.

"Zimmermann telegram," which might have been the work of someone within the U.S. or even British government, brazenly offered Mexico German help in taking back the states of Texas, Arizona, and New Mexico if it would go to war against its powerful neighbor. With more Americans killed in submarine attacks, Wilson used the telegram to bolster support for a declaration of war on April 6, 1917. Wilson promised a war that would "make the world safe for democracy." The United States turned its industrial might toward wartime production and drafted and trained an army that reached 4 million, of which half was in France by November 1918. The entry of the United States into the war tipped the balance fatally against Germany.

During 1917, German submarines sank one-fourth of all ships sailing to Britain. They sank 350 British ships in April alone. Half a million tons of shipping were sunk in February, three-quarters of a million in March, and nearly 1 million tons in April. But in the midst of despair, the British admiralty discovered that heavily escorted convoys could get through. Submerged mines at the entrances to the Channel also helped reduce the German U-boat threat. Within a few months, the first American troops reached the continent, along with a steady stream of supplies.

Russia Withdraws from the War

The second remarkable event of 1917 was the Russian Revolution (see Chapter 23). The eastern front had stabilized following the Russian offensive at the end of 1916, leaving the Russian and Austro-Hungarian armies depleted and exhausted. The Russian home front seemed on the verge of collapse, amid shortages of food far more serious than any faced by the other combatants. As liberals demanded political reforms, soldiers deserted in droves. In February 1917, strikes and bread riots in Petrograd (St. Petersburg had been renamed after the outbreak of the war in 1914 to a more Russian-sounding name) spread rapidly. Without troops of sufficient numbers or commitment to keep order, Tsar Nicholas II abdicated on March 15 (see Chapter 23). A provisional government promised the lands of the tsar and the Orthodox Church to the peasantry. In Petrograd, a Council (Soviet) of Workers and Soldiers also contended for power in the vacuum left by the sudden disappearance of autocracy. The head of the provisional government, Aleksandr Kerensky (1881–1970), had no intention of abandoning the war effort, and he ordered the commander in chief to launch another offensive on July 1. But "peace, land, and bread" became the motto of the soldiers. Many deserted or refused to obey their officers. Within a matter of weeks, the Germans had easily broken this last Russian offensive; a counterattack pushed the Russians back nearly 100 miles to Galicia.

In the months after the February Revolution of 1917, the well-organized Russian Communist Party, the Bolsheviks, grew in influence in the major cities and in the army. The Bolsheviks aimed to seize power and then take Russia out of the war as quickly as possible. They expected revolutions to break out in other countries as well, beginning with Germany, which had a far larger industrial proletariat than Russia. The German government desperately wanted to force the Russian provisional government to make peace immediately, so that the German high command could turn its full attention to the western front before the American entry into the war could turn the tide. With this in mind, they allowed exiled Bolshevik leader Vladimir Lenin (1870–1924) to return to Russia from neutral Switzerland through Germany and Finland.

On November 6 (October 24 by the Old Russian calendar), the Bolsheviks, who formed a majority within the powerful Petrograd Soviet, overthrew the provisional government they had helped save. They were supported by "soviets of workers and soldiers" in other cities. In the meantime, the German army, facing virtually no opposition, had captured the fortified town of Riga and was advancing along the Baltic coast. Now the Germans were happy to comply with Lenin's request for an immediate armistice. In return, the German government wanted the revolutionary government to agree to the independence of Finland, as well as that of Poland, Galicia, Moldavia, and the Baltic states of Estonia, Latvia, and Lithuania. Their goal was to create a series of small buffer states between Germany and Russia that they could dominate. These were strong demands. The Allies were understandably worried that such a peace between Germany and Russia could make it difficult to obtain peace in the west.

The Bolsheviks and German representatives talked into the new year. The French and British governments both rejected Lenin's call for an armistice, fearful of the effect Russia's withdrawal from the war might have on workers and socialists at home, as well as on the war's outcome. French Prime Minister Georges Clemenceau and British Prime Minister David Lloyd George denounced the Bolsheviks, but relatively few people in Russia wanted the war to continue. In December, the Bolsheviks unilaterally declared the war over and signed an armistice with Germany, although they did not accept the German conditions for a permanent peace. When the revolutionary Russian government did not agree to the German terms for a formal armistice, the German armies marched into the Russian heartland. They reached the Gulf of Finland—only 150 miles from Petrograd—as well as the Crimean peninsula in the south, and advanced far into Ukraine, stopped only by the need to turn full attention to the western front. The Germans then offered a cessation of hostilities in return for virtually all Russian war materiel they could carry with them. They also again demanded the independence of the border states of the Russian Empire, including Finland, Ukraine, Georgia, Lithuania, Latvia, Estonia, and Poland, which they would surely dominate. On March 3, 1918, the Bolshevik government agreed to the terms. The Treaty of Brest-Litovsk officially ended Russian participation in what the Allies called "the Great War for civilization."

Offensives and Mutinies

On the western front, 1917 brought another major Allied offensive. General Nivelle of France convinced his British counterpart in February that the long-awaited knockout punch was at last possible. A British attack would divert German forces from a French attack along the Aisne River. But the British attack ran headlong into the impenetrable German second line of defense, the "Hindenburg Line." On April 16, Nivelle sent 1.2 million soldiers into battle along the Aisne River in miserable weather. Allied tanks, which had been introduced into battle for the first time in 1916, became stuck in the mud or in shell craters. Ten days later, French losses totaled 34,000 dead, 90,000 wounded, and 20,000 missing. Soldiers sang, "If you want to find the old battalion, I know where they are, I know where they are—They're hanging on the old barbed wire. I've seen 'em, I've seen 'em, Hanging on the old barbed wire." Robert Graves wrote a poem, "The Dead Fox Hunter," in memory of a friend, a captain, who had been killed:

We found the little captain at the head;
    His men lay well aligned,
We touched his hand—stone cold—and he was dead,
    And they, all dead behind,

Had never reached their goal, but they died well;
They charged in line, and in the same line fell.

Nivelle again promised the increasingly anxious government in Paris that the breakthrough was just around the corner. Like other commanders, he reasoned that such failures occurred because the soldiers lacked sufficient *élan*. The next time, it would work. Without a pause, more troops were sent into the German meat grinder.

For the first time, soldiers resisted. Some French regiments were heard "baaing" like sheep led to the slaughterhouse as they marched past their commanding officers. On May 3, mutinies broke out. By the end of May, they had spread to other regiments, even though soldiers who refused to go over the top knew they could be summarily shot. They reasoned that they were going to die anyway. Some soldiers fired their rifles into the air and shouted, "Long live peace!" Some regiments elected spokesmen, who declared that they would defend the trenches against German attacks, but would not participate in any more foolish assaults. The mutinies affected half of the French divisions along the western front, and at the beginning of June, only two of twelve divisions holding the line in Champagne had been unaffected. One French commander estimated in June 1917 that he could count on the loyalty of no more than 50 percent of his troops. The loyalty of 35 percent was doubtful, and 15 percent could not be trusted.

Some soldiers were summarily shot where the officers retained the upper hand; 23,000 were court-martialed, 432 sentenced to death, and 55 executed. In all, more than 21,000 French soldiers deserted in 1917. The politicians and some of the generals blamed socialist "agitators" and peace propaganda. General Pétain, the hero of Verdun, knew otherwise, and at least tried to improve the conditions of daily life for the soldiers. The Nivelle offensive ground to a halt.

Despite this, the British commander, Haig, planned another offensive around Ypres, the "fields of Flanders." The goal was to push the Germans back from the coast to Ghent, depriving them of the Belgian railroads they used for supplies. The grim Haig had not bothered to inspect the front himself, nor did he pay attention to the pessimistic reports of his intelligence staff. He also had not reported estimates of German troop strength to the war cabinet in London. The battle began in heavy rain; the preliminary barrage turned the chalky soil into something of the consistency of quicksand. The third Ypres Offensive could claim only one success: the blowing up of the Messines Ridge by Welsh miners. In the Battle of Passchendaele ("They died in hell, they called it Passchendaele"), named after a devastated nearby village, the British gained four miles in exchange for 300,000 dead or wounded. One soldier determined that, in view of such gains, it would take 180 years to get to the Rhine River. An officer who rode up for the first time to see the devastated and virtually impassable terrain burst into tears, muttering "My God, did we really send men to fight here, in this?" before being told that it was even worse further up. British Prime Minister Lloyd George came to tour the front himself. The offensive ended. Haig kept his command.

The British then launched the first massive tank attack in the history of warfare, on drier ground near Cambrai on November 20, 1917. The tanks rolled over five miles, with few casualties. Like the virtual disappearance of the cavalry, it was a sign of things to come. Yet the Germans soon recaptured the land they had lost.

Morale plunged during the winter, particularly in Germany and France. A writer was surprised to see a soldier who had lost an arm drunkenly begging on a Parisian boulevard, muttering, "Peace, Peace." Shortages became worse, rationing more vexing. Occasionally in the south of France, sarcastic references were heard to "Paris's war," or to the blond refugees from the embattled northern departments as "the Krauts (*boches*) of the North." The French armaments minister faced shouts of "Down with the War!" when he visited a factory. There were waves of strikes in 1917. More calls for peace were heard, including one for a "peace of understanding" from the German Reichstag.

But Georges Clemenceau, a seasoned veteran of pre-war political battles and former prime minister, rallied the war effort in France after taking office again. He used troops against strikers, as he had before the war. He ordered the arrest of those calling for peace without victory, including his minister of the interior. "Domestic policy?" he shouted, "I wage war! Foreign policy? I wage war! I wage nothing but war!" A cartoon in Britain—unthinkable until 1917—pictured the encounter of two enlisted soldiers at the front. One said, "'Ow long you up for, Bill?" "Seven years," was the reply. First soldier, "You're lucky—I'm duration."

Compounding this bleak picture for the Allies was a combined Austrian and German offensive in Italy, strengthened by the arrival of German troops from the Russian front. They pushed the Italian army back seventy-five miles in the Battle of Caporetto on the Isonzo River. Despite 200,000 casualties and twice that many desertions, the Italians held along the Piave River, just twenty miles from Venice. The Allies finally moved to coordinate their war efforts. In October 1917, they established a Supreme War Council, which held regular meetings of the prime ministers of France, Britain, and Italy, as well as a representative sent by President Wilson.

Better news for the Allies came from the Middle East. The discovery of oil there prior to the war had dramatically increased the stakes for influence in the region. During the war, the British took advantage of Arab resentment—particularly by Muslim fundamentalists—of the Turks, who had ruled much of the Middle East for centuries, to stir up revolts. The writer and specialist on the Middle East, Colonel T. E. Lawrence (1888–1935), was among the British officers coordinating sudden attacks against the strategically important Turkish railway from the sacred city of Medina to Damascus, among other targets.

In the last decades of the nineteenth century, more Jews in Europe had begun to long for a homeland in Palestine, which was part of the declining Turkish Ottoman Empire, and by 1914, 85,000 Jews had moved there. The British government in principle supported the Zionist movement for a Jewish state, but it also hoped to add to Turkish troubles. On November 2, 1917, the Balfour Declaration, named for the British foreign secretary, Arthur Balfour, expressed British willingness to support the future creation of a "national home" for the Jews, a state in Palestine, once the Turks had been driven out, provided such a state would recognize the rights of the Arab populations who already lived there. This declaration partially contradicted the Sykes-Picot Agreement of 1916, which had secretly divided Syria and other parts of the Middle East into British and French zones of influence. The British government, however, realized that the eventual creation of a Jewish state in Palestine could serve as a buffer between the Suez Canal and Syria, the latter controlled by France. In December 1917, a British force took Jerusalem. The Central Powers' ally Turkey seemed on the verge of collapse.

The German Spring Offensive

In the spring of 1918, the Germans launched their "victory drive," their first major offensive since 1914. But Austria-Hungary showed signs of virtually dissolving, with major national groups openly calling for independence. Germany had lost its gamble that unrestricted submarine warfare could force Britain out of the war and prevent the United States from making an important contribution to the Allied side. By the spring, 325,000 American soldiers were in Europe. They were commanded by General John Pershing (1860–1948), who had won early fame for leading a "punitive expedition" (which turned out to be a wild-goose chase) against the Mexican bandit Pancho Villa. He had also served in campaigns against Geronimo and against the Sioux in the American West, and had fought in the Philippines and Cuba. Pershing, a tall, tough, stubborn commander who never softened an order with a smile, insisted that his troops remain independent, fearing that French and British generals would lead them to slaughter.

Ludendorff decided on a massive German assault along the Somme River, thereby avoiding the mud of Flanders and the hills and forts of eastern France around Verdun. His forces had been replenished by drafting younger and older men than before. On March 21, 1918, after a relatively brief bombardment of five hours in order to maintain some element of surprise, 1.6 million men attacked the Allied defenses in five separate offensives over a front of forty miles (see Map 22.7). When the weather cleared at noon and British planes could survey the front, the pilots observed that the Germans had succeeded in breaking through the Allied lines. Five days later, some German units had pushed forward forty miles. The Germans now advanced in Flanders, moving forward with relative ease against troops from Portugal, which had recently entered the war on the Allied side. Ludendorff hurled all available reserves into the battle. It looked as though the Germans would take the Channel ports, leading Haig to announce to his British troops that they must fight "with our backs to the wall and believing in the justice of our cause each of us must fight to the end." Once again, Paris was threatened. The Germans bombarded the French capital with their giant gun, "Big Bertha," which could lob shells each weighing up to a ton twenty-four miles into the air before they fell to earth with deadly impact. Late in May 1918, the offensive pushed the French back to Reims, and then as close to Paris as the Marne River in early June. American units

MAP 22.7 THE GERMAN OFFENSIVE, 1918   The spring offensive of 1918 in which the Germans attacked the Allies in five separate offensives along the western front.

engaged in their first sustained action near Château-Thierry in a frantic attempt to stop the German advance, and the French fought the Germans at Compiègne, stopping the German advance short of Paris. In the gloom of the Allied headquarters, French Marshal Ferdinand Foch (1851–1929) assumed command of the combined French, British, and American armies.

Soon the Germans again faced one of the dangers of trench warfare: they had outrun their cover and supplies, and faced fresh Allied reserves. On July 15, 1918, another major German offensive was repulsed. Ludendorff's offensive, which he viewed as the last chance to win the war, had failed. The French were not about to negotiate for an armistice. Morale plunged in Germany, which was faced with hundreds of thousands of new casualties and serious food shortages for the first time in the war. In January 1918, 250,000 German workers had defied the government by striking. They did so for economic reasons, however, not to stop the war. Some industrial sabotage occurred here and there. Carefully couched criticism of the war and of Kaiser William II began to appear in the press. The followers of the socialists Rosa Luxemburg and Karl Liebknecht, both imprisoned after the first public demonstration against the war, became bolder. Demonstrations took place in several cities, including Berlin. There were shortages of electricity and gas; food rationing, which had begun in 1915, became more severe. Inflation was rampant, pushed by the circulation of more paper money, as gold and silver were withdrawn to prevent hoarding. Black marketing spread, as people hoarded scarce goods and charged exorbitant, illegal prices for them.

Led by French forces, the Allies counterattacked in July 1918. The British used their tanks with increasing effectiveness to go over craters and barbed wire and to protect the advancing infantry. Coordinated attacks on the German lines began on August 8, 1918, the German army's darkest day, when the British moved forward eight miles along the front north of the Somme River. A month later, the Germans had been pushed back to the positions they had held at the start of the spring offensives.

The Allies were now confident that they would win the war, probably in 1919 if all went well. Ludendorff advised the kaiser to press for an armistice before it was too late. With the Allies gaining ground, on October 4, 1918, Germany's new chancellor, Prince Max von Baden (1867–1929), a liberal monarchist, asked President Wilson for an armistice based on the American president's call for "peace without victory." The Reichstag passed laws making ministers responsible to it and not to the kaiser. It was a revolution of sorts, but given the circumstances, Kaiser William II could do virtually nothing.

The situation for the Central Powers worsened on the Italian front. His armies in retreat, Austro-Hungarian Emperor Charles I seemed little inclined nor able to continue the war. Desertions from the Habsburg army mounted. When French and British troops moved into Bulgaria in September 1918, Bulgaria left the war and King Ferdinand abdicated in favor of his son, Boris III. There was now little doubt that the defeat of Germany and Austria-Hungary was near. On November 3, 1918, the Austro-Hungarian Empire withdrew from the war.

The Fourteen Points and Peace

On January 8, 1918, in an address to a joint session of the U.S. Senate and House of Representatives, President Wilson set out a blueprint for permanent peace. His "Fourteen Points" were based upon his understanding of how the Great War had begun and how future wars could be avoided. The first point called for "open covenants, openly arrived at," in place of the secret treaties whose obligations had pulled Europe into war. Wilson also called for freedom of the seas and freedom of trade, and the impartial settlement of colonial rivalries. Other points included the principle of nonintervention in Russia; the return of full sovereignty to Belgium and Alsace-Lorraine to France; autonomy—without mentioning independence—for the national groups within the Austro-Hungarian Empire; and the independence of Romania, Serbia, Montenegro, and Poland. The last of the Fourteen Points called for the establishment of an organization or association of nations to settle other national conflicts as they arose. If the desire of the European peoples to live in states defined by national boundaries had been one—if not the principal—cause of the war, then a peace that recognized these claims would be a lasting one. Or so thought Wilson, and many other people as well.

Germany appeared willing to accept Wilson's Fourteen Points as grounds for an armistice, hoping to circumvent the British and French governments, which clearly would demand unconditional surrender and were not terribly interested in Wilson's idealism. The British, for example, opposed the point calling for freedom of the seas. As Wilson considered what to do with the German proposal for an armistice, a number of U.S. citizens were killed when a U-boat again sank a British ship off the Irish coast. An angry Wilson then replied to Prince Max that the German military authorities would have to arrange an armistice with the British and French high command, and not with him. Germany called off unrestricted submarine warfare and tried to convince Wilson that recent changes in the civilian leadership in Berlin amounted to a democratization of the empire. But Foch and Clemenceau demanded unconditional surrender of the German fleet and occupation of the Rhineland by the French.

The collapse of the Central Powers accelerated. Bulgaria had signed an armistice in September 1918, and Turkey signed one the next month; the British occupied Damascus and Constantinople. When the Austro-Hungarian Empire followed the Germans in trying to get Wilson to negotiate an armistice based on the Fourteen Points, which trumpeted the sanctity of the nation-state, Czechs in Prague proclaimed an independent Czechoslovakia. Croats and Slovenes announced that they would join the Serbs in the establishment of a South Slav state of Yugoslavia. Hungary, too, proclaimed its independence, as if the Great War had been something forced on it by the Austrians. Facing no opposition, the Italian army finally managed to advance into Habsburg territory. Austria-Hungary signed an armistice on November 3, 1918. In the German Baltic port of Kiel, sailors mutinied. There were major riots in Berlin. An insurrection in Munich led to the declaration of a Bavarian Republic.

On November 7, 1918, an ad hoc German Armistice Commission asked the Allies for an end to hostilities. Two days later, a crowd proclaimed the German Republic in Berlin. William II followed Hindenburg's lead, blaming socialists and Jews for the overthrow of the empire. He then fled across the Dutch border and abdicated. On November 11, 1918, a representative of the provisional German government and General Foch signed an armistice in a railroad car in the middle of the forest near Compiègne, north of Paris. The celebrations in London, Paris, New York, and elsewhere on the Allied side went on for days. The mother of the poet Wilfred Owen received news that he had been killed as the church bells of her village were ringing for victory. A French veteran, tiring of the street festivities in his town, went at dusk to a cemetery. There he came upon a woman crying next to the tomb of her husband. Their small boy was with her, playing with a tricolor flag. Suddenly the boy cried out, "Papa, we've won!"

THE IMPACT OF THE WAR

There had been nothing like the Great War in history. About 6,000 people had been killed each day for more than 1,500 days. In more than four years of fighting, at least 74 million soldiers were mobilized. Of the 48 million men who served in the Allied armies, at least 18 million were casualties not including hundreds of thousands listed as missing. The Central Powers mobilized 25.5 million, and had 12.4 million casualties, again not counting the missing. There were approximately 8.5 million men killed and 22 million wounded (of whom an estimated 7 million may have been left permanently disabled). Another 12.6 million died from war-related causes. As Table 22.1 shows, the Austro-Hungarian, Russian, and French armies suffered proportionally more than the other major combatants.

But sheer numbers, however daunting, do not tell the whole story. Of the wounded who survived, many were condemned to spend the rest of their lives—shortened lives, in many cases—in veterans' hospitals. Soldiers who had lost limbs or who were mutilated in other ways became a common sight in European cities, towns, and villages after the war. Europe seemed a continent of widows and spinsters; so many men were killed in the prime of life that the birthrate fell markedly after the war. Support for families of the dead soldiers and invalids unable to work

A widow before her husband's grave at the end of World
War I.

strained national budgets. War cemeteries stretched across northern
France and Belgium. The carnage was not limited to the European continent: in an outbreak of ethnic hostility and in response to Armenian
demands for an independent state, the Turks forced 1.75 million Armenians to leave their homes in Turkey; more than a third of them perished
without water in the desert sun on the way to Syria, their bodies consumed
by wild animals. Furthermore, at least 21 million people (estimates have
ranged up to 100 million deaths) died in a worldwide influenza epidemic
in 1918–1919 that killed more people in Europe than did the war.

The flower of European youth—or much of it—had perished in the war.
There were other costs as well. The economic structure of northern
France and part of Belgium had been chewed up in the fighting. The German economy, which was devastated by the war, would be further crippled
by the terms of the peace treaty (see Chapter 24). The British economy
also suffered, though not to the same extent. The Carnegie Endowment
for International Peace made a brave attempt to calculate the war's actual
cost, and came up with a figure of $338 billion dollars after establishing a
rough value for property and even lives lost.

No one could begin to measure other dimensions of the war's impact. The psychological damage to the generation of survivors can hardly be measured. "Never such innocence again," observed the British writer Philip Larkin, referring to the period before the war. The post-war period, rampant with hard times and disappointments, caused many people to look back even more on the pre-war period as the "Belle Époque," the good old days.

Woodrow Wilson was not alone in thinking that the Great War was the war to end all wars. Many people came to believe that such a thing could never happen again. No one, they reasoned, could ever wish such a catastrophe on humanity. The American writer F. Scott Fitzgerald took a friend to a battlefield in the north of France: "See that little stream—we could walk to it in two minutes. It took the British a month to walk to it—a whole empire walking very slowly, dying in front and pushing forward

TABLE 22.1.   CASUALTIES IN THE GREAT WAR

ALLIED POWERS

Country	Mobilized	Dead	Wounded	POW/ Missing	Total	% Casualties
Russia	18,100,000	1,800,000	4,950,000	2,500,000	9,250,000	51.10
France	7,891,000	1,375,800	4,266,000	537,000	6,178,800	78.30
G.B., Emp. and Dom.	8,904,467	908,371	2,090,212	191,652	3,190,235	35.83
Italy	5,615,000	578,000	947,000	600,000	2,125,000	37.85
U.S.	4,273,000	114,000	234,000	4,526	352,526	8.25
Japan	800,000	300	907	3	1,210	0.15
Romania	1,000,000	250,706	120,000	80,000	450,706	45.07
Serbia	750,000	278,000	133,148	15,958	427,106	56.95
Belgium	365,000	38,716	44,686	34,659	118,061	32.35
Greece	353,000	26,000	21,000	1,000	48,000	13.60
Portugal	100,000	7,222	13,751	12,318	33,291	33.29
Montenegro	50,000	3,000	10,000	7,000	20,000	40.00
Total	48,201,467	5,380,115	12,830,704	3,984,116	22,194,935	46.05

CENTRAL POWERS

Country	Mobilized	Dead	Wounded	POW/ Missing	Total	% Casualties
Germany	13,200,000	2,033,700	4,216,058	1,152,800	7,402,558	56.08
Austria-Hungary	9,000,000	1,100,000	3,620,000	2,200,000	6,920,000	76.89
Turkey	2,998,000	804,000	400,000	250,000	1,454,000	48.50
Bulgaria	400,000	87,500	152,390	27,029	266,919	66.73
Total	25,598,000	4,025,200	8,388,448	3,629,829	16,043,477	62.67
Grand Total	73,799,467	9,405,315	21,219,152	7,613,945	38,238,412	51.81

Source: J. M. Winter, *The Great War and the British People* (London, Macmillan, 1985), p. 75.

behind. And another empire walked very slowly backward a few inches a day, leaving the dead like a million bloody rags. No European will ever do that again in this generation." He was wrong.

The heroic vocabulary of war that characterized all of Europe in 1914—and the press for the duration of the war—disappeared. As Ernest Hemingway put it in his novel *A Farewell to Arms,* the "abstract words such as glory, honor, courage, or hallow were obscene beside the concrete names of villages, the numbers of roads, the names of rivers, the numbers of regiments and the dates" associated with the deaths of so many people.

CONCLUSION

The Great War had several causes, with none alone standing as a sufficient cause. To be sure, the entangling alliances of the European great powers were undeniably a principal factor in the outbreak of hostilities. Aggressive nationalism spilled out of the opposing alliances during this period. Schoolchildren throughout much of Europe were taught that their country was the greatest nation in history, and that their enemies were craven reptiles. The imperial rivalries of the great powers—above all, in Africa—helped make the alliance system more rigid, sharpening rivalries between Germany and Britain and France. Nationalists strongly believed that having colonies helped define status as a great power: by such reasoning, states had to expand their military forces and be prepared to defend their empires as they would their own borders.

Military planners (who were, after all, nationalists themselves) in Germany, Austria-Hungary, France, and, to a lesser extent, Russia, all considered war not only inevitable but desirable. Military planners saw conflict between nations as a natural struggle for survival that diplomacy could postpone but not eliminate. To one British writer, "War . . . is the sovereign disinfectant, and its red stream of blood . . . cleans out the stagnant pools and clotted channels of the intellect." In Germany, an official in the chancellory wrote that "eternal and absolute enmity is fundamentally inherent in relations between peoples; and the hostility that we observe everywhere [is] the essence of the world and the source of life itself." War would be the ultimate test by which the fit—individuals and nations—would be measured. "Give me combat!" rang out from the dueling fraternities in Heidelberg to the gymnastic and shooting clubs of Paris. They got war, but, as we have seen, it turned out to be very different than had been anticipated.

For those who had been lucky enough to survive, how much greater the disappointment, disillusionment, and bitterness that would follow. One contemporary observer did not mince words: "The World War of 1914–1918 was the greatest moral, spiritual and physical catastrophe in the entire history of the English people—a catastrophe whose consequences, all wholly evil, are still with us." Many soldiers returned home to find skyrocketing prices and unemployment awaiting them. In Britain, parents whose sons had died as foot soldiers in France or Belgium learned that families of aristocratic officers had complained that their sons had been buried alongside ordinary people. Politicians who had put aside their differences during the war in a common effort for victory—such as the "Sacred Union" in France—reverted to bitter disagreements that were compounded by the dilemmas posed in the peace settlement. The problems of making peace and putting Europe back together again, as well as paying for the war, would not be easily resolved. U.S. participation in the war and, particularly, the Russian Revolution, which we will examine in the next chapter, would each have a profound impact on Europe's future. The Great War could not be relegated to the past. War became a continuing experience of the twentieth century.

CHAPTER 23

REVOLUTIONARY RUSSIA AND THE SOVIET UNION

When Nicholas II (1868–1918) was crowned tsar of Russia upon the death of Alexander III in 1894, he decided to hold a great popular festival on a huge field outside of Moscow, considered the sacred center of the empire. Convinced that it was his duty to uphold the principles of autocracy, Nicholas was sensitive to the tsar's traditional role as the Holy Father of all his people. He wanted to reaffirm the ties that bound his subjects to him, and he to them. The festival attracted enthusiastic crowds numbering in the hundreds of thousands. It featured rides, fortune telling, and other staples of Russian popular festivals. But in the stampede to get free beer and coronation souvenirs, more than 1,200 people were crushed to death and somewhere between 9,000 and 20,000 were injured. Celebration had turned to tragedy. And during the coronation itself the heavy chain of the Order of Saint Andrew dropped from Nicholas's shoulders to the ground. Many people—perhaps even the superstitious tsar himself—saw these events as bad omens for the tsar's reign.

Not bad omens, however, but rather the failure to implement meaningful political reform brought down Nicholas II and the Russian autocracy in 1917. First, the Revolution of 1905 led to reforms but did not alter the autocratic nature of the regime. This revolution forced Tsar Nicholas II to grant increased freedom of the press and to create an elected Duma (assembly). These reforms had disappeared, for all intents and purposes, when the tsar regained the upper hand, yet the Revolution of 1905 demonstrated the vulnerability of even a police state to popular mobilization. In February 1917, the tsar fell. Then, after six months of uncertainty and political division, the Bolshevik (October) Revolution overthrew the provisional government. Russia withdrew from the Great War. The "dictatorship of the proletariat" became that of Vladimir

Lenin's Communist Party. Upon Lenin's death in 1924, Joseph Stalin consolidated his personal authority in the Soviet Union, ruthlessly establishing state socialism.

The Russian Revolution of 1917, like that of 1905, was not the kind of revolution that the Russian populists or anarchists had predicted—massive uprisings of the peasant masses against lords and imperial officials— although peasant rebellion was an essential ingredient in both revolutions. Nor did it correspond to Karl Marx's prediction that a successful bourgeois revolution would be followed by a revolution undertaken by an industrial proletariat. War played a catalytic role in the Russian Revolution of 1917: Russia's shocking defeat in the Russo-Japanese War (1904–1905) and, above all, the horror of the Great War created hardships that increasingly undermined the legitimacy of the tsarist regime.

WAR AND REVOLUTION

Reformers were still biding their time when Russia went to war again in 1914. However, Lenin was dumbfounded when most socialists in other countries supported their country's mobilization for war. Among Russian socialists, "defensists" (Mensheviks and most Socialist Revolutionaries) argued that Russian workers should defend their country against German attack. "Internationalists" opposed the war, viewing it as a struggle between capitalist powers in which workers were but pawns.

Lenin took the war as a sign that capitalism might be ripe for what he thought was its inevitable fall. "Imperialism is the last stage," he wrote, "in the development of capitalism when it has reached the point of dividing up the whole world, and two gigantic groups have fallen into mortal struggle." He believed that if revolution were to break out in several countries, the fall of Russian autocracy and capitalism could be near, even without a true bourgeois revolution. Even if the Russian working class was less developed than those of Western nations, the corresponding weakness of the Russian bourgeoisie could facilitate a successful revolution. This revolution would be followed by the establishment of a dictatorship of the proletariat, that is, by a mobilized working class led by its most dedicated elements, the Bolsheviks. The revolution would then spread to other countries, where the working classes would follow the example of the first successful socialist revolution.

Russia at War

The Great War became a catalyst for demands for reform within Russia, first in the management of the war itself, and then in Russian political life. The war had begun with an upsurge of patriotism and political unity, with the tsar blessing icons and the faithful kneeling before him. A Bolshevik

Tsar Nicholas II, holding an icon, blesses his troops.

noted bitterly that amid shouts of " 'God Save the Tsar!' our class struggle went down the drain." Within a year, however, the war had shattered the "sacred union" that represented a patriotic consensus in 1914. Liberals renewed demands for political reform. Workers agitated for higher wages and better working conditions. By 1917, 15 million men had been drafted into the army, about 12 million of whom were poor peasants. It had proven difficult to transform peasants "who held rifles like rakes" into soldiers. Sent by high command into battle ill equipped, losses within the Russian army were staggering, even incalculable.

In the interest of the war effort, the government allowed national organizations to exist that earlier were forbidden. These groups became the organizational base for the liberal opposition. Liberal *zemstvo* representatives established a committee, the Union of *Zemstvos*, to organize relief of the sick and wounded; an organization of municipal governments, the Union of Towns, was also created.

In the spring of 1915, liberal Duma members began to express open dissatisfaction with the way the war was being run. Russia's factories experienced difficulties in meeting military needs; the army lacked sufficient rifles and artillery shells. The tsar permitted industrialists to form a War Industries Committee, to which delegations of workers were added, in order to expedite wartime production.

The war gradually transformed Petrograd, accentuating its social polarization. By 1916, most of Petrograd's workers, who made up 35 percent of the population, were producing war materiel, swelling the ranks of metal, textile, and chemical workers. More peasants flocked to the capital, as did some middle-class people seeking jobs and waves of refugees from the war zones of Russian Poland and the Baltic states.

As Russian society strained under the pressures of war, liberals demanded that the Duma be allowed to meet and that Tsar Nicholas dismiss a number of reactionary ministers. With military defeats weighing on him—none more disastrous than that at Tannenberg (August 1914), where 100,000 Russian troops were captured—followed by humiliating retreats, the tsar established a Council for National Defense. He summoned the Duma to meet in July 1915 and replaced four ministers. But the inept Nicholas had also assumed command of the army. Liberals feared this could lead to more military disasters, and would also take the tsar away from Petrograd, leaving imperial decision making even more subject to the influence of the hated Tsarina Alexandra.

The melancholy, ineffectual tsar remained extremely superstitious. Seventeen was his unlucky number: on January 17, 1895, the day of his first speech as tsar, an elderly noble had dropped a traditional gift of bread and salt, a bad omen, and on October 17, 1905, he had been forced to sign a constitution. But he may well have retained the respect and distant affection of most of the Russian people. Tsarina Alexandra, in contrast, was loathed by her subjects. Born in Germany, the granddaughter of Queen Victoria had been raised in England before marrying Tsar Nicholas in 1894. She had converted from Anglicanism to the Russian Orthodox Church. The illness of their only son, Alexei (1904–1918), a hemophiliac and the heir to the throne, increasingly weighed on the royal couple.

As she became ever more conservative, Alexandra extended her influence over her weak-willed husband. Nicholas dismissed ministers on the whims of the tsarina. ("Lovey, don't dawdle!" she wrote her husband, urging him to fire one.) Many people wrongly believed that Alexandra, "the German," was actively working for the interests of Germany. No German agent could have served Germany as well.

Tsarina Alexandra with Grigory Rasputin (center).

Alexandra's great favorite was Grigory Rasputin (1872–1916), a debauched "holy man." Claiming occult power and ability to heal the hemophiliac Crown Prince Alexei, Rasputin had moved gradually into the inner circle of court life. On one occasion, he predicted that one of Alexei's spells would shortly subside, and it did. To the consternation of the tsar's ministers, the influence enjoyed by the man the tsarina called "our friend" became a matter of state.

In December 1916, noble conspirators, who feared Rasputin's influence on military operations, put what they thought was enough poison into Rasputin's many drinks to kill a cow. When Rasputin seemed almost unfazed, they shot him repeatedly and smashed his skull in a protracted struggle. The assassins then weighted down his body and threw him into the Neva River.

The Progressive Bloc

In August 1915, some liberal members of the Duma, including Constitutional Democrats, had formed a Progressive Bloc that was committed to working with the tsar in the hope of encouraging reform. A strike at the enormous Putilov munitions factory in Petrograd—the largest factory in Europe with 30,000 workers—added to the tension. When he met in an emergency session with his Council of Ministers, the tsar followed Alexandra's instructions to clutch a religious icon in one hand and, with the other, to comb his hair using Rasputin's comb. Nicholas then dismissed his liberal ministers.

Food shortages eroded the revival of working-class patriotism that had accompanied the beginning stages of the war. The growth of public organizations, which opened up a larger public sphere for discussion and debate, helped mobilize opposition to autocracy. Cooperative associations formed by workers in order to resist high prices had 50,000 members by the end of 1916. Some workers on the War Industries Committee pushed for greater working-class militancy. The Bolsheviks again began to build support among industrial workers.

As Nicholas dismissed capable but strong-willed ministers and replaced them with less able (and sometimes corrupt) but pliant men, liberals remained paralyzed, cowed by tsarist repression amid increased worker militancy. Attacks on the management of the war rang out in the Duma, as well as in the Union of Towns and the Union of the *Zemstvos*. The latter in December 1916 passed a resolution calling on the Duma to stop cooperating with the tsar and demanded ministerial responsibility.

For the moment, however, the tsar and the liberals needed each other. Outright revolution or violent repression seemed equally dangerous to both. The state needed the continued participation of voluntary committees and agencies of local self-government in order to keep the country from collapsing into shortage-induced anarchy. Liberal-dominated committees and agencies required the centralized apparatus of the state to carry out their work.

Food shortages reached a peak during the harsh winter of 1916–1917 when peasants hoarded their grain. Police repression of strikes helped close the ranks of workers against the government. In Lithuania, nationalists demanded autonomy within the empire and some nationalist agitation occurred in other Russian borderlands as well. During the second half of 1916, Muslims in Turkistan in Central Asia rose up in arms against Russian rule after the government attempted to move a quarter of a million people to factories near the front. Increasing anger at the continued arrival of Russian settlers in Turkistan also played a role in the unrest. These occurrences revealed the complexity of the problem of nationalism in the Russian Empire. Yet the Petrograd garrison of about 160,000 soldiers still seemed adequate to the task of maintaining order, even though most were raw recruits.

The Socialist Revolutionary leader Aleksandr Kerensky (1881–1970), a lawyer, denounced the war in a speech whose daring rhetoric had never been heard in the Duma. Some loyal nobles now urged reforms. But Nicholas replaced members of the Progressive Bloc with uncompromising reactionaries. He and his family withdrew into retreat, leaving the government floundering like a rudderless boat in high seas.

The February Revolution

The Russian Revolution that began in Petrograd grew out of the massive discontent of hunger and deprivation, amid mounting frustration at tsarist intransigence against reform. Like most large European cities, Petrograd's neighborhoods reflected social segregation. The upper- and middle-class residential districts and the palatial buildings of imperial government lay on and near a long street called the Nevsky Prospect. This central artery was lined with banks, hotels, restaurants, cafés, a giant department store, and offices. The streetcars did not run as far as the muddy streets of the workers' districts, nor in many cases did the city's water mains or electric power lines. Epidemics were still frequent in Petrograd, as in Moscow and other Russian cities, which were characterized by acute overcrowding and inadequate standards of public health and sanitation.

Revolutionary organizations prepared a massive general strike for early January 1917, the anniversary of Bloody Sunday in 1905. During January and February, almost half of the capital's 400,000 workers went out on strike. Three weeks later, demonstrators demanded that a provisional government be appointed with the power to enact major reforms. Food lines stretched longer in Petrograd, Moscow, and other cities in temperatures that reached forty below zero. Demonstrations and bread riots, in which many women and young people participated, became a daily occurrence.

On February 23 (all subsequent dates here refer to the Old Russian calendar, which was thirteen days behind the Western calendar), International Women's Day, more determined demonstrators took to the streets. Workers in the Putilov munitions factory tore up factory rule books and created committees to represent their interests to the company. Female textile workers led the way out of the factories. Almost all of the large factories shut down in one industrial district. Demoralized Cossack cavalrymen sent to disperse the demonstrators reacted with none of their usual eagerness.

On February 25, a general strike closed down Petrograd. While Petrograd's Duma debated ways of dealing with severe food shortages, crowds of ordinary people (workers in blue caps, women wearing scarves, students wearing green and light blue caps) poured into Petrograd's center. The army had 400,000 troops available within thirty miles of the city, but military attention was focused on the front, not on Petrograd itself. Tsar Nicholas then ordered the commander of the garrison to suppress demonstrations. As street fighting began to spread in the city, some police and soldiers hesitated when ordered into the streets to disperse protesters.

The first news of the Russian Revolution hits the streets of Moscow in February 1917.

On February 26, the police arrested about a hundred Bolsheviks and other militants seeking to turn demonstrations into insurrection. The attitude of soldiers, most of whom were peasants or workers, now became crucial. Many were shocked and disillusioned that they were ordered to fire on insurgents. When a commanding officer tried to restore order by reading a telegram from the tsar, he was shot while trying to flee the barracks. Now thousands of soldiers and some officers went over to the insurgent side. "Do what you think is best," officers told soldiers when mutineers approached the Armored Car Division. Many soldiers loyal to the government received neither orders nor food. Government plans to overwhelm an uprising had not taken into consideration possible mutinies. Districts began to fall under the loose control of the insurgents; a number of officers and soldiers who continued to resist were summarily executed after being captured.

Miserable conditions of war, the unpopularity of the officers (who addressed the rank and file as masters had spoken to serfs), awful food, and empathy with the demands of the workers for "bread and peace" explain the massive defection of soldiers. Sailors mutinied on ships of the Baltic fleet, killing an admiral. In Petrograd, unrestrained crowds attacked symbols of the autocracy: the law courts, prisons, and the immense fortress of St. Peter and St. Paul. The capture of the arsenal put thousands of rifles and great quantities of ammunition into the hands of workers. "Red

Guards," factory militias whose members carried red flags, imprisoned tsarist officials.

Nicholas now ordered the Duma to dissolve. Some of its members, who were drawn from privileged society, obeyed, but the majority simply moved to a new meeting place. They voted to remain in Petrograd—a move not unlike the Tennis Court Oath of the third estate during the first period of the French Revolution, a precedent of which they were keenly aware. The Duma then elected a provisional committee, whose mandate was to restore order. In the meantime, the liberals, who had opposed revolution and tried to walk a tightrope between a desire for reform and their fear of the masses, now were in the position of trying to contain the revolution they had helped set in motion.

The Russian Revolution of February 1917 was unplanned and its outcome uncertain. But the soil was fertile. Experienced in strikes, Socialist Revolutionary, Menshevik, and Bolshevik activists helped impart a sense of direction to the movement. Their goal was the overthrow of the tsarist regime. Amid the turmoil of sudden change effected by groups who did not necessarily agree on what should happen next, the provisional committee began to function as a provisional government, organizing a food supply commission and a military commission to try to bring the soldiers roaming through the city under some control.

On February 27, in response to calls in the streets, the Petrograd Soviet of Workers' and Soldiers' Deputies was created. Members included several hundred workers, some of whom the demonstrators had freed from jail (where they had been placed for their political or trade union activities), as well as many soldiers. They elected officers, discussed ways to defend Petrograd against German military attack, and sent representatives to encourage the formation of soviets in other cities. Menshevik leaders took the lead in the Petrograd Soviet's creation as Bolshevik leaders held back, fearing that a large and effective soviet might make it more difficult for their party to direct worker militancy.

Hoping to overwhelm the rebellion with his presence, the tsar now decided to return to Petrograd from his sea resort, where he had gone to join his family. He spent almost two full days aboard his private train, critical moments in the February Revolution. As his train drew within a hundred miles of the capital, the tsar received an erroneous report that insurgent troops held the next stations and that they would refuse to let his train through. Nicholas then went to the northern military front, hoping to find a loyal army ready to march on Petrograd. In disbelief, he learned that Moscow, too, had fallen almost overnight to insurgents. His generals made no effort to save the regime. They believed the tsar's cause lost and that only his abdication could prevent civil war, and perhaps military defeat as well.

Nicholas II abdicated on March 2, 1917, leaving the throne to his brother, Prince Michael. He did so with characteristic calm that appeared to border on indifference—although he scribbled in his diary that day, "All around me—treason and cowardice and deceit." A few hours in revolutionary Petrograd convinced Prince Michael to refuse to succeed his brother. The Soviet placed the tsar and his family under house arrest until the summer, when they were taken by train to a small Siberian town.

The Russian autocracy had fallen in a matter of days, "with a sort of fabulous ease," in the words of a contemporary, and with only about a thousand people killed. No legions of faithful peasants had risen up from the land of the black earth to save the "Holy Father."

The Provisional Government and the Soviet

The provisional government and the Petrograd Soviet were left in the awkward position of serving as dual or parallel governments. The provisional government included Constitutional Democrats, liberals who had demanded only that the tsar initiate political reforms. The Petrograd Soviet, in contrast, consisted largely of workers and soldiers who had helped overthrow the tsar. The relationship between the moderate provisional government and the radical Soviet would ultimately affect the course of the Russian Revolution itself.

For the moment, the Petrograd Soviet promised to accept the provisional committee's authority. Several factors explain why the Soviet's Executive Committee ceded power to the provisional government. Some Mensheviks had an ideological reason for not seeking to override the provisional

Russian workers and soldiers guarding a government building, 1917.

government, seeing it as the expression of the Marxist bourgeois phase of the Revolution. Others, perhaps awed by the mass popular insurrection that appeared to have swept away tsardom, did not seem confident that they could run a government in precarious times (particularly as many of the most influential leaders of the revolutionary parties were still in exile). Furthermore, some leaders of the Soviet feared that radical opposition to the moderate provisional government would bring on an immediate military counter-revolution. For the moment, both the provisional government and the Soviet met in the same palace, with Aleksandr Kerensky, named minister of justice but also a member of the Soviet, running back and forth between the two bodies, trying to smooth relations between them.

On March 8, the provisional government granted civil liberties, including the right to strike, the amnesty of political prisoners, and the democratization of local government, and announced that it would convene a constituent assembly to establish a constitution. The Petrograd Soviet, now with 3,000 members and an executive committee meeting virtually around the clock, insisted on immediate economic and social reforms. The provisional government and the Soviet quickly became the focus of attention of competing political groups—Liberals, Socialist Revolutionaries, Mensheviks, and Bolsheviks—all of whom wanted to shape Russia's future.

The Army

In the meantime, the army was the last functioning imperial institution. With the war raging on, the Petrograd Soviet instructed soldiers to obey the provisional government's orders, unless they were countermanded by the Soviet. On March 1, the Soviet issued Order Number One, which claimed for the Petrograd Soviet the authority to countermand orders of the provisional government on military matters and called for the election of soldiers' committees in every unit. In fact, such elections had already widely occurred, a remarkable attempt to democratize army life. In some places on the front, soldiers had refused to obey officers and, in a few cases, had beat them up or even shot them. The soldiers wanted peace. The danger that the military front might collapse against German pressure seemed quite real. Desertions increased in the first month of the Revolution, though not as rapidly as one might have expected. Even the tempting Bolshevik promise of "land and peace" seemed a distant prospect. As soldiers put it, "What good is land to me if I'm dead?"

The United States, first, and then Great Britain, France, and Italy quickly gave diplomatic recognition to the provisional government, hoping that the Revolution would not drastically affect the Russian military commitment to hold the eastern front. But in a few places on the front, Russian troops fraternized with astonished German and Austro-Hungarian soldiers.

The Revolution Spreads

News of the Revolution and the abdication of Tsar Nicholas II spread rapidly, despite wartime disruptions of communication and transportation. People from seemingly all social classes attacked and disarmed police stations, freed political prisoners, and created provisional governing bodies.

In the distant reaches of the old empire, it sometimes took weeks for "commissars of the revolution" to arrive armed with the dramatic news. In some industrial regions, commissars found that workers had already occupied the factories, demanding higher wages, an eight-hour day, and worker control over production. But in most places, the situation remained unclear. One Russian's comment reflected this uncertainty: "We feel that we have escaped from a dark cave into bright sunlight. And here we stand, not knowing where to go or what to do."

With Petrograd and much of European Russia caught between war and revolution, some of the minority peoples of the empire began to demand more favorable political status. Their demands were as myriad and complicated as the old Russian Empire itself. Among the nationalities, some nationalists sought only cultural autonomy; others wanted some degree of political freedom within the context of a federal structure; still others demanded outright independence. Such demands soured relations between ethnic groups in regions where tensions had persisted, sometimes for centuries. In the Baltic states of Lithuania, Latvia, and Estonia, nationalist movements grew rapidly, at least partially because of the presence of a sizable minority of ethnic Russians who had benefited from centuries of Russian domination of those nations. In the steppes of Central Asia and in the northern Caucasus, fighting broke out between Russian settlers and Cossacks (who had begun to settle the regions in large numbers following the emancipation of the serfs in 1861), the Kazakh-Kirghiz, Bashkirs, and other Turkish peoples. Thousands of people perished in these struggles. In regions shared by more than one nationality or religion, disputes were inevitable.

The provisional government's goal was to hold the empire together until a constituent assembly could be elected to establish the political basis of the new state. Its declaration of civil rights for all peoples had made each nationality in principle equal. In some places, representatives of the new regime immediately turned over administrative responsibility to local committees or individuals. But elsewhere, local peoples set up their own institutions of self-rule, which tried to maintain order in the wake of the collapse of imperial institutions. In some places, nationalist movements competed with Socialist Revolutionaries, Mensheviks, and Bolsheviks for allegiance.

The provisional government announced that Poland, which had been an independent state until the Third Partition by Russia, Prussia, and Austria in 1795, would again become independent. But this gesture was meaningless, with German or Austro-Hungarian troops occupying most of Poland. In neighboring Byelorussia (Belarus)—like Poland, a battleground—a national committee led by Socialist Revolutionaries demanded autonomy and established a Rada (council).

The situation in Ukraine was particularly complicated. The provisional government feared that if it granted Ukrainian autonomy, other nationalities would demand similar treatment. Shortly after the tsar's abdication, Ukrainian socialists had formed a soviet. On March 4, 1917, nationalists and socialists established the Ukrainian Central Council. Centuries-old resentment of Russia, based on cultural and linguistic differences, rose to the surface. As more radical nationalists gathered in Kiev, the Rada summoned a Ukrainian National Congress, which began to draft a statute for autonomy. Ukrainian soldiers formed their own military units. Serving as a *de facto* provisional government in Ukraine, the Rada broadened its social and national base by including non-Ukrainian residents. In the meantime, nationalism began to grip Ukrainian peasants, and many of them began to occupy lands owned by Russian or Polish landlords.

In regions with sizable Muslim populations, national movements were divided between religious conservatives, Western-looking liberals, and leftist Socialist Revolutionaries. The first All-Russian Muslim Congress, which began on May 1, 1917, reflected these divisions; conservatives attempted to shout down speakers advocating rights for women. But Westernizers predominated, passing the measure. The congress announced the future formation of a religious administration that would be separate from the state.

In its first days, the provisional government in Petrograd gave top priority to assuring the food supply and insisted that the army curtail its unpopular policy of requisitioning grain. But the provisional government also had to confront two burning issues of even more immediate concern: pressure from the Soviet for economic and social reforms—particularly land reform—and holding the military front. The provisional government authorized the formation of local food supply committees and "land committees" in order to help gather information to formulate a land reform measure for the Constituent Assembly. Liberals wanted land reform, but insisted that it be carried out in a deliberate, legal manner. Peasants, however, wanted action, not committees.

An All-Russian Congress of Soviets began at the end of March 1917 in Petrograd. Bringing together representatives of other soviets that had sprung up after the Revolution, this congress transformed the Petrograd Soviet into a national body, establishing a central executive committee dominated by members of the Petrograd Soviet. This, too, increased popular pressure for a radicalization of the Revolution.

A groundswell of opposition to Russia's continued participation in the war, marked by popular demonstrations in Petrograd, gradually drove a

Aleksander Kerensky (front center) head of the provisional government, with troops in Petrograd, 1917.

wedge between workers and soldiers and the provisional government. Nonetheless, at the All-Russian Congress of Soviets, the Bolsheviks' call for an immediate end to the war was easily defeated. Mensheviks and the Socialist Revolutionaries (who enjoyed a broad base of support among peasants) were willing to continue the war, but on the condition that the provisional government work for peace without annexations of the land of Russia's enemies.

The issue of the war led to the provisional government's "April Crisis." The minister of foreign affairs, a leader of the Kadets (Constitutional Democratic Party), added a personal note to an official communication to the Allies that called for "war to decisive victory" and that cited Russia's "historic right" to take Constantinople. Protests by the Petrograd Soviet and demonstrations against the war led to his resignation from the government at the beginning of May.

The April Crisis led to the formation of the first coalition government, which reflected the push to the left. Aleksandr Kerensky emerged as the government's leading figure. The participation of socialist members of the Petrograd Soviet in this coalition government reinforced its authority by seeming to lend popular legitimacy, making it no longer merely a "bourgeois government."

The provisional government now accepted the Petrograd Soviet's demand that "peace without annexations" be the basis of Russian foreign policy. "Revolutionary defensism" seemed a middle position between those conservatives who wanted the war to continue until "decisive victory" had been reached, and radicals who were most concerned with protecting the Revolution itself. Supporting the provisional government, "revolutionary defensists" wanted "peace without annexations and indemnities," but they also demanded that Russian military capacity be fully maintained.

Worsening material conditions radicalized many workers, particularly in trade unions that had sprung up since February 1917. Workers organized factory committees and strikes in May. In the countryside, hundreds of thousands of peasants took news of the February Revolution as a promise of more land. The poorer peasants operated on the simplest principle of all: those who work the land ought to own it. Many children or grandchildren of former serfs began to occupy the land of the lords for whom they had previously worked, sometimes killing landlords or former imperial officials in the process (although generally peasants did not seem to have expropriated the land of the wealthier peasants in their own communities). The percentage of landless peasants may have fallen by half during the 1917–1920 period. Soviets were also formed in the countryside as civil authority began to disappear. In some places, the Orthodox Church could no longer compel obedience. A priest reported, "My parishioners will nowadays only go to meetings of the soviet, and when I remind them about the church, they tell me they have no time."

Lenin's Return

The German government wanted to expedite Lenin's return to Russia from Switzerland, where he had been in exile since 1900. The Bolshevik leader's return might exert further pressure on the provisional government to sue for peace, allowing the German army to concentrate its efforts on the western front. The Germans permitted Lenin to pass through German territory in a sealed railway car to assure that he had no contact with the German population. Lenin arrived in Petrograd in early April 1917.

Lenin gradually rallied the Bolshevik Party around his leadership, based on the following propositions: (1) Russian withdrawal from the war, the continuation of which he viewed as a serious obstacle to a Bolshevik victory; (2) no support for the provisional government; (3) a call for revolution in the other countries of Europe; and (4) the seizure of large estates by the peasantry.

In his "April Theses," Lenin argued that wartime chaos had allowed the bourgeois and proletarian revolutions to merge in a dramatically short period of time. The overthrow of the autocracy had suddenly and unexpectedly handed power to a weak bourgeoisie. The bourgeoisie, holding power through the provisional government, could be in turn overthrown by the proletariat, supported by the poorest peasants.

Local power would be held by workers, soldiers, and peasants through the soviets, but under party guidance. Lenin thus called the soviets "the embryo of a provisional revolutionary government," a basis on which a new state could be constructed through the "dictatorship of the proletariat and peasantry."

Aided by the provisional government's division and growing unpopularity, the Bolshevik Party gained support among the members of the factory committees, workers' militias, Red Guards (factory workers' militias), sailors at the naval base of Kronshtadt, and the soldiers within the Petrograd garrison. The failure of the existing provisional government to provide either peace or land undermined its support among peasants. It was powerless to resolve industrial disputes or to put an end to land seizures. In the meantime, Menshevik leaders warned that continued Bolshevik radicalism might push conservatives toward launching a coup d'état.

The July Days

Although neither troop morale nor the military situation boded well for a new Russian offensive, in mid-June Kerensky announced an offensive in Galicia. This was to reassure conservatives and moderates that military discipline had been restored, and to convince the Allies that Russia remained committed to winning the war.

On July 3, 1917, the Bolsheviks rose in insurrection. They had been encouraged by their increasing popularity among workers, the ongoing agrarian revolution, and widespread dissatisfaction with the war. The Bolshevik Central Committee, however, had initially opposed the revolt, fearing that it would be crushed. Nearly 100,000 soldiers who feared being sent to the front joined the chaotic insurrection. Sensing defeat, the Bolshevik Central Committee tried to call off the insurrection the next day. Most troops remained loyal to the provisional government, and the uprising failed.

These "July Days" hardened political lines in Russia. The provisional government ordered the arrest of Bolshevik leaders, and troops closed down party headquarters and the offices of the Bolshevik Party's newspaper, *Pravda* (Truth). Kerensky became prime minister of the second coalition government, depending even more on support from the Kadets. Lenin fled to Finland, certain that the premature insurrection had demonstrated that his party still lacked sufficient unity and support within the soviets.

The provisional government now believed that the Bolsheviks were finished. Kerensky tried to portray Lenin as a German agent, noting that the Bolsheviks in exile had received some German money. Kerensky's government disarmed army regiments it considered disloyal, reinstated the death penalty for disobedience at the front, and staged a state funeral, replete with national and religious symbolism, in honor of soldiers killed at the front.

But the repressive measures undertaken against the Bolsheviks were relatively ineffective because of the disorganization of the judicial apparatus, the rapid turnover of government officials, and the support the Bolsheviks enjoyed in the working-class districts. Many Bolshevik leaders escaped arrest; others were soon released from jail. The repressive measures further discredited the provisional government, which seemed to be using the July Days as an excuse to undertake a counter-revolution.

With Lenin hiding in Finland, several Petrograd Bolsheviks argued that the Bolshevik Party should seek common ground with the moderate socialists. Lenin would have none of that. From exile he tried to convince his party that because of the apparent power vacuum and his party's readiness, the next insurrection would succeed. Doubting the revolutionary potential of the soviets, many of whose members and leaders remained Mensheviks and Socialist Revolutionaries, the Bolsheviks turned to the factory committees to consolidate their support. Bolshevik newspapers and brochures again appeared in factories, denouncing the provisional government and accusing moderate socialists of counter-revolution.

The Kornilov Affair

Disillusioned by Kerensky's indecision, frustrated by the ineffectiveness of the repression against the Bolsheviks, and frightened by peasant land seizures, Russian conservatives, including some military officers and Kadets, as well, began to think in terms of a coup d'état.

General Lavr Kornilov (1870–1918), newly appointed commander in chief of the army, seemed the obvious candidate to overthrow the provisional government. He was a tough, decorated Cossack who had escaped from Hungary after being captured during the Great War and was a favorite of the Kadets. Prelates of the Orthodox Church sent him icons in the hope that the military could restore religious principles to Russia. In early August 1917, a "Conference of Public Figures," including influential leaders drawn from industry, commerce, banking, and the military, pledged Kornilov their support.

As Russian society became increasingly polarized, Kerensky organized a Moscow State Conference, which he hoped would mobilize support for his second coalition government. Most of the delegates (some of whom were leaders of trade unions, as well as bankers, representatives from the state dumas, military leaders, and professional people) now believed only a military dictatorship could save Russia from the soviets and from having to pull out of the war. Making matters worse, the Germans had captured Riga, a major Baltic seaport, and thus posed a direct threat to Petrograd.

Kerensky wanted Kornilov to form a military government that could restore order, but he believed that the general would remain loyal to him and to the idea of establishing a democratic republic. Kornilov was not nostalgic for the empire *per se*, but rather for its military style and authority. He probably wanted to seize power and impose a right-wing military regime. A confusing exchange led each leader to misconstrue what the other meant. Kerensky demanded Kornilov's resignation as commander in chief and, when the latter refused, called on the army to remain loyal to the provisional government. On August 27, Kornilov issued an ultimatum to the provisional government declaring that "the heavy sense of the inevitable ruin of the country commands me in this ominous moment to call upon all Russian people to come to the aid of the dying motherland."

Bolsheviks, Mensheviks, and Socialist Revolutionaries formed a committee for struggle against counter-revolution. Workers reinforced security around their factories. Bolsheviks were among those receiving arms at the arsenals in anticipation of a stand against a military coup. But no coup d'état took place, and probably none had been planned. By raising the specter of counter-revolution, however, the Kornilov Affair aided the Bolsheviks, who were able to portray themselves as the only possible saviors of the Revolution.

The October Revolution

Confronted by a growing political and social crisis, the provisional government seemed increasingly powerless. The workers of Petrograd were now organized and armed. Striking workers demanded "a minimum living wage," more control over hiring and firing, reduced factory hours, maternity leave for women workers, and worker "control" over management. Industrial workers believed that the soviets could bring them practical gains in their struggle for higher wages and generally better working conditions. The provisional government seemed incapable of solving the worsening economic crisis and unwilling to take Russia out of the war. Only the Bolsheviks promised in their program to turn over to the soviets some degree of political power. The All-Russian Executive Committee of the Soviets approved the Bolshevik demand that a "democratic" republic be declared by a government "of representatives of the revolutionary proletariat and peasantry" from which Kadets would be excluded.

The Bolsheviks Seize Power

Returning to Petrograd in disguise, Lenin on October 10 convinced the Bolshevik Central Committee that a second insurrection could succeed. Kerensky believed a Bolshevik insurrection imminent, but he vastly underestimated the party's influence with the Petrograd workers, the soviets, and within some army units. Bolshevik propaganda hammered away at the theme that their party, representing virtuous opposition, was untainted by support for the provisional government. Even if a majority of soldiers or of the population of Petrograd or of Russia did not necessarily favor the Bolsheviks, Lenin's assessment that they would not oppose their seizure of power proved correct. On October 16, 1917, the Bolsheviks formed a military revolutionary committee to coordinate the insurrection with factory committees and army regulars.

Late on October 24, 1917, Kerensky shut down Bolshevik newspapers and sent troops to hold the bridges over the Neva River. But the next day, Petrograd residents disarmed military cadets sent to one bridge. About 12,000 young Red Guards launched the insurrection.

Factory committees in Petrograd's industrial districts voted to support the uprising. It was coordinated by Leon Trotsky (Lev Davidovich Bronstein; 1879–1940). Trotsky, the revolutionary son of a wealthy Jewish farmer, had borrowed his alias from one of his prison guards. Bolsheviks repelled an attack by army cadets loyal to the provisional government, the only serious fighting of the October Revolution. The regiments upon which Kerensky had counted remained in their barracks, their neutrality striking a blow for the insurrection.

The provisional government simply collapsed. Kerensky left Petrograd the same day in a car borrowed from the U.S. embassy, hoping in vain to rally military support at the front. That night, the battleship *Aurora*, under the control of revolutionaries, lobbed a couple of shells toward the Winter Palace, where the last ministers of the provisional government were holding out. The provisional government surrendered after only about eight months of existence. The Bolsheviks now held power in Petrograd.

The October Revolution had occurred as if in slow motion. There were fewer people killed than in either the February Revolution or the July Days. Life went on in many districts of the city as if nothing unusual was occurring. Restaurants, casinos, theaters, and the ballet remained open as

The Bolsheviks seize the Winter Palace, October 1917.

usual, although banks closed, attendance was down somewhat at the theater, and streetcars were hard to find. The stock market, which had risen in anticipation of a military coup d'état during the Kornilov crisis, now fell. John Reed, an American sympathetic to the Bolshevik takeover, recalled that in Petrograd's fancy quarters "the ladies of the minor bureaucratic set took tea with each other in the afternoon, [each] carrying her little gold or silver or jeweled sugar-box, and half a loaf of bread in her muff, and wishing that the tsar were back, or that the Germans would come, or anything that would solve the servant problem . . . the daughter of a friend of mine came home one afternoon in hysterics because the woman streetcar conductor had called her 'Comrade.' "

Most Mensheviks and many Socialist Revolutionaries walked out of the All-Russian Congress of Soviets to protest the Bolshevik insurrection. On October 26, the remaining members approved the Bolshevik proposal that "all local authority be transferred to the soviets." The Central Committee of the Congress of Soviets, all Bolsheviks except for some leftist Socialist Revolutionaries, now ran the government.

In Moscow, Russia's second city, which was less socially polarized than Petrograd, the insurrection began after the first favorable reports from Petrograd arrived. There, too, the Bolsheviks found support in workers' neighborhoods. After a week of fighting, the forces of the provisional government surrendered.

In the vast reaches of the former Russian Empire, a "revolution by telegraph" took place. Commissars representing the Bolsheviks went into the provinces (see Map 23.1). In industrial regions, where the Bolsheviks already dominated some soviets, it was easy enough to establish a military revolutionary committee to assume local power. Socialist Revolutionaries believed that they could coexist with the new Bolshevik-dominated government. But the Bolsheviks manipulated ethnic, social, and political tensions, purging the soviets of non-Bolsheviks and pushing aside not only the local institutions of self-rule that had spontaneously sprung up after the February Revolution but also their nominal allies, the Socialist Revolutionaries. In the countryside, the Bolsheviks cultivated support among the poorest peasants.

In Ukraine, the situation remained calm at least partially because the Bolsheviks had early in the Revolution made an agreement with Ukrainian nationalists. In the distant borderlands where ethnic Russians were a minority, however, strong anti-Russian national feeling often made it extremely difficult for the Bolsheviks to take control.

The Bolsheviks remained a small minority in Russia at the time of the October Revolution. "We shall not enter into the kingdom of socialism in white gloves on a polished floor," Trotsky had warned shortly before the October Revolution. The revolutionary government, under Lenin's leadership, seized banks, closed down newspapers,

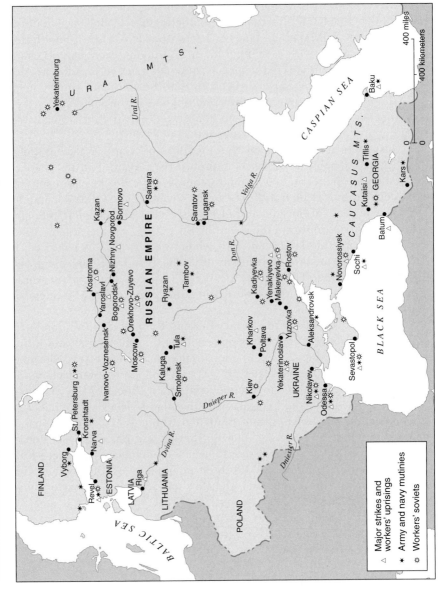

MAP 23.1 THE RUSSIAN REVOLUTION   Sites of strikes, uprisings, and army and navy mutinies during the Russian Revolution, as well as the cities in which soviets were established by the revolutionaries.

banned the Constitutional Democratic Party, and arrested some of its members, as well as a number of Mensheviks. In December, a new centralized police authority, the Cheka (All-Russian Extraordinary Commission), began to root out the Bolsheviks' enemies. It rapidly proliferated into a large organization with virtually unlimited power. Arbitrary arrests led the eminent writer Maxim Gorky to ask, "Does not Lenin's government, as did the Romanov government, seize and drag off to prison all those who think differently?"

In elections for the Constituent Assembly, the Bolsheviks were supported only by the left wing of the Socialist Revolutionaries. The Bolsheviks won just 29 percent of the vote, compared with 58 percent for the Socialist Revolutionaries, who maintained their support in the countryside. When the elected deputies arrived early in January 1918, the Bolsheviks forced the assembly to adjourn the next day. It never met again. Red Guards fired on a crowd of protesters.

That month, Lenin proclaimed the "Declaration of the Rights of the Toiling and Exploited People," which stated that the goal of the revolutionary government was "the socialist organization of society and the victory of socialism in all countries." The third All-Russian Congress of Soviets created the Russian Socialist Soviet Republic, a federation of "soviet republics." But, as in the Russian Empire, Russia's interests, even under socialism, remained paramount.

The Peace of Brest-Litovsk

After the Bolsheviks took power, Trotsky, the "People's Commissar for Foreign Affairs," offered Germany an immediate armistice. The German government accepted, and an armistice was signed early in December 1917. However, Trotsky broke off negotiations for a permanent peace agreement because of draconian German demands. In mid-February, German troops marched virtually unopposed into Russia, capturing Kiev and much of Ukraine and Crimea, as well as some of the Caucasus region. On March 3, 1918, the Bolshevik government signed the Treaty of Brest-Litovsk with Germany, giving up one-fourth of the surface of what had been imperial European Russia, containing some of its most fertile land and most of its iron and steel production. The Bolsheviks also agreed to German occupation of Estonia, Lithuania, and Latvia and acquiesced to pulling Russian troops out of Ukraine and Finland. Angered by the treaty and demanding rapid attention to the agrarian question, the leftist Socialist Revolutionaries ended their cooperation with the Bolsheviks. The Germans then occupied all of Finland and Ukraine, forcing the latter to sign a separate harsh peace, while setting up puppet regimes in both states.

MAP 23.2 THE RUSSIAN CIVIL WAR   Boundaries of areas controlled by the Whites and the Reds during the Russian Civil War, including advances by the White and foreign armies.

CIVIL WAR

The Russian Civil War began in 1918 when Kornilov and other generals raised armies to fight the Bolsheviks (see Map 23.2). The anti-Bolshevik forces became known as the "Whites" because they shared a common hatred of the Bolsheviks, the "Reds." The White armies held Central Asia and Siberia, the Kazan region east of Moscow, and the Caucasus Mountains. A legion of 50,000 Czechoslovak troops, which had surrendered earlier in the war, operated as an anti-Bolshevik force along an extensive stretch of territory into Siberia, holding the crucial trans-Siberian railway. The White army played upon anti-Semitism by denouncing Trotsky and other Bolshevik leaders because they were Jews. A wave of pogroms spread through Ukraine and parts of Russia. More than 2 million people fled abroad to escape the Russian Revolution and the ensuing Civil War.

Ukraine passed back and forth between Bolshevik and nationalist control in bloody fighting, falling again briefly into the hands of the Germans. A huge peasant army led by the anarchist Nestor Makno controlled parts of Ukraine after the Germans had fallen back. In Siberia, General Aleksandr Kolchak (1874–1920), backed by Britain and France, established a dictatorship, claiming to be the new government of Russia.

In February 1918, the Soviet government proclaimed the nationalization of all land. Food shortages and famine spread in the summer of 1918. The Bolsheviks reacted to the crisis by implementing "War Communism." The state appropriated heavy industries and gradually put an end to private trade. In June, the Bolsheviks established "committees of poor peasants" in order to "carry the class war to the village." As peasants refused to deliver produce to towns, the Bolsheviks forcibly requisitioned food and raw materials, turning poor peasants against wealthier ones, known as "kulaks." Peasants from whom grain was being taken sometimes reacted

Lenin addressing the troops leaving for the front during the Civil War, 1920. Trotsky is in uniform standing to the right of the podium, and was later removed from this famous photo after he was purged.

with shock—after all, before the October Revolution the Bolsheviks had loudly proclaimed their support for immediate land reform. Now Communist forces were taking their food. Many peasants resisted. In one village, a hungry crowd stormed the home of the local commissar, beat him to death, and stuffed his mouth full of food ration cards. War Communism may have saved the Revolution, but it took a terrible toll, leading to a dramatic decline in industrial production.

Bolshevik guards moved Nicholas II and his family to Ekaterinburg, a town in the Ural Mountains, as rumors spread that the Czech legion or monarchist generals were planning to rescue them. On July 17—again, the tsar's unlucky number—they were brutally executed on the orders of the local soviet, an act evidently approved by Bolshevik leaders.

The Allies, particularly Britain, supplied the White armies. In August 1918, British, American, and Canadian soldiers landed in the northern port of Murmansk, claiming that such measures were necessary to prevent Russia's northern ports from falling to the Germans. Allied suspicion of the new Bolshevik government strengthened their decision to intervene. British troops attacked Soviet forces, and American troops landed at the icy port of Archangel. Japanese troops established themselves in Siberia, where the Bolsheviks had little effective control, and they stayed there until 1922. In Ukraine, a Menshevik-leaning government opposed Bolshevik rule and permitted its territory to be used as a mobilization point for warfare against Russia's revolutionary government.

Allied intervention helped rally popular opinion against the Whites, whose wanton brutality, including routine rape and murder (some victims were forced to kneel and kiss portraits of the tsar before being killed), exceeded that of the Bolsheviks. Whites filled three freight cars with bodies of Red Guards, sending them along to the Bolsheviks, who were starving, with the wagons labeled "fresh meat, destination Petrograd." However, the Whites had no monopoly on savagery, as in some places Bolshevik forces massacred peasants and Cossacks. In Finland, after a bitter civil war between local Reds and Whites, the "White Terror" took 80,000 victims among those who had supported the Revolution.

Following attempts on the lives of several Bolshevik leaders, including Lenin, the "Red Terror" officially began in September 1918. Government decrees gave the Cheka almost unlimited authority and set up forced labor camps to incarcerate those considered enemies. While many victims were indeed working for the overthrow of the regime, many others were simply Mensheviks, Socialist Revolutionaries, or others who held political beliefs that displeased the Bolsheviks.

The Red Army defeated the largest White army, 150,000 strong under General Anton Denikin (1872–1947), in Ukraine during the summer of 1919 and turned back a final march on Moscow in October. General Aleksandr Kolchak's White army held out until late that year. The next year, the Red Army repelled a Polish invasion of Ukraine and continued on to

The White army executes suspected Bolsheviks during the Civil War.

the outskirts of Warsaw. A final attack launched from Crimea in 1920 ended in failure. Victory in the Civil War heightened Bolshevik determination not to tolerate movements for national autonomy. Commissars reestablished Bolshevik authority over the border lands such as Georgia, Ukraine, and Turkistan.

THE SOVIET UNION

The Revolution seemed to offer hope for peasants. Unleashed by the February Revolution, their rebellions continued in 1918. After destroying the authority of the imperial regime in the countryside, they then broke the power of the landlords. Many peasants feared the Whites, and they therefore went along with the demands of the Soviet regime, hoping that "peace and land" would follow. The Bolsheviks were able to install a centralized state authority to mobilize the countryside against the counter-revolution. Backed by a powerful army, they then destroyed the local soviets. Like the old imperial elites, the Bolsheviks mistrusted the peasants, their notions of family and village ownership of land, sense of collective responsibility, and eagerness to market what they produced. The Civil War reinforced Bolshevik prejudices against peasants, and it established a precedent for the use of mass terror to enforce the party's will in rural areas.

A constitution promulgated in July 1918 promised freedom of speech and assembly, as well as the separation of church and state. It also required all citizens to work. The "dictatorship of the proletariat" became that of the Bolsheviks. Marxist theory promised the "withering of the state" once socialism had been constructed, and Lenin himself warned against the growing power of the bureaucracy, which he had helped create. But the Soviet state did anything but wither.

The Union of Soviet Socialist Republics was created in 1922. It included Russia, Byelorussia (Belarus), Ukraine, and Transcaucasia (Georgia, Armenia, and Azerbaijan, which all became separate republics in 1936), to which Uzbek (Uzbekistan) was added in 1924, Turkmen (Turkistan) in 1925, Tadzhik in 1929, and Kazakh (Kazakhstan) and Kirghiz in 1936 (see Map 23.3). But in many places, the concept of the "national" borders of a republic meant absolutely nothing. In any case, Russian interests prevailed within the party, and thus within the government. The republics enjoyed virtually no autonomy, while the Soviet state claimed that communism had brought stability by eliminating ethnic tensions. The Soviets believed that ethnic claims were of only secondary importance in the long run; in the meantime, they encouraged the nationalities of the Soviet Union to develop their own identities, believing that ultimately nationalism would disappear in the new socialist world. It never did.

Democratic Centralism

For Lenin, "democratic centralism," which had referred to decisions taken by the Bolshevik Party, was also a goal in itself in the organization of the socialist state. In the summer of 1918, the Bolsheviks took the name of the Communist Party, a name Lenin had favored during the war as a way of more clearly differentiating the more radical Bolsheviks from the Mensheviks, their socialist rivals. Lenin's concept originally called for open and free discussion and debate on policy issues, but once party leaders made a decision all dissent had to end and all party members were to unite around the party line. Major decisions and discipline would thus come from the top. The structure suffocated the democratic apparatus on the local level, which henceforth received orders that flowed downward and outward from the central party apparatus in the name of the state.

The Communist government did not implement rights of nationalities or tolerate workers' self-management, two of the goals of many people who had helped overthrow the tsarist autocracy. A group called the Left Communists had opposed signing the Treaty of Brest-Litovsk with Germany, arguing that Russia should lead a revolutionary war against the capitalist powers. Furthermore, they denounced the growing centralization of power. In response, Lenin acidly denounced "Left Infantilism and the Petty Bourgeois Spirit" in the summer of 1918, referring to those who criticized the abandonment of the principles of workers' self-management. Now "workers' control" meant state control.

In June 1919, the Bolsheviks nationalized most of the large-scale industries. In early 1921, at the end of the Civil War, worker discontent

MAP 23.3 THE SOVIET REPUBLICS, 1922–1939 Soviet Socialist Republics (SSRs) and their capitals in the Union of Soviet Socialist Republics.

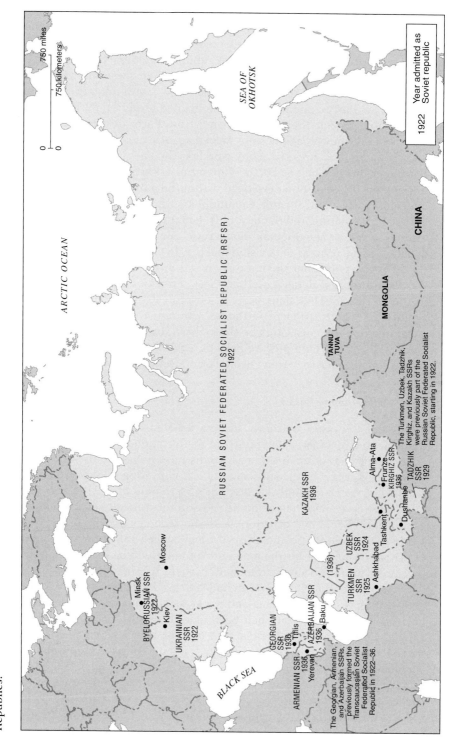

erupted in strikes and demonstrations in some industrial centers. In March 1921, the Red army crushed a revolt at the Kronshtadt naval base, where sailors demanded freely elected soviets. Massive strikes rocked Petrograd after Bolshevik authorities rebuffed workers' demands for better working conditions and more control over their shops and factories. A fundamental tension remained between the state—and therefore the Communist Party—and workers who remained loyal to their trade unions and wanted to run their plants themselves. Party officials pushed the soviets out of the way as the state turned against the idea of workers' self-management. This angered many workers, the vast majority of whom in Petrograd did not belong to the Communist Party. In 1920, then, two movements of opposition developed within the party: working-class opponents of party control, and Communists who objected to the party's authoritarian nature and the lack of freedom of speech. These opponents wanted to restore the original "democratic" element—free discussion and debate—to the process of decision making. In 1922, someone asked Trotsky, "Do you remember the days when you promised us that the Bolsheviks would respect democratic liberties?" Trotsky replied, "Yes, that was in the old days." That same year, when protests occurred in one region against the confiscation of Orthodox Church treasures, Lenin himself suggested that demonstrators be shot: "The more [of them] we manage to shoot, the better. Right now we have to teach this public a lesson, so that for several decades they won't even dare to think of resisting."

The New Economic Policy

Lenin and the other Bolshevik leaders debated how socialism could be implemented in a vast, poor country of many nationalities. The new Soviet government had to repair the massive disruption done to the economy by the Great War and by the subsequent Civil War. More then 7 million people died of starvation and sickness during a famine in 1921–1922. Moreover, the war against Poland and the loss of territory also accentuated the gravity of the economic situation. With the economy in near total collapse, Lenin recognized that communist ideology, which called for the abolition of private ownership, for the moment would have to be sacrificed. Market incentives would have to be tolerated, perhaps for some time.

Furthermore, War Communism had collapsed because of the resistance, active and passive, of peasants and workers. The cities and army had only been fed because the state had been able to requisition or commandeer supplies in the vast countryside. At a time of severe famine, the government needed to feed the population and build up a surplus of raw materials and food supplies. After the threat from the White armies had passed, some peasants had violently resisted grain requisitioning. Against this background, in March 1921, Lenin announced a "New Economic Policy" (NEP). Although the state maintained its centralized control over the economy, the NEP permitted peasants to use the land as if it were their own and

(*Left*) After the collapse of War Communism, a severe famine led to the starvation of millions, including the refugee children pictured here. (*Right*) As a result, Lenin instituted the New Economic Policy in 1921, which permitted free markets such as this one.

allowed trade of produce at market prices, although the state retained control of heavy industries. The goal was, above all, to encourage peasants to bring their crops to market. Lenin called this a temporary "retreat" on the road to socialism, a concession to peasant hostility to forced requisitioning. Some merchants whose stores had been nationalized during the Civil War were now allowed to manage them again, and the government permitted small-scale, privately owned manufacturing. Lenin even invited foreign investment in mining and other development projects.

The NEP was a success, making possible a revival of the economy. The amount of land under cultivation and industrial production gradually began to reach pre-war levels. In towns, small businesses run by "nepmen," prospered, and "kulaks" gained. But if the NEP brought economic concessions, there were virtually none in the political realm. The Bolsheviks further consolidated their hold over most government functions, claiming to be serving the interests of the working class by protecting them against the Western Allies, the middle class, and the kulaks. They declared all other political parties illegal, although Lenin claimed that this ban would be only a temporary measure, like the NEP itself. The Bolsheviks imprisoned Socialist Revolutionaries, whose base of support had been in the countryside, and exiled some Mensheviks. Moreover, officials began to limit the entrepreneurship of nepmen beginning in 1924 and of kulaks in 1927.

The Rise of Stalin

During the early 1920s, the influence of Joseph Stalin rose within the party. Stalin—an alias taken from the Russian word for "steel"—was born

Joseph (Soso) Dzhugashvili (1879–1953) in Georgia, beyond the Caucasus Mountains in the southern reaches of the Russian Empire. His father was a tough cobbler who may have been killed in a tavern brawl, his mother a religious and doting woman who worked as hard as his father drank. Stalin's early feelings of insecurity would eventually lapse into extreme paranoia.

The young Stalin entered an Orthodox seminary in 1894 in the Georgian capital of Tbilisi. Stalin, like many other seminarians, rebelled against the conservatism of the Orthodox Church. In the seminary, Stalin, who spoke Georgian, learned Russian, secretly read Marxist tracts, and joined a radical study circle, for which he was expelled from the seminary. Arrested in 1902 and exiled to Siberia the next year, Stalin escaped and returned to Georgia. There he sided with the Bolsheviks against the Mensheviks. The Bolsheviks' hardened secrecy appealed to the young Georgian's acerbic personality. More arrests, jail terms, exile to Siberia, and escapes followed in rapid succession over the next seven years. In 1912, Lenin appointed Stalin to the Bolshevik Central Committee, and, after yet another escape from prison, he became editor of *Pravda,* the Bolshevik Party newspaper.

At the time of the February Revolution, Stalin was a prisoner in Siberia, 600 miles from even the trans-Siberian railway. Stalin managed to return to Petrograd in March, 1917, and, after the October Revolution, helped Lenin draft the "Declaration of the Rights of the Peoples of Russia," which promised the peoples of the old Russian Empire self-determination. During the Civil War, he served with Lenin and Trotsky on the military revolutionary council and quarreled with the headstrong Trotsky over military tactics.

Stalin's differences with Trotsky went beyond their old rivalry. Trotsky had surprisingly little gift for the ruthless political infighting that was as natural to Stalin as breathing. Trotsky, an intense intellectual and powerful orator, considered Stalin a "mediocrity." Stalin considered himself a pragmatist, and he remained suspicious of "cosmopolitan"—often an anti-Semitic code word for Jewish—intellectuals such as Trotsky. The latter's caustic condemnation of bureaucrats in any guise irritated the old guard and undermined his support among them.

Trotsky espoused "permanent revolution," believing that socialism in the Soviet Union could only be victorious following world revolution and that the capitalist nations of the West were ripe to be overthrown by proletarian revolutions. The Communist International, which had been founded in 1919, aimed to help organize and assist revolutionary Communist parties in other countries. Lenin had believed that workers would overthrow one Western state after another. But this had not happened. The German Revolution of 1919 and the revolutionary government of Béla Kun in Hungary had been crushed (see Chapter 24). The International also promised to help colonial people free themselves from imperialist domination. "Colonial slaves of Africa and Asia!" the International proclaimed, "the hour of proletariat dictatorship in Europe will also be the hour of your own liberation."

In May 1922, Lenin suffered a stroke. His increasing incapacitation set off a struggle of succession infused with personal as well as ideological rivalries. Stalin was thus well placed as a potential successor to Lenin, who remained partially paralyzed and could speak only with difficulty. Stalin had demonstrated forceful independence while remaining loyal to the party, and he showed a capacity for organization. In April 1922, the Central Committee had named Stalin to the important, recently created post of general secretary, which allowed him to appoint allies to various important posts and to repress dissent within the party.

The problem of the role of the 180 nationalities in the Soviet Union became ever more pressing. Lenin's support for national self-determination had been principally intended to undermine the provisional government. Furthermore, concerned with the Soviet Union's image in the colonial world, he wanted to give the impression that the various republics enjoyed a degree of sovereignty. Yet Lenin believed that national differences posed a threat to "the dictatorship of the proletariat" and that they would become irrelevant in the new communist state.

Stalin, now commissar for nationalities, believed that the various peoples of the old imperial state should simply be incorporated into the existing Russian state. During the Civil War, he had returned to his homeland, Georgia, to crush "the hydra of nationalism," despite his earlier insistence that a communist regime would recognize national self-determination. Lenin, however, had rethought the national question during the bloody Civil War, retreating from his earlier stand. No longer having to concern

Vladimir Lenin (*left*) with Joseph Stalin (*right*) in a photo doctored by Stalin, who was eager to exaggerate his close association with Lenin.

himself with overthrowing the tsarist state but rather with building its socialist successor, he now denounced the "dominant nation chauvinism" of Russia, insisting that each major nationality have its own state, which would be incorporated into a union of Soviet peoples. In this way, he hoped, the various peoples of the Soviet Union would accept socialism without compulsion.

In the meantime, Stalin kept Lenin isolated as much as possible from visitors. In December 1922, a day after suffering another stroke, Lenin dictated his doubts about Stalin: "Comrade Stalin, on becoming general secretary, concentrated boundless power in his hands, and I am not sure whether he will always know how to use this power with sufficient caution." Lenin also now warned against the expansion of the bureaucracies of both the Communist Party and the state.

Lenin's death in January 1924 led Stalin to step up his efforts to consolidate his power. Stalin placed his own men on the Central Committee and made party appointments throughout the Soviet state. He took every occasion to leave the impression that Lenin had handpicked him to be the next Communist Party leader, later doctoring photos so that he appeared to have been constantly at Lenin's side as his chosen favorite. Stringing together quotations from Lenin, Stalin rushed into print his own *The Foundations of Leninism*, which suggested that he was the natural heir to the Marxist theorist.

The Left Opposition to Stalin was led by Trotsky and Grigory Zinoviev (1883–1936), the humorless but scrupulous curly-haired party secretary of Leningrad (Petrograd's name after Lenin's death). The Left Opposition believed that the Soviet Union ought to support independent—that is, non-Communist working-class organizations—and criticized Stalin for abandoning Communist internationalism. Stalin, in contrast, argued that the Bolsheviks first had to build "socialism in one country"—that is, the Soviet Union. Allying with the right wing of the party between 1925 and 1927, Stalin isolated leaders of the left by assigning their allies to inconsequential posts in distant places.

In 1927, the Left Opposition demanded worker mobilization against bureaucracy. Above all, they wanted accelerated industrialization in the state sector. They considered Lenin's NEP an unnecessary ideological compromise that might inadvertently bring back capitalism. Wealthier peasant proprietors, the Left Opposition argued, could be forced to provide the surplus that would sustain gradual industrialization. If the state, which controlled heavy industries, kept the prices of manufactured goods high, state revenue would increase, permitting further industrial development. But they opposed forced collectivization and other draconian policies of Stalin. In 1927, the Central Committee, with Stalin completely in charge, voted to expel Trotsky and Zinoviev from the Communist Party and refused to publish Lenin's "Political Testament," which had suggested that Stalin be replaced as general secretary. The Soviet Union entered the long period of the dictatorship of Joseph Stalin.

Five-Year Plans

Stalin believed that socialism could not be fully implemented until the Soviet Union had a stronger industrial base. After purging the Left Opposition, he openly favored their plan of accelerated industrialization. This would be paid for by extracting more resources from the peasantry. In 1928 and 1929, Stalin resumed the forced requisitioning of "surpluses" and expropriated the land of richer peasants. When this led to growing peasant opposition, he took the next step in 1930: the forced collectivization of agriculture—the elimination of private ownership of land and animals. The Five-Year Plan would mark a complete abandonment of Lenin's New Economic Policy, which Stalin believed would have allowed capitalism to be restored.

Nikolay Bukharin (1888–1938) objected to a policy of renewed requisitioning and immediate collectivization on the grounds that it would greatly undermine peasant support for the regime, ultimately slowing rather than speeding up industrialization. In 1928, he became the leader of the Right Opposition, which also disagreed with Stalin's abandonment of the principle of collective leadership. Stalin, with support from other top party leaders, accused Bukharin of trying to surrender to "capitalist elements." He ousted Bukharin from his position as editor of the Communist Party newspaper as well as from the International. By the end of 1930, Stalin had purged the Right Opposition from the party.

In formulating his Five-Year Plan, Stalin sought to take advantage of social tensions in Soviet society. He knew that workers believed that material progress was not coming fast enough and that they blamed peasants and smug bureaucrats. Stalin wanted to inspire workers to storm the "fortress" of remaining inequalities in Soviet society. He used the rhetoric of class struggle as a means of mobilizing effort, trying to turn workers against "bourgeois" managers and kulaks.

The first Five-Year Plan (1928–1933) led to a bloodbath in the countryside. Hundreds of thousands of peasants who refused to turn over their harvests, animals, or farms were killed. An officer in the secret police told a foreign journalist: "I am an old Bolshevik. I worked in the underground against the tsar and then I fought in the Civil War. Did I do all that in order that I should now surround villages with machine guns and order my men to fire indiscriminately into crowds of peasants?" Peasants resisted in many ways with determination and resourcefulness. There were waves of protest, often led by women, in which crowds demanded the repeal of decrees ordering the establishment of collective farms, the redistribution of land, or the introduction of new crop systems. In 1929, 30,000 fires were reported in Russia alone. Many peasants slaughtered livestock rather than allowing them to be taken by the collective farm. The number of horses fell from 36 million in 1929 to 15 million four years later, cattle from 67 million to 34 million during the same period.

Small plots were forcibly consolidated into collective farms. Peasants had to work a certain number of days each year for the collective farm; the

The deportation of prosperous peasants (kulaks) from a Russian village during land collectivization, 1930.

state supplied machinery, seed, and clothing. The free market disappeared, with the state establishing production quotas and setting prices. One of the primary goals of the collectivization of agriculture was to force peasants into industrial labor. During the first Five-Year Plan, the Soviet Union's industrial and urban populations doubled, as 9 million peasants were conscripted to work in factories.

In March 1930, Stalin signed an article in *Pravda* entitled "Dizzy with Success." He announced that his Five-Year Plan was succeeding beyond his wildest expectations and that the time had come for a pause. In fact, forced collectivization had catastrophically reduced Soviet agricultural production. Indeed, Stalin ordered officials to return expropriated animals to their owners. But he viewed this as a lull, not a change in theory.

The Five-Year Plan ended in 1932 (in part because of the effects of peasant resistance) after four years and three months, with 62 percent of the peasants now working for the state in collective farms. The campaign continued, though somewhat less brutally; four years later, the figure was 93 percent. Peasants were allowed to retain small private plots; the vegetables and fruits that they grew provided almost half of the produce reaching markets. Overall, however, living conditions deteriorated during the Five-Year Plan. Shortages of fuel and machine parts became severe. Hundreds of thousands of peasants had been killed, and perhaps 2 million had been exiled to Siberia or other distant places under the sentence of hard labor. Around 7 million people died of hunger between 1930 and 1933, and 4 to

5 million people starved during 1932 and 1933, most in Ukraine. In Kazakhstan in Central Asia, about 2 million people (one-tenth of the population) died or were killed between 1926 and 1933, including pastoral Kazakhs forced into a miserable, sedentary life in the collective farms.

The campaign for heavy industrialization proceeded successfully, if the human cost is conveniently forgotten. Despite inaccurate and sometimes misleading Soviet data, the state did meet some ambitious production targets in heavy industry (iron and steel), fuel production (oil and electricity), new industries (especially chemicals), and in the manufacture of tractors. While a harsh economic depression devastated Western economies, between 1929 and 1934 the Soviet economy may have had an annual growth rate of a remarkable 27 percent. These successes occurred despite inefficiency due to inadequate planning, chaotic reporting of figures (compounded by the mounting sense of urgency to report successes), and by the replacement of many of the most able technicians (because of their social class) by dedicated but semiliterate workers or peasants who sometimes mistook mud for oil.

Giant show projects such as the Dnieper Dam and the new industrial city of Magnitogorsk in the Ural Mountains attracted international attention. Foreign visitors found many workers who went to work with great initial enthusiasm. Party officials selected "heroes of labor" to be praised for surpassing their production targets by record amounts. A certain Andrei Stakhanov, a Don Basin miner, was credited in August 1935 with cutting 102 tons of coal during a single shift. A "Stakhanovite" became the idealized Soviet worker, working as fast as he or she could, and ready to step forward to denounce "Trotskyite wreckers and saboteurs."

The second Five-Year Plan (1933–1937) relied less on the shrill rhetoric of class warfare, despite ongoing collectivization. Stalin relaxed the ideologically charged campaign against "experts" of bourgeois origins, and technocrats again appeared in factories.

In the meantime, Stalin reinforced his dictatorship. Even with most consumer goods still wanting, 4.5 million radios in the Soviet Union broadcast Stalin's speeches in the 1930s. The grandson of a Soviet minister recalled, "Stalin was like a God for us. Somebody told me that Stalin could be the best surgeon. He could perform a brain operation better than anyone else, and I believed it." A poem from the 1930s, entitled "There Is a Man in Moscow," reflects this bizarre and troubling adulation:

Who is that man who appears to the toilers,
Spreading happiness and joy all around?
It is Stalin, I shout, so the whole world will hear,
It is Stalin, our Leader and Friend.

Soviet Culture

Many artists and writers were enthusiastic about the Revolution, and a spirit of utopianism survived into the early 1920s. The Communists wanted to build a unique culture based upon mass mobilization and commitment that would both reflect and accentuate the collectivization of life in the Soviet Union, helping forge consensus. The culture of utopianism would be defiantly proletarian and egalitarian.

In view of Stalin's determination that the Soviet Union rapidly industrialize, the machine and mechanization played major parts in Soviet imagery in the inter-war period. Soviet artists and writers believed that mechanization in the service of capitalists had further enslaved the masses but that technology could be potentially liberating. The state created art schools and provided assistance to struggling artists, hoping to enroll them in the service of the Revolution. In its first years, the Soviet state patronized futurists (see Chapter 20) as revolutionary artists who had embraced technological change and the machine and who would provide a novel aesthetic for socialism in the construction of an ideal society. Soviet futurists issued a manifesto in which they promised to "re-examine the theory and practice of Leftist art, to free it from individualist distortions, and develop its Communist aspects." Artists collaborated with designers in producing models for standardized clothing and household items.

As the Soviet state subsumed most aspects of public life, the initial mini-explosion of cultural forms that had occurred during the first years of the Soviet state gave way to repressive orthodoxy. Rejecting traditional and avant-garde art as bourgeois escapism, Stalin believed that art and literature should assume a social function. "The artist," he said in 1932, "must give first priority to the truthful presentation of life, and if he truly portrays our life, then he cannot but show that it leads to socialism. This will be socialist art. This will be socialist realism." Stalin preferred monumental murals that could be seen by many people, showing smiling workers toiling for the state. Artists who did not conform stood accused of pandering to "bourgeois values," an increasingly dangerous denunciation. The Union of Communist Youth (*Komsomol*) sent out members to preach cultural uniformity, disrupting plays considered "bourgeois."

The Polish-born poet Osip Mandelstam (1889–1938) mocked Stalin with a poem that he read to friends in 1933. He noted the rumor about Stalin's origins in Ossetia, in the mountains of Georgia, and, as dictator, the enormous weight of his words:

We live, deaf to the land beneath us,
Ten steps away no one hears our speeches,

But where there's so much as half a conversation
The Kremlin's mountaineer will get his mention

His cockroach whiskers leer
And his boot tops gleam.

Around him a rabble of thin-necked leaders—
Fawning half-men for him to play with.

They whinny, purr or whine
As he prates and points a finger,

One by one forging his laws, to be flung,
Like horseshoes at the head, the eye or the groin.

And every killing is a treat
For the broad-chested Ossete.

Mandelstam was arrested in 1934, sent to a camp for three years, and, after returning to Moscow, arrested again and sentenced to five years hard labor in another camp. There, in 1938, he died or was executed.

Stalin charmed and deceived many foreign statesmen and visitors, impressing them with the fact that millions of working-class children were now entering school for the first time. Some workers now attended night classes, or even university. Women obtained training and positions in fields from which they previously had been excluded, such as medicine. Soviet guides whisked foreign visitors around on Moscow's new subway to see the Soviet capital's improved housing, water supply, and sewage facilities. "Potemkin village" was a series of gleaming facades that impressed visitors, who did not realize that virtually nothing stood behind them. Although church and state had been officially separated in 1918, religious life went on as before, at least in rural areas, both in Orthodox regions and in the Islamic republics. Moreover, despite promoting atheism Stalin nonetheless discouraged unmarried couples from living together, banned abortion, and forbade homosexuality. Gradually in the 1930s, Stalin's early enthusiasm for equal opportunity for women waned; the state-approved image of the female as mother of committed Soviet children prevailed.

"Darkness at Noon": Stalin's Purges

By 1934, Stalin was no longer content to expel from the party those who did not share his views. In November, he may have ordered the murder of a trusted associate who ran the Communist Party in Leningrad because he believed the younger man might emerge as a rival. Four days after the murder, Stalin promulgated a state decree that expedited the punishment of those deemed to be "terrorists." Stalin ordered the arrest of Grigory Zinoviev, among others, for alleged complicity in the murder; he was sentenced to prison.

As arrests mounted in number, executions replaced sentences of hard labor. The charges became more and more outrageous—accusations of secretly plotting to overthrow the state, of "wrecking" Soviet industries, of trying to restore capitalism, of simply being "bourgeois," or even of being the wife of an "enemy of the people."

The first of the great show trials—staged before audiences and cameras—took place in 1936, the last in March 1938, when Bukharin and the remainder of the Right Opposition faced judges who sometimes appeared to be more nervous than they. Those on trial were forced to sign confessions in court, where sympathetic foreign observers sometimes nodded in agreement to absurd accusations. Children—who could be executed at age twelve—were encouraged to denounce their parents for crimes against the state. At least 680,000 people were sentenced to death in 1937–1938 and probably about 1 million people were executed in the camps (in addition of those who died of harsh conditions). Estimates of the number of prisoners in labor camps, colonies, and prisons have ranged from about 1.5 million to 7 million. These included an elderly woman sentenced to camp terms for having said things like "if people prayed they would work better." Stalin's long arm reached far beyond the boundaries of the Soviet Union to force Communist parties in Spain, France, and other nations to purge those who disagreed with his policies. Stalin's agents caught up with Trotsky, who had gone into exile in 1929 and lived outside Mexico City, and stabbed him to death with an ice pick as he sat in a garden in August 1940.

The first of the Stalinist show trials, complete with a contrite defendant on the left and dramatic lighting.

Stalin still feared that nationalism among the many peoples of the vast Soviet Union might threaten the functioning of the state and thus the centralized party apparatus he controlled. He purged "national deviationists" from the distant Muslim lands of Central Asia, and he sometimes applied this label to the Soviet Union's several million Jews as well. At the same time, Stalin encouraged the training of leaders among each of the peoples of the Soviet Union, publishing tomes of propaganda in each national language. Party leaders in the various republics, however, were subject to particularly close scrutiny from Moscow.

The purge of the "national deviationists" was an economic blow to the Soviet Union, eliminating many engineers and other people with needed technical expertise. Furthermore, at a time when the rise of Hitler to power in Germany was increasing international tensions, the purge weakened the Soviet armed forces. Behind Stalin's move against distinguished military leaders was his paranoid fear that they might one day oppose his conduct of foreign policy. Among the 30,000 to 40,000 officers who perished, all 8 Soviet admirals were executed, as were 75 out of 80 members of the Supreme Military Council.

CONCLUSION

"One of the most striking features of the year 1917," recalled a journalist, "was the speed with which the masses, after the overthrow of tsarism, created new forms of organization," including soviets of workers and soldiers, factory committees, military organizations among and between units at the front, peasant soviets that supplemented township committees, and land committees. But once the Bolsheviks seized power on behalf of the working class and poor peasants, they never relinquished it. They destroyed these popular organizations that had embodied the aspirations of millions of people. The Russian Revolution, which had begun as a quest for economic and social justice by intellectuals, workers, middle-class and lower-middle-class radicals, peasants, and non-Russian nationalists, turned into the dictatorship of the Communist Party.

Under the rule of Joseph Stalin, the Soviet Union's industrial capacity increased dramatically, but at a terrifying human cost. During the first Five-Year Plan and with Stalin's paranoid purges, the Soviet Union took on some of the murderous characteristics of the fascist regimes its leaders so bitterly denounced. This was the tragedy of the Russian Revolution.

CHAPTER 24

THE ELUSIVE SEARCH FOR STABILITY IN THE 1920S

In the preface to his novel *The Magic Mountain* (1924), Thomas Mann (1875–1955) wrote that it took place "in the long ago, in the old days, the days of the world before the Great War." Mann sets up a parallel between a Swiss sanatorium and contemporary European civilization. In that sanatorium, rationality (Enlightenment thought and democracy) confronts irrationality (the aggressive nationalism of the right-wing dictatorships that marched into power in many European states). In *The Magic Mountain,* which was an allegory for the post-war era, Mann expressed the mood of despair prevalent among European intellectuals in the 1920s: "For us in old Europe, everything has died that was good and unique to us. Our admirable rationality has become madness, our gold is paper, our machines can only shoot and explode, our art is suicide; we are going under, friends."

The Treaty of Versailles, signed in 1919 by a frail new German Republic, and the accompanying treaties signed by the victorious Allies and Germany's wartime partners, did not resolve national rivalries in Europe. Dark clouds of economic malaise, political instability, and international tension descended on Europe in the two decades that followed the war. Although Europe experienced a brief return to relative prosperity and political calm after 1924, the Wall Street Crash of 1929 ended that brief period of hope. The search for what U.S. senator and future president Warren G. Harding called "normalcy" proved elusive, if not impossible, in the 1920s.

The Great War helped unleash the demons of the twentieth century, as parties of the political extremes sprang up to threaten parliamentary governments. Nationalist groups, intolerant of those considered outsiders and committed to aggressive territorial expansion, carried their violence into the streets. Many members of these organizations were former soldiers

The Big Four deciding the future of Europe, 1919. Left to right: Vittorio Orlando of Italy, David Lloyd George of Great Britain, Georges Clemenceau of France, and Woodrow Wilson of the United States.

who vowed to replace democracies and republics with dictatorships. Moreover, ethnic rivalries within nations, many inflamed by the Treaty of Versailles, intensified social and political conflict in post-war Europe.

THE WAR'S END

The Great War swept away the Russian, German, Austro-Hungarian, and Ottoman Empires. Even before the war's end, the Russian Revolution destroyed the tsarist autocracy and took Russia out of the conflict. The specter of revolution frightened Europe's business and political leaders. Communist parties sprung up in one country after another.

Even before the representatives of the victorious Allies (along with those representing a host of smaller states) met in Versailles in 1919 for a peace conference, the German and Austro-Hungarian Empires had collapsed, rocked by revolutions. Amid social and political turmoil, the leaders of the great powers set out to reestablish peace in Europe, firmly believing that the Great War had been the "war to end all wars." But the Treaty of Versailles reflected the determination of Great Britain and France to punish Germany for its role in unleashing the conflict. Representatives of the new German Republic were forced to sign a clause essentially accepting full blame for the outbreak of the war, and to agree to pay an enormous sum in war reparations to the Allies.

Despite the idealistic belief of U.S. President Woodrow Wilson that an era of collective security had begun that would prevent future wars of a similar magnitude, the Paris Peace Conference left a legacy of bitterness and hatred that made it even more difficult for the German Republic to find stability because of massive dissatisfaction among nationalists with the terms of the treaty. Furthermore, the individual treaties between the Allies and Germany's wartime partners left several nationalities dissatisfied with the establishment of new states constituted out of the old empires; the newly drawn borders often left them on what they considered the wrong side of frontiers. In fact, the Treaty of Versailles and its accompanying smaller treaties left many significant problems unresolved. Groups of nationalists in Germany, above all, but also nationalists in some other countries, were determined to revise or abrogate the post-war peace settlements.

Revolution in Germany and Hungary

The end of the war brought political crises in Germany and Hungary. In the face of defeat, the German Empire started to come apart at the seams. In late October 1918, German sailors mutinied at two Baltic naval bases, demanding peace and the kaiser's abdication. In southern Germany, socialists led by Kurt Eisner proclaimed a Bavarian socialist republic in early November. The new chancellor, Prince Max von Baden, called on William II to abdicate, as the Socialists threatened to leave the emergency coalition cabinet if he did not do so. William abdicated on November 9. Von Baden then named Friedrich Ebert (1871–1925), a member of the left-wing Social Democratic Party, the largest party in the pre-war years, to succeed him as chancellor.

That same day, a German commission met with Allied representatives to begin drawing up terms for an armistice. On November 9, 1918, another Social Democrat, Philip Scheidemann (1865–1939), fearing that radical revolutionaries in Berlin and a few other cities would declare a socialist state, proclaimed the German Republic, without authorization from anybody. That night, William II fled across the border into the Netherlands.

On November 11, 1918, Germany signed the armistice with the Allies, ending the war. Chancellor Ebert named a provisional government, dominated by Social Democrats but with members of the more radical Independent Social Democratic Party also represented.

From its very beginning, the new German Republic was under siege from left and right. Inspired by the success of the Bolshevik Revolution in Russia, workers began to set up "workers' and soldiers' councils" and demanded higher wages and better work conditions, thereby antagonizing their employers. Workers also angered the army by calling for the dismissal of the right-wing General Paul von Hindenburg from the military high command on which he had served since 1916 and by demanding the abolition of the special military schools for officers that for generations had infused them with the elitism identified with Prussian militarism.

The right posed a more serious threat to the fledgling republic, a threat the Treaty of Versailles would strengthen. Germany had virtually no democratic traditions. Royalism and militarism ran deep, particularly in Prussia, the northern German state under whose auspices the unified German Empire had been forged in the 1850s and 1860s. Furthermore, demobilized soldiers, many of whom were anti-republican, still held their weapons. Ominously, a veteran wrote that he believed the bloodletting of 1914–1918 was "not the end, but the chord that heralds new power. It is the anvil on which the world will be hammered into new boundaries and new communities. New forms will be filled with blood, and might will be hammered into them with a hard fist."

The head of Germany's Supreme Army Command offered the chancellor the army's support, but on condition that the new government help the army maintain order and fight "Bolshevism." Ebert accepted and, in doing so, made the new republic virtually a prisoner of the army. Some generals had already begun to enlist demobilized soldiers into right-wing paramilitary units known as the "Free Corps."

Within the new government itself, a rift developed between the Social Democrats and the Independent Social Democrats, the latter demanding immediate assistance for workers. The Independent Social Democrats asked the government to organize a militia loyal to the republic. When Ebert refused, the Independent Socialist Democrats left the governing coalition, weakening the shaky government. The new minister of defense turned over security operations to the army, and continued to encourage the Free Corps. To the left, this seemed like leaving the fox to guard the hen house.

Workers in Berlin mounted huge demonstrations against the security police. In January 1919, police and soldiers put down an uprising by the Spartacists, a group of far-left revolutionaries who took their name from the leader of a revolt by Roman slaves in the first century B.C. Military units began to move against the Berlin Spartacists, hunting them down and murdering Karl Liebknecht and the Polish Marxist Rosa Luxemburg, two of their leaders, who had just founded the German Communist Party.

The German Republic's first elections in January 1919 provided a workable center-left coalition of Social Democrats (who held the most seats in the Reichstag), the Center Party, and the German Democratic Party. The members of the Reichstag elected Ebert president, and he in turn appointed Scheidemann to be the first premier of the Weimar Republic. The Reichstag gathered in Weimar, a small, centrally located town, chosen as the new republic's capital to counter the Prussian aristocratic and militaristic traditions identified with the old imperial capital of Berlin.

Following the breakup of the Habsburg monarchy in 1918 at the end of World War I, Hungary also soon became a battleground between the competing ideologies of the post-war period. Demobilized soldiers and former imperial officials were among those stirring up trouble. Hungarian nationalists feared, with good reason, that the victorious Allies would award disputed territories from pre-war Hungary to rival nationalities. With the collapse of the Austro-Hungarian Empire in the fall of 1918, Count Mihály Károlyi (1875–1955) led an unopposed revolution of liberals and socialists that proclaimed Hungarian independence. Károlyi favored a republic and initiated a program of land reform by turning over his own estate to peasants. Other wealthy landowners prepared to defend their vast estates against land-hungry peasants. In March 1919, Béla Kun (1886–c. 1937), a Communist journalist, took advantage of the post-war chaos and seized power and tried to impose a Soviet regime. He announced a more extensive land-reform policy, established collective farms and labor camps, and nationalized banks, insurance companies, and large- and medium-sized industries. Inflation and food rationing soared and the Hungarian currency lost 90 percent of its value. In July 1919, Kun attacked Romania, with the goal of retaking territory with a large Hungarian population. The Romanian army drove Kun's forces back, invading Hungary and marching to Budapest to help overthrow him. Admiral Miklós Horthy (1868–1957), a former Habsburg naval officer (with not much to do, as Hungary's new borders lacked access to the sea), seized power in 1920. He encouraged attacks against Jews, whose economic role in Hungary was considerable, claiming that they were Bolsheviks, and he ordered

(*Left*) Karl Liebknecht addresses his supporters in January 1919, shortly before his assassination. (*Right*) Leaders of the Hungarian Communist movement, including Béla Kun, on the right, after they were overthrown.

the execution of thousands of workers and Communists. Backed by the Hungarian upper classes, he marshaled support by declaring his determination to see Hungary regain its previous borders.

The Treaty of Versailles

In this volatile atmosphere, delegates from twenty-seven nations and the four British Dominions (Canada, South Africa, Australia, and New Zealand) gathered for the Paris Peace Conference in the château of Versailles outside Paris to make the peace that they believed would transform Europe. As they convened in January 1919, the representatives of the "Big Four"—Prime Minister David Lloyd George of Britain, Prime Minister Georges Clemenceau of France, President Woodrow Wilson of the United States, and Premier Vittorio Orlando of Italy—agreed that Germany, the nation they believed responsible for the war, should assume the financial burden of putting Europe back together again.

Beyond this area of agreement, the "Big Four" powers went to Versailles with different demands and expectations. France, which had suffered far greater losses than Britain, Italy, or the United States, demanded a harsh settlement that would eliminate Germany as a potential military threat. The diminutive, elderly, and thoroughly vindictive Clemenceau, a combative loner nicknamed "the Tiger," realized the dangers of a punitive peace settlement. But he was also mindful that the quest for security against Germany dominated French foreign relations and weighed heavily upon domestic politics. A French politician acknowledged a truth that no one wanted to hear and that would only gradually sink in: "France victorious must grow accustomed to being a lesser power than Germany vanquished." Defeated Germany was still potentially a stronger state because of its economic capacity and larger population.

France's victory had been Pyrrhic. More than 1.3 million Frenchmen were killed in the Great War, 16.5 percent of all soldiers mobilized. France seemed a country of crippled veterans, widows dressed in mourning black, and hundreds of thousands of children left without fathers, for whom pensions would have to be paid. Much of the north and northeast of the country lay in ruins; factories and railways had been destroyed in a region that included 70 percent of the country's coal. With the fighting ended, the state had to borrow money from its wartime allies and from its citizens at high interest rates in order to pay off those who had purchased war bonds.

Clemenceau demanded that Germany's military arsenal be drastically reduced and that French troops occupy the fertile Rhineland until Germany had paid its reparations to the Allies. These payments would be based on a rough estimate of damages caused to the victorious powers by the war. Many in France wanted to go further, demanding annexation of the left bank of the Rhine River, or at least the establishment of an independent state in the Rhineland as a buffer against further German aggression.

The British, represented by the Welsh Liberal David Lloyd George, came to Versailles with more flexible views than the French. Britain had been spared almost all the physical devastation suffered by its cross-Channel allies. Still, the British had suffered horrific loss of life, and they had borne more than their share of the war's financial costs. The British government thus supported France's position that Germany had to be contained in the future. At a time when the slogan "Squeeze the German lemon 'til the pip squeaks" was current, one of the British prime minister's campaign slogans had been "Hang the Emperor!" However Lloyd George now concluded that it was in Europe's interest to restore the fledgling German Republic to reasonable economic strength. In view of the perceived threat posed by the Russian Revolution, he reasoned that Germany could emerge as a force for European stability.

Italian Prime Minister Vittorio Orlando (1860–1952) came to Versailles assuming that his country would receive territories of the former Austro-Hungarian Empire promised by the Allies in 1915, when Italy had entered the war on their side: the port of Trieste; the strategically important Alpine region around Trent (the South Tyrol), which would give Italy a natural boundary; and Istria and northern Dalmatia on the Adriatic coast (see Map 24.1). President Wilson found acceptable Italian annexation of the first three; all had sizable—though, except in the case of Trieste, not majority—Italian populations. As a result, Italy was able to extend its frontiers to the Brenner Pass and to Trieste. But Wilson staunchly opposed Italian demands for Istria, northern Dalmatia, and the strategically important Adriatic port of Rijeka (known to its Italian minority as Fiume), which Italy had omitted from its demands in 1915, but now claimed. His reason for doing so was that Italians were only a minority in those territories. Italian nationalists denounced the "mutilated peace" that had not allowed annexation of all of the territories the Italian government had anticipated receiving for its role in the war.

Wilson's position on Italy's territorial demands reflected one of the broad principles this high-minded son of a Presbyterian minister brought with him to Versailles as representative of the United States. Wilson stood for national self-determination, the principle that ethnicity should determine national boundaries. He went to Versailles hoping to "make the world safe for democracy." This was manifest in his Fourteen Points, the blueprint of which Wilson had proclaimed in January 1918, and which he believed would bring lasting world peace. The U.S. president hoped that diplomacy would henceforth be carried out through "open covenants of peace," not secret treaties. Wilson believed that if the victorious powers applied "the principle of justice to all peoples and nationalities . . . whether they be strong or weak," Europe would enter an era of enduring stability.

Map 24.1 Territorial Settlements after World War I Territories lost by Germany, Bulgaria, Austria-Hungary, and Russia as a result of the treaties ending the Great War.

The U.S. president's main concern at Versailles was with the creation of a League of Nations to arbitrate subsequent international disputes. He was less concerned with specific conditions of peace or forcing a punitive settlement on Germany. In Wilson's opinion, the Great War had been fought largely over the competing claims of national groups, magnified by the commitments of great-power alliances, and it was not right to separate Rhineland Germans from Germany, as many people in Britain and France desired.

Wilson believed that the outbreak of the Great War had demonstrated that the diplomatic concept of a "balance of power," by which the predominant strength of one power was balanced by alliances between several other powers, was unequal to the task of maintaining peace. Henceforth, Wilson wanted the United States to assume an international role, joining Great Britain, France, Italy, and Japan as permanent members of the League of Nation's Council. By this reasoning, the League would stand for collective security against any power that would threaten the peace.

Yet idealism and reality were at odds at Versailles. Among the leaders of the three main victorious powers, Wilson's idealism contrasted with the determined realism of Lloyd George and Clemenceau. As they worked together for four months, they wrestled with public pressure, particularly in France, for a harsh peace, which they had to balance against the possibility that a draconian settlement might push defeated Germany, Austria, and Hungary in the direction of the Soviet Union.

The Covenant of the League of Nations, which Wilson insisted be added to the treaty, reflected the treaty's nod in the direction of Wilsonian idealism. Wilson had promulgated his Fourteen Points in January 1918, in the midst of the stalemate on the western front. But following the Allied victory, French and British realism prevailed in what was called the "victor's peace." Moreover, both Lloyd George and Clemenceau, unlike Wilson, enjoyed the full support of their constituents.

By the "war guilt clause," Article 231 of the treaty, Germany accepted full responsibility for "the loss and damage" caused the Allies "as a consequence of the war imposed upon them by the aggression of Germany and her allies." Many Germans were outraged in April 1919, when they learned of the harsh treaty that had been imposed on Germany. The Allies seemed to be punishing the new democratic German Republic for the acts of the old imperial regime. Premier Scheidemann resigned rather than sign the treaty. The next Social Democratic government signed it a week later, on June 28, 1919, but only after the Allies had threatened to invade Germany. The Treaty of Versailles returned to France Alsace and Lorraine, its two eastern provinces annexed by Germany after the Franco-Prussian War (see Map 24.2). French troops would occupy the parts of Germany that stood on the left, or western, bank of the Rhine River, as well as occupying for fifteen years a strategically critical strip of land along its right bank. These territories were to remain permanently demilitarized.

MAP 24.2 AREAS OF FRENCH AND GERMAN DISPUTES, 1920s Border areas, including the Rhineland and the Saar Basin, that were occupied by Allied troops or were part of a demilitarized zone after the Great War.

France would retain economic control over the rich coal and iron mines of the Saar border region (which would be administered by the League of Nations) for fifteen years, at which time the region's population would express by plebiscite whether it wished to remain German (which would be the result in 1935) or become part of France. Germany also had to cede small pieces of long-contested frontier territory to Belgium (Eupen and Malmédy).

In the east, Germany lost territory to Poland, which became independent for the first time since 1795. Poles had been forced to fight in the armies of the German, Austria-Hungarian, and Russian Empires during the war and both Russia and Germany had promised independence (the Central Powers had appointed a "Regency Council" in September 1917) in the quest for Polish support, while Polish nationalists had campaigned for support for Polish independence in Britain, France, and the United

States. On Armistice Day, November 11, 1918, German troops in Warsaw put down their arms and Poland became independent. The Treaty of Versailles awarded Poland the territory of Poznania and much of Pomerania, constituting the "Polish Corridor" that led to the Baltic Sea and divided East Prussia, which remained German, from the rest of Germany. The port city of Danzig (now Gdańsk) became a free city under the protection of the League of Nations.

The German army was to be reduced from millions of wartime troops to the minimal figure of 100,000 volunteer soldiers. The German navy, now blockaded by the British fleet, would be limited to twelve warships, with no submarines, and Germany would be allowed no air force.

Furthermore, Germany was to pay a huge sum—132 billion gold marks, the estimated cost of the war to the victorious Allies—in war reparations. (There was a precedent: France had been required to pay an indemnity to the German Empire following the French defeat in the Franco-Prussian War of 1870–1871.) The Weimar Republic would be required to turn over to the Allies much of its merchant fleet and part of its fishing fleet and railroad stocks, among other payments. The German Baltic shipyards were to build ships at no cost to the Allies. Each year, Germany was to give the Allies more than one-fourth of its extracted coal as further compensation.

But how was the new Weimar Republic to raise the remainder of the reparations? Tax revenues were low because the economy was so weak, and powerful German industrialists opposed the implementation of any new taxes on capital or business. The outflow of reparations payments in gold fueled inflation. Government expenses far outweighed income,

These boxes contain German currency that rapidly lost value due to out-of-control inflation.

exports rapidly declined, and prices began to rise far faster than in other countries, destabilizing the new Weimar government.

The English economist John Maynard Keynes (1883–1946) left the British delegation to Versailles in protest of the harsh treatment afforded Germany. He warned, "If we aim deliberately at the impoverishment of Central Europe, vengeance, I dare predict, will not limp." In particular he denounced the reparations payments in his book *The Economic Consequences of the Peace* (1919), prophesying accurately the failure of the Versailles settlement. Indeed, the reparations issue would poison international relations in the 1920s.

The Allies counted on German payments to help them remedy their own daunting economic problems of the post-war period. The promise of German reparations enabled the British and French governments to accede to conservative demands that taxes not be raised or levies imposed on capital. But, in fact, Germany paid only a small portion of the reparations. Germany received three times as much in loans from the Allies than it paid out. Reparations did not ruin the German economy, but their psychological impact in Germany damaged the very republic the Allies wanted to stabilize. The bitter resentment harbored by German right-wing parties toward the reparations compromised the ability of the Weimar Republic to survive.

France wanted the League of Nations to enforce the Treaty of Versailles and to ensure German payment of reparations. (Germany was not permitted to join the League of Nations.) But without an army, the League had no way of enforcing its decisions against member—or, for that matter, nonmember—states that chose to ignore its principles or decisions.

After his six-month stay at Versailles, President Wilson returned to the United States to fight for Senate ratification of the treaty. But the elections of November 1918 had given Wilson's Republican opponents control of the Senate. A mood of isolationism swept the country. A majority of senators opposed U.S. membership in the League of Nations, fearing that the treaty would commit the nation to entanglements in Europe. Influenced by the large numbers of German, Italian, and Irish American constituents, some senators believed the treaty to be too harsh on Germany, insufficiently generous to Italy, and irrelevant to Irish demands for independence from Britain. The U.S. government refused to participate in the various international organizations set up to enforce the treaty and to air economic and security concerns. In November 1919, the U.S. Senate rejected ratification of the Treaty of Versailles.

The absence of both the United States and the Soviet Union from the League doomed it to failure. The new Russian government had not even been invited to Versailles. There were two reasons for this: (1) the Bolsheviks had simply declared an end to the war in 1917 and withdrawn troops from the front; and (2) Great Britain, France, and the United States (distrusting the Bolsheviks, whose leader, Lenin, boldly predicted the worldwide victory of communism) had sent troops and military supplies to support the anti-Bolshevik forces in the Civil War in Russia.

Even among the victorious powers, the treaty generated some apprehension. It seemed a precarious peace. John Maynard Keynes recalled, "Paris was a nightmare, and every one there was morbid. A sense of impending catastrophe overhung the frivolous scene; the futility and smallness of man before the great events confronting him; the mingled significance and unreality of the decisions." When Marshal Ferdinand Foch of France read the treaty, he exclaimed, "This isn't a peace, it's a twenty year truce!" He was right.

Settlements in Eastern Europe

A series of individual treaties, each named after a suburb of Paris, sought to recognize the claims of ethnic minorities of each country, in some cases redrawing national boundaries (see Map 24.1). But each also left the defeated country feeling aggrieved, adding to the number of "revisionist" or "irredentist" states—that is, those nations that wanted the revision of the Versailles Settlement in order to award them territory they believed should be theirs.

Bulgaria, one of the German wartime allies, lost territory, including its Aegean coast, ceded to Greece by virtue of the Treaty of Neuilly (November 1919), as well as small pieces of land to Romania and parts of Thrace won in the Balkan Wars. By the Treaty of St. Germain (which specifically forbade Austrian union with Germany), Vienna was reduced to being the oversized capital of a small country, Austria, which now consisted of even less territory than the old German-speaking parts of the Habsburg domains. By the Treaty of Trianon (June 1920), Hungary lost two-thirds of its territory and three-fifths of its population, as lands with a sizable non-Hungarian population were shifted to other national states. Romania received more Hungarian territory than was left to Hungary and one-third of its population now consisted of Hungarians, but also Germans, Ukrainians, and Jews. The treaty left 3.4 million Hungarians living beyond the borders of Hungary, hardly Wilsonianism in action. About 1 million Bulgarians—16 percent of the population—now lived outside of Bulgaria.

The Treaty of Sèvres (August 1920), the most severe of the treaties with Germany's wartime allies, dismembered the Turkish Ottoman Empire. Britain, France, Italy, and Greece all coveted—as had the Russian and Habsburg empires in previous centuries—parts of the old Ottoman Empire that had stretched through much of the Middle East. Now the treaty awarded Smyrna, the region around present-day Izmir on the Anatolian peninsula, and Thrace to Greece; the island of Rhodes to Italy; Syria (then including Lebanon) to France, under mandate from the League of Nations; Iraq and Palestine to Britain, also under mandate from the League of Nations; and Saudi Arabia to Britain as a protectorate (see Map 24.3). Italian troops occupied Turkish territory even as the peace conference was proceeding; Greek forces moved into Smyrna and into Thrace.

In Turkey, the Italian and Greek occupations generated a wave of nationalist sentiment. Mustafa Kemal Pasha (1881–1938)—known as Atatürk—organized armed resistance against the foreign incursions. Turkish forces pushed Greek units out of Smyrna and threatened a neutral zone occupied by British troops. When the British government prepared to intervene, an exchange of populations was arranged. The Greeks were forced to withdraw from the Anatolian peninsula, and at least 1 million Greek refugees returned to Greece. Almost 400,000 Muslims left Greece for Turkey. The Treaty of Lausanne of 1923 left Turkey holding territory on both sides of the Bosporus, the sea of Marmara, and the Dardanelles Strait, which themselves were declared open to all nations. Italy and Greece had to settle for Turkish islands in the Aegean Sea. The Kurds, an ethnic minority within Turkey and Iraq, were still without an independent state. Atatürk became president of the Republic of Turkey, establishing his capital at Ankara in the interior of the Anatolian peninsula. The last Ottoman ruler left Turkey for the French Riviera. Seeking to westernize and secularize his country, Atatürk promulgated legal codes separating church and state, implemented compulsory education and the Latin alphabet, and prohibited Turks from wearing the fez (a traditional brimless hat).

NATIONAL AND ETHNIC CHALLENGES

President Wilson's espousal of ethnicity as the chief determinant of national boundaries had unleashed hopes among almost all the Eastern European peoples for independent states based on ethnic identities. The Treaty of Versailles accentuated the role of nationalism as a factor for political instability in Europe after the Great War. At the same time, the failure of the peacemakers at Versailles to address the demands of peoples colonized by the European powers left a legacy of mistrust.

The National Question and the Successor States

The Treaty of Versailles created "successor" states out of the ruins of the Austro-Hungarian Empire, as well as out of the territories that had belonged to defeated Germany and the defunct Russian Empire. The creation of these new states by the Treaty of Versailles followed the principle of nationalism—that ethnicity should be the chief determinant of national boundaries—which had helped cause the Great War. In the north, Finland finally gained its independence after having been for centuries subject to Swedish and, since the beginning of the nineteenth century, to Russian rule. The three Baltic states of Latvia, Estonia, and Lithuania also became independent of Russia (see Map 24.1). The largest of these successor states were Yugoslavia in the Balkans and Czechoslovakia and Poland in Central Europe. Referring to the new states and redrawn boundaries, Winston Churchill complained, "The maps are out of date!

The charts don't work any more!" The creation of smaller national states (which Lloyd George referred to as "five-foot-five nations") whose boundaries were largely determined by ethnicity added to the number of independent states in Europe. This number had decreased since 1500 as absolute monarchies had expanded their territories, and with German and Italian unification in the nineteenth century it had further decreased. But after the war, that trend was suddenly reversed. In 1914, there had been fourteen currencies in Europe; in 1919, there were twenty-seven.

The post-war treaties could not create states that satisfied all nationalities; in the new states of Central and Eastern Europe and the Balkans, nationalists felt aggrieved by the fact that some of those they considered their own lived as minorities in other states. The presence of ethnic minorities in each state would become a factor for nationalist discontent. In parts of Macedonia left inside Yugoslavia, Macedonians were forced to Serbianize their names, replacing "itch" with "off" at the end of them, which at least held out the possibility of assimilation.

Poland's extensive territorial claims brought it into conflict with other newly created states, including Lithuania, Czechoslovakia, and the Soviet Union. Religious differences compounded ethnic rivalries. Poland included about 1.5 million Byelorussians and 4 million Ukrainians, who, unlike the Catholic Poles, were largely Orthodox Christians. Moreover, about 1 million Germans, overwhelmingly Protestant, now lived in Poland. Life for a Croat or Hungarian in Serb-dominated Yugoslavia seemed not much different than it had been under the Austrian-dominated Habsburg monarchy before the war. Slovaks resented the domination of Czechoslovakia by the Czechs as much as they had resented the German-speaking bureaucrats of the Habsburg empire before the war.

The Allies also had the strategic containment of communism in mind when they created these new nation-states as buffers between the Soviet Union and Western Europe. After the armistice, the Allies allowed German armies to remain inside Russia, Ukraine, and Poland in order to prevent any attempt by the Red Army to carry the Russian Revolution into Central Europe. German troops continued to hold railway lines in the Baltic states in order to thwart any attempted Bolshevik takeover there.

Seeking security against Germany—as well as against the Soviet Union—Czechoslovakia, Romania, and Yugoslavia formed the Little Entente by signing alliances in 1920 and 1921. They also sought collective security against Hungary and Bulgaria, both of which demanded revision of the Treaty of Versailles in order to win back territory lost to their unwanted new neighbors. Moreover, all three states depended on a series of alliances that each had signed with France. (Poland sometimes worked with these states to achieve mutually beneficial goals but did not formally join the alliance.)

The Allies applied Wilson's idealized formula of "one people, one nation" unequally when it came to those states that had fought against them in the war. The Polish Corridor dividing East Prussia from the rest of Germany contained a sizable German population. Mineral-rich Upper Silesia, claimed by Poland, remained part of Germany after a plebiscite. But in parts of Austria, where German-speaking majorities might have wanted to join Germany, the Allies specifically disallowed plebiscites.

Carved for the most part out of the old Habsburg Balkan domains, Yugoslavia was the most ambitious attempt to resolve the national question through the creation of a multinational state in which the rights of several nationalities would be recognized. After complicated negotiations in 1917, the Serb government and a Yugoslav Committee made up of Croat and Slovene leaders in exile had agreed to form a new South Slav state when the war was concluded. They set up a provisional government even before an armistice had been signed. The new parliamentary monarchy would include Serbia, Montenegro, Croatia, and Slovenia (which lies between northern Italy and Austria), as well as Bosnia-Herzegovina and the smaller territory of Kosovo, two regions in which a majority of the population had converted to Islam during the centuries of Turkish domination. Yugoslavia also absorbed part of Macedonia, which was populated by Bulgarians, Greeks, and Macedonians.

From its beginning, Yugoslavia was caught in a conflict between the "Greater Serb" vision of Yugoslavia, in which Serbia would dominate, and a federalist structure in which all nationalities and religions would play equal, or at least proportional, roles. Serbs, who are Orthodox Christians, were the largest ethnic group in Yugoslavia, but they still only made up 43 percent of the total Yugoslav population, with the Catholic Croats accounting for about 23 percent. Belgrade became the capital of Yugoslavia, as it had been of Serbia. Middle-class Serbs held almost all of the key administrative, judicial, and military positions. Concentrations of Serbs lived in Croatia, and Croats in Serbia, further complicating the rivalry between the two major peoples of the new state, who spoke essentially the same language, although the Serbs use the Cyrillic alphabet. Other major ethnic groups within Yugoslavia included Hungarians, Romanians, Bulgarians, Greeks, and German-speaking Austrians, as well as gypsies.

The case of Czechoslovakia also illustrates the complexity of the national question. In 1917, a National Council, made up of both Czechs and Slovaks, became a provisional government. The Slovak philosopher Tomáš Masaryk (1850–1937), who had spent the war years making contacts in London in the hope of advancing the cause of an independent Czechoslovakia, became the president of the new state in 1918. He was extremely popular among both Czechs and Slovaks. But Czechs and Slovaks together made up only 65 percent of the population of the new country. Three million Germans living in the Sudetenland found themselves included within the borders of Czechoslovakia, as did 750,000 Hungarians. Furthermore, Slovaks complained that promises of administrative and cultural autonomy within the Czechoslovak state were never implemented.

Facing similar economic, social, and political tensions, Poland became a dictatorship. General Józef Pilsudski (1867–1935), one of the leaders of the Polish independence movement during the last decade of the Russian Empire, led a Polish legion that defended Warsaw in 1920 and drove the Soviet Red Army out of Poland. But the Polish economy lay in ruins. No rail links between Warsaw and other major cities survived the war; tracks from Germany and Austria simply stopped at the Polish border. Six currencies circulated simultaneously. Inflation was rampant: a dollar was worth 9 Polish zlotys at the end of the war, and 2.3 million in 1923! Deep divisions endured between nobles, who owned most of the land and had subverted central authority in virtually every period of Polish history, and the peasants, who demanded land reform. Fifty-nine different political parties existed in the early 1920s. As no party ever enjoyed a solid parliamentary majority, the government was run by an average of almost two parties a year. General Pilsudski, who had become chief of state in 1918, refused to stand for election for president in 1922 on the grounds that the constitution did not grant him sufficient executive authority. He denounced political parties, criticized the parliamentary regime, and called for a "moral regeneration" of Polish life. In 1926, Pilsudski, backed by wealthy landowners and the army, overthrew Poland's parliamentary government. After saying that he would have to wait to see whether Poland could be governed "without a whip," he imposed authoritarian rule.

Poland became the first of the Eastern European states to become a dictatorship in the post-war years. In Greece, which had remained neutral during the war, King Alexander had died in 1920, after being bitten by his pet monkey. When parliament deposed his successor, Greek political life lurched into an instability accentuated by the arrival of 1.5 million Greeks expelled from Bulgaria and Turkey. In Greek Macedonia, refugees now made up half of the population, which now consisted of 90 percent Greeks. In the small, backward Muslim state of Albania on the coast of the Adriatic Sea, moderate reformers battled proponents of the old ways against a backdrop of Italian territorial claims and bullying. Harvard-educated King Zog (Ahmed Zogu; ruled 1928–1939), fearing for his life, fled to Yugoslavia in 1924. The next year, he invaded his own country with an army, assumed the presidency of the Albanian Republic, and set up a dictatorial monarchy in 1928.

In Bulgaria, King Boris III (ruled 1918–1943) was head of the country in name only. Aleksandr Stamboliski (1879–1923), leader of the Agrarian Union Party, elbowed opponents aside to become premier in 1919. He signed the Treaty of Neuilly, agreeing to try to prevent Macedonian nationalists from using Bulgarian territory to organize attacks inside Greece. Stamboliski assumed dictatorial powers in 1920. Army officers helped engineer a coup d'état in 1923, with the support of the king. Stamboliski fell into the hands of Macedonian nationalists, who cut off his right arm, which had signed the Treaty of Neuilly, then stabbed him sixty times, decapitating him for good measure. The army killed about 20,000 peasants and workers who wanted reform. It was a sign of the times in the Balkans.

Colonial and National Questions

The peace treaties failed to address the rights—or lack of them—of people living in the colonies of the European powers. Some of these peoples demanded national independence, while others viewed themselves as being stateless. Representatives of ethnic, religious, and national groups— including the Irish, Persians, Jews, Arabs, Indians from the subcontinent, Vietnamese, Armenians, and American blacks—went to Versailles in the hope of attaining recognition of their national rights. Lloyd George belittled these outsiders as "wild men screaming through the keyholes." The Allies refused to allow Ho Chi Minh (1890–1969), a young Vietnamese, to read a petition that asked that the Rights of Man be applied to the French colonies. Only the representatives of Zionist groups—Jews who wanted the creation of a Jewish national state in Palestine—and their anti-Zionist Jewish rivals ever made it into the conference halls, and then only briefly. Women's groups, too, in vain sent representatives who hoped to be heard at Versailles.

Britain, still the world's largest colonial power, refused to accept President Wilson's plan that the League of Nations or some other international board arbitrate the future of colonies. The British government refused to recognize the right of self-determination. Still, the war had altered the relationship between Britain and its colonies, as well as that between France and its empire. The Dominions (Britain's original "settlement colonies" of Canada, South Africa, Australia, and New Zealand) had borne a great financial and material burden in the Great War, and a considerable loss of life as well. While they were not fully independent, a delegation from each had signed the Treaty of Versailles, each had a government responsible to its own citizens, and each became a member of the League of Nations. Discussions began to establish a "British Commonwealth," which was created in 1926 and formalized in 1931. In this union of Britain and the Dominions, each state would be independent and not subordinate to Britain but united by common allegiance to the crown.

The powers created the "mandate system" to deal with Germany's colonies. The latter were placed under the nominal authority of the League of Nations but were actually administered by Allied powers. Through this system, Britain increased the size of its empire by a million square miles, for example, by adding the former German colony of Tanganyika and parts of Togoland and the Cameroons as "mandate" colonies (see Map 24.3).

In Palestine, both Arabs and Jews had reason to be disappointed by the settlement. In 1915, the British government had promised some Arab

MAP 24.3 MANDATES UNDER THE LEAGUE OF NATIONS German colonies that were made mandates of the League of Nations and administered by Allied powers after the Great War.

Mandates

British
French
South African
Australian

Irish republicans behind a
barricade in Dublin.

leaders, in order to encourage Arab resistance against Germany's ally
Turkey, that after the war Britain would support an independent Arab
state. But a year later, the British and French governments had secretly
drawn up plans to divide the Middle East into two spheres of influence.
Moreover, in the 1917 Balfour Declaration (see Chapter 22), Britain had
promised to help Jews create a "national home" in Palestine, without necessarily promising to establish a Jewish state. Once the war ended, the
promises disappeared in smoke at Versailles. Britain established mandates
over Trans-Jordan (which would later become Jordan), as well as over Iraq
and Palestine, each of which was ruled by a viceroy responsible to the
colonial office in London. Britain maintained informal control over Egypt
and the Suez Canal even after nominal Egyptian independence in 1922.
France established a mandate over Lebanon as well as over Syria.

But the British government could no longer put aside the challenge of
the Irish movement for independence. The imposition of military conscription in Ireland in 1918 had angered Irish who felt no allegiance to the
empire. The Irish Republican Army, which was organized from remnants
of the rebel units disbanded after the ill-fated Easter Sunday insurrection
against Britain in 1916, gained adherents amid high unemployment,
strikes, and sectarian violence between Catholics and Protestants in
largely Protestant Ulster (the six counties of northeastern Ireland). In
a mood of mounting crisis, British Liberals wanted to begin negotiations
as soon as possible with Irish political leaders. Conservatives, in contrast,
wanted to crush the Irish Republicans. In the 1918 elections to the House
of Commons, Irish voters elected a majority of members of Sinn Féin
("We Ourselves" in Irish Gaelic), the Irish Republican political organization. The Sinn Féin members refused to take their seats in Parliament
and then unilaterally declared a republic. Parliament finally passed the

Government of Ireland Act in 1920, dividing Ireland into two districts. The Catholic district in the south—most of the island—was to become a crown colony. Protestant Ulster would remain part of Britain.

Many, if not most, Catholic Irish, however, wanted nothing less than complete independence. The British government kept about 50,000 troops and 10,000 police in Ireland, including the "Black and Tans," a special police force that terrorized the Irish population that supported the Irish Republicans. More than a thousand people were killed in fighting during 1921, half of whom were British policemen or soldiers ambushed by the Irish Republican Army. In January 1922, the British Parliament went a step further, creating the Irish Free State, a Dominion within the British Commonwealth, although many Irish republicans demanded the severance of all formal ties to Britain and the creation of a republic. Ulster, or Northern Ireland, remained within the United Kingdom. Continuing sporadic sectarian violence in Ulster proved that tensions between the Protestant majority and Catholic minority, which did not accept British rule, would not subside.

In colonies that were part of the empires of the European powers, the Great War accentuated nationalist movements for independence. For example, in India, which the British viewed as the key to sustaining the British Empire (it served, for one thing, as a vast reservoir of soldiers for the army), a growing Indian national movement developed. In 1919, Indians held a protest in Amritsar in Punjab against the Rowlatt Acts, which allowed the government to forgo juries in political trials. The British army retaliated by massacring 400 Indian civilians, enraging Indian nationalists, who pointed out the sacrifices Indians had made during the Great War. Like the Sepoy Mutiny of 1857 (see Chapter 21), the incident exacerbated the mutual suspicion and mistrust that had existed between Indians and British for decades. France also repressed revolutionary nationalist movements in its colonies of Indochina, Tunisia, Morocco, and the African island of Madagascar, and it curbed moderate groups asking only for the extension of political rights. During and following World War I (until the 1930s), most of the nationalist movements in the French colonies sought reform from within the colonial framework, not outright independence through revolution.

Japan strengthened its position as the only Asian great power. Japanese armies were already taking advantage of the turmoil that followed the Bolshevik Revolution to grab land from the old Russian Empire in Asia. Furthermore, Great Britain, France, and Italy had secretly agreed in 1917, in exchange for active Japanese support against the German navy, to back Japanese demands for concessions China had been forced to grant Germany in 1898 and 1899, when the great powers had taken advantage of China's relative weakness (see Chapter 21) during the "scramble for concessions." The members of the Chinese delegation to Versailles in 1919 had been unaware of the 1917 agreement; nor did the Chinese delegates know that their warlord premier had secretly agreed, in return for Japanese loans, to grant Japan a full concession to build railways in the northeast province of Shandong (Shantung). When the Allies publicly agreed to Japanese claims, demonstrations and riots erupted in China. The May 4 (1919) movement in China, named for the day of the first major demonstrations in Beijing against the Treaty of Versailles, accentuated the development of Chinese nationalism.

ECONOMIC AND SOCIAL INSTABILITY

Because of the relief and—for the victors—exhilaration with which many Europeans greeted the end of the Great War, the 1920s has often been described as "the roaring twenties." Europeans thrilled to quests for record speeds or landmark travel by air and automobile. They gathered around radios, lined up to attend movies, watched football games or bicycle races, dressed in more casual clothing styles than ever before, crowded into cabarets and clubs, and danced late into the night.

However, the two decades following the Great War were marked by tremendous economic and social instability. The continent was wracked by inflation and unemployment, factors that exacerbated international tensions and rivalries and poisoned domestic political life—particularly in

TABLE 24.1. WAR EXPENDITURE DURING THE GREAT WAR (1914–1919)
(BILLIONS OF DOLLARS)

	Normal Public Expenditure	War Expenditure	War Expenditure at 1913 Prices
France	5.0	28.2	9.3
Great Britain	4.7	43.8	21.2
Remainder of Empire	5.9	5.8	1.8
Italy	2.9	14.7	3.2
Russia	5.9	16.3	5.4
United States	2.9	36.2	17.1
Other Allies	3.3	2.0	(−0.3)
Allies	30.6	147.0	57.7
Germany	3.3	47.0	19.9
Austria-Hungary	5.4	13.4	4.7
Bulgaria, Turkey	1.4	1.1	0.1
Central Powers	10.1	61.5	24.7
All Belligerents	40.7	208.5	82.4

Source: Gerd Hardoch, *The First World War 1914–1918* (Berkeley: University of California Press, 1977), p. 153.

TABLE 24.2. INDEX OF WHOLESALE PRICES (1913=100)

	1914	1915	1916	1917	1918	1919
Germany	106	142	153	179	217	415
France	102	140	189	262	340	357
Great Britain	100	127	160	206	227	242
Italy	96	133	201	299	409	364
Canada	100	109	134	175	205	216
United States	98	101	127	177	194	206

Source: Gerd Hardoch, *The First World War 1914–1918* (Berkeley: University of California Press, 1977), p. 172.

Germany, but also in a number of other states reeling from the impact of the war. In Western Europe, after the long, bloody war finally ended and with the Russian Revolution fresh in mind, workers (and some women's groups as well) put forward demands for better living conditions. At the same time, economic and social elites were determined to overcome the challenge to their power launched by organized labor and the political parties of the left. But one of the results of the long ordeal of a war that had necessitated the mobilization of virtually all of the economic resources of the combatant powers was a growing determination among the parties of the political left that states ought to increase the services they provided their citizens. As such, the origins of the welfare state may in part be traced to the immediate post-war period.

Social Turmoil

The staggering economic disruption caused by the war contributed to the international disorder that ensued at its end. Soaring inflation and unemployment destabilized European political life. The conflict cost more than six times the national debts of all countries in the entire world from the end of the eighteenth century until 1914 (see Table 24.1).

Manufacturing and agricultural productivity fell dramatically during the conflict. Only countries far from the battlefields, such as the United States, Canada, India, and Australia, experienced economic growth. But they, too, could not escape high inflation and unemployment when the war ended. European states had borrowed vast sums of money to pay for the war; governments now began to print money to pay it back. This accelerated inflation (See Table 24.2). Prices were three times higher in 1920 in Britain than before the war, five times higher in Germany, and, in an ominous sign of things to come, 14,000 times higher in Austria and 23,000 times higher in Hungary! In Germany and France, bank accounts in 1929 were worth only between 15 percent and 20 percent of their value in 1913.

Workers resented what seemed to be a widening gap between themselves and the wealthy. The British press carried stories about well-placed entrepreneurs who had amassed fortunes selling war materials to the government, living it up while others died for their country and everyone else tightened their belts. The Conservative politician Stanley Baldwin referred to businessmen elected to Parliament in the first post-war election as "hard-faced men who looked as if they had done well out of the war."

Europe's business elite greeted the post-war era with some anxiety. Large-industry businessmen, including French steel magnates and German arms producers, had emerged from the war with huge profits. These were enhanced by cartel arrangements within their industries that allowed them to monopolize production and set prices. War production had benefited large companies more than small ones, as in Germany, where the War Raw Materials Corporations provided essential materials to certain large enterprises. The chemical giant I. G. Farben had been formed in Germany by joining together a number of smaller firms. Industrialists enjoyed greater prestige and political influence than ever before. With governments playing the leading role in establishing economic priorities, allocating resources, and recruiting labor during the war, fewer people now embraced the old classic liberal principle of laissez-faire. Some businessmen and state officials, particularly in Germany, Italy, and France, had been impressed by the degree of wartime cooperation between state, business, and labor. They now believed these arrangements should be permanent. They hoped that corporate entities could be established in each major industry to coordinate production, ending competition between companies. Sometimes calling themselves "corporatists" and their ideas "corporatism," they believed that such cartel arrangements might well reduce or even eliminate the social and political tensions inherent in capitalist economies by forging an organized alliance of interests, including those of the state, big business, and labor.

For more than a half century, European economic elites had worked to preserve their power against the mounting challenge of organized labor and the political parties of the left. They did so, for example, by trying to maintain the elite character of higher education, pressuring governments to maintain high tariff barriers at the expense of consumers, seeking to limit government intervention in factory conditions, or trying to maintain legislation that restricted the right to strike. Above all, many people of means had wanted to keep their countries from adopting universal male suffrage or even democracy. Despite their efforts, however, the role of parliamentary bodies had expanded in every Western country during the last decades before the war, as universal male suffrage had come to France, Italy, Belgium, Norway, Sweden, and even imperial Germany. By early 1921, the mobilization of workers, many of whom had wanted the socialization of key industrial resources and the participation of workers in factory decision making, had collapsed. The influence of business helped bring conservatives to power in Germany, Italy, and France in post-war elections.

Women's movements counted among the forces for democratization that gained considerably during the war. Having suspended their suffrage campaigns for the duration of the conflict, women's groups now demanded recognition for their wartime contributions—when they had taken the place of conscripts in factories and fields. After the war, women won the right to vote in Germany, Sweden, and several other countries in Western Europe, as well as in the newly created Eastern European states of Czechoslovakia, Poland, and Hungary. The legal position of women was probably strongest in Britain. Women voted for the first time in the British elections of December 1918, and the first woman was elected to the House of Commons soon after. The Sex Disqualification Act of 1919 opened the way for women to enter professions from which they had previously been excluded. But women who had taken men's jobs during the war gradually lost or abandoned their employment, many returning to domestic service. During the 1920s, the percentage of working women declined for the first time in many decades. Nonetheless, a greater variety of jobs became available to women. During the next two decades, many women found work in textile factories, commerce, transport, and in new jobs within the service sector (as hairdressers, department store clerks, or telephone operators). For many women, such jobs represented an advance in opportunity and conditions of work.

Some Britons began to think that their nation, which, unlike its continental rivals, had avoided insurgency and revolution in the nineteenth century, might now be vulnerable to an uprising by dissatisfied workers influenced by the Bolsheviks. In Glasgow, Scotland's largest city, workers demanding a forty-hour workweek raised the Communist red flag on the town hall. But an attempt to call a general strike, organized by the "triple alliance" of railway workers, miners, and dockworkers—the three largest unions—fizzled completely on April 15, 1921, "Black Friday" for British workers.

Conservative reaction in France to the Russian Revolution was similar. The French Employers Association printed thousands of posters showing a Bolshevik with a blood-stained knife between his teeth. The "National Block," drawing upon a wave of patriotism following the victory of the blue-clad French soldiers, won the 1919 elections, bringing a strongly nationalist majority to the "horizon blue" Chamber of Deputies. Many French conservatives, who before the war dreamed of a monarchical restoration or the overthrow of the republic by a military man, now supported the republic, as long as it was a conservative republic.

The labor movement gained strength in the immediate post-war period, but it failed to overcome the determined resistance of employers and national governments. In France, the General Confederation of Labor, which had recruited hundreds of thousands of new members after the war, reached 2 million members in 1920, although the proportion of unionized workers remained small when compared to the proportion in Britain. In Italy, more than 3 million workers joined unions in the first two years of peace. Unions mounted massive campaigns to make the economy more democratic, a goal that was more revolutionary than bread-and-butter issues like hours, wages, and conditions of work. Strikes spread in all Western countries. In France, a general strike collapsed in May 1920. Union efforts failed to obtain the nationalization of key industries, such as French railroads, or German and British coal mines. Factory councils, which workers hoped would meet with employers to set production targets, wages, and conditions, had

The French reaction to the Russian Revolution is illustrated by this anti-Bolshevik poster.

within a few years been eliminated in Germany, never got off the ground in France, and were quickly banned in Italy. Rates of unionization fell. "Corporatist" rhetoric gradually disappeared in Germany and France. Everywhere, with the notable exception of the Soviet Union, employers still called the shots.

The Left and the Origins of the Welfare State

The Great War was a devastating experience for the international socialist movement, which had in 1914 split into pro- and anti-war factions. The German Social Democrats and the socialist parties of France, Italy, and Belgium had rallied to the war effort of their respective countries despite internationalist opposition to what they saw as a war between capitalists. The Russian Revolution of 1917, too, divided socialists. The unexpected victory of the Bolsheviks in Russia suggested to some that socialists could come to power through a tightly organized, hierarchical party structure. In France, at the Congress of the French Socialist Party in Tours in December 1920, three-fourths of the delegates supported joining the Third Communist International, which had been founded in Moscow in 1919 to encourage the organization of Communist parties in all countries. They founded the French Communist Party. Those remaining loyal to the

French Socialist Party continued to accept reformism and thus loyalty to the republic, as well as to the democratic organization of their party.

Léon Blum (1872–1950) led the French Socialist Party. A Jew born into comfortable circumstances in Paris, Blum was a literary critic and intellectual who took a law degree and became a civil servant. Like his hero Jean Jaurès, the French socialist leader who had been assassinated in 1914 on the eve of the war, Blum was an idealist for whom socialism followed philosophically from what he considered the humanism of the French Revolution. Blum remained convinced that socialism would be achieved through the electoral process.

For Communists, the economic malaise of the 1920s seemed proof that capitalism's defeat was near. Furthermore, the defeat of most strikes after the war as well as conservative electoral victories in Britain, France, and Germany seemed to Communists to demonstrate that socialist participation in the political process or in conventional trade unions could only be self-defeating.

Within two years, the French Communist Party grew as large as the Socialist Party. In 1922, on orders from Moscow, the party purged intellectuals from its membership. The Communist Party attracted many followers in the grim industrial suburbs of Paris, the "red belt" around the capital. Communist-dominated municipalities provided social services, such as unemployment relief, as well as light and drinking water for residents living in hastily constructed and insalubrious dwellings. In contrast, the British Communist Party, founded in 1920 and repudiated by the Labour Party, never attracted more than a few thousand followers.

Reformism dominated the parties of the left in post-war Europe. The German Social Democratic Party and the French Socialist Party participated in parliamentary alliances that underlay, respectively, the Weimar Republic and French moderate center-left governments. Liberal parties, too, played a role in the three major states of Western Europe. The British Labour Party, closely allied with the trade unions, emerged as the second largest party in Britain after the war. All three parties depended, to a large extent, on the support of the reformist labor movements in their respective countries. In some ways, unions had become interest groups like any other, bargaining with governments and employers. To this extent, the communist critics of union reformism may have been correct when they warned that reformism served to integrate workers into the structure of the capitalist state.

The emerging outlines of the welfare state in the 1920s reflected the pressure of the parties of the left and of trade unions. At the same time, the origins of the welfare state must be seen in the context of earlier programs of social reform adopted in most countries in the decades before the Great War (see Chapter 20). While the Communist parties of Europe espoused, at least in principle, working-class revolution, socialists and most union members demanded that states provide certain minimum protection for workers. Scandinavia, Denmark, Sweden, and Norway evolved into social democracies, implementing pathbreaking social services. The socialist municipal government of Vienna constructed an attractive working-class apartment complex, providing communal facilities, such as laundries, bathhouses, and kindergartens. The fortress-like structure, which provided 64,000 new apartments, reflected the new sense of the political power of Viennese workers.

In Britain, Prime Minister David Lloyd George had promised demobilized soldiers "a country fit for heroes to live in." The reality was considerably less grand. However, pressured by the Labour Party, which now held the second largest number of seats in the House of Commons, the Housing and Town Planning Act of 1919 provided town councils with subsidies to encourage the construction of cheap row houses. This eliminated some slum overcrowding and provided many working-class families with centralized heating and bathrooms. Within old city limits, "council" flats paid for by town councils provided more modest lodgings for some of the poorest workers. In 1920, the British government expanded unemployment insurance coverage to include most industrial workers, and in 1925, Parliament granted pensions to war widows and orphans, major steps in the emergence of the British welfare state. In France, the Chamber of Deputies in 1930 provided insurance for 10 million workers.

POLITICAL INSTABILITY

In October 1919, the Italian prime minister, Vittorio Orlando, reflected the uncertainty prevalent in the immediate post-war period when he stated that the growing disillusionment threatened Europe "like a blind whirlwind of destruction and disordered violence." The economic crisis that followed the war and the political instability it helped engender were nowhere clearer and ultimately more damaging than in Germany, where the new Weimar Republic sought to steer an even course between threats from the left and the right. Moreover, in Britain and France, states with established parliamentary governments, the subsequent division between left and right was no less bitter, though ultimately it was less bloody.

Germany's Fragile Weimar Republic

The lasting impact of the war on domestic and international politics was most visible in the new German Republic. The newly elected Reichstag adopted the red, gold, and black flag of the ill-fated 1848 Frankfurt Parliament (see Chapter 16). The civil strife in which the Weimar Republic made its start influenced its constitution, approved by the Reichstag in July 1919. The constitution left the German president, who was to be popularly elected, considerable powers. Serving a term of seven years, he could dissolve the Reichstag and call for new elections. Although ministers would be responsible to the Reichstag, the president retained the power to suspend the constitution in order to restore order and to rule by decree, leaving the republic vulnerable to the president's authority.

Challenges to the republic came from the left and the right. In Bavaria, Kurt Eisner's rebel socialist republic collapsed. Following Eisner's murder by a rightist gunman in February 1919, Bavarian leftists rose up again in Munich in April to proclaim a Soviet-style republic. When a general strike paralyzed Berlin in early March, members of the Free Corps and regular German soldiers from Prussia gunned down several thousand workers and socialists.

The new republic desperately needed political stability. But many members of several key social groups, including bureaucrats and university professors who had received their posts under the empire, did not support the republic from the beginning. Several magistrates revealed their views by handing down absurdly light sentences to members of the Free Corps who had been arrested for murder.

Groups of army officers began to plot against the republic during the summer of 1919. Conservative politicians and businessmen attempted a coup d'état, or "putsch," led by Wolfgang Kapp, a former Prussian imperial bureaucrat, with the goal of overthrowing the republic. The Kapp Putsch occurred as the German army was about to be reduced radically in size according to the terms of the Treaty of Versailles. On March 20, 1920, the rebels took over Berlin. The conservative parties proclaimed their support for the new government. In Bavaria, right-wingers seized power after forcing the resignation of the socialist government that had taken power the previous April. With the republic on shaky ground, Chancellor Ebert appealed to the workers to defend the republic. They responded by launching a general strike that shut down much of the country. When some Berlin army units wavered, the Kapp Putsch collapsed.

But the threat to the republic was not over. The center and center-left parties of the Weimar coalition all suffered substantial losses in subsequent elections, while the conservative parties and radicals gained. When the Social Democrats withdrew from the government, the republic depended on a shaky coalition of Center Party politicians and moderate right-wing parties less committed than the Social Democrats to the republic they now governed. As Germany's economy floundered in ruinous inflation, political instability and violence mounted. In August 1921, two former army officers gunned down the Catholic Center Party leader who had signed the armistice ending the war.

Walther Rathenau (1867–1922), the new foreign minister, was determined to negotiate the reparations issue with British and French officials. He attempted to stop rampant German inflation by delivering goods to the Allies rather than gold as reparations. While a hastily arranged conference at Genoa took place, Rathenau shocked Britain and France by signing a statement of mutual friendship with the Soviet Union, the Rapallo Treaty

(April 1922), to counter Western pressure. The Soviet Union received German technical assistance, which it paid for by helping Germany evade some of the military stipulations of the Treaty of Versailles. Subsequently, German officers provided technical assistance to the Soviet army. The Soviets, winning diplomatic recognition and German acquiescence to its repudiation of debts contracted under tsarist rule, renounced any future war reparations from Germany. Two months later, right-wing nationalists murdered Rathenau.

The German mark plunged dramatically in value. The Weimar government informed the Allies that it could not meet the schedule of cash reparations payments, but that it would continue payments of coal and other natural resources. With the United States pressuring Britain and France to repay their war debts, the Allies grew all the more determined that Germany pay up. France's new premier, Raymond Poincaré (1860–1934), threatened a military occupation of the Ruhr Valley industrial district if Germany failed to meet the reparations schedule. He accused Germany of deliberately withholding payments and trying to force the Allies to make concessions by ruining its own currency.

Britain and France, however, could not agree on a common policy. The French refused a German request for a moratorium on reparations payments so that the German currency (the mark) could be stabilized. The resentful German government, backed by virtually all parties except the Communist Party, called on the miners of the Ruhr region to stop working for the Allies. This seemed to confirm Poincaré's contention that Germany was sabotaging repayment of its war debts.

On January 11, 1923, against the advice of the British government, French and Belgian troops occupied the Ruhr. When the German government began to finance the passive resistance in the Ruhr by simply printing more money with which to pay its miners not to work, inflation in Germany spiraled completely out of control, as Table 24.3 luridly demonstrates.

In 1923, Germans wheeled shopping carts filled with literally trillions of marks down the street in order to pay for a single loaf of bread. A half pound of apples went for 300 billion marks. Employees asked to be paid their wages each morning so that they could shop at noon before merchants posted the afternoon price rises. Spiraling inflation wiped out

The German mark being used as wallpaper during the period of extreme inflation after the Great War.

TABLE 24.3. THE MARK AND THE DOLLAR, 1914–1923

Date	Rate: 1 dollar =
July 1914	4.2 marks
January 1919	8.9
July 1919	14.0
January 1920	64.8
July 1920	39.5
January 1921	64.9
July 1921	76.7
January 1922	191.8
July 1922	493.2
January 1923	17,972.0
July 1923	353,412.0
August 1923	4,620,455.0
September 1923	98,860,000.0
October 1923	25,260,208,000.0
November 15, 1923	4,200,000,000,000.0

Source: Gordon Craig, *Germany 1866–1945* (New York: Oxford University Press, 1978), p. 450.

people with fixed incomes and small savings they had put aside for retirement. Many of those who believed that they had done their patriotic duty by buying war bonds during the war now blamed the Weimar Republic when those bonds became worthless. No salaries could possibly have kept pace with such runaway inflation. The poor found staples and other goods not only ridiculously expensive but often unavailable at the market as farmers hoarded produce. Nonetheless, those people who were able to pay off bank loans with wildly inflated currency or to invest in property did well. The rich got richer. In such an atmosphere, the German Communist Party attracted workers in great numbers, undercutting the Social Democrats.

In August 1923, Ebert turned to Gustav Stresemann (1878–1929) to form a government. Stresemann, a former monarchist, had been converted (principally by right-wing violence and political murders) to the republic. Governing by decree and supported by the Social Democrats, he convinced the miners to go back to work and to cease their passive resistance in the Ruhr Valley. France and Belgium ended the occupation after a nine-month period that had been as financially damaging to those nations as it was ruinous to Germany. German government printing presses stopped cranking out billion-mark notes and issued a new mark, which was equal to a trillion of the old marks. The hyperinflation ended.

Stresemann hoped to meet the Allied demands as much as possible, and in doing so, open the way for Germany's return to respectability as a European power. He hoped that this might clear the way for future Allied concessions, namely on Germany's disputed eastern frontier with the newly independent state of Poland. Stresemann convinced both Britain and France to provide loans to help Germany emerge from the economic crisis.

In 1924, a League of Nations commission, chaired by an American banker, Charles G. Dawes (1865–1951), extended the schedule for payment of German reparations. The Dawes Plan left the Reichsbank partially under the direction of an American commissioner who was to oversee German payments, but it did not lower the amount Germany was expected to pay. Meanwhile, the United States had reduced the debt the Allies owed it by percentages ranging from 30 percent (Britain) to 80 percent (Italy). Still, the Dawes Plan improved relations between the Allies and Germany and, with the revival of the European economy beginning in 1924, the reparations issue receded in importance. The Weimar Republic seemed to find stability as the economy finally began to improve. German industries became more competitive, and unemployment began to decline.

Stresemann's discreet and effective diplomacy, now as foreign minister, paid off. The Treaty of Locarno, signed in 1925 between Great Britain, France, Italy, Belgium, and Germany, signaled Germany's gradual return to international respectability. The following year, Germany became a council member of the League of Nations, in return for agreeing that it would not seek to alter its western boundaries with France and Belgium. The signatories at Locarno pledged to settle all future controversies peacefully. However, the Treaty of Locarno did not address the problem of Germany's eastern borders, which the German government refused to include in the agreement. European leaders and newspapers now began to use the phrase "the spirit of Locarno" to refer to a mood of increasing international cooperation.

Nonetheless, German right-wing parties could never forgive Stresemann for collaborating with the socialists. The opponents of the republic seemed almost more vehement in their denunciations of Weimar when it succeeded than when it failed. Success might generate stability and survival. Even after what appeared to be a diplomatic victory for Weimar, German elections reflected the renewed strength of the right; the old Prussian warrior General Paul von Hindenburg was elected president upon Ebert's death in 1925.

The Established Democracies: Britain and France

Britain and France were, to be sure, not immune from the political tensions of the post-war period. Britain, in particular, remained a class-segregated society, despite the intermarriage of aristocratic and industrial families at the top of the social hierarchy. Nowhere in Europe was the concentration of wealth so marked as in Britain. The top 1 percent of the population possessed two-thirds of the national wealth, and one-tenth of 1 percent owned a third of the land in England. Education, occupation, dress, accent, the newspapers one read, and leisure activities all defined and revealed the social class to which one belonged. The distance between the elegant country gentleman and the Yorkshire factory worker, or the top-hatted London banker and the cloth-capped East End docker, remained as great as in the eighteenth century.

Britain's Conservative Party swept to victory in the "khaki" elections (so called because of the color of British army uniforms) held in December 1918 following the armistice. The Labour Party benefited from the decline of the Liberal Party, whose major nineteenth-century issue, free trade, now appealed to relatively few voters. Labour gained the support of most new voters. In 1924, James Ramsay MacDonald (1866–1937), a skilled orator who moved in the most elegant social circles, formed the first Labour government. He preached "the inevitability of gradualness" and "the futility of violence."

The fall of MacDonald's Labour government after several months demonstrated the resilience of British Conservatives, as well as a widespread fear of communism. The Conservatives denounced MacDonald after his government became the first to accord official recognition to the Soviet Union. The press fanned the flames of a "red scare," similar to one then sweeping the United States. A newspaper published a letter it claimed had been written by Grigory Zinoviev, the head of the Communist International, detailing for British Communists ways of destabilizing the government. In fact, the letter was a forgery, the work of a Polish anti-Bolshevik. Returned to power, the Conservatives were determined to restore financial stability and to reject working-class demands. The government put Britain back on the gold standard in 1925, which meant that pounds sterling could be exchanged for gold according to a fixed rate of exchange. But this depleted the amount of gold reserves available to back the British currency and led to the pound's overvaluation. British products became more expensive on the international market, particularly when the other European powers stabilized their own currencies at lower rates. British manufacturing, the key to prosperity for more than a century, remained sluggish, its markets increasingly challenged by those of the United States and Japan. The United States had become the world's leading creditor nation. New York City was now the new center of international finance.

In Britain, tensions between industrialists and workers came to the fore in 1926. The mines still employed over 1 million workers, more than any other industry. After the war, the mining companies had reduced wages and lengthened the workday. A government commission in March 1926 recommended that firms implement safer working conditions, but that the miners accept lower wages. The miners rejected these conclusions with the slogan, "Not a minute on the day, not a penny off the pay." The Trade Union Council launched a general strike of miners in defense of the unions in May 1926. The vast majority of unionized workers in Britain went out in solidarity. The strike enraged the upper and middle classes,

A barricade during the London General Strike, 1926.

inconvenienced by the shutdown of all public transportation. Conservative Winston Churchill castigated the strikers as "the enemy," demanding
their "unconditional surrender" as if he were talking about a German
bunker in the war. The Labour Party was sympathetic to the plight of the
workers, but maintained a safe political distance. Businessmen and students from Oxford and Cambridge Universities drove buses and trucks
carrying people in and out of London while troops hauled food. After two
weeks, most workers had returned to their jobs (although the miners
remained on strike for seven months). The strike was broken. A year later,
Parliament passed the Trade Disputes Act, which forbade "sympathy
strikes," walkouts in support of striking workers by those in other industries, and which marked the defeat of labor militancy in Britain.

In France, too, conservatives held the upper hand in political life after
the war; with the exception of the period from 1924 to 1926, they held the
reins of government until 1934. That France had won the Great War suggested to many people that no pressing need existed to implement political
reforms. Social elites feared the left. Some increasingly blamed the institutional structure of the republic itself for France's malaise. Political
power rested in the Chamber of Deputies; the president, elected by the
chamber, had little power.

When the French franc, long considered to be invulnerable to economic
shocks, collapsed in value in a financial panic in 1924, the rightist government collapsed with it. A coalition of Radicals and Socialists, sharing little
more than anticlericalism, formed a left-center government. But this
alliance broke apart when the Socialists suggested a sizable tax on capital
as a solution to the economic crisis. The government fell in April 1925,
succeeded by ministries that came and went with bewildering regularity.

In 1926, the conservative Poincaré returned as premier. He raised taxes on consumption, which the wealthy preferred to levies on capital, because the burden did not fall on them. The franc stabilized, as wealthy Frenchmen brought assets back from abroad and began to buy francs, which then rose rapidly in value. Poincaré became known as the savior of the French currency. But his idea that political consensus existed in France was, like the belief that France was the most powerful country in Europe, only an illusion. Many ordinary French men and women believed that a "wall of money" still held the country hostage and, along with an entrenched bureaucracy, prevented social reform. The Chamber of Deputies increasingly came to be seen as a debating society incapable of responding effectively to domestic and international crises. Political and social tensions, which exceeded those in Britain, encouraged the disillusionment with democracy felt by parties of the political extremes such as the French Communist Party on the one hand, and the fledgling fascist movements intrigued by Benito Mussolini's seizure of power in Italy on the other.

ARTISTS AND INTELLECTUALS IN THE WASTE LAND

The effects of the Great War could also be easily seen in European intellectual and artistic life, as writers and painters wrestled with the consequences of a devastating struggle that stood as a great divide between the present and a world that was no more. Thus, a veteran of the trenches described the war's cataclysmic destruction as "a cyclopean dividing wall in time: a thousand miles high and a thousand miles thick, a great barrier laid across our life." Indeed, the resulting cultural uncertainty reflected the economic, social, and political chaos of the period.

The defiant modernism of artists and intellectuals in the wake of the war reflected a revolt against traditional cultural conventions within the arts but also against the strictures of bourgeois society. In Britain, for example, people still read Victorian novels and romantic poetry, but such texts seemed to offer no explanation for what had gone wrong in Europe. Horrified by the war, many artists and writers now rejected the social conventions that had inculcated the values of nationalism and blind obedience. In the wake of the war, the "outsiders" of the Belle Époque had become, at least in the realm of the arts, "insiders." To be sure, most of the dramatic changes in artistic expression that followed the war had their origins in the pre-war years—for example, the adoption of psychological, subjective themes and approaches to painting and writing. The war had destroyed not only millions of lives but many of the signposts by which artists and writers defined reality. The American writer Gertrude Stein (1874–1946), who bounced back and forth between her artist and writer friends in London and Paris, called the war's survivors "a lost generation." In a 1922 lecture, the French poet Paul Valéry (1871–1945) said, "The storm has died away and still we are restless, uneasy, as if the storm were about to break . . . among all these injured things is the mind. The mind has indeed been cruelly wounded. . . . It doubts itself profoundly."

The bleak 1922 poem *The Waste Land,* by American-born poet and critic T. S. Eliot (1888–1965), reflected the disintegrating impact that the war had on Europe.

> A heap of broken images, where the sun beats,
>
> And the dead tree gives no shelter, the cricket no relief,
> And the dry stone no sound of water. . . .
> . . . .
> Hooded hordes swarming . . .
> . . . .
> Falling towers
>
> Jerusalem Athens Alexandria
>
> Vienna London
>
> Unreal

The dadaists, a group of artists and writers who had gathered in Zurich in 1916, were the first to rebel against the absurdity of the slaughter of 1914–1918 by rejecting all artistic convention. They penned and painted nonsense; some wrote poems that consisted of words gathered from newspapers. It was all nonsense, but no more, they argued, than the war itself.

The artists and writers of the post-war generation stressed the primacy of subjectivism. Like soldiers emerging from the ghastly trenches, they looked into themselves in their quest to comprehend what seemed incomprehensible. Their subjectivism unleashed an imaginativeness that defined much of the new art.

The painters Piet Mondrian (1872–1944), Paul Klee (1870–1940), and Max Beckmann (1884–1950), among others, thumbed their noses at classical rules about painting, and even about what constituted art. Mondrian, a Dutch modernist painter, offered two-dimensional

A dada poster, 1920.

abstractions and straight lines forming grids. Klee's fantasies assumed unexpected shapes and distortions on the canvas; "the artist must distort," he contended, "for therein is nature reborn."

The expressionist movement, too, had its origins before the war. Beckmann rejected the label, but he defined the movement when discussing his own work, "What I want to show in my work is the idea which hides itself behind so-called reality. I am seeking the bridge which leads from the visible to the invisible." Expressionist poets rejected linguistic conventions in an attempt to communicate the emotion buried beneath the human exterior. Expressionist playwrights ignored long-established conventions of plot, character, and dialogue in order to represent what they considered to be unseen reality. In his modernist epic *Ulysses* (1922), the Irish writer James Joyce (1882–1941) abandoned long-accepted stylistic and narrative conventions to present the chaotic and seemingly unconnected—at least at first glance—"stream of consciousness" dialogue of three main characters, through which he revealed all their sensations and feelings. The novel's eroticism led it to be banned in Britain (but not in traditionally prudish Ireland), and in the United States until 1934.

In 1924, a group of nineteen painters and writers, led by the French artist and poet André Breton (1896–1966), published a "Surrealist Manifesto." In it they rejected "traditional humanism" and the respect for reason that seemed to have so manifestly betrayed mankind. They were not interested in rationality (which seemed defunct) but in what lay beneath it. The surrealists were obsessed with the crater-pocked landscape of churned-up earth, tree stumps, and the twisted rubble of northern France and Belgium. They sought to shock audiences and viewers by expressing themselves in a way that was spontaneous and deeply personal but still realistic. Breton's work sometimes defies interpretation because none was intended.

After four years in the trenches, the German surrealist Max Ernst (1891–1976) wrote that he had "died on the first of August 1914 and returned to life on the 11th of November 1918." Ernst joined a circle of dadaists in Cologne. His 1933 painting *Europe after the Rain (I)* depicts with oil and plaster what appears to be a distorted, disfigured, and unsettling aerial relief map of Europe. It suggests the mutilation of the continent, which appears to be slowly swallowing itself. The surrealists were militant leftists, and they were also among those few Europeans who opposed colonial domination.

For his part, the Viennese doctor Sigmund Freud, founding father of psychoanalysis, believed that the war demonstrated the irrational nature of mankind. Freud's scientific analysis of the unconscious, translated into many languages during the 1920s, had begun to influence sociologists, political scientists, and cultural anthropologists. They applied ideas drawn from psychoanalysis in order to try to understand group behavior and social conflict. The war lent a sense of urgency to that enterprise. Freud

Max Ernst's *Europe after the Rain (I)* (1933).

also greatly influenced surrealists such as Breton, who trained as an analyst and drew images and words from his dreams. Some of Freud's early ruminations about the role of the unconscious in art were based on the haunting experience of seeing shell-shocked soldiers.

THE RISE OF FASCISM

In 1912 in the "Manifesto of Futurism," the work of a small but influential avant-garde futurist movement, which was centered in Italy, had praised "the love of danger, the habit of energy and rashness." "Beauty exists only in struggle," the futurists insisted, seeking to glorify war as "the only cure for the modern world." In the context of the economic, social, political, and cultural chaos that followed the end of the Great War in 1918, this embrace of struggle and violence found its first institutionalized form in Italy, where the first fascist state was established in 1922.

Fascism has been defined as "a system of political authority and social order intended to reinforce the unity, energy, and purity" of national groups. Fascism proclaimed the supremacy of a race or a people (and, at the same time, the inferiority of others races or peoples, most seen in the anti-Semitism that characterized fascist regimes everywhere in Europe), and it vehemently opposed socialism and communism as ideologies that emphasized class differences instead of aggressive national unity. Fascists opposed parliamentary rule and particularly liberal democracies, which they viewed as promoting internal division (for example, by permitting unions and strikes) and national decline. Lining up behind dictators whom they believed, as natural, aggressive leaders, incarnated their national destiny, fascists trumpeted the historical rights of, and duties to, the nation, which they believed outweighed any other rights. In their view this gave them the right to exclude from the national community—and, for some fascists, to kill—those they considered outsiders, and to expand their national frontiers toward what they considered their proper "historical" limits. They placed such struggles in the context of what they conceived of as a Darwinian struggle of the fittest which they would win, celebrating what they considered to be the beauty of violence. Thus, fascism was less of an ideology *per se* than a violent plan of action.

Fascism created what has been called a "magnetic field" in Europe in the 1920s. Extreme right-wing movements won widespread support, first among some elites and then among millions of ordinary people, in many corners of Europe. For all the differences that existed between the right-wing movements that toppled one parliamentary government after another, they shared some striking similarities, as we shall see.

As Benito Mussolini's fascist party came to power in Italy in 1922, in Germany a right-wing anti-parliamentary movement—National Socialism, or Nazism—was gaining strength. It was built on nationalist frustrations resulting from defeat in the war. Adolf Hitler's Nazis also drew on widespread economic discontent and fear of socialism and communism. Nazis, like Italian fascists, espoused dictatorial rule. Whereas parliamentary government had been only superficially implanted in Italy, Germany had almost no democratic political traditions at all. Nazism was a mass movement, also like Italian fascism. It would draw on the support of hundreds of thousands of ordinary people in its assault on parliamentary government. However, the rise of fascism or other extreme right-wing political movements was in no way limited to Italy and Germany.

Mussolini and Fascism in Italy

The economic and social tensions of the immediate post-war period destabilized Italy's liberal government. The dissatisfaction of Italian nationalists with the Treaty of Versailles, which had awarded Istria and northern Dalmatia, territories along the Adriatic coast, to the new Yugoslav state, accentuated Italy's political crisis. This made Italy, in many ways unified in name only, vulnerable to a growing threat from the right.

Gabriele D'Annunzio (1863–1938), a bombastic, decadent poet, had in 1914 described war as perfect hygiene for the modern world. Having proclaimed, "I am not, and do not wish to be, a mere poet," he now took matters into his own hands. In September 1919, the decorated war veteran who had lost an eye in combat swept into the Adriatic city of Fiume (Rijeka). He led a force of 2,000 men, many of whom were demobilized soldiers like himself. D'Annunzio planted the Italian flag, forcing the Italian government to begin negotiations with the new Yugoslav state, which also claimed the port. Both countries agreed that Fiume would be independent, but that most of Istria and northern Dalmatia would remain in Yugoslavia, as the Treaty of Versailles had specified. D'Annunzio's little republic lasted sixteen months, until Italian ships lobbed a few shells in the general direction of the city and sent the poet and his small army packing.

Even in failure, D'Annunzio had stolen the thunder of another fervent Italian nationalist, Benito Mussolini (1883–1945). Mussolini was born to a family of modest means in the Romagna region in northern Italy. His father, a blacksmith, was something of a revolutionary; he had taught himself to read from socialist tracts and had named his son after the Mexican revolutionary Benito Juarez. The young Mussolini was a bully in school who was quick to raise his fists and pull a knife, once stabbing a girlfriend. He had no close friends—at least after the death of his brother in 1931—and was proud of it. ("Keep your heart a desert," he once advised.)

The young Mussolini read Karl Marx and Friedrich Nietzsche, whose espousal of daring revolt and the "will to power" intrigued him. After a stint in the army, Mussolini proclaimed himself a socialist and anti-militarist and became a political journalist. With other anti-militarists, he took to the streets to denounce Italy's colonial war against Libya (see Chapter 21). Late in 1912, Mussolini became editor of the Italian Socialist Party's newspaper, *Avanti!* At the outbreak of the Great War in 1914, Mussolini led a chorus of socialists demanding that Italy remain neutral.

During the first year of the war, Mussolini's views toward war changed. He wrote that the turmoil of the war might bring about social revolution; "only blood," he wrote, "makes the wheels of history turn." This chilling conclusion demonstrated that the influence of Nietzsche was overwhelming that of Marx in Mussolini's mind. Angered by the opposition his view encountered among socialists, Mussolini began another newspaper that would reflect his views alone.

In October 1914, a small number of syndicalists broke away from the Socialist Party, demanding that Italy join the war. They took the name "fascists" from the Latin word *fascio,* meaning a bundle of sticks, or, by extension, an association. When Italy entered the war in 1915, Mussolini joined the army. Lightly wounded in 1917, he returned to journalism. As the German and Austro-Hungarian armies suffered major defeats in 1918, Mussolini led the chorus of nationalist demands for a peace settlement favorable to Italian interests. In March 1919, he founded his own fascist organization, which he called the National Fascist Party.

The post-war crisis of Italy's liberal state aided the fascists. The major parties of Italy—the Liberals, the Socialists, and the new Catholic Popular Party—struggled in vain to find consensus. While governments formed and fell in quick succession, severe economic difficulties continued to plague Italy in the immediate aftermath of the armistice. Hundreds of thousands of demobilized troops joined the ranks of the unemployed. Following a brief post-war boom, inflation soared, eroding middle-class savings and undercutting the already low standard of living of workers and landless peasants. Agricultural depression compounded high unemployment.

As in Britain, France, and Germany, workers flocked to organized labor in Italy, and waves of strikes spread in 1919 and 1920. Peasant laborers demanded land and formed unions called "red leagues." In the south, thousands of poor families had begun to occupy some of the vast, often uncultivated holdings belonging to large landowners. Banditry became even more prevalent in southern Italy and Sicily.

During these "red years" of 1920–1922, many landowners and business-men turned against parliamentary government. In Italy more than in any other country, there was considerable interaction and interdependence between urban and rural elites. The Liberal government had alienated the wealthy by proposing a progressive tax on income and a high imposition on war profits, and it had outraged them by legalizing peasant land seizures. Uniformed squads of fascists intervened on behalf of wealthy landowners and businessmen, attacking syndicalists, Socialists, and Communists. Laborers and sharecroppers fought back against the fascist "black shirts," but had little chance because the landowners supplied these gangs with weapons. The left was divided and hesitant.

In contrast to France, where post-war strikes strengthened the conserv-ative republican government that had been elected in 1919, labor mili-tancy brought down the helpless Italian government. Mussolini, boasting

(*Left*) Mussolini (in back seat) on his way to the train station after being asked to form a government. (*Right*) The Duce and his sovereign, Victor Emmanuel III.

a private army and a sizable claque, or "applause squad," of paid supporters, praised the "bath of blood" that swept parts of Italy. He reveled in
rumors of a coup d'état associated with his name, cranking out violent
articles denouncing parliamentary government.

In 1921, the Liberals, hoping to find a parliamentary mandate to impose
order, offered the fascists qualified support and accepted them as electoral allies. Mussolini and several dozen other fascists were elected to the
Italian Parliament. The fascist leader now had an ideal soapbox for his
flamboyant oratory, as well as immunity from prosecution. The Liberal
government of Giovanni Giolitti resigned, succeeded by yet another coalition government.

The fascists were now a powerful political movement with prominent
allies, money, newspapers, and hundreds of thousands of members. Fascist thugs had carved out territories in which their word was law. They disrupted local political life, shattering the organization, confidence, and
support for the traditional parties. Mussolini, who took the title of the
Duce, or "the leader," presented himself as a defender of law and order,
blaming Socialists and the newly formed Communist Party for the turmoil. Fascists enjoyed the tacit support of many state and police officials,
as fascist violence went unpunished. Some prelates within the Church
hierarchy began to speak warmly of Mussolini.

For Mussolini, fascism was an ideology of violent confrontation, a
means of winning and maintaining political power, more than a coherent
doctrine of political philosophy. Fascists advocated a strong, virulently
nationalist, militarized state with which all Italians must identify: "Everything within the State, nothing outside the State, nothing against the
State" was how Mussolini put it. Italy would fulfill its "historic destiny."
However, Mussolini's conception of race depended on a historical and
cultural view and did not share Hitler's strange and pernicious obsession
with what he considered the biological basis of race.

In October 1922, Mussolini made his move. He pressured the diminutive, indecisive King Victor Emmanuel III (ruled 1900–1946), a shy man
who loved to hunt, wear military uniforms, and collect coins, to name him
and several other fascists to cabinet posts. The king remained out of Rome
for weeks at a time as the crisis built, hoping that it would simply go away.
As he planned a coup d'état, Mussolini charmed members of the royal
family. He told 40,000 fascists in Naples, "Either we are allowed to govern, or we will seize power by marching on Rome." The prime minister
asked the king to declare martial law and to use the army to restore order
by suppressing the fascists, who had seized control of several towns.

It was typical of the king, who combined indecision and fatalism, that he
declared a state of emergency, then changed his mind even as thousands of
black-shirted fascists began to surge toward Rome on the night of October
27, 1922. Mussolini took a comfortable night train to the capital. When
another aged politician refused the king's request to form a government,

Victor Emmanuel turned to Mussolini. On October 29, the Duce became prime minister. Fascists celebrated in the streets by beating up political enemies and closing down newspapers.

Despite the fact that his party held a small proportion of the seats in the chamber and could not claim the party allegiance of a single senator, Mussolini convinced both bodies to grant him full powers to rule by decree for a year. Many mainstream politicians endorsed him because the fascists promised to restore social order. They also assumed that Mussolini could not long survive once he was brought into respectable political life.

Mussolini's shrewd management of fascist newspapers and his ability to plant favorable articles in other papers through cajoling and bribery helped win further support. Aided by the intimidating tactics of the fascist militia, the National Fascist Party won enough votes in the 1923 elections to emerge as the majority party, at least with the support of the Catholic Popular Party.

Despite a major political crisis in 1924 that followed his implication in the murder of a Socialist deputy by fascists, Mussolini developed an almost cult-like following. The Duce encouraged the phrase "Mussolini is always right" and managed to convince millions of people that this was indeed the case. He was the first politician of the twentieth century to make use of modern communication techniques. He subsidized several films about his accomplishments; his rambling speeches, voluminous tomes, an autobiography, and several authorized biographies were sold in various glossy editions. By the early 1930s, Italian journalists were required to capitalize He, His, and Him when referring to Mussolini, as they did when mentioning God or Jesus Christ. All Italians at age eighteen had to take an oath to obey Mussolini. Italian press agents worked to enhance his image abroad. In Britain, playwright George Bernard Shaw thought well of the Duce; in Vienna, Sigmund Freud at first praised him; the American poet Ezra Pound remained an admirer. The U.S. ambassador saluted "a fine young revolution," and *Time* magazine put him on its cover eight times.

Not long after Mussolini took power, however, French newspapers began to describe him as a Carnival Caesar. The tag stuck. The Duce strutted about, boasting egregiously, his eyes rolling and his chin jutting out as he piled falsehood upon exaggeration. He insisted that officials and assistants sprint to his desk and ordered photographers to take pictures of him fencing, playing tennis, or running by troops he was reviewing. Mussolini obnoxiously boasted of his sexual energy and prowess. But despite his insistence that he be portrayed as dynamic, he was rather lazy and unable to concentrate on any one thing for very long. To some extent, the Italian dictator was an actor, and the balconies from which he thundered speeches were his stage.

Mussolini, who wore so many military decorations that a foreign journalist wrote that he "looked like a circus performer in off hours," planned an army of "eight million bayonets" and an air force that would "blot out the sun." But despite Mussolini's attempt to project an image of fascism that emphasized youthful physical vigor, relatively little military training actually took place in Italy. The Italian army remained beset by inadequate command structures and poor training.

The Duce took over the most important operations of the state and was like an orchestra conductor trying to play all of the instruments at once. He warned ministers not to disagree with him because they might divert him "from what I know to be the right path—my own animal instincts are always right." Officials reported only what they thought Mussolini wanted to hear. The consequences in international affairs would be catastrophic, as the gap between Mussolini's assessment of Italy's military strength and reality widened.

Mussolini treated domestic policy as an afterthought, once claiming that "to govern [Italy], you need only two things, policemen, and bands playing in the streets." Yet while it is easy to emphasize the farcical aspects of Mussolini's rule, in Italy, as in other fascist states, there was nothing comical about the brutality of the police or about his provocative foreign policy, which made Europe an increasingly dangerous place.

In order to placate a potentially powerful source of opposition, Mussolini made peace with the Catholic Church, which had previously denounced the regime after fascist squads smashed Catholic workers' cooperatives along with similar Socialist organizations. In 1929, the Duce signed the Lateran Pacts with the Church, a concordat that left the Vatican an independent papal enclave within Rome. In exchange, the papacy for the first time officially recognized Italy's existence. The Italian dictator returned religious instruction to all schools, and banned freemasonry, swearing in public, all literature that the Church considered obscene, and the sale of contraceptives. Mussolini won Catholic support with his pronatal campaign (which included a tax on "unjustified celibacy"), vague statements about the importance of the family, measures limiting Protestant publications, and fulminations against women participating in sports. The Duce himself now quickly had his grown children baptized and his marriage recognized by the Church, ten years after his civil marriage to a wife with whom he no longer lived. Pope Pius XI now called Mussolini "the man sent by Providence." Having found favor with the Church hierarchy and enjoying dictatorial power in Italy, Mussolini could turn to implementing an aggressive foreign policy, while dreaming of building another Roman Empire.

Hitler and the Rise of the Nazis in Germany

Like Italian fascism, the rise of the Nazis was closely identified with the rise to power of a charismatic leader, Adolf Hitler (1889–1945). Hitler was born in the small Austrian town of Braunau, on the border with Bavaria.

His father had risen to become a customs official of modest means. One teacher recalled "the gaunt, pale-faced youth . . . [Adolf Hitler] had definite talent, though in a narrow field. But he lacked self-discipline, being notoriously cantankerous, willful, arrogant, and bad-tempered. He had obvious difficulty in fitting in at school."

Hitler quit school in 1905. Turned down for admission to the Academy of Graphic Arts in Vienna, he nonetheless moved to the imperial capital where he worked as a paper-hanger and painted postcards, living in a hostel with little money and few friends. In the 1914 city directory, Hitler had himself listed as "painter and architect." He almost certainly must have absorbed the anti-Semitism rampant in Vienna, and he would later emphasize that period of his life in order to underline his claim that he had overcome adversity and had held his view of the world from the very beginning.

Hitler was of average height with a large head, dark hair, broad cheekbones, and an unusually high forehead. Wearing baggy clothes and sporting his characteristic trimmed mustache, he was not an impressive-looking man. He had bad teeth and poor eyesight. Hitler was compulsive about daily routines, did not drink coffee or smoke, was a vegetarian, and took only an occasional drink. He enjoyed the company of women—two of whom committed suicide out of love for him—but may, in fact, have been impotent.

At the outbreak of the Great War, Hitler can be seen in a picture of a large crowd cheering the proclamation of war in Munich enthusiastically. He joined the German army and was wounded in the leg in 1916, gassed in a British attack just before the end of the war, and decorated on three occasions for bravery. But his superiors found Hitler unfit for promotion to the officer corps, believing that he lacked leadership qualities.

Hitler would later recall "the stupendous impression produced on me by the war—the greatest of all experiences . . . the heroic struggle of our people." He had warned fellow soldiers that "in spite of our big guns victory would be denied" to Germany because of "the invisible foes of the German people," Marxists and Jews. The war accentuated Hitler's fanatical German nationalism.

Several influential German authors had also drawn similar conclusions from the war. In 1918, Oswald Spengler (1880–1936) had published the first volume of *The Decline of the West*. In it, he blamed Germany's defeat on the decay of Western civilization. "We no longer believe," he wrote, "in the power of reason over life. We feel that life rules over reason." He had anticipated that new, powerful leaders would emerge out of the maelstrom of subsequent wars; they would destroy the "impotent democracies." Spengler believed that German culture would be victorious in a biological struggle against its competitors. The result would be "the triumph of the idea of one race over all others." German culture would be

Some of the first Nazi storm troopers in 1922, with swastikas on their arms and flag.

embodied in a new state in which the individual would be subsumed in the nation.

By 1919, Hitler had constructed his view of the world. It was composed of racism, anti-Semitism, and extreme nationalism. His racism was based on the belief that Germans were "Aryans," descended from a superior Caucasian people. That year, Hitler joined the German Workers' Party, a newly formed right-wing nationalist organization. The following year, as Hitler rose to the head of the organization, he renamed it the National Socialist German Workers' Party, or Nazi Party. Impressed by Hitler's single-minded determination, some Nazis now referred to Hitler as the "Führer" or "leader." He was introduced into more elegant social circles, where cash for propaganda and guns could be found.

Nazis organized a paramilitary organization, the "storm troopers," known after 1921 as the S.A. (Stürmabteilungen), led by the hard-drinking, corpulent Bavarian Ernst Röhm (1887–1934). Like the Free Corps, the S.A. offered comradeship and an outlet for violence to frustrated war veterans. To its members and those of other paramilitary organizations organized in the wake of defeat, Hitler appeared to be a man of action, a survivor of the trenches, one of them, who promised to bring about rearmament and to expand military influence in Germany.

Emboldened by their success at attracting adherents, the Nazis marched out of a beer hall on November 9, 1923, planning to seize power in Munich and then march on Berlin. Troops loyal to the government put an end to the "Beer Hall Putsch." A lenient, anti-republican judge sentenced Hitler to five years in prison. He served only one year and emerged from prison a national figure. Hitler then turned to "legal" tactics, building up the Nazi Party.

In 1925, Hitler published *Mein Kampf* (*My Struggle*), which he had written in his comfortable jail quarters. Here he reiterated the claim, originally that of General von Hindenburg, that Germany had been stabbed in the back by Jews and Communists during the war. It was easy to forget that the military front had collapsed before the home front, a convenient collective amnesia. "If, at the beginning and during the war," Hitler wrote, "someone had only subjected about twelve or fifteen thousand of these Hebrew destroyers of the people to poison gas—as was suffered on the battlefield by hundreds of thousands of our best workers from all social classes and all walks of life—then the sacrifice of millions at the front would not have been in vain." He never strayed from the most salient themes of his appeal, believing that people could only absorb a few ideas that must be hammered in over and over again. Germany would rearm, then conquer "living space" at the expense of the "inferior" Slavic peoples to the east and south.

Beleaguered Germans look at a poster presenting Hitler as their savior.

Nazi propagandists portrayed Hitler as an energetic, devoted, and uncompromising leader who could unify Germans of all classes, who stood apart from the weakness, corruption, and compromise the right identified with the Weimar Republic. They pictured him as a God-fearing man (though, in fact, like Mussolini, he was not at all religious) who had overcome opposition to achieve great heights through personal sacrifice. Many Germans now believed that the problem was not that Germany had fought the war, but only that victory had been stolen from them.

In these early days, the Nazis, like Mussolini's fascists, appealed most to the lower middle class; later they would appeal to the entire spectrum of the German middle class. Many bourgeois families, which had been devastated by the hyperinflation of the early 1920s, stopped supporting the other conservative political parties and the Weimar Republic itself. Pensioners struggled to make ends meet; many small businessmen, shopkeepers, craftsmen, and clerks (some of whom now earned less than skilled workers) had to sell or pawn silver or other items of value that had been passed down in their families for generations. They looked to Hitler to protect them from "Bolsheviks" and did not care how he did so.

The Nazis won less than 3 percent of the vote in the 1928 elections. But German political life was moving to the right, led by the powerful National People's Party, most of whose members were increasingly anti-republican but not yet necessarily attracted to the Nazis. They preferred a monarchy or military dictatorship. The death in October 1929 of Gustav Stresemann, Germany's able and respected foreign minister, removed a powerful voice of support for the republic and gravely weakened the Weimar coalition in the Reichstag. Socialists, too, were divided. New political coalitions were based far more on makeshift convenience than determined loyalty to the republic. The political center disappeared as support for Weimar crumbled.

The American Wall Street Crash in late October 1929 compounded the social and political instability that had beset Europe since the end of the Great War more than ten years earlier. The economic hardship generated by the Depression swelled the ranks of parties committed to overthrowing parliamentary rule in Germany and other states. As support for the Nazis grew in Germany, Europe entered an even more dangerous period of instability.

CHAPTER 25

THE EUROPE OF DEPRESSION AND DICTATORSHIP

In the two decades following the Great War, one European dictator after another ended parliamentary democracy, imposing fascist rule and suppressing political opposition. These dictators poisoned international relations with nationalist bullying, making grandiose claims on the territories of other states.

In 1922, Benito Mussolini became the first dictator to take power. By the end of 1925, fascist parties demanding the imposition of dictatorships had sprung up in more than forty other nations. Other more traditional right-wing authoritarian movements, too, were on the rise. In Portugal, where junior army officers had overthrown the monarchy in 1910 and declared a republic, right-wing military officers staged a coup d'état in 1926. General Józef Pilsudski overthrew the Polish Republic the same year (see Chapter 24). All of the Eastern European and Balkan states became dictatorships in the 1920s and 1930s, with the exception of Czechoslovakia. By eliminating all opposition and consolidating power in 1929, Joseph Stalin transformed the Soviet Union into even more of an authoritarian state. In 1933, a right-wing government came to power in Austria, and Adolf Hitler became Nazi chancellor of Germany. The right-wing nationalist revolt against the republic of Spain began in 1936, starting a civil war that ended in 1939 with the victory of General Francisco Franco's right-wing nationalist forces. Britain and France were the only major powers in which parliamentary government was strong enough to resist the authoritarian tide. Yet democracy also survived in the smaller states of Belgium, the Netherlands, Switzerland, Denmark, Sweden, and Norway, despite the existence in each of these states of small fascist movements.

ECONOMIES IN CRISIS

The global depression that began in October 1929 had significant political consequences in Europe. Economic insecurity and accompanying social unrest undermined parliamentary rule in Germany, Austria, and in other Eastern European countries, and threatened it in France and Belgium. More and more people sought scapegoats who could be blamed for the frustrations of hard times: Jews, Socialists, Communists, other nationalities, big business. Under such circumstances, many people could be convinced that parliamentary government itself was to blame and that nationalistic dictatorships were the solution. Amid plunging confidence and general bewilderment, international cooperation became more difficult, particularly as the powers began to blame each other for adopting policies that adversely affected them. Many Germans castigated their wartime enemies for assessing massive, seemingly unjust reparations; many British and French citizens blamed Germany for not paying all the reparations; many Americans blamed their own allies, above all, Britain and France, for not paying back loans. The vicious cycle of mistrust grew.

The Great Depression

By 1924, prosperity seemed to have returned to much of post-war Europe, particularly Britain and France. But beneath the surface, the increasingly interdependent world economy had not recovered from the war. The wartime inflation continued for several years following the armistice. At the same time, the prices of steel and iron declined sharply after the war

(*Left*) The Wall Street Crash, October 1929. (*Right*) An unemployed Briton seeks work, 1930.

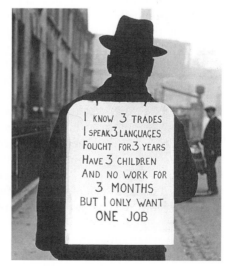

when demand plunged for tanks, artillery pieces, and munitions. Overproduction and the increasing use of hydroelectricity and oil caused the price of coal to fall rapidly. Slowly some industrial jobs began to disappear.

European agriculture was in a depressed state well before the Crash of 1929. The war had encouraged agricultural overproduction in Europe; in addition, more grain, meats, and other food supplies arrived on the continent during the 1914–1918 period from Australia, Argentina, Canada, and the United States, depressing the price of locally produced farm products. Lower farm incomes, aggravated by the burden of taxation, in turn reduced demand for manufactured goods.

European states reacted by erecting tariff barriers to try to protect their internal markets for domestic agricultural products. Countries like Bulgaria that depended on agricultural exports saw their foreign markets dry up, or they received less for what they sold. With less income and less Western investment, Eastern European and Balkan nations could not repay their wartime debts. Germany's defeat, the dismemberment of the Austro-Hungarian Empire, and the Russian Revolution significantly weakened the region's three largest pre-war trading partners.

The contraction of demand and price deflation probably would not have been enough to generate full-fledged economic disaster. But unrestrained financial speculation also eroded the world economy. In Germany, high interest rates attracted considerable foreign investment following the 1924 economic recovery. Credit was easily available, and companies issued huge amounts of stock shares based upon insufficient real assets. In the United States, a sizable reduction in demand for goods was already apparent by 1927. Wealthy people began to invest in highly speculative stocks.

Wartime loans and post-war debts made the finances of the larger powers more interdependent and helped destabilize the international economy. German reparations also adversely affected the world economy because, ironically, they accentuated the flow of capital into Germany. Following the Dawes Plan, which in 1924 extended the schedule of reparations, Germany borrowed $110 million from U.S. banks in order to meet its reduced reparations payments to the Allies, rather than paying them out of current income through higher taxes. German railroads served as collateral for the loans, which were immediately oversubscribed by ten times in New York. Like bonds and speculative investments, the reparation loans diverted investment away from industry and ignited further foreign lending. Besides loans to pay reparations, other loans also poured into Germany. Most of this debt was short term rather than long term, which made Germany even more vulnerable to a sudden calling in of those loans. In 1928, U.S. banks refused further loans to Germany, investing available funds instead in the Wall Street stock market, further undercutting German banks.

By early 1929, the U.S. economy was in recession. In late October, the New York stock market crashed, ruining many stockholders. Moreover, thousands of large and small investors also were ruined as stocks lost most of their value. American and British investors with assets still tied up in Germany now began to pull their money out as quickly as possible. German gold reserves were depleted, as banks owed far more money to creditors than they had assets. Table 25.1 shows the importance of the U.S.-German financial connection, which contributed to the fact that the Depression began earlier and production fell more in those two countries than in the other major powers.

As unemployment mounted to unprecedented levels, the "roaring twenties" became the "threadbare thirties." Jobs disappeared and families were compelled to spend the savings they had so painstakingly amassed over the previous five years, even as manufacturing and agricultural prices continued to fall because of the dramatic contraction of demand. Manufactured goods piled up on the docks.

Confronted by a catastrophic fall in production and prices, as well as unemployment approaching 20 percent of the workforce, British government officials and economists debated strategies that might revive their floundering economies. There were no easy answers. The economic orthodoxy of the day held that the way out of the crisis was to reduce public expenditures. The inflation of the immediate post-war period, particularly the hyperinflation that had ravaged Germany in 1922 and 1923, frightened statesmen and economists away from even limited financial or fiscal expansion.

National policy options, too, were further constrained by the interdependence of the international economy, especially under the gold standard. For example, Ramsey MacDonald's British Labour government first reacted to the Wall Street crash by increasing unemployment benefits and funding more public works, while raising taxes. These expenditures

TABLE 25.1. INDICES OF INDUSTRIAL PRODUCTION

Year	Germany	United States	France	Britain
1925	79.3	93.7	85.0	94.8*
1927	97.2	95.5	86.6	101.2
1929	101.4	107.2	109.4	106.0
1930	83.6	86.5	110.2	97.9
1931				
August	71.9	74.8	99.2	84.6
December	59.4	66.7	87.4	84.7
1932				
January	55.2	64.9	82.7	90.1
August	54.7	53.2	73.2	89.2

*For Great Britain, 1924.
Source: David E. Sumler, *A History of Europe in the Twentieth Century* (Homewood, IL: Dorsey Press, 1973), p. 145.

further increased the government deficit, already soaring because of reduced tax revenue and the payment of unemployment benefits. But the British government was then forced to reduce such benefits in order to be deemed creditworthy by New York and Parisian bankers in the hope of stabilizing the pound and maintaining the gold standard.

The international monetary system collapsed as the world economy plunged into dark depression. With the Depression, those banks and private interests that had loaned money to Germany began to call in debts. Already reeling from agricultural depression in Eastern Europe, the failure of the largest Austrian bank in May 1931 immediately entailed the collapse of several German banks to which it owed money and led to a general financial panic. U.S. President Herbert Hoover (1874–1964) suggested a moratorium on the repayment of all reparations and war debts, hoping that confidence and the end of the cycle of defaults would follow. The other powers accepted the moratorium in August 1931.

As the British economy floundered because of the decline in world trade, European bankers intensified the run on the pound. They exchanged their holdings of British pounds sterling for gold, £2.5 million worth per day during the summer of 1930, dangerously reducing Britain's gold reserves. As investors panicked, sterling quickly lost a third of its value.

In August 1931, MacDonald's government resigned, replaced by a "National Government," an inter-party coalition, though MacDonald stayed on as prime minister. Worsening conditions forced the National Government to take Britain off the gold standard in September 1931. This meant that the Bank of England would no longer remit gold in exchange for pounds. This seemed like a step into the economic unknown. Wild fluctuations in the values of other currencies followed. This further discouraged business, and international trade declined even more steeply, but it did permit some domestic recovery. In April 1933, the United States, too, went off the gold standard.

In Britain, the Conservatives' deflationary measures, which sought to reduce expenditures, seemed to British voters to be the only way out of the crisis; in the elections of October 1931, the Tories won an overwhelming majority of seats in the House of Commons. Neville Chamberlain (1869–1940) now became chancellor of the Exchequer. His aloof manner, inveterate dullness, rasping voice, and whiny disposition did little to inspire confidence—one critic suggested that he had been "weaned on a pickle." Chamberlain, who had successfully provided public housing for workers, promised a "doctor's mandate" to extract Britain from the economic crisis. The government imposed higher tariffs, further reducing consumer spending. Many Labourites, calling MacDonald a traitor to his party for going along with deflationary measures because they reduced unemployment benefits, still called for the nationalization of mining, the railways, and other essential industries as beginning steps toward the implementation of a more planned economy. But Labour's campaign ran headlong into traditional Conservative opposition and middle-class fear of socialism, as well as the orthodoxy of deflationary economic policies.

In the depths of the Depression, a fascist movement developed even in Britain, the home of parliamentary democracy. Oswald Mosley (1896–1980), born into a wealthy aristocratic family, had become the youngest member of Parliament in 1918. The vain Mosley, a skilled orator, had left the Conservative Party for a brief fling with Labour (leading the philandering Mosley to proclaim his new motto, "Vote Labour, Sleep Tory"). Attacking "international finance capital" and the Labour Party alike, he formed the British Union of Fascists in 1932 and began to deliver vehement speeches against Jews. An admirer of Mussolini, who provided funds for the British fascist movement, and Hitler, who served as best man at his second wedding, Mosley surrounded himself with black-shirted toughs. However, Mosley attracted more attention than followers (they never numbered more than 20,000). Considerable division existed in Britain as to which policies would best ease the effects of the Depression, but the British people, as throughout history, avoided political extremes.

Across the English Channel, smaller-scale industries, artisans, and family farmers in France at first were sheltered from the Depression because they depended, above all, on local markets. France also had considerable gold reserves, which helped maintain business and consumer confidence and helped keep consumer spending at a relatively high level. The run on the British pound and the German mark, too, at first aided France, as much of the gold exchanged by investors ended up in Paris. But gradually French prices also fell and unemployment rose, again revealing the interdependence of the world economy. French exports declined with the contraction of the world market, particularly because the franc, which had not plunged like the pound, was now overvalued, making French goods expensive abroad. But most French leaders considered devaluation to be anathema. "Who touches the franc," cautioned one newspaper, "touches France!" The French government, like that of Britain, stuck to classical economic remedies, ignoring demands for active state intervention to stimulate the economy from right-wing corporatists who sought support for cartels and from left-wing socialists who called for the nationalization of crucial industries and higher unemployment benefits.

Gradual European Economic Revival

In the rest of Europe, government leaders debated strategies that they hoped would pull their countries out of the Depression. One after another, the major powers acted in their own interests—establishing high tariffs and devaluing their currencies—without prior consultation with other governments. The U.S. government, like that of Britain, followed contemporary economic orthodoxy. Both sharply reduced government spending, cutting

Reflecting the enormity of class divisions in Britain during the Depression, these working-class boys look in amazement at two Eton students outside a cricket ground.

unemployment benefits and restricting credit. John Maynard Keynes, the maverick English economist, insisted that recovery would depend upon just the opposite strategy. He recommended an increase in government expenditures, including deficit spending—for example, on public works—to stimulate consumer spending by reducing unemployment. Keynes argued that deflationary measures, such as cutting government spending, reducing unemployment benefits, or encouraging companies to limit production and thus keep prices artificially high, were counterproductive. They could prolong the Depression by reducing the demand for goods. With one-quarter of the labor force out of work early in 1933 and wages falling, there was insufficient demand to generate a manufacturing upswing in Great Britain, the United States, or anywhere else. But Keynes was in a small minority, and most of his writing then still largely unknown.

Only very gradually did the Depression begin to recede in the industrialized countries. A modest recovery began in Britain in 1932. But it was not due to the dramatic improvement of British international trade upon which the Conservatives had counted. Rather, it followed a slow increase in consumer spending. Keynes had been right. Government decisions in 1934 and 1935 to increase unemployment benefits and restore government salaries to their pre-Depression levels helped. So did the subsidized construction of houses, which pumped money into the economy, restoring consumer confidence. While some inefficient steel and textile manufacturers went under, others consolidated and became more efficient, perhaps benefiting from the imposition of higher tariffs on industrial imports. Real wages slowly rose. The imposition of quotas on agricultural imports aided farmers. As industry and agriculture gradually returned to prosperity, unemployment began to fall.

The German economy also slowly improved, at least partially because, after Hitler came to power in 1933, rearmament created many jobs; business confidence slowly returned. In 1930, the Young Plan, named after its American originator, had extended the date to 1988 by which Germany was to have paid all reparations. Then the Lausanne Conference of 1932 simply declared the end of reparations payments. In France, the Depression lingered longer than in any other industrialized power, with the exception of the United States.

In the United States, where the Depression hit hardest, recovery came even more slowly. Franklin D. Roosevelt (1882–1945), elected president in 1932, implemented his "New Deal." It facilitated loans that saved banks, provided relief for the unemployed through public works programs, and provided assistance to farmers and to businesses. When Keynes learned of Roosevelt's plans, he jumped with glee, "Roosevelt was magnificently right" (he might have said, someone noted, that he was "magnificently left"). Gradually, a return of consumer confidence, boosted by the president's low-key "fireside chats" by radio to the American people, improved the economy. But only with the entry of the United States into the Second World War in 1941, with its massive mobilization of economic resources in the production of war materials, did the Depression finally end its grip on the United States. It is against this background of the Depression and hard times that the rise of fascism and other authoritarian movements must be seen both in the industrialized countries of Western Europe and in the largely agrarian states of Eastern Europe and the Balkans (see Map 25.1).

FASCIST MOVEMENTS

Anti-parliamentarianism, anti-communism, and anti-Semitism helped give fascism an international character. In 1935, there was even a short-lived attempt to create a fascist international, similar to the Communist International (Comintern) on the other end of the political spectrum. Mussolini contributed funds to the Belgian, Austrian, and British fascist movements. But the stridently nationalist aspect of fascism worked against such fascist internationalism. Yet fascist and right-wing authoritarian states found ready allies among similar regimes, as joint German and Italian assistance to the nationalist rebellion during the Spanish Civil War (1936–1939) solidified the alliance between Hitler and Mussolini.

There was no single fascist ideology, and not all of the right-wing authoritarian movements in Europe in the 1920s and 1930s can be qualified as fascist. In Spain, Francisco Franco imposed a military dictatorship like that of Antonio Salazar (1889–1970) in neighboring Portugal; both were predicated upon the influence of traditional elites, the Catholic Church, and the army. Yet, while sharing the anti-Bolshevism of fascist Italy and Nazi Germany, neither the Spanish nor the Portuguese dictatorship shared the expansionist ideology of those regimes, and both were distrustful of the kind of mass movement that helped sweep the Italian fascists and German Nazis to power. The agrarian populist dictatorships of Eastern Europe may also be described as fascist states, or at least "para-fascist" dictatorships.

MAP 25.1 DICTATORSHIPS IN EUROPE, 1932–1937   States ruled by dictators before 1932; states that became dictatorships after 1932; remaining democracies in 1937.

They, too, were characterized by aggressive, nationalist mass movements, anti-communism, anti-Semitism, and frenetic opposition to parliamentary rule. They also sought to maintain the social hierarchy within their states by violent means. Unlike the dictatorships in Germany and Italy, however, these other dictators, however much inspired in some ways by Mussolini and Hitler, had no illusions about expanding their states beyond what each claimed as the "historic" limits of their nationality. Moreover, Stalin's Soviet Union, too, had become a state dictatorship, like the fascist regimes, but one of the left, based on communist rhetoric about creating a workers' paradise. Stalin, casting aside the claims of the many non-Russian nationalities, and for that matter, of the workers themselves, tolerated no opposition to or within the Communist Party. Such states, then, were marked by centralized control of all political functions by a dictator ruling in the name of a single party. They used the police to enforce bans against the freedom of assembly and of the press, and to crush opposition through state-sponsored terror.

The Dynamics of Fascism

Several factors contributed to the rise of the extreme right, with none serving as a sufficient single explanation. If in the nineteenth century the middle class had stood as a bulwark of liberal values in Europe, this was no longer the case in the post-war climate. In Germany, Italy, and Austria, fascists found disproportionate support among the middle class, particularly the lower middle class. In Portugal, which had been ravaged by the Depression, conservative middle-class Catholics continued to support the dictatorship of Salazar, while applauding the policies of Mussolini and Hitler. By contrast, the British and French middle classes felt many of the same economic frustrations, but only in France did a good number turn to anti-parliamentarian political movements.

With the exception of the recovery of 1924–1929, the 1920s and 1930s were decades of economic crisis. When the American stock market crashed in October 1929, small savings accounts and pensions were wiped out. Many middle-class families watched in horror as their modest savings disappeared. They feared union leaders, Socialists, and Communists, who demanded an extension of public programs to aid unemployed workers and who espoused social revolution. But middle-class frustrations do not provide a sufficient explanation for the rise of authoritarian movements in Eastern Europe and the Balkans, where the middle classes were extremely small.

Fascist parties, in the largest sense, including the National Socialist German Workers' Party, developed in the 1920s as mass political movements. Yet, unlike those in democratic mass movements—for example, reform socialists—fascists rejected parliamentary rule. There was nothing democratic about fascist organizations: they were hierarchically structured, and aimed at dictatorship, ruled by one person. Fascist movements opposed trade unions, Socialists, and Communists with particular vehemence because all three espoused working-class internationalism. The trade unions' success in attracting members immediately after the war and incessant working-class demands for better conditions, backed up by strikes, frightened Europe's social and political elites.

Big business in Italy and Germany, as well as in France, aided the right by turning against parliamentary rule. Wealthy industrialists were key actors in the crisis that brought the Italian fascists and German Nazis to power in their respective states. Yet, at least in the beginning in Germany, many big businessmen were suspicious of Nazism's mass appeal. They preferred more traditional kinds of authoritarian ideas that appealed to their sense of social exclusiveness, such as a monarchy backed by the armed forces in the Prussian tradition. Smaller businessmen were more likely to back the Nazis. In Italy, the link between big business and fascism was more direct; in the industrial north, shipowners and iron and mining magnates, among others, provided funds for Mussolini's national movement or to local groups of fascists before the Duce came to power. Big business joined with smaller industrial and commercial concerns, as well as wealthy landowners, to facilitate the rise to power of a leader who promised to impose social and political order.

Fascists, Nazis, and other authoritarian right-wing groups blamed parliamentary government itself for the weaknesses and failures of their states in the post-war years. They believed parliamentary regimes to be unstable, chaotic, and soft by their very nature, weakened by factionalism and class divisions. Many of the states in which authoritarian dictators came to power lacked considerable support for parliamentary democracy. Moreover, the seeming instability of parliamentary regimes contributed to the attraction of a strong leader, a dictator, who would restore order and embody nationalist aspirations. The irony was, of course, that fascist gangs themselves were largely responsible for creating the political turmoil that ultimately led to the destruction of Central and Eastern Europe's nascent parliamentary governments.

Crowds saluted Mussolini, Hitler, and the dictators of smaller states with almost hysterical frenzy, believing that they embodied the aspirations of their people. They sought to identify themselves with strong leaders committed not only to imposing absolute order at home but also to territorial expansion and nationalistic aggrandizement. Propagandists orchestrated images of Mussolini and Hitler by using new techniques of communication, such as the mass press, radio, and even the cinema, to monopolize and manipulate their followers.

Fascists most often defined themselves by denouncing who and what they were against, rather than what they were for. Some proponents of fascism saw themselves as building a new social and political order based upon service to the nation. This idea of creating a new elite also distin-

An enthusiastic crowd, which includes many youths, greets Hitler at a rally at the Nuremberg stadium in 1937.

guished fascist from authoritarian movements in Spain and Portugal, where nationalists tried to affirm the domination of traditional elites, such as nobles and churchmen, and remained suspicious of mass movements in general. Fascists wanted a more powerful state that would expand its borders through conquest, fulfilling what they considered the "historic destiny" of their national group. Mussolini and Hitler appealed to the masses based on their support for a "national community" that joined all people of the nation, excluding those deemed to be outsiders. But their views and plans directly conflicted with the Versailles Peace Settlement in that they included the intention to undo the agreements signed by the German and Italian governments in 1919, which had left territory claimed by nationalists outside of the redefined borders of Italy and Germany. Nonetheless, they now pursued broadly expansionist goals that could only be met by absorbing the territories of other states.

In contrast, Socialists and Communists insisted that class tensions and conflicts were endemic in industrial society, and they based their political philosophies and appeal primarily on the perceived needs of the working class. Fascists, by contrast, viewed economic and social tensions as irrelevant, arguing that it was enough that all people shared a common national identity, and that this national community meant more than did economic disparities between social classes, and would make those divisions obsolete.

Mussolini and Hitler covered up the brutal realities of their rule by promising with vague rhetoric that the needs of the "national economic community" would be fulfilled. In the early 1920s, Mussolini had added "international finance capital" to his list of enemies, a holdover from the rhetoric of his days as a socialist before the war, a means of trying to convince workers that he spoke for their interests, too. Like Mussolini, authoritarian dictators Engelbert Dollfuss in Austria, and Antonio Salazar in Portugal, a former university lecturer in financial law, also added "corporatism" to their list of promises, announcing that associations of employers and workers would be formed within each industry that would be able to increase productivity and thus make class divisions obsolete. Such rhetoric was intended to appeal to employers and workers alike. But fascist states remained capitalistic in nature, with big business accruing great profits and workers lagging far behind.

The factors discussed above—middle-class economic frustration, upper-class fears of socialism, aggressive nationalism, anti-parliamentarianism, and the belief that a dictator could provide order and national fulfillment—were all present in European society before the Great War. But the cataclysmic experience of the war channeled them all in new and frightening directions, particularly in the cases of fascist Italy and Nazi Germany. The experience of the war itself contributed to the proliferation of aggressive nationalism. The war also had divided Europe into "victors" and "vanquished," countries that accepted the Versailles Settlement, and revisionist nations that did not. The latter included Germany, Hungary, and Bulgaria, but also Italy, which had joined the winning side in 1915 but received less at Versailles than Italian nationalists had demanded. In Germany, right-wing movements attracted demobilized soldiers, who had returned home with weapons, habits of military order, experience with violence, and the camaraderie of the trenches. Paramilitary squads, largely made up of war veterans, destabilized political life. The Free Corps in Germany, the Home Guard in Austria, and the Cross of Fire in France denounced the "decadence" and "softness" of parliamentary regimes.

Aggressive nationalism easily became racism. Germans were not alone in believing spurious literature proclaiming the superiority of their race and the degeneration of other races. In Eastern Europe, dictators identified other nationalities and ethnic groups that could be blamed for practically anything. The unique character of Hitler's National Socialism stemmed from its ideology of German racial supremacy, which went beyond the assertions of nationalist primacy of other right-wing dictators. From the beginning, Nazism manifested an unparalleled capacity for violence and destruction based upon the assumption that Nazis could assume the authority to determine who could live and who could die. This, too, took Nazi ideology and practice beyond other violent nationalist right-wing regimes. Yet anti-Semitism also characterized authoritarian movements in Austria, Poland, Romania, Yugoslavia, France, and Belgium, countries where Jews could, along with the parties of the left and the unions, be blamed for hard times. Finally, inspired by Hitler, Mussolini also added anti-Semitism to his nationalist rantings in 1938, though he did so in a haphazard way and never succumbed to Hitler's biological interpretation of race.

Fascism in Mussolini's Italy

By the time of the Depression, Benito Mussolini, who had seized power in 1922, had already transformed Italy into Europe's first fascist dictatorship (see Chapter 24). He made blustering promises about Italy becoming a Second Roman Empire, turning the Mediterranean into "our lake," and by uniting all Italians in fervent nationalism, bringing harmony and prosperity. To some foreign visitors, Mussolini's fascism seemed to offer a third way that lay between unchecked capitalism and the contentious challenge of socialism and communism. The Duce became famous abroad as the genius who managed to make Italian trains run on time, although, in fact, such a description applied only to those carrying tourists to the ski resorts in the Italian Alps.

Mussolini viewed corporatism (see Chapter 23) as a possible remedy to the economic problems that beset Italy. He established the outlines of a "corporative state," an idea borrowed from early modern guilds and Catholic religious organizations. In Germany and France, too, "corporatists" believed that by creating cartel-like corporations joining all people dependent upon one economic activity or industry, ruinous competition between companies and conflict between bosses and workers could be eliminated in the interest and prosperity of the "national economic community." The Duce created twenty-two corporations, or assemblies, overseen, at least in theory, by a National Council of Corporations, intended to cover every economic activity. Each corporation was based on a council of employers and employees. But Italian fascist corporatism had very little impact in Italy. Its chief practical consequence, at least until the early 1930s, was to swell the number of state bureaucrats hired to supervise creaky, inefficient, and largely superfluous organizations.

The paradox of Italian corporatism was revealed in Mussolini's rhetoric that there were no social classes in Italy, only Italians. The Duce cheerily proclaimed the end of class struggle and bragged that he had done more for workers than any other leader. But employers and workers were certainly not on an equal footing. Their trade unions destroyed (replaced by fascist trade unions), their conditions of life basically unimproved, and strikes now illegal, most workers remained skeptical about Mussolini. The fascist government did limit the workday in 1923, and in 1935 it introduced a five-day workweek. But employers broke contracts with impunity. The conditions of life for sharecroppers and other landless laborers worsened during the fascist period.

The Duce wanted to make Italy economically independent. State agencies invested in industries Mussolini considered crucial to the colonial and European wars he was planning. By 1935, no other European state, except Stalin's Soviet Union, controlled such a large portion of industry, with major shares in industries like steelworks and shipbuilding. Hydroelectricity and automobile manufacturing developed, but Italian industry still depended on raw materials imported from abroad, including copper, rubber, and coal.

Mussolini dubbed his most ambitious agricultural program the "battle for grain." But wheat production was uneconomical in many regions; by converting from labor-intensive crops to wheat, the Duce's pet program merely increased unemployment, while reducing pasture and fruit-growing lands and the number of farm animals. High tariffs on grain imports raised food prices. Land reclamation and irrigation projects also failed. While Mussolini's speeches celebrated "blood and soil" (a constant refrain on the fascist and authoritarian right in inter-war Europe), the number of Italian peasant proprietors fell.

The failures of Mussolini's economic policies were compounded by the demands of military spending, which absorbed a full third of Italian income by the mid-1930s. While the state spent heavily on planes and submarines, Italy's per capita income remained about that of Britain and the United States in the early nineteenth century. Illiteracy remained high, particularly in the south. The economy still depended upon traditional, small-scale agriculture. Under fascism, the gap between the more industrialized north and the poor south continued to grow.

Like Hitler and Stalin, Mussolini sought to eliminate the boundary between private and public life. He wanted the "new Italian woman" to espouse the values of, and serve, the nationalist state. With the fascist motto, "Everything within the State, nothing outside the State," he viewed the family as an essential component of fascism. "The Nation is served even by keeping the house swept. Civic discipline begins with family discipline," advised the *Decalogue of the Little Italian*. But fascism could never overcome the inevitable tensions between family obligations and what fascists considered national duties. Mussolini and the fascists believed they were restoring old values, but the very idea of service to the nation-state was very new—for example, the attempt to create mass fascist organizations of women ranging from after-work recreational clubs to female paramilitary squads. The Duce disliked the fact that women had obtained the right to vote in Great Britain, Germany, and several other countries, and that more Italian women were going to work. In Italy's fascist state, the place of women was to be in the home, obeying their husbands and having babies.

That not all Italians listened to Mussolini's bombastic rhetoric (nor to the Catholic Church) was demonstrated by the continuing fall of the birthrate (from 147.5 births per 1,000 in 1911 to 102.2 in 1936), despite the call of the Duce for more baby soldiers, and despite the state's ban on the sale of birth-control devices.

In the south, where peasants particularly resented and resisted the state, the Mafia provided an alternative allegiance, a parallel underworld government. Mussolini failed to destroy the power of the Neapolitan and Sicilian Mafias, even though the number of Mafia-related killings fell dramatically.

The Church, too, remained a strong alternative source of influence to fascism. Much of a Catholic revival, which included a rapid rise in the number of priests and nuns, continued to be independent of fascism. Pope Pius XI lost some of his enthusiasm for Mussolini's fascism, denouncing in the early 1930s "the pagan worship of the state." Few Italians paid attention to the Duce's attempts to convince Italians to stop singing in the streets, or his insistence that they dress babies in fascist black shirts. Massive emigration out of Italy continued throughout the 1920s and 1930s. Yet most Italians still supported Mussolini, if only passively.

Right-Wing Authoritarian Movements in Eastern Europe

Fascism was a Europe-wide phenomenon in no way limited to Nazi Germany and Mussolini's Italy. In Eastern and Central Europe, parliamentary governments did not survive the instability wrought by the economic dislocation of the 1920s and 1930s, nor the bitter ethnic rivalries within these nations, which included states that already existed at the outbreak of the war (Romania, Bulgaria, and Greece) and newly created states (Poland and Yugoslavia). Not including the new kingdom of Yugoslavia, each of

Italian women decked with gas masks line up for The Duce, as part of a parade of 70,000 fascist women and girls in celebration of the twentieth anniversary of fascism in 1939.

these multinational states had some sort of liberal constitution in the 1920s. Yet, by the end of the 1930s, right-wing dictatorships had overwhelmed political liberalism in each Eastern European nation except Czechoslovakia.

With the exception of Czechoslovakia, which included industrialized Bohemia, all of these countries were poor, heavily agricultural, and had high percentages of illiteracy. When compared with the countries of Western Europe, the countries of Eastern Europe had very small middle classes, except Czech Bohemia, parts of Serbia, and a few major cities, and they had virtually no traditions of parliamentary government.

A daunting variety of conflicting economic interests could be found among the people of Eastern Europe, ranging from those of wealthy Hungarian landowners to Bosnian mountain dwellers scratching out a meager living from thankless land. After the war, the governments of the Eastern European states implemented ambitious land reform programs that reduced the number and size of the large estates, adding to the ranks of small landholding farmers. But populist agrarian parties, such as the Peasant Party in Poland, the Smallholders in Hungary, and the Romanian National Peasant Party were essentially single-interest parties that fell under the sway of fascist demagogues playing on anti-urban prejudices. Such agrarian parties vilified Jews as ethnic outsiders, mobilizing resentment against their economic roles as bankers, small businessmen, and shopkeepers. In Bulgaria and, above all, in Hungary and Romania, wealthy landowners, desperate to protect their estates against further land reform and frightened by the rise of small Communist parties, turned toward authoritarian rule.

Poland was the first Eastern European state to become a right-wing dictatorship. General Józef Piłsudski seized power in 1926, imposing a military dictatorship that survived his death in 1935. The Yugoslav experiment in parliamentary rule ended abruptly in 1929, when King Alexander I (ruled 1921–1934) sent the assembly home from Belgrade and banned all political parties. That year, Croats established the Ustaša (Insurrection) Party, a right-wing nationalist party that demanded an independent Croatia. In 1934, Croatian nationalists assassinated King Alexander. Five years later, Croatia won status as an "autonomous" region with its own assembly, but this did not reduce Serb domination of the multinational state. In Yugoslavia, then, the principal battle was not between partisans of dictatorship and those of parliamentarian government, as in Germany, but between the authoritarian Serb government and right-wing Croat organizations.

In Hungary, Admiral Miklós Horthy appointed a fascist prime minister in 1932 but repressed the extreme right-wing parties when they threatened to seize power for themselves. Bulgarian political life was marked by assassinations and coups d'état followed by dictatorship in 1935. In Greece, republicans, monarchists, and military officers battled it out. And

King Alexander I of Yugoslavia and the French Foreign Minister Jean-Louis Bar-thou were assassinated while driving through Marseilles in 1934; the Croat separatist assassin was later lynched by the crowd.

in 1936, King George II (1890–1947) gave his blessing to the dictatorship of General Ioannis Metaxas (1871–1941), who, in the fascist style, took the title of "leader." In 1938, the Romanian King Carol II (1893–1953) established a dictatorship by suspending the constitution. He did so to protect his rule against a challenge from the fascist "Legion of the Archangel Michael" and particularly its murderous shock troops, the "Iron Guard," a fanatically Orthodox religious group with strong anti-Semitic prejudices. Romanian fascists drew upon peasant discontent created by Depression-era agricultural deflation. The king's bloody suppression of the Legion and the Iron Guard only postponed the victory of fascism in Romania.

In Eastern Europe, only Czechoslovakia, with a strong liberal tradition and a sizable Czech middle class, managed to achieve political stability as a parliamentary democracy. Despite differences between the country's Czechs and Slovaks, ethnic divisions had not yet necessarily become hatreds. The two largest political parties, the Agrarian Party and the Social Democratic Party, drew members from both peoples. By the late 1930s, it was apparent that the greatest threat to parliamentary rule in Czechoslovakia would come from Nazi Germany, as Hitler seized upon ethnic tensions in the Czech Sudetenland between the German-speaking population and the Czechs. Consequently, even Eastern Europe's most stable country was not immune from destabilizing ethnic rivalries.

Fascism in Austria

In Austria, the undersized, German-speaking remnant of the Habsburg empire, fascism was closely tied to German nationalism and anti-Semitism. Moreover, lying between Germany and Italy, Austria almost inevitably came under the influence of those states. During the 1930s, Mussolini wanted to absorb the Italian-speaking Tyrol, and Hitler wanted Germany to annex all of Austria. The Nazi Party of Austria was eager to help Hitler by destabilizing political life.

The split between left and right was particularly bitter in Austria, where on "Bloody Friday," July 15, 1927, police killed about a hundred striking workers during demonstrations by Socialists in Vienna protesting right-wing violence. Yet Vienna had a long tradition of social democracy, rooted in the politically active workers living in public housing on the edge of the city. The contrast between the stately inner city, where some of the old Habsburg nobles still lived, and its political "red belt" of working-class housing could not be missed. Much of the tax burden fell on the Viennese middle classes, which were for the most part socially conservative, fervently Catholic, and overwhelmingly supportive of the ruling Christian Social Party. Anti-Semitism had deep roots in Vienna—where the young Hitler had lived—as well as in provincial Austria. As everywhere, the Depression accentuated existing social and political tensions and violence.

The violent anti-parliamentary groups in neighboring Bavaria served as a point of attraction for the Austrian Nazis. Members of the Austrian right-wing Home Guard wore traditional green woolen coats, lederhosen, and Alpine hats, but carried quite modern machine guns. The socialist Social Democrats formed their own guard, determined to protect their members.

In 1933, Chancellor Engelbert Dollfuss (1892–1934), a diminutive, awkward man who wore traditional Austrian peasant garb because he was proud of his provincial origins, dissolved the Austrian Parliament because it stood in the way of an authoritarian state. In February 1934, after Home Guard raids on workers' organizations and newspapers, the workers of Vienna, led by the Social Democrats, began a general strike. Fighting erupted when Dollfuss unleashed the Home Guard and army against the left. Army units attacked the industrial suburbs with artillery fire, killing several hundred workers during four days of fighting. Police closed down all Social Democratic organizations, and tried and executed some of their leaders. Dollfuss then banned all political parties except the fascist Fatherland Front.

The Popular Front in France against the Far Right

Fascist parties in France had their origins in the anti-republican nationalism of the late nineteenth century. Here, too, the Great War and the economic and social frustrations of the post-armistice period contributed to the rise of the far right. War veterans were prominent in the Faisceau movement, which was founded in 1919 and which emulated the newly created Italian fascist organization, and in the Cross of Fire, established in 1929. French fascist leaders included two renowned producers of luxury products, the perfume magnate François Coty and the champagne baron Pierre de Taittinger. The latter's Patriotic Youth movement, founded in 1924, counted more than 100,000 members by the end of the decade.

The rise in immigration to France compounded the xenophobia and racism of the fascists. Beginning in 1935, more people died each year than were born in France, and its population grew only because of the arrival of immigrants—Italians, Poles, Spaniards, and Belgians, in order of number, but also Jews from Eastern Europe. About 7.5 percent of the French population in the late 1930s consisted of immigrants—the highest percentage in Europe. In Britain, by contrast, immigration was much less significant, which may have helped limit the appeal of the nationalistic far-right parties.

French fascists decried the very structure of the Third Republic, which seemed to them an anomaly in a continent of dictators. Political power in France lay not with a strong executive authority but with the Chamber of Deputies. The president, elected by the Chamber, was essentially a convener. Governments came and went in turn, increasing rightist dissatisfaction. In 1934, a seamy political scandal offered the extreme right an opening for action. The appearance of government complicity in a fraudulent bond-selling scheme engineered by Serge Stavisky (1886–1934), a Ukrainian-born Jew, led to increasingly violent rightist demonstrations against the republic. On February 6, 1934, right-wing groups rioted against the Chamber of Deputies. Communists, too, were there to protest. The rightists charged across the Seine River in Paris toward the Chamber of Deputies before being dispersed, with casualties on both sides. But, unlike the right in Germany, Italy, or Spain, the French right did not have a dominating figure capable of uniting opposition to parliamentary rule. On February 12, millions of French men and women marched in support of the republic. Although the government resigned, the republic was saved, to enjoy what some wags referred to as "another lease on death."

The formation of the Popular Front in France, an alliance between the Radical, Socialist, and Communist parties, must be seen in the context of the clear threat to parliamentary forms of government posed by the right not only in France but throughout Europe. Socialists and Communists had been at odds since the Congress of Tours in 1920. The split became policy when the Communist International (Comintern) of 1927 adopted the tactic of "class against class," which tolerated no concessions to "bourgeois" parties, including the Socialist Party. But in the 1930s, the reality of the threat of the right to France temporarily overcame ideology. Stalin's fear of German rearmament led the Comintern to repudiate the "class versus class" strategy in June 1934. The French Communist Party was now free to join forces with the Socialist and Radical parties in a Popular Front to defend the republic against fascism. The three parties prepared a compromise program incorporating tax reform, a shorter workweek, increased unemployment benefits, support for the League of Nations and international disarmament, and the dissolution of the fascist leagues.

The Popular Front won a clear victory in the subsequent elections of May 1936. But the Communists, despite having almost doubled their support, refused to participate in the ensuing government, on orders from Moscow. Léon Blum (1872–1950) became prime minister of the Popular Front government. That the Socialist leader was a Jew intensified the rage of the extreme right. "Better Hitler than Blum!" echoed in parts of Paris.

As unions, encouraged by the Popular Front's pre-election promises, put forward their demands, the largest strike wave in French history broke out across the country. For the first time, workers occupied plants, marching, singing, putting on theatrical productions, and staging mock trials of employers. The strikes, many by non-unionized workers, took both French labor federations and the Communist Party by surprise. The Communists tried to bring the strikes to a speedy conclusion, fearful that defeat might hurt their influence with workers, or help the Socialists. The Communist Party newspaper *L'Humanité* answered the workers' optimistic slogan "Everything is possible" with the headline "Everything is not possible!"

Blum convinced employers and union representatives to sign the "Matignon Agreements," establishing a forty-hour workweek, pay raises, and paid vacations. The strikes gradually ended. But the economy contin-

A riot outside of the Senate building in France in response to Premier Léon Blum's failure to secure power to rule by decree.

ued to falter, in the face of intransigent opposition from employers and wealthy families shipping assets out of France. Moreover, the reduced workweek undercut production. Blum declared a "pause" in his reform program, and cut back social benefits and other state expenditures.

The Popular Front began to unravel. In March 1937, police fired on workers demonstrating against the rightist Cross of Fire group. The Communists denounced the government, which they had helped bring to power but never joined. The government had to devalue the franc several more times because of the flow of gold abroad. Blum asked the Senate to grant him power to rule by decree. When the conservative-dominated Senate refused, he resigned in June 1937. For all intents and purposes, the Popular Front was over. A centrist government lurched on in France as the international situation worsened.

Fascism in the Low Countries

Fascism threatened the Belgium and the Netherlands, as well. In Belgium, the fascist party "Rex" (from the Latin for "Christ the King"), led by Léon Degrelle (1906–1994), drew on the frustrations of white-collar workers and shopkeepers, victims of the Depression, who blamed competition from department stores and socialist consumer cooperatives for their plight. Economic malaise compounded tensions generated by the linguistic division between French-speaking Walloons and the Flemish speakers of Flanders, some of whom demanded Flemish autonomy. Although a wave of strikes in Belgium in 1936, similar to that in France at the same time, frightened the middle class, the Belgian fascists never won more than 12 percent of the vote. The majority of the middle class remained loyal to parliamentary government. Banks and the Socialist and Catholic parties successfully pressured the government for action to assist the lower middle class by increasing credit available to small retailers and extending union rights to white-collar employees. The Catholic Church's condemnation of Rex in 1937 led many of the group's Catholic members to return to moderate Catholic parties.

Similarly, in the Netherlands, the Dutch National Socialist League, which emulated the Nazis, remained far too small to contemplate an overthrow of the government. The movement was condemned by both the Calvinist Reform Church and the Catholic Church and won the support of only 8 percent of Dutch voters in 1937.

NATIONAL SOCIALISM IN GERMANY

In Germany, the Depression helped swell the ranks of not only the Nazi Party but also other parties and groups (including powerful army officers and big businessmen) committed to the end of parliamentary government.

Political parties, labor unions, and voluntary associations crumbled before the Nazi onslaught. Nazi propaganda espoused the German "national community" that would make all social and political tensions obsolete. Nazi organizations enrolled millions of Germans. The army would loyally serve Hitler, the man some generals had not long before scornfully dismissed as an "Austrian corporal."

The Collapse of the Weimar Republic

The Depression increased opposition to the Weimar Republic, particularly among the middle classes. The Nazis in 1929 were but one of a number of extreme right groups determined to overthrow the republic. The Depression also further eroded the centrist coalition within the Reichstag upon which the republic had depended from the beginning. In March 1930, the last remnants of the Weimar coalition came apart under the pressure of the economic turmoil; the government, led by the Social Democrats, resigned. Thereafter social and political compromise seemed impossible. President Paul von Hindenburg began to rule by decree.

The new elections held in September 1930 confirmed the erosion of the parliamentary center. The Nazis received five times more votes than in the last elections, obtaining 18 percent of the popular vote and 107 seats in the Reichstag. The Communist Party, too, gained seats, while the Social Democratic Party lost seats, but remained the largest party with 143 deputies; the moderate conservative parties also lost representatives. Bolstered by rising numbers of supporters, in 1932 Hitler ran for president against Hindenburg, winning 13.5 million votes to the general's 19 million and the Communist candidate's 4 million. The Nazi Party now had more than 800,000 members.

Traditional conservatives, including a number of important generals, not the least of whom was Hindenburg himself, turned against the republic. Franz von Papen (1879–1969), power broker of the traditional antiparliamentarian right, became chancellor in June 1932. After elections for the Reichstag were held in November 1932, the Nazis became the largest party in the Reichstag (with 196 seats against 121 held by Social Democrats, 100 by Communists, and 90 by the Catholic Center Party). Between them, the Nazis and their bitter enemies, the Communists, both of whom rejected the Weimar Republic, had won more than half the votes cast. (Nonetheless, support for the Nazis had fallen by 2 million votes, reflecting the fact that some moderate conservatives were repelled by the murders and beatings carried out by Hitler's storm troopers, the S.A.)

Papen resigned as chancellor in December 1932. His successor, General Kurt von Schleicher (1882–1934), wanted to form a parliamentary majority by wooing some Nazis—but excluding Hitler—and even trade unionists, an improbable idea. When Schleicher's government resigned the next month, Papen sought to bring the Nazis into a coalition government. Hoping to transform Germany from a republic into a military authoritarian regime (perhaps through a monarchical restoration), Papen believed that Hitler could serve his purposes if the Nazis received only three of twelve cabinet posts (including one for Hitler). Once Hitler and the Nazis had helped assure the end of the Weimar Republic and the establishment of an authoritarian regime, they could be tossed aside. In Italy, Giolitti's Liberals had made the same fatal miscalculation in 1922 in their dealings with Mussolini.

Now joined by members of Hindenburg's family and staff, Papen convinced the old general to appoint Hitler as chancellor, believing that he could control Hitler in his capacity as vice-chancellor. On January 30, 1933, Adolf Hitler formed the seventeenth—and last—Weimar government. "We've boxed Hitler in," was the way Hindenburg memorably put it. "We have hired him," Papen assured his friends.

Many Prussian nobles and generals still mistrusted Hitler. To the former, he seemed a vulgar commoner, a painter of tourist postcards in Vienna; to the latter, a mere foot soldier who made boastful claims of military expertise. But the generals had been taught, above all, to obey orders. Furthermore, Hitler's denunciations of Bolshevism appealed to their dislike of Russia, their enemy on the eastern front during the Great War.

Most wealthy businessmen still preferred more traditional nationalists like Hindenburg and Papen and worried about Hitler's unpredictability. Hitler's early denunciations of capitalists and promises to create a new political elite irritated industrialists. The Nazi Party found but one major donor among big businessmen—the Rhineland steel magnate Fritz Thyssen—and a group of industrialists even tried to convince Hindenburg to leave Hitler out of the cabinet. The Nazis boasted that small donors and modest membership fees financed their party. Although some big businessmen shared the Nazis' virulent anti-Semitism, they were uneasy with the foreign condemnation it brought, and concerned that it might one day undercut their markets abroad. A one-day boycott in April 1933 called by the Nazis against Jewish businesses in Germany backfired, failing to attract mass support.

But big business nonetheless contributed to the fall of Weimar. Most Rhineland industrialists were no more in favor of parliamentary government than were Prussian Junkers. Hitler flattered business leaders, telling them that they had "worked their way to the top . . . which again only proves their higher race—they have the right to lead." Big businessmen were not about to oppose Hitler, as he promised public order, which was good for business, even if achieved at gunpoint.

The Nazi State

The Nazi state was predicated upon Hitler's eagerness to use violence to fortify his power. In this he shared much with the Italian fascist dictator

Communists under arrest after the Reichstag fire of 1933, which was most likely set by the Nazis themselves.

Benito Mussolini and with Joseph Stalin, who made terror an essential part of the bureaucratic apparatus of the Communist Party and who more and more identified the interests of the party with his own rule. In Germany, Hitler's appointment as chancellor sparked a wave of systematic and brutal Nazi attacks on union members, Socialists, Communists, Jews, and some Catholics who opposed Nazism.

Mussolini had consolidated his power over the Italian state in about three years. It took Hitler less than three months. During the night of February 27, 1933, a fire caused considerable damage to the Reichstag building in Berlin. The police arrested a deranged, homeless Dutch Communist, charging him with arson. Although the debate on the origins of the Reichstag fire continues, it was probably set by someone working in the Prussian ministry of the interior with the intention of blaming the Communists.

Citing an imaginary Communist plot, Hitler convinced sympathetic members of the Reichstag to vote an emergency decree suspending virtually all individual rights. Hitler suspended the rights of those accused of crimes against the state. Penalties of imprisonment and even death could be imposed without due legal process as police arrested thousands of Communists. Hermann Göring (1893–1946), one of Hitler's long-time disciples and now minister of the interior in Prussia, authorized the creation of an auxiliary police force made up of members of the S.A. and other paramilitary groups.

But the parliamentary elections of March 5, 1933, which Hitler promised would be the last held in Nazi Germany and which took place amid enormous Nazi intimidation, did not give Hitler the overwhelming majority he had anticipated—the Nazis emerged with only 44 percent of the vote. Nonetheless, Hitler proceeded as if the vote had been unanimous. On March 23, the cowed Reichstag approved an Enabling Act, which extended the unlimited "emergency" powers of the Nazis and transferred power from the legislative to the executive branch of government. The liberal political parties of the Weimar Republic simply disbanded in late June. In July 1933, Hitler banned all political parties except the Nazi Party. Hundreds of thousands of Germans now stampeded to join it. The party grew tripled in size, with 2.5 million members by the end of 1933, adding so many people that the "old fighters" who had joined early in the 1920s began to grumble that the party was losing its so-called elite character.

The Nazis implemented the apparatus of a dictatorial state. In May 1933, they organized the state-controlled German Labor Front to replace the unions they had decimated. With labor parties and unions destroyed and strikes now illegal, workers had no way of opposing decrees that made them legally subordinate to their employers. Hitler dissolved the state parliaments and took away the remaining autonomy of the individual German states, appointing Nazis to take over state governments. A new law empowered officials to dismiss subordinates whom they considered potentially disloyal to the Nazis, or who could not prove that they were of pure "Aryan" racial stock.

Despite Nazi rhetoric about a racially pure community of Germans, Hitler was far from envisioning social equality, which he associated with socialism and communism. Still, for some Germans, the Nazi Party, and particularly the S.S. (*Schutzstaffel,* security units that guarded Hitler), provided a means of social mobility; military trappings conveyed the respectability many people associated with a uniform. Joining the Nazis provided status for young Germans whose economic aspirations had been blocked by the Depression and whose contributions to the party would be recognized. Although the Nazis drew support from virtually all of German society (although proportionately less support from workers), the Depression drove more desperate middle-class Germans into the Nazi fold.

Hitler needed the loyalty of Germany's professional army so that his power would remain unchallenged and to carry out his foreign policy ambitions. But many German officers were becoming increasingly wary of the S.A., which was now almost 3 million strong and which seemed out of control. Its members openly competed with Nazi officials for local influence and appointments. Ernst Röhm believed that his S.A. represented the second wave of the Nazi revolution. He announced that henceforth members of his force could not be tried by courts, and that they were to be immune from police authority. Foolishly bragging that he would free Hitler from his "stupid and dangerous" advisers, Röhm complained bitterly, "Adolf is a swine. He will give us all away."

The S.S. and the Gestapo (the Nazi secret police) crushed the S.A. on June 30, 1934. They killed at least eighty people, including Röhm. The "night of the long knives" also swept up some noted conservatives and military officers, as Hitler had feared trouble from the old right as well as from the S.A. Hitler convinced President von Hindenburg that the gory purge had saved the German Third Reich (Third Empire) from a plot. Hindenburg concurred, expressing the view that "he who wants to make history like Hitler must be prepared to let guilty blood flow and not be soft."

Hindenburg's death in August 1934, allowed Hitler to combine the titles of chancellor and Führer ("leader"), which replaced that of "president," a title that smacked of the republic. The army agreed to take an oath of personal allegiance to the man now considered "the executor of the whole people's will." In August, 90 percent of those voting in a plebiscite approved Hitler's assumption of both functions.

The Nazi program of "coordination" was applied to most aspects of civil society, such as organized groups and activities outside the family. In order to prevent any challenge to their monopoly of power, the Nazis had already gradually taken over associational life—organizations based, for example, on occupation and universities attended, as well as sports clubs. The Nazis worked to convert schools into mouthpieces for Hitler's state, providing new textbooks with instructions for teachers as to what should be taught, including "racial theory" and "Teutonic prehistory." Pictures of Hitler went up in every classroom and radios were provided so that his speeches could be heard. Physical education and sports became more prominent subjects. Instead of students fearing their teachers, as had often been the case in German schools, now non-Nazi teachers had reason to fear their students; members of the Hitler Youth organization were quick to report to Nazi Party members if a teacher seemed recalcitrant.

While the Nazi Party provided many people with a sense of national commitment, to disdain politics came to be seen as a virtue. An old German proverb says, "He who has choice has torment." In such dictatorships, people have no choices left. In this way, the Nazis appropriated

Hitler paying homage to Hindenburg shortly before the latter's death.

fears and suspicions of political life held by residents of small towns. Depoliticized, closely monitored voluntary associations and churches could remain the center of local public life without threatening Nazi domination.

The Nazis brought hundreds of thousands of active Germans into carefully controlled Nazi organizations, the goal of each being to "reach toward Hitler"—that is, to share the racist, nationalist goals of the Führer. The Hitler Youth by 1936 included almost half the German boys between ten and fourteen years of age; a League of German Girls also flourished. The Nazis reduced social life to its most basic component, the family. (At the same time, however, the Nazis encouraged children to denounce their parents for being disloyal to the fatherland, and the party even sponsored "Aryan breeding" programs outside the family unit.) Vicarious participation in the mass ceremonies and rituals of Nazism also helped augment a sense of national identity.

Hitler implemented the Nazi "leadership principle," which he defined as a "doctrine of conflict." He applied a strategy of "divide and rule" to the higher echelons of government, such as the three chancellories that replaced the cabinet. He tolerated and even encouraged open, aggressive competition between his most trusted subordinates and between branches of government. Those who enjoyed Hitler's confidence ruthlessly and aggressively carved out personal fiefdoms. Unlike Stalin, who watched over even the most minor details with obsessive care, the Führer provided little supervision to government agencies. Occasionally something would catch Hitler's attention and frenzied activity would follow. But he missed meetings, worked irregular hours, and was often disorganized. Hitler valued personal loyalty far more than efficiency and purposely kept the exact functions of some of his most important officials undefined.

The "doctrine of conflict" adversely affected the economic goals Hitler set for the state. The army and the air force quarreled over resources, the S.S. and the police over jurisdiction. The Four-Year Plan launched in 1936 under Hermann Göring's direction illustrated the functioning of the Nazi state. Hitler wanted to stimulate economic development, above all in industries necessary for rearmament: steel, iron, and synthetic fuel and rubber. Göring spent far too much time warring with other branches of government. Furthermore, although government contracts appealed to industrialists, they resisted state intervention in their businesses. The Four-Year Plan failed to achieve its lofty goals.

Hitler realized that sheer terror was not enough to maintain popular support. Although he knew or cared very little about economics, Hitler correctly determined that the rapid rearmament of Germany would help create jobs. Food shortages remained severe until 1936, but public works projects also helped reduce unemployment and inflation. Big industrial concerns prospered, particularly those manufacturing war materials. Hitler bragged that he had wrought an "economic miracle."

More consumer goods, such as radios, reached the consumer market, contributing to a sense of optimism about material conditions of life. The Labor Front organized cut-rate Nazi vacations. Some families of modest means, many of whom had never had the opportunity to travel before, took cruises in the Baltic or even in the Mediterranean Sea. Hitler named this program "Strength Through Joy," perhaps taking the idea from Mussolini, whose fascists inaugurated the "Afterwork" program of recreational trips in Italy in the mid-1920s. However, production of Hitler's planned low-cost "Volkswagen," or "people's wagon" was postponed because factories were needed for military production.

Yet sectors of the German economy remained weak. German industry, particularly the armaments manufacturers, depended on imports of iron ore, copper, oil, rubber, and bauxite. Many Germans found that their share in the "national community" was small. And although Hitler liked to identify the German people with what he considered rural virtues—"blood and soil," as he, like Mussolini, frequently put it—the number of small farms continued to decline, and the income of farmers stagnated. There was no marked return to the soil. Germany continued to urbanize under the Third Reich.

Like Mussolini, the Führer preached that women's place was in the kitchen or in the delivery room. The state offered attractive financial benefits to families with children, and the German birthrate continued to rise, bolstered by an improving economy. Just months after becoming chancellor, Hitler forced women to give up industrial jobs and excluded them from public service and teaching. Certain occupations were classified as "women's work," primarily those involving traditional textile or handicraft production or farmwork. But, despite the slogan "women at home," the reality in Nazi Germany, as in Mussolini's Italy, was increasingly otherwise. The campaign to remove women from paid employment ended in the late 1930s, as women were needed to replace men conscripted into the army. The number of women working in German industry rose by a third between 1933 and 1939.

Some intellectuals and artists jumped on the Nazi bandwagon. Very few members—though the novelist Thomas Mann, who had moved from being an angry conservative to a supporter of the republic by 1922, was one—resigned from the prestigious Prussian Academy of Arts when called upon to pledge allegiance to Hitler. The philosopher Martin Heidegger (1889–1976) saluted the Führer as "guided by the inexorability of that spiritual mission that the destiny of the German people forcibly impresses upon its history." Hitler hauled out Heidegger on formal occasions to claim that Germany's finest scholars had become Nazis. In fact, some of the finest German minds were already leaving.

The Nazis burned books that espoused ideas of which they disapproved. This policy began in May 1933, when storm troopers coordinated the burning of books by Jews, Communists, Socialists, and other disapproved

The 1937 "Entartete Kunst" (Degenerate Art) exhibition.

authors. In 1937, posters in the municipal library of Essen actually boasted that in the four years that had elapsed since the book burnings, there had been a "healthy" decline in books borrowed and in the use of the reading room.

Hitler waged war against what he called "decadent" art and its new experimental forms, ordering many works removed from museums. During the Weimar period, Berlin, a city with 40 theaters and 120 newspapers, had become a center of daring and successful experimentation by artists, writers, and composers, as well as scholars. In 1919, the architect Walter Gropius (1883–1969) had begun a school that combined art and applied arts in the town of Weimar. The Bauhaus—Architect's House—set the architectural and decorative style of Weimar, stressing simplicity and beauty, expressing function through form, combining art and craft. By using the most modern materials available in the quest for "total architecture," Gropius hoped to reconcile art and industry. The Bauhaus's modernism and the presence of foreign architects, artists, and designers made it suspect to Nazis. Hitler, the former aspiring artist, detested modernism. He closed the Bauhaus as a symbol of "cultural Bolshevism."

In 1937, the Nazis in Munich staged an "Exhibition of Degenerate Art," including expressionist and dadaist paintings, among other modernist works. A Great German Art Show opened at the same time, offering samples of officially approved painting. While Stalin's preferred style of "socialist realism" emphasized work, Nazi art celebrated being German. Nazi artists offered sentimental portraits of German families tilling the land or at home, blond youths hiking in the Pomeranian forests, and square-jaw soldiers portrayed as medieval Teutonic knights.

In their attacks upon modernist composers, the Nazis reserved particular vehemence for the works of Jewish composers such as Gustav Mahler (1860–1911) and Arnold Schoenberg (1874–1951), while the

late-nineteenth-century compositions of the anti-Semitic Richard Wagner delighted Hitler. The theater, too, suffered from censorship, as well
as from the departure of a number of Germany's leading playwrights.
Hitler himself preferred light plays, such as a rustic comedy that earned
the Critic's Prize in Berlin in 1934, in which the leading character was a
pig. Anti-modernism could be seen in Nazi attacks on the supposed
hedonism of the "roaring twenties," which Nazis associated with licen-
tiousness, homosexuality, neon lights, jazz, and modern dances. Nazis
did not do the Charleston.

Joseph Goebbels (1897–1945), Hitler's minister of propaganda, permitted movie producers and newspaper editors to exercise self-censorship.
They were aware of the costs of making a slip. In Germany, as in all of
Western Europe, films—first silent movies and then "talkies"—had
become by far the most popular form of entertainment. Like Muzak on
elevators, which was invented during the Depression, films provided a
temporary escape from hard times. Nazism encouraged the production of
a number of virulently anti-Semitic films, above all *The Jew Suess* (1940),
the story of an eighteenth-century Jewish financier who betrays a German
state and is executed, to the cheers of Nazi audiences.

Hitler commissioned the popular, star-struck filmmaker Leni Riefen-
stahl (1902–2003) to produce *Triumph of the Will*, a remarkable propaganda film that depicts the carefully orchestrated Nuremberg rally of
1934, with its uniforms, banners, and impeccable regimentation.

Hitler's New Reich and the Jews

Central to Hitler's perverted view of the world was anti-Semitism, which
he made a cornerstone of Nazi ideology and of state policy. Nazism was
largely based on the quest for racial "purity," the establishment of a hierarchy of races, and the determination to carry out genocide, the planned
destruction of an entire race. Arguably the centrality of anti-Semitism in
Nazi ideology and practice distinguishes Hitler's Nazi regime from other
fascist and authoritarian regimes, in which anti-Semitism played a lesser
(though still awful) part. In 1935, the Nuremberg Laws, which made the
swastika the official symbol of Nazi Germany, deprived Jews (defined by
having had at least one Jewish grandparent) of citizenship, declaring them
to be "subjects." Jews were forced to wear a yellow Star of David prominently on their clothing when they left their homes. The laws also forbade
marriage or sex between non-Jewish Germans and Jews. Signs in restaurants, movie houses, and parks proclaimed that Jews were not allowed. Yet
some Jewish businesses, including banks, at first continued to operate, if
only because Hitler feared the economic consequences if they were
closed. Some of these were "Aryanized" (purged of Jewish owners and
managers) by the spring of 1938. Shortly thereafter, the German state
forced Jewish families to list the value of what they owned and to turn over

their assets to Gentile trustees, who could dispose of these estates as they wanted. Decrees established a list of professions and occupations from which Jews were to be excluded.

When Hitler came to power, some Jews emigrated immediately, or made plans to do so. With Jews unable to teach in universities after early 1933 or to attend university as of 1937, many distinguished Jewish scholars and artists left for Britain or the United States, including the brilliant physicist Albert Einstein (1879–1955). More than 1,600 scholars and scientists had lost, resigned, or left their positions. Other intellectual exiles from Hitler's Germany were not Jewish, among them the poet Stefan George, the writer Thomas Mann, and the painter Max Beckmann. But one had to have some place to go. The borders of Hungary and Yugoslavia were closed to refugees. One by one, countries that had accepted Jewish refugees began refusing to do so. In 1938, the French government greatly tightened restrictions on the admission of refugees, claiming that France was being "saturated" with them. Britain, where 80 percent of refugees now were Jewish, made it harder for Jews to get into Britain, or to go to Palestine, which Britain controlled. Switzerland, which had been known as a haven for political exiles, that same year closed the door on Jews fleeing Germany or Austria. Moreover, the Swiss government suggested that German passport officials stamp "non-Aryan" on passports of Jews so that they could be turned back at the frontier. The Swiss police hunted down refugees living in Switzerland whom they deemed illegal residents, putting them across the German border, or other frontiers.

On the evening of November 9, 1938, following the assassination of a German embassy official in Paris by a Polish Jew, S.S. and other Nazi activists launched planned attacks on specific Jewish businesses and homes throughout Germany. They destroyed stores, killed several hundred Jews and beat thousands. Thirty thousand Jews were imprisoned in camps. The terrifying night became known as *Kristallnacht*, because the

Nazis post placards in a Jewish shop window. The notice reads "It is forbidden to buy from this Jewish shop."

sound of shattering glass windows resounded throughout Berlin that night. Few Germans protested.

Hitler's Foreign Policy

Hitler had never concealed his goal of shattering the Treaty of Versailles. German foreign policy, then, came to dominate European international affairs. Hitler planned to rearm Germany, and he demanded the return of the Saar Basin, whose rich mines the French held north of their border, and of German parts of Upper Silesia on the border of Poland, the remilitarization of the Rhineland, and the absorption of the Polish (or Danzig) Corridor, which divided Prussia from East Prussia. But Hitler's long-term goals, which were far greater, were inseparable from his megalomaniacal determination to expand Germany by armed conquest, which he had made clear in *Mein Kampf*, published in 1925.

Hitler's foreign policy was predicated upon his determination that Germany conquer "living space" (*Lebensraum*) in Eastern Europe and his theory, based on spurious biological premises, that the Aryan race was superior to any other and therefore had the right, indeed the obligation, to assert its will on the "inferior" Slav peoples. A week after becoming chancellor in January 1933, Hitler told German generals of his plans to rearm Germany and to conquer land for agricultural production and German settlements in central, southeastern, and eastern Europe. The Slavic peoples of the Soviet Union, Poland, and Czechoslovakia would serve the German "master race" as slaves.

Once Hitler came to power, he was less open about his previously stated goals because of Germany's vulnerability to invasion, but these goals did not change. Hitler had to move with particular caution to avoid confrontation with Britain and particularly with France, with whom he considered war to be inevitable. For the moment, Poland and Czechoslovakia each had a stronger army than Germany. So Hitler had to carry out his foreign policy with patience and resourcefulness. He left in place the foreign minister and much of the old diplomatic corps, although he viewed them as weak and suspected their loyalty. In May 1933, he declared that he had no intention of rearming Germany, assuring the other powers that he wanted only peace. That October, however, Hitler announced that Germany would walk out of the Geneva Disarmament Conference, which had begun the previous year, and that it would leave the League of Nations. Once again, he insisted that Germany wanted peace and respect and would take only legal steps to "break the chains of Versailles."

Hitler signed a nonaggression agreement with Poland in January 1934. To the surprised generals who knew he intended to wipe Germany's neighbor off the map, he assured them that he had no intention of respecting the agreement. The German-Polish nonaggression pact was a blow to France's plans to maintain Germany's diplomatic isolation by a collective treaty system directed against Hitler. These military alliances with the Eastern European states of Poland, Czechoslovakia, Romania, and Yugoslavia would have left Germany surrounded by potential enemies, albeit relatively small ones, closely tied to France. The Polish dictator Józef Pilsudski did not trust Hitler, but he believed that he might be able to profit from Poland's strategic position between Germany and the Soviet Union and could take advantage of a possible German attack on either Austria or Czechoslovakia to take disputed territories.

Hitler's pact with Poland chilled Russian relations with Germany. It led Stalin to seek security against Hitler. The Soviet Union joined the League of Nations in September 1934; Stalin signed a defense treaty with France in May 1935, and quickly another with Czechoslovakia, which bound the Soviets to defend that country in case of a German attack, but only if France fulfilled its treaty obligations.

Hitler and Mussolini

While France scurried to find allies, Germany had none. Hitler had long admired Benito Mussolini. The two dictators had much in common. Both had taken advantage of economic and social crisis to put themselves in a position of unchallenged authority. Both intended to revise the Treaty of Versailles. Hitler's territorial ambitions in Eastern Europe did not conflict with Mussolini's goal of possible empire-building in the Balkans and North Africa. But because of possible conflicting interests, notably Hitler's long-range intention to annex Austria and Mussolini's claim of the Austrian Tyrol for Italy, both men at first viewed each other with some suspicion. Yet fascist Italy and Nazi Germany seemed natural allies, sharing France as an enemy. The Duce had proclaimed in 1933, the year Hitler came to power: "The victory of Hitler is also our victory."

Mussolini had reduced Albania, the small, impoverished nation across the Adriatic, to a virtual Italian protectorate, although it had almost no Italian population. In the South Tyrol, absorbed under the terms of the post-war settlement, Mussolini ordered a policy of Italianization, forbidding the use of the German and Slovene languages in schools. In Somalia, the country at the horn of Africa that Italy had conquered before the war, he ordered villages burned and residents slaughtered, turning the country into a military base from which new conquests could be launched. In Libya, Italian forces routinely ordered the use of mustard gas and public hangings to try to solidify their control.

Mussolini worked to increase international tensions wherever possible in the hope of taking advantage of instability. The Duce had signed the Kellogg-Briand Pact in 1928, in which the major powers renounced war as an instrument of national policy, not because he believed in its principles, but because he wanted Britain and France to treat Italy as a great power. Meanwhile, Italy funneled secret arms to Germany and trained its pilots in violation of post-war treaties and the policies of the League of Nations, to which Italy, but not Germany, belonged. In the Balkans, Italian agents provided financial support to right-wing terrorist groups, including ethnic Hungarians and Croats plotting against the Yugoslav government.

Hitler's plan to absorb Austria required Italian support, or at least neutrality, until Hitler had fully rearmed Germany. But for the moment, Germany was still in no position to antagonize France, whose army could have occupied much of Germany with only minimal resistance. But the German dictator took a calculated risk in 1934. Austrian Chancellor Dollfuss had made himself dictator and waged war on the left, but he intended to maintain Austrian independence. He had also banned the Austrian Nazi Party, which was funded and supplied by German Nazis, and had signed alliances with Italy and Hungary. Austrian Nazis, backed by Hitler, retaliated by assassinating Dollfuss during a badly organized coup attempt. The steely Kurt von Schuschnigg (1897–1977) replaced Dollfuss as leader of an authoritarian government closely tied to the Catholic Church. Schuschnigg, like his predecessor, believed he could maintain right-wing rule in Austria without German help. These dual allegiances—to Austrian independence and to an institutional role for the Catholic Church—here separated Austria's authoritarian regime from that in Germany.

Mussolini had sent tanks to the Austro-Italian frontier at the time of the attempted coup. A Nazi takeover of Austria would leave a potentially aggressive power at Italy's northern frontier. But, for the moment, Mussolini was absorbed in preparing for war against the African state of Ethiopia.

Hitler thus correctly assessed that it was unlikely that Britain, France, and Italy would mount an effective, concerted response to blatant German moves to overthrow the Austrian government. Each government limited itself to a protest against German meddling in Austrian internal politics, asserting its interest in Austria's independence. The attempted putsch in Vienna alarmed the British government. But it was convinced that conciliatory moves toward Germany might keep Hitler in line, particularly if, as a good many British conservatives believed, Hitler wanted no more than to be recognized as a power and to be able to defend Germany's borders. Nor was the French government willing to do more than express irritation, as it was confronting a fascist threat in France itself.

In 1935, however, Hitler's foreign policy entered a new and more aggressive phase. He defied the Versailles Treaty in March by announcing that Germany's army would be increased to half a million men, that military service would become compulsory, and that the German air force had already been rebuilt, despite the prohibition of the peace agreement. British, French, and Italian representatives met in Stresa, Italy, in April 1935 to discuss and denounce Germany's violation of the Treaty of Versailles—as did the League of Nations itself—and to reaffirm the Treaty of Locarno of 1925, in which the German government had joined Britain, France, and Italy in pledging to resolve future inter-

Ethiopian soldiers use donkeys to carry machine guns to confront the Italian invasion, 1935.

national disputes peacefully. Hitler then made the usual reassuring noises, stating that he would sign bilateral agreements with any of the powers (as opposed to the collective security agreements he had already helped shred), uphold the Treaty of Locarno, and recognize the territorial integrity of Austria.

Great Britain reflected wariness by signing a naval agreement with Germany in June 1935, establishing a ratio of 100:35 between the two navies. This agreement, however, enraged the French government; Britain had not even informed its ally of the hasty negotiations that led to the agreement. France then signed a secret treaty with Italy, the goal of which was to protect Austrian independence.

In October 1935, Mussolini's armies invaded Ethiopia, where Italian forces had suffered humiliating defeat in 1896. Determined to expand Italy's fledgling empire, a quarter of a million Italian women, including the queen, pawned their wedding rings (women who turned in their gold rings received in exchange tin ones blessed by the pope) to help raise money for the war of conquest fought with bombs, machine guns, and poison gas. Although the wave of popular enthusiasm Mussolini had anticipated in Italy failed to materialize, the Duce correctly assessed that Britain and France would do little more than denounce the invasion because they still desired Mussolini's support against Hitler. Realizing this, Hitler had encouraged Italy to attack Ethiopia.

Ethiopian Emperor Haile Selassie appealed to the League of Nations for help for his country, which had been a member nation since 1923. The League imposed economic sanctions against Italy, but left them weak by excluding oil from the list of products affected, and it did not try to prevent passage of Italian ships through the Suez Canal on the way to Ethiopia. The British government made it clear that it considered the appeasement of Italy the only way to end the crisis and placed an embargo against the sale of arms to Ethiopia, effectively letting Mussolini have his way. U.S. President Franklin Roosevelt even offered Italy American loans in order to develop the conquered colony.

Italian troops took the Ethiopian capital of Addis Ababa in May 1936. Over 500,000 Ethiopians were killed in the one-sided fighting. Italy lost only 5,000 soldiers, a number Mussolini decried as so small that it seemed to cheapen his victory. On July 15, 1936, the League of Nations formally lifted all sanctions against Italy. The Stresa agreement, which had been made with the goal of containing Hitler, collapsed as Mussolini defied the League of Nations. The Duce now began referring to himself as the "invincible Duce."

Remilitarization and Rearmament

On March 7, 1936, German troops moved into the Rhineland, which had been declared by the Treaty of Versailles to be a demilitarized zone. Hitler had secretly promised his anxious generals that he would order German forces to pull back if the French army intervened. Whether or not an armed British and French response might have stopped Hitler at this point has long been debated.

German ambassadors in the European capitals then claimed that the move had been necessitated by the destruction of the Locarno agreements by France's pact with the Soviets. The blustering, lazy Joachim von Ribbentrop (1893–1946), the German ambassador to Britain (who had simply added the aristocratic "von" to his name), attempted without success to browbeat the British into an alliance with Germany. France pushed the British government to react sharply against Hitler's brazen move, but would not act alone. France's unwillingness to act without British support in the crisis was a legacy of its failed occupation of the Rhineland in 1923, when it was forced to act with only Belgian assistance (see Chapter 24). In Germany, Hitler's prestige soared. He had delivered as promised, facing down the powers that had imposed the Treaty of Versailles and destroying the Locarno Treaty.

Hitler now speeded up the pace of German rearmament, particularly of the air force. By 1938, armament production absorbed 52 percent of state expenses and 17 percent of Germany's gross national product. German rearmament forced Britain to modernize its armed forces. Prodded by the Labour Party, British military expenses more than doubled between 1934 and 1937, though this was far less than what Germany spent at the same time (see Table 25.2).

Germany had the advantage of rearming with the most up-to-date war materials, while the arsenals of the other powers included old weapons

TABLE 25.2. DEFENSE EXPENDITURES OF THE GREAT POWERS, 1930–1938 (IN MILLIONS OF CURRENT DOLLARS)

Year	Japan	Italy	Germany	U.S.S.R.	U.K.	France	U.S.
1930	218	266	162	772	512	498	699
1933	183	351	452	707	333	524	570
1934	292	455	709	3,479	540	707	803
1935	300	966	1,607	5,517	646	867	806
1936	313	1,149	2,332	2,933	892	995	932
1937	940	1,235	3,298	3,446	1,245	890	1,032
1938	1,740	746	7,415	5,429	1,863	919	1,131

Source: Paul Kennedy, *The Rise and Fall of the Great Powers* (New York: Vintage, 1989), p. 296.

and equipment. Steel had gradually replaced wood in the construction of airplanes. Slotted wings made landings safer by reducing the speed upon approach. Some advanced fighters could now fly up to 400 miles per hour. Bombers with four engines had greatly enhanced range. Aircraft carriers further revolutionized air warfare. There were changes on the ground, too. Both German and French tanks were now much more powerful, protected by thick armor, and they had radios and carried heavy guns.

THE SPANISH CIVIL WAR

The German army and air force would try out their new weapons in Spain, which, although neutral in the Great War, became the battlefield of European ideologies during the bloody civil war that lasted from 1936 to 1939. For the first time since the Peninsular War during the Napoleonic era, the world's attention turned to Spain.

Indeed, there was relatively little to distinguish the Spain of 1920 from that of more than a century earlier. The days of empire and glory had long since passed, symbolized by the loss of Cuba and the Philippines to the United States in 1898. With the exception of relatively industrialized Catalonia and the Basque provinces in the northwestern corner of the country, Spain remained an overwhelmingly agricultural society. Coalitions and alliances between the nobility, the Catholic Church, and the army determined political power in Madrid.

Social and Political Instability

The ineffectual King Alfonso XIII (ruled 1886–1931) confronted social and political problems that defied solution. Catalonian and Basque regional separatism challenged the domination by the Spanish government in Madrid. Chronic political and social instability helped push the army into the role of chief arbiter of political life. Labor strife, assassinations, street battles, and police violence became the order of the day in the early 1920s. Spain had declared a protectorate over northern Morocco in 1912 and had begun to use poison gas against Moroccan insurgents who wanted independence. In 1921 Moroccans inflicted a shocking defeat on Spanish forces, costing the lives of 10,000 Spanish soldiers. This increased pressure from socialists and republicans on the monarchy.

In 1923, General Miguel Primo de Rivera (1870–1930) seized power with the support of the army and even the king. Four years later, espousing "nation, church and king," Primo set out to "modernize" Spain, ordering the construction of dams, sewers, roads, and prisons. He became a familiar sight in the cafés and bars of Madrid, such tours occasionally being followed by gushing, incoherent bulletins to the Spanish people drafted on his return home. Primo de Rivera antagonized the political left by promulgating a constitution in 1927 that made ministers no longer responsible to the Cortes and upset army officers (so numerous that they made up one-sixth of the army) by intervening in promotions. The weak Spanish economy eroded middle-class support for his regime. Primo de Rivera resigned in 1930.

The following year, Alfonso XIII abdicated after elections returned an anti-monarchist majority to the Cortes. The army refused to save the monarchy, because most officers now hoped to impose authoritarian rule. The nobles, upon whose support the kings of Spain had for centuries depended, "observed the fall of the monarchy as they might have watched a bad film."

A coalition of republicans and moderate Socialists established the Second Spanish Republic in April 1931. The government of Manuel Azaña (1880–1940) enacted a series of anticlerical measures, including the formal separation of church and state, imposed new taxes, passed labor reforms, and enacted land reform, including the outright expropriation of some of the largest estates. More strikes, land seizures by peasants, and attacks on churches and convents drove wealthy landowners and churchmen toward the anti-parliamentary right. Although assailed from the right, the Spanish Republic was unable to count on the support of the unions, which wanted even more far-reaching social reforms, or of anarchists, who wanted the abolition of the state itself. Azaña fell from power in September 1933.

Thus began the republic's two "black years," marked by increasing social and political violence. The inclusion of the right in a more conservative republican government brought a violent reaction from the left. During the "October Revolution" of 1934, leftists in Madrid, Catalan autonomists, and miners in the northern province of Asturias rose up, quickly setting up local "soviets" throughout their region. They held out for two weeks before being brutally crushed by Moroccan troops commanded by General Francisco Franco (1892–1975).

MAP 25.2 THE SPANISH CIVIL WAR, 1936–1939   The growing domination of Spain by the nationalists, as well as arrows showing nationalist and republican loyalist attacks during the Spanish Civil War.

In 1935, Radicals, Socialists, Communists, and some anarchists formed a "Popular Front" in defense of the republic against the right. It barely won a majority in elections held at the beginning of the next year, then quickly fell apart because of ideological differences amid high unemployment and political violence. The Falange, a small paramilitary fascist movement begun in 1933, further destabilized the republic. The Falange emulated the Italian fascist "black shirts" and German Nazis. In response to a wave of violence against republicans, the government declared the Falange illegal and arrested its leader in March 1936.

A military insurrection against the republic began in Morocco on July 17, 1936, quickly followed by garrison uprisings in most of Spain's major cities (see Map 25.2). German and Italian planes then carried the insurgents to the Spanish mainland. Right-wing nationalist rebels overwhelmed loyalist troops and workers in several key cities and soon held the traditionally conservative regions of Castile, Galicia, and Navarre.

The fragility of the loyalist alliance compromised the loyalist defense of the Spanish Republic. In Madrid, Socialist trade unions held the upper hand. In Catalonia and Andalusia, anarchist peasants and workers were a majority; they took the outbreak of the war as a signal to begin a social revolution, expropriating land, occupying factories, and establishing cooperatives. Workers' committees, holding power in some regions, unleashed terror against the upper classes. The Socialists now were in the awkward position of trying to rein in the social revolution for which they had originally called. Communists feared that an attempted social revolution from below would compromise the attempt to save the republic and, furthermore, that it might undercut support for their party. The Communist Party grew sixfold in less than a year, adopting the centralized, hierarchical structure upon which Stalin insisted. It purged members who had joined the Workers' Party of Marxist Unification (P.O.U.M.), which supported Trotsky against Stalin. The Communists, determined to destroy their allies on the loyalist side, withheld supplies and ammunition from anarchist and Socialist units.

Whereas the loyalists suffered the consequences of disunity, the nationalists benefited from increasing unity behind General Franco. Short, portly, and bald, Franco did not look the part of an officer who had risen rapidly through the ranks. Franco blamed freemasons (members of anticlerical Masonic lodges) for Spain's problems as Hitler blamed Jews for those of Germany. Franco considered himself a warrior king struggling against infidels who deserved no mercy.

The Struggle between Loyalists and Nationalists

The Spanish Civil War was fought with a savagery unseen in Western Europe since the seventeenth-century wars of religion. At least 580,000 people, and probably many more, died as a result of the war. Of these, only about one-sixth were killed on the battlefield. Ten thousand died in (largely nationalist) air raids on civilians, and thousands more died from disease and malnutrition. During the war, nationalists executed at least 200,000 loyalists (not counting those killed after Franco's victory), and about that same number died at the hands of the loyalist forces or from disease in prison. Throughout the first two months of the war, in areas controlled by the loyalists, age-old social and political tensions exploded in violence and death. Members of the Falange and monarchists were taken from their cells in the Madrid prison and shot; in the province of Catalonia alone, more than 1,000 clergy and nuns perished. The nationalists made effective propaganda use of loyalist atrocities, real or imaginary, as the pro-nationalist London *Daily Mail* proclaimed "Reds Crucify Nuns." The nationalists organized "fiestas of death" in bull rings, machine-gunning loyalists, including prominent intellectuals, Basque priests, and workers.

The Spanish Civil War polarized Europe because it pitted against each other the political extremes that had emerged in Europe since the Great War. For the political right, religion and social hierarchy were at stake in a pitched battle against socialism, communism, and anarchism. Those supporting the Spanish Republic saw the civil war as a struggle against international fascism. Foreign volunteers, including 20,000 Britons and Irish and many refugees from Nazi Germany, joined the loyalist forces. The volunteers of the Abraham Lincoln Brigade from the United States fought with idealism and determination—but with only occasional effectiveness. However these "International Brigades" were largely responsible for the heroic defense of Madrid that began on November 7, 1936. The writers who fought in the Spanish Civil War, virtually all on the loyalist side, produced some of the most remarkable and surprisingly objective literature about war written in the twentieth century, including the American novelist Ernest Hemingway's *For Whom the Bell Tolls* (1940) and the British writer George Orwell's *Homage to Catalonia* (1938), an account of his service on the loyalist side and of the damaging divisions between the major political factions, above all, the damaging role of the communists.

Franco's forces enjoyed a significant military advantage over the loyalists because their forces included the bulk of the armed forces at the outbreak of the civil war. The loyalist army lacked such necessities as field glasses and good maps. Orwell recalled his amazement at being issued an 1896 model German Mauser rifle and at the seemingly insurmountable difficulties of forging an able fighting force out of a motley crew of illiterate peasants, anarchist workers, shop clerks, and foreign volunteers, many of whom did not speak Spanish and for whom the only word known in common was "comrade."

The republican loyalists counted on receiving arms, munitions, and other supplies from the Western democracies. But the British government wanted to maintain peace at all costs, and many of its prominent political figures admired Franco. In France, Premier Léon Blum's Popular Front government hesitated to take any steps that would widen the Spanish conflict and further polarize his own country. Without tanks, airplanes, and other supplies from the Soviet Union, the Spanish Republic probably would have almost immediately collapsed in the face of the nationalist forces.

German and Italian assistance proved decisive. While Britain, France, and the United States abided by nonintervention agreements, Italy sent 100,000 soldiers to Spain. The loyalists easily defeated the ill-equipped Italian forces, who relied on Michelin tourist maps, in a spring 1937 ground battle. The Italians fared somewhat better in the air, where they faced virtually no opposition, and Mussolini's pilots helped destroy loyalist supply lines. Hitler used the Spanish Civil War as a military training ground, sending planes, guns, munitions, and other supplies through Portugal. German advisers trained nationalist pilots and military personnel.

The pilots of the German Condor Legion flew bombing runs against loyalist Spanish forces, as well as against civilians. On April 26, 1937, German and Italian planes bombed and strafed the small town of Guernica, killing more than 100 residents. Within a month, the Spanish-born painter Pablo Picasso had immortalized the martyrdom of Guernica in his large canvas depicting the horrors of modern warfare.

When the nationalists attacked Madrid at the end of August 1937, the Communist militant Dolores Ibarruri, known as "La Pasionaria" (1895–1989), rallied loyalists with her defiant shout, "They shall not pass!" In the north, the nationalists reached the Atlantic Ocean, cutting off the loyalist Basque provinces from France. By October 1937, Franco's forces controlled all of the north coast. The loyalists struggled along an imposing front that stretched from the Mediterranean south of Granada to the Pyrenees. When Franco's army reached the Mediterranean Sea, it isolated Catalonia from remaining loyalist territory; republican supplies dwindled. Barcelona fell in January 1939. Britain and France (where the Popular Front had fallen from power) quickly recognized the Franco regime. Republican refugees carried what they could through the mountains and snows of the Pyrenees to France. Those who fled into Portugal, in which the republic had been overthrown in 1926, were returned to Spain by the dictatorship of Salazar, who, like Franco, claimed to have saved his nation. In Portugal, the cult of Fátima, where the Virgin Mary was said to have appeared, was closely tied at this time to anti-communism. (Salazar, whose police and censorship reigned surpreme, encouraged the slogan "Fátima for religion, *fado* songs for nostalgia, and football for the glory of Portugal!") Despite assurances to Britain and France to the contrary, bloody reprisals against loyalists in Spain began immediately.

Pablo Picasso's *Guernica* (1937), mourning a German and Italian air attack on the Basque village.

(*Left*) Communist leader Dolores Ibarruri, "La Pasionaria." (*Right*) General Francisco Franco.

Franco, now known as "Caudillo," or "leader"—like the Italian Duce and the German Führer—established an authoritarian dictatorship based on the support of the army, the Church, and wealthy landowners, three groups that had opposed the republic. But recognizing Spain's weakness, Franco declined to pursue a policy of expansion that characterized Italian fascism or German national socialism. Furthermore, as in Salazar's Portugal, Franco's dictatorship allowed the Catholic Church an institutional role that would have been unthinkable in Nazi Germany and was less significant in Italy.

THE COMING OF WORLD WAR II

Determined to achieve his territorial goals and willing to go to war if necessary to do so, Hitler in 1936 allied with Italy and Japan. He sent German troops into Austria and then Czechoslovakia, believing that Great Britain and France would not resist, but prepared to go to war if they did so. Finally, Germany and the Soviet Union astonished the world by signing a mutual nonaggression pact, clearing the way for Hitler to launch a murderous attack on Poland. Attempting to avoid war at all costs, Britain and France accepted the occupation of Austria and Czechoslovakia but drew the line at Poland, leading to the confrontation that would begin the Second World War.

The Axis

Joint participation in support of the Spanish nationalists moved Germany and Italy closer together. The Italian dictator no longer dismissed Hitler as a "gramophone that plays only seven tunes," and he made it clear that he was willing to agree to Austria's loss of independence for a closer relationship with Hitler's Germany. Coming to the conclusion that German military strength could further Italian aims, in October 1936, Mussolini signed a pact with Hitler, forming what the Italian dictator called an "Axis." During Mussolini's visit to Berlin in the fall of 1937, Hitler flattered the Duce, afterward entertaining aides with imitations of Mussolini's strutting speeches. Hitler made clear that Germany's interests lay to the east; Mussolini could have the Mediterranean, and a free hand in Yugoslavia, Albania, and Greece.

The Duce now openly borrowed from Hitler's Nazis in other ways. The Duce ordered his soldiers to goose-step like the Germans, claiming that it was the military stride of ancient Rome. This led to considerable embarrassment for the elderly King Victor Emmanuel III, who could not attempt it without falling down. Mussolini also ordered his countrymen to stop shaking hands and take up the ancient Roman military salute of an outstretched arm at a 45-degree angle.

Racial theories had hitherto never played more than a minor part in Mussolini's rise to power or his daily bombast. The Duce, who had a Jewish mistress, had mocked Hitler's "delirium of race," and Mussolini at first enjoyed widespread support among Italian Jews—about one of every three had first joined the Fascist Party. But in 1938 Mussolini began a campaign against Italian Jews, who numbered no more than 50,000 in a country of 40 million people. These measures managed only to irritate many Italians in a country in which Jews seemed perfectly well assimilated.

Germany found another authoritarian partner in Japan. Over the last half of the nineteenth century, Japan had made itself an industrial and military power. In need of raw materials such as oil and rubber, the Japanese government sought to create an empire in Southeast Asia. By the late 1930s, the Japanese army had reached 1 million men, with reserves of twice that number. The Japanese air force had 2,000 fighter planes, including the new "Zero" fighter, as fast as any in the world. In 1931, Japan embarked on a piecemeal conquest of Manchuria at the expense of China. Since Japan has virtually no natural resources, its goal was to create a resource base, which would be necessary for fighting the total war that many young Japanese generals eagerly anticipated. A year later, the Japanese government created the client state of Manchukuo, declaring the last emperor of China, Henry Pu-Yi, to be its emperor.

Fearing that the Soviet Union might try to hinder its military expansion, Japan late in 1936 signed a formal friendship treaty with Germany, the "Anti-Comintern" (anti-Communist International) Pact, hoping also to discourage possible British and American intervention in Asia. In 1937, Japanese forces began to conquer chunks of northern China in order to establish a buffer zone between Manchukuo and the Soviet Union. This brought conflict with China. Japan then embarked on a major naval expansion program, exceeding both in number and size the limits stipulated by the Washington Naval Conference (1921–1922) to which Japan, among the other powers, had agreed. The United States was entrenched in isolationism and still suffering from the Depression. Angered by Japanese aggression and Japan's alliance with Nazi Germany, Britain and the other Western powers joined the United States in imposing an embargo on the sale of oil and other vital raw materials to Japan.

Aggression and Appeasement

In November 1937, Hitler unveiled to the generals his plans to absorb Austria and Czechoslovakia, perhaps as early as the following year if political unrest in France or a war in the Mediterranean between France and Italy reduced the chances of a French military response (see Map 25.3). Hitler's confidence derived partly from information he had received that Neville Chamberlain, the new Conservative British prime minister, who in a speech had once called Hitler's National Socialism "a great social experiment," might accept Germany's annexation of Austria and the Czech Sudetenland as inevitable. Chamberlain was concerned only that the

Prisoners of the war between China and Japan over the Japanese invasion of Manchuria, 1931.

MAP 25.3 GERMAN AND ITALIAN EXPANSION, 1935–1939   Aggression by Germany
and Italy against their neighbors.

annexation occur without strife. Chamberlain feared that if Britain went
to war against Germany, Hitler's allies Italy and Japan would strike British
imperial interests in the Middle and Far East—for example, in Egypt and
Burma. Furthermore, he viewed German ambitions toward the German-
speaking parts of Austria and Czechoslovakia, as well as toward the Polish

Corridor, as in keeping with the principle of nationalism, believing that Germany had been treated too harshly by the Treaty of Versailles.

Convinced that Britain would not act, Hitler bullied Austrian Chancellor Kurt von Schuschnigg to legalize the Austrian Nazi Party. When Schuschnigg announced that a plebiscite on the question of his nation's independence would be held, Hitler ordered German troops into Austria, justifying the invasion with the improbable claims that German citizens were being mistreated there and that Austria was plotting with Czechoslovakia against Germany. On March 12, 1938, most of the Austrian population greeted German troops not as conquerors, but as liberators. Hitler thus effected the unification (*Anschluss*) of Germany and Austria that had been specifically forbidden by the Versailles Peace Settlement. The Nazis arrested more than 70,000 people and frenzied Viennese crowds beat up Jews. Britain and France sent official protests, but the British government permitted the German Reichsbank to confiscate funds that the Austrian National Bank had deposited in the Bank of England, allowing the Nazis to gain valuable gold and foreign currency reserves.

Czechoslovakia was next on Hitler's list. During the summer of 1938, he orchestrated a campaign against the Czech government, particularly against President Edvard Beneš (1884–1948). At issue was the status of the Sudetenland Germans of Czechoslovakia, but Hitler was also furious that some anti-Nazi Germans had found refuge in Prague. Beneš, with Poland casting a covetous eye on the long-disputed coal-mining region of Teschen, now desperately sought reassurance from France and the Soviet Union, which were obliged by separate treaties to defend Czechoslovakia against attack. But the Soviets refused to act unless joined by France, and France refused to act without the British. In any case, France could really only help its Eastern European allies by attacking Germany itself.

Chamberlain had already decided not to act at all. In April 1938, the British prime minister had warned France that, in case of war with Germany, Britain would not send to the continent military help comparable to that which helped save France and Belgium in 1914. In May, German troops began to mass along the Czechoslovak border. Thus abandoned, the Czech government agreed to a series of German demands regarding the status of the Sudeten Germans.

On September 15, 1938, Chamberlain flew to the Führer's mountain retreat in southern Germany. When Hitler informed him that he would fight a world war in order to unite the Sudeten Germans to their fatherland, Chamberlain agreed to try to convince the French and Czech governments that Germany's absorption of the Sudetenland was the best hope for peace. Hitler promised Chamberlain that this would be the last territorial revision of the Treaty of Versailles that Germany would demand. But the German dictator continued to encourage Slovak demands for autonomy and Polish and Hungarian claims on the Czech borderlands. On September 19, 1938, Britain and France virtually ordered the Prague government to cede to Germany territories where the 3 million ethnic Germans formed a majority. Chamberlain returned to Germany to see Hitler again on September 22. He informed the Führer that Czechoslovakia, as well as France, had agreed to the annexation of the Sudetenland, asking only that the new borders of Czechoslovakia be protected by a joint agreement.

Faced with the kind of collective security agreement he loathed, Hitler now threatened that Germany would occupy the Sudetenland by October 1 and would recognize Polish and Hungarian claims on territory ceded to Czechoslovakia in 1918. This would have dismembered Czechoslovakia for all practical purposes. Chamberlain was perplexed. The French government balked, demanding Hitler's original terms as presented to Chamberlain. Hitler then seemed to draw back, offering hope that the crisis might be ended peacefully. He agreed to Chamberlain's proposal that Hitler, Mussolini, Édouard Daladier (1884–1970; the French prime minister), and Chamberlain meet to settle everything once and for all. Back in London, Chamberlain confronted mounting skepticism. The British government ordered preliminary measures for civil defense in case of war. Chamberlain tried to rally British public opinion with a speech on September 27: "How horrible, fantastic, incredible it is that we should be digging trenches and trying on gas masks here because of a quarrel in a faraway country between people of whom we know nothing. It seems still more impossible that a quarrel which has already been settled in principle should be the subject of war."

At the multilateral conference at Munich in September 1938, Hitler refused to allow representatives of the Soviet Union to attend. Czech officials were not even allowed to assist at the dismemberment of their own

Austrians salute Germany's annexation of Austria, March 1938.

country. Chamberlain and Daladier agreed to immediate German occupation of the Sudetenland (the most industrialized part of the country),
Poland's annexation of Teschen, the transfer of parts of Slovakia to Hungary, all in exchange for Hitler's personal guarantee of the redrawn borders of the partitioned nation. Hitler had taken another significant step in
the revision of the Treaty of Versailles. Chamberlain stepped off the plane
in London announcing to cheering crowds that he had brought his country "peace in our time."

In France, popular opinion did not want another war, and the military
expressed apprehension about taking on the refurbished and expanded
German armed forces. The French government felt abandoned by Britain,
and by neighboring Belgium, which three years earlier had abrogated its
1920 military agreement with France and proclaimed neutrality. France,
which had completed a line of bunker-like fortifications—the Maginot
Line—to the Belgian frontier and counted on Belgium's ability to defend
against a German attack, was now more exposed to a German attack
because of Belgian neutrality. The French government also feared that
Hitler might convince Franco of Spain to join Germany in a war against
republican France from the other side of the Pyrenees.

The appeasement of Hitler at Munich provided the German army with
more time to prepare for the conquest of what remained of Czechoslovakia. Appeasement—the term would subsequently take on a negative
sense—had characterized both British and French foreign policy in dealing with Mussolini (as the Ethiopian invasion demonstrated) and Hitler.
Appeasement as foreign policy was influenced by the sheer horror of the
Great War and many Europeans' unwillingness to contemplate a new conflict while preoccupied with the effects of the Depression. Appeasement
did not mean peace at any price, but rather the belief that if Germany, in
particular, was appeased on one or two minor demands, then it would be
placated. Hitler would then, so the reasoning went, be satisfied, and
Europe would be safe from war. It was pure illusion.

On March 16, 1939, Hitler shattered the Munich agreements, putting
an end to the policy of appeasement. German troops marched across the
Czech border and occupied Prague, establishing the "Protectorate of
Bohemia-Moravia." Again, as in the case of Austria, the British government helped Hitler out by allowing the transfer of 6 million pounds of
Czech gold deposits from London banks to the German-occupied state.
Even more important, Germany strengthened its forces with the addition
of the Czech air force and army, and it no longer had to maintain strong
defenses on its southern border. Even for Chamberlain, this marked the
end of illusions.

Hitler's brazen move shocked Mussolini, who complained, "Each time
Hitler occupies a country, he sends me a message." In April 1939, Italian
troops invaded and annexed Albania, while the Duce expressed confidence
that he could force France to give up Corsica and Tunisia. With war on

the horizon, British factories began turning out fighter planes as quickly as possible.

Looking east, the euphoric Hitler now demanded that Lithuania relinquish the Baltic port of Memel, which had been given to Lithuania by the Treaty of Versailles. Lithuania did so. He then demanded that Poland relinquish the port of Danzig and international access to the Polish Corridor that had by virtue of the Treaty of Versailles separated East Prussia from the rest of Germany. As always, Hitler offered a concession that would prove empty as soon as it had served its purpose: this time it was support against the Soviet Union's claim to parts of Poland that bordered on Ukraine.

The Polish government, which had been in a state of crisis since Józef Pilsudski's death in 1935, readied its military defenses. The British government, which had refused to consider any alliances with the small states of Central Europe, now hurriedly signed a pact with Poland on April 6, 1939, guaranteeing Polish independence and assistance in case of German aggression. On April 26, Chamberlain told the House of Commons that conscription of men twenty and twenty-one years of age would begin. France (which was committed to Poland by alliance) and Britain then signed pacts with Romania and Greece and offered military support to Turkey. Hitler himself probably hoped that rapid Polish capitulation in the face of a German invasion might present its Western allies with a *fait accompli* that might discourage their military response. Perhaps Poland would be convinced to join in a war against the Soviet Union. But Hitler accepted the strong possibility that war would follow any German move against Poland, even though he knew that the German economy could not reach full capacity for war production until 1943.

Few statesmen in France or Great Britain still harbored any illusions about what was next. British public opinion rapidly turned against appeasement. Winston Churchill (1874–1965), one of the few members of the House of Commons who had been convinced since 1936 that Britain would have to go to war against Hitler, called for an alliance with the Soviet Union against Germany. Chamberlain agreed, but moved slowly, at least partially because he did not trust Stalin. Discussions with Soviet diplomats dragged on, stumbling inevitably on the refusal of either Poland or Romania to accept Soviet troops on their territory, necessary to any effective defense against a German attack. Chamberlain then heard rumors that Stalin and Hitler, bitter enemies, were conducting diplomatic discussions, but laughed them off: "I cannot bring myself to believe that a real alliance between Russia and Germany is possible."

In early April 1939, Hitler had ordered the German army to prepare for an invasion of Poland on the following September 1. He shored up his alliance with Italy, signing in May 1939 the Pact of Steel, a formal military alliance between the two countries. Mussolini, who called the pact "absolute dynamite," nonetheless thought that he could continue to play

Neville Chamberlain promises "peace in our time" after his return from Munich in September 1938.

off Germany, Britain, and France against each other. He had believed Hitler when he said that he would not begin a war with Poland for several more years. But knowing that doctored statistics could not hide the fact that Italy was unprepared for war, and now tied by a formal alliance to Hitler, the Duce had painted Italy into a corner.

The Unholy Alliance

Stalin himself no longer had doubts about Hitler's ultimate intentions toward the Soviet Union. But the Russian army needed time to prepare for war. Stalin had decimated the officer corps during the purges of the past three years. In the short run, Hitler wished to avoid war with the Soviet Union while he was fighting in Poland; in the longer run, anticipating war with the Western powers, he sought to avoid fighting a war on two fronts. Stalin did not trust the Western Allies to maintain their commitment to resist Hitler and did not think that even a Soviet pact with Britain and France would prevent Hitler from attacking Poland, Russia's old enemy.

In one of the most astonishing diplomatic turnarounds in history, Hitler announced on August 23, 1939, that Germany had signed a nonaggression pact with the Soviet Union, the Molotov-Ribbentrop Pact, named for the two foreign ministers. The man Stalin had called "the bloody assassin of the workers" signed an agreement with the leader Hitler had referred to as "the scum of the earth," a Communist who dominated a state that he planned to conquer. Hitler believed that a German pact with the Soviet Union would smash the will of Britain and France to defend Poland.

Stalin had reasons not to trust Britain or France. After German armies marched into Austria in 1938, the British had rejected a Soviet call for a meeting of the powers to discuss a collective response. Furthermore, the Western Allies had not bothered to consult with the Soviet Union while appeasing Hitler at Munich. Now Hitler assured Stalin that "in the event of a territorial and political rearrangement," the small, independent states of Latvia and Estonia, coveted by Russia, as well as Finland and eastern Poland, would be fair game for the Soviet Union. From Stalin's point of view, it was in the Soviet Union's interest to avoid war as long as possible, the assumption being that the imperialist powers, all of them enemies of the Communists, ultimately would destroy each other.

Many—perhaps even most—Germans seemed prepared to follow Hitler into a new war. A popular German magazine in April 1939 had cheerfully run the headline, "Gas Masks for German Children Now Ready." Undeterred by Britain's reaffirmation of its commitment to defend Polish independence, or by doubts expressed by some of his confidants, Hitler ordered the German invasion of Poland.

CONCLUSION

The collapse of the political center in Europe under the stress of the Treaty of Versailles and the Depression helped create the Europe of dictatorships. German aggression finally brought a response from Great Britain and France, the two powers that remained parliamentary governments. World War II began. In retrospect, given the deterioration of the political climate, the rise of dictatorships, and the violence of the inter-war period in the Europe of extremes, one can even ask whether the entire period between 1914 (when World War I began) and 1945 (when World War II finally ended after the deaths of millions of people) can be viewed as a thirty years' war.

CHAPTER **26**

WORLD WAR II

For the second time in just twenty-five years, a conflict began in Europe that would soon become a world war. It would be even more devastating than World War I, wreaking destruction on a global scale. Germany's invasion of Poland in September 1939, like its invasion of Belgium twenty-five years before, started a chain reaction that brought all the world powers into the conflict. The Soviet Union occupied eastern Poland, the Baltic rstates of Lithuania, Latvia, and Estonia, and Finland. Japan joined Germany and Italy, and the United States entered the war on the side of Great Britain and the free French government exiled in London. Following Hitler's attack on the Soviet Union in June 1941, the communist state became an ally of Britain and the United States.

The Second World War was the first in which civilian populations became strategic targets and the first in which systematic genocide became part of the war effort. The technology of warfare developed rapidly; existing weapons were perfected and, by the end of the war, new, terrible weapons of mass destruction had taken a terrible toll on human life. When the war ended in 1945, Europe seemed to be entering an even more threatening era. Unlike the end of World War I in 1918, few people now dreamed that World War II would be the "war to end all wars."

THE WAR IN EUROPE BEGINS

The war for which Hitler had prepared for so long began with a rapid, brutal German attack on Poland on September 1, 1939. Stalin's Soviet Union, having just signed a nonaggression pact with Nazi Germany, stood by, and then sent an occupying force into eastern Poland. As Nazi troops overran Poland, the latter's Western allies, Great Britain and France, protested, but took no military action. Soviet troops soon invaded Finland, and German forces occupied Denmark and then Norway. Hitler next turned his attention to the west, invading France, the Netherlands, and Belgium, and launching massive bombing attacks against Britain in preparation for an invasion.

German soldiers attack the German-Polish border on the first day of the Nazi invasion of Poland, September 1, 1939.

The German Invasion of Poland

On September 1, 1939, about 1.5 million German troops, led by an armored division, poured into Poland. Fighters and light bombers thundered overhead, carefully coordinating their attacks to protect the infantry. Britain and France responded two days later by declaring war on Germany, following agreements concluded with the Polish government earlier that year.

Hitler wanted Polish resistance crushed quickly enough that Britain, and possibly France as well, would limit their reaction to a declaration of war. But he was prepared to fight the Western Allies if necessary, despite the lingering doubts of some of his generals about Germany's preparedness for war on such a massive scale.

Poland had a large and well-trained army of more than 1 million soldiers. But it made no difference that the Polish cavalry was the finest in Europe when enemy tanks arrived. The German air force destroyed half of Poland's planes in the first attacks on its bases. Bombers battered Warsaw. Poland's frontier defenses quickly crumbled before the onslaught of motorized columns of the German *Blitzkrieg* ("lightning war"), which were attacking from three directions. The Polish government fled Warsaw for London on September 7, and its capital fell on September 27, 1939.

Following the German invasion of Poland, Soviet armies invaded Poland from the east. They did so with Hitler's blessing, under a secret agreement made between Stalin and Hitler as part of the Molotov-Ribbentrop

Nonaggression Pact signed on August 23, 1939. Poland, which had lost its independence after being partitioned for the third time by its powerful neighbors in 1795, once again was divided up. On Stalin's orders, almost 15,000 Polish officers were executed in the forest of Katyn about 200 miles southwest of Moscow. The Soviet dictator ordered the transfer of Poles in cattle wagons as "special settlers" to the eastern reaches of the Soviet Union.

The "Phony War"

As Hitler had hoped, Britain and France took no military action. Few people seemed willing to "die for Danzig (Gdańsk)," the Polish port Germany had lost by the Treaty of Versailles. British and French military experts, shocked by the speed of the German victory over Poland, overestimated the strength of Hitler's armies. An immediate French and British attack on Germany from the west might have been successful, as long as the Germans were tied up in Poland, where the German army and air force had seriously depleted its supply of munitions. Britain and France had more than twice as many divisions ready and the German air force had few planes in the west. French troops made one brief, unopposed excursion fourteen miles into Germany, and then retreated. The British Royal Air Force flew over Germany, but dropped only leaflets calling for peace. Both the British and French governments believed that an attack on Germany would fail. They were stunned by Hitler's pact with Stalin; unlike in World War I, it now appeared that Germany would only have to fight a war on one front.

Hitler confidently announced to his generals on September 12, 1939, that he planned to order an invasion of France in the near future. The German army and air force were readied, while the French army dug in behind the supposedly impregnable fortifications of the Maginot Line, a row of bunkers stretching from Switzerland to the Belgian border (see Map 26.1).

Planned first for November and then for January, the German invasion of Western Europe was finally postponed until the spring of 1940. The winter months that followed the Polish invasion became immediately known as the "phony war." French troops stared into the rain, mist, and fog from their bunkers. Fearing German bombing attacks, the British government issued Londoners gas masks and imposed a nighttime blackout. Italian dictator Benito Mussolini had developed cold feet just before Hitler's invasion of Poland, because he knew that Italy lacked enough coal, oil, iron, and steel to wage a lengthy war. But he now believed a German invasion of France was inevitable. Mussolini announced that Italy's status would be one of "non-belligerence," a term he selected to avoid comparisons with the "neutrality" against which he had vociferously campaigned before Italy entered World War I in 1915.

MAP 26.1 THE GERMAN AND ITALIAN ADVANCE, 1939–1942   The opening of the war included advances by the Germans into Poland, the U.S.S.R., the Scandinavian countries, the Balkans, and North Africa. The Italians sent troops into Albania, and from there into Greece. The British unsuccessfully attempted to take a stand against the Germans in Norway, and British and French troops were evacuated from the continent at Dunkirk.

The War in the Frozen North

Although the "phony war" continued in the west, fighting began in northern Europe. The Russian border with Finland, an independent state since the Russian Revolution, lay only fourteen miles from Leningrad. Stalin demanded that the Finnish government cede strategically important territories to the Soviets. When the Finnish government refused in November 1939, the Red army invaded. Badly outnumbered Finnish soldiers fought bravely in subzero temperatures, sometimes on skis, carrying light machine guns against Russian tanks and temporarily holding back the Soviet forces. Finland harbored no illusions about winning the "Winter War," but, like Poland, hoped to be saved by British and French diplomatic or military intervention. France now favored, at least in principle, armed intervention on behalf of Finland. So did Britain's Winston Churchill, the Conservative politician who had angered his party by opposing appeasement of Hitler at Munich. But Finnish resistance soon was broken. Finland suffered 20,000 deaths and 500,000 wounded in the short, bloody war. By the Peace of Moscow, signed March 12, 1940, the Soviet Union annexed about 10 percent of Finnish territory as almost 500,000 Finns fled their country.

In April 1940, British ships mined the Norwegian harbor of Narvik, despite the objections of the government of Norway, in an attempt to stop Swedish iron ore from being shipped to Germany. In order to prevent the British from intervening, the Germans first landed in Denmark, which surrendered without a fight (see Map 26.1). Taking the Allies by surprise, German paratroopers landed at Oslo and other Norwegian port cities, followed by reinforcements put ashore by ships. German troops repelled Allied troops who arrived at the end of April with sketchy orders and inadequate weapons. Vidkun Quisling (1887–1945), organizer of a fascist party in the 1930s, became the puppet head of state in Norway, his name entering the dictionary as synonymous with traitor.

Prime Minister Chamberlain had assured the British House of Commons that Germany "had missed the bus" by waiting so long to attack. But Germany's victory in Norway, followed by a lightning occupation of Denmark, brought down the Chamberlain government. Churchill, who had sat in the House of Commons off and on since 1900, became prime minister on May 10, 1940, at the age of sixty-five. The outspoken Churchill was an unpopular choice among even some Conservatives, who held an overwhelming majority in Parliament. Many remembered his impulsive and stubborn attachment to far-fetched military operations during the First World War, which had led to the catastrophic defeat of British troops at Gallipoli in 1915. Even one of his trusted advisers said that Churchill had ten new ideas each day, but that nine of them were bad. Still, his resilience, determination, and dedication would make Churchill an extraordinary wartime leader.

The Fall of France

German troops stared confidently across the Rhine River at their French opponents. The German army could simply sidestep the French Maginot

Line, which stopped at the Belgian frontier. Germany enjoyed vast superiority over France in the air (France had only about 500 first-line fighter planes, Germany about 4,000). Furthermore, the German army and air force were already well-practiced, having launched their invasion of Poland.

The French army seemed unequal to the task of holding off a German attack. Soldiers had become demoralized by the winter months in the damp bunkers along the Maginot Line. The plan of the French high command to engage the enemy forces as they moved into the Low Countries was undermined by the Belgian and Dutch governments; both, hoping to remain neutral, had been unwilling to coordinate defense planning with the French army. The French generals lacked confidence in the strength of their forces and—at least some—in the Third Republic itself. French tanks were as good as those of Germany but lacked fuel and were dispersed among infantry divisions, instead of concentrated in tank divisions. Teams of horses still pulled French artillery pieces. French communications networks along the front were inadequate. After eight months of "phony war," many people in France were uncertain as to why they might be once again fighting Germany.

Compounding serious military problems, the British and French governments were already sniping at each other. The French resented the fact that their ally had sent a relatively small army to France; the British government seemed willing to defend France down to the last Frenchman. On the other hand, the French had irritated the British by opposing Allied

Hitler takes a triumphant stroll through Paris in June 1940.

bombing of Germany, fearing that the expected swift reprisals would strike them, not Britain.

On May 10, 1940, the "phony war" in the west suddenly ended. In a carefully rehearsed attack that astonished the Allies, German gliders landed troops that captured a massive Belgian fortress. Airborne divisions took the airport and central bridges of the Dutch port of Rotterdam; German bombers then destroyed ships, docks, and the heart of the old city, killing 40,000 people. The German assault on France began through the Ardennes Forest on the Belgian border; ten tank divisions pushed seventy miles, brushing aside the lighter French tanks. German planes, controlling the air, swept down on French troops and destroyed half the planes of the British Royal Air Force within three days of the invasion. Mussolini, a portly vulture circling above the wounded French prey, had declared war on France on May 10, but an Italian army managed to advance only about a hundred yards across the border toward Nice.

French commanders then foolishly sent most of their armored reserves into the Netherlands while German tanks, having reached the Meuse River in eastern France, now turned west and began moving toward the English Channel. They were vulnerable to an Allied counterattack, but only a minor challenge by a tank column commanded by French General Charles de Gaulle (1890–1970) slowed the German drive to the Channel. The British Expeditionary Force, instead of attacking the exhausted German tank columns, retreated from Belgium into France, heading toward the Channel. German columns reached the Channel on May 21, 1940, cutting the Allied forces in half. The Netherlands surrendered on May 15, Belgium on May 28. By now the roads of northern France were choked, not only with retreating British and French troops, but also with Belgian and French refugees fleeing the battle zones, diving into ditches to escape strafing German fighters.

France's defeat was by now only a matter of time. On June 3 and 4, every available English vessel, including fishing trawlers and pleasure craft, evacuated almost 340,000 British and French troops from the northern French port city of Dunkirk, as Allied soldiers also escaped the continent from other ports. The German army now wheeled to confront the French troops still uselessly holding the Maginot Line. The French government left Paris for Bordeaux in the southwest, as it had in 1870. The German army occupied the capital on June 14. With its troops in disarray and with morale completely broken by the loss of more than 100,000 men (compared to 40,000 German dead), the French military command was ready to surrender. But France and Britain had several months earlier agreed that neither ally would ask for an armistice without the approval of the other. The British wanted the French government to move to North Africa and to continue fighting. On June 16, Marshal Philippe Pétain, hero of the Battle of Verdun in 1916, became premier. The next day, he asked Germany for an armistice. On June 22, 1940, the gleeful Hitler accepted the French surrender in a railway car in the spot where Germany had signed a similar document in November 1918. Hitler danced a jig of joy, and then set out to tour Paris.

The Battle of Britain

Britain would fight on. For the moment, it did so alone. Addressing the House of Commons, Churchill declared, "I have nothing to offer but blood, toil, tears, and sweat. . . . You ask, what is our policy? I will say: it is to wage war, by sea, land, and air, with all our might and with all the strength that God can give us."

Hitler now considered whether an invasion of Britain, "Operation Sea Lion," could succeed. Germany held both the French and Belgian Channel ports, a position it had never achieved during World War I. Furthermore, with Ireland having proclaimed its neutrality, Britain no longer had the use of southern Irish ports.

Fearing a German attack, the British government interned German subjects, including some of the 50,000 Jewish refugees from Nazism. In some places, officials took down road signs and place names, and shopkeepers shredded local maps to disorient any German invading army. The German admirals, however, advised Hitler that attacks against British interests in North Africa and the Mediterranean would be the best way of defeating Britain, drawing on Italian and possibly Spanish help.

For Germany to invade Britain, the German air force (the Luftwaffe) had to control the skies. The ensuing Battle of Britain, fought over the Channel and above southern England, lasted four dramatic months, from the last day of July until October 31, 1940, although most of the climactic duels in the sky took place from the second week of August until the end of September. Against the Luftwaffe's 1,200 bombers and 1,000 fighters, the Royal Air Force could counter with only about 900 fighters, not all of which could be put into the air at once. The British used radar, first developed in 1935, to detect oncoming German attacks. Recently built British Spitfires and Hurricanes reached greater speeds than the German Messerschmitt fighters and could break through the fighter escorts to get to the cumbersome German bombers. Frustrated, Hitler ordered the bombing of key industries and aircraft factories in England even as British bombers appeared over Berlin in August, demonstrating that Britain was far from defeated. The German bombing "blitz" of London began on September 7. Londoners took to the subway stations and underground air-raid shelters for protection.

Britain lost 650 fighters, but factories were producing replacements and new pilots were being trained. As German air losses mounted, the Luftwaffe turned to less accurate night bombing to keep the British fighters out of the air. At the end of September 1940, Hitler was forced to abandon

(*Left*) Evacuating children from London during the German bombing "blitz" 1940. (*Right*) British Prime Minister Winston Churchill amid the rubble outside of St. Paul's Cathedral, 1940.

his plan to invade England. Churchill called the Battle of Britain his country's "finest hour."

A Global War

World War II rapidly spread to almost all corners of the globe. Total war absorbed national resources on an unprecedented scale. In Britain, factories began to turn out weapons, munitions, and wartime materiel. The government assumed considerable control over the economy, coordinating production, raising taxes, and imposing rationing. Scientists were put to work in the war effort. World War II would require similar efforts from each of the great powers.

Hitler counted among his allies Italy, Romania, Hungary, and Bulgaria, as well as Japan, each eager for territorial acquisitions. But Nazi troops had to bail out the Italians in Greece, which Mussolini had ordered attacked in October 1940. After invading Egypt, the Duce soon found his small North African empire reeling from British attacks.

In June 1941, Germany launched an air and ground attack on the Soviet Union, shattering the Molotov-Ribbentrop Pact of August 1939. However, Hitler failed to reckon with determined Russian resistance, as well as with the harsh Russian winter. The largest invading army in history ground to a halt in the frozen snow. Finally, on December 7, 1941, Japanese planes carried out a surprise attack on the U.S. naval and air force base at Pearl

Harbor, Hawaii. The raid inflicted great damage on the U.S. Pacific Fleet, and brought the United States into what had become a global conflict fought on an unprecedented scale.

Total War

Britain was the first combatant in World War II to find itself engaged in a total war. As the war expanded, other states confronted similar challenges. German military planners counted on Hitler's confident assertion that the United States would stay out of the war, and that Germany could bring the British to their knees. But the United States, where British resistance won sympathy and admiration, could help Britain in other ways. On December 29, 1940, President Franklin D. Roosevelt announced that the United States would be "the arsenal of democracy," despite its official position of neutrality. Since direct loans might recall for many Americans the defaults by those in debt to the United States after World War I, Congress passed the Lend-Lease Act in March 1941. It authorized the president to lend destroyers, trucks and other equipment, and food to Great Britain, which in exchange would lease naval bases in the Caribbean to the United States.

Unlike Germany, which had been preparing for war virtually since Hitler came to power, Britain had to start almost from scratch. The British government succeeded in rallying the king's subjects to wartime sacrifices. Because very few people had any doubts about the extent of the Nazi threat to Britain itself, including possible invasion, military conscription at the beginning of the war brought less protest than it had in World War I in a nation with a long tradition of resistance to the idea of a standing army. Before the war began, the British armed forces comprised 500,000 people; at the end of the war, 5 million. Women took the places in industry vacated by departing troops, accounting for 80 percent of the increase in the labor force between 1939 and 1943. In 1939, 7,000 women worked in ordnance factories in Britain; in October 1944, there were 260,000.

The British War Cabinet imposed more governmental control on the economy, and by 1942 it had achieved a high degree of coordination in wartime production. The government imposed higher taxes, implemented rent control, and established rationing (limiting purchases of such English staples as jams and candy), and called for voluntary restraints on wage raises. Pants came without cuffs or zippers; a suspicious gray "utility loaf" replaced white bread. In order to feed a population expanded by the arrival of wartime refugees from France and other countries, British farmers augmented agricultural production by increasing the amount of land under cultivation by a full third.

In October 1940, Churchill established a scientific advisory committee to put some of Britain's most eminent scientists to work designing more powerful and reliable weapons. One of the most significant breakthroughs of the war was not a technological innovation but the solving of the complex puzzle of a secret code. British intelligence officers, aided by mathematicians, deciphered communications between Hitler and his high command during the Battle of Britain. This subsequently allowed the Allies to know many German moves in advance. British intelligence officers then broke the German communications code, facilitating, among other things, the identification of spies. The code breakers by the end of 1943 were reading more than 90,000 messages a month. The British Psychological Warfare Division, along with their U.S. counterpart, also put the science of psychology into the service of modern warfare, waging radio and leaflet campaigns in an attempt to weaken the will of the enemy to continue fighting. Germany and Japan countered by employing two Americans ("Axis Sally" and "Tokyo Rose," respectively) to broadcast messages to U.S. troops, trying to convince them that they could never win the war.

Hitler's Allies

Realizing that Germany could not successfully invade Britain, Hitler sought other allies in an attempt to win the war quickly. Seeking to discourage the United States, Japan's rival in the Pacific, from entering the war on the Allied side against Germany and Italy, the two Axis powers signed the Tripartite Pact with Japan in September 1940. By this treaty, Germany and Italy recognized Japan's interests in Asia, while Japan acknowledged those of Germany and Italy in Europe. The treaty specified that each power agreed to cooperate should any one of them be attacked by "a Power at present not involved in the European war or in the Chinese-Japanese conflict." Hitler then tried to convince Francisco Franco, whose victory in the Spanish Civil War Hitler had helped make possible, to join the war of the "Axis" powers against Britain. The German dictator envisioned a Spanish seizure of Gibraltar and German use of naval bases in the Spanish Canary Islands. The Spanish dictator pleaded the poverty of his country and, as if to emphasize the point, arrived at the meeting with Hitler hours late on a plodding train. The German dictator then made exorbitant demands for future territorial considerations in North Africa. After spending eight hours cajoling Franco, Hitler said, "I would prefer to have three or four teeth extracted rather than go through that again." Franco's Spain, however much ideologically in tune with some aspects of Hitler's Germany, remained neutral.

In Romania, King Carol II was powerless in the face of his greedy neighbors, who were encouraged by Germany. He surrendered to Hungary a part of Transylvania that had been awarded to Romania by the Treaty of Versailles but that included a considerable Hungarian population. Stalin forced Romania to hand over to the Soviet Union northern Bukovina and

Bessarabia, which had once been part of the Russian Empire. Bulgaria, too, helped itself to Romanian territory. As a result, the fascist Iron Guard rebelled and forced King Carol to abdicate in favor of his son Michael in September 1940.

Now convinced it was facing a long war, Germany hurried to secure a supply of raw materials by occupying Romania and its rich oil fields in October 1940. A right-wing general, Ion Antonescu (1882–1946), ran the country with the help of the Iron Guard, which served German interests and unleashed its fury against Romania's Jews and Communists. Both Romania and Hungary formally joined the Axis in November 1940, Bulgaria in March 1941.

From the beginning, it appeared that Italy's contributions to the German war effort would be minimal at best. Mussolini, who had promised the Italian people new victories, now aimed to take as much territory in North Africa as possible before the British surrender upon which he counted. After having failed to launch air attacks, as Hitler had wanted, on British bases on the Mediterranean island of Malta, Mussolini now invaded Egypt in September 1940, refusing a German offer to supply tanks because he wanted Italy to claim victory on its own. Unable to provide troops with air cover, Italian forces suffered a series of humiliating defeats at the hands of British forces.

Desperate for victory somewhere, on October 28, 1940, the Duce surprised Hitler—as well as his own generals, with whom he rarely consulted—by ordering the Italian army to invade Greece from Albania. Having paid large bribes to Greek generals and officials not to resist invasion, Mussolini anticipated an easy victory. But a Greek patriot army drove the Italians back into Albania, where resistance movements made life difficult for Mussolini's troops. The Italian army took out its frustrations against the Croatian population of Dalmatia on the Adriatic coast. In the meantime, British forces battered the Italian fleet.

Italy's imperial holdings in East Africa rapidly crumbled in the spring. A British and French force took Addis Ababa, Ethiopia's capital, in April 1941. Italian troops retreated through the North African desert. Hitler sent General Erwin Rommel (1891–1944), commander of a tank division to North Africa, to bail them out. Mussolini vowed to continue the war "until the last Italian is killed."

The German Invasion of Russia

Hitler always intended to invade and defeat the Soviet Union, despite the Molotov-Ribbentrop Nonaggression Pact of August 1939. After occupying eastern Poland following the German invasion of Poland, Soviet troops had occupied the Baltic republics of Estonia, Latvia, and Lithuania during the summer of 1940, claiming that they had been illegitimately detached from Russia after World War I, when they had become independent.

German interest in Finland and moves in Romania now made Soviet Foreign Minister Vyacheslav Molotov (1890–1986) anxious. The Soviets
sought reassurance in a new pact, one that Mussolini would sign as well.
Molotov went to Berlin. Assured personally by Hitler that Britain lay
defeated, Molotov replied, "Then whose bombers are those overhead, and
why are we in this bomb shelter?"

Hitler intended "Operation Barbarossa," the invasion of Russia, to be a
"quick campaign" of no more than ten weeks' duration. He hoped that
Japan would attack Siberia, thereby forcing Stalin to divert troops there.
The German generals held the Russian army in such contempt that they
ordered no serious assessment of Russia's existing or potential military
strength. If the Finns on skis had been able to hold off Russian divisions
with seemingly little more than snowballs, how could German fighters and
tanks fail to break through with relative ease? Some of Hitler's generals
were not so sure.

The opening of a Balkan front delayed Hitler's invasion of the Soviet
Union, which had been planned for May 1941. Britain had sent forces to
Greece following the Italian invasion, which made German bases in
Yugoslavia even more crucial. An anti-German faction had overthrown the
Yugoslav government in March and refused to join the Axis or to allow
German troops into the country. Hitler ordered a German invasion of
Yugoslavia in April, which then pushed into Greece. As in World War I,
Bulgaria cast its fate with Germany. Bulgarian troops occupied parts of
Greek Macedonia and Thrace. The German army forced a British with-
drawal from the Greek mainland to the Aegean island of Crete, which
soon fell to German paratroopers on May 27. By the end of May 1941,
Hitler's armies held all of the Balkans.

Hitler could now concentrate on an invasion of the Soviet Union.
Stalin, however, failed to heed warnings from Britain and the United
States that Russia was Germany's next target. Believing these warnings,
including some of his own army's military reports, to be part of a conspiracy to turn him against his German ally, Stalin ordered the execution of
some of his intelligence officers.

On June 22, 1941, German planes, tanks, and more than 3 million
troops attacked the Soviet Union. When the news came at 4 A.M., Stalin
was so numb with shock at news of Hitler's betrayal that he did not order
resistance for two hours and left it to Molotov to address the Soviet people
by radio.

The Soviets had many more men, field artillery, tanks, and aircraft than
Germany, and for the most part their weapons were of quality equal to or
even superior to that of the Germans. But German forces quickly devastated Soviet defenses, communication, and transportation networks. One
army pushed toward Leningrad, reaching its suburbs in July 1941 and
undertaking a siege of the city. But Leningrad held. The battleship *Aurora*,
which had served the Bolshevik cause in the Revolution of 1917, was

pressed into service, its guns commandeered from a museum. A second German army captured more than 250,000 prisoners near Minsk, 250 miles northeast of Warsaw; a third, finding support from anti-Russian Ukrainians, took Kiev on September 24, 1941. Hitler rejected his generals' suggestion that the attack on Moscow be given priority. Instead, armored units were transferred to the northern army besieging Leningrad.

The scorched-earth tactics of the German troops left Russian towns and villages in ruins, and hundreds of thousands of civilians dead. But despite enormous battlefield casualties, as well as half a million captured prisoners dying of hunger and cold in German camps, Russian resistance stiffened. News of Nazi atrocities helped rally virtually the entire population. German armies bogged down in the face of determined resistance around Smolensk. Soviet state-run factories were easily converted to wartime production, soon turning out tanks of equal quality to those of the invader. The United States, still officially neutral in the conflict, now extended the Lend-Lease policy to the Soviet Union.

Their drive to victory stalled, despite having captured more than a million square miles of Soviet territory, the German troops, like Napoleon's armies in 1812, found that a frozen winter, the coldest in a century, followed the chilly Russian fall. "Hitler no more resembles Napoleon than a kitten resembles a lion," Stalin taunted. Oil for tanks and guns froze. So did soldiers. The German high command, so certain of a quick victory, had not bothered to provide them with warm clothing and blankets for temperatures reaching far below zero.

Fallen Nazi soldiers during the German invasion of Russia, 1942.

After ordering a halt in the push toward Moscow, Hitler, fearing the consequences of retreat on German morale, ignored the advice of his generals to pull back and await spring weather. Early in December 1941, a desperate German attack stalled twenty miles from Moscow. The German army never got closer. During the first year of the Russian campaign, German casualties reached 1.3 million, or 40 percent of the original invading force, the greatest losses of any single military operation in history. Hitler may have conquered Poland, France, Belgium, the Netherlands, and much of the Balkans, but he had failed to defeat Britain and the Soviet Union.

Japan's Attack on the United States

Four years of Japanese aggression in Asia brought the resource-poor island nation to the point of confrontation with the United States. Since invading Manchuria in 1931 and proclaiming it the puppet state of Manchukuo a year later, Japan had sought to expand its influence and territory in the Pacific region. Southeast Asian oil was one Japanese target, particularly after the economic boycott imposed by the United States, Great Britain, and the Netherlands following the Manchurian invasion. The Japanese quest for rubber, tin, and other raw materials threatened British economic interests in Burma and Malaya, as well as those of the Dutch in Java and of the United States in the Philippine Islands.

In 1937, Japan had joined the Anti-Comintern Pact that Germany and Italy had signed in November 1936. This further undermined its relations with the United States. In 1937, the Japanese army invaded China and occupied the main Chinese ports, moves that the American government viewed with great alarm. The Molotov-Ribbentrop Nonaggression Pact between the Soviet Union and Germany had voided the Anti-Comintern Pact (since the Soviet Union was a Communist state). In September 1940, Japan concluded the Tripartite Pact with Germany and Italy. Japanese aggression in Asia continued. In an effort to stop the flow of Allied supplies to Chinese forces over the railway from Hanoi and a long dirt road from Burma, Japan had assumed a "protective" occupation of French Indochina in July 1941. A nonaggression pact with the Soviet Union, signed in April 1941, two months before the German invasion of Russia, bolstered Japanese confidence that it could attack and inflict a stinging defeat on the United States.

On Sunday morning, December 7, 1941, a Japanese force of fighters and dive-bombers surprised the American naval and air force base at Pearl Harbor, Hawaii. Three U.S. battleships were sunk, and five were severely damaged; ten other vessels were destroyed or disabled. In addition, 188 planes were destroyed, and many others were damaged. The attack killed 2,403 naval and other military personnel, and more than 1,000 were wounded. However, three aircraft carriers were at sea, and therefore

View from a Japanese bomber during the attack on Pearl Harbor.

escaped the attack and could still be readied to take on the Japanese fleet in the Pacific Ocean. Vast stocks of oil, too, survived. Japan quickly followed with successful invasions of Malaya, the Philippines, Singapore (where almost 60,000 British soldiers surrendered), and Pacific islands as far distant as the Aleutians near Alaska (see Map 26.2).

Because American intelligence officers had deciphered Japan's coded messages, President Roosevelt had known that Japan was planning to launch a war against the United States. The emperor believed that a rapid Japanese victory would force the Americans to a negotiated settlement. Yet the attack on Pearl Harbor came as a surprise, in part because U.S. intelligence services were swamped with messages suggesting attacks at other locations. Calling December 7, 1941, "a day that will live in infamy," Roosevelt declared war on Japan.

Hitler, bound by treaty to Japan, then declared war against the United States on December 11, to the surprise and consternation of some of his generals. Hitler believed that public opinion in the United States was against American involvement in another European war. In fact, he knew amazingly little about the United States, viewing it from his strange vantage point as a nation corrupted by racial mixing.

Upon hearing the news of Pearl Harbor, Churchill is reported to have exclaimed, "We have won the war!" The entry of the United States into the war against Germany provided, as in 1917, a crucial material advantage to the Allies. Despite its slow recovery from the Depression, which hit it harder than any other nation, the United States was the largest industrial power in the world, producing more than the next six powers combined. American factories, though privately owned, were quickly converted to

MAP 26.2 THE JAPANESE ADVANCE AND ALLIED COUNTEROFFENSIVE, 1941–1945   After launching a surprise attack against the U.S. naval and air force base at Pearl Harbor, Hawaii, the Japanese successfully invaded most of the Southeast Asian countries and many of the Pacific islands.

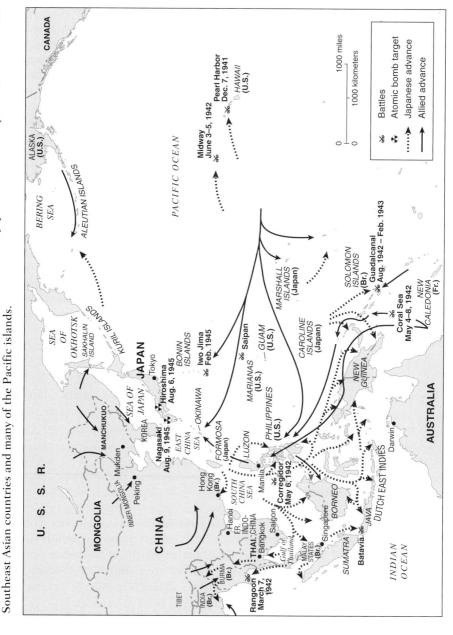

military production. In response to wartime demand, industrial production in the United States doubled by the end of 1943.

Despite the patronizing attitude of the aristocratic, self-assured, cigar-smoking British prime minister, a warm personal relationship gradually developed between Churchill and Roosevelt. Their rapport helped overcome the tension that had developed between the two powers because of the original unwillingness of the United States to join Britain in the war. The Japanese attack on Pearl Harbor ended U.S. isolationism. American citizens rallied to the war effort, particularly against the Japanese. "Remember Pearl Harbor!" struck a chord in the United States that "Remember Belgium" or "France" could not have.

The fact that an Asian power had attacked the United States galled Americans, many of whom believed that Asians were inferior. Amid rumors that Japanese citizens and Japanese Americans were preparing to carry out acts of sabotage in the United States, the U.S. government interned in "relocation centers" about 40,000 Japanese citizens residing in the United States and 70,000 of its Japanese Americans, who were citizens by birth living on the West Coast. American citizens of German descent, in contrast, were not interned. The playwright Arthur Miller noticed that the men with whom he worked at the Brooklyn Navy Yard had no "comprehension of what Nazism meant—we were fighting Germany because she had allied herself with the Japanese who had attacked us at Pearl Harbor."

The first of several meetings between the British and American military chiefs of staff took place in Washington, D.C., in January 1942. The Allied commanders decided to give the European theater of war the highest priority. An immediate concentration of attacks against Japanese forces seemed less urgent. In any case, it would take considerable time to dislodge the Japanese from the Southeast Asian countries and Pacific islands they had conquered.

HITLER'S EUROPE

Whether or not each conquered state retained some autonomy, German policies were primarily directed at extracting useful raw materials needed to wage an extended war. The exact nature of the relationship between Germany and each occupied state varied from country to country. Yet everywhere the Nazis carried out Hitler's policy of genocide against Jews and others belonging to what he considered to be inferior races.

In every country overrun by German troops, people could be found who were eager or willing to collaborate with the Nazis. These ranged from Marshal Philippe Pétain, head of the Vichy state in France, to ordinary people whose political biases or hope for gain or even just survival led them to help the Nazis. Yet, in many countries, resistance movements bravely opposed the rule of the Nazis or their allies. The largest and most successful resistance was in mountainous Yugoslavia, where resisters were able to take on entire German divisions, and, to a lesser extent, in France, where groups of guerrilla fighters undertook hit-and-run attacks against the Germans and against the Vichy government. In Germany, resistance to Hitler and the Nazis was extremely limited, notwithstanding a courageous attempt by disenchanted army officers to assassinate Hitler in July 1944. To the end, most Germans remained loyal to the Führer, or at least did not resist.

The Nazi "New European Order"

Hitler sought to exploit the economic resources of the countries his armies had conquered and to assure that no effective opposition could emerge in any of them. Germany annexed the disputed Polish territories it had claimed, including Poznan, Upper Silesia, and the Polish Corridor, because Hitler considered them German in the first place. Direct German administration was extended to Ukraine and Byelorussia (Belarus). Germans who lived in Poland, Lithuania, or those parts of the Soviet Union that were behind German lines were "repatriated" to Germany, or settled in the newly conquered territories (see Map 26.3).

German policies were different in Poland and Russia, whose peoples Hitler considered to be racial inferiors. Following the capture of Warsaw, Hitler had sent five special "action" squadrons to Poland with orders to wipe out the Polish upper class. All over the country, businessmen, political leaders, intellectuals, and teachers were executed or sent to extermination camps.

Norway and Denmark, deemed by Hitler to be sufficiently "Nordic" or "Aryan" to be "Germanized," were allowed relative autonomy. In Denmark, where the only elections in any country under a Nazi regime took place, the Danish Nazi Party won a paltry 2 percent of the vote. Hitler left Germany's central and southern European "independent" allies with some autonomy, depending on the extent to which they followed his wishes. Admiral Horthy ruled Hungary under increasingly close German supervision, particularly after Hitler learned that he had tried to play both sides by getting in touch with the Allies in 1942. Slovakia, which had been denied independence by the Versailles Settlements, had become autonomous when Germany marched into Czechoslovakia in 1938, splitting the country into two parts. Pro-German nationalist fascists held power in Slovakia. In wartime Romania, Ion Antonescu and his fascist Iron Guard ruled. Hitler divided Yugoslavia into the states of Serbia, Montenegro, and Croatia, allowing Hungary to annex Yugoslav territory awarded by the Versailles Settlements. Placing Serbia under direct German administration, he put Croatia and Montenegro under the rule of an authoritarian leader informally responsible to Mussolini.

MAP 26.3 HITLER'S EUROPE, 1942   Hitler's expansion to the east and west, showing the greatest extent of the German occupation of Europe and major battle sites.

The Germans imposed crushing obligations on conquered lands, including enormous financial indemnities and exchange rates that strongly favored the German currency. Germans operated factories and shipping companies in occupied lands. In France, the Germans first took movable raw materials and equipment useful for war production. As the war went on, German demands became greater; the occupation authorities closely regulated the armament, aircraft, mining, and metal industries. Some French businesses made the best of the situation, eagerly working with German firms. Others quietly subverted German demands and expectations for cooperation.

The "Final Solution"

Hitler's obsessive racial theories had become official policy in Nazi Germany before the war (see Chapter 25). For the Nazis, the process of forging the "national community" meant the elimination of groups they considered to be "outsiders." They made a temporary exception of foreign laborers, upon whom the economy depended during the war. In 1939, Hitler had ordered the killing, often by injection, of Germans who were mentally deficient and handicapped. At least 70,000 mentally retarded people perished, including children, before public objections that the victims were German halted this practice in August 1941. In addition, the Nazis sterilized between 320,000 and 350,000 German "outcasts" between 1934 and 1945; these included people determined by Nazi doctors to manifest "hereditary simple-mindedness," alcoholism, homosexuality, chronic depression, schizophrenia, or those who were deemed "work shy." Hitler also mandated experiments to determine how thousands of people could be killed "efficiently" in assembly-line fashion.

In 1939, Hitler told Heinrich Himmler (1900–1945), the leader of the S.S., to plan for the occupation of Poland and the Soviet Union. Himmler, a short, stout man whose glasses gave him the appearance of a schoolteacher, was obsessed with the pagan Germans of pre-history, establishing several spurious academic institutes to investigate his crackpot theories. Himmler welcomed Hitler's order to "eliminate the harmful influence of such alien parts of the population." Hitler announced to the Reichstag on January 30, 1939, that the result of the anticipated war would be "the annihilation of the Jewish race in Europe," the "final solution" to what Hitler considered to be the Jewish problem.

Nazi plans to exterminate Jews took shape as German military defeats mounted in Russia, where the massacre of Slavs had already begun. In January 1941, Himmler announced to S.S. leaders a change in policy. Hitler no longer wanted to transform the Slavs into a slave labor force, but rather to destroy at least 30 million of them, so that Germans eventually could occupy their lands. German troops and death squads began mass executions of Russian prisoners and civilians, killing by shooting, starvation,

Jews being massacred in Lithuania, 1942.

or exposure. Before the war ended, at least 3.3 million Soviet prisoners of war—of 5.7 million captured—died or were executed in German prisoner-of-war camps.

In October 1941, the Nazis began to prepare for the Holocaust, the genocide of European Jews. Hermann Göring ordered Reinhard Heydrich (1904–1942), the chief of the secret police, to prepare "with regard to organization, substantive, and financial viewpoints for a total solution of the Jewish question in the German sphere of influence in Europe." Even earlier, a Gestapo directive on July 17, 1941, ordered commanders of prison camps in the east to liquidate "all the Jews." By the end of 1941, 1 million Jews had been massacred. As the European conflict became a world war in December 1941, Hitler's anti-Semitic program led to the decision to destroy all Jews. Heydrich and other Nazi officials met in Wannsee, a Berlin suburb, in January 1942. There they drew up even more systematic plans for genocide.

The murders of Jews began, first in mobile vans, using carbon monoxide gas, then in the extermination camp of Auschwitz in Poland. By 1942, the Nazis had built other extermination camps, including Treblinka, surrounded by barbed-wire, electrified fences, and watchtowers (see Map 26.4). Gallows stood in an open space near the prisoners' wooden huts. But most victims were exterminated in air-tight gas chambers with Zyklon B gas, chosen because it killed with assembly-line efficiency. The victims' eyeglasses, gold from their teeth, and all other valuables became the property of the Reich.

Inmates of the camps wore tattered striped uniforms, and they were identified by numbers tattooed on their arms. They were ordered to file past an officer, who selected those deemed "unfit" for hard work. He sent them toward a building marked "shower" or "bath," and each was given, in the ultimate cynical gesture, a small piece of soap. A recent, unknowing arrival at Auschwitz inquired of another prisoner as to the whereabouts of his friend. " 'Was he sent to the left side?' . . . 'Yes,' I replied. 'Then you can see him there,' I was told. 'Where?' A hand pointed to the chimney a few hundred yards off, which was sending a column of flame up into the gray sky of Poland. It dissolved into a sinister cloud of smoke." Those people—mostly the young in relatively good health—sent toward the right would continue to live until they dropped dead of fatigue or were subsequently sent to the left side in the next "selection." At Auschwitz, the daily death count reached as high as 15,000 victims. One of the granddaughters of Alfred Dreyfus, the Jewish French lieutenant falsely accused of treason in the 1890s, perished at Auschwitz in 1944.

MAP 26.4 NAZI DEATH CAMPS   Sites of the death camps in Europe.

The fascist states of Croatia and Romania, both Germany's allies, carried out the mass murder of Jews themselves. The Romanian government killed 300,000 Jews in the provinces that the Soviets had occupied in 1940, but few in what the Romanians considered the heartland of the country. Many Lithuanian Jews were slaughtered by other Lithuanians. And in a Polish village in 1941, German troops encouraged but did not assist in the massacre of Jews by their neighbors.

Some people protected the Jews. A small French town took in Jewish children, producing identity cards for them that made them family members. In Marseille, Varian Fry, an American editor, journalist, and member of the American Refugee Committee, relentlessly planned escape routes, purchased tickets, and, where possible, obtained transit and other visas and found sponsors for about 1,000 Jews early in the war, including the painter Marc Chagall and the poet André Breton. In Amsterdam, a Christian family hid a bourgeois Dutch Jewish family in a secret apartment in their house for several years. In her resolutely cheerful diary, the young Anne Frank described her family's hiding place as "a paradise compared with how other Jews who are not in hiding must be living." It frightened her to think of her friends who had fallen into the clutches of "the cruelest brutes that walk the earth." Several months after her fourteenth birthday, the Germans discovered the Jews hidden in the secret apartment, the girl and her family were deported to Auschwitz and then Bergen-Belsen, where she and most of her family died late in 1944.

Danes saved virtually the entire Jewish population of their country in October 1943. When word came that the German occupying forces were preparing to deport Danish Jews, Danes ferried Jews across the straits to nearby neutral Sweden. Perhaps fearing that mass deportations might spark Danish resistance, in this case German authorities looked the other way. In Bulgaria, King Boris and his government, although allied with Nazi Germany, simply abandoned plans to deport the country's 50,000 Jews, despite the fact that they had been forced since early in the war to wear yellow stars (yet Bulgaria had willingly handed over to the Nazis and thus to certain death Greek and Yugoslav Jews). In Hungary, which had the largest community of Jews in Europe, 63,000 Jews had died early in the war after being deported or sent to work for the Nazis after Hungary entered the war in 1941. For three years, Admiral Horthy resisted German demands that the Jews of Hungary be sent to death camps, probably because he was concerned with the fate of Hungarian-born Jews. After German occupation in 1944, he ordered the deportations of Jews that had begun to be stopped. Yet Hungarian police killed tens of thousands of Jews in Hungary. In Croatia, where Italy had established an occupation zone, some Italian army officers protected Jews (and Serbs as well) from Croatian death squads. But when in August 1942, Germany requested that the Italians turn the Croatian Jews over to the Nazis, Mussolini wrote "no objection" across the letter. Mussolini's administrative incapacity,

Dutch Jews on their way to the trains for transport from Amsterdam to a concentration camp.

however, may have saved many Italian Jews. Furthermore, as news of more German defeats came, the Italian authorities had little interest in rounding up Italian Jews. They ignored German directives, or they could be bribed to look the other way. Some non-Jewish Romans contributed their jewelry to help raise a ransom demanded by the Germans from Jews, under threat of deportation. Others helped Jews hide. Despite the courage, determination, and luck that saved many lives, continental European Jews were, as a whole, at the mercy of the Nazis. By the end of the war, 6 million Jews had been transported in cattle cars to death camps and exterminated.

Nazi doctors performed barbaric experiments on prisoners. These included measuring the pain a patient could survive when being operated on without anesthesia; how long one could live in subfreezing temperatures; or whether prisoners would allow themselves to be killed if they thought their children might be spared. Gypsies were also Nazi targets, viewed as "biological outsiders" who were both "alien" by virtue of not being "Aryan" and "asocial," because they were nomadic. During the war, the Nazis killed about 500,000 European gypsies. Communists, socialists, and repeat criminal offenders were also considered "asocial." Many of them perished as well. Himmler persecuted homosexuals ruthlessly, in part because they would not, through procreation, help redress the losses of Germans in World War I.

One of the most haunting questions of World War II is at what point the leaders of the Allies and of neutral states actually learned that the Nazis were undertaking the extermination of an entire people. In Germany, persistent rumors of the death camps and other atrocities could be disbelieved or ignored because most of the camps themselves were outside the country, in Poland, and elsewhere. Many Germans, in any case, simply did not care. ("Who, after all, speaks today of the annihilation of the Armenians [by the Turks in 1915]?" Hitler exclaimed shortly before the outbreak of the war in 1939.) Rumors of mass exterminations had begun to reach Britain and the United States in 1942, although the details were not known. Even after confirmation provided by four young Jews who escaped from Auschwitz in the summer of 1942, and by information arriving via the Polish underground and diffused by the Polish government in London, many people—including even some leaders of the Jewish communities in Britain, Palestine, and the United States—refused to believe "the terrible secret." Articles in British, Swiss, and U.S. newspapers exposed the mass killings of Jews. Pope Pius XII (pope 1939–1958), who had served as the Vatican's representative in Berlin before his election as pope and who issued no papal encyclicals condemning anti-Semitism, knew of the death camps by the end of 1943. Yet, despite the efforts of some clergy in a number of countries to help Jews or to call attention to what was happening, the pope limited his action to occasional reminders of the necessity of "justice and charity" in the world.

The U.S. and British governments had no official reactions to the terrifying news. Some officials expressed disbelief—"wild rumors inspired by Jewish fears"—or believed reports to be exaggerated. A head of the British intelligence service claimed that Poles and Jews were exaggerating "in order to stoke us up." President Roosevelt certainly knew by the summer of 1942, but he rejected the idea of retaliatory bombing of German civilians. He believed that only a sustained military effort could defeat the Nazis. With Hitler's invasion of Russia having gone awry, it looked as though the tide was beginning to turn against Germany. The Allied governments feared that if too much publicity was given to the disappearance of hundreds of thousands of Jews—millions seemed simply too many to believe—it might generate calls to aid them directly. This, they worried, might undercut the united war effort. Hitler's "final solution"—the Holocaust—went on until the very end of the war.

Resistance to the Nazis

Everyone in German-occupied territories knew the potential cost of resistance. In Czechoslovakia, the assassination in May 1942 of Reinhard Heydrich brought savage reprisals, including the destruction of the village of Lidice, where the men were executed, the women were sent to extermination camps, and the children were scattered. When in a Yugoslav town in October 1941 partisans (loyalists) killed ten Germans, the Nazis retaliated by massacring 7,000 men, women, and children.

Resistance movements were most effective where hills and mountains offered protection from German troops, as in central and southern France, Greece, and Yugoslavia. Active and effective resistance was least possible in the flatlands of Holland, western Belgium, Moravia, and northern France, areas in which it was difficult to hide and where there were heavy concentrations of German troops, and many collaborators as well. German military strength made civilian resistance extremely difficult in Poland and in conquered regions of the Soviet Union. Wherever possible, the Allies dropped supplies to resistance groups. But only in Yugoslavia and, to a lesser extent, France, did the resistance movements help bring about Germany's military defeat.

In Yugoslavia, the tenacious Croatian Communist Josip Broz (1892–1980), who became known by his code name of Tito, formed the first army of partisans able to engage the Germans effectively in combat. Tito had worked in Germany before World War I. He had served in the Austro-Hungarian army during World War I and was badly wounded and captured. Returning in 1920 to newly independent Yugoslavia, Tito became an active trade unionist and in 1923 joined the Yugoslav Communist Party. After spending six years in prison, he went to Moscow and then returned to Yugoslavia as general secretary of the Communist Party there.

Tito's partisans fought courageously against the collaborationist Yugoslav puppet states. The Croatian puppet state killed 300,000 Serbs (sparing some deemed "redeemable" because they may have had some Croat ancestors) and sought to convert survivors by force to Catholicism. The minister of education voiced the opinion that a third of the Serbs should be forced to convert, a third expelled from Croatia, and a third killed. Use of the Cyrillic alphabet became illegal. When asked if he did not fear the punishment of God for what he had done, a fascist (Ustaša) guard retorted, "Don't talk to me about that. . . . For my past, present and future deeds I shall burn in hell, but at least I shall burn for Croatia." At the same time, members of the conservative Serb resistance (Chetniks) killed thousands of non-Serbs.

Tito insisted on cooperation between Serb and Croat resisters, and maintained contacts with non-Communist groups. Protected by the rugged mountains of Croatia, Tito commanded 20,000 men by 1943. Despite being hounded by German, Italian, Bulgarian, and both Croatian and Serb fascist troops, he managed to carve out entire zones under his control. Late in the war, the British government ended support for the Chetniks and began to supply Tito's forces with heavy equipment. Yugoslav partisans tied up entire Italian and German divisions. Tito established local Communist committees to serve as governing authorities in each liberated region, and gained support from the Western Allies.

In Western Europe, the Nazis found leaders willing to follow German directives obediently and often enthusiastically. In Belgium, principally in Flanders, the Dutch-speaking part of the country, the German occupation gave the fascist leagues influence they had not had before the war. France, by its armistice with Germany in June 1940, had been divided into an occupied zone and a much smaller southern zone that retained independence through collaboration with the Nazis. The free zone had its capital in the spa town of Vichy in central France, although in November 1942 German troops occupied this so-called free zone. The xenophobia and anti-Semitism of the right-wing French politicians and writers of the 1930s came to fruition in Vichy. Traditional conservatives dissatisfied with the Third Republic for religious and political reasons also lent their support to Vichy.

The elderly Marshal Pétain served as the head of state of the Vichy government, which the United States officially recognized. He remained popular, at least until late 1942, because many people in France shared his anti-Marxism and anti-Semitism. He was widely credited with having saved the French state from extinction at the hands of the German invaders.

But although Vichy may have temporarily saved the French state, Pétain and other collaborators sacrificed the French nation. In the "new order," "Country, Family, Work" replaced "Liberty, Fraternity, Equality" on French coins. Vichy proclaimed a "spiritual revival" against "decadence." Pétain dissolved the Chamber of Deputies and favored the Catholic

Marshal Tito (Josip Broz), pictured on the right, Communist head of the Yugoslav Resistance, with his wartime staff in the mountains of Yugoslavia, 1944.

Church by banning Masonic lodges and divorce. Vichy attempted to impose a new structure of "corporatism" on the French economy and society; these vertical economic structures were intended to eliminate social conflict and replace trade unions, which, as in Germany, became illegal.

Vichy's policies toward Jews revealed the extent of its collaboration with the Nazis. Vichy enacted restrictions on Jews similar to those in force in Germany. Beginning in October 1940, a series of laws forbade Jews from holding jobs in public service, education, or cultural affairs, or in professions such as medicine and law. A law promulgated in July 1941 sought "to eliminate all Jewish influence in the national economy"; the state appointed a trustee who could sell any property or liquidate any business owned by Jews.

These exclusions were only the beginning. French police cooperated with German soldiers after Hitler's May 1941 order to round up 3,600 Polish Jews in France. In December, the Vichy government proclaimed that it would collaborate with the Nazis with "acts, not words." In July 1942, the French police seized 13,000 Jews, most of them foreign-born, in Paris, sending them to extermination camps in Germany. Premier Pierre Laval (1883–1945) insisted that children be sent with their parents to the German death camps. A Parisian woman later recalled, "I saw a train pass. In front, a car containing French police and German soldiers. Then came cattle cars, sealed. The thin arms of children clasped the grating. A hand waved outside like a leaf in a storm. When the train slowed down, voices cried, 'Mama!' And nothing answered except the squeaking of the springs of the train." Vichy France was the only territory in Europe in which local authorities deported Jews without the presence of German occupying forces.

The legacy of French resistance to German occupation and to Vichy France was ultimately more significant than that of collaboration. On June 18, 1940, General Charles de Gaulle, broadcasting from London, called on the French people to resist German rule. The next month, Churchill established an agency in London to provide material assistance to resistance groups.

Churchill grudgingly respected de Gaulle, but he also detested him. The same room could not hold the two domineering personalities, a fact compounded by Churchill's bad French. Roosevelt, who considered the towering general "well-nigh intolerable," believed de Gaulle dangerously ambitious, a potential thorn in the Allied side. In December 1941, de Gaulle had surprised the Allies by sending a small force to capture the French islands of Saint Pierre and Miquelon off the coast of Newfoundland, which were controlled by Vichy France.

Roosevelt believed that there was nothing to be gained from recognizing de Gaulle's London-based "Free French" movement as the legitimate French government. The U.S. government hoped that Vichy might be convinced to collaborate less openly with Nazi Germany and, above all, to try

The Vichy *milice* (police) raiding a French farmhouse looking for *maquis*.

to keep French North Africa out of German hands. The British and U.S. governments worried that recognizing de Gaulle's movement might alienate most of the French population. Anti-British Vichy propaganda repeatedly reminded the public that 1,300 French sailors had been killed when the British navy, fearing that they might fall into German hands, had sunk a battleship, a battle cruiser, and several destroyers in July 1940 as they lay in port at Mers el-Kébir in Algeria.

Several resistance movements in France were united only by a hatred of Nazi occupation and Vichy collaboration. Communists, despite not officially turning against Vichy until Germany attacked the Soviet Union in June 1941, formed a well-organized and effective resistance force in France. Jean Moulin, a former departmental prefect during the Third Republic, led de Gaulle's Free French resistance in France. Moulin managed early in May 1943 to unify the resistance groups within the National Council of Resistance. He was betrayed by a collaborator and died under torture in July 1943 without revealing the names of others in the resistance network.

Resistance spread when the Germans in 1943 began to force France to provide workers for factories in Germany. Many of those refusing to go to Germany fled into the hills and mountains of France. These resistance bands came to be called the *maquis*, a name for rugged brush in the south of France that could conceal them.

Better armed by airplane drops of guns, the *maquis* grew bolder. On the three occasions they challenged German troops in open conflict, the results were disastrous. But by 1944, the *maquis* controlled several regions of southern France, at least at night, vulnerable only to the arrival of German military columns, diversions that the German army could by then ill afford. General Dwight Eisenhower (1890–1969), commander of Allied forces in the European theater of operations, later perhaps exaggerated when he said that the resistance in France was the equivalent of fifteen military divisions. The French resistance would enable de Gaulle, who would perpetuate the myth that all resistance had been in his name, to emerge from the war with great personal prestige that would contribute to France's rebuilding.

Against Hitler in Germany

The vast majority of Germans remained loyal to their Führer, even as the war dragged on and defeats mounted. The German minister of propaganda, Joseph Goebbels (who once said "a lie told over and over again becomes a truth") sought to maintain civilian commitment and confidence in ultimate victory, even as Allied bombers frequently droned overhead and news of horrendous losses on the Russian front became known. Disgruntlement and bitter jokes were common, but they did not threaten the regime. Those who had never approved of Hitler retreated into family life and the daily economic struggle to get by. When wartime deprivation left people grumbling, Germans tended to blame Hitler's subordinates, not the Führer.

German resistance against Hitler was fragmented and ineffective. Courts sentenced 15,000 Germans to death for crimes against the state, under an expanded definition of capital crimes, which included listening to BBC radio broadcasts from London. Trade union and Communist groups, earlier smashed by the S.S., emerged again as economic conditions worsened in 1942 and 1943. Some students in Munich and Communists in Berlin bravely distributed anti-Nazi propaganda, but such courageous acts were not widespread. About 250,000 people in Germany were imprisoned or forced to emigrate because of their political opposition and at least 150,000 German Communists were put in extermination camps, and a good many other people were tortured and killed before they got that far. The active connivance of ordinary Germans, who continued to step forward to denounce neighbors for being Jewish or for their political beliefs or statements, aided the S.S. and the Gestapo in rooting out potential sources of opposition. Even humane gestures toward Jews or foreign workers were dangerous. Here and there, young people responded to Nazism by adopting a counterculture of nonconformity, refusing to join the Hitler Youth, listening to American music deemed decadent by Hitler, and scrawling anti-Nazi graffiti on walls. The Nazis publicly hanged several sixteen-year-old boys for such actions. But this dissident subculture represented no more than a mild irritation to the Nazis.

The only serious plot against Hitler came among traditional conservatives within the army. Opposition among officers emerged, not out of a hatred for Nazi ideals or because they did not share Hitler's territorial ambitions, but rather from growing anxiety that Hitler's military decisions would lead to German defeat.

On July 20, 1944, Colonel Claus von Stauffenberg (1907–1944) carried a bomb in his briefcase to a staff meeting with Hitler near the Russian front. Stauffenberg, who had been badly maimed in battle, was a conservative aristocrat appalled by the systematic Nazi murder of Jews and Soviets and by what he considered Hitler's amateur management of the war. He hoped that Hitler's assassination would allow the army to impose a fascist state similar to that of Italy. He placed the bomb under the table beneath Hitler, who instinctively shoved the briefcase out of his way, moving it to the other side of a heavy table support. The bomb exploded, wounding Hitler slightly. Those implicated in the plot were quickly arrested and slowly strangled by nooses of piano wire as they writhed on meat hooks. Movie cameras recorded their agonizing death for the later amusement of Hitler, his mistress, and friends. Hitler also ordered the execution of about 5,000 other Germans in positions of authority whose loyalty seemed suspect. A decree of "liability of next of kin" led to the arrest of family members of leading conspirators. Thousands of Germans turned out in several major cities to celebrate their Führer's escape from death. Until the very end, Hitler appeared to hold the allegiance of most Germans.

THE TIDE TURNS

By the end of 1942, the Germans were on the defensive on the high seas, in the Soviet Union, and in North Africa, where Italian forces were routed and German forces pushed back (see Map 26.5). The entry of the United States into the Second World War helped turn the tide against Germany. American war supplies and then armed forces strengthened the Allied cause as they had in World War I. The German war machine was chaotically managed and German resources increasingly inadequate to fighting a war on so many fronts.

Hitler's invasion of Russia turned into a full-fledged military disaster, culminating in the crushing, costly defeat and surrender of German forces at Stalingrad in February 1943. As Hitler's Balkan allies one by one pulled out of the war, the Allies launched an invasion of Italy from North Africa, forcing the king of Italy to agree to a secret armistice and pushing German troops to retreat to the north. On June 6, 1944, Western Allied forces launched a massive invasion of France, landing on the beaches of Normandy, and forcing the German army to pull back, fighting all the way. The Allies first reached the Rhine River in March 1945.

MAP 26.5 THE DEFEAT OF GERMANY, 1942–1945 Allied advances and Axis withdrawal up to the end of World War II.

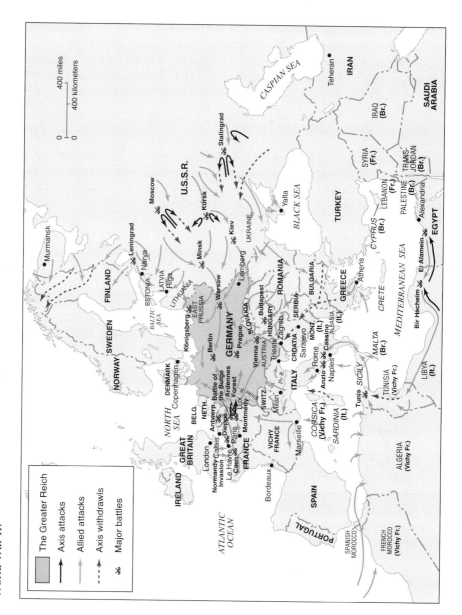

Now confident of victory over Hitler, the Big Three (Churchill, Roosevelt, and Stalin) began to plan for the end of the war. As the Soviet army began to push the Germans back across a broad front in July 1943, it became clear that when the war ended, the Red Army could control large parts of Eastern and Central Europe. This probability brought dissension to the Big Three, particularly as Churchill feared that the Red Army might never leave the Eastern European nations it liberated from German occupation.

Germany on the Defensive

With the majority of German men between the ages of eighteen and fifty in the army, Germany's war machine required new workers. By late 1941, there were already 4 million foreigners working in Germany, including prisoners of war (in violation of international agreements), and in May 1944, almost twice that number, the majority of whom were Soviet citizens. More German women now worked in the factories, despite Hitler's view that women should only be housekeepers and bearers of Aryan warriors. German industry increasingly depended upon conscript labor from conquered countries.

In the meantime, Germany's day-to-day operation of the war effort remained chaotic, as ministries, military branches, and Hitler's favored henchmen competed against each other. In the spring of 1942, Hitler named the architect Albert Speer to be minister of armaments production. Speer's organizational skill helped triple German armaments production within two years. But not until 1944 did Hitler grant Speer responsibility for the needs of the air force, Göring's personal preserve. Hitler then awarded Göring "plenipotentiary powers" over the entire war effort. Unlike his enemies, Hitler thus resisted carefully coordinated state planning, which he believed smacked of communism. German war supplies remained inadequate to the enormous goals Hitler had set. Gradually, realists like Speer began to see a German military victory as difficult, even improbable.

As in World War I, German military commanders placed their hopes on closing Allied shipping lanes across the Atlantic, thereby preventing supplies from reaching Britain. Many American ships and crews went down in the icy Atlantic. However, most got through. German U-boats, the hunters, became the hunted. New submarine-detecting devices enabled airplanes and destroyers to sink German submarines with depth charges.

The War in North Africa

With the failure of the submarine campaign against Allied shipping, Germany now had to depend on its army's success on land. In North Africa, the German tank division commanded by Erwin Rommel, by now known as the "Desert Fox" because of his quick judgment and daring tactical improvisations, had forced British troops back from Libya into Egypt. Victories in the spring of 1942 at Bir Hacheim and Tobruk, where the Germans captured a garrison of 35,000 British troops, put Rommel only sixty miles from Alexandria. However, at the end of August 1942, the British tank force of General Bernard Montgomery (1887–1976) pushed back another Rommel offensive. Montgomery knew his enemy's plan of attack in advance through reports from British intelligence services. The Allied forces, enjoying superior strength and controlling the skies, then attacked Rommel's forces, breaking through the German and Italian defenses at El Alamein (in Egypt) in early November 1942. For the next ten weeks they pursued the German armored division across the desert all the way to Tunisia.

The Allies now faced major strategic decisions. Churchill wanted to strike at what he called the "soft underbelly" of the axis through Italy, the Balkans, and the Danube Basin after driving Hitler's armies from North Africa. This would leave British forces in an excellent position to protect British interests in the Middle East. Stalin, however, continued to insist on a major Allied attack against Germany in the west to force Hitler to divert resources from the Russian campaign. Stalin pointed out that the Red Army had borne the brunt of the war against Hitler, inflicting 90 percent of the losses the German armed forces had suffered in battle since June 1941. Churchill, however, feared that a direct confrontation with the largest concentration of German troops might be disastrous and wanted to postpone a cross-Channel invasion of France as long as possible.

Royal British Marines attacking the beach of North Africa, 1944.

With the Axis reeling in North Africa and British troops now controlling Egypt and Libya, the Allied commanders now decided first to drive all German and Italian troops out of North Africa before contemplating an invasion of France from Britain. They had been sobered by a disastrous cross-Channel raid by Canadian troops against the French port of Dieppe in August 1942 and feared that a massive invasion in France might fail.

In November 1942, the Allies launched "Operation Torch." A British and American force commanded by American General Dwight Eisenhower landed on the coast of French Algeria and Morocco and easily overcame Vichy resistance. To his shock and consternation, de Gaulle now learned that the Allies were negotiating with the Vichy commander in North Africa, Admiral Jean Darlan (1881–1942). Despite Pétain's order that Vichy forces in North Africa continue to oppose the Allied invasion, Darlan ordered his troops to accept a cease-fire after three days of fighting. Hitler used Darlan's capitulation in North Africa as an excuse in November 1942 for German forces to occupy the "free" zone of Vichy France. Little now remained of Vichy's illusion of independence. French naval commanders scuttled their own ships to prevent them from being used by the German navy.

The Allies named Darlan as "the head of the French state" in return for his promise that French troops in North Africa would now join the Allies. Darlan's extreme right-wing views and close association with Vichy collaborators soon left him without much British or American support, however. De Gaulle demanded that Britain and the United States recognize his French Committee of National Liberation as France's legitimate government. But Churchill, an old imperialist, viewed with concern de Gaulle's pressing determination to maintain France's empire, especially in the context of the two powers' long-standing imperial rivalry. Churchill feared that if the British government recognized de Gaulle as the head of the French state, it would be committing itself to supporting a new France, the direction of which could hardly then be seen. A French monarchist solved part of the Allied dilemma by assassinating Darlan. The Allies forced de Gaulle to share leadership of Free France with another general, a slap in the face that de Gaulle neither forgot nor forgave. After the defeat of a vigorous German counterattack, by the end of May 1943, no German or Italian troops remained in North Africa.

The Allies' strategic bombing campaign, the goal of which was to sap German morale as much as to hamper the production of planes and guns, began to take its toll in 1943. The American poet Randall Jarrell remembered, "In bombers named for girls, we burned / The cities we had learned about in school." The Royal Air Force could now strike at night with reasonable accuracy, while scrambling German radar, thereby reducing losses. British bombers dumped tons of bombs during night raids over the industrial Ruhr area and major cities. Many American bombers were lost despite fighter escorts because the U.S. Air Force preferred daytime attacks, when pilots could more easily find their targets. The impact of the strategic bombing campaign on German wartime industrial production was far below Allied expectations, however, particularly given the great number of planes and crews lost.

Hitler's Russian Disaster

On the eastern front, Hitler's invasion of the Soviet Union turned into a military disaster. Defeats in Russia during the last months of 1942 and in 1943 sent the German invaders reeling. Hitler's armies had been forced to retreat from the Moscow region. The Red Army was now receiving better and more plentiful supplies from the Allies through the icy northern port of Murmansk and from Iran in the south. By now Soviet factories were turning out a steady supply of tanks and trucks equipped to fight in the snow and ice. German tanks faced not only improved Soviet tanks but also handmade incendiary bombs consisting of bottles, gasoline, and cloth fuses that became known as "Molotov cocktails," after the Soviet foreign minister Vyacheslav Molotov.

Improvements in the organization and discipline of the Red Army also made their mark. Unlike Hitler, Stalin delegated authority to efficient and trusted party members during the war, holding in abeyance the ideological indoctrination and murderous purges that had characterized much of the Soviet Union's post-revolutionary period. The Soviet army that Hitler had once mocked, now larger and more effectively deployed than his own, wore down German forces.

In the north, Leningrad, first reached by German troops in July 1941, held on against a German siege that lasted 506 days, the longest in modern history, and that killed at least 650,000 Russian civilians. Hitler's printed invitations to celebrate Leningrad's fall could never be sent out. Further defeats in the north made Germany's drive to the Soviet oil fields of the Caucasus Mountains, and the Donets Basin industrial region in the south, all the more critical. In the south, the Red Army slowed the German advance toward Stalingrad, a strategically located industrial city on the Volga River.

The battle of Stalingrad was a great turning point in the European war. The Soviets had begun concentrating a huge force around the city, even as early German successes deluded Hitler into thinking Stalingrad's fall was inevitable. In November 1942, as Soviet troops held off the German assault in house-to-house fighting, Hitler confidently began to transfer some of his exhausted troops to the north. The Soviet army counterattacked on November 19, trapping the weakened German armies as Soviet tanks moved easily across the frozen ground. From Berlin, Hitler ordered his troops to hold out until the last man. By the time German survivors surrendered on February 2, 1943, the German army had lost more than 300,000 soldiers.

Red Army soldiers pick their way through the rubble of Stalingrad.

Soviet troops then fought their way into Leningrad, which had been besieged by the German army. In July 1943, in a battle involving more than 9,000 tanks, the Red Army won a great victory in and around the city of Kursk, 500 miles south of Moscow. The Soviets repelled a massive German attack against an exposed Soviet line of defense and then pushed the Germans back, with a huge loss of life. The greatest tank battle ever fought further depleted the German armored divisions that had once seemed invincible, putting an end to the tactic of *Blitzkrieg*. The Soviets were now battering their enemy on three fronts, even as Hitler was forced to divert troops to Italy and the Balkans. The Red Army recaptured all of the Crimea in the south by May 1943, pushing the Germans back to Ukraine in the summer.

In February 1944, Soviet troops reached what had been the eastern Polish border before the German invasion. In the meantime, waves of British and American bombers devastated German cities; over 40,000 people perished in attacks on Hamburg in July 1943, during which more than 9,000 tons of bombs rained down on the port city.

One by one, Germany's Balkan allies bailed out. Romanian troops had greatly aided the Nazi campaign in Odessa and the Crimea; Romanian oil and wheat had fueled the German war effort. Now, in March 1944, seeing the writing on the wall, the Romanian government approached the Allies, hoping to arrange a separate peace. In August, King Michael finally ended Ion Antonescu's military dictatorship, and the new government declared war on Germany. The Red Army soon poured into the country, occupying Bucharest in late August 1944.

Hitler intended Bulgaria to serve as a buffer against a possible Allied invasion from Turkey. Bulgaria enjoyed the most autonomy of any Nazi-held Eastern European state because it provided Germany with badly needed grain, had permitted the establishment of military bases on its territory, and had declared war on Britain and the United States in 1941. Hitler had allowed Bulgaria to annex Thrace from Greece (where Bulgarian forces executed thousands of Greeks and banned the Greek language) and to take Greek and Yugoslav Macedonia. Now, as Germany's defeat appeared increasingly likely, the Bulgarian government brazenly announced its war against the Allies had ended. But the Soviet Union declared war on Bulgaria on September 5, 1944. Following a popular insurrection, the Soviet Union controlled the resulting coalition government, as in the case of Romania. Soviet domination of the Balkan states began to take shape.

The Allied Invasion of Italy

With North Africa and its airfields secure, the Allies decided to invade Sicily as a first step in an invasion of southern Italy. The plunging morale and material conditions of the Italian population, who had been promised an empire by Mussolini but had received only hardship, contributed to the Allied decision.

In July 1943, Palermo and Messina quickly fell to Allied troops. The fascist Grand Council asked King Victor Emmanuel III to end Mussolini's dictatorship. The king, eager to save his throne and fearing a complete German takeover, dismissed and arrested the stunned Mussolini as prime minister. The new government, while announcing that Italy would continue to fight alongside of Germany, had begun secret negotiations with the Allies. When Hitler learned this in September 1943, he ordered his troops to occupy Italian airfields.

Churchill remained determined that the Allies should now invade Italy's mainland. At a minimum, such an invasion would tie up considerable numbers of German troops and probably knock Italy completely out of the war. Romanian oil fields would be within reach of bombers taking off in Italy. The Italian resistance had gained momentum. Socialists, Catholic groups, and, above all, Communists began to print clandestine newspapers and organize scattered attacks against fascists. The United States, still pushing for a full-scale landing in France, reluctantly agreed to the Italian invasion. The German high command hoped to stop the Allied offensive in northern and central Italy, near Florence. In the meantime, the Italian king, fearing Hitler's wrath, reassured Germany of Italy's loyal participation in the war as an ally. However, the new Italian government signed an armistice with the Allies on September 3, 1943. Victor Emmanuel naively hoped that Italy could make peace with both

Germany and the Allies, and that his monarchy would survive the end of the war.

On the same day that the armistice was signed between Italy and the Allies, British and Canadian troops crossed the Strait of Messina, beginning an invasion of the Italian peninsula. The king and his family fled Rome with the prime minister, leaving a million Italian soldiers with the choice of being interned by the Germans or deserting their units. Most deserted, and 80,000 Allied prisoners of war escaped from camps in Italy.

The Allies set up a new government in the south, its members drawn from the resistance groups. In the meantime, on September 12, 1943, a daring German commando raid had freed Mussolini from a mountaintop prison. In Berlin, Hitler proclaimed the Duce head of the "Italian Social Republic," a puppet regime. Mussolini ordered the execution of the members of the Grand Council who had opposed him and denounced the Italian people for having betrayed him.

The Germans slowly retreated behind one river after the next, with both sides taking large losses. The new front settled on a series of fortifications a hundred miles south of Rome, over which stood the old monastery of Monte Cassino. In January 1944, two Allied divisions landed behind the German lines at Anzio. They did so at the instigation of Churchill, who sought the capture of Rome as quickly as possible. Only in the spring, after terrible losses, were Allied troops able to break through the German defenses to free their armies still trapped near Anzio. The Allies took Rome on June 4, 1944. The German armies fell back to establish a new defensive perimeter south of the Po River between Pisa and Florence.

(*Left*) Hamburg Germany, after Allied bombing. (*Right*) The devastated Stuttgart after Allied bombing.

The Big Three

Soviet advances against German forces increasingly focused Western attention on the future of Central and Eastern Europe once Hitler's Germany had been defeated. At their Casablanca meeting in January 1943, Churchill and Roosevelt had concerned themselves only with military strategy and not with the future of Europe. With Stalin absent, the British and American governments agreed to put off discussions of the territorial settlements that would follow Germany's defeat. Churchill and Stalin had already informally agreed to Soviet absorption of the Baltic states after the war. They did so despite the opposition of Roosevelt, who argued that Stalin had joined the war against the Nazis only after Hitler had attacked the Soviet Union.

Stalin's insistence that the United States and Britain open another front in the west by invading France in part stemmed from his fear that his allies wanted to see the Red Army slowed in its drive westward. As deliveries of Allied supplies to Russia through Murmansk trickled to a halt, Stalin seemed confirmed in his suspicions.

Meeting at Moscow in October 1943, the British, American, and Soviet foreign ministers reaffirmed an agreement that the Allies would accept nothing less than Germany's unconditional surrender. The Allies also reaffirmed their intention, originally stated in the Atlantic Charter of August 1941 signed by Roosevelt and Churchill, that a United Nations organization replace the ineffective, moribund League of Nations. But again they left open the thorny question of the political future of Central and Eastern Europe after the war.

Stalin finally met Churchill and Roosevelt in Teheran in November 1943. Amid heavy meals and clinking glasses, the leaders formulated harsh plans for post-war Germany. Stalin stated that the Soviet Union was not about to contemplate any change in its border with Poland as it existed in June 1941, the result of the Soviet invasion and absorption of much of eastern Poland in 1939. Yet, despite the occasional flurry of improvisational map-making—using knives, forks, and matchboxes on the tablecloths—the Big Three left the essential specifics of the proposed outlines of post-war Europe for the future.

The D-Day Invasion of France

At Teheran, Stalin and Roosevelt convinced Churchill to accept a plan for the invasion of France. General Dwight Eisenhower coordinated the "D-Day" landing in France, dubbed "Operation Overlord." Born in a small town in Kansas, Eisenhower was a forthright man of integrity. Beneath his sparkling blue eyes, folksy manner, and smile ("He had only to smile at you," Montgomery once said, "and there was nothing you would not do for him") lay shrewdness, cunning, and a remarkable ability

A modern armada of ships puts ashore military supplies following the D-Day invasion, June 1944.

for organization. The plan was for 150,000 troops to attack the English Channel beaches of Normandy in western France, followed in the next days and weeks by almost 500,000 more. About 4 million tons of support materiel would have to be landed as well. Floating caissons and old ships sunk off the coast would provide three makeshift harbors. In the meantime, German commanders believed that the most likely place for an all-out assault was near Calais to the north, offering the closest crossing points from England.

The first hours of Operation Overlord would be crucial. The Allies needed to take and protect a beachhead that would allow the bulk of their troops to get ashore quickly. Planes would drop squadrons of parachutists behind German lines. Hitler had assigned General Rommel to organize the German defense against the Allied invasion. His defenders would depend on the rapid arrival of armored units to back up the coastal batteries and infantry units trying to hold their positions against attacking Allied troops.

After a one-day postponement because of a gale, at dawn on the morning of June 6, 1944, Allied troops struggled ashore in shallow water from landing craft and established beachheads on the coast of Normandy. They confronted murderous fire from the cliffs above, taking heavy losses. But the landing succeeded, at least partially because the German air force was outnumbered by 20 to 1, preventing rapid German reinforcement. As more men, tanks, trucks, and materiel came ashore, German troops gradually fell back. By the end of July 1944, despite fierce resistance, the Allies held most of Normandy. After seven weeks, the Allies had landed 1.3 million troops and sustained over 120,000 casualties. The Germans lost 500,000 men trying to defend Normandy. Hitler allowed Rommel, discovered to have known about the plot against the Führer's life, to escape execution by committing suicide.

On August 15, 1944, another Allied army landed on the French Mediterranean coast and moved up the Rhône Valley with little opposition. The main Allied army pushed toward Paris. On August 19, an uprising of the resistance movement began in Paris. Because de Gaulle demanded that a French unit be the first to reach the capital, French forces reached Paris on August 22, 1944. De Gaulle himself entered Paris on August 25. Finally, in October the British government recognized de Gaulle's administration as the legitimate government of France.

German resistance stiffened at the Rhine River and the first Allied attempts to cross into Germany failed. Hitler, whose moods varied between wild optimism and resigned depression, had aged rapidly and trembled through recurring bouts with illness. Now, although Germany's collapse seemed imminent, he again seemed confident, telling Albert Speer in November 1944, "I haven't the slightest intention of surrendering. Besides, November has always been my lucky month." In December, Hitler ordered a massive counterattack in the hills and forests of the Ardennes in Belgium and Luxembourg, with the goal of pushing rapidly toward the Belgian river port of Antwerp. At Montmédy, a German S.S. unit massacred captured American soldiers. News of the incident spread rapidly along the front. After retreating forty-five miles, the U.S. army pushed the Germans back in the Battle of the Bulge.

As the Nazi army retreated in northern Italy, the Red Army approached Germany from the east. On every front, Allied troops increasingly found that their enemies turned out to be boys and elderly men who had been rushed to the front with virtually no training. German cities burned, notably Dresden, which American planes fire-bombed early in 1945. About 50,000 residents of Berlin died in Allied air attacks. The Allies dropped 315 tons of bombs on Germany for every 1 ton the Luftwaffe had dropped on Britain in 1940. In 1993, about one World War II bomb every day was still being discovered unexploded in Berlin. The American army crossed the Rhine River on March 8 and on April 25, 1945, met up with Soviet troops at the Elbe River just sixty miles south of Berlin.

Hitler, expressing confidence that the Big Three alliance would break up, held out hope for Germany's newly developed weapons, in which he had earlier expressed no interest: the deadly V-1 jet-propelled "flying bomb" could strike targets from 3,000 feet at speeds of 470 miles per hour; the terrifying V-2 rocket could fly faster than the speed of sound. Launched from France, the first V-1 struck London on June 12, 1944, doing considerable damage. The first jet- and rocket-propelled fighter planes, the former reaching speeds of 500 miles per hour, arrived in time to join the Battle of the Bulge, but without significant effect.

With defeat ever closer, Hitler accepted, even desired, the total destruction of Germany, considering it better than the shame of surrender: "If the war is lost, the people will be lost also. It is not necessary for us to worry about what the German people will need in order to survive. On the contrary, it is best for us to destroy even these things."

ALLIED VICTORY

Romania and Bulgaria had surrendered in August and September 1944, respectively. With the Red Army in control of much of the Balkans, the question was not if Berlin would be taken, but when, and by whom. Though worried that the Soviets sought a preponderant role in Central Europe, Eisenhower was prepared to allow Stalin the prestige of capturing Berlin. The much greater problem still remained: the future of Germany and Eastern Europe. As the Red Army moved closer to Berlin, the meetings of the Big Three in the waning months of the year proved exceptionally important for the future of Europe. Churchill and Stalin met in Moscow in October 1944 and worked out a rough division of post-war Western and Soviet interests in Central and Eastern Europe. By the time the Big Three came together at Yalta in Crimea in March 1945, German armies were falling back rapidly on every front, and the Red Army was closing in on Berlin.

Victory in Europe

Churchill was determined to work out an informal agreement with the Soviets as to the respective spheres of influence in the Balkans when the war ended. In October 1944, he met with Stalin in Moscow. This time Roosevelt, who suspected Churchill of trying to maintain the British Empire at all costs, did not participate. Churchill later described the conference with Stalin: "I said, 'Let us settle about our affairs in the Balkans. . . . How would it do for you to have ninety percent of the say in Romania, for us to have ninety percent of the say in Greece, and go fifty-fifty about Yugoslavia?' " After adding 75 percent for the Soviet Union in Bulgaria and fifty-fifty for Hungary, the British prime minister pushed the paper across to Stalin. "There was a slight pause. Then he took his blue

Joseph Stalin, Franklin Roosevelt, Winston Churchill, and Vyacheslav Molotov at the Yalta Conference, 1945.

pencil and made a large tick upon it, and passed it back to us. It was all settled in no more time than it takes to sit down."

When the Big Three met in the Black Sea resort of Yalta in February 1945, the Red Army had drawn within 100 miles of Berlin. The Yalta meeting, then, would be crucial for the future of post-war Europe. Churchill agreed to the post-war division of Germany into British, American, Soviet, and French zones of military occupation. Already in Eastern Europe, Communist Party members were working feverishly to expand Soviet influence. Stalin feared that his wartime Allies might lead a post-war campaign against communism, which had been the case after World War I. He agreed to Roosevelt's demand that the Soviet Union declare war on Japan, which the U.S. president believed would expedite Japan's defeat in Asia. But, in exchange, Stalin asked for and received Allied promises that the Soviet Union would control Outer Mongolia, the Kurile Islands, and the southern half of Sakhalin Island, both north of Japan.

In Poland, the Soviets had established a provisional government dominated by Polish Communists. At Yalta, the other Allies went along with Stalin's insistence that the provisional government (to which would be added representatives from the non-Communist Polish government, which had been functioning in London during the war) would become Poland's new government. Churchill and Roosevelt also went along with Stalin's insistence that the Soviet Union would keep the parts of eastern Poland that had been absorbed by the Soviet invasion in 1939. Poland's western frontier with Germany was to be left to a future conference, one that was never held. The Big Three all agreed that free elections would be held in Eastern Europe.

At Yalta, the Allies agreed that the League of Nations had been doomed in its attempts to keep the peace by the nonparticipation of the then-isolationist United States and by the exclusion of the Soviet Union from the League. They now agreed that the United States and the Soviet Union would be permanent members of the Security Council of the new United Nations. Roosevelt wanted to avoid committing the United States to an active role in post-war Europe; he counted instead on the proposed United Nations to resolve future problems. He also took a dim view of Churchill's commitment to the maintenance of the British Empire, which Roosevelt thought not in keeping with the principle of self-determination.

The awful war now moved toward an end. The Red Army launched a final attack on Berlin in April 1945. Italian partisans captured Mussolini near the Swiss frontier. They executed him and his mistress, hanging their bodies upside down at a gas station. Himmler, von Ribbentrop, and Göring now agreed that Germany must end the war. As Soviet tanks drew near on the night of April 28–29, 1945, Hitler married his longtime mistress, Eva Braun, in the depths of a fortified bunker in central Berlin. Then they committed suicide on April 30 as the rumble of Russian tanks

Soldiers from the Red Army hoist the Soviet flag over the German Reichstag in Berlin.

could be heard above. Joseph Goebbels poisoned his six children, shot his wife, and killed himself. Admiral Karl Dönitz, to whom Hitler had delegated authority, surrendered to the Allies on behalf of Germany on May 8, 1945. The Reich that Hitler had once bragged would last for a thousand years lay in ruins twelve years after its creation.

The Defeat of Japan

The German collapse in North Africa, Russia, and Eastern Europe now allowed the Allies to turn their attention more fully to the war in the Pacific. The sheer scope of Japanese military operations, spread from the Aleutian Islands southwest of Alaska to the South Pacific, put Japan on the defensive. Troops and supplies poured into the Pacific from the United States, which had speedily reconstituted its fleet after the Pearl Harbor disaster. Victory in the Battle of the Coral Sea (May 1942), which turned back Japanese ships carrying troops to the southern coast of New Guinea, protected Australia from possible invasion. A month later, the American fleet and torpedo bombers inflicted a major defeat on the Japanese navy at the Battle of Midway, an island almost a thousand miles northeast of Hawaii (see Map 26.2). Four Japanese aircraft carriers were sunk.

In August 1942, an American offensive had begun against Guadalcanal, one of the South Pacific Solomon Islands. Guadalcanal fell on February 8,

1943, the first of the Japanese wartime conquests to be recaptured. American assaults in New Guinea and far north in the Aleutian Islands also succeeded. General MacArthur's forces began driving the Japanese from New Guinea in January 1943, completing the task early in 1944. From then on, the Americans adopted the strategy of driving Japanese forces from one island to another, "leapfrogging" through the Pacific. Some Japanese forces were still tied down in China, and others were scattered on the islands of the Pacific Ocean. Gradually, the U.S. navy gained control of the seas, its submarines picking off Japanese supply ships. A Japanese invasion of India, begun from Burma in March 1944, failed in July. With the help of a Chinese attack from the north, British troops recaptured Burma. Hard-earned summer victories brought U.S. troops within 1,400 miles of Tokyo. On October 20, 1944, MacArthur's forces attacked the Philippines, defeating the Japanese fleet and the demoralized Japanese troops. There, the Japanese first used kamikaze tactics, suicide missions flown by pilots who crashed their planes into American ships.

The American capture of the island of Iwo Jima on March 27, 1945, brought U.S. planes to within 700 miles of Japan. On Okinawa, the next stop, piles of bleached human bones could still be seen on the beaches a decade after the war's end. A U.S. marine remembered, "Replacements [got] hit before we even knew their names. They came up confused, frightened, and hopeful, got wounded or killed, and went right back to the rear on the route by which they had come, shocked, bleeding, or stiff." Saipan and Guam provided bases from which American long-range bombers could reach Japan. As the Japanese army reeled back in China, American "superfortress" bombers showered Japanese cities with incendiary bombs that turned wooden buildings into fiery death traps. One attack destroyed 40 percent of Tokyo within three hours. Japan's five largest cities lay in ruins. American forces prepared to invade the southern islands of Japan itself. With the American fleet off Okinawa confronting suicide missions by Japanese pilots, it was clear that such an invasion would cost many lives.

Meanwhile, the United States was readying a new weapon of hitherto unimaginable proportions with which it hoped to force an unconditional Japanese surrender. In 1938, a German scientist in Berlin had achieved nuclear fission, splitting the atom and releasing tremendous energy. This meant that if a means could be found to set off a nuclear chain reaction, a bomb of enormous destructive power could be built. During the first years of the war, British and American scientists had worked separately to achieve this powerful nuclear reaction. German scientists, too, were working in the same direction. In the United States, German scientists who had fled the Nazis first discovered that an isotope of uranium could set off the anticipated chain reaction. The United States detonated the first atomic bomb on July 16, 1945, in the New Mexico desert.

Nine days later, President Harry Truman (Roosevelt died of a cerebral hemorrhage in April 1945) presented Japan with an ultimatum warning

that it faced "prompt and utter destruction" if it did not surrender unconditionally. When Japanese resistance continued, an American air force
plane, the *Enola Gay*, dropped an atomic bomb on the Japanese port city
of Hiroshima on August 6, 1945, engulfing the city in a mushroom cloud
of fire and radiation that killed 80,000 people. Two days later, another
plane dropped a second atomic bomb that destroyed much of Nagasaki,
killing 36,000 people in a storm of fire. Thousands more would die of radiation sickness in the days, months, and years to follow. The night of the
Nagasaki attack, the Japanese emperor called on his cabinet to surrender.
On September 2, 1945, Japanese representatives signed documents of
unconditional surrender on the battleship *Missouri*. The Second World
War was over. But a new and potentially even more dangerous atomic age
had begun.

CONCLUSION

The first Soviet troops arriving at the Nazi death camps discovered nightmarish horrors: technology harnessed to the task of genocide to create factories of death; piles of corpses and of children's shoes; and the few lucky
survivors—the living dead—barefoot human skeletons fortunate enough
to have been liberated before their turn to be exterminated had come. The

(*Left*) A mushroom cloud envelopes Nagasaki after the U.S. Army's deployment of
an atomic bomb. (*Right*) The destruction after the atomic blast at Hiroshima.

death camps became perhaps the most awful symbol of the total war that was World War II. About 6 million Jews perished during the war. The Nazis killed about 2.7 million Polish Jews; at the end of the war, only about 40,000 to 50,000 Polish Jews had survived the Holocaust.

World War II brought mass military mobilization and mass death. At least 17 million people were killed in the fighting and another 20 million civilians perished, half in the Soviet Union; Germany lost more than 6 million people, Japan 2 million, and Britain and France lost about 250,000 and 300,000 respectively. Part of the horror of the period is that we will never really know the full extent of human loss. Millions had been wounded, many crippled for life. Millions of survivors had been carried by luck, good and bad, far from home. Husbands, wives, children, and other relatives were often lost forever. Europe became a continent of "displaced persons," as they were called.

The psychological damage to those who lived through night bombing in shelters, those who spent years waiting for definitive news about missing loved ones, or those who had somehow survived extermination camps, cannot be calculated. Europe seemed haunted by the sad memories of last conversations and letters. Among the hundreds of thousands who emerged with physical or psychological wounds, there were relatively few left to tell the story of Auschwitz or Dachau. One survivor recalled his determination to hold on against all odds "to tell the story, to bear witness; and that to survive, we must force ourselves to save at least the skeleton, the scaffolding, the form of civilization."

A combination of factors had brought Europe and the world to war for the second time in less than thirty years. The end of World War I had left Europe divided between "victors" and revisionist states bitterly unhappy with the settlements imposed by the Versailles treaties. Germany, in particular, was resentful, open to the challenges posed by aggressive nationalist parties on the right. Eastern Europe had been notoriously unstable during the 1920s and 1930s. The Depression ravaged Europe, compounding the challenges faced by states with parliamentary rule. One dictatorship after another came to power. Mussolini's Italy and Hitler's Germany pursued policies of expansionism. At the same time, at least until German troops moved into Prague in March 1939, the British and French governments carried out foreign policies based on appeasement. World War II began when it became clear upon the German invasion of Poland that only military defeat could stop Hitler. The Soviet Union had joined the Allied cause only when Hitler's army invaded it in June 1941, and the United States entered the war only when Japanese planes attacked Pearl Harbor six months later. World War II assumed an even more global dimension than had World War I.

After World War II, in contrast to the end of World War I, there seemed little optimism that such a total war could not occur again. Two factors, in particular, contributed to this new feeling of angst. First was the rising tension even before the war ended between the Soviet Union and the Western Allies. The second was the development of rockets, the jet plane, and, above all, the atomic bomb, a terrifying weapon for a new age.

The cataclysmic experience of the Second World War weighed heavily on the social, political, and cultural climate of the post-war era. In every country, those who resisted Nazi rule played a major part in the reconstitution of their nations after the war. Politicians, intellectuals, and virtually everyone else would try to come to grips with what had happened to Europe, to assess blame, and to find hope. For the moment, however, for many, it seemed enough to have survived.

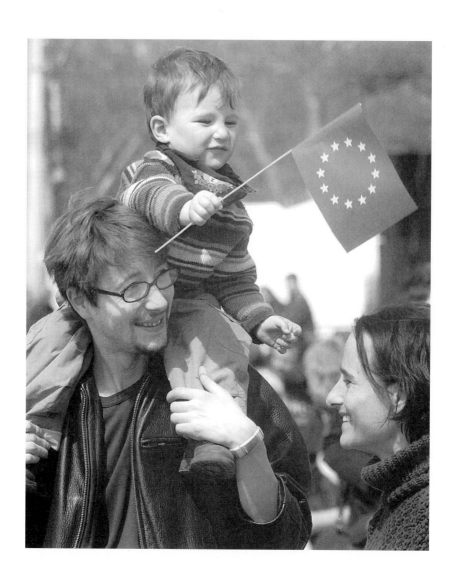

PART SEVEN

EUROPE IN THE POST-WAR ERA

Following the devastation of World War II, Europe rebuilt under the growing shadow of the Cold War. The dawn of the nuclear age added to rising tensions between the Western powers (now led by the United States) and the Soviet Union. The Soviet Red Army, which had liberated Eastern Europe from the Nazis, became an occupying force. In Poland, Czechoslovakia, Bulgaria, and the other states of Eastern Europe, Soviet-backed Communists pushed other political parties aside until they held unchallenged authority in each state. They nationalized industries and undertook massive forced collectivization of agriculture. Germany, devastated by total defeat, was divided into a western zone, which became the German Federal Republic, and an eastern zone, which became the Communist German Democratic Republic. Berlin, lying within East Germany, remained divided between East and West, and quickly became a particular focus of Cold War rivalry.

Several major crises seemed to bring the United States and the Soviet Union dangerously close to open conflict. Soviet intervention in 1956 to crush a revolt against Communist rule in Hungary and in 1968 to clamp down on Communist reformers in Czechoslovakia strained relations between East and West in Europe, even as the Soviet Union and Communist China began to go their own ways in the late 1950s. The Cuban Missile Crisis of 1962 brought the United States and the Soviet Union to the brink of nuclear war.

In the meantime, Western Europe slowly recovered from the ordeal of total war, and the relative peace and new prosperity engendered a "baby boom," as in the United States. More and more people lived in cities, with fewer working the land, and a burgeoning culture of consumption took hold, increasingly influenced by America. The status of and opportunities for women, who had played a vital role in the war effort, gradually improved. In Britain, the Labour government laid the foundations for the modern welfare state. Other Western states, too, increased the number of social services provided by their governments. The age of empire ended with decolonization. Britain granted independence to its former colonies. France, the Netherlands, Belgium, and Portugal also lost their empires, but often after nationalist insurrections and bloody fighting.

In West Germany and France, Socialist parties came to power in the early 1970s and 1980s, respectively. In Greece, Spain, and Portugal, repressive dictatorships gave way to parliamentary regimes. Parties concerned with the environment—the "Greens"—made sizable political inroads in West Germany. But, at the same time, terrorism brought a new, unsettling dimension to political life. Terrorist groups threatened security in such areas as Northern Ireland and the Basque region of Spain, where nationalists were demanding independence, and in the Middle East, where militant organizations opposed Israel's policy toward the Palestinian people.

In the Soviet Union, following his rise to head of state in 1985, Soviet leader Mikhail Gorbachev initiated a bold series of economic and political reforms, hoping to maintain communism by eliminating its authoritarian nature and encouraging greater political participation and economic prosperity. When movements for reform arose in the countries of the Eastern European bloc, beginning in Poland and Hungary, Gorbachev made clear that the Soviet Union would not intervene. Communism collapsed in one Eastern European state after another in 1989. Throngs of East Germans pouring through the Berlin Wall in November 1989 symbolized the fall of communism in Eastern Europe. Germany became a unified state once again. The Soviet Union itself then broke apart, as one former Soviet republic after another declared independence. The Cold War, which had largely defined international relations since the end of World War II, ended. The collapse of the Soviet Union left the United States as the world's only superpower.

In every one of the former communist states, the challenges of achieving democratic rule and a successful market economy were daunting. The ethnic complexity of these states compounded the difficulties. In the former Yugoslavia, a bloody civil war began in Bosnia in 1992. The war brought atrocities on a scale unseen since World War II, most of which were perpetuated against Muslims by Serb forces.

European economic cooperation had begun in the years following World War II, with the founding of the Organization for European Economic Cooperation in 1948, the creation of the Common Market in 1959, and the European Community in 1967. The Treaty of Maastricht, signed in 1992 by the twelve members of the European Community, created the European Union, which has as a base a partnership between two old enemies, France and Germany. The single market that began for member states in 1993 led to the creation of a common currency—the "euro"—in 2002 (although three states have retained their former currencies). Ten more states (eight of which had been within the Soviet bloc) will join the European Union in 2004.

The globalization of the world economy, reflecting remarkable improvements in transportation and communication, has brought the continents of the world closer together, facilitating the movement of people, ideas, and products across the globe. Migrants from Africa and Asia began to arrive in Europe in ever greater numbers, attracted by the possibility of jobs and a better life. Many fled political turmoil at home, arriving as political refugees or simply crossing borders without detection. Immigrants from the Balkans also headed west in great numbers. Periods of economic downturn have left immigrants unwanted by many in their adoped countries, subject to xenophobia and targeting by political parties. Even as Europe now enjoys peace, the question of immigration remains a challenge, particularly in Western Europe. And so does the specter of increased terrorism across the globe, in the wake of the attacks in New York City and Washington, D.C., on September 11, 2001. Finally, Europe confronts another challenge, as well. Many Europeans believe that international cooperation, embodied in the multilateralism inherent in the United Nations and the European Union, must be defended in the face of the seeming determination of the United States to go its own way with or without allies.

CHAPTER 27

REBUILDING DIVIDED EUROPE

The Second World War ended with little of the optimism that had followed the conclusion of the First World War. Winston Churchill, for one, was pessimistic, "What is Europe now? A rubble heap, a charnel house, a breeding ground of pestilence and hate." About four times more people had been killed in World War II (as a direct or indirect result of the fighting) than had died in World War I, which had been "the war to end all wars." As the smoke of war cleared, Europeans struggled to comprehend the devastation around them: flattened cities, crippled industry, and millions of refugees. Jews who were fortunate enough to have survived the death camps returned to their homes in France, Belgium, the Netherlands, and Germany to find that more than 6 million Jews had been exterminated by the Nazis. Countries that the German armies had occupied or that had been Nazi allies had to determine how to deal with collaborators, and they also faced the challenge of establishing democratic political institutions. In almost every country, the shift from a wartime to a peacetime economy would pose a great challenge.

As Europe counted its millions of dead, the hot war gave way to the Cold War between East and West. The Red Army's drive into Central Europe in the waning months of the war had left Eastern Europe and the Balkans under Soviet domination. In a speech in Missouri in May 1945, Churchill lamented that "an iron curtain is drawn down upon their front. We do not know what is going on behind." The division of Europe into two camps—Communist, dominated by the Soviet Union, and Western democracies, under the influence of the United States—was formalized by the creation of corresponding military alliances after the war. That both the United States and the Soviet Union had at their disposal atomic and hydrogen bombs, weapons of unparalleled mass destruction, made enormous the risks of possible conflict. The Cold War helped put an end to any possible return of the relative isolationism that had characterized the United States during the interwar period.

In part as a result of the Communist challenge, during the immediate post-war years France, Italy, and the German Federal Republic (West Germany) elected right-center governments supported by Catholic parties. Moreover, by 1951, the Conservative Party, rejected by voters in 1945, was back in power in Britain. In the meantime, Social Democratic parties tried to distance themselves from Marxism as parties for reform. Movements for independence in the Asian and African colonies of the European powers led to rapid decolonization and further loss of European authority. Yet, at the same time, the European economy grew in the immediate post-war years, and then took off at a remarkable pace during the 1950s.

Despite the shadow of the Cold War and decolonization, the period between 1950 and 1973 was a period of great economic growth in Western Europe. The number of people working in manufacturing or the service sector increased dramatically, and the percentage of people working the land fell rapidly. Reflecting the wartime experience, economic and social planning played an important part in the recovery of the European economy, in its rapid expansion, and in the construction of welfare states in several West European countries. The welfare state emerged in part out of the experience of state planning and social solidarity during World War II, as many countries began wide-ranging social services to aid and protect their people. Finally, the post-war era brought the beginnings of European economic cooperation.

IN THE WAKE OF DEVASTATION

Putting Europe back together proved a daunting task. By the time World War II ended in 1945, probably as many as 60 million people had been killed as a result of the war. Although fewer people from France and Great Britain were killed in the Second World War than the First World War (620,000 and 400,000, respectively), the death tolls in Central and Eastern Europe during the Second World War were almost beyond comprehension. In the Soviet Union, deaths due to the war can only be estimated at between 15 and 25 million people—even more, if one includes the millions who were victims of Joseph Stalin's purges. Moreover, 1,700 cities and towns and 70,000 villages were completely destroyed. About 6 million Germans died in Hitler's war. More than 20 percent of the Polish population perished (and 90 percent of Poland's Jews), and 10 percent of the population of Yugoslavia was killed. Damage to property from air raids, ground warfare, and reprisals by retreating German forces was incalculable. German air raids in the first year of the war devastated sections of London and Coventry in Britain, Leningrad and Kiev in the Soviet Union, and the Dutch port of Rotterdam. The German army completely leveled Warsaw in retaliation for the 1944 uprising there. In turn, Allied bombing

Displaced persons in post-war Europe.

runs left Berlin, Dresden, and the industrial cities of the Rhineland in ruins, and key French industrial and port cities were severely damaged as well.

Only recently have historians become aware of tragedies stemming from what would in the 1990s be known as "ethnic cleansing" during and immediately after the war. For example, between April 1943 and August 1947 in the lands that would become Communist Poland and the Soviet republic of Ukraine about 100,000 civilian Poles and Ukrainians were killed and another 1.4 million were forced from their lands by the invading Red Army. During the period of Nazi and then Soviet occupation (for the second time, as the Soviets had occupied these territories during 1939–1941), first Ukrainians and then Poles themselves undertook "ethnic cleansing." Ukranian nationalists killed Poles in Volhynia and Galicia in 1943, and the Poles committed atrocities when civil war between the two ethnic groups followed with the liberation of Poland.

The Potsdam Settlement

Decisions taken by the Allies toward the end of the war brought a radical restructuring of the national boundaries of Central and Eastern Europe. The restructuring was largely determined by the Soviet military advance. By the time of the German surrender in May 1945, the Red Army had occupied all of the states of Eastern Europe except Yugoslavia and Greece. For his part, Churchill had urged that the British and American armies quickly move into Central Europe before the Red Army could get there. But the Western armies held back. In Germany, Soviet troops controlled what became the eastern zone; the British held the industrial Rhineland and Ruhr Basin, as well as much of the north; American and French armies held southern Germany; and the four powers divided Berlin.

In July 1945, Stalin, Churchill, and the new president of the United States, Harry Truman (1884–1972), met in the Berlin suburb of Potsdam to consider the fate of defeated Germany. (Roosevelt had died the previous April.) Rejecting several plans, including one that would have divided Germany into a number of small, de-industrialized states, little more than "tomato patches," the Allied leaders agreed that Germany should be reunified, despite the original opposition of de Gaulle. The Four Power Allied Control Council (France had joined the Potsdam powers) planned to establish a new, disarmed, and de-Nazified Germany.

The dawn of the nuclear age added drama to the end of the war. The development of the atomic bomb (and its more lethal successor, the hydrogen bomb, first tested by the United States in 1954) had its origins in theories developed by Albert Einstein (see Chapter 21). A series of subsequent scientific discoveries demonstrated that if the nucleus of the atom could be split, a tremendous explosion of energy would result. During World War II, to work on the atomic bomb, the United States had assembled a team of scientists, many of whom had escaped from Nazi Germany. Hitler's own scientists had already begun similar research and were close to reaching some of the same conclusions. Soviet scientists were frantically trying to come up with the atomic bomb, but they were several crucial years behind American scientists. In 1945, nuclear theory became reality, and the first atomic bomb was exploded in a desert in New Mexico on July 16.

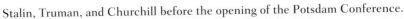

Stalin, Truman, and Churchill before the opening of the Potsdam Conference.

President Truman learned of the successful atomic bomb test the day before the opening of the Potsdam Conference in July 1945. It seemed clear that the use of the bomb against Japan might hasten the end of the war in the Pacific, and thus negate the usefulness of Russia's agreeing to join the war against Japan. The news of the American atomic bomb made Stalin more hostile toward the United States, which had no intention of sharing its new military secret. The unbelievable devastation wrought by the dropping of atomic bombs on Hiroshima and Nagasaki in Japan on August 6 and 9, 1945, carried Europe and the world into a new and frightening era. Truman, who had gone to Potsdam with idealism inspired by the principles of democracy and nationalism, now confronted grave international tensions. These made any hope of an American isolationist retreat to the Western Hemisphere impossible.

The growing mistrust between the Western Allies and the Soviet Union affected the Potsdam Conference. Stalin's territorial demands included not only regions previously considered part of Germany, Russia, Romania, and Czechoslovakia, but also strategically crucial parts of Turkey. The latter would give the Soviet Union virtual control of the straits of Constantinople—which Russian tsars had sought since the eighteenth century. The Soviet Union acquired the three Baltic states (which the Red Army had occupied in 1940) of Estonia, Latvia, and Lithuania, a large chunk of East Prussia, and parts of Finland, Czechoslovakia, and Romania (Bessarabia and some of Bukovina). Poland, which lost much of its eastern territory to the Soviet Union, also gained at Germany's expense (see Map 27.1).

Other territorial adjustments came at the expense of Germany's wartime allies, such as Italy, from which Yugoslavia acquired a small border region. As the Allies dictated the new alignments, little attention was paid to the fact that the new borders, as after World War I, left various nationalities dissatisfied. Hungarians living in Transylvania did not want to be left within the redrawn borders of Romania, and Romanians who found themselves inside Hungary resented what they considered to be punishment for having been forced by the Nazis and their wartime dictators to fight on the side of Germany. Austria, which Hitler had annexed to his Reich in 1938, had its independence and neutrality restored; military occupation by the victorious World War II powers ended in 1955 with the withdrawal of Soviet troops in exchange for Austria's declaration of neutrality. In northern Europe, Finland, where the Communist Party did not do well in postwar elections, retained its independence, despite sharing a border with the Soviet Union, which accepted Finnish neutrality.

Other issues accentuated the split between the wartime allies. As after the end of World War I, the Western Allies disagreed on the question of war reparations. The Soviet Union, which had suffered far more than Great Britain and the United States, demanded that Germany be forced to pay for the costs of the war. Specifically, Stalin wanted the equivalent of

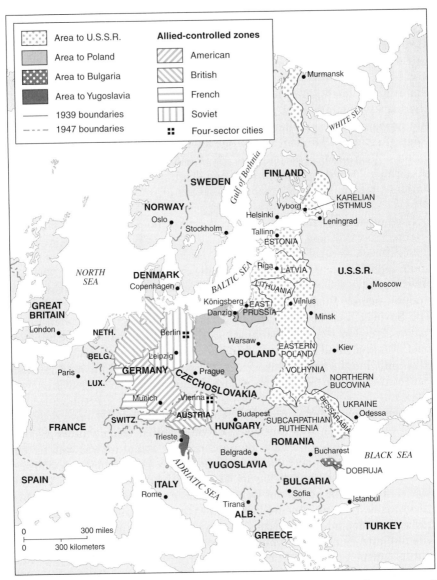

MAP 27.1 POST-WAR TERRITORIAL SETTLEMENTS Territorial changes as of 1947, including American, British, French, and Soviet zones in Germany, as well as boundaries of the Soviet Union, Poland, Bulgaria, and Yugoslavia after the war.

$20 billion in reparations, as well as German industrial equipment. The Soviet Union eventually received half the amount of money demanded (although in greatly inflated currency), as well as about 25 percent of industrial equipment from the German zones occupied by Britain, France, and the United States. In the meantime, Soviet trains and trucks began to haul German machinery and other industrial materials from the eastern zone back to Russia. By now fully suspicious of Soviet intentions in Eastern Europe, Truman eliminated the Soviet Union from the list of nations eligible for U.S. loans to help with rebuilding their economies.

The Western Allies concurred that the victors should negotiate peace treaties with Germany's former allies (Italy, Hungary, Romania, and Bulgaria), which were to be represented by "recognized democratic governments." But it was soon clear that the governments of the last three nations were anything but democratically elected.

The United Nations and Cold War Alliances

In November 1944, the Dumbarton Oaks Conference in Washington, D.C., planned the United Nations, which would replace the League of Nations. It would serve to protect the freedom and self-determination of member nations. An international conference in San Francisco in 1945 drew up its Charter. The UN headquarters was placed in New York, where a secretary-general would coordinate its activities. The United Nations would consist of a General Assembly of member nations (fifty-one at the organization's inception), each of which would have one vote, and a Security Council of eleven (fifteen after 1965) members. The United States, Great Britain, the U.S.S.R., France, and the Republic of China (Taiwan) were designated as "permanent members of the Security Council," each with a veto over deliberations, and the other five (ten after 1965) seats would be filled on a revolving basis by states chosen by the General Assembly. When China was admitted to the UN in 1971, it received the Republic of China's permanent seat on the Security Council.

The United Nations became a battleground for the Cold War. Yet it was an arena for verbal battles—hostile words and strident denunciations were still better than wars. The United Nations helped the European state system reemerge after the war. Furthermore, in some cases the United Nations provided necessary mediation in disputes between nations. However limited its powers, the United Nations, unlike the defunct League of Nations, could send peacekeeping forces to various hot spots on the globe, although the accomplishments of these efforts would vary considerably. Moreover, the UN provided emergency relief funds in the immediate postwar period to Czechoslovakia, Poland, Italy, and Greece.

As a reaction to the horrors of World War II, in 1948 the General Assembly of the United Nations adopted the Universal Declaration of Human Rights, which has subsequently served as the basis for efforts to protect the rights of individuals. Building in part on the Bill of Rights of the United States and the Declaration of the Rights of Man and of Citizen of the French Revolution, the Declaration proclaimed civil and political rights; the right to a fair trial; the freedoms of assembly, belief, and speech; and the rights to education, an adequate standard of living, and to participation in cultural life. Moreover, slavery and torture were acknowledged as violations of human rights. The Genocide Convention, also of 1949, made genocide a crime under international law.

Besides founding the United Nations to mediate disputes, the states of Europe also hedged their bets by establishing military alliances, whereby they pledged to come to the defense of their allies in case any one of them was attacked. Thus, in March 1948, Great Britain, France, Belgium, the Netherlands, and Luxembourg signed the Pact of Brussels. It served as the military component of the subsequent Council of Europe to which most of the nations of Western Europe adhered. The United States joined members of the Pact of Brussels in the North Atlantic Treaty Organization (NATO) in 1949, which subsequently added Italy, Denmark, Norway, Iceland, Portugal, Canada, Greece, and Turkey (see Map 27.2). Directed against the Soviet Union, the treaty bound all of the member countries to defend jointly any of the signatories who were attacked, creating a unified command for a common army and placing NATO's headquarters in Paris. NATO became the cornerstone of the alliance between the United States and Western Europe.

The Soviets and their Eastern European allies countered the Western powers in 1955 by signing the Warsaw Pact, which offered its members similar guarantees to those of NATO against attack. It formalized and internationalized the individual pacts of mutual defense that the Soviet Union had signed with its client states during or immediately following World War II, providing a new justification for the stationing of Soviet troops in Poland, Hungary, Czechoslovakia, and East Germany.

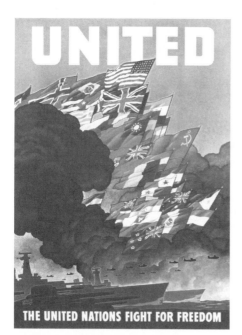

THE UNITED NATIONS FIGHT FOR FREEDOM

A poster from 1943 promoting the United Nations, with the flags of its member nations rising above ships and planes of war.

Confronting Turmoil and Collaborators

The European economy lay in ruins. Bombing on both sides had been systematic, destroying with increasing accuracy the industrial structure of Europe. Sunken ships blocked port harbors. Almost all bridges over the major rivers had been destroyed. Only fragments of Europe's transportation and communication networks remained in service, making the distribution of the meager

MAP 27.2 EASTERN AND WESTERN BLOCS, 1955 NATO and the Warsaw Pact were the military alliances that defined the post-war world.

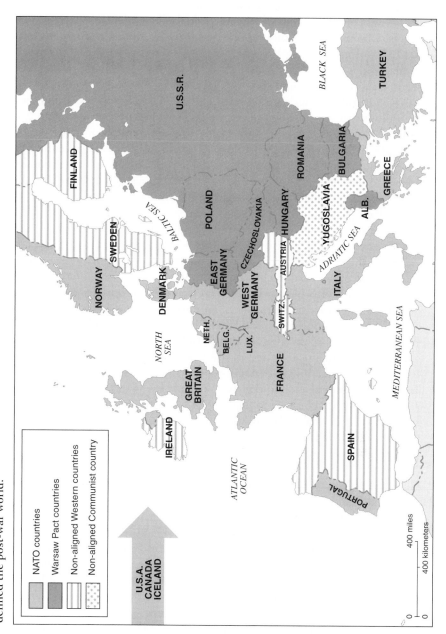

harvests of 1944 difficult. In Britain, gold and silver reserves had sunk dramatically, and the government had been forced to take out large loans, initiating a long period of virtual British dependence on the United States, which provided the bulk of these funds. Nonmilitary manufacturing had plunged during the war. The markets for British manufactured goods, which had all but disappeared during the war, could not be quickly reconstituted.

Agricultural production in every war zone had fallen by about half, leaving millions of people without enough to eat. Inflation was rampant; the value of European currencies plunged. As after World War I, the German currency became virtually worthless. German housewives picked through the rubble of bombed-out buildings looking for objects of value, combing forests for mushrooms and berries for their families to eat. The black market supplied not only luxuries but also necessities.

The European continent had become a world of "displaced persons," as well as of widows and orphans. After World War I, the leaders of the victorious powers had redrawn the borders of Poland, Hungary, Yugoslavia, and the other new or redefined Eastern European nations with regard to the location of national majorities and minorities. Now national minorities within newly redrawn boundaries were forced into boxcars and moved— displaced—to new locations so as to correspond more or less to newly drawn national frontiers. In all, there were about 50 million refugees in the immediate post-war period. Furthermore, millions of prisoners of war, such as Germans incarcerated in the Soviet Union, had to be repatriated. In the meantime, the Red Army carried out massacres and systematic rapes of German women and girls. Germans living in Lithuania, which in 1940 had been incorporated against its will into the Soviet Union, were sent back to Germany. In addition, tens of thousands of Germans were forcibly expelled from Czechoslovakia during the period from May to August of 1945 and during the organized transfers of January through November 1946. Thousands died during this period. About 1.5 million Germans still lived in camps for displaced persons in 1947. In all, about 12 million Germans were forced to leave their homes. Almost 4 million returned to Germany, most arriving with virtually nothing from the U.S.S.R. and Poland. In Germany, one of every six persons was a refugee. Signs of gnawing poverty were not hard to find in every country in the post-war period. Only half of the houses in France had running water, and only a third of those in Austria, Spain, and Italy. Providing decent housing became a goal of governments in most countries.

Stalin repopulated East Prussia with about 1 million people hauled from Russia, Byelorussia (Belarus), Ukraine, and even distant Kazakhstan. Germany gave up territory to Poland to compensate that battered nation for land lost to the Soviet Union. Poles whose homeland had become part of the Soviet Union now moved back into western Poland, which had been conquered during the war. At the same time, almost 500,000 Ukrainians were forced by Poland to head eastward to the Soviet Union. Several hundred thousand Jews from Eastern Europe who had been fortunate enough to survive the Holocaust now headed west, some fleeing new pogroms in Poland in 1946. In all, about 7 million members of Eastern European ethnic groups faced resettlement. The result was a dramatic decrease in the percentage of ethnic minorities living in Poland, Czechoslovakia, and Romania, declining from 32 percent to 3 percent in the first case. Churches, synagogues, and even a few mosques were razed, depending on the location; towns and streets received new names to reflect the brutal transfer of ethnic minorities.

The punishment of those who had collaborated with the Nazis began as soon as the occupied territories were liberated (and, in some cases, had begun during the war itself). In France, resistance forces summarily executed (sometimes after quick trials) about 10,000 accused collaborators—"justice at the crossroads." Courts sentenced about 2,000 people to death (about 800 were executed) and more than 40,000 to prison. Vichy Prime Minister Pierre Laval was executed. Marshal Philippe Pétain was found guilty of treason, but because of his age and stature as the "hero of Verdun" during the First World War, he was imprisoned on a small island off the western coast of France, where he died in 1951. Women who had slept with German soldiers had their heads shaved and were paraded through their towns in shame.

In countries that had been occupied by Hitler's armies, people struggled to determine degrees of guilt. In Belgium, courts prosecuted 634,000 people for their part in the German occupation—a staggering figure in a country of only 8 million people. Moreover, the disproportionate role of Flemish collaborators further increased the division between the Flemish and Walloon (French-speaking) populations of Belgium. In Norway, 55,000 members of the Norwegian Nazi Party were put on trial after the war, and, although many drew jail terms, only 25 were executed. On the other hand, in Austria, where much of the population had seemed to welcome union with Hitler's Germany with frenzied enthusiasm, only 9,000 people were put on trial and only 35 collaborators were executed. (More than forty years after the end of World War II, it was revealed that Kurt Waldheim, who had served as general secretary of the United Nations and later was elected president of Austria, had known about and may have encouraged atrocities committed against Yugoslavs by the German army in which he proudly served.) In Italy, where reprisals against Nazi collaborators at the war's end had been carried out with speed and efficiency (about 15,000 executions between 1943 and 1946), there were few trials of fascists after the war. This was in part because the Italian fascists had been, at least when compared to the Nazis, relatively mild in their treatment of their enemies. Furthermore, millions of people had joined fascist organizations or unions because they felt obliged to, and questions of guilt were ambiguous. In Eastern Europe, purges of former collaborators with the

A French collaborator whose head has been shaved is paraded through a village near Cherbourg following liberation of the region by Allied troops, 1944.

Nazis took on a high profile, such as in Yugoslavia, where Tito's victorious forces executed thousands of Serbs, Croats, and Slovenes who had collaborated.

The most dramatic post-war trial occurred in Nuremberg in August 1945 when the Allies put twenty-four high-ranking German officials on trial before an international tribunal. Defendants included Hermann Göring, Alfred Rosenberg, and several generals. The court found twenty-one of the defendants guilty of war crimes, and ten were executed. Göring committed suicide in his cell shortly before he was to be executed. The remainder of those found guilty were imprisoned, including Rudolf Hess, who at the time of his suicide in 1987 was the only inmate in Berlin's Spandau Prison. Less spectacular trials of more minor Nazi figures went on in Germany for years.

Many war criminals, however, escaped or were let free after the war. Doctor Josef Mengele, who had carried out brutal experiments on living patients, including children, managed to get to Paraguay. A good many found a warm welcome from right-wing dictatorships. The U.S. government facilitated the escape of a few Nazi war criminals in exchange for information about Communists in Germany and elsewhere in Europe. Indeed growing anti-communism put a brake on purges of wartime collaborators in Western Europe. Other war criminals managed to fade into the chaos of post-war Europe, some with new names and identities. Some did not even bother to change their names, and more than a few eventually served in the West German government. In 1959, Israeli agents kidnapped in South America Adolf Eichmann, who had participated in the massacre of thousands of Jews, and took him to Israel, where he was tried, convicted, and executed. In the mid-1980s, a French court convicted Klaus Barbie, a Nazi war criminal who had fled after the war, sentencing him to life in prison. The justice meted out to Nazis and collaborators may have been imperfect, and sometimes came quite late, but it was better than no justice at all.

POLITICAL REALIGNMENTS

Backed by the Soviet Union, Communist governments took power in every Eastern European state in the post-war period. After first declaring support for the constitution of parliamentary democracies, calling for a union of "anti-fascist" political groups, and participating in elections, in each case Communist parties elbowed the other parties aside. At the same time, Communist parties grew in strength in several Western European states, most notably gaining members among industrial workers in Italy and France. Communists dominated the major trade-union organizations in those countries; they entered post-war governments in Belgium and Denmark. Communist wartime resistance against Nazi Germany helped swell the prestige of Communist parties, even as their close identification with the Soviet Union began to engender suspicion among political elites. France, Italy, and the German Federal Republic had right-center governments in which Catholic parties played a major role, although Communist parties were large and influential in France and Italy.

As a response to the growing Communist influence, in March 1947 President Truman announced the "Truman Doctrine," which proclaimed "the policy of the United States to support free people who are resisting attempted subjugation by armed minorities or by outside pressures." While pressuring France and Italy to keep Communists from being named to government posts, the United States undertook a program of massive economic aid to Western Europe. Through the Marshall Plan, named after the American secretary of state, George Marshall, who devised it, the United States contributed $13 billion between 1948 and 1951 toward the rebuilding of the Western Allies' economies (see below). The Marshall Plan was intended to help Western Europe resist communism and to make Europe a powerful trading partner for American industry.

Divided Germany

Germany became the focal point for Cold War tensions. The failure of the Soviet, British, French, and U.S. foreign ministers to agree on the nature of a peace treaty with Germany in the spring of 1947 began the Cold War. That year Stalin, who had in 1943 officially announced the end of the

Comintern, which had been established with the goal of fomenting world-wide revolution, inaugurated its successor organization, the Cominform. It was intended to consolidate Soviet authority in the states of Eastern Europe. This, too, accentuated tensions with the Western powers. In 1949, the Soviet-occupied eastern zone, in which large landholdings had been seized in 1945, became the German Democratic Republic; the American, British, and French occupation zones became the German Federal Republic. The barbed wire and minefields that divided these zones reflected the ideological division between them. In the meantime, both the Soviet Union and the Western powers worked quickly to create intelligence agencies of great size to spy on the other.

The Allies oversaw the development of the political institutions of what became the German Federal Republic. Until 1951, when the occupation statute of 1949 was revised, all legislation passed by the Federal Republic had to be approved by the Western Allies. They carried out a process of de-Nazification, beginning with schools, but did not undertake any major social reforms. This meant that the powerful industrial cartels remained in place, despite the Allies' agreement to the contrary at Potsdam. In part, the devastation of the German economy seemed to necessitate leaving what was left of Germany's industrial base intact. The constitution of the German Federal Republic stated that parties obtaining a minimum of 5 percent of the popular vote in an election could be represented in the Federal Parliament (the Bundestag). This kept small parties, principally those of the extreme right, out of the parliament. (During the Weimar Republic, many small parties had contributed to political instability.) The Federal Constitutional Court banned neo-Nazi parties, and the Communist Party was outlawed as well. In fact, this federalism was very much in keeping with the long traditions of German particularism: many independent German states had existed until German unification in 1871, and local political and cultural traditions remained entrenched.

The Allies insisted that the German president's powers be limited in order to avoid the unrestricted executive power that had existed in Hitler's Germany, as well as at the very end of the Weimar period, when the chancellor ruled by decree. The president would be elected by a federal assembly consisting of all members of the Bundestag and about the same number of delegates from each state for a term of five years. The chancellor, appointed by the president, became the effective head of state. The states of the Federal Republic elected representatives to an upper house (Bundesrat). Because the upper house could block legislation, this electoral process, too, strengthened the decentralization of political power in West Germany.

Konrad Adenauer (1876–1967), the Catholic mayor of Cologne, served as chancellor of the German Federal Republic until 1963. His wartime opposition to the Nazis, hostility to the Soviets and to East Germany, and his social conservatism reassured the Allies, even as he handed out positions to former Nazis. The centrist Christian Democratic Union Party, the largest party in the Bundestag, with its sister party, the Bavarian Social Union, shaped political life in the Federal Republic. Supported by smaller parties on the right, the Christian Democrats held power from 1949 until 1969, with the Social Democratic Party the chief opposition party. Adenauer forged a close alliance with France intended to serve as a bulwark against the Soviet Union.

In the meantime, the Cold War hastened the acceptance by the Western powers of the German Federal Republic and its rearmament in the Western alliance. British and U.S. military authorities proposed West German rearmament as early as 1950, over the understandable objections of France, which Germany had invaded twice in less than forty years. That year, the Federal Republic became a nonvoting member of the Council of Europe. Moreover, bolstered by economic recovery and the total discrediting of the extreme political right wing, the German Federal Republic achieved full sovereignty and diplomatic respectability, joining NATO in 1955.

The Soviet-occupied eastern zone of Germany became in 1949 the German Democratic Republic (GDR, also commonly known as East Germany). Walter Ulbricht (1893–1973), who was the solemn son of a Saxon tailor and who had spent the war years in the Soviet Union, returned to Berlin with the Red Army and became secretary of the Communist Party. He remained, for all practical purposes, head of state until his forced retirement in 1971.

The GDR took over the administration of the eastern zone in 1955 from the Soviets, although its government continued to follow Soviet instructions.

Soldiers march near the frigid border dividing the British and Soviet sectors of Germany.

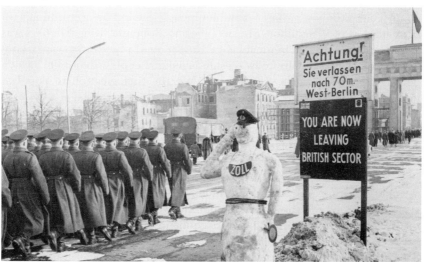

The Communist Party controlled most facets of cultural life. Many writers and artists left for West Germany, although the talented playwright Bertolt Brecht (1898–1956) remained.

Eastern Europe under the Soviet Shadow

One by one, the states of Eastern Europe fell under the domination of Soviet-backed Communist parties, which benefited from Soviet prestige of having defeated the Nazis and from Stalin's claims that the Soviet Union had brought impressive economic and social gains to its people. The Bulgarian Communist Party had about 14,000 members in late 1944 and 422,000 in 1946; that of Poland 20,000 in mid-1944 and 300,000 a year later (despite the historical unpopularity of Russia and the Soviet Union). Moreover, the Soviet Union at first played into the hands of nationalism in Eastern Europe, supporting, for example, the annexation of Transylvania by Romania, at the expense of Hungary. During 1945–1946, coalition governments (in which Communists participated) took over large estates and distributed land to peasants, about half of the land of Poland and a third of that of Hungary.

From the beginning, parties that had collaborated with the Nazis and other right-wing groups were excluded from power. The Communists pushed aside partners in coalitions, as in Czechoslovakia and Hungary, including progressive socialist and peasant agrarian parties, or absorbed them. Coalition governments elected or otherwise constituted at the end of the war disappeared one by one, until the Communists controlled each state. In Hungary in 1947, two years after the Communist Party had been roundly defeated in elections, the Communist Party ousted the Smallholders, or Peasant Party, which had won 57 percent of the vote. During the next six years the Communists in Hungary executed some political opponents among the more than 1.3 million people hauled before tribunals (of a population of 9.5 million). In neighboring Romania, King Michael was forced out in similar circumstances. Bulgarian Communists won a contested victory in a plebiscite that established a "Peoples' Republic," which quickly became a single party state. After the first election in post-war Poland, Communists gradually pushed aside the Socialists, who constituted the other major party. Thereafter, Communist governments controlled the bureaucracies that burgeoned with state management of the economy—above all, the police—and began to implement strict censorship.

The Eastern European countries suffered the absence of solid parliamentary traditions, as well as the mood of defeatism and emerging Cold War tensions. Czechoslovakia had not only been the most industrialized of the Central and Eastern European countries but also the most stable between the wars. Czechoslovakia alone had not become a dictatorship. In the first post-war elections in May 1946, Communists won more than a third of the vote in the elections. Two non-Communists, Eduard Beneš (1884–1948) and Jan Masaryk (1886–1948), served as president and foreign minister respectively in a coalition government. But in 1948, after protesting the Czechoslovakian government's overtures to the United States for financial assistance, the Communists seized power, shutting down other political parties. Masaryk died after he jumped—or was pushed—from his office window, and Beneš soon died after resigning from office. The Communist coup d'état accentuated Western suspicion of and hostility to the Soviet Union.

From Moscow, Stalin engineered purges that swept away even loyal party members in the Eastern European nations (half a million in Czechoslovakia alone). Arrests in Hungary have been estimated at 200,000, 180,000 in Romania, and 80,000 in tiny Albania. Show trials (including those of popular Catholic prelates in Hungary and Czechoslovakia, in the latter case including a "Trial of Vatican Agents"), prison sentences, labor camps, and many executions followed. Stalin also tightened Moscow's grip on the fourteen non-Russian republics in the Soviet Union, purging "bourgeois nationalists" in several of them. While Stalin promoted economic growth in the Communist states of Eastern Europe, economic policies furthered a division of labor whereby some of the Soviet "satellite" states produced agricultural products and others manufactured particular goods. The Soviet Union used the Eastern European economies to further Soviet economic interests through unfavorable trade arrangements. One by one, beginning with Bulgaria and Czechoslovakia in 1949, the states of Eastern Europe launched five-year plans based on the Soviet model. However, consumer goods of all kinds were de-emphasized until the mid-1950s, sacrificed, as had been the case in the Soviet Union, to the drive for heavy industrialization that gave birth to enormous plants producing steel and iron. The collectivization of agriculture began in earnest, but this sharply reduced productivity, this, too, to the detriment of the populations of each country. Like peasants in the Soviet Union during the early 1930s, hundreds of thousands of peasants in Eastern Europe resisted by rebellion, arson, sabotage, and simply by dragging their feet. Yet by 1960, state farms accounted for 84 percent of the land of Romania and 87 percent in Czechoslovakia (though only about 12 percent of land in Poland and Yugoslavia).

Stalin's Soviet Union, however, did not dominate all states in Eastern Europe. In Yugoslavia, Communist leader Tito, whose determined resistance army had freed his country from German occupation without Soviet military assistance, refused to permit Soviet domination of his multinational country. In 1948, Tito took advantage of Stalin's stinging denunciation of his country to break with the Soviet Union. Over the next decades, Yugoslavia received millions of dollars in Western aid. The Yugoslav economy remained "mixed" in the sense that the private sector coexisted with state planning and collectivization.

A Greek soldier stands guard during the Civil War in 1947.

In Greece, the departure of German troops led to an extremely bloody civil war that lasted until 1949, pitting Greek Communists against an alliance of forces that supported the monarchy. The Soviet Union held to an agreement made with Churchill in 1944 not to intervene militarily, but it provided the Communists with considerable material assistance. The United States and Britain aided the monarchist forces, which finally prevailed in 1949. Between 1947 and 1963, the United States poured more than 3 billion dollars in assistance into Greece, in which the Communist Party was banned.

Stalin's Successors in the Soviet Union

In the Soviet Union, Joseph Stalin had emerged from the war with his authority within the Communist Party unchallenged and his prestige enormous. Statues, pictures, and other images of Stalin seemed to be everywhere. But weakened by arteriosclerosis, Stalin's paranoia became virtually psychotic as he ordered more purges in the name of the Communist Party. The ruthless Lavrenty Beria (1899–1953), head of the omnipresent secret police, used a gold-plated phone to order arrests. Between 1948 and 1952, some prominent Jewish intellectuals and artists, including members of a Soviet Jewish Anti-Fascist Committee which had worked to mobilize Jews against the German invasion during World War

II, were tried and executed or simply disappeared. They were targeted both because of Stalin's anti-Semitism and because some were believed to have had contacts with the West. In 1953, Stalin suffered a stroke and died. Beria's subsequent arrest, trial, and execution signaled an end to the Stalinist period.

After Stalin's death, the Soviet Union entered a period of "collective leadership," a concept that had been abandoned during Stalin's personal dictatorship. Decisions were made by the fourteen members of the Presidium (a permanent executive committee) of the Communist Party, which included Georgy Malenkov (1902–1988), a pragmatist who had been trained as an engineer and who believed that Stalin's dictatorship had hampered the Soviet economy. Meanwhile, the coarse, rotund Nikita Khrushchev (1894–1971), the son of a miner in a family of peasants, advanced within the Communist Party. He was part of the pragmatic, or technocratic, faction, but he was also a successful party organizer. In 1955, Khrushchev, with support within the Soviet bureaucracy, won the upper hand in his struggle with Malenkov for power. While maintaining an emphasis on heavy industry, Khrushchev also concentrated on planning and investing in Soviet agriculture, a sector that had never recovered from the effects of forced collectivization. He understood that the production of consumer goods would have to take a more prominent place in economic planning. He ordered the rapid expansion of land under cultivation. The quality of life for most Soviet citizens began to improve gradually, although not as fast as that of highly placed Communist Party members, who had automobiles and comfortable country houses.

The Soviet people were largely unaware of the power struggles fought in secrecy within the Kremlin. Like Western sovietologists, they could only chart the waxing and waning of party leaders' authority by their appearances, by the ranking or the omission of their names on official lists, or by their placement among the gray heads on the giant reviewing stand in Red Square during the annual May Day military parade.

In February 1956, Khrushchev denounced Stalin's "cult of personality" and his ruthless purges in an unpublished but widely cited speech delivered at the Twentieth Party Congress. Such direct criticism was unprecedented in the history of the Soviet Union. Furthermore, Khrushchev accepted the fact that different paths to socialism could exist in different countries. Khrushchev allowed the national republics within the Soviet Union more authority over their own affairs. He gave intellectuals and artists in the republics more freedom to develop non-Russian cultural interests. A brief relaxation of censorship permitted the publication of books that offered brutally frank critiques of the Stalin years.

However, democratic centralism—the strict centralization of government and its domination by the Communist Party—continued. The Communist Party's authority over the republics remained for the most part in the hands of ethnic Russians. The thaw in censorship soon ended.

Censors banned *Doctor Zhivago* (completed in 1956 and translated in 1958) by Boris Pasternak (1890–1960). Published in Italy and winning the Nobel Prize for literature, it offered a nuanced picture of tsarist Russia and therefore implicitly stood as a criticism of the Soviet regime. Soviet artists and filmmakers, too, were reined in, although some remained daring and imaginative within the confines of official toleration.

As the Soviet Union's economic difficulties continued and the sixth Five-Year Plan floundered badly, Khrushchev blamed its failure on excessive centralization of planning and administration. His political rivals, however, blamed him. In 1957, Khrushchev overcame a group that challenged his leadership, ousting Malenkov, Molotov, and Bulganin from key party positions. In 1961, Khrushchev ordered Stalin's remains to be removed from the Kremlin mausoleum and placed less conspicuously in the Kremlin Wall.

ECONOMIC RECOVERY, THE WELFARE STATE, AND EUROPEAN ECONOMIC COOPERATION

The European economy revived with impressive, unanticipated speed (see Table 27.1). The Marshall Plan contributed to the revival of Western Europe. However, the European economic recovery was already well under way by the time the Marshall Plan began in 1948. Britain and France had already matched their industrial production of the pre-war period and Italy, the Netherlands, and Belgium followed within a year.

Moreover, the monies provided by the Marshall Plan amounted to only 6.5 percent of France's gross national product (GNP), 2.5 percent of that of Britain, and 5.3 percent of that of Italy. The Marshall Plan helped Western European states purchase raw materials, fuel, and machinery for industry; in Britain, about a third of the aid went to the purchase of food. Funds from the Marshall Plan also allowed Western European governments some margin to pay for the beginnings of social programs emerging with the construction of welfare states (see below, p. 1234). At the same time, the United States offered loans and credits to a number of European countries, with an eye toward encouraging anti-communism by bolstering the coalition of centrist political parties, as in the case of France.

European economic growth followed a combination of state involvement in the economy and liberalization of trade, creating mixed economies. The most successful mix seemed to be a combination of state planning, timely nationalizations, notably of railroads, coal, and steel, and encouragement of private industry. Nationalized railroads aided the process of rebuilding and expansion in West Germany, France, Belgium, and Britain, carrying prodigious amounts of freight and millions of passengers each year. The Italian government played a major role in Italy's economy, owning almost 30 percent of Italian industry. The government of the

TABLE 27.1. INDICES OF INDUSTRIAL PRODUCTION, 1946–1950
(1938 = 100)

	1946	1947	1948	1949	1950
Belgium	91	106	120	129	139
Britain	106	114	128	137	148
France	79	95	111	122	125
Italy	75	93	99	105	119
Netherlands	74	94	113	126	137
W. Germany	29	34	51	75	90

Source: William I. Hitchcock, *The Struggle for Europe: The Turbulent History of a Divided Continent, 1945–2002* (New York: Doubleday, 2003), p. 135.

German Federal Republic took a lesser role in economic planning than that of France, but it imposed short-term tariffs and encouraged agricultural modernization.

In France, the state played a significant role in the country's economic revival. After the war, France benefited from the importation of West German raw materials. The state had assumed control of the airlines, the largest banks, the Renault automobile plants (whose owner had collaborated with the Germans), natural resources (such as gas and coal), and steel and electricity. The brilliant French economist Jean Monnet (1888–1979) headed an Office of Planning, which encouraged and coordinated voluntary plans for modernizing business enterprises and agriculture, drawing on the capital and expertise of government technocrats. Despite mounting inflation and government deficits exacerbated by the unprofitability of newly nationalized industries, the French gross national product doubled in ten years.

The continued concentration of industrial production in large companies characterized the post-war period. Western Europe, slowly following the lead of the United States, entered the world of conglomerates. A single Belgian company controlled from 50 to 80 percent of Belgian bank deposits, 60 percent of insurance business, 40 percent of the iron and steel produced, 30 percent of coal, and 25 percent of Belgian electrical energy. This virtual monopoly did not seem to slow the development of the Belgian economy, which expanded rapidly. In Italy, the role of the state in orchestrating industry, encouraged by Mussolini's fascism, survived the war. The Institute for Industrial Reconstruction, which had been founded in 1933, survived with state encouragement to control an increasing number of enterprises. The National Agency for Hydrocarbons, which was similarly encouraged and assisted by the state emerged as a veritable cartel in itself, drawing huge profits from a variety of activities, including construction, chemicals, and textile production. Government investment helped the emergence of the Italian steel industry and a state-owned petroleum company provided industry with inexpensive fuel.

The Western Allies recognized that the economic recovery of West Germany was essential in achieving political stability in Central Europe and resisting Soviet communism implanted a short distance away in East Germany. An infusion of American aid—$1.5 billion between 1948 and 1952 primarily through the Marshall Plan—contributed to the rebuilding of key industries in West Germany. The western zones of Germany, which contained most of the nation's natural resources, contributed to a recovery that surprised even the most optimistic economists. The German Federal Republic also had the advantage (one, to be sure, bought at horrific cost during the war) of starting from scratch and building new factories that utilized the most modern equipment. West Germany's other advantages included the presence of many engineers, a skilled labor force, and its protection by the Western Allies (it did not have to spend much for defense). Moreover, the influx of refugees from East Germany contributed to the remarkable growth of the West German economy. West Germany attracted streams of migrant workers from Spain, Italy, Greece, Yugoslavia, and, above all, Turkey. The German Federal Republic also did not have a colonial empire to dismantle.

Ludwig Erhard (1897–1977), the minister of economic affairs who maintained his integrity as staunchly anti-Nazi during the war, was the architect of West German economic success. Aided by the implementation in 1948 of a free-market economy and a stable political life, the German Federal Republic reformed its battered currency, the mark (which was launched with new bills that year). Price controls and rationing ended. This all helped restore confidence, which in turn helped fuel the economic resurgence. Black-marketeering gradually ended as inflation and unemployment were brought under control. West Germany developed a combination of laissez-faire economics and business responsibility for the social welfare of its people, "the social market economy." France and Italy did not duplicate the West German economic "miracle," but made considerable progress nonetheless.

The emergence of welfare states within the context of market capitalism has been one of the most significant evolutions in the post-war period. State economic and military planning during World War II helped shape expectations of continued government assistance. During the war, the British government had provided school meals and subsidized the cost of milk. A wartime committee undertook some hypothetical planning for social reforms, including unemployment and illness benefits. In 1943, British Conservatives and Liberals had joined the Labour Party in supporting a proposal for establishing a system of national welfare once the war ended. With the war over, in response to popular desire for social reforms, the British Parliament, spurred by the Labour Party, passed bills implementing new social benefits. These included the National Health Service, funds for the unemployed, retirement pensions, and assistance for widows. It also enacted a series of bills nationalizing the Bank of England, airlines, the railways, roads, canals, buses, London's subway, and the coal and steel industries. Economic growth and a low rate of unemployment made such programs, financed through taxation, easier than they would have been in a period of economic slowdown. Popular support was such that it was the Conservatives, in power between 1951 and 1964, who expanded the services of the British welfare state, even though Conservative policy was, in principle, against such powerful government.

In other countries, too, the general appreciation of the sacrifices ordinary people had made during the long, hard conflict contributed to a growing sense that states should provide services to citizens in the name of solidarity. The welfare state thus also reflected the assumption that the monopoly of wealthy people over the economy had contributed to the rise of fascist movements in Europe between the wars.

European states greatly expanded subsidized social services for their citizens. This was true in Western states, in which laissez-faire economic theory had long held the upper hand, as well as in Communist states, in which the role of centralized state economic planning was a major part of Communist ideology and practice. "Welfare states" would provide cradle-to-grave social services. In many countries, social legislation provided government assistance to the sick and impoverished. Government insurance programs covered health-care costs in Britain, Sweden, Denmark, France, Italy, the Soviet Union, and the other Communist nations. Most countries in the West provided financial assistance to the unemployed; in

German minister of economic affairs Ludwig Erhard (head of table) addressing a session of the World Bank and International Monetary Fund.

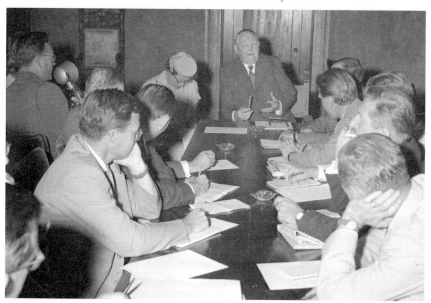

Communist states, where there was not supposed to be any unemployment, menial jobs were found for almost everyone. In all, states expended four times more funds for social services in 1957 than in 1930. Progressive taxation helped raise funds to provide these services. In most European countries, education was made free, or fees were kept at modest rates. The prevalence of social programs in most European countries led to the characterization of welfare states as part of a "European" model of society, which was often contrasted with the United States.

The post-war era also brought international economic cooperation among Western states, encouraged by the Cold War. The Organization for European Economic Cooperation (OEEC) was founded in 1948 with seventeen member states (which the United States later joined; it was succeeded in 1961 by the Organization for Economic Cooperation and Development, OECD, which was expanded to include Australia, Canada, and New Zealand). The OEEC helped plan European economic reconstruction after World War II. Cooperation among the Western states also led to the creation of the European Coal and Steel Community (ECSC; 1952). This was the inspiration of the French statesman Robert Schuman (1886–1963), and it reflected the thinking of U.S. Secretary of State Dean Acheson and of Jean Monnet, both of whom believed that it was in France's interest to move toward better relations with West Germany. The ECSC, which overcame strenuous British objections, coordinated production of French and German coal and steel in the interest of efficiency, but it also was intent on forging a new relationship that ultimately would place France and West Germany at the center of the new Europe. Despite inevitable problems stemming from sometimes competing interests, the ECSC first raised the possibility of serious European economic integration.

Communist Economies

Rebuilding the Soviet economy after World War II was a monumental task. After the Soviet Union's decidedly Pyrrhic victory, those who had managed to flee the war zones returned to devastated cities. Successive years of harvest failure from 1946 to 1947 compounded the extreme suffering. The highly centralized planning of the fourth Five-Year Plan, which began in 1945, allowed the Soviets to concentrate on key industries like coal and steel. Soviet planners benefited from the commandeering of industrial capital goods from Germany and Eastern Europe. Large-scale industrial production exceeded pre-war levels in 1950 by a comfortable margin, although such results were only modestly reflected in the quality of life of Soviet citizens. Collectivized farms permitted some degree of efficient planning, but they also generated peasant resistance.

Once they recovered from being forced to contribute resources to Soviet economic growth and from buying Soviet products at inflated prices, the

Communist states of Eastern Europe benefited from Soviet technological assistance. In 1949, the Soviet Union and its Eastern European allies formed the Council of Mutual Economic Assistance (COMECON). This organization sought to coordinate economic planning so that, for example, only the German Democratic Republic and Poland would build ships, because Poland and Germany both had long traditions of shipbuilding. Industrial production rose most rapidly in Eastern Europe in the German Democratic Republic and Czechoslovakia. Bulgaria, Romania, and Yugoslavia, the least industrialized of the Eastern European countries, also developed manufacturing bases. Romania, however, more than any other of the Soviet Union's client states (with the exception of Yugoslavia), managed to retain considerable autonomy in economic matters, although large-scale industry and agricultural collectivization were emphasized as in the other Eastern European states.

The economic development of the German Democratic Republic, however short on freedom, was nonetheless at first impressive. Before Soviet occupation, the eastern zone of Germany had had a small industrial base, but this industrial infrastructure had been pillaged after the war by the Soviet extraction of raw materials and machinery. The collectivization of industrial production then proceeded rapidly and by 1952 the state employed three of every four workers. Despite the loss of many skilled workers to the German Federal Republic, East Germany emerged with the strongest economy of the Soviet Union's Eastern bloc; only Hungary boasted a similar standard of living by the 1960s. Steel production and shipbuilding, particularly, expanded rapidly in the 1950s and 1960s, as the German Democratic Republic fulfilled its assigned role in the Soviet government's plan for economic development in the Communist states. Nonetheless, to many East Germans conditions of life seemed more attractive in West Germany than in East Germany. Hundreds of thousands of people voted with their feet and left for West Germany. When the leader of East Germany, Communist hard-liner Walter Ulbricht, announced in 1952 that the government would begin collectivizing farms, about 20,000 farmers immediately fled to West Germany. By 1965, collective farms tilled 85 percent of the land in East Germany.

The planned economies of the Soviet Union and its Eastern European allies could count some accomplishments, although adequate attention to the desires of their citizens was not one of them. The Soviet gross national product, which had stood at 36 percent of that of the United States in 1957, rose to about 50 percent of that of its great rival in 1962, and it edged closer in the subsequent two decades. Above all, the Soviet economy remained haunted by daunting inefficiency. The housing shortage remained acute into the 1960s. Although in the Soviet Union housing construction tripled between 1953 and 1969, families still had long waits for better apartments. Existing apartments were often horrendously overcrowded, with several families sharing accommodations.

The U.S. airlift to Berlin, 1948–1949.

In Yugoslavia, which Tito had succeeded in making virtually indepen-dent of the Soviet Union, workers were permitted more self-administra-tion through workers' councils or committees. In the 1950s, the collectivization of agriculture, which had begun after the war, was aban-doned, with farmers retaking their old plots. Yugoslavia's economy, in par-ticular, improved, despite shortages and great inequalities among its six republics.

COLD WAR CRISES

Each international crisis between the Soviet Union and the United States took on great significance because scientists had developed weapons of mass destruction many times more powerful than those that had leveled Hiroshima and Nagasaki. During the 1950s, children in the United States participated in mock air raid drills, putting their heads between their knees to practice bracing for the shock of a nuclear explosion, as if such a position would make the slightest difference in the case of a nuclear attack. The United States and the Soviet Union drew up plans to evacuate American and Soviet leaders into elaborate shelters from which they could order the launching of more missiles and bombs. Plans followed to evacu-ate civilians from urban centers. Britain exploded its first atomic bomb in 1952, France in 1960. And so did China, although its capacity to employ them seemed uncertain. In the 1970s, Israel, probably India, and perhaps Pakistan as well, gained nuclear capability.

The Cold War focused on a series of crises that, drawing world attention, exacerbated tensions between the United States and the Soviet Union. The Soviet Union claimed that the Western Allies had unilaterally broken the agreements reached at the Potsdam Conference. In July 1948, Soviet troops blocked trains and truck routes through the Soviet zone of occupation in Berlin in order to prevent supplies from reaching the Allied half of the city. The Allies began a massive airlift of supplies to West Berlin; at times, planes landed in Berlin every three minutes, bringing much-needed food, medicine, and other necessities. After secret negotiations, Stalin backed down, allowing trucks to roll through the German Democratic Republic beginning in 1949, the year of that state's creation. Berlin remained divided between East and West.

The Cold War reached Asia, as well. Japan's defeat left China divided between the nationalist government of Chiang Kai-shek (1887–1975), which held the south, and the forces of the Communist leader Mao Zedong (1893–1976). In the civil war that followed, Mao's Communist forces gradually pushed the nationalist forces out of China. In full retreat by 1949, Chiang Kai-shek's army occupied the large island of Formosa (Taiwan). There Chiang established a government that claimed to represent all of China. On the mainland, Mao proclaimed the People's Republic of China. The Soviet Union quickly recognized the new, giant Communist state, while the United States recognized the nationalist government of Taiwan as China's legitimate government.

Riots in East Germany in 1953 and what became a full-scale insurrection in Hungary in 1956 revealed mounting dissatisfaction in Eastern Europe with Communist rule. In each case, armed Soviet intervention drew scathing Western denunciations. The arms race between the United States and the Soviet Union heated up. In 1961, the Soviets and the German Democratic Republic tried to stem the tide of East Germans leaving East Berlin for the West by constructing a wall between the zones,

Chinese children read intently from the works of Chairman Mao.

making escape an often deadly undertaking. In 1962, U.S.–Soviet relations reached a dangerous nadir when American aerial photographs revealed the presence of Soviet nuclear warheads in Cuba, whose Communist leader was Fidel Castro (1926–   ). The crisis, which brought the two superpowers dangerously close to nuclear war, was diffused when Soviet leader Khrushchev agreed to remove the missiles. U.S. involvement in a protracted struggle between South Vietnam and Communist North Vietnam further strained U.S.–Soviet relations. In the meantime, the Soviet Union and China, once allies, had gone their own ways, as they competed with each other for the allegiance of newly independent Third World states. However, with Leonid Brezhnev (who had helped force out Khrushchev in 1964) in power in the Soviet Union, there seemed little hope for any significant reduction in Cold War tensions.

The Korean War

After the confrontations between the West and the East in Germany came the first Cold War crisis outside of Europe. China had been divided into a Communist state, supported by the Soviet Union, and a Nationalist state, supported by the United States. Similarly, Korea had a Communist "people's republic" in the north, supported by the Soviet Union, and in the south, a republic created under the patronage of the United States.

In June 1950, North Korean troops, upon Stalin's go-ahead, invaded the southern zone. General Douglas MacArthur took command of the U.S. forces defending South Korea, backed by small contingents sent by other members of the United Nations, which had passed a resolution condemning the Communist invasion. For the first time (with the exception of events in Greece), Communist and non-Communist forces engaged in open warfare, a conflict fought with conventional weapons, but with the risk of nuclear bombs lurking in the background.

Although Chinese troops were aiding the northern side, U.S. forces pushed back the Communist forces in 1951. In any case, neither side wanted to see the war expand beyond Korea. A peace settlement left the division between North and South Korea almost the same as before the war, but at the cost of 3 million casualties (including 140,000 U.S. troops killed and wounded).

Because of Chinese participation and Russian support for North Korea, the Korean War heightened Cold War tensions in Europe. To the Allies, the war raised the outside possibility of a Soviet-led invasion of the German Federal Republic, similar to that launched by North Korean troops. In the United States, the war contributed to a mood of anti-communism and fear of "the enemy within" that bordered on mass hysteria, orchestrated by Senator Joseph McCarthy. "McCarthyism" entered the dictionary as a term for political name-calling and persecution. In Europe, the Cold War undermined Socialist parties, most of which had been bitter

North Korean prisoners of war being harassed by Seoul residents as South Korean soldiers look on.

enemies of the Communist parties during the inter-war years, a rivalry that continued in the post–World War II era.

Stirrings in Eastern Europe

Following Stalin's death in 1953, East German workers, whose trade unions were powerless in the face of state control, complained loudly about high quotas, low wages, and food shortages. On June 17, 1953, Berlin workers rioted, led by construction workers after production quotas had been again raised without commensurate compensation. East German troops, backed by Soviet tanks, ended the disturbances, and a wave of repression followed. That year alone, more than 330,000 East Germans fled to the West.

The East German Communist government realized that state planning had to provide more consumer goods. Ideology alone could not generate commitment. The Soviet Union sent material assistance to the German Democratic Republic and let it write off most of the war reparations owed from the eastern zone. Despite inadequate housing, too few automobiles, and occasional food shortages due to poor planning, more consumer goods gradually became available in the 1960s.

Long rows of drab apartments sprang up near the Brandenburg Gate that divided East and West Berlin. State-sponsored clubs for children provided recreation, as well as ideological indoctrination. Through intensive training and programming—and, in some cases, steroids—East Germany began in the late 1960s to produce athletes of great accomplishment in international sporting events, particularly in swimming and track and field.

Khrushchev's denunciation of Stalin and the "thaw" in foreign and domestic policies had repercussions in Eastern Europe in 1956. In March 1956, the Communist government of Poland reined in the secret police and gave amnesty to thousands of political prisoners. However, strikes in June led to military repression. In October 1956, Wladyslaw Gomulka (1905–1982), a moderate imprisoned during the Stalin era, returned from oblivion to head the government by the Polish Politburo. A reformer, Gomulka purged Stalinists and reached accommodation with the enormously influential Polish Catholic Church. Furthermore, Gomulka halted the collectivization of agriculture in his country. Independent peasants held three-quarters of the nation's arable land, a far greater percentage of privately held farms than in any other country in the Eastern bloc. However, Gomulka also reassured the Soviet Union that Poland had no intention of abandoning the Warsaw Pact or turning its back on socialism.

Soviet concessions to Yugoslavia and Poland encouraged a movement for reform in Hungary, where liberal Communists were already eager to turn their backs on Stalinism. Imre Nagy (c. 1895–1958), a liberal, had risen to become prime minister of Hungary. He had sought to move Hungarian manufacturing away from the Stalinist obsession with heavy industry in order to increase production of consumer goods. Nagy also tolerated peasant resistance to the implementation of agricultural collectivization. In 1955, Nagy's policies drew opposition from Communist hard-liners, and he was ousted from office. A profound movement for reform now took root in Hungary. Intellectuals and students held meetings to discuss possible paths to liberalization. A hard-line response from the new prime minister led to a demonstration of 50,000 people on October 23, 1956. Protesters smashed a statue of Stalin. Police opened fire on a crowd trying to storm a radio station. But Hungarian troops sent to rout the demonstrators refused to fire, in some cases joining those now protesting communism itself. That night, the Hungarian Communist leadership requested Soviet assistance but also named Nagy as prime minister in the hope of ending the demonstrations. Western radio broadcasts heard in Hungary hinted that outside help might be forthcoming and firmed popular resolve. Nagy named a new coalition government that included liberal Communists. He began to negotiate with the Soviet government, but he made clear that he intended to end the one-party system by adding several non-Communists to his government. Furthermore, he called for Hungarian withdrawal from the Warsaw Pact and asked that Soviet troops be removed from his country.

To the Soviet government, Hungary's defection was unthinkable because it might spark similar movements in other Eastern European nations and destabilize the republics of the Soviet Union. On November 4, Nagy announced that Hungary would withdraw from the Warsaw Pact. While the French, British, and U.S. governments were preoccupied with the Suez Canal crisis (see Chapter 28), the Soviet government, after first withdrawing its troops beyond the Hungarian border at the end of October, sent soldiers and tanks into Budapest and other major Hungarian cities to crush Hungarian resistance. Nagy, who had been refused asylum by the Yugoslav embassy, was tried and executed, along with about 2,000 other people. More than 200,000 Hungarians fled to Western Europe and the United States. Soviet intervention ended hope that Stalin's death might bring about change in Eastern Europe and end the Cold War. János Kádár (1912–1989) became Hungary's new leader, backed by Soviet military strength. Over the long run, Kádár skillfully liberalized the Communist regime, while remaining careful not to antagonize unnecessarily the Soviet Union with any ideological justification for his policies. He relaxed government control if the party's interests were not at stake. Hungary's "goulash communism" included market-oriented, decentralized reforms, and toleration of some degree of entrepreneurship and profit. The result was a higher standard of living than existed elsewhere in the Communist world.

With their hands full with Hungary, the Soviets were in no position to move aggressively against Poland. In any case, Gomulka was careful to give them no excuse for military action (for example, he never proclaimed a "Polish road to socialism"). He gradually rescinded some of the relatively liberal policies, including toleration of free artistic and political expression, and put workers' councils that had sprung up in 1956 under party control. In the meantime, Poland remained economically dependent on the Soviet Union.

In Yugoslavia, despite its determined independence of the Soviet Union, open political opposition was not tolerated. One of the distinguished founders of post-war Yugoslavia, the Bosnian intellectual Milovan Djilas (1911–1995), was expelled from the party in 1954 for having contended in his book *The New Class: An Analysis of the Communist System* (1961) that privileged party officials had become a ruling caste with little in common with ordinary people.

The liberal agitation in Poland and the Hungarian Revolution in 1956 threatened Khrushchev's authority in the Soviet Union. Stalinists claimed that Khrushchev's attack on Stalin at the Twentieth Party Congress in 1956 was to blame for agitation in those countries. Furthermore, Soviet aid to stabilize its Eastern European client states undermined economic development at home. But, at the same time, the failure of the Western powers to intervene on behalf of Hungary—because they feared nuclear war with the Soviet Union—seemed to the Soviets to legitimize the division of Europe into spheres of influence dominated by the United States and the Soviet Union.

Soviet–U.S. Tensions

Khrushchev was responsible for a mild thaw in the Cold War. In 1955, the Soviet leader, who wanted to improve relations with the West, met with U.S. President Dwight Eisenhower (1890–1969) in Geneva, the first of the "summit" meetings between the two great powers. At the Twentieth Party Congress the following year, Khrushchev rejected Stalin's contention that Communist and capitalist powers would inevitably go to war, and he now claimed that "peaceful coexistence" was possible between the two political worlds. Soviet foreign policy entered a less contentious and somewhat more flexible period. Looking to the Third World for allies, the Soviet leader courted India, Egypt, and Syria, as well as a number of smaller states, winning their friendship with technical and material assistance. Soviet foreign policy was carried out with the aim of detaching countries from the direct influence of the United States.

As Soviet armed intervention in Hungary in 1956 increased mutual suspicion between East and West, rapid advances in Soviet military science further augmented the rivalry with the West. In October 1957, the Soviets launched the first satellite (*Sputnik*) after developing an intercontinental ballistic missile (ICBM). Space exploration became part of the Cold War. The United States won the race to the moon, when American astronauts landed on the lunar surface in July 1969, an event seen by millions on television. Bilateral negotiations between the Soviet Union and the United States to reduce their respective nuclear capabilities failed in 1955 and again in 1958. When Nikita Khrushchev visited the United States in 1959, he provocatively told Vice President Richard Nixon, "We will bury you!"

In May 1960, the Soviets shot down a U-2 American plane taking spy photos from high over the Soviet Union. The Soviets demanded an apology for this violation of Soviet air space and received none. Khrushchev then refused to participate in a Geneva summit meeting (perhaps also because Soviet relations with China were rapidly deteriorating).

In Europe, Berlin stood divided between Soviet and Western zones of occupation. The United States, Britain, and France still refused either to recognize officially the GDR's existence or to pull out of West Berlin. In 1958, the hot-tempered Khrushchev threatened to take over the administration of all of Berlin, but backed down in the face of Allied intransigence. In the meantime, streams of East Germans—about 2.6 million people between 1950 and 1962—continued to leave for the West, most to the Federal Republic. Between 1950 and 1964, about 500,000 West Germans moved to the East, some fleeing the persecution of Communists in the German Federal Republic, and others simply wanting to be with their families in the East. But this number pales when compared to the number of Germans who moved from East to West. The exodus included many doctors and other trained specialists vital to East Germany. During the first half of August 1961 alone, more than 47,000 people fled to the West.

On August 17, 1961, Berliners awoke in the morning to find East German workers building a wall to divide the eastern sector from the western one. Ground floor windows that permitted escape from East to West were boarded up. Telephone lines leading to West Berlin were cut.

The Berlin Wall became a symbol of the Cold War. U.S. President John F. Kennedy visited Berlin later that summer to view the wall, proclaiming in a speech that he, too, was a "Berliner" (not realizing that a Berliner was also a popular name for a sweet pastry). Enforcement was brutal, although a subsequent relaxation of East German controls allowed Germans on both sides to visit their relatives (it was much easier, however, for East Germans over sixty-five years of age to gain approval to visit West Germany, for if they stayed, the Federal government would have to pay their pension and medical costs). Guards checked car trunks and even the bottoms of cars looking for hidden passengers trying to escape. Western tourists climbed stairs strategically placed in West Berlin to have a look at East German guards staring back from watchtowers behind barbed wire on the other side. Still, people tried to escape and many succeeded: they sprinted across no-man's-land, defying a hail of bullets, swam across rivers, flew small planes or homemade balloons into West Germany, dug tunnels, and hid in trucks and cars. Some did not make it: hundreds were killed attempting to escape.

(*Left*) The Berlin Wall goes up in 1961. (*Right*) U.S. President John F. Kennedy addresses West Berliners, 1961.

Because of the threat of nuclear war, the Cuban Missile Crisis of 1962 was the world's most dangerous moment since the end of World War II. The island of Cuba, which had been a virtual protectorate of the United States since the Spanish-American War in 1898, became a Communist state in 1959 after Fidel Castro led a guerrilla attack that succeeded in ousting the corrupt American protégé, Fulgencio Batista (1901–1973). Batista's supporters, with the help of the U.S. military, launched an ill-conceived invasion of Cuba at the "Bay of Pigs" in 1961. It failed miserably. In October 1962, American aerial photographs revealed that Soviet missiles capable of being armed with nuclear warheads were stationed on the island of Cuba. The U.S. government demanded the removal of the missiles and threatened to destroy them if this demand was not met. Some knowledgeable advisers to President John F. Kennedy estimated the chances of the outbreak of a nuclear war at between one-third and one-half, dangerous odds indeed. Debates in the United Nations helped buy time while negotiations proceeded. The world breathed a collective sigh of relief as Khrushchev ordered the missiles removed, a Soviet defeat.

In 1963, Khrushchev seemed to be more inclined to negotiate at the disarmament conference in Geneva. In contrast, the U.S. government seemed determined to hold the line against concessions to the Soviets. The Soviet negotiating team at the conference stormed out in anger. Khrushchev banged his shoe on the table for emphasis while denouncing the United States at the United Nations.

Despite the fact that the United States and Soviet Union both signed a 1963 treaty banning nuclear tests, the arms race had accelerated. Soviet and American naval vessels and submarines closely monitored each other's movements. Both sides used spies and informers, not only in the "enemy" camp, but in neutral countries as well. The Soviet secret police (KGB) and the American Central Intelligence Agency (CIA) spread their well-financed spy networks worldwide. Periodic spy scandals occurred in the West, most notably in Britain, where several prominent intellectuals turned out to have been spying for the Soviet Union. The growing number of colonies receiving their independence from Britain and France fostered increased competition between the two systems in Africa and Asia (see Chapter 28).

By the mid-1960s, the rivalry between the United States and the Soviet Union spread to Southeast Asia. In 1964, the United States officially became involved in the civil war in Vietnam. When President Lyndon B. Johnson (1908–1973) announced that an American naval vessel had been attacked off the coast of Vietnam (which in fact never occurred), the American Congress passed the so-called Tonkin Gulf Resolution against the North Vietnamese government. The United States committed more and more men and material in support of the South Vietnamese government against the North Vietnamese Communist troops of Ho Chi Minh, and their allies, the Vietcong guerrillas fighting in the south. As in Greece

(*Left*) Soviet leader Nikita Khrushchev and Cuban leader Fidel Castro meet in Moscow, 1963. (*Right*) U.S. Ambassador to the United Nations Adlai Stevenson reads a statement to Security Council members as an aide points to the location of Soviet missiles in Cuba.

after World War II and in the Korean War, the Soviets backed the Communist forces. The costly American role in the civil war came under increasing opposition at home and in Europe, particularly from university students. The Vietnam War badly divided public opinion in the United States and strained U.S. relations with its allies.

Sino-Soviet Rivalry

The alliance between Mao's China and the Soviet Union, cemented by the Korean War, began to break apart. A common Communist ideology could not gloss over issues of power politics between the two giants. Not only did they share an immense frontier, but certain border regions—above all, Mongolia—had long been claimed by both states. In addition, Soviet initiatives to India threatened Chinese relations with the subcontinent. Khrushchev's turn away from Stalinism angered Mao Zedong, the Chinese Communist leader, as did the Soviet leader's overtures for support among Asian political leaders. In China, a "cult of personality" focused on Chairman Mao just as that in the Soviet Union had celebrated Stalin. Furthermore, attempts to modernize China's traditional subsistence economy had been heavily influenced by Stalin's five-year plans, which had emphasized heavy industry, while at the same time proceeding with the rapid, ruthless collectivization of all industrial and agricultural production. Moreover, Chinese economic growth would certainly make the Chinese less dependent on Soviet technical advisers.

The Chinese government grew increasingly uneasy about Russia's nuclear weapons. Mao believed Stalin's contention that war between capitalism and socialism was inevitable. He resented the unwillingness of the Soviets under Khrushchev, who had abandoned that particular tenet of Communist thought, to share their military secrets with their Chinese counterparts. Khrushchev's attempts to relax tensions with the West—and particularly his visit to Washington, D.C., in 1959—irritated Mao, who used the perceived threat from the West as a means of pushing the Chinese to make more sacrifices to modernize the economy. Numerous Soviet technical advisers in China were sent home. In 1964, Mao accused the Soviet Union of itself being an "imperialist" power because it dominated the smaller states of Eastern Europe. A series of incidents on the border between the two powers in 1969 generated considerable tension.

Chinese and Russian diplomats and advisers now competed as rivals for the ears of Third World leaders. The Chinese Communists received support from an unlikely place. Albania, the small, backward, largely Muslim state squeezed between Yugoslavia and the Adriatic Sea, broke with the Soviet Union, denying the Soviet claim that Moscow should be the center of communism. The Albanian voice in Europe, Radio Tirana, praised Mao and Chinese socialism while denouncing the Soviet Union for "revisionism." The Soviet Union broke off diplomatic relations with Albania in 1961. This represented an embarrassing rejection of Soviet authority, particularly when put into the context of the ongoing Sino-Soviet split. However, Albanian Communist leader Enver Hoxha (1908–1985) broke with the Chinese Communist leadership in 1978, criticizing China's improved relations with the United States.

The Brezhnev Era

Soviet economic stagnation and the humiliation of the Cuban Missile Crisis contributed to Khrushchev's sudden fall from power in 1964. Some military leaders had opposed Khrushchev's support of economic planning that emphasized consumer goods over heavy industry. However, despite Khrushchev's cocky assurances that the Soviet Union would within four years produce more meat, milk, and butter than the United States, severe shortages further alienated many Soviet citizens. Old Stalinists surfaced again, resistant to any reform. The army, wary of the Chinese situation, accused Khrushchev of having taken too great a risk by establishing missile sites in Cuba. In October 1964, Khrushchev returned to Moscow for a meeting called by his enemies only to find out that he was being retired into honorable obscurity.

Leonid Brezhnev (1906–1982), who had risen in the Communist Party bureaucracy with Khrushchev's assistance, became general secretary of the Communist Party. Brezhnev, far less impulsive than Khrushchev, returned to Communist orthodoxy. He affirmed the authority and prestige of party bureaucrats and of the KGB, but he stopped well short of Stalinism. While building up Soviet military capability, the Soviet leader ordered an increase in the production of consumer goods. Nonetheless, centralized planning and agricultural collectivization remained the basis of the inefficient and technologically backward Soviet economy.

There was little talk of a "thaw" either inside or outside the Soviet Union during the Brezhnev era. Cynicism mounted within the Soviet Union, even among committed Communists who had long awaited the day when the corner would be turned and prosperity would arrive. That day never came.

CONCLUSION

In many ways, the Cold War defined the history of Europe—and of the United States, China, and many other states—for four decades following World War II. The ideological and power struggles between the Soviet Union and the United States greatly affected the political histories of each state. This was also true of the smaller Eastern European states dominated by the Soviet Union. The rivalry between the two great powers and their allies inevitably affected the political life and foreign policies of the Western European states, as well as those of the emerging states of the Third World. In the meantime, two major changes that will be described in the next chapter had begun to transform Western Europe in the decades that followed the end of World War II. Western powers freed their colonies either by choice or because of the movements for national independence

Medium-range Soviet strategic missiles taking part in a military parade in Moscow on November 7, 1963, in a Soviet show of strength.

that emerged in Africa and Asia. And the countries of Western Europe entered a period of unprecedented prosperity, marked by a rising—and more urban—population, a revolution in transportation and communication, the emphatic proliferation of a culture of consumption, and an increasingly global economy.

28

DECOLONIZATION AND
A NEW PROSPERITY

The post-war period brought two major developments to Western Europe, in addition to the Cold War and the attempts of intellectuals and artists to come to grips with the tragedy of World War II. One was decolonization. Since even before the time of Christopher Columbus, European powers had begun to colonize the rest of the world. Spain, England (and then Britain), France, and Portugal established vast empires across the seas. During the period of the "new imperialism" that lasted from the mid-1880s until World War I, Germany, Italy, and even Belgium had, like Britain and France, absorbed large chunks of Africa into their domains. Now, during the first two decades following World War II, most of the colonies of the Western powers achieved independence, sometimes after protracted wars of independence. The decline of Britain as a great power was itself symbolic: the sun finally set on the British Empire as its colonies became independent states. The other major development was a new prosperity, as the economies of the Western nations recovered from the war—indeed from the period since 1929—with remarkable speed and entered a period of spectacular economic growth. The consumer age began. Economic growth came even as superpower competition between the United States and the Soviet Union made the European powers less important in the world, as did the growing prodigious economic might of Japan and the rise of China as a great power. In the meantime, during the late 1960s Asians and Africans seeking a better life began to arrive in unprecedented numbers in Western Europe.

POLITICS IN THE WEST IN THE POST-WAR ERA

With Germany, Italy, and Vichy France defeated, political continuity with pre-war governments could be found only in Britain among the major Western European powers. Yet, even in Britain, political change occurred as voters in the first post-war election turned against the Conservatives and brought the Labour Party to power in July 1945. Labour's victory was a repudiation of the Conservative government's pre-war economic policies and its inadequate reaction to Hitler's aggressive moves in Central Europe in the late 1930s. Clement Attlee (1883–1967), a hard-working but uninspiring man who lacked Churchill's charisma, became prime minister. Attlee was once described as "a sheep dressed in sheep's clothing." Churchill had allegedly disparaged him in remarking, "An empty cab pulled up to 10 Downing Street, and Attlee got out." Nonetheless, Attlee proved to be an effective leader.

The British economy slowly revived following the war. Industrial production reached pre-war levels by 1946 and grew by a third by the end of the decade, despite increasingly obsolete factories and low rates of investment and savings. However, British share in international trade declined sharply during the next three decades. West Germany and France passed Britain in most economic categories. Some conservatives blamed the welfare state and the strength of the unions for Britain's relative economic decline, arguing that both forced the government and private companies to pay higher wages. Yet British welfare costs were less than those of France, and British citizens paid proportionally fewer taxes than the Germans or French. Rather, the costs of maintaining the British Empire undercut the government's quest for austerity as it faced enormous trade deficits and debts to the United States. To an extent, the Attlee government had to choose between financing domestic economic recovery and maintaining the British Empire. It chose the former.

Conservatives returned to power in 1951 on a wave of impatience with the slowness of the economic recovery. The Tories were committed to undoing the nationalizations undertaken by Labour after the war. But they found it difficult to privatize such nationalized industries as iron and steel because they had become unprofitable and therefore failed to attract private interest. Privatization (including the sale of most steel and iron companies to private companies) barely scratched the surface. Furthermore, any move against the welfare system of Labour would have been generally unpopular. Labour returned to power in 1964 with the support of the trade unions, in the wake of a juicy scandal (John Profumo, the Conservative minister of defense, had been associating with a Russian agent and a prostitute at the same time). But led by Edward Heath, the Conservatives returned to power in 1970.

In some ways, France emerged from World War II in better shape than it had from World War I, which had taken far more French lives. And although industrial cities and ports had been pounded by bombing raids— German in 1940 and Allied in the last years of the war—the systematic devastation that had taken place in northern and northeastern France during 1914–1918 had not been repeated, in part because the French armies had collapsed so rapidly before German tanks in 1940.

(*Left*) British Prime Minister Winston Churchill with his deputy, the future Prime Minister Clement Attlee. (*Right*) Charles de Gaulle returns to France after the German occupation.

In the eighteen months that followed his triumphant march down the Champs-Elysées to Paris's town hall in August 1944, Charles de Gaulle ruled virtually alone. But his inattention to France's precarious economic situation and the unwillingness of centrists to support tough measures to constrict the money supply (such as by taxing wealth) only exacerbated shortages.

In October 1945, the vast majority of French men and women voted against a return to the political institutions of the Third Republic, identified with France's defeat in 1940. This referendum was the first election in which French women could vote after receiving the suffrage that year. In the subsequent elections for the Constituent Assembly, Communists—whose contributions to the resistance had been essential—took the greatest percentage of seats, with the Socialists (led by former Prime Minister Léon Blum, who had been imprisoned during the war by the Vichy government) only a few percentage points behind. The Popular Republican Movement (MRP), a new center-right party, also did well by building on de Gaulle's reputation and the Catholic resistance, and by opposing Communist political strength.

Frustrated that the new regime would have a weak executive authority, reflecting Socialist and Communist fears of Caesarism, however, de Gaulle resigned from government in January 1946.

After voters overwhelmingly rejected the Constituent Assembly's proposed constitution in May, a second Constituent Assembly was elected the following month to write a new constitution. This was approved by a narrow majority of voters in October 1946. Like the Third Republic, the political institutions of the new Fourth Republic seemed conducive to governmental instability and immobility. Between 1946 and 1958, France would have twenty-four different governments, most based on left-center coalitions centered on the MRP, the Socialists, and smaller parties. The president and the prime minister had influence, but little power. While de Gaulle cooled his heels in his village in eastern France, awaiting a call for him to return to power, a new Gaullist party (the Rally of the French People, or RPF) became the opposition party of the right.

In Italy, a new regime had to be constructed after the war. The monarchy's passive capitulation to fascism had discredited King Victor Emmanuel III, who compounded his unpopularity by trying to blame the Italian people for fascism. In June 1946, more than half of those voting repudiated the monarchy (although most southerners voted for it), despite the abdication of the king in favor of his son and the efforts of the pope to influence the election. Italy became a republic.

In the elections for a Constituent Assembly, women were eligible to vote for the first time, as in France. The new constitution provided for the election of the president by the two houses of parliament, both of which were to be elected by popular vote. The president would have little power, and regional governments would have their own assemblies. Most Italians feared a powerful centralized state, at least partially because it would seem a continuity of fascism, but also because it seemed antithetical to long-standing regional identities. Futhermore, the Church vigorously opposed the development of a more centralized state, fearful of losing influence.

The new Italy was to be built on values associated with the resistance. But the Italian south had been

An Italian woman votes in the first election open to both sexes, 1946.

liberated by the Allies with very little participation by the resistance movement. Therefore, what many Italians referred to as a "cleansing wind from the north," where the resistance had been strong, did not extend into southern Italy and Sicily, both of which largely remained dominated not only by powerful landowners but also by the Mafia. Furthermore, many fascist officials in the south simply held on to their positions, weakening the republic's prestige.

The government of Italy remained rooted in the center-right. The Christian Democratic Party, a staunchly anti-Communist centrist force with close ties to the Catholic Church and powerful economic interests, dominated political life in post-war Italy, dispensing patronage and bribes. Like its counterparts in West Germany and France, the Italian Christian Democratic Party reflected the accommodation of most Catholics with democracy. The Communist Party became the second-largest political party, claiming the allegiance of as much as a quarter of the population. In the 1960s, Italian governments undertook modest social reforms. Moreover, the popular Pope John XXIII (pope 1958–1963) called for social reform. This encouraged the Christian Democrats to form coalitions with the Socialists. Beginning in 1963, control of the government passed from the center-right to the center-left.

DECOLONIZATION

The Third World had been on the periphery of international politics since the age of the "new imperialism" that began in the 1880s. The Second World War accelerated the independence movements that had developed after World War I. In the colonies in Africa, Asia, and Southeast Asia, the rise of nationalism led to movements demanding national independence. Thus, beginning in the 1950s, European colonies became central actors in some of the dramas of international politics. The peacemakers at Versailles (particularly President Wilson) in 1919 had espoused nationalism as a principle for the territorial organization of states. But France and Britain, in particular, had been unwilling to grant freedom to their colonies, both viewing their empires as part of their national identities. During and after the war, the U.S. government had made clear its unwillingness to support the maintenance of the British and French colonial empires.

For his part, Winston Churchill had believed that if Britain was to remain a world power, it had to retain its empire, despite the opposition of Eisenhower to colonialism. However, succeeding prime ministers realized that it would be better to grant colonies independence than to have to confront massive insurrections. Britain's former colonies achieved independence peacefully, for the most part. In contrast, France (particularly in the case of Algeria) and Portugal struggled to retain their colonies even in the face of popular insurgency. The Netherlands and Belgium both resisted nationalist movements briefly before recognizing the independence of their former colonies. In many colonies, educated and active groups stood ready in the quest for independence. By 1980, more than half of the 154 members of the United Nations had been admitted to membership since 1956.

The end of the colonial era reflected the relative decline of the European powers in international affairs. Britain and France, in particular, left important traditions of government, culture, and language in Africa, Asia, and the Middle East (for example, French prestige in Lebanon). But during the 1960s and 1970s, the United States and the Soviet Union aggressively competed for the allegiance of these young states.

Decolonization in South and Southeast Asia

India, a densely populated, vastly complex subcontinent of many peoples, languages, cultures, and several major religions, was the largest colony in the world. Hindus formed the largest religion, but there were millions of Muslims as well, particularly in Bengal and Punjab in the north. Great Britain's political domination of the subcontinent dated to the eighteenth century. During the 1920s and 1930s, Indian nationalism developed among an Indian elite, many of whom had been educated in England. When World War II began, the British government asked the Congress Party, the largest Indian political organization, for its support against the Japanese. The Congress Party was not a religious party, and it included many non-Hindus, including Sikhs and Muslims—among them, Muhammad Ali Jinnah, who would emerge as the founding father of Pakistan. The Congress Party called for the creation of a secular state. Yet many of the leaders of the Congress Party were Hindu, and it made use of Hindu symbolism as a means of winning mass support. This in itself added to the strength of the Muslim League, a party intended to represent Muslim interests. When the Hindu leaders of the Congress Party, Mohandas Gandhi (1869–1948) and Jawaharlal Nehru (1889–1964), refused to offer unqualified support during the war, the British government ordered them jailed. In 1942, the British government informed them that India would receive full status within the British Commonwealth at the end of the war if India fully cooperated with the British government in the meantime. However, Gandhi and Nehru demanded complete independence for India. Gandhi, in particular, became a symbol of Indian resolution to win independence by peaceful means. When he threatened a massive campaign of nonviolent resistance to British rule, the British government sent him to jail again.

With the British Conservative Party out of government after the war, Labour Prime Minister Clement Attlee announced in 1946 that India would be granted full independence. A year later, he made clear that the

Mohandas Gandhi steps from a third-class train after Indian independence.

responsibility for organizing a transition to independence would lie with the people of India. Bitter fighting followed between Hindus and Muslims as India became independent in 1947. The Muslim League insisted on the creation of a separate Muslim nation, which the Hindu Congress Party rejected outright. Hindus and Muslims battled in much of India. Finally, Britain agreed to form two independent states: India, which would be largely Hindu, and Pakistan, divided between East Pakistan and West Pakistan on either side of India, which would be Muslim. Since millions of Muslims lived in India and many Hindus lived in Pakistan, however, it proved impossible to draw state boundaries so that they exactly corresponded to ethnic and religious differences.

In August 1947, India and Pakistan became fully independent. However, fighting between Hindus and Muslims continued. Hindus drove millions of Muslims out of India; many of them starved to death during forced marches to Pakistan. Likewise, about the same number of Hindus and Sikhs were expelled from Pakistan. A Hindu extremist assassinated Gandhi in 1948 because he had accepted the establishment of Pakistan.

India became the world's largest democracy (its population reached 900 million by 1990), but many of its daunting problems remained unsolved: poverty compounded by a phenomenally high birthrate, an insufficient structure of democratic institutions, and bitter religious rivalries. Pakistan, too, faced the challenges of poverty and the lack of a democratic tradition. The awkward division of Pakistan into East and West, separated by Hindu India, ended in 1971 when East Pakistan rebelled against Pakistani authority. After Indian troops intervened against Pakistani forces, Bangladesh became an independent state, one of the poorest nations in the world. Meanwhile, the British government had also granted independence to other British colonies in Asia: the island of Ceylon (Sri Lanka) and Burma (Myanmar) in 1948, and Singapore in 1965.

In Southeast Asia, the end of Japanese occupation during World War II served as a catalyst for decolonization, leaving the way open for independence movements. The Japanese conquests had provided a kind of charade of liberation with the arrival of Japanese forces and the public humiliation of white colonizers they had defeated. In French Indochina, which had until 1945 survived as Vichy France's only colony (the others had fallen to the Allies), colonizers sought to command the allegiance and compliance of the indigenous populations by imposing a harsher colonialism, orchestrated by an authoritarian colonial regime that trumpeted Marshal Pétain's "National Revolution" in France. At the same time, Vichy France had encouraged the revival of local historical and cultural traditions. The carrot-and-stick approach of such strategies backfired, increasing the number of people who wanted independence.

With the economies of the Western European nations still suffering the effects of the war, the costs of resisting independence movements seemed high. Opposition to colonialism came not only from the colonized peoples but also from intellectuals, students, and political parties of the left at home.

The Japanese occupation had driven the British out of the Malay Peninsula and the Dutch colonists out of Indonesia. The states on the Malay Peninsula formed the Federation of Malaya after the war, granted partial independence by Britain. Communists battled British troops off and on during the 1940s and 1950s, until Britain granted complete independence in 1957 to what became Malaysia in 1963. In Indonesia, the nationalist leader Sukarno (1901–1970) took advantage of the Dutch absence from the region to proclaim Indonesian independence. Negotiations arranged by the United Nations led the Netherlands to grant Indonesian independence in 1949. Eight years later, the Indonesian government expelled Dutch citizens and confiscated their property. Sukarno called his government a "guided democracy," assuming the presidency for life in 1963. As the economy floundered, however, the Indonesian Communist Party grew in size. The Indonesian government maintained neutrality in the Cold War, accepting large sums of money from the Soviet Union and the United States. In 1965, Lieutenant General Suharto (1921–) seized power. Undertaking a bloody campaign of terror against Communists, he consolidated his dictatorship, with the support of the armed forces. In 1998, riots in the capital of Jakarta led to his resignation.

Britain and the Middle East

The Second World War initiated a period of decline in British influence in the Middle East. Egypt had achieved independence after World War I.

But in 1945 the British government still controlled Palestine, which had an Arab majority. Jews, however, considered Palestine their promised land. During the 1920s and 1930s, many Jews had emigrated there, hoping one day to construct a Jewish state. In the wake of World War II, they were joined by hundreds of thousands of Jews—Holocaust survivors—from Europe. In 1947, the British government, already facing attacks from militant Jews committed to ending British occupation, asked the United Nations to resolve Palestine's future. In its first major international decision, the United Nations called for the division of Palestine into the Jewish state of Israel and an Arab state. That land intended for a new Arab state was incorporated into the neighboring states of Jordan and Egypt, as well as Israel. Although outnumbered, Israeli forces took over much of the British mandate in 1948, achieving independence. Jerusalem, a holy city for Jews, Arabs, and Christians, was to remain temporarily under the control of the United Nations.

Fighting had begun between Palestinian Arabs and Jews following the UN resolution. On May 14, 1948, Arab forces from Egypt, Syria, Lebanon, and Jordan attacked the newly established state of Israel, but were defeated in 1949. Many Arabs had left lands that became part of Israel after having been assured that they could return to them when Arab forces had defeated Israel. The victorious Israeli army expelled large numbers of Arabs from their lands, although about 150,000 Palestinian Arabs remained in Israel. At least 700,000 Palestinians became refugees when they fled to Jordan, which had become independent in 1946. The seeds were sown for future conflicts. The Arab states refused to recognize the existence of a separate Palestinian Arab identity, although Palestinians retained some rights, such as being able to vote and to serve in the Israeli Parliament. Those Palestinians remaining in Israel believed that they had been relegated to the status of second-class citizens, and they remained under military rule until 1965. After 1948, no new Arab towns were established in Israel, although the population of Palestinians increased fivefold, and until recently it remained the policy of Israel that no land "redeemed" by Jews could be sold to non-Jews.

The Suez Canal Crisis

Growing European dependence on oil as a source of energy would make the Middle East increasingly important in international politics. The Suez Canal had been the centerpiece of British interests and defenses in the Middle East since British troops first occupied Egypt in 1882. Although the British withdrawal from India in 1947 had somewhat reduced its strategic importance to Britain, about two-thirds of the oil from the Middle East on which Britain and Western Europe depended was transported through the canal. Egypt had been independent since 1922, but Britain maintained considerable influence there. Furthermore, the canal itself was owned by the British (more than 40 percent) and French governments, as well as by stockholders, primarily British.

In 1952, when Egyptian nationalist sentiment against Britain ran high (in part because the British government refused to allow Egypt to occupy Sudan), a group of young nationalist military officers overthrew Egyptian King Farouk in a bloodless coup. Gamal Abdel Nasser (1918–1970), the head of the new Egyptian government, emerged as one of the most influential figures in rising Pan-Arab nationalism. Nasser established Egyptian neutrality in the tug-of-war between East and West. He refused to sign a treaty with the United States (which had been quick to recognize the new state of Israel in 1948), and he castigated Iran and Turkey for their pro-American policies.

As Egyptian nationalism mounted, the Egyptian government (which had renounced the Anglo-Egyptian alliance treaty of 1936) demanded British withdrawal from the narrow zone along the Suez Canal. In 1954, the Egyptian and British governments signed an agreement (vehemently opposed by some British Conservatives) by which British troops would begin a phased withdrawal that would be completed in June 1956. Britain would retain the right to send military forces back should the canal be attacked (presumably by the Soviet Union); the British and Egyptian governments would respect the freedom of navigation through the canal. Many Egyptians (particularly a radical organization, the Muslim Brotherhood) opposed this agreement, which seemed to maintain some degree of British control over the Suez Canal. They sought to end once and for all Egypt's semicolonial status.

Egypt became a pawn in the struggle between the United States and the Soviet Union for the allegiance of non-aligned nations. Gradually, Nasser, who denounced the British and French role in the Middle East, turned

(*Left*) A Russian cartoon salutes Nasser's seizure of the Suez Canal in July 1956. The banner reads "Shares of the Suez Canal Company Ltd." (*Right*) Sunken ships block the Suez Canal.

toward the Soviet Union for economic support, resenting the United States for its close ties to Israel and spurning Britain's defensive pact with Turkey and Iraq (the Baghdad Pact, 1955). The Soviet Union sought to increase its reach in the Middle East, capitalizing on considerable dissatisfaction among Arab nationalists with the role of the United States in the construction of a Middle East treaty association similar to NATO. The Soviet government signed an agreement with Egypt, promising to exchange weapons for Egyptian cotton. Egypt planned to construct the Aswan High Dam on the Upper Nile River, which Nasser believed would help modernize the Egyptian economy. The World Bank had agreed to finance the construction of the dam if Britain and the United States would contribute. But the U.S. government was increasingly suspicious of British goals. Indeed, the British government was planning to overthrow Nasser. On July 19, 1956, the United States suddenly withdrew its offer when it seemed that the Egyptian government would accept a Soviet offer to finance the dam's construction. On July 26, Nasser announced the nationalization of the Suez Canal, with the assurance, however, that shareholders, many of whom were British, would be compensated.

The British government, pushed by staunch Conservatives who feared that Nasser would undermine British interests in the Middle East, decided on armed intervention. France, too, wanted Nasser out of power because of French interests in the canal. More than this, Nasser supported the Algerian National Liberation Front, which sought Algerian independence from France. In the meantime, the U.S. government, which opposed military action against Egypt, sought to diffuse the crisis through negotiation.

The government of Israel, which was still technically at war with Egypt and had been since 1948, was also concerned about emerging ties between Egypt and the Soviet Union. Moreover, the arrival of Soviet arms in Egypt raised fears of a possible Egyptian invasion. In October 1956, the British government came around to the French view that they should agree to an Israeli invasion of Egypt, which would provide both powers with an excuse to intervene militarily and occupy the Suez Canal Zone. (The U.S. government was kept unaware of these difficult negotiations.) Israel sent an invasion force into Egypt on October 29. The Egyptian army put up stiff resistance. A Franco-British ultimatum then demanded that Israeli and Egyptian forces withdraw to ten miles from the canal. Indeed, the Israeli government halted the military drive within Egypt. An Anglo-French force then landed in Egypt and occupied the Canal Zone after Nasser ordered the scuttling of ships to block the canal. On November 3, the General Assembly of the United Nations called for a cease-fire (supported by both the United States and the Soviet Union), and a day later, it authorized a peacekeeping force. On November 5, British and French troops parachuted into Port Said, followed by troops put ashore the next day. That day, November 6, 1956, Britain agreed to accept the cease-fire. Pressure on both Israel and Egypt from the United States and the Soviet

Union (which had reason to be pleased that the world's attention could be diverted from Hungary, where Russian tanks were crushing an anti-Communist revolt; see pp. 1242–1243) brought an end to the Suez crisis. U.S. pressure proved decisive, particularly with Britain, as the U.S. government refused to support British sterling (its currency), which fell dramatically in the face of fears of a cut-off of oil from the Middle East. British and French troops withdrew. The Suez Canal crisis had demonstrated that Western powers could no longer impose their will on the Middle East. Thereafter, the process of decolonization proceeded rapidly.

In Britain, Prime Minister Sir Anthony Eden (1897–1977) suffered a nervous breakdown and resigned from office in January 1957. Harold Macmillan (1894–1986), who succeeded Eden as prime minister and who had been a proponent of the Suez action, then undertook what one Conservative leader called the "most spectacular retreat from Suez since the time of Moses." Following the salvaging of the forty ships that Egypt had sunk in the canal, the Suez Canal reopened in April 1957 under Egyptian control. In 1958, British ally King Faisal II was overthrown and assassinated in Iraq. When the island of Cyprus gained its independence in 1960, Britain lost its last base in the Middle East.

French Decolonization

France, too, lost its colonial empire in the post-war era, but not without bloody struggles. The French had begun their conquest of North Africa in 1830 and had held modern-day Laos, Cambodia, and Vietnam since the 1880s. The French left Syria and Lebanon in 1946 by agreement with the United States and Britain. In 1947, French troops put down a massive insurrection in Madagascar, with an enormous loss of life. The island finally received its independence in 1960, one of fourteen former French colonies in Africa. In Vietnam, Ho Chi Minh (Nguyen Tat Thanh or Nguyen Ai Quoc, or "the Patriot," as he called himself before taking power; 1890–1969) had become president of the Democratic Republic of Vietnam after the war. His father was an official under the French who had resigned from his position because of his Vietnamese nationalism. Ho Chi Minh himself worked as a kitchen helper on a French passenger liner before becoming a Communist activist. After founding the Indochinese Communist Party in 1929, he unified three groups of Vietnamese Communists under his leadership. Following his condemnation to death by the French government, Ho was saved by the refusal of the British government in Hong Kong to turn him over to French authorities. Nonetheless, the British arrested him in 1931, and he remained in prison in Hong Kong for two years. During World War II, he led the Vietminh, an organization of Vietnamese Communists.

The French had lost their control of Indochina to the Japanese in March 1945, but they soon began the attempt to reconquer their former

(*Left*) A Vietminh fighter is taken prisoner by a French soldier in 1952. (*Right*) A French patrol in Vietnam in 1954.

colony. In November 1946, the French army attacked the port of Haiphong, killing 6,000 Vietnamese, and captured Hanoi, the Vietnamese capital. France restored the nominal authority of a playboy emperor, Bao Dai (1913–1997). Nonetheless, war between Ho Chi Minh's Vietnamese army, which held most of the countryside, and the French continued. Ho, supported by the Chinese, prophesied, "You will kill ten of our men, but we will kill one of yours and you will end up by wearing yourselves out." The Korean War, which began in 1950, increased U.S. interest in the ongoing struggles in Vietnam, bringing U.S. military assistance to the French effort. Early in 1954, the French army suffered a crushing defeat at the hands of the Vietnamese at Dien Bien Phu, a well-fortified French outpost that fell to a Vietnamese attack. Pierre Mendès-France (1907–1982), the new Socialist premier, succeeded in extracting France from war in Vietnam (he would later prove less successful in encouraging the French to drink milk instead of wine, a more hopeless task). At the Geneva Convention that year, France agreed to the division of Vietnam into two states. North Vietnam became a Communist regime led by Ho Chi Minh; South Vietnam became a republic run by a succession of corrupt leaders who carried out U.S. policy in exchange for a free hand. France had lost more than 20,000 soldiers in Vietnam.

The end of French colonialism was even more wrenching in North Africa. There were 1.2 million French citizens in Algeria, 300,000 in Morocco, and 200,000 in Tunisia. These French residents were called *pieds noirs* ("black feet") because of the black boots worn by French soldiers. Morocco and Tunisia were French protectorates, although nominally ruled by a sultan and bey (sovereign), respectively. Algeria, in contrast, was a colony, directly administered by French officials. During the inter-war period, a small nationalist movement developed in Algeria, some of whose members demanded independence, not just an extension of rights. In 1945, French troops put down an uprising in Algeria, at the cost of 40,000 Algerian lives. During the early 1950s, movements for national independence continued to develop in France's North African colonies.

The writer Albert Camus, who was born in Algeria, summed up the difficult choices for some French families who lived there; he said that if given the choice between justice and his mother, he would take his mother. Many of the French living in North Africa had become wealthy; some had successfully developed land taken from the Arab population over the past century. Others were of modest means, including café owners in Algiers, government functionaries, and farmers with small plots of land.

In 1954, the National Liberation Front (Front de Libération Nationale, the FLN) called for Algerian independence. An uprising for independence began just four months after the French defeat at Dien Bien Phu. Fearing that the movement might spread to Tunisia and Morocco (where, in fact, some fighting followed), the French government granted virtual independence to both states in 1956, despite protests of French residents and the vigorous opposition of the French officer corps, which believed its honor was at stake.

In Algeria, the struggle between the FLN and the French army intensified in scale. As guerrilla actions and bombings increased and losses mounted, many people in France began to accept Algerian independence as both inevitable and desirable. In February 1956, French residents in Algiers rioted against the government when French Premier Guy Mollet came to introduce his newly appointed governor of Algeria. In October, the newly crowned king of Morocco met with leaders of the FLN, enraging the French right. Mollet, fearing the political consequences of the war, then ordered the kidnapping of Ahmed Ben Bella (1919–   ), a leader of the Algerians, and launched a repression in France of critics of the French Algerian policy. In November 1956, France joined Britain in the ill-fated invasion of Egypt, in part because of French anger at Egyptian support for the Algerian insurrection. In 1957, French troops undertook a brutal campaign that included torture against militants and civilians alike, culminating in "the battle of Algiers" fought in the Arab quarters of the Algerian capital. In France, the left increasingly demanded an end to the war; intellectuals, like the philosopher Jean-Paul Sartre and the novelist Camus, denounced the torture of Algerians by the French army. In the meantime, casualties mounted in the French army (which, unlike the French war in Vietnam, included conscripts). Throughout the Algerian war of independence, the FLN successfully played off Cold War rivalries, using mass communication and building support in Algerian communities abroad, while winning support within international organizations. Their campaign helped accentuate division in France over the Algerian war, while isolating France internationally.

After humiliating defeats at the hands of the German army in 1940 and by the Vietnamese at Dien Bien Phu in 1954, some French military officers saw the fight in Algeria as a last stand for their honor. A decline in military salaries and living conditions—particularly housing—had followed the decline of the prestige of the French army in France and around the world. Citations for bravery and even the lists of those killed and wounded stopped appearing in government publications. Early in 1958, by which time French troops in Algeria numbered 500,000, French planes attacked FLN camps on the other side of the border with Tunisia. When a new premier was rumored to be willing to negotiate with the insurgents, on May 13, 1958, a demonstration by French settlers in Algiers protesting against any compromise turned into a military-led insurrection against the French government. A "Committee of Public Safety" of rightists seized power, led by General Jacques Massu. On May 24, another right-wing Committee of Public Safety seized power in Corsica. A military coup d'état seemed possible on the mainland of France.

Charles de Gaulle, who had been waiting in self-imposed exile for something like this to happen, announced that he was ready to serve France again. Many politicians, fearing a military seizure of power, believed that de Gaulle alone could prevent chaos. On May 29, 1958, President René Coty appointed de Gaulle premier, a move approved by the National Assembly early in June. The general accepted, on the condition that he could rule by emergency decree for six months and could then ask the

Algerian rioters face off against the police force called out to suppress a demonstration against French Premier Guy Mollet's arrival in Algiers, 1956.

nation to approve a new constitution. The right, including army officers, was delighted with de Gaulle's return to power, thinking that the general would never allow Algerian independence.

The new constitution greatly increased the authority of the president, whose term was set at seven years to end revolving-door ministries. Presidents under the Fifth French Republic would conduct foreign policy, appoint prime ministers, and dissolve the French parliament. In September 1958, 80 percent of French voters approved the constitution of the French Fifth Republic.

But what about Algeria? De Gaulle went to Algiers and, in a remarkably noncommittal speech, told the settlers in June 1958, "I have understood you, I know what you have tried to do here." But he had already decided that the costs of continuing the war in Algeria were too great, too divisive. He removed the generals responsible for the coup in Algeria from their posts. For a man whose nationalism underlay his political philosophy, it seemed an astonishing turnaround.

To some military officers, de Gaulle's actions seemed an incredible betrayal, a stab in the back by a fellow military man. As the Dreyfus Affair had revealed in the 1890s and the Vichy years had confirmed, a right-wing anti-democratic tradition survived in the officer corps. Many officers now felt betrayed not only by de Gaulle but also by much of the population in France. They enjoyed some support among rightist parties. When de Gaulle recalled General Massu to Paris in January 1960, right-wing riots took place in Paris. In Algeria, *pieds noirs* began a general strike and put up barricades. De Gaulle made an appeal to the rioters by television and radio, rallying public opinion to what had clearly become a policy of allowing Algerians to decide their own future.

Negotiations between Algerian leaders and De Gaulle's government began in the spring of 1961. In the meantime, a secret group within the army, the OAS (Secret Army Organization) had formed in January 1961, determined at all costs to keep Algeria French. In April it staged a coup d'état and held power in Algiers and in the city of Oran for three days, without winning the support of the army. In Paris, the political parties of the left and center threw their support to de Gaulle. The general once again went on television and again assumed emergency powers, this time for a year. The OAS twice tried to assassinate de Gaulle, once nearly succeeding, riddling his car with machine-gun fire. Members planted bombs in Algerian cities and in Paris in order to terrorize the civilian population. Given the chance to vote on their future, the Algerians opted for independence; in France, the vote for Algerian independence in July 1961 was 15 million to 5 million. On March 19, 1962, the Algerian War officially ended, with the French people overwhelmingly ratifying the peace terms. In July 1962, Algeria became independent.

De Gaulle believed that France had a special historic mission, and he never doubted for a moment the part he was to play in it. He feared the domination of Europe and France by Britain and the United States. He insisted that France maintain an independent nuclear capability (the *force de frappe*, a nuclear bomb first tested in 1960). Moreover, de Gaulle sought a closer diplomatic relationship with the German Federal Republic. Ending decades of animosity, the close partnership between Germany and France formed the cornerstone of the new Europe. In the meantime, although no longer a great power, France maintained considerable prestige in the Third World.

Throughout his political career, de Gaulle's speeches were full of references to France's "grandeur." Although much of his political support came from the right, the general stated, "De Gaulle is not on the left. Or on the right. Or in the center. De Gaulle is above." The general's political style was more that of a monarch than of a president. He often referred to himself in the third person, occasionally using the royal "we." Not long after there had been attempts on his life, one of his aides informed de Gaulle that he ran great risks by plunging into crowds of people during his visits to provincial towns. The general replied, "Get one thing into your head. De Gaulle interests me only as a figure of history."

De Gaulle refused to cooperate with the other Western powers. He never forgot the humiliation of France's exclusion from the Allied conferences at Yalta and Potsdam. In 1966, France left NATO's military command, forcing it to transfer its headquarters from Paris to Brussels. U.S. army and air force bases in France were closed. De Gaulle angered the U.S. government by refusing to support its policies in Vietnam. He outraged many Canadians during a state visit in 1967 by shouting, "Long live Free Quebec!" (Quebec is a predominantly French-speaking province of Canada in which there has been considerable sentiment for independence.) Although de Gaulle remained vehemently anti-Communist, he wanted France to provide leadership as a third force that stood between the Soviet Union and the United States.

Decolonization in Sub-Saharan Africa

At the end of World War II, only Egypt, Liberia, and Ethiopia had achieved independence in Africa. Nationalist groups in Africa were less organized than had been their counterparts in India and Southeast Asia. In the subsequent decades, British rule ended in one African colony after another. In 1957, Ghana (formerly the Gold Coast) became the first British colony in Africa to become independent after the Second World War, with Kwame Nkrumah (1909–1972) its president. Others soon followed, including Nigeria in 1960, Sierra Leone and Tanganyika in 1961, Uganda in 1962, and Kenya in 1963. Sixteen states in Africa became independent in 1960, including the Ivory Coast, Senegal, and Cameroon, former French colonies (see Map 28.1) that had belonged to the French Union, an organization established in Africa in 1946.

Map 28.1 Decolonization The map shows movements for decolonization in Africa, Asia, and the Far East, giving the dates at which each of the colonies achieved independence.

The Republic of South Africa left the British Commonwealth in 1961. With a white population of 21 percent (with 68 percent African, 2 percent of mixed race, and 2 percent Asian) in 1950, South Africa continued the system of apartheid, an official policy of racial inequality and segregation that was supported by the ultraconservative white Afrikaner population of Dutch origin. In 1965 Rhodesia, which had been a self-governing colony, declared its independence from Britain. It did so, in part, so that its white minority would not have to share power with the black majority population. The British government then led a campaign of international economic sanctions against the white regime of its former colony. In 1980, Rhodesia was divided into the independent states of Zimbabwe and Zambia, where blacks obtained political rights.

In the Belgian Congo in central West Africa, the Belgian government first tried to placate nationalists with concessions in the late 1950s and then to repress them following rioting in 1959. A year later, the Belgian government suddenly pulled out of its former colony (although the Congo's army retained Belgian officers), declaring the Congo independent in June 1960. Before independence, however, preliminary elections had revealed considerable political division. Civil war began between two nationalist leaders, a bloody conflict complicated by ethnic and tribal loyalties. Soldiers mutinied against their Belgian commanders and began to attack Europeans remaining in the Congo. The Congo's wealthiest province, Katanga, then declared its independence. At the request of the Congo's premier, the United Nations sent troops to restore order. After a year, the civil war ended. Katanga did not end its succession until 1963.

In 1965, Colonel Mobutu Sese Seko (1930–1997) imposed military rule in the Congo. He nationalized his country's wealthy mines. The old colonial capital of Leopoldville became Kinshasa. Mobuto renamed Lake Albert after himself and set about amassing enormous personal wealth. In 1971, the country became known as Zaire.

Portugal was another small European state that held colonies many times its size. It struggled to retain its colonies of Angola and Mozambique, which lie on the southwestern and southeastern coasts, respectively, of Africa. A nationalist uprising for independence (led by the Popular Movement for the Liberation of Angola) lasted from 1961 to 1975, when the new Portuguese government, which a year earlier had overthrown the dictatorship that had ruled Portugal for decades, granted independence to Angola. However, as in the case of the former Belgian Congo, fighting broke out between a Marxist group and an extreme right-wing military faction, the former backed by the Soviet Union, the latter by the United States. The war lasted until 1991, when the Popular Movement, aided by Cuban funds and soldiers, won the war. Nonetheless, the rightists continued to battle the new government. In Mozambique, following independence in 1975 after a long insurrection, warfare between left and right also began. There, too, the far-left faction won, while the right,

The Duchess of Kent delivers a message from the Queen of England to
the Ghanaian Parliament in 1957, the year that Ghana became the first
British colony in Africa to become independent.

assisted by the South African government, launched a campaign of terror.
Ordinary people, the vast majority of them impoverished, suffered untold
horrors of famine and slaughter, complicated by increasing tension
between Mozambique's leftist government and Zimbabwe.

Independence in many cases proved to be no panacea for new African
nations. Many post-colonial administrations proved unable or unwilling to
provide a decent quality of life to people. Some new states fell into bloody
and debilitating civil wars. These conflicts were compounded by the multiplicity of ethnic groups, tribalism, and a lack of political experience—
problems that still stand as daunting impediments to the construction of
modern political systems in developing nations. Even with the departure
of colonial governments, European companies still controlled valuable
raw materials, as in the case of Zaire. And a good many African rulers have
abused their power by enriching themselves at the expense of their people,
while adopting, as in the case of Robert Mugabe of Zimbabwe, anticolo-
nial rhetoric to justify their plunder.

A NEW PROSPERITY

Thus, the difficult but still encouraging years in the immediate post-war
period gave way to a period of considerable economic growth from 1950 to

1973. European economies benefited from the ongoing globalization of trade, the availability of a labor supply, and more state planning (at least in the case of Italy and France). Oil rapidly replaced coal as the principal source of fuel for industrial growth. This fact alone dramatically increased the strategic importance of the Middle East. Natural gas, much of which was imported into Europe from the Soviet Union, offered another source of energy.

Foreign trade within and beyond Europe boomed: West Germany's imports multiplied during the 1950s by four times and its exports by six times. By 1960, the German Federal Republic was the world's second leading exporter of goods, including machinery, appliances, radios, chemicals, and automobiles—the Volkswagen conquered some of the European market and appeared with increasing frequency in the United States.

Table 28.1 provides comparative rates of industrial productivity for the major nations of Europe, as well as for Japan and the United States. In France, industrial production in 1959 was twice that of 1938. Smaller nations also thrived. Norway, Denmark, and Sweden all became more prosperous nations thanks largely to the development of fishing, agriculture, industry, and a booming service sector.

Great disparities remained between and within European nations. By the end of the 1960s, the German Federal Republic, Switzerland, and Sweden were the most prosperous European countries; Ireland, Portugal, Greece, and Spain were the poorest in Western Europe. Romania and Albania were the poorest Communist states. In Table 28.1, Britain's relative decline sticks out.

As a result of the German economic "miracle," West Germany's gross national product tripled between 1950 and 1964, aided by the Korean War, which increased demand for war-related industries. German industrial

TABLE 28.1. INDEX OF INDUSTRIAL PRODUCTION

	1938	1948	1952	1959	1963	1967
United States	33	73	90	113	133	168
West Germany	53	27	61	107	137	158
France	52	55	70	101	129	155
Italy	43	44	64	112	166	212
Holland	47	53	72	110	141	182
Belgium	64	78	88	104	135	153
Britain	67	74	84	105	119	133
Austria	39	36	65	106	131	151
Spain				102	149	215
Sweden	52	74	81	106	140	176
Japan	58	22	50	120	212	347

Source: Walter Laqueur, *Europe Since Hitler* (New York: Penguin, 1982), p. 194.

production more than doubled between 1948 and 1951, and it increased by six times from 1948 to 1964. West Germany assumed pre-war Germany's role as a major producer of steel and machinery. The chemical industry, strong in Germany since the late nineteenth century, continued to develop rapidly. Italy, which had also been defeated in the war, also enjoyed a boom. Between 1959 and 1963 its exports increased by more than 14 percent per year and industrial production rose by 8 percent. Real wages in Italy in 1954 were more than 50 percent higher than they had been before the war, as the Italian economy also grew rapidly with the help of considerable U.S. financial assistance.

Cooperation between countries contributed to economic growth in Western Europe. The Treaty of Rome (1957) laid the groundwork for the European Atomic Energy Community and the European Economic Community (EEC, which was also sometimes known as the European Common Market). It began in 1958, with member nations including France, Italy, the German Federal Republic, Belgium, Luxembourg, and the Netherlands. The European Economic Community gradually eliminated trade barriers between member states in Western Europe, established common customs tariffs, and worked toward equalizing wages and social-security arrangements among the member countries. The result was to help increase trade within member states, contributing to their prosperity. By helping reduce trade barriers, the European Economic Community aided Europe's new prosperity.

The boom of the 1950s and 1960s elevated the standard of living for most Europeans, although great gaps between social classes remained. It brought increased material comfort previously unimaginable in most sectors of European society, including veritable symbols of the post-war age: automobiles, refrigerators, and televisions. New synthetic products (like plastic), some of which had been developed or improved by wartime scientific research, engendered a consumer revolution.

The resulting rise in the standard of living for Western industrial workers gradually reduced any possibility that workers might be a revolutionary force in Europe. At the same time, the growth in managerial and lower-level white-collar employment (as opposed to the "blue-collar" industrial workers) decreased the proportional size of the industrial workforce. White-collar workers, including shop and bank clerks, insurance agents, business assistants, hotel staff, and secretaries, now outnumbered factory workers in an increasing number of countries. The old trade unions lost some of their clout; union leaders looked increasingly to clerical workers for new members.

European states maintained a commitment to comprehensive welfare programs. Between 1965 and 1981, the proportion of government expenditures in Britain that went to social welfare rose from 16 to 25 percent, and in Sweden from 19 to 33 percent. Everywhere, the increase in government services added to the size of bureaucracies in most European countries, most notably in France, the Scandinavian nations (above all, Sweden), and the Eastern bloc countries. Yet the advent of welfare states was predicated on economic growth. When economies do not grow, however, social-welfare costs become drains on national budgets. Countries like Great Britain, France, and Sweden, would later find, for instance, that rising medical costs would threaten to outstrip the ability of government programs to pay for them.

A CHANGING CONTINENT

While intellectuals grappled with the horror of what World War II had wrought, a remarkable economic revival was under way in the 1950s, engendering increased prosperity and a growing population. This was the "baby boom." Moreover, people lived longer and longer, due to improvements in medicine and diet. Mechanization and commercialization augmented agricultural production, which became more efficient. Because of this "Green Revolution," more and more rural people left the land for cities, which grew rapidly. Industries, financial services, and the service sector concentrated in the continent's emerging urban world.

Intellectual Currents in the Post-War Era

Outside of a sense of relief, there seemed little about which to be optimistic at the end of World War II. The British writer George Orwell summed up the general feeling when he wrote, "Since about 1930, the world had given no reason for optimism whatsoever. Nothing in sight except a welter of lies, cruelty, hatred, and ignorance." Cynicism seemed to prevail. Unlike the period immediately following World War I, few people now believed that another total war was inconceivable. Many writers and artists seemed overwhelmed with pessimism, even hopelessness, in the face of the atomic age and the Cold War. Claiming "alienation" from the society they increasingly criticized, many Western intellectuals withdrew into introspection. However, for some, communism seemed to offer a plan for the harmonious organization of society. Communist parties in Western nations attracted many enthusiastic intellectuals who believed that the Soviet Union offered a successful model to be emulated in their own countries.

French existentialism became an influential cultural current during the first two decades following the war. The French philosopher Jean-Paul Sartre (1905–1980) believed that in the wake of the unparalleled destruction of World War II, the absurdity of life was the most basic discovery one could make. Denying the existence of God, existentialists like Sartre posited that life has no meaning. Their conclusion was that a person could only truly find any fulfillment while living "a suspended death" by becoming aware of his or her freedom to choose and to act. Sartre titled one of his plays *Huis clos* (*No Exit*), as he believed there was nothing beyond this life. Sartre's novels glorify the individual spirit seeking freedom, not through Enlightenment rationalism, but rather through a comprehension of life's irrationality. However, more than this, Sartre believed that violent revolution could free the individual from the human condition by allowing him or her to find truth by redefining reality. To this end, he joined the French Communist Party when the war was over. However, existentialism slowly lost its grip on French intellectual life, at least partially because of growing disillusionment with the Soviet Union among many leftist intellectuals.

The Algerian-born French writer Albert Camus (1913–1960) shared Sartre's view of mankind's tragic situation, but broke with Sartre in 1952 over the latter's enthusiasm for Stalin's Soviet Union. Camus's answer to the dark world of brutality reflected by the war (during which he participated in the resistance) and the frustrations of the post-war period was for the individual to search for meaning in life by choosing a path of action—even revolt—against absurdity, irrationality, and tyrannies of all kinds. The rebel should act, according to Camus, from a personal sense of responsibility and moral choice that are independent of belief in God or any political system. Confronting the arrival of murderous disease in the

A gathering of intellectuals after the war, including Jean-Paul Sartre (seated left), Albert Camus (seated center), Pablo Picasso (standing with arms folded), and Simone de Beauvoir (to the far right and standing next to some of Picasso's work).

Algerian city of Oran, Dr. Rieux, the central figure in Camus's *The Plague* (1947), does not believe in God or absolute standards of morality, but he nonetheless helps people take action to cope with the epidemic.

The "theater of the absurd," which also reflected intellectuals' reaction to the horrors of the war, was centered in Paris and had a following from 1948 to about 1968. It offered highly unconventional and antirational plays. The Irish-born Samuel Beckett (1906–1989) and other playwrights sought to shock audiences with provocative themes and by stringing together seemingly unrelated events and dialogue in order to demonstrate that existence is without purpose and absurd. They rejected plots, conventional settings, and individual identities. Their clownish, mechanical characters are perpetual exiles alienated in a bizarre, nightmarish world that makes no sense. The lack of causality in these plays is a commentary on life itself. Beckett's *Waiting for Godot* (begun in 1948 but not published in French until 1952 and in English two years later) is the best known of the absurdist plays. It tells a disconnected tale of two old derelicts, Vladimir and Estragon (although they call themselves by childish nicknames). They meet night after night in anticipation of the arrival of a certain Godot (perhaps intended to be a diminutive of God), though it is never clear what difference in their lives his arrival would ever make, if any. He never comes, so we never know.

Other intellectuals of the left also reacted to what they perceived as the lack of moral absolutes in a world that had experienced total war. They too were preoccupied by the possibilities of social liberation. Frantz Fanon (1925–1961), a black French social critic from Martinique, explored the revolutionary potential of the "Third World" (that is, relatively underdeveloped countries, some of whom were unaligned in the Cold War) in *The Wretched of the Earth* (1961). The French anthropologist Claude Lévi-Strauss (1908–) espoused cultural relativism, moving anthropology away from a Western-centered view of "peripheral" or "underdeveloped" regions with his work on Brazil and Southeast Asia. Lévi-Strauss's interest in how communities behave, too, led away from the emphasis on the individual that characterized both Freudianism and existentialism.

Change also occurred in the research and writing of history. The French *Annales* (the name of a scholarly journal) school, founded by the medievalist and wartime resistance hero and martyr Marc Bloch (1886–1944), treated political and diplomatic events as mere foam on the waves of history. Instead, these historians espoused a "total history" that would describe and analyze the lives of ordinary people in the context of major economic and social changes of the past.

In contrast to the intellectuals in the West, intellectuals in the Soviet Union were stymied by the state. Writers, artists, and filmmakers confronted a state apparatus that made the costs of free expression so high that voluntary adherence to state-dictated norms followed. "Socialist realism" (art and literature of generally horrendous quality, intended to inspire the population by showing smiling Soviet citizens at work; see Chapter 23) was the only authorized form of artistic expression; the works of most Western artists were condemned as tools of capitalism. Art was intended to encourage devotion to and sacrifice for the state. But while he rejected the ideas of Freud and Einstein out of hand, Stalin gave official approval to the crackpot theories of the geneticist Trofim Lysenko (1898–1976), who insisted that knowledge or beliefs that were experienced by one generation could be genetically inherited. Stalin's particular interest in this theory was that it suggested that party members who learned official orthodoxy and experienced conformity in social behavior would pass the same characteristics on to their offspring.

In the 1950s and 1960s, artistic talent was often channeled into films rather than into the traditional arts. Western European filmmakers made important contributions to cinema. While most American film producers emphasized light entertainment (such as westerns and war movies with special effects and love stories), Italy's Federico Fellini (*La Strada*, 1956, and *La Dolce Vita*, 1959) and Sweden's Ingmar Bergman (*The Seventh Seal*, 1956) turned out serious art films (although European audiences, too, flocked to see Hollywood films). French New Wave directors, including Jean-Luc Godard (*Breathless*, 1959) and François Truffaut (*400 Blows*, 1959), rebelled against traditional cinematographic techniques and used innovations such as jump cuts and disruptive editing to create a sense of dislocation and to remind the viewer that he or she was watching

Italian filmmaker Federico Fellini on the set of his 1956 film *La Strada*.

a film, not reality. Their experimental films explored human relationships and often portrayed antiheroes. In contrast, the English producer and director Alfred Hitchcock (1899–1980) frightened and intrigued generations of audiences with riveting suspense films like *Psycho* (1960).

The Post-War Baby Boom

Following the war, a veritable "baby boom" occurred in Europe, as in the United States. Europe's population grew from 264 million in 1940 to 320 million by the early 1970s. The increase in the birthrate after the war more than made up for the loss of hundreds of thousands of emigrants to North America and Latin America, particularly from Italy. Europeans also lived longer, aided by improvements in diet and in health.

Increases in industrial and agricultural productivity, opening up new jobs, encouraged families to have more children, as did government policies that aided families that had children. In France, where leaders had openly worried about the low birthrate, special incentives were offered to families that had more than two children. Medical advances (such as the virtual elimination of polio by the end of the 1950s) and an increase in the number of doctors further reduced infant mortality. The birthrate increased between 1950 and 1966 in every country in Western Europe, with Switzerland, the Netherlands, the German Federal Republic, and France leading the way. The Soviet Union and Poland, too, saw high annual natural increases. Nonetheless, because of virtually unchecked population growth in India, China, and other Third World nations, Europe's percentage of the world population fell to 16 percent in 1990.

The increase in the birthrate had a far-reaching social and political impact. British, French, and German eighteen-year-olds received the right to vote in the early 1970s. Moreover, governments had to increase spending dramatically on education to prepare the young for jobs in an economy that was rapidly becoming more complex. Laws obliged parents to send their children to school from the time they were about six until they were fourteen or sixteen years old, depending on the country. Illiteracy became quite uncommon in Europe by the 1960s. University education came within reach of a larger proportion of the population. But despite the tripling of the number of university students in Britain, France, and Italy between 1938 and 1960, there was relatively little democratization of university attendance, which remained the preserve of the upper classes. In 1967, fewer than 10 percent of French university students were the children of workers or peasants. In Great Britain, particularly, but also in the other countries of the West, working-class and farm families could not afford to send their children to university because time away from earning represented an economic hardship. In Eastern Europe and the Balkan countries, the number of students in higher education rose rapidly, as well.

The plight of the elderly was often lost in the emphasis on youth. As the life expectancy of people increased with improvements in diet and medical advances, there were more old people than ever before and social-service budgets began to sag under the weight of an aging population.

With the rapid development of the service sector of Western economies, the proliferation of white-collar jobs lifted the expectations, status, and income of hundreds of thousands of families. A more equitable distribution in taxation helped remove some of the tax burden from ordinary people. But enormous economic and social gaps remained between rich and poor, particularly in Britain and France. In 1960, 5 percent of the British population owned about 75 percent of the nation's wealth.

The Green Revolution

In the two decades that followed World War II, Western European agriculture was transformed by the "Green Revolution." Large-scale, commercialized agriculture permitted most nations to produce almost all of the food consumed by their populations. Agricultural productivity rose by 30 percent between the end of the war and 1962. In the German Federal Republic, agricultural production increased by two-and-a-half times between 1950 and 1964.

There were several reasons for these changes in farming. First, mechanized agriculture was increasingly widespread, particularly use of the tractor. Second, fertilizers augmented farm yields in northern Europe, while pesticides—a mixed blessing because of the long-term ecological costs—prevented blight. Advances in types of seeds, animal husbandry (particularly artificial insemination), and irrigation also contributed to greater productivity. Third, the size of many farms increased as smaller and less productive plots were consolidated into larger units.

Governments programs encouraged the cooperative use of tractors, and they often provided agricultural information to farmers. State-sponsored land reform in Sicily turned over formerly unfarmed large estates to people eager to work the land. In many countries, government assistance facilitated reforestation, electrification, irrigation projects, and road building that would have been beyond the means of private initiatives.

The Green Revolution was spread unevenly across Europe. Agriculture became most efficient in the more prosperous northern states of Western Europe: Great Britain, the Netherlands, Belgium, West Germany, Denmark, and northern France. Denmark, France, and other European nations generated agricultural surpluses and became major exporters of food during the 1970s and 1980s.

Fewer farmers fed a much larger population. The continued commercialization of agriculture accentuated the exodus from the land to the rapidly growing cities of Europe. In Italy, the farming population fell from about 40 percent after the war to 24 percent in 1966. In Great Britain, the first European nation in which agriculture was substantially mechanized even before the war, less than 4 percent of the population worked the land by the early 1970s. Before World War II, 76 percent of the population of Romania worked the land and 11 percent had been employed in industry; by 1986, only 28 percent still tilled the soil, and the percentage employed in manufacturing had risen to 45 percent. Before World War I, about half the population of Europe worked in agriculture, a figure that included fishermen and foresters. In 1955, the percentage had fallen to about 24 percent, and it has continued to decline, although it remains higher in southern Europe. In every country, agriculture's share of the gross national product has fallen.

In the 1950s, Western European peasants started to join organizations to lobby for assistance and favorable tariffs. Peasants blocked traffic in Rome and Paris with tractors and farm animals to protest government policies; in Brittany in the late 1970s, they filled the courtyard of a prefecture with artichokes to protest low prices. Ironically, this phenomenon came at a time when peasants, because of the rural exodus in Western Europe, have lost most of their political voice.

In the Communist countries of Eastern Europe, the collectivization of agriculture proceeded during the 1950s and 1960s. Somewhat greater efficiency (which, to be sure, did not necessarily mean acceptance of the Communist system by landowners whose land had been expropriated by the state) permitted substantial movement of the rural population into cities and factories. In the German Democratic Republic and Bulgaria, 85 percent of the land had been collectivized by the mid-1960s. In Poland at about the same time, more than 85 percent of the land remained in private hands because the Polish Communist leadership feared open popular resistance to massive agricultural collectivization.

An Urban World

Europe rapidly urbanized in the decades following World War II. Great Britain, the Netherlands, and the German Federal Republic led the way. In the German industrial Rhineland, it became difficult to tell where one city ended and another began. In Eastern Europe, the population living in cities increased from 37.5 million at the end of the 1940s to 58 million twenty years later.

Modern architects confronted the challenge of designing large, functional buildings at a reasonable cost. The necessity of housing millions of new urban residents contributed to a uniformity of architectural style. Tall, drab, uniform towers filled with small apartments sprang up in and around major urban centers, providing adequate lodging, but not much more, in

The clash of old and new in Europe's changing cities.

cramped quarters with thin walls. Commuting became a fact of urban life in much of Europe. By the 1980s, almost 20 percent of the French population resided in Paris and its surroundings. Of these, only about 3 million lived in the City of Light itself, the rest inhabiting sprawling suburbs.

In the early 1960s, the Soviets began to build new suburbs and satellite towns to accommodate the population seeking to live in Moscow, which grew from 2 million in 1926 to more than 5 million in 1959. Leningrad's population increased from 1.7 million to 3.3 million during the same period, despite the death of hundreds of thousands of its residents as a result of the German siege during the war.

Rapid urban growth, closely tied to the concentration of large-scale industries, posed problems of health and safety. Factories increasingly polluted the air of industrial regions. Nonetheless, projects of urban renewal enhanced the quality of life in cities and towns. Again, Paris provides a good example. Much of its historic center was refurbished, dilapidated seventeenth-century noble residences were sandblasted clean, and some of them were transformed into fancy apartments and shops catering to visitors. West German, Belgian, French, and Dutch cities, among others, sported shining urban centers, with some streets reserved for beleaguered pedestrians tired of dodging onrushing cars and suffering the chaos of honking horns.

Western Europe's burgeoning cities became increasingly clogged with automobiles, which, in addition to factory pollution, dirtied the air. The automobile had an enormous impact on work and leisure in Europe, however, particularly in the West. The production of automobiles soared on the continent. Moreover, the number of cars on the road increased from 5 million in 1948 to 44 million in 1965; in France the number rose from 1.7 million in 1950 to about 11 million by the mid 1960s. The construction of new freeways and toll roads could not begin to keep up with the increase of traffic. The traffic jam in Europe began.

CHANGING CONTOURS OF ECONOMIC LIFE

Since World War II, the economic transformations in Europe have engendered several major social changes. Trade and technology led to an increasing interconnectedness and interdependence of global economies. The workforce changed as the percentage of population working the land fell sharply and more and more women began to work outside the home in careers that had traditionally been off-limits to them. Consumerism began to thrive, and goods that might have been considered luxury items just a few decades earlier became readily available.

Oil and the Global Economy

The Six-Day Arab-Israeli War of 1967 and the 1973 Yom Kippur War both resulted in easy Israeli victories over their Arab rivals. Israel expanded its territory, absorbing Jerusalem, a holy city for Christians, Jews, and Arabs, and occupying Arab land on the West Bank and in the Gaza Strip. Western support for Israel, particularly that of the United States, was matched by Soviet support for the Arab states and for the stateless Palestinian people. An embargo by the oil-producing Arab states of the Middle East (undertaken by the Organization of Petroleum Exporting Countries, or OPEC) in 1973 had disastrous consequences for the economies of Western nations, particularly in Europe, which was more dependent on Middle Eastern oil than was the United States.

The Arab oil embargo interrupted the supply of oil from the Middle East. It led to a rapid rise in the price of oil and contributed to the high inflation that undermined Western economies for the rest of the 1970s. Dependency on oil led states to urge people to consume less gasoline (for example, by encouraging greater use of public transportation and, in the United States, by reducing speed limits). Britain and Norway each began to extract oil in the stormy North Sea. European countries,

Israeli soldiers dance in front of the wailing wall in Old Jerusalem during the Six-Day Arab-Israeli War, 1967.

especially France, had already begun to develop nuclear installations to generate more energy.

The oil crisis helped bring an end to what had been a long period of relative prosperity and stability. It also was one of the sources of the economic recession that gripped Western Europe from the mid-1970s to the mid-1980s. Inflation, which had been at modest levels during the 1950s and 1960s but had been accentuated by the U.S. war in Vietnam, began to soar. The oil embargo contributed to the high rates of unemployment, which strained European welfare budgets.

Advances for Women

In the decades following World War II, the status of women gradually improved, although the amount of improvement varied across the continent. While women lost some skilled jobs to men returning from service after the war, economic expansion and the creation of ever more white-collar jobs (for example, in travel agencies and department stores) provided new employment possibilities. Simone de Beauvoir's *The Second Sex* (1949) helped mobilize movements for the rights of women in the United States and, more slowly, in Europe. In Western countries, the important contribution of working women made it difficult to continue to deny half the population the right to vote. During the period from 1944 to 1948, women received the suffrage in France, Italy, Belgium, and Portugal. Women probably were more equal in the countries of the Soviet bloc (where there were no free elections) in terms of employment opportunities, although in practice this often meant that they bore the dual burden of wage earning and domestic duties. In the Soviet Union, 43 percent of workers were women in the 1950s. In Western Europe, more and more middle-class women began to work full-time. Beginning in 1977, French women no longer needed their husbands' permission to work. In Communist countries, women more easily entered the medical profession, but men dominated the state bureaucracies. Women were most successful in reaching rough equality in the Scandinavian countries, least so in the Mediterranean lands where traditional biases remained more difficult to overcome.

At the same time, the number of female university students rose dramatically, and so did the number of women in the professions. Women received legal protection against job discrimination in England in the late 1960s, and in France the government created a Ministry for the Status of Women.

Feminism, reviving during the 1968 protests, helped the cause of women's rights. Gradually the percentage of women serving in legislatures increased. In the Soviet Union and Sweden, women made up more than half of all employees, and more than a third in every European country. Moreover, gays and lesbians gained more rights beginning in the 1970s, even if some countries have retained laws permitting discrimination against them.

Living Better, Consumer Culture

With a gradual reduction in the workday and higher wages, families had more time and money for leisure. Travel became an essential part of middle-class and, increasingly, working-class life. Air travel linked European cities to each other and to other continents. Gradually, particularly with the introduction of the passenger jet in the late 1950s, the airplane replaced the passenger ship for cross-Atlantic travel. The era of the shipboard romance was almost over.

Telephones facilitated business and family life. By the late 1950s, hardly any large enterprises could afford to be without one. Household phones became more common in the 1960s in most of Western Europe. The telephone's diffusion came slower in France, however, where the minister of communication in 1964 actually referred to the telephone as a "gimmick."

The radio and then television helped shape a mass consumer culture, catapulting entertainers to fame and making household names of politicians who could be heard instead of simply imagined. The first television sets were viewed at the World's Fair in New York City in 1939. By the late 1960s, a majority of Western European households had a television and by the mid-1970s, relatively few were without one. Television without question played a role in the spread of discontent in the Soviet Union and the Communist nations of Eastern Europe and the Balkans, first bringing little by little views of ways of life and relative prosperity in Western states, and then carrying news of the mobilization against and then the fall of one regime after another. During the past several decades, television has continued to expand horizons, making the world more interconnected. In the mid-1980s, the U.S.-based CNN network began to reach across the world. Just as television coverage of dramatic news events (for example, the death of Princess Diana of England in 1997 or the terrorist attacks of September 11, 2001) could be instantaneously seen around the world, so sports took on an increasingly global dimension as well (above all, the World Cup and the Olympics).

The era of television and radio ended the great age of the newspaper. During the first years after the war, Europeans read more—and arguably better—newspapers than ever before or since. As Europeans increasingly received their news and their entertainment from television and radio, however, newspapers merged and many folded. With the exception of the stately, serious dailies like *Le Monde* of Paris, the *Manchester Guardian*, the *Frankfurter Allegemeine* in the German Federal Republic, and *La Stampa* of Milan, an increasing number of tabloid papers relied upon sensationalism, scandals, and the proclamation of juicy unsubstantiated rumor as truth to attract readers. In the Soviet Union, where the state was the only source of printed news, more than 7 million copies of *Pravda* were printed every day. As in the 1930s, conservative publishers controlled the majority of newspapers in Western Europe.

World War II brought only a brief hiatus in the export of Hollywood films to Europe. American film stars became those of the continent (at the same time, some European actors and actresses, such as Marlene Dietrich, Sophia Loren, Audrey Hepburn, and Elizabeth Taylor became stars in the United States). While American films had broad appeal, Italian, British, French, Russian, German, and Czech filmmakers nonetheless turned out some movies of artistic quality.

In France, some films took subjects from recent and sometimes painful history, notably Gilles Pontecorvo's *The Battle of Algiers* (1961), which used some actual participants in the Algerian insurrection (see pp. 1263–1265), to which the film is highly sympathetic. Marcel Orphuls's documentary about collaboration and resistance in World War II France, *The Sorrow and the Pity* (1969), helped spur the rethinking of French collaboration with the Nazis during the Vichy years.

The transportation and communications revolutions have made the world a much smaller place. The cost of transatlantic phone calls fell rapidly with the advent of optical fibers in the 1980s. Then in the 1990s the computer revolution and the Internet brought hundreds of millions of people within range of each other, putting a world of information at their fingertips (although Web sites remain censored in China and some other countries). Credit cards and then personal computers transformed the way people make purchases, and cell phones changed the way people communicate (to the annoyance of drivers, other passengers, and fellow diners). In the context of the ongoing revolution in communications, the advent of computer viruses demonstrated the extent to which the world has become increasingly interconnected. The apparent vulnerability of even the most sophisticated computer systems to knowledgeable hackers has led to fears for national security systems.

A reaction among many European intellectuals against post-war consumerism, closely identified with the United States, generated anti-Americanism. The latter reflected hostility to U.S. foreign and nuclear policy during the Cold War and fear of American domination of NATO. The U.S. placement of nuclear weapons in Western Europe, beginning with West Germany in 1955, generated both anti-nuclear organizations and anti-Americanism. Intellectuals criticized U.S. culture as reeking of vulgar materialism. A prominent French sociologist called the U.S. publication *Reader's Digest* "a pocket-sized stupefier" whose translation into French risked debasing French culture. French governments, too, viewed Americanization as a threat to French culture. There was an economic dimension to this struggle, as U.S. companies and products dramatically augmented their presence in Western Europe. None generated more controversy than Coca-Cola. During the early 1950s, the French government feared the

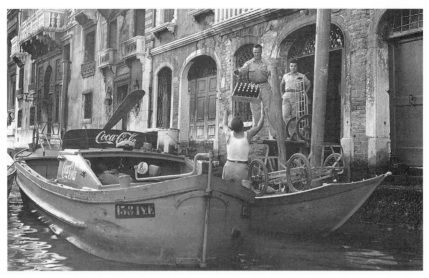

Delivering Coca-Cola in Venice.

competition that Coca-Cola could give the wine industry. Encouraged by the powerful wine lobby, the French government tried—ultimately without success—to keep Coca-Cola from the French market as Coke bottles began to sweep across Europe beginning in the late 1940s. In contrast, anti-Americanism seemed less pronounced in Germany and Austria, which had embraced Nazism and arguably were seeking new identities.

The partial "Americanization" of European consumer culture could readily be seen, however, by the late 1960s. Supermarkets began to put many small grocery stores out of business. American words and terms crept into European languages (such as *le week-end* and *le snack-bar* in French, leading purists to denounce such terms as *franglais*).

The fast-paced "American way of life" exerted a growing attraction on European business and consumers. Television, radio, and billboards promoted material comfort. Some intellectuals at first believed that "Americanization" might erode what they considered Western Europe's moral stature, although they were attracted by the relative affluence of American society. Europeans gradually discovered American "management techniques," using them in both business and government. Thus, French technocrats trained in the *Grandes Écoles*, the most prestigious schools in France, began to take their place in the 1950s in the highest government circles, espousing greater efficiency.

American consumerism and popular culture found favor in European societies. By the late 1970s, McDonald's had already begun to dot European capitals and gradually smaller cities as well. In the 1980s, EuroDisney (now called Disneyland-Paris), which one French theatrical director called "a cultural Chernobyl" (referring to the nuclear accident in Ukraine in 1986), opened its doors outside of Paris. The first Starbuck's opened its doors in Paris in 2003.

The rapid rise of international tourism offers another example of economic globalization in the post–World War II era, as well as a result of increased prosperity and more leisure time. In particular, the advent of the jumbo jet in the late 1960s increased the number of passengers who could be squeezed into a single plane, reducing the cost of tickets. The era of the charter flight began. North American, Asian, and African destinations became more common.

Each July and August, millions of Western Europeans began to take to the road, the majority heading toward the sunny beaches of southern Europe. Paid vacations became an expected part of the "good life." Tourism became essential to the economies of the sunny Mediterranean countries—above all, Spain—visited by millions of people each year, but also Italy, France, Portugal, and Greece. The French and British governments collaborated on the development of the supersonic Concorde, which, in the late 1970s, began to fly a small number of extremely wealthy passengers from Paris and London to New York and Washington, D.C. in three hours and fifteen minutes, less than half the time of a regular jet. An aging fleet, a disastrous crash, and years of financial losses

A demonstration against the Euro Disneyland theme park in Paris: "We don't want to be the Indians of Euro Disneyland!".

ended supersonic travel by Concorde in 2003. The railroad equivalent of the Concorde—and a far greater economic success—was the French "Train of Great Speed" (TGV), which carries passengers at speeds well over 170 miles per hour in comfort. Other countries, too, developed faster trains. Air travel beyond Europe and rail travel within the continent helped take millions of vacationers each summer to new and exciting places. Tourists from the United States and, in the 1980s and early 1990s, from Japan, arrived in Europe in droves. In 1994, the "Chunnel" opened, a thirty-mile tunnel linking France and Great Britain by trains running under the English Channel, putting London just a few hours away from Paris and Brussels. In 2001 a bridge and tunnel linking Denmark and Sweden began service.

One distressing effect of the transportation revolution, however, has been the rapid spread of AIDS (indeed, one interpretation is that it was first spread by an airline steward who travelled between continents). AIDS has ravaged Europe (although not nearly to the same extent as Africa, where it is now the number one killer) and has increased the cost of health care. As of 2003, more than 60 million people worldwide have been infected by the HIV virus, at least a third of whom have died. Although many AIDS victims live longer than before, no cure has yet been found.

Sizable challenges as well as exciting opportunities have accompanied the greater global interconnectedness brought by the transportation and communication revolution. From the post-war period to the present day, the pace of change has increased just as distances have seemed to decrease.

CHAPTER 29

THE EMERGENCE OF CONTEMPORARY EUROPE AND THE COLLAPSE OF COMMUNISM

After almost two decades of growing prosperity and relative political and social calm, domestic political conflict erupted in Europe—above all, in France—and the United States in 1968. The social, political, and cultural revolts that exploded that year seemed to pit young people, especially students, against those entrenched in power. Many "baby boomers" born after the war saw their revolt as one of an entire generation against its elders. They blamed them for a world that seemed unresponsive to demands for social justice and political change on behalf of the under-privileged and the oppressed. Many felt alienated (a word then much in vogue) from materialistic, industrial, bureaucratic society, and even from the universities where they studied. Feminism, too, was a significant undercurrent during the protests of 1968, but then largely remained a movement of middle-class intellectuals and students.

Demonstrations and protest brought political reaction. The turmoil in France ended amid government repression and a conservative show of force. Demonstrations subsided elsewhere in Western Europe, although they continued in the United States. In Western Europe, conservative or centrist parties dominated the governments of Britain, the German Fed-eral Republic, and Italy for most of the 1970s and 1980s, while the Social-ists held power in France between 1981 and 1995. And, in southern Europe, democratic rule came to Portugal, Spain, and Greece.

A period of détente between the United States and the Soviet Union in the 1970s was followed by a chill as a result of Soviet intervention in Afghanistan in 1979. Then in 1989, dramatic change occurred in Eastern Europe. Mikhail Gorbachev, the leader of the Soviet Union, had in the mid-1980s undertaken a dramatic series of reforms liberalizing the economy and political life in the Communist state. His bold moves encouraged further demands for reform, as well as stimulating nationalist movements in the Soviet Union's republics. The impact was soon felt in Eastern Europe. As campaigns for liberalization started up again in Poland and Hungary, it became clear that the Soviet leadership would not intervene to crush movements for reform. Furthermore, Gorbachev made it clear that he viewed reform in Eastern Europe as desirable.

Throughout Eastern Europe, one Communist government fell after another. These revolutions ranged from the "velvet revolution" in Czecho-slovakia to the violent overthrow of Nicolae Ceaușescu in Romania, until there were no Communist regimes left in Eastern Europe (although in Bulgaria, Romania, and Albania, former Communists retained power). The fall of communism was achieved through a remarkably peaceful process of change in most of Eastern Europe. However, in 1989, Yugoslavia began to break apart in a cacophony of ethnic hatred generated by the very question that the polyglot state's creation after World War I could not resolve: the national question. In Bosnia, civil war raged. Finally, the Soviet Union itself collapsed in 1991. The American official

Adulation of Mikhail Gorbachev in Stuttgart, West Germany, for his bold moves toward reform and liberalization in the Soviet Union.

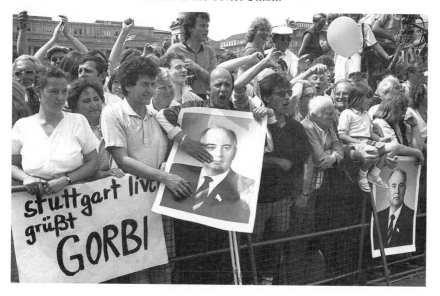

George Kennan's prediction in 1947 that the Soviet system "bears within it the seeds of its own decay" turned out to be correct.

POLITICS IN A CHANGING WESTERN WORLD

During the late 1960s, a loosely connected movement for political and social change swept across university campuses in a number of Western countries. Youth increasingly trumpeted sexual freedom, aided by the availability of birth control (notably the pill, beginning in the 1960s and 1970s) and the legalization of abortion in some countries, including Britain in 1967. Based largely but not exclusively in the surging generation of baby boomers born after World War II (in the United States, the student age population increased from 16 million in 1960 to 26 million in 1970), the youth revolt challenged long-established hierarchies, party politics, and even consumerism. From Berkeley, California, to Paris, Berlin, and Amsterdam, students protested against American involvement in the Vietnamese civil war, where, despite government claims of a high-minded struggle against communism, the United States seemed to be supporting a corrupt political regime against determined nationalists, albeit Communists. In the United States, particularly, the movements of the 1960s were closely tied to the civil rights movement, as students protested against social injustice and racism. Long hair, sexual freedom, rock music, and marijuana seemed part of the idealistic youth rebellion against the state and capitalism. The British impact on popular culture was never greater than in the 1960s, when the Beatles, Mick Jagger and the Rolling Stones, and the Who, among other rock groups, became phenomenally popular across much of the globe. The Beatles, who toured the United States in 1964, wore their hair long, and long hair became a symbol of youth rebellion. In France, student demonstrations, insurgency, and strikes shook the country, challenging the government of Charles de Gaulle. Demonstrations also rocked Italy, West Germany, and other Western European countries.

Western European states began to turn away from U.S. foreign policy domination. European governments no longer automatically accepted U.S. Cold War rhetoric, which had encouraged the arms race. They reasoned that if the two superpowers went to war, the battlefields (in conventional warfare) or the targets (in case of "limited" nuclear warfare) would be in Europe. Thus, a groundswell of popular opposition emerged in 1983 in the German Federal Republic and Britain, in particular, to NATO's planned deployment of new nuclear missile systems on European soil.

Student Protests Challenge Gaullist France

In the spring of 1968, demonstrations began in Paris against the rigid, overcrowded, and underfunded French university system, which largely remained the preserve of the elite. Intellectual ferment was heightened by the opposition of intellectuals and students to American participation in the war in Vietnam. In France, students rebelled against those in political power, inequality, and even modern technology, which seemed to them dehumanizing. Graffiti in the Latin Quarter (where students attended the Sorbonne) proclaimed, "Comrades, the Revolution is daily, it is a fête [festival], an explosion."

Early in May 1968, a student radical, Daniel Cohn-Bendit, was expelled from the University of Paris. To protest, students, joined by young faculty members, occupied university buildings at the Sorbonne. After the police entered the university and began arresting students, the demonstrators fanned out and were joined by more students. Several students were killed and hundreds injured when police attacked hastily improvised barricades.

Unlike in the United States, where most workers found student demands too radical and many supported U.S. participation in the war in Vietnam, many French workers took to the streets in support of the students. A general strike began on May 13, 1968, in protest against police brutality. It became the largest wave of French strikes since 1936. Strikers demanded raises, rights of self-management, and better working conditions. Union organizations and the Communist Party, which had considerable prestige among industrial workers, had little to do with the movement. The tail seemed to be wagging the dog. If anything, trade union and Communist leaders tried to bring the movement under their control in its first days. Gaullist Prime Minister Georges Pompidou (1911–1974) hurriedly returned from a state visit to Afghanistan to confront the growing crisis.

After a hurried and even strange flight to West Germany, presumably to assure himself of the loyalty of French army units stationed there, the French president Charles de Gaulle dissolved the National Assembly on May 30, 1968, and announced that new elections would be held on June 23. Gaullists organized counter-demonstrations in support of the government, capitalizing on the hostility of many middle-class citizens and peasants in traditionally conservative regions to the turmoil in Paris. The strike movement ebbed, in part because the government and many private companies agreed to raise the wages of workers. This left the students standing alone. De Gaulle dismissed Pompidou as prime minister.

While de Gaulle won what amounted to a referendum on his rule, his towering presence seemed increasingly anachronistic. Speeches about national "grandeur" rang hollow as French influence in the world declined. De Gaulle's answer to a general crisis of confidence was to call for more "participation" in the political process, as a way of expressing French "national ambition," which he believed was slipping away. "The French think of nothing but increasing their standard of living," he once complained. "Steak and French fries are fine. A family car is useful. But all that does not add up to national ambition." In 1969, the president

(*Left*) Students battling police in the streets of Paris, May 1968. (*Right*) A counter-demonstration by the well-dressed.

announced another national referendum, this one on local administrative reform. This seemed an unlikely issue for de Gaulle, who believed in an efficiently centralized state and cared little about regional liberties (he once asked rhetorically how one could rule a country with several hundred different kinds of cheese). De Gaulle lost what turned into a plebiscite on his government. The general curtly announced his retirement from political life, and withdrew for the final time to his village in eastern France.

The contentious year 1968 brought student demonstrations and riots to Italy and West Germany, as well. The University of Rome had been built to accommodate 5,000 students and that year enrolled 60,000 students. Thousands of university graduates were frustrated because they could not find jobs. But, unlike the initial movement in France, the Italian students found no support from workers, who had their own complaints, and the movement quickly collapsed. West Berlin was the center of the student movement in West Germany, which also had seen a rapid rise in the number of university students. Many of them were alienated from mainstream politics and castigated German leaders for having Nazi antecedents.

Shifts in Western European Politics after 1968

During the 1970s, a decade of improved relations between the Western powers and the Soviet Union, European domestic politics underwent a shift from the right to centrist governments. This change was apparent not only in the German Federal Republic and Britain (where Labour was in power from 1974 to 1979) but also in France, where the Gaullist government was replaced by a centrist government. In Italy, the strikes of 1968 and 1969 generated further political instability, although the Christian

Democrats, forming a series of center-left coalition governments, continued to dominate Italian politics. In West Germany, the Christian Democrats refused any negotiations of consequence with the German Democratic Republic or the Soviet Union. However, following waves of student protest in the German Federal Republic, Social Democrats first bucked the European tide and came to power in 1969. They were helped by an alliance with the centrist Free Democrats, who abandoned their Christian Democrat allies. Willy Brandt (1913–1992), who had fled Nazi Germany and fought with the Norwegian resistance during the Second World War before becoming mayor of Berlin, took office as chancellor. In 1970, Brandt signed a nonaggression pact with the Soviet Union, paving the way for the development of trade between the two states. Brandt also moved to resolve the remaining diplomatic and territorial disputes in Central and Eastern Europe after World War II, while remaining solidly in the Western bloc. With an eye toward entering into formal relations with Poland, he signed the Treaty of Warsaw, which recognized the frontier between Poland and East Germany as redrawn after the war. Furthermore, Brandt succeeded in establishing normal relations—at least as much as possible given the circumstances—with East Germany. While echoing his predecessors' commitment to NATO, Brandt improved relations with the German Democratic Republic, meeting with East German leaders and calling for an "opening toward the East." He described his policy as "two states, one nation." Millions of people were allowed to cross the wall to visit the other side, overwhelmingly West Germans allowed to visit East Berlin.

Brandt resigned in 1974 following the discovery that one of his aides was a spy for East Germany. Helmut Schmidt (1918–), a more conservative Social Democrat, became chancellor. Schmidt weathered subsequent political storms, but drew the wrath of environmentalists and anti-nuclear groups in 1979 (which had begun to spring up in the 1950s) when he asked the United States to station medium-range nuclear missiles on West German soil to counter similar Soviet missiles. Schmidt and centrist French president Valéry Giscard d'Estaing (1926- ; president 1974–1981) believed that Germany and France had to become the center of Western Europe. However, economic recession, rising unemployment, and Schmidt's refusal to reduce welfare payments (alienating the Social Democrats' coalition partner, the Free Democrats), led to the return to power in 1982 of the Christian Democrats. They were led by Helmut Kohl (1930–), who cut taxes and reduced government spending. Thus, the Christian Democrats continued to dominate the political life of the German Federal Republic. In September 1998, elections swept Gerhard Schröder into the chancellorship, based on a coalition between Social Democrats and the German ecological party, known as the Greens, replacing Kohl, who resigned two years later as chairman of the Christian Democratic Party in the wake of a financial scandal. Schröder was reelected in September 2002.

In Britain, under the pressure of the oil crisis and following bitter mining strikes, the Conservative government fell in 1974. But the subsequent Labour governments of Harold Wilson (1916–1995) and James Callaghan (1912–   ) were buffeted by soaring inflation, which was exacerbated by a series of major union victories in prolonged strikes during the Callaghan government.

Upper- and middle-class Britons turned against Callaghan, claiming that the unions now held their country hostage. In 1979, Conservative leader Margaret Thatcher (1925–   ), the daughter of a prosperous grocer from the English Midlands, became prime minister. She was the first woman to hold the position (although she vociferously repudiated feminism).

Prime Minister Thatcher was committed to putting into effect a tight monetary policing ("monetarism"). She promised to slash government expenses with cutbacks. Within three years, 1 million jobs in manufacturing had disappeared. Although overall public spending remained about the same over the next decade, the Conservative government eliminated some of the health and education measures Labour had implemented. Thatcher, who earned the sobriquet "the Iron Lady," sold off nationalized industries, reduced inheritance and capital taxes, and waged war against the trade unions. She reduced the government's role in industry by selling off some nationalized industries, notably the rail system, with disastrous results for service. Without government subsidies, many factories closed down and unemployment rose rapidly. By 1983, Britain's 3 million unemployed workers (about 12 percent of the workforce) received reduced unemployment benefits. Cuts in housing subsidies left hundreds of thousands without adequate places to live. She had, after all, once advised Britons to "glory in inequality." In the meantime, rail service, once a pride of Britain, became increasingly inefficient and even dangerous. Yet Thatcher retained the support of the upper and middle classes, as well as the backing of a segment of the working-class population—"Tory workers," who proudly displayed pictures of the royal family in their modest residences.

Margaret Thatcher, the first woman to hold the position of British Prime Minister, shakes hands with West German Chancellor Helmut Schmidt.

As Conservatives sought to weather the storms of a floundering economy, in May 1982, the military government of Argentina, seeking to reverse a decline in its popularity at home, invaded the Falkland Islands. Although the British occupied the sparsely populated Falklands, which lie about 300 miles from the coast of Argentina in the Atlantic Ocean, Argentina had claimed them since the nineteenth century. British forces, benefiting from superior military technology, easily recaptured the Falklands. The short war encouraged a burst of patriotism, boosting the prime minister's standing at home. Furthermore, the British economy began to recover in the early 1980s and inflation slowed down.

With the Conservative Party in power, the Labour Party became increasingly divided between radicals and reformers. The creation of the small Social Democratic Party (allied with the Liberal Party) added to the disarray on the left. Thatcher and the Conservatives rolled to another impressive victory in the general elections of 1983 over the bitterly divided Labour Party. In 1985, she outlasted a long strike by coal miners. However, fearing the revival of the Labour Party, Conservative leaders unseated Thatcher in 1990, replacing her with the colorless John Major (1943–   ), who became prime minister following elections two years later. Meanwhile, Tony Blair moved the Labour Party toward the center. "New Labour" championed "modern liberal social democracy." Turning away from the class politics of the old Labour Party and its rhetorical embrace of socialism, "New Labour" reached out toward liberals and even moderate conservatives. Blair emphasized a commitment to economic progress and to practical policies in place of shrill rhetoric. At the same time, in sharp contrast to most Conservatives, Blair made clear that he believed that Britain's future lay with Europe. The sweeping victory of "New Labour" in 1997 brought Blair to 10 Downing Street as prime minister. It was the worst Conservative defeat in Britain since 1832. In contrast, elections in Poland and Bulgaria brought conservative parties to power. In 2001, Blair's Labour Party swept to another easy victory in Britain, leaving Socialist or Social Democratic parties in power in 9 of the 15 member states of the European Union (see Chapter 29).

Blair's policies increasingly could have been confused with those of his Conservative rivals, whose share of the electorate plunged further in the national elections of 2001. In the meantime, the death of Princess Diana (1961–1997) in a high-speed car crash in a Paris tunnel on August 31, 1997, plunged Britain into mourning. This was just the latest of a series of reverses for the British monarchy, including Diana's separation and then divorce from Prince Charles in 1996. Despite the attachment of many people to the monarchy as an institution and the fascination with the royal family perpetuated by coverage in tabloid newspapers, to an increasing percentage of the British population, the monarchy seemed an expensive and irrelevant atavism. Yet, to fervent British royalists, Prince William (heir to the throne after his father, Charles) and his younger brother, Harry, offered hope for the future.

In France, the economic slump that began with the oil crisis of 1973 and financial scandals undercut the presidency of the centrist Valéry Giscard d'Estaing, a technocrat committed to economic modernization. In 1981, the pragmatic Socialist François Mitterrand (1916–1996) won election as president, drawing on a wide spectrum of support. Other Socialists, too, bucked the conservative tide. Social Democratic parties maintained power in Scandinavia. Andreas Papandreou (1919–1996), became Greece's first Socialist premier in 1981. Italy and Spain also had moderately left-wing governments. Yet, in France and other countries, Socialist governments governed with moderation, abandoning traditional agendas of the left in the interest of practical politics. In every country, the old role of unions to push Socialist governments to enact left-wing agendas declined with the reduction in the number of industrial workers. Abandoned factories in the German Ruhr region, northeastern France, northern England, and the Czech Republic stood as rusty symbols of an old industrial world that no longer existed.

By nationalizing large corporations and more banks and initiating ambitious social reforms, Mitterrand confronted determined opposition from the business community. The French franc plunged on the international currency market, as wealthy people began to remove their assets from France. A year after taking office, the Socialist government was forced to devalue the franc and freeze prices and wages. Pressure from the right mounted from the Gaullists and their ambitious leader, Jacques Chirac (1932–   ), the mayor of Paris. The inability of the Socialist government to revive the economy undercut its popularity, as did its anticlerical educational measures.

In the 1986 elections for the Chamber of Deputies, the right triumphed, leading to an awkward period of government known as "cohabitation." This required Mitterrand to select a rightist premier, Chirac, and ministers drawn from the right and center. The new government sold off some nationalized banks and businesses and ended wage and price controls. Cohabitation worked fairly well, in part because Mitterrand and Chirac shared similar views on some aspects of foreign policy.

Given a slight majority in the elections for the National Assembly in 1988, Mitterrand appointed Socialist prime ministers, but the right swept into office with the legislative elections of 1993. When his second term ended in 1995, Mitterrand had become the longest serving head of state in France since Napoleon III (emperor 1852–1870). Chirac was elected president in 1995. He began his presidency by authorizing the resumption of French nuclear testing in the South Pacific, leading to considerable international opposition, particularly in Australia, New Zealand, and Japan. Facing a high unemployment rate and a growing economic deficit that threatened to undercut the value of the French franc, in November

1995 Prime Minister Alain Juppé announced reductions in health, retirement, and other benefits. Strikes forced the government to make some concessions. In 1997, however, Chirac called elections a year early in hopes of receiving a sweeping mandate. Socialists dominated the elections, forcing Chirac to name the Socialist Lionel Jospin as prime minister, bringing another uncomfortable period of "cohabitation" with a conservative president and a Socialist prime minister.

In Italy, political instability and corruption continued to characterize political life. In some ways, Italy remains what Austrian Prince Metternich called it well before national unification in the nineteenth century—a "geographical expression." Despite a general increase in prosperity, inflation and high unemployment left many Italians still dissatisfied with all political parties. A 1970 European survey reported that 72 percent of Italians were "highly" or "completely" unhappy with their democracy. Union militancy increased in the face of intransigence from employers and the state.

The government of Bettino Craxi (1934–   ) from 1983 to 1986 was the longest and in many ways most stable of the post-war period. Socialists replaced the Communists as Italy's second largest party, forcing the Christian Democrats to accept them as coalition partners in 1986. Craxi himself was convicted of corruption, however, and fled in 1993 to Tunisia. Giulio Andreotti (1919–   ), Christian Democrat prime minister on six different occasions, stood accused not only of corruption, but was eventually found guilty of arranging the murder of a journalist who had uncovered evidence of wrongdoing. More than 2,500 Italian politicians and businessmen were arrested for corruption in one eighteen-month period. Campaigns against the Mafia have been periodic (including, most vigorously, following the assassination in 1992 of a public prosecutor who had devoted himself to the difficult legal war against the Mafia). In the 1994 elections, conservative financier and media tycoon Silvio Berlusconi became prime minister of Italy. His new right-wing party, Forza Italia, came out of the elections as Italy's most successful party, with two parties of the extreme right as allies, both denouncing the increase in the immigrant population: the Northern League, which campaigned on a program of independence for northern Italy, provocatively describing the south as a weight around the neck of the north, and the neo-fascist National Alliance. The remnants of the old Communist Party came in second. Cynicism and mistrust of politicians has become even more common in Italy.

In every Western country, a new political force began to be felt. "Green" parties, political groups of militant environmentalists angered by the deterioration of the environment, emerged in Western Europe during the 1980s. In the German Federal Republic, the Greens, Europe's largest environmental party, were alarmed by industrial pollution, which was slowly killing their country's forests. Environmental parties stridently opposed nuclear power, even before the Soviet nuclear

A nuclear power plant dwarfs a more traditional source of power.

disaster at Chernobyl in Ukraine in 1986. Green votes proved pivotal in a number of local elections, and they won twenty-seven seats in the German parliamentary elections of 1983. Furthermore, environmentalists protested that virtually uncontrolled tourism was taking a great ecological toll, largely because of the litter and pollution generated by hundreds of thousands of campers, particularly in and around rivers, seas, and oceans. Greens helped push for agreements that have led to some cleaning up of the Rhine River and Mediterranean beaches.

Finally, in almost all Western states, economic slumps have accentuated complaints that state-subsidized programs are too expensive. In Sweden and Denmark, Social Democratic parties were ousted after decades of rule by conservatives calling for sharp reductions in the tax rates that financed cradle-to-grave social programs. With the recession of the early 1990s reducing tax revenue, Western European governments have tried to reduce social benefits—for example, by reducing unemployment payments.

The Transition to Democracy in Southern Europe

During the 1970s, three southern European dictatorships underwent a process of democratization: Greece, Portugal, and Spain. Greece, the cradle of democracy, had been controlled by a series of right-wing governments since its civil war in the late 1940s. In 1967, military officers overthrew Greece's first post-war government of the left, ruthlessly crushed dissent, imprisoning and even torturing political opponents. The military dictators planned to seize the island of Cyprus, which lies off the coast of Turkey and which both Greece and Turkey had claimed for centuries. Bitter disagreements over the form of a new constitution led to fighting between Greeks and Turks. The Greek Cypriot National Guard overthrew the government of Cyprus. Meanwhile, the Cypriot Turks defeated the Greeks and declared the northeastern, predominantly Turkish part of the island to be independent. Further fighting ended in a cease-fire, and the former government returned to power. Meanwhile, in Greece, the government of the Greek generals, which had not sent help to the Greek Cypriot insurgents, collapsed in 1974. Greece became a republic in which conservative and Socialist parties took turns in power. The country's major problems remained a relatively undeveloped, inefficient economy still largely dependent on tourism, and hostile relations with Turkey.

In Portugal, Antonio Salazar, who had been dictator from 1932 to 1968 and who had ordered flags flown at half-mast upon hearing of Hitler's death in 1945, died in 1970. His authoritarian successors struggled inefficiently with economic backwardness. Thousands of Portuguese went abroad as seasonal workers each year or emigrated to other countries in Western Europe or to the Western Hemisphere. At the same time, the dictatorship was determined to hold on to Portugal's African colonies at all costs. The Portuguese army became entangled in a long, bitter war with nationalist rebels in its African colonies of first Angola, beginning in 1961, and then Mozambique, conflicts that Portugal could neither afford (at the annual cost of half the nation's budget) nor win (see Chapter 28). A group of liberal army officers had begun to have serious doubts that the war could ever be won. In April 1974, they overthrew the dictatorship by moving tanks into the center of Lisbon. The Socialist Party emerged victorious in elections the following year, Angola and Mozambique became independent, lapsing into bloody civil wars. Despite a series of brief governments, including another coup two years later by a group of officers who feared the Communists, the Portuguese transition to democracy occurred without bloodshed. Portugal attempted collectivization and a program of state nationalizations, but political turmoil forced the government to abandon both in 1976. That year, Mário Soares took office as the first democratically elected prime minister in Portugal in fifty years, and he dominated Portuguese political life into the 1990s. In 1986, Portugal joined the European Common Market, which immediately opened the Spanish market to Portuguese products and ended Britain's long role as its primary trading partner.

In Spain, General Francisco Franco survived as dictator long after his friends Hitler and Mussolini had gone to their graves. After World War II, the United Nations had considered imposing sanctions against Spain because of Franco's support of the Axis powers, but the United States prevented this. Franco maintained Spain's authoritarian political structure. His police kept the left at bay, while he undercut political challenges from other conservative groups—monarchists, Falangists (a fascist group dating to the 1930s), the army, and the Catholic Church (particularly its militant lay organization, Opus Dei). Trade unions and political parties remained illegal. Franco would accept economic modernization, but not if it served as a Trojan horse for secular values, which he vehemently opposed.

In the late 1960s, opposition to Franco's regime mounted in Catalonia and the Basque country, Spain's most industrial regions, each with an entrenched separatist movement. Franco struck hard against Basque and Catalan separatists; the Catalan language, for example, remained illegal in print. But Franco retained popularity in traditionally religious regions, such as Navarre and his native Galicia.

Franco agreed that Juan Carlos (1938–   ), the son of the heir to the throne before the civil war, would succeed him as head of state. The general assumed that following his death, Spain would remain an authoritarian country. Within the Spanish government, however, many officials already believed political reform inevitable, even desirable. Socialist and Communist parties existed, although they were illegal. Government censorship itself had become more lax in the 1970s.

In 1975, Franco died after a long illness. Juan Carlos became king, and to the surprise of many people, including Franco's disciples, he accepted the transformation of Spain into a constitutional monarchy with a democratic political structure. Spain emerged from authoritarian rule and international isolation. The government foiled several subsequent plots by rightists to overthrow the republic, including the invasion of the Spanish Parliament by gunmen who briefly held members hostage in 1978.

Spectacular economic growth and increasing prosperity helped the centrist Adolfo Suarez (1932–   ) keep a series of governments afloat through skillful political negotiation, even without a parliamentary majority. But Suarez's party lost support because some of its leaders had loyally supported Franco. The charismatic Felipe González and the Socialists swept Suarez aside, winning an overwhelming victory in the 1982 elections and emerging victorious again in 1989. In 1996, José Maria Aznar became Spain's first conservative prime minister since the time of Franco.

Catholicism in Modern Europe

Like the nations of Western Europe, the Catholic Church, for centuries a major force in European life, had to respond to pressures for change. It retained considerable allegiance in much of Europe, particularly Italy, Spain, Portugal, and Ireland. Yet even these solidly Catholic countries have legalized divorce, despite ecclesiastical opposition. In France, most Catholics depended on the Church only for life's basic rites of passage: baptism, first communion, marriage, and burial, and thus they were known as "four-wheel Catholics," for the carriages identified with each ceremony.

Within the Catholic Church, a liberal current of thought and action developed in response to some of the social problems of modern life.

"Worker priests" entered factories in the 1950s, trying to win back workers to the Church, while supporting their demands for better working conditions, until the pope condemned the movement. The election in 1958 of the smiling, more liberal Pope John XXIII signaled a new direction, marked by the opening of dialogue with other religions. Pope John presided over a council (Vatican II) that undertook significant changes in Church practices, allowing the Mass to be said in local languages and appointing more cardinals from other places than Europe and North America, without altering dogma.

Pope John's successor Paul VI continued the move toward ecumenism, visiting Istanbul and Jerusalem to meet with leaders of the Eastern Orthodox churches. But several notable theologians who challenged Church doctrine drew the wrath of Rome. In 1978, Paul died, as did his successor, John Paul I, after only two months on the throne of Saint Peter. The puffs of white smoke rising from the Vatican chimney then announced the first non-Italian pope since the sixteenth century, the Polish-born Pope John Paul II (Karol Wojtyla; 1920–   ). While remaining conservative on matters of faith and doctrine, the new pope traveled far and wide across the world, calling for social justice while visiting Latin America, Asia, Africa, the Soviet Union, and the United States. He became a symbol of hope for millions of oppressed people. Yet, at the same time, the pope frustrated liberal Catholics, some of whom want to end the papal interdiction on contraception and allow the ordination of women as priests.

An industrial chaplain speaks with a factory worker in Scotland, in an effort to liberalize the Catholic Church and bring it into modern life.

THREATS TO PEACE

Europeans in the first four decades following the end of World War II lived under the shadow of several considerable threats to peace. First and foremost, the enormous nuclear arsenals of the Soviet Union and the United States, as well as Britain and France among the latter's European allies, made the possibility of any armed conflict between East and West potentially catastrophic. However, the 1970s brought a period of détente between the Soviet Union and the United States, leading to serious negotiations between the two powers to reduce nuclear arms. In the meantime, ethnic and religious conflicts burst out in several countries, including violence between Catholics and Protestants in Northern Ireland, the Basque separatist movement in Spain, and Serb aggression against Albanians in the Yugoslav province of Kosovo.

Nuclear Weapons and Superpower Tensions

The phased U.S. withdrawal from Vietnam beginning in 1973 (followed two years later by the victory of the Communist North Vietnamese and their southern allies, the Vietcong) removed one thorny issue between the United States and the Soviet Union, then the world's two superpowers. Continued tension between the Soviet Union and China (accompanied by a concentration of Soviet forces along the disputed borders in Manchuria and Siberia) gradually eroded the old U.S. view of communism as a monolithic force, engendering more realistic diplomatic assessments of international politics. Furthermore, both Western powers and the Soviet Union faced daunting economic problems that partially shifted the focus of government to domestic concerns.

In 1972, Soviet leader Leonid Brezhnev and U.S. President Richard Nixon signed an arms-reduction agreement known as SALT I (Strategic Arms Limitation Talks), by which they agreed to maintain parity in nuclear offensive weapons systems. However, as military technology continued to advance rapidly, both sides began to defy the spirit of the agreement by developing new systems. Nixon was forced to resign as U.S. president in 1974 because of the Watergate Affair: he had approved illegal operations against Democratic headquarters and then lied about what he knew. His successors sought to link further arms-reduction talks to Soviet progress in human rights. Both the Soviet Union and the United States deployed new missiles in Europe. President Jimmy Carter stressed support of human rights in his foreign policy. He and Brezhnev signed a new agreement, SALT II, by which the Soviets agreed to limit missile launchers and nuclear warheads and the United States agreed not to develop a new missile. Carter, however, had to withdraw the agreement from consideration by the Senate in January 1980 because of political opposition, primarily from conservatives who feared that SALT II would leave the

Soviets with greater nuclear capability than that of the United States. As the number of nuclear weapons increased in Europe, anti-nuclear movements revived, particularly in Britain and Germany.

The Soviet invasion of Afghanistan in December 1979 put an end to détente. Soviet troops were sent in support of the pro-Soviet government, which was besieged by a variety of rebels, including Islamic fundamentalists. (One of the motives of the Soviet invasion of Afghanistan was to forestall fundamentalist movements in Soviet republics with sizable Muslim populations.) Reacting to the Soviet invasion, the United States limited grain sales to the Soviet Union and boycotted the Olympic Games in Moscow in 1980. Soviet military action in Afghanistan took a great toll in lives. It also demonstrated that the Soviet Army was not invincible. The Soviet-American chill lasted into the mid-1980s.

Timeless Religious and Ethnic Divisions

Compared to the sixteenth, seventeenth, and eighteenth centuries, religious conflicts have diminished in modern Europe. In Great Britain, Scottish nationalists won 30 percent of the votes in the 1974 elections, but thereafter their total fell off rapidly. Scotland received its own legislature in 1997, the first since its union with England in 1707. However, in Northern Ireland, the bitter centuries-old rivalry between Catholics and Protestants generated fighting and terror. Although the Catholic Republic of Ireland obtained independence in 1922, Northern Ireland is primarily Protestant (two-thirds of the population) and remains part of Britain. The Irish Republican Army, claiming to represent Ulster Catholics, struck at the British army and Protestants alike. Several weeks of disturbances in 1969 unleashed decades of violence. Secret Protestant paramilitary organizations, claiming that the British army inadequately protected Protestants, struck back against Catholics. Ian Paisley, a Protestant clergyman, heightened tension by speaking out provocatively against any compromise. On January 30, 1972—"Bloody Sunday"—British troops killed thirteen demonstrators in the Northern Irish town of Londonderry.

The economic crisis of the 1970s compounded Northern Ireland's problems, making Catholics even more disadvantaged compared to Protestants, in part because they suffered discrimination. The IRA, buying guns on the world weapons market with money stolen from banks or contributed by sympathetic Irish Americans, struck not only in Northern Ireland but also periodically in England. In 1988, after the British army gunned down several members of the IRA in Gibraltar, two incidents symbolized the tragedy of Northern Ireland. Protestant gunmen from an Ulster paramilitary force hurled grenades and shot at mourners at a Catholic funeral for IRA members; and at the subsequent funeral for one of the Catholics who had been killed, mourners dragged two British soldiers from their car and murdered them.

The aftermath of a bomb planted by the Irish Republican Army in Belfast, Northern Ireland, 1972.

In 1994, the IRA agreed to a cease-fire, and for the first time in many years, hope surfaced that a political solution to one of Europe's oldest religious and national conflicts was possible. But the IRA claimed responsibility for a bomb attack in London in 1996. Another cease-fire in 1997 could not still the violence that continued periodically, particularly during the period of the traditional Protestant summer marches. On April 10, 1998, Protestant and Catholic representatives signed the Belfast Agreement (or Good Friday Agreement), which provided for a National Assembly for Northern Ireland in which both religions would be represented. A month later, the people of Northern Ireland and of the Irish Republic overwhelmingly approved the Belfast Agreement. However, in July 1998, three young Catholic brothers were killed by a firebomb tossed into their house in Northern Ireland. Several weeks later, a car bomb exploded in the Northern Ireland town of Omagh, killing twenty-nine people. In December 1999, the British Parliament granted substantial power to the Northern Ireland Assembly, with a Catholic moderate as deputy first minister and David Trimble, a Protestant, as first minister. However, in February 2000, the British government suspended the Catholic and Protestant power-sharing government of Northern Ireland when the IRA refused to establish a timetable for the disarmament of its members. Trimble resigned in July 2001 because the IRA had not given up its weapons. Peace in Northern Ireland remained fragile. "The Troubles" showed few signs of being over.

Demands by ethnic minorities, "nations without states," surfaced in several countries. A small movement existed among German speakers in the Italian Tyrol, who wanted to be included in Austria. Spanish Basque separatists (the ETA), sometimes hiding in the French Basque country, moved across what they considered an arbitrary frontier to attack Spanish government, army, and police installations. Popular support for the separatists in the Spanish Basque region waned in the 1980s, after the constitution of 1978 recognized "autonomous communities" within Spain. The ETA campaign of bombs and assassinations has continued off and on, interrupted by occasional cease-fires.

In France, small separatist movements existed in Brittany; in Alsace, where the few separatists were linked to right-wing German extremists; in the French south, where there was a smattering of left-wing "Occitan" separatists; and, above all, on the Mediterranean island of Corsica, where several nationalist groups opposed continued French rule with occasional bombs and assassinations, even as they feuded among themselves. In 2000, the French government offered some autonomy to Corsica. In Belgium, a new federal constitution in 1993 divided Belgium into three regions: Flemish, Walloon, and Brussels.

Two world wars and the loss of millions of people did not end problems stemming from unresolved questions and claims based upon nationality. Nowhere was this more dramatically evident and more tragic than in Yugoslavia. During the years of Communist rule, Yugoslavs had lived in relative peace. But tensions persisted between Serbs and Croats, the country's two largest ethnic groups. They shared a common spoken language (though the Serbs use the Russian Cyrillic alphabet and Croats use the Latin alphabet). Yugoslavia's capital, Belgrade, was also that of Serbia. Serbs enjoyed disproportionate representation in the Communist state bureaucracy.

Regional disparities in economic development and prosperity compounded Yugoslav ethnic divisions. In the north, the republic of Slovenia, which was by far the most ethnically homogeneous of Yugoslavia's republics, enjoyed a standard of living not far below that of its neighbors, Austria and Italy. In the south, the republic of Macedonia remained backward and relatively impoverished. Adjacent to Albania, the territory of Kosovo had been largely peopled by ethnic Albanians who were Muslims. Yet the minority Serbs—only about 15 percent of the population—viewed Kosovo as sacred Serb soil, because the Ottoman Turks had defeated them there in 1389. Kosovo had become part of Serbia during the Balkan Wars (1912–1913). At a minimum, ethnic Albanians claimed the right to be the seventh Yugoslav republic.

Other countries in Eastern Europe were not immune to national tensions either, despite official ideology holding that such rivalries were irrelevant in Communist societies. Hungarians living in Romania deeply resented their minority status. Many Greeks, left by chance on the Bulgarian side of the frontier after World War II, or in Albania, were also unhappy with their lot. In the Soviet Union, ethnic nationalism surfaced in many of the republics, particularly in the Baltic states of Lithuania, Estonia, and Latvia, which the Soviet Union had absorbed during World War II and where a sizable Russian minority now lived. In Ukraine, nationalists kept their movement alive with poetry and literary manuscripts in Ukrainian, passed from hand to hand.

THE FALL OF COMMUNISM

In 1975, the leaders of European states gathered in Helsinki, Finland, to sign the Helsinki Accords, which concluded the first Conference on Security and Cooperation. All European states, with the exception of Albania, signed the accords, which recognized as valid the national borders drawn up after World War II. The thirty-five signatories also pledged to respect human rights and to cooperate in economic and scientific matters. To some critics, the Helsinki Accords seemed to recognize Soviet domination of Eastern Europe since the war. To other observers, they were a significant step forward because the heads of Communist states agreed to respect human rights. The accords seemed a healthy pause in the renewed tension between East and West.

Hardly anyone at the time could have anticipated the fact that fourteen years later, communism would collapse in Eastern Europe, nor that in 1991 communism would fall in the Soviet Union, which would disintegrate shortly thereafter. As Mikhail Gorbachev undertook reform in the Soviet Union in an attempt to save the Communist state, communism in Eastern Europe collapsed abruptly in 1989 (see Map 29.1). It took ten years in Poland, ten months in Hungary, ten weeks in East Germany, ten days in Czechoslovakia, and ten hours in Romania, almost in inverse proportion to the size and effectiveness of opposition to Communist rule within each Eastern European country. The Warsaw Pact dissolved in March 1991. However, the euphoria that arose from the realization that the Cold War had suddenly ended proved to be brief. New challenges and problems, among them those that had beset Europe for centuries, presented themselves. Decades of Communist rule had prevented the emergence of healthy political organizations. Civil society in each country remained seriously undeveloped. Changing from planned economies with varying degrees of collectivization to free-market economies would prove extremely difficult and disruptive. Long-simmering ethnic conflicts exploded in Yugoslavia, and these ethnic divisions also complicated the fall of communism in Romania, Hungary, Czechoslovakia, and Bulgaria.

MAP 29.1 THE FALL OF COMMUNISM IN EASTERN EUROPE AND THE SOVIET UNION, 1989–1991   With the fall of communism came the reunification of Germany and the breakup of the Soviet Union.

Countries affected by boundary changes
‑‑‑‑‑ Old 1989 boundaries
‑ ‑ ‑ New 1993 boundaries

Resistance to Soviet Domination

Calls for change echoed loudly in Communist Czechoslovakia in 1968. Intellectuals and writers accused the leadership of the Communist Party of clinging to Stalinism. The party leadership also acknowledged the need for change. In January 1968, party leaders named Alexander Dubček (1921–1992), a liberal Slovak, to be first secretary of the Communist Party, and thus head of state. During the "Prague Spring," Dubček tried to implement "socialism with a human face" by implementing reforms but as he did so he glanced anxiously over his shoulder toward Leonid Brezhnev's Soviet Union. Crucial to these reforms was a democratization of decision making and greater freedom of expression. But, as in the case of Hungary in 1956, the Soviet leadership feared that, despite Dubček's assurances to the contrary, Czechoslovakia might attempt to move away from the Warsaw Pact. On August 21, 1968, Soviet tanks and troops moved rapidly across the border, rolling into Prague. They brutally put an end to the Prague Spring.

The Soviet invasion of Czechoslovakia initiated another chill in Soviet-Western relations. Moreover, the Communist parties of Italy and France criticized the invasion. In the mid-1970s, Western Communist leaders, particularly in Spain and Italy, began to call themselves "Euro-communists." Accepting the fact that the Western nations had taken different paths of historical development than had the Soviet Union, they stressed their own independence—for example, by collaborating with Socialists and other left-wing parties. However, Eurocommunism proved unable to slow the decline in membership in the Communist parties of Western Europe, although the Communist Party of Italy retained many followers.

Under the "Brezhnev Doctrine," the Soviet leadership tried to justify the invasion of Czechoslovakia and left open the possibility of future intervention in any of the satellite states of Eastern Europe. For almost two decades following the Soviet invasion of Czechoslovakia, the countries of Eastern Europe suffered stifling domination by their Communist parties, which were backed by the Soviet Union. With the exception of Albania, which remained closed to virtually all foreign contact during the rigid dictatorship of Enver Hoxha, only Yugoslavia retained real independence. The "Yugoslav experiment" still comprised a mixed economy that combined state-owned and private enterprise. The Soviet invasion of Czechoslovakia disenchanted even more Communists in Eastern European countries. Many now no longer believed that communism could be reformed.

Opposition to Communist rule and Russian influence mounted in all of the Eastern European states during the 1980s. Following Stalin's death in 1953, the Soviet Union had been willing to countenance the revival of nationalism in Eastern Europe, as long as it remained within the context of communism dominated by the Soviets. The overwhelming economic failures of the Communist regimes grew ever more apparent, particularly in comparison with the standard of living in Western states. Television and radio carried images and reports of the consumer culture of the more prosperous people across the Iron Curtain; this became an important part of the arsenal of the West in the Cold War. In the meantime, Eastern European Communist states continued to borrow massively from the West, which merely patched over huge problems without bringing economic reform. Debt owed by Eastern European countries in hard currency rose from 6 billion dollars in 1971 to 66 billion dollars in 1980 and over 95 billion dollars in 1988. Well-developed social services could not compensate for economic inefficiency and massive demoralization. Reassurance from leaders that all was well fell on increasingly deaf ears. Membership in the Communist Party declined, particularly among young people, while the age of the leadership increased dramatically. Popular dissatisfaction thus lay not far below the surface in most Eastern European countries.

Massive unrest led to strikes in Poland in 1970, generating increasingly vocal and organized political opposition. Edward Gierek (1913–2001), who became first secretary of the Polish United Workers' (Communist) Party in 1970, made some political concessions while attempting to stimulate economic growth. However, despite massive foreign loans and credits that assisted in creating something of an economic boom in the early 1970s, by 1976 Poland again had lapsed into economic stagnation. In 1980, strikes and riots in protest of living conditions spread rapidly in industrial areas, particularly in the vast shipyards of Gdańsk. Solidarity, a

(*Left*) Communist leaders meet shortly before the Russian invasion of Czechoslovakia. Participants include Walter Ulbricht and Erich Honecker of East Germany (first two on the left), and Soviet Communist Party chief Leonid Brezhnev conferring with Premier Alexei Kosygin (first two on the right). (*Right*) Soviet armies occupy Prague, 1968.

new, independent, illegal organization of trade unions, gained 10 million members. It was led by Lech Walesa (1943–   ), an electrician from Gdańsk. The Catholic Church (whose prestige became even greater with the election in 1978 of John Paul II, a Pole, as pope) helped mobilize opposition to the Communist government. In response, the Polish government agreed to tolerate the creation of new unions as long as they did not engage in political activity, and thereby challenge the domination of the Communist Party.

In September 1980, the Communist Central Committee responded to the ongoing crisis by forcing Gierek to resign as head of state. Two months later, the government officially recognized Solidarity's existence. However, accommodation between the government and the non-Communist trade unions did not last long, particularly after Solidarity members called for free elections. In December 1981, General Wojciech Jaruzelski (1923–   ), the new head of state, imposed martial law and replaced some key Communist Party officials in government with military officers. He suspended Solidarity and put hundreds of leading dissidents under arrest, including Lech Walesa. During this period, the police murdered a priest active in Solidarity. Troops brutally crushed strikes that broke out in response to the repression. In 1982, the government declared Solidarity illegal again, although martial law ended a year later. But Poland was stuck in the quicksand of economic stagnation, and the regime's opponents remained organized and active beneath the surface.

In the meantime, East Germany, Bulgaria, and Czechoslovakia were the Eastern European nations that were most loyal to the Soviet Union. The German Democratic Republic's chief, Erich Honecker (1912–1994), who came to power in 1971, proved as intransigent to reform as his predecessor, Walter Ulbricht. The Lutheran Church provided a center for some dissidents, organizing weekly "prayers for peace" in Leipzig. A sizable peace group formed in the early 1980s. In Czechoslovakia, the one state in Eastern Europe that had remained a democracy during the inter-war period, the state campaign against dissidents was more intense. Unlike Poland, opposition in Czechoslovakia was limited to students, intellectuals, artists, and clergy. In 1977, about 1,200 writers, philosophers, intellectuals, and musicians signed a protest against government limitation of freedoms in an attempt to force the government to respect the Helsinki human-rights convention it had signed. Despite the fact that this was anything but a revolutionary document (those who signed pledged not to engage in political activity), the members of the "Charter 77" group suffered repression, political trials, and harassment, and they were prevented from holding decent jobs.

Gradual economic liberalization helped make Hungary the most free and the second (after the German Democratic Republic) most prosperous of the Eastern bloc countries. The gradual development of a market economy and a private agricultural sector helped stabilize the

Communist regime, while Soviet subsidies aided the Hungarian economy. The Hungarian Communist leadership tolerated limited organized political opposition, and in 1985 Hungary became the first Communist state to declare political pluralism to be an ideal. However, unlike Poland, Hungary had no organized and tested opposition force such as Solidarity.

In sharp contrast, there was no liberalization of any kind in Romania. Nicolae Ceauşescu (1918–1989), head of the Romanian Communist Party, had brazenly adopted a position of relative independence, or "national communism," with respect to the Soviet Union, criticizing the Soviet invasion of Czechoslovakia, remaining neutral in the Sino-Soviet conflict, and refusing to participate in Warsaw Pact maneuvers. Although the Soviet Union had assigned Bulgaria and Romania the role of concentrating on agricultural production for the Eastern bloc nations, Ceauşescu had forged ahead with grandiose plans to generate industrial development. The results were disastrous. Romania became, after Albania, the poorest country in Europe, while caught in the increasingly mad grip of Ceauşescu's "cult of personality." The dictator ordered the destruction of 1,500 villages in Transylvania. These were largely in areas where many Hungarians resided, whom he targeted while trying to garner support from Romanians with nationalist appeals against the largest ethnic minority in the country. He also ordered some of old Bucharest torn down to forge enormous boulevards that would lead to his reviewing stand.

The Gorbachev Era

In the Soviet Union, Leonid Brezhnev reinforced the powers of the oppressive Soviet bureaucracy (with the motto "trust in cadres") and the prestige of the army and the KGB (the secret police). Reflecting the chill in relations with the United States, the Soviet Union, like its rival, poured more money into the manufacture of arms. After Brezhnev died in 1982, he was succeeded as general secretary of the Soviet Communist Party (and thus as head of state) by Yuri Andropov (1914–1984), who, despite his long years in the KGB, was somewhat more liberal than Brezhnev. Unlike his predecessor, Andropov acknowledged that there was widespread inefficiency and corruption in Soviet economic planning and government. He called for greater popular participation in economic decision making, purged incompetent party hacks from important positions, and promised a war on alcholism. But in 1983 Andropov suffered a heart attack, and until his death early the following year he could only hope that the mild reforms he had begun would have some effect. Andropov's successor, Konstantine Chernenko (1911–1985), had been a Brezhnev aide and was more in the Brezhnev mold than Andropov. Chernenko was seventy-three and chronically ill when he came to power, however, and both he and the Soviet state treaded water until his death in March 1985.

Mikhail Gorbachev (1931–   ) succeeded Chernenko as general secretary of the Communist Party and head of the Soviet Union in 1985. Born in southern Russia, Gorbachev had worked his way up in the party youth organization and studied law at the University of Moscow. Both his grandfathers had been arrested on false charges during the Stalin era while he was a boy. Gorbachev became secretary of the Communist Central Committee and assumed responsibility for Soviet agriculture. Less instinctively xenophobic than other Soviet leaders, he was the first Soviet leader since Lenin to have a university degree. Relatively young, charming, flexible, and determined, Gorbachev was a master of Communist Party machinations. When he received a medal at a televised awards ceremony, he was the only member of the Central Committee to say thank you without reading from note cards.

Gorbachev began by exorcizing some remaining ghosts from the Stalinist past, which he believed had destroyed the Communist dream. Like a number of optimistic party officials and intellectuals, Gorbachev believed that the Prague Spring could come to Moscow, but that the Communist Party should continue to dominate political life in the Soviet Union. He embraced a policy of liberation known in Russian as *glasnost*: openness in government combined with a greater degree of free expression. He put some liberals in positions of responsibility and ordered the relaxation of censorship. Artists and writers brought forth new work, including strident criticisms of the Soviet regime. At the same time, more forthright accounts of life in the West appeared on the television news, which served to put the Soviet economy and its living standards in a particularly unflattering light.

The Soviet leader increasingly spoke openly about the failure of economic planning without sufficient material incentives for workers. However, he still remained convinced that communism could be rescued by necessary reforms once the inefficiency and brutality of Stalinism had been completely eliminated. Moreover, in the Soviet Union, because collective farms had failed, state agricultural planning would have to be scrapped in favor of a free-market economy. For the moment, Gorbachev bided his time, although he summarily cashiered some corrupt or incompetent local party officials and launched a full-fledged campaign against alcoholism, which had taken on epidemic proportions in the demoralized Soviet Union.

Gorbachev espoused *perestroika*: a restructuring of the Soviet system in order to make it more efficient and responsive to the needs of Soviet citizens. His model may well have been Lenin's implementation of the New Economic Policy in 1921 (see Chapter 23), which had revived the Soviet economy without sacrificing Communist authority. Gorbachev had seen Prime Minister Alexei Kosygin's attempt to have the Soviet economy turn out more consumer goods in the mid-1960s (only about 33 percent of Soviet households had a refrigerator in 1970, in contrast to about 70 percent in Britain) overwhelmed by a conservative backlash in the wake of the Prague Spring of 1968. Gorbachev insisted that "we need a revolution of the mind." In 1987, he reduced the role state corporations played in the Soviet economy, paving the way for increasing economic privatization. The state accepted private cooperatives and permitted state companies to sell their products on the open market (which encouraged luxury goods, not daily necessities). Furthermore, Gorbachev sought foreign investment in the Soviet Union. However, decades of economic inefficiency would clearly have to be overcome. Black marketeering remained a way of life for millions of people. The enormous costs of social programs weighed heavily on the sagging economy. The Communist countries of Eastern Europe, which had been exploited to economic advantage during the immediate post-war period, now represented an expensive drain on Soviet finances because of subsidies and the cost of maintaining Soviet troops there.

In 1988, Gorbachev began to sponsor a series of remarkable political reforms. Dissidents within the Communist Party or even non-Communists could now be elected to the Congress of People's Deputies. He expressed determination to continue the "thaw" with the West that Khrushchev had begun but that had ended during the Brezhnev era, which he ridiculed as the "era of stagnation." In 1985, Gorbachev replaced Andrey Gromyko, a mainstay of the Brezhnev years, as foreign minister with an old friend, Eduard Shevardnadze (1928–   ), a wily Georgian whom he had known since both were officials in the Young Communist League.

Three factors converged in the late 1980s to bring about the fall of communism. First, nationalist movements gained momentum within the Soviet Union, particularly in Lithuania, Latvia, Estonia, Moldavia, Armenia, Ukraine, and Georgia, where soldiers in 1989 bludgeoned to death nineteen demonstrators demanding independence. These movements, encouraged by the growing vulnerability of the Soviet state to a weak economy, were not placated by the belated toleration of greater cultural autonomy. Moreover, in some of the republics, long-festering conflicts between nationalities began to come to the surface, further undermining Soviet authority. In Azerbaijan, for instance, Muslim Azerbaijanis began a pogrom against Christian Armenians in 1990.

Second, in 1989, a forceful democratic opposition to communism emerged, led in Russia by the Nobel Prize–winning Russian physicist Andrey Sakharov (who had helped develop the hydrogen bomb). Gorbachev's encouragement of participation in public life (in the hope of benefiting from a groundswell of support for reform) increased the ranks of Soviet citizens demanding reform. For many people, tales of the Gulag became increasingly powerful, exposed by the exiled Russian writer Aleksandr Solzhenitsyn's *The Gulag Archipelago*. Moreover, the campaign for human rights, led by Sakharov, discredited the regime, even if the Gulag itself no longer existed. The Helsinki Accords, signed by the Soviet Union as well as by the Western powers, encouraged dissidents because they linked human rights to trade and nuclear limitation. Increasingly, Russian dissidents managed to reach a large audience through the circulation of handwritten, typed, or clandestinely printed manuscripts, as well as through the medium of Western radio broadcasts. Groups of young people formed to discuss current problems, the talk inevitably turning to the need for reform. The result was a de facto alliance between reformers and nationalists within the Soviet Union.

Third, the aggravation of the economic crisis beginning in 1988 increased the number of Soviet citizens convinced that a Communist government could not bring about a meaningful improvement in the quality of their lives. At the same time, television broadcasts from Finland day after day showed the advantages of a free-market economy. In the Soviet Union, economic plan followed economic plan, with Gorbachev vacillating between free-market policies and traditional Communist state controls. The result was a further weakening of the economy, replete with shortages and undermined by enormous military spending. Moreover, Soviet subsidies to bolster the economies of Poland and other Eastern European states had taken their toll on the Soviet economy.

As the Soviet economy was virtually collapsing, Gorbachev determined that the Soviet Union could not afford to continue the arms race with the United States. He therefore moved to improve relations with the U.S. government. In the early 1980s, Soviet–U.S. relations had continued to sour dangerously. Following the U.S. ban on the export of oil and gas to the Soviet Union after the Soviet invasion of Afghanistan in 1979, the U.S. government had tried to prevent the Soviet Union from constructing a long pipeline that would bring Siberian natural gas to Central Europe by threatening sanctions against any state or company that assisted the endeavor. Then U.S. President Ronald Reagan backed a plan to construct a space-based missile-defense shield, dubbed "Star Wars" (Strategic Defense Initiative), provoking an outcry by the Soviet Union and by some U.S. allies as well. In 1983, a Russian fighter shot down a Korean Airlines passenger plane that had entered Soviet air space, killing 169 people, including Americans. The Soviet Union boycotted the 1984 Olympics, which were held in Los Angeles, as the United States had done four years earlier in Moscow.

Gorbachev now resumed arms-limitation negotiations with the United States, but he refused to sign an agreement because Reagan would not include the "Star Wars" experiments in negotiations. Highly successful visits to Washington, D.C., and New York in 1987 gave the Soviet leader considerable world television exposure, leading to great personal popularity. He charmed Western leaders, notably British Prime Minister Margaret Thatcher, by promising to establish a free-market economy in the Soviet Union. That year the United States and the Soviet Union agreed to reduce the number of medium-range missiles, and two years later they signed

A worker measures radioactivity around the destroyed reactor after the Chernobyl explosion in 1986, the most serious nuclear accident in history.

another arms-control agreement, as well. In 1988, the Soviet Union agreed to recall troops from Afghanistan after nine years of bloody fighting against rebels there. For the first time in anyone's memory, government publications admitted the severe economic and social problems that troubled the Soviet Union. The Soviet Union began to allow Soviet Jews to emigrate abroad in greater numbers than ever before. In 1989, almost 70,000 Jews emigrated, most leaving for Israel or the United States.

In 1986, the most serious nuclear accident in history occurred in Ukraine, when a nuclear reactor exploded at Chernobyl, near Kiev, sending radioactive material pouring into the atmosphere. Thousands of people in the vicinity were killed or suffered grave illnesses. A nuclear cloud passed above Ukraine, Russia, and the Scandinavian states, among other countries. Following an initial official attempt to deny the seriousness of the disaster, Gorbachev discussed the situation with unexpected openness. The Soviet leader's push toward accommodation with the West took Western political leaders by surprise.

Meanwhile, in Eastern Europe early in 1989, some reform-minded government officials joined opposition leaders in Poland and Hungary in the belief that economic and political liberalization was urgent. Communist rule slowly floundered under the weight of economic decline and popular dissatisfaction. In Bulgaria, Czechoslovakia, East Germany, Albania, and Romania, entrenched Communist leaders sought desperately to hold on to power. The East German and Czech governments reverted to force in an attempt to halt popular movements for change. Romania's Ceauşescu predictably tried massive repression before being swept aside.

A crucial factor made the outcome of this wave of demands for reform in Eastern Europe in 1989 different from those occurring earlier (in East Germany in 1953, Hungary in 1956, and Czechoslovakia in 1968): the Soviet government no longer was determined to preserve its empire. Indeed the shout "Gorbi, Gorbi, Gorbi!" rang out from the ranks of protesters. Even if in Czechoslovakia, East Germany, and Romania, particularly, Communist leaders were determined to overwhelm dissent, Soviet tanks would no longer back them up. Indeed, in a speech to the Council of Europe in Strasbourg in July 1989, Gorbachev made clear that he rejected the Brezhnev doctrine that had brought Soviet intervention in Czechoslovakia in 1968: "Any interference in domestic affairs and any attempts to restrict the sovereignty of states, both friends and allies or any others, are inadmissible." The Soviet leader called events in Eastern Europe "inspiring," adding "What the Poles and Hungarians decide is their affair, but we will respect their decision whatever it is."

Transition to Parliamentary Government in Poland and Hungary

Poland became the first test case for the new Soviet relationship with its former satellites. The trade union organization Solidarity had virtually achieved the status of an unofficial opposition party. The Catholic Church, too, remained a source of organized opposition to communism. But although these organizations exerted some pressure on the government, it was the continued pitiful performance of the economy that fatally undermined communism. In 1987, the Polish government held a referendum, asking Poles to support price rises. When they were overwhelmingly voted down, the government imposed them anyway. Strikes followed, and demands mounted for the relegalization of Solidarity. A year later, popular frustration with widespread shortages and a grotesquely inflated currency was manifested in more strikes and demonstrations. The government could no longer meet the interest payments on its massive debt to Western banks. In August 1988, the government invited Solidarity to negotiate with it. The opposition agreed to participate in exchange for government recognition of the legal status of Solidarity as the legitimate representative of Poles opposed to Communist rule. Negotiations between Solidarity representatives and the government in 1989 led to the first relatively free elections in Poland since the immediate post-war period (even though 65 percent of the seats in the lower house of the Polish parliament would be reserved for Communists). The addition of a senate to the parliament and the creation of the position of president of Poland reflected Solidarity's reach. Still, General Jaruzelski confidently believed he could orchestrate liberalization on his own terms. He badly underestimated the unpopularity of the Communist Party in Poland.

Solidarity's candidates swept to victory. The extent of Communist humiliation was such that candidates supported by Solidarity (with the support of the Catholic Church) won all 161 parliamentary seats contested in the elections. Moreover, Communist candidates won only 2 of 35 seats in elections in which they ran unopposed. As a result, the Communists could not put together a government acceptable to Solidarity. When parliament elected Solidarity leader Tadeusz Mazowiecki (1927–   ) as premier, Poland had a non-Communist premier for the first time since Stalin imposed communism in Poland. The Polish Communist Party, pressured by Gorbachev, accepted the *fait accompli*: the election of the first non-Communist government in Eastern Europe since 1948. However, Solidarity leaders, still wary that popular momentum once again could lead to heavy-handed repression, supported the election by the Polish parliament of General Jaruzelski as president.

In 1990, the Communist era ended in Poland when the Polish Communist Party changed its name and started espousing pluralist politics. In the wake of a split within Solidarity between the followers of Mazowiecki and Walesa, the latter was elected president in December 1990. The Democratic Union, a party formed by Mazowiecki's followers within Solidarity, won the largest number of seats in the lower house and the senate. Economic reforms, aimed at introducing a full-fledged free-market economy, were slow to take effect, however. Poland began a long struggle for economic stability with mounting unemployment and a dramatically increased crime rate.

In Hungary, the Hungarian Democratic Forum and several smaller opposition groups began to emerge in 1988 out of café and living-room gatherings of longtime dissidents. Gorbachev's reforms in the Soviet Union greatly encouraged opposition groups. But as the government struggled with the floundering Hungarian economy and resisted implementing a full market economy, reform-minded Communists realized that communism would have to be reformed or it would disappear. In 1988, liberals ousted longtime leader János Kádár from power and established a new leadership that was intent on reforming Hungary.

In 1989, a combination of economic deterioration (marked by a decline in productivity and rampaging inflation) and organized opposition convinced the Communist leadership in Hungary (as in Poland) to seek political compromise with opposition leaders. For the Hungarian Communists, an insurrection, such as the one that had been crushed by Soviet tanks in 1956, had to be avoided at all costs. Yet, at least in the beginning, opposition groups, with the memory of Soviet intervention still looming large, hesitated to call the legitimacy of the Communist regime into question.

In the summer of 1989, confronted by the intransigence of hard-liners, the Hungarian opposition formed an "Opposition Round Table" and negotiated with the government. Candidates of the Democratic Forum won free elections. Faced with continuing popular mobilization (for example, a massive commemoration of the Hungarian revolution in 1848 against Habsburg rule, which had been crushed by a Russian army), the

Communist leadership decided to try to outbid the Hungarian liberals by initiating reforms. In this way, the government, increasingly dominated by reformers, began to distance itself from the Communist Party. Political opposition forced the Communist Party to acknowledge that it would play no part in Hungary's future. In May 1989, the government ordered the removal of barbed wire that defined the border with Austria. In June, the Communist Party itself admitted that the 1956 trial and execution of reform leaders had been illegal. The former premier Imre Nagy, who had been executed after the 1956 insurrection, was reburied with national honors. That month, the Hungarian Communist Party changed its name to the Hungarian Socialist Party. It espoused democratic principles and encouraged the development of opposition parties, and it accepted a new constitution proclaimed later that year. The transition from communism to multiparty parliamentary rule in Hungary was therefore peaceful, with the Hungarian Democratic Forum leading a subsequent coalition government.

The Collapse of the Berlin Wall and of East German Communism

As pressure for change mounted in Poland and Hungary, East Germans fled the German Democratic Republic in record numbers. Many travelled to the German Federal Republic via Czechoslovakia and then Hungary,

Border guards cut down the Hungarian "Iron Curtain."

whose government in May 1989 had opened its border with Austria. About 150,000 East Germans reached the West during the first nine months of 1989 alone. Eschewing the reforms undertaken by Gorbachev in the Soviet Union, East German Communist leader Erich Honecker in June 1989 had praised the Chinese army and police for crushing the pro-democracy demonstrations in Beijing's Tiananmen Square. Hundreds of activists were killed and thousands imprisoned. While other Communist governments negotiated with determined reformers, the East German leadership stood firm until it was too late. Honecker retreated into ideological orthodoxy with tired slogans, "Always forward [with socialism], never back!" He demanded that Hungary return fleeing East Germans to their country, as specified in an old treaty between the two Communist states. The Hungarian government refused to do so. East Germans who were returning from Prague on board a train passing through Dresden and Leipzig received permission to emigrate to West Germany. Learning of this, other East Germans frantically tried to climb aboard the train. About 1.5 million East Germans applied for exit visas. Most of these refugees were young workers and their families, very much like those the first East German Communist leaders had believed would always remain loyal to communism.

When Gorbachev visited East Berlin early in October 1989, demonstrators chanted his name, which had virtually become synonymous with opposition to the East German regime. When demonstrations spread to other major cities, Honecker ordered the police to attack demonstrators, but Egon Krenz, the Politburo member responsible for state security, refused to do so. On October 18, 1989, Honecker, old, ill, and ignored, was forced out in favor of Krenz, who was more moderate, but no reformer. In Leipzig, anxious opposition leaders and fearful Communist officials had met and resolved that peace must be maintained at all costs.

On October 23, 1989, the Soviet foreign minister Eduard Shevardnadze, who shared many of Gorbachev's views, declared that each country in Eastern Europe "has the right to an absolute, absolute freedom of choice." Such words further encouraged demonstrations and meetings in East Germany. On November 4, Krenz announced that East Germans were free to leave for West Germany via Czechoslovakia. A wholesale exodus began. On November 9, Krenz capitulated to the inevitable, announcing a sweeping change in government and promising to initiate legislation that would grant East Germans the right to travel where and when they wanted. He ordered that the Berlin Wall, which had divided East Berlin from West Berlin since August 1961, be torn down. Around 3 million East Germans (out of a population of 16 million) poured over the demolished wall, or crossed into West Germany at once-forbidden checkpoints. An East German poet remarked, "I must weep for joy that it happened so quickly and simply. And I must weep for wrath that it took so abysmally long."

When Egon Krenz announced that East Germans could travel where and when they wanted, people gathered at the Berlin Wall to forge openings with whatever tools they had.

Krenz, however, still hoped that his promise that free elections would follow could keep the Communists in power. But lacking popular support, Krenz's government fell on December 3, succeeded by a series of committees until the elections of March 1990. In the meantime, angry East German citizens demonstrated in front of the offices of the Communist Party and the secret police.

In the elections, conservatives favoring German reunification (led by the equivalent of the West German Christian Democrats) won a surprisingly easy victory over Social Democrats and the remnants of the (now renamed) Communist Party. A number of East German leaders already expressed eagerness for German reunification. Here, again, there would be no Russian opposition (a policy announced by Gorbachev in February 1990, though not without some misgivings) to what had seemed for decades to be unthinkable because of the fear in Russia that one day Germany might again threaten the peace. In the meantime, the German Democratic Republic began selling off state-owned companies. In May 1990, East and West Germany agreed to closer economic cooperation; the West German mark became the currency of both Germanies. In September, Britain, France, and the United States, viewing reunification as inevitable, renounced their rights in Berlin. Unification took effect on October 3, 1990. In December, the first elections in the newly unified Germany returned the Christian Democrats to power, with Helmut Kohl now chancellor. In this way, German unification was effected with speed, but at great financial cost to the former German Federal Republic, which would for years have to allocate a substantial part of its budget to modernizing the former Communist state and providing public services to new citizens (including unemployment benefits in the wake of the collapse of state-run industries). In 1999, Berlin again became the capital of Germany.

The "Velvet Revolution" in Czechoslovakia

In Czechoslovakia, where the Communist leadership resisted the forces for change as vehemently as their counterparts in East Germany, the regime was swept aside in ten days. As the economy weakened and news arrived of the fall of the Berlin Wall, the number of determined dissidents rapidly swelled beyond the ranks of intellectuals who had courageously demonstrated in 1988 on the twentieth anniversary of the Soviet invasion. Czechs and Slovaks alike signed petitions calling for reform. On November 17, 1989, students staged a demonstration in honor of a student executed by the Nazis fifty years earlier. But speakers quickly ignored the program censors had approved and began to call for academic freedom and government respect for human rights. Then, instead of disbanding to outlying squares as promised, the crowd started to march toward the giant St. Wenceslas Square in the center of Prague. A squad of riot police (who may or may not have had the authorization of the government) moved into the crowd, throwing canisters of tear gas and beating some students with clubs. Outraged demonstrators, now including workers and employers, protested the police violence.

The next day, a crowd assembled on the spot where police had beaten protesters. Students called for a general strike to begin ten days later. As the demonstrations continued to grow, protesters prepared for a potentially bloody repression. Indeed, the minister of defense announced that the army was "ready to defend the achievements of socialism" amid rumors that troops were being mobilized around Prague.

Yet, without the support of the Soviet Union, the Czechoslovak Communist government took no steps to repress the movement for freedom. On November 19, 1989, the entire Politburo resigned. In a Prague theater, a group of leading dissidents, including students, formed the "Civic Forum," calling on the government to negotiate with them over four demands: the resignation of two Communist officials blamed for the police attack two days earlier, the establishment of a commission to investigate the police attack, the release of political prisoners, and the resignation of Communist leaders responsible for the Soviet invasion in 1968. Civic Forum was led by Václav Havel (1936–   ), a popular playwright (whose plays had been banned by the government but circulated in manuscript) and a veteran of the Charter 77 group. He had been imprisoned several times for dissent, once nearly dying from mistreatment. In 1979, he had chosen to spend time in jail rather than leave Czechoslovakia.

On November 21, 1989, the elderly Aleksandr Dubček, the Slovak reformer who led the Communist Party of Czechoslovakia during the 1968 events and had called for "socialism with a human face" before being sent packing by the Soviet army, addressed a throng assembled in St. Wenceslas Square. The crowds, however, did not want any kind of socialism. Students went to factories in search of support from workers. Thereafter, crowds poured into the streets almost every day, waving national flags and calling for freedom of speech and the release of political prisoners. Throngs heard speeches calling for the end to communism; they lay wreaths on the spot where a Czech student burned himself to death in 1968 in protest of the Soviet invasion. On November 24, 1989, the Communist Central Committee narrowly voted against using the army to put an end to demonstrations. But with the security police in disarray, only ordinary police directing traffic were seen in the streets. In the meantime, in Slovakia, intellectuals formed an organization called "Public Against Violence," the Slovak equivalent of the Czech Civic Forum.

In Czechoslovakia, the Communist government now had no choice but to negotiate with its opponents who demanded free elections. Yet, unlike Poland and Hungary, where political opposition was well developed within the constraints of the system, there were virtually no reform-minded Communists within Czechoslovakia, which had one of the most rigid Communist governments in Eastern Europe. From Moscow, Gorbachev advised the Czechoslovak leaders not to use force. Negotiations between the government and Havel and other representatives of Civic Forum began on November 26. That day, more than half of the top leadership within the party was purged. On November 28, Civic Forum demanded the formation of a new government. A Communist Party official admitted, "We are aware of the fact that we don't have the trust of the people. We simply lost it—this trust. We are aware of it, I say it quite openly." It was quite an understatement.

Confronted by the success of the general strike, the government accepted five non-Communist members on December 3, 1989. The Communist-dominated Federal Assembly voted to end the party's domination of political life. On December 10, the first cabinet in Czechoslovakia since 1948 not dominated by Communists was sworn in. The general strike ended, and more than one-third of the members of the Communist Party resigned during the first two weeks of December. On December 29, the Federal Assembly unanimously elected Havel president of Czechoslovakia.

As in most places in Eastern Europe, there were very few calls for revenge against the Communist leadership (Romania would be a notable exception). Even Havel was surprised by the speed of it all, declaring that "the end of communism took us all by surprise." Sweeping away communism itself had not been the aim of Civic Forum; rather, it seemed possible only to press for the creation of a new government in which non-Communists would play a major role. But a bloodless revolution, what Havel called a "velvet revolution," had succeeded, led by writers, actors, and students in tune with the country's inter-war democratic traditions. Free elections in December 1990 gave Civic Forum and its allies a majority of seats. In the spring, the government ended price controls. Havel quickly announced that Czechoslovakia "must return to Europe," suggesting that, like Poland, its future lay with the West.

The new government of Czechoslovakia immediately faced not only the problem of creating a viable democracy but also greater tensions between Czechs and Slovaks. Although the two peoples shared seventy years of common political history, much separated them. The Czech part of the state was more urban, Protestant, and industrial than Slovakia, which was more rural and Catholic. (When Pope John Paul II visited the Slovak capital of Bratislava in the spring of 1990, the crowd of 1 million people represented 20 percent of the entire Slovak population.) Many Slovak nationalists called for the creation of an independent Slovakia. On January 1, 1993, the "velvet divorce" took place. The Czech Republic and Slovakia became two separate states. As everywhere in Eastern Europe, their weak economies compounded the problems of creating viable democratic institutions and establishing market economies.

Václav Havel, leader of the Civic Forum and first president elected under free elections in Czechoslovakia after the fall of the Communists in 1989, reads the names of members of Czechoslovakia's first non-Communist government since 1948.

Revolutions in Bulgaria, Romania, and Albania

Communist regimes also fell in Bulgaria, Romania, and Albania, the three Eastern European states without significant movements for reform. In Bulgaria, there had been little organized opposition to the regime from intellectuals or anyone else. Yet, there too, long-suppressed unrest began to emerge in response to pressure for reform in other Eastern European countries. Todor Zhivkov (1911–1998), the first secretary of the Communist Party of Bulgaria since 1954 and the head of state since 1971, could boast a record of modest economic growth, at least until the late 1970s. He also had orchestrated several cover-ups of the misdeeds of his family members (including the implication of his hard-drinking and -gambling son in the death of a television announcer and a sexual assault for which his grandson stood accused). When a Bulgarian airliner crashed at the Sofia airport, killing most passengers, Zhivkov ordered that his jet leave at once for his Black Sea vacation, flying over the burning jet and its victims. Furthermore, the Bulgarian secret police had achieved international notoriety, being blamed for an attempt to assassinate Pope John Paul II in Rome in 1981, as well as for a James Bond–like murder of a Bulgarian dissident, killed by the deadly jab of a poison-tipped umbrella in London.

The Bulgarian economy faltered badly in the late 1980s. Middle Eastern nations owing Bulgaria money could not pay their debts because of falling oil prices. At the same time, Bulgarian exports (principally agricultural produce and light manufactured goods) had difficulty finding markets, particularly as the economic crisis deepened in the Soviet Union. Rural migrants poured into Sofia and other Bulgarian cities in search of work.

As the economy deteriorated, Zhivkov and the Communist leadership sought to displace popular anger in the direction of the country's large and rapidly growing Turkish minority, most of whom lived in central and eastern Bulgaria. From time to time during the past several decades, the Turks had been the target of discriminatory government measures, including a law in 1984 requiring them to adopt Bulgarian names and forbidding the practice of Islam (the religion of most Turks). Just what the Bulgarian government hoped to achieve by such measures remains unclear (although this was hardly the first time in the often violent history of the region that an ethnic group had been targeted for discrimination in the hope of deflecting public opinion). After launching a harsh campaign against Turkish customs, Zhivkov's government encouraged the ethnic Turks to emigrate to Turkey, which further destabilized the Bulgarian economy. More than 300,000 of them left for Turkey within three months in 1989. Many, however, soon returned, disappointed that conditions of life in Turkey seemed even worse than in Bulgaria.

With news of dramatic political changes occurring in the other Eastern European states, the Bulgarian Politburo surprised Zhivkov by suddenly demanding his resignation on November 10, 1989, the day after the Berlin

Wall had been breached. The ease with which this was accomplished suggests that some party bureaucrats, army officers, and even members of the notorious government security force now believed change to be inevitable. Gorbachev, too, believed that Zhivkov had to go. The new government purged Stalinists, announced the end of the Communist monopoly on political power, and welcomed back Turks, contributing to a nationalist backlash among many Bulgarians. Zhivkov was tried for misuse of government funds and sentenced to prison.

In January 1990, the Communist monopoly on political power ended, and the Bulgarian Communist Party changed its name to the Bulgarian Socialist Party. However, in June, the former Communists, capitalizing on resurgent ethnic rivalries and fear of change in the countryside, won a majority of seats in the New National Assembly. A new constitution followed in October 1991. The Bulgarian Socialist Party and the Union of Democratic Forces remained the two largest parties, both confronting a poor economy and the lack of foreign investment, with industry remaining for the most part still under state control. After weeks of protests over the economic situation, riots broke out in 1997 in Sofia when the ruling Socialist Party refused to allow a vote that called for early elections. Elections brought the Union of Democratic Forces back to power with Ivan Kostov as prime minister in 1997. Loans from the World Bank then helped stabilize the Bulgarian economy. In an amazing turnaround in 2001, former King Simeon II (Simeon Saxe-Coburg-Gotha, who ruled from age six in 1943 until 1946) became prime minister following an electoral victory over Kostov.

In Romania, the fall of the Ceauşescu clan and communism was anything but bloodless. Ceauşescu, who had enriched his family (at least thirty of whom held high office), vowed that reform would come to Romania "when pears grow on poplar trees." He awarded himself titles such as "Genius of the Carpathians" and the "Danube of Thought." His wife, Elena, fraudulently claimed to be a brilliant chemist, presenting papers that had been prepared by Romanian scientists, and then refusing to answer questions about them. On the occasion of a state visit to Britain, when the Queen of England knighted the Romanian leader, Ceauşescu and his wife virtually pillaged a suite at London's Buckingham Palace, carting away everything of value they could. In order to begin to pay back $10 billion in foreign loans, Ceauşescu cut back food imports, increased food exports, rationed electricity, and banned abortion and the sale of contraceptives in the hope of increasing the Romanian population.

Ceauşescu's downfall began in 1989 in the Transylvanian town of Timisoara, where ethnic Hungarians resented their second-class status. Ceauşescu had ordered the razing of 8,000 largely Hungarian villages and the relocation of their residents. A popular Hungarian pastor loudly denounced the regime and called for democracy. After the Romanian security police broke into the pastor's home and beat him up, people

(*Left*) A Romanian prays for countrymen executed on the orders of dictator Nicolae Ceauşescu in Timisoara, Romania. (*Right*) A Romanian militiaman watches the execution of Ceauşescu and his wife on television.

formed a human chain around his home. Crowds rioted, smashing store windows and burning Ceauşescu's books and portraits. Romanians joined Hungarians in the protests. Army units refused to fire on demonstrators. The feared security forces (the Securitate, 180,000 strong) stepped in, shooting three army officers for disobeying orders and firing on crowds, killing a number of children.

Discontent spread rapidly. As another cold Romanian winter approached and Romanians suffered the usual severe food and fuel shortages, Hungarian and Yugoslav television showed events rapidly transpiring in other Eastern European countries. Demonstrations now spread to various Romanian towns. Ceauşescu returned from a trip to Iran in December 1989 and called for a massive demonstration of support in Bucharest. Orchestrated cheers from the crowd soon became jeers, drowning out the dictator's pathetic speech blaming riots on Hungarian nationalists. From the safety of his palace, Ceauşescu ordered troops to fire on the crowds below. But most units refused to obey and, as a result, the minister of defense was executed on Ceauşescu's orders. The hated secret police eagerly fired on the assembled crowds; tanks crushed protesters in a scene hauntingly reminiscent of Beijing's Tiananmen Square earlier that year. After soldiers battled the security forces outside the presidential palace, hundreds of bodies lay in the streets.

Several of the dictator's top officials now decided that Ceauşescu's days of iron rule were numbered. Ceauşescu and his wife left their stately residence on December 22, 1989, through secret tunnels, and then commandeered a helicopter. They were captured and immediately charged with murder and embezzlement of government funds. On Christmas Day, they were tried by a hastily convoked tribunal (which, in fact, had no legal authority) and condemned to death. They were then taken behind the building and shot, their bloody bodies left lying stiffly in the snow for a worldwide television audience to see while members of the security forces continued their resistance. More than 1,000 Romanians died during the revolution that overthrew Ceauşescu.

A number of political parties quickly formed, including the National Salvation Front, which consisted in large part of anti-Ceauşescu Communists. In the elections of May 1990, the National Salvation Front won an overwhelming victory, drawing votes of peasants and party members. Ion Iliescu (1930–   ), a reformer who had befriended Gorbachev while studying at a technical institute in Moscow, became president of Romania. Former Communists have continued to play a major role, however, in what remains one of Europe's poorest countries. The old Securitate apparatus, essentially intact despite the fall of Ceauşescu, in June 1990 aided Romanian miners, many of whom remained loyal to the Communists, in a violent attack on demonstrators (several of whom were killed), who were protesting what they considered the National Salvation Front's neo-communism. Romania tottered in uncertainty.

Communism was swept away even in Albania, which had remained largely isolated from change in Eastern Europe by sealed borders. Ramiz Alia, first secretary of the Communist Party of Labor and president of Albania, confidently asserted in December 1989, "There are people abroad who ask: Will processes like those taking place in Eastern Europe also occur in Albania? We answer firmly and categorically: No, they will not occur in Albania."

In Europe's poorest country, where food shortages had generated sullen anger, news of the fall of Ceauşescu in December 1989 emboldened dissidents. Riots occurred in the northern Albanian city of Shkodër. As a crisis mounted, Alia announced greater openness in the selection of government leaders and a larger role for workers in choosing managers. Moreover, agricultural cooperatives for the first time would be allowed to sell surplus produce. Alia then announced the right to travel abroad and an abrogation of the long-standing ban on "religious propaganda," and he expressed interest in establishing normal diplomatic ties with Washington and Moscow. A group of Albanian intellectuals demanded the end of the Communist monopoly on power. Several thousand Albanians adopted the East German tactic of entering foreign embassies and legations in the hope of gaining the right to emigrate. Students went on strike. In late 1990, veterans' and youth organizations were declared independent of the Communist Party of Labor. Elections were scheduled for February 1991. Like other Communist leaders, Alia believed that he could maintain control, placating Albanians with minor reforms.

Confronted by demonstrations that began in December 1990, Alia announced that henceforth the Communist Party would cease to be the only approved political party. The Democratic Party quickly constituted itself, and opposition newspapers began to publish, although the Communist Party of Labor retained control of radio and television. In February

1991, a crowd of 100,000 demonstrated in Tirana, pulling down a large statue of former strongman Enver Hoxha. In early March, 20,000 Albanians tried to force their way onto boats departing for Italy. This event, which focused international attention on Albania, produced a Communist backlash, particularly in the countryside, where Hoxha had been a cult figure. In elections that month, the Communists won 68 percent of the vote. Despite this victory, the handwriting was on the wall. In June 1991, the Communist government resigned. For the first time since 1944, a coalition government came to power. Albania, too, entered the post-Communist world with most of its people convinced that economic and political reforms alone could save Albania from grinding poverty and isolation. Elections in 1992 gave the Democratic Party a majority of the seats in the National Assembly, and Alia resigned as Albania's president. For the next decade, the Democratic Party and the Socialist Party battled it out, against the background of economic hardship, the arrival of tens of thousands of refugees from Kosovo, political corruption and assassination, and the bizarre events of 1997, when a series of pyramid investment schemes collapsed on naive purchasers. The latter led to riots, violence, and the arming of a considerable percentage of the population with some of the 1 million military arms that had fallen into civilian hands. Greek troops had to intervene to maintain peace in what remains in many ways an unstable country.

The Collapse of the Soviet Union

As one by one the former Eastern European satellites of the Soviet Union abandoned communism, unhappiness with communism became more vocal within the Soviet Union itself. In March 1990, the Communist government voted to permit non-Communist parties in the Soviet Union, and it created the office of president. State restrictions on religious practice ended. That month, the Congress of People's Deputies elected Mikhail Gorbachev president of the Soviet Union, a significant change since previously the head of the Communist Party was the titular head of state.

Pressure for the breakup of the Soviet Union mounted from the republics. In Estonia, Latvia, and Lithuania a human chain of more than 1 million people formed to support the independence of their nations. In June 1990, the Russian Republic declared that laws passed by its legislature could override those of the Soviet Union. The other republics followed suit with similar legislation. Gorbachev's attempt to enhance government decentralization fell short of what nationalists in the republics sought. In June 1990, Lithuania unilaterally declared its independence from the Soviet Union; Gorbachev responded by ordering an embargo on Soviet oil and gas shipped to the Baltic state.

Gorbachev remained fundamentally skeptical of democracy. He still wanted to maintain a role for the Communist Party in the new era, and he wanted to ensure the existence of the Soviet Union itself. In 1990, he appointed several hard-line government officials and ordered a crackdown on nationalist movements in the Baltic states. This led to the dramatic resignation of Eduard Shevardnadze, the popular foreign minister.

In Russia, the charismatic, hard-drinking, impulsive Boris Yeltsin (1931–   ) had risen to positions of authority in the Communist Party as an efficient and honest administrator. He had several years earlier been elected to the Moscow council and now was elected to the Russian Congress of People's Deputies in March. Committed to reform and claiming that Gorbachev was not, he challenged the latter's authority and the very legitimacy of the Soviet state. As chair of the Supreme Soviet, he announced that henceforth Russia would be a sovereign, independent state. Unlike Gorbachev, Yeltsin had no illusions about the survival of communism; he harbored grave doubts that the Soviet Union itself would survive and was willing to ally with the other republics against Gorbachev. When reactionary Communists attempted to unseat Yeltsin as chairman in the Russian Parliament, he received a show of support from several hundred thousand Moscovites. He retained the democratic pedigree Gorbachev lacked.

As he tried to steer an impossible middle course between the reformers and those committed to maintaining a role for the Communist Party, Gorbachev now seemed to move away from reform, possibly encouraging right-wing officials within the Communist Party, army, and KGB, who believed their positions threatened by a reduction in hostility with the United States. The hard-line group had begun putting pressure on Gorbachev in September 1990, and the army undertook mysterious maneuvers around Moscow.

In January 1991, Gorbachev may have approved an attempt to overthrow the democratically elected government of Lithuania, beginning with an attack on a television installation in the capital of Vilnius. The clumsy plot, which involved army and KGB agents pretending they were a Lithuanian dissident group, failed miserably, costing thirteen lives. A month later, in a referendum deemed by the Soviet government to be illegal, 90 percent of those voting in Lithuania expressed their support for independence, as did 77 percent of those voting in both Estonia and Latvia (the difference is explained by the fact that many Russians live in Estonia and Latvia).

In a nationally televised speech in February 1991, Yeltsin called for his rival Gorbachev to resign from office. Gorbachev, in turn, responded by ordering Soviet troops to surround the Kremlin in a show of force against the more liberal Yeltsin. However, the latter had begun to undermine the army and security forces, where he counted followers, whereas Gorbachev's turn toward conservatives cost him supporters.

However, Gorbachev's conservative retrenchment proved short-lived. In April, he abandoned his commitment to preserving the Soviet Union at all costs and accepted the idea of autonomy for the republics. In June 1991, Yeltsin, a Russian nationalist, was elected president of the "Russian Federation," another sign of how quickly the Soviet Union was changing. The Communists now had little support in Russia, the Soviet Union's largest republic.

It became increasingly clear that Gorbachev was losing control, and that the Soviet Union was vulnerable to a rightist coup. Gorbachev, who had been meeting with Western leaders in London, returned to Moscow and announced a new Communist Party platform, which eliminated Marxism and Leninism in favor of "humane and democratic socialism." He then left for an August vacation in Crimea.

Intransigent Communists were now firmly convinced that Gorbachev's policies threatened communism and the existence of the Soviet Union. In August 1991, hard-liners within the Communist Party, army, KGB, and some members of Gorbachev's own cabinet (including the minister of defense) placed the Soviet leader under house arrest in his own Crimean residence in an attempted coup d'état that looked more like a comic opera. Setting up an "Emergency Committee," the conspirators apparently hoped that they could convince or force Gorbachev to throw his prestige against reform, believing that he would agree to declare a state of emergency. Gorbachev agreed to do so, but only if such a move were approved "constitutionally" by the Supreme Soviet. The conspirators then publicly declared the president to be "incapacitated," announcing that the vice president would take charge.

In Moscow, where KGB officials had refused the conspirators' order to arrest Boris Yeltsin, the Russian leader courageously defied the coup. He stood on a tank outside the Russian Parliament in Moscow and encour-

(*Left*) Atop a tank in front of the Russian Parliament building, Boris Yeltsin urges the Russian people to resist the coup d'état of August 1991. (*Right*) Yeltsin seems to be reprimanding Mikhail Gorbachev in the wake of the failed coup d'état.

aged resistance. The coup fell apart, its leaders having underestimated the strength of both Yeltsin's and Gorbachev's popular support. They also had overestimated their own support within the army, which in fact remained loyal to Gorbachev, despite the resentment of many officers and enlisted men about deteriorating conditions of life in the once-proud force that had long been closely identified with the Soviet state. Moreover, six years of political debate in the Soviet Union had increased the number of ordinary people committed to reform. Yeltsin was able to mobilize the Moscow public by calling for resistance and the restoration of Gorbachev as the legitimate Soviet leader. This appeal to constitutionality revealed how much had changed in a very short time.

Gorbachev returned in August to Moscow a hero, and again took a more reformist stance. Yeltsin, as head of the Russian Parliament, used that body to validate a number of decrees he had announced during the crisis. Even as Gorbachev continued to defend the Communist Party before the Supreme Soviet, Yeltsin suspended the Communist Party and its newspaper *Pravda*. These bold moves amounted to the dismantling of communism in Russia. Yeltsin reiterated his commitment to national self-determination.

The failed coup accelerated the collapse of the Soviet Union. Gorbachev appointed new people to key ministries. Some KGB officers were pensioned off, and television and radio were freed from the constraints of censorship. The Soviet government finally recognized the outright independence of the Baltic republics just months after Gorbachev had insisted on retaining the structure of the Soviet Union.

Gorbachev himself accepted the legitimacy of Yeltsin's decrees. Moreover, at the end of August 1991, the Supreme Soviet voted to put an end to the extraordinary powers previously accorded Gorbachev and to suspend the Communist Party in the entire Soviet Union. Yeltsin quickly moved to initiate a market economy in Russia.

One by one, the republics took steps to leave the Soviet Union, in which Russians constituted only about half of the population. Moldavia, Uzbekistan, and Azerbaijan declared their independence. Other Soviet republics held or planned plebiscites, all of which led to declarations of independence from the Soviet Union. In December 1991, Ukraine declared its independence after 90 percent of the population voted to leave the Soviet Union. By the end of the year, thirteen of the fifteen Soviet republics had declared their independence. Yeltsin and the presidents of Belarus and Ukraine created the Commonwealth of Independent States, declaring the Soviet Union dissolved. Gorbachev now acknowledged that the Soviet Union no longer existed. Symbolically, Leningrad again assumed its old name of St. Petersburg. On December 25, 1991, Gorbachev resigned, closing one of the most remarkable political eras in modern European history.

Challenges in the Post-Communist World

The end of communism in the Soviet Union and Eastern Europe has not guaranteed an easy transition to parliamentary, democratic rule. The lack of democratic traditions, economic turmoil, and ethnic rivalries posed daunting challenges. Until the fall of communism, Russia itself had been first a tsarist autocracy and then a Communist dictatorship. Indeed, the history of the inter-war years demonstrates the danger that aggressive nationalism poses to parliamentary government.

Nowhere are the stakes higher for a peaceful transition to democracy than in Russia. The president of Ukraine put it this way: "When there's frost in Russia on Thursday, by Friday there's frost in Kiev." As rivalry between Yeltsin and the Congress of People's Deputies grew in 1992 and early 1993, Yeltsin declared a "special presidential regime," dissolving the legislature and overriding opposition to his reform program. Yeltsin insisted that the Russian presidency should have considerable authority, whereas the Congress feared too much presidential power, remembering well the dictatorship of the Communist Party. A deputy prime minister of Turkmenistan admitted, "We're praying day and night for Yeltsin to stay in power. Any of those who might come after him, all of them have an ax in their hand." In 1996, Yeltsin became the first democratically elected president of Russia. In ill health, his resignation at the end of 1999 brought Vladimir Putin, a former KGB officer, to power, first as acting president and then as elected president of Russia. President Putin faced a great tragedy in 2000, when the Russian nuclear submarine *Kursk* sank with 118 men lost in the frigid Berents Sea north of Murmansk.

While the West breathed a sigh of relief with the collapse of communism, the existence of nuclear weapons in several of the former states of the Soviet Union became a considerable concern. Kazakhstan's possession of nuclear arms makes events there particularly important. Ukraine's nuclear arsenal and its claim to the remnants of the Soviet Black Sea Fleet docked in Crimea raised tension between Russia and Ukraine, by far the two most powerful of the old Soviet republics. In 1992, Ukraine, Russia, Belarus, and Kazakhstan all agreed that nuclear weapons stored on their territory would either be destroyed or turned over to Russia within a few years. In 1996, nuclear warheads were shipped to Russia for destruction. However, the problem of preventing the theft and sale of nuclear materials, particularly to potential terrorists, remains one of the most important concerns for the future.

The end of communism has left other problems. Among them, the rapid industrialization in East Germany, Romania, and Czechoslovakia under communism left horrendous pollution from coal-burning furnaces and virtually unregulated factories. Acid rain has destroyed forests, killed rivers, and compromised the health of residents. It will take decades and massive financial investment to clean it all up. Moreover, the 1986 Chernobyl dis-

An automobile heads toward smog and smokestacks, a tableau of the pollution in Eastern Europe.

aster clearly demonstrated the vulnerability of the rest of Europe to nuclear fallout.

Suddenly freed from Soviet domination, the newly independent states faced the challenge of putting their own foreign relations on a firm footing. For many of the former Soviet republics, relations with Russia are complicated by centuries of animosity. Soviet rule had favored Russian interests and brought the settlement of large Russian populations, as well as troops (250,000 Soviet troops were stationed in Soviet republics other than Russia at the time of the Soviet Union's dissolution).

Like the Soviet Union, the Eastern European Communist states were largely atomized societies of one-party rule without political infrastructures, traditions of political parties, civic cultures, or adequately developed voluntary associations. Only in Poland and Hungary had non-Communist political leadership gradually emerged in the 1980s. As we have seen, the Polish Solidarity movement and several Hungarian associations provided a basis for the emergence of party politics following the dismantling of one-party rule. In 1989, Civic Forum in Czechoslovakia served the same function.

In the first free elections held in Eastern Europe since the late 1940s, two distinct trends were seen in the 1990s. Nationalist right-center parties emerged victorious in eastern Germany, Poland, and Hungary, where the parties of the left, including those formed by former Communists (some of them, to be sure, converted reformers), fared badly. On the other hand, in

Bulgaria and Romania, which had virtually no democratic traditions, former Communist parties (hurriedly renamed and claiming the mantle of reform) came out better than any other parties. They did particularly well in the countryside, where reform movements had been absent and Communist officials maintained considerable prestige, identified with the modest increase in living standards that had occurred during the decades since the war. In late 1995, the Communist Party emerged as the biggest winner in the legislative elections in Russia. Six years after the fall of the Berlin Wall, Bulgaria, Hungary, Lithuania, and Poland, where Lech Walesa was turned out of office in 1995, were now led by former Communists. Many of them benefited from being familiar faces able to draw on old political networks and from protest votes from people exasperated by economic woes. In 1996, Romania elected its first non-Communist government since the end of the Ceauşescu regime seven years earlier. However, after several years of political instability, Ion Iliescu, the former Communist who was president from 1990 to 1996, was re-elected in 2000, marking the defeat of the far-right Great Romania Party.

However, the former Communist states have accepted the necessity of creating modern economic systems based on private enterprise. Western economic advisers provided some of the expertise as the nationalized sector of Eastern European economies was drastically reduced within about five years. Yet in former Communist countries where collectivization was a way of life (except in Poland and Hungary), economic privatization has not been easy. Some collectivized farms resisted decollectivization, while some former owners of property collectivized by Communist regimes demanded their lands back. Throughout Eastern Europe, as well as the former Soviet Union, weak economies and a relatively low standard of living continued to generate political instability. Policy changes came with numbing speed. The utilization of free-market "shock therapy," including the end of price controls on most consumer goods, brought chaos to Russia and Poland. Economic output in both countries fell drastically. In the region as a whole, industrial production fell by between 20 percent and 40 percent. Widespread unemployment and the sudden end of the massive welfare system under which entire populations had grown up left bewilderment, hardship, and anger. Furthermore, in most of the former Communist countries, the end of authoritarian rule led to major increases in violent crime—above all, in Russia, where organized crime burgeoned.

Foreign investment was far from adequate. Galloping inflation (up to 20 percent a month in Russia and 40 percent in Ukraine, where economic measures were halfhearted) engendered bitterness. Despite the fact that its Western creditors in March 1991 canceled half of the debts owed by Poland, the economic outlook in that country seemed bleak. The Russian economy virtually collapsed in the 1990s and by the end of the decade about 30 percent of the population of Russia was classified as impoverished. With taxpayers simply not paying, Russia barely avoided bankruptcy in 1998, postponing paying off $43 billion in short-term loans. In 1997, the new Romanian government undertook major economic reforms, with the help of loans from the World Bank and the International Monetary Fund. These included the reduction of state subsidies to companies and the privatization of many state-run businesses.

Ethnic tensions in Eastern Europe remain. Winston Churchill's comment after the Treaty of Versailles in 1919 still rings true: "Injuries were wrought to the structure of human society which a century will not efface." About 600,000 ethnic Hungarians live in Slovakia, 500,000 in Serbia, and 200,000 in Ukraine. Tensions remain between Turks and Bulgarians in Bulgaria and between Hungarians and Romanians in Romania. The potential for ethnic violence in Russia and the other former Soviet republics also remains. Fighting between Azerbaijanis and Armenians in an Armenian enclave of Nagorno-Karabakh reflected long-standing Islamic religious and cultural ties with Turkey, as well as historical links between Armenia and Russia. In Georgia, too, fighting was widespread between Eduard Shevardnadze's government and supporters of a former dissident elected president in 1991. One observer called the Caucasus "a Yugoslavia that has already begun to happen." Furthermore, Russia's role in such conflicts (particularly in states with sizable Russian minorities) could remain a source of tension, potentially threatening the honeymoon between Russia and the former republics of the Soviet Union. Since 1994, Russian troops first sent by Boris Yeltsin have battled nationalist Muslim insurgents in Chechnya (which lies north of Georgia and west of the Caspian Sea). The revolt, which has taken the lives of thousands of civilians, has generated a harsh repression, while generating terrorist attacks orchestrated by rebels inside Chechyna and inside Russia. The Russian government proposed greater Chechen autonomy, but not independence. Russian troops captured Grozny, the capital of the breakaway republic, in February 2000. In October 2002, Chechen rebels held an entire theater audience captive in Moscow, demanding an end to Russian occupation of their land, until Russian forces used poison gas and an assault to free most of the hostages, 117 of whom were killed.

Moreover, 25 million Russians lived in other republics within the Soviet Union at the time of the latter's disintegration. It was telling that in Estonia and Romania, no sooner had Communist rule ended than new governments established language tests to determine who was a "real" Estonian or Romanian. The newly independent Baltic republics established laws that classified Russians and Byelorussians (who make up nearly half of the population of Latvia and 40 percent of that of Estonia) as foreigners. Nation-states, which many liberals long assumed were necessary before constitutional rights and equality could be assured, have not always turned out to be liberal and tolerant. In Russia, the xenophobic Liberal Democratic Party won almost a quarter of the vote in Parlimentary elections in 1993; its leader, Vladimir Zhirinovsky, promised wars of conquest in the name of Russia, insisting that Russia maintain control over the Crimea, now part of Ukraine, and northern Kazakhstan. In 1996 Zhirinovsky, a virulent anti-Semite who talked of reconquering Alaska, won 4 million votes in the presidential election.

The Disintegration of Yugoslavia

The story of the disintegration of Yugoslavia most tragically illustrates the complexity of the past, the impact of ethnic politics on the post-Communist era in Eastern Europe and the Balkans, and the challenges and hopes for the future. Marshal Josip Broz ("Tito"), a Croat, had believed that communism in Yugoslavia could end ethnic rivalries and Serb domination and had repressed nationalist groups. Following Tito's death in 1980, a collective presidency that rotated every year among the republics governed Yugoslavia.

In the mid-1980s, the Yugoslav government, dominated by Serbs, launched a brutal repression of Albanians living in Kosovo, claiming that Albanian nationalism posed a threat to communism. In April 1987, Slobodan Milošević, the leader of the Serb Communist Party, addressed a throng of 15,000 Serbs and Montenegrins in Kosovo. When the Albanian-dominated police moved in to break up the mass gathering, Milošević made a provocative speech, telling the Serbs and Montenegrins that the land of Kosovo was theirs, and that they should remain at all costs.

Boosted by this public relations success among Serbs, Milošević soon emerged as the dominant figure in Yugoslavia. He turned the Communist Party and state apparatus into instruments serving Serb nationalist interests, preparing to establish a "Greater Serbia" should Yugoslavia break up. Milošević undertook what amounted to a military occupation of Kosovo, ending its administrative autonomy. In 1989, fighting broke out in Kosovo between ethnic Albanians, Serbs, and Montenegrins. Milošević also pushed aside party leaders in several other provinces. Regional Communist Party hierarchies only weakly resisted or completely capitulated under the pressure of Serb nationalism, which was further inflamed by Albanian resistance in Kosovo. That year, the legislature of Serbia ended even the very limited autonomy Tito had awarded Kosovo and restricted the use of the Albanian language.

Yugoslavia quickly disintegrated (see Map 29.2). The movement for political reform began in January 1990 in Slovenia, the wealthiest and most homogeneous of Yugoslavia's six republics (with over 90 percent of its population consisting of Slovenes). New parties formed in each of the six republics, including in Serbia, where Communist leaders were most opposed to reform. Non-Communists won a majority of the parliamentary seats in Bosnia-Herzegovina, Croatia, Slovenia, and Macedonia. The Communist Party changed its name to the Socialist Party and won a majority in Milošević's Serbia and in Montenegro, Serbia's ally.

In Slovenia and Croatia, calls by nationalists for succession from Yugoslavia grew louder, although some reformers still wanted the state to survive with a federalist structure. In response, Milošević denounced Croatian nationalists as Ustaša (World War II Croatian fascists). Yet, even within Serbia, Milošević's authority drew increasing criticism from those who wanted reform.

In December 1990, almost 90 percent of Slovenes who voted in a referendum expressed their desire for national independence. In Croatia, the nationalist Franjo Tudjman, who had been a general, won a clear electoral victory, accentuating tensions between Croatia and the wider Yugoslav state. Milošević loudly espoused the creation of a Greater Serbia that would include all territories populated by Serbs. Along the Croatian coast

MAP 29.2 THE DISINTEGRATION OF YUGOSLAVIA, 1995 The fall of the Communists in Yugoslavia led to the breakup of the Yugoslav federation and to civil war between Croats, Serbs, and Bosnian Muslims. This map reflects the settlement reached in the Dayton Peace Accords, signed in November 1995.

of Dalmatia, Serb nationalist groups raided police stations, killing several Croatian policemen and seizing guns and ammunition.

In May 1991, Serbia prevented the succession of a Croat to the rotating presidency of Yugoslavia. Attempted intervention by the Yugoslav army in Slovenia was met by determined resistance and was short-lived. But when Croatia declared its independence from Yugoslavia in June 1991, as did Slovenia, violent conflicts between Croats and Serbs intensified. Serb militias, supported and armed by Yugoslav army units, began occupying large chunks of Croatia that had sizable Serb populations. Within several months they held about one-third of Croatian territory. Croats were driven from their villages in an extended series of Serb operations that killed thousands of people. From the heights above, Serbs shelled the walled Croatian city of Dubrovnik on the Adriatic coast, damaging one of Europe's most beautiful cities. Croatia became independent in January 1992, although parts of Croatia still remained under Serb control.

Macedonia declared its independence in September 1991, despite tensions between the Slavic majority and its Albanian Muslim minority. In Bosnia-Herzegovina, ethnic rivalries brought violence. The Yugoslav army occupied parts of Bosnia, allegedly to protect Serbs. In March 1992, a majority of Bosnian Muslims and ethnic Croats voted for independence. However, Bosnian Serbs refused to recognize the legality of the plebiscite. They declared their own independence and attacked Sarajevo, the capital of Bosnia. Milošević's surviving Yugoslav state, as well as Serb minorities within each republic, viewed declarations of independence as unacceptable provocations. A bloody civil war broke out in Bosnia-Herzegovina, and in parts of Croatia. In some regions, Bosnian Serbs carried out "ethnic cleansing," a term they invented. Ethnic cleansing by Bosnian Serbs recalls Nazi atrocities committed during World War II, as well as the Turkish slaughter of Armenians in 1895 and again during World War I, the Serbian massacre of thousands of Albanian civilians who lived in what had been Ottoman Kosovo during the First Balkan War of 1912, the execution of thousands of Serbs by Austro-Hungarian troops in 1914, and Turkish outrages against Greeks in Anatolia in 1921 and 1922.

Serbs forced at least 170,000 non-Serbs from their homes and drove them away or imprisoned them. Bosnian Serb militias perpetuated atrocities against Bosnian Muslims, including rapes and mass executions. Thousands of Muslims were massacred in fields outside the town of Srebrenica. In the meantime, in predominantly Croat parts of Bosnia, Croats also carried out brutal measures against Muslims, who sometimes reciprocated against Serbs and Croats.

Milošević, presiding over what remained of Yugoslavia (Serbia and Montenegro), eliminated constitutional guarantees given by the Yugoslav republic to the provinces of Kosovo and Vojvodina. Although Yugoslav armies withdrew, fearing international intervention, Bosnian Serb forces, supplied by the Yugoslav army, surrounded Sarajevo, lobbing mortar and

(*Left*) A Kosovo Albanian refugee released from the custody of the Yugoslav Army collapses. (*Right*). Yugoslav president Slobodan Milošević brandishes a mace, a gift from his supporters.

cannon shells from the heights above and shooting at civilians, including elderly people, women, and children. In response to assistance given the Bosnian Serbs by Milošević's government, the United Nations placed an economic embargo on the rump Yugoslav state. But the NATO alliance stood by and allowed Serbian nationalists to conquer more than 70 percent of Bosnia-Herzegovina. "Europe is dying in Sarajevo," warned a poster in Germany. "The Bosnian crisis has been the major post–Cold War turning point in Europe, and we missed the turn," sadly noted one French leader. To make things even worse, Croats and Muslims in Bosnia now began to fight each other.

The Bosnian conflict took a terrible toll, creating hundreds of thousands of refugees, including half of the population of Bosnia. Croatia entered the conflict not only with the goal of protecting the United Nations "safe zones" for Bosnian Muslims but also with an eye toward taking Bosnian territory that it considered Croatian. This moved the region close to a full-scale Balkan war. Germany, a nation with historically antagonistic relations with the Slavs and which during World War II turned loose Croatian fascists on the Serbs, was the first state to recognize the independence of Croatia (as well as Slovenia and Bosnia), and it lobbied effectively against the imposition of economic sanctions against Croatia.

Early in 1994, a cease-fire agreement took hold. Bosnian Muslim and Croatian leaders met in Washington, D.C., forming a Muslim-Croat Federation within Bosnia-Herzegovina. However, the Bosnian Serbs refused to respect either the cease-fire or an international plan for peace. The arrival of blue-helmeted UN peacekeepers at first made little difference, the first international attempt ever to stop ethnic cleansing. NATO launched air strikes against Serb targets in Bosnia. In June 1995, the Bosnian Serbs humiliated the United Nations by taking some of its peacekeepers hostage. In August 1995, the Croats recaptured Krajina, contested territory bordering on Bosnia, which Croatian Serbs had declared to be independent in 1991. Now tens of thousands of Serbs from Krajina took to the roads as refugees, heading toward Serb strongholds in Bosnia.

By the Dayton Peace Accords orchestrated in November 1991 by the U.S. government, Bosnia was to be a single state that included a Bosnian-Croat federation and a Serb republic. This agreement would be supervised by a NATO peacekeeping force, including U.S. troops. However, Bosnian Serbs overran free zones that NATO forces had established to provide safe haven to Bosnian Muslims driven from their villages by Serbs. Mass murders perpetrated against Muslims in 1995 (including thousands in a so-called UN-protected safe zone) led to the indictment of Bosnian Serb leader Radovan Karadžić by the International Criminal Tribunal, a UN tribunal that was established in The Hague (in the Netherlands) to judge those accused of crimes against humanity and genocide. Europe's bloodiest conflict since World War II went on, with the United Nations standing by helplessly.

In Kosovo, where Albanians made up 80 percent of the population, Albanians had formed the Kosovo Liberation Army with the goal of obtaining freedom from Yugoslavia. In 1998 and 1999, Milošević unleashed Serb forces against ethnic Albanians in the Serbian province of Kosovo. Thousands of Albanians were massacred and about 800,000 were forced to leave Kosovo. In the meantime, a cease-fire arranged by the United States in October 1998 quickly collapsed and peace talks in Paris early the next year fell apart because Serb negotiators would not discuss autonomy for Kosovo and because Milošević refused to allow NATO peacekeepers into the province. Serb troops brutally attacked Albanian villages in Kosovo and undertook ethnic cleansing, killing several thousand Albanians. Serb forces drove at least 860,000 Albanians from Kosovo into Albania and Macedonia. When Serb forces did not withdraw from Kosovo, NATO forces in March 1999 began attacking Serb military targets in Serbia itself with missiles launched from U.S. ships and bombers based in Great Britain, Germany, and Italy. In May 1999, the International Criminal Tribunal in The Hague issued a warrant for Milošević's arrest, charging him with crimes against humanity. The bombing campaign, which lasted into June, forced Serb forces to withdraw from Kosovo and to allow 50,000 NATO peacekeepers into Kosovo. Russian troops also moved into Kosovo and into Pristina, and they were integrated into peacekeeping forces. NATO forces then oversaw the return of about 720,000 ethnic Albanian refugees to Kosovo, as about 50,000 Serbs now fled possible reprisals.

In 2000, Kosovo enjoyed its first free elections since the war began in 1999. Yet events in Macedonia reflected the fragility of peace and the depth of ethnic tensions. Attacks launched by Albanian rebels against Macedonian police in the former Yugoslavian republic led to more fighting, and NATO troops were sent to Macedonia as peacekeepers, authorized to monitor an agreement between the two sides.

Milošević's government in Yugoslavia collapsed in October 2000 in the face of mass demonstrations. It gave way to a transitional government that included members of his old party. In 2000, Vojislav Kostunica became president of Yugoslavia, winning about 65 percent of the votes in legislative elections. Milošević was arrested in April 2001 on charges of abuse of power and was transferred to the International Criminal Tribunal in The Hague to face charges of crimes against humanity and genocide, violations of the Geneva Convention of 1949. In the meantime, the new Yugoslav government worked quickly to end the international isolation brought about by Milošević's vicious policies. The United States and other states terminated economic sanctions against Yugoslavia, and the World Bank and the European Union promised economic aid. Early in 2003, even the name Yugoslavia disappeared, replaced by Serbia-Montenegro, the only two of the seven provinces of Yugoslavia that remained together. The assassination in March 2003 of the prime minister of Serbia, Zoran Djindjic,

Ethnic Albanians cheer a French soldier with the NATO peacekeeping force in Kosovo, 1999.

who had been one of the forces behind the ouster of Milošević in 2000, attested to the continuing volatility of states in the former Yugoslavia.

Conclusion

The Western European nations failed to act effectively to resolve the Bosnian crisis, but the cooperation between states in the former Soviet bloc and the West is reassuring. In addition, Russia and the United States signed an arms treaty in 2002 and have cooperated in space ventures, notably a space station, although the tragic destruction of the *Columbia* space shuttle on entering the earth's atmosphere in February 2003 raised some doubts about the cost and risks to astronauts of space travel.

Freed from Communist rule, some of the Eastern European states lobbied to join NATO. In 1997, NATO announced that it would expand its membership to include eventually Poland, the Czech Republic, and Hungary, hoping that the adherence of former Communist states would help consolidate democracy. Furthermore, it was also announced that a Permanent Joint Council in Brussels would bring together NATO members and Russia to consider joint actions, including arms control and peacekeeping. This is a remarkable turnabout, as NATO had been originally established with the goal of containing the Soviet Union. This, too, has been a sign of new times.

CHAPTER 30

GLOBAL CHALLENGES, EUROPEAN COOPERATION, AND THE UNCERTAINTIES OF A NEW AGE

The dramatic increase in the movement of peoples from one part of the world to another has been one dimension of globalization. After centuries of sending millions of European emigrants to other continents, the past decades have reversed the trend, bringing streams of people seeking better lives in Europe. Yet while immigrants have contributed enormously to the economies of many European states, their presence and the cultural differences they bring with them have generated xenophobia and an increase in the political influence of nationalist parties of the extreme right in many states. Immigration thus poses a challenge to the new Europe, raising difficult issues of identity and the very question of what it means to be European.

Globalization has brought other difficult challenges as well. Europe has ceased to be the center of global political concern and conflict, a title that has arguably passed to the Middle East. Globalization has made Europe, like other parts of the world, vulnerable to the tensions tied to conflicts in the Middle East. Terrorist attacks have carried the struggles in that part of the world to Europe itself, among other continents. Moreover, with the collapse of the Soviet Union, European unity and the traditional Western alliance have been challenged by the domination of the United States. Yet the European Union (EU) in the 1990s carried cooperation between European states to a level barely imaginable a decade or two before.

1343

Within the European Union, a single market led to the inauguration of a single currency—the "euro"—in 2002.

IMMIGRATION TO EUROPE

For centuries, Europeans had left their continent and migrated to the Western Hemisphere, primarily the United States. In the last decades of the twentieth century, the direction of the flow reversed. More than ever before, the world's population is on the move. Millions of people have immigrated to Western Europe. Africans, Asians, Turks, and people from the Middle East have arrived, legally or illegally, in Western European countries, in search of a better life. To be sure, immigration within Europe, particularly from the poorer countries of southern and eastern Europe has also continued to be significant. The mass movement of people from the "Third World," particularly from Africa and Asia, must be seen in the context of the rapid growth of the world's population. The population of Africa in 1950 had been half that of Europe; by 1985, the two populations stood about even, and within several decades the population of Africa will probably be three times that of Europe. In some cases, it was newly independent colonies that sent emigrants to their former colonizers (for example, the case of Congo and Belgium, and the East Indies and the Netherlands).

North African immigrants captured by a patrol boat after trying to enter Spain illegally.

Beginning in the late 1960s, foreign-born "guest workers" (as they are called in Germany) made up an increasing proportion of the workforce in every Western European state. They infused expanding European economies, which suffered from a shortage of labor, with energy, taking up a variety of jobs, some skilled but most unskilled. Europe now has an estimated 15 million to 18 million foreign workers. A steady stream of immigrants arrived in Britain, many from India and Pakistan, former colonies. The newcomers to Britain were attracted by the need for labor, and their presence was encouraged, as in other Western countries, by the government. Italian workers had begun to emigrate to Sweden and Switzerland in the 1950s; the West German government established recruiting offices in southern Europe and North Africa, hoping to encourage immigration. The number of foreigners living in Western Europe, particularly in large cities such as Paris, Berlin, London, and Brussels, tripled in thirty years. In Switzerland, foreign workers make up 17 percent of the workforce. The ethnic composition of this workforce varies from country to country. Turks have settled in Germany in great numbers because of the relative proximity and historically close ties between Turkey and Germany. Portuguese make up the largest group of foreign residents in France, followed closely by Moroccans, Algerians, and Tunisians, and an increasing number of West Africans. In Great Britain, Irish, Indian, and Central and Eastern European immigrants are the largest groups of foreign residents. The percentage of ethnic minorities living in Britain rose from 6 percent to 9 percent in the decade between 1991 and 2001. In the latter year, 1.5 million Muslims lived in England and Wales, representing more than 3 percent of the population. In France, the number of mosques rose from 130 in 1976 to more than 1,000 twenty years later.

Immigration became potentially one of the most explosive problems Western European governments faced. When economic recession sharply reduced the number of available jobs, the political tide began to turn even more against foreign workers. Beginning in the late 1960s and in the 1970s, states began to make it more difficult for foreigners to immigrate. The British government put laws restricting immigration (targeting non-white arrivals) in place in 1968 and 1971. In the former year, Enoch Powell, a Conservative MP (Member of Parliament), caused a storm when he warned that unchecked immigration would swamp Britain, leading to bloodshed. When the economic recession began in the mid-1970s, other European states began to enact more restrictive immigration policies. While many foreign-born workers, recruited as single young men before the economic recession, became permanent residents of the countries where they worked (and some became citizens), they were joined by hundreds of thousands of illegal workers.

Nations put into effect stricter border controls in an attempt to reduce illegal immigration. This has been true even as the birthrates of many countries have continued to decline. Early in the twenty-first century,

Table 30.1.   Foreign-Born Population and Percentage of Total Population, 1995

Country	Population	Percentage
Austria	724,000	9
Belgium	910,000	9
Denmark	223,000	4.2
Finland	69,000	1.3
France	3.5 million	6.3
Germany	7.1 million	8.8
Ireland	96,000	2.7
Italy	991,000	1.7
Luxembourg	138,000	33.4
Spain	500,000	1.2
Switzerland	1.3 million	18.9
U.K.	2 million	3.4
U.S.	24.6 million	10

Source: *World Book, 1998* (Chicago: World Book, 1999), p. 245.

fourteen countries are no longer reproducing themselves (with Italy and Spain leading the way in restricting births, followed by Germany and Sweden); in other countries, population growth is zero, or not far above that. This trend of low birthrates began following World War I, but the baby boom of the post–World War II period put an end to that. At the end of the twentieth century, economic uncertainty was certainly related to the continued fall in the number of births. The birthrate now shows no sign of reversing the trend of decline. Many Western European countries will lose population without significant immigration and their economies will continue to require the labor of immigrants, legal and otherwise (as that of West Germany, which depended on arrivals from East Germany and other places in the immediate post-war era). Furthermore, declining populations could undercut national economies in the future.

Yet, because immigration has become a political lightning rod, immigrants are placed in a different situation than citizens of countries in the European Union, even if the borders of continental European countries are extremely difficult to police. EU nations have continued to build on the Schengen Agreement (1985), which initiated the exchange of information about immigration, moving toward common policies of border policing.

Following the collapse of communism, the opening of Eastern European borders and the elimination of border controls between many Western European states increased the number of people trying to reach Western Europe from Asia, Africa, and Eastern Europe, seeking a better life in Western nations. As social services sagged under the additional weight of impoverished and often clandestine newcomers, some Europeans felt themselves overwhelmed by immigrants.

Between 1990 and 1993, 200,000 Albanians crossed the mountains to reach Greece. Thousands of others, desperately attempting to flee violence and economic ruin in their country, making the dangerous trip across the Adriatic Sea to Italy. Romanians were among those hiding in trucks, trying to pass into the West. Between 1980 and 1992, 15 million immigrants arrived in Western Europe. The number of people seeking asylum rose from about 65,000 in 1983 to over 500,000 in 1991—many from Yugoslavia, torn by ethnic conflict, Romania, and Turkey. By the latter year, estimates assessed the number of illegal residents in Western countries at about 3 million people. In response, Western European governments have adopted new laws and strategies in order to reduce the number of immigrants, establishing tougher tests for claims of political asylum and sending illegal immigrants back to their countries. The percentage of asylum seekers whose cases are judged favorably by government authorities has been decreasing. With 7 percent of its population now made up of foreigners (60 percent of them non-European), France has turned away from its long-held belief that being born in that country was enough to become a French citizen; it now requires that children born in France to non-French parents must apply for citizenship between the ages of sixteen and twenty-one. Moreover, the government has made it more difficult for foreigners to acquire French citizenship through marriage. Yet massive migration to Europe will certainly continue. Referring to the smuggling of migrants into his country, the Austrian director of immigration put it memorably, "There are no distances any longer in this world. There are no islands."

The 1980s and 1990s brought a massive movement of desperate people seeking a better life somewhere else. Haitians took to the seas in dangerously flimsy boats, attempting to reach the United States. Kurds fled Iraq and Turkey for Europe, as North Africans left Algeria (ravaged by a bloody civil war following the army's seizure of power in 1992 and the rise of militant Islamic fundamentalist groups), Tunisia, and Morocco, trying to reach France via Spain, if they did not drown first on the way to Spain. An Albanian journalist spoke for millions worldwide, "There is no bread in the bakeries, no milk. There is a shortage of salt. . . . All are disillusioned. There is no money and no hope."

While some foreign workers have been assimilated in their countries of residence, many have not and have maintained the customs of their homelands. For example, in many countries tensions remain between Christians and Muslims (in the early twenty-first century, more than 12 million Muslims lived in Western Europe). In such countries, including Britain, France, and Germany, Muslims have been viewed with suspicion and have been subject to discrimination. In France, when Muslim schoolgirls went to school wearing the traditional headscarf of Muslim women, they were expelled; a lengthy court process ensued until a compromise was found.

As in the inter-war years, economic weakness has encouraged hostility to those some consider to be outsiders, and a perceived lack of security against crime became a central focus of electoral campaigns. In 1987, foreign and minority prisoners accounted for one-third of those locked up in France, Belgium, and Switzerland. In Britain, the devastating social effects of economic decline have been particularly felt in Manchester, Liverpool, Sheffield, Leeds, and other northern manufacturing cities of the nineteenth-century Industrial Revolution. In the 1990s, riots by—but also against—immigrants (principally Indians, Pakistanis, Bangladeshi, and West Indians) rocked several industrial cities and East London.

Polls have reflected popular fears (without any foundation) that the quality of education declines when too many immigrants and asylum seekers are present in the classroom. Many Europeans believe that immigrants abuse existing social welfare programs (indeed, they are more apt to draw disproportionately upon them), and that most of those asking for political asylum were fleeing economic hardship, not political persecution. At the same time, the emigration of many educated people with special training deprives poor countries of much-needed talent.

Even if most countries are now multicultural, multiculturalism has been slow in coming. (Indeed, it is instructive that if in the United States the very term "multiculturalism" in general has a positive sense, in Germany it means "a disarray of cultures, in which each individual culture is stripped of its richness and uniqueness.") Difficulties in learning the language of the new country of residence has compounded the problem, making it harder to find and maintain employment. This has often put the younger generation of foreign workers, born in their countries of residence, in the uncomfortable position of being excluded from mainstream life where they reside and not wishing to return to their parents' country of origin.

In the meantime, rising intolerance, racism, and xenophobia—hallmarks of the rise of fascism during the inter-war years—have become apparent in both Western and Eastern Europe. In Western Europe, the backlash against immigration has been marked by rising xenophobic opposition orchestrated by extreme right-wing nationalist parties, directed against foreign workers and their families. Brutal and even murderous attacks against foreigners proliferated in Germany (including the tragic firebombing of a hostel for foreign workers and asylum seekers), France, and Britain, as well as in virtually all other Western European countries. German Chancellor Helmut Kohl warned that "the evil spirits that have come to life again in the Balkans are not unique to that area." The severe recession of the early 1990s, the worst since World War II, contributed to this explosive situation, causing high unemployment rates (in 1993 over 10 percent in the European Union) and increased discouragement among young people; disproportionately affected by unemployment, they fear that they will not find jobs and that they will be the first generation in the post-war period to do less well economically than their parents.

Right-wing political parties, such as the National Front in Britain (founded in 1967) and the party of the same name in France (founded in

A prayer demonstration by Muslims to protest the opposition to the construction of a mosque in Nice, France, an example of cultural tensions across a multicultural Europe.

1972), adopted aggressive anti-immigrant stances. In Germany, where tiny parties of the extreme right had either been banned by the government (by virtue of the German Basic Law) or did very badly at the polls, the party known as the Republicans started up in 1983 and was subsequently joined by the German People's Union, which has bitterly denounced legal changes in 1999 that made it somewhat easier for longtime foreign-born residents to become citizens. Xenophobia has also been seen in such traditionally liberal, open-minded countries as Sweden and Denmark.

In France, Jean-Marie Le Pen emerged as the leader of the far-right National Front. Le Pen, a staunch nationalist who had been accused of torture after a stint in the army in Algeria and who once said that the death camps were "a minor detail" of World War II, was elected to the European Parliament in 1984 and won 14 percent of the vote in the first round of the presidential election in 1988 and gained another percentage point seven years later. In 2002, he finished second on the first balloting in the presidential election with about 17 percent of the vote (4.8 million ballots), before winning only 18 percent of the vote in the second balloting against Jacques Chirac, as the left rallied to the fight against Le Pen. The National Front first carved out support in the Mediterranean region of France, where many *pieds noirs* (former French settlers in North Africa) families resent the presence of a considerable number of North African residents. In 1995, the National Front won control of three southeastern French towns. In Austria, Jorg Heider, head of the Austrian Freedom

Party, became prime minister in 1999 after joining the conservative People's Party in a coalition. Despite (or perhaps because of) his obvious affection for the Nazis, his party won 28 percent of the vote in 1997, in which immigration was a central issue. In the Netherlands, long a haven of toleration for immigrants, Pim Fortuyn, a candidate for the post of prime minister, caused an uproar by stating that his country had been saturated by immigration, and that there was no room left (he was assassinated in 2002). In Switzerland, too, a party of the extreme right made its mark, as the Swiss People's Party gained almost 25 percent of the votes in 1999. The Danish People's Party, the Norwegian Progress Party, and the Flemish Bloc in Belgium reflect the close association of extreme right-wing parties and anti-immigrant sentiments. To counter a rise in racism with calls for toleration and solidarity, grassroots organizations sprang up in many countries, such as "SOS-Racism" in France.

European Community, European Union

As politics in the countries of Western Europe shifted back and forth between left and right, the need for coordination in both economics and politics became apparent to farsighted leaders. Some believed that ultimately European political unification and a common foreign policy and security might be achieved. To this end, the European Community (EC) was created in 1967, when the European Atomic Energy Community, the European Coal and Steel Community (ECSC), and the European Economic Community (the EEC, or European Common Market) merged their organizations. The original members were Belgium, France, West Germany, Italy, Luxembourg, and the Netherlands (see Map 30.1). The government of Great Britain had first been disinclined to join the EC, fearing the flooding of its internal market by less expensive agricultural produce. But after British voters overwhelmingly approved their country's application for membership, Britain joined the EC in 1973. Britain's membership had twice been rejected by virtue of France's veto, because of de Gaulle's forceful objections to Britain's membership. With de Gaulle's departure from political life, Edward Heath, a Conservative but one who believed that his nation's future lay with Europe, took Britain into the EC. However, Harold Wilson, Heath's Labour successor as prime minister, sought to renegotiate the terms of Britain's membership, and Britain remained a hesitant, skeptical member. In the meantime, the close relationship between France's president Valéry Giscard d'Estaing and West Germany's premier Helmut Schmidt lent stability to the EC, as Britain pouted across the Channel. The advent of staunchly Conservative and vigorously anti-European Margaret Thatcher as British prime minister in 1979 put her country's membership at risk, until an urgent EC meeting agreed to reduce British financial contributions. In the meantime, Denmark and Ireland had also joined the EC in 1973, followed by Greece in 1981, and Spain and Portugal in 1986.

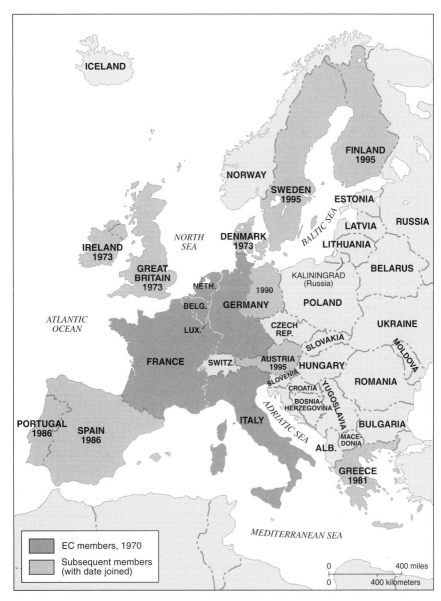

MAP 30.1 MEMBERS OF THE EUROPEAN COMMUNITY   The original six members of the European Community—France, West Germany, the Netherlands, Belgium, Luxembourg, and Italy—were later joined by Denmark, Great Britain, the Irish Republic, Spain, Portugal, and Greece.

The EC eliminated troublesome tariffs. This aided the most efficient producers, who were able to specialize and sell their products easily beyond the borders of their country. But it put smaller producers at a disadvantage. The Danish dairy industry profited greatly from sales of milk and cheese to other member countries, as did their French counterparts in Normandy; but dairy farmers elsewhere often found that they could not compete with larger, more productive competitors. The problem of wine revealed the challenges posed by EC agricultural policy. New members Spain and Portugal produced great amounts of wine, threatening vintners producing cheap wine in southern France. They protested the arrival of even cheaper Italian wine by blocking roads at the frontier. Moreover, they bitterly opposed Spain's entry into the EC for the same reason. The EC initially imposed tariffs and quotas to keep out agricultural exports from the fledgling democracies of Eastern Europe.

Jacques Delors (1925–), a former minister of finance under French President François Mitterrand, became president of the European Commission in 1985. Delors led the campaign for a unified Europe unburdened by wrenching national divisions that could undercut the EC's economic clout in the face of Japanese and U.S. economic strength. In 1986, member states signed the Single Europe Act. Calling for the termination of all obstacles to the free movement of capital, goods, workers, and services, it pointed toward the anticipated establishment of a single market within member states. Moreover, from the beginning Delors believed that the EC should build a "social dimension."

Delors had in 1988 indicated his hope that in the future a single currency could be used by member states, further accentuating trade within the EC, while eliminating fluctuations in the value of individual currencies. From the outset, Thatcher and British Conservative "Euroskeptics" opposed the plan, partially out of fear that Germany's then-booming economy and currency would dominate the other EC members. Thatcher's departure from office in 1990 did not end vehement opposition from British Conservatives.

The Treaty of Maastricht, signed in that southern Dutch city in 1992 by the twelve members of the European Community, transformed the EC into the European Union. The new name took effect in 1993, when the single market began operation. France barely approved the treaty in a referendum called by President Mitterrand in late 1992 and it took a second vote to obtain the same result in Denmark. The European Union opened all borders within the European Community and committed the European Community to "economic and monetary union" by 1999. In 1994, Austria, Norway, Sweden, and Finland were asked to join, although Norway, which early in the 1970s had turned down membership in the EC, rejected the treaty.

The European Commission became the executive institution of the European Union. Headquartered in Brussels, it consists of members appointed by each member state. The European Commission is headed by a rotating president and proposes legislation to the Council of Ministers, whose members are also delegated by each member state and which also has a rotating presidency. Each participating state elects representatives to the European Parliament, which has its headquarters in Strasbourg, and can reject a proposed budget. The European Court of Justice rules on disputes between member states and between individual plaintiffs and the European Union. The European Council consists of the heads of each member state and meets twice a year (or more), along with the president of the European Commission. Finally, the European Union even has a small army, established by virtue of the Amsterdam Treaty of 1999.

The European Union, comprising 370 million people in fifteen member states, now accounts for almost 18 percent of the world's exports, more than that of the United States. One of the most daunting challenges of creating a single market has been to establish an effective agricultural policy that takes into consideration the tremendous variety of agricultural production within the member states. As part of the common agricultural policy (known as CAP), EU subsidies to farmers accounted for nearly half of the annual budget in 1995. Subsidies have protected member states by limiting the importation of products from outside the EU, but they also have generated overproduction, such that many farmers are paid not to produce, or for the surpluses they produce. Besides this, considerable European Union funds are diverted in the attempt to aid the continual development of the poorer member states, including Greece and Portugal, and disadvantaged regions within other countries, such as southern Italy and Sicily. The admission of Poland and other Eastern European nations will require enormous agricultural subsidies, although certainly the level of such funding will be kept below those expended on behalf of older members. In the meantime, the European Union maintains strict guidelines for agricultural producers (for example, on how cheese can be produced).

Member states of the European Union are required to keep their budget deficits down to no more than 3 percent of gross domestic product. Anticipation of a common currency spurred government efforts to control national deficits, leading, as in the case of France, to protests and strikes from unions. In 1998, the European Central Bank began operations; it is charged with the task of managing the new currency, the euro, setting interest rates for the euro zone of eleven nations and working to keep down inflation. The euro was launched at the beginning of 1999 (without the participation of Britain, Sweden, or Denmark, which all chose not to participate, and Greece, which failed to meet the financial criteria for monetary union that the EU had set for member states). The euro became the official currency in member states on January 1, 2002. A relatively smooth transition was made possible by considerable preparations, including effective publicity campaigns by governments, banks, and shopping centers, the conversion of machines accepting bills and coins, and assistance to the elderly, immigrants, and other groups. In its first year of existence, the euro, which had weakened vis-à-vis the U.S. dollar, began to rise, overtaking the weakening American currency.

The European Union has engendered not only feelings of ambivalence toward supranational economic and political organizations but also a nationalist response, as in the case of some British Conservatives, who object to the ceding of sovereignty (as well as operational costs) to bureaucrats working in Brussels. Many ordinary people believe themselves disconnected from the workings of Brussels. Even some farmers who receive subsidies from the EU are unaware that they come from Brussels and not their own ministries of agriculture. Moreover, the grim economic situation in Europe in the early years of the twenty-first century casts something of a shadow over EU plans for expansion.

In 2002, the European Commission approved a report recommending the admission of ten more states in 2004, in anticipation of referendums in each country: Poland, the Czech Republic, Lithuania, Latvia, Estonia, Hungary, Slovakia, Slovenia, Malta, and Cyprus (in all likelihood without the Turkish Republic of Northern Cyprus, which constitutes about 20 percent of the population). Such expansion would give the European Union twenty-five member states and a single market encompassing about 450 million people.

Future members can look to the example of Ireland, whose economy has received a major boost from its EU membership, largely through the biotech revolution. High unemployment (averaging about 10 percent in EU countries in 1998), low agricultural productivity, the necessity of institutional reform, and the great cost of becoming a member of the European Union, as well as the extremely limited democratic experience of some of the new members, will pose challenges to new members and to the European Union itself. The economic gap between the wealthiest countries—Britain, France, and Germany—and the states of Central and Eastern Europe seeking the advantage of greater access to markets remains considerable. Anticipating an ultimate membership of twenty-five states (with twenty-one official languages, up from eleven), the very structure of the Union and its administration could prove unwieldy. The subsequent admission of Bulgaria and Romania seems likely as well, assuming that they meet the economic, political, and other criteria (including environmental considerations) for EU membership. That the citizens of the three most prosperous members of the European Union—Great Britain, France, and Germany—have expressed the greatest skepticism about adding new members could pose problems in the future, because of high rates of unemployment and continued dependence on traditional agriculture. The question of the possible admission of Turkey may well generate considerable debate, in part because of some doubts that the country is really European, in part because of recent successes of fundamentalist Islamic groups in elections in a country that is overwhelmingly Muslim. In

1995, Necmettin Irbakan became the first Islamic prime minister of Turkey, a republic since 1923, with the Islamic party "Welfare" as a coalition partner. However, he resigned a year later, accused of undermining the nonreligious basis of the Turkish republic.

Each prospective new member must accept certain treaties, court decisions, and regulations in order to obtain admission to the European Union. The challenges for each country include reducing extremely high levels of unemployment and sizable trade deficits, financing the expensive entry into the European Union while meeting its budgetary constraints, and convincing skeptics or the ambivalent that membership can provide advantages. Yet, at the same time, the number of citizens of countries within the European Union who describe themselves as feeling "European" has increased, suggesting that multiple identities are indeed possible. The effective existence of the European Economic Union has encouraged regionalism, assisting the revival of such languages as Catalan and Welsh. This, too, may help reduce ethnic tension and conflicts. Moreover, many on the left in Europe have reason to hope that the European Union will guarantee the rights of individuals through its Charter of Fundamental Social Rights of Workers. Despite the hesitation of some continental conservatives and of Great Britain, which has not accepted the European Convention on Human Rights—always fearful of relinquishing any of its prerogatives as a nation-state—the EU is likely to uphold and defend human rights. Indeed, the EU allocates considerable funds to humanitarian causes.

Irish farmers clog the streets of Dublin with their tractors to protest the reforms proposed by the Common Agricultural Policy of the European Union that would reduce their income.

The European Union tries to protect member states by maintaining standards for the importation of agricultural and food products. For example, "mad cow" disease, which struck cattle in Britain in the 1990s and infected a few human beings with a degenerative disease of the brain, led not only to the slaughter of millions of animals in Britain but also to the European Union's ban on the import of British beef to the continental countries of the European Union for thirty-two months. Likewise, the EU in 1997 began labeling products made from genetically modified soybeans and corn. Such imports, principally from the United States, are more resistant to damage by insects, but the long-range effect of their consumption is still unknown.

OPPOSITION TO GLOBALIZATION

Globalization became the target of protests and demonstrations in the 1990s. Giant companies and banks, multinational in their structure and interests, have enormous economic power, for better or for worse. Huge sums can be sent, traded, or invested with the push of a button. Global finance has brought volatility to the world economy, as the sharp decline in the U.S. stock market that began in 2000 revealed. International dependence on oil, too, has increased, with prices rising and falling, often in tune with international events (such as the Arab oil boycott of 1973–1974).

To its critics, globalization could be identified with corporate greed and indifference to the fate of the poor of the Third World. A French farmer (who had spent part of his childhood in California), José Bové (1953–   ), became a symbol of protest when in 1999 he led an attack on a McDonald's in the southern French town of Millau, damaging the fast-food restaurant as a means of calling attention to globalization. Cases of corporate greed and deception—such as that of the giant Enron corporation in the United States, whose corporate officers had lied and deceived, unloading their shares before the fall and leaving employees with nothing—cast a shadow over big multinational corporations. Demonstrations turned into riots in Seattle during the meeting of the World Trade Organization in 1999 and in Nice in 2000 at protests during the European Union summit meetings. During the summer of 2001, protestors demonstrated at the summit in Gothenburg (Sweden) and then in Genoa (Italy), the site of the G-8 meeting, an informal association of the world's leading industrial nations. Battles between thousands of protestors and police left one dead and hundreds hurt.

Two events at the very end of 2002 seemed to put into context the distance between attitudes of powerful companies (and states) and opponents of unrestrained globalization who fear the consequences for Third World people in the new global economy. A Swiss-based chocolate

The 1999 meeting of the World Trade Organization in Seattle, Washington, was greeted with protests against the negative effects of globalization.

company announced that it would sue Ethiopia, one of the world's poorest nations, for 6 million dollars to compensate for earnings of which it had been deprived in the mid-1970s when its assets had been nationalized by a leftist government. As an estimated 14 million Ethiopians now were vulnerable to starvation, the announcement of the suit before an international court generated outrage, leading to the company's decision to invest what money it might gain in Ethiopia. At about the same time, to protect the interests of U.S. pharmaceutical companies, the United States vetoed a plan that would have provided generic drugs that combat diseases such as tuberculosis at reduced cost to poor countries.

Damage to the environment is itself linked to global interconnectedness. The oceans have become veritable highways for the shipment of oil in huge tankers, a good many of which are old and badly maintained. Periodic oil spills have damaged coasts catastrophically, such as that in the English Channel in 1967 or another off the Atlantic coast of Spain in 2003. The diffusion of nuclear power (to say nothing of the threat of nuclear weapons) presents great risks, for all the advantage in generating electricity. The first nuclear reactor that was used to generate electric power started up in the Soviet Union in 1954. By the end of the twentieth century, nuclear reactors, many of them old, generated about one-third of Europe's electricity. France led the way in adopting nuclear technology in the production of electricity and by the end of the twentieth century nuclear reactors produced 75 percent of its electricity. Nuclear power generated 60 percent of Belgium's electricity and 45 percent of that of Sweden. In 1979, an accident at Three Mile Island in Pennsylvania helped mobilize anti-nuclear groups. The horrendous explosion at Chernobyl in Ukraine in 1986 demonstrated clearly the risks of reactors that are old, badly maintained, or both. Chernobyl helped further mobilize opposition to nuclear power. And as the threat from international terrorism becomes more real, nuclear reactors stand as potentially inviting targets for terrorists intent on taking as many lives and causing as much damage as possible. International organizations such as Greenpeace have actively opposed potential threats to the environment by nuclear power.

Opposition to globalization has centered on profits Western-based companies earn selling products produced at low wages in, for example, Southeast Asia. Caps or jerseys with logos from NBA basketball teams, brand-name tennis shoes, and T-shirts with the names of U.S. universities became part of popular culture around the globe. Some of the products that are sold for high prices in the West are produced by destitute people in Asia (or elsewhere) for pitiful wages.

THE THREAT OF TERRORISM

During the 1970s and 1980s, small groups on the extreme left and right turned to political terrorism. Violence seemed to them the only means of destabilizing political elites in the hope of taking power. Some terrorist groups were militant nationalists seeking independence from what they considered foreign occupying powers. Such groups included factions within the Irish Republican Army committed to ending British rule in Northern Ireland, militant Basque separatists (the ETA) seeking independence from Spain, and Kurdish rebels in Turkey, wanting their own state.

Between 1969 and 1982, political terrorists killed at least 1,119 people, the most notorious case being the bombing of the railroad station of Bologna in 1980 by fascists in which 85 people died. In the early 1970s, left-wing extremists (organized into perhaps as many as 100 separate groups) launched deadly attacks. Unlike rightist terrorists, who struck out more randomly, seeking to create a climate of fear that they hoped would bring a right-wing coup, leftist extremists began to attack prominent political and business leaders. The Red Brigades, founded in 1970, kidnapped and killed former Italian premier Aldo Moro in 1978. But by the early 1980s, Italian terrorism had ebbed, the campaigns at political destabilization having failed. Italian politicians put aside their usual differences long enough to back a vigorous campaign that led to the arrest of a number of militants.

In the German Federal Republic, small groups of left-wing terrorists lashed out with bombings, bank robberies, kidnappings, assassinations, and even a plane hijacking. The most notorious of these groups, the Baader-Meinhof gang, had links to terrorist groups in France and other Western countries. Several of their members were imprisoned.

Other extremists also undertook terrorist acts in Europe. Attacks included the massacre of Israelis by Palestinian militants at the 1972 Olympic Games in Munich and the seizure of a cruise ship in 1985. Terrorists who were thought to be receiving support from the governments of Iran, Iraq, Syria, or Libya staged several attacks in the mid-1980s. A terrorist bomb in 1989 blew up a U.S. passenger jet over Scotland, killing all 259 people aboard. In 1995, an Algerian Islamic fundamentalist group claimed responsibility for placing on subways and underground trains in Paris several bombs that exploded during rush hour, killing and maiming. Islamic fundamentalist groups based in the Middle East have been active recruiting adherents in European states that have large concentrations of Muslims. Thus, the continued rise of Islamic fundamentalism has had repercussions in Europe, most notably in France.

Islam is not the only religion in which aggressive fundamentalism has emerged. In the United States, groups of Protestant fundamentalist extremists have targeted groups they do not like. In Israel, Jewish fundamentalist groups, in coalition with the right-wing Likud party, have helped shape Israeli hard-line policies toward Palestinian demands for an independent state. Moreover, extremists willing to use terror have not been limited to religious groups. In 1995, a right-wing extremist bombed a government building in Oklahoma City, killing 168 people, including many small children.

Members of a Chechen terrorist group occupy a Moscow theater, holding 700 people hostage to demand the end of the war in Chechnya, 2002.

An Israeli policeman and Palestinian civilian clash in Jerusalem.

Since the collapse of the Soviet Union and the end of the Cold War, the threat of nuclear war has receded. However, another threat has emerged. Terrorism has posed an increasing threat in Western Europe, as extremist political groups and Islamic fundamentalist groups launched attacks.

One of the consequences of globalization has been the increased vulnerability of Europe, as well as the United States, to political struggles and events occurring far away and to the terrorism these events have generated. Terrorists detonated cars packed with bombs in front of U.S. embassies in Dar es Salaam, Tanzania, and Nairobi, Kenya, in the summer of 1998, killing 213 people and wounding more than 5,000 in the latter attack. Islamic fundamentalists were also responsible for terrorist attacks in Arab states where fundamentalists wanted to impose strict religious government.

The Palestinian question divides public opinion in Europe. In Israel, the Palestinian minority demands an independent Palestinian state. Groups of Palestinian militants have undertaken murderous attacks on Israelis. In a cycle of violence that has become tragically common, the Israeli government often responds by razing villages or by further restricting the rights of Palestinians. The assassination of Yitzhak Rabin by a right-wing Israeli in 1995 was a blow to peace in the Middle East, which may well hinge on the Palestinian situation. In 1996, the Palestinian leader Yasir Arafat struck from the Palestine Liberation Organization's charter the call for destroying Israel. This seemed to be a step in the right direction. However, the "peace process"—as U.S. officials refer to it optimistically—began to break down in 2000. The combination of a revival of Palestinian militancy, including bomb attacks and then suicide bombings, and the advent of hard-line Ariel Sharon as prime minister of Israel in 2000 seemed to make the creation of a Palestinian state and peace itself even more difficult, if not unlikely.

The collapse of the Soviet empire left the United States as the world's single superpower. In the late 1990s, a more aggressive U.S. foreign policy increased fears in Europe about U.S. foreign unilateralism and a rush to use force. On a continent ravaged by two devastating world wars, this has not gone down well, and it has merged with a residual anti-Americanism. Moreover, the U.S. refused in 2001 to sign the Kyoto Protocol, an agreement that requires countries to reduce the harmful greenhouse gas emissions that have caused global warming. President George W. Bush contended that such environmental measures could undermine the U.S. economy, but many Europeans sharply criticized the action.

U.S. policy has drawn other European attacks, as well. During the mid-1980s, many Europeans had opposed the U.S. intention to create a missile defense system (dubbed "Star Wars") in violation of the U.S.–Russian Antiballistic Missile (ABM) Treaty, from which the United States withdrew. In 2003, the U.S. government announced its intention to resume testing of the proposed missile defense system, despite earlier failures. Moreover, in 2002, the U.S. government announced that it would not accept the jurisdiction of a proposed new international court, which was being set up to try those accused of crimes against humanity. Some saw this as evidence that the United States felt itself to be above the law.

On a day of horror, September 11, 2001, hijackers commandeered four U.S. jetliners shortly after they took off from several airports in the morning. Two were crashed into the World Trade Center in lower Manhattan in New York City and a third into the Pentagon outside Washington, D.C. The fourth airliner plunged to earth in eastern Pennsylvania after heroic passengers fought the hijackers for control of the plane. Nearly 3,000 people were killed, the vast majority perishing in the World Trade Center, both towers of which collapsed in a heap of rubble. A massive manhunt began for the Saudi Arabian–born Osama bin Laden (1957–), leader of the Al Qaeda ("The Base") movement, which claimed responsibility for the attacks. Many of its members had trained in Afghanistan, which was ruled by an Islamic fundamentalist militia called the Taliban. Late that fall, the United States launched massive air strikes against Taliban installations in Afghanistan, and troops on the ground searched the rugged mountains near the border with Pakistan. An interim government took power in Afghanistan, backed by U.S. forces, facing the chronic problems of tribalism and poverty. The Al Qaeda organization had spread almost worldwide, with cells in Germany, Italy, France, and Britain, as well as in Malaysia and the Philippines. European states supported and assisted the U.S. campaign to uproot the structure of the Al Qaeda network in their countries. International police cooperation led to the arrests of Al Qaeda members in Germany, France, Spain, Britain, and Italy but the search for others continued.

September 11 may in fact have brought a bigger backlash against immigrants in some European countries than in the United States. In a poll taken in 2002 in EU member states, 39 percent of those responding said that they believed that unemployed immigrants should be returned to the countries of their origin. September 11 put a temporary end to discussions within the European Union about bringing in line existing laws and regulations in member countries for the movement of immigrants within EU countries.

European Responses to U.S Policy

Frustrated by the failure to capture bin Laden, the Bush administration then turned its attention to Saddam Hussein in Iraq, arguing that he was continuing to produce and to hide "weapons of mass destruction" and that he had links to Al Qaeda. At the same time, North Korea announced in 2002 that it had maintained its nuclear weapons program, perhaps as a way of trying to increase the flow of foreign assistance. While British prime minister Tony Blair and a number of other states actively supported the U.S. position, Germany (with a socialist government), France (a conservative government), and Russia disagreed with the Bush administration's position, arguing that Iraq could be disarmed without war and that UN weapons inspectors should have more time. In the meantime, the weapons inspectors found no "weapons of mass destruction," including chemical weapons that Saddam Hussein had been long-suspected of using in his war against Iran in the 1980s, and subsequently against the Kurdish minority living in Iraq. Moreover, the Iraqis began to destroy missiles whose range exceeded that permitted by the United Nations following the Gulf War of 1991, when U.S. troops drove Iraqi forces from Kuwait, which Saddam Hussein had invaded. Eastern European states that had been under Soviet domination for almost half a century supported U.S. policy, while Turkey sought to trade the use of its territory by U.S. troops and planes for a multi-billion-dollar aid package. In the meantime, skeptics speculated about the real reason for the U.S. government's insistence that Saddam Hussein threatened its national interests: some believed it to be Iraqi oil; others evoked the American president's determination to finish the war his father, former president George H. W. Bush, had not; and some felt it was motivated by the primacy of internal U.S. politics and preparation for the next presidential election.

The outpouring of European sympathy and goodwill toward the United States following the terrorist attacks in New York and Washington, D.C., in 1999 seemed to have been dissipated. U.S. Defense Secretary Donald Rumsfeld's remarks in 2003 that his country held "Old Europe" in contempt led to a vigorous response. A former French official criticized the "arrogance of the U.S. that wants to govern the world by itself with fewer and fewer rules." Many Europeans agreed.

The U.S. administration's determination to proceed against Iraq (with the support of a small coalition, most notably Britain, whose prime minister, Tony Blair, faced a growing split in his own Labour Party and a loss of public support) generated the greatest crisis in NATO's history, threatening the Western alliance. President Bush's rhetorical evocation of a "crusade" against terrorism called to mind the medieval aggressive wars of European Christians against Islam. The Iraq crisis threatened the prestige and effectiveness of the United Nations, because of the determination of the United States government to go it alone, despite the opposition and potential vetoes of Russia, France, and China—permanent members (each with a veto) on the Security Council of the United Nations. Indeed, Russia announced that it viewed a U.S. war on Iraq without the approval of the Security Council as a violation of the UN Charter, which the U.S. had signed.

Citing "immediate danger" from Iraqi "weapons of mass destruction" and claiming some of the latter could be readied to attack other countries within forty-five minutes, the U.S. and British leaders launched an invasion of Iraq that began in March 2003. The major combat lasted only a couple of weeks. Iraqi resistance collapsed; Saddam Hussein and his family disappeared. The short war killed only several hundred U.S. and British troops, but bombing by the "coalition" took the lives of about 6,000 Iraqi civilians. The United States set up military authority in Iraq, along with a British zone, anticipating that it would eventually give way to some sort of democratic Iraqi government (assuming religious, ethnic, and other tensions could be overcome). However, even several months after the official end of the war no nuclear, biological, or chemical weapons had been discovered in Iraq. This left the impression that some of the U.S. and British

United States policy toward Iraq polarized Europe in 2003, with (*left*) Prime Ministers Tony Blair of Britain, José Maria Aznar of Spain, and José Durao Barroso of Portugal aligning themselves with U.S. President George W. Bush (second from right), against the opposition of French President Jacques Chirac (*right*), German Chancellor Gerhard Schroder, and Russian President Vladimir Putin.

intelligence documents used to reach the conclusion that the regime of Saddam Hussein posed an immediate threat to the region or to U.S. interests—thus justifying the invasion—had been exaggerated, misrepresented, or even possibly fabricated. Saddam Hussein's odious, brutal regime had fallen, but the debate over U.S. and British credibility and the challenge to multilateral international cooperation went on. In the meantime, Iraq remained an unstable and dangerous place amid attacks on U.S. occupation forces by Saddam loyalists and probably by terrorists from abroad. Rebuilding Iraq would prove to be an expensive process.

CONCLUSION

As Europe moves through the first decade of the twenty-first century, its influence over the rest of the world has been reduced. Yet Europeans now for the most part live in peace, a situation that seems likely to remain for the foreseeable future (despite conflicts here and there—notably in Northern Ireland—that have gone on for decades). Conditions of life have continued to improve for most Europeans, thanks to ongoing advances in medicine and the production of food. This has not been the case for many (if not most) immigrants, particularly those living clandestinely, from hand to mouth. Europe still confronts the challenges of finding enough safe energy while protecting the environment.

As in other regions, European economies must continually adapt to the challenges of globalization. With no more Communist states in Europe, the victory of capitalism, which parties of the left contested so vigorously for 150 years, cannot really be doubted. In Asia, even China has embraced some aspects of capitalism. But at the same time high unemployment rates in Europe have demonstrated that capitalism leaves many people vulnerable to the vicissitudes of the market, marginalizing millions of people. Finding an appropriate balance between the free market and state intervention remains essential, particularly in former Communist states, where the shock therapy of wide-open market forces has left many people in a precarious position. Determined protests against globalization reflect the fact that global interconnectedness has not benefited everyone, and that hundreds of millions of desperately poor people in Asia and Africa, and on other continents as well, have left behind.

Human rights around the world stand as a European concern. Human-rights groups have grown up in many parts of Europe, as elsewhere in the world. New York–based Amnesty International has been a force for identifying countries in which human rights are not respected, as has Human Rights Watch in New York and the International Commission of Jurists, based in Geneva. European states were among those that put enormous pressure on South Africa in the 1970s and early 1980s, as it defied the world by maintaining its now dismantled official system of racial apartheid. Genocide in the African nation of Rwanda, ethnic cleansing in Kosovo, starvation in Ethiopia, and the thorny situation in the Middle East have also been the focus of human-rights groups, as well as states. The European Union has made support of human rights one of its priorities. Human-rights abuses by Serbs were cited as a reason for Western military intervention in Bosnia in the 1990s.

Europeans have many reasons to be optimistic about the future. German unification was achieved peacefully. Two old enemies, Germany and France, stand as a stable center for the continent's future. Even during the reunification of Germany, no one was heard talking about the creation of a "Greater Germany" that would include Austria. Despite divisions over policy toward Iraq, NATO has adapted to the fall of communism and expanded toward the east. Signs of greater toleration can be found in Eastern Europe and the Balkans, as well. In 1997, for the first time, ethnic Hungarians living in Romania could use their own language in their dealings with government officials and in education. And in 2000 the Bulgarian government finally allowed the state television network to broadcast a weekly news program in Turkish. However, ethnic and religious rivalries, as in centuries past, have by no means been eliminated. In Eastern Europe and the Balkans, it has proven easier to tear down the existing order than to construct a new one. Yet we can be optimistic. In most of Europe, nationalist irredentist claims have largely subsided.

The Cold War is no more and in Europe there is seemingly little risk of a hot one. The European Union has brought a single market to much of Europe and will continue to expand, with the help of the single currency, the euro. This in itself has made the continent smaller, making it even easier for people to travel and giving them increasingly more in common. All this should carry Europe into an even more prosperous future, one that can be built on lasting peace.

GLOSSARY

by Richard Van Nort, Queens College, CUNY

abstract art   art that abandons the traditional system of perspective that artists began using during the Renaissance and replaces it with depictions of objects as an artist visualizes them in his mind, rather than as his eye perceives them.

Act of Union   (1707) act passed by the Parliaments of both England and Scotland that created the kingdom of Great Britain, consisting of England, Scotland, and Wales.

Dante Alighieri   (1265–1321) great Florentine poet of the Middle Ages and author of the poems *The Inferno, The Purgatorio,* and *The Paradiso,* which describe the medieval Christian cosmological view of the afterlife.

Amicable Grant   English tax on the revenues of both the church and laity, assessed in 1525 by Cardinal Wolsey, minister of King *Henry VIII.*

Anabaptists   radical Protestants who, in 1525, rejected the baptism of infants because they could find no reference to it in the Bible. They believed that only adults could manifest true faith and therefore be worthy of baptism.

anarchism   political philosophy that calls for the overthrow of society and the end of the state and all political organization.

apartheid   policy of segregation and racial inequality in South Africa that maintained the power and prestige of the white minority.

appeasement   policy of France and Britain in the 1930s to avoid confrontation with the fascist governments of Italy and Germany over their expansion and conquest of their weaker neighbors.

Arminianism   Sixteenth-century Protestant movement in Holland and England that rejected the Calvinist idea of predestination and held that an individual could achieve salvation through free will. Arminians also accepted the institutions, rites, and rituals of the Church of England.

Ashantis   a tribe of native Africans who established a kingdom in west Africa in the early-eighteenth century, and remained independent until they were absorbed by the British Empire in 1901.

Augsburg Confession   (1530) summary of the beliefs of Martin Luther that his friends presented to the German Imperial Diet in 1530, stating that one's salvation was due to grace extended by God and was gained by faith alone, not through the performance of good works.

avant-garde   a small group of people who see themselves in the forefront of artistic expression and achievement.

Avignon Papacy   (1309–1378) period after the death of Pope Boniface VIII when the papacy was controlled by the king of France and located in Avignon, France.

Axis   military alliance between Nazi Germany, fascist Italy, and Japan that was designed to support these nations' goals of regional and world domination.

Aztecs   Native Americans who ruled an empire of tribes in the valley of Mexico. At the time of first European contact, the last Aztec ruler, Montezuma, controlled an empire of 25 million people from his capital city of Tenochtitlán.

Balfour Declaration   (1917) statement passed by the English Parliament on November 2, 1917, that expressed the British willingness to support the future creation of a Jewish state in Palestine once the Turks were driven out.

barometer   instrument that detects changes in atmospheric pressure and is used in weather prediction.

Bastille   fortress and arsenal in Paris that also functioned as a prison for political dissidents. On the morning of July 14, 1789, thousands of people stormed the Bastille and liberated the prisoners.

Battle of Culloden   (April 1746) the last battle fought on the soil of Great Britain, in which forces loyal to *Charles Edward Stuart* were annihilated by the English army, led by the Duke of Cumberland, William Augustus.

bayonet   a razor-sharp knife that, when attached to a musket, converts the musket into a makeshift spear.

Beer Hall Putsch   (1923) the first attempt, on November 9, 1923, of Adolf Hitler and the Nazi party to seize power in Munich and march on Berlin. Troops loyal to the government broke the attempt and sent Hitler to jail.

Jeremy Bentham   (1748–1832) founder and most influential proponent of the liberal philosophy of utilitarianism, which posited that all laws should be judged by their social utility—that is, whether they provide the greatest good for the greatest number of people.

Berlin Conference   (1884–1885) meeting called by General Bismarck that divided the territory of the Congo basin between Belgium and France.

bills of exchange   promissory notes, used in place of gold and silver, that could be sold to third parties.

Bill of Rights   (1689) law signed by William and Mary, as a condition to becoming monarchs of England, that limited their power in several ways: it required that the monarch be a member in good standing of the Church of England and stated that he could not suspend the nation's laws, levy taxes, or maintain an army without the consent of Parliament. He also could not interfere in Parliamentary elections or impinge on the free speech of members of Parliament.

Black Death   also known as the bubonic plague, the first serious European outbreak was in the sixth century A.D.; it reemerged on a major scale in the thirteenth and fourteenth centuries. It causes a swelling and blackening of the lymph glands and is often carried by the fleas of the brown rat.

Blitzkrieg   (German: lightning war) term used by the Germans in World War II to describe the coordination of airpower, mechanized infantry, and armor used to attack and overwhelm an adversary before that adversary could react.

Jean Bodin   (1530–1596) the first French philosopher to advocate the doctrine of absolute monarchy in *The Six Books of the Republic* (1576). Bodin pictured the monarch as a lawgiver who applied the rule of law to his subjects with or without their consent.

Boers   (Dutch: farmers) Dutch Calvinists who settled in South Africa.

Bolsheviks   followers of Lenin who rejected the common Marxist view that the entire working class should attain a revolutionary consciousness. They believed instead that only a select minority of workers should be trained as professional revolutionaries, to join intellectuals in directing the masses toward a proletariat revolution.

Cesare Bonesana (1738–1794) marquis of Beccaria and author of the book *On Crimes and Punishment* (1764), which put forth the concept that the accused is innocent until proven guilty, a cornerstone of Western judicial systems, and the notion that punishment should be determined by an assessment of the damage done to society.

bourgeoisie property-owning non-noble townspeople, usually engaged in commerce, trade and manufacturing, includes people from wealthy businessmen to struggling retail merchants and innkeepers.

Boxers a secret anti-foreigner Chinese society that led a rebellion in 1900 against the occupying western powers.

Brezhnev Doctrine policy that stated that the Soviet Union would use military means if necessary to prevent a client state from following ideas and practices outside standard Moscow doctrine; it was developed as the justification for the Soviet Union's invasions of Czechoslovakia and later Afghanistan.

Edmund Burke (1729–1797) a leading member of the English Parliament in the late-eighteenth century who argued that political parties should be the basis of representative government and the political order.

Byzantine Empire realm that began as the eastern half of the Roman Empire with its capital at Constantinople (founded in 325 A.D.). The eastern Empire survived the fall of the western Empire in 476 A.D. and persisted until 1453, when its much-reduced territory was captured by the Turks.

John Calvin (1509–1564) Protestant leader who, while in Switzerland, developed the doctrine of predestination, whereby God decides who is worthy of grace and who of eternal damnation. Calvinism became the foundation of Protestant movements in France, Holland, Scotland, and England.

canon law the system of laws governing activities in the medieval Christian Church.

cartel formal agreement by which competitors within the same industry protect profits by sharing markets, regulating output, fixing prices, or taking other measures to limit competition, which enables a few large companies to dominate production and distribution of certain goods.

cast iron result of heating iron to its melting point, alloying it with carbon, and pouring the liquid into a mold to cool until it solidifies.

Robert Castlereagh (1769–1822) British Prime Minister at the end of the Napoleonic wars who took part in the negotiations at the *Congress of Vienna*.

Baldassare Castiglione (1478–1529) author of *The Courtier* (1528), which described the ideal Renaissance man.

Catherine the Great of Russia (ruled 1762–1796) tsarina who embraced the ideas of the Enlightenment in the hopes of making her rule more effective and, in 1785, formalized the relationship between the autocratic state and the nobles with the the Charter of Nobility.

Catholic Emancipation Act (1829) law passed by the English Parliament that removed all legal restrictions preventing English Catholics from holding office or serving in Parliament.

Catholic League   alliance of French Catholics who fought the French Protestants during the religious struggles of the sixteenth century.

Cavaliers   supporters of King *Charles I* in the English Civil War.

Camillo di Cavour   (1810–1861) Prime Minister of the kingdom of Sardinia who, from 1852 until his death, built the unification of Italy around the constitutional monarchy of Piedmont-Sardinia, the peninsula's strongest and most liberal state.

Miguel de Cervantes   (1547–1616) author of *Don Quixote*, the first part of which was published in 1605 and the second in 1615.

Charles I   of England (Stuart, ruled 1625–1649) son of *James I* and, like his father, an advocate of absolute monarchy. He attempted to rule England without the consent of Parliament, which led to the English Civil War. Charles lost that war and was ultimately tried by Parliament and executed.

Charles II   of England (Stuart, ruled 1661–1685) son of *Charles I* who, after Oliver Cromwell's death, was restored to the crown and gave England a reprieve from years of violent turmoil.

Charles V   of Spain (Habsburg, ruled Spain 1516–1558, Holy Roman Empire 1519–1558) emperor of the Holy Roman Empire and also king of Spain he ruled until 1558, when he retired to a monastery.

Charles VI   of Austria (Habsburg, ruled 1711–1740) Holy Roman emperor who attempted to keep the remaining lands ruled by the house of Habsburg together after the War of Spanish Succession. He died in 1740 without a male heir.

Charles IX   of France (Valois, ruled 1560–1574) became king of France at age ten; his mother, Catherine de' Medici, ruled as regent while he was a minor.

Charles X   of France, (Bourbon, ruled 1824–1830) reactionary monarch who attempted to undo the effects of the French Revolution and produced an outpouring of opposition in 1830, which forced him to abdicate.

Charter of 1814   law signed by *Louis XVIII* that restored monarchy to France while upholding the concept of equality before the law and the Napoleonic Civil Code.

Chartist Movement   early-nineteenth-century English political movement that supported the Great Charter, a document that called for reducing the power of Britain's elite via universal suffrage for men, annual elections, equally populated electoral districts, secret ballots, and salaries for members of Parliament, which would allow more ordinary people to serve.

Church of England   founded in 1533 at the request of King *Henry VIII*, it maintains the tradition of apostolic succession and merges the essential tenets of Protestant reform with aspects of orthodox Catholic doctrine, such as transubstantiation.

Civic Forum   a group of Czechoslovakian dissidents, led by Vaclav Havel, that opposed the Communist Czechoslovakian government at the end of the Cold War.

Jean Baptiste Colbert   (1619–1683) Comptroller General of France under *Louis XIV*, best known as the chief proponent of *mercantilism* in France.

common law   system of law that emerged in medieval England and was based on custom and past court decisions instead of on statutes.

compass   instrument for determining direction, consisting of a freely moving piece of iron which points to either magnetic north or south. It was first invented by the Chinese and brought to the West in the late Middle Ages.

Concert of Europe alliance between Russia, Great Britain, Prussia, Austria, and France from 1815 until 1854, whose aim was to maintain the rule of monarchy and the balance of power in Europe.

Concordat of Bologna (1516) agreement between the papacy and the king of France that gave control of ecclesiastic appointments to the king, subject to papal confirmation.

Congress of Vienna (1815) meeting of the allies who defeated Napoleon (Austria, Prussia, Russia, and Great Britain); it restored the French monarchy and created the international alliance called the *Concert of Europe*.

Congress Party the largest single Indian political organization devoted to achieving Indian independence from Britain; two of its major leaders were Mohandas Gandhi and Jawaharlal Nehru.

corporatism economic policy that creates cartel-like corporations to unite everyone dependent upon one activity or industry and eliminate competition in the interest of the prosperity of the national economic community. This policy was adopted by fascist Italy, among others.

conquistadors Spanish soldiers and sailors who explored and then conquered Central and South America in the sixteenth century.

condottieri professional mercenaries who operated in Renaissance Italy.

Nicholas Copernicus (1473–1543) Polish philosopher and astronomer who rejected the geocentric theory, that the sun and planets revolve around the earth, and argued for the heliocentric theory, that the earth and other planets revolve around the sun.

Cossacks a semi-nomadic people of the Ukraine who were skilled in cavalry warfare and became the lead combat units in the Russian army and enforcers of the Russian tsar's power.

cottagers English farmers and rural workers in cottage industries who were provided with shelter and furnishings as a part of their pay.

Council of Trent (1545) meeting of Catholic leaders to assess the condition of the Catholic Church and define its doctrines. It rejected most points raised by the Protestant movement and reaffirmed the authority of the pope and bishops, the seven sacraments, and the presence of Christ in the Eucharist.

Oliver Cromwell (1599–1658) member of Parliament who opposed *Charles I* during the English Civil War and commanded the army that defeated the Royalists; he became Lord Protector of England in 1653.

crop rotation farming method whereby landowners planted fodder and root plants, such as clover and turnips, instead of leaving a portion of their land fallow, as in the three field system. This regenerated the soil and provided food for animals and humans.

Crusades military expeditions undertaken by Christian Europe under papal sanction whose purpose was to recover the Holy Land from the rule of Muslims; they would later include military expeditions within Europe itself.

Dawes Plan a debt-restructuring proposal for Germany after World War I, named for the chairman of the International Banking Committee, American banker Charles Dawes. The plan called for Germany to make yearly debt payments from 1924 until 1929, in return for which France and Belgium would recall their troops from Germany.

Declaration of the Rights of Man   statement passed by the National Assembly of France in 1791 that denounced aristocratic privilege and stated that all citizens were equally eligible for all public offices (according to their abilities), that every citizen had the right to free speech, and that no person could be imprisoned except according to the law.

Defenestration of Prague   on May 23, 1618, a crowd of Protestant protesters carried a petition for the right to worship to the Hradcany palace, stormed into the council chamber, and engaged the Bohemian royal Catholic officials in a debate that resulted in the Protestant mob hurling the royal delegates from the window.

René Descartes   (1596–1650) French philosopher and mathematician who advocated the use of deductive reasoning to discover truth.

détente   policy pursued by the Nixon administration that advocated dialogue between the United States and the Soviet Union on the premise that this dialogue would resolve issues that were in their mutual interests, while still allowing for non-military competition.

devots   fanatical French Catholics who opposed any reconciliation with French Protestants.

Denis Diderot   (1713–1784) French philosopher who compiled the *Encyclopedia*, an attempt at a complete survey of all intellectual knowledge in eighteenth-century Europe. The *Encyclopedia* took twenty-five years to produce and spread Enlightenment thought throughout Europe and America.

Dominion status   term established by the statute of Westminster in 1931, to be applied to self-governing divisions of the British Empire as freely associating members of the British Commonwealth bound only by allegiance to the British sovereign.

double-entry bookkeeping   method of financial accounting in which each financial transaction is entered twice in a ledger. One entry is marked as a debit from one account and the other entry as a credit to a different account.

Edict of Nantes   (1598) signed by King *Henry IV* (Henry of Navarre) of France, this edict made Catholicism the official religion of France, but also granted religious tolerance to the nation's 2 million Protestants.

Edict of Toleration   (1779) issued by Emperor Joseph II of Austria that extended tolerance to non-Catholics, including Jews, in Austria-Hungary.

Edward VI   of England (Tudor, ruled 1547–1553) son of *Henry VIII* and Jane Seymour; a Protestant, he undertook an aggressive campaign to reinforce the power of the Church of England created by his father.

Elizabeth I   of England (Tudor, ruled 1558–1603) daughter of *Henry VIII* and Anne Boleyn, she never married and was known as the "Virgin Queen." During her reign England became a major power, strong enough to defeat the Spanish Armada of *Philip II*.

Enclosure Acts   laws that allowed seventeenth- and eighteenth-century British landowners to appropriate communally owned lands for private use. Ultimately, landowners enclosed over 7 million acres of land—more than 25 percent of England's total farmland.

Desiderius Erasmus   (1466–1536) Dutch philosopher who spearheaded a movement to apply the principles of humanistic philosophy to Christianity and biblical study.

Estates General   assembly of representatives from each of the three estates—the clergy, the nobility and the commoners—that was established in the fourteenth century as an advisory council to the king of France.

European Economic Community   (EEC, also called the Common Market) established in 1958 by France, West Germany, Italy, Belgium, Luxembourg, and the Netherlands as a free trade area in which people, goods, and money could move across natural borders without hindrance. The Common Market approved a 10 percent mutual reduction in tariffs and, in 1959, the free exchange of national currencies, which was a first step toward the creation of the European Union.

extra-territoriality   the right granted by the Imperial Chinese government to Westerners that meant they were subject to the laws of their own nation, not to the Chinese Imperial law and judicial system.

Factory Act   (1875) law enacted by the English Parliament to reduce the work week in large factories to fifty-six hours.

feudalism   the distribution of land (called fiefs) by European monarchs to those who were obliged to perform military service in return.

Francis I   of France (Valois, ruled 1515–1547) Renaissance prince, patron of *Leonardo da Vinci*, and rival of Holy Roman Emperor *Charles V* for domination of Europe. He signed the *Concordat of Bologna* in 1516 with Pope Leo X.

Francis II   of France (Valois, ruled 1559–1560) succeeded his father, *Henry II,* to the French throne at age fifteen, but died after a reign of only eighteen months.

Frederick the Great   of Prussia (ruled 1740–1786) also known as Frederick II, one of the "enlightened despots" who used the ideas of the Enlightenment to make his government function more efficiently and justly.

French Royal Academy of Science   scholarly group founded in Paris in 1666 for the purpose of scientific exchange and debate.

Fronde   revolt against the growth in royal authority in France that lasted from 1648 to 1653. Both powerful nobles and the lower classes fought against the young King *Louis XIV*, who ultimately overcame them.

Galen   (129–c.199 A.D.) Greek doctor who practiced in the Roman Empire and whose works became one of the foundations of medieval medicine.

Galileo Galilei   (1564–1642) Italian Renaissance mathematician and astronomer whose work disproved the geocentric theory, which held that the earth is the center of the solar system. He produced evidence supporting the heliocentric theory, which claimed that the sun is the center, but the papacy ultimately forced him to recant his views under the threat of torture.

galleon   a large seagoing vessel used in the fifteenth and sixteenth centuries and equipped with several sails and usually a number of cannons to shoot at an enemy craft rather than to ram it.

galley   an early seagoing craft propelled by oars or by oars and sail. It could be equipped with a ram for use against enemy ships and was used mainly in the Mediterranean Sea by both Christian and Muslim navies.

Giuseppe Garibaldi   (1807–1882) revolutionary fighter and leader of popular military movements aimed at the unification of Italy.

gentry   the English rural elites, both noble and non-noble, who owned large parcels of land.

George I   of Britain (Hanover, ruled 1714–1727) a German prince who inherited the British throne and established the Hanover dynasty, which still rules Britain today under the name of Windsor.

George II   of Britain (Hanover, ruled 1727–1760) British king who involved England in a number of Central Europe's disputes to safeguard his family's German interests.

George III   of Britain (Hanover, ruled 1760–1820) king who presided over many defining moments in Britain's history: the formal establishment of the British Empire, the loss of its American colonies, and Britain's struggle and ultimate triumph against Napoleonic France.

Gestapo   secret police of Nazi Germany.

glasnost   term used by Mikhail Gorbachev's government in the Soviet Union to describe a policy of openness in government and a greater degree of free expression for the people.

Good Friday Agreement   (1998) agreement signed on April 10, 1998, by representatives of the Protestant and Catholic radical movements that formed the basis for the current coalition government of Northern Ireland.

Gordon Riots   (1788) riots in which Protestant London crowds attacked the property of Catholics.

Grand Alliance   the eighteenth-century alliance between England, Holland, Austria, Prussia, and Portugal against France.

Grand Remonstrance   (1641) law passed by the English Parliament that presented a history of the Stuart monarchy's misdeeds and affirmed the *Magna Carta* and the *Petition of Right*.

Great Game   the diplomatic and military struggle between the British and Russian empires for the domination of the Near East and Asia.

guild   a medieval organization of people with common professional skills that set standards for training and workmanship. One entered a guild for training as an apprentice at an early age, and only after being tested could one be admitted as a full member of the guild.

habeas corpus   rule of law passed by the English Parliament in 1679 that stated that a judge may issue a writ requiring that an imprisoned person must be either put on trial or released.

Hanseatic League   a commercial alliance of towns and cities in northern Germany during the Middle Ages.

Henry II   of France (Valois, ruled 1547–1559) son of *Francis I*, signed the *Peace of Cateau-Cambresis* with Spain in 1559 to end decades of war. While celebrating peace with Spain in 1559, Henry took part in a jousting tournament and was accidentally killed, leaving his wife, Catherine de' Medici, as regent.

Henry III   of France (Valois, ruled 1574–1589) succeeded his brother *Charles IX*. During his reign Henry attempted to walk a fine line between earning the support of Catholics and attempting some rapprochement with Protestants. In 1588 he had Henry, Duke of Guise, assassinated. Some months later a Catholic monk assassinated Henry III himself, ending the Valois dynasty.

Henry IV   of France (Bourbon, ruled 1589–1610) also known as Henry of Navarre, founder of the Bourbon dynasty. He was a man of pragmatic religious outlook who declared the *Edict of Nantes*, which attempted to end years of strife between Protestants and Catholics in France.

Henry VII of England (Tudor, ruled 1485–1509) became king of England by defeating King Richard III of York at the Battle of Bosworth Field and established the Tudor dynasty.

Henry VIII of England (Tudor, ruled 1509–1547) initially a prominent Catholic during the Reformation, but broke with the pope and established the Church of England in order to obtain a divorce from his wife, Catherine of Aragon.

The Herero an indigenous people living in modern-day Tanzania who rebelled against the German Empire in 1903.

Thomas Hobbes (1588–1679) English philosopher who zealously advocated the rule of absolute monarchy in his book *Leviathan* (1651). He argued that only by placing absolute power in the hands of one man could society prevent human affairs from lapsing into a "state of nature" where each man warred against every other man.

William Hogarth (1697–1764) English artist who created paintings and prints of everyday life in eighteenth-century London.

Holy League alliance between Spain, Venice, and the papacy against the Ottoman Turks.

Huguenots French Protestants who rebelled against Catholic domination and struggled for the right to practice their own religion.

humanism philosophical school of the Renaissance that shifted the curriculum of schools from away from scholasticism and towards Latin grammar, rhetoric, and metaphysics. The underlying principle of humanism is that "man is the measure of all things."

Hundred Years' War a series of wars between England and France that began in the fourteenth century and continued into the fifteenth century. These wars were fought over territory in modern France that was claimed by both kings, and they ended with the explusion of the English from France.

Jan Hus (1369–1415) Bohemian theologian who criticized the worldliness of many priests and rejected the authority of the papacy, his teachings led to the Hussite Wars in Central Europe.

husbandmen farmers who owned the smallest parcels of land in England.

Ignatius of Loyola (1491–1556) Basque noble who founded the Society of Jesus (whose members are known as the Jesuits), which became a major force in the Counter-Reformation.

Independents militant Puritans who wished to see a loose alliance of congregations that would choose their own ministers instead of a national, centralized church in England, they opposed any compromise with the Stuart monarchy.

Index of Forbidden Ideas and Books a list, formulated by Pope Paul IV in 1559, of books and ideas considered to be incompatible with the practice of Roman Catholicism.

Intendants the title given to various public officials in the French Royal bureaucracy in the eighteenth century.

Investiture Crisis massive struggle, mainly led by the Holy Roman emperor, between the ecclesiastical government of the pope and the secular governments of Europe. Although the contest was officially over the appointment of bishops by secular rulers, the real issue was the subservience of one government to the other.

Irish Republican Army (or IRA) a resistance movement that began in protest of the British of occupation Ireland during the First World War and is still active in Northern Ireland today.

Iron Curtain   term coined by Sir Winston Churchill in a 1946 speech for the Soviet Union's military occupation of Eastern Europe.

Isabella of Castile   (ruled Castile 1474–1504, Aragon 1479–1504) Queen of Castile who married Ferdinand of Aragon in 1469 to create the nation of Spain. Under Ferdinand and Isabella's rule in 1492 the Spanish finished their long effort to drive the Islamic Moors from the Iberian Peninsula.

Ivan IV   of Russia (ruled 1533–1584) also known as Ivan the Terrible, he expanded the Duchy of Moscow by conquering territory from the Muslim Tartars and the Mongols, thereby creating the foundation for modern Russia. He was noted for paranoid rages and massacres of dissidents.

James I   of England (Stuart, ruled 1603–1625) son of Mary, Queen of Scots, succeeded *Elizabeth I* to the English throne. James was an advocate of absolute monarchy and had many conflicts with the English Parliament.

James II   of England (Stuart, ruled 1685–1688) brother of *Charles II* and assumed the crown after his brother's death. Unlike his brother, James openly espoused both absolute monarchy and sympathy for the Catholic faith, which resulted in the Glorious Revolution, a coup d'état executed by Parliament that placed William of Orange and his wife, *Mary Stuart*, on the throne.

janissary   member of an elite Turkish infantry corps composed of slaves who were taken at birth from Christian villages in the Turkish Empire.

jingoism   chauvinism in foreign policies, based on military superiority. The term came from the phrase "by jingo," often used to follow a vehement assertion. It was particularly associated with the conservative supporters of British Prime Minister Benjamin Disraeli's imperialistic policies.

joint-stock partnerships   invented by the English in 1600, they provide long-term capital funding by selling shares in a company.

Junkers   the hereditary feudal land-owning class in Prussia from which the army traditionally drew most of its officers and generals.

Justices of the Peace   English officials, usually from prosperous gentry families, who dispensed justice, collected taxes, raised troops and maintained order.

Immanuel Kant   (1724–1804) the foremost proponent of the philosophical school of German idealism as put forth in his book *Critique of Pure Reason* (1781). He claimed that reason alone was not the basis of knowledge and that each person understands the world around him through concepts that cannot be separated from his experience.

Kellogg–Briand Pact   (1928) treaty in which the United States, Great Britain, and France renounced war as an instrument of national policy.

Johannes Kepler   (1571–1630) scientist who persuasively proved that *Copernicus's* idea of planetary motion was correct by using data gathered by Tycho Brahe. He also showed that the motion of the planets was due to the force of gravity.

Levellers   radical British group within Cromwell's Parliamentary Army who demanded new laws to protect the poor as well as the wealthy and wanted to broaden the electoral franchise.

John Locke   (1632–1704) English politician and political philosopher who was active during the Glorious Revolution. His theory of natural rights to life, liberty, and property were the intellectual foundation of the American Declaration of Independence.

longbow a six-foot-tall bow capable of accurately shooting a yard-long arrow 300 yards. The longbow was the national weapon of the English, who used it with devastating effect against the French during *Hundred Years' War*.

Louis XIII of France (Bourbon, ruled 1610–1643) centralized the power of the monarchy with the aid of his able minister, *Cardinal Richelieu*. During the *Thirty Years' War* Louis became allied to England and the Dutch Republic against the Habsburg Empire.

Louis XIV of France (Bourbon, ruled 1643–1715) overcame the resistance of both the nobility and peasants during the *Fronde* revolt to emerge as the most powerful monarch in Europe. Throughout his reign, Louis centralized power and government in France around his person.

Louis XV of France (Bourbon, ruled 1715–1774) continued his father's policies of absolute monarchy and aggressive war, pushing France towards bankruptcy in the process.

Louis XVI of France (Bourbon, ruled 1774–1792) continued his father's spendthrift policies, ultimately bankrupting France and bringing on the French Revolution.

Louis XVIII of France (Bourbon, ruled 1814–1824) restored to the French throne in 1814 after the defeat of Napoleon.

Louis-Philippe (Bourbon, ruled 1830–1848) Duke of Orleans who was installed as king of France in 1830 and ruled as a consitutional monarch until 1848.

Luddites English workers who wanted to return to the economic and social order of pre-Industrial Revolution England.

Luftwaffe the Air Force of Nazi Germany.

Maginot Line a continuous set of massive fortresses along the French border that was meant to contain the attack of Nazi Germany on France. In World War II, the Germans simply went around the Maginot Line by invading Holland and Belgium.

Marshall Plan economic plan named after the U.S. Secretary of State George Marshall that was designed to aid and support the rebuilding of Western European economies after the end of World War II.

Martin Luther (1483–1546) dean of the theological seminary in Wittenberg who began to question publicly the abuses committed by the Catholic Church. His protests and calls for reform ultimately precipitated the Protestant Reformation and the creation of the Lutheran Church.

Niccolò Machiavelli (1469–1527) Italian writer who was exiled when the Medicis reinstated their rule in Florence; while in exile he wrote *The Prince* (1513), which described the art of ruling a state as a benevolent tyrant.

Magna Carta (1215) charter that the English barons forced King John Plantagenet to sign in 1215. The charter included the crown's promise that no one could be arrested, imprisoned, or punished in any way except after a trial by his peers and in accordance with the law of the land. Furthermore, the king could only level new taxes with the consent of a great counsel, which became what we call Parliament.

Mahdi ("the expected one") a nineteenth-century Sudanese religious leader who led a successful revolt against Egyptian governance and the British involvement in the Sudan.

Thomas Malthus (1766–1834) English economist who, in his book *Essay on the Principle of Population* (1798), argued that natural checks on the human population would become less significant and that the population would multiply exponentially while the food supply would grow only arithmetically, leading to ultimate crisis for all of humanity.

manor a large tract of land owned by a nobleman who occupied it with his family and all of his dependents.

Maria Theresa of Austria (Habsburg, ruled 1740–1780) crowned archduchess of Austria and queen of Hungary and Bohemia, but was barred from becoming the Holy Roman emperor. She continued the struggle of her father, *Charles VI*, to retain the Habsburg lands against her adversary, *Frederick the Great* of Prussia, in a series of wars.

Karl Marx (1818–1883) German intellectual philosopher who formed the Communist League and in 1848 published *The Communist Manifesto*.

Giuseppe Mazzini (1805–1872) considered to be the guiding spirit of the movement for Italian unification.

Cosimo de' Medici (1389–1464) one of the wealthiest and most powerful bankers and manufacturers of textiles in Renaissance Florence. In 1434 he seized control of Florentine politics; his family maintained that control throughout the fifteenth century.

Mensheviks members of the Russian Social Democratic Workers Party (Marxists) who believed that a proletariat revolution would occur after a bourgeois uprising succeeded in overthrowing the tsarist state. They stood against the high degree of Communist Party centralization upon which Lenin insisted.

mercantilism theory that global wealth was static and that a nation became wealthier at the expense of other nations. A nation's wealth was increased by importing more gold and silver into its economy than it sent out.

Methodism English Protestant movement begun by John Wesley that stressed that all people are equal before God's eyes.

Clemens von Metternich (1773–1859) Chancellor of Austria who dominated both the *Congress of Vienna* and the *Concert of Europe*. Metternich believed that Europe would only find peace if its monarchs suppressed the forces of liberalism and nationalism.

James Mill (1773–1836) Scottish economist and philosopher who emerged as the political champion of the middle class in his 1820 "Essay on Government."

John Stuart Mill (1806–1873) son of *James Mill* and author of *On Liberty* (1859), which argued that the individual is the best judge of his or her own interests. Mill also espoused the causes of women's rights and union formation.

Harriet Taylor Mill (1807–1858) English feminist and wife of *John Stuart Mill*, who advocated that in her time, "for the first time in the world, men and women are really companions."

Molotov-Ribbentrop Pact (1939) named for the foreign ministers of Nazi Germany and the Soviet Union and termed a nonaggression pact, it was actually a *de facto* alliance for the partition of Poland; it was signed on August 23, 1939.

monopoly government grant for exclusive control of a commodity or service issued to a single party in a nation's economy.

Montagnards French Democratic socialists, drawn mainly from France's largest cities, who were prominent in the revolutions of 1848.

Montesquieu (1689–1755) a French nobleman and lawyer who wrote *The Spirit of Laws* (1748). Montesquieu examined each form of government in history in order to determine its merits and concluded that a government combining the elements of monarchy, aristocracy, and democracy, where the elements would exist in a system of checks and balances, would be best.

Thomas More (1478–1535) English Catholic intellectual who wrote *Utopia* (1516) and died a martyr for refusing, in 1534, to take an oath of loyalty to *Henry VIII* as head of the then-newly established Church of England.

Muslim League Indian political organization, ultimately led by Mohammed Ali Jinnah, that called for the creation of a Muslim state in the northwest corner of the Indian subcontinent. This state was founded in 1947 and named Pakistan.

mustard gas a poisonous gas first developed and used by Germany in World War I; inhaling it subjects the lungs to a burning irritant that ultimately destroys lung tissue.

National Assembly established in France on June 17, 1789, when the third estate overwhelmingly approved a motion stating that it was the true representative of national sovereignty. The National Assembly absorbed the remainder of the *Estates General* and became the fundamental government of revolutionary France.

Navigation Acts laws requiring that all goods brought into England be shipped by either English ships or ships from the goods' country of origin.

New Deal a set of programs initiated by U.S. President Franklin D. Roosevelt in 1932 to try to end the Great Depression. These programs facilitated loans that saved banks, provided relief for the unemployed through public works programs, and gave assistance to farmers and businessmen.

Isaac Newton (1642–1727) English scientist and mathematician who established the laws of motion, which constituted the foundation of physics up until the work of Albert Einstein.

nihilists Russian revolutionary intellectuals who rejected the materialistic doctrines of the West as well as many Russian traditions.

nobles the first estate in the *Estates General* in France; the term designated the upper class of Europe before the French Revolution.

nominalists followers of William of Occam who rejected papal authority and the hierarchical structure of the church and believed that individual piety should be the cornerstone of religious life.

North Atlantic Treaty Organization (NATO) an organization of Western nations designed to coordinate the defense of Western Europe against attack, originally against Soviet and *Warsaw Pact* forces.

Open Door Policy title of the 1899 statement by U.S. Secretary of State John Hayes that proclaimed that China's territorial sovereignty was to be preserved and that merchants of all nations were to be treated equally everywhere in China.

Opium War (1839–1842) when the Chinese emperor attempted to stop the spread of opium addiction by completely ending trade with foreigners, the British Navy sent gunboats to China and forced the emperor to capitulate.

Organization of Petroleum-Exporting Countries (OPEC) organization originally formed by Iran, Iraq, Kuwait, Saudi Arabia, and Venezuela in 1960 to control petroleum production, prices, and competition.

Pan-Slavism movement that seeks to unify all the Slavic nations in the Balkans and promote their interests.

Peace of Augsburg (1555) compromise agreed to by the Holy Roman emperor *Charles V* and the Imperial representative assembly that stipulated that the religion of each of the Empire states would follow the religion of the ruler of that state.

Peace of Cateau-Cambresis (1559) treaty between the Habsburg empire and France that secured Habsburg domination of Italy.

Peace of Dresden (1745) treaty that secured the withdrawal of Prussia, after it had gained the province of Silesia, from the *War of the Austrian Succession*.

Peace of Karlowitz (1699) treaty that ended the war between Austria and the Turks; the Turks ceded lands to Austria, Venice, and Poland.

Peace of Vienna (1606) treaty that guaranteed religious freedom in Hungary and recognized Prince Mathias as the head of the Habsburg family and heir to the Holy Roman Empire.

perestroika economic policy of the Gorbachev administration that restructured the Soviet economy to allow for more open markets and privatization.

Peter the Great of Russia (Romanov, ruled 1682–1725) tsar who transformed Russia into the Russian Empire by using Enlightenment ideas to make his government more efficient and adding new territory to his realm. Peter reoriented Russia toward the West by building a new capital city that he called St. Petersburg.

Petition of Right (1628) act passed by Parliament and presented to *Charles I* that reaffirmed the *Magna Carta* and declared the loans to the crown and taxes levied by the crown without Parliament's consent to be in violation of that charter.

Francesco Petrarch (1304–1374) Florentine intellectual poet who was influential in the rediscovery of the classics of Latin antiquity.

Philip II of Spain (Habsburg, ruled 1556–1598) his kingdom included Spain, the Netherlands, parts of Italy, and colonies in the Americas, making him the ruler of the first superpower in modern history. Philip was a religious extremist who fought against the Islamic Turks and Protestants, whom he considered heretics.

physiocrats eighteenth-century economic thinkers who argued that land, not gold and silver, was the source of wealth. They wanted the state to stop interfering in agriculture and the commerce of farm goods.

pietism a seventeenth-century Protestant movement in northern Germany that emphasized preaching and the study of the Bible and stressed the primacy of the one's individual conscience.

pike a twelve- to eighteen-foot long spear, first used in the late fourteenth century. When many men carried pikes in a close formation, they could defeat armored cavalry.

pikemen soldiers who carried *pikes* in close formation.

plebiscite a direct vote by the people of a country or municipality to determine an important political issue—for example, the determination of political economy or affiliation with another political unit.

Politiques   moderate French Catholics who pushed for reconciliation with the French Protestants.

positivism   the view that human progress is inevitable and moves in a linear manner, continuously bringing improvements over time.

Pragmatic Sanction   (1713) asserted the indivisibility of the Habsburg domains and recognized the right of inheritance of both females and males to the monarchy should *Charles VI* die without having any sons. Charles did die without a male heir, leaving *Maria Theresa* to rule Habsburg territory.

Presbyterians   Protestant sect whose followers were the majority in the Parliamentary faction during the English Civil War. They wished to see the establishment of the Calvinist church in England and were inclined to compromise with the king.

Price Revolution   a massive inflation of prices in the sixteenth century, caused by the rise in population and economic boom, in which the cost of living greatly exceeded wage increases.

Pride's Purge   the Parliamentary army's coup against Parliament, led by Colonel Pride, that expelled Presbyterians from Parliament, leaving only 20 percent of Parliament's members still in office. Those members of Parliament then tried King *Charles I* for treason and had him executed.

primogeniture   tradition in which the eldest son inherits the entire estate.

printing press   machine for printing on paper using movable type. It was first invented in China, and then developed in northern Europe in the late-fifteenth century.

Privy Council   advisory board to the English monarch that consisted of between twelve and eighteen members drawn from the nobility, the gentry, and royal officers; they also oversaw military and judicial administration.

protectorate   nation or people who are dominated by a militarily stronger nation; it implies that the stronger nation controls the foreign policy and much of the domestic policy of the weaker nation while leaving its government intact.

psychoanalysis   method developed by Sigmund Freud in the 1890s to better understand the workings of the subconscious mind; it dominated the emerging field of psychology for decades.

Ranters   one of the factions that arose during the English Civil War, they rejected the ideas of heaven, hell, and sin and called for salvation based upon the indulgence of sex and liquor.

Reform Act of 1832   law that lowered the minimum franchise requirement in order to broaden the English electorate; it almost doubled the size of the electorate.

Reign of Terror   a bloody stage of the French Revolution, lasting from September 1793 to July 1794, that was presided over by the ruthless Committee of Public Safety.

Cardinal Richelieu   (1585–1642) minister of *Louis XIII* who expanded the administrative authority and fiscal reach of the crown.

Roman law   the system of law established by the Roman Empire and still in effect in the Byzantine Empire throughout the Middle Ages. In medieval Western Europe it formed the basis of statute law.

romanticism   artistic and cultural movement that emerged in Western Europe in the late-eighteenth century. It emphasized the individual living within the natural world, using his imagination and emotion to achieve personal development.

rotten borough   a sparsely populated rural electoral district that was still represented in the English Parliament. The most notorious of these districts was the district of Dunwich, which had been submerged beneath the sea since the twelfth century.

Roundheads   supporters of the Parliamentary party in the English Civil War; the term was in derision of their closely cropped haircuts.

Jean-Jacques Rousseau   (1712–1778) French Enlightenment author and philosopher. His works include *Heloise* (an early novel), *Emile, On Education,* and *The Social Contract*. He condemned the inequality found in civilized societies and was a major inspiration for the ideology of the French Revolution.

Royal assize courts   the English courts charged with enforcing Parliamentary laws and the orders of the *Privy Council* as well as trying felony cases.

St. Bartholomew's Day Massacre   Paris massacre that occurred on August 24, 1572 and lasted six days, killing 2,000 Protestants. Throughout France another 10,000 Protestants perished.

St. Thomas Aquinas   (1225–1274) fourteenth-century Franciscan monk who used Aristotelian logic to deduce the existence of God in a set of rational proofs that moved from one premise to the next.

Girolamo Savonarola   (1452–1498) charismatic Dominican monk who predicted the French invasion of Italy and opposed the Medici in Florence and the papacy on grounds of corruption. After helping drive the Medici from power he took control of the Florentine Republic.

Frederick von Schiller   (1759–1805) German romantic poet.

Great Schism   (1378–1417) period when there was a pope elected in Avignon, a pope elected in Rome, and a third pope elected in Pisa. Each of these popes claimed total authority over the Christian Church and refused to recognize the authority of the others.

scholasticism   system of thought that applies logical reasoning to philosophical and theological questions. The scholastic curriculum centered on law, medicine, and theology and focused on reconciling the Greek classics to Christian theological questions.

Sepoy Mutiny   (1857) a massive revolt that almost threw the British out of India and led to a complete reorganization of British rule there.

Seven Years' War   (1756–1763) also known as the French and Indian War in the United States, it was fought between France, Prussia, Britain, and Spain. This war was the first global conflict in modern history, with battles in North America, the Caribbean, and India, as well as Europe. France lost the war and as a result lost most of its colonial holdings to England and Spain.

seignorial rights   the rights of the nobility over the peasantry. They included income from rent, kind, and dues, as well as the right to dispense justice on their lands in their own courts.

Sickness Insurance Law   (1883) law passed by the English Parliament that provided income protection for all workers for up to thirteen weeks if their income fell below a certain level, with the monies coming from deductions withheld from the workers' wages.

Abbé Emanuel Joseph Sieyes   (1748–1836) the major advocate of the third estate during the French Revolution who led the movement to establish the *National Assembly*.

simony   the sin of selling church offices and positions.

slash and burn agriculture   method of burning plants on farmland to enrich the soil with the ash.

Adam Smith   (1723–1790) economist who argued against mercantilism and formulated the concept of capitalism. He opposed *guild* restrictions, *monopolies*, and trade barriers and instead believed that the market should be allowed to set its own prices and be free of interference from the government.

social Darwinism   the attempt to apply Darwin's theory of evolution to human history. It held that stronger people prevailed over weaker ones and that governments should not interfere with the "survival of the fittest."

Society for the Abolition of the Slave Trade   group founded in 1787 by independent English abolitionists.

Society of Jesus   (Jesuits) a religious order approved by the papacy in 1540. Jesuits underwent rigorous intellectual and physical training and undertook a special oath of allegiance to the pope. They became a major force in the Counter-Reformation.

Society of the Thirty   a group of liberal French nobles and lawyers who met to discuss and debate politics and distribute liberal political pamphlets before the French Revolution. They argued that the Third Estate, which represented the commoners, was entitled to twice as many representatives in the *Estates General* as the nobility and clergy.

socket bayonet   the result of fusing a metal socket to a razor sharp knife. The socket *bayonet* could then be attached over the barrel of a musket, converting the gun into a spear.

Solidarity   an independent organized movement of Polish trade unions at the end of the Cold War. Led by Lech Walesa, it was instrumental in the collapse of the Soviet domination of Eastern Europe.

Spanish Road   a military corridor that began in Genoa and passed across the Alps to end in the Netherlands. Along this road flowed the troops, provisions, and munitions necessary to supply the Spanish army occupying the Netherlands in the sixteenth century.

Special Theory of Relativity   theory of physics published by Albert Einstein in 1905 that stated that the velocity of light was both constant and independent of the velocities of both the source of that light and the light's observer, and that mass and energy were equivalent. This was expressed in the now famous equation, $e=mc^2$.

spinning jenny   an early spinning machine with more than one spindle that allowed one person to spin a number of yarns at the same time.

Sputnik   the satellite launched by the Soviet Union's rocket program in October 1957. The launch of *Sputnik* marked the first major achievement of the Soviet space program, which in turn spurred the United States to develop its own space program, NASA.

Star Chamber   English court that judged dissenters charged with offenses against the crown, named for a room in Westminster with a blue ceiling spangled with stars.

stadholder   the chief official of the Dutch Republic who in times of emergency was commander-in-chief of the military forces of Holland. In times of peace he had more influence than actual power and could not declare war, enact legislation, or even officially participate in debates on policy.

Strategic Arms Limitation Talks   (SALT I) conference between U.S. President Nixon and Soviet Union Premier Brezhnev that produced the first treaty to limit the size of the superpowers' nuclear arsenals.

Mary Stuart   of England (ruled 1688–1694) the Protestant daughter of *James II* who ascended to the throne of England with her husband, William of Orange, in 1688, but died without children.

Anne Stuart   of England (ruled 1702–1714) the Protestant daughter of *James II* who succeeded her brother-in-law, William of Orange, to the throne, but died without any surviving children.

James Stuart III   (1688–1766) Catholic half-brother of *Anne Stuart* who challenged the succession of *George I* to the throne of England. He led an unsuccessful revolt in 1715.

Charles Edward Stuart   (1720–1788) the last pretender to the English crown from the Stuart family. In 1745 he landed in Scotland and marched on London to overthrow the Hanoverian dynasty. He found no support in England and was defeated in 1745 at the *Battle of Culloden*.

sumptuary regulations   laws designed to control and limit the purchase of luxury items to particular social classes.

Suez Canal   Egyptian canal that, when completed in 1869, allowed ships to sail from the Mediterranean Sea through the Red Sea to India and the East, thereby vastly reducing travel time from Europe to East Asia.

taille   the French Royal tax on land.

Charles Maurice Talleyrand   (1754–1838) French career diplomat who served both Napoleon and the restored Bourbon monarchy.

Taylorism   scientific management of assembly line production, named after the American engineer who developed its techniques.

Thirty Years' War   a series of wars in Central Europe between Protestant and Catholic forces over control of the Holy Roman Empire. More than one million men fought in these wars, which resulted in desolation throughout Germany. The conflict ended with the *Treaty of Westphalia* in 1648.

telescope   an optical instrument in which the optical lenses are placed apart from each other in a tube in such a way as to magnify the image of a distant object.

three fields system   system of planting farmland in which one field is left fallow while the other two fields are cultivated.

tithes   payment owed to the Catholic Church from the laity, usually 10 percent of one's income before taxes.

Tories   faction that supported a powerful English monarchy in the late-seventeenth and eighteenth centuries.

Treaty of Adrianople   (1829) treaty that separated Moldavia and Wallachia from the Ottoman Empire and made them *protectorates* of Russia.

Treaty of Aix-la-Chapelle   (1668) treaty that enabled France to extend its northern border to annex Lille and part of Flanders.

Treaty of Andrussovo   (1667) treaty that ended the war between Russia and Poland. Russia annexed the Ukraine east of the Dneiper River.

Treaty of London   (1827) treaty between Britain, France, and Russia that threatened the Ottoman Empire with military intervention if the Ottomans did not accept the *de facto* independence of Greece. Greece gained its formal independence in 1832.

Treaty of Munster   (1648) part of the *Treaty of Westphalia*, which officially recognized Dutch independence.

Treaty of Nanking   (1842) treaty that granted the British the ability to establish a number of treaty ports open to British trade (including Shanghai) and authority over Hong Kong, and gave the right of extra territoriality to the British and other Europeans.

Treaty of Nysdat   (1721) treaty by which Russia added Estonia and Livonia to *Peter the Great*'s empire.

Treaty of Paris of 1763   treaty that ended the *Seven Years' War*. Austria recognized Prussia's 1740 absorption of Silesia, while Canada became British and the Louisiana territory was given to Spain.

Treaty of Paris of 1783   treaty between Great Britain and the United States that recognized America's independence.

Treaty of Ryswick   (1697) treaty by which France gained territory in Alsace.

Treaty of Utrecht   (1713) treaty that ended the War of Spanish Succession. Austria received the Southern Netherlands, Lombardy, and Naples. Phillip V of the Bourbon family became king of Spain while renouncing French succession. Spain lost all European territory beyond the Pyrenees. France surrendered Newfoundland, Nova Scotia, and Hudson Bay to Britain.

Treaty of Versailles   (1783) treaty between Great Britain, France, and Spain that ended the war that existed between those countries as a result of France and Spain's support of the American Revolution.

Treaty of Westphalia   (1648) treaty that ended the *Thirty Years' War*. Among other points, the treaty recognized the independence of the Dutch Republic of the United Provinces and Switzerland and gave the German states more independence from the weakened Holy Roman Empire. Lutherans and Calvinists were granted religious tolerance.

Triple Alliance   military alliance of Germany, the Austro-Hungarian Empire, and Italy, forged in 1882 against the military threat of France and Russia. Italy left the alliance before World War I and ultimately joined the Allies.

Triple Entente   military alliance between France, England, and Imperial Russia against the potential threat from Germany and Austria-Hungary. This alliance was known during World War I simply as the "Allies."

True Levellers   one of the factions of the English Civil War, also known as Diggers. They rejected Parliament's claims to speak for the country and opposed the private ownership of land.

Truman Doctrine   policy announced by U.S. President Truman in 1948 that determined that the United States was going "to support free people who are resisting subjugation when armed minorities were applying outside pressures." In other words, the United States would resist all attempts by the Soviet Union to expand its sphere of influence.

Mary Tudor   of England (ruled 1553–1558) also known as Bloody Mary, the daughter of *Henry VIII* and Catherine of Aragon who launched an aggressive campaign to restore the Catholic Church in England and persecuted many Protestants.

U-boats   submarines used by the German Navy during World War I and World War II.

Ultra-royalists   also known as Ultras, fanatical aristocratic royalists who were opposed to the French Revolution and who, after Waterloo, launched the "white" terror, a purge of those who had supported Napoleon.

utopian socialism   philosophy that envisioned a gentle world of cooperation and rejected as egotistic the individualism of liberalism. Most utopian socialists were French and attempted to produce a critique of social changes brought about by nineteenth-century capitalism.

vassalage   legal relationship where one man who has greater wealth and power bestows some of his land on another in exchange for military service.

Vatican II   a council of the Catholic Church presided over by Pope John XXIII from 1962 to 1965. It undertook massive revisions of church practices, most particularly allowing the mass to be said in the local vernacular language.

Andreas Vesalius   (1514–1564) the founder of modern biological science who published his work on the fabric of the human body.

Vichy France   the French government, headed by Marshal Petain, that surrendered two-thirds of its territory to Nazi Germany on June 22, 1940. Petain headquartered his government in the southern French city of Vichy, where his government acted as a *de facto* ally of the Nazis.

Victor Emanuel II   (Savoy, ruled 1849–1878) rule of the kingdom of Sardinia who supported various movements aimed at unifying Italy that would gradually extend his control over the Italian peninsula.

Viet-Cong   the Communist guerrilla movement in South Vietnam that fought first the U.S.-supported governments of South Vietnam and then, from 1965 until 1975, the U.S. military itself.

Voltaire   (Francis-Marie Arouet, 1694–1778) one of the most famous philosophes, a crusader for religious tolerance, and proponent of deism.

Robert Walpole   (1667–1745) Chancellor of the British Exchequer from 1721 to 1741 who perfected a system of political patronage by which he managed the British House of Commons.

Warsaw Pact   (1955) a military alliance between the Soviet Union and the nations of Eastern Europe, then under Soviet domination.

War of the Austrian Succession   war that pitted Prussia and England against Austria, France, and Russia over the German province of Silesia. It ended in 1748 with the *Treaty of Aix-la-Chapelle*.

Whigs   members of Parliament who were critical of the English monarchy and advocated Parliamentary supremacy.

Workmen's Compensation Law   (1897) English law that made employers responsible for bearing the cost of on-the-job injuries.

John Wycliffe   (1328–1384) English priest and scholar whose studies led him to challenge Christian orthodoxy. Wycliffe stressed the role of faith in reaching salvation and insisted that reading the Scriptures should form the basis of faith.

yeomen   independent landowners and tenant farmers of some means who had political rights and could vote in Parliamentary elections but ranked below the gentry on the social ladder.

Young Turks   a group of nationalist intellectuals, influenced by Western political ideas, who wished to restore the greatness of the Ottoman Empire by modernizing and unifying the empire.

Zulu   a collection of South African tribes organized into a military empire by the charismatic and ruthless king Chaka in the early nineteenth-century. The Zulu fought both the British and the Dutch in a series of wars that lasted into the late-nineteenth century.

Huldrych Zwingli   (1484–1531) Swiss pastor who preached salvation by virtue of faith alone. His ideas flourished in parts of Switzerland and some German states.

FURTHER READINGS

GENERAL

Feroz Ahmad, *The Making of Modern Turkey* (1993).

Michael Anderson, *Approaches to the History of the Western Family, 1500–1914* (1980).

Philippe Ariès, *Centuries of Childhood: A Social History of Family Life* (1962).

Philippe Ariès and Georges Duby, eds., *A History of Private Life* (5 vols., 1987–1993).

Geoffrey Barraclough, *The Origins of Modern Germany* (1979).

Geoffrey Best, *War and Society in Revolutionary Europe, 1770–1870* (1982).

David Blackbourn, *The Long Nineteenth Century: A History of Germany, 1780–1918* (1997).

Jerome Blum, *The End of the Old Order in Rural Europe* (1978).

———, *Lord and Peasant in Russia from the Ninth to the Nineteenth Century* (1961).

Richard Bonney, *The European Dynastic States, 1494–1660* (1991).

John Bossy, *Christianity in the West, 1400–1700* (1985).

Fernand Braudel, *The Mediterranean World in the Age of Philip II* (1992).

Peter Brown, *The Rise of Western Christendom: Triumph and Diversity, A. D. 200–1000* (2003).

Peter Burke, *Popular Culture in Early Modern Europe* (1978).

Franco Cardini, *Europe and Islam* (2001).

S. G. Checkland, *British Public Policy, 1776–1939: An Economic, Social, and Political Perspective* (1985).

Carlo Cipolla, *Before the Industrial Revolution: European Society and Economy, 1000–1700* (1980).

Carlo Cipolla, ed., *The Fontana Economic History of Europe* (6 vols., 1976–1977).

Martin Clark, *Modern Italy, 1871–1982* (1984).

Eric Cochrane, *Italy, 1530–1630* (1988).

Linda Colley, *Captives: Britain, Empire, and the World, 1650–1800* (2002).

Norman Davies, *A History of Poland: God's Playground* (2 vols., 1981).

David Brion Davis, *The Problem of Slavery in the Age of Revolution, 1770–1823* (1975).

Georges Duby and Michelle Perrot, eds., *A History of Women in the West* (5 vols., 1992–1994).

Christopher Duggan, *A Concise History of Italy* (1994).

Richard Dunn, *The Age of Religious Wars, 1559–1715* (1979).

Elizabeth Eisenstein, *The Printing Revolution in Early Modern Europe* (1993).

Norbert Elias, *The Civilizing Process* (1994).

William Ferguson, *Scotland: 1689 to the Present* (1968).

Orlando Figes, *Natasha's Dance: A Cultural History of Russia* (2002).

R. F. Foster, *Modern Ireland, 1600–1972* (1988).

François Furet and Jacques Ozouf, *Reading and Writing: Literacy in France from Calvin to Jules Ferry* (1983).

Peter Gay, *Education of the Senses: The Bourgeois Experience: Victoria to Freud, Vol. I* (1999).

———, *The Cultivation of Hatred: The Bourgeois Experience: Victoria to Freud, Vol. III* (1994).

———, *The Tender Passion: The Bourgeois Experience: Victoria to Freud, Vol. II* (1999).

Felix Gilbert and David Clay Large, *The End of the European Era, 1890 to the Present* (2002).

Robert Gildea, *Barricades and Borders: Europe, 1800–1914* (1987).

John Gillis, *Youth and History: Tradition and Change in European Age Relations, 1770 to the Present* (1981).

Jack Goldstone, *Revolution and Rebellion in the Early Modern World* (1991).

E. J. Hobsbawm, *The Age of Revolution, 1789–1848* (1962).

Paul Hohenberg and Lynn Lees, *The Making of Urban Europe, 1000–1950* (1985).

Geoffrey Hosking, *Russia and the Russians: A History* (2001).

Lynn Hunt, ed., *The New Cultural History* (1989).

Charles Ingrao, *The Habsburg Monarchy, 1618–1815* (1994).

Barbara Jelavich, *History of the Balkans* (2 vols., 1983).

Henry Kamen, *European Society, 1500–1700* (1984).

John Keegan, *The Face of Battle* (1976).

———, *A History of Warfare* (1993).

Tom Kemp, *Industrialization in Nineteenth-Century Europe* (1985).

Paul Kennedy, *The Rise and Fall of the Great Powers* (1987).

V. G. Kiernan, *European Empires from Conquest to Collapse, 1815–1960* (1982).

Tony Kushner and Katharine Knox, *Refugees in the Age of Genocide* (2001).

H. G. Koenigsberger, *Early Modern Europe, 1500–1789* (1987).

———, *The Habsburgs and Europe, 1516–1660* (1971).

E. H. Kossman, *The Low Countries, 1780–1940* (1978).

Dominick LaCapra and Steven L. Kaplan, eds., *Modern European Intellectual History: Reappraisals and New Perspectives* (1982).

C. A. Macartney, *The Habsburg Empire, 1790–1918* (1969).

Roger Magraw, *France, 1815–1914: The Bourgeois Century* (1983).

Mary Jo Maynes, *Schooling in Western Europe: A Social History* (1985).

Mark Mazower, *The Balkans: A Short History* (2000).

Peter McPhee, *A Social History of France, 1780–1880* (2004).

John M. Merriman, *The Stones of Balazuc: A French Village in Time* (2002).

Alec Reginald Meyers, *Parliaments and Estates in Europe to 1789* (1975).

Joel Mokyr, *Twenty-Five Centuries of Technological Change: An Historical Survey* (1990).

P. K. O'Brien and C. Keyser, *Economic Growth in Britain and Europe, 1780–1914* (1978).

Geoffrey Parker, *The Military Revolution: Military Innovation and the Rise of the West, 1500–1800* (1988).

Kenneth Pomerantz, *Great Divergence: Europe, China, and the Making of the Modern World Economy* (2000).

Colin Russell, *Science and Social Change in Britain and Europe, 1700–1900* (1983).

Peter Sahlins, *Boundaries: The Making of France and Spain in the Pyrenees* (1989).

Joan W. Scott, *Gender and the Politics of History* (1988).

Hugh Seton-Watson, *The Russian Empire, 1801–1917* (1967).

Stanford J. Shaw, *History of the Ottoman Empire and Modern Turkey*, (2 vols., 1976–1977).

James Sheehan, *German History, 1770–1866* (1990).

Quentin Skinner, *Foundations of Modern Political Thought* (1978).

Yuri Slezkine, *Arctic Mirrors: Russia and the Small Peoples of the North* (1994).

Bonnie G. Smith, *Changing Lives: Women in European History since 1700* (1989).

Timothy Snyder, *The Reconstruction of Nations: Poland, Ukraine, Lithuania, Belarus, 1569–1999* (2003).

A. J. P. Taylor, *The Struggle for Mastery in Europe, 1848–1918* (1954).

Charles Tilly, *Coercion, Capital, and European States, AD 990–1990* (1990).

———, *The Contentious French: Four Centuries of Popular Struggle* (1986).

Richard Vinen, *A History in Fragments: Europe and the Twentieth Century* (2001).

Mack Walker, *German Home Towns: Community, State, and General Estate, 1648–1871* (1971).

Piotr Wandycz, *The Price of Freedom: A History of East Central Europe from the Middle Ages to the Present* (1992).

Robert K. Webb, *Modern England from the Eighteenth Century to the Present* (1968).

Eric R. Wolf, *Europe and the People without History* (1983).

Isser Woloch, ed., *The Ambiguities of Freedom* (1996).

Stuart Woolf, *A History of Italy, 1700–1860* (1986).

E. A. Wrigley, *Population and History* (1969).

Theodore Zeldin, *France, 1848–1945* (5 vols., 1978–1981).

CHAPTER 1. MEDIEVAL LEGACIES AND TRANSFORMING DISCOVERIES

Kenneth R. Andrews, *Trade, Plunder and Settlement: Maritime Enterprise and the Genesis of the British Empire, 1480–1630* (1984).

Robert Bartlett, *The Making of Europe: Conquest, Colonization and Cultural Change 950–1350* (1993).

M. W. Beresford, *New Towns of the Middle Ages* (1988).

Marc Bloch, *Feudal Society* (2 vols., 1961).

Brenda Bolton, *The Medieval Reformation* (1983).

John Boswell, *Christianity, Social Tolerance, and Homosexuality: Gay People in Western Europe from the Beginning of the Christian Era to the Fourteenth Century* (1980).

———, *The Kindness of Strangers: The Abandonment of Children in Western Europe from Late Antiquity to the Renaissance* (1988).

Rosalind B. and Christopher Brooke, *Popular Religion in the Middle Ages* (1984).

Alfred W. Crosby, *Ecological Imperialism: The Biological Expansion of Europe, 900–1900* (1986).

R. O. Crummey, *The Formation of Muscovy, 1404–1613* (1987).

Georges Duby, *Rural Economy and Country Life in the Medieval West* (1968).

Edith Ennen, *The Medieval Woman* (1989).

Robert Fossier, *Peasant Life in the Medieval West* (1988).

Bernard Hamilton, *Religion in the Medieval West* (1986).

Denys Hay, *Europe in the Fourteenth and Fifteenth Centuries* (1989).

———, *Europe, the Emergence of an Idea* (1968).

Norman Housley, *The Later Crusades, 1274–1580* (1992).

William C. Jordan, *Europe in the High Middle Ages* (2001).

Emmanuel Leroy Ladurie, *Montaillou: The Promised Land of Error* (1979).

Malcolm David Lambert, *Medieval Heresy: Popular Movements from Bogomil to Hus* (1976).

Robert S. Lopez, *The Commercial Revolution of the Middle Ages, 950–1300* (1971).

Angus MacKay, *Society, Economy and Religion in Late Medieval Castile* (1987).

Richard Mackenney, *Sixteenth-Century Europe: Expansion and Conflict* (1993).

H. E. Mayer, *The Crusades* (1988).

Michel Mollat, *The Poor in the Middle Ages* (1986).

R. I. Moore, *The First European Revolution, c. 970–1215* (2000).

John H. Mundy, *Europe in the High Middle Ages, 1150–1309* (1991).

J. H. Parry, *The Age of Reconnaissance: Discovery, Exploration and Settlement, 1450–1650* (1981).

Fritz Rorig, *The Medieval Town* (1967).

CHAPTER 2. THE RENAISSANCE

William J. Bouwsma, *The Waning of the Renaissance, 1550–1640* (2002).

Judith Brown, *In the Shadow of Florence* (1982).

Eugene Brucker, *Renaissance Florence* (1983).

Peter Burke, *The Italian Renaissance: Culture and Society in Italy* (1987).

———, *Popular Culture in Renaissance Europe, 1450–1620* (1986).

A. G. Dickens, *The Age of Humanism and Reformation: Europe in the Fourteenth to Sixteenth Centuries* (1972).

Carlo Ginzburg, *The Cheese and the Worms: The Cosmos of a Sixteenth-Century Miller* (1982).

———, *Night Battles* (1985).

Richard Goldthwaite, *The Building of Renaissance Florence* (1981).

Anthony Grafton and Lisa Jardine, *From Humanism to the Humanities: Edu-*

cation and the Liberal Arts in Fifteenth- and Sixteenth-Century Europe (1986).

J. R. Hale, *Renaissance Europe* (1977).

———, *War and Society in Renaissance Europe, 1450–1620* (1986).

Denys Hay and John Law, *Italy in the Age of the Renaissance, 1380–1530* (1989).

Dale Kent, *The Rise of the Medici* (1979).

Margaret King, *Women in the Renaissance* (1991).

Lauro Martines, *Power and Imagination: City-States in Renaissance Italy* (1988).

Garrett Mattingly, *Renaissance Diplomacy* (1988).

Harry A. Miskimin, *The Economy of Early Renaissance Europe, 1300–1460* (1975).

———, *The Economy of Later Renaissance Europe, 1460–1600* (1977).

J. G. A. Pocock, *The Machiavellian Moment: Florentine Political Thought and the Atlantic Republican Tradition* (1975).

John Stephens, *The Italian Renaissance: The Origins of Intellectual and Artistic Change before the Reformation* (1990).

Hugh Thomas, *The Conquest of Mexico* (1993).

Chapter 3. The Two Reformations

Cornelis Augustijn, *Erasmus: His Life, Works, and Influence* (1991).

Philip Benedict, *Christ's Churches Purely Reformed: A Social History of Calvinism* (2002).

William J. Bouwsma, *John Calvin: A Sixteenth-Century Portrait* (1987).

Euan Cameron, *The European Reformation* (1991).

Anwar Chejne, *Islam and the West: The Moriscos: A Cultural and Social History* (1983).

William A. Christian, Jr., *Local Religion in Sixteenth-Century Spain* (1981).

A. G. Dickens, *The English Reformation* (1989).

Carlos Eire, *From Madrid to Purgatory: The Art and Craft of Dying in Sixteenth-Century Spain* (1995).

———, *War Against the Idol: The Reformation of Worship from Erasmus to Calvin* (1986).

Ronnie Po-Chia Hsia, *Social Discipline in the Reformation: Central Europe, 1550–1750* (1989).

———, *Society and Religion in Munster, 1535–1618* (1984).

Lisa Jardine, *Erasmus, Man of Letters: The Construction of Charisma in Print* (1993).

David Kirby, *Northern Europe in the Early Modern Period: The Baltic World, 1492–1772* (1990).

Sherrin Marshall, ed., *Women in Reformation and Counter-Reformation Europe: Public and Private Worlds* (1989).

Bernd Moeller, *Imperial Cities and the Reformation* (1982).

John W. O'Malley, *Trent and All That: Renaming Catholicism in the Early Modern Period* (2000).

Steven E. Ozment, *Flesh and Spirit: Private Life in Early Modern Germany* (1999).

————, *The Reformation in the Cities: The Appeal of Protestantism to Sixteenth-Century Germany and Switzerland* (1975).

————, *When Fathers Ruled: Family Life in Reformation Europe* (1983).

Eugene R. Rice, Jr., and Anthony Grafton, *The Foundations of Early Modern Europe 1460–1559* (1994).

Thomas Robisheaux, *Rural Society and the Search for Order in Early Modern Germany* (1989).

Robert W. Scribner, *For the Sake of Simple Folk: Popular Propaganda for the German Reformation* (1984).

Lewis Spitz, *The Protestant Reformation* (1987).

Keith Thomas, *Religion and the Decline of Magic* (1971).

Tessa Watt, *Cheap Print and Popular Piety, 1550–1640* (1991).

Merry E. Weisner, *Women and Gender in Early Modern Europe* (1993).

CHAPTER 4. THE WARS OF RELIGION

Susan Dwyer Amussen, *An Ordered Society: Gender and Class in Early Modern England* (1988).

Stuart Clarke, *Thinking with Demons: The Idea of Witchcraft in Early Modern Europe* (1997).

Natalie Zemon Davis, *The Gift in Sixteenth-Century France* (2000).

————, *The Return of Martin Guerre* (1983).

Eamon Duffy, *The Voices of Morebath: Reformation and Rebellion in an English Village* (2001).

J. H. Elliott, *Europe Divided, 1559–1598* (1968).

Bruce Gordon, *The Swiss Reformation* (2002).

Mark Greengrass, *France in the Age of Henry IV: The Struggle for Stability* (1995).

Brad S. Gregory, *Christian Martyrdom in Early Modern Europe* (1999).

R. J. Knecht, *Francis I* (1992).

————, *The French Civil Wars* (2000).

Geoffrey Parker, *Europe in Crisis, 1598–1648* (1979).

Geoffrey Parker, ed., *The Thirty Years' War* (1988).

N. M. Sutherland, *The Massacre of St. Bartholomew and the European Conflict, 1559–1572* (1973).

CHAPTER 5. THE RISE OF THE ATLANTIC ECONOMY: SPAIN AND ENGLAND

Ralph Davis, *The Rise of the Atlantic Economies* (1973).

Jan De Vries, *The Economy of Europe in an Age of Crisis, 1600–1750* (1978).

J. H. Elliott, *The Count-Duke of Olivares: The Statesman in an Age of Decline* (1987).

————, *Imperial Spain, 1469–1714* (1964).

G. R. Elton, *England Under the Tudors* (1991).

Felipe Fernandez-Armesto, *The Spanish Armada: The Experience of War in 1588* (1989).

John Guy, *Tudor England* (1988).

Henry Kamen, *Spain's Road to Empire: The Making of a World Power, 1492–1763* (2002).

John Lynch, *Spain, 1516–1598* (1994).

———, *Spain under the Habsburgs, 1516–1700* (2 vols., 1964–1969).

Colin Martin and Geoffrey Parker, *The Spanish Armada* (1988).

Geoffrey Parker, *The Grand Strategy of Philip II* (2000).

———, *Philip II* (1978).

Carla Rahn Philips, *Galleons for the King of Spain* (1986).

Immanuel Wallerstein, *The Modern World System* (1974).

Penry Williams, *The Tudor Regime* (1979).

Joyce Youings, *Sixteenth-Century England* (1984).

CHAPTER 6. ENGLAND AND THE DUTCH REPUBLIC IN THE SEVENTEENTH CENTURY

Bruce R. Galloway, *The Union of England and Scotland, 1603–1608* (1986).

Pieter Geyl, *The Revolt of the Netherlands, 1555–1609* (1966).

Christopher Hill, *God's Englishman: Oliver Cromwell and the English Revolution* (1975).

———, *The World Turned Upside Down* (1972).

Derek Hirst, *Authority and Conflict: England, 1603–1658* (1986).

Ronald Hutton, *The British Republic, 1649–1660* (1990).

Jonathan I. Israel, *The Dutch Republic: Its Rise, Greatness, and Fall, 1477–1806* (1995).

J. R. Jones, *The Revolution of 1688 in England* (1972).

Mark Kishlansky, *A Monarchy Transformed: Britain, 1603–1714* (1996).

Peter Laslett, *The World We Have Lost: England before the Industrial Age* (1983).

Brian P. Levack, *The Formation of the British State: England, Scotland, and the Union, 1603–1707* (1987).

John Morrill, *The Revolt of the Provinces: Conservatism and Revolution in the English Civil War, 1630–1650* (1980).

Geoffrey Parker, *The Army of Flanders and the Spanish Road, 1567–1659* (1972).

J. L. Price, *Culture and Society in the Dutch Republic during the Seventeenth Century* (1974).

Conrad Russell, *The Causes of the English Civil War* (1990).

Simon Schama, *An Embarrassment of Riches: An Interpretation of Dutch Culture in the Golden Age* (1988).

J. A. Sharpe, *Early Modern England: A Social History, 1550–1760* (1990).

Kevin Sharpe, *The Personal Rule of Charles I* (1995).

Lawrence Stone, *The Causes of the English Revolution, 1629–1642* (1990).

———, *The Crisis of the Aristocracy, 1558–1641* (1967).

David Underdown, *Fire from Heaven: Life in an English Town in the Seventeenth Century* (1992).

———, *Revel, Riot, and Rebellion: Popular Politics and Culture in England, 1603–1660* (1985).

Keith Wrightson, *Earthly Necessities: Economic Lives in Early Modern Britain* (2000).

———, *English Society, 1550–1760* (1982).

CHAPTER 7. THE AGE OF ABSOLUTISM, 1650–1720

Perry Anderson, *Lineages of the Absolutist State* (1974).

William Beik, *Absolutism and Society in Seventeenth-Century France: State Power and Provincial Aristocracy in Languedoc* (1985).

Joseph Bergin, *Cardinal Richelieu: Power and the Pursuit of Wealth* (1985).

Paul Bushkovitch, *Peter the Great* (2001).

James B. Collins, *The State in Early Modern France* (2001).

J. H. Elliott, *Richelieu and Olivares* (1984).

Richard J. Evans, *The Making of the Habsburg Empire, 1550–1770* (1979).

Pierre Goubert, *Louis XIV and Twenty Million Frenchmen* (1972).

Ragnhild Hatton, *Europe in the Age of Louis XIV* (1979).

Sharon Kettering, *French Society, 1589–1715* (2001).

Robert Mandrou, *Introduction to Modern France, 1500–1640* (1975).

Roland Mousnier, *Peasant Uprisings in Seventeenth-Century France, Russia, and China* (1970).

David Parker, *The Making of French Absolutism* (1983).

Theodore Rabb, *The Struggle for Stability in Early Modern Europe* (1975).

Orest Ranum, *The Fronde: A French Revolution* (1993).

———, *Paris in the Age of Absolutism* (2003).

Nicholas Riasanovsky, *The Image of Peter the Great in Russian History and Thought* (1985).

CHAPTER 8. THE NEW PHILOSOPHY OF SCIENCE

Herbert Butterfield, *The Origins of Modern Science, 1300–1800* (1965).

John Fauvel, Raymond Flood, Michael Shortland, and Robin Wilson, eds., *Let Newton Be! A New Perspective on His Life and Works* (1988).

A. R. Hall, *The Revolution in Science, 1500–1750: The Formation of the Modern Scientific Attitude* (1983)

Margaret Jacobs, *The Cultural Meaning of the Scientific Revolution* (1988).

Hugh Kearney, *Science and Change, 1500–1700* (1971).

Alexandre Koyr, *The Formation of the Modern Scientific Attitude* (1983).

T. S. Kuhn, *The Structure of Scientific Revolution* (1989).

Robert K. Merton, *Science, Technology, and Society in Seventeenth-Century England* (1970).

Londa Schiebinger, *The Mind Has No Sex? Women and the Origins of Modern Science* (1990).

R. S. Westfall, *Never at Rest: A Biography of Issac Newton* (1993).

B. H. G. Wormald, *Francis Bacon: History, Politics, and Science, 1561–1626* (1993).

CHAPTER 9. ENLIGHTENED THOUGHT AND THE REPUBLIC OF LETTERS

Keith Baker, *Inventing the French Revolution: Essays in the Political Culture of Eighteenth-Century France* (1990).

Roger Chartier, *The Cultural Origins of the French Revolution* (1991).

Maurice Cranston, *The Noble Savage: Jean-Jacques Rousseau, 1754–1762* (1991).

———, *Philosophers and Pamphleteers: Political Theorists of the Enlightenment* (1986).

Thomas E. Crow, *Painters and Public Life in Eighteenth-Century Paris* (1985).

Robert Darnton, *The Business of Enlightenment* (1979).

———, *The Great Cat Massacre* (1985).

———, *The Literary Underground of the Old Regime* (1985).

Peter Gay, *The Enlightenment: An Interpretation* (2 vols., 1966–1969).

———, *Voltaire's Politics: The Poet as Realist* (1988).

Dena Goodman, *The Republic of Letters: A Cultural History of the French Enlightenment* (1984).

Norman Hampson, *A Cultural History of the Enlightenment* (1969).

Carla Hesse, *The Other Enlightenment: How French Women Became Modern* (2001).

Darrin M. McMahon, *Enemies of the Enlightenment: Anti-Philosophes and the Birth of the French Far Right, 1778–1830* (1998).

J. M. McManners, *Death and Enlightenment: Changing Attitudes to Death among Christians and Unbelievers in Eighteenth-Century France* (1982).

Roy Porter and Mikulás Teich, eds., *The Enlightenment in National Context* (1981).

Franco Venturi, *Italy and the Enlightenment: Studies in a Cosmopolitan Century* (1972).

CHAPTER 10. EIGHTEENTH-CENTURY ECONOMIC AND SOCIAL CHANGE

M. S. Anderson, *Europe in the Eighteenth Century, 1713–1783* (1982).

C. A. Bayly, *Imperial Meridian: The British Empire and the World, 1780–1830* (1989).

David A. Bell, *The Cult of the Nation in France: Inventing Nationalism, 1680–1800* (2001).

Maxine Berg, *The Age of Manufacturers, 1700–1820: Industry, Innovation, and Work in Britain* (1985).

Peter Borsay, *The English Urban Renaissance: Culture and Society in the Provincial Town, 1660–1770* (1989).

P. J. Corfield, *The Impact of English Towns, 1700–1800* (1982).

Douglas Hay et al., *Albion's Fatal Tree: Crime and Punishment in Eighteenth-Century England* (1975).

Steven L. Kaplan, *Provisioning Paris: Merchants and Millers in the Grain and Flour Trade during the Eighteenth Century* (1984).

Emmanuel LeRoy Ladurie, *The Peasants of Languedoc* (1974).

Paul Langford, *A Polite and Commercial People: England, 1727–1783* (1989).

G. E. Mingay, *Land and Society in England, 1750–1980* (1994).

J. H. Parry, *Trade and Dominion: The European Overseas Empires in the Eighteenth Century* (1971).

Roy Porter, *English Society in the Eighteenth Century* (1986).

George Rudé, *Paris and London in the Eighteenth Century* (1971).

Bernard Semmel, *The Methodist Revolution* (1973).

Lawrence Stone, *The Family, Sex, and Marriage in England, 1500–1800* (1977).

E. P. Thompson, *Whigs and Hunters: The Origins of the Black Act* (1975).

Isser Woloch, *Eighteenth-Century Europe: Tradition and Progress, 1715–1789* (1982).

CHAPTER 11. EIGHTEENTH-CENTURY DYNASTIC RIVALRIES AND POLITICS

Paul Avrich, *Russian Rebels, 1600–1800* (1972).

Bernard Bailyn, *The Ideological Origins of the American Revolution* (1992).

C. B. A. Behrens, *The Ancien Régime* (1967).

———, *Society, Government, and the Enlightenment: The Experiences of Eighteenth-Century France and Prussia* (1985).

David Bell, *Lawyers and Citizens: The Making of a Political Elite in Old Regime France* (1994).

John Brewer, *Party Ideology and Popular Politics at the Accession of George III* (1976).

———, *The Sinews of Power: War, Money, and the English State, 1688–1783* (1989).

J. C. D. Clark, *English Society, 1688–1832* (1985).

Linda Colley, *Britons: Forging the Nation, 1707–1837* (1992).

———, *In Defiance of Oligarchy: The Tory Party, 1714–1760* (1982).

Olwen Hufton, *The Poor of Eighteenth-Century France, 1750–1789* (1974).

Isabel de Madariaga, *Catherine the Great: A Short History* (1990).

Sara Maza, *Private Lives and Public Affairs: The Causes Celebres of Prerevolutionary France* (1993).

Neil McKendrick, John Brewer, and J. H. Plumb, *The Birth of a Consumer Society: The Commercialization of Eighteenth-Century England* (1982).

Edmund Sears Morgan, *Benjamin Franklin* (2003).

———, *The Birth of the Republic, 1763–1789* (1977).

Daniel Roche, *The People of Paris* (1987).

Robert M. Schwartz, *Policing the Poor in Eighteenth-Century France* (1988).

Wayne Te Brake, *Regents and Rebels: The Revolutionary World of an Eighteenth-Century Dutch City* (1989).

Franco Venturi, *The End of the Old Regime in Europe, 1776–1789* (2 vols., 1991).

Ernst Wangermann, *The Austrian Achievement, 1700–1800* (1973).

CHAPTER 12. THE FRENCH REVOLUTION

Nigel Aston, *Religion and Revolution in France, 1780–1804* (2000).

Jean-Paul Bertaud, *The Army of the French Revolution: From Citizen-Soldiers to Instrument of Power* (1988).

T. C. W. Blanning, *The French Revolutionary Wars, 1787–1802* (1996).

Jack R. Censer, *The French Press in the Age of Enlightenment* (1994).

Richard Cobb, *The Police and the People: French Popular Protest, 1789–1820* (1972).

Wiliam Doyle, *Origins of the French Revolution* (1988).

Marianne Elliott, *Partners in Revolution: The United Irishmen and France* (1982).

Alan Forrest, *Conscripts and Deserters: The Army and French Society during the Revolution and Empire* (1989).

———, *The French Revolution and the Poor* (1981).

Francois Furet, *Interpreting the French Revolution* (1992).

David Garrioch, *The Making of Revolutionary Paris* (2002).

Dominique Godineau, *The Women of Paris and Their French Revolution* (1998).

Carla Hesse, *Publishing and Cultural Politics in Revolutionary Paris, 1789–1810* (1991).

Patrice Higonnet, *Sister Republics: the Origins of French and American Republicanism* (1988).

Lynn Hunt, *The Family Romance of the French Revolution* (1992).

———, *Politics, Culture, and Class in the French Revolution* (1984).

Peter Jones, *The Peasantry in the French Revolution* (1988).

Georges Lefebvre, *The Coming of the French Revolution* (1989).

Ted W. Margadant, *Urban Rivalries in the French Revolution* (1992).

Peter McPhee, *The French Revolution, 1789–1799* (2002).

Sarah E. Meltzer and Leslie W. Rabine, eds., *Rebel Daughters: Women and the French Revolution* (1989).

Mona Ozouf, *Festivals and the French Revolution* (1988).

R. R. Palmer, *The Age of the Democratic Revolution: A Political History of Europe and America, 1760–1800* (2 vols., 1959–1964).

———, *Twelve Who Ruled: The Year of the Terror in the French Revolution* (1989).

Jeremy D. Popkin, *Revolutionary News: The Press in France, 1789–1799* (1990).

Georges Rudé, *The Great Fear of 1789* (1973).

William H. Sewell, Jr., *A Rhetoric of Bourgeois Revolution: the Abbé Sieyès and "What is the Third Estate?"* (1994).

Donald Sutherland, *France, 1789–1815: Revolution and Counterrevolution* (1986).

Timothy Tackett, *Religion, Revolution, and Regional Culture in Eighteenth-Century France: The Ecclesiastical Oath of 1791* (1986).

———, *When the King Took Flight* (2003).

Charles Tilly, *The Vendée* (1964).

Isser Woloch, *The New Regime: Transformations of the French Civic Order, 1789–1820s* (1994).

CHAPTER 13. NAPOLEON AND EUROPE

Louis Bergeron, *France under Napoleon* (1981).

Michael Broers, *Europe under Napoleon* (1996).

————, *The Politics of Religion in Napoleonic Italy: The War against God, 1801–1814* (2002).

Steven Englund, *Napoleon: A Political Life* (2004).

J. Christopher Herold, *The Age of Napoleon* (1985).

Felix Markham, *Napoleon* (1963).

Gunther Rothenberg, *The Art of Warfare in the Age of Napoleon* (1978).

Alan Schom, *One Hundred Days: Napoleon's Road to Waterloo* (1992).

Jakob Walter, *The Diary of a Napoleonic Foot Soldier* (1991).

Stuart Wolfe, *Napoleon's Integration of Europe* (1991).

D. G. Wright, *Napoleon and Europe* (1984).

CHAPTER 14. THE INDUSTRIAL REVOLUTION, 1800–1850

W. L. Blackwell, *The Beginnings of Russian Industrialization, 1800–1860* (1968).

Michel Foucault, *Madness and Civilization* (1973).

W. O. Henderson, *The Industrialization of Europe, 1780–1914* (1970).

Colin Heywood, *Childhood in Nineteenth-Century France: Work, Health, and Education among the Classes Populaires* (1988).

E. J. Hobsbawm, *The Age of Extremes: The Short Twentieth Century, 1914–1991* (1994).

E. J. Hobsbawm and George Rudé, *Captain Swing* (1975).

Gareth Stedman Jones, *Languages of Class: Studies in English Working-Class History* (1983).

David J. V. Jones, *Rebecca's Children: A Study of Rural Society, Crime, and Protest* (1989).

David Landes, *The Unbound Prometheus: Technological Change and Industrial Development in Western Europe from 1750 to the Present* (1976).

Lynn Hollen Lees, *Exiles of Erin: Irish Migrants to Victorian London* (1979).

David McLellan, *Karl Marx: His Life and Thought* (1977).

John M. Merriman, *The Margins of City Life: Explorations on the French Urban Frontier, 1815–1851* (1991).

Joel Mokyr, *The Gift of Athena* (2003).

Claire Goldberg Moses, *French Feminism in the Nineteenth Century* (1984).

John Roach, *History of Secondary Education in England, 1800–1870* (1987).

William H. Sewell, Jr., *Work and Revolution in France: the Language of Labor from the Old Regime to 1848* (1980).

E. P. Thompson, *The Making of the English Working Class* (1963).

Louise A. Tilly and Joan W. Scott, *Women, Work, and Family* (1978).

Clive Trebilcock, *The Industrialization of the Continental Powers, 1780–1914* (1989).

CHAPTER 15. CHALLENGES TO RESTORATION EUROPE: THE MIDDLE CLASSES IN THE AGE OF LIBERALISM

Michael Brock, *Great Reform Act* (1973).

Clive H. Church, *1830 in Europe: Revolution and Political Change* (1983).

Gordon A. Craig, *The Triumph of Liberalism: Zurich in the Golden Age, 1830–1869* (1988).

Leonore Davidoff and Catherine Hall, *Family Fortunes: Men and Women of the English Middle Class, 1780–1850* (1991).

Friedrich Engels, *The Condition of the Working Class in England* (1993).

Eric J. Evans, *Britain before the Reform Act: Politics and Society, 1815–1832* (1989).

Norman Gash, *Aristocracy and People: Britain, 1815–1865* (1979).

Hugh Honour, *Romanticism* (1979).

Clara M. Lovett, *The Democratic Movement in Italy, 1830–1876* (1982).

R. J. Morris, *Class, Sect and Party: The Making of the British Middle Class: Leeds, 1820–1850* (1990).

Harold Perkin, *The Origins of Modern English Society, 1780–1880* (1972).

Pamela M. Pilbeam, *The Middle Classes in Europe, 1789–1914: France, Germany, Italy and Russia* (1990).

Leon Plantinga, *Romantic Music: A History of Musical Style in Nineteenth-Century Europe* (1984).

Barbara Taylor, *Eve and the New Jerusalem: Socialism and Feminism in the Nineteenth Century* (1983).

Dror Wahrman, *Imagining the Middle Class: The Political Representation of Class in Britain, c. 1780–1840* (1995).

William Weber, *Music and the Middle Class: The Social Structure of Concert Life in London, Paris and Vienna* (1975).

CHAPTER 16. THE REVOLUTIONS OF 1848

Maurice Agulhon, *The Republican Experiment, 1848–1852* (1983).

T. J. Clark, *The Absolute Bourgeois: Artists and Politics in France, 1848–1851* (1973).

István Deák, *The Lawful Revolution: Louis Kossuth and the Hungarians, 1848–1849* (1979).

Ted W. Margadant, *French Peasants in Revolt: The Insurrection of 1851* (1979).

John M. Merriman, *The Agony of the Republic: The Repression of the Left in Revolutionary France, 1848–1851* (1978).

Peter McPhee, *The Politics of Rural Life: Political Mobilization in the French Countryside, 1845–1852* (1992).

Jonathan Sperber, *The European Revolutions, 1848–1851* (1993).

———, *Rhineland Radicals: The Democratic Movement and the Revolution of 1848–1849* (1991).

CHAPTER 17. THE ERA OF NATIONAL UNIFICATION

David Blackbourn and Geoff Eley, *The Peculiarities of German History: Bourgeois Society and Politics in Nineteenth-Century German History* (1984).

István Deák, *Beyond Nationalism: A Social History of the Habsburg Officer Corps, 1848–1918* (1990).

Lothar Gall, *Bismarck: The White Revolutionary* (2 vols., 1986).

Denis Mack Smith, *Cavour* (1985).

———, *Cavour and Garibaldi, 1860: A Study of Political Conflict* (1985).

———, *Victor Emanuel, Cavour, and the Risorgimento* (1971).

Lucy Riall, *Sicily and the Unification of Italy* (1998).

Adrien Shubert, *A Social History of Modern Spain* (1990).

Helmut Smith, *German Nationalism and Religious Conflict: Culture, Ideology, Politics, 1870–1914* (1995).

Fritz Stern, *Gold and Iron: Bismarck, Bleichröeder, and the Building of the German Empire* (1977).

CHAPTER 18. THE DOMINANT POWERS IN THE AGE OF LIBERALISM: BRITAIN, RUSSIA, AND FRANCE

Robert Anderson, *Education and Opportunity in Victorian Scotland* (1983).

Abraham Ascher, *The Revolution of 1905* (2 vols., 1992).

Jeffrey A. Auerbach, *The Great Exposition of 1851: A Nation on Display* (1999).

Edward Berenson, *The Trial of Madame Caillaux* (1992).

Victoria E. Bonnell, *Roots of Rebellion: Workers' Politics and Organizations in St. Petersburg and Moscow, 1900–1914* (1983).

Asa Briggs, *Victorian Cities* (1977).

———, *Victorian People* (1954).

Jeffrey Brooks, *When Russia Learned to Read: Literacy and Popular Literature, 1861–1917* (1985).

Michael Burns, *Dreyfus: A Family Affair, 1789–1945* (1992).

David Cannadine, *The Decline and Fall of the British Aristocracy* (1990).

H. J. Dyos and Michael Wolff, *The Victorian City: Images and Realities* (2 vols., 1983).

Michael Freeman, *Railways and the Victorian Imagination* (1999).

Norman Gash, *Aristocracy and People: Britain, 1815–1865* (1979).

David M. Goldfrank, *The Origins of the Crimean War* (1994).

Sudhir Hazareesingh, *From Subject to Citizen: The Second Empire and the Emergence of Modern French Democracy* (1998).

Gertrude Himmelfarb, *Poverty and Compassion: The Moral Indignation of the Late Victorians* (1991).

E. J. Hobsbawm, *The Age of Capital, 1848–1875* (1976).

Steven L. Hoch, *Serfdom and Social Control in Russia: Petrovskoe, a Village in Tambov* (1986).

Walter Houghton, *The Victorian Frame of Mind* (1957).

Michael Howard, *The Franco-Prussian War: The German Invasion of France, 1870–1871* (1981).

Paula Hyman, *From Dreyfus to Vichy: The Remaking of French Jewry, 1906–1939* (1979).

William Irvine, *The Boulanger Affair Reconsidered: Royalism Boulangism, and the Origins of the Radical Right in France* (1989).

Gareth Stedman Jones, *Languages of Class: Studies in English Working Class History, 1832–1982* (1983).

G. Kitson Clark, *The Making of Victorian England* (1962).

James F. McMillan, *Napoleon III* (1991).

Alain Plessis, *The Rise and Fall of the Second Empire, 1852–1871* (1985).

Roger Price, *The French Second Empire: An Anatomy of Political Power* (2001).

Norman Rich, *The Age of Nationalism and Reform, 1850–1890* (1970).

Bertrand Semmel, *John Stuart Mill and the Pursuit of Virtue* (1984).

Alan Sked, *The Decline and Fall of the Habsburg Empire* (1989).

F. M. L. Thompson, *The Rise of Respectable Society, 1830–1900* (1986).

Robert Tombs, *The War Against Paris, 1871* (1981).

Frank M. Turner, *John Henry Newman: The Challenge to Evangelical Religion* (2002).

Martha Vicinus, *Suffer and Be Still: Women in the Victorian Age* (1973).

Eugen Weber, *Peasants into Frenchmen: The Modernization of Rural France, 1870–1914* (1986).

Steven Wilson, *Ideology and Experience: Anti-Semitism in France at the Time of the Dreyfus Affair* (1982).

G. M. Young, *Portrait of an Age: Victorian England* (1980).

Theodore Zeldin, *The Political System of Napoleon III* (1971).

Reginald E. Zelnick, *Labor and Society in Tsarist Russia: The Factory Workers of St. Petersburg, 1855–1870* (1971).

CHAPTER 19. RAPID INDUSTRIALIZATION AND ITS CHALLENGES, 1870–1914

Lenard Berlanstein, ed., *Rethinking Labor History* (1993).

David Blackbourn, *Margingen: Apparitions of the Virgin Mary in Bismarckian Germany* (1993).

Alain Corbin, *Women for Hire: Prostitution and Sexuality in France after 1850* (1990).

David F. Crew, *Town on the Ruhr: A Social History of Bochum, 1860–1914* (1979).

Geoffrey Crossick and Heinz-Gerhard Haupt, ed., *Shopkeepers and Master Artisans in Nineteenth-Century Europe* (1984).

Nancy Green, *The Pletzl of Paris: Jewish Immigrant Workers in the Belle Époque* (1986).

Ruth Harris, *Lourdes: Body and Spirit in the Secular Age* (1999).

Paul M. Hohenberg and Lynn Hollen Lees, *The Making of Urban Europe, 1000–1950* (1985).

David P. Jordan, *Transforming Paris: The Life and Labors of Baron Haussmann* (1995).

Thomas A. Kselman, *Miracles and Prophecies in Nineteenth-Century France* (1983).

Thomas Laqueur, *Religion and Respectability: Sunday Schools and Working-Class Culture, 1780–1850* (1976).

William C. Lubenow, *Parliamentary Politics and the Home Rule Crisis* (1988).

John Lukacs, *Budapest, 1900: A Historical Portrait of a City and Its Culture* (1988).

Mary Jo Maynes, *Taking the Hard Road: Life Course in French and German Workers' Autobiographies in the Era of Industrialization* (1995).

Michael B. Miller, *The Bon Marché: Bourgeois Culture and the Department Store, 1869–1920* (1981).

Alan S. Milward and S. B. Saul, *The Development of the Economies of Continental Europe, 1850–1914* (1977).

Leslie Moch, *Moving Europeans: Migration in Western Europe since 1650* (1993).

Donald Reid, *Paris Sewers and Sewermen: Realities and Representations* (1991).

Jonathan Schneer, *London, 1900: The Imperial Metropolis* (1999).

Bonnie G. Smith, *Ladies of the Leisure Class: The Bourgeoises of Northern France in the Nineteenth Century* (1982).

Gareth Stedman Jones, *Outcast London: A Study in the Relations between Classes in Victorian Society* (1992).

Frank M. Turner, *John Henry Newman: The Challenge to Evangelical Religion* (2002).

Judith R. Walkowitz, *Prostitution and Victorian Society: Women, Class, and the State* (1983).

CHAPTER 20. POLITICAL AND CULTURAL RESPONSES TO A RAPIDLY CHANGING WORLD

Steven E. Aschheim, *The Nietzsche Legacy in Germany, 1890–1990* (1992).

Laura Engelstein, *The Keys to Happiness: Sex and the Search for Modernity in Fin-de-Siècle Russia* (1992).

Peter Gay, *Freud: A Life for Our Time* (1988).

Ruth Gay, *The Jews of Germany: A Historical Portrait* (1992).

Steven C. Hause and Anne R. Kenney, *Women's Suffrage and Social Politics in the French Third Republic* (1984).

E. H. Hunt, *British Labour History, 1815–1914* (1981).

James Joll, *The Anarchists* (1981).

John M. Merriman, *The Red City: Limoges and the French Nineteenth Century* (1991).

Peter G. Pulzer, *The Rise of Political Anti-Semitism in Germany and Austria* (1988).

Charles Rearick, *Pleasures of the Belle Époque* (1985).

Carl E. Schorske, *Fin-de-Siècle Vienna: Politics and Culture* (1980).

Jerrold Seigel, *Bohemian Paris: Culture, Politics, and the Boundaries of Bourgeois Life, 1830–1930* (1986).

Roger Shattuck, *The Banquet Years: The Origins of the Avant-Garde in France 1885 to World War I* (1988).

Debora L. Silverman, *Art Nouveau in Fin-de-Siècle France: Politics, Psychology, and Style* (1989).

Mikulás Teich and Roy Porter, eds., *Fin-de-Siècle and Its Legacy* (1990).

Eugen Weber, *France, Fin-de-Siècle* (1986).

CHAPTER 21. THE AGE OF EUROPEAN IMPERIALISM

Imran Ali, *The Punjab under Imperialism* (1988).

W. Baumgart, *Imperialism: The Idea and Reality of British and French Colonial Expansion 1880–1914* (1982).

Raymond Betts, *The False Dawn: European Imperialism in the Nineteenth Century* (1975).

Henri Brunschwig, *French Colonialism, 1871–1914: Myths and Realities* (1966).

David Cannadine, *Orientalism: How the British Saw Their Empire* (2001).

Richard Drayton, *Nature's Government: Science, Imperial Britain and the "Improvement" of the World* (2000).

Adam Hochschild, *King Leopold's Ghost: A Story of Greed, Terror, and Heroism in Colonial Africa* (1998).

Alan Hodgart, *The Economics of European Imperialism* (1977).

Dane Kennedy, *Hill Stations and the British Raj* (1996).

———, *Islands of White: Settler Society and Culture in Kenya and South Rhodesia, 1890–1939* (1987).

Patricia M. E. Lorcin, *Imperial Identities: Stereotyping, Prejudice and Race in Colonial Algeria* (1995).

Timothy Mitchell, *Colonizing Egypt* (1988).

Bernard Porter, *The Lion's Share: A Short History of British Imperialism, 1850–1983* (1984).

Ronald Robinson, John Gallagher, and Alice Denny, *Africa and the Victorians* (1981).

Edward Said, *Orientalism* (1979).

Megan Vaughan, *Curing Their Ills: Colonial Power and African Illness* (1991).

Gwendolyn Wright, *The Politics of Design in French Colonial Urbanism* (1991).

Chapter 22. The Great War

Stéphane Audoin-Rouzeau, *Men at War, 1914–1918: National Sentiment and Trench Journalism in France during the First World War* (1992).

Jean-Jacques Becker, *The Great War and the French People* (1985).

Margaret H. Darrow, *French Women and the First World War: War Stories of the Home Front* (2000).

Modris Eksteins, *Rites of Spring: The Great War and the Birth of the Modern Age* (1989).

Niall Ferguson, *The Pity of War: Explaining World War I* (1999).

Paul Fussel, *The Great War and Modern Memory* (1975).

Peter Gatrell, *A Whole Empire Walking: Refugees in Russia during World War I* (1999).

Ross Gregory, *The Origins of American Intervention in the First World War* (1971).

David G. Herrmann, *The Arming of Europe and the Making of the First World War* (1996).

Alister Horne, *The Price of Glory: Verdun, 1916* (1963).

Michael Howard, *The First World War* (2002).

Samuel Hynes, *A War Imagined: The First World War and English Culture* (1990).

James Joll, *The Origins of the First World War* (1992).

John Keegan, *The First World War* (1998).

George F. Kennan, *The Fateful Alliance: France, Russia, and the Coming of the First War* (1992).

Paul Kennedy, *The Rise of Anglo-German Antagonism, 1860–1914* (1980).

Vejas G. Liulevicius, *War Land on the Eastern Front: Culture, National Identity and German Occupation in World War I* (2000).

Lyn Macdonald, *1915: The Death of Innocence* (1993).

——, *Somme* (1983).

Arthur Marwick, *The Deluge: British Society and the First World War* (1966).

——, *Women at War, 1914–1918* (1977).

Justin McCarthy, *The Ottoman People and the End of Empire* (2001).

George Robb, *British Culture and the First World War* (2002).

Kenneth Silver, *Esprit de Corps: Avant-Garde Art and the First World War in France* (1990).

Leonard V. Smith, *Between Mutiny and Obedience: The Case of the French Fifth Infantry Division during World War I* (1994).

Leonard V. Smith, Stéphane Audoin-Rouzeau, and Annette Becker, *France and the Great War* (2002).

Nigel Steel and Peter Hart, *Passchendaele: The Sacrificial Ground* (2000).

James Stokesbury, *A Short History of World War I* (1981).

Norman Stone, *The Eastern Front, 1914–1917* (1998).

John W. Wheeler-Bennett, *Brest-Litovsk: The Forgotten Peace* (1971).

J. M. Winter, *The Great War and the British People* (1986).

——, *Sites of Memory, Sites of Mourning: The Great War in European Cultural History* (1995).

J. M. Winter and Jean-Louis Robert, *Capital Cities at War: Paris, London, Berlin, 1914–1919* (1997).

CHAPTER 23. REVOLUTIONARY RUSSIA AND THE SOVIET UNION

Abraham Ascher, *The Revolution of 1905* (2 vols., 1992).

Paul Avrich, *Kronstadt, 1921* (1991).

Victoria E. Bonnell, *Roots of Rebellion: Workers' Politics and Organizations in St. Petersburg and Moscow, 1900–1914* (1983).

Robert Conquest, *The Great Terror: A Reassessment* (1990).

R. W. Davies, Mark Harrison, and S. G. Wheatcroft, eds., *The Transformation of the Soviet Union, 1913–1945* (1994).

Terence Emmons, *The Formation of Political Parties and the First National Elections in Russia* (1983).

Orlando Figes, *Peasant Russia, Civil War* (1989).

Sheila Fitzpatrick, *Everyday Stalinism: Ordinary Life in Extraordinary Times: Soviet Russia in the 1930s* (1999).

——, *The Russian Revolution, 1917–1932* (1982).

Tsuyoshi Hasegawa, *The February Revolution: Petrograd, 1917* (1981).

Peter Holquist, *Making War, Forging Revolution: Russia's Continuum of Crisis, 1914–1921* (2002).

Geoffrey Hosking, *The First Socialist Society: A History of the Soviet Union from Within* (1993).

John L. H. Keep, *The Russian Revolution: A Study in Mass Mobilization* (1976).

Diane Koenker, *Moscow Workers and the 1917 Russian Revolution* (1982).

Stephen Kotkin, *Magnetic Mountain: Stalinism as a Civilization* (1995).

W. Bruce Lincoln, *Red Victory: A History of the Russian Civil War, 1918–1921* (1999).

Richard Pipes, *Russia under the Bolshevik Regime* (1994).

Alexander Rabinowitch, *The Bolsheviks Come to Power: The Revolution of 1917 in Petrograd* (1978).

William G. Rosenberg, *Liberals in the Russian Revolution: The Constitutional Democratic Party, 1917–1921* (1974).

S. A. Smith, *Red Petrograd: Revolution in the Factories, 1917–1918* (1983).

Richard Stites, *Revolutionary Dreams: Utopian Vision and Experimental Life in the Russian Revolution* (1988).

CHAPTER 24. THE ELUSIVE SEARCH FOR STABILITY IN THE 1920s

R. J. B. Bosworth, *The Italian Dictatorship: Problems and Perspectives in the Interpretation of Mussolini and Fascism* (1998).

Victoria De Grazia, *How Fascism Ruled Women: Italy, 1922–1945* (1992).

Peter Gay, *My German Question: Growing up in Nazi Berlin* (1998).

———, *Weimar Culture: The Outsider as Insider* (1968).

Robert Graves, *Goodbye to All That* (1960).

Robert Graves and Alan Hodge, *The Long Week-End: A Social History of Great Britain, 1918–1939* (1963).

Adrian Gregory, *A Silence of Memory: Armistice Day, 1919–1946* (1994).

Pierre-Jakez Hélias, *The Horse of Pride: Life in a Breton Village* (1978).

Martin Kitchen, *Europe between the Wars: A Political History* (1988).

MacGregor Knox, *Mussolini Unleashed, 1939–1941: Politics and Strategy in Fascist Italy* (1982).

Richard F. Kuisel, *Capitalism and the State in Modern France* (1983).

Gregory M. Luebbert, *Liberalism, Fascism, or Social Democracy: Social Classes and the Political Origins of Regimes in Interwar Europe* (1991).

Denis Mack Smith, *Italy and Its Monarchy* (1989).

———, *Mussolini: A Biography* (1983).

Charles Maier, *Recasting Bourgeois Europe: Stabilization in France, Germany, and Italy in the Decade after World War I* (1975).

Sally Marks, *The Illusion of Peace: Europe's International Relations, 1918–1933* (1976).

Walter A. McDougall, *France's Rhineland Diplomacy, 1914–1924* (1978).

Detlev J. K. Peukert, *The Weimar Republic* (1989).

Antoine Prost, *In the Wake of War: "Les Ancien Combattants" and French Society* (1992).

Joseph Rothschild, *East Central Europe between the Two World Wars* (1974).

Steven A. Schuker, *The End of French Predominance in Europe: The Financial Crisis of 1924 and the Adoption of the Dawes Plan* (1976).

Alan Sharp, *The Versailles Settlement: Peacemaking in Paris* (1991).

Daniel J. Sherman, *The Construction of Memory in Interwar France* (1999).

Dan P. Silverman, *Reconstructing Europe after the Great War* (1982).

Robert Soucy, *Fascism in France: The First Wave, 1924–1933* (1986).

A. J. P. Taylor, *English History, 1914–1945* (1965).

Zerv Sternhell, *The Birth of a Fascist Ideology: From Cultural Rebellion to Political Revolution* (1994).

Mark Trachtenberg, *Reparation and World Politics* (1980).

CHAPTER 25. THE EUROPE OF DEPRESSION AND DICTATORSHIP

William Sheridan Allen, *The Nazi Seizure of Power: The Experience of a Single German Town, 1922–1945* (1984).

Pierre Azéma, *From Munich to the Liberation, 1938–1944* (1985).

George Baer, *Test Case: Italy, Ethiopia and the League of Nations* (1976).

Ivo Banac, *The National Question in Yugoslavia* (1985).

P. M. H. Bell, *The Origins of the Second World War* (1986).

Richard Bessel, ed., *Life in the Third Reich* (1987).

Karl Dietrich Bracher, *The German Dictatorship: The Origins, Structure, and Effects of National Socialism* (1970).

Gerald Brenan, *The Spanish Labyrinth: An Account of the Social and Political Background of the Civil War* (2001).

Michael Burleigh, *The Third Reich: A New History* (2000).

Jane Caplan, *Government without Administration: State and Civil Service in Weimar and Nazi Germany* (1988).

Helmut Gruber, *Red Vienna: Experiments in Working-Class Culture, 1919–1934* (1991).

H. Stuart Hughes, *Consciousness and Society: The Reorientation of European Social Thought, 1890–1930* (1979).

Gerald Jackson, *The Spanish Republic and the Civil War, 1931–1939* (1974).

Julian Jackson, *The Popular Front in France: Defending Democracy, 1934–1938* (1988).

Ian Kershaw, *Hitler* (2 vols., 1999–2000).

———, *The "Hitler Myth": Image and Reality in the Third Reich* (1991).

Charles Kindleberger, *The World in Depression, 1929–1939* (1986).

MacGregor Knox, *Common Destiny: Dictatorship, Foreign Policy and War in Fascist Italy and Nazi Germany* (2000).

Rudy Koshar, *Social Life, Local Politics, and Nazism: Marburg, 1880–1935* (1986).

David Clay Large, *Between Two Fires: Europe's Path in the 1930s* (1990).

Detlev J. K. Peukert, *Inside Nazi Germany: Conformity, Opposition, and Racism in Everyday Life* (1987).

George Orwell, *Homage to Catalonia* (1955).

Anthony Read and David Fisher, *The Deadly Embrace: Hitler, Stalin and the Nazi-Soviet Pact, 1939–1941* (1989).

Joachim Remak, *The Origins of the Second World War* (1979).

Robert Soucy, *Fascism in France: the Second Wave, 1933–1939* (1995).

Peter Stansky and William Abrahams, *Journey to the Frontier: Julian Bell and John Cornfield, Their Lives and the 1930s* (1966).

Fritz Stern, *The Politics of Cultural Despair: A Study in the Use of the Germanic Ideology* (1974).

Hugh Thomas, *The Spanish Civil War* (2001).

Henry A. Turner, Jr., *German Big Business and the Rise of Hitler* (1985).

———, *Hitler: Thirty Days to Power* (1996).

Eugen Weber, *France: The Hollow Years* (1995).

Gerhard L. Weinberg, *The Foreign Policy of Hitler's Germany: Diplomatic Revolution in Europe, 1933–1936* (1970).

———, *Starting World War II, 1937–1939* (1980).

Susan Zuccotti, *Under His Very Windows: The Vatican and the Holocaust* (2002).

CHAPTER 26. WORLD WAR II

Omer Bartov, *Hitler's Army: Soldiers, Nazis, and War in the Third Reich* (1992).

Marc Bloch, *Strange Defeat* (1968).

Sarah Farmer, *Martyred Village: Commemorating the 1944 Massacre at Oradour-sur-Glane* (1999).

Paul Fussell, *Wartime: Understanding and Behavior in the Second World War* (1989).

Robert Gellately, *Backing Hitler: Consent and Coercion in Nazi Germany* (2001).

———, *The Gestapo and German Society: Enforcing Racial Policy, 1933–1945* (1990).

Jan Tomasz Gross, *Neighbors: The Destruction of the Jewish Community in Jedwabne, Poland* (2001).

Raul Hilberg, *Perpetrators, Victims, Bystanders: The Jewish Catastrophe, 1933–1945* (1992).

Peter Hoffmann, *The History of the German Resistance, 1933–1945* (1977).

Julian Jackson, *France: The Dark Years, 1940–1944* (2002).

Eric T. Jennings, *Vichy in the Tropics: Pétain's National Revolution in Madagascar, Guadaloupe, and Indochina, 1940–1944* (2001).

H. R. Kedward, *In Search of the Maquis: Rural Resistance in Southern France, 1942–1944* (1993).

John Keegan, *The Second World War* (1989).

———, *Six Armies in Normandy* (1982).

Martin Kolinsky, *Britain's War in the Middle East: Strategy and Diplomacy, 1936–1942* (1999).

Walter Laqueur, *The Terrible Secret: Suppression of the Truth about Hitler's "Final Solution"* (1980).

David Clay Large, *And the World Closed Its Doors: One Family's Struggle to Escape the Holocaust* (2003).

Michael Marrus, *The Holocaust in History* (1988).

Arthur Marwick, *The Home Front: The British and the Second World War* (1977).

Ernest R. May, *Strange Victory: Hitler's Conquest of France* (2000).

Mark Mazower, *Inside Hitler's Greece: The Experience of Occupation, 1941–1944* (1993).

Alan S. Milward, *War, Economy, and Society, 1939–1945* (1977).

Norman Naimark, *The Russians in Germany: A History of the Soviet Zone of Occupation, 1945–1949* (1995).

Robert O. Paxton, *Vichy France: Old Guard and New Order, 1940–1944* (1972).

Robert O. Paxton and Michael R. Marrus, *Vichy France and the Jews* (1981).

Henry Rousso, *Vichy Syndrome: History and Memory in France since 1944* (1991).

Jonathan Steinberg, *The Axis and the Holocaust, 1941–1943* (1990).

John F. Sweets, *Choices in Vichy France* (1986).

Donald Cameron Watt, *How War Came* (1989).

Gerhard L. Weinberg, *A World at War: A Global History of World War II* (1994).

CHAPTER 27. REBUILDING DIVIDED EUROPE

John Lewis Gaddis, *The United States and the Origins of the Cold War, 1941–1947* (2000).

———, *We Know Now: Rethinking Cold War History* (1997).

Paul Ginsborg, *A History of Contemporary Italy: Society and Politics, 1943–1988* (1990).

Michael Harrison, *Reluctant Ally: France and Atlantic Security* (1981).

Stanley Hoffmann, *Decline or Renewal? France since the Popular Front: Government and the People, 1936–1986* (1988).

Michael J. Hogan, *The Marshall Plan: America, Britain and the Reconstruction of Western Europe, 1947–1952* (1987).

Tony Judt, *Past Imperfect: French Intellectuals, 1944–1956* (1993).

George F. Kennan, *The Nuclear Delusion: Soviet-American Relations in the Atomic Age* (1983).

Lothar Kettenacher, *Germany since 1945* (1997).

Richard Kuisel, *Seducing the French: The Dilemma of Americanization* (1993).

Bruce R. Kuniholm, *The Origins of the Cold War in the Near East: Great Power Conflict and Diplomacy in Iran, Turkey, and Greece* (1994).

Arthur Marwick, *British Society since 1945* (1982).

Vojtech Mastny, *Helsinki, Human Rights, and European Security* (1986).

Alan S. Milward, *The European Rescue of the Nation-State* (1992).

———, *The Reconstruction of Western Europe, 1945–1951* (1984).

Kenneth O. Morgan, *Labour in Power, 1945–1951* (1984).

———, *The People's Peace: British History, 1945–1990* (1991).

Norman M. Naimark, *A History of the Soviet Zone of Occupation, 1945–1949* (1995).

Robert A. Pollard, *Economic Security and the Origins of the Cold War* (1985).

Frank Prochaska, *Royal Bounty: The Making of a Welfare Monarchy* (1995).

Paul Preston, *Franco: A Biography* (1993).

Henry Rousso, *Vichy Syndrome: History and Memory in France since 1944* (1991).

Haig Simonian, *The Privileged Partnership: Franco-German Relations in the European Community, 1969–1984* (1985).

William Taubman, *Khrushchev: The Man and His Era* (2003).

Henry A. Turner, Jr., *Germany from Partition to Reunification* (1992).

CHAPTER 28. DECOLONIZATION AND A NEW PROSPERITY

Franz Ansprenger, *The Dissolution of Colonial Empires* (1989).

P. J. Cain and A. G. Hopkins, *British Imperialism: Crisis and Deconstruction, 1914–1990* (1993).

Muriel Evelyn Chamberlain, *Decolonization: The Fall of the European Empires* (1985).

Matthew Connelly, *A Diplomatic Revolution: Algeria's Fight for Independence and the Origins of the Post–Cold War Era* (2002).

Jacques Dalloz, *The War in Indochina* (1990).

Prosser Gifford and William Roger Louis, eds., *Decolonization and African Independence: The Transfers of Power, 1960–1980* (1988).

John D. Hargeaves, *Decolonization in Africa* (1988).

Alistair Horne, *A Savage War of Peace: Algeria, 1954–1962* (1978).

Robert J. Lieber, *Oil and the Middle East: Europe in the Energy Crisis* (1976).

Chapter 29. The Emergence of Contemporary Europe and the Collapse of Communism

Paul Arthur and Keith Jeffery, *Northern Ireland since 1968* (1988).

Ivo Banac, *Eastern Europe in Revolution* (1992).

Corelli Barnett, *The Pride and the Fall: The Dream and Illusion of Britain as a Great Nation* (1987).

Serge Berstein, *The Republic of De Gaulle, 1958–1969* (1993).

George W. Breslauer, *Gorbachev and Yeltsin as Leaders* (2002).

David Caute, *The Year of Barricades: A Journey through 1968* (1989).

David Childs, *Britain since 1945* (2001).

Robert Darnton, *Berlin Journal: 1989–1990* (1991).

Karen Dawisha and Bruce Parrott, *Russia and the New States of Eurasia: The Politics of Upheaval* (1994).

Timothy Garton Ash, *In Europe's Name: Germany and the Divided Continent* (1993).

———, *The Polish Revolution: Solidarity, 1980–1982* (1983).

Paul Ginsborg, *Italy and its Discontents: Family, Civil Society, State 1980–2001* (2001).

Robert O. Keohane, Joseph S. Nye, and Stanley Hoffmann, *Europe after the Cold War* (1993).

Stephen Kotkin, *Armageddon Averted: The Soviet Collapse, 1970–2000* (2001).

Walter Laqueur, *Europe since Hitler* (1983).

Carol Skalnick Leff, *The Czech and Slovak Republics: Nation versus State* (1997).

Anatol Lieven, *The Baltic Revolution: Estonia, Latvia, Lithuania and the Path to Independence* (1999).

Martin E. Malia, *The Soviet Tragedy: A History of Socialism in Russia, 1917–1991* (1993).

Kenneth Maxwell, *The Making of Portuguese Democracy* (1995).

Paul Preston, *The Triumph of Democracy in Spain* (1986).

Peter Riddell, *The Thatcher Era and Its Legacy* (1991).

Joseph Rothschild, *Return to Diversity: A Political History of East Central Europe since World War II* (1993).

Alan Sked and Chris Cook, *Postwar Britain: A Political History* (1990).

Ronald Grigor Suny, *The Revenge of the Past: Nationalism, Revolution, and the Collapse of the Soviet Union* (1993).

George Weigel, *The Final Revolution: The Breaking of Communist Europe* (1991).

CHAPTER 30. GLOBAL CHALLENGES, EUROPEAN COOPERATION, AND THE UNCERTAINTIES OF A NEW AGE

Martin Baldwin-Edwards and Martin A. Schain, eds., *The Politics of Immigration in Western Europe* (1994).

Rogers Brubaker, *Citizenship and Nationhood in France and Germany* (1992).

Desmond Dinan, *Ever Closer Union? An Introduction to the European Community* (1994).

Françoise Gaspard, *A Small City in France* (1995).

Daniel Gros and Niels Thygesen, *European Monetary Integration* (1992).

Alec G. Hargraves, *Immigration, Race, and Ethnicity in Contemporary France* (1995).

Bernard Lewis, *Islam and the West* (1993).

Barbara Marshall, *The New Germany and Migration in Europe* (2000).

Jorgen Nielsen, *Muslims in Western Europe* (1992).

John Pinder, *The Building of the European Union* (1998).

Larry Siedentop, *Democracy in Europe* (2001).

Derek Urwin, *The Community of Europe: A History of European Integration since 1945* (1995).

John Wrench and John Solomos, eds., *Racism and Migration in Western Europe* (1993).

CREDITS

Frontispiece: P. Borgomano (17th–18th c.), *The Market of Saluzzo*, Left Section. Detail. © Alinari/Art Resource, NY.

Part One (p. xxxvi) Hans Holbein the Younger, *Jean de Dinteville and Georges de Selve ("The Ambassadors"),* National Gallery, London; **Part Two (p. 174)** Marcus Gheeraerts the Younger, *Elizabeth I (The Ditchley Portrait),* 1592 (2561), By courtesy of the National Portrait Gallery, London; **Part Three (p. 308)** *Allegory of Europe* by Solimena, Francesco (1657–1747), Leeds Museums and Art Galleries (Temple Newsam House) UK/Bridgeman Art Library; **Part Four (p. 466)** Barricades in the Rue Saint-Antoine, Bildarchiv Preussischer Kulturbesitz, Berlin; **Part Five (p. 702)** Paris communards, Bettmann Archive; **Part Six (p. 940)** Trench warfare, Hulton-Deutsch Collection; **Part Seven (p. 1208)** Associated Press/AP.

Chapter 1: p. 4 (left) Staatliche Museen Preussischer Kulturbesitz; (right) Ampliaciones y Reproducciones MAS, Barcelona; **p. 9** Bibliothèque de l'École des Beaux Arts, Giraudon/Art Resource, NY; **p. 11** Juniano Majo from *De Majestate*, Art Archive/Bibliotheque Nationale Paris/Dagli Orti; **p. 13** The Art Archive/Museo Catedràlicio Zamora Spain/Dagli Orti; **p. 15** Hans Wertinger, 1530, Germanisches Nationalmuseum, Nürnberg; **p. 17** From a painting by Bruegel, Metropolitan Museum, New York; **p. 21** Lorenzo Lotto, *Master Marsilio and his Wife,* 1523, © Erich Lessing/Art Resource, NY; **p. 23** Gerini Niccolo' di Pietro, *Storie di S. Matteo* (Banchieri), Scala/Art Resource, NY; **p. 24** Crispin de Passe, woman spinning from *Deliciarum Libeleus,* Hulton-Deutsch Collection Ltd; **p. 30** The Art Archive/British Library/HarperCollins Publishers; **p. 33** MEPC Print Collection, Miriam and Ira D. Wallach Division of Art, Prints & Photographs, New York Public Library, Astor, Lenox, and Tilden Foundations; **p. 39** Kobe Museum, Japan; **p. 42** Illustration from Lienzo de Tlaxcala, *Antiguedades Mexicanas* (1892), Tozzer Library, Harvard University.

Chapter 2: p. 47 Ghilandaio Domenico, 1485, Sessetti Chapel, Santa Trinita, Scala/Art Resource, NY; **p. 49** Hulton|Archive by Getty; **p. 52** Bonifacio Bembo, *Francesco Sforza,* © Scala/Art Resource, NY; **p. 55** Pianta della Catena, *Firenze,* 1490, Scala/Art Resource, NY; **p. 57** Giorgio Vasari, *The Signory Discuss the War against Pisa,* Palazzo Vecchio, Florence, Soprintendenza alle Gallerie, Florence; **p. 59** (left) Petrarch, Alinari/Art Resource, NY; (right) Ambrosius Holbein, *Aushängeschild eines Schulmeister,* Oeffentliche Kunstsammlung, Basel, Kunstmuseum, Inv. 311; **p. 63** (left) Leonardo da Vinci, *Foetus in the womb,* Her Majesty Queen Elizabeth II/Royal Collection Enterprises Ltd; (right) Leonardo da Vinci, *Divine proportion,* Alinari /Art Resource, NY; **p. 67** Raphael, *Leo X and His Cardinals,* Uffizi Gallery, Florence, Alinari/Art Resource, NY; **p. 68** Andrea Mantegna, fresco, Palazzo Ducale, Mantua (Sadea-Sansoni) Alinari/Art Resource, NY; **p. 71** Masaccio, *The Expulsion of Adam and Eve from Eden,* Brancacci Chapel, Florence, Alinari/Art Resource, NY; **p. 73** Andrea Mantegna, *The Dead Christ,* Brera, Milan, Alinari/Art Resource, NY; **p. 74** Sandro Botticelli, *Birth of Venus,* Uffizi Gallery, Florence, Alinari/Art Resource, NY, © Erich Lessing; **p. 76** Leonardo da Vinci, *The Last Supper,* Sta. Maria delle Grazie, Alinari/Art Resource, NY; **p. 80** © Alinari/Art Resource, NY; **p. 82** Bust of Niccolò Machiavelli from Palazzo Vecchio, Florence, Scala.

Prince of Wales, © Her Majesty Queen Elizabeth II/Royal Collection Enterprises, Ltd.; **p. 227** After A. Van Dyck, *William Laud* (# 171), By courtesy of the National Portrait Gallery, London; **p. 230** From John Vicar's *Sight of the Transactions of These Latter Years*, etching by Wencelaus Hollar, British Library; **p. 231** John Pym (# 1425), By courtesy of the National Portrait Gallery, London; **p. 235** Sir Peter Lely, *Oliver Cromwell*, Galleria Palatina, Florence, Photo supplied by British Information Services; **p. 237** Hulton|Archive by Getty; **p. 240** Weesop, *An Eyewitness Representation of the Execution of King Charles I (1600–49) of England, 1649*, The Bridgeman Art Library; **p. 244** *England's Memorial of its Wonderful Deliverance from French Tyranny and Popish Oppression*, The Bridgeman Art Library; **p. 246** *William and Mary*, Colonial Williamsburg Foundation; **p. 251** J. Berckheyde, *The Amsterdam Bourse, 1668*, Amsterdams Historisch Museum; **p. 252** Gerrit Berckheyde, *The Waag and Crane on the Spaarne at Haarlem*, © Rijksmuseum-Stichting, Amsterdam; **p. 253** Rembrandt van Rijn, *Jews in the Synagogue in Amsterdam*, The Bridgeman Art Library; **p. 254** Romeyn de Hooghe, *The Dike-break at Coevorden*, Engraving, Bodleian Library, Oxford; **p. 256** Rembrandt van Rijn, *Syndics of the Cloth Guild*, © Rijksmuseum-Stichting, Amsterdam; **p. 259** Jean Paul, "Siege of Maastricht by the Armies of King Louis XIV", © Réunion des Musées Nationaux/Art Resource, NY.

Chapter 7: p. 262 Title page from T. Hobbes, *Leviathan*, 1651, New York Public Library Rare Book Division, Astor, Lenox, and Tilden Foundations; **p. 269** from *Memoire Turcheseche*, The Art Archive/Museo Correr Venice/Dagli Orti; **p. 271** Hyacinthe Rigaud, *Louis XIV*, Louvre, Paris, Giraudon/Art Resource, NY; **p. 273** (left) Rousselet, Le Prince de Condé, Empereur des Turcs, from *Courses de Testes et de Bagues faites par le Roy*, 1670, Gift of Mrs. Herbert L. Stern, Courtesy of the Art Institute of Chicago; (right) Philippe de Champagne, *Portrait of Mazarin*, Chantilly, Photographie Bulloz; **p. 276** Gobelins after Le Brun, *Louis XIV visiting the Gobelins Factory*, Versailles, © R.M.N.; **p. 279** French school, 17th Century, The Château of Versailles, Photographie Bulloz; **p. 281** (left) French figurative plaque of the Sun, Cabinet des Médailles, © cliché Bibliothèque Nationale de France, Paris; (right) Louis XIV as the Exterminator of Protestantism, Departement des Imprimés, © cliché Bibliothèque Nationale de France, Paris; **p. 287** G. Lauch, Engraving of Leopold I, Trustees of the British Museum; **p. 288** The Art Archive/Museum der Stadt wien/Dagli Orti; **p. 291** Frederick William I, Warder Collection; **p. 292** Mathieu Merian the Younger, Engraving of Ivan the Terrible in Novgorod, © cliché Bibliothèque Nationale de France, Paris; **p. 295** (left) T. H. Wedekind, *Charles XII*, Armémuseum, Stockholm, Photograph by Bo Michaëlsson; (right) Sebastian Bourdon, *Queen Christina of Sweden on Horseback*, Museo del Prado, Madrid, Spain, © Scala/Art Resource, NY; **p. 296** Jean Marc Nattier, *Peter I the Great, Emperor of Russia, 1715*, Chateaux de Versailles et de Trianon, Versailles, France, © Réunion des Musées Nationaux/Art Resource, NY; **p. 304** Aveline, *The Rock of Gibraltar*, Mary Evans Picture Library.

Chapter 8: p. 314 Copernican heliocentricism, Warder Collection; **p. 316** Jan Stephan van Calcar, title page from Vesalius' *De humani corporis fabricia*, 1543, Kupferstichkabinett, Basel; **p. 318** (left) Kepler, Warder Collection; (right) J. Kepler, *Prodromus Dissertationum*, Tubingen, 1596, Rare Book Collection, New York Public Library, Astor, Lenox, and Tilden Foundations; **p. 320** (left) Francis Bacon, Trustees of the British Museum; (right) Galileo, Dr. G. B. Pineider, Florence; **p. 323** Unknown artist, *Portrait of Descartes*, Photographie Bulloz; **p. 324** Sir Isaac Newton (# 2881), By courtesy of the National Portrait Gallery, London; **p. 327** Tapestry of Testelin after a cartoon by Le Brun, *Establishment of the Academy of Science*, Musée de Versailles, Giraudon/Art Resource, NY; **p. 328** Frontispiece to *Nature's Pictures Drawn by Fancies Pencil*, 1656, By permission of the Houghton Library, Harvard University; **p. 331** **Padua University**, Science Photo Library; **p. 333** Royal Observatory, London, The Science Museum/Science and Society Picture Library.

Chapter 9: p. 336 (left) Sir Godfrey Kneller, *Portrait of John Locke*, Philip Mould, Historical Portraits Ltd., London, UK, The Bridgeman Art Library; (right) Francois Hubert Drouais, *Portrait of Comte George-Louis Buffon, 1753*, Chateaux de Versailles et de Trianon, Versailles, France, The Bridgeman Art Library; **p. 339** The *philosophes*, Bibliothèque Nationale, Paris; **p. 341** Montesquieu, Photographie Bulloz; **p. 344** Illustration from Diderot's *Encyclopedia, Hunting Traps*, Mary Evans Picture Library; **p. 348** (left) Q. de la Tour, *Jean Jacques Rousseau*, Photographie Bulloz; (right) Rousseau and Voltaire fighting, Bibliothèque

Yermakov, *Princess Lasarev in Tatar costume*, Tbilisi, c. 1890, Moscow State Historical Museum; **p. 785** Hulton|Archive by Getty; **p. 790** Bloody Sunday, Roger-Viollet; **p. 793** Czar Nicholas opens the Duma, © Hulton-Deutsch Collection/Corbis; **p. 795** (left) Napoleon III caricature, © Corbis; (right) Napoleon III, Hulton|Archive by Getty; **p. 797** "The Inauguration of the Suez Canal," 1869, after Riou, *Passage at El Guisr,* British Library; **p. 800** Édouard Manet, *Execution of Emperor Maximilian,* 1867, Städtische Kunsthalle, Mannheim, Germany, Photograph © Erich Lessing, Art Resource, NY; **p. 804** Caricature on the cession of Alsace-Lorraine, Photographie Bulloz; **p. 805** Execution during Paris Commune, Bibliothèque Nationale, Paris; **p. 807** Champs Elysées in Paris during the Commune, Photoworld/FPG; **p. 809** Suicide of Boulanger, from *Le Petit Journal,* 10 October 1891, © cliché Bibliothèque Nationale de France, Paris; **p. 811** (left) Emile Courtet, "The Qualities of the Jew after Gall's Method," *La Libre Parole Illustrée,* 23 December 1893, The Jewish Museum, NY; (right) Alfred Dreyfus, Roger-Viollet.

Chapter 19: p. 815 (left) Eiffel Tower at Paris Exposition of 1900, Bibliothèque Historique de la Ville de Paris, photo by Gerard Leyris; (right) Palace of Electricity at the Paris Exhibition of 1900, Collection George Sirot, Paris; **p. 817** Louis Pasteur, Photographie Giraudon; **p. 819** "The Stroke of Midnight," © cliché Bibliothèque Nationale de France, Paris; **p. 826** Automobile assembly line, © 1914 Ford Motor Co.; **p. 827** Telephone switchboard, Photoworld/FGP; **p. 829** (left) The Curies, English Caricature Lithograph, 1904; (right) Ernest Rutherford, Cambridge University Library, Rutherford Collection, courtesy AIP Emilio Segrè Visual Archives; **p. 830** Albert Einstein, The Hebrew University of Jerusalem; **p. 834** Lewis W. Hine, *Immigrants on Ellis Island,* 1905, Museum of the City of New York; **p. 837** Pit Boys, Warder Collection; **p. 839** Henri de Toulouse-Lautrec, *In the Salon at the Rue des Mouins, 1894,* Musee Toulouse-Lautrec, Albi, France, The Bridgeman Art Library; **p. 841** (left) High Street, Glasgow, The Mansell Collection; (right) Company housing near the Mines of Bruay, 1889, © cliché Bibliothèque Nationale, Paris; **p. 842** Emperor Napoleon III and Georges Haussmann, Photographie Bulloz; **p. 843** La rue Traversine, Archives Nationales, C.R.D.P. de Paris, © B.H.V.P.; **p. 847** Clerks in Cadbury's General Office, 1912, Photo courtesy Cadbury Ltd.; **p. 849** Protest against admission of women to Cambridge University, 1881, © Hulton-Deutsch Collection/Corbis; **p. 851** A. Deroy, *The Grotto at Lourdes,* © Archivo Iconografico, S.A./Corbis; **p. 852** Parisian department store, Éditions Tallandier; **p. 854** Sarah Bernhardt photographed in a coffin, Bettmann Archive; **p. 856** (left) Grecian Olympics, © Bettmann/Corbis; (right) Robert Baden-Powell, © Hulton-Deutsch Collection/Corbis.

Chapter 20: p. 860 Dinnertime in an English workhouse, Warder Collection; **p. 865** Socialist League at Hammersmith, © The Board of the Trustees of the Victoria & Albert Museum, London/Art Resource, NY; **p. 868** (left) Socialist Baptism, Mary Evans Picture Library; (right) Pope Leo, © Bettmann/Corbis; **p. 871** (left) Assassination of French President Carnot, Photos12.com–Oasis; (right) Peter Kropotkin's *The Spirit of Revolt,* Houghton Library, Harvard University; **p. 874** Emily Davison's death at the Derby, 1913, Mansell Collection; **p. 876** Felix Tournachon Nadar, Portrait of Charles Baudelaire, 1855, Photos12.com–ARJ; **p. 877** Jean-François Millet, *The Gleaners,* 1857, The Louvre, Paris, Gift of Mme Pommery, photo courtesy of Musées Nationaux, Photographie Bulloz; **p. 878** Gustave Courbet, *The Bather,* 1853, Musée Fabre, Montpellier, Lauros-Giraudon/Art Resource, NY; **p. 880** Édouard Manet *Déjeuner sur l'herbe,* 1863, Musée d'Orsay, Erich Lessing/Art Resource, NY; **p. 881** Edgar Degas, *L'Absinthe,* 1877, Musée d'Orsay, Paris, Giraudon/Art Resource, NY; **p. 883** Georges Moreau de Tours, *Morphiamania,* Archives Charmet/Bridgeman Art Library; **p. 885** Nietzsche, © Corbis/Bettmann; **p. 887** Sigmund Freud, © Austrian Archives/Corbis; **p. 889** Frederick Hollyer, Portrait of Sir Edward Burne-Jones and William Morris, © Stapleton Collection/Corbis; **p. 890** *The Rite of Spring,* 1913, Warder Collection; **p. 892** Georges Seurat, *A Sunday Afternoon on the Island of the Grande Jatte,* 1884, © The Art Institute of Chicago, Helen Birch Bartlett Memorial Collection; **p. 894** (left) Antoni Gaudí i Cornet, *Casa Batlló,* 1905–07, Ampliaciones y Reproducciones MAS, Barcelona; (right) Gustav Klimt, *Judith II (Salomé),* 1909, Museum of Modern Art of Ca' Pesaro, Venice, © Cameraphoto Venezia/Art Resource, NY; **p. 896** (left) Pablo Picasso, © cliché Réunion des Musées Nationales, Paris; (right) Pablo Picasso, *Les Demoiselles d'Avignon,* 1907, Museum of Modern Art, Lillie P. Bliss Bequest, © 1996 Museum of Modern Art, NY/ARS, NY.

Chapter 21: p. 899 Anton von Werner, *Der Kongreß zu Berlin,* 1881, photo by Klaus Göken, 1993, Bildarchiv Preussischer Kulturbesitz; **p. 901** Colonization of the Congo, Hulton|Archive by Getty; **p. 903** Germany and France establish their colonial borders in the Congo, From *Le Petit Journal,* 9 November 1913, © cliché Bibliothèque Nationale de France, Paris; **p. 906** The British fleet anchored off Alexandria, 1882, Mansell Collection; **p. 908** (left and right) Caricatures of Germans in Africa, From *Jugend,* 1896, Warder Collection; **p. 910** The charge of the dervishes at the Battle of Omdurman in the Sudan, Mansell Collection; **p. 913** (left) British Soldiers Marching Through Pretoria, © Corbis; (right) Boer Commandos, © Bettmann/Corbis; **p. 915** IMP/GEH Warder Collection; **p. 917** (left) The ruins of Lucknow, © the Board of Trustees of the Victoria & Albert Museum/Art Resource, NY; (right) Viceroy Lord Curzon and Lady Curzon enter Delhi, 1903, Mansell Collection; **p. 920** Boxers in Peking, Photos12.com–Oasis; **p. 922** J. Macfarlane from *The Kipling Reader,* 1908, © British Library; **p. 926** Trading ships in Calcutta, India Office Library; **p. 928** Ashanti Royalty Submitting to British from *The Graphic,* Hulton|Archive by Getty; **p. 932** Thomas Jones Barker, *Queen Victoria Presenting a Bible at Windsor,* 1861, By courtesy of the National Portrait Gallery, London (#4969); **p. 935** Natives with Ivory, Dar Es Salaam, Tanganyika, Library of Congress, Prints and Photographs Division, Frank and Frances Carpenter Collection, LC-USZ62-102973.

Chapter 22: p. 944 *Simplicissimus* cartoon, Warder Collection; **p. 945** (left) *Simplicissimus* cartoon, Warder Collection; (right) Emperor Francis Joseph, Hulton-Deutsch Collection Ltd.; **p. 950** John Tenniel in *Punch* 20 September 1884, Bismarck and Puppets, Mary Evans Picture Library; **p. 954** Broadside about Morocco, c. 1906, © cliché Bibliothèque Nationale de France, Paris; **p. 959** Enver Bey and the Young Turks Party, Photos12.com; **p. 963** David Wilson, *The Vortex: Will the Powers Be Drawn In?,* 1912, The Mansell Collection; **p. 965** Archduke Ferdinand and his wife in Sarajevo, UPI; **p. 969** (left) Marshal Joseph Joffre, Canadian War Museum #19810152-012; (right) Alfred von Schlieffen, © Bettmann/Corbis; **p. 973** (left) Soldiers depart for war, Warder Collection; (right) Southwark Town Hall, London, December 1915, Hulton-Deutsch Collection Ltd.; **p. 975** Old combat and new in World War I, Imperial War Museum; **p. 978** Paul Nash's *We Are Making New World,* Imperial War Museum; **p. 980** (left) French soldiers wearing gas masks, Roger-Viollet; (right) Victims of a German gas attack, National Archives; **p. 982** Dogfight, Warder Collection; **p. 984** (left) Poster of Lord Kitchener, Canadian War Museum, 56-04-11-078; (right) "Women of Britain say—Go!", Canadian War Museum, 56-04-11-074; **p. 989** © Hulton-Deutsch Collection/Corbis; **p. 995** Battlefield of the Somme, UPI/Bettmann; **p. 997** Russian sharpshooters, Canadian War Museum; **p. 999** German-Russian Comradeship, © Hulton-Deutsch Collection/Corbis; **p. 1000** Citizens of Berlin hunt for food, Ullstein Bilderdienst; **p. 1003** (left) Allied tanks, Canadian War Museum, 0.1568, Acq# 1981–692/3; (right) German U-Boat, © Hulton-Deutsch Collection/Corbis; **p. 1013** A widow at the cemetery of Maroeil, Photos12.com–Oasis.

Chapter 23: p. 1019 Tsar Nicholas II blessing the troops, 1915, Popperfoto; **p. 1020** Tsarina Alexandra and Grigory Rasputin, Warder Collection; **p. 1023** Nevsky Prospect, Courtesy George Eastman House; **p. 1025** Workers and soldiers guarding a government building, 1917, Bildarchiv Preussischer Kulturbesitz; **p. 1029** Kerensky with troops, Petrograd, 1917, Sovfoto; **p. 1034** Bolsheviks seize the Winter Palace, October, 1917, Warder Collection; **p. 1039** Lenin addressing troops, 1920, Warder Collection; **p. 1041** White army executes suspected Bolsheviks, UPI/Bettmann; **p. 1045** (left) Starving refugee children, 1921, Hulton-Deutsch Collection Ltd; (right) Free market during NEP, 1921, Warder Collection; **p. 1047** Lenin and Stalin, Photoworld/FPG; **p. 1050** Deportation of kulaks, 1930, The Illustrated London News Picture Library; **p. 1054** Show Trials, ©Bettmann/Corbis.

Chapter 24: p. 1057 The Council of Four, 1919, Imperial War Museum; **p. 1060** (left) Karl Liebknecht, 1919, Photograph by Willy Römer, Berlin, Ullstein Bilderdienst; (right) Bolsheviks, Hulton|Archive by Getty; **p. 1066** Devalued German currency, Archiv für Kunst und Geschichte (Katherine Young); **p. 1075** Irish Republicans in Dublin, Warder Collection; **p. 1081** Anti-Bolshevik Poster, Photos12.com–Oasis; **p. 1085** © Hulton-Deutsch Collection/Corbis; **p. 1089** A barricade during the London General Strike, 1926, Warder Collection; **p. 1091** John Heartfield, cover collage for *Der Dada,* No. 3, April 1920, Courtesy Merrill C. Berman Collection; **p. 1093** Max Ernst, *Europe after the Rain (I),* 1933, private collection; **p.** 1096 (left) Mussolini leaving the Quirinale, Centro Anni a Roma, Fratelli Palombi Editori, Roma; (right) Mussolini and Victor Emmanuel III, Keystone/Hulton-Deutsch Collection Ltd; **p.** 1101 Nazi storm troopers, 1922, Ullstein Bilderdienst; **p.** 1102 Plebiscite propaganda, 1934, Photoworld/FPG.

Chapter 25: p. 1105 (left) James N. Rosenberg, *October 29, Dies Irae,* 1929, Philadelphia Museum of Art, Purchased: Lila Dowin Peck Fund; (right) Briton seeks work, 1930, Hulton-Deutsch Collection Ltd; **p.** 1110 Outside Lords Cricket Ground, 1937, Hulton-Deutsch Collection Ltd; **p.** 1115 Hitler Youth Saluting the Fuhrer, 1937, ©Hulton-Deutsch Collection/Corbis; **p.** 1119 Italian Women Soldiers, © Bettmann/Corbis; **p.** 1121 Assassination of King Alexander Karadjordjevic I, Hulton|Archive by Getty; **p.** 1124 Red Riots in Paris, © Bettmann/Corbis; **p.** 1128 Communists arrested after Reichstag Fire, 1933, Bundesarchiv, Koblenz; **p.** 1130 Hitler and Hindenburg, Warder Collection; **p.** 1133 Entartete Kunst Exhibition, 1937, Photos12.com–Keystone Pressedienst; **p.** 1135 Targeting of Jewish-owned shops, Hulton-Deutsch Collection Ltd; **p.** 1139 Italian-Abyssinian War, Hulton|Archive by Getty; **p.** 1146 Pablo Picasso, *Guernica* (mural), 1937, Museo del Prado; **p.** 1147 (left) "La Pasionaria," UPI/Bettmann; (right) Francisco Franco, Hulton|Archive by Getty; **p.** 1149 Japanese Occupation of Manchuria, Hulton|Archive by Getty; **p.** 1152 Austria after annexation, 1938, Hulton-Deutsch Collection Ltd; **p.** 1155 Neville Chamberlain, 1938, Hulton-Deutsch Collection Ltd.

Chapter 26: p. 1158 Germany Invades Poland, Associated Press, AP; **p.** 1162 Hitler in Paris, 1940, Canadian War Museum,19910172-001, Grossdeutschland im Weltgeschehen 1940; **p.** 1165 (left) Children evacuated from London, 1940, The Illustrated London News Picture Library; (right) Churchill at St. Paul's Cathedral after the blitz, 1940, Warder Collection; **p.** 1170 German Invasion of Russia, © Bettmann/Corbis; **p.** 1172 Pearl Harbor Attack, Hulton|Archive by Getty; **p.** 1178 Lithuanians slaughtering Jews, 1942, Marx-Verlag GmbH, Allgemeine Wochenzeitung der Juden in Deutschland; **p.** 1181 Dutch Jews before transport to a concentration camp, Warder Collection; **p.** 1184 Partisan headquarters in Yugoslavia, 1944, Camera Press Ltd, London; **p.** 1186 Vichy raid against Maquis, 1944, Roger-Viollet; **p.** 1191 North Africa, 1944, Associated Press, U.S. Army; **p.** 1194 Stalingrad, Hulton|Archive by Getty; **p.** 1196 (left) Hamburg after Allied bombing, Ullstein Bilderdienst; (right) Stuttgart after Allied bombing, Ullstein Bilderdienst; **p.** 1198 D-Day, June 1944, Maritime Administration; **p.** 1200 Yalta, 1945, National Archives; **p.** 1202 Soviet Flag mounted on Reichstag, Photograph by Yevgeny Chaldey/Voller Ernst; **p.** 1204 (left) Nagasaki, Associated Press, Office of War Information; (right) Hiroshima, Associated Press, AP.

Chapter 27: p. 1215 Displaced persons, 1945, Henri Cartier-Bresson/Magnum Photos, New York; **p.** 1216 Potsdam, 1945, U.S. Signal Corps; **p.** 1220 United Nations Poster, © Swim Ink/Corbis; **p.** 1224 Collaborator escorted out of Cherbourg, 1944, Robert Capa/ Magna Photos, New York; **p.** 1227 Soldiers Marching into Soviet Zone of Germany, © Bettmann/Corbis; **p.** 1230 Sentry Overlooking Athens, © Hulton-Deutsch Collection/ Corbis; **p.** 1235 © Bettmann/Corbis **p.** 1238 Berlin airlift, Wide World Photos; **p.** 1239 Cult of Mao, Camera Press Ltd.; **p.** 1241 Korean War POW, Associated Press; **p.** 1245 (left) Building the Berlin Wall, 1961, German Information Service, New York; (right) Kennedy in Berlin, 1963, AP/Wide World Photos; **p.** 1247 (left) Khrushchev and Castro, 1963, Novosti, London; (right) UN Security Council during Cuban Missile Crisis, 1962, Neal Boenzi/NYT Pictures; **p.** 1249 May Day Parade, 1963, Camera Press Ltd.

Chapter 28: p. 1253 (left) Churchill and Attlee, Associated Press, AP; (right) Charles de Gaulle, © Bettmann/Corbis; **p.** 1254 Elderly Italian Woman Voting, © Bettmann/Corbis; **p.** 1257 Gandhi, Information Service of India; **p.** 1260 (left) Russian cartoon of Suez Canal seizure, School of Slavonic and Eastern European Studies, University of London; (right) Sunken ships block the Suez Canal, 1956, Hulton-Deutsch Collection Ltd; **p.** 1263 (left) French in Vietnam, 1952, L'Illustration/Sygma; (right) French patrol, Vietnam, © 1954 Robert Capa/Magnum Photos, New York; **p.** 1265 Demonstration in Algiers, © Bettmann/Corbis; **p.** 1270 Ghana Independence Ceremony, Associated Press; **p.** 1274 Cast of Picasso's play *Le Desir Attrapé* in his Paris studio, 1944, Photographie Brassai © copyright Gilberte Brassai; **p.** 1276 Fellini on the set of *La Strada,* Ponti-De Laurentiis/The

Kobal Collection; **p. 1280** Housing in Czechoslovakia, Warder Collection; **p. 1281** Six Day War, Associated Press; **p. 1285** Coca-Cola delivery, Venice, © 1950 David Seymour/Magnum Photos, New York; **p. 1286** Anti Euro Disney Demonstration, © Pierre Vauthey/Corbis Sygma.

Chapter 29: p. 1289 Germans greet Gorbachev, 1989, AP/Wide World Photos; **p. 1292** (left) Students revolt in Paris, © 1968 Bruno Barbey/Magnum Photos Inc.; (right) Conservatives counter-demonstrate, Roger-Viollet; **p. 1294** Margaret Thatcher and Helmut Schmidt, © Bettmann/Corbis; **p. 1298** Nuclear power plant and windmill, U.N. Photo; **p. 1301** © Hulton-Deutsch Collection/Corbis; **p. 1304** IRA bombing, Belfast, 1972, © 1995 Abbas/Magnum Photos, New York; **p. 1309** (left) Communist Party summit, 1968, AP/Wide World Photos; (right) Tanks in Prague, 1968, © 1968 Josef Koudelka/Magnum Photos Inc.; **p. 1315** Chernobyl, © Kostin Igor/Corbis Sygma; **p. 1318** Cutting down the Iron Curtain, AP Photo/Bernhard J. Holzner; **p. 1320** The Berlin Wall falls, © Alexandra Avakian/Woodfin Camp; **p. 1323** Václav Havel, 1989, AP/Wide World Photos; **p. 1326** (left) Mass grave in Timisoara, © Gilles Saussier/Gamma Liaison; (right) Militiaman watching Ceauçescu's execution on the presidential television set, © 1989 David C. Turnley/Black Star; **p. 1330** (left) Yeltsin resisting the coup, 1991, AP/Wide World Photos; (right) Yeltsin and Gorbachev, Photo by Shone/Gamma Liaison; **p. 1333** Pollution in Eastern Europe, © Giansanti Gianni/Corbis Sygma; **p. 1339** (left) Albanian Refugee, © AFP/Corbis; (right) Slobodan Milosevic, Associated Press, AP; **p. 1341** NATO in Kosovo, © AFP/Corbis.

Chapter 30: p. 1344 Illegal African Immigrants, © Reuters NewMedia Inc./Corbis; **p. 1349** Muslims in Nice, © AFP/Corbis; **p. 1355** Farmers Protest in Dublin, © Reuters NewMedia Inc./Corbis; **p. 1357** World Trade Organization Protest in Seattle, Associated Press, AP; **p. 1359** Chechen Rebels, © AFP/Corbis; **p. 1360** © Reuters NewMedia Inc./Corbis; **p. 1363** (left) Coalition of the Willing, Associated Press, AP; (right) Jacques Chirac, Associated Press, AFP Pool.

Tables: Table 1-1 (p. 19) European Population in the Sixteenth and Seventeenth Centuries, in Richard MacKenney, *Sixteenth-Century Europe: Expansion and Conflict* (New York: Macmillan, 1993), p. 51; **Table 7.1 (p. 267)** The Size of European Armies, 1690–1814, in Paul Kennedy, *The Rise and Fall of the Great Powers* (New York: Vintage, 1989), p. 99; **Table 10.1 (p. 392)** European Population, 1700–1800, in Paul Kennedy, *The Rise and Fall of the Great Powers* (New York: Vintage, 1989), p. 99; **Table 10.2 (p. 406)** Europe's Largest Cities at the end of the Eighteenth Century; **Table 14.1 (p. 557)** Estimated Populations of Various European Countries from 1800–1850, in Carlo M. Cipollo, ed., *The Fontana Economic History of Europe: Vol. 3, The Industrial Revolution* (London: HarperCollins, 1973), p. 29; **Table 14.2 (p. 566)** Manufacturing Capacity throughout Europe, in Carlo M. Cipolla, ed., *The Fontana Economic History of Europe: Vol. 4(1), The Emergence of Industrial Societies* (London: HarperCollins, 1973), p. 165; **Table 14.3 (p. 576)** Population of Major European Cities; **Table 17.1 (p. 742)** Ethnic Composition of the Austro-Hungarian Empire in 1910; **Table 19.1 (p. 820)** Annual Output of Steel, in Carlo M. Cipolla, ed., *The Fontana Economic History of Europe: Vol. 4(2), The Emergence of Industrial Societies* (London: HarperCollins, 1973), p. 775; **Table 19.2 (p. 828)** Production of Coal and Steel in Russia, in Arcadius Kahan, *Russian Economic History: The Nineteenth Century* (Chicago: University of Chicago Press, 1989) p. 21; **Table 19.3 (p. 835)** Population Growth in Major States between 1871 and 1911, in Colin Dyer, *Population and Society in Twentieth Century France* (New York: Holmes and Meier, 1978), p. 5; in M. Huber, *La Population de L'Europe Pendant la Guerre* (Paris: P.U.F., 1931), p. 7; **Table 19.4 (p. 836)** The Decline in Family Size (Number of Children) in England and Wales, in E. A. Wrigley, *Population and History* (New York: McGraw-Hill, 1969), p. 197; **Table 19.5 (p. 839)** Emigration to the United States, 1871–1910, in Leonard Dinnerstein and David M. Reimers, *Ethnic Americans: A History of Immigration and Assimilation* (New York: HarperCollins, 1977), p. 11; **Table 19.6 (p. 850)** Number of Public Servants (Non-Military), in Norman Stone, *Europe Transformed, 1878–1919* (Cambridge, MA: Harvard University Press, 1984), p. 130; **Table 22.1 (p. 1014)** Casualties in the Great War, in J. M. Winter, *The Great War and the British People* (London: Macmillan, 1985), p. 75; **Table 24.1 (p. 1077)** War Expenditure during the Great War, in Gerd Hardoch, *The First World War 1914–1918* (Berkeley: University of California Press, 1977), p. 153; **Table 24.2 (p. 1078)** Index of Wholesale Prices, in Gerd Hardoch,

The First World War 1914–1918 (Berkeley: University of California Press, 1977), p. 172; **Table 24.3 (p. 1086)** The Mark and the Dollar, 1914–1923, in Gordon Craig, *Germany 1866–1945* (New York: Oxford University Press), p. 450; **Table 25.1 (p. 1107)** Indices of Industrial Production, in David E. Sumler, *A History of Europe in the Twentieth Century* (Homewood, IL: Dorsey Press, 1973), p. 145; **Table 25.2 (p. 1141)** Defense Expenditures of the Great Powers, 1930–1938, in Paul Kennedy, *The Rise and Fall of the Great Powers* (New York: Vintage, 1989), p. 296; **Table 27.1 (p. 1233)** Indices of Industrial Production, in William I. Hitchcock, *The Struggle for Europe: The Turbulent History of a Divided Continent, 1945–2002* (New York: Doubleday, 2003), p. 135; **Table 28.1 (p. 1271)** Index of Industrial Production, in Walter Laqueur, *Europe Since Hitler* (New York: Penguin, 1982) p. 194; **Table 30.1 (p. 1346)** Foreign-born Population and Percentage of Total Population, in *World Book, 1998* (Chicago: World Book, 1999), p. 245.

Poetry: pp. xxxi Bertolt Brecht, "A Worker Reads History," from *Selected Poems*, by Bertolt Brecht, translated by H. R. Hays, copyright 1947 by Bertolt Brecht and H. R. Hays and renewed 1975 by Stefan S. Brecht and H. R. Hays, reprinted by permission of Harcourt Inc. and the Ann Elmo Agency, Inc.; **p. 994** Isaac Rosenberg's "Break of Day in the Trenches," from *The Collected Poems of Isaac Rosenberg*, ed. Denys Harding and Gordon Bottomley, copyright 1937 by Denys Harding and Gordon Bottomley, in acknowledgment of the Literary Estate of Isaac Rosenberg and Chatto and Windus, Ltd.; **p. 998** "The Hero," from *Collected Poems of Siegfried Sassoon*, by Siegfried Sassoon, copyright 1918, 1920, by E. P. Dutton, copyright 1936, 1946, 1947, 1948, by Siegfried Sassoon, used by permission of Viking Penguin, a division of Penguin Books USA Inc., and by permission of George Sassoon; **p. 1005–6** Excerpt from Robert Graves' "The Dead Fox Hunter," from Robert Graves, *Collected Poems*, 1975, Carcanet Press Limited, copyright 1975 by Robert Graves; **p. 1051** Excerpt from Tvorchestro Narodof's "There Is a Man in Moscow," 1937, in Robert H. McNeal, *Stalin: Man and Ruler* (New York: New York University Press, 1988), p. 228; **p. 1052–53** Excerpt from poem by Osip Mandelstam; **p. 1091** Excerpt from T. S. Eliot's "The Waste Land" in *Collected Poems, 1909–1962*, by T. S. Eliot, copyright 1936 by Harcourt Brace and Company, copyright © 1964, 1963 by T. S. Eliot, reprinted by permission of Faber and Faber Ltd.; **p. 1192** Excerpt from Randall Jarrell's "Losses," in *The Complete Poems* (New York: Farrar, Straus, & Giroux, 1969), p. 145, copyright 1943–1944, 1946, 1947, 1948, by Mrs. Randall Jarrell, copyright renewed 1969, 1970, 1971, 1973, 1975 by Mrs. Randall Jarrell, reprinted by permission of Farrar, Straus, & Giroux, Inc., and by Faber and Faber Ltd.

Index